AutoCAD 2018:
A Problem-Solving Approach, Basic and Intermediate

(24th Revised and Updated Edition)

Sham Tickoo
Professor
Purdue University Northwest
Hammond, Indiana, USA

Contributing Authors
CADCIM Technologies, USA
Tickoo Institute of Emerging Technologies (TIET), India

BPB PUBLICATIONS

ISBN: 978-93-86551-63-4
24th Revised and Updated Edition
(For distribution in SAARC countries only)

Limits of Liability and Disclaimer of Warranty

Distributors

BPB PUBLICATIONS
20, Ansari Road, Darya Ganj
New Delhi-110002
Ph: 23254990/23254991

BPB BOOK CENTRE
376 Old Lajpat Rai Market
DELHI-110006
Ph: 23861747

DECCAN AGENCIES
4-3-329, Bank Street
HYDERABAD-500195
Ph: 24756967/24756400

COMPUTER BOOK CENTRE
12, Shrungar Shopping Centre
M.G. Road
BENGALURU–560001
Ph: 25587923/25584641

MICRO MEDIA
Shop No. 5, Mahendra Chambers
150 DN Rd. Next to Capital Cinema
V.T (C.S.T.) Station
MUMBAI-400001
Ph: 22078296/22078297

Published by Manish Jain for BPB Publications, 20 Ansari Road, Darya Ganj
New Delhi-110002 and Printed by Repro India Ltd, Mumbai

DEDICATION

To teachers, who make it possible to disseminate knowledge
to enlighten the young and curious minds
of our future generations

To students, who are dedicated to learning new technologies
and making the world a better place to live in

SPECIAL RECOGNITION

A special thanks to Mr. Denis Cadu and the ADN team of Autodesk Inc.
for their valuable support and professional guidance to
procure the software for writing this textbook

THANKS

To employees of CADCIM Technologies and
Tickoo Institute of Emerging Technologies (TIET)
for their valuable help

Note
If you are a faculty member, you can register by clicking on the following link to access the teaching resources: ***http://www.cadcim.com/Registration.aspx***. The student resources are available at ***http://www.cadcim.com***. We also provide **Live Virtual Online Training** on various software packages. For more information, write us at ***sales@cadcim.com***.

Table of Contents

Dedication iii
Preface xxi

Chapter 1: Introduction to AutoCAD

AutoCAD Screen Components 1-2
- Start Tab 1-2
- Drawing Area 1-2
- Command Window 1-3
- Navigation Bar 1-5
- ViewCube 1-6
- In-canvas Viewport Controls 1-6
- Status Bar 1-6

Invoking Tools in AutoCAD 1-10
- Keyboard 1-10
- Ribbon 1-11
- Application Menu 1-12
- Tool Palettes 1-13
- Menu Bar 1-13
- Toolbar 1-13
- Shortcut Menu 1-13
- File Tabs 1-14

AutoCAD Dialog Boxes 1-17
Starting a New Drawing 1-18
- Open a Drawing 1-19
- Start from Scratch 1-19
- Use a Template 1-19
- Use a Wizard 1-20

Saving Your Work 1-24
- Save Drawing As Dialog Box 1-25

Automatic Timed Save 1-27
Creating Backup Files 1-28
- Changing Automatic Timed Saved and Backup Files into AutoCAD Format 1-28
- Using the Drawing Recovery Manager to Recover Files 1-28

Closing a Drawing 1-29
Opening an Existing Drawing 1-29

Opening an Existing Drawing Using the Select File Dialog Box 1-30
Opening an Existing Drawing Using the Startup Dialog Box 1-32
Opening an Existing Drawing Using the Drag and Drop Method 1-33
Quitting AutoCAD 1-33
Creating and Managing Workspaces 1-33
Creating a New Workspace 1-34
Modifying the Workspace Settings 1-34
AutoCAD Help 1-35
Autodesk CLOUD 1-37
Autodesk App Store 1-39
Design Feed 1-41
Additional Help Resources 1-45
Self-Evaluation Test 1-45
Review Questions 1-46

Chapter 2: Getting Started with AutoCAD

Dynamic Input Mode 2-2
Enable Pointer Input 2-2
Enable Dimension Input where possible 2-3
Show command prompting and command input near the crosshairs 2-4
Show additional tips with command prompting 2-5
Drafting Tooltip Appearance 2-5
Drawing Lines in AutoCAD 2-6
The Close Option 2-7
The Undo Option 2-8
Invoking Tools Using Dynamic INPUT/Command Prompt 2-8
Coordinate Systems 2-9
Absolute Coordinate System 2-9
Relative Coordinate System 2-12
Direct Distance Entry 2-18
Erasing Objects 2-21
Canceling and Undoing Operation 2-21
Object Selection Methods 2-22
Window Selection Method 2-22
Crossing Selection Method 2-23
Lasso Selection Method 2-23
Drawing a Circle 2-25
Basic Display Commands 2-29
Zooming Drawings 2-29
Moving the view 2-30
Setting Units Type and Precision 2-30
Specifying the Format 2-31
Specifying the Angle Format 2-31
Setting the Direction for Angle Measurement 2-32
Specifying Units for the Drawing or the Block to be Inserted 2-33
Sample Output 2-33
Specifying Units for Lighting 2-33

Setting the Limits of a Drawing 2-35
  Setting Limits 2-36
  Limits for Architectural Drawings 2-36
  Limits for Metric Drawings 2-38
Introduction to Plotting Drawings 2-39
Modifying AutoCAD Settings by Using the Options Dialog Box 2-41
Self-Evaluation Test 2-45
Review Questions 2-46

Chapter 3: Getting Started with Advanced Sketching

Drawing Arcs 3-2
Drawing Rectangles 3-10
Drawing Ellipses 3-14
Drawing Regular Polygons 3-18
Drawing Polylines 3-20
Drawing Donuts 3-25
Placing Points 3-27
  Changing the Point Style and Size 3-27
  Placing Multiple Points 3-28
  Placing Points at Equal Distance 3-28
  Placing Points at Specified Intervals 3-28
Drawing an Infinite Line 3-28
  Drawing Construction Lines 3-29
  Drawing Ray 3-31
Writing a Single Line Text 3-32
Working With Templates 3-32
Self-Evaluation Test 3-33
Review Questions 3-34

Chapter 4: Working with Drawing Aids

Introduction 4-2
Understanding the Concept and Use of Layers 4-2
Working with Layers Enhanced 4-3
  Creating New Layers 4-4
  Making a Layer Current 4-4
  Controlling the Display of Layers 4-5
  Arranging Layers in Increasing Order 4-9
  Arranging Layers in Increasing Order with Respect to First Digit 4-10
  Merging Layers 4-11
  Deleting Layers 4-12
  Managing the Display of Columns 4-13
  Selective Display of Layers 4-13
  Layer States 4-15
  Reconciling New Layers 4-16
  Isolating and Unisolating Layers 4-16
  Controlling the Layer Settings 4-17

Object Properties 4-21
Changing the Color 4-22
Changing the Linetype 4-22
Changing the Lineweight 4-23
Changing the Plot Style 4-24
Changing Object Properties using the Properties Palette 4-24
Changing Object Properties using the Quick Properties Palette 4-25
Global and Current Linetype Scaling 4-26
LTSCALE Factor for Plotting 4-26
Changing the Linetype Scale Using the Properties Palette 4-27
Working with the DesignCenter 4-27
Drafting Settings Dialog Box 4-28
Setting Grid 4-29
Setting Snap 4-30
Snap Type 4-30
Drawing Straight Lines Using the Ortho Mode 4-31
Working with Object Snaps 4-32
Running Object Snap Mode 4-44
Overriding the Running Snap 4-45
Cycling through Snaps 4-45
Setting the Priority for Coordinate Entry 4-46
Using AutoTracking 4-47
Object Snap Tracking 4-47
Polar Tracking 4-48
AutoTrack Settings 4-48
Function and Control Keys 4-49
Self-Evaluation Test 4-49
Review Questions 4-50

Chapter 5: Editing Sketched Objects-I

Creating a Selection Set 5-2
Editing Sketches 5-7
Moving Sketched Objects 5-7
Copying Sketched Objects 5-8
Creating Multiple Copies 5-9
Creating an Array of Selected Objects 5-9
Creating a Single Copy 5-10
Pasting Contents from the Clipboard 5-11
Pasting Contents Using the Original Coordinates 5-11
Offsetting Sketched Objects 5-11
Through Option 5-12
Erase Option 5-12
Layer Option 5-13
Rotating Sketched Objects 5-13
Scaling the Sketched Objects 5-15
Filleting the Sketches 5-17
Chamfering the Sketches 5-20

Blending the Curves 5-23
Trimming the Sketched Objects 5-24
Extending the Sketched Objects 5-28
Stretching the Sketched Objects 5-30
Lengthening the Sketched Objects 5-31
Arraying the Sketched Objects 5-32
Rectangular Array 5-33
Polar Array 5-40
Path Array 5-45
Mirroring the Sketched Objects 5-48
Text Mirroring 5-49
Breaking the Sketched Objects 5-50
Placing Points at Specified Intervals 5-51
Dividing the Sketched Objects 5-53
Joining the Sketched Objects 5-53
Self-Evaluation Test 5-58
Review Questions 5-59

Chapter 6: Editing Sketched Objects-II

Introduction to Grips 6-2
Types of Grips 6-2
Adjusting Grip Settings 6-3
Editing Objects by Using Grips 6-5
Stretching the Objects by Using Grips (Stretch Mode) 6-5
Moving the Objects by Using Grips (Move Mode) 6-6
Rotating the Objects by Using Grips (Rotate Mode) 6-7
Scaling the Objects by Using Grips (Scale Mode) 6-9
Mirroring the Objects by Using Grips (Mirror Mode) 6-10
Editing a Polyline by Using Grips 6-11
Loading Hyperlinks 6-13
Editing Gripped Objects 6-13
Changing the Properties Using the Properties Palette 6-13
Matching the Properties of Sketched Objects 6-14
Quick Selection of Sketched Objects 6-15
Cycling Through Selection 6-17
Managing Contents Using the DesignCenter 6-17
Folders Tab 6-19
Open Drawings Tab 6-20
History Tab 6-20
Autodesk Seek design content Link 6-20
Making Inquiries About Objects and Drawings 6-22
Measuring Area of Objects 6-23
Measuring the Distance between Two Points 6-26
Identifying the Location of a Point 6-27
Listing Information about Objects 6-27
Listing Information about all Objects in a Drawing 6-28
Checking Time-Related Information 6-28

Obtaining Drawing Status Information 6-29
Displaying Drawing Properties 6-30
Basic Display Options 6-30
Redrawing the Screen 6-31
Regenerating Drawings 6-31
Zooming Drawings 6-32
Panning Drawings 6-39
Creating Views 6-41
Understanding the Concept of Sheet Sets 6-44
Creating a Sheet Set 6-44
Adding a Subset to a Sheet Set 6-48
Adding Sheets to a Sheet Set or a Subset 6-49
Archiving a Sheet Set 6-49
Resaving all Sheets in a Sheet Set 6-51
Placing Views on a Sheet of a Sheet Set 6-51
Self-Evaluation Test 6-52
Review Questions 6-53

Chapter 7: Creating Texts and Tables

Annotative Objects 7-2
Annotation Scale 7-2
Assigning Annotative Property and Annotation Scales 7-2
Customizing Annotation Scale 7-3
Multiple Annotation Scales 7-3
Assigning Multiple Annotation Scales Manually 7-3
Assigning Multiple Annotation Scales Automatically 7-4
Controlling the Display of Annotative Objects 7-5
Creating Text 7-6
Writing Single Line Text 7-6
Entering Special Characters 7-11
Creating Multiline Text 7-11
Editing Text 7-29
Editing Text Using the TEXTEDIT Command 7-29
Editing Text Using the Properties Palette 7-29
Modifying the Scale of the Text 7-30
Aligning Text 7-31
Combine Text New 7-32
Inserting Table in the Drawing 7-32
Creating a New Table Style 7-38
Setting a Table Style As Current 7-41
Modifying a Table Style 7-41
Modifying Tables 7-42
Creating Text Styles 7-47
Creating Annotative Text 7-49
Checking Spelling 7-50
Text Quality and Text Fill 7-51
Finding and Replacing Text 7-52

Creating Title Sheet Table in a Sheet Set 7-53
Self-Evaluation Test 7-55
Review Questions 7-56

Chapter 8: Basic Dimensioning, Geometric Dimensioning, and Tolerancing

Need for Dimensioning 8-2
Dimensioning in AutoCAD 8-2
Fundamental Dimensioning Terms 8-3
Dimension Line 8-3
Dimension Text 8-3
Arrowheads 8-3
Extension Lines 8-4
Leader 8-4
Center Mark and Centerlines 8-5
Alternate Units 8-5
Tolerances 8-5
Limits 8-6
Associative Dimensions 8-6
Definition Points 8-7
Annotative Dimensions 8-8
Selecting Dimensioning Tools 8-8
Dimensioning a Number of Objects Together 8-9
Creating Linear Dimensions 8-10
Creating Aligned Dimensions 8-14
Creating Arc Length Dimensions 8-15
Creating Rotated Dimensions 8-16
Creating Baseline Dimensions 8-17
Creating Continued Dimensions 8-18
Creating Angular Dimensions 8-19
Creating Diameter Dimensions 8-23
Creating Jogged Dimensions 8-23
Creating Radius Dimensions 8-24
Creating Jogged Linear Dimensions 8-25
Generating Center Marks and Centerlines 8-25
Creating Associative Centermarks 8-26
Creating Associative Centerlines 8-27
Creating Ordinate Dimensions 8-28
Maintaining Equal Spacing between Dimensions 8-29
Creating Dimension Breaks 8-30
Creating Inspection Dimensions 8-32
Working with True Associative Dimensions 8-33
Removing the Dimension Associativity 8-34
Converting a Dimension into a True Associative Dimension 8-34
Drawing Leaders 8-35
Multileaders 8-39

Drawing Multileaders 8-39
Adding Leaders to Existing Multileader 8-42
Removing Leaders from Existing Multileader 8-42
Aligning Multileaders 8-42
Collecting Multiple Leaders 8-45
Geometric Dimensioning and Tolerancing 8-47
    Geometric Characteristics and Symbols 8-47
Adding Geometric Tolerance 8-48
Complex Feature Control Frames 8-50
    Combining Geometric Characteristics 8-50
    Composite Position Tolerancing 8-51
Using Feature Control Frames with Leaders 8-52
Projected Tolerance Zone 8-53
Creating Annotative Dimensions, Tolerances, Leaders, and Multileaders 8-56
Self-Evaluation Test 8-57
Review Questions 8-57

Chapter 9: Editing Dimensions

Editing Dimensions Using Editing Tools 9-2
    Editing Dimensions by Stretching 9-2
    Editing Dimensions by Trimming and Extending 9-4
    Flipping Dimension Arrow 9-5
Modifying the Dimensions 9-5
Editing the Dimension Text 9-7
Updating Dimensions 9-8
Editing Dimensions with Grips 9-8
Editing Dimensions Using the Properties Palette 9-8
Model Space and Paper Space Dimensioning 9-12
Self-Evaluation Test 9-14
Review Questions 9-14

Chapter 10: Dimension Styles, Multileader Styles, and System Variables

Using Styles and Variables to Control Dimensions 10-2
Creating and Restoring Dimension Styles 10-2
New Dimension Style Dialog box 10-3
Controlling the Dimension Text Format 10-11
Fitting Dimension Text and Arrowheads 10-16
Formatting Primary Dimension Units 10-19
Formatting Alternate Dimension Units 10-22
Formatting the Tolerances 10-24
Dimension Style Families 10-28
Using Dimension Style Overrides 10-31
Comparing and Listing Dimension Styles 10-33
Using Externally Referenced Dimension Styles 10-33

Creating and Restoring Multileader Styles 10-34
Modify Multileader Style Dialog Box 10-35
Self-Evaluation Test 10-42
Review Questions 10-42

Chapter 11: Adding Constraints to Sketches

Introduction 11-2
Adding Geometric Constraints 11-2
Applying the Horizontal Constraint 11-2
Applying the Vertical Constraint 11-3
Applying the Coincident Constraint 11-4
Applying the Fix Constraint 11-4
Applying the Perpendicular Constraint 11-5
Applying the Parallel Constraint 11-5
Applying the Collinear Constraint 11-6
Applying the Concentric Constraint 11-6
Applying the Tangent Constraint 11-6
Applying the Symmetric Constraint 11-7
Applying the Equal Constraint 11-7
Applying the Smooth Constraint 11-8
Controlling the Display of Constraints 11-8
Applying Constraints Automatically 11-13
Applying Dimensional Constraints 11-14
Converting a Dimensional Constraint into an Annotational Constraint 11-15
Concept of a Fully-Defined Sketch 11-16
Under-defined 11-16
Fully-defined 11-16
Over-defined 11-16
Controlling the Display of the Dimensional Constraint 11-17
Working with Equations 11-22
Adding Equations while Applying Dimensional Constraints 11-22
Adding Equations Using the Parameters Manager 11-22
Self-Evaluation Test 11-27
Review Questions 11-27

Chapter 12: Hatching Drawings

Hatching 12-2
Hatch Patterns 12-2
Hatch Boundary 12-2
Hatching Drawings Using the Hatch Tool 12-3
Panels in the Hatch Creation Tab 12-4
Creating Annotative Hatch 12-17
Hatching the Drawing Using the Tool Palettes 12-18
Drag and Drop Method 12-18
Select and Place Method 12-18

Modifying the Properties of the Predefined Patterns available in the Tool Palettes 12-19
Hatching Around Text, Dimensions, and Attributes 12-20
Editing Hatch Patterns 12-20
Using the Hatch Editor Tab 12-20
Using the Edit Hatch Tool 12-21
Using the Properties Tool 12-22
Editing the Hatch Boundary 12-24
Using Grips 12-24
Trimming the Hatch Patterns 12-25
Using AutoCAD Editing Tools 12-27
Hatching Blocks and Xref Drawings 12-27
Creating a Boundary Using Closed Loops 12-28
Other Features of Hatching 12-29
Self-Evaluation Test 12-30
Review Questions 12-31

Chapter 13: Model Space Viewports, Paper Space Viewports, and Layouts

Model Space and Paper Space/Layouts 13-2
Model Space Viewports (Tiled Viewports) 13-2
Creating Tiled Viewports 13-2
Making a Viewport Current 13-5
Joining Two Adjacent Viewports 13-5
Splitting and Resizing Viewports in Model Space 13-7
Paper Space Viewports (Floating Viewports) 13-7
Creating Floating Viewports 13-8
Creating Rectangular Viewports 13-9
Creating Polygonal Viewports 13-10
Converting an Existing Closed Object into a Viewport 13-11
Temporary Model Space 13-11
Editing Viewports 13-13
Controlling the Display of Objects in Viewports 13-13
Locking the Display of Objects in Viewports 13-13
Controlling the Display of Hidden Lines in Viewports 13-14
Clipping Existing Viewports 13-14
Maximizing Viewports 13-15
Controlling the Properties of Viewport Layers 13-16
Controlling the Layers in Viewports Using Layer Properties Manager 13-18
Paper Space Linetype Scaling (PSLTSCALE System variable) 13-20
Inserting Layouts 13-21
Importing Layouts to Sheet Sets 13-24
Inserting a Layout Using the Wizard 13-24
Defining Page Settings 13-24
Working with the MVSETUP Command 13-26

Converting the Distance Between Model Space and Paper Space 13-30
Controlling the Display of Annotative Objects in Viewports 13-31
Self-Evaluation Test 13-33
Review Questions 13-34

Chapter 14: Plotting Drawings

Plotting Drawings in AutoCAD 14-2
Plotting Drawings Using the Plot Dialog Box 14-2
Adding Plotters 14-10
Editing the Plotter Configuration 14-11
Importing PCP/PC2 Configuration Files 14-13
Setting Plot Parameters 14-13
    Working with Page Setups 14-13
    Importing a Page Setups 14-16
Using Plot Styles 14-17
    Adding a Plot Style 14-17
    Plot Style Table Editor 14-19
    Applying Plot Styles 14-23
    Setting the Current Plot Style 14-24
Plotting Sheets in a Sheet Set 14-27
Self-Evaluation Test 14-28
Review Questions 14-28

Chapter 15: Template Drawings

Creating Template Drawings 15-2
Standard Template Drawings 15-2
Loading a Template Drawing 15-7
Customizing Drawings with Layers and Dimensioning Specifications 15-9
Customizing a Drawing with Layout 15-13
Customizing Drawings with Viewports 15-16
Customizing Drawings According to Plot Size and Drawing Scale 15-18
Self-Evaluation Test 15-22
Review Questions 15-23

Chapter 16: Working with Blocks

The Concept of Blocks 16-2
Converting Entities into a Block 16-2
Inserting Blocks 16-5
Creating and Inserting Annotative Blocks 16-12
    Block Editor 16-14
Dynamic Blocks 16-16
Adding Parameter and Action Simultaneously Using Parameter Sets 16-33
Inserting Blocks Using the DesignCenter 16-34
Using Tool Palettes to Insert Blocks 16-34

Inserting Blocks in the Drawing 16-35
Modifying Properties of the Blocks in the Tool Palettes 16-35
Adding Blocks in Tool Palettes 16-36
Drag and Drop Method 16-37
Shortcut Menu 16-37
Modifying Existing Blocks in the Tool Palettes 16-37
Layers, Colors, Linetypes, and Lineweights for Blocks 16-38
Nesting of Blocks 16-39
Inserting Multiple Blocks 16-41
Creating Drawing Files Using the Write Block Dialog box 16-43
Defining the Insertion Base Point 16-45
Editing Blocks 16-45
Editing Blocks in Place 16-45
Exploding Blocks Using the XPLODE Command 16-48
Renaming Blocks 16-50
Deleting Unused Blocks 16-51
Applying Constraints to Blocks 16-51
Self-Evaluation Test 16-58
Review Questions 16-58

Chapter 17: Defining Block Attributes

Understanding Attributes 17-2
Defining Attributes 17-2
Editing Attribute Definition 17-7
Using the Properties Palette 17-8
Inserting Blocks with Attributes 17-8
Managing Attributes 17-11
Extracting Attributes 17-17
Controlling the Attribute Visibility 17-35
Editing Block Attributes 17-36
Editing Attributes Using the Enhanced Attribute Editor 17-36
Editing Attributes Using the Edit Attributes Dialog Box 17-38
Global Editing of Attributes 17-40
Redefining a Block with Attributes 17-45
In-place Editing of Blocks with Attributes 17-45
Inserting Text Files in the Drawing 17-46
Self-Evaluation Test 17-47
Review Questions 17-48

Chapter 18: Understanding External References

External References 18-2
Dependent Symbols 18-2
Managing External References in a Drawing Enhanced 18-4
The Overlay Option 18-12
Attaching Files to a Drawing 18-16

Working with Underlays 18-16
Editing an Underlay 18-17
Opening an Xreffed Object in a Separate Window 18-19
Using the DesignCenter to Attach a Drawing as an Xref 18-19
Adding Xref Dependent Named Objects 18-20
Clipping External References 18-21
Displaying Clipping Frame 18-23
Demand Loading 18-24
Editing References In-Place 18-26
Self-Evaluation Test 18-27
Review Questions 18-28

Chapter 19: Working with Advanced Drawing Options

Understanding the Use of Multilines 19-2
Defining the Multiline Style 19-2
Drawing Multilines 19-6
Editing Multilines by Using Grips 19-8
Editing Multilines by Using Dialog Box 19-8
Cross Intersection (CC/OC/MC) 19-9
Tee Intersection (CT/OT/MT) 19-10
Corner Joint (CJ) 19-11
Adding and Deleting Vertices (AV/DV) 19-11
Cutting and Welding Multilines (CS/CA/WA) 19-12
Creating Revision Clouds 19-15
Rectangular Revision Cloud 19-15
Polygonal Revision Cloud 19-15
Freehand Revision Cloud 19-15
Creating Wipeouts 19-16
Creating NURBS 19-17
Editing Splines 19-20
Editing Splines using 3D Edit Bar 19-24
Self-Evaluation Test 19-24
Review Questions 19-25

Chapter 20: Grouping and Advanced Editing of Sketched Objects

Grouping Sketched Objects Using the Object Grouping Dialog Box 20-2
Grouping Sketched Objects Using the Group Button 20-7
Selecting Groups 20-7
Changing Properties of an Object 20-8
Exploding Compound Objects 20-14
Editing Polylines 20-15
Editing Single Polyline 20-16
Editing Multiple Polylines 20-29
Undoing Previous Commands 20-30
Reversing the Undo Operation 20-35
Renaming Named Objects 20-35

Removing Unused Named Objects 20-36
View items you can purge 20-37
View items you cannot purge 20-37
Setting Selection Modes Using the Options Dialog Box 20-38
Self-Evaluation Test 20-42
Review Questions 20-42

Chapter 21: Working with Data Exchange & Object Linking and Embedding

Understanding the Concept of Data Exchange in AutoCAD 21-2
Creating Data Interchange (DXF) Files 21-2
Creating a Data Interchange File 21-2
Information in a DXF File 21-3
Converting DXF Files into Drawing Files 21-3
Importing CAD Files 21-4
Other Data Exchange Formats 21-4
DXB File Format 21-4
Creating and Using an ACIS File 21-4
Importing PDF Files Enhanced 21-5
Importing 3D Studio Files 21-7
Creating and Using a Windows Metafile 21-7
Creating and Using a V8 DGN File 21-8
Creating a BMP File 21-8
Raster Images 21-8
Attaching Raster Images 21-9
Managing Raster Images Enhanced 21-10
Editing Raster Image Files 21-13
Clipping Raster Images 21-13
Adjusting Raster Images 21-14
Modifying the Image Quality 21-15
Modifying the Transparency of an Image 21-15
Controlling the Display of Image Frames 21-16
Changing the Display Order 21-16
Other Editing Operations 21-16
Scaling Raster Images 21-17
DWG Convert 21-17
Conversion Setup Options 21-18
Working with PostScript Files 21-21
Creating PostScript Files 21-21
Object Linking and Embedding (OLE) 21-24
Self-Evaluation Test 21-32
Review Questions 21-33

Chapter 22: Conventional Dimensioning and Projection Theory Using AutoCAD

Dimensioning 22-2
Dimension Units 22-2
Inch Units 22-2
The Decimal-Inch System 22-2
The Fraction-Inch System 22-3
SI (Metric) Units 22-3
Dimensioning Components 22-4
Common Rules For Dimensioning 22-4
Dimensioning of Rounds, Fillets, and Chamfers 22-13
Dimensioning of Repetitive Features 22-14
Working Drawings 22-14
Detail Drawing 22-14
Assembly Drawing 22-15
Bill of Materials 22-16
Multiview Drawings 22-16
Understanding the X, Y, and Z Axes 22-17
Orthographic Projections 22-18
Positioning Orthographic Views 22-21
Sectional Views 22-26
Auxiliary Views 22-37
Self-Evaluation Test 22-42
Review Questions 22-43

Chapter 23: Concepts of Geometric Dimensioning and Tolerancing

History of Tolerances and Allowances 23-2
Methods of Tolerancing 23-2
Limit Dimensioning 23-3
Plus and Minus Tolerancing 23-4
Geometric Tolerances 23-4
Form Tolerances 23-10
Profile Tolerances 23-19
Orientation Tolerances 23-22
Location Tolerances 23-25
Runout Tolerances 23-29
Fits 23-33
Hole Basis System 23-33
Shaft Basis System 23-34
Standards of Fits 23-39
Standard Inch Fits 23-39
Standard Metric Fits 23-42
Self-Evaluation Test 23-49
Review Questions 23-49

Chapter 24: Isometric Drawings

Isometric Drawings 24-2
Isometric Projections 24-2
Isometric Axes and Planes 24-3
Setting the Isometric Grip and Snap 24-3
Drawing Isometric Circles 24-7
Creating Fillets in Isometric Drawings 24-8
Dimensioning Isometric Objects 24-8
Isometric Text 24-10
Self-Evaluation Test 24-11
Review Questions 24-12

Index **I-1**

Preface

AutoCAD 2018

AutoCAD, developed by Autodesk Inc., is the most popular PC-CAD system available in the market. Today, over 7 million people use AutoCAD and other AutoCAD-based design products. 100% of the Fortune 100 firms and 98% of the Fortune 500 firms are Autodesk customers. AutoCAD's open architecture allows third-party developers to write application software which has significantly added to its popularity. For example, the author of this book has developed a software package "**SMLayout**" for sheet metal products that generates a flat layout of various geometrical shapes such as transitions, intersections, cones, elbows, tank heads, and so on. Several companies in Canada and United States are using this software package with AutoCAD to design and manufacture various products. AutoCAD also facilitates customization that enables the users to increase their efficiency and improve their productivity.

The **AutoCAD 2018: A Problem-Solving Approach, Basic and Intermediate** textbook contains a detailed explanation of AutoCAD commands and their applications to solve drafting and design problems. Every AutoCAD command is thoroughly explained with the help of examples and illustrations. This makes it easy for the users to understand the functions and applications in the drawing. After reading this textbook, you will be able to use AutoCAD commands to make a drawing, dimension a drawing, apply constraints to sketches, insert symbols as well as create text, blocks and dynamic blocks. In this book concepts of GD&T have been explained in detail.

The book also covers basic drafting and design concepts that provide you with the essential drafting skills to solve the drawing problems in AutoCAD. These include dimensioning principles, and assembly drawings. While going through this textbook, you will discover some new unique applications of AutoCAD that will have a significant effect on your drawings. In addition, you will be able to understand why AutoCAD has become such a popular software package and an international standard in PC-CAD.

Symbols Used in the Textbook

Note

The author has provided additional information to the users about the topic being discussed in the form of notes.

Tip

Special information and techniques are provided in the form of tips that will increase the efficiency of the users.

New

This symbol indicates that the command or tool being discussed is new.

Enhanced

This symbol indicates that the command or the tool being discussed has been enhanced in AutoCAD 2018.

Formatting Conventions Used in the Textbook

Refer to the following list for the formatting conventions used in this textbook.

- Command names are capitalized and written in boldface letters.

  Example: The **MOVE** command

- A key icon appears when you have to respond by pressing the ENTER or the RETURN key.

  Enter

- Command sequences are indented. The responses are indicated in boldface. The directions are indicated in italics and the comments are enclosed in parentheses.

  Command: **MOVE**
  Select object: **G**
  Enter group name: *Enter a group name (the group name is group1)*

- The methods of invoking a tool/option from the **Ribbon**, **Menu Bar**, **Quick Access Toolbar**, **Tool Palettes**, **Application menu**, toolbars, Status Bar, and Command prompt are enclosed in a shaded box.

Ribbon:	Draw > Line
Menu Bar:	Draw > Line
Tool Palettes:	Draw > Line
Toolbar:	Draw > Line
Command:	LINE or L

Naming Conventions Used in the Textbook

Tool

If you click on an item in a toolbar or a panel of the **Ribbon** and a command is invoked to create/edit an object or perform some action, then that item is termed as **tool**.

For example:
To Create: **Line** tool, **Circle** tool, **Extrude** tool
To Edit: **Fillet** tool, **Array** tool, **Stretch** tool
Action: **Zoom** tool, **Move** tool, **Copy** tool

If you click on an item in a toolbar or a panel of the **Ribbon** and a dialog box is invoked wherein you can set the properties to create/edit an object, then that item is also termed as **tool**, refer to Figure 1.

For example:
To Create: **Define Attributes** tool, **Create** tool, **Insert** tool
To Edit: **Edit Attributes** tool, **Block Editor** tool

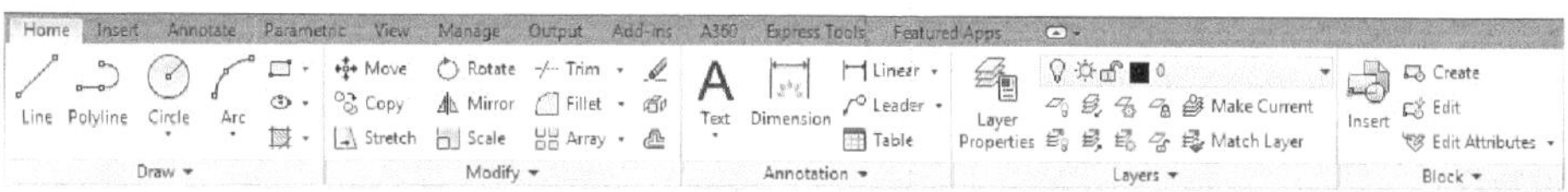

Figure 1** Various tools in the **Ribbon

Button

If you click on an item in a toolbar or a panel of the **Ribbon** and the display of the corresponding object is toggled on/off, then that item is termed as **button**. For example, **Grid** button, **Snap Mode** button, **Ortho Mode** button, **Properties** button, **Tool Palettes** button, and so on; refer to Figure 2.

Figure 2** Various buttons displayed in the Status Bar and **Ribbon

The item in a dialog box that has a 3d shape is also termed as **button**. For example, **OK** button, **Cancel** button, **Apply** button, and so on.

Dialog Box

The naming conventions used for the components in a dialog box are mentioned in Figure 3.

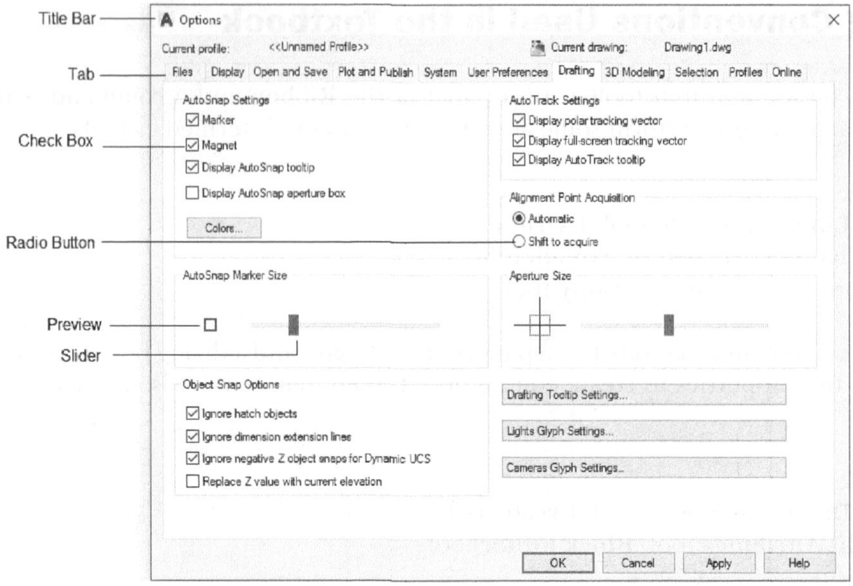

Figure 3 The components of a dialog box

Drop-down

A drop-down is the one in which a set of common tools are grouped together. You can identify a drop-down with a down arrow on it. These drop-downs are given a name based on the tools grouped in them. For example, **Circle** drop-down, **Fillet** drop-down, and so on; refer to Figure 4.

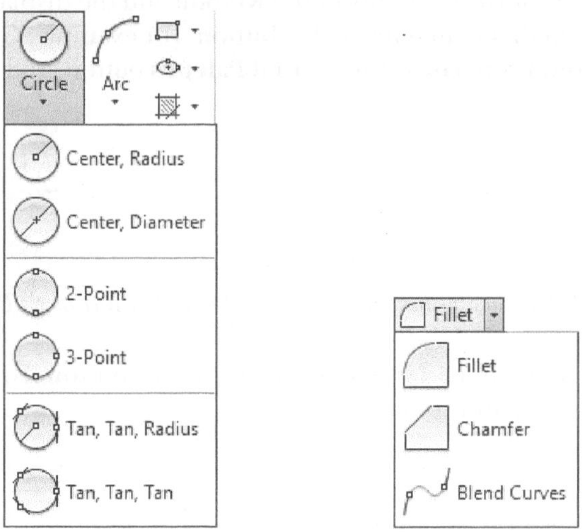

*Figure 4 The **Circle** and **Fillet** drop-downs*

Drop-down List

A drop-down list is the one in which a set of options are grouped together. You can set various parameters using these options. You can identify a drop-down list with a down arrow on it. To know the name of a drop-down list, move the cursor over it; its name will be displayed as a tool tip. For example, **Lineweight** drop-down list, **Linetype** drop-down list, **Object Color** drop-down list, **Visual Styles** drop-down list, and so on; refer to Figure 5.

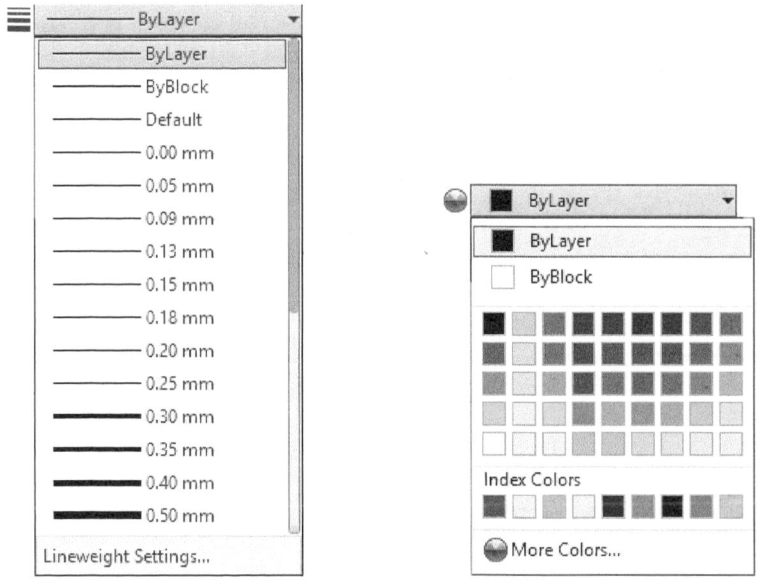

Figure 5 The ***Lineweight*** *and* ***Object Color*** *drop-down lists*

Options

Options are the items that are available in shortcut menu, drop-down list, Command prompt, **PROPERTIES** palette, and so on. For example, choose the **Properties** option from the shortcut menu displayed on right-clicking in the drawing area; refer to Figure 6.

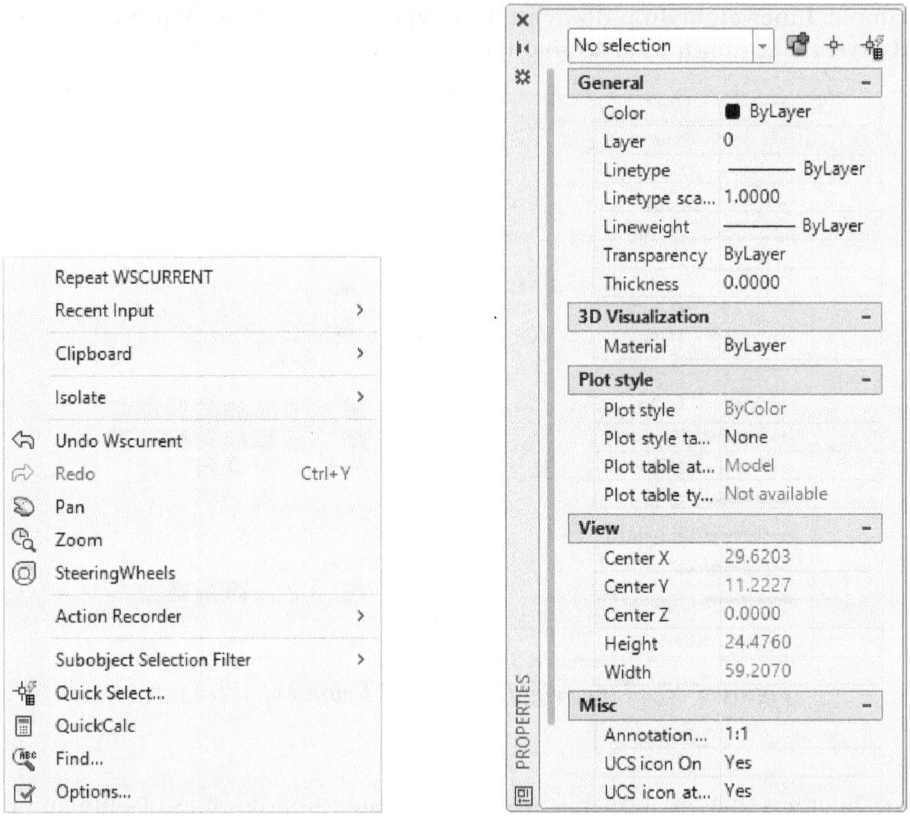

*Figure 6 Options in the shortcut menu and the **PROPERTIES** palette*

Tools and Options in Menu Bar

A menu bar consists of both tools and options. As mentioned earlier, the term **tool** is used to create/edit something or to perform some action. For example, in Figure 7, the item **Box** has been used to create a box shaped surface, therefore it will be referred to as the **Box** tool.

Similarly, an option in the menu bar is the one that is used to set some parameters. For example, in Figure 7, the item **Linetype** has been used to set/load the linetype, therefore it will be referred to as an option.

Figure 7 Tools and options in the menu bar

Free Companion Website

It has been our constant endeavor to provide you the best textbooks and services at affordable price. In this endeavor, we have come out with a Free Companion website that will facilitate the process of teaching and learning of AutoCAD 2018. If you purchase this textbook, you will get access to the files on the Companion website.

The following resources are available for the faculty and students in this website:

Faculty Resources

- **Technical Support**
  The faculty can get online technical support by contacting ***techsupport@cadcim.com***.

- **Instructor Guide**
  Solutions to all review questions and exercises in the textbook are provided in this guide to help the faculty members test the skills of the students.

- **PowerPoint Presentations**
  These slides provide the basis for a lecture outline and help you present concepts and material. The key points and concepts can be graphically highlighted for student retention.

- **Part Files**
  The part files used in illustrations, examples, and exercises are available for free download.

- **Input Files**
  The input files used in examples are available for free download.

Student Resources

- **Technical Support**
  You can get online technical support by contacting ***techsupport@cadcim.com***.

- **Part Files**
  The part files used in illustrations and examples are available for free download.

- **Input Files**
  The input files used in examples are available for free download.

You can access additional learning resources by visiting ***http://allaboutcadcam.blogspot.com***.

If you face any problem in accessing these files, please contact the author at ***stickoo@pnw.edu*** or ***tickoo525@gmail.com***.

Stay Connected

You can now stay connected with us through Facebook and Twitter to get the latest information about our textbooks, videos, and teaching/learning resources. To stay informed of such updates, follow us on Facebook (***www.facebook.com/cadcim***) and Twitter (***@cadcimtech***). You can also subscribe to our You Tube channel (***www.youtube.com/cadcimtech***) to get the information about our latest video tutorials.

Chapter 1

Introduction to AutoCAD

Learning Objectives

After completing this chapter, you will be able to:

- *Start AutoCAD*
- *Understand the usage of the components of the initial AutoCAD screen*
- *Invoke AutoCAD commands from the keyboard, menus, toolbars, shortcut menus, Tool Palettes, and Ribbon*
- *Work with File Tabs*
- *Understand the usage of components of dialog boxes in AutoCAD*
- *Start a new drawing using the New tool, File Tabs, and the Startup dialog box*
- *Save the work using various file-saving commands*
- *Close a drawing*
- *Open an existing drawing*
- *Quit AutoCAD*
- *Understand various options of AutoCAD help*
- *Understand the concept of Design Feed*

Key Terms

- *Initial Setup*
- *AutoCAD Screen Components*
- *Ribbon*
- *Application Menu*
- *Tool Palettes*
- *Menu Bar*
- *Toolbar*
- *New*
- *Save*
- *Save As*
- *Close*
- *STARTUP*
- *Open*
- *Partial open*
- *Drawing Recovery Manager*
- *Workspaces*
- *Help*
- *Autodesk App Store*
- *Autodesk 360*
- *Autodesk Cloud*
- *Design Feed*
- *File Tabs*

AutoCAD SCREEN COMPONENTS

When you install AutoCAD 2018, the AutoCAD 2018 - English shortcut icon is created on the desktop. You can start AutoCAD by double-clicking on this icon. The initial AutoCAD screen comprises of drawing area, command window, menu bar, several toolbars, Model and Layout tabs, and Status Bar, refer to Figure 1-1. A title bar that has an AutoCAD symbol and the current drawing name is displayed on top of the screen.

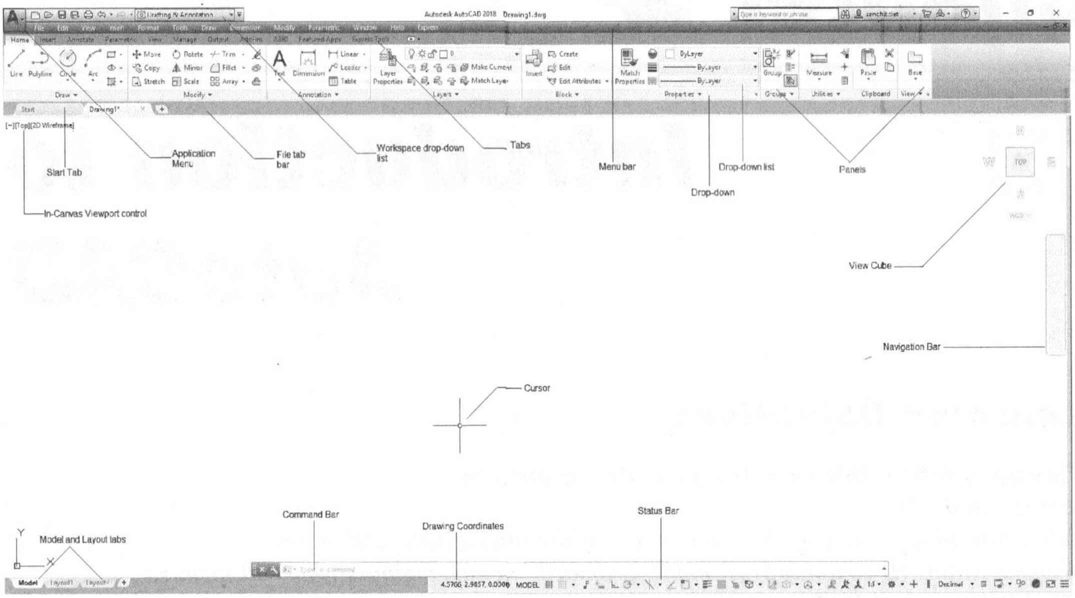

*Figure 1-1 AutoCAD screen components in AutoCAD **Drafting & Annotation** workspace*

Start Tab

In AutoCAD, the **Start** tab is displayed in the AutoCAD environment when you close all the drawing templates or when there are no drawings open. The **Start** tab contains two sliding frames, **CREATE** and **LEARN**, refer to Figure 1-2. These frames are discussed next.

CREATE

The **CREATE** page is displayed by default. In the **CREATE** page, you can access sample file, recent files, templates, product notifications as well as connect with the online community. The **CREATE** page is divided into four areas: **Get Started**, **Recent Documents**, **Notifications**, and **Connect**.

LEARN

When you click on **LEARN**, the **LEARN** page is displayed. The **LEARN** page provides tools to help you learn AutoCAD. It is divided into three columns: **What's New**, **Getting Started Videos**, and **Learning Tips/Online Resources**.

Drawing Area

The drawing area covers the major portion of the screen. In this area, you can draw the objects and use the commands. To draw the objects, you need to define the coordinate points, which can be selected by using your pointing device. The position of the pointing device is represented on the screen by the cursor. The window also has the standard Windows buttons such as Close, Minimize, and Restore Down on the top right corner. These buttons have the same functions as in any other standard Window.

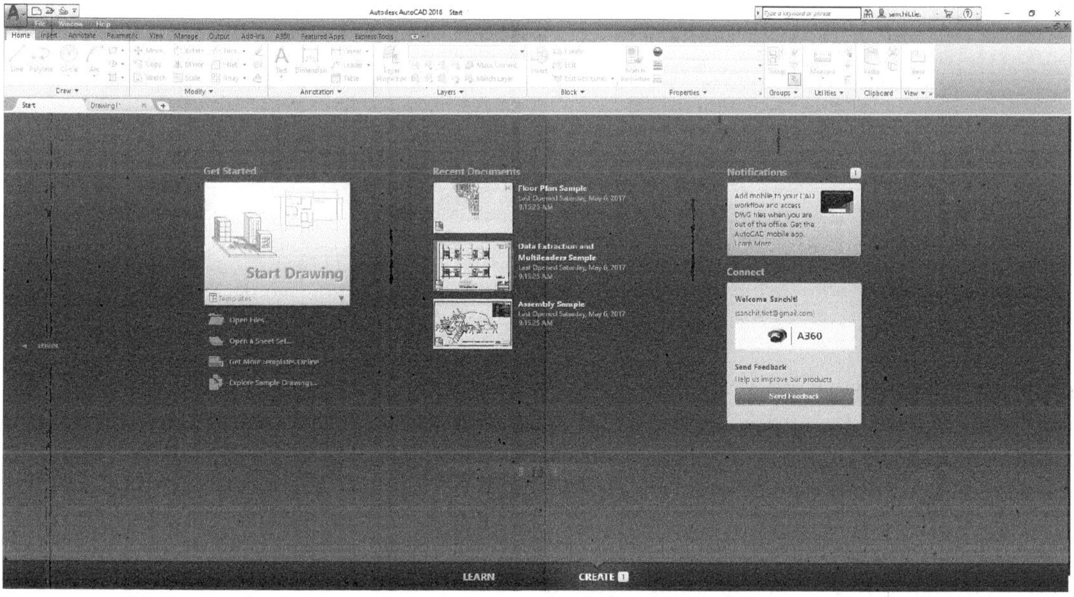

*Figure 1-2 The **Start** tab in AutoCAD 2018*

Command Window

The command window at the bottom of the drawing area has the command prompt where you can enter the commands. It also displays the subsequent prompt sequences and the messages. You can change the size of the window by placing the cursor on the top edge (double line bar known as the grab bar) and then dragging it. This way you can increase its size to see all the previous commands you have used. You can also press the F2 key to display **AutoCAD Text Window**, which displays the previous commands and prompts.

Tip

*You can hide all toolbars displayed on the screen by pressing the CTRL+0 keys or by choosing **View > Clean Screen** from the menu bar. To turn on the display of the toolbars again, press the CTRL+0 keys. You can also choose the **Clean Screen** button in the Status Bar to hide all toolbars.*

Auto Correct the Command Name

In AutoCAD, if you type a wrong command name at the command prompt, a suggestion list with most relevant commands will be displayed, refer to Figure 1-3. You can invoke the desired command by selecting the required option from this list.

Auto Complete the Command Name

When you start typing a command name at the command prompt, the complete name of the command will be displayed automatically. Also, a list of corresponding commands will be displayed, as shown in Figure 1-4. The commands that have not been used for a long time will be grouped in folders at the bottom of the list.

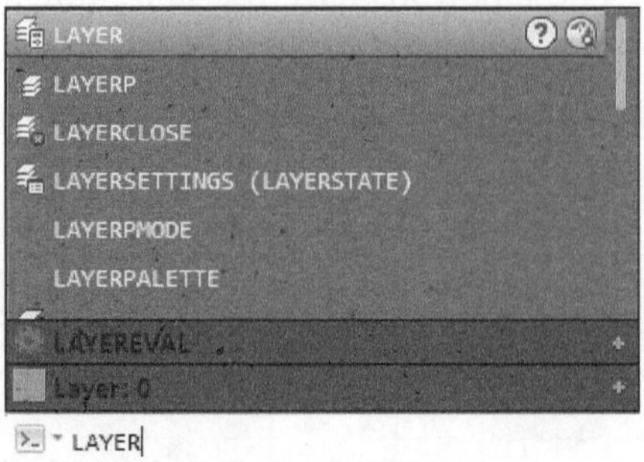

Figure 1-3 *Suggestion list with relevant commands*

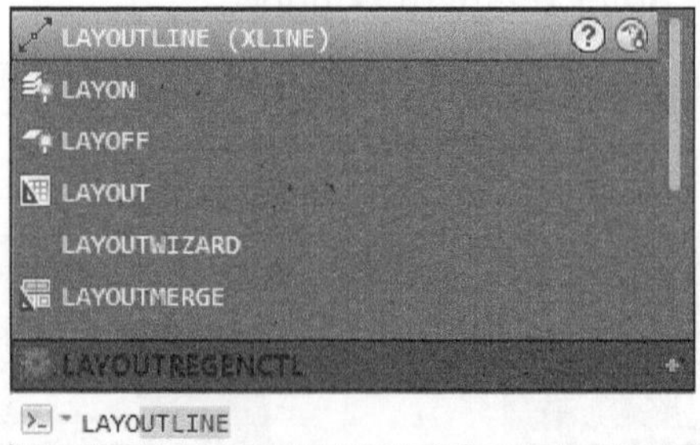

Figure 1-4 *Command bar displaying complete command name automatically*

Internet Search

You can get more information about a command by using the **Search in Help** and **Search on Internet** buttons available adjacent to the command name in the command line, refer to Figure 1-5. If you choose the **Search in Help** button, the **Autodesk AutoCAD 2018-Help** dialog box will be displayed. In this dialog box, you can find information about the command. By using the **Search on Internet** button, you can find information about the command on internet. Note that these buttons will be available adjacent to the selected command name in the suggestion list.

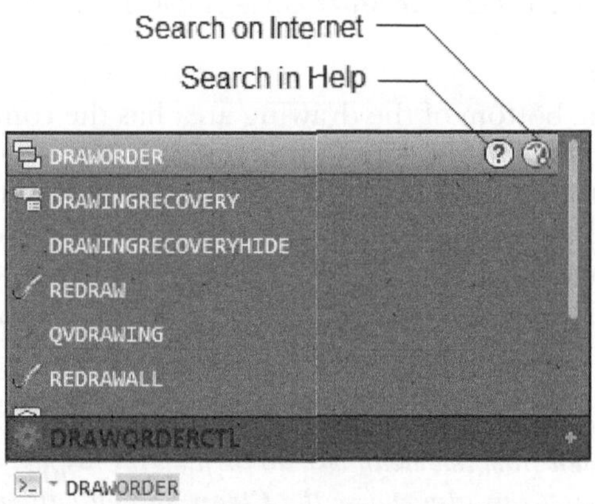

Figure 1-5 *The **Search in Help** and **Search on Internet** buttons displayed in the suggestion list*

Synonym Suggestions

In AutoCAD, you can invoke a command by entering synonyms of the command name. By entering the synonym at the command prompt, the command related to the synonym entered will be displayed. For example, if you enter **ROUND** at the command prompt, then the **FILLET** command will be displayed, as shown in Figure 1-6.

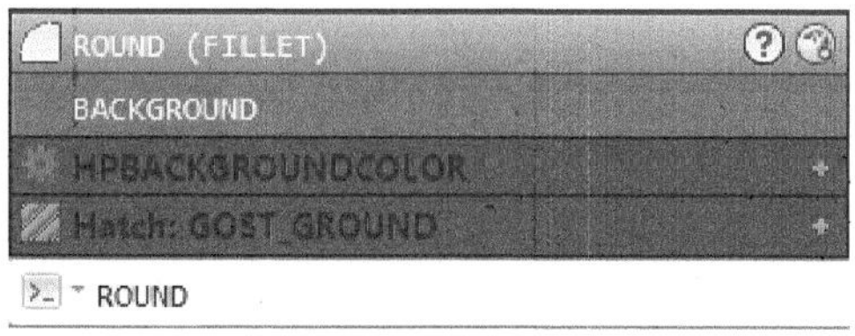

Figure 1-6 *Suggestion list displayed after entering a synonym of command name at the command prompt*

Input Search Options

In AutoCAD, you can enable or disable the functions such as Auto Complete and Auto Correct by using the options available in the **Input Search Options** dialog box. To invoke this dialog box, right-click at the command prompt; a shortcut menu will be displayed. Next, choose **Input Search Options** from the shortcut menu; the **Input Search Options** dialog box will be displayed, as shown in Figure 1-7. You can now enable or disable the required functions by using this dialog box.

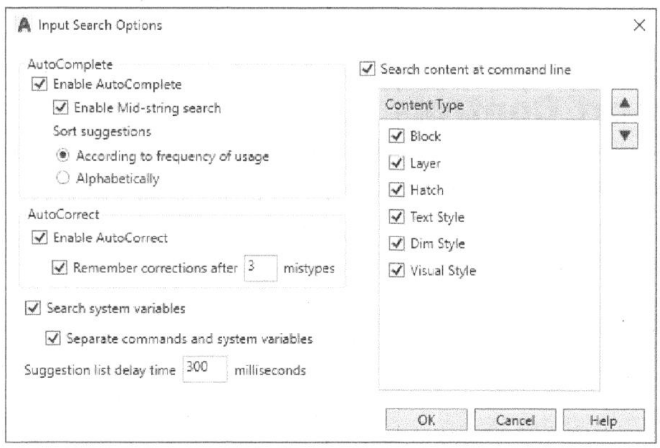

Figure 1-7 *The* ***Input Search Options*** *dialog box*

Navigation Bar

The **Navigation Bar** is displayed in the drawing area and contains navigation tools. These tools are grouped together, refer to Figure 1-8, and are discussed next.

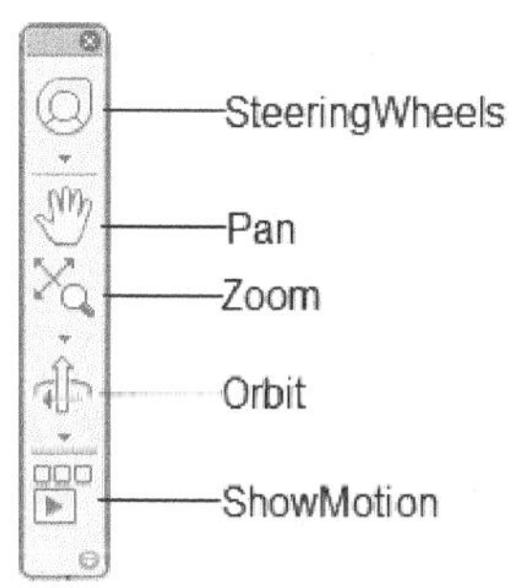

Figure 1-8 *Tools in the* ***Navigation Bar***

SteeringWheels

The SteeringWheels has a set of navigation tools such as pan, zoom, and so on. You will learn more about the SteeringWheels in the later chapters.

Pan

This tool allows you to view the portion of the drawing that is outside the current display area. To do so, choose this tool, press and hold the left mouse button, and then drag the drawing area. Press ESC to exit this command.

Zoom Tools

Zoom tools are used to enlarge the view of the drawing on the screen without affecting the actual size of the objects. These tools are grouped together in the **Zoom** drop-down. You will learn more about zoom tools in later chapters.

Rotate Tools

Rotate tools are used to rotate the view in 3D space. These tools are grouped together in the **Rotate** drop-down.

ShowMotion

Choose this button to capture different views in a sequence and animate them when required.

ViewCube

ViewCube is available on the top right corner of the drawing area and is used to switch between the standard and isometric views or roll the current view. The ViewCube and its options are discussed in later chapters.

In-canvas Viewport Controls

In-canvas Viewport Controls is available on the top left corner of the drawing screen. It enables you to change the view, visual style as well as the viewport.

Status Bar

The Status Bar is displayed at the bottom of the screen and is called Application Status Bar, refer to Figure 1-9. It contains some useful information and buttons that make it easy to change the status of some AutoCAD functions. You can toggle between the on and off states of most of these functions by choosing them. You can add or remove these buttons in the Status Bar by selecting respective option from the **Customization** flyout.

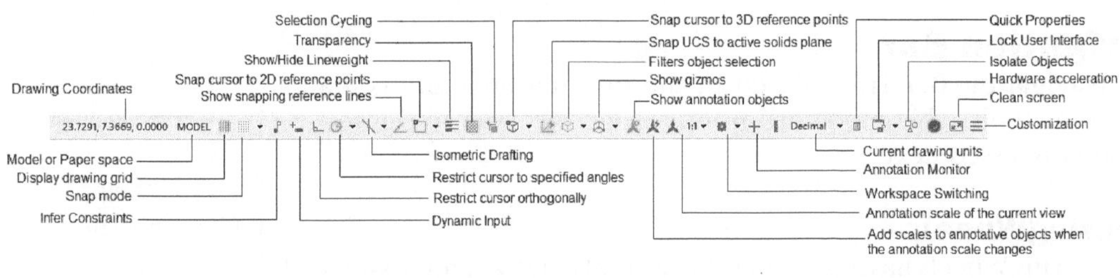

*Figure 1-9 The Status Bar displayed in the **Drafting & Annotation** workspace*

Coordinates

The information about the coordinates is displayed on the left corner of the Status Bar near the **Model** and **Layout** tabs. You can choose the coordinate button to toggle between the on and off states. The **COORDS** system variable controls the type of display of the coordinates. If the value of the **COORDS** variable is set to 0, the coordinate display is static, that is, the coordinate values displayed in the Status Bar change only when you specify a point. If the value of the **COORDS** variable is set to 1, 2, or 3, the coordinate display is dynamic. When the variable is set to 1, AutoCAD constantly displays the absolute coordinates of the graphics cursor with respect to the UCS origin. The polar coordinates (length<angle) are displayed if you are in

an AutoCAD command and the **COORDS** variable is set to 2. The geographic (latitude and longitude) coordinates are displayed if the **COORDS** variable is set to 3. Note that geographic coordinates will only be displayed if their are any in the current drawing. By default, the **COORDS** variable is set to 1.

Model Space

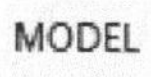

This button is chosen by default because you are working in the model space to create drawings. You will learn more about the model space in later chapters.

Grid

In AutoCAD, the grid lines are used as reference lines to draw objects. If this button is chosen, the Display of drawing grid will turn on and the grid lines are displayed on the screen. The F7 function key can be used to turn the grid display on or off.

Snap Mode

If the **Snap Mode** button is chosen, the snap mode will turn on. So, you can move the cursor in fixed increments. The F9 key acts as a toggle key to turn the snap on or off.

Infer Constraints

If this button is chosen then some of the geometric constraints will be automatically applied to sketch when it is drawn. You can use CTRL+SHIFT+I as a shortcut key to toggle this button.

Dynamic Input

This button is used to turn the **Dynamic Input** on or off. Turning it on facilitates the heads-up design approach because all commands, prompts, and dimensional inputs will now be displayed in the drawing area and you do not need to look at the command prompt all the time. This saves the design time and also increases the efficiency of the user. If the **Dynamic Input** mode is turned on, you will be allowed to enter the commands through the **Pointer Input** boxes, and the numerical values through the **Dimension Input** boxes. You will also be allowed to select the command options through the **Dynamic Prompt** options in the graphics window. To turn the **Dynamic Input** on or off, use the F12 key.

Ortho Mode

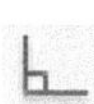
If this button is chosen, you can draw lines at right angles only. You can use the F8 function key to turn ortho on or off.

Polar Tracking

If you turn the polar tracking on, the movement of the cursor is restricted along a path based on the angle set as the polar angle. Choose this button to turn the polar tracking on. You can also use the F10 function key to turn on this option. Note that turning the polar tracking on, automatically turns off the ortho mode.

Isometric Drafting

In AutoCAD, you can activate the required working plane. To activate the required working plane, choose the **Isometric Drafting** button from the Status Bar. On choosing this button, a flyout is displayed with the **isoplane Left**, **isoplane Top,** and **isoplane Right** options. You can choose the required option from this flyout to activate the respective work plane.

Object Snap Tracking

When you choose this button, the inferencing lines will be displayed. Inferencing lines are dashed lines that are displayed automatically when you select a sketching tool and track a particular keypoint on the screen. Choosing this button turns the object snap tracking on or off. You can also use the F11 function key to turn the object snap tracking on or off.

2D Object Snap

When this button is chosen, you can use the running object snaps to snap on to a point. You can also use the F3 function key to turn the object snap on or off. The status of **OSNAP** (off or on) does not prevent you from using the immediate mode object snaps.

LineWeight

Choosing this button in the Status Bar allows you to turn on or off the display of lineweights in the drawing. If this button is not chosen, the display of lineweight will be turned off.

Transparency

This button is available in the Status Bar and is chosen to turn on or off the transparency set for a drawing. You can set the transparency in the **Properties** panel or in the layer in which the sketch is drawn.

Selection Cycling

When this button is chosen, you can cycle through the objects to be selected, if they are overlapping or close to other entities. On selecting an entity when this button is chosen, the **Selection** list box with a list of the entities that can be selected will be displayed. You can use CTRL+W as a shortcut key to toggle this button.

3D Object Snap

When this button is chosen, you can snap the key point on a solid or a surface. You can also use the F4 function key to turn on or off the 3D object snap.

Dynamics UCS

Choosing this button allows or disallows the use of dynamic UCS. Allowing the dynamic UCS ensures that the XY plane of the UCS got dynamically aligned with the selected face of the model. You can also use the F6 function key to turn this button on or off.

Selection Filtering

In AutoCAD, you can filter objects as per your requirement by using this button. If you want to select only **Vertex**, **Edge**, **Face**, **Solid History**, or **Drawing View Components** of a 3D object, then you can choose the required option from the flyout which is invoked by clicking on the small arrow at right side of this button. You can also select multiple objects through selection window.

The **Drawing View Component** option is used to select the components of an assembly or parts in a multi body. Using this option, you can select components either individually, or through window selection. You can also turn off the filters by choosing this button again.

Gizmo

You can move, rotate and scale a 3D object by choosing this button from the Status Bar. When you click on the small arrow available at the right side of this button, a flyout will be displayed with the **Move Gizmo**, **Rotate Gizmo**, and **Scale Gizmo** options.

Annotation Visibility

This button is used to control the visibility of the annotative objects that do not support the current annotation scale in the drawing area.

AutoScale

This button, if chosen, automatically adds all the annotation scales that are set current to all the annotative objects present in the drawing.

Annotation Scale

The annotation scale controls the size and display of the annotative objects in the model space. This button has a flyout that displays all the annotation scales available for the current drawing.

Workspace Switching

In AutoCAD, you can switch between different environments or workspaces by using the **Workspace Switching** button that is available at the right of the Status Bar. On clicking the **Workspace Switching** button, a flyout will be displayed with the list of all available workspaces. You can select the required workspace to invoke. You will learn more about workspaces later in this chapter.

Annotation Monitor

This button is used to turn the **Annotation Monitor** on or off. If it is turned on, all the non-associative annotations will get highlighted by placing a badge on them, as shown in Figure 1-10.

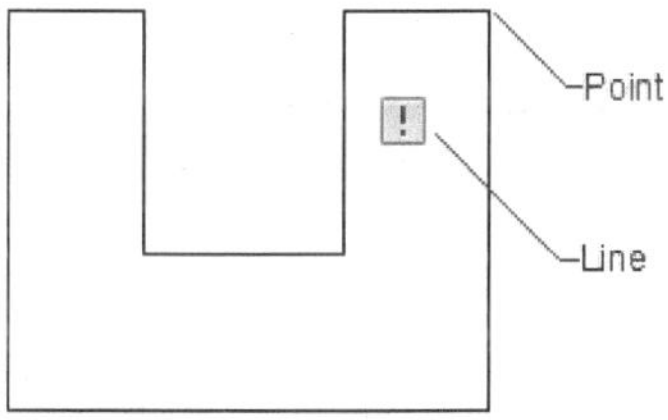

Figure 1-10 *The non-associative annotation*

Units

This button displays and controls the units of drawing. It has a flyout that displays all the unit systems available for drawing.

Quick Properties

If you select a sketched entity when this button is chosen in the Status Bar, the properties of the selected entity will be displayed in a panel. You can use CTRL+SHIFT+P as a shortcut key to toggle this button.

Lock UI

This button is used to dock/undock the toolbars, panels, and windows.

Isolate Objects

This button is used to hide or isolate objects from the drawing area. On choosing this button, a flyout will be displayed with two options. Choose the **Isolate Objects** option from this flyout and then select the objects to hide or isolate. To end isolation or display a hidden object, click this button again and choose the **End Object Isolation** option.

Graphics Performance

This button is used to set the performance of the software to an acceptable level.

Clean Screen

This button is available at the right corner of the Status Bar. This button, when chosen, displays an expanded view of the drawing area by hiding all the toolbars except the command window, Status Bar, and menu bar. The expanded view of the drawing area can also be displayed by choosing **View > Clean Screen** from the menu bar or by using the CTRL+0 keys. Choose the **Clean Screen** button again to restore the previous display state.

Customization

The **Customization** button is available at right corner of the Status Bar. Using this button, you can customize to add or remove tools in the Status Bar.

Plot/Publish Details Report Available

This icon is displayed in the Status Bar when some plotting or a publishing activity is performed in the background. When you click on this icon, the **Plot and Publish Details** dialog box, which provides the details about the plotting and publishing activity, will be displayed. You can copy this report to the clipboard by choosing the **Copy to Clipboard** button from the dialog box.

Manage Xrefs

The **Manage Xrefs** icon is displayed in the Status Bar whenever an external reference drawing is attached to the selected drawing. This icon displays a message and an alert whenever the Xreffed drawing needs to be reloaded. To find detailed information regarding the status of each Xref in the drawing and the relation between the various Xrefs, click on the **Manage Xrefs** icon; the **External References Palette** will be displayed. The Xrefs are discussed in detail in Chapter 18, Understanding External References.

INVOKING TOOLS IN AutoCAD

On starting AutoCAD, when you are in the drawing area, you need to invoke AutoCAD tools to perform an operation. For example, to draw a line, first you need to invoke the **Line** tool and then define the start point and the endpoint of the line. Similarly, if you want to erase objects, you must invoke the **Erase** tool and then select the objects for erasing. In AutoCAD, you can invoke the commands using the Keyboard, Ribbon, Application Menu, Tool Palettes, Menu bar, Shortcut menu, and Toolbar.

Keyboard

You can invoke any AutoCAD command from the keyboard by typing the command name and then pressing the ENTER key. As you type the first letter of command, AutoCAD displays all available commands starting with the letter typed. If the **Dynamic Input** is on and the cursor is in the drawing area, by default, the command will be entered through the **Pointer Input** box. The **Pointer Input** box is a small box displayed on the right of the cursor, as shown in Figure 1-11. However, if the cursor is currently placed on any toolbar or menu bar, or if the **Dynamic Input** is turned off, the command will be entered through the command prompt. Before you enter a command, the command prompt is displayed as the last line in the command window area. If it is not displayed, you must cancel the existing command by pressing the ESC (Escape) key.

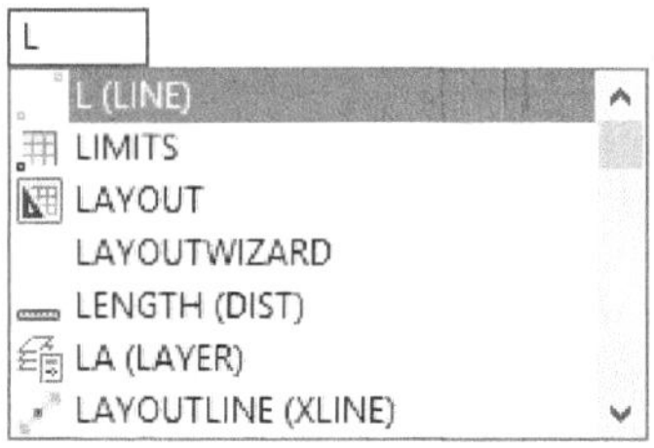

***Figure 1-11** The **Pointer Input** box displayed when the **Dynamic Input** is on*

The following example shows how to invoke the **LINE** command using the keyboard:

Command: **LINE** or **L** Enter (L is command alias)

Ribbon

In AutoCAD, you can also invoke a tool from the **Ribbon**, refer to Figure 1-12. The tools for creating, modifying, and annotating the 2D and 3D designs are available in the panels instead of being spread out in the entire drawing area in different toolbars and menus.

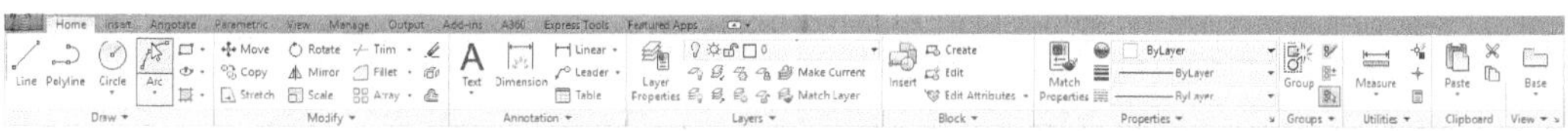

***Figure 1-12** The **Ribbon** for the **Drafting & Annotation** workspace*

When you start the AutoCAD session for the first time, by default the **Ribbon** is displayed horizontally below the **Quick Access Toolbar**. The **Ribbon** consists of various tabs. The tabs have different panels, which in turn, have tools arranged in rows. Some of the tools have small black down arrow. This indicates that the tools having similar functions are grouped together. To choose a tool, click on the down arrow; a drop-down will be displayed. Choose the required tool from the drop-down displayed. Note that if you choose a tool from the drop-down, the corresponding command will be invoked and the tool that you have chosen will be displayed in the panel. For example, to draw a circle using the **2-Point** tool, click on the down arrow next to the **Center, Radius** tool in the **Draw** panel of the **Home** tab; a flyout will be displayed. Choose the **2-Point** tool from the flyout and then draw the circle. You will notice that the **2-Point** tool is displayed in place of the **Center, Radius** tool.

Choose the down arrow to expand the panel. You will notice that a push pin is available at the left end of the panel. Click on the push pin to keep the panel in the expanded state. Also, some of the panels have an inclined arrow at the lower-right corner. When you left click on an inclined arrow, a dialog box is displayed. You can define the setting of the corresponding panel in the dialog box.

You can reorder the panels in the tab. To do so, press and hold the left mouse button on the panel to be moved and drag it to the required position. To undock the **Ribbon**, right-click on the blank space in the **Ribbon** and choose the **Undock** option. You can move, resize, anchor, and auto-hide the **Ribbon** using the shortcut menu that will be displayed when you right-click on the heading strip. To anchor the floating **Ribbon** to the left or right of the drawing area in the vertical position, right-click on the heading strip of the floating **Ribbon**; a shortcut menu is displayed. Choose the corresponding option from this shortcut menu. The **Auto-hide** option will hide the **Ribbon** into the heading strip and will display it only when you move the cursor over this strip.

You can customize the display of tabs and panels in the **Ribbon**. To customize the **Ribbon**, right-click on any one of the tools in it; a shortcut menu will be displayed. On moving the cursor over one of the options, a flyout will be displayed with a tick mark before all options and the corresponding tab or panel will be displayed in the **Ribbon**. Select/clear appropriate option to display/hide a particular tab or panel.

Application Menu

The **Application Menu** is available at the top-left of the AutoCAD window. It contains some of the tools that are available in the **Standard** toolbar. Click on the down arrow on the **Application Menu** to display the tools, as shown in Figure 1-13. You can search for tools or commands by using the search field on the top of the **Application Menu**. To search a tool or command, enter its complete or partial name in the search field; the list of related tools and commands will be displayed. If you click on a tool from the list, the corresponding command will get activated.

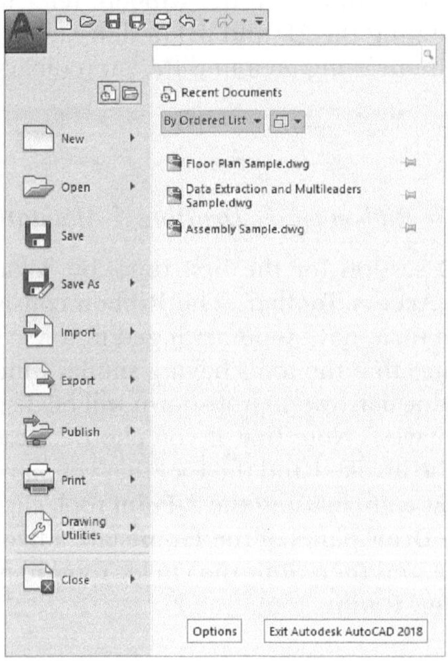

*Figure 1-13 The **Application Menu***

By default, the **Recent Documents** button is chosen in the **Application Menu**. Therefore, the recently opened drawings will be listed. If you have opened multiple drawing files, choose the

Open Documents button; the documents that are opened will be listed in the **Application Menu**. To set the preferences of the file, choose the **Options** button available at the bottom-right of the **Application Menu**. To exit AutoCAD, choose the **Exit Autodesk AutoCAD 2018** button next to the **Options** button.

Tool Palettes

AutoCAD has provided **Tool Palettes** as an easy and convenient way of placing and sharing hatch patterns and blocks in the current drawing. By default, the **Tool Palettes** are not displayed. Choose the **Tool Palettes** button from the **Palettes** panel in the **View** tab or choose the CTRL+3 keys to display the **Tool Palettes** as a window in the drawing area. You can resize the **Tool Palettes** using the resizing cursor that is displayed when you place the cursor on the top or bottom extremity of the **Tool Palettes**. The **Tool Palettes** are discussed in detail in Chapter 12, Hatching Drawings.

Menu Bar

You can also select commands from the menu bar. Menu bar is not displayed by default. To display the menu bar, click on the down arrow in the **Quick Access Toolbar**; a flyout is displayed. Choose the **Show Menu Bar** option from it; the menu bar will be displayed. As you move the cursor over the menu bar, different tabs are highlighted. You can choose the desired item by left-clicking on it; the corresponding menu is displayed directly under the title. For example, to draw an ellipse using the **Center** option, choose the **Draw** menu and then choose the **Ellipse** option; a cascading menu will be displayed. From the cascading menu, choose the **Center** option. In this text, the command selection sequence will be referenced as choosing **Draw > Ellipse > Center** from the menu bar.

Toolbar

Toolbars are not displayed by default. To display a toolbar, choose **Tools > Toolbars > AutoCAD** from the **Menu Bar**; a list of toolbars will be displayed. Select the required toolbar. Figure 1-14 shows the **Draw** toolbar invoked.

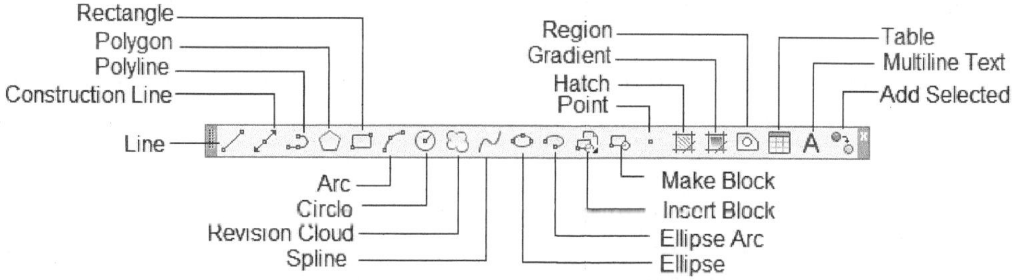

*Figure 1-14 The **Draw** toolbar*

Shortcut Menu

AutoCAD has provided shortcut menus as an easy and convenient way of invoking the recently used tools. These shortcut menus are context-sensitive, which means that the tools in shortcut menus are dependent on the place/object for which they are displayed. A shortcut menu is invoked by right-clicking and is displayed at the cursor location. You can right-click anywhere in the drawing area to display the general shortcut menu. It generally contains an option to select the previously invoked tool again, apart from the common tools for Windows, refer to Figure 1-15.

If you right-click in the drawing area while a command is active, a shortcut menu is displayed, containing the options of that particular command. Figure 1-16 shows the shortcut menu when the **Polyline** tool is active.

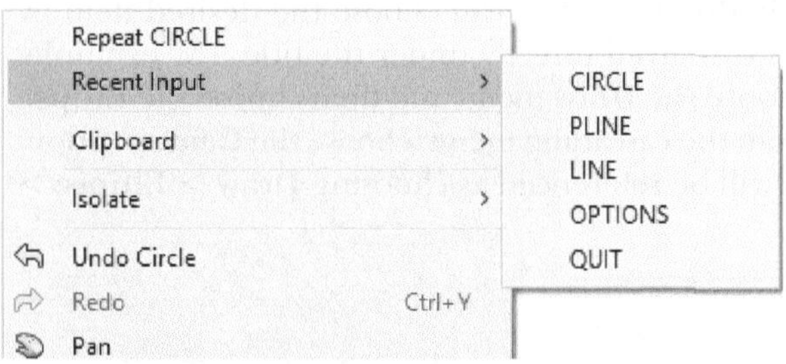

Figure 1-15 Partial view of the shortcut menu with the recently used tools

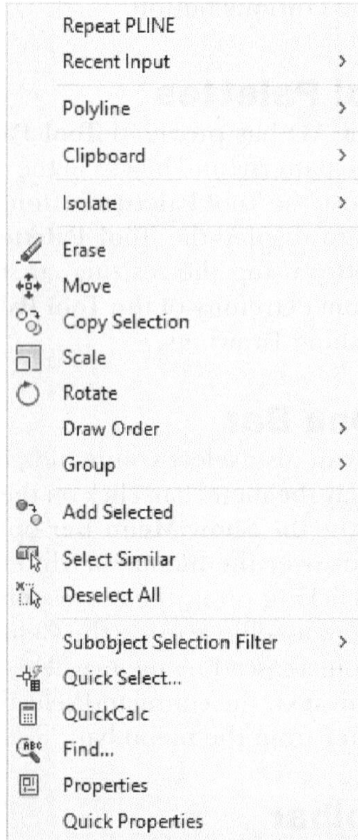

Figure 1-16 *Shortcut menu with the* ***Polyline*** *tool active*

File Tabs

The **File Tabs** button is available in the **Interface** panel of the **View** tab. It is used to toggle the display of the File tab bar which displays all opened files. You can easily switch between multiple opened drawings by clicking on them.

You can also create a new drawing file by clicking on the (+) sign available at the end of the File tab bar. When you click on the (+) sign, the **New Tab** will be displayed. You can create a new drawing by clicking on the **Start Drawing** icon on the left side of the **New Tab** in **Get Started** area. Figure 1-17 shows the **File Tabs** button chosen in the **Ribbon**.

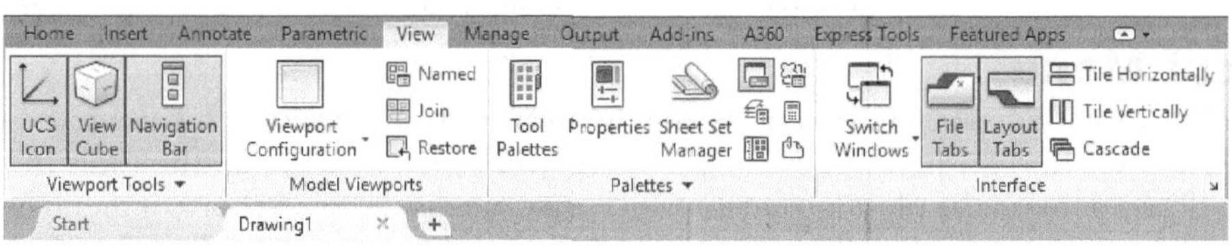

Figure 1-17 *The* ***File Tabs*** *button chosen in the* ***Ribbon***

In the File tab bar, all the added tabs get arranged in the sequence in which the respective drawings are opened or created. You can change the sequence of tabs in the File tab bar by using the left mouse button. To do so, press and hold the left mouse button on any tab and drag it to the desired location, refer to Figure 1-18.

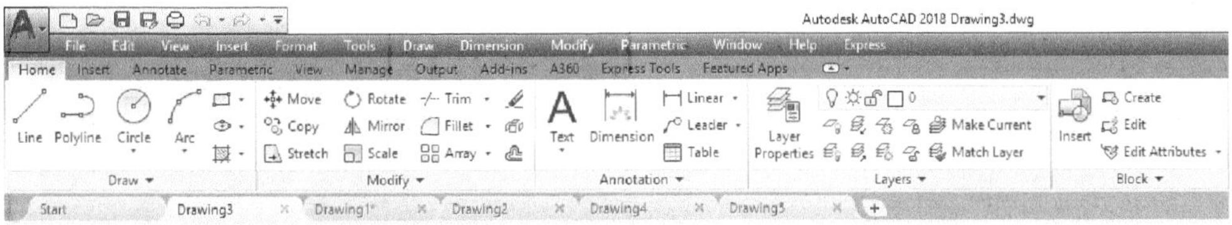

Figure 1-18 *Tab dragged in the File tab bar*

In AutoCAD if a large number of files are opened, some of the files will not be visible in the File tab bar and therefore an overflow symbol will be displayed on its right end, refer to Figure 1-19. To open any tab which is not visible in the File tab bar, click on the overflow symbol; the names of all the tabs will be displayed in a flyout, refer to Figure 1-19. Also, when you move the cursor on a tab name, previews of the Model, Layout1, Layout2 will be displayed, refer to Figure 1-19. You can open the desired environment by clicking on its preview.

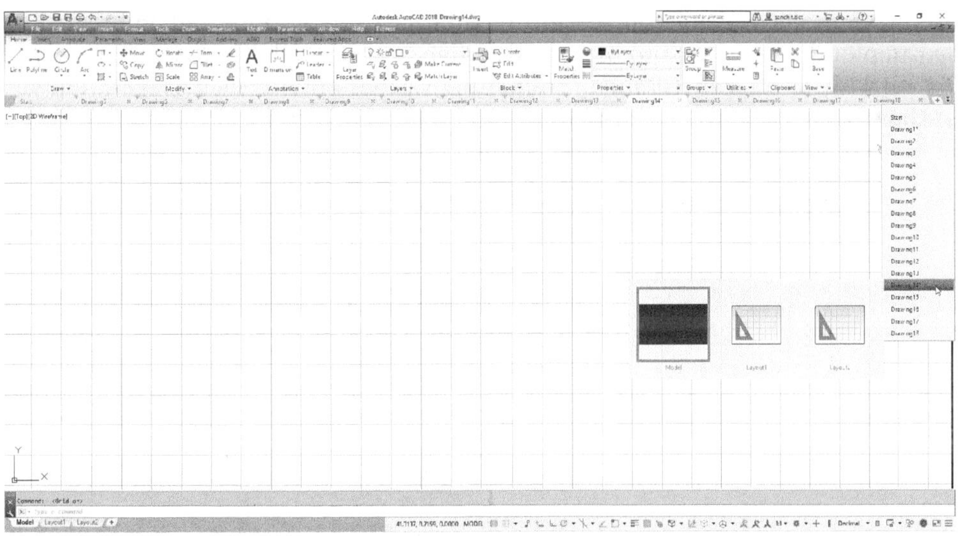

Figure 1-19 *Flyout with file tab names and preview of their respective drawings*

If you move the cursor over a file tab, the preview of the model and layouts will be displayed. When you move the cursor over any preview, the corresponding preview will be displayed in the drawing area, refer to Figure 1-20.

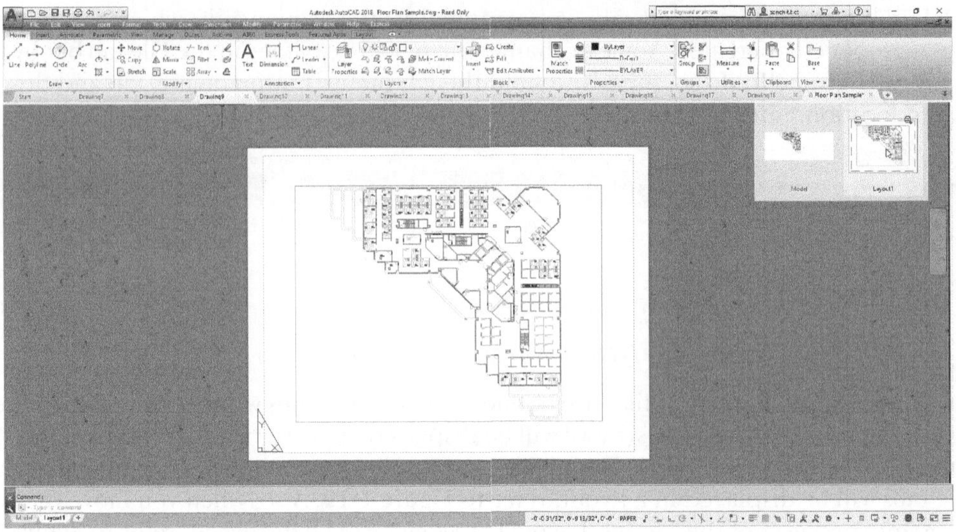

Figure 1-20 *Previews of model and layouts*

There are two buttons available on the top of preview window: **Plot** and **Publish**. By using **Plot**, you can plot the drawing, and by using **Publish**, you can publish the drawing. When you right-click on a file tab, a shortcut menu containing various options such as **New**, **Open**, **Save**, **Save As**, **Close**, and so on will be displayed, refer to Figure 1-21. You can choose the option from the shortcut menu as per your requirement.

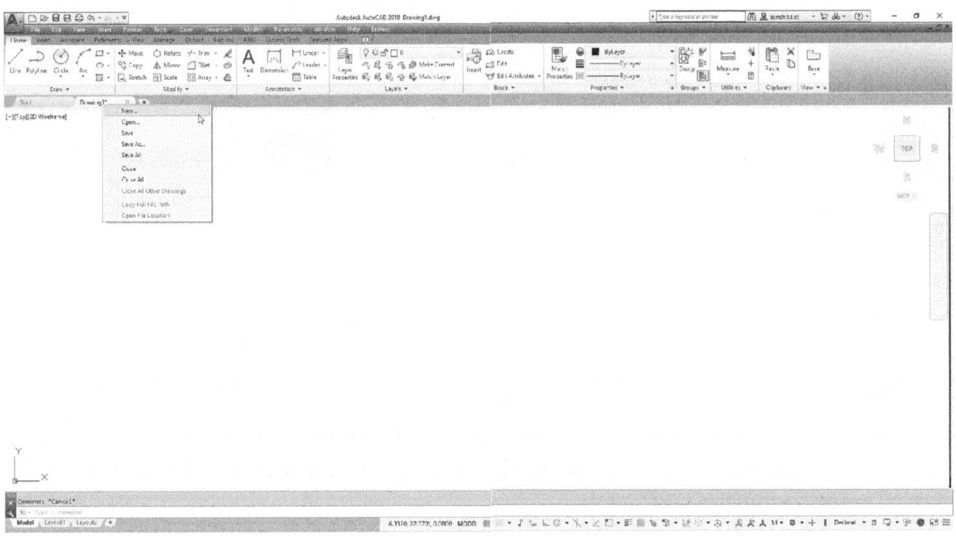

Figure 1-21 *Shortcut menu displayed on right-clicking on the File tab bar*

There are two icons displayed on the file tab: Asterisk icon and Lock icon. The Asterisk icon * indicates that the file is modified but not saved. The Lock icon indicates that the file is locked and the changes cannot be saved with the original file name, although you can use the **Save As** tool to create another copy.

To open a drawing as a locked file, first choose the **Open** option from the shortcut menu displayed on right-clicking over the file tab; the **Select File** dialog box will be displayed. Select the desired file and then select the **Open Read-Only** option from the **Open** drop-down list, as shown in Figure 1-22. On doing so, the file will be opened as a locked file in the drawing area. You can also open the file as a locked file by using the **Open** button from the **Quick Access Toolbar**.

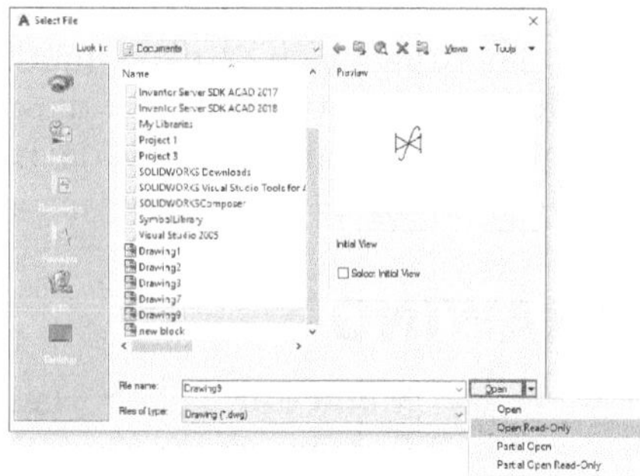

Figure 1-22 *Selecting the **Open Read-Only** option*

AutoCAD DIALOG BOXES

There are certain commands, which when invoked, display a dialog box. A dialog box is a convenient method of a user interface. When you choose an item in the menu bar with the ellipses [...], it displays the dialog box. For example, the **Options** option in the **Tools** menu displays the **Options** dialog box. A dialog box contains a number of parts like the dialog label, radio buttons, text or edit boxes, check boxes, slider bars, image boxes, and command buttons. These components are also referred to as tiles. Some of the components of a dialog box are shown in Figure 1-23.

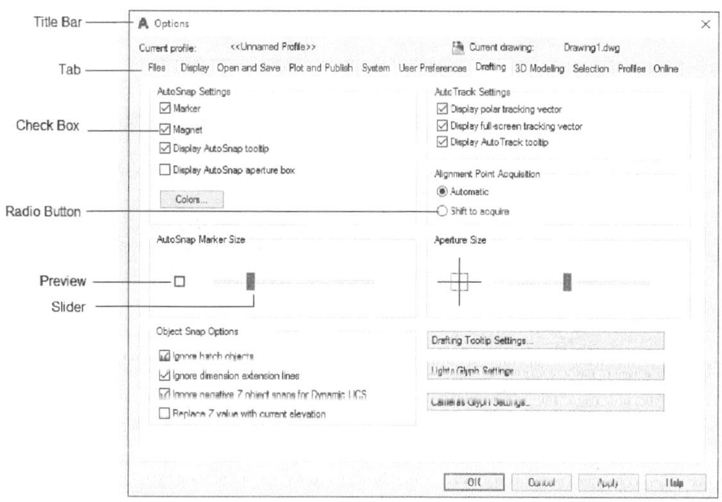

Figure 1-23 *The components of a dialog box*

You can select the desired tile of the dialog box by using the pointing device, which is represented by an arrow when a dialog box is invoked. The titlebar displays the name of the dialog box. The tabs specify the various sections with a group of related options under them. The check boxes are toggle options for making the particular option available or unavailable. The drop-down list displays an item and an arrow on the right which when selected displays a list of items to be chosen from.

You can make a selection in the radio buttons. Only one can be selected at a time. The image displays the preview image of the item selected. The text box is an area where you can enter a text such as a file name. It is also called an edit box because you can make changes to the text entered. In some dialog boxes, there is the [...] button, which displays another related dialog box. There are certain buttons (**OK**, **Cancel**, **Help**) at the bottom of the dialog box. The function of each of these buttons is implied in their name. The button with a dark border is the default button. The dialog box has the **Help** button for getting help on the various features of the dialog box.

STARTING A NEW DRAWING

Application Menu: New > Drawing	**Menu Bar:** File > New
Quick Access Toolbar: New	**Command:** NEW or QNEW

You can open a new drawing using the **New** tool in the **Quick Access Toolbar**. When you invoke the **New** tool, by default AutoCAD will display the **Select template** dialog box, as shown in Figure 1-24. This dialog box displays a list of default templates available in AutoCAD. The default selected template is ***acad.dwt***, which starts the 2D drawing environment. You can select the ***acad3D.dwt*** template to start the 3D modeling environment. Alternatively, you can select any other template to start a new drawing that will use the settings of the selected template. You can also open any drawing without using any template either in metric or imperial system. To do so, choose the down arrow on the right of the **Open** button and choose the **Open with no Template-Metric** option or the **Open with no Template-Imperial** option from the drop-down.

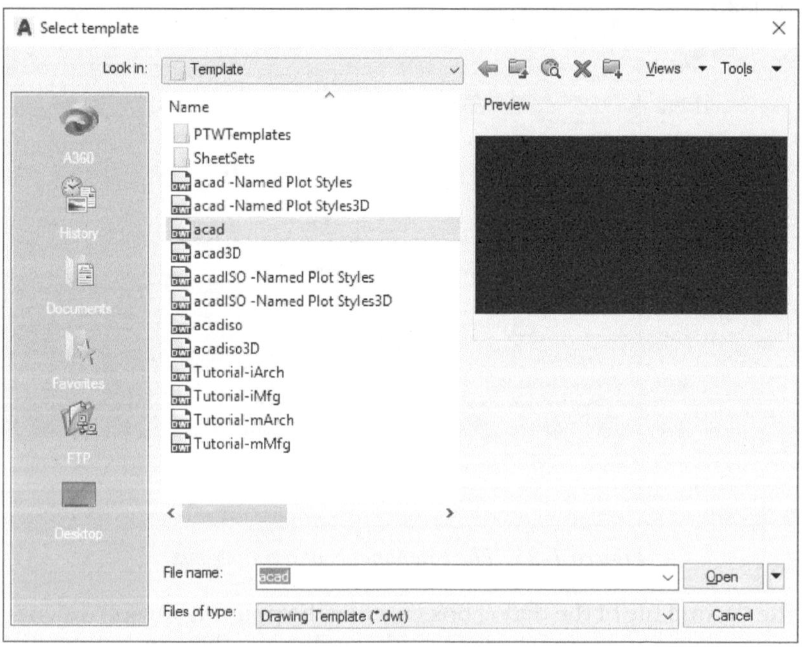

Figure 1-24 *The* ***Select template*** *dialog box*

You can also open a new drawing using the **Start from Scratch**, **Use a Template**, or **Use a Wizard** option from the **Create New Drawing** dialog box. By default, this dialog box is not invoked. To invoke the **Create New Drawing** dialog box, enter **STARTUP** in the command window and then enter **1** as the new value for this system variable. After setting **1** as the new value for the system variable, whenever you invoke the **New** tool, the **Create New Drawing** dialog box will be displayed, as shown in Figure 1-25. The options in this dialog box are discussed next.

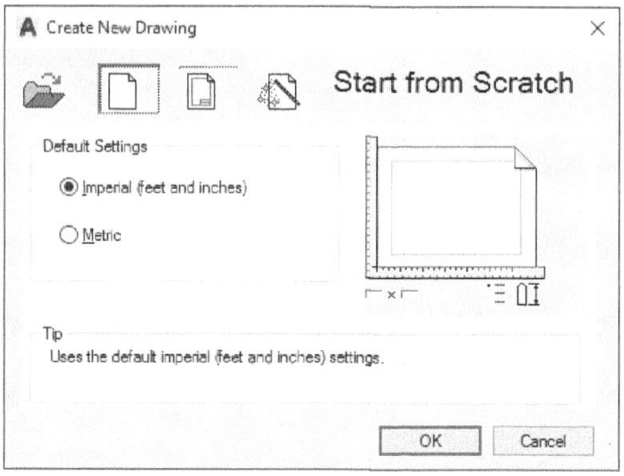

***Figure 1-25** The **Create New Drawing** dialog box*

Open a Drawing

By default, this option is not available. This option will be available when you start a new session of AutoCAD. This option is discussed later in this chapter.

Start from Scratch

When you choose the **Start from Scratch** button, AutoCAD provides you with options to start a new drawing that contains the default AutoCAD setup for Imperial (*Acad.dwt*) or Metric drawings (*Acadiso.dwt*). If you select the Imperial default setting, the limits are 12X9, text height is 0.20, and dimensions and linetype scale factors are 1.

Use a Template

When you choose the **Use a Template** button in the **Create New Drawing** dialog box, AutoCAD displays a list of templates, as shown in Figure 1-26. The default template file is *Acad.dwt* or *Acadiso.dwt*, depending on the installation. You can directly start a new file in the 2D sketching environment by selecting the *acad.dwt* or *acadiso.dwt* template. If you use a template file, the new drawing will have the same settings as specified in the template file. All the drawing parameters of the new drawing such as units, limits, and other settings are already set according to the template file used. The preview of the template file selected is displayed in the dialog box. You can also define your own template files that are customized to your requirements (refer to Chapter 15, *Template Drawings*). To differentiate the template files from the drawing files, the template files have a *.dwt* extension whereas the drawing files have a *.dwg* extension. Any drawing file can be saved as a template file. You can use the **Browse** button to select other template files. When you choose the **Browse** button, the **Select a template file** dialog box is displayed with the **Template** folder open, displaying all the template files.

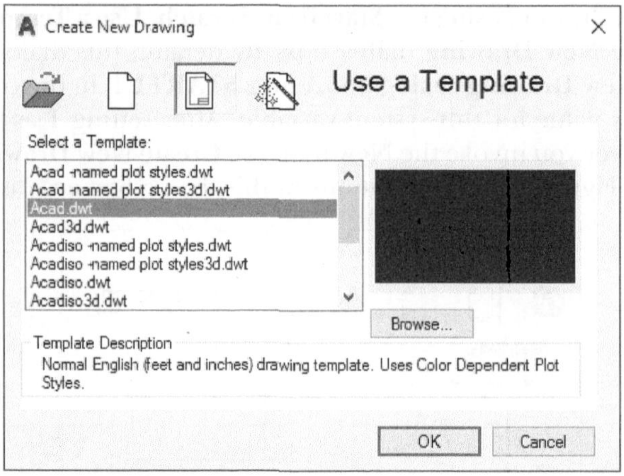

***Figure 1-26** The default templates displayed on choosing the **Use a Template** button*

Use a Wizard

The **Use a Wizard** option allows you to set the initial drawing settings before actually starting a new drawing. When you choose the **Use a Wizard** button, AutoCAD provides you with the option for using the **Advanced Setup** or **Quick Setup**, as shown in Figure 1-27. In the **Advanced Setup**, you can set the units, limits, and the different types of settings for a drawing. In the **Quick Setup**, you can specify the units and the limits of the work area.

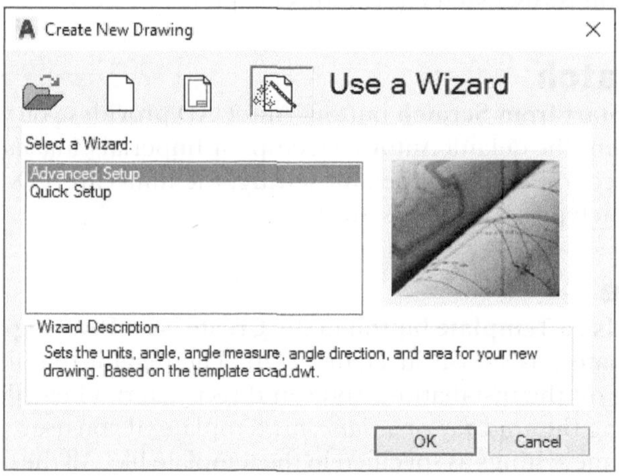

***Figure 1-27** The wizard options displayed on choosing the **Use a Wizard** button*

Advanced Setup

This option allows you to preselect the parameters of a new drawing such as the units of linear and angular measurements, type and direction of angular measurements, approximate area desired for the drawing, precision for displaying the units after decimal, and so on. When you select the **Advanced Setup** option from the **Create New Drawing** dialog box and choose the **OK** button, the **Advanced Setup** wizard is displayed. In the wizard, the **Units** page is displayed by default, as shown in Figure 1-28.

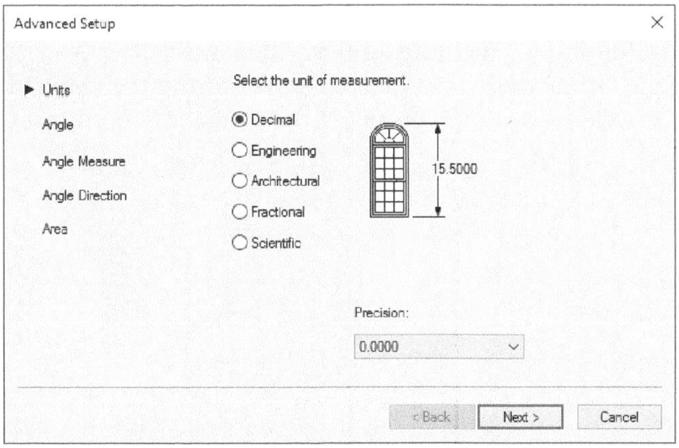

Figure 1-28 The ***Units*** *page of the* ***Advanced Setup*** *wizard*

This page is used to set the units for measurement in the current drawing. You can select the required unit of measurement by selecting the respective radio button. You will notice that the preview image is modified accordingly. The different units of measurement you can choose from are Decimal, Engineering, Architectural, Fractional, and Scientific. You can also set the precision for the measurement units by selecting the required option from the **Precision** drop-down list.

Choose the **Next** button to open the **Angle** page, as shown in Figure 1-29. You will notice that an arrow appears on the left of **Angle** in the **Advanced Setup** wizard. This implies that this page is current.

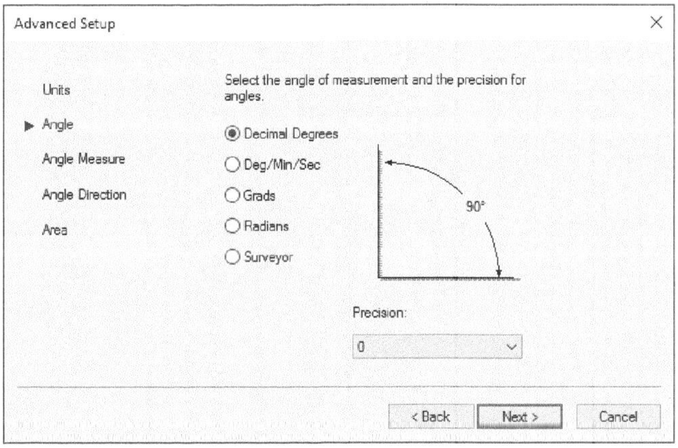

Figure 1-29 The ***Angle*** *page of the* ***Advanced Setup*** *wizard*

This page is used to set the units for angular measurements and its precision. The units for angle measurement are Decimal Degrees, Deg/Min/Sec, Grads, Radians, and Surveyor. The units for angle measurement can be set by selecting any one of these radio buttons as required. The preview of the selected angular unit is displayed on the right of the radio buttons. The precision format changes automatically in the **Precision** drop-down list depending on the angle measuring system selected. You can then select the precision from the drop-down list.

The next page is the **Angle Measure** page, as shown in Figure 1-30. This page is used to select the direction of the baseline from which the angles will be measured. You can also set your own direction by selecting the **Other** radio button and then entering the value in the corresponding edit box. This edit box is enabled when you select the **Other** radio button.

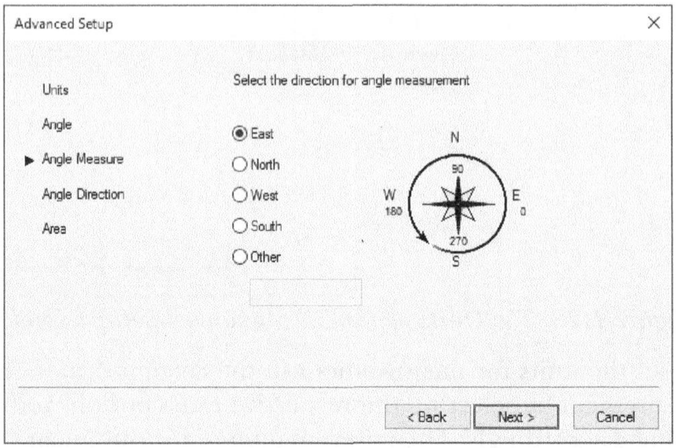

***Figure 1-30** The **Angle Measure** page of the **Advanced Setup** wizard*

Choose the **Next** button to display the **Angle Direction** page, as shown in Figure 1-31, to set the orientation for the angle measurement. By default, the angles are positive, if measured in a counterclockwise direction. This is because the **Counter-Clockwise** radio button is selected. If you select the **Clockwise** radio button, the angles will be considered positive when measured in the clockwise direction.

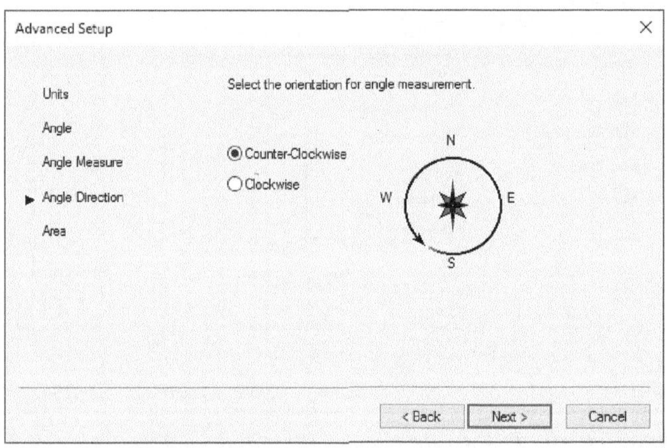

***Figure 1-31** The **Angle Direction** page of the **Advanced Setup** wizard*

To set the limits of the drawing, choose the **Next** button; the **Area** page will be displayed, as shown in Figure 1-32. You can enter the width and length of the drawing area in the respective edit boxes.

Note

*Even after you increase the limits of the drawing, the drawing display area is not increased. You need to invoke the **Zoom All** tool from the Navigation Bar to increase the drawing display area.*

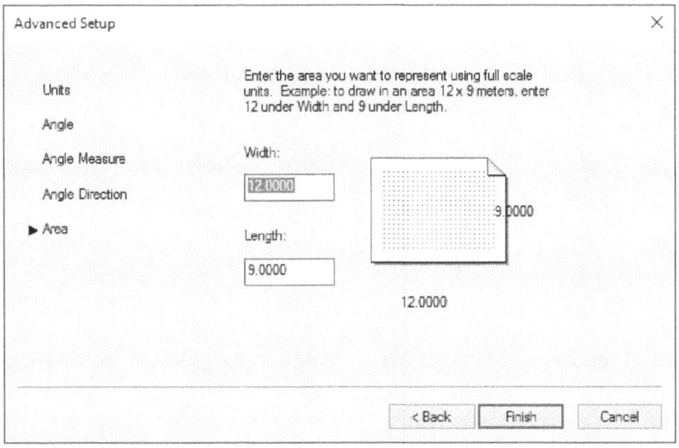

***Figure 1-32** The **Area** page of the **Advanced Setup** wizard*

Quick Setup

When you select the **Quick Setup** option from the **Create New Drawing** dialog box and choose the **OK** button, the **QuickSetup** wizard is displayed. This wizard has two pages: **Units** and **Area**. The **Units** page is opened by default, as shown in Figure 1-33. The options in the **Units** page are similar to those in the **Units** page of the **Advanced Setup** wizard. The only difference is that you cannot set the precision for the units in this wizard.

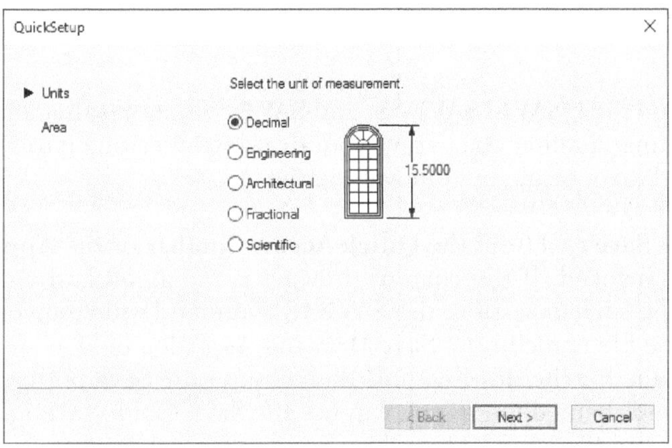

***Figure 1-33** The **Units** page of the **QuickSetup** wizard*

Choose the **Next** button to display the **Area** page, as shown in Figure 1-34. The **Area** page of the **QuickSetup** wizard is similar to that of the **Advanced Setup** wizard. In this page, you can set the drawing limits.

Tip

*When you open an AutoCAD session, a drawing opens automatically. But you can open a new drawing using options such as **Start from Scratch** and **Use a Wizard** before entering into AutoCAD environment using the **Startup** dialog box. As mentioned earlier, the display of the **Startup** dialog box is turned off by default. Refer to the section of **Starting a New Drawing** to know how to turn on the display of this dialog box.*

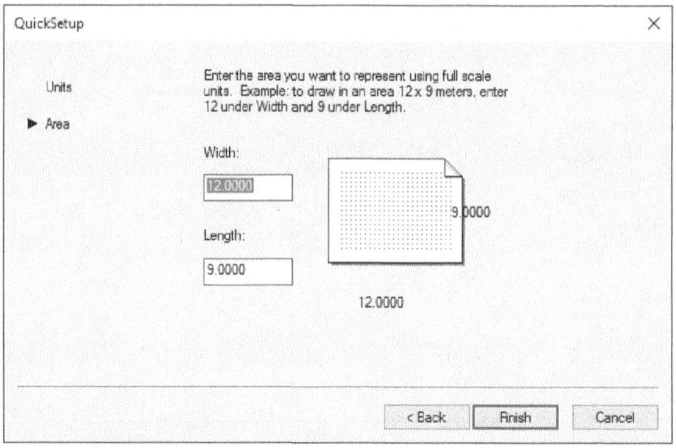

*Figure 1-34 The **Area** page of the **QuickSetup** wizard*

SAVING YOUR WORK

Application Menu: Save, Save As	**Menu Bar:** File > Save or Save As
Quick Access Toolbar: Save or Save As	**Command:** QSAVE, SAVEAS, SAVE

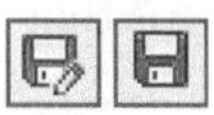

You must save your work before you exit the drawing editor or turn off your system. Also, it is recommended that you save your drawings in regular intervals, so that in the event of a power failure or an editing error, all work saved before the problem started is retained.

AutoCAD has provided the **QSAVE**, **SAVEAS**, and **SAVE** commands that allow you to save your work. Also, these commands allow you to save your drawing by writing it to a permanent storage device, such as a hard drive or in any removable drive.

When you choose the **Save** tool from the **Quick Access Toolbar** or the **Application Menu**, the **QSAVE** command is invoked. If the current drawing is unnamed and you save the drawing for the first time in the current session, the **SAVEAS** command will be invoked and you will be prompted to enter the file name in the **Save Drawing As** dialog box, as shown in Figure 1-35. You can enter the name for the drawing and then choose the **Save** button. If you have saved a drawing file once and then edited it, you can use the **Save** tool to save it, without the system prompting you to enter a file name. This allows you to do a quick save.

When you choose the **Save As** tool from the **Application Menu** or the **Quick Access Toolbar**, the **Save Drawing As** dialog box is displayed, similar to that shown in Figure 1-35. Even if the drawing has been saved with a file name, this tool gives you an option to save it with a different file name. In addition to saving the drawing, it sets the name of the current drawing to the file name you specify, which is displayed in the title bar. This tool is used when you want to save a previously saved drawing with a different file name. You can also use this tool when you make certain changes to a template and want to save the changed template drawing but leave the original template unchanged.

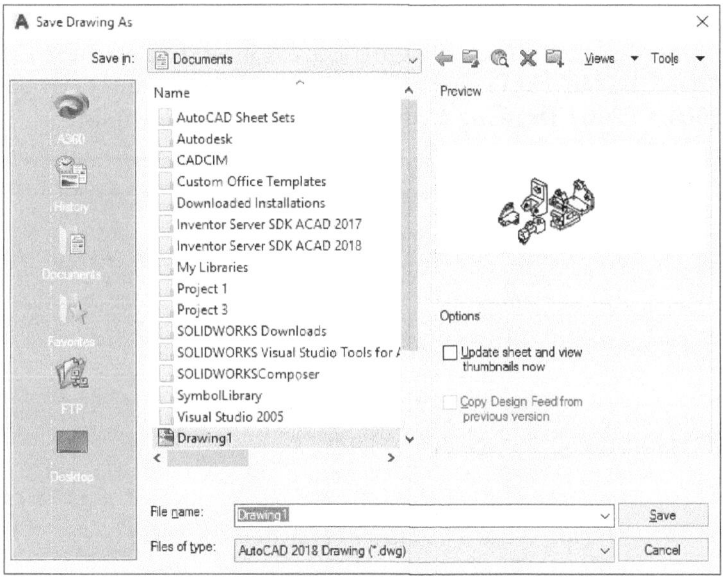

***Figure 1-35** The **Save Drawing As** dialog box*

Save Drawing As Dialog Box

The **Save Drawing As** dialog box displays the information related to the drawing files on your system. The various components of the dialog box are described next.

Places List

A column of icons is displayed on the left side of the dialog box. These icons contain the shortcuts to the folders that are frequently used. You can quickly save your drawings in one of these folders. The **History** folder displays the list of the most recently saved drawings. You can save your personal drawings in the **Documents** or the **Favorites** folder. The **FTP** folder displays the list of the various FTP sites that are available for saving the drawing. By default, no FTP sites are shown in the dialog box. To add a FTP site to the dialog box, choose the **Add/Modify FTP Locations** option from the **Tools** drop-down. The **Desktop** folder displays the list of contents on the desktop. You can add a new folder in this list for an easy access by simply dragging the folder on to the Places list area. You can rearrange all these folders by dragging them and then placing them at the desired locations. It is also possible to remove the folders, which are not in frequent use. Right-click on the particular folder and then select **Remove** from the shortcut menu. Now, you can also save the document to a new location of Autodesk Cloud. The option for saving the document is discussed next.

File name Edit Box

To save your work, enter the name of the drawing in the **File name** edit box by typing the file name or selecting it from the drop-down list. If you select the file name, it automatically appears in the **File name** edit box. If you have already assigned a name to the drawing, the current drawing name is taken as the default name. If the drawing is unnamed, the default name *Drawing1* is displayed in the **File name** edit box. You can also choose the down arrow located on the right of the edit box to display the names of the previously saved drawings and choose a name here.

Files of type Drop-down List

The **Files of type** drop-down list, refer to Figure 1-36, is used to specify the drawing format in which you want to save the file. For example, to save the file as an AutoCAD 2004 drawing file, select **AutoCAD 2004/LT2004 Drawing (*.dwg)** from the drop-down list.

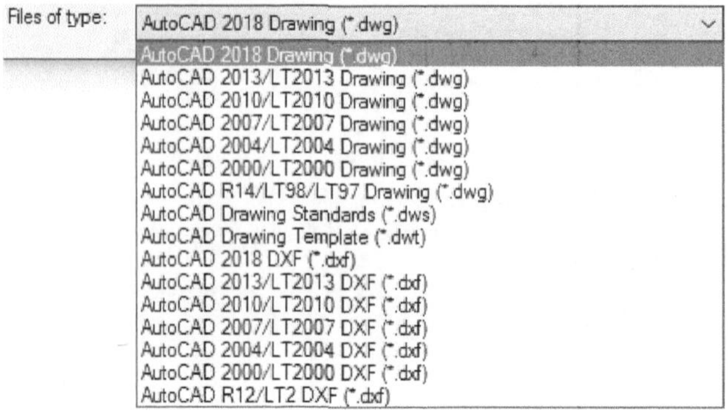

***Figure 1-36** The **Files of type** drop-down list*

Save in Drop-down List

The current drive and path information is listed in the **Save in** drop-down list. AutoCAD will initially save the drawing in the default folder, but if you want to save the drawing in a different folder, you have to specify the path. For example, to save the present drawing as *house* in the *C1* folder, choose the arrow button in the **Save in** drop-down list to display the drop-down list. Select **C**: from the drop-down list; all folders in the C drive will be listed in the **Name** list box. Double-click on the **C1** folder, if it is already listed there or create a folder C1 by choosing the **Create New Folder** button. Select *house* from the list, if it is already listed there, or enter it in the **File name** edit box and then choose the **Save** button. Your drawing (*house*) will be saved in the *C1* folder (*C:\C1\house.dwg*). Similarly, to save the drawing in the D drive, select **D:** in the **Save in** drop-down list.

Tip

The file name you enter to save a drawing should match its contents. This helps you to remember the drawing details and make it easier to refer them later. Also, the file name can be 255 characters long and can contain spaces and punctuation marks.

Views drop-down list

The **Views** drop-down list has the options for the type of listing of files and displaying the preview images, refer to Figure 1-37.

List, Details, and Thumbnails Options

If you choose the **Details** option, it will display the detailed information about the files (size, type, date, and time of modification) in the **Name** list box. In the detailed information, if you click on the **Name** label, the files are listed with the names in alphabetical order. If you double-click on the **Name** label, the files will be listed in the reverse order. Similarly, if you click on the **Size** label, the files are listed according to their size in ascending order. Double-clicking on the **Size** label will list the files

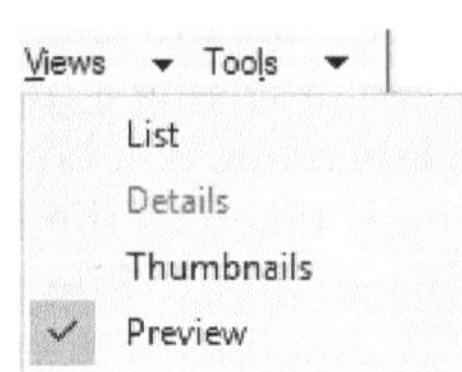

***Figure 1-37** The **Views** drop-down list*

in descending order of size. Similarly, you can click on the **Type** label or the **Date modified** label to list the files accordingly. If you choose the **List** option, all files present in the current folder will be listed in the **File** list box. If you select the **Thumbnails** option, the list box displays the preview of all the drawings, along with their names displayed at the bottom of the drawing preview.

Create New Folder Button

If you choose the **Create New Folder** button, AutoCAD creates a new folder under the name **New Folder**. The new folder is displayed in the **Name** list box. You can accept the name or change it to your requirement. You can also use the ALT+5 keys to create a new folder.

Up one level Button

The **Up one level** button displays the folders that are up by one level. For example, if you are in the *Sample* subfolder of the *AutoCAD 2018* folder, then choosing the **Up one level** button will take you to the *AutoCAD 2018* folder. You can also use the ALT+2 keys to do the same.

Search the Web Button

It displays the **Browse the Web - Save** dialog box that enables you to access and store AutoCAD files on the Internet. You can also use the ALT+3 keys to browse the Web when this dialog box is available on the screen.

Tools drop-down list

The **Tools** drop-down list, refer to Figure 1-38, has an option for adding or modifying the FTP sites. These sites can then be browsed from the FTP shortcut in the Places list. The **Add Current Folder to Places** and **Add to Favorites** options add the folder displayed in the **Save in** edit box to the Places list or to the Favorites folder. The **Options** button displays the **Saveas Options** dialog box where you can save the proxy images of the custom objects. It has the **DWG Options** and **DXF Options** tabs. The **Digital Signatures** button displays the **Digital Signatures** dialog box, which is used to configure the security options of the drawing.

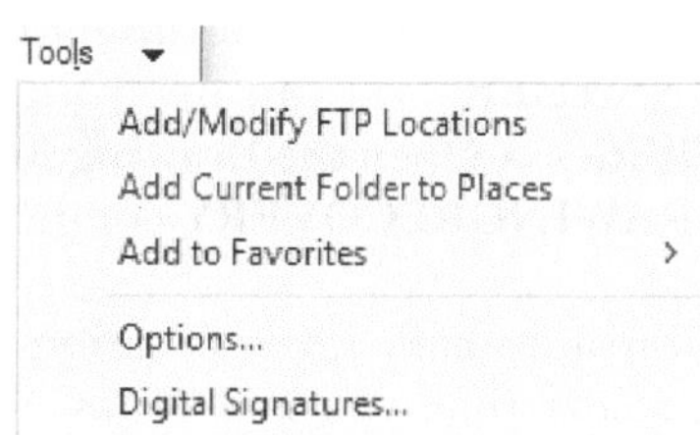

Figure 1-38 *The **Tools** drop-down list*

AUTOMATIC TIMED SAVE

AutoCAD allows you to save your work automatically at specific intervals. To change the time intervals, you can specify the intervals duration in minutes in the **Minutes between saves** edit box in the **File Safety Precautions** area in the **Options** dialog box (**Open and Save** tab). This dialog box can be invoked by choosing the **Options** button from the **Application Menu**. Depending on the power supply, hardware, and type of drawings, you should decide on an appropriate time and assign it to this variable. AutoCAD saves the drawing with the file extension *.sv$*. You can also change the time interval by using the **SAVETIME** system variable.

Tip

*Although the automatic save feature saves your drawing after a certain time interval, you should not completely depend on it because the procedure for converting the ac$ file into a drawing file is cumbersome. Therefore, it is recommended that you save your files regularly using the **QSAVE** or **SAVEAS** commands.*

CREATING BACKUP FILES

If the drawing file already exists and you use **Save** or **Save As** tool to update the current drawing, AutoCAD creates a backup file. AutoCAD takes the previous copy of the drawing and changes it from a file type *.dwg* to *.bak*, and the updated drawing is saved as a drawing file with the *.dwg* extension. For example, if the name of the drawing is *myproj.dwg*, AutoCAD will change it to *myproj.bak* as a backup file and save the current drawing as *myproj.dwg*.

Changing Automatic Timed Saved and Backup Files into AutoCAD Format

Sometimes, you may need to change the automatic timed saved and backup files into AutoCAD format. To change a backup file into AutoCAD format, open the folder, in which you have saved the backup or the automatic timed saved drawing. Choose the **View** tab and select the **File name extensions** check box from the **Show/hide** area. Rename the automatic saved drawing or the backup file with a different name and also change the extension of the drawing from *.sv$* or *.bak* to *.dwg*.

Using the Drawing Recovery Manager to Recover Files

The files that are saved automatically can also be retrieved by using the **DRAWING RECOVERY MANAGER**. You can open the **DRAWING RECOVERY MANAGER** by choosing **Drawing Utilities > Open the Drawing Recovery Manager** from the **Application Menu** or by entering the **DRAWINGRECOVERY** command at the command prompt.

If the automatic save operation is performed in a drawing and the system crashes accidentally, the next time you run AutoCAD, the **Drawing Recovery** message box will be displayed, as shown in Figure 1-39. The message box informs you that the program unexpectedly failed and you can open the most suitable among the backup files created by AutoCAD. Choose the **Close** button from the **Drawing Recovery** message box; the **DRAWING RECOVERY MANAGER** is displayed on the left of the drawing area, as shown in Figure 1-40.

The **Backup Files** rollout lists the original files, the backup files, and the automatically saved files. Select a file; its preview will be displayed in the **Preview** rollout. Also, the information corresponding to the selected file will be displayed in the **Details** rollout. To open a backup file, double-click on its name in the **Backup Files** rollout. Alternatively, right-click on the file name and then choose **Open** from the shortcut menu. It is recommended that you save the backup file at the desired location before you start working on it.

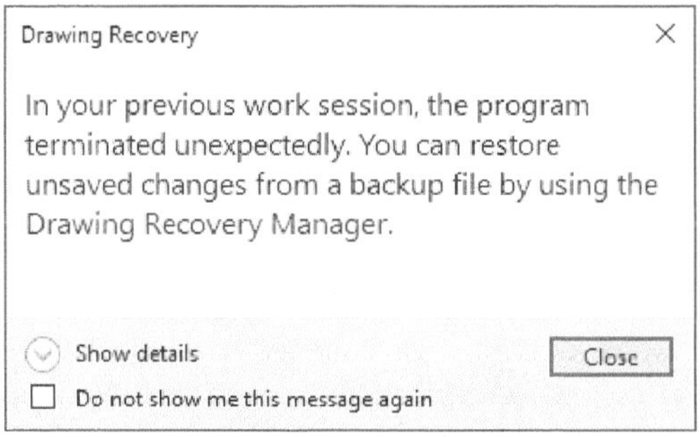

*Figure 1-39 The **Drawing Recovery** message box*

*Figure 1-40 The **DRAWING RECOVERY MANAGER***

CLOSING A DRAWING

You can close the current drawing file without actually quitting AutoCAD by choosing **Close > Current Drawing** from the **Application Menu** or by entering **CLOSE** at the command prompt. If multiple drawing files are opened, choose **Close > All Drawings** from the **Application Menu**. If you have not saved the drawing after making the last changes to it and you invoke the **CLOSE** command, AutoCAD displays a dialog box that allows you to save the drawing before closing. This box gives you an option to discard the current drawing or the changes made to it. It also gives you an option to cancel the command. After closing the drawing, you are still in AutoCAD from where you can open a new or an already saved drawing file. You can also use the close button (**X**) of the drawing area to close the drawing.

OPENING AN EXISTING DRAWING

Application Menu: Open > Drawing	**Quick Access Toolbar:** Open
Menu Bar: File > Open	**Command:** OPEN

You can open an existing drawing file that has been saved previously. There are three methods that can be used to open a drawing file: by using the **Select File** dialog box, by using the **Create New Drawing** dialog box, and by dragging and dropping.

Opening an Existing Drawing Using the Select File Dialog Box

If you are already in the drawing editor and you want to open a drawing file, choose the **Open** tool from the **Quick Access Toolbar**; the **Select File** dialog box will be displayed, refer to Figure 1-41. You can select the drawing to be opened using this dialog box. This dialog box is similar to the standard dialog boxes. You can choose the file you want to open from the folder in which it is stored. You can change the folder from the **Look in** drop-down list. You can then select the name of the drawing from the list box or you can enter the name of the drawing file you want to open in the **File name** edit box. After selecting the drawing file, you can choose the **Open** button to open the file. Here, you can choose *Drawing1* from the list and then choose the **Open** button to open the drawing.

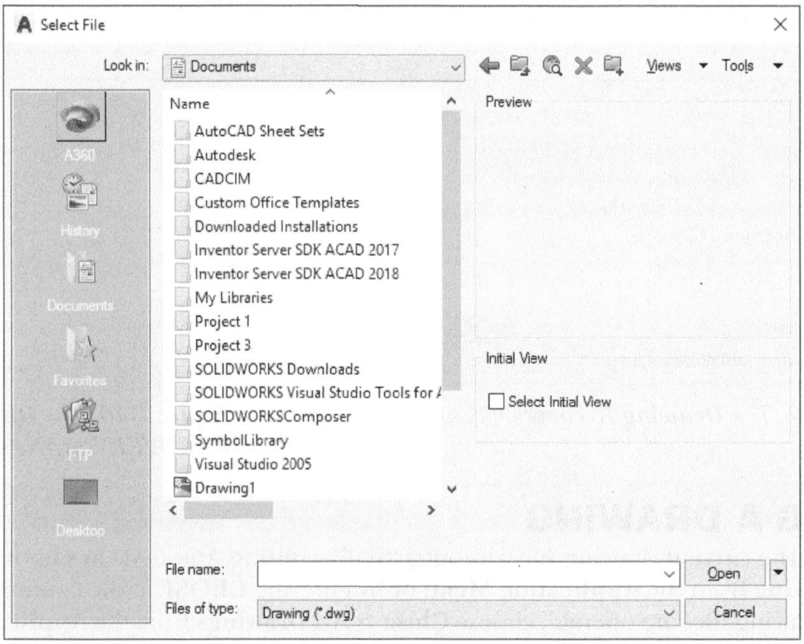

*Figure 1-41 The **Select File** dialog box*

When you select a file name, its image is displayed in the **Preview** box. If you are not sure about the file name of a particular drawing but know the contents, you can select the file names and look for the particular drawing in the **Preview** box. You can also change the file type by selecting it in the **Files of type** drop-down list. Apart from the *dwg* files, you can open the *dwt* (template) files or the *dxf* files. You have all the standard icons in the Places list that can be used to open drawing files from different locations. The **Open** button has a drop-down list, as shown in Figure 1-42. You can choose a method for opening the file using this drop-down list. These methods are discussed next.

*Figure 1-42 The **Open** drop-down list*

Open Read-Only

To view a drawing without altering it, you must select the **Open Read-Only** option from the drop-down list. In other words, read only protects the drawing file from changes. AutoCAD does not prevent you from editing the drawing, but if you try to save the opened drawing with the original file name, AutoCAD warns you that the drawing file is write protected. However, you can save the edited drawing to a file with a different file name using the **Save Drawing As** dialog box. This way you can preserve your drawing.

Partial Open

The **Partial Open** option enables you to open only a selected view or a selected layer of a selected drawing. This option can be used to edit small portions of a complicated drawing and then save it with the complete drawing. When you select the **Partial Open** option from the **Open** drop-down list, the **Partial Open** dialog box is displayed, as shown in Figure 1-43, which contains different views and layers of the selected drawing.

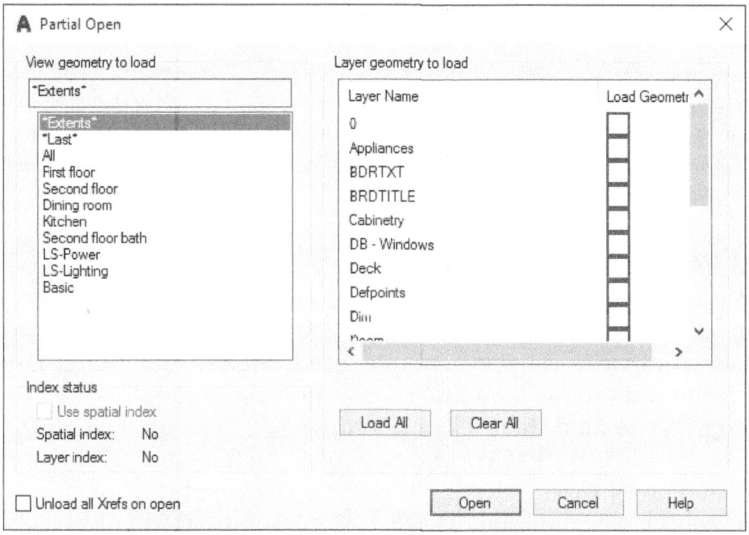

*Figure 1-43 The **Partial Open** dialog box*

When you select a check box for a layer and then choose the **Open** button, only the objects drawn in that particular layer for the drawing are displayed in the new drawing window. You can make the changes and then save it. For example, in the *C:/Program Files/Autodesk/AutoCAD 2018* folder, double-click on the **Sample** folder and then **Mechanical Sample** and select *Mechanical - Xref* from the list. Now, choose the down arrow on the right of the **Open** button to display the drop-down list and choose **Partial Open**. All the views and layers of this drawing are displayed in the **Partial Open** dialog box (click **Yes**, if AutoCAD prompts for read-only files). Select the check box on the right of the layer that you want to open. When you choose the **Open** button, after selecting the layers, only the selected layers of the drawing will be opened.

Note

The concept of layers is discussed in Chapter 4, Working with Drawing Aids.

Loading Additional Objects to Partially Opened Drawing

Once you have opened a part of a drawing and made the necessary changes, you may want to load additional objects or layers on the existing ones. This can be done by using the **PARTIALOAD** command, which can be invoked by choosing **File > Partial Load** from the menu bar or by entering **PARTIALOAD** at the command prompt. This command displays the **Partial Load** dialog box, which is similar to the **Partial Open** dialog box. You can choose another layer and the objects drawn in it will be added to the partially loaded drawing.

Note

1. *The **Partial Load** option is not enabled in the **File** menu unless a drawing is partially opened.*
2. *Loading a drawing partially is a good practice when you are working with objects on a specific layer in a large complicated drawing.*
3. *In the **Select File** dialog box, the preview of a drawing which was partially opened and then saved is not displayed.*

Tip

If a drawing was partially opened and saved previously, it is possible to open it again with the same layers and views. AutoCAD remembers the settings so that while opening a previously partially opened drawing, a dialog box is displayed prompting for an option to fully open it or restore the partially opened drawing.

Select Initial View

A view is defined as the way you look at an object. Select the **Select Initial View** check box if you want to load a specific view initially when AutoCAD loads the drawing. This option will work, if the drawing has saved views. This is generally used while working on a large complicated drawing, in which you want to work on a particular portion of the drawing. You can save that particular portion as a view and then select it to open the drawing next time. You can save a desired view by using AutoCAD's **VIEW** command (refer to "Creating Views" topic, Chapter 6). If the drawing has no saved views, selecting this option will load the last view. If you select the **Select Initial View** check box and then the **OK** button, AutoCAD will display the **Select Initial View** dialog box. You can select the view name from this dialog box, and AutoCAD will load the drawing with the selected view displayed.

Tip

*1. Apart from opening a drawing from the **Startup** dialog box or the **Select File** dialog box, you can also open a drawing from the **Application Menu**. By default, the **Recent Documents** option is selected in the **Application Menu**. As a result, the most recently opened drawings will be displayed and you can open the required file from it.*

2. It is possible to open an AutoCAD 2000 drawing in AutoCAD 2018. However, when you save this drawing, it is automatically converted and saved as an AutoCAD 2018 drawing file.

Opening an Existing Drawing Using the Startup Dialog Box

If you have configured the settings to show the **Startup** dialog box by setting the **STARTUP** system variable value as **1**, the **Startup** dialog box will be displayed every time you start a new AutoCAD session. The first button in this dialog box is the **Open a Drawing** button. When you choose this button, a list of the recently opened drawings will be displayed for you to select from it, as shown in Figure 1-44. Note that this button is activated only when this dialog box is displayed by default on starting a new session of AutoCAD. The **Browse** button displays the **Select File** dialog box, which allows you to browse another file.

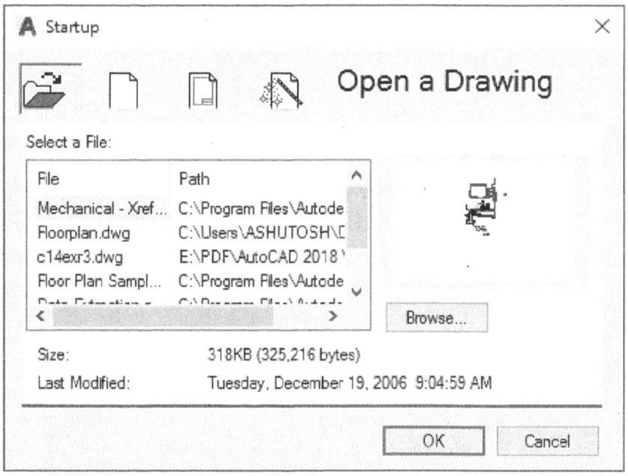

Figure 1-44 *List of the recently opened drawings*

Note

The display of the dialog boxes related to opening and saving drawings will be disabled, if the ***STARTUP*** *and the* ***FILEDIA*** *system variables are set to 0. The initial value of these variables is 1.*

Opening an Existing Drawing Using the Drag and Drop Method

You can also open an existing drawing in AutoCAD by dragging it from the Window Explorer and dropping it into AutoCAD. If you drop the selected drawing in the drawing area, the drawing will be inserted as a block and as a result, you cannot modify it. But if you drag the drawing from the Window Explorer and drop it anywhere other than the drawing area, AutoCAD will display the selected drawing.

QUITTING AutoCAD

You can exit the AutoCAD program by using the **EXIT** or **QUIT** commands. Even if you have an active command, you can choose the **Exit Autodesk AutoCAD 2018** from the **Application Menu** to quit the AutoCAD program. In case the drawing has not been saved, it allows you to save the work first through a dialog box. Note that if you choose **No** in this dialog box, all the changes made in the current drawing till the last save will be lost. You can also use the **Close** button (**X**) of the main AutoCAD window (present in the title bar) to end the AutoCAD session.

CREATING AND MANAGING WORKSPACES

A workspace is defined as a customized arrangement of **Ribbon**, toolbars, menus, and window palettes in the AutoCAD environment. You can create your own workspaces, in which only specified toolbars, menus, and palettes are available. When you start AutoCAD, by default, the **Drafting & Annotation** workspace is displayed as the current workspace. You can select any other predefined workspace from the **Workspace** drop-down list available in the title bar, next to the **Quick Access Toolbar**, refer to Figure 1-45. You can also set the workspace from the flyout that will

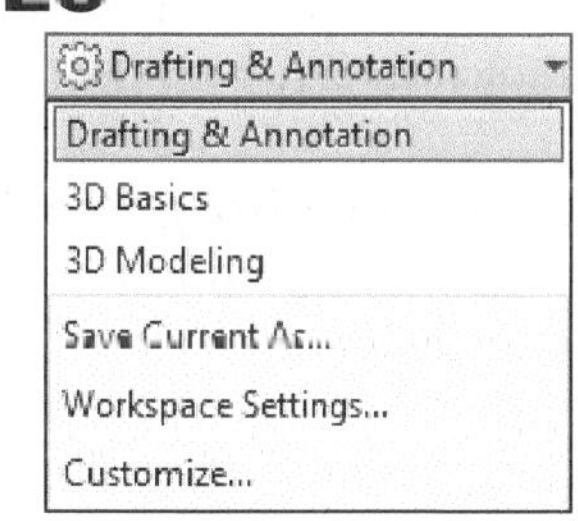

Figure 1-45 *The predefined workspaces*

be displayed on choosing the **Workspace Switching** button on the Status Bar or by choosing the required workspace from the **Quick Access Toolbar**.

Creating a New Workspace

To create a new workspace, customize the **Ribbon** and invoke the palettes to be displayed in the new workspace. Next, select the **Save Current As** option from the **Workspace** drop-down list in the titlebar; the **Save Workspace** dialog box will be displayed, as shown in Figure 1-46. Enter the name of the new workspace in the **Name** edit box and choose the **Save** button.

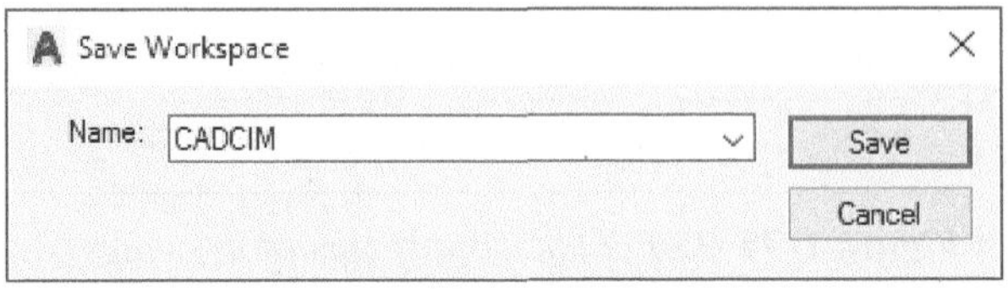

Figure 1-46 *The* ***Save Workspace*** *dialog box*

The new workspace is now the current workspace and is added to the **Workspace** drop-down list in the **Quick Access Toolbar**. Likewise, you can create workspaces based on your requirement and switch from one workspace to the other by selecting the name from the drop-down list in the **Workspaces** toolbar or the drop-down list in the **Quick Access Toolbar**.

Modifying the Workspace Settings

AutoCAD allows you to modify the workspace settings. To do so, select the **Workspace Settings** option in the **Workspace** drop-down list in the title bar; the **Workspace Settings** dialog box will be displayed, as shown in Figure 1-47. All workspaces are listed in the **My Workspace** drop-down list. You can make any of the workspaces as My Workspace by selecting it from the **My Workspace** drop-down list. You can also choose the **My Workspace** button from the **Workspaces** toolbar to change the current workspace to the one that was set as My Workspace in the **Workspace Settings** dialog box. The other options in this dialog box are discussed next.

Menu Display and Order Area

The options in this area are used to control the display and the order of display of workspaces in the **Workspace** drop-down list. By default, workspaces are listed in the sequence of their creation. To change the order, select a workspace and choose the **Move Up** or **Move Down** button. To control the display of the workspaces, you can select or clear the check boxes. You can also add a separator between workspaces by choosing the **Add Separator** button. A separator is a line that is placed between two workspaces in the **Workspace** drop-down list in the title bar, as shown in Figure 1-48.

When Switching Workspaces Area

By default, the **Do not save changes to workspace** radio button is selected in this area. This ensures that while switching the workspaces, the changes made in the current workspace will not be saved. If you select the **Automatically save workspace changes** radio button, the changes made in the current workspace will be automatically saved when you switch to the other workspace.

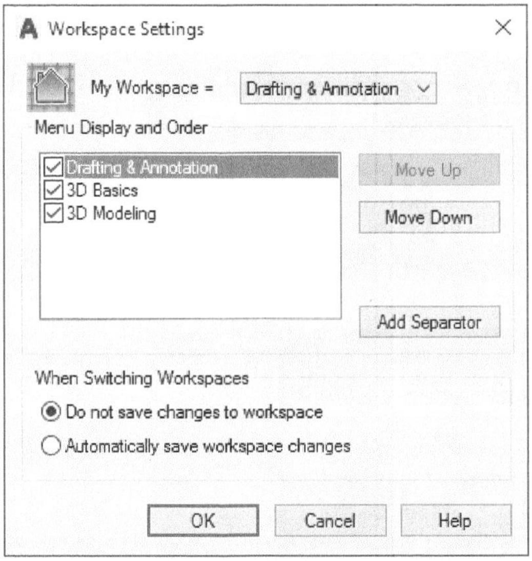

*Figure 1-47 The **Workspace Settings** dialog box*

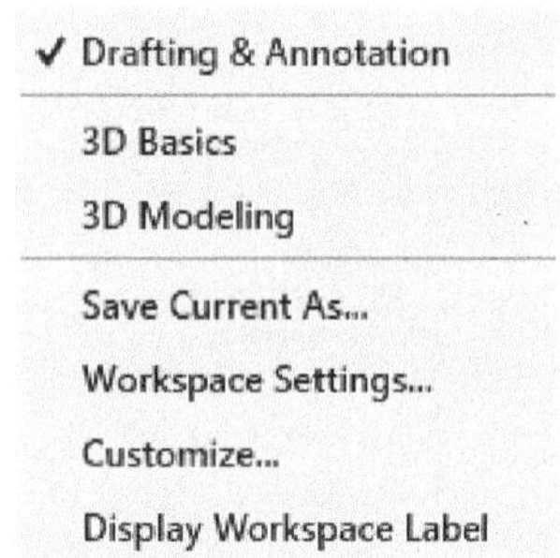

*Figure 1-48 The **Workspace** drop-down list after adding separators*

AutoCAD HELP

Titlebar: ? > Help **Shortcut Key:** F1 **Command:** HELP or ?

You can get the on-line help and documentation about the working of AutoCAD 2018 commands from the Help menu in the title bar, refer to Figure 1-49. You can also access the Help menu by pressing the F1 function key. An InfoCenter bar is displayed at the top right corner in the title bar that will help you to sign into the Autodesk Online services, refer to Figure 1-50. You can also access AutoCAD community by using certain keywords. Some important options in the Help menu are discussed next.

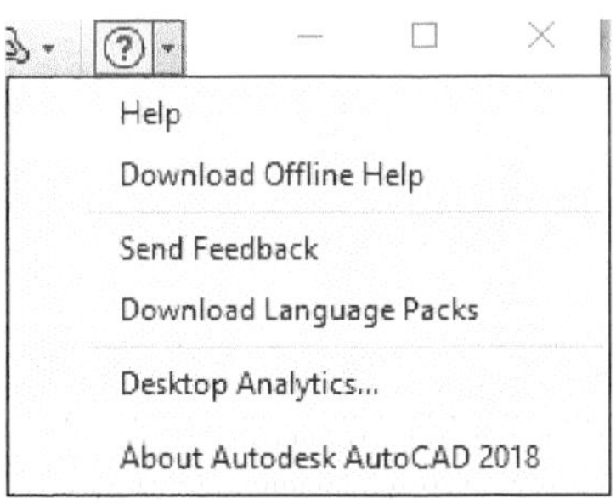

*Figure 1-49 The **Help** menu*

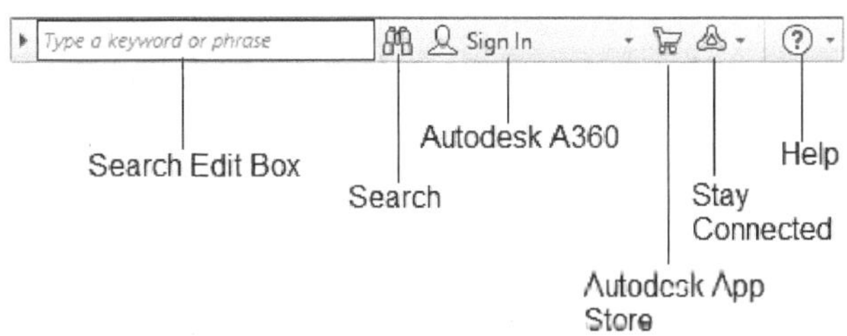

*Figure 1-50 The **InfoCenter** bar*

In the **Autodesk AutoCAD 2018 - Help** window, refer to Figure 1-51, you can choose the **Help Home** button to explore new features in AutoCAD 2018. In this window, you can browse videos, tutorials, and documentation for beginners and advanced users in the **Learn** and **Resources** sections. You can download sample files and offline help database from the **Downloads** section. You can also connect to other users of Autodesk community and discussion groups using the **Connect** section.

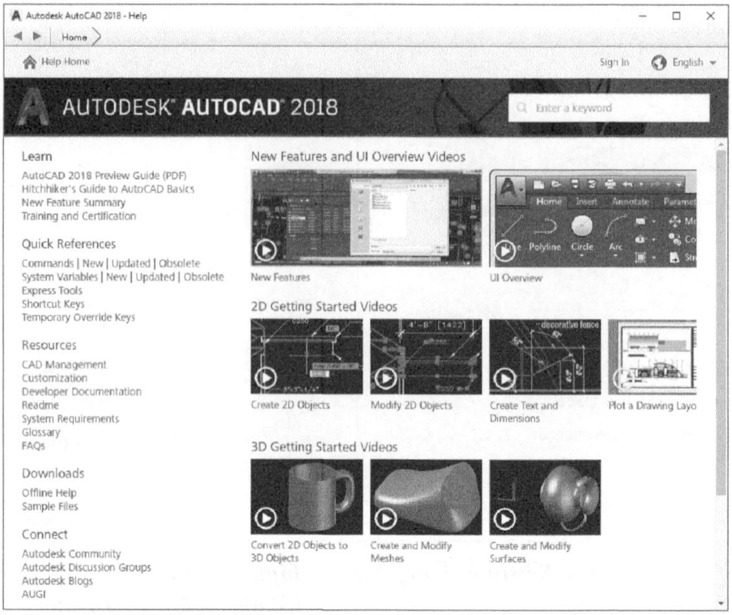

Figure 1-51 ***The Autodesk AutoCAD 2018 - Help*** *window*

In the **Autodesk AutoCAD 2018 - Help** window, you can search about any keyword related to AutoCAD by using the Search edit box, as shown in Figure 1-52. You can further refine your search by selecting the desired link using the **REFINE BY** section of the help window.

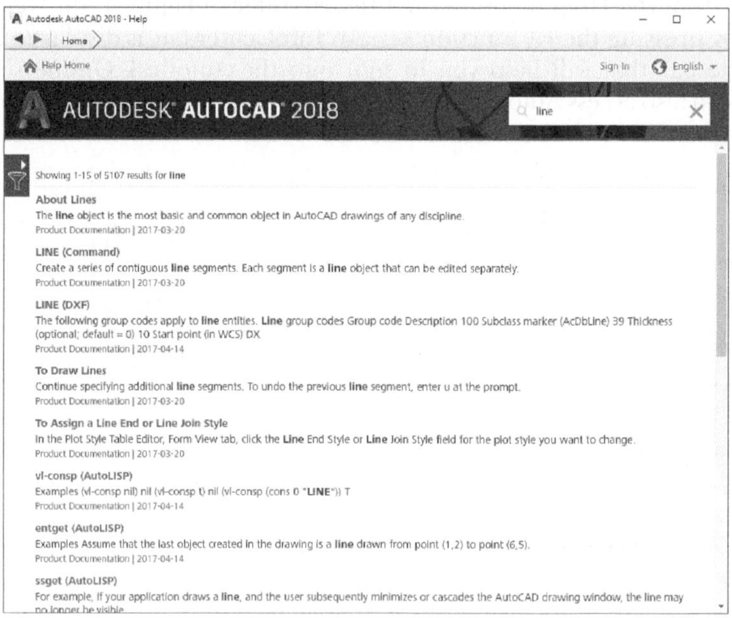

Figure 1-52 *Searching the keyword using the Search edit box*

Download Offline Help

This option is used to read the help contents and topics when the user has no internet access. (AutoCAD prompts you to download help file, user can save this file and then use it later on.)

Send Feedback

You can also directly contact Autodesk regarding support, discussion, or any consulting work. When you click on this option, a page will be displayed asking for the required queries and contact details. After entering the contact details, you can press **Submit** to exit.

Download Language Packs

Once AutoCAD is installed, you can also install the AutoCAD language pack to run AutoCAD in your preferred language by choosing this option.

Desktop Analytics

When you choose this option, the **Data collection and use** dialog box will be displayed. In the dialog box, Autodesk will prompt you to participate in a program to simply collect nonpersonal product usage information from the Autodesk software.

About Autodesk AutoCAD 2018

This option gives you information about the release, serial number, licensed to, and also the legal description about AutoCAD.

Autodesk CLOUD

The Autodesk Cloud is used to save and share the documents online. Using this technology, you can also view and update other user's documents available on Autodesk Cloud. To share a document, you first need to login to the Autodesk account. To do so, choose the **Sign In to Autodesk account** option from the **Sign In** flyout in the InfoCenter bar; the **Sign In** window will be displayed. Now, login to the account using the Autodesk ID and password; the **Default A360 Settings** window will be displayed. Choose the **OK** button from the window; your account name will be displayed in place of **Sign In** in the **Sign In** flyout. Next, choose the **A360** option from the **Sign In** flyout; the **A360 Drive** window will be displayed in the default browser, refer to Figure 1-53. To upload a document on Autodesk Cloud, choose the **Upload** button from the top right corner of the browser window; the **Open** dialog box will be displayed. Next, select the document to be uploaded and choose the **Open** button; the document will get uploaded in the cloud. Now, you can share the document in the Autodesk Cloud by selecting suitable options. There are two ways to share a document: Private Sharing and Public Sharing. To share a file, hover the cursor over that file and choose the **Share** button from the highlighted options, refer to Figure 1-54; the **Share** window will be displayed, as shown in Figure 1-55. In the **Get Link** tab, you can specify the settings for sharing the file.

Figure 1-53 The A360 DRIVE window

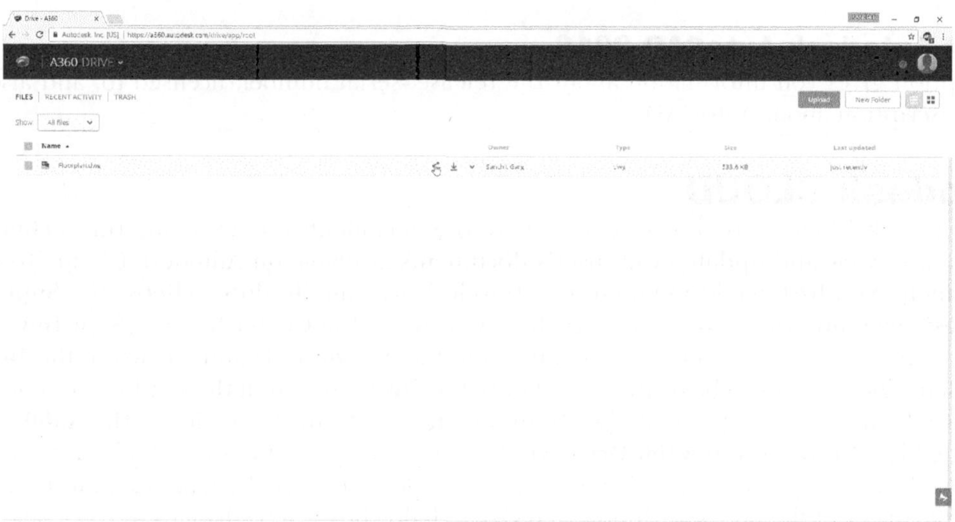

Figure 1-54 Options highlighted on hovering the cursor on a file

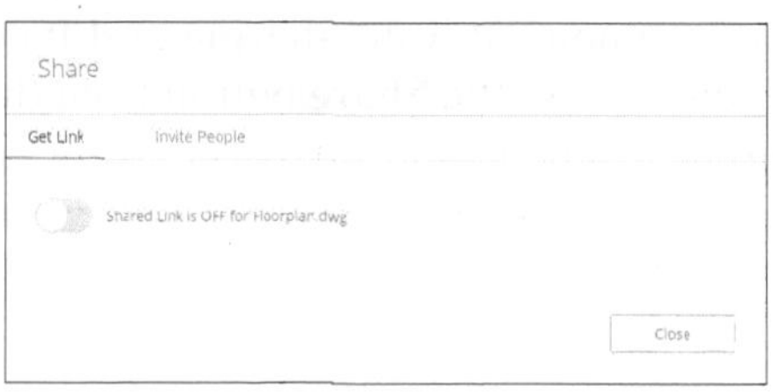

Figure 1-55 The Share window

You can also invite other users to view, download, or update the files in the A360 Drive. To do so, choose the **Invite People** tab in the **Share** window and enter a valid email address of the user whom you want to invite. Next, select the required options from the **Permission** drop-down list to specify whether the user can view, view and download, download and update, or have a full access of the shared file, refer to Figure 1-56.

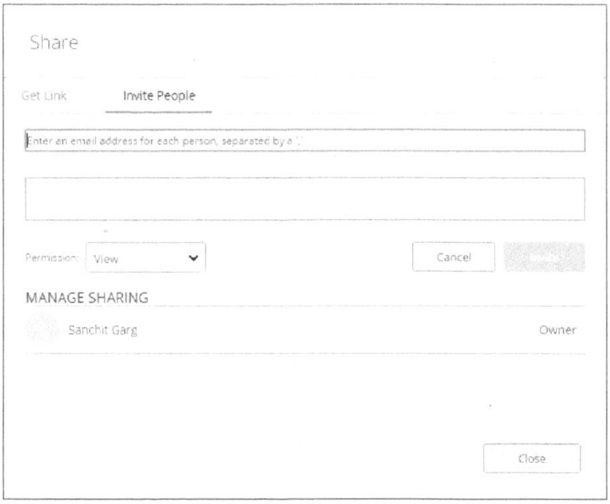

***Figure 1-56** The **Invite People** tab in the **Share** window*

Autodesk App Store

Autodesk App Store helps you to download various applications for AutoCAD, get connected to the AutoCAD community, share information and designs, and so on. You can download the AutoCAD apps from the **Featured Apps** panel of the **Featured Apps** tab in the **Ribbon**, refer to Figure 1-57. To download the AutoCAD apps, choose the required apps from the **Featured Apps** panel of the **Featured Apps** tab; the default browser will open with icons of apps that you can download, as shown in Figure 1-58. Now, you can download the apps by clicking the **Download** button.

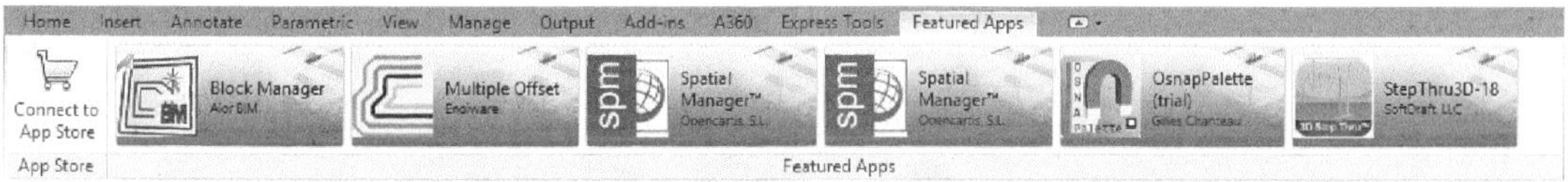

Figure 1-57** The **Featured Apps** tab in the **Ribbon

You can also download the apps other than the apps available in the **Featured Apps** panel. To do so, choose the **Connect to App Store** button from the **App Store** panel of the **Featured Apps** tab; the **AUTODESK APP STORE** window will be displayed, as shown in Figure 1-59. Now, you can download the required apps from the window. Some of the apps are paid and some of them are free to download. You can download various Autodesk apps such as StepThru3D-18, DDAttMod, and so on from this page. You can also publish your own Autodesk products for other users of Autodesk 360.

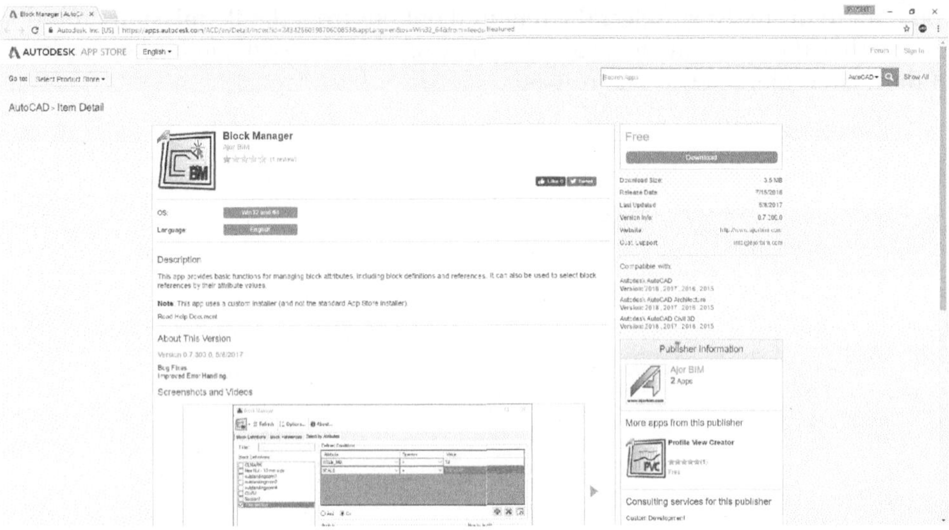

Figure 1-58 *The **AUTODESK APP STORE** window open with apps to be downloaded*

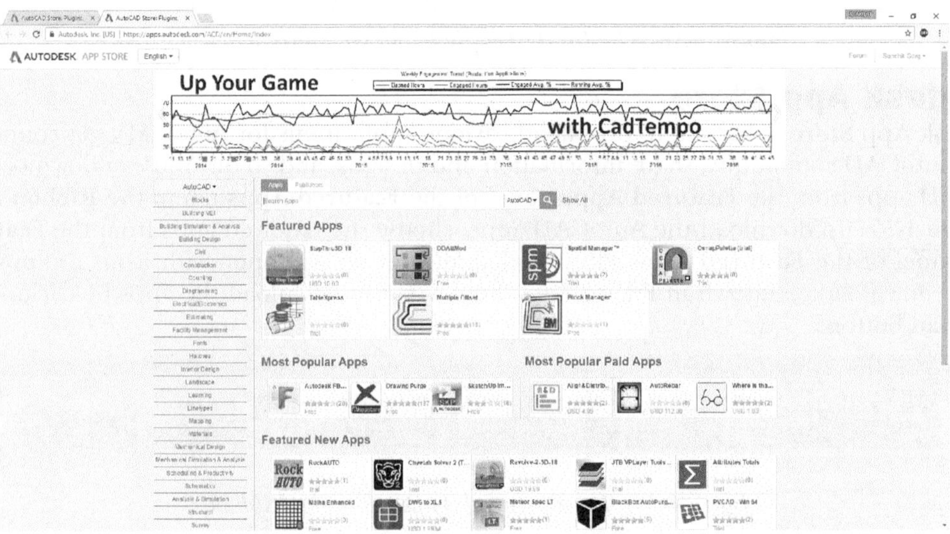

Figure 1-59 *The **AUTODESK APP STORE** window*

In addition to AutoCAD apps, you can also download apps for software other than AutoCAD such as Autodesk Alias, Revit, Simulation, and so on. You can also search for the apps by entering the name of the app in the **Search Apps** text box.

After downloading and installing the apps, the apps will be available in the **Add-ins** tab. You can choose the required app to work with. Also, you can manage the apps by choosing the **App Manager** button available in the **App Manager** panel of the **Add-ins** tab. To manage the app, choose the **App Manager** button; the **Autodesk App Manager** dialog box will be displayed, as shown in Figure 1-60. In the dialog box, all the installed apps are displayed. To manage a particular app, right-click on it; a shortcut menu will be displayed, Now, you can choose the required option to manage it.

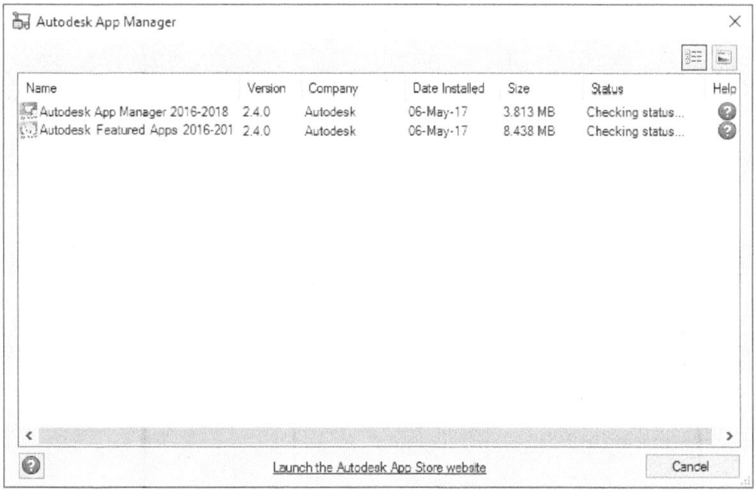

Figure 1-60 The ***Autodesk App Manager*** *dialog box*

Design Feed

In AutoCAD, the **DESIGN FEED** palette is used to share a document with the people who have Autodesk 360 account. It can be invoked by entering **DESIGNFEEDOPEN** in the command bar. **The DESIGN FEED palette is shown in Figure 1-61. In this palette, click on the Login link in the palette; the Autodesk-Sign-In window will be displayed. Enter your Autodesk ID and password to sign in. On doing so, you will notice that the DESIGN FEED palette gets modified, as shown in Figure 1-62.** Next, click the **Invite People** link to display the **Design Feed - Invite People** dialog box, as shown in Figure 1-63. In this dialog box, specify the mail address with which you want to share the file. Also, the drawing file will be saved in **A360**. The other options of the **DESIGN FEED palette** are discussed next.

Create a new post Text Box

This text box is used to enter a message for the post. You can enter any query related to any specific area or point in a drawing by using this text box and then share it. Note that everyone can view your post but only the Autodesk A360 registered users can reply to your post.

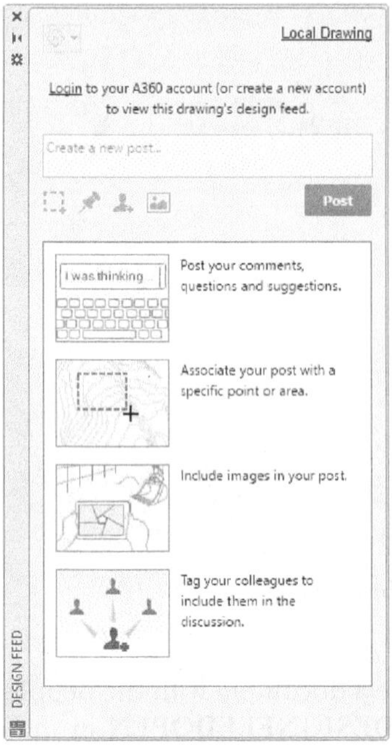

Figure 1-61 The ***DESIGN FEED*** *palette*

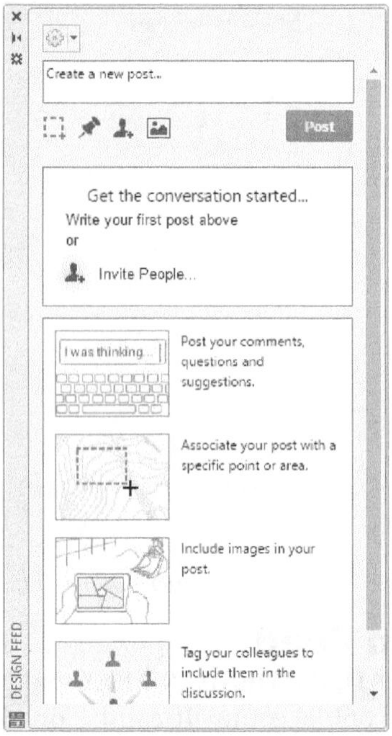

Figure 1-62 The ***DESIGN FEED*** *palette with all options activated*

Figure 1-63 The ***Design Feed - Invite People*** *dialog box*

Associate this post to an area in the drawing

This button is used to associate the post entered in the **Create a new post** text box to the desired area in a drawing. To post a message/query associated with a specific area in the drawing, choose this button and then specify the required area by using the cross selection method; a blue dashed rectangle enclosing the selected portion along with the design feed bubble is displayed in the drawing area, refer to Figure 1-64. Once the area has been specified for the post, you need to post it so that other users of Autodesk A360 account working on the same drawing, can view and reply to your post. To post the text, choose the **Post** button from the **DESIGN FEED** palette. Figure 1-65 shows a drawing with the added post. Note that in the drawing area, every post is represented with its serial number assigned in the **DESIGN FEED** palette.

Figure 1-64 *Drawing with enclosed area and design feed bubble*

Figure 1-65 *Post with the number assigned in the **Design Feed** palette*

Associate this post to a point in the drawing

This button is used to associate the post entered in the **Create a new post** text box to the desired point in the drawing. To do so, choose this button and then specify the point by clicking the left mouse button in the drawing area; the post will be assigned to the specified point and a design feed bubble will be displayed in the drawing area. Once the point has been specified for the post, you need to publish the post so that other users of Autodesk A360 account working on the same drawing can get updated with the post. To publish the post, choose the **Post** button from the **DESIGN FEED** palette. Note that in the drawing area, every post is represented with its serial number assigned in the **DESIGN FEED** palette.

Tag in this post

This button is used to tag the people with whom you want to share the post through Autodesk A360. To add people to the sharing list, you need to choose this button before posting the message. On doing so, the **Invite People** button will be displayed in the **DESIGN FEED** palette. If you already have the connections with whom you want to share the post, select the check boxes adjacent to their E-mail ids from the **DESIGN FEED** palette and then choose the **Post** button.

You can also share the post with the new connections that are not listed in the **DESIGN FEED** palette by choosing the **Invite People** button. To do so, choose the **Invite People** button; the **Design Feed - Invite People** dialog box will be displayed, refer to Figure 1-63. To add people in sharing list, enter their E-mail ids in the **To** text box and then choose the **Invite** button at the bottom of the **Design Feed - Invite People** dialog box; the E-mail ids will be added in your connection and will be displayed in the **DESIGN FEED** palette. Choose the **Post** button to publish the post.

Attach image(s) to this post

This button is used to attach images to your posts. Using this button, you can attach different image file formats such as *.bmp*, *.dib*, *.jpg*, *.jpeg*, *.jpe*, *.jfif*, *.jif*, and *.png* to your post. To attach an image with the post, choose the **Attach image(s) to this post** button; the **Select File** dialog box will be displayed. Browse to the desired file, select it and then choose the **Open** button from the dialog box; the selected image file will be attached. Now, you can publish your post with the attached image file.

Design Feed Settings

The options in this drop-down list are used to display and hide the design feed bubbles and resolved posts from the drawing. These options are discussed next.

Hide All

This option is used to hide all design feed bubbles and posts attached in the drawing area.

Show Bubbles

This option is used to display the design feed bubbles in the drawing.

Note

When you click on the bubble, the post will be displayed along with the blue colored dashed rectangle in the drawing area. Note that if you press the ESC key, the post gets disappeared but the bubble remains available.

Show Extended bubbles

This option is used to display the post with the preview of the message in the drawing area along with its bubble. Note that if you press the ESC key, the preview of the post remains available in the drawing area.

show resolved

This check box is used to toggle the display of resolved posts and their respective design feed bubbles in the drawing area.

ADDITIONAL HELP RESOURCES

1. You can get help for a command while working by pressing the F1 key. The help window containing information about the command is displayed. You can exit the window and continue with the command.

2. You can get help about a dialog box by choosing the **Help** button in that dialog box.

3. Autodesk has provided several resources that you can use to get assistance with your AutoCAD questions. The following is a list of some of the resources:

   a. Autodesk website *http://www.autodesk.com*
   b. AutoCAD technical assistance website *http://knowledge.autodesk.com*
   c. AutoCAD discussion groups website *https://forums.autodesk.com/t5/autocad-forum/bd-p/706*

4. You can also get help by contacting us at *techsupport@cadcim.com* and *sales@cadcim.com*.

5. You can download AutoCAD drawings, programs, and special topics by registering yourself at the faculty's website by visiting: *http://cadcim.com/Registration.aspx*

Self-Evaluation Test

Answer the following questions and then compare them to those given at the end of this chapter:

1. The ________ button is used to set the performance of the software to an acceptable level.

2. If the __________ variable is set to 1 and you invoke the **New** tool, the **Create New Drawing** dialog box will be displayed.

3. If you want to work on a drawing without altering the original drawing, you must select the __________ option from the **Open** drop-down list in the **Select File** dialog box.

4. The __________ option enables you to open only a selected view or a selected layer of the current drawing.

5. You can use the __________ command to close the current drawing file without actually quitting AutoCAD.

6. The __________ system variable can be used to change the time interval for automatic save.

7. By using the __________ button, you can find information about a command on internet.

8. You can enable or disable the functions such as AutoComplete, AutoCorrect, and so on by using the options available in the __________ dialog box.

9. The __________ button is used to toggle the display of the File tab bar which displays all opened files.

10. The __________ palette is used to share a document with the users who have Autodesk 360 account.

11. You can press the F3 key to display the **AutoCAD Text Window**, which displays the previous commands and prompts. (T/F)

12. If you do not have internet connection, you cannot access the Help files. (T/F)

13. If a drawing was partially opened and saved previously, it is not possible to open it again with the same layers and views. (T/F)

14. If the current drawing is unnamed and you save the drawing for the first time, the **Save** tool will prompt you to enter the file name in the **Save Drawing As** dialog box. (T/F)

Review Questions

Answer the following questions:

1. Which of the following combination of keys should be pressed to hide all toolbars displayed on the screen?

   (a) CTRL+3 (b) CTRL+0
   (c) CTRL+5 (d) CTRL+2

2. Which of the following combination of keys should be pressed to turn on or off the display of the **TOOL PALETTES**?

   (a) CTRL+3 (b) CTRL+0
   (c) CTRL+5 (d) CTRL+2

3. Which of the following commands is used to exit the AutoCAD program?

   (a) **QUIT** (b) **END**
   (c) **CLOSE** (d) None of these

4. Which of the following options in the **Startup** dialog box is used to set the initial drawing settings before actually starting a new drawing?

   (a) **Start from Scratch** (b) **Use a Template**
   (c) **Use a Wizard** (d) None of these

5. When you choose the **Save** tool from the **File** menu or choose the **Save** tool from the **Quick Access Toolbar**, which of the following commands is invoked?

   (a) **SAVE** (b) **LSAVE**
   (c) **QSAVE** (d) **SAVEAS**

6. AutoCAD has provided __________ as an easy and convenient way of placing and sharing hatch patterns and blocks in the current drawing.

7. By default, the angles are positive if measured in the __________ direction.

8. The __________ check box is used to toggle the display of resolved posts.

9. The shortcut menu invoked by right-clicking in the command window displays the most recently used commands and some of the window options such as **Copy**, **Paste**, and so on. (T/F)

10. You can open an AutoCAD 2004 drawing in AutoCAD 2018. (T/F)

11. The file name that you enter to save a drawing in the **Save Drawing As** dialog box can be 255 characters long, but cannot contain spaces and punctuation marks. (T/F)

12. You can close a drawing in AutoCAD even if a command is active. (T/F)

Answers to Self-Evaluation Test

1. Graphics Performance, **2.** STARTUP, **3.** Open Read-Only, **4.** Partial Open, **5.** CLOSE, **6.** SAVETIME, **7.** Search on Internet, **8.** Input Search Options, **9.** File Tabs, **10.** Design Feed, **11.** F, **12.** F, **13.** F, **14.** T

Chapter 2

Getting Started with AutoCAD

Learning Objectives

After completing this chapter, you will be able to:

- *Draw lines by using the Line tool*
- *Understand the coordinate systems used in AutoCAD*
- *Clear the drawing area by using the Erase tool*
- *Understand the two basic object selection methods: Window selection and Crossing selection methods*
- *Draw circles by using various tools*
- *Use the Zoom and Pan tools*
- *Set up units by using the Units tool*
- *Set up and determine limits for a given drawing*
- *Plot drawings by using the basic plotting options*
- *Use the Options dialog box and specify settings*

Key Terms

- *Dynamic Input*
- *Line*
- *Coordinate Systems*
- *Absolute Coordinate System*
- *Relative Coordinate System*
- *Direct Distance Entry*
- *Erase*
- *Object Selection*
- *Circle*
- *Zoom*
- *Pan*
- *Units Format*
- *Limits*
- *Plot*
- *Options*

DYNAMIC INPUT MODE

In AutoCAD, the **Dynamic Input** mode allows you to enter the commands through the pointer input and the dimensions using the dimensional input. When this mode is turned on, all the prompts are available at the tooltip as dynamic prompts and you can select the command options through the dynamic prompt. The settings for the **Dynamic Input** mode are done through the **Dynamic Input** tab of the **Drafting Settings** dialog box. To invoke the **Drafting Settings** dialog box, right-click on the **Dynamic Input** button in the Status Bar; a shortcut menu will be displayed. Choose the **Dynamic Input Settings** option from the shortcut menu; the **Drafting Settings** dialog box will be displayed, as shown in Figure 2-1. The options in the **Dynamic Input** tab are discussed next.

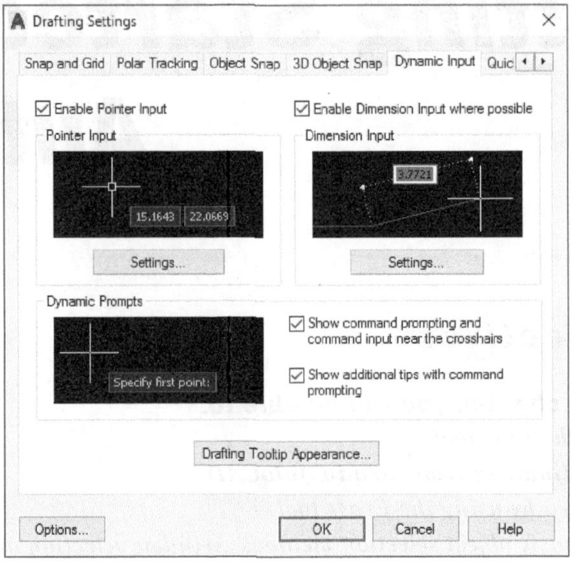

*Figure 2-1 The **Dynamic Input** tab of the **Drafting Settings** dialog box*

Enable Pointer Input

If the **Enable Pointer Input** check box is selected, you can enter the commands through the pointer input. Figure 2-2 shows the **CIRCLE** command entered through the pointer input. If this check box is cleared, the Dynamic Input will be turned off and commands have to be entered through the command prompt. If you enter any alphabet in the Dynamic Input prompt, all tools whose names start with the entered alphabet will be displayed in a list at the pointer, refer to Figure 2-2.

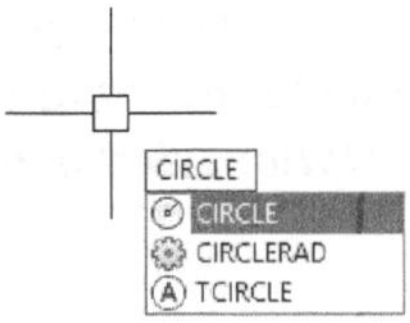

Figure 2-2 Entering a command using the pointer input

If you choose the **Settings** button from the **Pointer Input** area, the **Pointer Input Settings** dialog box will be displayed, as shown in Figure 2-3. The radio buttons in the **Format** area of this dialog box are used to set the default settings as either Polar or Cartesian format for specifying the second or next points of entities. By default, the **Polar format** and **Relative coordinates** radio buttons are selected. As a result, the coordinates will be specified in the polar form and with respect to the relative coordinates system. You can select the **Cartesian format** radio button to enter the coordinates in Cartesian form. Similarly, if you select the **Absolute coordinates** radio button, the coordinate's values will be measured with respect to the absolute coordinate system.

The options in the **Visibility** area of the **Pointer Input Settings** dialog box are used to set the visibility of the coordinate tool tips. By default, the **When a command asks for a point** radio button is selected. You can select the other radio buttons to modify this display.

Enable Dimension Input where possible

The **Enable Dimension Input where possible** check box is selected by default. As a result, the dimension input field is displayed in the graphics area showing a preview of that dimension. Figure 2-4 displays the dimension input fields. The options under the Dynamic prompt will be available when you press the down arrow key from the keyboard. The dotted lines show the geometric parameters like length, radius, or diameter corresponding to that dimension. Figure 2-4 shows a line being drawn using the **PLINE** command. The two dimension inputs that are shown are for the length of the line and the angle with the positive direction of the X axis.

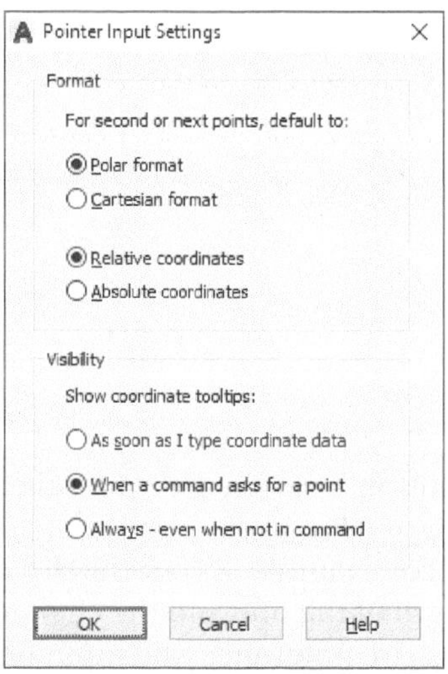

Figure 2-3 *The **Pointer Input Settings** dialog box*

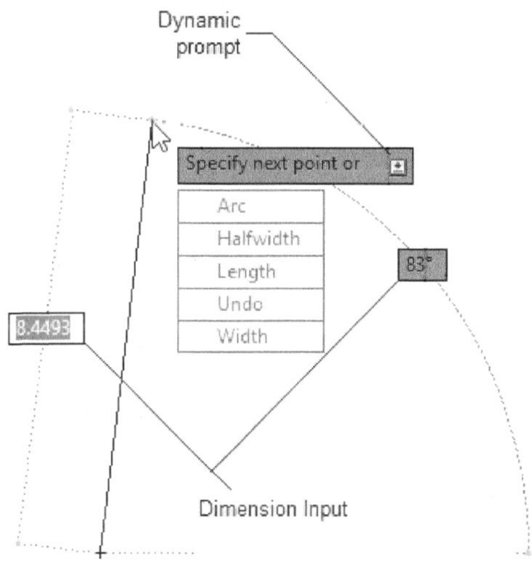

Figure 2-4 *Input fields displayed when the **Enable Dimension Input where possible** check box is selected*

Using the TAB key, you can toggle between the dimension input fields. As soon as you specify one dimension and move to the other, the previous dimension will be locked. If the **Enable Dimension Input where possible** check box is cleared, the preview of dimensions will not be displayed. You can only enter the dimensions in the dimension input fields below the cursor, as shown in Figure 2-5. Choose the **Settings** button from the **Dimension Input** area to display the **Dimension Input Settings** dialog box, as shown in Figure 2-6.

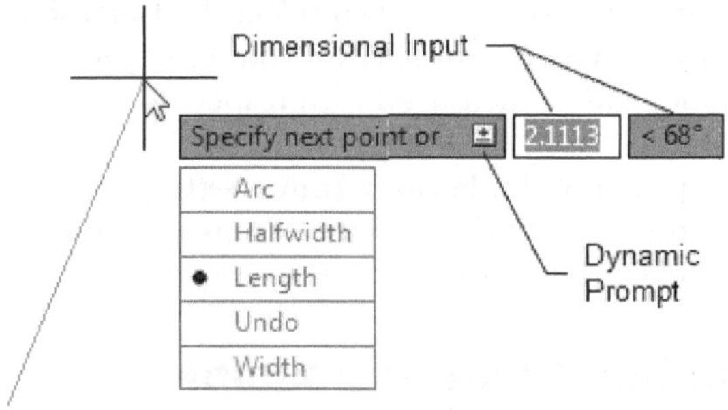

***Figure 2-5** Input fields displayed when the **Enable Dimension Input where possible** check box is cleared*

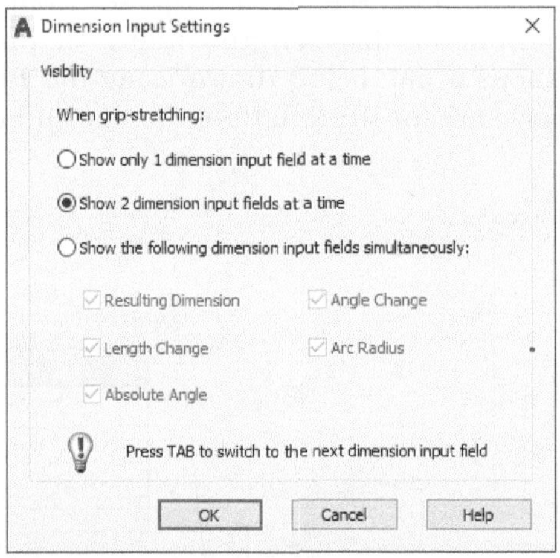

***Figure 2-6** The **Dimension Input Settings** dialog box*

By default, the **Show 2 dimension input fields at a time** radio button is selected. As a result, two dimension input fields will be displayed in the drawing area while stretching a sketched entity. The two input fields will depend on the entity that is being stretched. For example, if you stretch a line using one of its endpoints, the input field will show the total length of the line and the change in its length. Similarly, while stretching a circle using the grip on its circumference, the input fields will show the total radius and the change in the radius. You can set the priority to display only one input field or various input fields simultaneously by selecting their respective check boxes.

> **Tip**
> *If multiple dimension input fields are available, use the TAB key to switch between the dimension input fields.*

Show command prompting and command input near the crosshairs

If this check box is selected, the prompt sequences will be dynamically displayed near the crosshairs. Whenever a black arrow appears at the pointer input, it suggests that the other options are also available. To access these options, press the down arrow key to see the dynamic prompt listing all options. In the dynamic prompt, you can use the cursor or the down arrow key to jog through the options. A black dot will appear before the option that is currently active. In Figure 2-5, the **Length** option is currently active. Press ENTER to confirm the polyline creation using the **Length** option.

Show additional tips with command prompting

In AutoCAD, on selecting the **Show additional tips with command prompting** check box available in the **Dynamic Input** tab of the **Drafting Settings** dialog box, refer to Figure 2-1, the display of tips for the grip manipulation will be turned on.

Drafting Tooltip Appearance

When you choose the **Drafting Tooltip Appearance** button, the **Tooltip Appearance** dialog box will be displayed, as shown in Figure 2-7. This dialog box contains the options to customize the tooltip appearance.

You can choose the **Colors** button to change the color of the tooltip in the model space or layouts. The edit box in the **Size** area is used to specify the size of the tooltip. You can also use the slider to control the size of the tool tip. Previews are displayed in the **Model Preview** and the **Layout Preview** areas as the value is changed in the **Size** edit box.

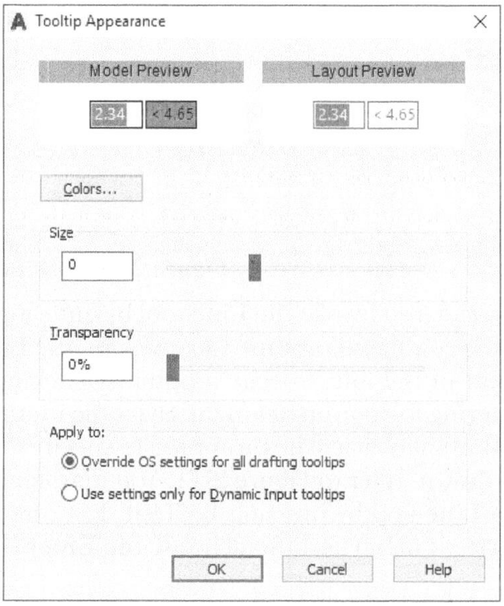

Figure 2-7 The ***Tooltip Appearance*** *dialog box*

Similarly, the transparency of the tooltip can be controlled using the edit box or the slider in the **Transparency** area. In the **Apply to** area, the **Override OS settings for all drafting tooltips** radio button is selected by default which ensures that the changes made in the **Tooltip Appearance** dialog box will be applied to all drafting tooltips. If you select the **Use settings only for Dynamic Input tooltips** radio button, the changes will be applied only to the **Dynamic Input** tooltips. For example, if you change any of the parameters using the **Tooltip Appearance** dialog box and select the **Use settings only for Dynamic Input tooltips** radio button, the tooltips for the dynamic input will be modified but for the polar tracking it will consider the original values.

On the other hand, if you select the **Override OS settings for all drafting tooltips** radio button, the tooltips displayed for the polar tracking will also be modified based on the values in the **Tooltip Appearance** dialog box.

DRAWING LINES IN AutoCAD

Ribbon: Home > Draw > Line **Toolbar:** Draw > Line **Menu Bar:** Draw > Line
Tool Palettes: Draw > Line **Command:** LINE/L

The most commonly used fundamental object in a drawing is line. In AutoCAD, a line is drawn between two points by using the **Line** tool. You can invoke the **Line** tool from the **Draw** panel of the **Home** tab in the **Ribbon**, refer to Figure 2-8. Besides this, you can choose the **Line** tool from the **Draw** tab of the **Tool Palettes**. To invoke the **Tool Palettes**, choose the **Tool Palettes** button from the **Palettes** panel in the **View** tab, as shown in Figure 2-9. Alternatively, you can invoke the **Line** tool from the **Draw** toolbar, as shown in Figure 2-10. However, the **Draw** toolbar is not displayed by default. To invoke this toolbar, choose **Tools > Toolbars > AutoCAD > Draw** from the Menu Bar.

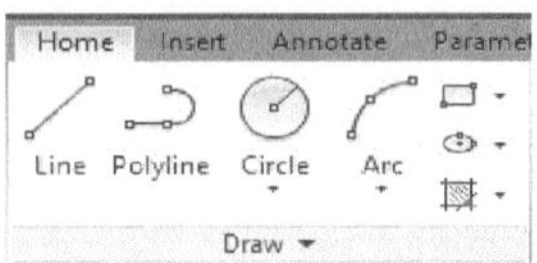

*Figure 2-8 The **Line** tool in the **Draw** panel*

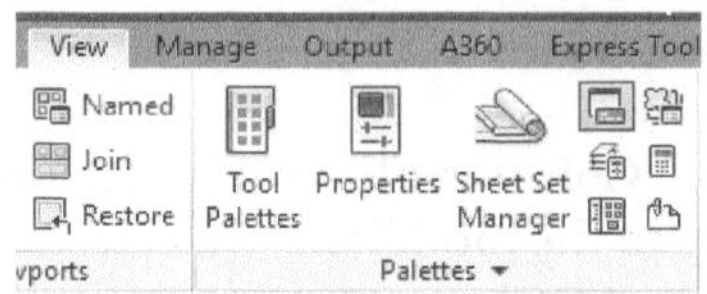

*Figure 2-9 Invoking the **Tool Palettes** from the **Palettes** panel*

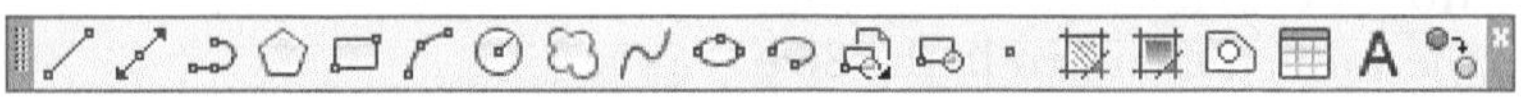

*Figure 2-10 The **Line** tool in the **Draw** toolbar*

You can also invoke the **Line** tool by entering **LINE** or **L** (L is the alias for the **LINE** command) at the command prompt. On invoking the **Line** tool, you will be prompted to specify the starting point of the line. Specify a point by clicking the left mouse button in the drawing area or by entering its coordinates in the Dynamic Input fields or the command prompt. After specifying the first point, you will be prompted to specify the second point. Specify the second point; a line will be drawn, refer to Figure 2-11. You may continue specifying points and draw lines or terminate the **Line** tool by pressing ENTER, ESC, or SPACEBAR. You can also right-click to display the shortcut menu and then choose the **Enter** or **Cancel** option from it to exit the **Line** tool.

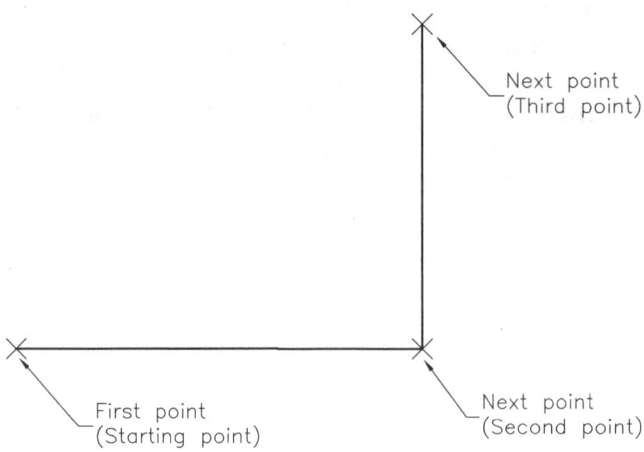

*Figure 2-11 Drawing lines using the **Line** tool*

Start a new file with the ***acad.dwt*** template in the **Drafting & Annotation** workspace and choose the **Line** tool from the **Draw** tab. The prompt sequence for the drawing the sketch shown in Figure 2-11 is given next.

*Choose the **Line** tool*

Specify first point: *Move the cursor (mouse) and left-click to specify the first point.*

Specify next point or [Undo]: *Move the cursor horizontaly toward the right and left-click to specify the second point.*

Specify next point or [Undo]: *Specify the third point.*

Specify next point or [Close/Undo]: Enter *(Press ENTER to exit the **Line** tool.)*

Note

When you specify the start point of the line by pressing the left mouse button, a rubber band line stretches between the selected point and the current position of the cursor. This line is sensitive to the movement of the cursor and helps you select the direction and the placement of the next point for the line.

Note that in the command prompt the **Close** and **Undo** options will be displayed while creating lines using the **Line** tool. Both these options are discussed next.

The Close Option

After drawing two continuous lines by using the **Line** tool, you will notice that the **Close** option is displayed at the command prompt. The **Close** option is used to join the current point to the start point of the first line when two or more continuous lines are drawn. If you specify the endpoint by using the mouse, then click at the start point of the first line or enter **C** at the command prompt, as given in the command prompt below.

*Choose the **Line** tool.*

LINE Specify first point: *Pick the first point.*

Specify next point or [Undo]: *Pick the second point.*

Specify next point or [Undo]: *Pick the third point.*

Specify next point or [Close/Undo]: *Pick the fourth point.*

Specify next point or [Close/Undo]: **C** Enter *(The fifth point joins with the first point).* Refer to *Figure 2-12.*

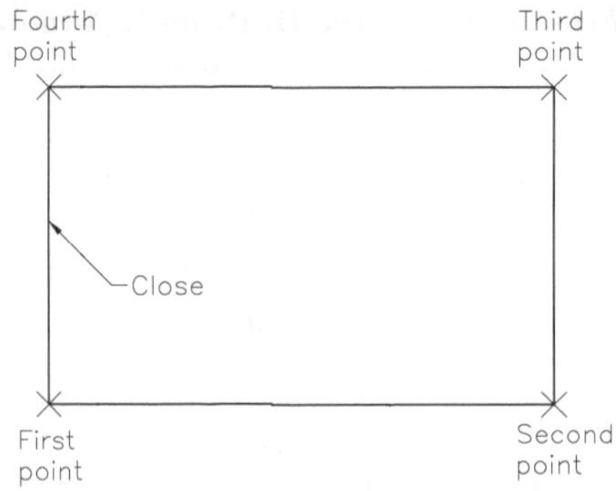

*Figure 2-12 Using the **Close** option of the **Line** tool*

You can also choose the **Close** option from the shortcut menu displayed on right-clicking in the drawing area.

> **Tip**
> *After exiting the **Line** tool, to draw another line starting from the endpoint of the previous line, press ENTER twice; a new line will start from the endpoint of the previous line. You can also type the @ symbol to start the line from the last point. For example, after drawing a circle if you invoke the **Line** tool, the @ symbol will snap to the center point of the circle.*

The Undo Option

While drawing a line, if you specify a wrong endpoint, then you can undo the last specified point and go back to the previous stage by using the **Undo** option of the **Line** tool. You can use this option multiple times. To use this option, type **Undo** (or just **U**) at the **Specify next point or [Undo]** prompt. You can also right-click to display the shortcut menu and then choose the **Undo** option from it.

> **Note**
> *Whenever you open a new drawing, you need to modify the drawing display area. To modify the display area, select the required tool from the **Zoom** drop-down in the **Navigator** bar; the drawing display is modified. You will learn more about the **Zoom** tools later in this chapter.*

INVOKING TOOLS USING DYNAMIC INPUT/COMMAND PROMPT

In AutoCAD, if you enter any alphabet at the command prompt or Dynamic Input, all the tools whose name start with the entered alphabet will be displayed in a list at the command prompt or Dynamic Input. For example, if you enter **L** at the command prompt or Dynamic Input, all the tools whose names start with the alphabet L will be displayed, refer to Figure 2-13. In this way, you can view all the tool names starting with a particular alphabet and select the required tool.

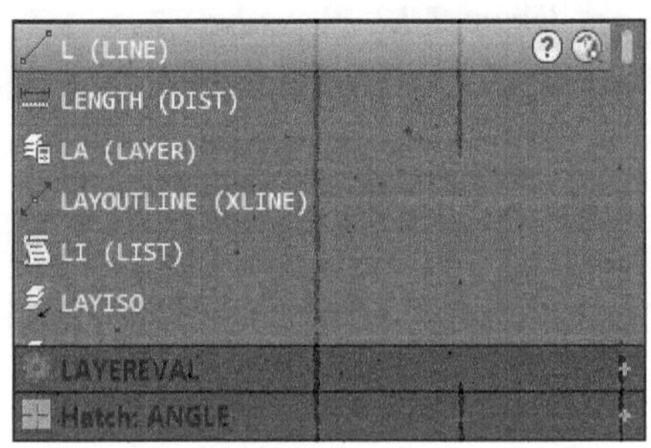

Figure 2-13 List displayed after typing L at the command prompt

COORDINATE SYSTEMS

In AutoCAD, the location of a point is specified in terms of Cartesian coordinates. In this system, each point in a plane is specified by a pair of numerical coordinates. To specify a point in a plane, take two mutually perpendicular lines as references. The horizontal line is called the *X* axis and the vertical line is called the *Y* axis. The *X* and *Y* axes divide the *XY* plane into four parts, generally known as quadrants. The point of intersection of these two axes is called the origin and the plane is called the XY plane. The origin has the coordinate values of X = 0, Y = 0. The origin is taken as the reference for locating a point on the *XY* plane. Now, to locate a point, say P, draw a vertical line intersecting the X axis. The horizontal distance between the origin and the intersection point will be called the X coordinate of P. It will be denoted as P(x). The *X* coordinate specifies how far the point is to the left or right from the origin along the *X* axis. Now, draw a horizontal line intersecting the Y axis. The vertical distance between the origin and the intersection point will be the Y coordinate of P. It will be denoted as P(y). The *Y* coordinate specifies how far the point is to the top or bottom from the origin along the *Y* axis. The intersection point of the horizontal and vertical lines is the coordinate of the point and is denoted as P(x,y). The *X* coordinate is positive if measured from the right of the origin and is negative if measured from the left of the origin. The *Y* coordinate is positive if measured above the origin and is negative if measured below the origin, refer to Figure 2-14.

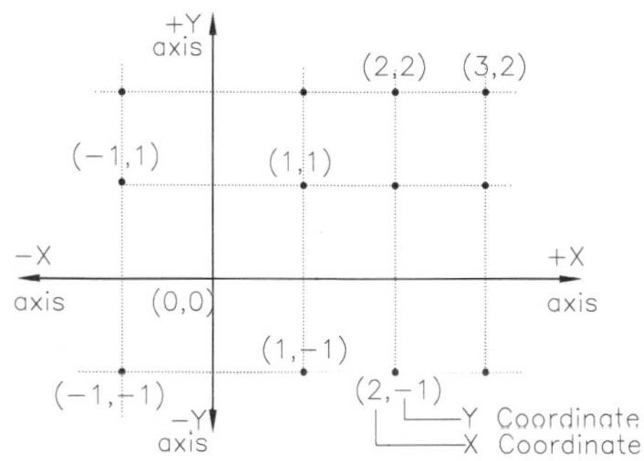

Figure 2-14 *Cartesian coordinate system*

In AutoCAD, the default origin is located at the lower left corner of the drawing area. AutoCAD uses the following coordinate systems to locate a point in the XY plane.

1. Absolute coordinate system
2. Relative coordinate system
    a. Relative rectangular coordinate system
    b. Relative polar coordinate system
3. Direct distance entry

If you are specifying a point by entering its location at the command prompt then you need to use any one of the coordinate systems.

Absolute Coordinate System

In the Absolute Coordinate System, points are located with respect to the origin (0,0). For example, a point with coordinates, X = 4 and Y = 3 is measured 4 units horizontally (distance along the *X* axis) and 3 units vertically (distance along the *Y* axis) from the origin, as shown in Figure 2-15. In AutoCAD, the absolute coordinates are specified at the command prompt by entering *X* and *Y* coordinates, separated by a comma. However, remember that if you are specifying the coordinates by using the **Dynamic Input** mode, you need to add # as the prefix to the X coordinate value. The following example illustrates the use of absolute coordinates at the command prompt to draw the rectangle shown in Figure 2-16.

*Choose the **Line** tool (Ensure that the **Dynamic Input** button is not chosen)*

LINE Specify first point: **1,1** [Enter] *(X = 1 and Y = 1.)*

Specify next point or [Undo]: **4,1** [Enter] *(X = 4 and Y = 1.)*

Specify next point or [Undo]: **4,3** [Enter]

Specify next point or [Close /Undo]: **1,3** [Enter]

Specify next point or [Close/Undo]: **C** [Enter]

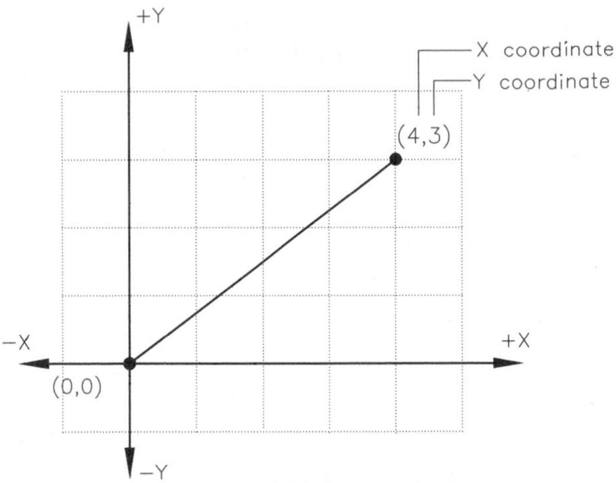

***Figure 2-15** Absolute Coordinate System*

***Figure 2-16** Rectangle created by using absolute coordinates*

Example 1 — *Absolute Coordinate System*

Draw the profile shown in Figure 2-17 by using the Absolute Coordinate system. The absolute coordinates of the points are given in the table given below. Save the drawing with the name *Exam1.dwg*.

Point	Coordinates
1	3,1
2	3,6
3	4,6
4	4,2

Point	Coordinates
5	5,2
6	6,3
7	7,3
8	7,1

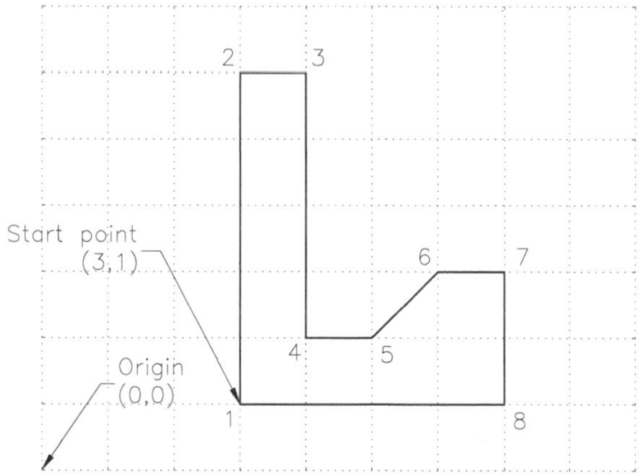

Figure 2-17 *Drawing a figure using the absolute coordinates*

Start a new file with the ***acad.dwt*** template in the **Drafting & Annotation** workspace. Once you know the coordinates of the points, you can draw the sketch by using the **Line** tool.

Choose the ***Zoom All*** *tool*

Choose the ***Line*** *tool*

The prompt sequence is given next.

LINE Specify first point: **3,1** Enter *(Start point.)*

Specify next point or [Undo]: **3,6** Enter

Specify next point or [Undo]: **4,6** Enter

Specify next point or [Close/Undo]: **4,2** Enter

Specify next point or [Close/Undo]: **5,2** Enter

Specify next point or [Close/Undo]: **6,3** Enter

Specify next point or [Close/Undo]: **7,3** Enter

Specify next point or [Close/Undo]: **7,1** Enter

Specify next point or [Close/Undo]: **C** Enter

Choose the **Save** tool from the **Quick Access Toolbar** to display the **Save Drawing As** dialog box. Enter **Exam1** in the **File name** edit box and then choose the **Save** button. The drawing will be saved with the specified name in the default *Documents* folder.

Exercise 1 Absolute Coordinate System

Draw the profile shown in Figure 2-18. The distance between the dotted lines is 1 unit. Enter absolute coordinates of the points given in the following table. Then, use these coordinates to draw the same figure.

Point	Coordinates	Point	Coordinates
1	2, 1	6	________
2	________	7	________
3	________	8	________
4	________	9	________
5	________		

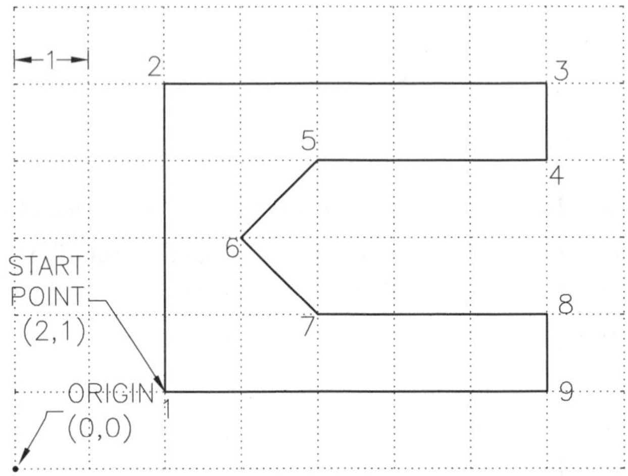

Figure 2-18 Drawing for Exercise 1

Relative Coordinate System

There are two types of relative coordinate system:
1. Relative Rectangular System
2. Relative Polar System

Relative Rectangular Coordinate System

In the Relative Rectangular Coordinate system, the location of a point is specified with respect to the previous point, not with respect to the origin. To enter coordinate values in terms of the Relative Rectangular Coordinate system, check whether the **Dynamic Input** is on or not. If the **Dynamic Input** is turned on, then by default the profile will be drawn using the Relative Rectangular Coordinate system. Therefore, in this case, enter the X coordinate, type comma (,), and then enter the Y coordinate. However, if the **Dynamic Input** is turned off, the coordinate values have to be prefixed by the @ symbol, so that the profile will be drawn using the Relative Rectangular Coordinate system. For example, to draw a rectangle of length 4 units and width 3 units and the lower left corner at the point (1,1) using the Relative Rectangular Coordinate system, refer to Figure 2-19, you need to use the following prompt sequence:

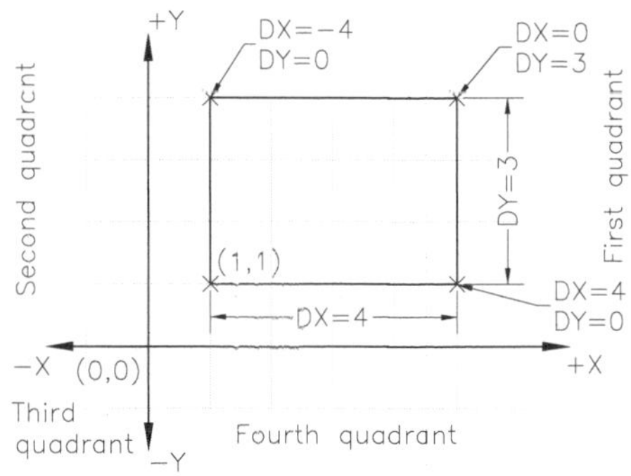

***Figure 2-19** Drawing lines using the relative rectangular coordinate*

*Choose the **Line** tool (make sure that the **Dynamic Input** is turned off)*

LINE Specify first point: **1,1** Enter *(Start point)*

Specify next point or [Undo]: **@4,0** Enter

Specify next point or [Undo]: **@0,3** Enter

Specify next point or [Close/Undo]:**@-4,0** Enter

Specify next point or [Close/Undo]: **@0,-3** Enter

Specify next point or [Close/Undo]: Enter

Remember that if the **Dynamic Input** is on, you need to use a comma (,) after entering the first value in the Dynamic Input boxes. Else, AutoCAD will take coordinates in relative polar form.

Sign Convention: As mentioned, in the Relative Rectangular Coordinate system, the distance along the X and Y axes is measured with respect to the previous point. To understand the sign convention, imagine a horizontal line and a vertical line passing through the previous points so that you get four quadrants. If the new point is located in the first quadrant, then both the distances (DX and DY) will be specified as positive values. If the new point is located in the third quadrant, then both the distances (DX and DY) will be specified as negative values. In other words, the point will have a positive coordinate values, if it is located above or right of an axis. Similarly, the point will have a negative coordinate value, if it is located below or left of the axis.

Example 2 — *Relative Rectangular Coordinate*

Draw the profile shown in Figure 2-20 using Relative Rectangular Coordinates. The coordinates of the points are given in the table below.

Point	Coordinates	Point	Coordinates
1	3,1	8	-1,-1
2	4,0	9	-1,1
3	0,1	10	-1,0
4	-1,0	11	0,-2
5	1,1	12	1,-1
6	0,2	13	-1,0
7	-1,0	14	0,-1

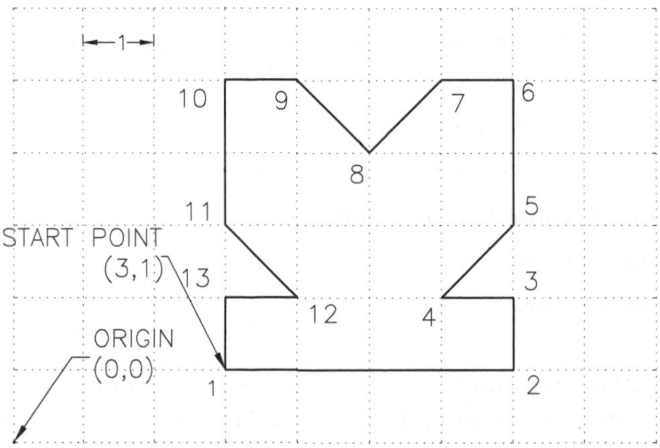

Figure 2-20 *Profile for Example 2*

Start a new file with the ***acad.dwt*** template in the **Drafting & Annotation** workspace. Before you proceed, you need to make sure that the **Dynamic Input** is turned on.

Choose the ***Zoom All*** tool

Next, *choose the **Line** tool*

LINE Specify first point: *Type* **3,1** *in the dynamic input boxes and press* Enter *(Start point)*

Specify next point or [Undo]: *Type* **4,0** *in the dynamic input boxes and press* Enter

Specify next point or [Undo]: *Type* **0,1** *in the dynamic input boxes and press* Enter

Specify next point or [Close/Undo]: *Type* **-1,0** *in the dynamic input boxes and press* Enter

Specify next point or [Close/Undo]: *Type* **1,1** *in the dynamic input boxes and press* Enter

Specify next point or [Close/Undo]: *Type* **0,2** *in the dynamic input boxes and press* Enter

Specify next point or [Close/Undo]: **-1,0** *and press* Enter

Specify next point or [Close/Undo]: **-1,-1** *and press* Enter

Specify next point or [Close/Undo]: **-1,1** *and press* Enter

Specify next point or [Close/Undo]: **-1,0** *and press* Enter

Specify next point or [Close/Undo]: **0,-2** *and press* Enter

Specify next point or [Close/Undo]: **1,-1** *and press* Enter
Specify next point or [Close/Undo]: **-1,0** *and press* Enter
Specify next point or [Close/Undo]: **0,-1** *and press* Enter
Specify next point or [Close/Undo]: Enter

Exercise 2 *Relative Rectangular Coordinate*

For Figure 2-21, enter the relative rectangular coordinates of the points in the table given below. Then, use these coordinates to draw the figure. The distance between the dotted lines is 1 unit.

Point	Coordinates	Point	Coordinates
1	2, 1	12	________
2	________	13	________
3	________	14	________
4	________	15	________
5	________	16	________
6	________	17	________
7	________	18	________
8	________	19	________
9	________	20	________
10	________	21	________
11	________	22	________

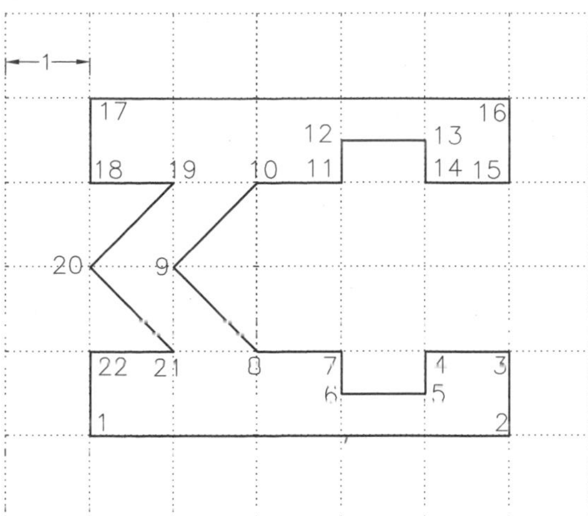

Figure 2-21 Drawing for Exercise 2

Relative Polar Coordinate System

In the relative polar coordinate system, the location of a point is specified by defining the distance of the point from the current point and the angle between the two points with respect to the positive *X* axis. The prompt sequence to draw a line of length 5 units whose start point is at 1,1 and inclined at an angle of 30 degrees to the *X* axis is given next, as shown in Figure 2-22.

Choose the ***Line*** *tool*
Specify first point: **1,1** Enter
Specify next point or [Undo]: **@5<30** Enter

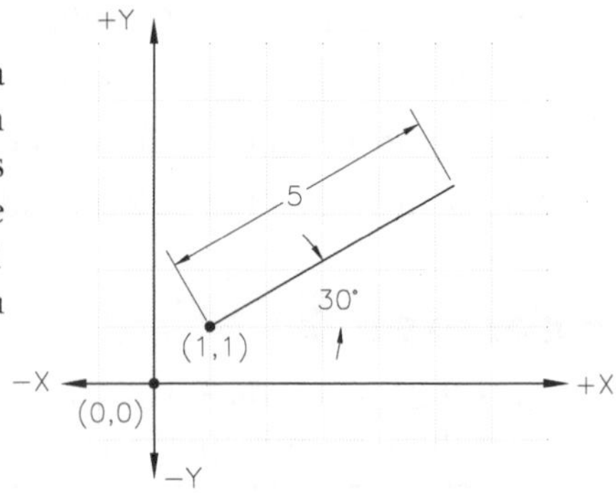

Figure 2-22 *Drawing a line by using relative polar coordinates*

If the **Dynamic Input** is on, by default the relative polar coordinate mode will be activated. Therefore, when you invoke the **Line** tool and specify the start point, two input boxes will be displayed. The second input box shows the angle value, preceded by the **<** symbol. Now, enter the distance value and press the TAB key to shift to the second input box, and then enter the angle value.

Sign Convention. By default, in the relative polar coordinate system, the angle is measured from the horizontal axis as the zero degree. Also, the angle is positive if measured in counter clockwise direction and is negative if measured in clockwise direction. Here, it is assumed that the default setup of the angle measurement has not been changed.

Note

You can modify the default settings of the angle measurement direction by using the ***Units*** *tool from the* ***Format*** *tab of the Menu Bar which is discussed later in this chapter.*

Example 3 — Relative Polar Coordinate

Draw the profile shown in Figure 2-23 by using the relative polar coordinate system. The relative coordinate values of each point are given in the table. The start point is located at 1.5, 1.75. Save this drawing with the name *Exam3.dwg*.

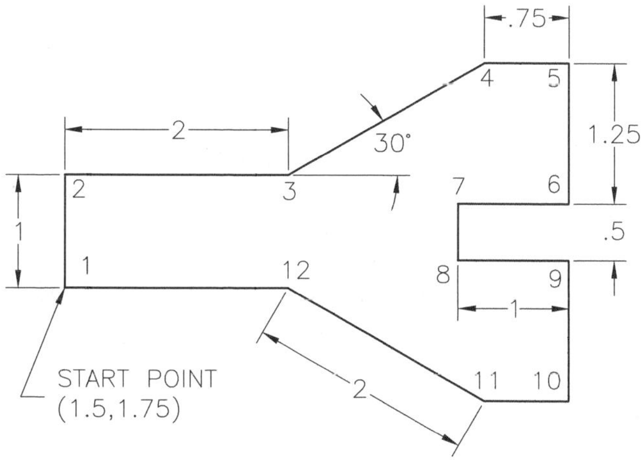

Figure 2-23 *Drawing for Example 3*

Point	Coordinates
1	1.5,1.75
2	@1.0<90
3	@2.0<0
4	@2.0<30
5	@0.75<0
6	@1.25<-90 (or <270)

Point	Coordinates
7	@1.0<180
8	@0.5<270
9	@1.0<0
10	@1.25<270
11	@0.75<180
12	@2.0<150

Start a new file with the ***acad.dwt*** template in the **Drafting & Annotation** workspace. Next, you need to modify the drawing display area. To do so, choose the **Zoom Extents** or **Zoom All** tool from the **Navigation bar**. Next, turn off the **Dynamic Input** option by choosing the **Dynamic Input** button from the Status Bar.

*Choose the **Line** tool*

LINE Specify first point: **1.5,1.75** Enter *(Start point)*

Specify next point or [Undo]: **@1<90** Enter

Specify next point or [Undo]: **@2.0<0** Enter

Specify next point or [Close/Undo]: **@2<30** Enter

Specify next point or [Close/Undo]: **@0.75<0** Enter

Specify next point or [Close/Undo]: **@1.25<-90** Enter

Specify next point or [Close/Undo]: **@1.0<180** Enter

Specify next point or [Close/Undo]: **@0.5<270** Enter

Specify next point or [Close/Undo]: **@1.0<0** Enter

Specify next point or [Close/Undo]: **@1.25<270** Enter

Specify next point or [Close/Undo]: **@0.75<180** Enter

Specify next point or [Close/Undo]: **@2.0<150** Enter

Specify next point or [Close/Undo]: **C** Enter *(The last point joins with the first point)*

To save this drawing, choose the **Save** tool from the **Quick Access Toolbar**; the **Save Drawing As** dialog box will be displayed. Enter **Exam3** in the **File name** edit box and then choose the **Save** button; the drawing will be saved with the specified name in the default *Documents* folder.

Exercise 3 Specifying Points using Coordinates

Draw the profile, as shown in Figure 2-24 by specifying points using the relative polar coordinate system. Do not dimension the profile.

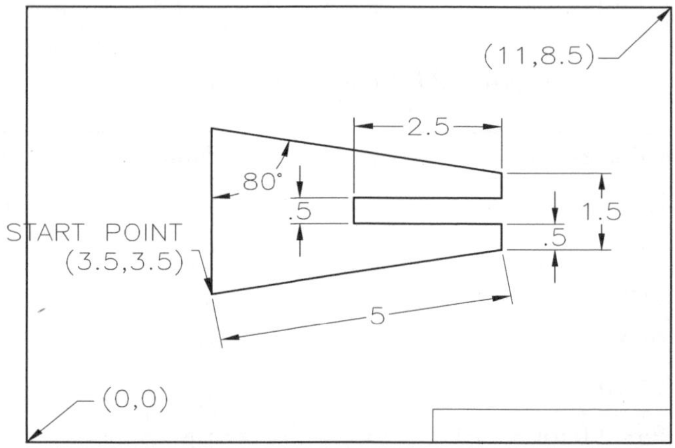

Figure 2-24 *Drawing for Exercise 3*

Direct Distance Entry

The easiest way to draw a line in AutoCAD is by using the Direct Distance Entry method. Before drawing a line by using this method, ensure that the **Dynamic Input** button is chosen in the Status Bar. Next, choose the **Line** tool; you will be prompted to specify the start point. Enter the coordinate values in the text box and press ENTER; you will be prompted to specify the next point. Now, enter the absolute length of the line and its angle with respect to the last point in the corresponding text boxes, as shown in Figure 2-25. Note that you can use the TAB key to toggle between the text boxes. If the **Ortho** mode is on while drawing lines using this method, you can position the cursor only along the *X* or *Y* axis. If the **Dynamic Input** button is not chosen, then you need to enter the length of the line at the command prompt. Therefore, position the cursor at the desired angle, type the length at the command prompt, and then press ENTER, refer to Figure 2-25.

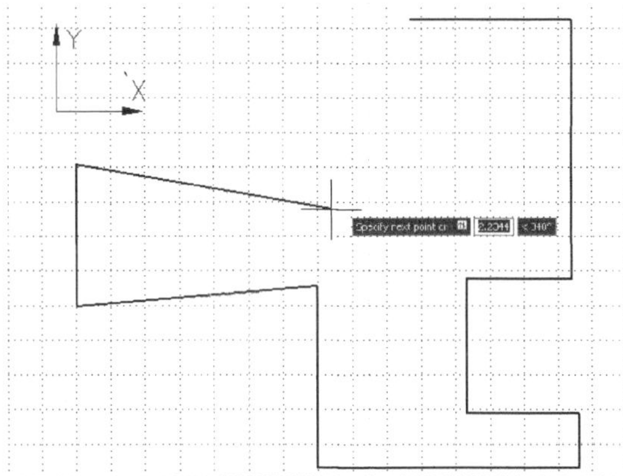

Figure 2-25 Drawing lines using the Direct Distance Entry method

Example 4 Direct Distance Entry

In this example, you will draw the profile , as shown in Figure 2-26, by using the Direct Distance Entry method. The start point is 2,2.

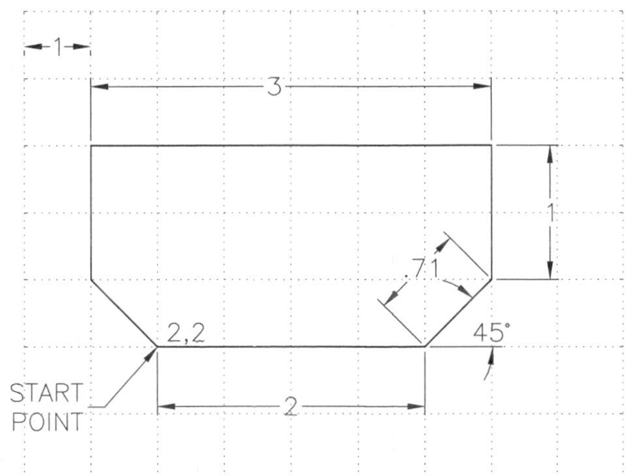

Figure 2-26 Drawing for Example 4

Also, you can use the **Polar Tracking** button to draw lines. The **Polar Tracking** button allows you to track the lines at specified angles. The default angle specified for polar tracking is 90 degrees. Therefore, by default, you can track lines at an angle that is multiple of 90 degrees, such as 90, 180, 270, and 360. In this example, you need to draw lines at the angles that are multiples of 45 degrees such as 45, 90, 135, and so on. Therefore, first you need to set the polar tracking angle as 45 degrees.

Note
You will learn more about polar tracking in Chapter 4.

1. Start a new file with the ***acad.dwt*** template in the **Drafting & Annotation** workspace.

2. Right-click on the **Polar Tracking** button on the Status Bar and then choose **45** from the shortcut menu displayed. Again, choose the **Polar Tracking** button in the Status Bar to turn polar tracking on if it is not turn on by default.

3. Choose the **Line** tool from the **Draw** panel of the **Home** tab; you are prompted to specify the start point.

4. Enter **2,1** at the command prompt and press ENTER; you are prompted to specify the next point.

5. Move the cursor horizontally toward the right and when the tooltip displays 0 as polar angle, type **2** and press ENTER; you are prompted to specify the next point.

6. Move the cursor at an angle close to 45 degrees and when the tooltip displays 45 as polar angle, type **0.71** and press ENTER; you are prompted to specify next point.

7. Move the cursor vertically upward and when the tooltip displays 90 as polar angle, type **1** and press ENTER; you are prompted to specify the next point.

8. Move the cursor horizontally toward the left and when the tooltip displays 180 as polar angle, type **3** and press ENTER; you are prompted to specify the next point.

9. Move the cursor vertically downward and when the tooltip displays 90 polar angle, type **1** and press ENTER; you are prompted to specify the next point.

10. Type **C** and press ENTER.

Tip
You can add more angular values in the shortcut menu displayed on right clicking the ***Polar Tracking*** *button in the Status Bar. To do so, choose the* ***Tracking Settings*** *option from the shortcut menu; the* ***Drafting Settings*** *dialog box will be displayed. Next, in the* ***Polar Angle Settings*** *area choose the* ***New*** *button and then enter the new angle value in the edit field that appears in the* ***Additional angles*** *box of the dialog box. Similarly, you can specify multiple angle values. Once you are done, choose the* ***OK*** *button.*

EXERCISE 4 Direct Distance Entry

Use the Direct Distance Entry method to draw a parallelogram. The base of the parallelogram equals 4 units, the side equals 2.25 units, and the angle equals 45 degrees. Draw the same parallelogram using the absolute, relative, and polar coordinates. Note the differences and the advantages of using this method over the Relative and Absolute Coordinate methods.

ERASING OBJECTS

Ribbon: Home > Modify > Erase
Toolbar: Modify > Erase
Menu Bar: Modify > Erase
Tool Palettes: Modify > Erase
Command: ERASE/E

Sometimes, you may need to erase the unwanted objects from the drawing. You can do so by using the **Erase** tool. This tool is used exactly the same way as an eraser is used in manual drafting to delete the unwanted lines. To erase an object, choose the **Erase** tool from the **Modify** panel, refer to Figure 2-27.

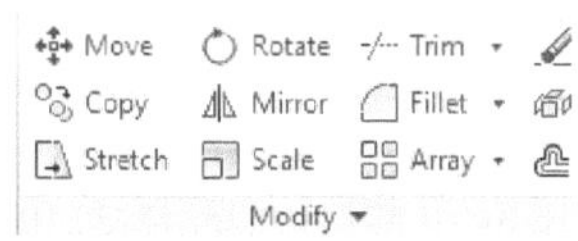

***Figure 2-27** The **Erase** tool in the **Modify** panel*

You can also choose the **Erase** tool from the **Modify** toolbar, as shown in Figure 2-28. To invoke the **Modify** toolbar, choose **Tools > Toolbars > AutoCAD > Modify** from the Menu Bar. On invoking the **Erase** tool, a small box, known as Pick box, replaces the screen cursor. To erase the object, select it by using the pick box, refer to Figure 2-29; the selected object will be displayed in transparent lines and the **Select objects** prompt will be displayed again. You can either continue selecting the objects or press ENTER to terminate the object selection process and erase the selected objects. The prompt sequence is given next.

*Choose the **Erase** tool*

Select objects: *Select the first object.*

Select objects: *Select the second object.*

Select objects: press ENTER

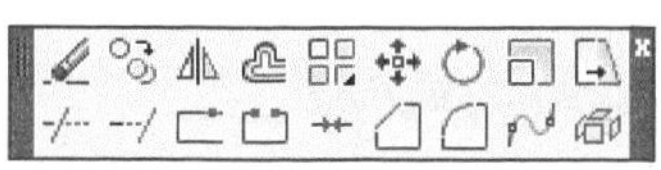

***Figure 2-28** The **Erase** tool in the **Modify** toolbar*

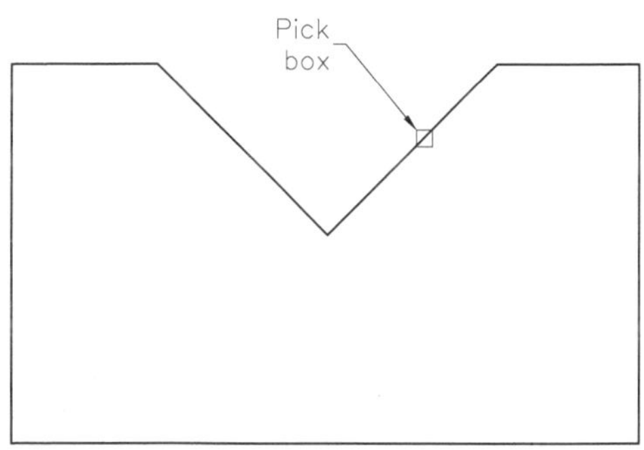

***Figure 2-29** Selecting the object by positioning the pick box at the top of the object*

If you enter **ALL** at the **Select objects** prompt, all objects in the drawing area will be selected, even if they are outside the display area. Now, if you press ENTER, all the selected objects will be erased. To erase the objects, you can also first select the objects to be erased from the drawing and then choose the **Erase** option from this shortcut menu that is displayed on right-clicking in the drawing area.

CANCELING AND UNDOING OPERATION

To restore the erased object, enter the **OOPS** or **UNDO** command. The **OOPS** command is used to restore the last erased object from the drawing area. The **UNDO** command is used to undo the action of the previously performed command. You can also choose the **Undo** tool from the **Quick Access Toolbar**. To cancel or exit a command, press the ESC (Escape) key on the keyboard.

OBJECT SELECTION METHODS

The usual method to select objects is by selecting them individually. But it will be time-consuming, if you have a number of objects to select. This problem can be solved by creating a selection set that enables you to select several objects at a time. The selection set options can be used with those tools that require object selection, such as **Erase** and **Move**. There are many object selection methods, such as **Window**, **Crossing**, and so on. In this chapter, you will learn about two methods: **Window** and **Crossing**. The remaining options are discussed in Chapter 5.

Window Selection Method

The window selection is one of the selection methods in which an object or group of objects are selected by drawing a window. The objects that are completely enclosed within the window are selected and the objects that lie partially inside the boundaries of the window are not selected. To select the objects by using the Window selection method, specify first corner point of a polygon and then type **WP** at the command prompt. Next, draw a polygon to select the object and then press ENTER. As you move the cursor, a blue color window of continuous line will be displayed. The size of this window changes as you move the cursor. Figure 2-30 shows the window drawn to select objects by using the Window selection method. The objects that will be selected are shown in light blue shaded lines.

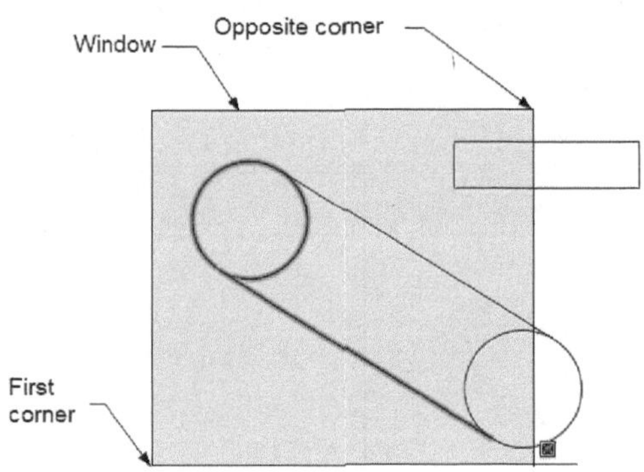

Figure 2-30 *Selecting objects using the Window selection method*

You can also use the **Window** option without entering **WP** at the command prompt. To do so, specify a point on the screen. This is considered as the first corner of the window. Moving the cursor to the right will display a blue-shaded window. After enclosing the required objects, specify the other corner of the window. The objects that are completely enclosed within the window will be selected and displayed in shaded blue lines. The following is the prompt sequence for window selection method after invoking the **Erase** tool:

Select objects: *Select a blank point as the first corner of the window*

Select objects: Specify opposite corner: *Drag the cursor to the right to select the other corner of the window*

Select objects: Enter

Crossing Selection Method

The crossing selection is one of the selection methods in which an object or group of objects that are completely or partially enclosed by the selection window are selected. The objects to be selected should touch the window boundaries or completely enclosed within it. To select the objects by using the Crossing selection method, specify first corner point of a polygon and then type **CP** at the command prompt and draw a polygon to select the objects and then press ENTER. As you move the cursor, a green color window with dashed outline will be displayed. Figure 2-31 shows a window drawn to select objects by using the Crossing selection method. The selected objects are shown in shaded blue lines.

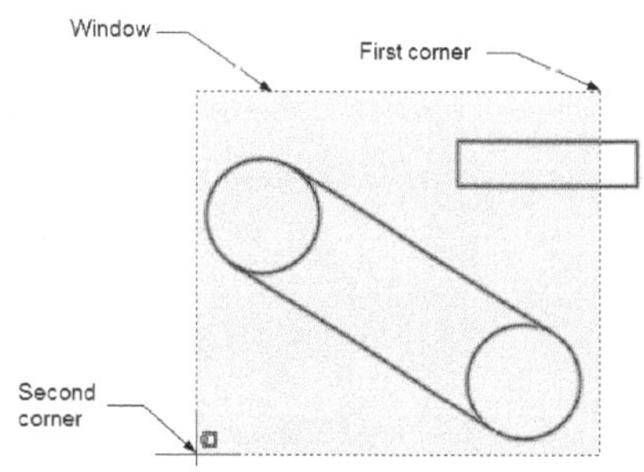

***Figure 2-31** Selecting objects using the Crossing selection method*

You can also invoke the Crossing selection method without entering **CP** at the command prompt. To do so, specify a point in the drawing area and move the cursor to the left. As you move the cursor, a green color window with dashed outline will be displayed. Specify the opposite corner of the window; the objects touching the window boundary and enclosed within this window will be selected and displayed in shaded blue lines.

The prompt sequence for the crossing selection method when you choose the **Erase** tool is given next.

Select objects: *Select a blank point as the first corner of the crossing window*

Select objects: Specify opposite corner: *Drag the cursor to the left to select the other corner of the window*

Select objects: Enter

If you do not invoke any tool and click to specify the first corner of the window for window selection or crossing selection, the command prompt provides you with three selection options: **Fence**, **WPolygon**, and **CPolygon**. If you enter **FENCE** or **F** at the command prompt, you can select objects by drawing a fence around them. If you enter **WP** or **CP** at the command prompt, you can select objects by drawing a polygon around them. These options will be discussed in detail in Chapter 5.

Lasso Selection Method

The lasso's selection is one of the selection methods in which an object or group of objects which are completely or partially enclosed by the selection area are selected. The objects to be selected should touch the window boundaries or completely enclosed within it. To select the objects by using the Lasso method, press and hold the left mouse button and drag the cursor; a selection area will be displayed, as shown in Figure 2-32.

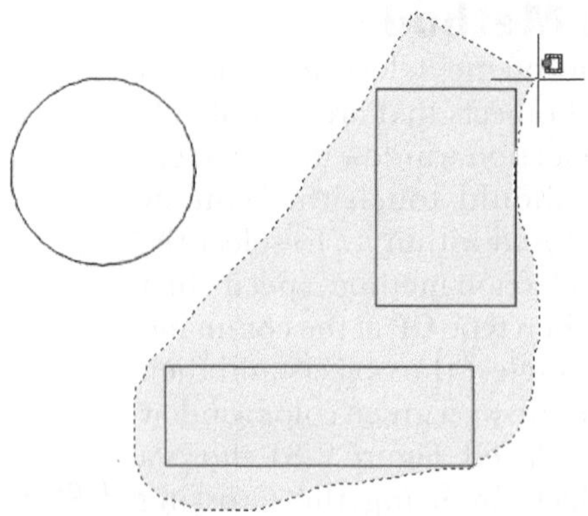

Figure 2-32 *Selecting objects using the lasso selection method*

Note that if you drag the cursor from left to right, only the objects enclosed in the area will be selected. And, if you drag the cursor from right to left, the objects touching the boundary of the lasso selection area will also be selected.

To activate the Lasso selection method, if it is not activated by default, invoke the **Options** dialog box and choose the **Selection** tab; the options available in the **Selection** tab will be displayed. Select the **Allow press and drag for Lasso** check box available in the **Selection modes** area of the dialog box; the Lasso selection will be activated, refer to Figure 2-33.

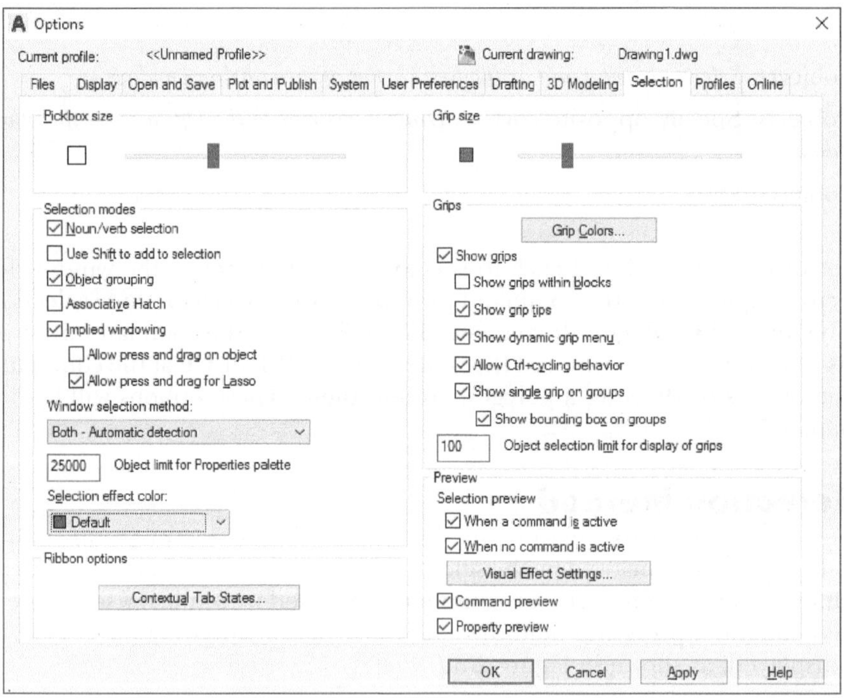

Figure 2-33 *The **Allow press and drag for Lasso** check box selected from the **Options** dialog box*

DRAWING A CIRCLE

Ribbon: Home > Draw > Circle
Toolbar: Draw > Circle **Menu Bar:** Draw > Circle
Tool Palettes: Draw > Circle **Command:** CIRCLE/C

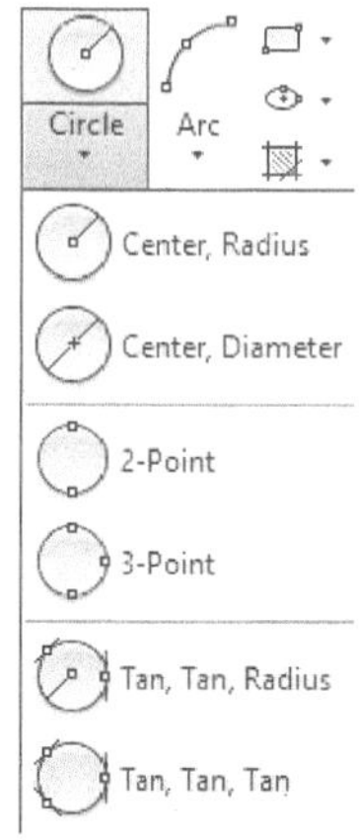

Figure 2-34 *Tools in the **Circle** drop-down*

In AutoCAD, you can draw a circle by using six different tools. All these tools are grouped together in the **Draw** panel of the **Ribbon**. To view these tools, choose the down arrow below the **Circle** tool in the **Draw** panel, as shown in Figure 2-34; all tools will be listed in the drop-down. Note that the name of the tool chosen last will be displayed in the **Draw** panel. You can also invoke the **Circle** tool from the **Draw** tab in the **Tool Palettes** or by entering **C** in the command prompt. The different tools to draw a circle are discussed next.

Drawing a Circle by Specifying Center and Radius

Ribbon: Home > Draw > Circle drop-down > Center, Radius
Menu Bar: Draw > Circle> Center, Radius **Command:** CIRCLE/C

To draw a circle by specifying its center and radius when the **Dynamic Input** button is chosen, choose the **Center, Radius** tool from the **Circle** drop-down of the **Draw** panel; you will be prompted to specify the center of the circle. Type the coordinates and press ENTER or specify the center by using the left mouse button. After specifying the center of the circle, move the cursor to define its radius; the current radius of the circle will be displayed in a dimension input box, as shown in Figure 2-35. This radius value will change as you move the cursor. Type a radius value in the dimension input box or click to define the radius; a circle of the specified radius value will be drawn. If the **Dynamic Input** is not chosen, you need to specify the input values in the command prompt.

Drawing a Circle by Specifying Center and Diameter

Ribbon: Home > Draw > Circle drop-down > Center, Diameter
Menu Bar: Draw > Circle> Center, Diameter

To draw a circle by specifying its center and diameter, when the **Dynamic Input** button is chosen, choose the **Center, Diameter** tool from the **Circle** drop-down of the **Draw** panel; you will be prompted to specify the center. Type the coordinates and press ENTER or specify the center by using the left mouse button. After specifying the center of the circle, move the cursor to define its diameter; the current diameter of the circle will be displayed in the dimension input box, as shown in Figure 2-36. This diameter value will change as you move the cursor. Type a diameter value in the dimension input box or click to define the diameter; a circle of the specified diameter value will be drawn. If the **Dynamic Input** is not chosen, you need to specify the input values in the command prompt.

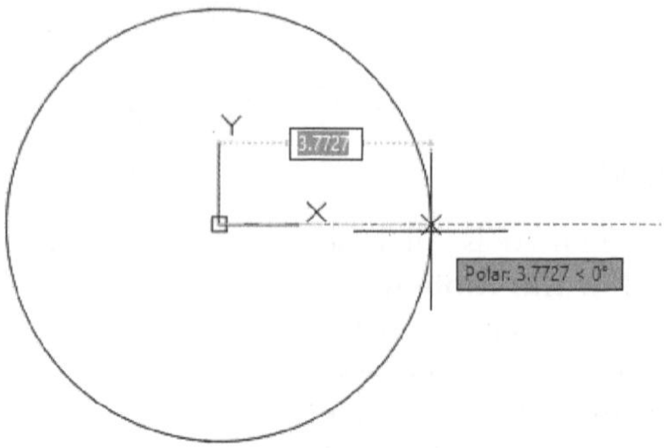

Figure 2-35 Drawing a circle by specifying the center and the radius

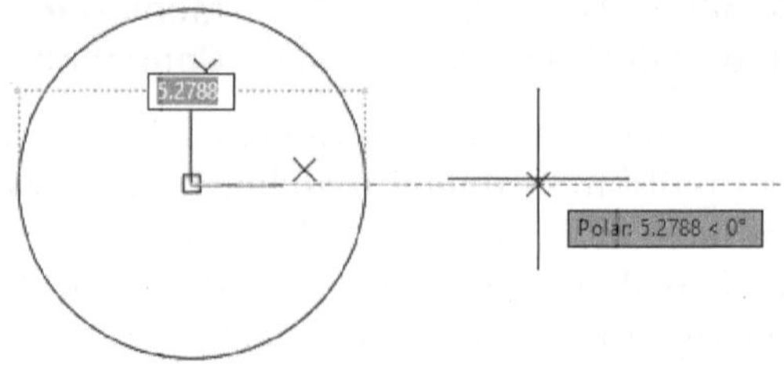

Figure 2-36 Drawing a circle by specifying the center and the diameter

Drawing a Circle by Specifying Two Diametrical Ends

Ribbon: Home > Draw > Circle drop-down > 2-Point
Menu Bar: Draw > Circle> 2 Points **Command:** CIRCLE/C > 2P

You can also draw a circle by specifying its two diametrical ends, refer to Figure 2-37. To do so, choose the **2-Point** tool from the **Circle** drop-down of the **Draw** panel; you will be prompted to specify the first end of the diameter. Type the coordinates and press ENTER. After specifying the first end point of the diameter of the circle you will be prompted to specify second end point of the circle's diameter. Type the coordinates and press ENTER or click in the drawing area to specify the second point of the circle's diameter.

Drawing a Circle by Specifying Three Points of a Circle

Ribbon: Home > Draw > Circle drop-down > 3-Point
Menu Bar: Draw > Circle> 3 Points **Command:** CIRCLE/C > 3P

To draw a circle by specifying three points on its periphery, choose the **3-Point** tool from the **Circle** drop-down of the **Draw** panel and specify the three points in succession. You can type the coordinates of the points or specify them by using the left mouse button.

The prompt sequence to enter three coordinates on choosing the **3-Point** tool is given below.

Specify center point for circle or [3P/2P/Ttr(tan tan radius)]: _3p
Specify first point on circle: **3,3**
Specify second point on circle: **3,1**
Specify third point on circle: **4,2** *(refer to Figure 2-38)*

You can also use the relative rectangular coordinates to define the points.

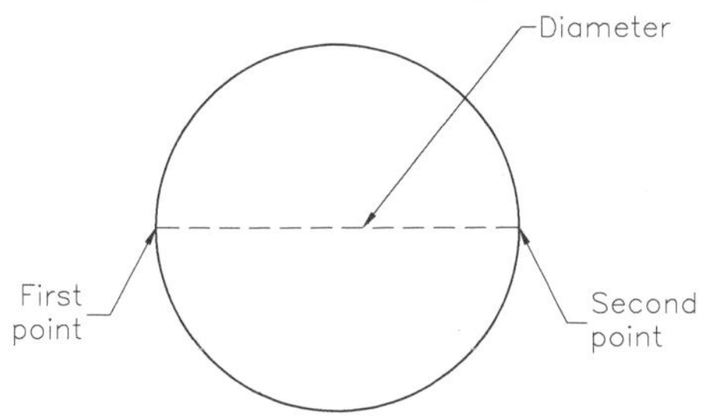

*Figure 2-37 A circle drawn by using the **2-Point** tool*

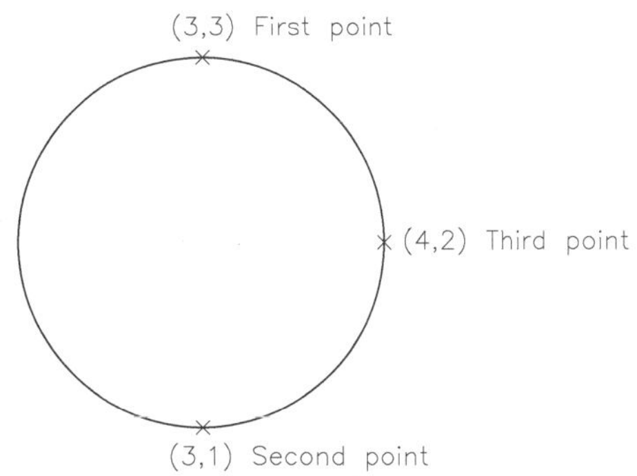

*Figure 2-38 A circle drawn by using the **3-Point** tool*

Drawing a Circle Tangent to Two Objects

Ribbon: Home > Draw > Circle drop-down > Tan, Tan, Radius
Menu Bar: Draw > Circle> Tan, Tan, Radius **Command:** CIRCLE/C > T

An object (line, circle, or arc) is said to be tangent to a circle or an arc if it touches the circumference of the circle or the arc at only one point. To draw a circle that has specified radius and is tangent to two objects, choose the **Tan, Tan, Radius** tool from the **Circle** drop-down of the **Draw** panel; you will be prompted to specify a point on the first object to be tangent to the circle. Move the cursor near the object to be made tangent to the circle; a tangent symbol will be displayed. Specify the first point; you will be prompted to specify a point on the second object to be made tangent to the circle. Move the cursor near the second object that is to be tangent to the circle; a tangent symbol will be displayed. Specify the second point; you will be prompted to specify the radius. Type the radius value in the dimension input box and press ENTER; a circle of the specified radius and tangent to two specified objects will be drawn.

In Figure 2-39 through Figure 2-42, the dotted circle represents the circle that is tangent to two objects. The circle actually drawn depends on how you select the objects to be made tangent to the new circle. The figures show the effect of selecting different points on the objects. If you specify too small or large radius, you may get unexpected results or the "**Circle does not exist**" prompt.

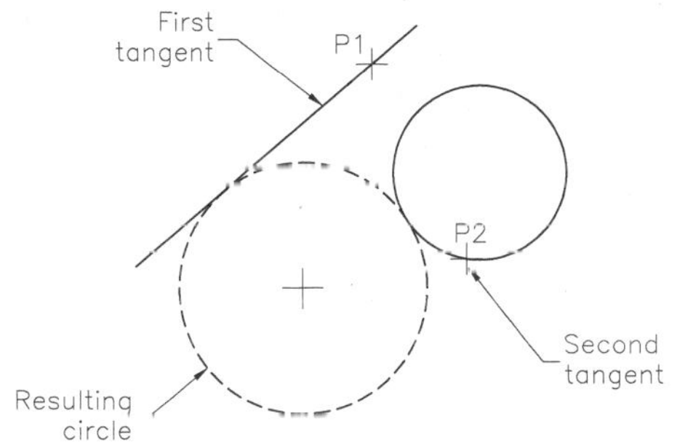

***Figure 2-39** Drawing a circle tangent to two objects*

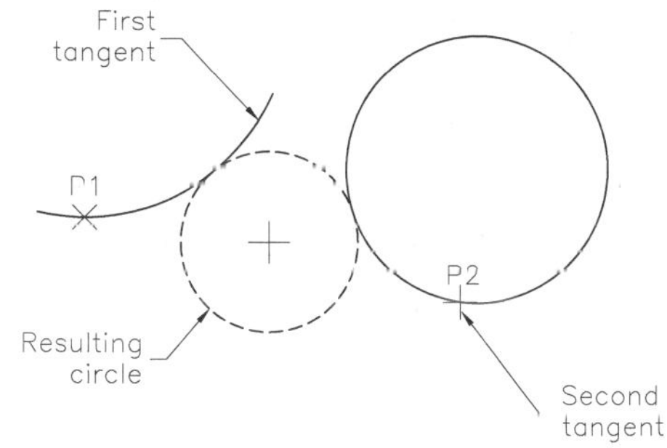

***Figure 2-40** Drawing a circle tangent to two objects*

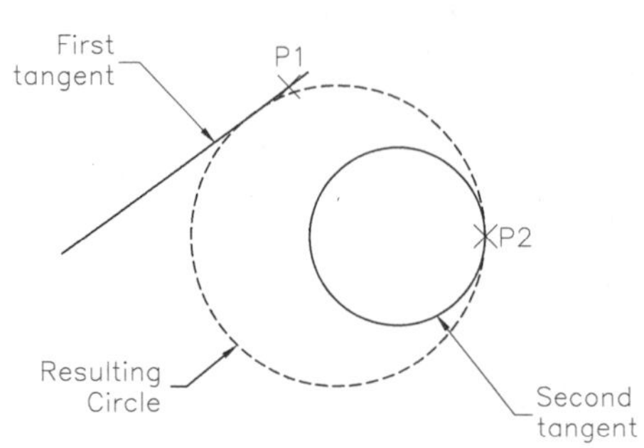

Figure 2-41 Drawing a circle tangent to two objects

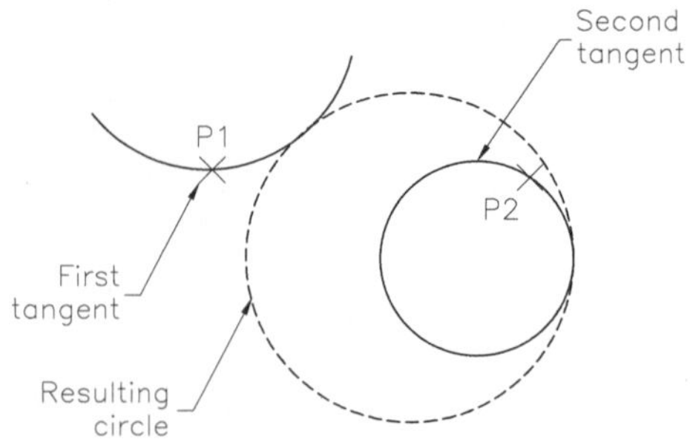

Figure 2-42 Drawing a circle tangent to two objects

Drawing a Circle Tangent to Three Objects

Ribbon: Home > Draw > Circle drop-down > Tan, Tan, Tan
Menu Bar: Draw > Circle> Tan, Tan, Tan

You can also draw a circle that is tangent to three objects. To do so, choose the **Tan, Tan, Tan** tool from the **Circle** drop-down of the **Draw** panel and select the three objects in succession to which the resulting circle is to be tangent; the circle will be drawn, as shown in Figure 2-43.

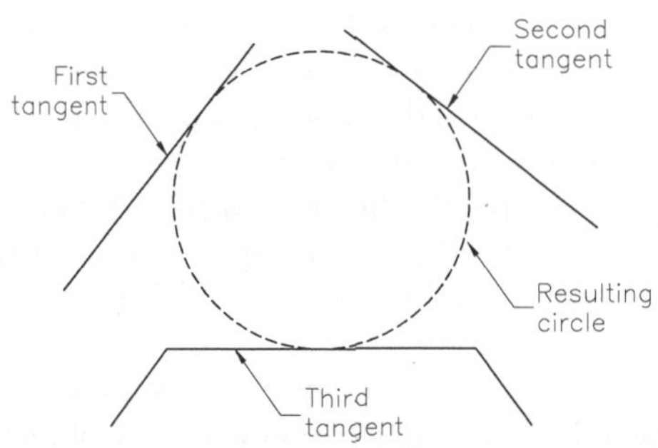

Figure 2-43 Drawing a circle tangent to three objects

Exercise 5 — Line and Circle

Draw the profile shown in Figure 2-44 using various options of the **Line** and **Circle** tools. Use the absolute, relative rectangular, or relative polar coordinates for drawing the triangle. The vertices of the triangle will be used as the centers of the circles. The circles can be drawn by using the **Center, Radius**, or **Center, Diameter**, or **Tan, Tan, Tan** tools.

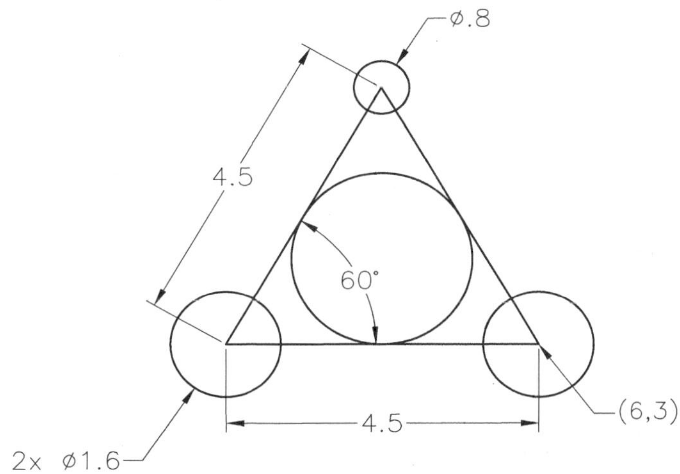

Figure 2-44 Drawing for Exercise 5

BASIC DISPLAY COMMANDS

Sometimes while drawing a sketch, it may be very difficult to view and alter minute details. You can overcome this problem by viewing only a specific portion of the drawing. This is done by using the **Zoom** tools. These tools let you enlarge or reduce the size of the drawing displayed on the screen. Similarly, you may need to slide the drawing view. This can be done by using the **Pan** tool. These are called display commands and are discussed next.

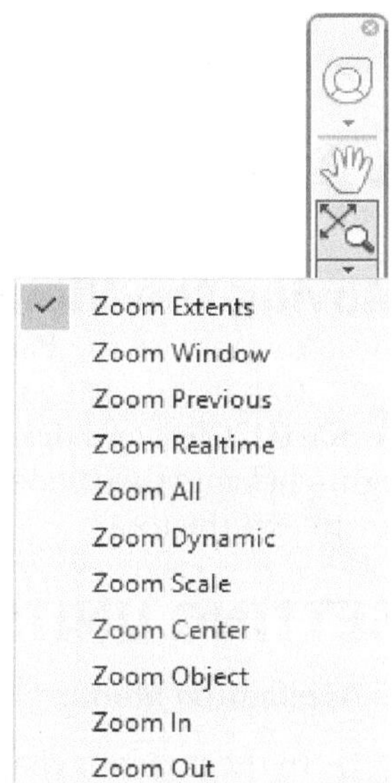

Figure 2-45** Zoom tools in the **Navigator Bar

Zooming Drawings

The **Zoom** tools are used to enlarge or reduce the view of a drawing on the screen, without affecting the actual size of entities. These tools are grouped together and are available in the Navigator Bar. To invoke different Zoom tools, click on the down arrow at the bottom of the **Zoom Extents** tool in the Navigator Bar; the **Zoom** drop-down will be displayed with different Zoom tools, as shown in Figure 2-45. You can also invoke the Zoom tools by choosing **View > Zoom** from the Menu Bar. To display the Menu Bar, click on the down arrow in the **Quick Access Toolbar** and then select **Show Menu Bar** option from the drop-down displayed. Some Zoom tools are also available in the **Standard** toolbar. These tools are discussed next.

Zoom Extents

Choose the **Zoom Extents** tool to increase or decrease the drawing display area so that all sketched entities or dimensions fit inside the current view.

Zoom Window

This is the most commonly used tool of the **Zoom** drop-down. On choosing this tool, you need to draw a window by specifying its two opposite corners. The center of the zoom window becomes the center of the new display area and the objects in this window are magnified.

Zoom Realtime

The **Zoom Realtime** tool is used to dynamically zoom in or out of a drawing. When you choose this tool, the cursor will be replaced by the zoom cursor. To zoom out a drawing, press and hold the left mouse button and drag the cursor downward. Similarly, to zoom in a drawing, press and hold the left mouse button and drag the cursor upward. As you drag the cursor, the display of drawing changes dynamically. After you get the desired view, exit this tool by right-clicking and then choosing **Exit** from the shortcut menu displayed. On exiting this tool, the zoom cursor will change into crosshairs. You can exit the **Zoom Realtime** tool by pressing the ESC key. You can also use the scroll wheel to zoom in/out the drawing.

Zoom Previous

While working on a complex drawing, you may need to zoom in a drawing multiple times to edit some minute details. After completing the editing, if you want to view the previous views, choose the **Zoom Previous** tool. You can view up to the last ten views by using the **Zoom Previous** tool.

Zoom In / Zoom Out

Choose the **Zoom In / Zoom Out** tool to increase/decrease the size of the drawing view twice/half of the original drawing size, respectively.

Note

You will learn about the other Zoom tools in detail in Chapter 6.

Moving the View

You can use the **Pan** tool to move a view by sliding and placing it at the required position. To pan a drawing view, invoke the **Pan** tool from the Navigator Bar; a hand cursor will be displayed. Click and drag the cursor in any direction to move the drawing. To exit the **Pan** tool, right-click and then choose **Exit** from the shortcut menu. You can also press the ESC or ENTER key to exit the tool.

SETTING UNITS TYPE AND PRECISION

Application Menu: Drawing Utilities > Units **Command:** UNITS/UN

In the previous chapter, you learned to set units while starting a drawing by using the **Use a Wizard** option in the **Startup** dialog box. But, if you are drawing a sketch in an existing template or in a new template, you need to change the format of the units for distance and angle measurements. To do so, choose **Format > Units** from the Menu Bar; the **Drawing Units** dialog box will be displayed, as shown in Figure 2-46. You can also invoke this dialog box by choosing **Drawing Utilities > Units** from the **Application Menu**. The procedure to change the units format is discussed next.

*Figure 2-46 The **Drawing Units** dialog box*

Specifying the Format

In the **Drawing Units** dialog box, you can select the desired format of units from the **Type** drop-down list available in the **Length** area. You can select any one of the five formats given next.

Architectural (0'-01/16")	Decimal (0.0000)	Engineering (0'-0.0000")
Fractional (0 1/16)	Scientific (0.00E+01)	

If you select the scientific, decimal, or fractional format, you can enter the values for distance or coordinate in any of these three formats. But, if you select the engineering or architectural format, you can enter the values for distance or coordinate in any of the five formats.

Note

The inch symbol (") is optional. For example, 1'1-3/4" is same as 1'1-3/4 and 3/4" is same as 3/4.

Specifying the Angle Format

You can select any one of the following five angle measuring formats:

1. Decimal Degrees (0)
2. Deg/min/sec (0d)
3. Grads (0g)
4. Radians (0r)
5. Surveyor's Units (N 0d E)

If you select any one of the first four measuring formats, you can specify the angle in the Decimal, Degrees/minutes/seconds, Grads, or Radians formats, but you cannot enter the angle in the Surveyor's Units system. However, if you select the Surveyor's Units system, you can enter angle values in any of the five systems. To enter a value in another system, use the appropriate suffixes and symbols, such as r (Radians), d (Degrees), or g (Grads). If you enter an angle value without indicating the symbol of a measuring system, it is taken in the current system.

In Surveyor's Units, you must specify the angle that the line makes with respect to the north-south direction, as shown in Figure 2-47. For example, if you want to define an angle of 60-degree with north, in the Surveyor's Units the angle will be specified as N 60d E. Similarly, you can specify angles such as S 50d E, S 50d W, and N 75d W, refer to Figure 2-47. You cannot specify an angle that exceeds 90-degree (N 120 E). Angles can also be specified in radians or grads; for example, 180-degree is equal to π(3.14159) radians. You can convert degrees into radians, or radians into degrees by using the equations given below.

radians = degrees X 3.14159/180;
degrees = radians X 180/3.14159

Grads are generally used in land surveys. There are 400 grads or 360 degree in a circle. 90 degree angle is equal to 100 grads.

In AutoCAD, the angles are measured from the positive X axis. If measured in a counterclockwise direction, then angles are positive and vice-versa, refer to Figure 2-48. If you want the angles to be measured as positive in the clockwise direction, select the **Clockwise** check box from the **Angle** area. You can specify the precision for the length and angle in the respective **Precision** drop-down lists in this dialog box.

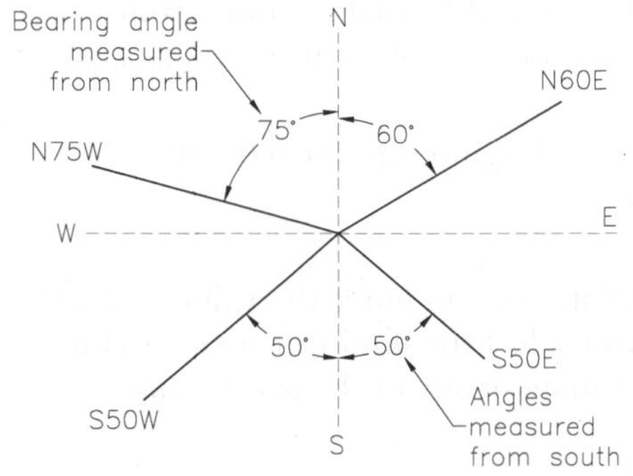

Figure 2-47 *Specifying angles in Surveyor's Units*

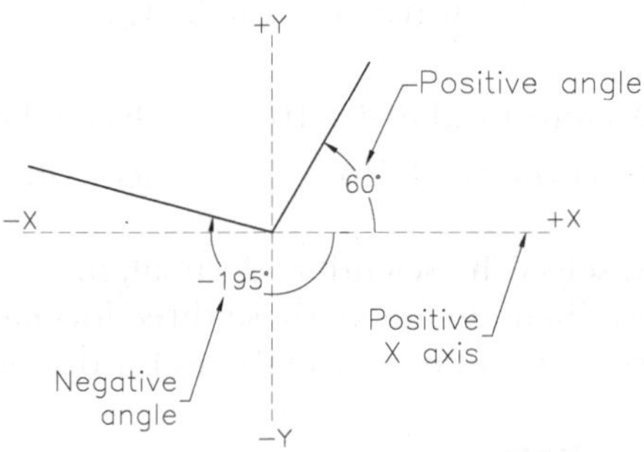

Figure 2-48 *Measuring angles*

Setting the Direction for Angle Measurement

As mentioned above, angles are measured about the positive X axis. This means the base angle (0-degree) is set along the east direction, refer to Figure 2-49. To change this base angle, choose the **Direction** button in the **Drawing Units** dialog box; the **Direction Control** dialog box will be displayed, as shown in Figure 2-50. Select the appropriate radio button to specify the direction for the base angle (0-degree).

If you select the **Other** option, you can set the direction of your choice for the base angle (0-degree) by entering a value in the **Angle** edit box or by choosing the **Pick an angle** button and picking two points to specify the angle. After specifying the base angle direction, choose the **OK** button to apply the settings.

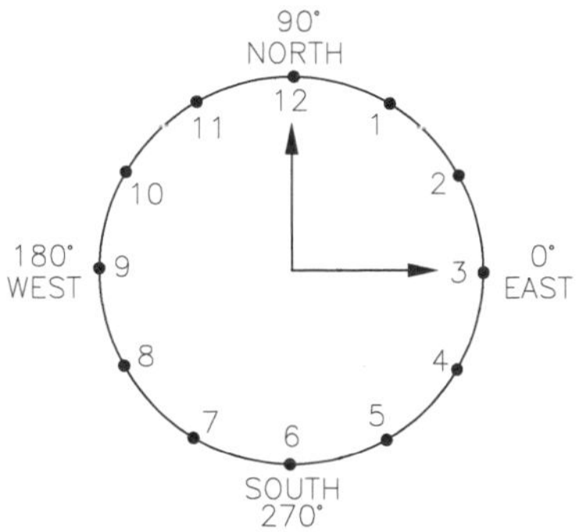

Figure 2-49 North, South, East, and West directions

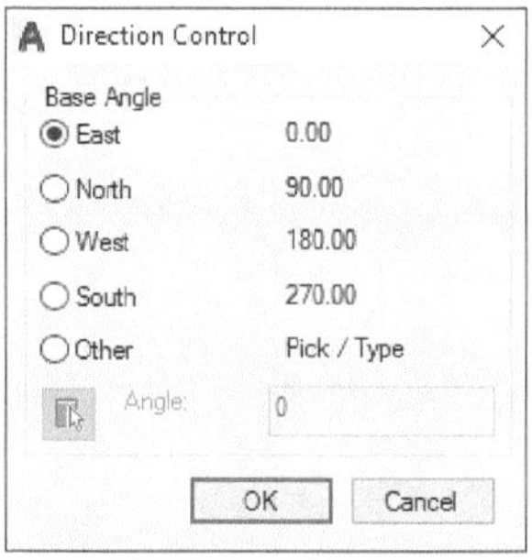

Figure 2-50 The ***Direction Control*** *dialog box*

Tip

If you are entering values by using the dimension input boxes that are displayed when the ***Dynamic Input*** *option is on, then you are not required to set the base angle.*

Specifying Units for the Drawing or Block to be Inserted

To set units for a block or a drawing to be inserted, select a unit from the **Units to scale inserted content** drop-down list. Now, if you insert a block or a drawing from the **DesignCenter**, the specified unit will be applied to the block. Even if the block was created using a different measuring unit, AutoCAD scales it and inserts it using the specified measuring unit. If you select **Unitless** from the drop-down list, then the units specified in the **Insertion Scale** area of the **User Preferences** tab in the **Options** dialog box will be used.

Note

Inserting blocks in a drawing is discussed in detail in Chapter 16.

Sample Output

The **Sample Output** area in this dialog box shows the example of the current format used for specifying units and angles. When you change the type of length and angle measure in the **Length** and **Angle** areas of the **Drawing Units** dialog box, the corresponding example is displayed in the **Sample Output** area.

Specifying Units for Lighting

You can also specify the units to be used for the measurement of intensity of photometric lights. Photometric lights are used for rendering the objects. Select the desired unit system from the **Units for specifying the intensity of lighting** drop-down list in the **Lighting** area of the **Drawing Units** dialog box.

Example 5 Setting Units

In this example, you will set units for a drawing based on the specifications given below and then draw Figure 2-51.

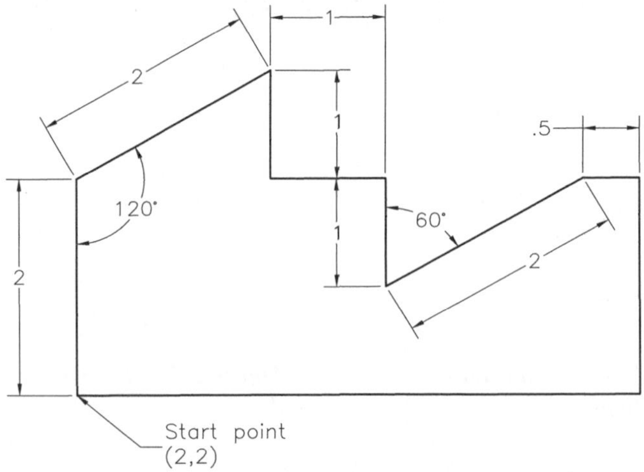

Figure 2-51 *Drawing for Example 5*

a. Set the units of length to decimal with precision equal to 0.
b. Set the angular measurement to Surveyor's Units with precision equal to N 0d E.
c. Set the base angle (0-degree) to North and the direction of measurement of angles to clockwise.

The following steps are required to complete this example:

1. Start a new file with the ***acad.dwt*** template in the **Drafting & Annotation** workspace and invoke the **Drawing Units** dialog box by choosing **Drawing Utilities > Units** from the **Application Menu**. You can also invoke this dialog box by choosing **Format > Units** from the Menu Bar.

2. In the **Length** area of this dialog box, select **Decimal** from the **Type** drop-down list. Select **0** from the **Precision** drop-down list.

3. In the **Angle** area of this dialog box, select **Surveyor's Units** from the **Type** drop-down list. From the **Precision** drop-down list, select **N 0d E** if not already selected. Also, select the **Clockwise** check box to set the clockwise angle measurement to positive.

4. Choose the **Direction** button to display the **Direction Control** dialog box. Next, select the **North** radio button. Choose the **OK** button to exit the **Direction Control** dialog box.

5. Choose the **OK** button to exit the **Drawing Units** dialog box.

6. With the units set, you need to draw Figure 2-51 using the relative polar coordinates. Turn off the dynamic input. The prompt sequence to complete the sketch is as follows:

   *Choose the **Line** tool*
   LINE Specify first point: ***2,2*** Enter
   Specify next point or [Undo]: ***@2<0*** Enter
   Specify next point or [Undo]: ***@2<60*** Enter

Specify next point or [Close/Undo]: ***@1<180*** Enter
Specify next point or [Close/Undo]: ***@1<90*** Enter
Specify next point or [Close/Undo]: ***@1<180*** Enter
Specify next point or [Close/Undo]: ***@2<60*** Enter
Specify next point or [Close/Undo]: ***@0.5<90*** Enter
Specify next point or [Close/Undo]: ***@2<180*** Enter
Specify next point or [Close/Undo]: ***C*** Enter

Here, the units are decimal and the angles are measured from north (90-degree axis). Also, the angles are measured as positive in a clockwise direction and negative in a counterclockwise direction.

7. Choose the **Zoom All** tool from the Navigator Bar; the drawing display area gets modified.

SETTING THE LIMITS OF A DRAWING

Menu Bar: Format > Drawing Limits **Command:** LIMITS

In AutoCAD, limits represent the drawing area and it is endless. Therefore, you need to define the drawing area before starting the drawing. In the previous chapter, you learned to set limits while starting a drawing by using the **Use a Wizard** option in the **Startup** dialog box. If you are working in a drawing by using the default template, you need to change the limits. For example, the template **acad.*dwt*** has the default limits set to 12,9. To draw a rectangle of dimension 15x10 in this template, you need to change its limits to 24x18. To do so, choose **Format > Drawing Limits** from the Menu Bar; you will be prompted to specify the lower left corner. The following is the prompt sequence of this tool for setting the limits to 24,18 for the ***acad.dwt*** template which has the default limits 12,9.

*Choose the **Drawing Limits** tool*
Reset Model space limits:
Specify lower left corner or [ON/OFF]<0.0000,0.0000>: **0,0** Enter
Specify upper right corner <12.0000,9.0000>: **24,18** Enter

Tip
*Whenever you reset the drawing limits, the display area does not change automatically. To change the display area, use the **Zoom All** tool from the **Zoom** drop down.*

The limits of the drawing area are usually determined by the following factors:

1. The actual size of drawing.
2. The space needed for adding dimensions, notes, bill of materials, and other necessary details.
3. The space between various views so that the drawing does not look cluttered.
4. The space for the border and title block, if any.

Setting Limits

To get a good idea of how to set up limits, it is better to draw a rough sketch of a drawing. This will help in calculating the required drawing area. For example, if an object has a front view size of 5 X 5, a side view size of 3 X 5, and a top view size of 5 X 3, the limits should be set so that the drawing and everything associated with it can be easily accommodated within the set limit. In Figure 2-52, the space between the front and side views is 4 units and between the front and top views is 3 units. Also, the space between the border and the drawing is 5 units on the left, 5 units on the right, 3 units at the bottom, and 2 units at the top. (The space between the views and between the borderline and the drawing depends on the drawing.)

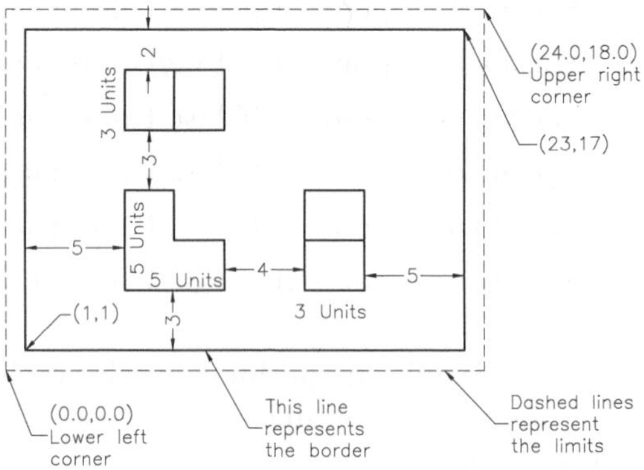

Figure 2-52 *Setting limits in a drawing*

After knowing the size of different views, the space required between views, the space between the border and the drawing, and the space required between the borderline and the edges of the paper, you can calculate the space in the following way:

Space along (*X* axis) = 1 + 5 + 5 + 4 + 3 + 5 + 1 = 24
Space along (*Y* axis) = 1 + 3 + 5 + 3 + 3 + 2 + 1 = 18

This shows that the limits you need to set for this drawing are 24 X 18. Once you have determined the space, select the sheet size that can accommodate your drawing. In the case just explained, you will select a D size (34 X 22) sheet. Therefore, the actual drawing limits will be 34,22.

Tip

To display the grid, choose the ***Display drawing grid*** *button from the Status Bar. By default, the grid will be displayed beyond the limits. To display the grid up to the limits, use the* ***Limits*** *option of the* ***GRID*** *command and set the* ***Display grid beyond Limits [Yes/No] <Yes>:*** *to* ***No****; the grids will be displayed only up to the limits set.*

Limits for Architectural Drawings

Most architectural drawings are drawn at the scale of 1/4" = 1', 1/8" = 1', or 1/16" = 1'. You must set the limits accordingly. The following example illustrates how to calculate the limits of an architectural drawing.

Given

Sheet size = 24" X 18"
Scale is 1/4" = 1'

Calculate limits

Scale is 1/4" = 1'
or 1/4" = 12"
or 1" = 48"

X limit = 24" X 48"
= 1152" or 1152 Units
= 96'
Y limit = 18" X 48"
= 864" or 864 Units
= 72'

Thus, the scale factor is 48 and the limits are 1152",864" or 96',72'.

Example 6 Setting Limits

In this example, you will calculate the limits and determine an appropriate drawing scale factor for the drawing shown in Figure 2-53. You will plot the drawing on a 12" X 9" sheet.

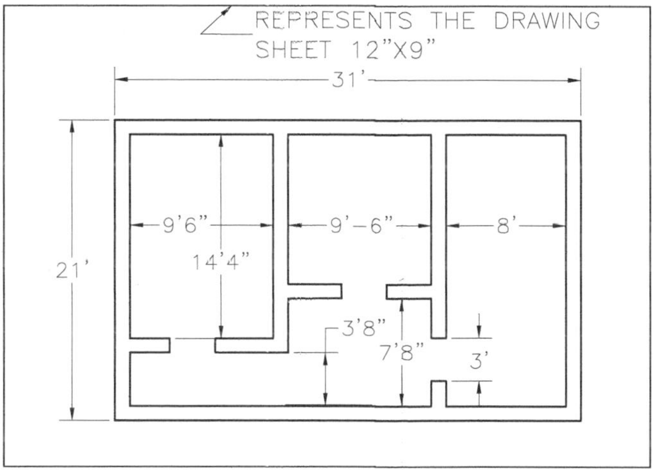

Figure 2-53 Drawing for Example 6

The calculation for the scale factor is given next.

Given or known

Overall length of the drawing = 31'
Length of the sheet = 12"
Approximate space between the drawing and the edges of the paper = 2"

Calculate the scale factor

To calculate the scale factor, you have to try various scales until you find the one that satisfies the given conditions. After some experience, you will find this fairly easy to do. For this example, assume a scale factor of 1/4" = 1'.

Scale factor 1/4" = 1' or 1" = 4'

Thus, a line 31' long will be = 31'/4' = 7.75" on paper. Similarly, a line 21' long = 21'/4' = 5.25". Approximate space between the drawing and the edges of paper = 2".

Therefore, the total length of the sheet = 7.75 + 2 + 2 = 11.75"

Similarly, the total width of the sheet = 5.25 + 2 + 2 = 9.25"

Because you selected the scale 1/4" = 1', the drawing will definitely fit in the given sheet of paper (12" x 9"). Therefore, the scale for this drawing is 1/4" = 1'.

Calculate limits

Scale factor = 1" = 48" or 1" = 4'
The length of the sheet is 12"
Therefore, X limit = 12 X 4' = 48' and Y limit = 9 X 4' = 36'

Limits for Metric Drawings

When the drawing units are in metric, you must use the standard metric size sheets or calculate limits in millimeters (mm). For example, if the sheet size is 24 X 18, the limits, after conversion to the metric system, will be 609.6,457.2 (multiplying length and width by 25.4). You can round these numbers to the nearest whole numbers 610,457. Note that the metric drawings do not require any special setup, except for the limits. Metric drawings are like any other drawings that use decimal units. Similar to architectural drawings, you can draw metric drawings to a scale. For example, if the scale is 1:20, you must calculate the limits accordingly. The following example illustrates how to calculate limits for metric drawings:

Given

Sheet size = 24" X 18"
Scale = 1:20

Calculate limits

Scale is 1:20
Therefore, scale factor = 20
X limit = 24 X 25.4 X 20 = 12192 units
Y limit = 18 X 25.4 X 20 = 9144 units

Exercise 6 — *Setting Units and Limits*

Set the units of the drawing according to the specifications given below and then make the drawing shown in Figure 2-54 (leave a space of 3 to 5 units around the drawing for dimensioning and title block). The space between the dotted lines is 1 unit.

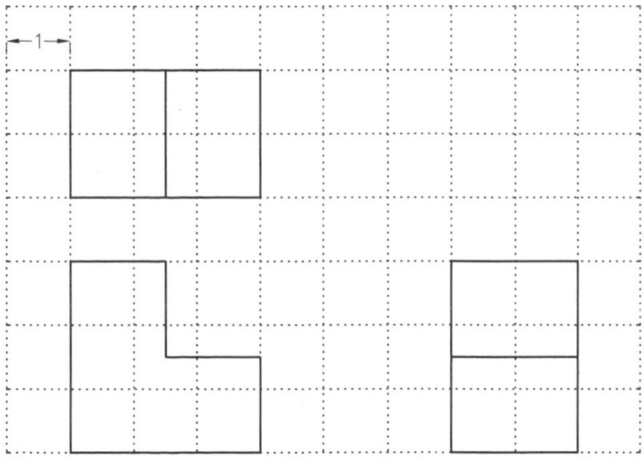

Figure 2-54 *Drawing for Exercise 6*

1. Set UNITS to decimal units, with two digits to the right of the decimal point.
2. Set the angular measurement to decimal degrees, with the number of decimal places for display of angles equal to 1.
3. Set the direction to 0-degree (east) and the direction of measurement of angles to counterclockwise (angles measured positive in a counterclockwise direction).
4. Set the limits leaving a space of 3 to 5 units around the drawing for dimensioning and title block.

INTRODUCTION TO PLOTTING DRAWINGS

Ribbon: Output > Plot > Plot	**Quick Access Toolbar:** Plot
Application Menu: Print > Plot	**Command:** PLOT or PRINT

After creating a drawing of an architectural plan or a mechanical component, you may need to send it to the client or have a hard copy for reference. To do so, you need to plot the drawing. To plot the drawing, choose **Plot** from the **Quick Access Toolbar**; the **Plot-Model** dialog box will be displayed. If the dialog box is not expanded by default, choose the **More Options** button at the lower right corner of the dialog box to expand it, refer to Figure 2-55.

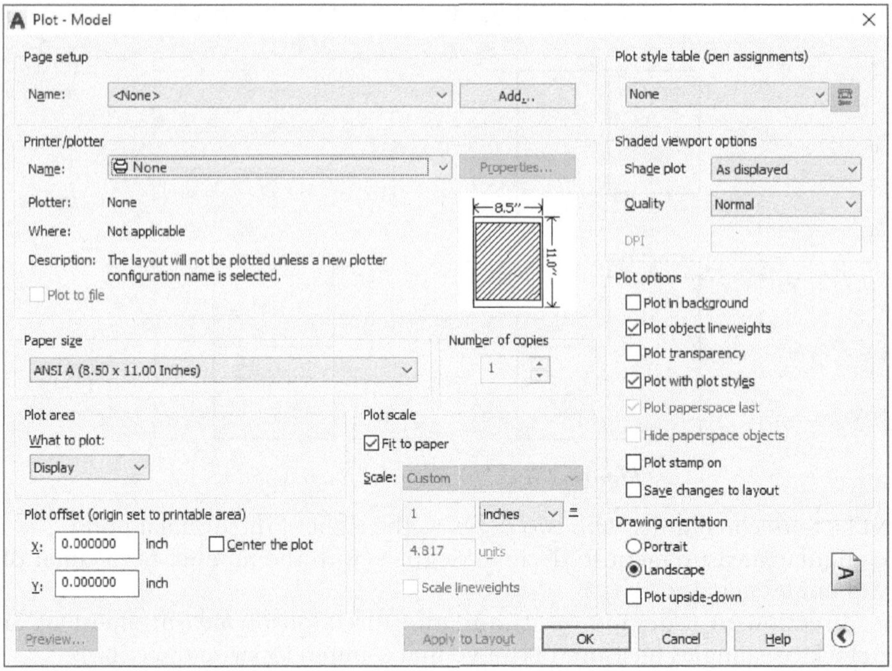

*Figure 2-55 The **Plot-Model** dialog box*

Basic Plotting

Basic plotting involves selecting the correct output device (plotter), specifying the area to plot, selecting the paper size, specifying the plot origin, orientation, and the plot scale.

To learn the basic plotting, you will plot the drawing drawn in Example 3 of this chapter. It is assumed that AutoCAD is configured for two output devices: Default Windows System Printer and 53436DrawingMaster DM800.

1. Invoke the **Plot** dialog box by choosing the **Plot** tool in the **Quick Access Toolbar**.

2. The name of the default system printer is displayed in the **Name** drop-down list in the **Printer/plotter** area. Select the printer to be used from the **Name** drop-down list.

3. Select the **Window** option from the **What to plot** drop-down list in the **Plot area**. The dialog box will close temporarily and the drawing area will appear. Next, select two opposite corners to define a window that can enclose the entire area you want to plot. Note that the complete drawing along with the dimensions should be enclosed in the window. Once you have defined the two corners, the **Plot** dialog box will reappear.

4. To set the size of the plot, you need to select a paper size from the drop-down list in the **Paper size** area. After selecting the paper size, you need to set the orientation of the paper. To set the orientation, expand the **Plot** dialog box by choosing the **More Options** button at the lower right corner of the dialog box. You can set the orientation as **Landscape** or **Portrait** by selecting the appropriate radio button from the **Drawing orientation** area. The sections in the **Plot** dialog box related to the paper size and orientation are automatically

revised to reflect the new paper size and orientation. For this example, you will specify the **A4** paper size and the **Portrait** orientation.

5. You can also modify values for the plot offset in the **Plot offset (origin set to printable area)** area; the default value for X and Y is 0. For this example, you can select the **Center the plot** check box to get the drawing at the center of the paper.

6. In AutoCAD, you can enter values for the plot scale in the **Plot scale** area. Clear the **Fit to paper** check box if it is selected and then click on the **Scale** drop-down list in the **Plot scale** area to display various scale factors. From this list, you can select a scale factor based on your requirement. For example, if you select the scale factor **1/4" = 1'-0"**, the edit boxes below the drop-down list will show 0.25 inches = 12 units. If you want the drawing to be plotted so that it fits on the specified sheet of paper, select the **Fit to paper** check box. On selecting this check box, AutoCAD will determine the scale factor and display it in the edit boxes. For this example, you will plot the drawing so that it scales to fit the paper. Therefore, select the **Fit to paper** check box and notice the change in the edit boxes. You can also enter arbitrary values in the edit boxes.

7. To preview a plot, choose the **Preview** button. You can preview the plot on the specified paper size. In the preview window, the realtime zoom icon will be displayed. If needed, you can zoom in or zoom out the preview image for better visualization.

8. If the plot preview is satisfactory, you can plot your drawing by right-clicking and then choosing **Plot** from the shortcut menu displayed. If you want to make some changes in the settings, choose **Exit** in the shortcut menu or press the ESC or ENTER key to get back to the dialog box. Change the parameters and choose the **OK** button in the dialog box to plot the drawing.

MODIFYING AutoCAD SETTINGS BY USING THE OPTIONS DIALOG BOX

Application Menu: Options **Command:** OPTIONS/OP

You can use the **Options** dialog box to change the default settings and customize them to your requirements. For example, you can use this dialog box to turn off the settings that are used to display the shortcut menu, change the display color of the objects, or specify the support directories containing the files you need.

To invoke the **Options** dialog box, right-click at the command prompt or in the drawing area when no command is active or no object is selected and then choose **Options** from the shortcut menu; the **Options** dialog box will be displayed, as shown in Figure 2-56. The name of the current profile and the current drawing names will be displayed below the title bar. You can save a set of custom settings in a profile to be used later for other drawings. The different tabs in the **Options** dialog box are discussed next.

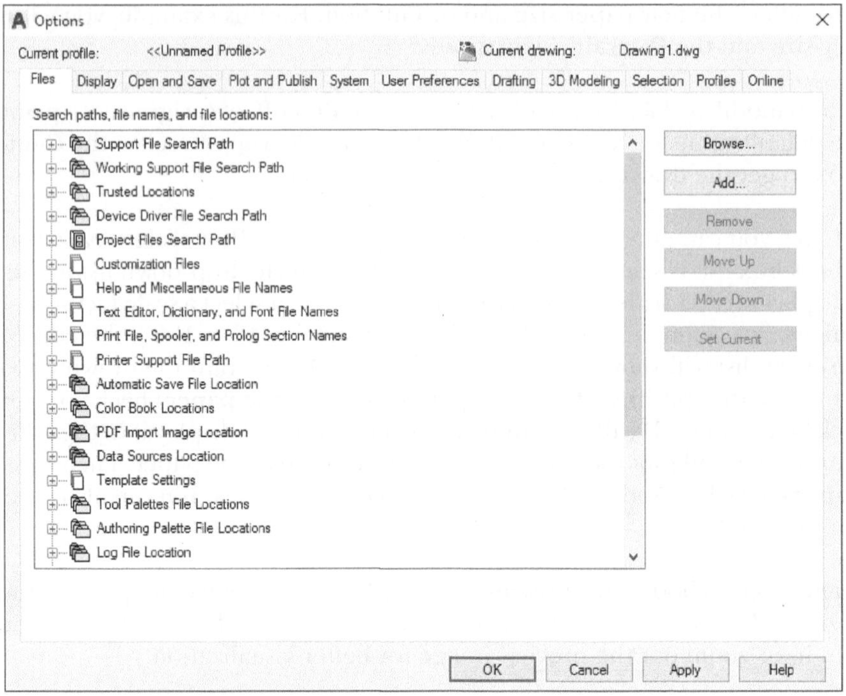

*Figure 2-56 The **Options** dialog box*

Files

This tab stores the directories in which AutoCAD looks for the driver, support, menu, project, template, and other files. It uses three icons: folder, paper stack, and file cabinet. The folder icon is for a search path, the paper stack icon is for files, and the file cabinet icon is for a specific folder. Suppose you want to know the path of the font mapping file. To do so, you need to click on the **+** symbol before the **Text Editor**, **Dictionary, and Font File Names** folders and then select the **Font Mapping File** node, refer to Figure 2-56. Similarly, you can define a custom hatch pattern file and then add its search path.

Display

This tab is used to control the drawing and window settings like screen menu display and scroll bar. For example, to display scroll bars in the drawing window to scroll up and down, select the **Display scroll bars in drawing window** check box from the **Window Elements** area. You can change the background color of the graphics window, layout window, and command line as well as the color of the command line text by using the **Drawing Window Colors** dialog box that is displayed on choosing the **Colors** button. In the **Display** tab, you can specify the parameters to set the display resolution and display performance. You can also set the smoothness and resolutions of certain objects such as circle, arc, rendered object, and polyline curve.

You can also toggle on and off the display performance such as pan and zoom with raster images, apply the solid fills, and so on. In this tab, you can toggle on and off the various layout elements such as the layout tabs on the screen, margins, paper background, and so on.

Open and Save

This tab is used to control the parameters related to the opening and saving of files in AutoCAD. You can specify the file type while saving the file using the **SAVEAS** command. The various formats available are **AutoCAD 2018 Drawing (*.dwg)**, **AutoCAD 2013/LT2013 Drawing (*.dwg)**, **AutoCAD 2010/LT2010 Drawing (*.dwg)**, **AutoCAD 2007/LT2007 Drawing (*.dwg)**, **AutoCAD 2004/LT 2004 Drawing (*.dwg)**, **AutoCAD 2000/LT2000 Drawing (*.dwg)**, **AutoCAD R14/LT98/LT97 Drawing (*.dwg)**, **AutoCAD Drawing Template(*.dwt)**, **AutoCAD 2018 DXF(*.dxf)**, **AutoCAD 2013/LT2013 DXF(*.dxf)**, **AutoCAD 2010/LT2010 DXF (*.dxf)**, **AutoCAD 2007/LT2007 DXF (*.dxf)**, **AutoCAD 2004/LT2004 DXF (*.dxf)**, **AutoCAD 2000/LT2000 DXF(*.dxf)**, and **AutoCAD R12/LT2 DXF (*.dxf)**. You can also set various file safety precautions such as the Automatic Save feature or the creation of a backup copy. On selecting the **Display digital signature information** check box, you can view the digital signature information when a file with a valid digital signature is opened. You can change the number of the recently saved files to be displayed in the **File Open** area. You can also set the various parameters for external references and the ObjectARX applications.

Plot and Publish

The options in this tab are used to control the parameters related to plotting and publishing of the drawings in AutoCAD. You can set the default output device and also add a new plotter. You can set the general parameters such as the layout or plot device paper size and the background processing options while plotting or publishing. It is possible to select the spool alert for the system printer and also the OLE plot quality. You can also set the parameters for the plot style such as the color-dependent plot styles or the named plot styles.

System

This tab contains AutoCAD system settings options such as the adjusting graphic performance and pointing device settings options where you can choose the pointing device driver. Here you can also set the display of the **OLE Properties** dialog box and beep for wrong user input. You also have options to set the parameters for database connectivity.

User Preferences

The parameters in this tab are used to control the settings such as the right-click customization to change the shortcut menus according to the user's preferences. You can set the units parameters for the blocks or drawings that are inserted as well as the priorities for various coordinate data entry methods. You can also set the lineweight options.

Drafting

The options in this tab are used to control the settings such as autosnap settings and aperture size. Here you can also set the toggles on and off for the various autotracking settings. Using this tab, you can also set the tool tip appearance of **Dynamic Input** mode in the Model and Paper space.

3D Modeling

This tab is used to control the settings related to 3D modeling such as the display of cursor in the 3D modeling environment, visual styles, 3D navigation, and so on.

Selection

This tab is used to control the methods of object selection, grips, grip colors, and the grip size. You can also set the various selection modes.

Profiles

This tab is used to save and restore the system settings. To save a profile and have different settings, choose the **Add to List** button; the **Add Profile** dialog box will be displayed. Enter the name and description of the profile and then choose the **Apply & Close** button. Next, make the new profile current and then change the settings in each tab. The settings thus applied will be saved in the new profile and can be restored anytime by making the profile current.

Note

*The options in various tabs of the **Options** dialog box have been discussed throughout the book wherever applicable.*

Tip

*Some options in the **Options** dialog box have drawing file icon on their left. For example, the options in the **Display resolution** area of the **Display** tab have drawing file icons. This specifies that these parameters are saved with the current drawing only; therefore, it affects only that drawing. The options without the drawing file icon are saved with the current profile and affect all the drawings present in that AutoCAD session or future sessions.*

Example 7 Modifying the Default Options

In this example, you will create a profile with specific settings by using the **Options** dialog box.

1. Choose the **Options** button from the **Application Menu** to invoke the **Options** dialog box. Alternatively, right-click in the drawing area to display the shortcut menu, and then choose **Options** to invoke this dialog box.

2. Choose the **Profiles** tab, and then choose the **Add to List** button to display the **Add Profile** dialog box. Enter **CADCIM** as the name of the new profile and **Profile created for chapter 2, Example 7** as the description of the new profile, and then choose the **Apply & Close** button to exit.

3. Select the **CADCIM** profile and then choose the **Set Current** button to make this profile current. You will notice that the **Current Profile** name above the tabs displays *CADCIM*.

4. Choose the **Display** tab and then choose the **Colors** button; the **Drawing Window Colors** dialog box is displayed. Select **2D model space** in the **Context** area and **Uniform background** in the **Interface element** area. Select **White** from the **Color** drop-down list; the background color of the model tab will change into white. Choose the **Apply & Close** button to return to the **Options** dialog box.

5. Choose the **Drafting** tab and then change **AutoSnap Marker Size** to the maximum using the slider bar. Choose the **Apply** button and then the **OK** button to exit the dialog box.

6. Draw a line and then choose the **Object Snap** button from the Status Bar if not already chosen. Again, invoke the **Line** tool and move the cursor on the previously drawn line; a marker will be displayed at the endpoint. Notice the size of the marker now.

7. Invoke the **Options** dialog box again and choose the **Profiles** tab. Double-click on the default profile to reload the default settings and choose **OK**; the screen settings will change as specified in the default profile.

Self-Evaluation Test

Answer the following questions and then compare them to those given at the end of this chapter:

1. You can erase a previously drawn line by using the _________ option of the **Line** tool.

2. Choose the _________ tool from the **Circle** drop-down to draw a circle that is tangent to two previously drawn objects.

3. The _________ tool is used to enlarge or reduce the view of a drawing without affecting the actual size of entities.

4. After increasing the drawing limits, you need to choose the _________ tool from the Navigator Bar to display the complete area inside the drawing area.

5. In _________ units, you must specify the bearing angle that a line makes with the north-south direction.

6. You can preview a plot before actually plotting it by using the _________ button in the **Plot** dialog box.

7. You can draw a line by specifying the length and direction of the line using the Direct Distance Entry method. (T/F)

8. While using the Window Crossing method of object selection, only those objects that are completely enclosed within the boundaries of the crossing box are selected. (T/F)

9. Choose the **3-Point** tool from the **Circle** drop-down to draw a circle by specifying the two endpoints of the circle's diameter. (T/F)

10. If you choose the engineering or architectural format for units in the **Drawing Units** dialog box, you can enter distances or coordinates in any of the five formats. (T/F)

Review Questions

Answer the following questions:

1. Which of the following keys is not used to terminate the **Line** tool at the **Specify next point or [Close/Undo]:** prompt?

   (a) SPACEBAR (b) BACKSPACE
   (c) ENTER (d) ESC

2. Which of the following tools is used to zoom a drawing up to the limits or the extents, whichever is greater?

   (a) **Zoom Previous** (b) **Zoom Window**
   (c) **Zoom All** (d) **Zoom Realtime**

3. How many formats of units can be chosen from the **Drawing Units** dialog box?

   (a) Three (b) Five
   (c) Six (d) Seven

4. Which of the following input methods cannot be used to invoke the **Options** tool for displaying the **Options** dialog box?

   (a) Menu (b) Toolbar
   (c) Shortcut menu (d) command prompt

5. When you define direction by specifying angle, the output of the angle does not depend on which of the following factors?

   (a) Angular units (b) Angle value
   (c) Angle direction (d) Angle base

6. The __________ option of the **Line** tool can be used to join the current point with the initial point of the first line when two or more lines are drawn in succession.

7. The __________ option of drawing a circle cannot be invoked by entering the command at the command prompt.

8. When you select any type of unit and angle in the **Length** or **Angle** area of the **Drawing Units** dialog box, the corresponding example is displayed in the __________ area of the dialog box.

9. If you want a drawing to be plotted so that it fits on the specified sheet of paper, select the __________ option in the **Plot** dialog box.

10. The __________ tab in the **Options** dialog box is used to store the details of all profiles available in the current drawing.

11. You can use the __________ command to change the settings that affect the drawing environment or the AutoCAD interface.

12. In the relative rectangular coordinate system, the displacements along the X and Y axes (DX and DY) are measured with respect to the previous point and not with respect to the origin. (T/F)

13. In AutoCAD, by default, angles are measured along the positive X axis and it will be positive if measured in the counterclockwise direction. (T/F)

14. You can also invoke the **Plot** dialog box by choosing the **Plot** option from the shortcut menu displayed on right-clicking in the command prompt. (T/F)

15. The **Files** tab of the **Options** dialog box is used to store the directories in which AutoCAD looks for the driver, support, menu, project, template, and other files. (T/F)

Exercise 7 *Relative Rectangular & Absolute Coordinates*

Invoke the **Line** tool and use the following relative rectangular coordinate values to draw the object.

Point	Coordinates
1	3.0, 3.0
2	@3,0
3	@-1.5,3.0
4	@-1.5,-3.0
5	@3.0,5.0
6	@3,0
7	@-1.5,-3
8	@-1.5,3

Exercise 8 *Relative Rectangular & Polar Coordinates*

Draw the profile shown in Figure 2-57 by using the relative rectangular and relative polar coordinates of the points given in the following table. The distance between the dotted lines is 1 unit. Save this drawing with the name *C02_Exer8.dwg*.

Point	Coordinates	Point	Coordinates
1	3.0, 1.0	9	______
2	______	10	______
3	______	11	______
4	______	12	______
5	______	13	______
6	______	14	______
7	______	15	______
8	______	16	______

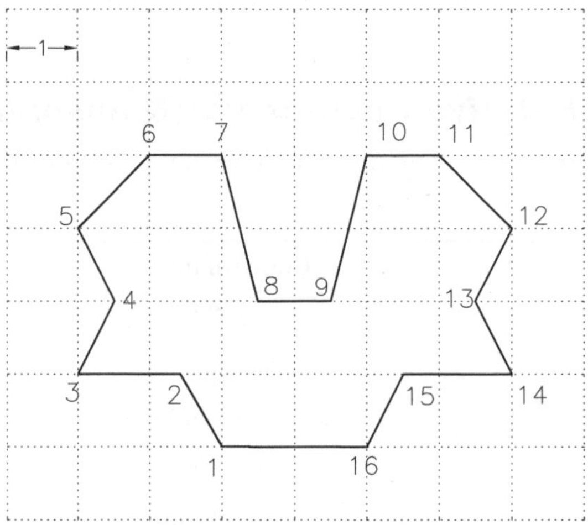

Figure 2-57 Drawing for Exercise 8

Exercise 9 — *Relative Polar Coordinates*

For the drawing shown in Figure 2-58, enter the relative polar coordinates of the points in the following table. Next, use these coordinates to create the drawing. Do not dimension the drawing.

Point	Coordinates	Point	Coordinates
1	1.0, 1.0	6	______
2	______	7	______
3	______	8	______
4	______	9	______
5	______		

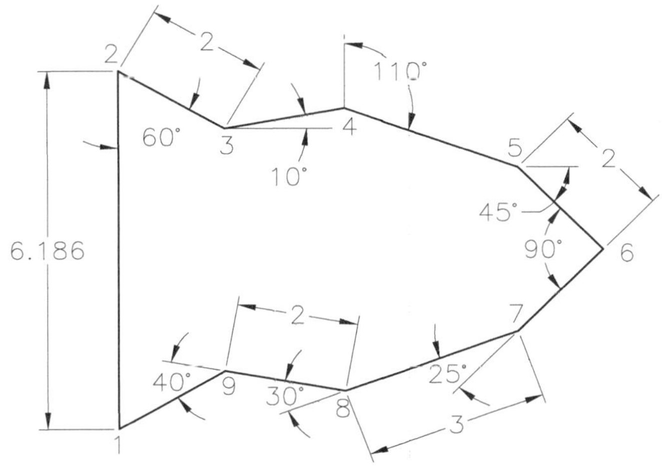

Figure 2-58 Drawing for Exercise 9

Exercise 10 — Line and Circle

Draw the sketch shown in Figure 2-59 by using the **Line** and **Center, Radius** tools. The distance between the dotted lines is 1.0 unit.

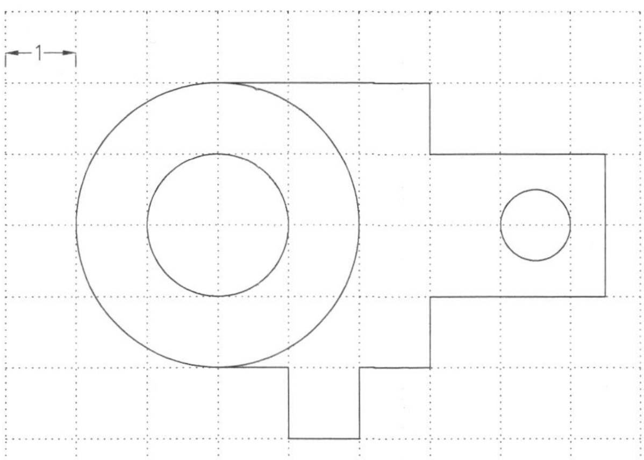

Figure 2-59 Drawing for Exercise 10

Exercise 11 Line and Circle Tangent to Two objects

Draw the sketch shown in Figure 2-60 using the **Line** and **Tan, Tan, Radius** tools.

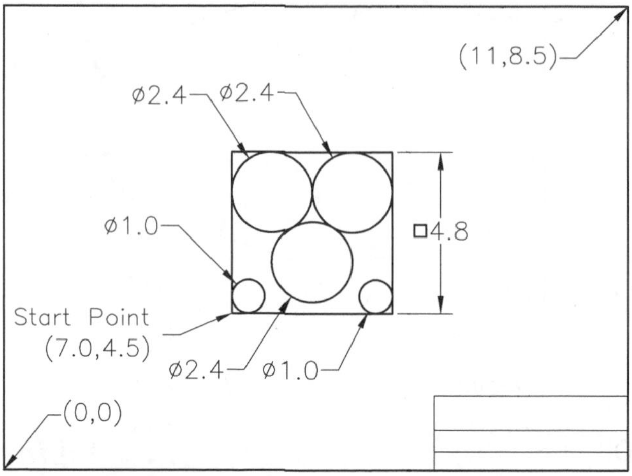

Figure 2-60 *Drawing for Exercise 11*

Exercise 12 Setting Units

Set the units for a drawing based on the following specifications.

1. Set the units to architectural with the denominator of the smallest fraction equal to 16.
2. Set the angular measurement to degrees/minutes/seconds with the number of fractional places for the display of angles equal to 0d00'.
3. Set the direction to 0-degree (east) and the direction of measurement of angles to counterclockwise (angles measured positive in counterclockwise direction).

Based on Figure 2-61, determine and set the limits for the drawing. The scale for this drawing is 1/4" = 1'. Leave enough space around the drawing for dimensioning and title block. (HINT: Scale factor = 48 sheet size required is 12 x 9; therefore, the limits are 12 X 48, 9 X 48 = 576, 432. Expand the **Zoom** drop-down and then select the **Zoom All** tool to display the new limits.)

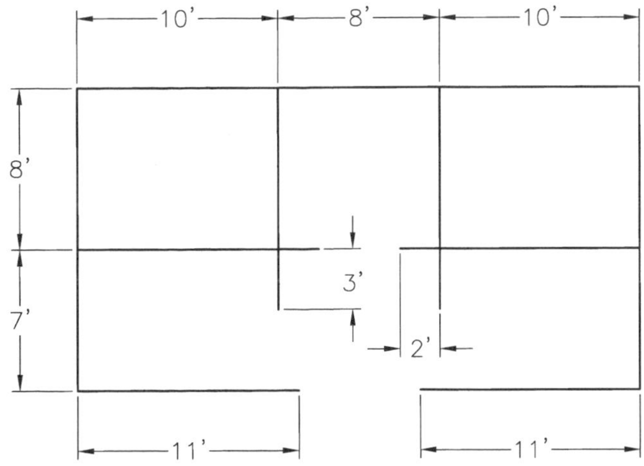

Figure 2-61 Drawing for Exercise 12

Exercise 13

Draw the object shown in Figure 2-62. The distance between the dotted lines is 1 unit. Determine the limits for this drawing and use the Decimal units with 0.00 precision.

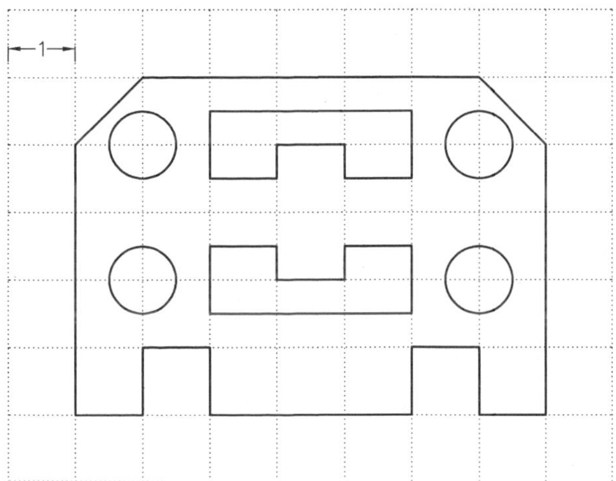

Figure 2-62 Drawing for Exercise 13

Exercise 14

Draw the object shown in Figure 2-63. The distance between the dotted lines is 10 feet. Determine the limits for this drawing and use the Engineering units with 0'0.00" precision.

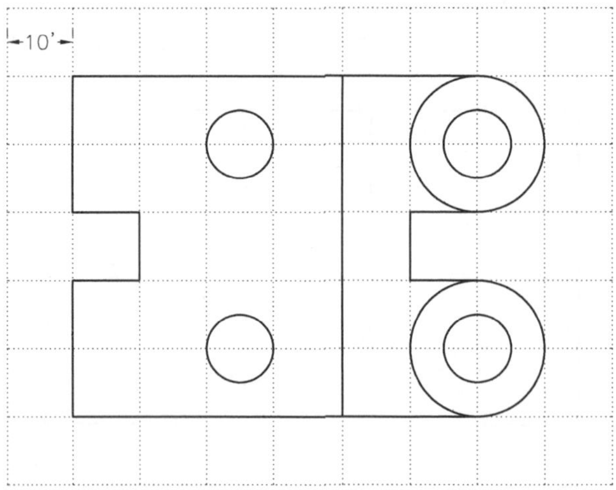

Figure 2-63 Drawing for Exercise 14

Problem-Solving Exercise 1

Draw the object shown in Figure 2-64, using the **Line** and **Center, Diameter** tools. In this exercise only the diameters of the circles are given. To draw the lines and small circles (Dia 0.6), you need to find the coordinate points for the lines and the center points of the circles. For example, if the center of concentric circles is at 5,3.5, then the *X* coordinate of the lower left corner of the rectangle will be 5.0 - 2.4 = 2.6.

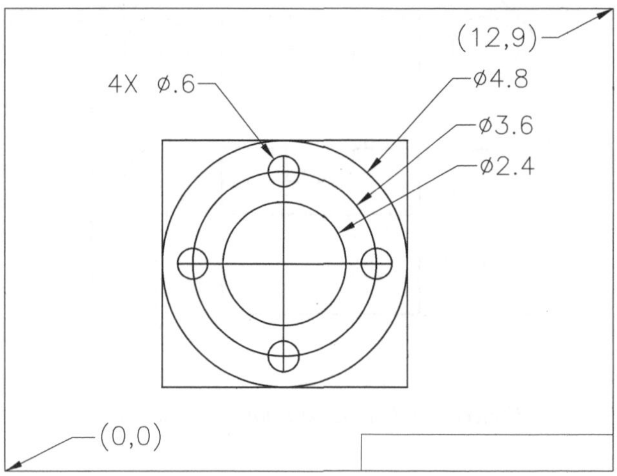

Figure 2-64 Drawing for Problem-Solving Exercise 1

Answers to Self-Evaluation Test

1. **Undo**, **2**. **Tan, Tan, Radius**, **3**. **ZOOM**, **4**. **Zoom All**, **5**. Surveyor's, **6**. **Preview**, **7**. T, **8**. F, **9**. F, **10**. T

Chapter 3

Getting Started with Advanced Sketching

Learning Objectives

After completing this chapter, you will be able to:

- *Draw arcs using various options*
- *Draw rectangles, ellipses, elliptical arcs, and polygons*
- *Draw polylines and donuts*
- *Place points and change their style and size*
- *Draw an infinite line*
- *Write simple text*
- *Use different templates*

Key Terms

- *Arc*
- *Rectangles*
- *Explode*
- *Ellipse*
- *Elliptical Arc*
- *Polygon*
- *Polylines*
- *Donut*
- *Points*
- *Construction Line*
- *Text*
- *Ray*
- *FILLMODE*
- *PDMODE*
- *DDPTYPE*

DRAWING ARCS

Ribbon: Home > Draw > Arc drop-down **Toolbar:** Draw > Arc
Menu Bar: Draw > Arc **Command:** ARC/A

An arc is defined as a segment of a circle. In AutoCAD, an arc is drawn by using the tools available in the **Arc** drop-down. There are eleven different tools to draw an arc. The tools to draw an arc are grouped together in the **Arc** drop-down of the **Draw** panel in the **Ribbon**, refer to Figure 3-1. You can choose the appropriate tool depending upon the parameters known and then draw the arc. Remember that the tool that was used last to create an arc will be displayed in the **Draw** panel. The different methods to draw an arc are discussed next.

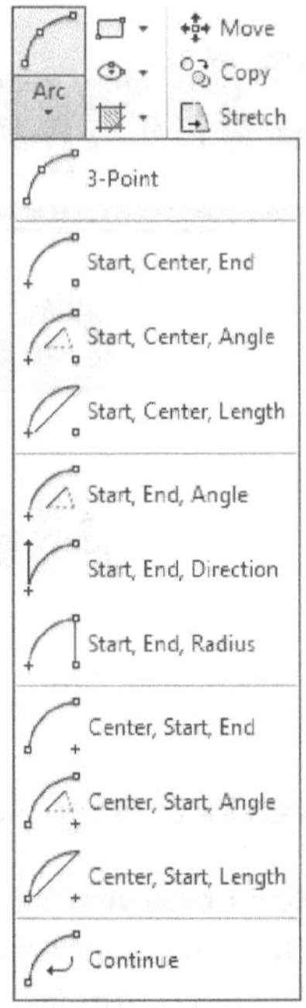

Figure 3-1 *The tools in the* ***Arc*** *drop-down*

Drawing an Arc by Specifying Three Points

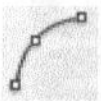

To draw an arc by specifying the start point, endpoint, and another point on its periphery, choose the **3-Point** tool from the **Arc** drop-down in the **Draw** panel, refer to Figure 3-1. On doing so, you will be prompted to specify the start point. Specify the first point or specify coordinates for the first point. Then, specify the second point and endpoint of the arc, refer to Figure 3-2.

Following is the prompt sequence to draw an arc by specifying three points (You can also specify the points by using the mouse).

Choose the ***3-Point*** *tool from the* ***Arc*** *drop-down in the* ***Draw*** *panel (Ensure that dynamic input is off)*
Specify start point of arc or [Center]: **2,2** Enter
Specify second point of arc or [Center/End]: **3,3** Enter
Specify end point of arc: **3,4** Enter

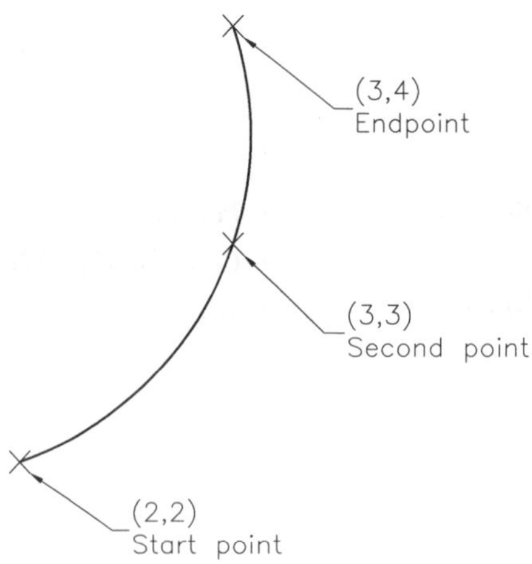

Figure 3-2 *Drawing an arc using the* ***3-Point*** *tool*

Exercise 1 — 3-Point

Draw several arcs by using the **3-Point** tool. The points can be selected by entering coordinates or by specifying points on the screen. Also, try to create a circle by drawing two separate arcs and a single arc and notice the limitations of the **Arc** tools.

Drawing an Arc by Specifying its Start Point, Center Point, and Endpoint

If you know the start point, endpoint, and center point of an arc, choose the **Start, Center, End** tool from the **Arc** drop-down in the **Draw** panel and then specify the start, center, and end points in succession; the arc will be drawn. The radius of the arc is determined by the distance between the center point and the start point. Therefore, the endpoint is used to calculate the angle at which the arc ends. Note that in this case, the arc will be drawn in a counterclockwise direction from the start point to the endpoint around the specified center, as shown in Figure 3-3.

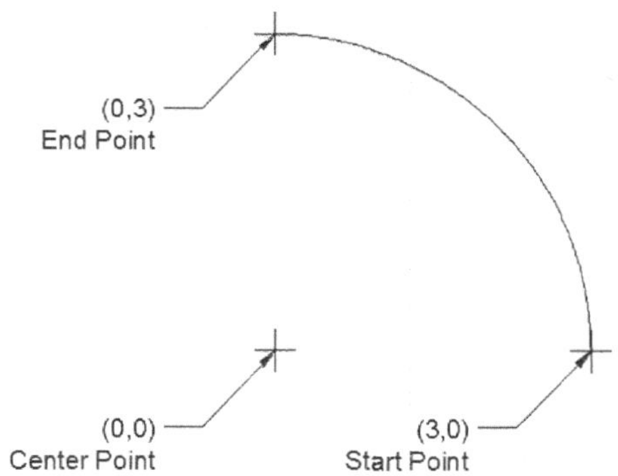

*Figure 3-3 Drawing an arc using the **Start, Center, End** tool*

Drawing an Arc by Specifying its Start Point, Center Point, and Included Angle

Included angle is the angle between the start and end points of an arc about the specified center. If you know the location of the start point, center point, and included angle of an arc, choose the **Start, Center, Angle** tool from the **Arc** drop-down in the **Draw** panel and specify the start point, center point, and included angle; the arc will be drawn in a counterclockwise direction with respect to the specified center and start point, refer to Figure 3-4.

If you enter a negative angle value, the arc will be drawn in a clockwise direction, refer to Figure 3-5. Following is the prompt sequence to draw an arc by specifying the center point at (2,2), start point at (3,2), and an included angle of -60 degrees:

*Choose the **Start, Center, Angle** tool from the **Draw** panel (Ensure that dynamic input is off)*
Specify start point of arc or [Center]: **3,2** Enter
Specify center point of arc: **2,2** Enter
Specify included angle (hold Ctrl to switch direction): **-60** Enter , refer to Figure 3-5.

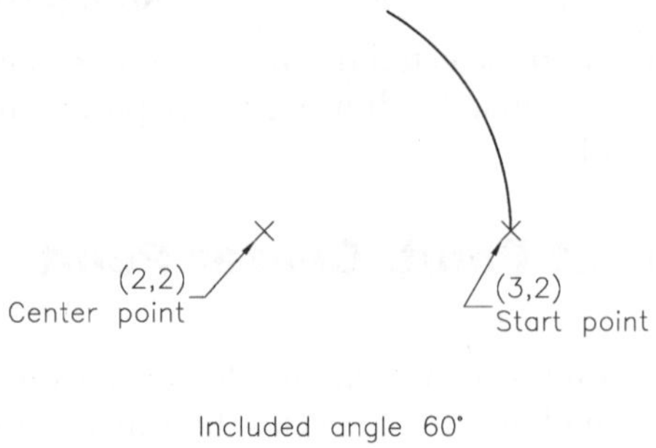

Figure 3-4 Drawing an arc using the ***Start, Center, Angle*** *tool*

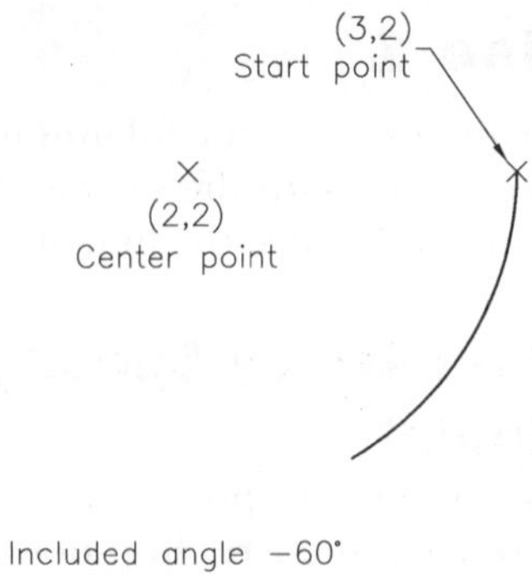

Figure 3-5 Drawing an arc by specifying a negative angle using the ***Start, Center, Angle*** *tool*

In AutoCAD, while creating an arc, you can flip the direction of the arc for specifying a point on the arc circumference using the CTRL key. To do so, while creating the arc if you press and hold the CTRL key and move the cursor, you will notice that the direction of arc has been flipped. Now, you can specify the parameters of the arc in different direction. Note that if you release the CTRL key, the direction of arc creation will switch back to the previous direction.

Exercise 2 — Start, Center, Angle

a. Draw an arc whose start point is at 6,3, center point is at 3,3, and the included angle is 240 degrees.

b. Draw the profile shown in Figure 3-6. The distance between the dotted lines is 1.0 unit. Create the arcs by using different arc command options as indicated in the figure.

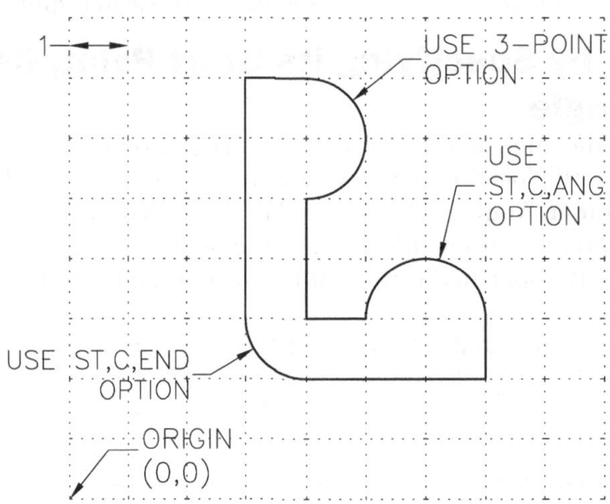

Figure 3-6 Drawing for Exercise 2

Drawing an Arc by Specifying the Start Point, Center Point, and Chord Length

A chord is defined as a straight line connecting the start point and endpoint of an arc. To draw an arc by specifying its chord length, choose the **Start, Center, Length** tool from the **Arc** drop-down in the **Draw** panel and specify the start point, center point, and length of the chord in succession. On specifying the chord length, AutoCAD will calculate the included angle and an arc will be drawn in the counterclockwise direction from the start point. A positive chord length gives the smallest possible arc with that length, as shown in Figure 3-7. This arc is known as minor arc. The included angle in a minor arc is less than 180 degrees. A negative value for the chord length results in the largest possible arc also known as major arc, as shown in Figure 3-8.

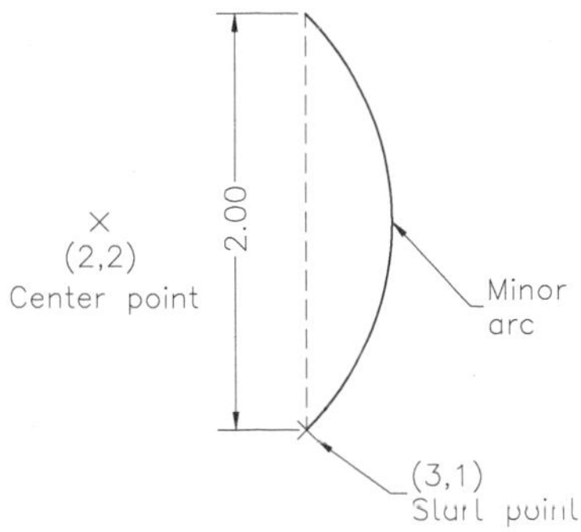

*Figure 3-7 Drawing a minor arc by specifying a positive chord length using the **Start, Center, Length** tool*

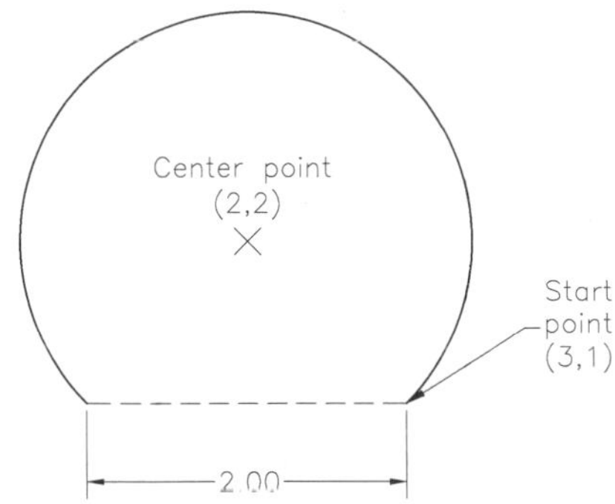

*Figure 3-8 Drawing a major arc by specifying a negative chord length using the **Start, Center, Length** tool*

Drawing an Arc by Specifying its Start Point, Endpoint, and Included Angle

To draw an arc by specifying its start point, endpoint, and the included angle, choose the **Start, End, Angle** tool from the **Arc** drop-down in the **Draw** panel and specify the start point, endpoint, and the included angle in succession; the arc will be drawn. A positive included angle value draws an arc in the counterclockwise direction from the start point to the endpoint, as shown in Figure 3-9. Similarly, a negative included angle value draws the arc in clockwise direction.

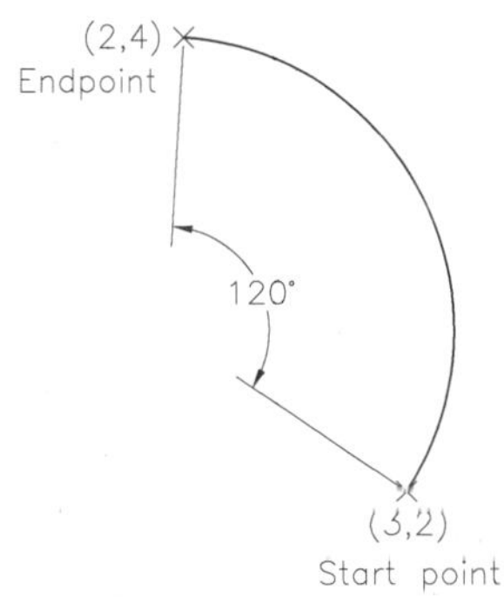

*Figure 3-9 Drawing an arc using the **Start, End, Angle** tool*

Drawing an Arc by Specifying its Start Point, Endpoint, and Direction

This option is used to draw a major or minor arc, whose size and position are determined by the distance between the start point and endpoint and the direction specified. You can specify the direction by selecting a point on a line that is tangent to the start point or by entering an angle between the start point of the arc and the end point of the tangent line.

To draw an arc by specifying its direction, choose the **Start, End, Direction** tool from the **Arc** drop-down in the **Draw** panel and specify the start and end points in succession; you will be prompted to specify the direction. Specify a point on the line that is tangent to the start point or enter an angle between the start point of the arc and the end point of the tangent line; an arc will be drawn.

In other words, on using this option, the arc will start in the direction you specify (the start of the arc is established tangent to the direction you specify). The prompt sequence to draw an arc, whose start point is at 3,6, endpoint is at 4.5,5, and direction of -40 degrees is given next.

Choose the ***Start, End, Direction*** *tool from the* ***Arc*** *drop-down (Ensure that dynamic input is off)*
Specify start point of arc or [Center]: **3,6** Enter
Specify end point of arc: **4.5,3** Enter
Specify tangent direction for the start point of arc (hold Ctrl to switch direction): **-40** Enter, refer to Figure 3-10.

The prompt sequence to draw an arc, whose start point is at 4,3, endpoint is at 3,5, and direction of 90 degrees, is given next.

Choose the ***Start, End, Direction*** *tool from the* ***Arc*** *drop-down (Ensure that dynamic input is off)*
Specify start point of arc or [Center]: **4,3** Enter
Specify end point of arc: **3,5** Enter
Specify tangent direction for the start point of arc (hold Ctrl to switch direction): **90** Enter, refer to Figure 3-11.

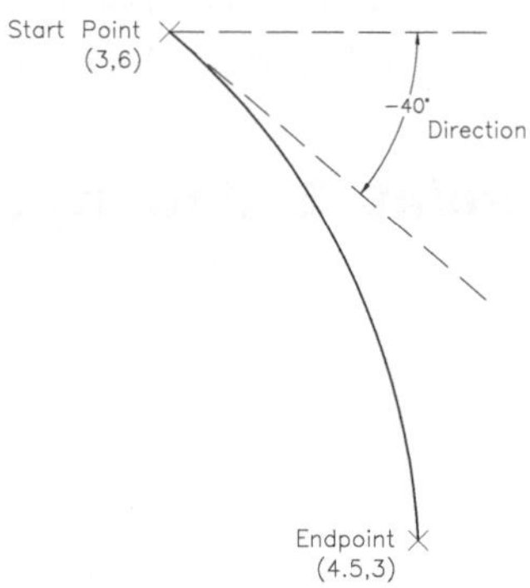

Figure 3-10 *Drawing an arc in negative direction using the* ***Start, End, Direction*** *tool*

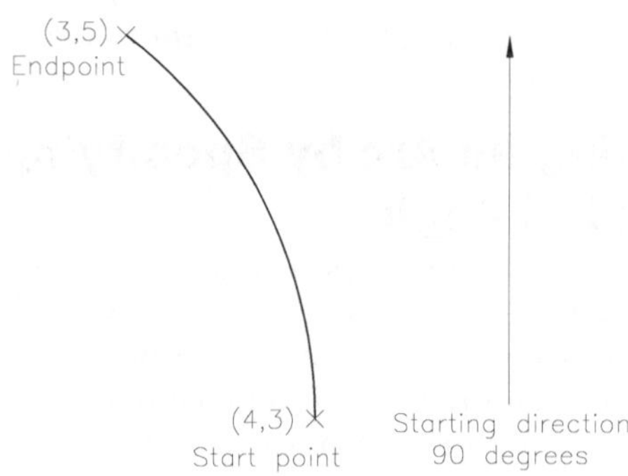

Figure 3-11 *Drawing an arc in positive direction using the* ***Start, End, Direction*** *tool*

Exercise 3 — Start, End, Direction

a. Specify the directions and coordinates of two arcs in such a way that they form a circular figure.

b. Draw the profile shown in Figure 3-12. Create the curves by using the **Start, End, Direction** tool. The distance between the dotted lines is 1.0 unit and the diameter of the circles is 1 unit.

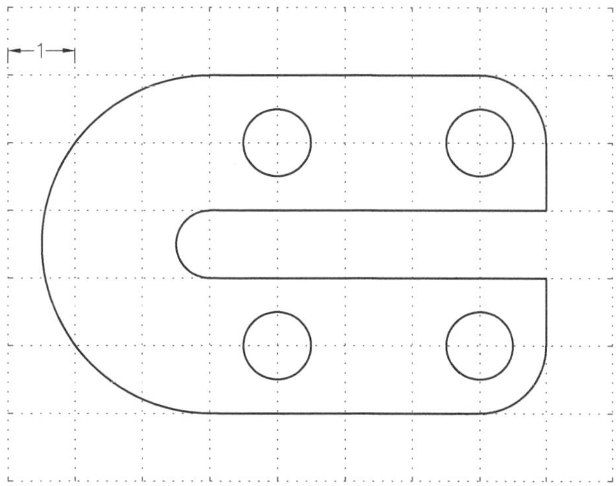

Figure 3-12 Drawing for Exercise 3

Drawing an Arc by Specifying its Start Point, Endpoint, and Radius

If you know the location of the start point, endpoint, and radius of an arc, choose the **Start, End, Radius** tool from the **Arc** drop-down in the **Draw** panel and specify the start and end points; you will be prompted to specify the radius. Enter the radius value; the arc will be drawn. In this case, the arc will be drawn in counterclockwise direction from the start point. This means that a negative radius value results in a major arc (the largest arc between the two endpoints), refer to Figure 3-13(a). A positive radius value results in a minor arc (smallest arc between the start point and the endpoint), refer to Figure 3-13(b).

Drawing an Arc by Specifying its Center Point, Start Point, and Endpoint

The **Center, Start, End** tool is the modification of the **Start, Center, End** tool. Use this tool, whenever it is easier to start drawing an arc by establishing the center first. Here, the arc is always drawn in a counterclockwise direction from the start point to the endpoint, around the specified center. The prompt sequence for drawing the arc shown in Figure 3-14, which has a center point at (3,3), start point at (5,3), and endpoint at (3,5), is given next.

*Choose the **Center, Start, End** tool from the **Draw** panel. (Ensure that dynamic input is off)*
Specify center point of arc: **3,3** Enter
Specify start point of arc: **5,3** Enter
Specify end point of arc (hold Ctrl to switch direction) or [Angle/chord Length]: **3,5** Enter

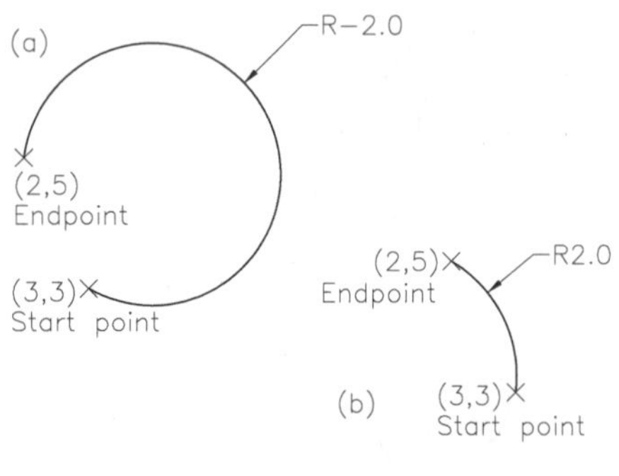

Figure 3-13 Drawing an arc using the ***Start, End, Radius*** *tool*

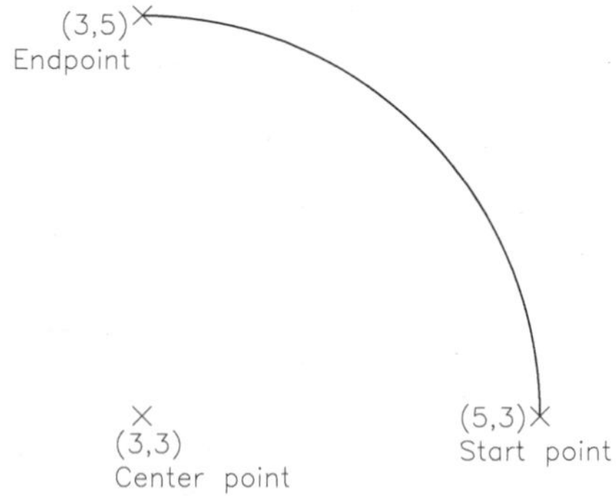

Figure 3-14 Drawing an arc using the ***Center, Start, End*** *tool*

Drawing an Arc by Specifying its Center Point, Start Point, and Angle

You can use the **Center, Start, Angle** tool if you need to draw an arc by specifying the center first. The prompt sequence for drawing the arc shown in Figure 3-15, which has a center point at (4,5), start point at (5,4), and included angle of 120 degrees, is given next.

Choose the ***Center, Start, Angle*** *tool from the* ***Arc*** *drop-down (Ensure that dynamic input is off)*
Specify center point of arc: **4,5** Enter
Specify start point of arc: **5,4** Enter
Specify included angle (hold Ctrl to switch direction): **120** Enter, refer to Figure 3-15.

Drawing an Arc by Specifying the Center Point, Start Point, and Chord Length

The **Center, Start, Length** tool is used whenever it is easier to draw an arc by establishing the center first. The prompt sequence for drawing the arc shown in Figure 3-16, which has a center point at (2,2), start point at (4,3), and length of chord as 3, is given next.

Choose the ***Center, Start, Length*** *tool from the* ***Arc*** *drop-down (Ensure that dynamic input is off)*
Specify center point of arc: **2,2** Enter
Specify start point of arc: **4,3** Enter
Specify length of chord (hold Ctrl to switch direction): **3** Enter, refer to Figure 3-16.

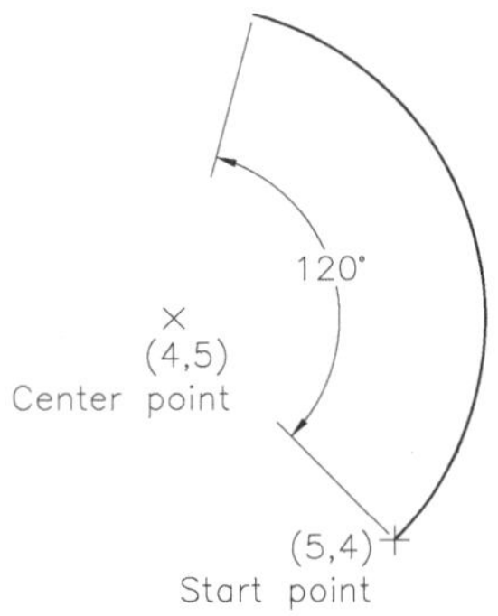

Figure 3-15 *Drawing an arc using the **Center, Start, Angle** tool*

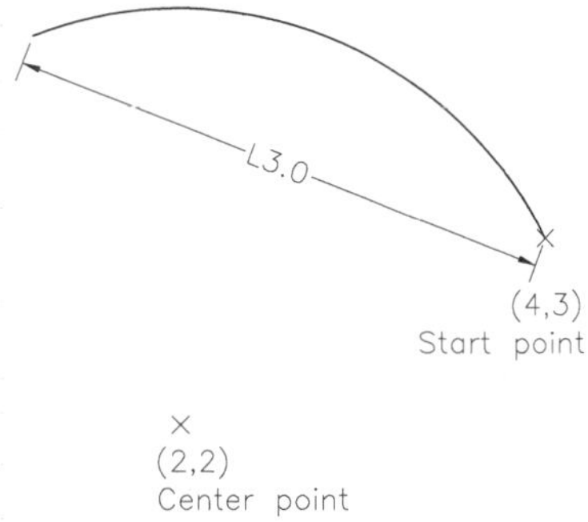

Figure 3-16 *Drawing an arc using the **Center, Start, Length** tool*

Exercise 4 **Center, Start, Length**

Draw a minor arc with the center point at (3,4), start point at (4,2), and chord length of 4 units.

Drawing an Arc by Using the Continue Tool

To create an arc that is tangent to a previously drawn arc or line, choose the **Continue** tool from the **Arc** drop down in the **Draw** panel; the start point and the direction of the arc will be taken from the endpoint and the ending direction of the previous line or arc. Next, specify the endpoint to draw an arc.

Tip

*The **Continue** tool can also be invoked automatically by first drawing a line or an arc, then choosing a tool from the **Arc** drop-down in the **Draw** panel, and finally pressing ENTER at the **Specify start point of arc or [Center]** prompt (not valid for the **Center, Start, End; Center, Start, Angle;** and **Center, Start, Length** tools).*

Exercise 5

a. Use the **Center**, **Start**, **Angle**, and **Continue** tools to draw the profiles shown in Figure 3-17.

b. Draw the profile shown in Figure 3-18. The distance between the dotted lines is 1.0 unit. Create the radii as indicated in the drawing by using the **Arc** tools.

Figure 3-17 *Drawing for Exercise 5(a)*

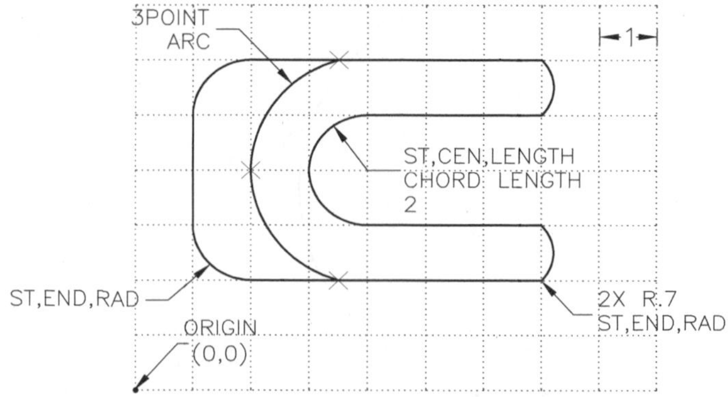

Figure 3-18 *Drawing for Exercise 5(b)*

DRAWING RECTANGLES

Ribbon: Home > Draw > Rectangle **Toolbar:** Draw > Rectangle
Tool Palettes: Draw > Rectangle **Command:** RECTANG/REC

A rectangle is drawn by choosing the **Rectangle** tool, refer to Figure 3-19, from the **Draw** panel of the **Home** tab. In AutoCAD, you can draw rectangles by specifying two opposite corners of the rectangle by specifying the area and the size of one of the sides or by specifying the dimensions of the rectangle. All these methods of drawing rectangles are discussed next.

Drawing Rectangles by Specifying Two Opposite Corners

On invoking the **Rectangle** tool, you will be prompted to specify the first corner of the rectangle. Enter the coordinates of the first corner or specify the first corner by using the mouse; you will be prompted to specify the other corner. The first corner can be any one of the four corners. Specify the diagonally opposite corner by entering the coordinates or by using the left mouse button, as shown in Figure 3-20.

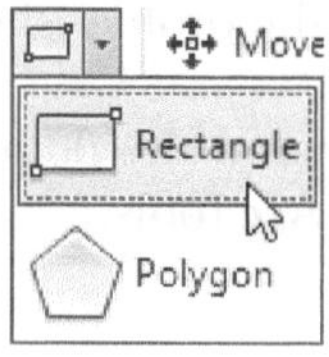

Figure 3-19 *Invoking the* ***Rectangle*** *tool from the* ***Draw*** *panel*

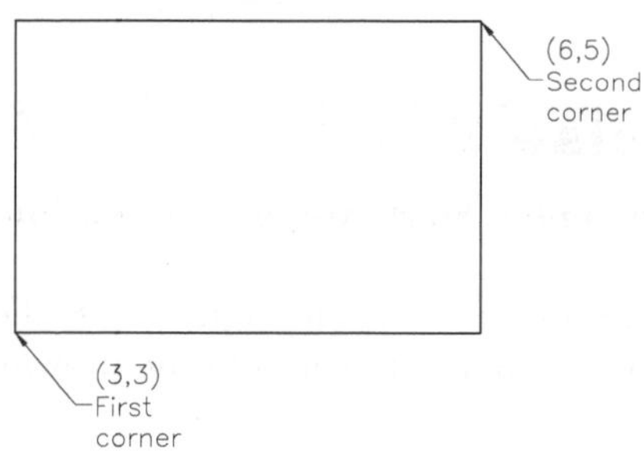

Figure 3-20 *Drawing a rectangle by specifying two opposite corners*

Drawing Rectangles by Specifying the Area and One Side

To draw a rectangle by specifying its area and the length of one of the sides, first specify the start point. Next, invoke the shortcut menu by right-clicking and then choose the **Area** option. Next, specify the parameters; the rectangle is drawn. Following is the prompt sequence to draw a rectangle whose start point is at 3,3, has an area of 15 units and length of 5 units:

*Choose the **Rectangle** tool from the **Draw** panel*
Specify first corner point or [Chamfer/Elevation/Fillet/Thickness/Width]: **3,3** [Enter]
Specify other corner point or [Area/Dimensions/Rotation]: **A** [Enter]
Enter area of rectangle in current units <100.000>: **15** [Enter]
Calculate rectangle dimensions based on [Length/Width] <Length>: **L** [Enter]
Enter rectangle length <10.0000>: **5** [Enter]

In the above case, the area and length of the rectangle were entered. The system automatically calculates the width of the rectangle by using the following formula:

Area of rectangle = Length x Width
Width = Area of rectangle/Length
Width =15/5
Width =3 units

Drawing Rectangles by Specifying their Dimensions

You can also draw a rectangle by specifying its dimensions. This can be done by choosing the **Dimensions** option from the shortcut menu at the **Specify other corner point or [Area/Dimensions/Rotation]** prompt and entering the length and width of the rectangle. The prompt sequence for drawing a rectangle whose start point is at 3,3 with a length of **5** units and width of **3** units is given next.

*Choose the **Rectangle** tool from the **Draw** panel*
Specify first corner point or [Chamfer/Elevation/Fillet/Thickness/Width]: **3,3** [Enter]
Specify other corner point or [Area/Dimensions/Rotation]: **D** [Enter]
Specify length for rectangles <0.0000>: **5** [Enter]
Specify width for rectangles <0.0000>: **3** [Enter]
Specify other corner point or [Area/Dimensions/Rotation]: *Click on the screen to specify the orientation of rectangle.*

Here, you are allowed to choose any one of the four locations for placing the rectangle. You can move the cursor to see the four quadrants. Depending on the location of the cursor, the corner point that is specified first holds the position of either the lower left corner, the lower right corner, the upper right corner, or the upper left corner. After deciding the position, you can click to place the rectangle.

Drawing Rectangle at an Angle

You can also draw a rectangle at an angle. This can be done by choosing the **Rotate** option from the shortcut menu, at the **Specify other corner point or [Area/Dimensions/Rotation]** prompt and entering the rotation angle. After entering the rotation angle, you can continue sizing the rectangle using any one of the above discussed methods. The prompt sequence for drawing a rectangle at an angle of 45-degree is:

*Choose the **Rectangle** tool from the **Draw** panel*
Specify first corner point or [Chamfer/Elevation/Fillet/Thickness/Width]: *Select a point as lower left corner location.*
Specify other corner point or [Area/Dimensions/Rotation]: **R** [Enter]

Specify rotation angle or [Pick points] <current>: **45** Enter
Specify other corner point or [Area/Dimensions/Rotation]: *Select a diagonally opposite point.*

While specifying the other corner point, you can place the rectangle in any of the four quadrants. Move the cursor in different quadrants and then select a point in the quadrant in which you need to draw the rectangle. Figure 3-21 shows a rectangle drawn at an angle of 45-degree.

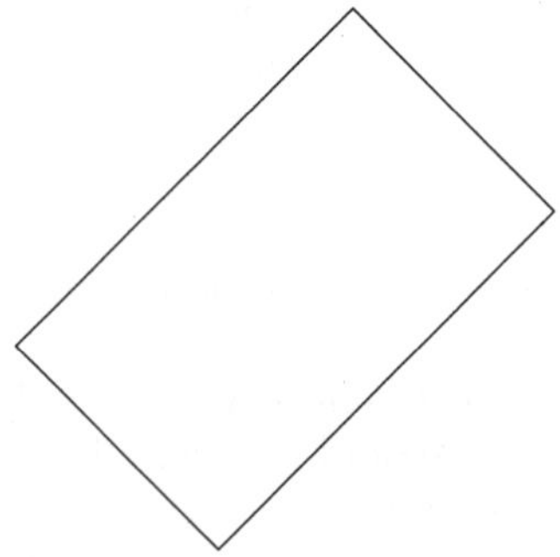

Figure 3-21 *Rectangle drawn at an angle*

Note
Once the rotation angle has been specified, the subsequent rectangles will be drawn at the specified angle. If you do not want to draw the subsequent rectangles at an angle, you need to reset the rotation angle to zero.

You can also set some of the parameters of a rectangle before specifying the start point. These parameters are available as options in the command Prompt and are discussed next.

Chamfer

The **Chamfer** option is used to create a chamfer, which is an angled corner, by specifying the chamfer distances, refer to Figure 3-22. The chamfer is created at all four corners. You can give two different chamfer values to create an unequal chamfer.

*Choose the **Rectangle** tool from the **Draw** panel*
Specify first corner point or [Chamfer/Elevation/Fillet/Thickness/Width]: **C** Enter
Specify first chamfer distance for rectangles <0.0000>: *Enter a value, d1.*
Specify second chamfer distance for rectangles <d1>: *Enter a value, d2.*
Specify first corner point or [Chamfer/Elevation/Fillet/Thickness/Width]: *Select a point as lower left corner.*
Specify other corner point or [Area/Dimensions/Rotation]: *Select a point as upper right corner.*

Note
The sequence of d1 is calculated clockwise while the sequence of d2 is calculated counterclockwise from the corners of the rectangle.

Fillet

The **Fillet** option is used to create a filleted rectangle, refer to Figure 3-23. You can specify the required fillet radius. The following is the prompt sequence for specifying the fillet:

*Choose the **Rectangle** tool from the **Draw** panel*
Specify first corner point or [Chamfer/Elevation/Fillet/Thickness/Width]: **F** Enter
Specify fillet radius for rectangles <0.0000>: *Enter a value.*
Specify first corner point or [Chamfer/Elevation/Fillet/Thickness/Width]: *Select a point as lower left corner.*
Specify other corner point or [Area/Dimensions/Rotation]: *Select a point as upper right corner.*

Note that the rectangle will be filleted only if the length and width of the rectangle are equal to or greater than twice the value of the specified fillet. Otherwise, AutoCAD will draw a rectangle without fillets.

Note

You can draw a rectangle with chamfers or fillets. If you specify the chamfer distances first and then specify the fillet radius in the same rectangle, the rectangle will be drawn with fillets only.

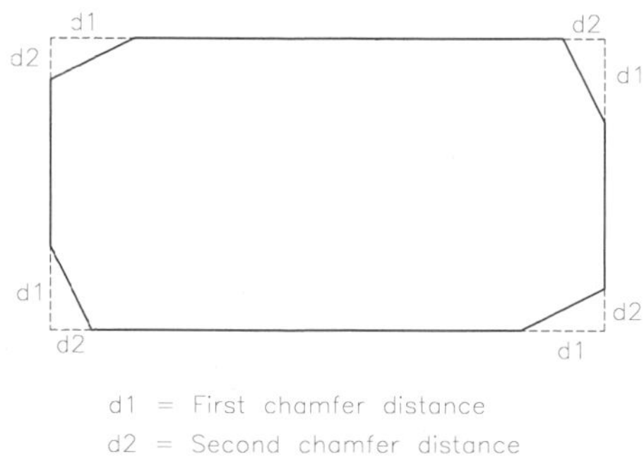

***Figure 3-22** Drawing a rectangle with chamfers*

***Figure 3-23** Drawing a rectangle with fillets*

Width

The **Width** option is used to create a rectangle whose line segments have some specified width, as shown in Figure 3-24.

Specify first corner point or [Chamfer/Elevation/Fillet/Thickness/Width]: **W** Enter
Specify line width for rectangles <0.0000>: *Enter a value.*

Thickness

The **Thickness** option is used to draw a rectangle that is extruded in the Z direction by a specified value of thickness. For example, if you draw a rectangle with thickness of 2 units, you will get a cuboid whose height is 2 units, refer to Figure 3-25. To view the cuboid, choose the **Home** option of the **ViewCube** from the drawing area or choose **SE Isometric** from **View** > **Views** panel. To restore the view to the plan view, choose **Top** from **View** > **Views** panel or choose **Top** from the **ViewCube** in the drawing area.

Specify first corner point or [Chamfer/Elevation/Fillet/Thickness/Width]: **T** Enter
Specify thickness for rectangles <0.0000>: *Enter a value.*

Elevation

The **Elevation** option is used to draw a rectangle at a specified distance from the *XY* plane along the *Z* axis. For example, if the elevation is 2 units, the rectangle will be drawn two units above the *XY* plane. If the thickness of the rectangle is 1 unit, you will get a rectangular box of 1 unit height, located 2 units above the *XY* plane, refer to Figure 3-25.

Figure 3-24 Drawing a rectangle of specified width

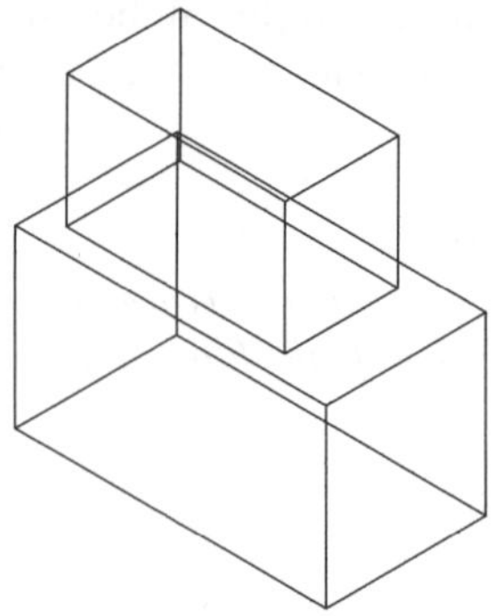

Figure 3-25 Drawing rectangles with thickness and elevation specified

Specify first corner point or [Chamfer/Elevation/Fillet/Thickness/Width]: **E** Enter
Specify elevation for rectangles <0.0000>: *Enter a value.*

Note

1. The values you enter for chamfer, fillet, width, elevation, and thickness become the current values for the rectangles drawn subsequently. Therefore, you need to reset the values based on the requirement.

*2. A rectangle generated by using the **Rectangle** tool is treated as a single object. To edit the individual lines of the rectangle, you need to explode the rectangle by using the **Explode** tool from the **Modify** panel of the **Home** tab and then edit them.*

Exercise 6 — Rectangle

Draw a rectangle of length 4 units, width 3 units, and start point at (1,1). Draw another rectangle of length 2 units and width 1 unit, with its first corner at 1.5,1.5, and which is at an angle of 65-degree.

DRAWING ELLIPSES

Ribbon: Home > Draw > Ellipse drop-down **Toolbar:** Draw > Ellipse
Tool Palettes: Draw > Ellipse **Command:** ELLIPSE/EL

If you cut a cone by a cutting plane at an angle and view the cone perpendicular to the cutting plane, the shape created is called an ellipse. An ellipse can be created by using different tools available in the **Ellipse** drop-down of the **Draw** panel, refer to Figure 3-26. In AutoCAD, you can create a true ellipse also known as a NURBS-based (Non-Uniform Rational Bezier Spline) ellipse. A true ellipse has center and quadrant points. If you select it, grips (small blue squares) will be displayed at the center and quadrant points of the ellipse. If you move one of the grips located on the perimeter of the ellipse, the size of the ellipse will be changed.

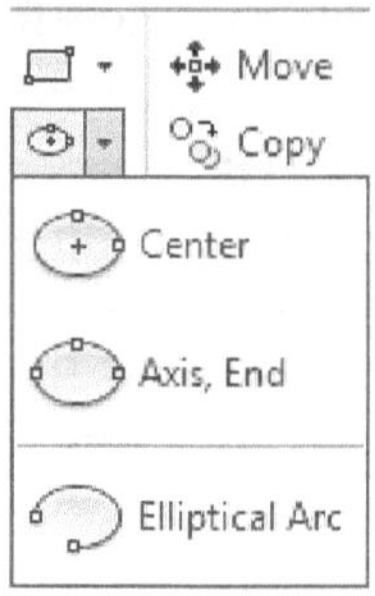

*Figure 3-26 Tools in the **Ellipse** drop-down of the **Draw** panel*

Once you invoke the **Ellipse** tool, the **Specify axis endpoint of ellipse or [Arc/Center]** or **Specify axis endpoint of ellipse or [Arc/Center/Isocircle]** (if isometric snap is ON) prompt will be displayed. The response to this prompt depends on the option you choose. The various options are explained next.

Note

*By default, the **Isocircle** option is not available for the **Ellipse** tool. To display this option, you have to select the **Isometric snap** radio button in the **Snap and Grid** tab of the **Drafting Settings** dialog box.*

Drawing Ellipse Using the Center Option

To draw an ellipse by specifying its center point, endpoint of one of its axes, and endpoint of other axis, choose the **Center** tool from the **Ellipse** drop-down in the **Draw** panel; you will be prompted to specify the center of the ellipse. The center of an ellipse is defined as the point of intersection of the major and minor axes. Specify the center point or enter coordinates; you will be prompted to specify the endpoint. Specify the endpoint of the major or minor axis; you will be prompted to specify the distance of the other axis. Specify the distance; the ellipse will be drawn.

After specifying the endpoint of one axis, you can enter **R** at the **Specify distance to other axis or [Rotation]** prompt to specify the rotation angle around the major axis. In this case, the first axis specified is considered as the major axis. On specifying the rotation angle, the ellipse will be drawn at an angle with respect to the major axis. Note that the rotation angle should range between 0 and 89.4-degrees. Figure 3-27 shows the ellipse created at different rotation angles.

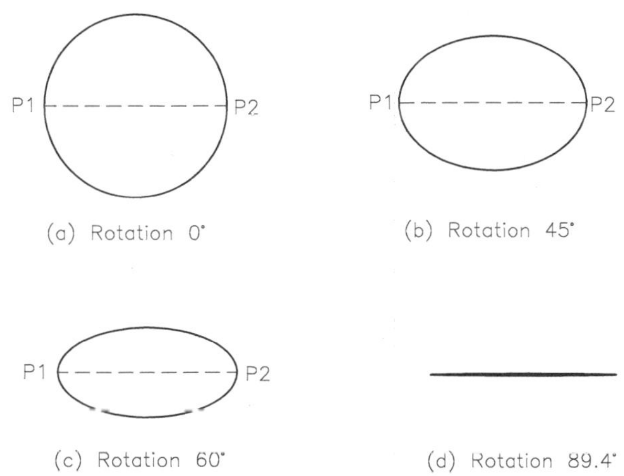

Figure 3-27 Rotation about the major axis

Drawing an Ellipse by Specifying its Axis and Endpoint

To draw an ellipse by specifying one of its axes and the endpoint of the other axis, choose the **Axis, End** tool from the **Ellipse** drop-down of the **Draw** panel; you will be prompted to specify the axis end point. Specify the first endpoint of one axis of the ellipse; you will be prompted to specify the other endpoint of the axis. Specify the other endpoint of the axis. Now, you can specify the distance to other axis from the center or specify the rotation angle around the specified axis.

Figure 3-28 shows an ellipse with one endpoint of the axis located at (3,3), the other at (6,3), and the distance to the other axis as 1 unit. Figure 3-29 shows an ellipse with one endpoint of the axis located at (3,3), the other at (4,2), and the distance to the other axis as 2 units.

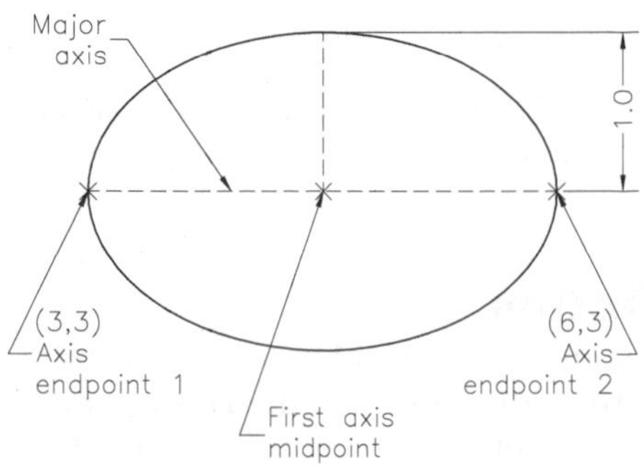

Figure 3-28 Drawing an ellipse using the Minor axis and end points on the Major Axis

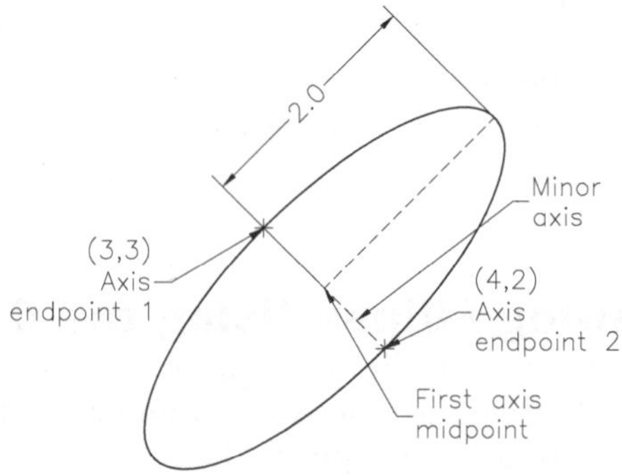

Figure 3-29 Drawing an ellipse using the Major axis and end points on the Minor Axis

Exercise 7 — *Ellipse*

Draw an ellipse whose major axis is 4 units and the rotation around this axis is 60 degrees. Draw another ellipse whose rotation around the major axis is 15 degrees.

Drawing Elliptical Arcs

Ribbon: Home > Draw > Ellipse drop-down > Elliptical Arc **Toolbar:** Draw > Ellipse Arc
Tool Palettes: Draw > Ellipse Arc **Command:** ELLIPSE > Arc

In AutoCAD, you can draw an elliptical arc by choosing the **Elliptical Arc** tool from the **Ellipse** drop-down of the **Draw** panel. On choosing this tool, you can specify the endpoints of one of the axes, the distance to other axis from the center and any one of the following information:

1. Start and End angles of the arc.
2. Start and Included angles of the arc.
3. Start and End parameters.

Remember that in case of elliptical arcs, angles are measured from the first point and in a counterclockwise direction.

In this section, you will draw an elliptical arc by using the information given below.

a. Start angle = -45, end angle = 135
b. Start angle = -45, included angle = 225
c. Start parameter = @1,0, end parameter = @1<225

Specifying the Start and End Angles of the Elliptical Arc [Figure 3-30(a)]

*Choose the **Elliptical Arc** tool from the **Ellipse** drop-down*
Specify axis endpoint of elliptical arc or [Center]: *Select the first endpoint*
Switch on the Ortho mode by pressing F8, if it is not already chosen
Specify other endpoint of axis: *Select the second point to the left of the first point*
Specify distance to other axis or [Rotation]: *Select a point or enter a distance*
Specify start angle or [Parameter]: **-45** Enter
Specify end angle or [Parameter/Included angle]: **135** Enter *(Angle where arc ends)*

Specifying the Start and Included Angles of the Elliptical Arc [Figure 3-30(b)]

*Choose the **Elliptical Arc** tool from the **Ellipse** drop-down*
Specify axis endpoint of elliptical arc or [Center]: *Select the first endpoint*
Specify other endpoint of axis: *Select the second point to the left of the first point*
Specify distance to other axis or [Rotation]: *Select a point or enter a distance*
Specify start angle or [Parameter]: **-45** Enter
Specify end angle or [Parameter/Included angle]: **I** Enter
Specify included angle for arc<current>: **225** Enter *(Included angle)*

Specifying the Start and End Parameters [Figure 3-30(c)]

*Choose the **Elliptical Arc** tool from the **Ellipse** drop-down*
Specify axis endpoint of elliptical arc or [Center]: *Select the first endpoint*
Specify other endpoint of axis: *Select the second endpoint to the left of the first point*
Specify distance to other axis or [Rotation]: *Select a point or enter a distance*
Specify start angle or [Parameter]: **P** Enter
Specify start parameter or [Angle]: **@1,0** Enter
Specify end parameter or [Angle/ Included angle]: **@1<225** Enter

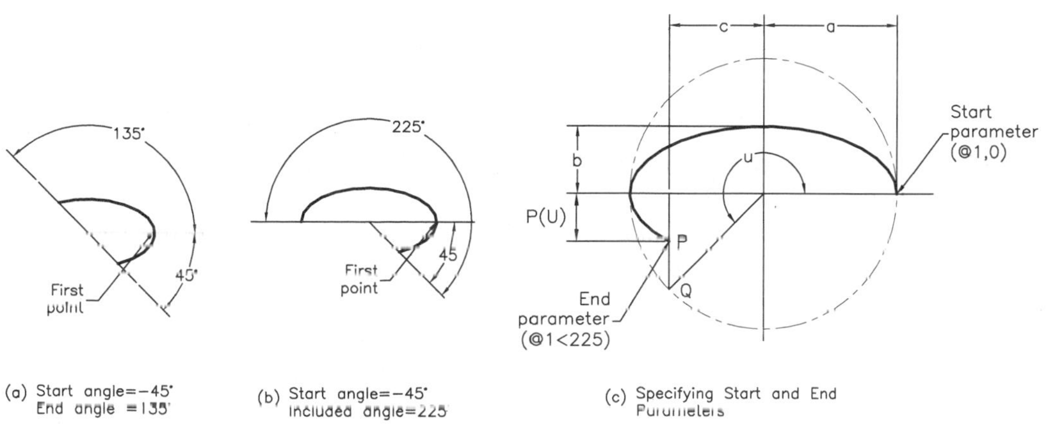

Figure 3-30 *Drawing elliptical arcs*

Exercise 8 *Elliptical Arc*

a. Construct an ellipse with center at (2,3), axis endpoint at (4,6), and the other axis endpoint at a distance of 0.75 unit from the midpoint of the first axis.

b. Draw the profile shown in Figure 3-31. The distance between the dotted lines is 1.0 unit.

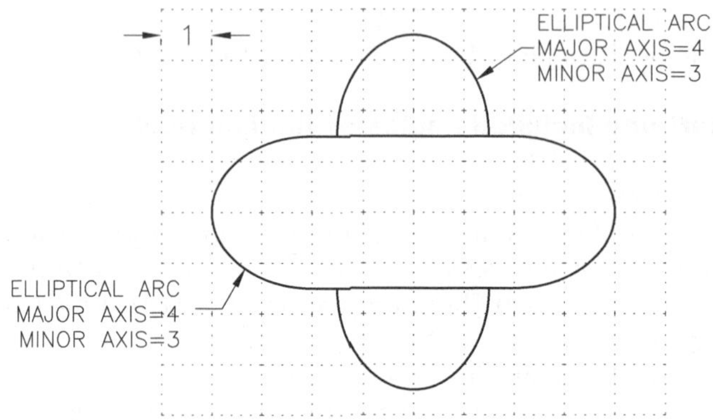

Figure 3-31 *Drawing for Exercise 8*

DRAWING REGULAR POLYGONS

Ribbon: Home > Draw > Rectangle drop-down > Polygon **Toolbar:** Draw > Polygon
Tool Palettes: Draw > Polygon **Command:** POLYGON/POL

A regular polygon is a closed geometric entity with equal sides. The number of sides of a polygon vary from 3 to 1024. For example, a triangle is a three-sided polygon and a pentagon is a five-sided polygon. To draw a regular 2D polygon, choose the **Polygon** tool from the **Rectangle** drop-down of the **Draw** panel; you will be prompted to specify the number of sides. Type the number of sides and press ENTER. Now, you can draw the polygon by specifying the length of an edge or by specifying the center of the polygon. Both these methods are discussed next.

Drawing a Polygon by Specifying the Center of Polygon

After you specify the number of sides and press ENTER, you will be prompted to specify the center of polygon. Specify the center point; you will be prompted to specify whether the polygon to be drawn is inscribed in a circle or circumscribed about an imaginary circle. A polygon is said to be inscribed when it is drawn inside an imaginary circle such that the vertices of the polygon touch the circle, refer to Figure 3-32. A polygon is said to be circumscribed when it is drawn outside the imaginary circle such that the sides of the polygon are tangent to the circle, refer to Figure 3-33. Type **I** or **C** to draw an inscribed or a circumscribed polygon respectively, and press ENTER; you will be prompted to specify the radius. Specify the radius and press ENTER; a polygon will be created.

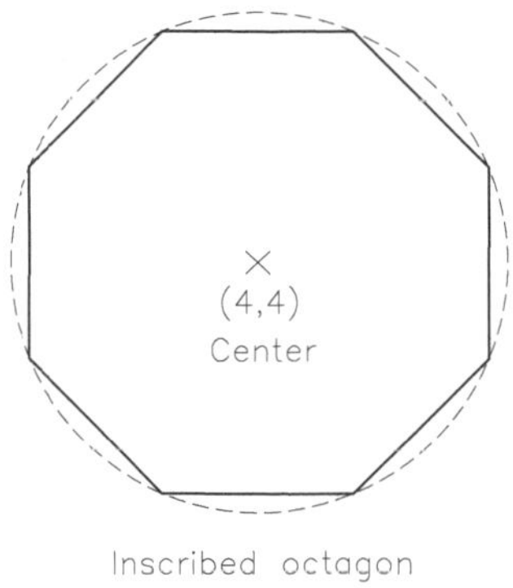

Figure 3-32 *Drawing an inscribed polygon using the* ***Center of Polygon*** *option*

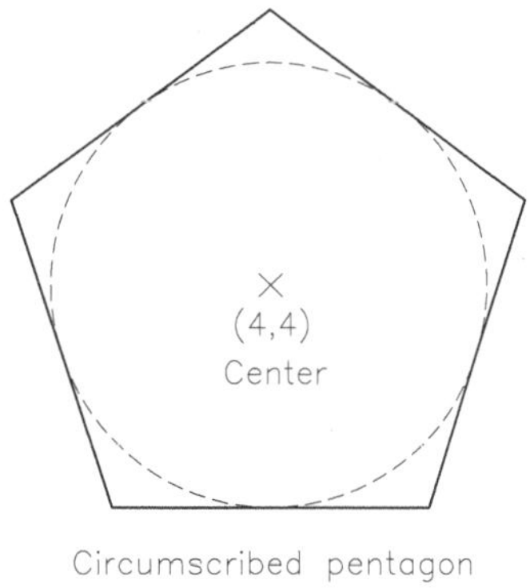

Figure 3-33 *Drawing a circumscribed polygon using the* ***Center of Polygon*** *option*

Drawing a Polygon by Specifying an Edge

To draw a polygon by specifying the length of an edge, you need to type **E** at the **Specify center of polygon or [Edge]** command prompt and press ENTER. Next, specify the first and second endpoints of the edge in succession; the polygon will be drawn in a counterclockwise direction, as shown in Figure 3-34.

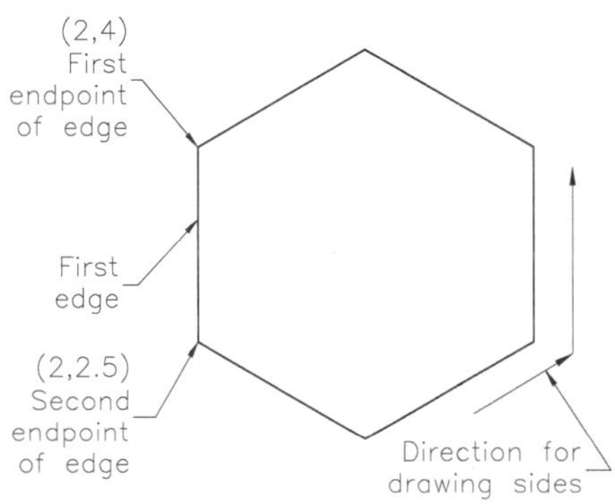

Figure 3-34 *Drawing a polygon (hexagon) using the* ***Edge*** *option*

Exercise 9

Draw a circumscribed polygon of eight sides by using the **Center of Polygon** method.

Exercise 10

Draw a polygon of ten sides by using the **Edge** option and an elliptical arc, as shown in Figure 3-35. Let the first endpoint of the edge be at (7,1) and the second endpoint be at (8,2).

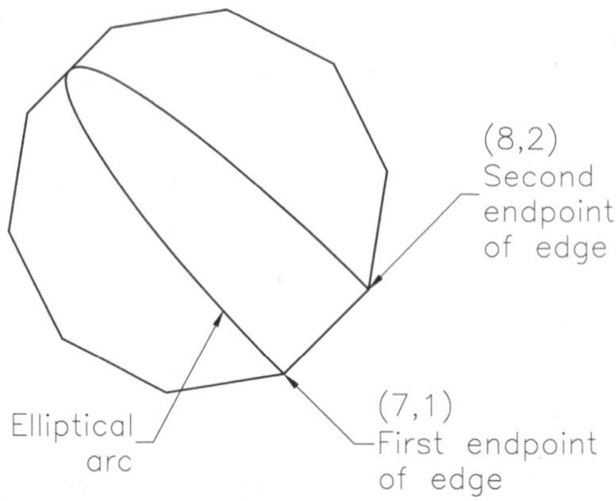

Figure 3-35 Polygon and elliptical arc for Exercise 10

DRAWING POLYLINES

Ribbon: Home > Draw > Polyline	**Toolbar:** Draw > Polyline
Tool Palettes: Draw > Polyline	**Command:** PLINE/PL

Generally, polylines means many lines. Some of the features of a polyline are listed below.

1. Polylines are thick lines with desired width. They are very flexible and can be used to draw any shape, such as a filled circle or a donut.
2. Polylines can be used to draw objects in any linetype (for example, hidden linetype).
3. Polylines are edited by using the advanced editing tools such as the **Edit Polyline** tool from the **Modify** panel of the **Home** tab.
4. A single polyline object can be formed by joining polylines and polyarcs of different thickness.
5. It is easy to determine the area or perimeter of a polyline feature.

To draw a polyline, choose the **Polyline** tool from the **Draw** panel, refer to Figure 3-36. The **Polyline** tool functions fundamentally like the **Line** tool except that some additional options are provided and all segments of the polyline form a single object. After invoking the **Polyline** tool and specifying a start point, the following prompt is displayed.

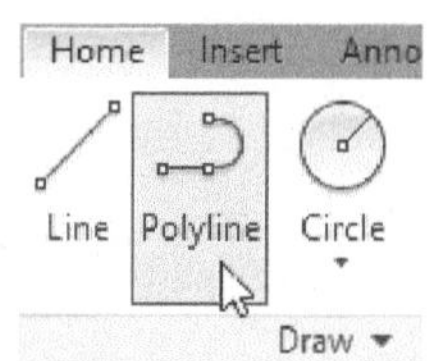

*Figure 3-36 Choosing the **Polyline** tool from the **Draw** panel*

Specify start point: *Specify the starting point or enter its coordinates.*
Current line-width is 0.0000
Specify next point or [Arc/Halfwidth/Length/Undo/Width]:

Note that the message **Current line-width is 0.0000** is displayed automatically indicating that the polyline drawn will have 0.0000 width.

When you are prompted to specify the next point, you can continue specifying the next point and draw a polyline, or depending on your requirements, the other options can be invoked. All these options are discussed next.

Next Point of Line

This is the default set option that is displayed after specifying the start point and is used to specify the next point of the current polyline segment. If additional polyline segments are added to the first polyline, AutoCAD automatically makes the endpoint of the previous polyline segment as the start point of the next polyline segment. The prompt sequence is given next.

Choose the ***Polyline*** *tool from the* ***Draw*** *panel*
Specify start point: *Specify the start point of the polyline.*
Current line-width is 0.0000.
Specify next point or [Arc/Halfwidth/Length/Undo/Width]: *Specify the endpoint of the first polyline segment.*
Specify next point or [Arc/Close/Halfwidth/Length/Undo/Width]: *Specify the endpoint of the second polyline segment, or press ENTER to exit the tool.*

Width

To change the current width of a polyline, enter **W** (width option) at the last prompt. You can also right-click and choose the **Width** option from the shortcut menu. On doing so, you will be prompted to specify the width at the start and end of the polyline. Specify the widths of the polyline and press ENTER; the polyline will be drawn with the specified width.

The starting width value is taken as the ending width value by default. Therefore, to have a uniform polyline, you need to press ENTER at the **Specify ending width < >** prompt. However, if you specify a different value for the ending width, the resulting polyline will be tapered.

For example, to draw a polyline of uniform width 0.25 unit, start point at (4,5), endpoint at (5,5), and the next endpoint at (3,3), use the following prompt sequence:

Choose the ***Polyline*** *tool from the* ***Draw*** *panel*
Specify start point: **4,5** Enter
Current line-width is 0.0000
Specify next point or [Arc/Halfwidth/Length/Undo/Width]: **W** Enter
Specify starting width <current>: **0.25** Enter
Specify ending width <0.25>: Enter
Specify next point or [Arc/Halfwidth/Length/Undo/Width]: **5,5** Enter
Specify next point or [Arc/Close/Halfwidth/Length/Undo/Width]: **3,3** Enter
Specify next point or [Arc/Close/Halfwidth/Length/Undo/Width]: Enter. *Refer to Figure 3-37.*

Similarly, to draw a tapered polyline of starting width 0.5 units and an ending width 0.15 units, a start point at (2,4), and an endpoint at (5,4), use the prompt sequence given next.

Choose the ***Polyline*** *tool from the* ***Draw*** *panel*
Specify start point: **2,4** Enter
Current line-width is 0.0000
Specify next point or [Arc/Halfwidth/Length/Undo/Width]: **W** Enter
Specify starting width <0.0000>: **0.50** Enter
Specify ending width <0.50>: **0.15** Enter
Specify next point or [Arc/Halfwidth/Length/Undo/Width]: **5,4** Enter
Specify next point or [Arc/Close/Halfwidth/Length/Undo/Width]: Enter. *Refer to Figure 3-38.*

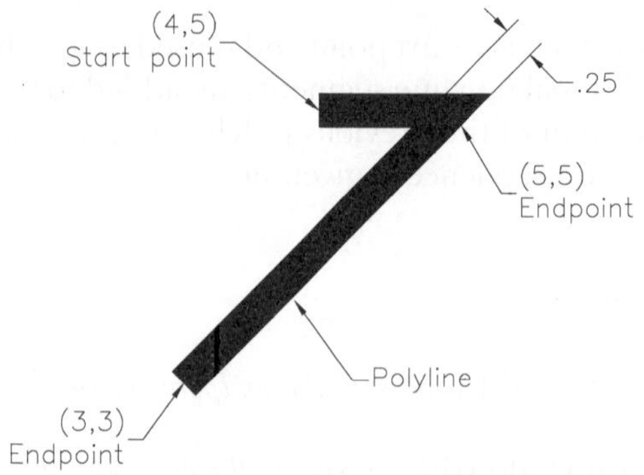

*Figure 3-37 Drawing a uniform polyline using the **Polyline** tool*

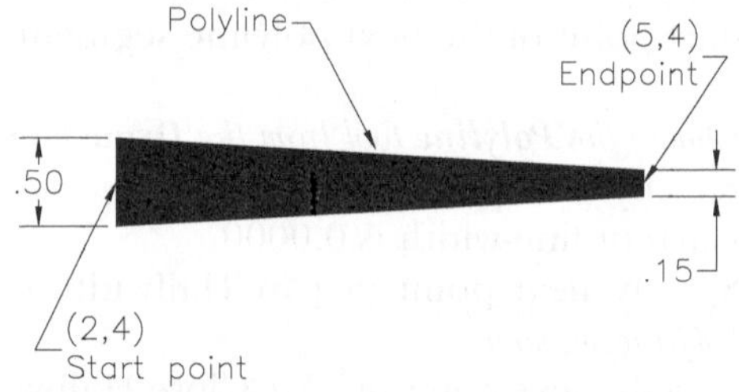

*Figure 3-38 Drawing a tapered polyline using the **Polyline** tool*

Halfwidth

The halfwidth is equal to the half of the actual width of a polyline. This option is invoked by entering **H** or choosing **Halfwidth** from the shortcut menu. The prompt sequence to specify the starting and ending halfwidths of a polyline is given next.

Specify next point or [Arc/Halfwidth/Length/Undo/Width]: **H** Enter
Specify starting half-width <0.0000>: **0.12** Enter *(Specify the desired starting halfwidth)*
Specify ending half-width <0.1200>: **0.05** Enter *(Specify the desired ending halfwidth)*

Length

The **Length** option is used to draw a new polyline segment of specified length and at the same angle as the last polyline segment or tangent to the previous polyarc segment. This option is invoked by entering **L** at the following prompt or by choosing **Length** from the shortcut menu.

Specify next point or [Arc/Close/Halfwidth/Length/Undo/Width]: **L** Enter
Specify length of line: *Specify the desired length of the Pline*

Undo

This option erases the most recently drawn polyline segment. It can be invoked by entering **U** at the **Specify next point or [Arc/Close/Halfwidth/Length/Undo/Width]** prompt. You can use this option repeatedly until you reach the start point of the first polyline segment. If you use this option again, the message **All segments already undone** will be displayed.

Close

This option will be available only when at least one segment of a polyline is drawn. It closes the polyline by drawing a polyline segment from the most recent endpoint to the initial start point.

Arc

This option is used to switch from polylines to polyarcs. You can also set the parameters associated with polyarcs. By default, the arc segment is drawn tangent to the previous segment of the polyline. The direction of the previous line, arc, or polyline segment is the default direction for the polyarc. On invoking the arc option, you need to choose the sub-options to draw the polyarc. Some of the sub-options to draw a polyarc are similar to that of drawing an arc. The sub-options that are different are discussed next.

CLose

This option will be available only when you specify two or more than two points for creating the polyline segments. To join the start and last points of a polyline in the form of an arc, type **CL** at the **Specify endpoint of arc (hold Ctrl to switch direction) or [Angle/CEnter/CLose/Direction/Halfwidth/Line/Radius/Second pt/Undo/Width]** command prompt and press ENTER; an arc will be created that will close the loop.

Direction

Usually, the arc drawn by using the **Arc** option of the **Polyline** tool is tangent to the previously drawn polyline segment. In other words, the starting direction of the arc depends upon the ending direction of the previous segment. The **Direction** option is used to specify the direction of the tangent for the arc segment to be drawn. You need to specify the direction by specifying a point. The prompts are given next.

Specify tangent direction for the start point of arc: *Specify the direction.*
Specify endpoint of arc (hold Ctrl to switch direction): *Specify the endpoint of arc.*

Halfwidth

The use of this option is similar to the option used for the polyline segment. It is used to specify the starting and ending halfwidths of an arc segment.

Line

This option is used to invoke the **Line** mode again.

Radius

This option is used to specify the radius of the arc segment. The prompt sequence for specifying the radius is given next.

....Specify endpoint of arc or [Angle/CEnter/CLose/Direction/Halfwidth/Line/Radius/Second pt/Undo/Width]: **R**
Specify radius of arc: *Specify the radius of the arc segment.* Enter
Specify endpoint of arc (hold Ctrl to switch direction) or [Angle]: *Specify the endpoint of arc or choose an option.*

If you specify a point, the arc segment will be drawn. If you use the angle option, you will have to specify the angle and the direction of the chord at the **Specify included angle** and **Specify direction of chord for arc (hold Ctrl to switch direction) <current>** prompts, respectively.

Second pt

This option is used to select the second point of an arc while using the **3-Point arc** option. The prompt sequence is given next.

Specify second point of arc: *Specify the second point on the arc*
Specify end point of arc: *Specify the third point on the arc*

Width

This option is used to enter the width of the arc segment. The prompt sequence for specifying the width is the same as that of the polyline. To draw a tapered arc segment, as shown in Figure 3-39, you need to enter different values at the starting width and ending width prompts.

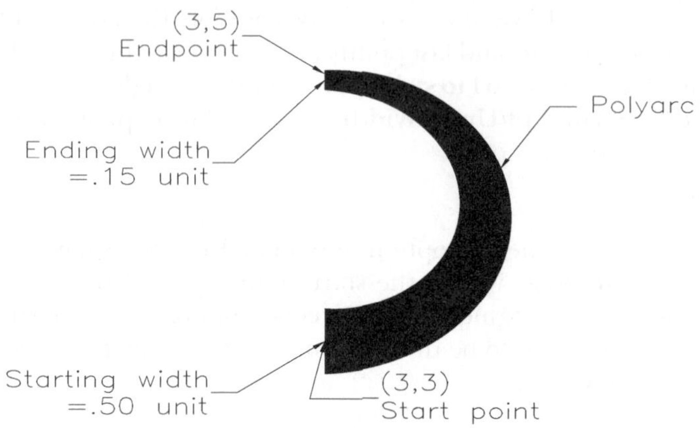

***Figure 3-39** Drawing a polyarc*

The prompt sequence to draw an arc, whose start point is at (3,3), endpoint is at (3,5), starting width is 0.50 unit, and ending width is 0.15 unit, is given next.

*Choose the **Polyline** tool from the **Draw** panel*
Specify start point: **3,3** Enter
Current line-width is 0.0000
Specify next point or [Arc/Halfwidth/Length/Undo/Width]: **A** Enter
Specify endpoint of arc (hold Ctrl to switch direction) or [Angle/CEnter/CLose/Direction/Halfwidth/Line/Radius/Second pt/Undo/Width]: **W** Enter
Specify starting width <current>: **0.50** Enter
Specify ending width <0.50>: **0.15** Enter
Specify endpoint of arc (hold Ctrl to switch direction) or [Angle/CEnter/Direction/Halfwidth/Line/Radius/Second pt/Undo/Width]: **3,5** Enter
Specify endpoint of arc (hold Ctrl to switch direction) or [Angle/CEnter/CLose/Direction/Halfwidth/Line/Radius/Second pt/Undo/Width]: Enter

Tip

*In AutoCAD, you can close an open polyline using the **Fillet** tool (by defining radius as zero). To do so, choose the **Fillet** tool from the **Modify** panel of the **Home** tab and select the two open ends of the polyline. Figure 3-40 shows an open polyline and Figure 3-41 shows closed polyline after selecting both ends.*

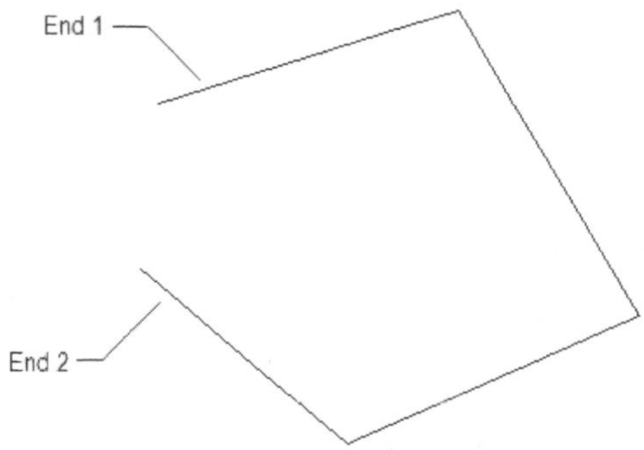

Figure 3-40 Open polyline with two ends

Figure 3-41 Final closed polyline

Exercise 11

Draw the objects shown in Figures 3-42 and 3-43 by using the polylines of different widths.

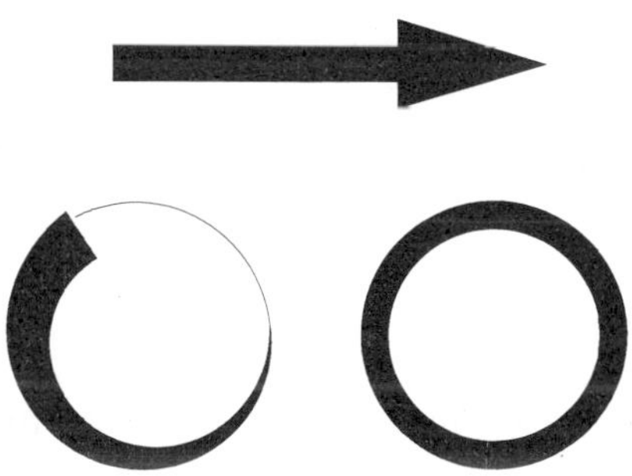

Figure 3-42 Drawing for Exercise 11

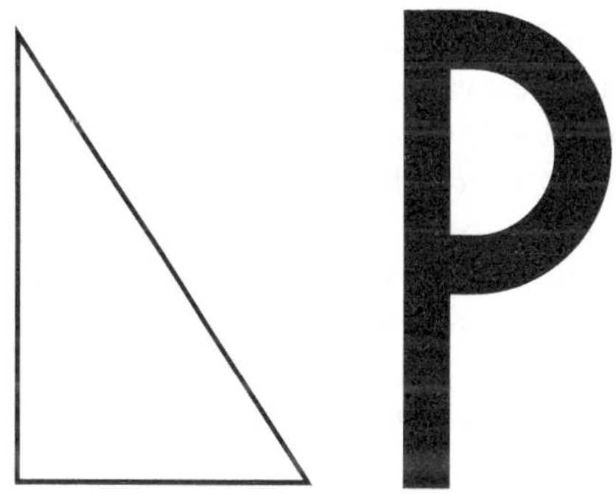

Figure 3-43 Drawing for Exercise 11

DRAWING DONUTS

Ribbon: Home > Draw > Donut **Command:** DONUT/DOUGHNUT/DO

In AutoCAD, the **Donut** tool is used to draw an object that looks like a filled circular ring called donut. AutoCAD's donuts are made of two semicircular polyarcs with a certain width. Therefore, the **Donut** tool allows you to draw a thick circle. The donuts can have any inside and outside diameters. If **FILLMODE** is off, a donut will look like a circle (if the inside diameter is zero) or a concentric circle (if the inside diameter is not zero). On invoking the **Donut** tool, you will be prompted to specify the diameters. After specifying the two diameters, the donut gets attached to the crosshairs. Specify a point for the center of the donut in the drawing area to place the donut. In this way, you can place as many donuts as required without exiting the tool. Press ENTER to exit the tool.

The default values for the inside and outside diameters of donuts are saved in the **DONUTID** and **DONUTOD** system variables. A solid-filled circle is drawn by specifying the inside diameter as zero, if **FILLMODE** is on.

Example 1 — Donut

You will draw an unfilled donut shown in Figure 3-44 with an inside diameter of 0.75 unit, an outside diameter of 2.0 units, and centered at (2,2). You will also draw a filled donut and a solid-filled donut with the given specifications.

The following is the prompt sequence to draw an unfilled donut shown in Figure 3-44.

Command: **FILLMODE** Enter
New value for FILLMODE <1>: **0** Enter
Command: *Choose the **Donut** tool from the **Draw** panel*
Specify inside diameter of donut<0.5000>: **0.75** Enter
Specify outside diameter of donut <1.000>: **2** Enter
Specify center of donut or <exit>: **2,2** Enter
Specify center of donut or <exit>: Enter

The prompt sequence for drawing a filled donut with an inside diameter of 0.5 unit, outside diameter of 2.0 units, which is centered at a specified point is given below:

Command: **FILLMODE** Enter
Enter new value for FILLMODE <0>: **1** Enter
Command: *Choose the **Donut** tool from the **Draw** panel*
Specify inside diameter of donut<0.5000>: **0.5** Enter
Specify outside diameter of donut <1.000>: **2** Enter
Specify center of donut or <exit>: *Specify a point*
Specify center of donut or <exit>: Enter. *Refer to Figure 3-45*

To draw a solid-filled donut with an outside diameter of 2.0 units, use the following prompt sequence:

*Choose the **Donut** tool from the **Draw** panel*
Specify inside diameter of donut <0.50>: **0** Enter
Specify outside diameter of donut <1.0>: **2** Enter
Specify center of donut or <exit>: *Specify a point*
Specify center of donut or <exit>: Enter. *Refer to Figure 3-46*

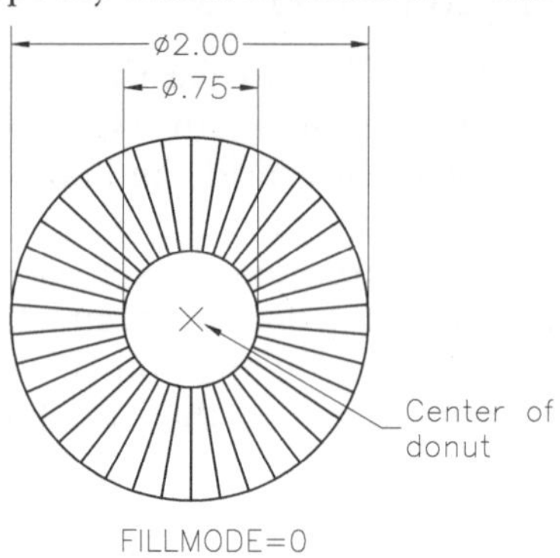

Figure 3-44 *Unfilled donut*

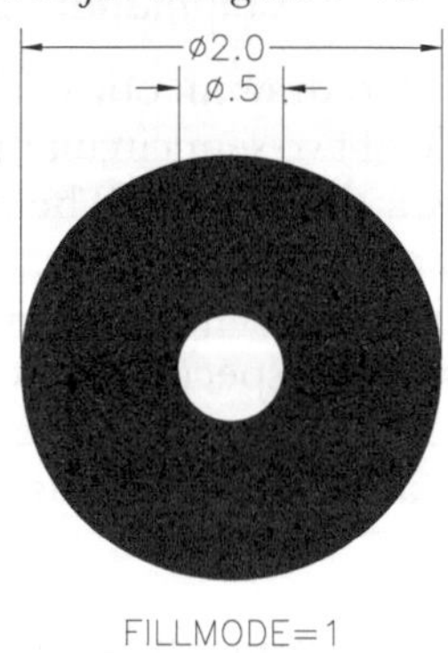

Figure 3-45 *Filled donut*

Figure 3-46 *Solid-filled donut*

PLACING POINTS

A point is one of the basic drawing objects and is specified as a dot (a period). A point is defined as a geometric object that has no dimension and properties, except location. However, in AutoCAD, you can control the size and appearance (style) of a point. You will first learn to change the point style and size and then about various methods to place a point.

Changing the Point Style and Size

Ribbon: Home > Utilities > Point Style **Command:** DDPTYPE or PTYPE

To change the style and size of a point, choose the **Point Style** tool from the **Utilities** panel of the **Home** tab; the **Point Style** dialog box will be displayed, as shown in Figure 3-47. Select any one of the twenty point styles in the **Point Style** dialog box. You can specify the point size as a specified percentage of the drawing area or as an absolute size by selecting the **Set Size Relative to Screen** or **Set Size in Absolute Units** radio button respectively. After selecting the appropriate radio button, enter the point size in the **Point Size** edit box. Choose the **OK** button after specifying the parameters. Now, the points will be drawn according to the selected style and size, until you change the style and size. You can also change the point style and the point size by using the **PDMODE** and **PDSIZE** system variables, respectively. The different values of **PDMODE** and the resulting style are shown in Figure 3-48.

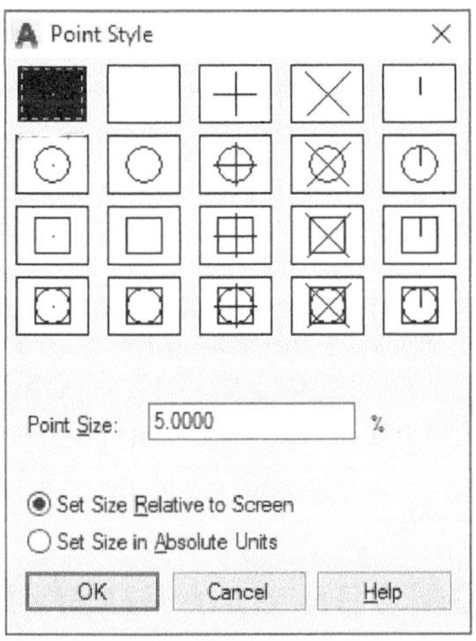

*Figure 3-47 The **Point Style** dialog box*

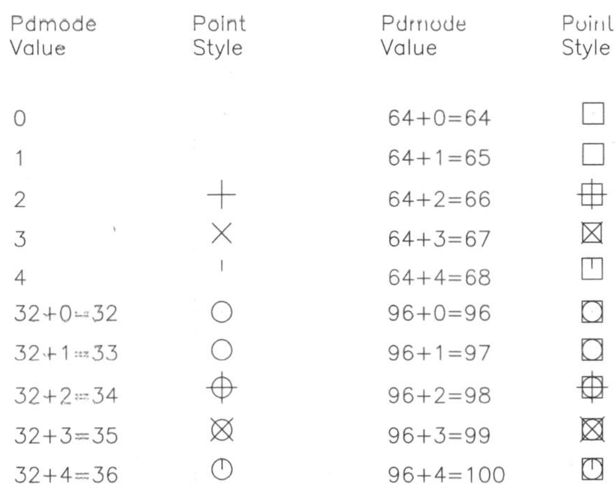

*Figure 3-48 Different point styles for **PDMODE** values*

Note

*On selecting the **Set Size Relative to Screen** radio button, the point size will not change when you zoom in or zoom out the drawing (type **REGEN** and press enter once you zoom in or zoom out the drawing). However, on selecting the **Set Size in Absolute Units** radio button, the size of the point will change when you zoom the drawing in or out.*

Placing Multiple Points

Ribbon: Home > Draw > Multiple Points	**Toolbar:** Draw > Point
Menu Bar: Draw > Point > Multiple Point	**Tool Palettes:** Draw > Point

To place points, choose the **Multiple Points** tool from the **Draw** panel, refer to Figure 3-49; the current **PDMODE** and **PDSIZE** values will be displayed and you will be prompted to specify a point. Left-click to place a point.

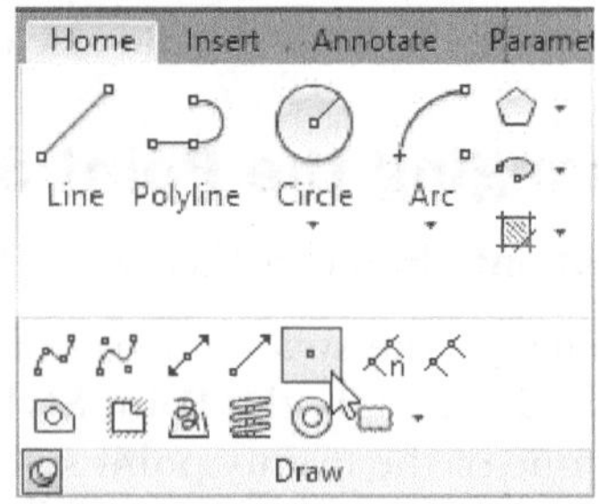

*Figure 3-49 Choosing the **Multiple Points** tool from the **Draw** panel*

Next, continue placing as many points as needed and then press ESC to exit the command. You can also enter the coordinate value and place a point at a particular location.

Placing Points at Equal Distance

Ribbon: Home > Draw > Divide	**Command:** DIVIDE/DIV

To place points at an equal distance on an object, choose the **Divide** tool from the **Draw** panel; you will be prompted to select an object to divide. Select an object; you will be prompted to specify the number of segments. Enter the number of segments; the points will be created on the object.

Placing Points at Specified Intervals

Ribbon: Home > Draw > Measure	**Command:** MEASURE/ME

You can place points at specified intervals on an object by selecting the object and specifying the length of the segment between two points. To do so, choose the **Measure** tool from the **Draw** panel; you will be prompted to select the object to measure. Select the object; you will be prompted to specify the length of the segment. Specify the length of the segment; the points will be placed at specified intervals.

Exercise 12 — *PDMODE and PDSIZE*

a. Try various combinations of the **PDMODE** and **PDSIZE** variables.

b. Check the difference between the points generated by using the negative values of **PDSIZE** and the points generated by using positive values of **PDSIZE**.

DRAWING AN INFINITE LINE

In AutoCAD, you can draw a construction line or a ray that aids in construction or projection. A construction line (xline) is a 3D line that extends to infinity at both ends. As line is infinite in length and does not have any endpoint, Whereas, a ray is a 3D line that extends to infinity at only one end. The other end of the ray is a finite endpoint. The xlines and rays have zero extents. This means that the extents of the drawing will not change if you use the **Zoom All** tool. Most of the object snap modes work with both xlines and rays with some limitations. You cannot use the **Endpoint** object snap with the xline because by definition an xline does not have any endpoints. However, for rays, you can use the **Endpoint** snap on one end only. Also, xlines and rays take the properties of the layer in which they are drawn.

Tip

Sometimes, Xlines and rays when plotted like any other object may create confusion. Therefore, it is recommended to create the construction lines in a different layer altogether so that you can recognize them easily. You will learn about layers in the later chapters.

Drawing Construction Lines

Ribbon: Home > Draw > Construction Line	**Toolbar:** Draw > Construction Line
Tool Palettes: Draw > Construction Line	**Command:** XLINE/XL

To draw a construction line that extends to infinity from both sides, invoke the **Construction Line** tool from the **Draw** panel. The prompt sequence that is displayed on choosing this tool is as follows:

Specify a point or [Hor/Ver/Ang/Bisect/Offset]: *Specify an option or select a point through which the xline will pass.*

The various options displayed on invoking the **Construction Line** tool are discussed next.

Point

If you use the default option, you need to specify two points through which the xline will pass. After specifying the first point, move the cursor; a line will be attached to the cursor. On specifying the second point, an xline will be created that passes through the first and second points, refer to Figure 3-50.

Specify a point or [Hor/Ver/Ang/Bisect/Offset]: *Specify a point.*
Specify through point: *Specify the second point.*

You can continue to select more points to create more xlines. All these xlines will pass through the first point you had selected at the **Specify a point** prompt. This point is also called the root point. Right-click or press ENTER to exit the tool.

Horizontal

This option is used to create horizontal xlines of infinite length that pass through the selected points. The xlines will be parallel to the *X* axis of the current UCS, refer to Figure 3-51. On invoking this option, a horizontal xline will be attached to the cursor and you will be prompted to select a point through which the horizontal xline will pass. Specify a point. You can continue specifying more points to draw more horizontal xlines. To exit the tool, right-click or press ENTER.

Vertical

This option is used to create vertical xlines of infinite length that pass through the selected points. The xlines will be parallel to the *Y* axis of the current UCS, refer to Figure 3-51.

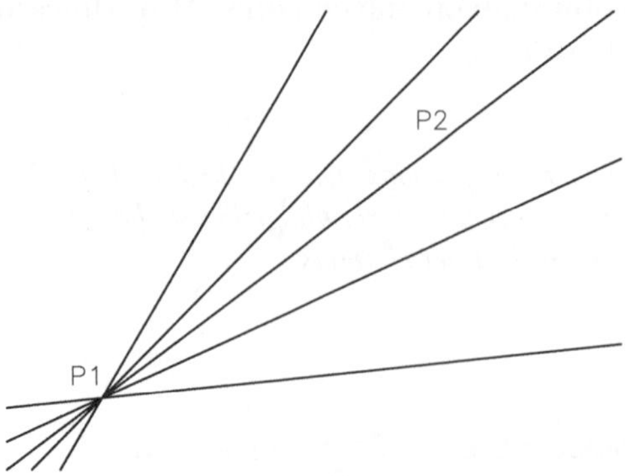

Figure 3-50 *Drawing the xlines*

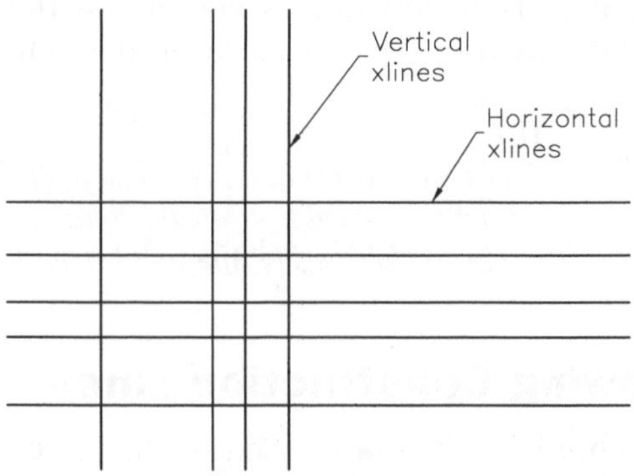

Figure 3-51 *Horizontal and vertical xlines*

Angular

This option is used to create xlines of infinite length that pass through the selected point at a specified angle, refer to Figure 3-52. The angle can be specified by entering a value. You can also invoke the **Reference** option by selecting an object and then specifying an angle relative to it. The **Reference** option is useful when the actual angle is not known, but the angle relative to an existing object can be specified.

*Choose the **Construction Line** tool from the **Draw** panel*
XLINE Specify a point or [Hor/Ver/Ang/Bisect/Offset]: **A** Enter
Enter angle of xline (0) or [Reference]: **R** Enter *(Use the **Reference** method to specify the angle)*
Select a line object: *Select a line.*
Enter angle of xline <0>: *Enter angle (the angle will be measured counterclockwise with respect to the selected line)*
Specify through point: *Specify the second point* Enter.

Bisect

This option is used to create an xline that bisects an angle. In this case, you need to specify the vertex, start point, and endpoint of the angle. The xline will pass through the vertex and bisect the angle specified by selecting two points. The xline created using this option will lie on the plane defined by the selected points. The following is the prompt sequence for this option, refer to Figure 3-53.

*Choose the **Construction Line** tool from the **Draw** panel*
XLINE Specify a point or [Hor/Ver/Ang/Bisect/Offset]: **B** Enter
Specify angle vertex point: *Enter a point (P1).*
Specify angle start point: *Enter a point (P2).*
Specify angle end point: *Enter a point (P3).*
Specify angle end point: *Select more points or press ENTER or right-click to end the tool.*

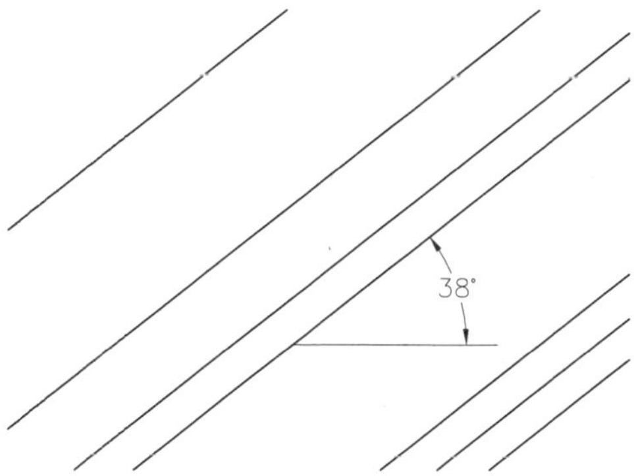

Figure 3-52 The angular xlines

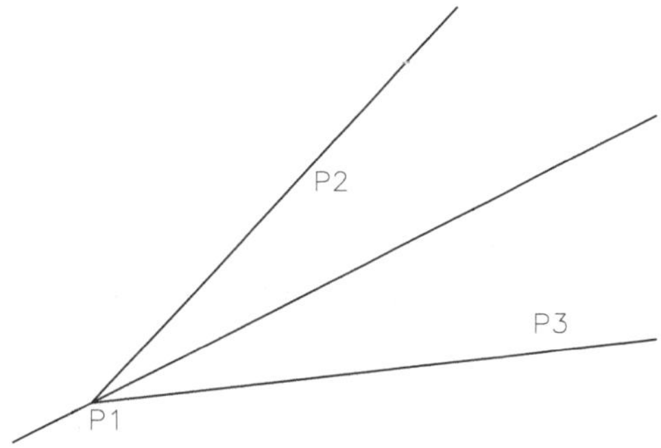

*Figure 3-53 Using the **Bisect** option to draw xlines*

Offset

The **Offset** option is used to create xlines that are parallel to a selected line/xline at a specified offset distance. You can specify the offset distance by entering a numerical value or by selecting two points on the screen. If you choose the **Through** option, the offset line will pass through the selected point. The following is the prompt sequence for this option:

*Choose the **Construction Line** tool from the **Draw** panel*
XLINE Specify a point or [Hor/Ver/Ang/Bisect/Offset]: **O** Enter
Specify offset distance or [Through] <Through>: *Press ENTER to accept the **Through** option or specify a distance from the selected line object at which the xline shall be drawn.*
Select a line object: *Select the object to which the xline is drawn parallel and at a specified distance.*
Specify through point: *Select a point through which the xline should pass.*

After specifying the offset distance and selecting a line object, you need to specify the direction in which the xline has to be offset. You can continue drawing construction lines or right-click or press ENTER to exit the tool.

Drawing Ray

Ribbon: Home > Draw > Ray **Command:** RAY

A ray is a 3D line similar to the xline with the difference being that it extends to infinity only in one direction. It starts from a specified point and extends to infinity through the specified point. The prompt sequence is given next.

Specify start point: *Select the start point for the ray.*
Specify through point: *Specify the second point.*

Press ENTER or right-click to exit the tool.

WRITING A SINGLE LINE TEXT

Ribbon: Home > Annotation > Multiline Text drop-down > Single Line
Command: TEXT/DT

The **Single Line** tool is used to write a single line text. Although you can write more than one line of text using this command, but each line will be a separate text entity. To write text, choose the **Single Line** tool from **Home > Annotation > Multiline Text** drop-down. This tool is also available in the **Multiline Text** drop-down available in the **Text** panel of the **Annotate** tab. After invoking this tool, you need to specify the start point for the text. Next, you need to specify the text height and the rotation angle. As you enter the characters, they start appearing on the screen. After typing a line if you press ENTER, the cursor will be automatically placed at the start of the next line and the prompt for entering another line will be repeated. Type another line or press ENTER again to exit the tool. You can use the BACKSPACE key to edit the text on the screen while writing it. The prompt sequence is given next.

*Choose the **Single Line** tool from the **Draw** panel*
Current text style: "Standard" Text height: 0.2000 Annotative: No Justify: Left
Specify start point of text or [Justify/Style]: *Specify the starting point of the text.*
Specify height<current>: *Enter the text height.*
Specify rotation angle of text <0>: Enter
Enter the first line of the text in the text box displayed in the drawing window.
Enter the second line of the text in the text box displayed in the drawing window.
Press ENTER twice to exit.

Note
The other tools to enter text are discussed in detail in Chapter 7.

WORKING WITH TEMPLATES

In AutoCAD, you can use various templates to make your drawings. AutoCAD comes with standard drawing templates such as *acad.dwt, acadiso.dwt, acad3D.dwt, acadiso3D.dwt, acad-Named Plot Styles.dwt, acadISO-Named Plot Styles.dwt,* and so on. The ISO template drawings are based on the drawing standards developed by ISO (International Organization for Standardization). To use these template drawings, select the required template from the **Templates** drop-down of the **Get Started** area in the **Start** tab, as shown in Figure 3-54. You will learn more about templates in Chapter 15.

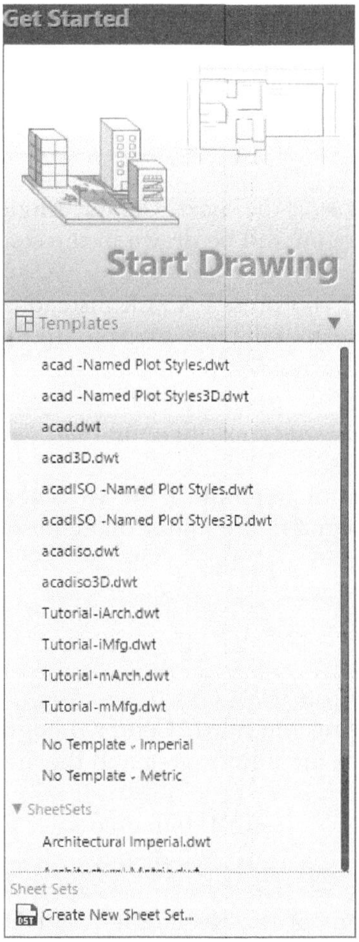

Figure 3-54 *Various templates in the **Templates** drop-down*

Self-Evaluation Test

Answer the following questions and then compare them to those given at the end of this chapter:

1. The __________ option of the **Rectangle** tool is used to draw a rectangle at a specified distance from the XY plane along the Z axis.

2. If the **FILLMODE** is set to __________, only the outlines for the new polyline will be drawn.

3. You can get a __________ polyline by entering two different values at the starting width and ending width prompts.

4. Choose the __________ tool from the **Draw** panel to place points at specified intervals on an object.

5. Choose the __________ tool from the **Draw** panel to draw as many points as you want in a single command.

6. The size of a point will be taken as a percentage of the viewport size if you enter a __________ value for the **PDSIZE** variable.

7. While drawing an arc by choosing the **Start, Center, Angle** tool if you enter the included angle with a negative value, an arc will be drawn in the clockwise direction. (T/F)

8. After choosing the **Arc** tool if you press ENTER instead of specifying the start point, the start point and direction of the arc will be taken from the endpoint and ending direction of the previous line or the arc drawn. (T/F)

9. By using the **Single Line** tool, you can write more than one line of text. (T/F)

10. The start and end parameters of an elliptical arc are determined by specifying a point on the circle whose diameter is equal to the minor diameter of an ellipse. (T/F)

Review Questions

Answer the following questions:

1. On drawing an arc by choosing the **Start, Center, Length** tool, a positive chord length generates the smallest possible arc (minor arc), and the arc is always less than:

   (a) 90 degree (b) 180 degree
   (c) 270 degree (d) 360 degree

2. Which of the following options of the **Rectangle** tool is used to draw a rectangle that is extruded in the Z direction by a specified value?

   (a) **Elevation** (b) **Thickness**
   (c) **Extrude** (d) **Width**

3. Which of the following tools should be used to draw a line in 3D space that starts from a specified start point and the other end extends to infinity?

   (a) **Polyline** (b) **Ray**
   (c) **Construction Line** (d) **Multiline Text**

4. A polygon is said to be __________ when it is drawn inside an imaginary circle and its vertices touch the circle.

5. If additional polyline segments are added to the first polyline, the __________ of the first polyline segment becomes the start point of the next polyline segment.

6. By using the **Donut** tool, you can draw a solid-filled circle by specifying the inside diameter as __________ and keeping the **FILLMODE** on.

7. The _________ option of the **Construction Line** tool is used to create construction lines of infinite length that are parallel to the *Y* axis of the current UCS.

8. You can use the _________ key to edit text on the screen while writing it using the **Single Line** tool.

9. While drawing an arc by choosing the **Start, End, Angle** tool, a negative included angle value draws the arc in clockwise direction. (T/F)

10. When the **Continue** option of the **Arc** tool is used to draw arcs, each successive arc is perpendicular to the previous one. (T/F)

11. If you specify the chamfer distances first and then specify the fillet radius of the same **Rectangle** tool, the rectangle will be drawn with chamfers only. (T/F)

12. A rectangle drawn using the **Rectangle** tool is treated as a combination of different objects, therefore, the individual sides can be edited independently. (T/F)

Exercise 13 Arc

Draw the sketch shown in Figure 3-55. The distance between the dotted lines is 1.0 unit. Create arcs by choosing appropriate tools from the **Arc** drop-down.

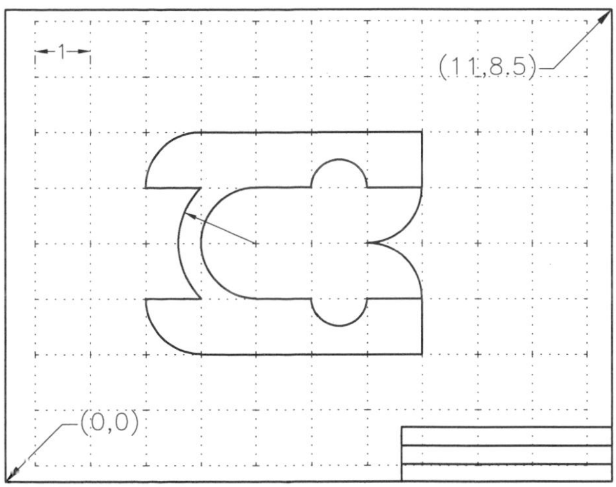

Figure 3-55 *Drawing for Exercise 13*

Exercise 14 *Ellipse*

Draw the sketch shown in Figure 3-56. The distance between the dotted lines is 0.5 unit. Create ellipses using the tools in the **Ellipse** drop-down.

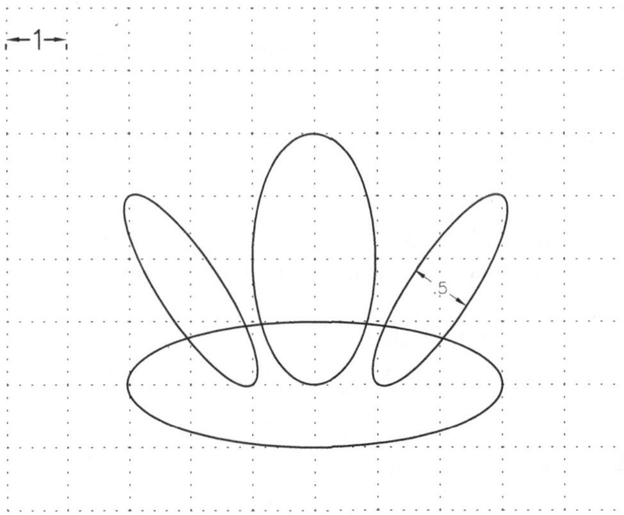

Figure 3-56 *Drawing for Exercise 14*

Exercise 15

Draw the sketch shown in Figure 3-57 using the **Line**, **Circle**, and **Arc** tools. The distance between the dotted lines is 1.0 unit and the diameter of the circles is 1.0 unit.

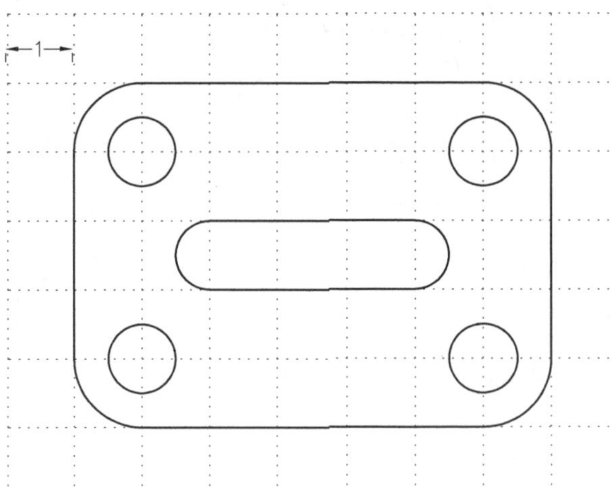

Figure 3-57 *Drawing for Exercise 15*

Exercise 16

Draw the sketch shown in Figure 3-58 using the **Line**, **Circle**, and **Arc** tools or their options. The distance between the grid lines is 1.0 unit and the diameter of the circle is 1.0 unit.

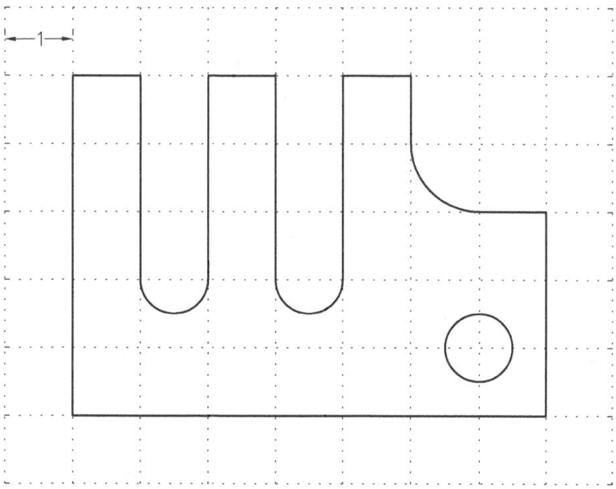

Figure 3-58 *Drawing for Exercise 16*

Exercise 17

Draw the object shown in Figure 3-59. The distance between the dotted lines is 5 inches. Determine the limits for this drawing and use the Fractional units with 0 1/16 precision.

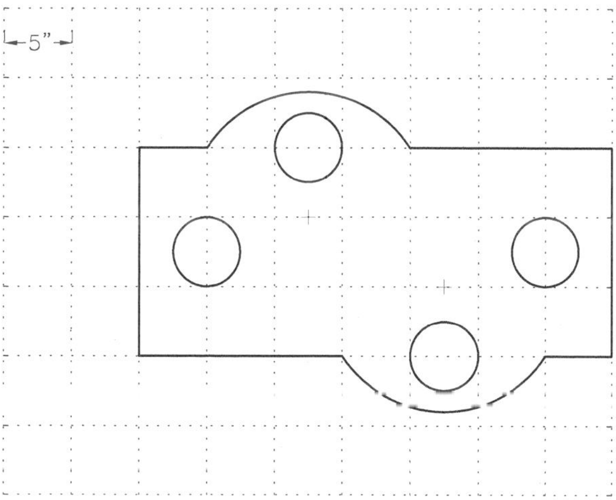

Figure 3-59 *Drawing for Exercise 17*

Problem-Solving Exercise 1 — *Arc*

Draw the sketch shown in Figure 3-60. Next, create arcs by using the **Arc** tools indicated in the drawing. (Use the @ symbol to snap to the previous point. Example: Specify start point of arc or [Center]: @)

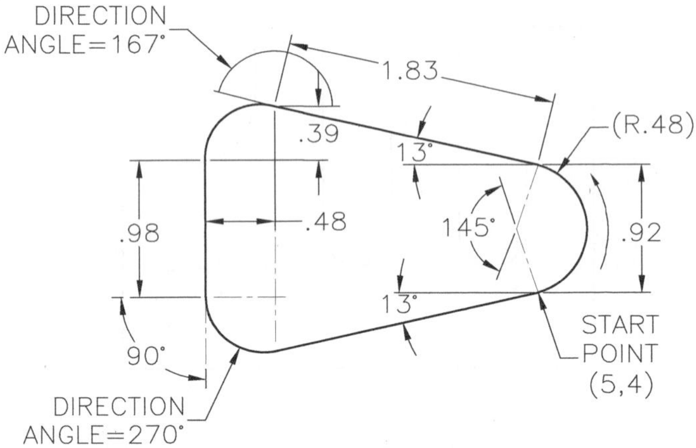

Figure 3-60 *Drawing for Problem-Solving Exercise 1*

Problem-Solving Exercise 2 — *Arc*

Draw the sketch shown in Figure 3-61. Create arcs by using the **Arc** tools. The distance between the dotted lines is 0.5 unit.

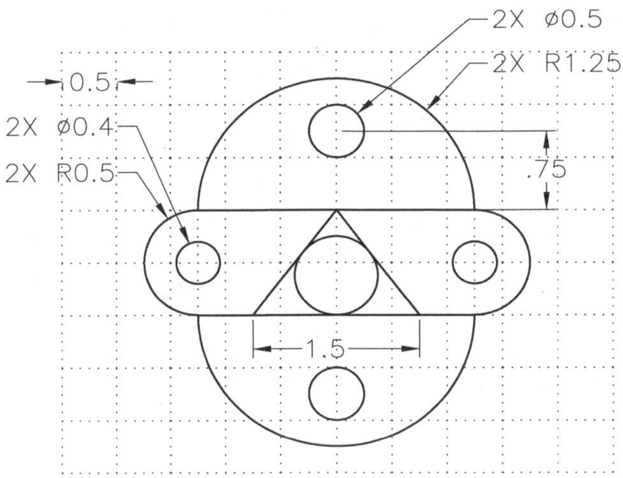

Figure 3-61 *Drawing for Problem-Solving Exercise 2*

Problem-Solving Exercise 3 Arc

Draw the sketch shown in Figure 3-62 by using different tools in the **Draw** panel. Note, Sin30=0.5 and Sin60=0.866. The distance between the dotted lines is 1 unit.

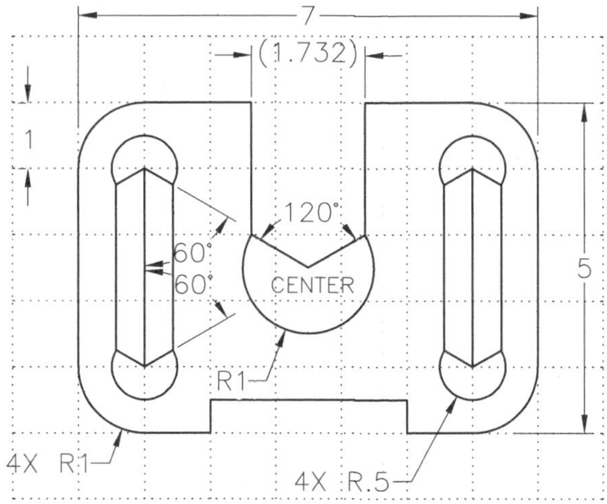

Figure 3-62 Drawing for Problem-Solving Exercise 3

Problem-Solving Exercise 4

Draw the sketch shown in Figure 3-63 using the **Polygon**, **Circle**, and **Line** tools.

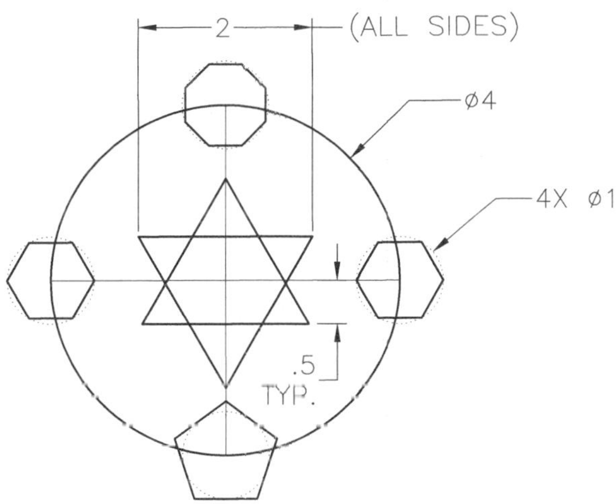

Figure 3-63 Drawing for Problem-Solving Exercise 4

Problem-Solving Exercise 5

Draw the sketch shown in Figure 3-64 by using different tools in the **Draw** panel. Also, draw the hidden lines and center lines as continuous lines. Note that the dimensions are given only for your reference.

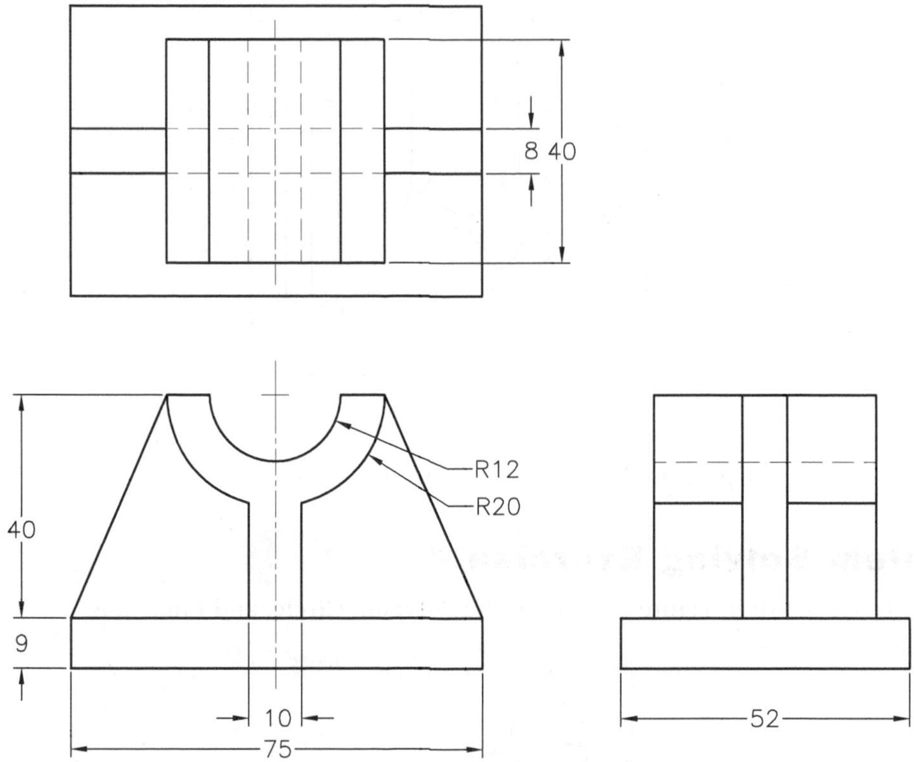

Figure 3-64 *Drawing for the Problem-Solving Exercise 5*

Problem-Solving Exercise 6

Draw the sketch shown in Figure 3-65 in the paper space area of the **Manufacturing Metric** template. Note that the dimensions are given only for your reference.

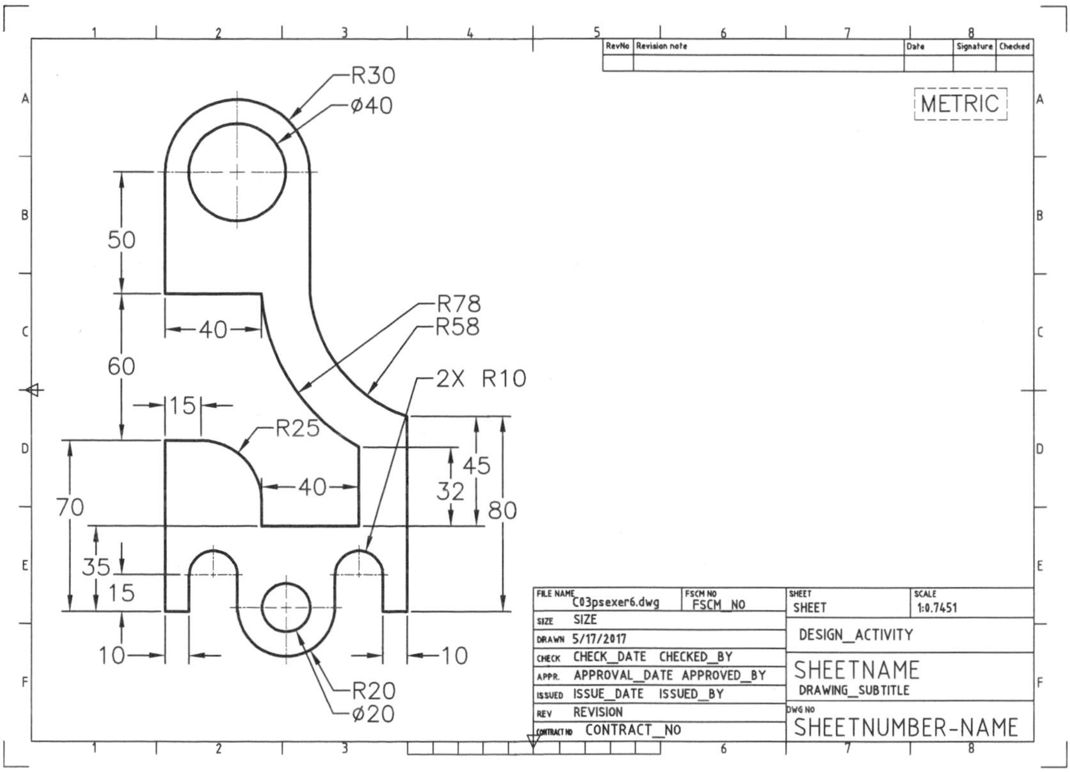

Figure 3-65 Drawing for the Problem-Solving Exercise 6

Problem-Solving Exercise 7

Draw the sketch shown in Figure 3-66.

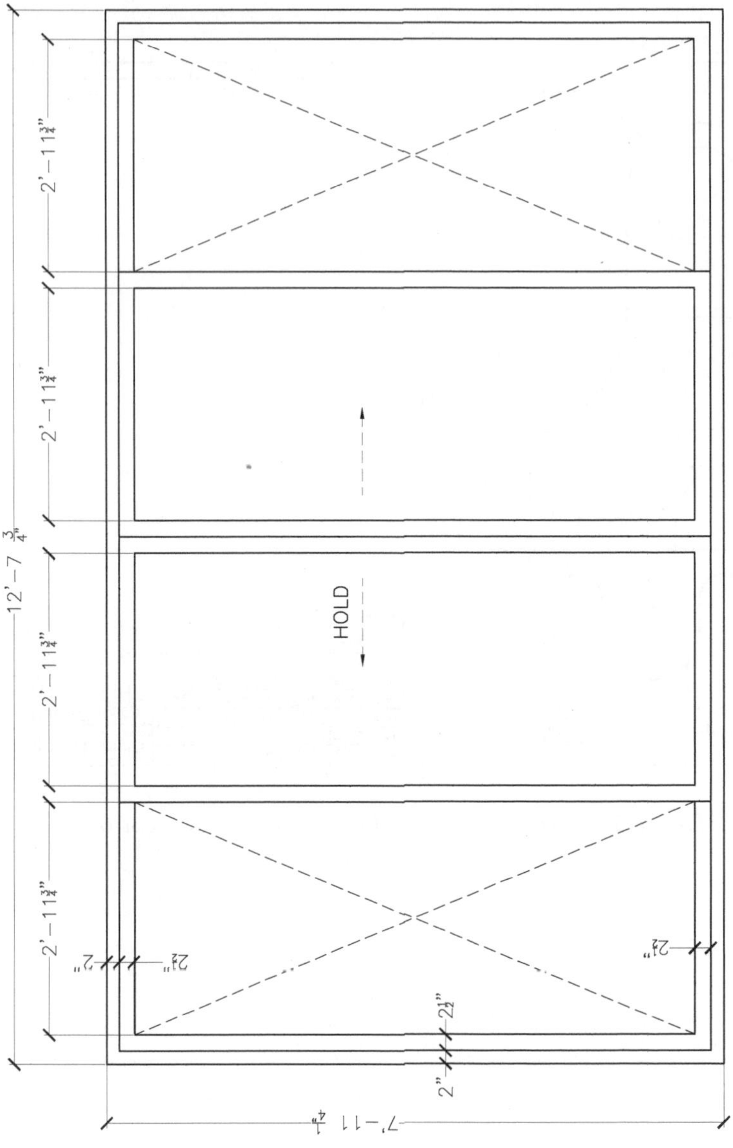

Figure 3-66 Drawing for the Problem-Solving Exercise 7

Answers to Self-Evaluation Test

1. **Elevation**, **2.** 0, **3.** Tapered, **4.** **Measure**, **5.** **Multiple Point**, **6.** Negative, **7.** T, **8.** T, **9.** T, **10.** F

Chapter 4

Working with Drawing Aids

Learning Objectives

After completing this chapter, you will be able to:

- *Set up layers, and assign colors and linetypes to them*
- *Change general object properties using the Properties panel*
- *Change object properties using the Properties tool*
- *Determine the line type scaling and the LTSCALE factor for plotting*
- *Set up Grid, Snap, and Ortho modes*
- *Use the object snaps and run the Object Snap modes*
- *Use AutoTracking to locate keypoints in a drawing*

Key Terms

- *Layer*
- *Freeze*
- *Thaw*
- *Plot Style*
- *Reconciling Layers*
- *Isolating Layers*
- *Quick Properties*
- *Global Linetype scaling*
- *Current Linetype scaling*
- *DesignCenter*
- *DSETTINGS*
- *OSNAP*

INTRODUCTION

In this chapter, you will learn about the drawing setup and the factors that affect the quality and accuracy of a drawing. This chapter contains a detailed description of the procedure of setting up a layer. You will also learn about some other drawing aids, such as Grid, Snap, and Ortho. These aids will help you create drawings accurately and quickly.

UNDERSTANDING THE CONCEPT AND USE OF LAYERS

The concept of layers can be best explained by using the concept of overlays in manual drafting. In manual drafting, different details of a drawing can be drawn on different sheets of paper or overlays. Each overlay is perfectly aligned with the others. Once all of them are placed on top of each other, you can reproduce the entire drawing. For example, in Figure 4-1, the object lines are drawn in the first overlay and the dimensions in the second overlay. You can place these overlays on top of each other and get a combined look of the drawing.

In AutoCAD, instead of using overlays, you can use layers. Each layer is assigned a name. You can also assign a color and a line type to a layer. For example, in Figure 4-2, the object lines are drawn in the OBJECT layer and the dimensions are drawn in the DIM layer. The object lines will be red because red has been assigned to the OBJECT layer. Similarly, the dimension lines will be green because green has been assigned to the DIM layer. You can display the layers together, individually, or in any combination.

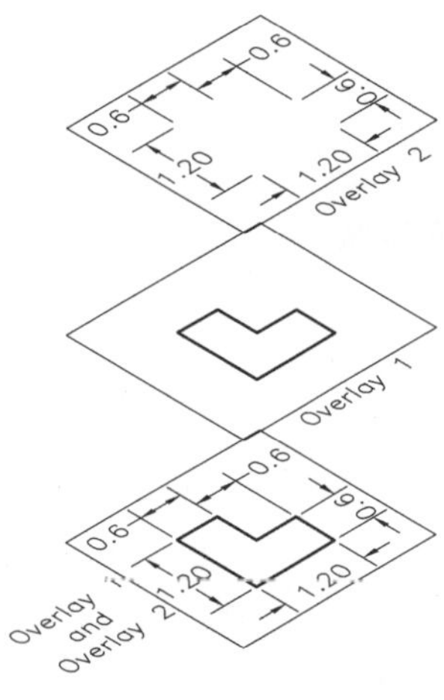

Figure 4-1 Drawing lines and dimensions in different overlays

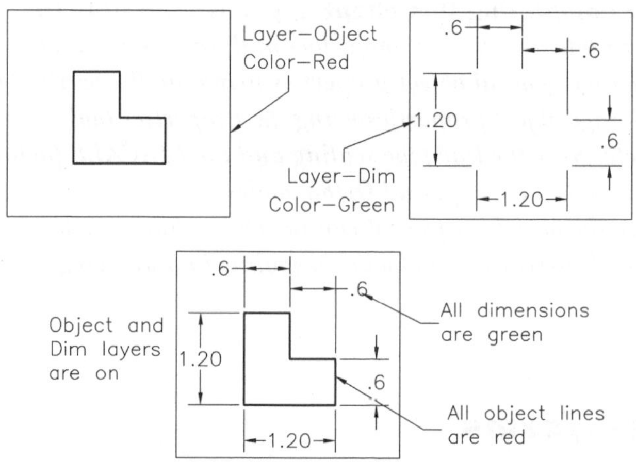

Figure 4-2 Drawing lines and dimensions in different layers

Advantages of Using Layers

1. Each layer can be assigned a different color. Assigning a particular color to a group of objects is very important for plotting. For example, if all object lines are red, then at the time of plotting, you can assign the red color to a slot (pen) that has the desired tip width. Similarly, if the dimensions are green, you can assign the green color to another slot (pen) that has a thin tip. By assigning different colors to different layers, you can control the width of lines while plotting the drawing. You can also make a layer plotable or non-plotable.

2. Layers are also useful for performing some editing operations. For example, to erase all dimensions in a drawing, you can freeze or lock all layers except the dimension layer, then select all objects by using the Window Crossing option, and erase all dimensions.
3. You can turn off a layer or freeze a layer that you do not want to be displayed or plotted.
4. You can lock a layer to prevent the user from accidentally editing the objects in it.
5. Colors also help you distinguish different groups of objects. For example, in architectural drafting, the plans for foundation, floors, plumbing, electrical work, and heating systems may be made in different layers. In electronic drafting and in PCB (printed circuit board), the design of each level of a multilevel circuit board can be drawn on a separate layer. Similarly, in mechanical engineering, the main components of an assembly can be made in one layer, other components such as nuts, bolts, keys, and washers can be made in another layer, and the annotations such as datum symbols and identifiers, texture symbols, Balloons, and Bill of Materials can be made in yet another layer.

WORKING WITH LAYERS

Ribbon: Home > Layers > Layer Properties **Command:** LAYER/LA
Toolbar: Layers > Layer Properties Manager

You can freeze, thaw, lock, unlock, and so on by using the **Layers** panel in the **Ribbon**, as shown in Figure 4-3. However, to add new layers, to delete the existing layers, or to assign colors and linetypes to layers, you need to invoke the **LAYER PROPERTIES MANAGER.**

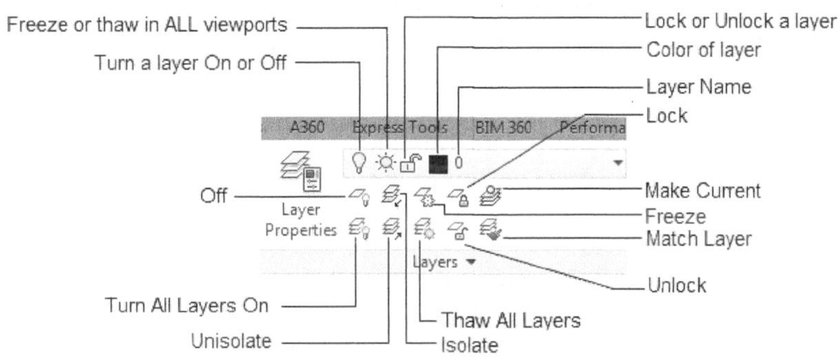

***Figure 4-3** The **Layers** panel*

To invoke the **LAYER PROPERTIES MANAGER**, choose the **Layer Properties** button from the **Layers** panel of the **Home** tab, or invoke it from the **Layers** toolbar, as shown in Figure 4-4.

***Figure 4-4** The **Layers** toolbar*

On invoking the **LAYER PROPERTIES MANAGER**, a default layer with the name 0 is displayed. It is the current layer and any object you draw is created in it. The current layer can be recognized by the green colored tick mark in the **Status** column. There are certain features such as color, linetype, and lineweight that are associated with each layer. The **0** layer has the default color as white, linetype as continuous, and lineweight as default.

Creating New Layers

To create new layers, choose the **New Layer** button in the **LAYER PROPERTIES MANAGER**; a new layer, named Layer1, with the same properties as that of the current layer will be created and listed, as shown in Figure 4-5. Alternatively, right-click anywhere in the **Layers** list area of the **LAYER PROPERTIES MANAGER** and then choose the **New Layer** option from the shortcut menu to create a new layer. If there are more layers and you right-click on a layer other than the current layer and then choose **New Layer** from the shortcut menu, a new layer will be created with the properties similar to the layer on which you right-clicked. To create a new layer that is automatically frozen in all viewports, choose the **New Layer VP Frozen in All Viewports** button in the **LAYER PROPERTIES MANAGER**.

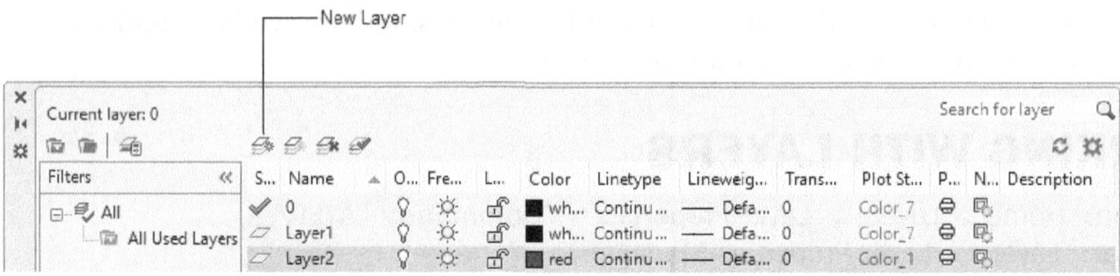

***Figure 4-5** Partial view of the **LAYER PROPERTIES MANAGER** with the new layers created*

Naming a New Layer

New layers are created with the name layer 1, layer 2, and so on. To change or edit the name of a layer, select it, then click once in the field corresponding to the **Name** column, and enter a new name. Some of the points to be remembered while naming a layer are given below.

1. A layer name can be up to 255 characters long, including letters (a-z), numbers (0-9), special characters ($ _ -), and spaces. Any combination of lower and uppercase letters can be used while naming a layer. However, characters such as <>^;:,?*|"=, and so on are not valid characters while naming a layer.
2. Layers should be named to help the user identify the contents of the layer. For example, if a layer name is HATCH, a user can easily identify it and its contents. On the other hand, if a layer's name is X261, it is hard to identify its contents.
3. Layer names should be short but should also convey a meaning.

> **Tip**
> *If you exchange drawings or provide drawings to consultants or others, it is very important that you standardize and coordinate layer names and other layer settings.*

Making a Layer Current

To draw an object in a particular layer, you need to make it the current layer. There are different methods to make a layer current and these are listed below.

1. Double-click on the name of a layer in the list box in the **LAYER PROPERTIES MANAGER**; the selected layer is made current.
2. Select the name of the layer in the **LAYER PROPERTIES MANAGER** and then choose the **Set Current** button in the **LAYER PROPERTIES MANAGER**.

3. Right-click on a layer in the **Layer** list box in the **LAYER PROPERTIES MANAGER** and choose the **Set current** option from the shortcut menu displayed, see Figure 4-6.
4. Select a layer from the **Layer Control** drop-down list in the **Layers** toolbar.
5. Select a layer from the **Layer** drop-down list in the **Layers** panel or from **Quick Access Toolbar.**
6. Choose the **Make Current** button from the **Layers** panel; you will be prompted to select the object whose layer you want to make current. Select the required object; the layer associated with that object will become current.

Note

*In AutoCAD 2018, you can add **Layer** drop-down list to **Quick Access Toolbar** by selecting the **Layer** option from the **Customize Quick Access Toolbar**.*

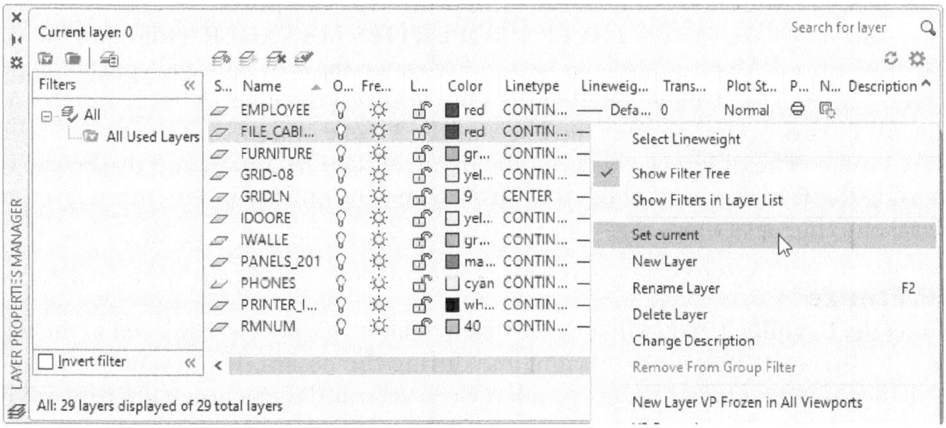

*Figure 4-6 The **LAYER PROPERTIES MANAGER** with the shortcut menu*

On making a layer as the current layer, a green color tick mark will be displayed in the **Status** column of that layer and the name of the current layer will be displayed at the upper-left corner of the **LAYER PROPERTIES MANAGER**. The name and properties of the current layer will be displayed in the **Layers** toolbar.

Note

*If you select more than one layer at a time using the SHIFT or CTRL key, the **Set Current** option appears inactive in the shortcut menu in the **LAYER PROPERTIES MANAGER**. This is because only one layer can be made current at a time.*

Controlling the Display of Layers

You can control the display of layers by using the display options from the **LAYER PROPERTIES MANAGER**. These options are discussed next.

Turn a layer On or Off

Choose the **Turn a layer On or Off** toggle icon (bulb) to turn a layer on or off. You can also turn the layer on or off by clicking on the **Turn a layer On or Off** toggle icon located in the **Layer** drop-down list from the **Layers** panel or from the **Quick Access Toolbar,** as shown in Figure 4-7. The objects in the layers that are turned on are displayed and can be plotted, while the objects in the layers that are turned off are not displayed and cannot be plotted. However, you can perform the operations such as drawing and editing of the objects in the layer that has been turned off. You can turn the current layer off, but AutoCAD will display a message box informing you that the current drawing layer has been turned off.

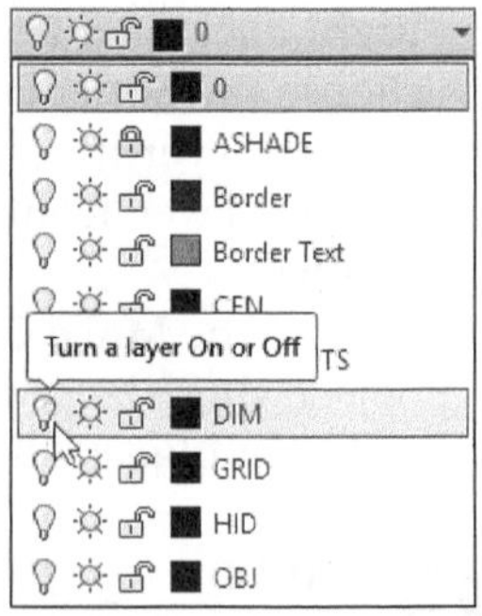

*Figure 4-7 Turning off the **DIM** layer*

Freeze or thaw in ALL Viewports

Sometimes, in an architectural drawing, you may not need the door tag, window tag, or surveyor data to be displayed, so that they are not changed. These types of information or entities can be placed in a particular layer and that layer can be frozen. You cannot edit the entities in the frozen layer. Also, frozen layers are invisible and cannot be plotted. To freeze a layer, choose the **Freeze or thaw in ALL viewports** toggle icon (sun/snowflakes) in the **LAYER PROPERTIES MANAGER**. Note that the current layer cannot be frozen. You can also choose the **Freeze or thaw in ALL viewports** toggle icon in the **Layers** panel of the **Ribbon** or from the **Quick Access Toolbar** to freeze or thaw a layer. The **Thaw All Layers** option negates the effect of the **Freeze** option, and the frozen layers are restored to normal. The difference between the usage of the **Off** option and the **Freeze** option is that in using the **Freeze** option, the layer is frozen and the entities in the frozen layer are not regenerated and thus save time.

New VP Freeze

On choosing the **Layout** tab, you will observe that a default viewport is displayed in the drawing area. You can also create new viewports anytime during the design. If you want to freeze some layers in all the subsequent new viewports, select the layers, and then choose the **New VP Freeze** toggle icon. The selected layers will be frozen in all the subsequently created viewports, without affecting the existing viewports.

VP Freeze

This icon will be available only if you invoke the **LAYER PROPERTIES MANAGER** in the **Layout** tab, refer to Figure 4-8. The **Freeze or thaw in current viewport** toggle icon will also be available in the **Layer** drop-down list in the **Layers** panel of the **Ribbon** or in the **Layers** toolbar. If there are multiple viewports, make a viewport as the current viewport by double-clicking in it and freeze or thaw the selected layer in it by choosing the **VP Freeze** icon in the **LAYER PROPERTIES MANAGER**. However, a layer that is frozen in the model space cannot be thawed in the current viewport.

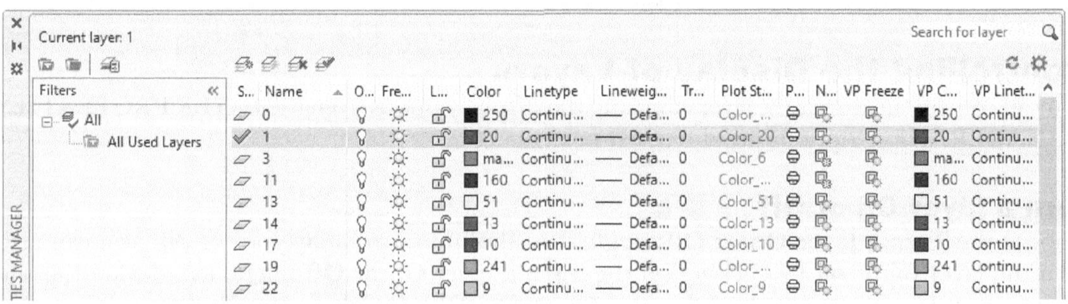

*Figure 4-8 Partial view of the **LAYER PROPERTIES MANAGER** with the **VP Freeze** icon*

Lock or Unlock a Layer

While working on a drawing, if you want to avoid editing some objects on a particular layer but need to have them visible, use the Lock/Unlock toggle icon to lock the layer. However, you can still use the objects in the locked layer for Object Snap and inquiry tools such as **List**. You can also make the locked layer as the current layer and draw objects on it. Note that you can also plot a locked layer. The **Unlock** option overrules the **Lock** option and allows you to edit objects on the layers that were previously locked.

Make a Layer Plotable or Non plotable

By default, you can plot all layers, except the layers that are turned off or frozen. If you do not want to plot a layer that is not turned off or frozen, select the layer and choose the **Plot** icon (printer). This is a toggle icon, therefore you can choose this icon again to plot the layer.

Assigning Linetype to a Layer

By default, continuous linetype is assigned to a layer, if no layer is selected while creating a new layer. Otherwise, new layer takes the properties of the selected layer. To assign a new linetype to a layer, click on the name of the linetype under the **Linetype** column of that layer in the **LAYER PROPERTIES MANAGER**; the **Select Linetype** dialog box with the linetypes loaded on your computer will be displayed. Select the new linetype and then choose the **OK** button; the selected linetype will be assigned to the layer. If you are opening the **Select Linetype** dialog box for the first time, only the **Continuous** linetype will be displayed, as shown in Figure 4-9.

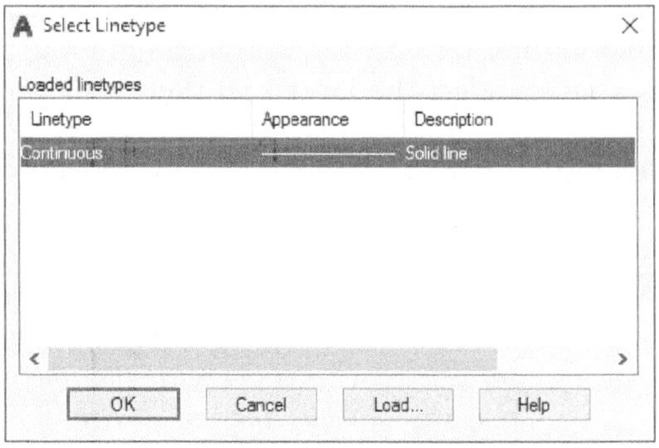

Figure 4-9 *The* ***Select Linetype*** *dialog box*

You need to load linetypes and then assign them to layers. To load linetypes, choose the **Load** button in the **Select Linetype** dialog box; the **Load or Reload Linetypes** dialog box will be displayed, see Figure 4-10. This dialog box displays all linetypes in the *acad.lin* or *acadiso.lin* file. In this dialog box, you can select a single linetype, or a number of linetypes by pressing and holding the SHIFT or CTRL key and then selecting the linetypes. After selecting the linetypes, choose the **OK** button; the selected linetypes are loaded in the **Select Linetype** dialog box. Now, select the desired linetype and choose the **OK** button; the selected linetype is assigned to the selected layer.

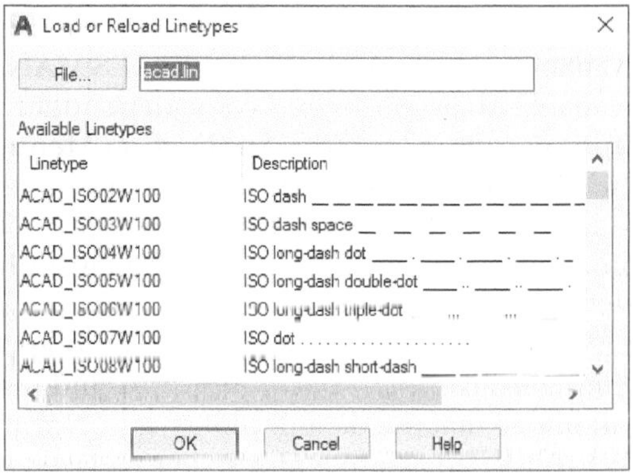

Figure 4-10 *The* ***Load or Reload Linetypes*** *dialog box*

Assigning Transparency to a Layer

By default, no transparency is assigned to a layer, if **Layer 0** is selected while creating that layer. Otherwise, new layer takes the transparency of the selected layer. To assign transparency to a layer, click on the **Transparency** field of that layer; the **Layer Transparency** dialog box will be displayed. Select the required transparency level from the **Transparency value (0-90)** drop-down list and choose **OK**. You can also enter a value in the edit box. Now, if you place an object on this layer, the object will have a faded color according to the specified transparency value.

Assigning Color to a Layer

To assign a color to a layer, select the color swatch in that layer in the **LAYER PROPERTIES MANAGER**; the **Select Color** dialog box will be displayed. Select the desired color and then choose the **OK** button; the selected color will be assigned to the layer.

Assigning Lineweight to a Layer

Lineweight is used to give thickness to objects in a layer. For example, if you create a sectional plan, you can assign a layer with a larger value of lineweight to create the objects through which the section is made. Another layer with a lesser lineweight can be used to show the objects through which the section does not pass. This thickness is displayed on the screen if the display of the lineweight is on. The lineweight assigned to an object can also be plotted. To assign a lineweight to a layer, select the layer and then click on the lineweight associated with it; the **Lineweight** dialog box will be displayed, as shown in Figure 4-11. Select a lineweight and then choose the **OK** button from this dialog box to return to the **LAYER PROPERTIES MANAGER**.

> **Tip**
>
> *Remember that the Linetype Control, Lineweight Control, Color Control, and Plot Style Control list boxes in the **Properties** panel should display **ByLayer** as the current property of the objects. This is to ensure that the objects drawn in a layer take the properties assigned to the layer in which they are drawn.*

Assigning Plot Style to a Layer

The plot style is a group of property settings such as color, linetype, and lineweight that can be assigned to a layer. The assigned plot style affects the drawings while plotting only. The drawing in which you are working should be in the named plot style mode (*.stb*) to make the plot style available in the **LAYER PROPERTIES MANAGER**. If the **Plot Style** icon in the dialog box is not available, then you are in a color-dependent mode (*.ctb*). To make this icon available, choose the **Options** button from the **Application Menu**; the **Options** dialog box will be displayed. Choose the **Plot and Publish** tab from this dialog box. Next, choose the **Plot Style Table Settings** button to invoke the **Plot Style Table Settings** dialog box. In this dialog box, select the **Use named plot styles** radio button from the **Default plot style behavior for new drawings** area and then exit both the dialog boxes. After changing the plot style to named plot style dependent, you have to start a new AutoCAD session to apply this setting. Start a new AutoCAD session with templates like *acad -Named Plot Styles* and invoke the **LAYER PROPERTIES MANAGER**. You will notice that the default plot style is **Normal**, in which the color, linetype, and lineweight are BYLAYER. To assign a plot style to a layer, select the layer and then click on its plot style; the **Select Plot Style** dialog box will be displayed, as shown in Figure 4-12. In this dialog box, you can select a specific plot style from the **Plot styles** list of available plot styles. Plot styles need to be created before you can use them (see Chapter 14, *Plotting Drawings*). Choose the **OK** button to return to the **LAYER PROPERTIES MANAGER** .

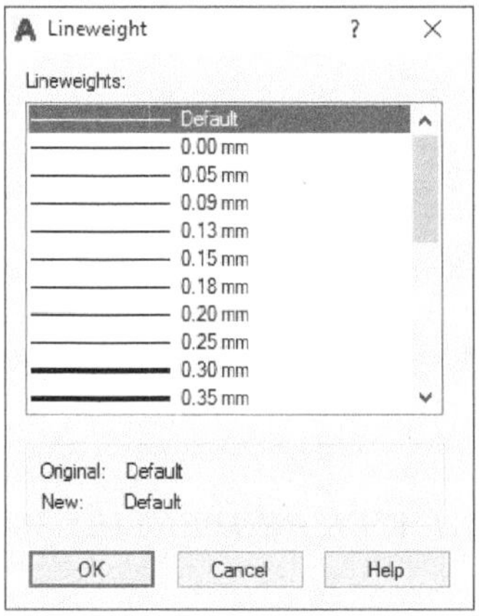

Figure 4-11 *The* ***Lineweight*** *dialog box*

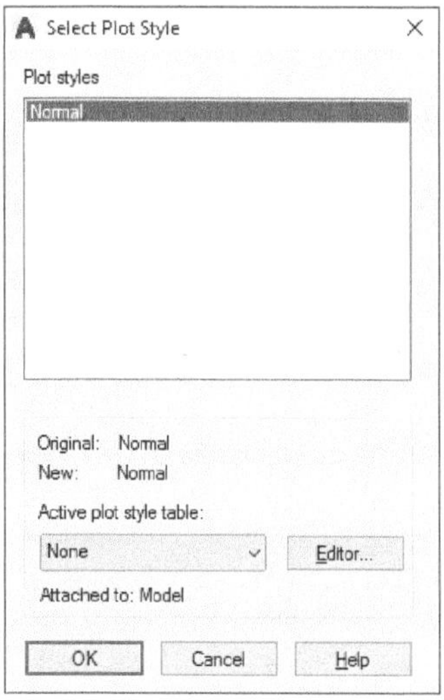

Figure 4-12 *The* ***Select Plot Style*** *dialog box*

Tip

You can also change the plot style mode from the command line by using the CPLOTSTYLE system variable. If the current drawing in is in color-dependent mode, CPLOTSTYLE has a value of BYCOLOR. If the drawing is in named plot styles mode, CPLOTSTYLE can be set to the following values (BYLAYER is the default):

"BYLAYER"
"BYBLOCK"
"NORMAL"

Note

When you are in a viewport, you can override the color, linetype, lineweight, and plot style settings assigned to a selected layer for the particular viewport (current viewport). These settings for all other viewports and model space will remain unaffected. All these overrides are highlighted in different background colors. Also, the icon of the selected layer under the ***Status*** *column will change indicating that some of the properties of the selected layer have been overridden by the new ones (see Chapter 13, for Model Space Viewports, Paper Space Viewports, and Layouts).*

Arranging Layers in Increasing Order

In AutoCAD, the layers in the **LAYER PROPERTY MANAGER** get arranged automatically in the numerical and alphabetical order. For example, if the layers created are in numeric form 0, 1, 3, 2, 20, 25, 17, then they will be automatically arranged as 0, 1, 2, 3, 17, 20, 25, refer to Figure 4-13. Similarly, if the layers are created in the form of 0, 4, 2, 1, 3, A, C, D, B, then the numerical values will take precedence over the alphabetical values and the layers will be arranged as 0, 1, 2, 3, 4, A, B, C, D, refer to Figure 4-14. Note that, if the layers are not arranged in an order, then you need to choose the **Refresh** button available on the top right corner of the **LAYER PROPERTIES MANAGER** to get them arranged.

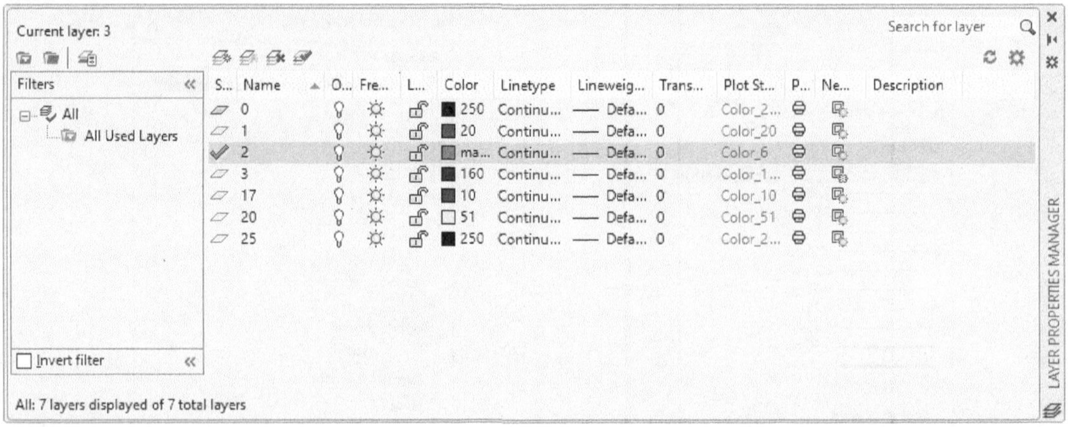

*Figure 4-13 The layers arranged in increasing order in the **LAYER PROPERTIES MANAGER***

Note

*You can reverse the order of layers by clicking on the **Name** column in the **LAYER PROPERTIES MANAGER**.*

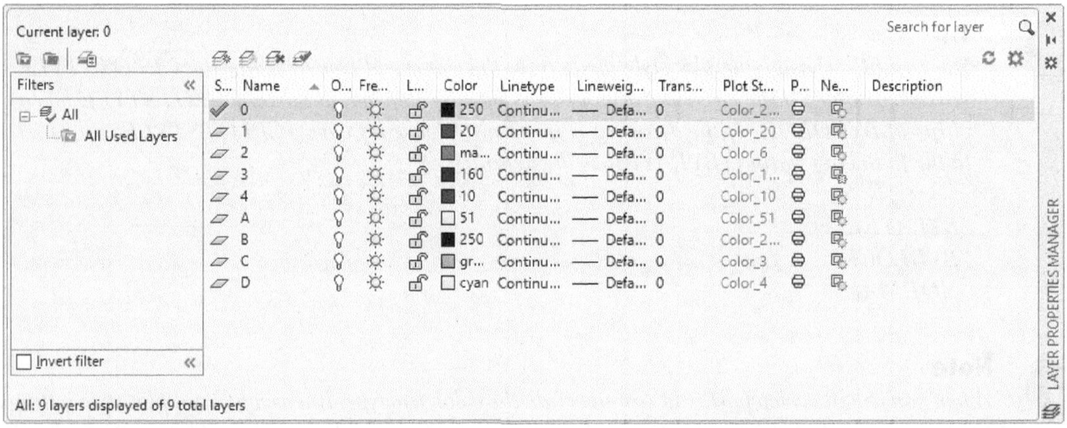

*Figure 4-14 The layers arranged automatically in the **LAYER PROPERTIES MANAGER***

Arranging Layers in Increasing Order with Respect to First Digit

The layers in the **LAYER PROPERTIES MANAGER** can be assigned numeric names. In AutoCAD, you can assign numeric name to layers in **LAYER PROPERTIES MANAGER** and then arrange them in increasing order on the basis of the first digit of the numeric names assigned. For example, if there are layers in the **LAYER PROPERTIES MANAGER** with the name 1, 4, 10, 12, and 50. The name of the layers will be arranged in increasing order with respect to their values. To arrange the names of layers in increasing order with respect to their first digits, specify the value of SORTORDER system variable at the command prompt. Figure 4-15 and Figure 4-16 show the layers arranged with the SORTORDER value as 1 and 0 respectively.

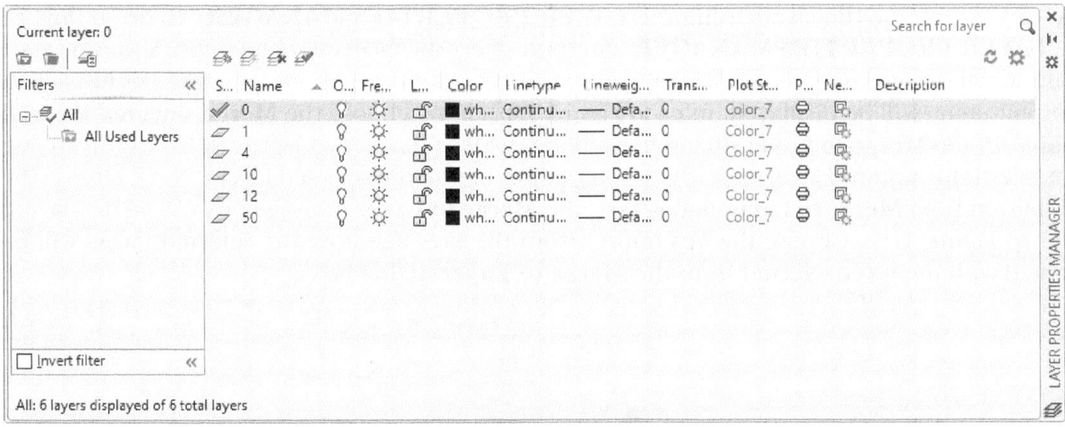

***Figure 4-15** The layers arranged with the value of SORTORDER system variable as 1*

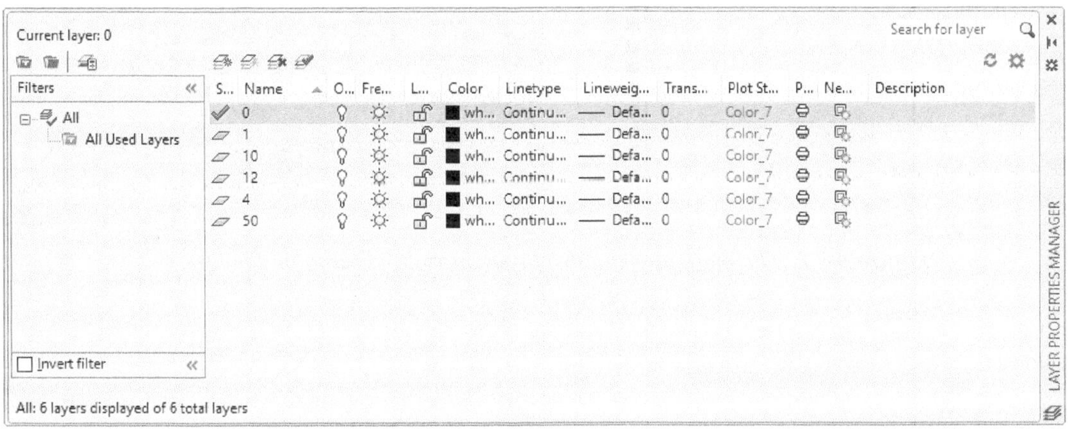

***Figure 4-16** The layers arranged with the value of SORTORDER system variable as 0*

Merging Layers

Ribbon: Home > Layers > Merge **Command:** LAYMRG

In AutoCAD, you can merge objects of different layers to a specific layer. On doing so, the layers of the objects to be merged will be deleted and properties of the objects to be merged will be modified as per the newly specified layer. To merge objects of different layers to a specific layer, choose the **Merge** tool from the **Layers** panel of the **Home** tab; you will be prompted to select objects of different layers that are to be merged. The following is the prompt sequence displayed on invoking this tool.

Select object on layer to merge or [Name] : Select objects whose layer you want to merge Enter
Select object on target layer or [Name] : Select the target object with which you want to merge the layers Enter
Do you wish to continue? [Yes/No] <No>: Enter the required option or press Enter

You can also merge the layers using the **LAYER PROPERTIES MANAGER**. To do so, invoke the **LAYER PROPERTIES MANAGER** and then select the layers to be merged. You can select multiple layers by using the CTRL key. After selecting the layers to be merged, right-click; a shortcut menu will be displayed, refer to Figure 4-17. Now, choose the **Merge selected layer(s) to** option; the **Merge to Layer** dialog box will be displayed, refer to Figure 4-18. In this dialog box, select the required layer with which you want to merge the selected layers. Next, choose the **OK** button from **Merge to Layer** dialog box; the **Merge to Layer** message box will be displayed, refer to Figure 4-19. Choose the **Yes** button from the message box; the selected layers will be merged with the layer selected from the **Merge to Layer** dialog box.

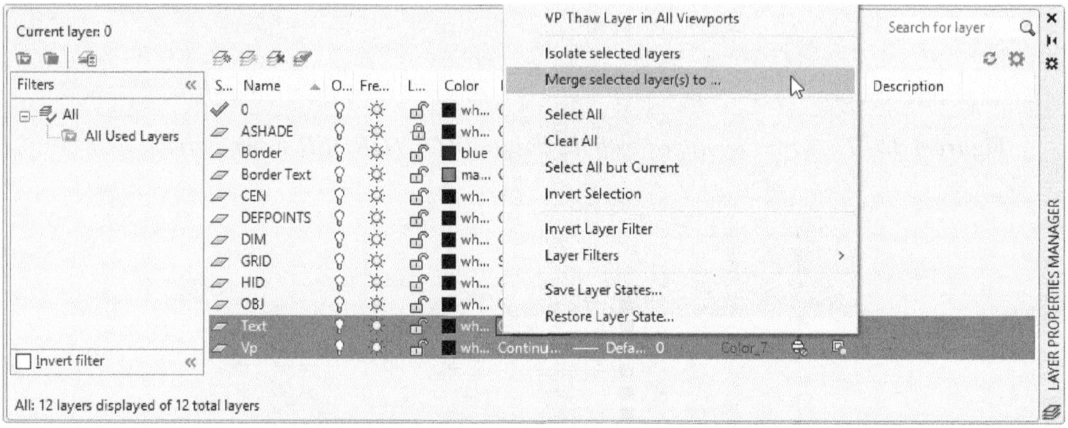

Figure 4-17 The shortcut menu displayed on right-clicking on the layers

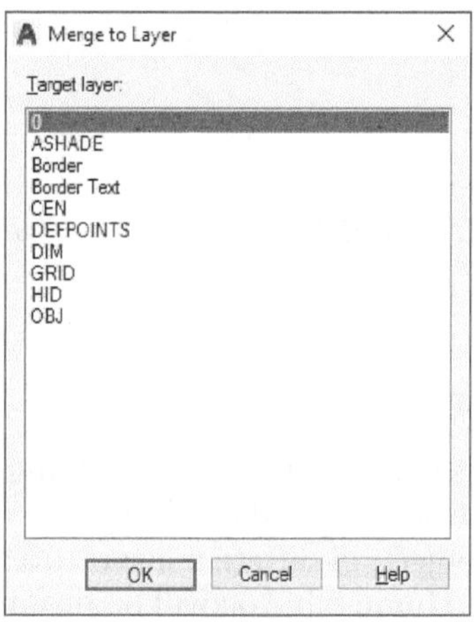

Figure 4-18 The ***Merge to Layer*** *dialog box*

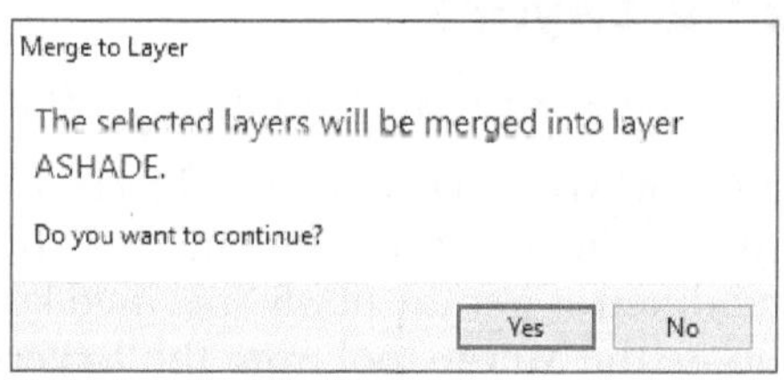

Figure 4-19 The ***Merge to Layer*** *message box*

Deleting Layers

To delete a layer, select it and then choose the **Delete Layer** button from the **LAYER PROPERTIES MANAGER**. Remember that you cannot delete a layer that contains an object. Additionally, you cannot delete layers 0, Defpoints (created while dimensioning), Ashade (created while rendering), current layer, and an Xref-dependent layer.

Managing the Display of Columns

You can change the display order of columns in the **LAYER PROPERTIES MANAGER**. To do so, drag and drop the desired column head to the desired location. You can also change the display order by right-clicking on the column head and choosing the **Customize** option from the shortcut menu, as shown in Figure 4-20. On choosing this option, the **Customize Layer Columns** dialog box will be displayed, as shown in Figure 4-21. Select the desired column from the list and then choose the **Move Up** or **Move Down** button to change the display order.

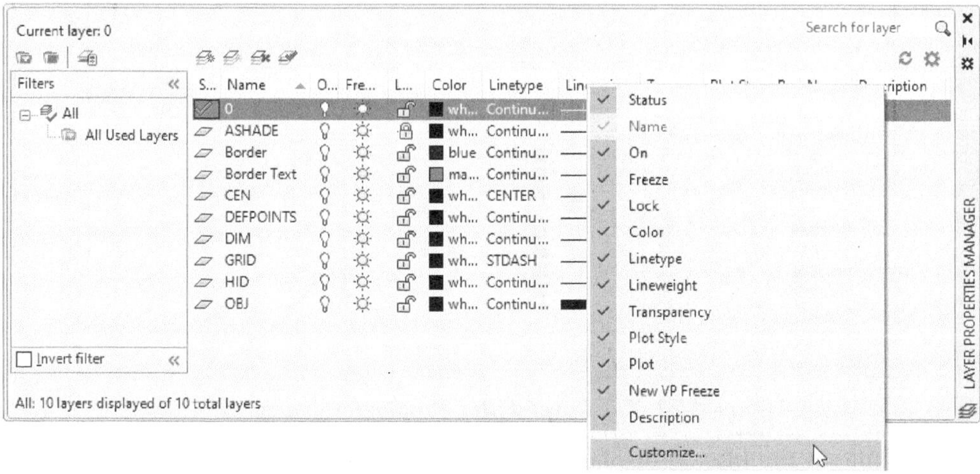

Figure 4-20 *The shortcut menu to manage column heads*

You can also control the column heads to be displayed in the **LAYER PROPERTIES MANAGER** by using the shortcut menu shown in Figure 4-20. The tick marked entries in the shortcut menu will be displayed in the list. Choose the entry that you want to display in the **LAYER PROPERTIES MANAGER** from the shortcut menu.

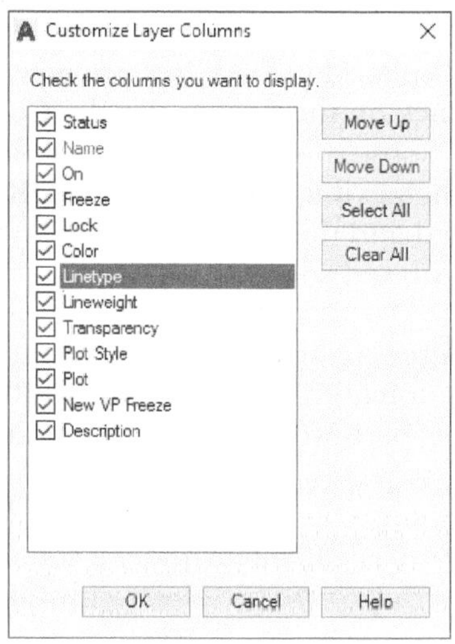

Figure 4-21 *The* ***Customize Layer Columns*** *dialog box*

Selective Display of Layers

If a drawing has a limited number of layers, it is easy to scan through them. However, if the drawing has a large number of layers, it is sometimes difficult to search through the layers. To solve this problem, you can use layer filters. By defining filters, you can specify the properties and display only those layers in the **LAYER PROPERTIES MANAGER** that match the properties in the filter. By default, the **All** and **All Used Layers** filters are created. The **All** filter is selected by default, and therefore, all layers are displayed. If you select the **All Used Layers** filter, only the layers that are used in the drawing will be displayed.

AutoCAD allows you to create a layer property filter or a layer group filter. A layer group filter can have additional layer property filters. To create a filter, choose the **New Property Filter** button, which is the first button on the top left corner of the dialog box. When you choose this button, a new property filter will be added to the list and the **Layer Filter Properties** dialog box will be displayed, as shown in Figure 4-22.

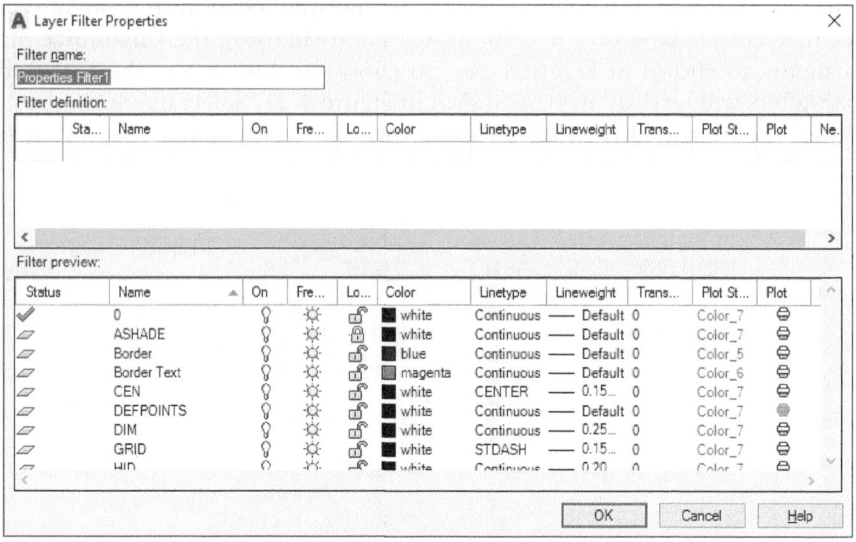

Figure 4-22 The ***Layer Filter Properties*** *dialog box*

The default name of the filter is displayed in the **Filter name** edit box. You can enter a new name for the filter in this edit box. Using the **Layer Filter Properties** dialog box, you can create filters based on any property column in the **Filter definition** area. The layers that will be actually displayed in the **LAYER PROPERTIES MANAGER** based on the filter that you create will be displayed in the **Filter preview** area. For example, to list only those layers that are red in color, click on the field under the **Color** column; a swatch **[...]** button will be displayed in this field. Choose this button to display the **Select Color** dialog box. Select **Red** from this dialog box and then exit it by choosing the **OK** button. You will notice that the filter row color has changed to red and the display of layers in the **Filter preview** has been modified such that only the layers with red color are displayed.

After creating the filter, exit the **Layer Filter Properties** dialog box. The layer filter is selected automatically in the **LAYER PROPERTIES MANAGER** and only the layers that satisfy the filter properties are displayed. You can restore the display of all layers again by clicking on the **All** filter.

Choose the **New Group Filter** button (second button on the top left corner of the dialog box) to group all filters under a common group name. You can create groups and subgroups of filters to categorize the filters with similar criteria.

Note

To modify a layer filter, double-click on it; the ***Layer Filter Properties*** *dialog box will be displayed. Modify the filter and then exit the dialog box.*

In the **LAYER PROPERTIES MANAGER**, when you select the **Invert filter** check box, the selected filter parameters are inverted. For example, if you have selected a filter to show all layers, none of the layers will be displayed. Note that in the **LAYER PROPERTIES MANAGER**, the current layer is not displayed in the list box if it is not among the filtered layers.

Layer States

While working in a drawing, you can save the properties of all layers under one name and restore the properties later. The properties thus saved can also be imported to other drawings. This saves time in setting the layer properties again in a new drawing. To save the properties of all layers in a drawing, choose the **Layer States Manager** button in the **LAYER PROPERTIES MANAGER**; the **Layer States Manager** dialog box will be displayed, as shown in Figure 4-23. Choose the **New** button to invoke the **New Layer State to Save** dialog box. Specify the name and description related to the state of a layer in the **New layer state name** and **Description** edit boxes respectively, and then choose the **OK** button. Choose the **More Restore Options (Alt+ >)** button next to the **Help** button; the dialog box will expand. Specify different states and properties of the layers by selecting the corresponding check boxes in the **Layer properties to restore** area. Choose the **Restore** button to save the layer state. However, this layer state is saved only for the current file. If you want to use the current layer state in other files also, you need to save them. To do so, choose the **Export** button; the **Export layer state** dialog box will be invoked. Enter a name for the layer state. The layer state will be exported with the *.las* extension.

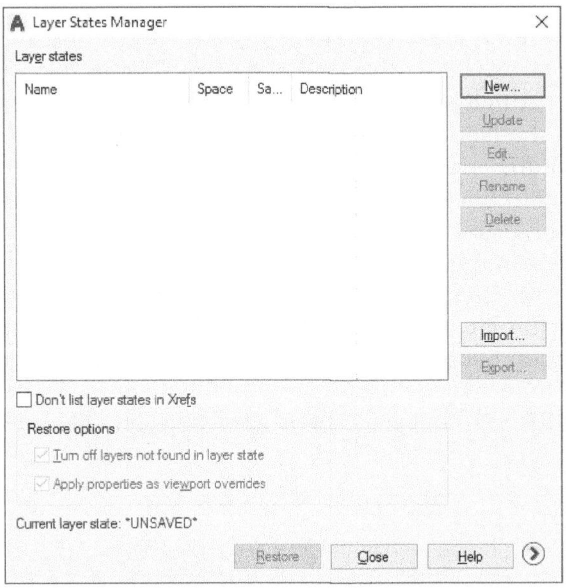

Figure 4-23 *The* ***Layer States Manager*** *dialog box*

You can also import a layer state later in any other file by using the **Layer States Manager** dialog box. On importing a layer state, you can edit the states and properties of the imported layer state. You can also rename and delete a layer state.

Select the **Don't list layer states in Xrefs** check box; the layer states that are defined in an externally referenced drawing will be referenced from the **Layer states** list box. Select the **Turn off layers not found in layer state** check box to turn off the newly created layers (that were created after defining the layer state) so that the drawing appears the same as it was when the layer state was saved. The **Apply properties as viewport overrides** check box is used to apply the layer property overrides to the current viewport. This check box is selected by default and is available only when a viewport is active.

Note

*1. Select the **New Layer State** option from the **Layer State** drop-down list in the **Layers** panel of the **Home** tab to invoke the **New Layer State to Save** dialog box and save the new layer state. Similarly, select the **Manage Layer States** option from the **Layer State** drop-down list to invoke the **Layer States Manager** dialog box.*

*2. The linetypes will be restored with the layer state in a new drawing file only if the linetypes are already loaded using the **Select Linetype** dialog box.*

Reconciling New Layers

When you save or plot a drawing for the first time, AutoCAD compiles a list of existing layers. These layers are known as reconciled layers. When new layers are inserted or an external reference is attached to the current drawing, AutoCAD compares these new layers (unreconciled layers) with the previously created list. This helps prevent any new layers from being added to the current drawing without user's permission.

If you need AutoCAD to notify the unreconciled layer, choose the **Settings** button from the **LAYER PROPERTIES MANAGER**; the **Layer Settings** dialog box will be displayed. Select the **Evaluate new layers added to drawing** check box and then select the **Evaluate all new layers** radio button and the **Notify when new layers are present** check box from the **Layer Settings** dialog box. You also need to select the check boxes under this check box based on your requirement. After selecting the **Notify when new layers are present** check box and the corresponding options, the **Unreconciled New Layers** notification is displayed see Figure 4-24, whenever new unreconciled layers are found in the current drawing or in the externally referenced drawings. As soon as the unreconciled layers are found in the drawing, an **Unreconciled New Layers** filter is automatically created in the **LAYER PROPERTIES MANAGER**. Click on the blue link in the information bubble or open the **LAYER PROPERTIES MANAGER** to view the unreconciled layers. To reconcile the layers, select all the unreconciled layers in the **LAYER PROPERTIES MANAGER**, right-click on them, and choose the **Reconcile Layer** option from the shortcut menu displayed.

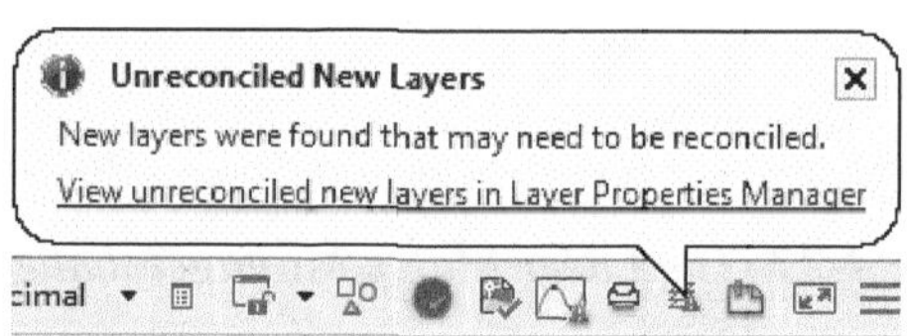

Figure 4-24 *The information bubble for unreconciled layers*

Isolating and Unisolating Layers

Ribbon: Home > Layers > Isolate/Unisolate **Command:** LAYISO/LAYUNISO
Toolbar: Layers II > Layer Isolate/Layer Unisolate

Isolating and unisolating layers are used to lock or turn off all the layers except those for the selected objects. To isolate a layer, choose the **Isolate** tool from the **Layers** panel; you will be prompted to select the objects. Select one or more objects and press the ENTER key; the layers corresponding to the selected objects will get isolated and unlocked. All other layers will be turned off or frozen in the current viewport or locked depending on the current settings.

The unisolated layers (locked) will appear faded. This will help you to differentiate between the isolated and unisolated layers. You can change the settings by choosing the **Settings** option from the shortcut menu at the **Select objects on the layer(s) to be isolated or [Settings]** prompt. The options at the **Settings** prompt are discussed next.

Off

This option is used to turn off or freeze all layers except the selected layers. Choose the **Off** sub option to turn off all layers, except the selected one in all viewports, and choose the **Vpfreeze** sub option to freeze all layers, except the selected one only in the current floating viewport.

Lock and fade

This option is used to lock all layers except the selected one and prompts you to enter the fade value to specify the fading intensity. You can also control the fading intensity by dragging the **Locked layer fading** sliding bar in the **Layers** panel. You can also turn off or on the fading effect by choosing the **Locked Layer Fading** button from the **Layers** panel.

To unisolate the previously isolated layer, choose the **Unisolate** tool from the **Layers** panel.

Controlling the Layer Settings

The **Settings** button in the **LAYER PROPERTIES MANAGER** is used to control the new layer notification settings. You can also change the background color used to highlight the layer properties that are overridden in the current viewport. Choose the **Settings** button in the **LAYER PROPERTIES MANAGER**; the **Layer Settings** dialog box will be displayed, as shown in Figure 4-25. The options in the **Layer Settings** dialog box are discussed next.

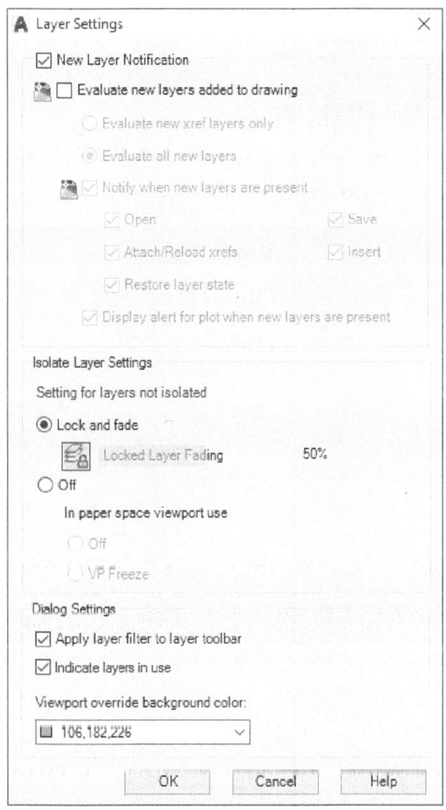

*Figure 4-25 The **Layer Settings** dialog box*

New Layer Notification Area

By default, the **Evaluate new layers added to drawing** check box is cleared. Therefore, the new layers will not be evaluated. Also, the user will not be informed about the unreconciled layers. Select the **Evaluate new layers added to drawing** check box; all other options in this area will be available. The **Evaluate new xref layers only** radio button is selected by default and allows AutoCAD to evaluate the new layers added only to the externally referenced drawings. Select the **Evaluate all new layers** radio button to evaluate all the layers in the drawing, including the unreconciled layers of the externally referenced drawings. This setting can also be controlled by setting the **LAYEREVAL** system variable to 2.

The **Notify when new layers are present** check box is selected by default and is used to specify the operations after which AutoCAD will evaluate the unreconciled files. These operations include open, save, attach/reload xrefs, insert, and restore layer states. Select the respective check boxes to specify your preferences. These settings can also be specified by using the **LAYERNOTIFY** system variable. The values for this system variable are 0, 1, 2, 4, 8, 16, and 32. The respective operations after which an information bubble will be displayed are Off, Open, Reload/Attach for xrefs, Restore layer state, Save, and Insert.

Isolate Layer Settings Area

The options in this area are used to set the display state of the unisolated layers. If you need to display a locked layer in a faded mode, select the **Lock and fade** radio button and set the intensity of fading by using the slider. Similarly, you can make the unisolated layers turned off or VP Freeze in the viewport by selecting the **Off** radio button and the corresponding option.

Dialog Settings Area

You can apply the current layer filter to the **Filter applied** drop-down list in the **Layers** toolbar. To do so, invoke the **Layer Filter Properties** dialog box by choosing the **New Property Filter** button from the **LAYER PROPERTIES MANAGER**. Select the layer state or property from the **Filter definition** list box and choose the **OK** button. Only the filtered layers will be displayed in the **Layer Control** drop-down list of the **Layers** toolbar.

Example 1 *Layers*

Set up three layers with the following linetypes and colors. Then, create the drawing shown in Figure 4-26 (without dimensions).

Layer Name	Color	Linetype	Lineweight
Obj	Red	Continuous	0.012”
Hid	Yellow	Hidden	0.008”
Cen	Green	Center	0.006”

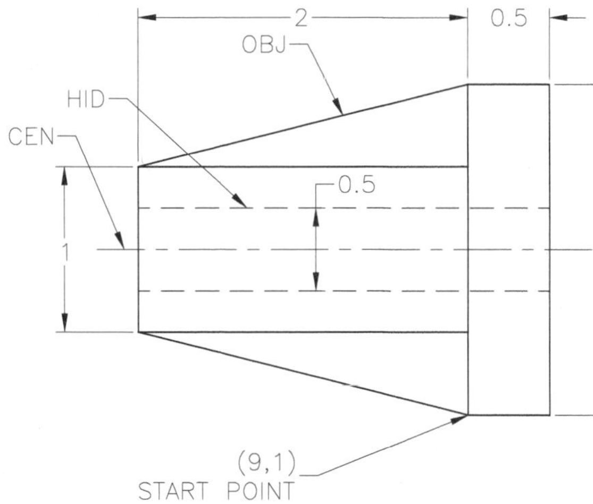

Figure 4-26 *Drawing for Example 1*

In this example, assume that the limits and units are already set. Before drawing the lines, you need to create layers and assign colors, linetypes, and lineweights to them. Also, depending on the objects that you want to draw, you need to set a layer as the current layer. In this example, you will create layers by using the **LAYER PROPERTIES MANAGER**. You will use the **Layer** drop-down list in the **Layers** panel to set a layer as the current layer and then draw the figure.

1. As the lineweights specified are given in inches, first you need to change their units, if they are in millimeters. To do so, invoke the **Lineweight Settings** dialog box by right-clicking on the **Show/Hide Lineweight** button on the Status Bar and then choose the **Lineweight Settings** option from the shortcut menu. Select the **Inches (in)** radio button in the **Units for Listing** area of the dialog box and then choose the **OK** button.

2. Choose the **Layer Properties** button from the **Layers** panel in the **Home** tab of the **Ribbon** to display the **LAYER PROPERTIES MANAGER**. The layer **0** with default properties is displayed in the list box.

3. Choose the **New Layer** button; a new layer (Layer1) with the default properties is displayed in the list box. Change the default name, **Layer1** to **Obj**.

4. Left-click on the **Color** field of this layer; the **Select Color** dialog box is displayed. Select the **Red** color and then choose the **OK** button; red color is assigned to the **Obj** layer.

5. Left-click on the **Lineweight** field of the **Obj** layer; the **Lineweight** dialog box is displayed. Select **0.012"** and then choose the **OK** button; the selected lineweight is assigned to the **Obj** layer.

6. Again, choose the **New Layer** button; a new layer (Layer1) with properties similar to that of the **Obj** layer is created. Change the default name to **Hid**.

7. Left-click on the **Color** field of this layer; the **Select Color** dialog box is displayed. Select the **Yellow** color and then choose the **OK** button.

8. Left-click on the **Linetype** field of the **Hid** layer; the **Select Linetype** dialog box is displayed. If the **HIDDEN** linetype is not displayed in the dialog box, choose the **Load** button; the **Load or Reload Linetypes** dialog box is displayed. Select **HIDDEN** from the list and choose the **OK** button from the **Load or Reload Linetypes** dialog box. Next, select **HIDDEN** from the **Select Linetype** dialog box and then choose the **OK** button.

9. Left-click on the **Lineweight** field of the **Hid** layer; the **Lineweight** dialog box is displayed. Select **0.008"** and then choose the **OK** button; the selected lineweight is assigned to the **Hid** layer.

10. Similarly, create the new layer **Cen** and assign the color **Green**, linetype **CENTER**, and lineweight **0.006"** to it.

11. Select the **Obj** layer and then choose the **Set Current** button to make the **Obj** layer current, refer to Figure 4-27. Choose the **Close** button to exit the **LAYER PROPERTIES MANAGER**.

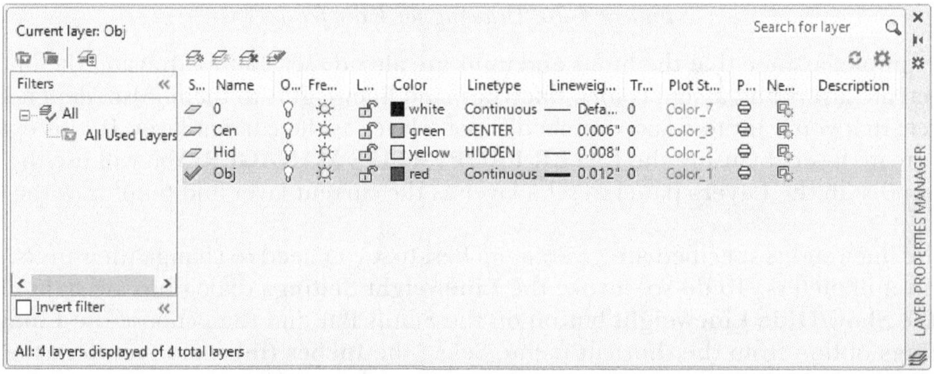

Figure 4-27 Layers created for Example 1

12. Choose the **Show/Hide Lineweight** button from the Status Bar to turn on the display of the lineweights of the lines to be drawn.

13. Choose the **Dynamic Input** button from the Status Bar to turn it on.

14. Choose the **Line** tool from the **Draw** panel and draw solid lines in the drawing, refer to Figure 4-26. Make sure that the start point of the line is at 9,1. You will notice that a continuous line is drawn in red color. This is because the **Obj** layer is the current layer and red color is assigned to it.

15. Click the down arrow in the **Layer** drop-down list available in the **Layers** panel to display the list of layers and then select the **Hid** layer from the list to make it current, as shown in Figure 4-28.

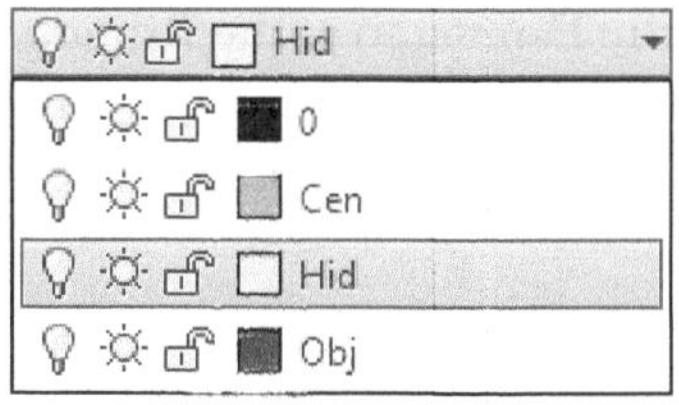

***Figure 4-28** Selecting the **Hid** layer from the **Layers** panel to set it as the current layer*

16. Draw two hidden lines; the lines are displayed in yellow color with hidden linetype.

17. Draw the center line; the centerline is displayed in yellow color with hidden linetype. This is because the **Hid** layer is the current layer.

18. Now, select the centerline and then select the **Cen** layer from the **Layer** drop-down list available in the **Layers** panel; the color and linetype of the centerline are changed.

Exercise 1 — *Layers*

Set up layers with the following linetypes and colors. Then make the drawing (without dimensions), as shown in Figure 4-29. The distance between the dotted lines is 1.0 unit.

Layer Name	Color	Linetype
Object	Red	Continuous
Hidden	Yellow	Hidden
Center	Green	Center
Dimension	Blue	Continuous

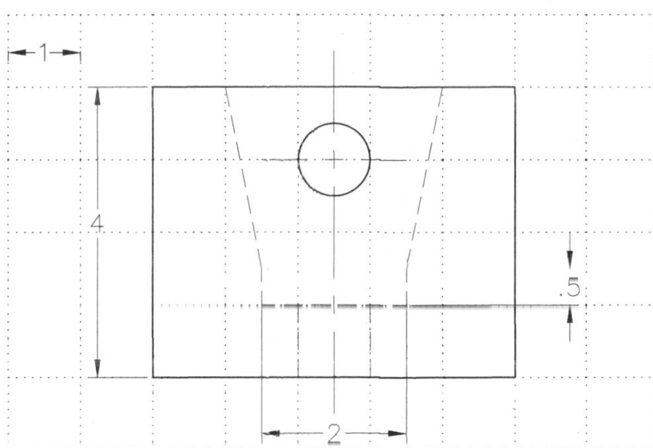

***Figure 4-29** Drawing for Exercise 1*

OBJECT PROPERTIES

Drawing entities have properties such as color, linetype, lineweight, and plot style based on the layer it is associated with. However, you can change these properties by using the **PROPERTIES** palette or the **Properties** panel in the **Home** tab of the **Ribbon**. By default, the **By Layer** option will be selected in the **Object Color**, **Lineweight**, and **Linetype** drop-down lists of the **Properties** panel in the **Ribbon**. Therefore, the properties set in the current layer will be applied to the entities in it. The procedure to change the properties of the selected objects is discussed next.

Changing the Color

Select the object whose color you want to change; the current color of the object will be displayed in the **Object Color** drop-down list. To change this color, select the down arrow in the **Object Color** drop-down list, as shown in Figure 4-30, and select a new color; the selected color will be applied to the object. If you want to assign a color that is not displayed in the list, select the **More Colors** option; the **Select Color** dialog box will be displayed. You can select the desired color in this dialog box, and then choose the **OK** button.

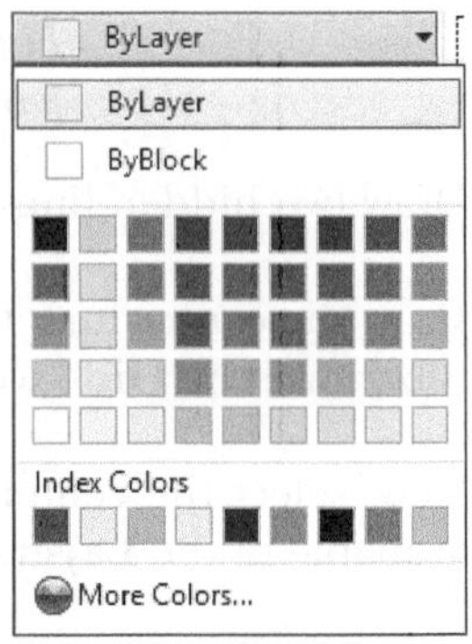

*Figure 4-30 Different colors in the **Object Color** drop-down list*

To set a color other than the one set in the current layer as the current color, select a color from the **Object Color** drop-down list without selecting an object. Now, all new objects will be drawn in this color.

Changing the Linetype

To set a linetype other than the one set in the current layer as the current linetype, select a linetype from the **Linetype** drop-down list in the **Properties** panel from the **Home** tab, as shown in Figure 4-31. Now, all objects will be drawn in this linetype.

To assign a linetype that is not displayed in the list, choose the **Other** option; the **Linetype Manager** dialog box will be displayed, as shown in Figure 4-32. By default, the **ByLayer**, **ByBlock**, and **Continuous** linetypes will be listed in this dialog box. To load other linetypes, choose the **Load** button; the **Load or Reload Linetypes** dialog box will be displayed. Select a linetype in this dialog box and choose the **OK** button; they will be displayed in the **Linetype Manager** dialog box. Next, select the required linetype from this dialog box and choose the **OK** button. You can also make a linetype current by using the **Current** button in the **Linetype Manager** dialog box.

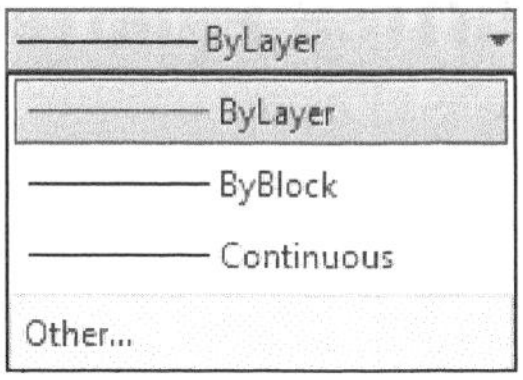

*Figure 4-31 The **Linetype** drop-down list*

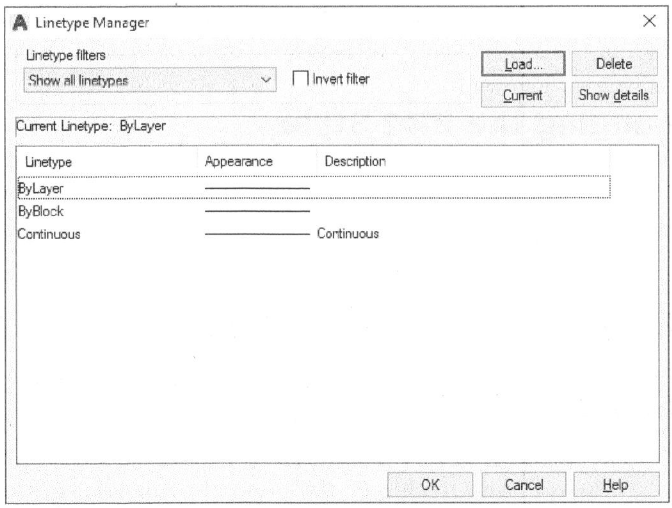

*Figure 4-32 The **Linetype Manager** dialog box*

Changing the Lineweight

To change the lineweight of a selected object, select a different lineweight value from the **Lineweight** drop-down list in the **Properties** panel. Also, you can set a new lineweight as current by selecting it from the list. To assign a lineweight value that is not listed in the drop-down list, select the **Lineweight Settings** option from the **Lineweight** drop-down list; the **Lineweight Settings** dialog box will be displayed, as shown in Figure 4-33. You can also invoke this dialog box by choosing the **Lineweight Settings** option from the shortcut menu that is displayed on right-clicking on the **Hide/Show Lineweight** button in the Status Bar. In this dialog box, set the current lineweight for the objects.

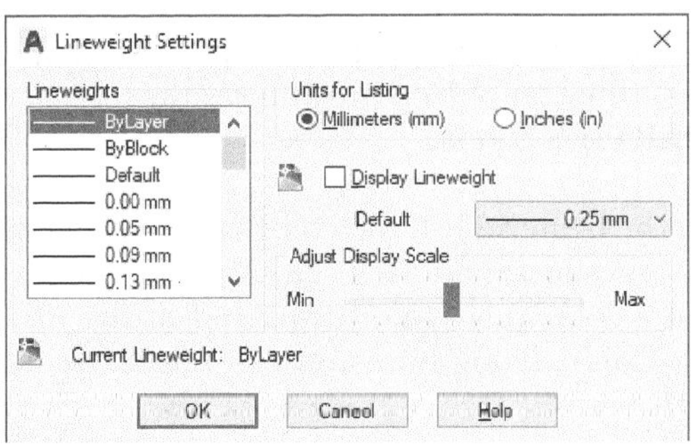

*Figure 4-33 The **Lineweight Settings** dialog box*

You can change the units for the lineweight and also the display of lineweights for the current drawing. Lineweights are displayed in pixel width, which depend on the value of lineweight chosen. You can select the **Display Lineweight** check box to display lineweight in the drawing. For a large drawing, displaying lineweight increases the regeneration time, and therefore the corresponding check box should be cleared. As mentioned earlier, you can also turn the display of lineweights to on or off directly from the Status Bar by choosing the **Show/Hide Lineweight** button. The value set in the **Adjust Display Scale** slider bar also affects the regeneration time.

You can keep the slider bar at **Max** for getting a good display of different lineweights on the screen in the Model space; otherwise keep it at **Min** for a faster regeneration.

Changing the Plot Style

The options in this drop-down list will be available only if you are using the named plot style modes. To change the plot style, select a plot style from the **Plot Style** drop-down list in the **Properties** panel. Also, you can set a new plot style as current by selecting it from the drop-down list.

Changing Object Properties Using the PROPERTIES Palette

Ribbon: View > Palettes > Properties **Command:** PROPERTIES/CH/MO/PR
Toolbar: Standard > Properties

The **PROPERTIES** palette is used to set the current properties and to change the general properties of the selected objects. The **PROPERTIES** palette is displayed on choosing the **Properties** tool from the **Palettes** panel of the **View** tab, as shown in Figure 4-34. It can also be invoked by selecting and right-clicking on an object and then choosing the **Properties** option from the shortcut menu. Right-clicking in the **PROPERTIES** palette displays a shortcut menu from where you can choose **Allow Docking** or **Auto-hide** to dock or hide the palette.

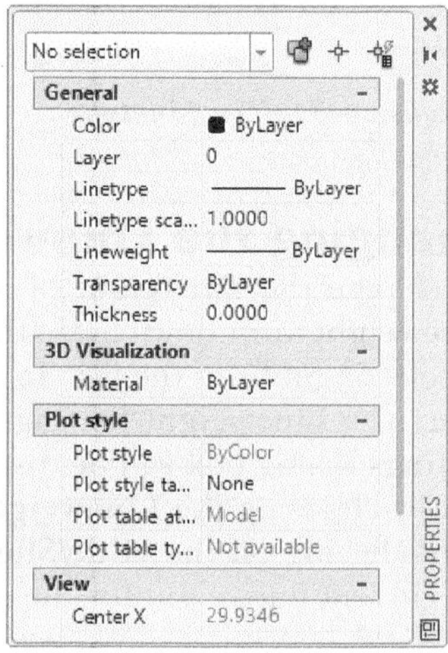

Figure 4-34 *The* ***PROPERTIES*** *palette*

When you select an object, the **PROPERTIES** palette displays the properties of the selected object. Depending on the object selected, the properties differ. If you change the properties in the **PROPERTIES** palette without selecting any object, the current properties will be changed in the **Properties** panel of the **Home** tab. Now, if you draw an object, it will have the properties set in the **PROPERTIES** palette.

When you select **Color** from the **General** list, the color of the selected object is displayed, along with a down arrow. Click the down arrow and select a color from the list to assign to the selected object. If you want to assign a color that is not displayed in the list, choose the **Select Color** option to display the **Select Color** dialog box. You can select the desired color in this dialog box, and then choose the **OK** button.

Similarly, you can set current the linetype, lineweight, linetype scale, and other properties for the other objects individually. You can also assign a hyperlink to an object. The **Hyperlink** field in this window displays the name and description of the hyperlink, if any, assigned to the object. If there is no hyperlink attached to the object, this field will be blank. To add a hyperlink to a selected object, click on this field; the button will be displayed in this field. Choose the button; the **Insert Hyperlink** dialog box will be displayed where you can enter the path of the URL or the file that you want to link to the selected object.

Exercise 2 — Object Properties

Draw a hexagon on the **Obj** layer in red. Keep the linetype hidden. Now, use the **PROPERTIES** palette to change the layer, the color to yellow, and the linetype to continuous.

Changing Object Properties using the Quick Properties Palette

Status Bar: Quick Properties **Command:** QP

In AutoCAD, you can view some of the properties of the selected entity in the Quick Properties palette or in the **PROPERTIES** palette. To view the properties, keep the **Quick Properties** button chosen in the Status Bar and then select an entity; some of the properties of the selected entity will be displayed in the Quick Properties palette. Alternatively, enter **QP** at the command prompt or the **Dynamic Input** to invoke the Quick Properties palette. You can change the properties that are displayed in the Quick Properties palette. Figure 4-35 shows the Quick Properties palette that is displayed on selecting a line.

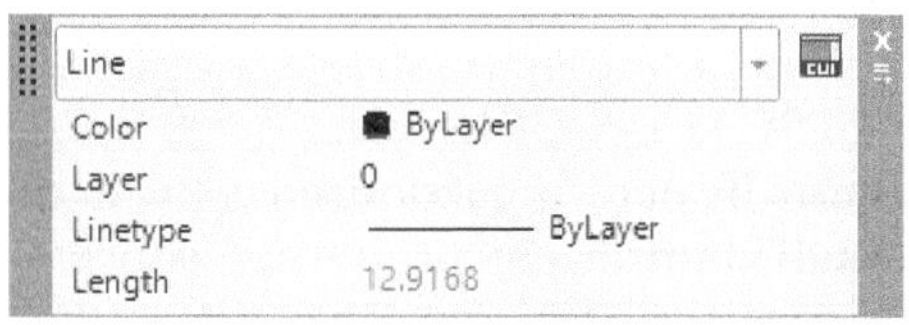

Figure 4-35 *The Quick Properties palette*

If you select multiple objects of different types, then in the drop-down list available in the Quick Properties palette, the name of the objects will be defined as **All** and the number of selected entities will be displayed in parenthesis. After selecting multiple entities, you can also select a particular type of object from the drop-down list to view the properties of the particular object type.

To set the properties displayed in the Quick Properties palette, right-click on the **Quick Properties** button in the Status Bar and choose the **Quick Properties Settings** option; the **Drafting Settings** dialog box will be displayed with the **Quick Properties** tab chosen. You can specify the display of the object type, the position of palette on invoking, and the height of palette by selecting a suitable option in this dialog box.

You can customize the Quick Properties palette such that it displays the required properties of a selected entity. To do so, choose the **Customize** button available next to the drop-down list; the **Customize User Interface** dialog box will be displayed. In the dialog box, different object types and their corresponding properties will be displayed on the right. If you select an object type, you will notice that the check boxes of some of the properties are selected. The properties, whose check boxes are selected will be listed in the Quick Properties palette. You can also select the check boxes of the properties that you want to be displayed in the Quick Properties palette.

If you place the cursor over an entity and pause, a tooltip, called the rollover tooltip, will be displayed. You can synchronize the properties displayed in the rollover tooltip and the **Quick Properties** panel. To do so, invoke the **Customize User Interface** dialog box, right-click on the **Rollover Tooltips** sub node in it, and choose the **Synchronize with Quick Properties** option from the shortcut menu.

GLOBAL AND CURRENT LINETYPE SCALING

The **LTSCALE** system variable controls the global scale factor of the lines in a drawing. For example, if **LTSCALE** is set to 2, all lines in the drawing will be affected by a factor of 2. Like **LTSCALE**, the **CELTSCALE** system variable controls the linetype scaling with the only difference that **CELTSCALE** determines the current linetype scaling. For example, if you set **CELTSCALE** to 0.5, all lines drawn after setting the new value for **CELTSCALE** will have the linetype scaling factor of 0.5. The value is retained in the **CELTSCALE** system variable. For example, line (a) in Figure 4-36 is drawn with a **CELTSCALE** factor of 1 and line (b) is drawn with a **CELTSCALE** factor of 0.5. The length of the dash is reduced by a factor of 0.5 when **CELTSCALE** is 0.5. The net scale factor is equal to the product of **CELTSCALE** and **LTSCALE**. Figure 4-36(c) shows a line that is drawn with **LTSCALE** of 2 and **CELTSCALE** of 0.25. The net scale factor = **LTSCALE** X **CELTSCALE** = 2 X 0.25 = 0.5. You can also change the global and current scale factors by entering a desired value in the **Linetype Manager** dialog box. If you choose the **Show details** button, the properties associated with the selected linetype will be displayed, as shown in Figure 4-37. You can change the values according to your drawing requirements.

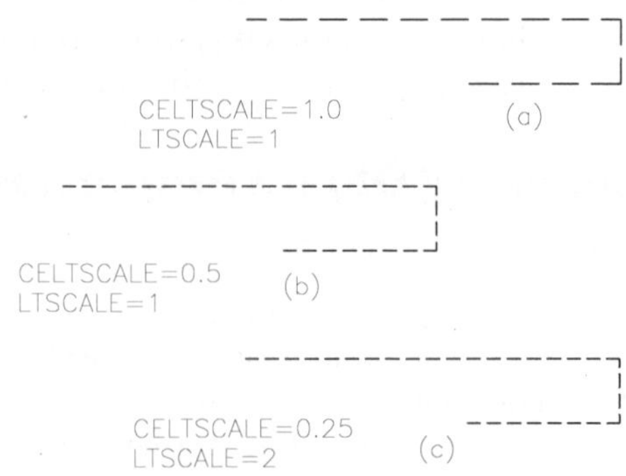

Figure 4-36 Using ***CELTSCALE*** *to control current linetype scaling*

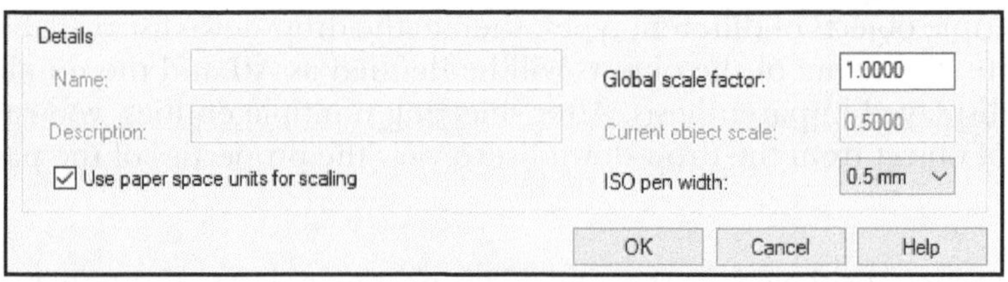

Figure 4-37 The ***Details*** *area of the* ***Linetype Manager*** *dialog box*

LTSCALE FACTOR FOR PLOTTING

The **LTSCALE** factor for plotting depends on the size of the sheet you use to plot the drawing. For example, if the limits are 48 by 36, the drawing scale is 1:1, and to plot the drawing on a 48" by 36" size sheet, then the **LTSCALE** factor is 1. If you check the specification of the **Hidden** linetype in the *acad.lin* file, the length of each dash is 0.25. Hence, when you plot a drawing with 1:1 scale, the length of each dash in a hidden line will be 0.25.

However, if the drawing scale is 1/8" = 1' and you want to plot the drawing on 48" by 36" paper, the **LTSCALE** factor must be 8 X 12 = 96. The length of each dash in the hidden line will increase by a factor of 96, because the **LTSCALE** factor is 96. Therefore, the length of each dash will be (0.25 X 96 = 24) units. At the time of plotting, the scale factor must be 1:96 to plot the 384' by 288' drawing on 48" by 36" paper. Each dash of the hidden line that was 24" long on the drawing will be 24/96 = 0.25" long when plotted. Similarly, if the desired text size on the paper is 1/8", the text height in the drawing must be 1/8 X 96 = 12".

LTSCALE factor for PLOTTING = Drawing Scale

Sometimes your plotter may not be able to plot a 48" by 36" drawing, or you might like to decrease the size of the plot so that the drawing fits within the specified area. To get the correct dash length for hidden, center, or other lines, you must adjust the **LTSCALE** factor. For example, if you want to plot the previously mentioned drawing in a 45" by 34" area, the correction factor is:

Correction factor = 48/45
= 1.0666

New **LTSCALE** factor = **LTSCALE** factor x Correction factor
= 96 x 1.0666
= 102.4

New **LTSCALE** factor for PLOTTING = Drawing Scale x Correction Factor

Note

If you change the ***LTSCALE*** *factor, all lines in the drawing will be affected by the new ratio.*

Changing the Linetype Scale Using the PROPERTIES Palette

You can also change the linetype scale of an object by using the **PROPERTIES** palette. To do so, select the object and then invoke the **Properties** option; the **PROPERTIES** palette will be displayed. Next, locate the **Linetype scale** edit box in the **General** list and enter a new linetype scale value in the edit box. The linetype scale of the selected objects is changed as specified.

WORKING WITH THE DESIGNCENTER

Ribbon: View > Palettes > DesignCenter **Command:** ADC/ADCENTER
Toolbar: Standard > DesignCenter

The Design Center allows you to reuse and share contents in different drawings. You can use this palette to locate the drawing data with the help of search tools and then use it in your drawing. You can insert layers, linetypes, blocks, layouts, external references, and other drawing content in any number of drawings. Hence, if a layer is created once, it can be used repeatedly any number of times.

Open the **DESIGNCENTER** palette and then choose the **Tree View Toggle** button to display the **Tree pane** and the **Palette** side by side (if they are not already displayed). Open the folder that contains the drawing having the required layers and linetypes to be inserted. You can use the **Load** and **Up** buttons to open the folder. For example, to insert some layers and linetypes from the drawing *c4d1* saved at the *c:\AutoCAD 2018\c04_ACAD_2018*, browse to the folder and open *c4d1* to display its contents. Select **Layers**; the layers created in *c4d1* will be displayed in the **Palette**. Press and hold the CTRL key and select the **Border** and **CEN** layers. Right-click to display the shortcut menu and choose **Add Layer(s)**, as shown in Figure 4-38; the two layers are added to the current drawing. You can also drag and drop the desired layers into the current drawing. If you open the drop-down list in the **Layers** toolbar, you will notice that the two layers are listed there. Similarly, you can insert other elements such as linetypes, blocks, dimension styles, and so on. You will learn more about Design Center in later chapters.

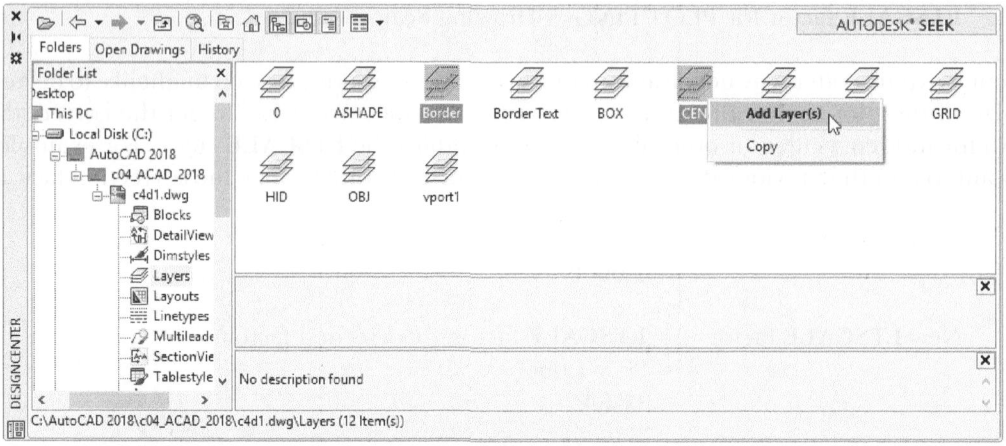

*Figure 4-38 The **DESIGNCENTER** palette with the shortcut menu*

DRAFTING SETTINGS DIALOG BOX

Command: DSETTINGS/DS

You can use the **Drafting Settings** dialog box to set the drawing modes such as Grid, Snap, Object Snap, Polar, Object Snap tracking, and Dynamic Input. All these modes help you draw accurately and also increase the drawing speed. You can right-click on the **Snap mode**, **Display drawing grid**, **Restrict cursor orthogonally**, **Restrict cursor to specified angles**, **Snap cursor to 2D reference points**, **Snap cursor to 3D reference points**, **Object Snap Tracking**, **Dynamic Input**, **Quick Properties**, or **Selection Cycling** button in the Status Bar to display a shortcut menu. In this shortcut menu, choose the respective **Settings** to display the **Drafting Settings** dialog box, as shown in Figure 4-39. This dialog box has seven tabs: **Snap and Grid**, **Polar Tracking**, **Object Snap**, **3D Object Snap**, **Dynamic Input**, **Quick Properties**, and **Selection Cycling**. On starting AutoCAD, these tabs have default settings. You can change them according to your requirements.

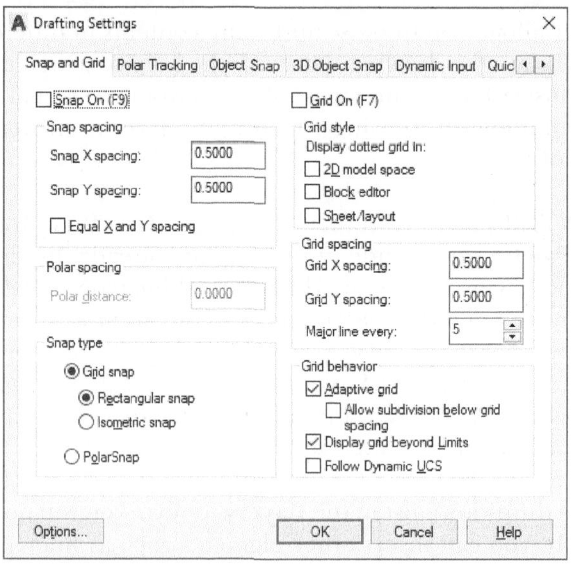

*Figure 4-39 The **Drafting Settings** dialog box*

Note

In AutoCAD 2018, you can resize the ***Drafting Settings*** *dialog box by dragging any side or corner of this dialog box.*

Setting Grid

Grid lines are the checked lines on the screen at predefined spacing, see Figure 4-40. In AutoCAD, by default, the grids are displayed as checked lines. You can also display the grids as dotted lines, refer to Figure 4-41. To do so, set the **2D model space** check box in the **Grid style** area of the **Snap and Grid** tab of the **Drafting Settings** dialog box. These dotted lines act as a graph that can be used as reference lines in a drawing. You can change the distance between grid lines as per your requirement. If grid lines are displayed within the drawing limits, it helps to define the working area. The grid also gives you an idea about the size of the drawing objects. By default, the grid will be displayed beyond the limits. To display the grid up to the limits, right-click on the **Display drawing grid** button in the Status Bar and then choose the **Grid Settings** option from the shortcut menu displayed; the **Drafting Settings** dialog box will be displayed. In this dialog box, clear the **Display grid beyond Limits** check box from the **Grid behavior** area. Now, the grids will be displayed only up to the limits set.

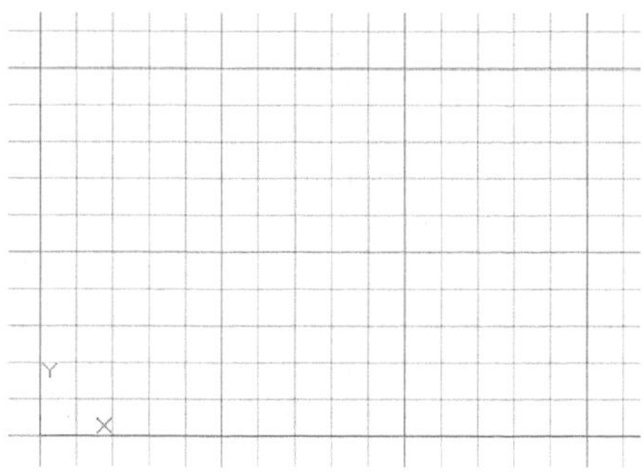

Figure 4-40 *Grid as checked lines*

Figure 4-41 *Grid as dots*

Grid On (F7): Turning the Grid On or Off

You can turn the grid display on/off by using the **Grid On** check box in the **Drafting Settings** dialog box. You can also turn the grid display on/off by choosing the **Display drawing grid** button in the Status Bar or by using the F7 key. **Display drawing grid** is a toggle button. When the grid display is turned on after it has been turned off, the grid is set to the previous grid spacing.

Grid X Spacing and Grid Y Spacing

The **Grid X spacing** and **Grid Y spacing** edit boxes in the **Drafting Settings** dialog box are used to define the desired grid spacing along the X and Y axes. For example, to set the grid spacing to 0.5 units, enter **0.5** in the **Grid X spacing** and **Grid Y spacing** edit boxes. You can also enter different values for the horizontal and vertical grid spacing, refer to Figure 4-42. If you specify only the grid X spacing value and then choose the **OK** button in the dialog box, the corresponding Y spacing value will automatically be set to match the X spacing value, as shown in Figure 4-42. Therefore, if you want different X and Y spacing values, clear the **Equal X and Y spacing** check box in the **Snap spacing** area, and enter different X and Y spacing values to create unequal Grid Spacing, as shown in Figure 4-43.

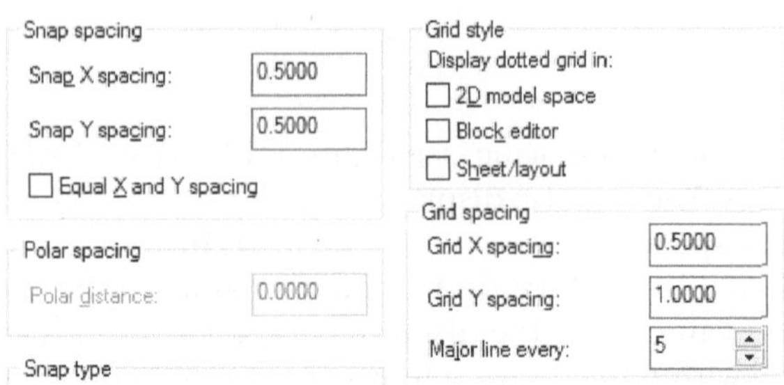

*Figure 4-42 The **Grid Spacing** area of the **Drafting Settings** dialog box*

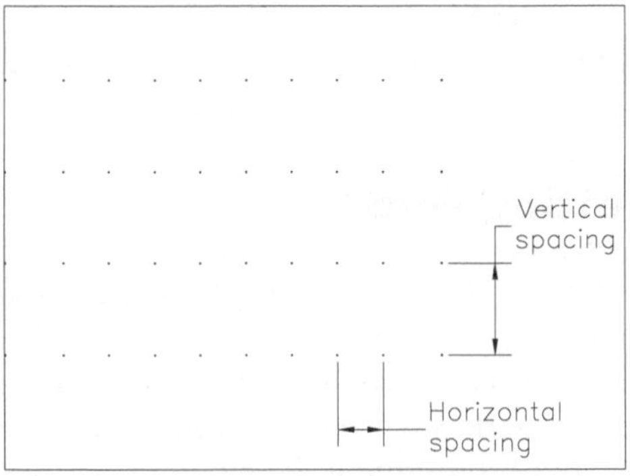

Figure 4-43 Creating unequal grid spacing

Note

Grids are especially effective in drawing when the objects in the drawing are placed at regular intervals.

Setting Snap

After displaying the grid, you need to switch on the snap mode so that the cursor snaps to the snap point. The snap points are invisible points that are created at the intersection of invisible horizontal and vertical lines, refer to Figure 4-44. A snap point is independent of the grid spacing and the two can have equal or different values. Therefore, when the snap mode is on, the cursor moves at specified intervals from one point to another. You can turn on the snap mode even when the grid lines are invisible. To set snap spacing, enter the X and Y values in the corresponding edit boxes in the **Snap spacing** area of the **Snap and Grid** tab in the **Drafting Settings** dialog box, refer to Figure 4-42. You can turn the snap mode on/off by selecting the **Snap On** check box from the **Drafting Settings** dialog box. You can also turn the snap on or off by choosing the **Snap mode** button in the Status Bar, or from the shortcut menu displayed by right-clicking on the **Snap mode** button in the Status Bar, or by using the function key F9 as a toggle key.

Snap Type

There are two snap types, **PolarSnap** and **Grid snap**. On selecting **Grid snap**, the cursor snaps along the grid. The **Grid snap** is either of the **Rectangular snap** type or of the **Isometric snap** type. Rectangular snap is the default snap and has been discussed earlier. The other types are discussed next.

Isometric Snap

The isometric mode is used to make isometric drawings. In isometric drawings, the isometric axes are at angles 30, 90, and 150 degrees. The isometric snap/grid enables you to display the grid lines along these axes, as shown in Figure 4-45. Select the **Isometric snap** radio button in the **Snap type** area of the **Drafting Settings** dialog box to set the snap grid to the isometric mode. Once you select the **Isometric snap** radio button and choose **OK** in the dialog box, the cursor aligns with the isometric axis. You will notice that the X spacing is not available for this option. You can change the vertical snap and grid spacing by entering values in the **Snap Y spacing** and **Grid Y spacing** edit boxes. While drawing in the isometric mode, you can adjust the cursor orientation to the left, top, or right plane of the drawing by using the F5 key. The procedure to create drawings using the **Isometric snap** option is discussed in the later chapters.

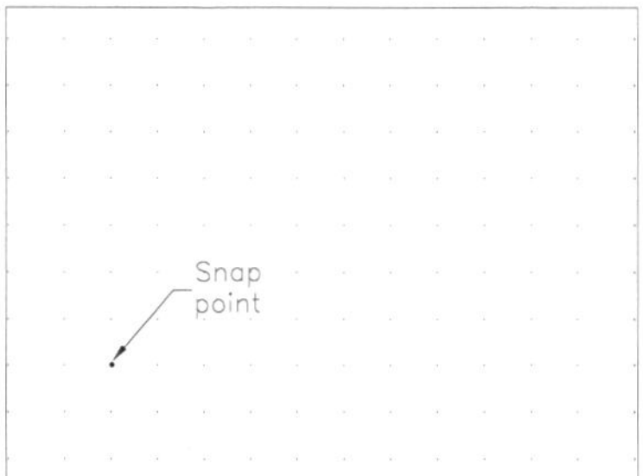

Figure 4-44 *Invisible Snap grid*

Figure 4-45 *Isometric Snap grid*

PolarSnap

The polar snap is used to snap points at a specified distance along the polar alignment angles. To set the snap mode as polar, select the **PolarSnap** radio button in the **Snap type** area; the **Polar distance** edit box will be enabled and the snap spacing options will be disabled. Enter a value for the distance in the **Polar distance** edit box and choose the **OK** button. If this value is zero, AutoCAD takes the same value as specified for Snap X spacing earlier. Now, if you draw a line, the cursor snaps along an imaginary line according to the Polar tracking angles that are relative to the last point selected. The polar tracking angle can be set in the **Polar Tracking** tab of the **Drafting Settings** dialog box (discussed later in this chapter).

For example, select the **PolarSnap** radio button and enter **0.5** in the **Polar distance** edit box. Choose the **Polar Tracking** tab and enter **30** in the **Increment angle** drop-down list and then choose the **OK** button. Choose the **Snap Mode** and **Polar Tracking** buttons in the Status Bar. Invoke the **Line** tool and select the start point anywhere on the screen. Now, if you move the cursor at angles in multiples of 30-degree, a dotted line will be displayed and if you move the cursor along this dotted line, a small cross mark will be displayed at a distance of 0.5 (polar snap).

DRAWING STRAIGHT LINES USING THE ORTHOMODE

The **ORTHOMODE** is used to draw lines at right angles only. You can turn the **ORTHOMODE** on or off by choosing the **ORTHOMODE** button in the Status Bar, by using the function key F8, or by using the **ORTHO** command. When the **ORTHOMODE** is on and you move the cursor to specify the next point, a rubber-band line is connected to the cursor in horizontal (parallel to the *X* axis) or vertical (parallel to the *Y* axis) direction. To draw a line in the Ortho mode, specify the start point at the **Specify first point** prompt. To specify the second point, move the cursor and specify a desired point. The line drawn will be either vertical or horizontal, depending on the direction in which you move the cursor, see Figure 4-46 and Figure 4-47.

Tip

*You can use the buttons in the Status Bar (at the bottom of the graphics area) to toggle between on or off for different drafting functions like **Snap**, **Grid**, and **Ortho**.*

Figure 4-46 Drawing a horizontal line using the ***Ortho*** *mode*

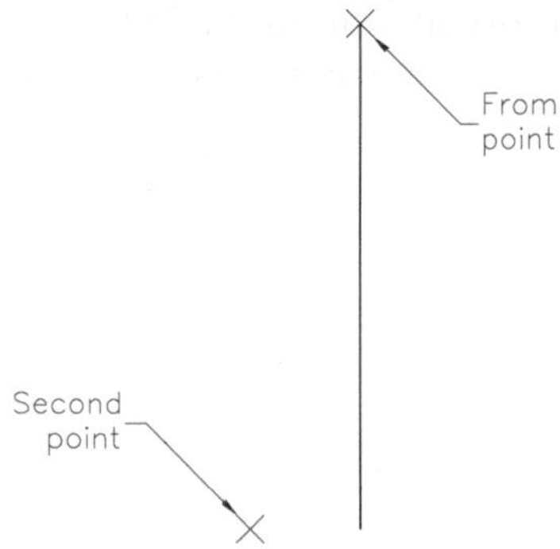

Figure 4-47 Drawing a vertical line using the ***Ortho*** *mode*

WORKING WITH OBJECT SNAP

Toolbar: Object Snap

The term object snap refers to the cursor's ability to snap exactly to a geometric point on an object. The advantage of using object snaps is that you do not have to specify an exact point. For example, to snap the midpoint of a line, use the **Midpoint** object snap and move the cursor closer to the object; a marker (in the form of a geometric shape, a triangle for Midpoint) will automatically be displayed at the mid point. Click to snap the mid point.

Object snaps recognize only the objects that are visible on the screen, These objects include the objects on the locked layers. The objects on the layers that are turned off or frozen are not visible, and they cannot be used for object snaps.

Object snapping can be done by using the **Object Snap modes** shortcut menu. To invoke this shortcut menu, choose a tool, press and hold the SHIFT key, and then right-click, as shown in Figure 4-48. You can also do object snapping by using the **Object Snap** toolbar shown in Figure 4-49. Alternatively, you can invoke the **Object Snap modes** shortcut menu when you are inside any other sketching tool. For example, invoke the **Center, Radius** option from the **Draw** panel and then right-click to invoke the shortcut menu. From the shortcut menu, choose the **Snap Overrides** option to display the **Object Snaps** shortcut menu. The following are the object snap modes in AutoCAD.

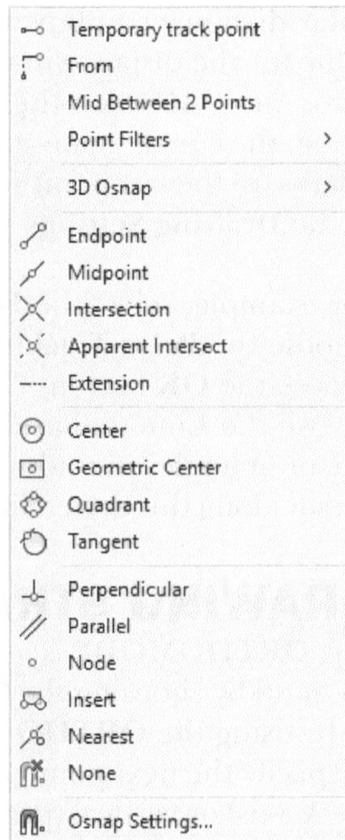

Figure 4-48 The ***Object Snap modes*** *shortcut menu*

Endpoint	Center
Perpendicular	Nearest
Midpoint	Quadrant
Parallel	None
Intersection	Tangent
Insertion	From
Apparent Intersection	Extension

Geometric center
Node
Midpoint Between two points

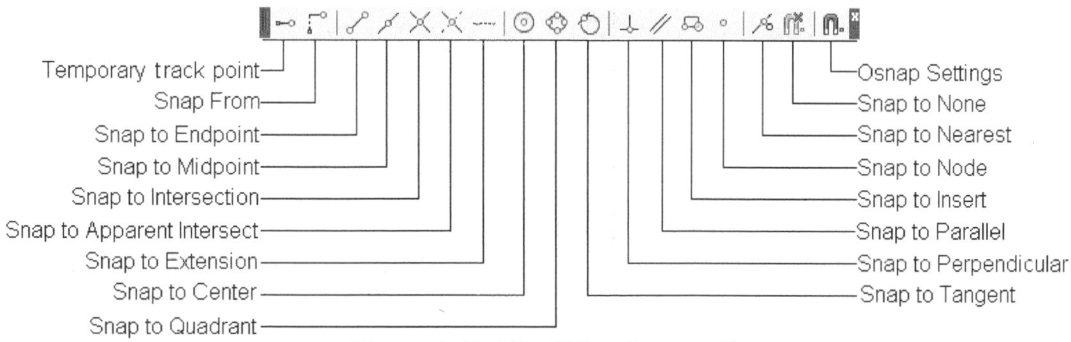

*Figure 4-49 The **Object Snap** toolbar*

AutoSnap

The AutoSnap feature controls various characteristics for the object snap. As you move the target box over the object, AutoCAD displays the geometric marker corresponding to the shapes shown in the **Object Snap** tab of the **Drafting Settings** dialog box. You can change different AutoSnap settings such as attaching a target box to the cursor when you invoke any object snap, or change the size and color of the marker. These settings can be changed from the **Options** dialog box (**Drafting** tab). You can invoke the **Options** dialog box from the **Application Menu**, or by choosing the **Options** button in the **Drafting Settings** dialog box. After invoking the **Options** dialog box, choose the **Drafting** tab in this dialog box; the **AutoSnap Settings** area will be displayed, as shown in Figure 4-50.

Select the **Marker** check box to toggle the display of the marker. Select the **Magnet** check box to toggle the magnet that snaps the crosshairs to the particular point of the object for that object snap. You can use the **Display AutoSnap tooltip** and **Display AutoSnap aperture box** check boxes to toggle the display of the tooltip and the aperture box. Note that if the **Display AutoSnap tooltip** check box is selected in the **Options** dialog box and you move the cursor over an entity, after invoking a tool, the autosnap marker will be displayed. Now, do not move the cursor; the name of the object snap will be displayed. You can change the size of the marker and the aperture box by moving the **AutoSnap Marker Size** and **Aperture Size** slider bars, respectively. You can also change the color of the markers by choosing the **Colors** button. The size of the aperture is measured in pixels (short form of picture elements). Picture elements are dots that make up the screen picture. The aperture size can also be changed by using the **APERTURE** command. The default value for the aperture size is 10 pixels. The display of the marker and the tooltip is controlled by the **AUTOSNAP** system variable. The following are the bit values for **AUTOSNAP**.

Bit Values	**Functions**
0	Turns off the Marker, AutoSnap Tooltip, and Magnet
1	Turns on the AutoSnap marker
2	Turns on the AutoSnap tooltips
4	Turns on the AutoSnap magnet

8	Turns on polar tracking
16	Turns on object snap tracking
32	Turns on tooltips for polar tracking, object snap tracking, and Ortho mode

The basic functionality of Object Snap modes is discussed next.

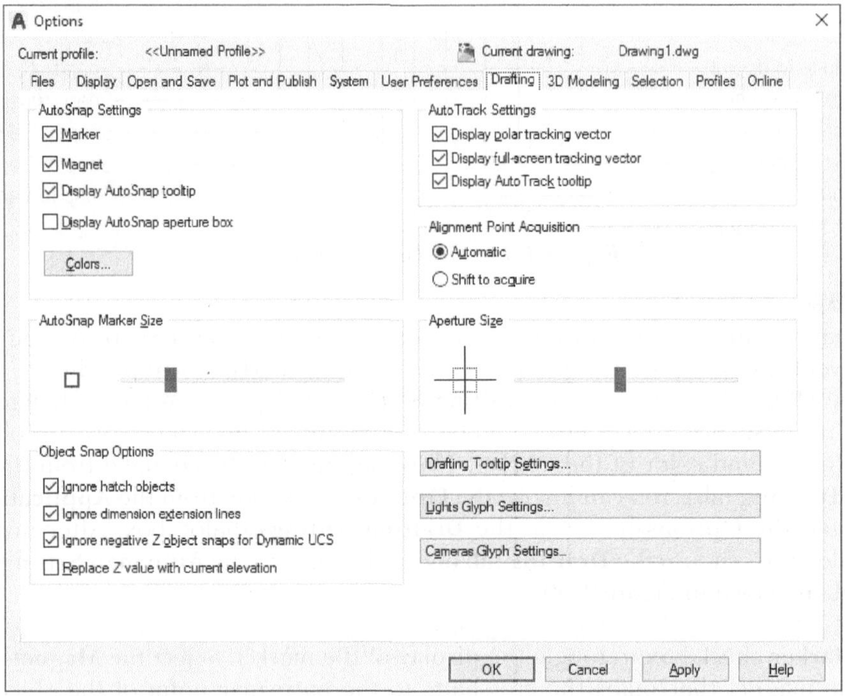

*Figure 4-50 The **Drafting** tab of the **Options** dialog box*

Endpoint

The **Endpoint** Object Snap mode is used to snap the cursor to the closest endpoint of a line or an arc. To use this Object Snap mode, invoke a draw tool such as **Line** and choose the **Snap to Endpoint** button and move the cursor (crosshairs) anywhere close to the endpoint of the object; a marker will be displayed at the endpoint. Click to select that point; the endpoint of the object will be snapped. If there are several objects near the cursor crosshairs, the endpoint of the object that is closest to the crosshairs will be snapped. However, if the **Magnet** is on, you can move to grab the desired endpoint. Figure 4-51 shows the cursor snapping the end point of a circle. The dotted line is the proposed line to be drawn.

Midpoint

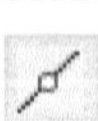

The **Midpoint** Object Snap mode is used to snap the midpoint of a line or an arc. To use this Object Snap mode, choose the **Snap to Midpoint** button and select an object anywhere; the midpoint of the object will be snapped. Figure 4-52 shows the cursor snapping to the midpoint of a line. The dotted line is the proposed line to be drawn.

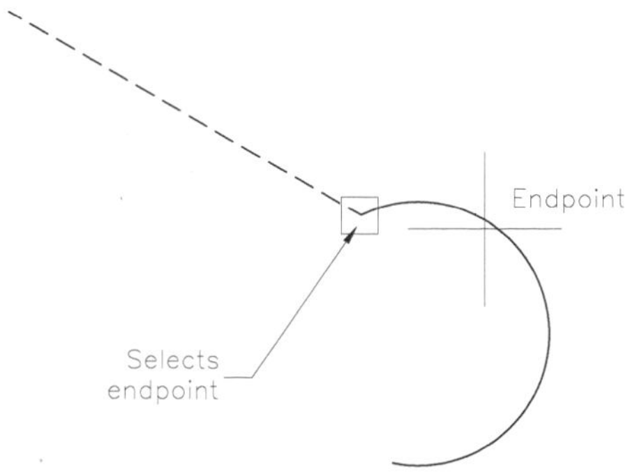

*Figure 4-51 The **Endpoint** Object Snap mode*

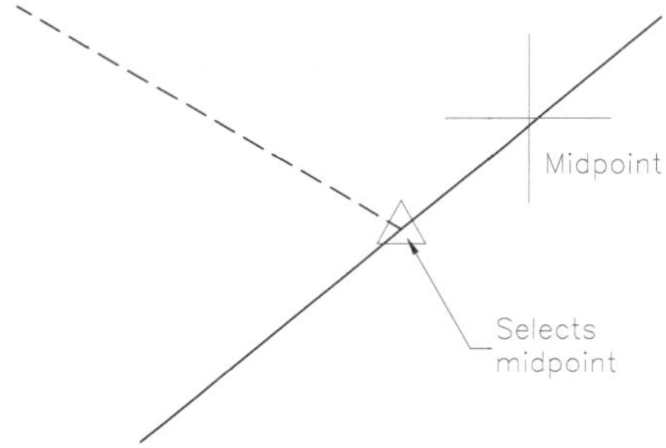

*Figure 4-52 The **Midpoint** Object Snap mode*

Nearest

The **Nearest** Object Snap mode is used to select a point on an object (line, arc, circle, or ellipse) that is visually closest to the crosshairs. To use this mode, invoke a tool, choose the **Nearest** object snap, and then move the crosshairs near the intended point on the object; a marker will be displayed. Left-click to snap that point. Figure 4-53 shows the cursor snapping the point in a line. The dotted line is the proposed line to be drawn.

Center

The **Center** Object Snap mode is used to snap the cursor to the center point of an ellipse, circle, or arc. After choosing this option, move the cursor on the circumference of a circle or an arc; a marker will be displayed at the center of the circle. Left-click to snap the center of the circle. Figure 4-54 shows the cursor snapping the center point of a circle. The dotted line is the proposed line to be drawn.

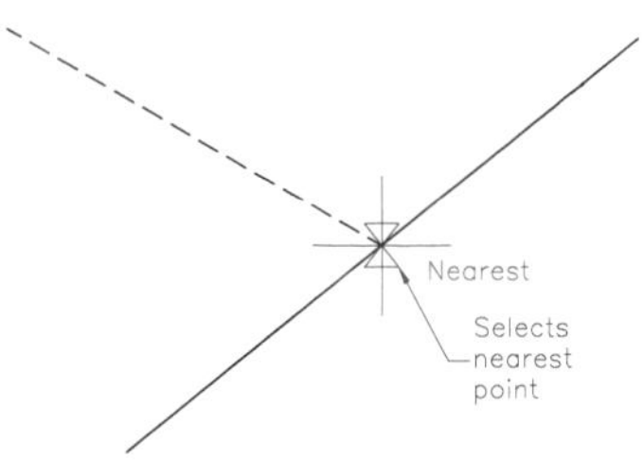

*Figure 4-53 The **Nearest** Object Snap mode*

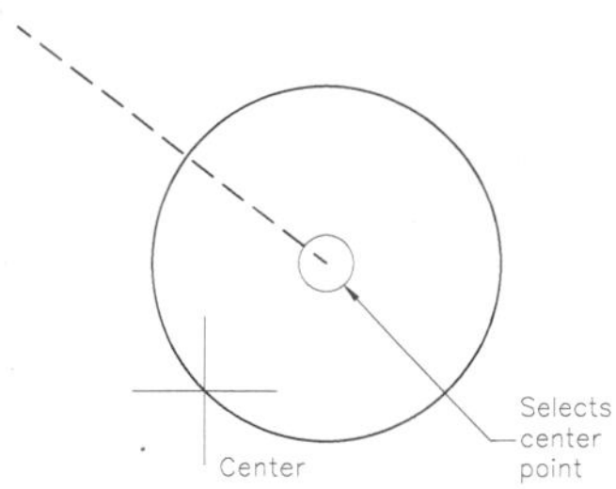

*Figure 4-54 The **Center** Object Snap mode*

Tangent

The **Tangent** Object Snap mode is used to snap the cursor to the tangent point of an existing ellipse, circle, or arc. To use this mode, invoke a tool, choose the **Tangent** Object Snap and place the cursor on the circumference of a circle or an arc and select it. Figure 4-55 shows the cursor selecting the circle. The dashed line is the proposed tangential line. Figure 4-56 shows the use of the **Nearest**, **Endpoint**, **Midpoint**, and **Tangent** Object Snap modes.

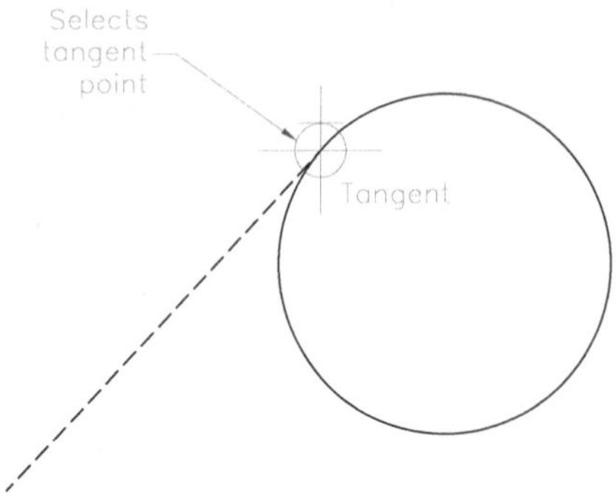

Figure 4-55 *The* ***Tangent*** *Object Snap mode*

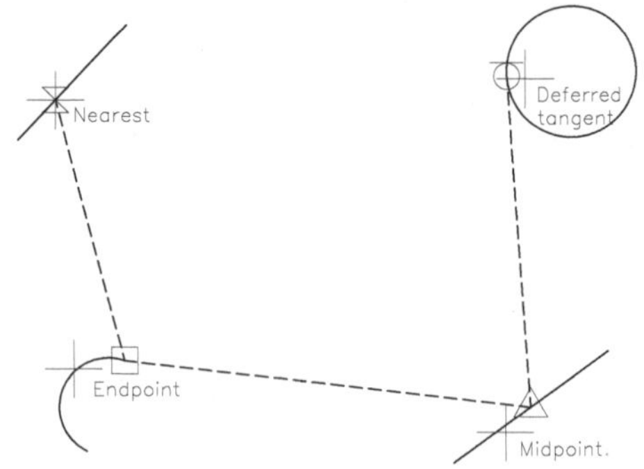

Figure 4-56 *Using the* ***Nearest, Endpoint, Midpoint,*** *and* ***Tangent*** *Object Snap modes*

Note

If the start point of a line is defined by using the ***Tangent*** *Object Snap, the tip shows* ***Deferred Tangent****. However, if you end the line using this Object Snap, the tip shows* ***Tangent****.*

Quadrant

The **Quadrant** Object Snap mode is used to snap the cursor to the quadrant point of an ellipse, an arc, or a circle. A circle has four quadrants, and each quadrant subtends an angle of 90 degrees. Therefore, the quadrant points are located at **0**, **90**, **180**, and **270**-degree positions. If the circle is inserted as a block (see Chapter 16) and rotated, the quadrant points will also be rotated by the same degree, as shown in Figure 4-57 and Figure 4-58.

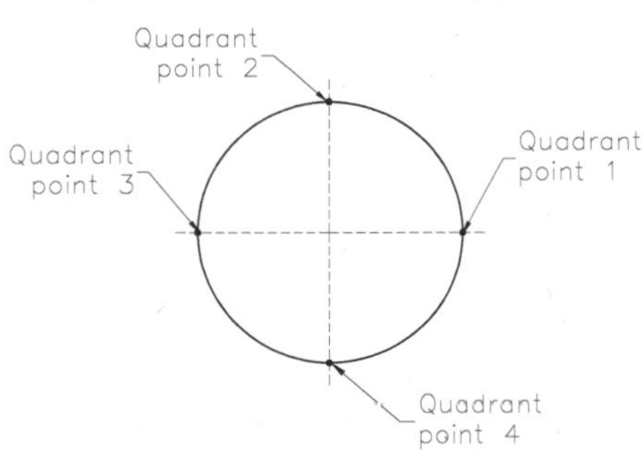

Figure 4-57 *Location of the circle quadrants*

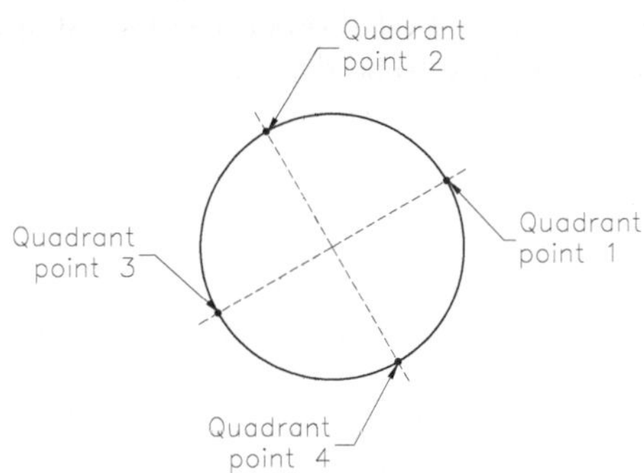

Figure 4-58 *Quadrants in a rotated circle*

To use this object snap, position the cursor on the circle or arc closest to the desired quadrant and click when the marker is displayed. Figure 4-59 shows the cursor selecting the third quadrant and the proposed line.

Intersection

The **Intersection** Object Snap mode is used to snap the cursor to a point where two or more lines, circles, ellipses, or arcs intersect. To use this mode, invoke a tool, choose the **Intersection** Object Snap and move the cursor to the desired intersection point such that the intersection is within the target box and click when the intersection marker is displayed.

Figure 4-60 shows the cursor selecting the intersection point and the proposed line is in dotted line.

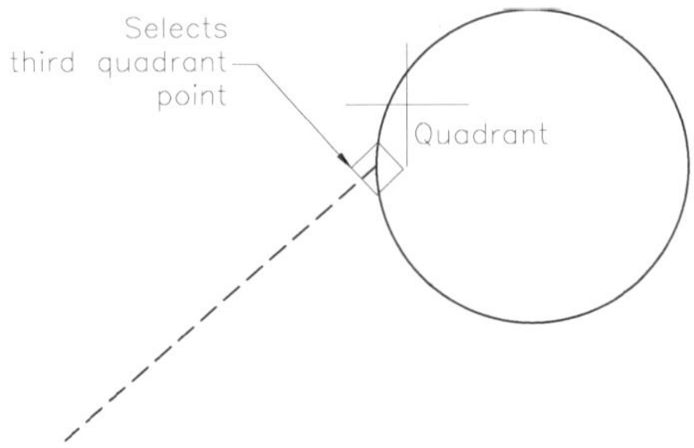

*Figure 4-59 The **Quadrant** Object Snap mode*

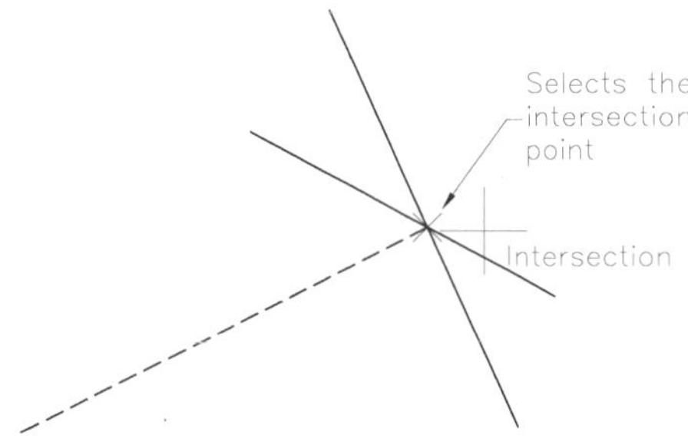

*Figure 4-60 The **Intersection** Object Snap mode*

After setting the **Intersection** Object Snap mode, if the cursor is close to an object and not close to actual intersection, the **Extended Intersection** tooltip will be displayed. If you select this object, you need to select another object. Move the cursor close to another object; the intersection point will be snapped. Left-click to select the intersection point. But if the object selected second does not intersect with the object selected first, then the cursor will snap to the extended intersection point, as shown in Figure 4-61. The extended intersections are the intersections that do not exist but are imaginary and formed if a line or an arc is extended.

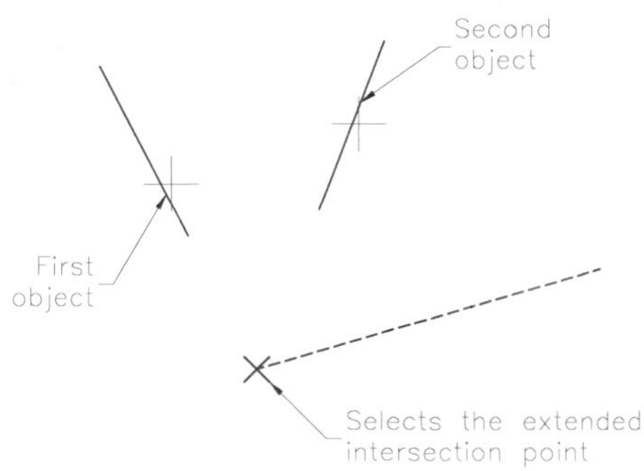

*Figure 4-61 The **Extended Intersection** Object Snap mode*

Apparent Intersection

The **Apparent Intersection** Object Snap mode is used to select the projected intersections of two objects in 3D space. Sometimes, two objects appear to intersect one another in the current view, but in 3D space they do not actually intersect. The **Apparent Intersection** snap mode is used to select such intersections. This mode works on wireframes in 3D space. If you use this object snap mode in 2D, it works like an extended intersection.

Perpendicular

The **Perpendicular** Object Snap mode is used to draw a line perpendicular to or from another line, or normal to or from an arc or a circle, or to an ellipse. After invoking the **Line** tool, if you invoke this mode and then select an object, a perpendicular line will be attached to the cursor. Move the cursor and place the line, as shown in Figure 4-62. But after invoking the **Line** tool, if you select the start point of the line first and then invoke the **Perpendicular**

Object Snap mode, you need to select an object. On doing so, AutoCAD selects a point such that the resulting line is perpendicular to the selected object, as shown in Figure 4-63.

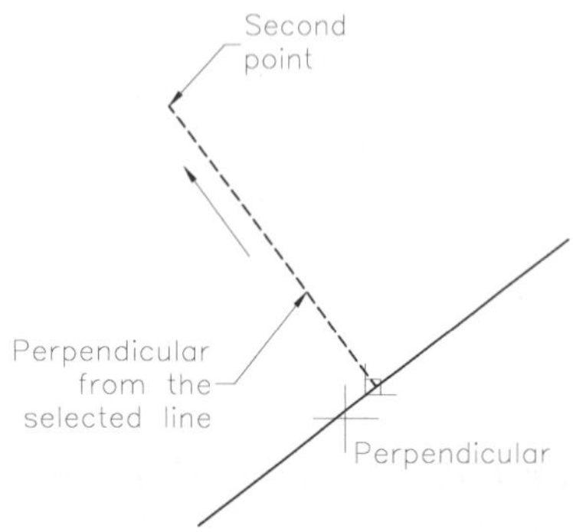

Figure 4-62 *Selecting the* ***Perpendicular*** *snap first*

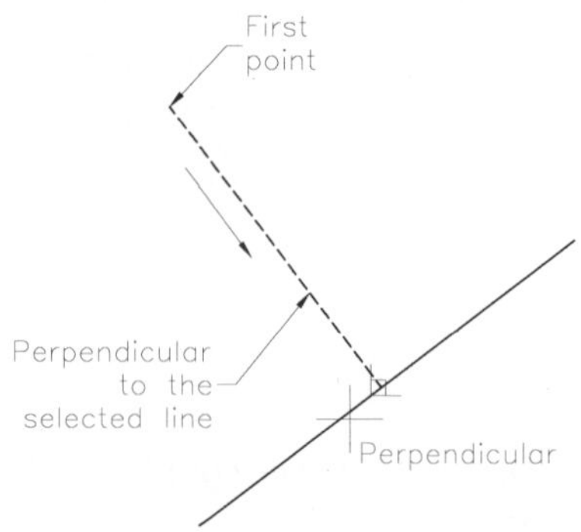

Figure 4-63 *Selecting the start point and then the* ***Perpendicular*** *snap*

Figure 4-64 shows the use of various object snap modes.

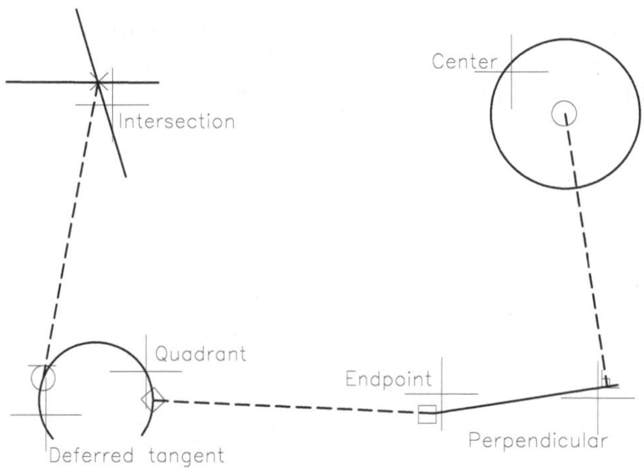

Figure 4-64 *Using various object snap modes to locate points*

Exercise 3 — Quadrant & Tangent

Draw the sketch shown in Figure 4-65. P1 and P2 are the center points of the top and bottom arcs. The space between the dotted lines is 1 unit.

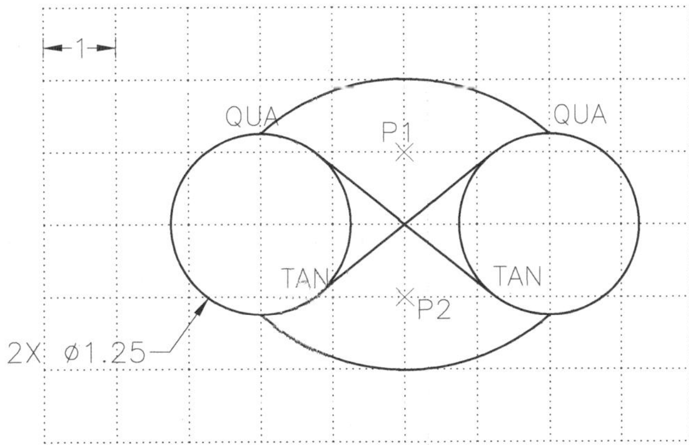

Figure 4-65 Drawing for Exercise 3

Node

You can use the **Node** Object Snap mode to snap the points placed by using the **Multiple Points**, **Divide**, or **Measure** tools. Figure 4-66 shows the three points placed by using the **Multiple Points** tool. The dotted line indicates the proposed line to be drawn and the **Node** tooltip displayed on moving the cursor close to a point.

Insertion

The **Insertion** Object Snap mode is used to snap to the insertion point of a text, shape, block, attribute, or attribute definition. The insertion point is the point with respect to which a text, shape, or a block is inserted. Figure 4-67 shows the insertion point of the text and the block. The dotted line is the proposed line to be drawn.

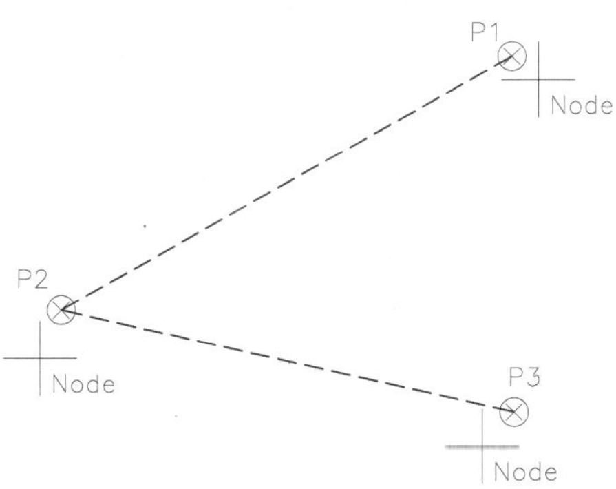

*Figure 4-66 Using the **Node** Object Snap*

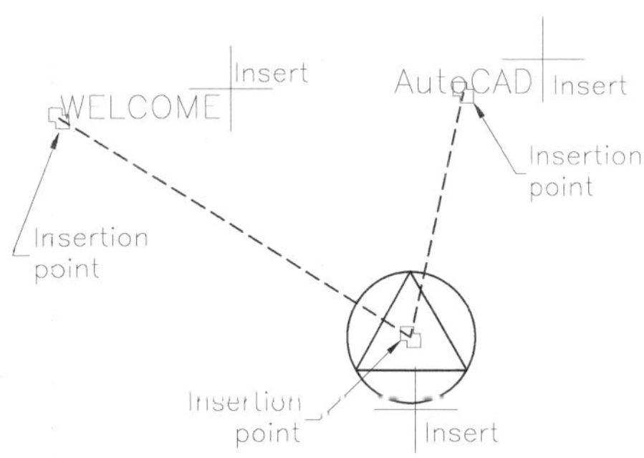

*Figure 4-67 The **Insertion** Object Snap*

Snap to None

The **Snap to None** Object Snap mode is used to turn off any running object snap (see the section "Running Object Snap Mode" that follows) for one point only. The following example illustrates the use of this Object Snap mode.

Invoke the **Drafting Settings** dialog box and choose the **Object Snap** tab. Select the **Midpoint** and **Center** check boxes. This sets the object snap to midpoint and center. Now, to draw a line whose start point is closer to the endpoint of another line, invoke the **Line** tool and move the cursor to the desired position on the previous line. The cursor automatically snaps to the midpoint of the line. You can disable this automatic snap by choosing the **Snap to None** object snap from the **Object Snap** toolbar.

Parallel

When you need to draw a line parallel to a line or a polyline, use the **Parallel** Object Snap. For example, when you are in the middle of the **Line** tool, and you have to draw a line parallel to the one already drawn, you can use the **Parallel** object snap mode as discussed next.

1. Choose **Line** from the **Draw** toolbar.
2. Select a point on the screen.
3. Choose the **Parallel** button from the **Object Snap** toolbar.
4. Move the cursor close to the reference object and pause for a while; the parallel tooltip appears on it, indicating that the line has been selected.
5. Now, move the cursor at an angle parallel to the line; an imaginary parallel line (construction line) appears, on which you can select the next point. As you move the cursor on the construction line, a tooltip with relative polar coordinates is displayed near the cursor. This helps you to select the next point. The line thus drawn is parallel to the selected object, as shown in Figure 4-68.

Extension

The **Extension** Object Snap mode is used to locate a point on the proposed extension path of a line or an arc (Figure 4-69). It can also be used with intersection to determine the extended intersection point. To snap a point by using this snap mode, choose the **Line** tool from the **Draw** toolbar, and then choose the **Snap to Extension** button from the **Object Snap** toolbar. Briefly pause at the end of the line or the arc; a small plus sign (+) or a tooltip will appear at the end of the line or the arc, indicating that it has been selected. If you move the cursor along the line, a temporary extension path will be displayed and the tooltip displays the relative polar coordinates from the end of the line. Select a point or enter a distance to begin a line and then select another point to finish the line.

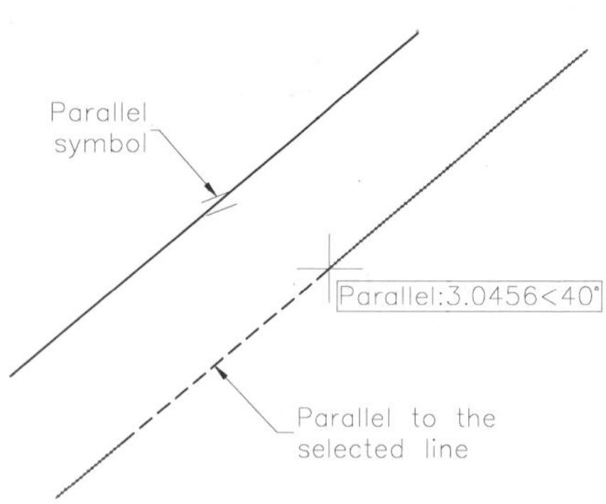

***Figure 4-68** The **Parallel** Object Snap mode*

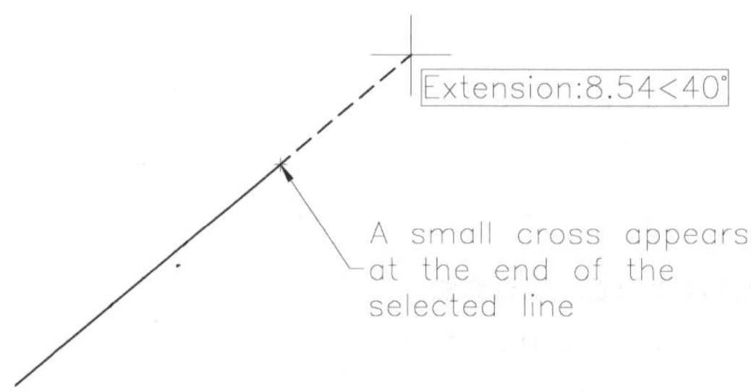

***Figure 4-69** The **Extension** Object Snap mode*

> **Tip**
>
> *1. While using the **Parallel** object snap mode, you can choose more than one line as reference line which is indicated by a plus sign. Depending upon the direction in which you move the cursor, AutoCAD will choose any one of these reference lines and the chosen line will be marked with the parallel symbol in place of the plus sign.*
>
> *2. Similarly, while using the **Extension** object snap mode, you can choose more than one endpoint as the reference.*

From

The **From** Object Snap mode is used to locate a point relative to a given point (Figure 4-70). For example, to locate a point that is 2.5 units up and 1.5 units right from the endpoint of a given line, you can use the **From** Object Snap as follows:

*Choose the **Line** tool.*
Specify first point: *Choose the **Snap From** button from the **Object Snap** toolbar.*
Specify first point: _from Base point: *Specify the base point.*
Spccify first point: _from Basc point: <Offsct>: **@1.5,2.5**

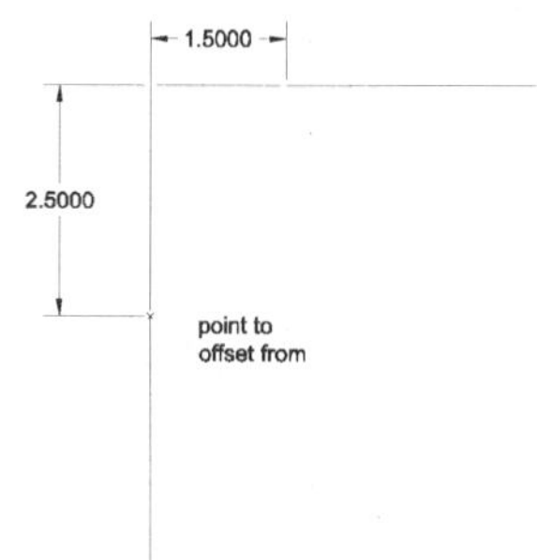

Figure 4-70 *Using the **From** Object Snap mode to locate a point*

> **Note**
>
> *The **From** Object Snap mode cannot be used as the running object snap.*

Geometric Center

The **Geometric center** Object Snap mode is used to snap the cursor to the Geometric center point of the Geometric entities. After choosing this option, move the cursor on the Geometric entity; a marker will be displayed at the Geometric center of the entity. Figure 4-71 shows the cursor snapping the Geometric center of a Rectangle.

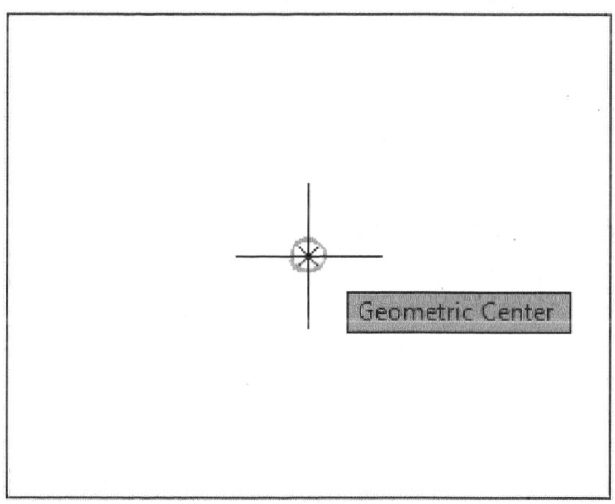

Figure 4-71 *The **Geometric center** Object Snap mode*

Mid Between 2 Points

This Object Snap mode is used to select the midpoint of an imaginary line drawn between two selected points. Note that this Object Snap mode can only be invoked from the shortcut menu. To understand the working of this Object Snap mode, refer to the sketch shown in Figure 4-72. In this sketch, there are two circles and you need to draw another circle with the center point at the midpoint of an imaginary line drawn between the center points of two existing circles. The following is the prompt sequence:

*Choose the **Center, Radius** tool*
Specify center point for circle or [3P/2P/Ttr (tan tan radius)]: *Right-click and choose **Mid Between 2 Points** from the **Snap Overrides** cascading menu*
_m2p First point of mid: *Snap the center of the left circle*
Second point of mid: *Snap the center of the right circle*
Specify radius of circle or [Diameter] <current>: *Specify the radius of the new circle*

Temporary Track Point

The **Temporary track point** is used to locate a point with respect to two different points. If you choose this button and then select a point and move the cursor, an orthogonal imaginary line will be displayed either horizontally or vertically. Then, you need to select another point to display another orthogonal imaginary line in the other direction. The required point will be located where these two imaginary lines intersect. You can also use this option along with the other Object Snap modes. To locate a point, invoke the **Line** tool from the **Draw** toolbar and then use the temporary tracking as follows.

Specify first point: *Choose the **Temporary track point** button from the **Object Snap** toolbar.*
Specify temporary OTRACK point: *Choose the **Snap to Midpoint** button from the **Object Snap** toolbar.*
Select the midpoint of the line and move the cursor horizontally toward the right.
Specify first point: *Choose the **Temporary Tracking Point** button from the **Object Snap** toolbar.*
Specify temporary OTRACK point: *Choose the **Snap to Endpoint** button from the **Object Snap** toolbar.*
Select the upper endpoint of the line and move the cursor vertically down.

As you move the cursor down, both the horizontal and vertical imaginary lines will be displayed, as shown in Figure 4-73. Select their intersection point and then draw the line.

Combining Object Snap Modes

You can also combine the snaps from the command line by separating the snap modes with a comma. In this case, AutoCAD searches for the specified modes and grabs the point on the object that is closest to the point where the object is selected. The prompt sequence for using the **Midpoint** and **Endpoint** object snaps is given next.

*Choose the **Line** tool*
LINE Specify first point: **MID, END** Enter *(MIDpoint or ENDpoint object snap.)*
Of: *Select the object*

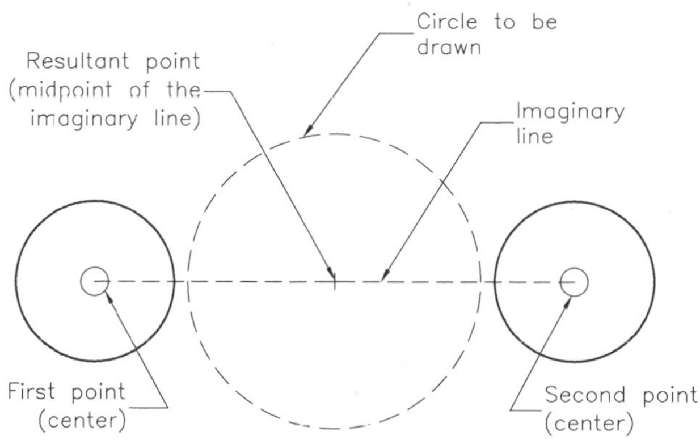

Figure 4-72 *Using the **Midpoint Between 2 Points** Object Snap mode to locate a point*

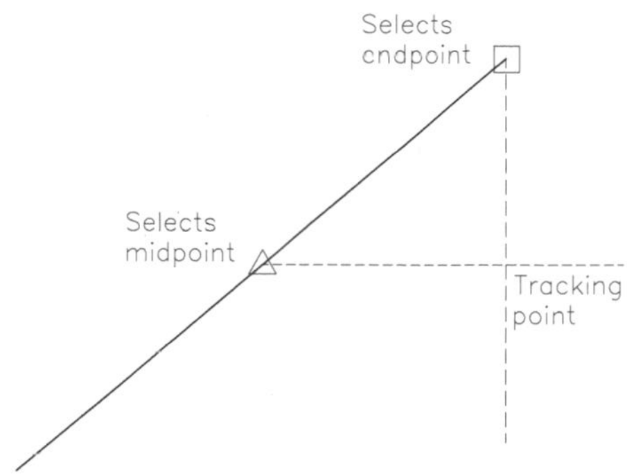

Figure 4-73 *Using temporary tracking point*

Note

In reference to object snaps, "line" generally includes xlines, rays, and polyline segments, and "arc" generally includes polyarc segments.

Exercise 4

Draw the sketch shown in Figure 4-74. The space between the dotted lines is 1 unit.

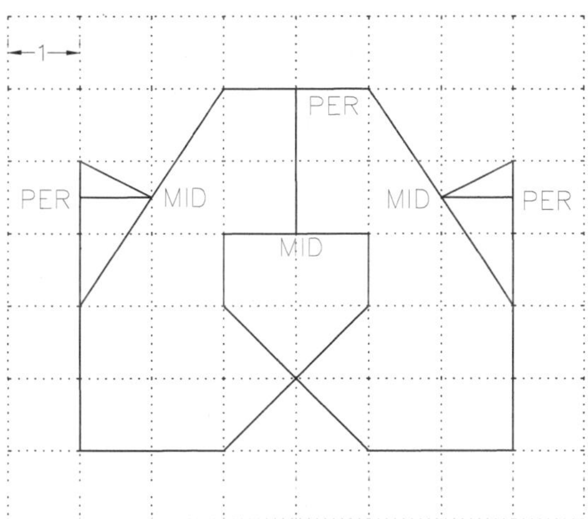

Figure 4-74 *Drawing for Exercise 4*

Using Coordinate Filters

Coordinate filters are also known as Point filters and allow you to align objects by filtering the coordinate of the existing geometrics.

To invoke the point/coordinate filters (.X, .Y, .Z, .XY, .XZ, and .YZ filters), press the SHIFT key and then right click; a shortcut menu will be invoked. Next, move the cursor over the **Point Filters** option; a cascading menu will be displayed. In this cascading menu, you can select the required type of filter. On invoking the **.X** point filter, you can click on a point in the drawing area whose X coordinate needs to be defined. After defining the X coordinate, you will be prompted to define Y or Z coordinate. Click on another point in the drawing area to define the Y or Z coordinate.

For example, if you want to draw a circle at the center of a rectangle, you can use the point filters. To do so, invoke the **Circle**, **Radius** tool and then press the SHIFT key and right click to invoke the shortcut menu. Next, move the cursor over the **Point Filter** option, a cascading menu appears. Select the **.X** option; you will be prompted to specify the X coordinate (**.X** of). Click on the midpoint of a horizontal line; you will be prompted to specify the y coordinate [**.X** of (need **YZ**)]. Click on the midpoint of a vertical line; the center point of the circle is specified. Next, specify the radius or diameter of the circle by entering a value at the command prompt; the circle will be created.

RUNNING OBJECT SNAP MODE

Toolbar: Object Snap > Osnap Settings **Command:** OS/OSNAP

In the previous sections, you learned to use object snaps to snap to different points of an object. The object snaps are to be selected from the toolbar or from the shortcut menu. One of the drawbacks of this method is that you have to select them every time, even if you are using the same snap mode again. This problem can be resolved by using Running Osnap. The Running Osnap can be invoked by using the **Object Snap** tab of the **Drafting Settings** dialog box, as shown in Figure 4-75. If you choose the **Osnap Settings** button from the toolbar, or enter **OSNAP** at the command prompt, or choose **Settings** from the shortcut menu displayed on right-clicking on the **OSNAP** button in the Status Bar, then the **Object Snap** tab will be displayed in the **Drafting Settings** dialog box. In this tab, you can set the running object snap modes by selecting the check boxes next to the snap modes. For example, to set **Endpoint** as the running Object Snap mode, select the **Endpoint** check box and then the **OK** button to exit the dialog box.

Once you set the running Object Snap mode, a marker will be displayed when you move the crosshairs over the key points. If you have selected a combination of modes, AutoCAD selects the mode that is closest to the crosshairs. For example, if you have selected the **Endpoint**, **Midpoint**, and **Center** check boxes in the dialog box and move the cursor over a line, the endpoint or the midpoint will be displayed, depending upon the position of the crosshair. Similarly, if you place the cursor over the circumference of a circle, the center will be displayed. The running Object Snap mode can be turned on or off without losing the object snap settings by choosing the **OSNAP** button in the Status Bar. You can also accomplish this by pressing the function key F3 or CTRL+F keys.

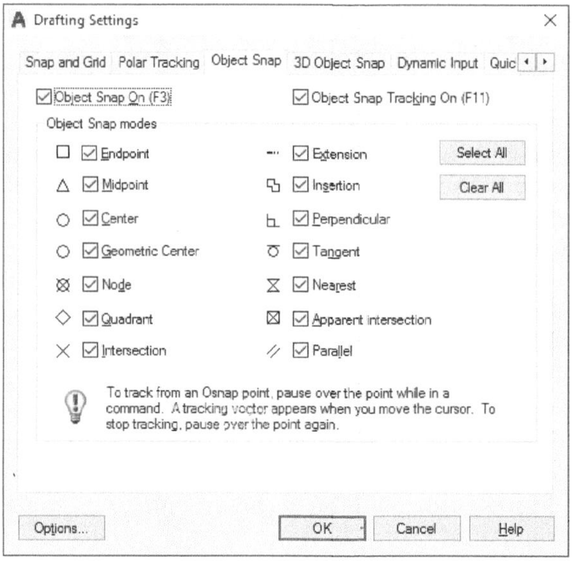

Figure 4-75 The ***Drafting Settings*** *dialog box (****Object Snap*** *tab)*

Overriding the Running Snap

When you select the running object snaps, all other Object Snap modes are ignored unless you select another Object Snap mode. Once you select a different osnap mode, the running OSNAP mode is temporarily overruled. After the operation has been performed, the running OSNAP mode becomes active again. If you want to discontinue the current running Object Snap mode completely, choose the **Clear All** button in the **Drafting Settings** dialog box. If you want to temporarily disable the running object snap, choose the **OSNAP** button (off position) in the Status Bar.

If you override the running object snap modes for a point selection and do not find a point to satisfy the override Object Snap mode, AutoCAD displays a message to this effect. For example, if you specify an override Object Snap mode of Center and no circle, ellipse, or arc is found at that location, AutoCAD will display the message "**Point or option keyword required**".

Cycling through Snaps

AutoCAD displays the geometric marker corresponding to the shapes shown in the **Object Snap** tab of the **Drafting Settings** dialog box. You can use the TAB key to cycle through the snaps. For example, if you have a circle with an intersecting rectangle, as shown in Figure 4-76 and you want to snap to one of the geometric points on the circle, you can use the TAB key to cycle through geometric points. The geometric points for a circle are the center point, quadrant points, and intersecting points with the rectangle. To snap to one of these points, first you need to set the running object snaps (center, quadrant, and intersection object snaps) in the **Drafting Settings** dialog box. Then, invoke a tool and move the cursor over the objects; AutoSnap displays a marker and a tooltip. You can cycle through the snap points by pressing the TAB key. For example, if you press the TAB key while the aperture box is on the circle and the rectangle (near the lower left intersection point), the intersection, center, and quadrant points will be displayed one by one. Left-click to select the required key point.

Setting the Priority for Coordinate Entry

Sometimes you may want the keyboard entry to take precedence over the running Object Snap modes. This is useful when you want to locate a point that is close to the running osnap. By default, when you specify the coordinates (by using the keyboard) of a point located near a running osnap, AutoCAD ignores the point and snaps to the running osnap. For example, if you have selected the **Intersection** object snap in the **Object Snap** tab of the **Drafting Settings** dialog box and if you enter the coordinates of the endpoint of a line very close to the intersection point, refer to Figure 4-77 (a), the line will snap to the intersection point and ignore the keyboard entry point.

Therefore, to set the priority between the keyboard entry and the object snap, select the **Keyboard entry** radio button in the **User Preferences** tab of the **Options** dialog box, see Figure 4-78, and then choose **OK**. Now, if you enter the coordinates of the endpoint of a line very close to the intersection point, refer to Figure 4-77 (b), the start point will snap to the coordinates specified and the running osnap (intersection) is ignored. This setting is stored in the **OSNAPCOORD** system variable and you can also set the priority through this variable. A value **0** gives priority to running osnap, value **1** gives priority to the keyboard entry, and value **2** gives priority to the keyboard entry except scripts.

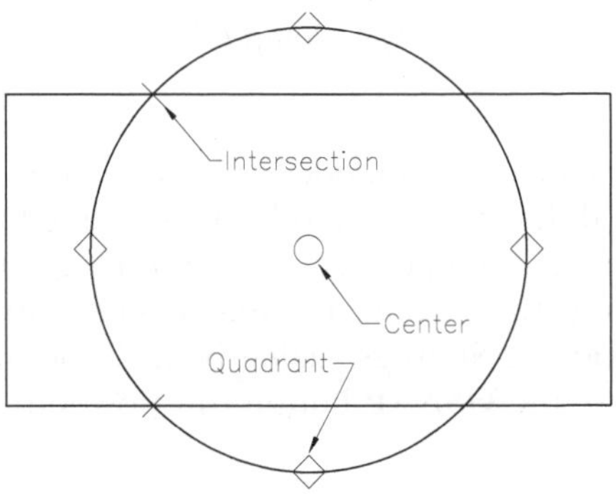

Figure 4-76 *Using the TAB key to cycle through the snaps*

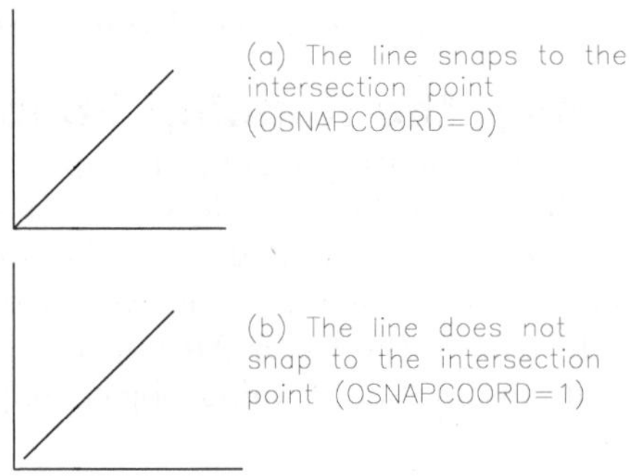

Figure 4-77 *Setting the coordinate entry priority*

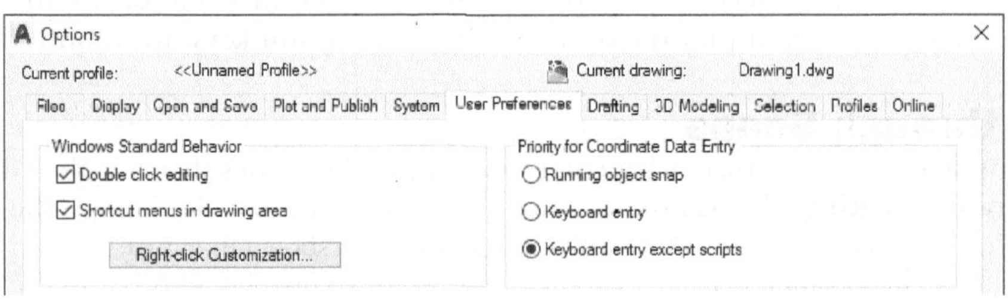

Figure 4-78 *Setting priority for coordinate data entry in the* ***Options*** *dialog box*

Tip

If you do not want the running osnap to take precedence over the keyboard entry, you can simply disable the running osnap temporarily by choosing the ***OSNAP*** *button in the Status Bar. Now, you can specify a point close to a running osnap without changing the settings for coordinate entry in the* ***Options*** *dialog box.*

USING AUTOTRACKING

While using AutoTracking, the cursor moves along temporary paths to locate key points in a drawing. It can be used to locate points with respect to other points or objects in the drawing. There are two types of AutoTracking options: Object Snap Tracking and Polar Tracking.

Object Snap Tracking

Object Snap Tracking is used to track the movement of the cursor along the alignment paths based on the Object Snap points (running osnaps) selected in the **Object Snap** tab of the **Drafting Settings** dialog box. You can set the object snap tracking on by selecting the **Object Snap Tracking On (F11)** check box in the **Object Snap** tab of the **Drafting Settings** dialog box or by choosing the **Object Snap Tracking** button in the Status Bar or by using the function key F11.

The direction of a path is determined by the motion of the cursor or the point you select on an object. For example, to draw a circle whose center is located at the intersection of the imaginary lines passing through the center of two existing circles (Figure 4-79), you can use AutoTracking. To do so, select **Center** check box in the **Object Snap** tab of the **Drafting Settings** dialog box and turn on the **Object Snap** button in the Status Bar. Now, activate the object tracking by choosing the **Object Snap Tracking** button in the Status Bar. Choose the **Center,Radius** option from the **Draw** toolbar and pause the cursor at the center of the first circle till the marker or a plus sign is displayed. Then, move it horizontally to get the imaginary horizontal line. Move the cursor toward the second circle; the horizontal path disappears. Now, place the cursor for a while at the center of the second circle and move it vertically to get the imaginary vertical line. Move the cursor along the vertical alignment path and when you are in line with the other circle, the horizontal path will also be displayed. Select the intersection of the two alignment paths. The selected point becomes the center of the circle. Then, enter radius or specify a point.

Similarly, you can use AutoTracking in combination with the **Midpoint** object snap to locate the center of the rectangle and then draw a circle, refer to Figure 4-80.

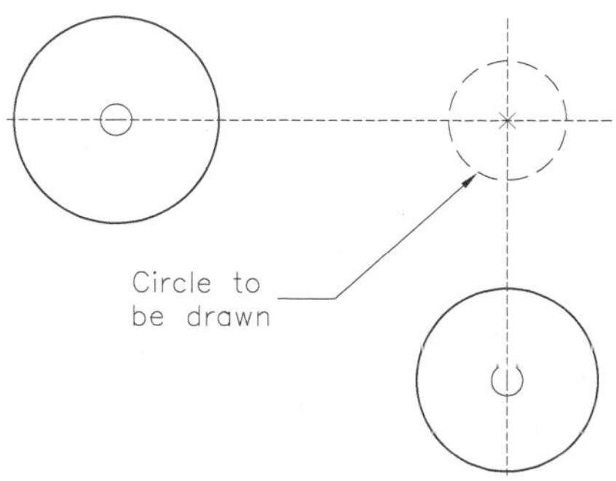

***Figure 4-79** Using **AutoTracking** to locate a point (center of circle)*

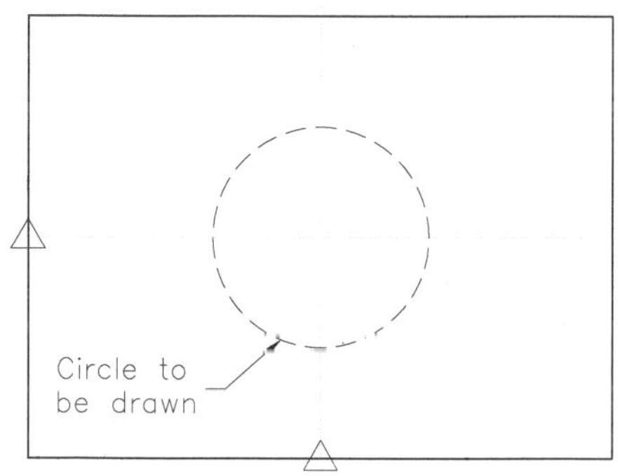

***Figure 4-80** Using **AutoTracking** to locate a point (midpoint of rectangle)*

Note

*Object tracking works only when **OSNAP** is on and some running object snaps have been set.*

Polar Tracking

Polar Tracking is used to locate points on an angular alignment path. Polar tracking can be selected by choosing the **Polar Tracking** button in the Status Bar by using the function key F10, or by selecting the **Polar Tracking On (F10)** check box in the **Polar Tracking** tab of the **Drafting Settings** dialog box, as shown in Figure 4-81. Polar Tracking constrains the movement of the cursor along a path that is based on the polar angle settings. For example, if the **Increment angle** list box value is set to 15-degree in the **Polar Angle Settings** area, the cursor will move along the alignment paths that are multiples of 15-degree (0, 15, 30, 45, 60, and so on) and a tooltip will be displayed specifying the distance and angle. Selecting the **Additional angles** check box and choosing the **New** button allows you to add an additional angle value. The imaginary path will also be displayed at these new angles, apart from the increments of the increment angle selected.

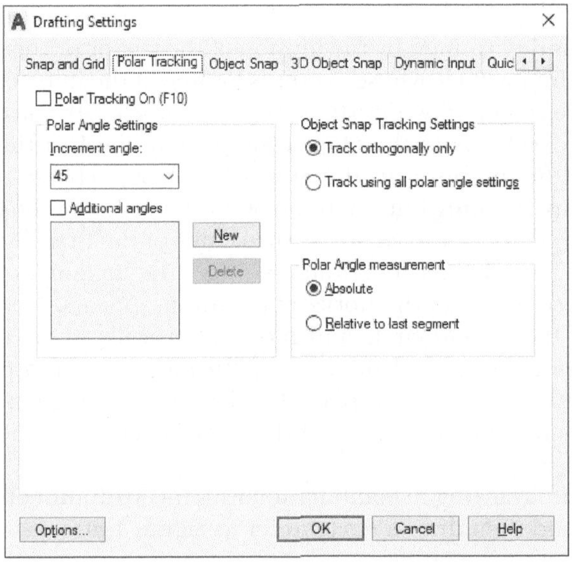

*Figure 4-81 The **Polar Tracking** tab in the **Drafting Settings** dialog box*

For example, if the increment angle is set to **15** and you add an additional angle of **22**, the imaginary path will be displayed at 0, 15, 22, 30, 45, and the increments of 15. Polar tracking is used only when the Ortho mode is off.

In the **Drafting Settings** dialog box (**Polar Tracking** tab), you can set the polar tracking to absolute or relative to the last segment. If you select the **Absolute** radio button, the base angle is taken from 0. If you select the **Relative to last segment** radio button, the base angle for the increments is set to the last segment drawn. You can also use Polar tracking together with Object tracking. You can select the **Track using all polar angle settings** radio button in the dialog box.

AutoTrack Settings

You have different settings while working with autotracking. These settings can be specified in the **Drafting** tab of the **Options** dialog box, as shown in Figure 4-82. If you choose the **Options** button in the **Polar Tracking** tab of the **Drafting Settings** dialog box, the **Options** dialog box with the **Drafting** tab chosen will be displayed. You can use the **Display polar tracking vector** check box to toggle the display of the angle alignment path for Polar tracking. You can also use the **Display full-screen tracking vector** check box to toggle the display of a full-screen construction line for Otrack. You can use the **Display Auto Track tooltip** check box to toggle the display of tooltips with the paths. You can also use the **TRACKPATH** system variable to define the path display settings.

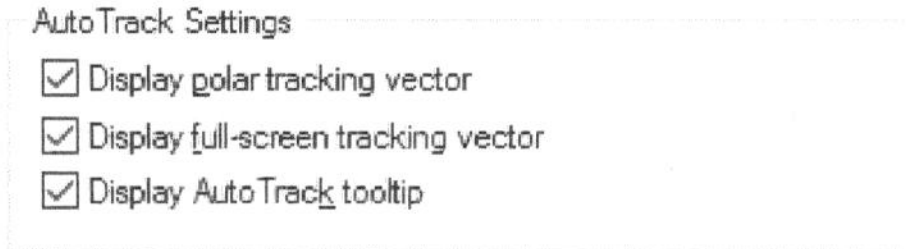

Figure 4-82 *The **AutoTrack Settings** area in the **Options** dialog box (**Drafting** tab)*

Tip

*You need the **Options** dialog box quite frequently to change different drafting settings. To invoke this dialog box, choose the **Options** button from the **Drafting Settings** dialog box; the **Options** dialog box will be displayed with the **Drafting** tab chosen. After making changes in the dialog box, choose the **OK** button to get back to the **Drafting Settings** dialog box.*

FUNCTION AND CONTROL KEYS

You can also use the function and control keys to change the status of the coordinate display, Snap, Ortho, Osnap, tablet, screen, isometric planes, running Object Snap, Grid, Polar, and Object tracking. The following is a list of functions and their control keys.

F1 Help
F2 Graphics Screen/AutoCAD Text Window
F3 Osnap On/Off (CTRL+F)
F4 3DOsnap On/Off
F5 Isoplane top/right/left (CTRL+E)
F6 Dynamic UCS On/Off (CTRL+D)
F7 Grid On/Off (CTRL+G)
F8 Ortho On/Off (CTRL+L)
F9 Snap On/Off (CTRL+B)
F10 Polar tracking On/Off
F11 Object Snap tracking
F12 Dynamic Input On/Off

Self-Evaluation Test

Answer the following questions and then compare them to those given at the end of this chapter:

1. You can change the plot style mode from the command prompt by using the __________ system variable.

2. The __________ button enables you to set up an invisible grid that allows the cursor to move in fixed increments from one snap point to another.

3. The __________ snap works along with polar and object tracking only.

4. The __________ Object Snap mode is used to select the projected or visual intersections of two objects in 3D space.

5. The __________ can be used to locate a point with respect to two different points.

6. You can set the priority between the keyboard entry and the object snap through the __________ tab of the **Options** dialog box.

7. The layers that are turned off are displayed on the screen but cannot be plotted. (T/F)

8. The drawing in which you are working should be in the named plot style mode (*.stb*) to make the plot style available in the **LAYER PROPERTIES MANAGER**. (T/F)

9. The grid pattern appears within the drawing limits which help define the working area. (T/F)

10. If a circle is inserted as a rotated block, the quadrant points are not rotated by the same amount. (T/F)

Review Questions

Answer the following questions:

1. Which of the following options is not displayed in the shortcut menu displayed on right-clicking on a layer in the **LAYER PROPERTIES MANAGER** when you select more than one layer by using the SHIFT key?

   (a) **New Layer** (b) **Select All**
   (c) **Make Current** (d) **Clear All**

2. Which of the following function keys acts as a toggle key for turning the grid display on or off?

   (a) F5 (b) F6
   (c) F7 (d) F8

3. Which one of the following object snap modes is used to turn off any running object snap for one point only?

   (a) **NODE** (b) **NONE**
   (c) **FROM** (d) **NEAREST**

4. Which of the following object snap modes cannot be used as the running object snap?

   (a) **EXTENSION** (b) **PARALLEL**
   (c) **FROM** (d) **NODE**

5. Which of the following keys can be used to cycle through different running object snaps?

   (a) ENTER (b) SHIFT
   (c) CTRL (d) TAB

6. While working on a drawing, you can save all layers with their current properties settings anytime under one name and then restore them later using the __________ button in the **LAYER PROPERTIES MANAGER**.

7. You can use the __________ window to locate the drawing data with the help of the search tools and then use it in your drawing.

8. The __________ function key is used to turn on/off the Osnap.

9. The difference between the usage of the **Off** option and the **Freeze** option is that in the **Freeze** option, the frozen layers are not __________ by the computer while regenerating the drawing.

10. The size of the aperture is measured in __________.

11. In the **Extension** object snap mode, when you move the cursor along a path, a temporary extension path and the tooltip is displayed with the cursor. The tooltip displays __________ coordinates from the end of the line.

12. You cannot enter different values for the horizontal and vertical grid spacing. (T/F)

13. You can lock a layer to prevent a user from accidentally editing the objects in it. (T/F)

14. When a layer is locked, you cannot use the objects in it for Osnaps. (T/F)

15. The thickness given to the objects in a layer by using the **Lineweight** option is displayed on the screen and can be plotted. (T/F)

Exercise 5 — *Line type and Object Color*

Set up layers with the following linetypes and colors. Then make the drawing, as shown in Figure 4-83. The distance between the dotted lines is 1.0 unit.

Layer name	Color	Linetype
Object	Red	Continuous
Hidden	Yellow	Hidden
Center	Green	Center

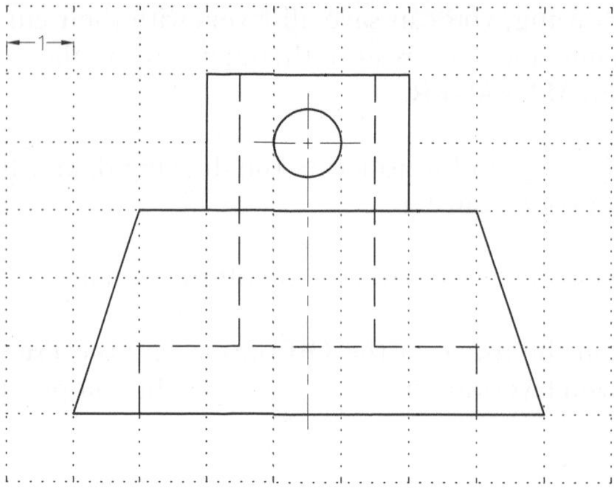

Figure 4-83 *Drawing for Exercise 5*

Exercise 6 — *Line type and Object Color*

Set up layers, linetypes, and colors and then make the drawing shown in Figure 4-84. The distance between the dotted lines is 1.0 unit.

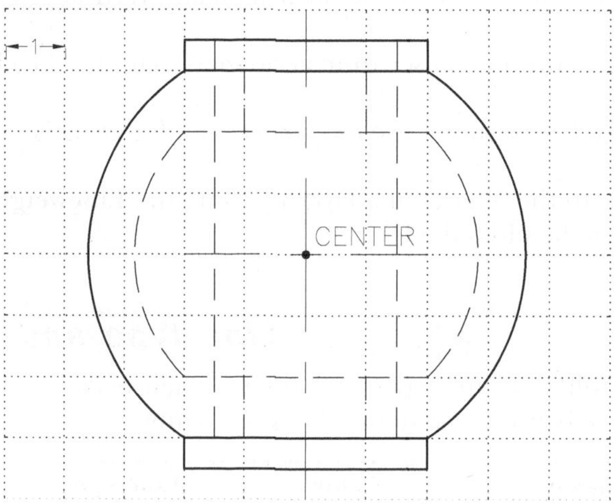

Figure 4-84 *Drawing for Exercise 6*

Exercise 7 Line type and Object Color

Set up layers, linetypes, and colors and then make the drawing shown in Figure 4-85. Use the object snaps as indicated.

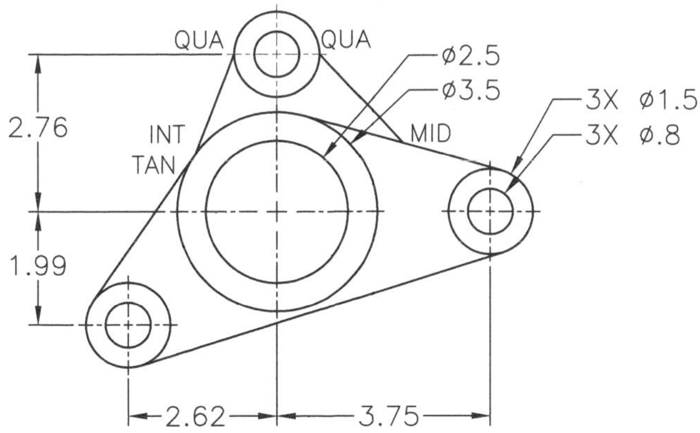

Figure 4-85 Drawing for Exercise 7

Problem-Solving Exercise 1

Draw the object shown in Figure 4-86. First draw the lines and then draw the arcs using the appropriate Arc tools.

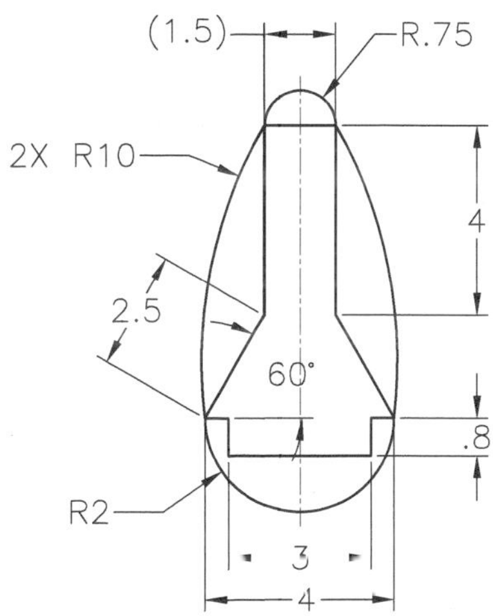

Figure 4-86 Drawing for Problem-Solving Exercise 1

Problem-Solving Exercise 2

Draw the object shown in Figure 4-87. First draw the front view (bottom left) and then the side and top views.

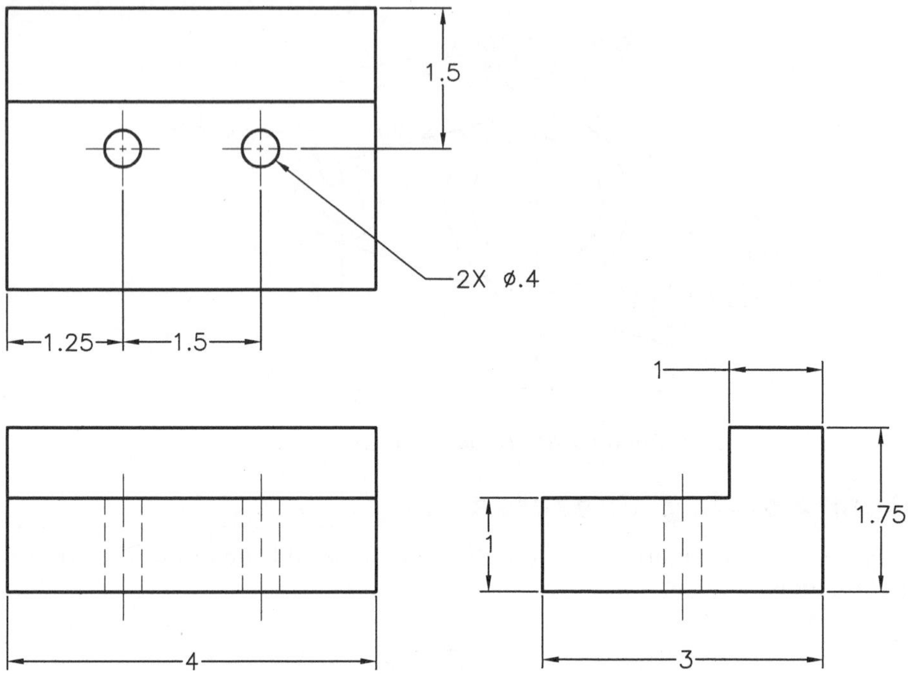

Figure 4-87 Drawing for Problem-Solving Exercise 2

Problem-Solving Exercise 3

Draw the sketch shown in Figure 4-88 in the paper space area of the **Manufacturing Metric** template. Note that the dimensions are given only for your reference.

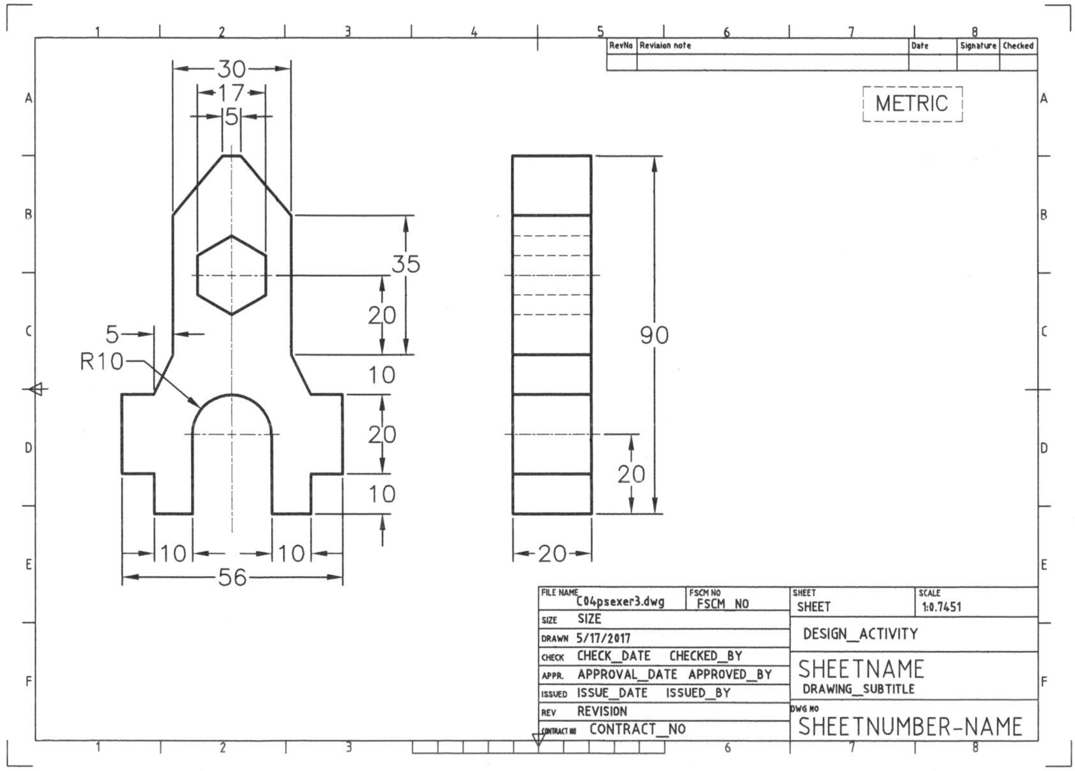

Figure 4-88 *Drawing for Problem-Solving Exercise 3*

Problem-Solving Exercise 4

Set up layers, linetypes, and colors and then make the drawing shown in Figure 4-89.

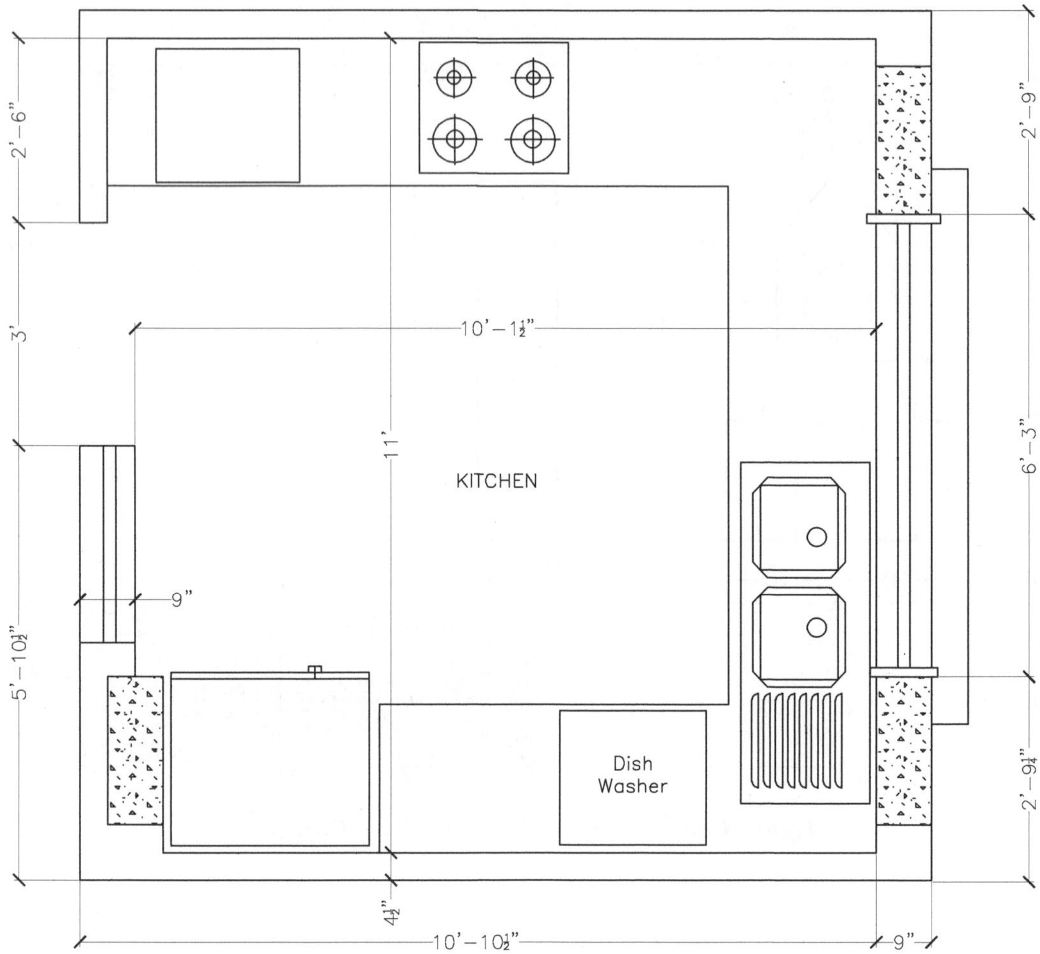

Figure 4-89 Drawing for Problem-Solving Exercise 4

Answers to Self-Evaluation Test

1. CPLOTSTYLE, **2. SNAP**, **3.** Polar, **4. Apparent Intersection**, **5.** Temporary Tracking, **6. User Preferences**, **7.** F, **8.** T, **9.** T, **10.** F

Chapter 5

Editing Sketched Objects-I

Learning Objectives

After completing this chapter, you will be able to:

- *Create selection sets using various object selection options*
- *Use the Move and Copy tools*
- *Copy objects using the Array tool*
- *Understand various editing and measuring tools*

Key Terms

- *Move*
- *Copy*
- *Break*
- *Offset*
- *Chamfer*
- *Trim*
- *Extend*
- *Stretch*
- *Array*
- *Rotate*
- *Mirror*
- *Scale*
- *Lengthen*
- *Measure*
- *Divide*
- *Blend*

CREATING A SELECTION SET

For most of the tools, the default object selection method is to use the pick box (cursor) and select one entity at a time. You can also click in blank area and select objects by using the **Window** option or the **Crossing** option. In Chapter 2, these two options were discussed. The other options used for selection are listed below and are discussed in this chapter.

Last	CPolygon	Add	Undo	Previous	SUbobject
Fence	Box	SIngle	ALL	Group	AUto
WPolygon	Remove	Multiple	Object		

Last

This option is used to select the last drawn object, which is partially or fully visible in the current display. This is the most suitable option to select the last drawn object while editing it. Keep in mind that if the last drawn object is not in the current display, the last drawn object in the current display will be selected. Although a selection can be made using the **Last** option, only one object is selected at a time. However, you can use the **Last** option a number of times but it will require you to start the command again. You can use the **Last** selection option with any tool that requires the selection of multiple objects (for example, **Copy**, **Move**, and **Erase**). To select the last drawn object by using this option, invoke a particular tool, and then enter **LAST** or **L** at the **Select objects** prompt to use this object selection method.

Exercise 1 — *Erase*

Draw the profile shown in Figure 5-1(a) by using the **Line** tool. Then, use the **Last** option of the **Erase** tool to erase the three most recently drawn lines to obtain Figure 5-1(d).

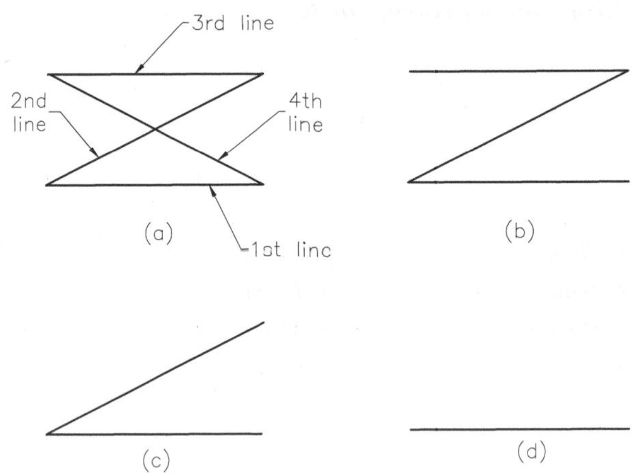

Figure 5-1 The initial and final profiles for Exercise 1

Previous

The **Previous** option is used to select the objects that were selected in the previous selection set. Generally, AutoCAD saves the previous selection set; therefore, you can select those objects again by using the **Previous** option, instead of invoking the same selection method. In other words, with the help of the **Previous** option, you can select the previous set without selecting the objects individually. The prompt sequence for doing so is given next.

*Choose the **Copy** tool from the **Modify** panel*
Select objects: *Select the objects* Enter
Specify base point or [Displacement mOde] <Displacement>: *Specify the base point*
Specify second point or [Array] <use first point as displacement>: *Specify the point for displacement*
*Choose the **Move** tool from the **Modify** panel*
Select objects: **P** Enter
found

The previous selection set is cleared by various deletion operations and the tools associated with them, like **Undo**. You cannot select objects in the model space and then use the same selection set in the paper space, or vice versa. This is because AutoCAD keeps the record of the space (paper space or model space), in which the individual selection set is created.

WPolygon

This option is similar to the **Window** option with the only difference that by using this option, you can define a window consisting of an irregular polygon. You can specify the selection area by specifying points around the object that you want to select, refer to Figure 5-2. Similar to the window method, the objects to be selected by using this method should be completely enclosed within the polygon. The polygon is formed as you specify points and can take any shape except a self-intersecting profile. The last segment of the polygon is automatically drawn to close the polygon. The polygon can be created by specifying the coordinates of the points or by specifying the points with the help of a pointing device. With the **Undo** option, the most recently specified WPolygon point can be undone. To use the **WPolygon** option with the object selection tools such as **Erase**, **Move**, **Copy**, invoke a tool, enter **WP** at the **Select objects** prompt, and then specify the vertices of the polygon.

Exercise 2 — *WPolygon*

Draw several objects, select some of them using the **WPolygon** option, and then erase them.

CPolygon

This option is similar to the **Window** option with the only difference that by using this option you can define a window consisting of an irregular polygon. The procedure to create a polygon is the same as discussed above. In this option, in addition to the objects that are completely enclosed within the polygon, an object lying partially inside the polygon or even touching it are also selected, refer to Figure 5-3.

CPolygon is formed as you specify the points. The points can be specified at the Command line or by specifying points using the mouse. Just as in the **WPolygon** option, the crossing polygon can take any shape except a self-intersecting profile. As the last segment of the polygon is drawn automatically, the CPolygon is closed at all times.

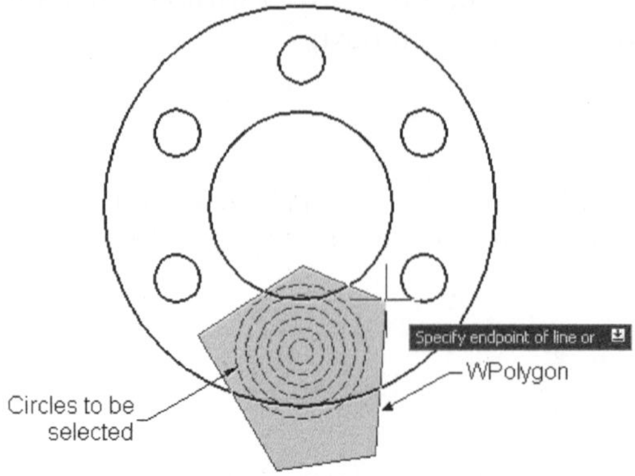

Figure 5-2 *Selecting objects using the* ***WPolygon*** *option*

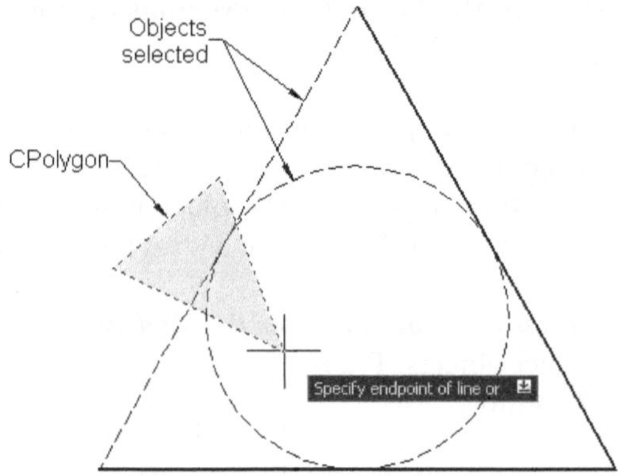

Figure 5-3 *Selecting objects using the* ***CPolygon*** *option*

Remove

The **Remove** option is used to remove the objects from a selection set, but not from the drawing. The following is the prompt sequence used for removing the objects from the selection set shown in Figure 5-4.

Choose the ***Erase*** *tool from the* ***Modify*** *panel of the* ***Home*** *tab*
Select objects: *Select objects (a), (b), and (c)*
Select objects: **R** Enter
Remove objects: *Select object (a)*
1 found, 1 removed, 2 total
Remove objects: Enter

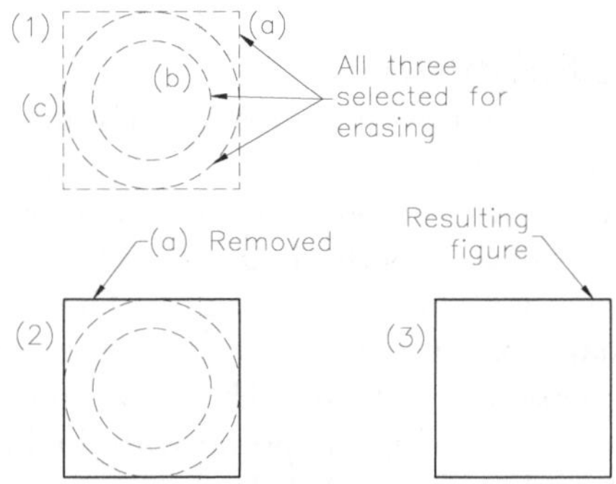

Figure 5-4 *Removing objects using the* ***Remove*** *option*

Tip
Objects can also be removed from a selection set by using the SHIFT key. For example, pressing the SHIFT key and selecting an object (a) with the pointing device will remove the object from the selection set. On doing so, the message: ***1 found, 1 removed, 2 total*** *will be displayed.*

Add

You can use the **Add** option to add objects to a selection set. When you start creating a selection set, you are in the **Add** mode. Once you create a selection set by using any selection method, you can add more objects by simply selecting them with the pointing device, if the system variable **PICKADD** is set to 2 (default). If it is set to 0, you need to press the SHIFT key and then select the objects to add objects to the selection set.

ALL

The **ALL** selection option is used to select all objects in the current working environment of the current drawing. Note that the objects in the "OFF" layers can also be selected by using the **ALL** option. However, you cannot select the objects that are in the frozen layers by using this method. You can use this selection option with only those tools that require object selection. After invoking a tool, enter **ALL** at the **Select objects** prompt. Once you enter this option, all the objects drawn on the screen will be highlighted. For example, if there are four objects on the screen and you want to erase all of them, follow the prompt sequence given next.

*Choose the **Erase** tool from the **Modify** panel of the **Home** tab*
Select objects: **ALL** Enter
4 found
Select objects: Enter

You can also use this option in combination with the other selection options. For example, consider that there are five objects on the drawing screen and you want to erase three of them. To do so, invoke the **Erase** tool, enter **ALL** at the **Select objects** prompt. Then, press the SHIFT key and select the two objects that you want to remove from the selection set. Next, press ENTER; the remaining three objects will be erased.

Fence

In the **Fence** option, a selection set is created by drawing an open polyline through the objects to be selected. In such a case, any object touched by the polyline is selected, refer to Figure 5-5. The selection fence can be created by entering the coordinates at the Command line or by specifying the points with the pointing device. With this option, more flexibility of selection is provided because a fence can intersect itself. The **Undo** option can be used to undo the most recently selected fence point. Like the other selection options, this option is also used with the tools that need an object selection. The prompt sequence to use the **Fence** option after choosing the **Erase** tool is given next.

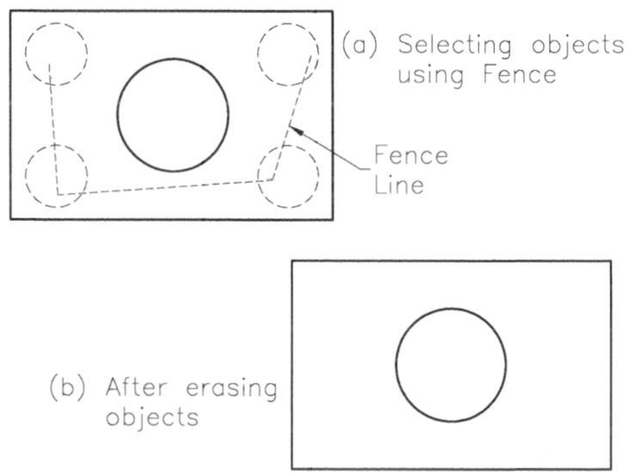

***Figure 5-5** Erasing objects using the **Fence** option*

Select objects: **F** Enter
Specify first fence point or pick/drag cursor: *Specify the first point*
Specify next fence point or [Undo]: *Specify the second point*
Specify next fence point or [Undo]: *Specify the third point*
Specify next fence point or [Undo]: *Specify the fourth point*
Specify next fence point or [Undo]: Enter
Select object: Enter

Group

The **Group** option enables you to select a group of objects by their group name. You can create a group and assign a name to it with the help of the **Group** tool in the **Groups** panel of the **Home** tab (see Chapter 20, *Grouping and Advanced Editing of Sketched Objects*). Once a group has been created, you can select it by using the **Group** option for editing. This makes the object selection process easier and faster, since a set of objects can be selected by just entering the name of their group. The prompt sequence to use the **Group** option is given next.

*Choose the **Move** tool*
Select objects: **G** [Enter]
Enter group name: *Enter the name of the predefined group you want to select*
4 found
Select objects: [Enter]

Exercise 3 — *Erase*

Draw six circles and then erase all of them by using the **ALL** option of the **Erase** tool. Next, use undo command so that all the circles are displayed in the drawing area. Now, use the **Fence** selection set option with the **Erase** tool and remove alternate circles.

Box

If the system variable **PICKAUTO** is set to 1, the **Box** selection option is used to select the objects inside a rectangle. After you have entered **Box** at the **Select objects** prompt, you need to specify the two corners of a rectangle at the **Specify first corner** and **Specify opposite corner** prompts. If you define the box from right to left, it will be equivalent to the **Crossing** option. Therefore, it also selects the objects that touch the rectangle boundaries, in addition to the ones that are completely enclosed within the rectangle. If you define the box from left to right, this option will be equivalent to the **Window** option and will select only those objects that are completely enclosed within the rectangle.

The prompt sequence after choosing the **Box** option is given next.

Specify first corner: *Specify a point*
Specify opposite corner: *Specify the opposite corner point of the box*
Select objects: [Enter]

AUto

The **AUto** option is used to establish an automatic selection. Using this option, you can select either a single object or a number of objects by creating a window or a crossing. If you select a single object, it will be selected. If you specify a point in the blank area, you are automatically in the **Box** selection option, and the point you have specified becomes the first corner of the box. **AUto** and **Add** are the default selection methods in such cases.

Multiple

On entering **M** (Multiple) at the **Select objects** prompt, you can select multiple objects at a single **Select objects** prompt. In this case, the selected objects will not be highlighted. Once you press ENTER at the **Select objects** prompt, all selected objects will be highlighted together.

Undo

This option removes the most recently selected object from the selection set.

SIngle

When you enter **SI** (SIngle) at the **Select objects** prompt, the selection takes place in the **SIngle** selection mode. Once you select an object or a number of objects using the **Window** or **Crossing** option, the **Select objects** prompt does not repeat. AutoCAD proceeds with the tool for which the selection has been made.

*Choose the **Erase** tool*
Select objects: **SI** [Enter]
Select objects: *Select the object to erase; the selected object is erased*

SUbobject

This option is used to select sub-entities of an object such as the edges and faces. This option can also be used to select the individual members of a composite solid created by applying Boolean operations such as union, intersection, and so on. You can use this option on solid models with modify operations such as erase, move, rotate, and so on.

> **Tip**
> *Sub-objects can also be selected by pressing and holding the CTRL key when you are prompted to select objects for a selection set.*

Object

This option is used to exit the **SUbobject** option and it enables you to select objects as a whole again.

You can also create a selection set by using the **SELECT** command. The prompt sequence to do so is given next.

Command: **SELECT** [Enter]
Select objects: *Use any selection method*

EDITING SKETCHES

To use AutoCAD efficiently, you need to know the editing tools and how to use them. In this section, you will learn about the editing tools. These tools can be invoked from the **Ribbon**, or toolbar, or by entering them at the command prompt. Some of the editing tools or commands such as **ERASE** and **OOPS** have been discussed in Chapter 2 (Getting Started with AutoCAD).

MOVING SKETCHED OBJECTS

Ribbon: Home > Modify > Move	**Toolbar:** Modify > Move
Command: MOVE/M	

The **Move** tool is used to move one or more objects from their current location to a new location without changing their size or orientation. On choosing this tool from the **Modify** panel, refer to Figure 5-6, you will be prompted to select the objects to be moved. Select the object by using any one of the selection techniques discussed earlier; you will be prompted to specify the base point. The base point is the reference point with respect to which the object will be picked and moved. It is recommended to select the base point on the object selected to be moved. On specifying the base point, you will be prompted to specify the second point of displacement. This is the new location where you want to move the object. On specifying this point, the selected objects will move to this point. Figure 5-7 shows objects moved by using the **Move** tool.

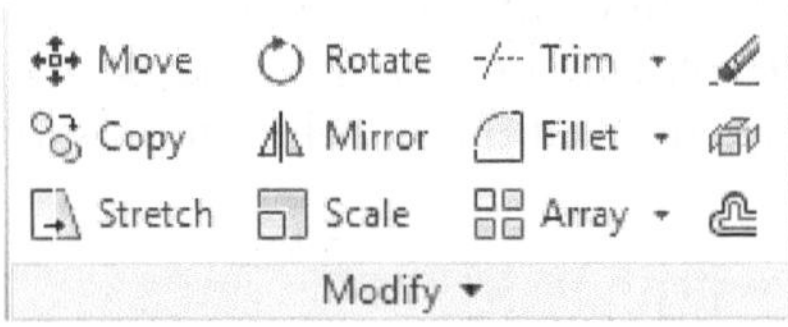

Figure 5-6 *The* ***Modify*** *panel*

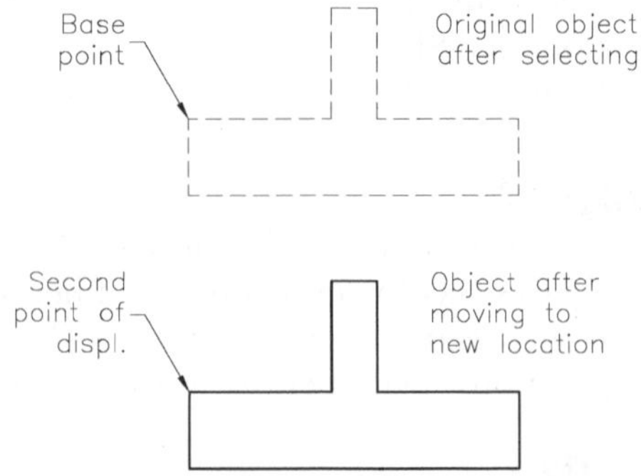

Figure 5-7 *Moving the object to a new location*

The prompt sequence that will be followed on choosing the **Move** tool from the **Modify** panel is given next.

Select objects: *Select the objects to be moved*
Specify base point or [Displacement] <Displacement>: *Specify the base point to move the selected object(s)*
Specify second point or <use first point as displacement>: *Specify the second point or press ENTER to use the first point*

If you press ENTER at the **Specify second point of displacement or <use first point as displacement>** prompt, AutoCAD interprets the first point as the relative value of the displacement in the *X* axis and *Y* axis directions. This value will be added in the *X* and *Y* axis coordinates and the object will be automatically moved to the resultant location. For example, draw a circle with its center at (3,3) and then select the center point of the circle as the base point. Now, at the **Specify second point or <use first point as displacement>** prompt, press ENTER. You will notice that the circle is moved such that its center is now placed at 6,6. This is because 3 units (initial coordinates) are added along both the X and Y directions.

COPYING SKETCHED OBJECTS

Ribbon: Home > Modify > Copy	**Toolbar:** Modify > Copy
Command: COPY/CO	

The **Copy** tool is used to copy an existing object. This tool is used to make the copies of the selected objects and place them at the specified location. To copy an object, you need to invoke this tool, select the objects and then specify the base point. Next, you need to specify the second point where the copied objects have to be placed. Figure 5-8 shows the objects copied by using this tool. The prompt sequence that will be followed when you choose the **Copy** tool from the **Modify** panel is given next.

Select objects: *Select the objects to copy*
Specify base point or [Displacement/mOde]<Displacement>: *Specify the base point*

Specify second point or [Array] <use first point as displacement>: *Specify a new position on the screen using the pointing device or by entering coordinates*
Specify second point or [Array/Exit/Undo] <Exit>: Enter

Creating Multiple Copies

On specifying the second point, the copy of the selected object will be created and you will be prompted again to specify the second point. You can continue specifying the second point for creating multiple copies of the selected entities, as shown in Figure 5-9. You can use the **U (Undo)** option to undo the last copied instance at any stage of the **Copy** tool. After entering **U**, you can again specify the position of the last instance. The prompt sequence for creating multiple copies of an object by using the **Copy** tool is given next.

Select objects: *Select the objects to copy* Enter
Specify base point or [Displacement/mOde]<Displacement>: **O** Enter
Enter a copy mode option [Single/Multiple]<current>: **M** Enter
Specify base point or [Displacement/mOde]<Displacement>: *Specify the base point*
Specify second point or [Array] <use first point as displacement>: *Specify a point for placement*
Specify second point or [Array/Exit/Undo] <Exit>: *Specify another point for placement*
Specify second point or [Array/Exit/Undo] <Exit>: *Specify another point for placement*
Specify second point or [Array/Exit/Undo] <Exit>: Enter

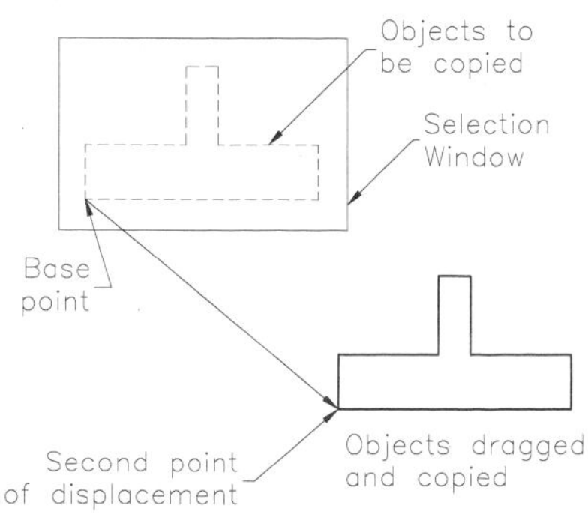

***Figure 5-8** The objects copied by using the **COPY** tool*

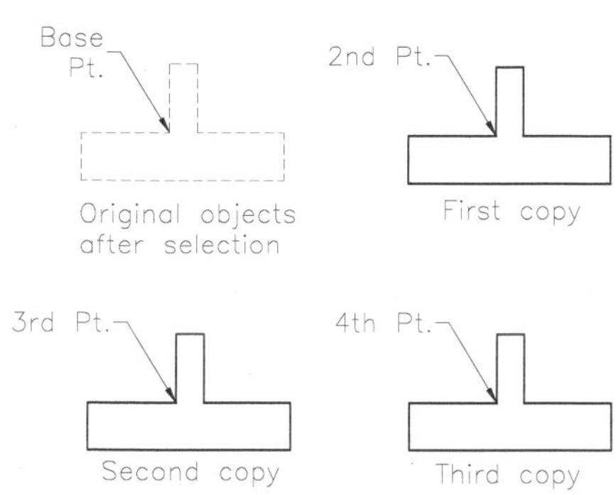

***Figure 5-9** Making multiple copies*

Creating an Array of Selected Objects

After specifying the base point, you will be prompted to specify the second point (where the copied object will be placed). You can create an array (multiple copies arranged in linear manner) of the selected objects by entering **ARRAY** or **A** at the **Specify second point or [Array] <use first point as displacement>:** command prompt. On entering the required command at the command prompt, you will be prompted to specify the number of items to array. Enter the number of items and press ENTER; you will be prompted to specify the second point and the preview of the array of selected items will be displayed attached to the cursor. Click to specify the second point; the linear array of selected object will be created, refer to Figure 5-10. In this array, the distance between any two consecutive items will be equal to the distance specified between the first and second points. If you enter **FIT** at the **Specify second point or [Fit]** command prompt, all array items will fit inside the first and second points, refer to Figure 5-11.

The prompt sequence for creating a linear array of a rectangle with the second point option of the **Copy** tool is given next, refer to Figure 5-10.

*Choose the **Copy** tool from the **Modify** panel of the **Home** tab*
Select objects: 1 found
Select objects: Enter
Current settings: Copy mode = Multiple
Specify base point or [Displacement/mOde] <Displacement>: *Specify the base point*
Specify second point or [Array] <use first point as displacement>: **A** or **ARRAY**
Enter number of items to array: **3**
Specify second point or [Fit]: *Specify another point for placement*

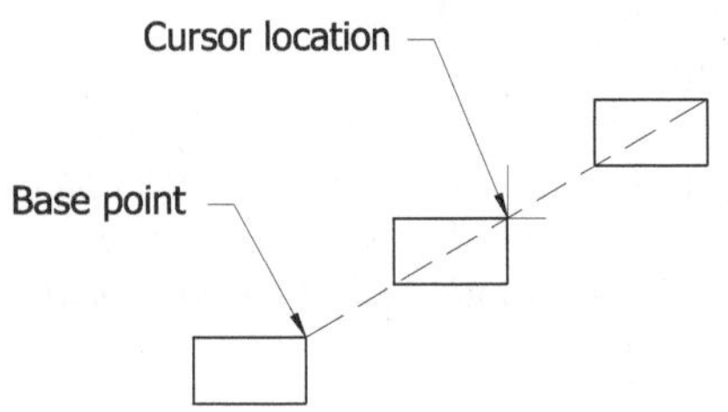

***Figure 5-10** Linear array created by using the **Copy** tool*

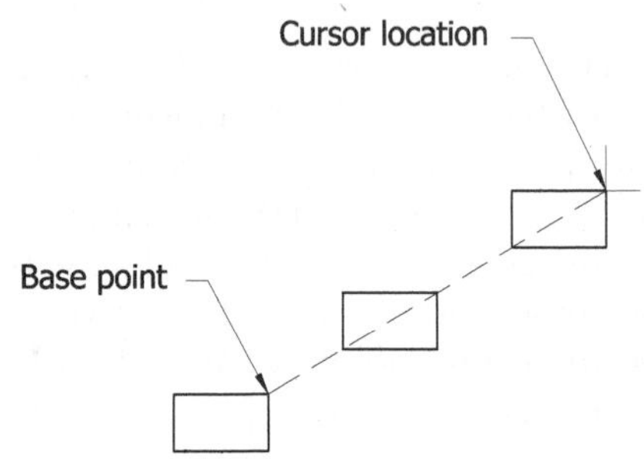

***Figure 5-11** Array created by using the **Fit** option of the **Copy** tool*

The prompt sequence for creating the linear array of a rectangle by using the **Fit** option of the **Copy** tool is given next, refer to Figure 5-11.

*Choose the **Copy** tool*
Select objects: 1 found
Select objects: Enter
Current settings: Copy mode = Multiple
Specify base point or [Displacement/mOde] <Displacement>: *Specify the base point*
Specify second point or [Array] <use first point as displacement>: **A** or **ARRAY**
Enter number of items to array: **3**
Specify second point or [Fit]: **F** or **FIT**
Specify second point or [Array]: *Specify another point for placement*

Creating a Single Copy

By default, AutoCAD creates multiple copies of the selected objects. However, you can also create a single copy of the selected object. To create a single copy of the selected object, choose the **mOde** option from the shortcut menu at the **Specify base point or [Displacement/mOde]** <current> prompt. Next, choose the **Single** option from the shortcut menu at the **Enter a copy mode option [Single/Multiple] <current>** prompt. On specifying the second point of displacement, a copy will be placed at that point.

Note

You can also copy an object by using CTRL+C. The copied content will be stored in the clipboard.

Exercise 4 Copy

In this exercise, you will create the drawing shown in Figure 5-12. Use the **Copy** tool for creating the drawing.

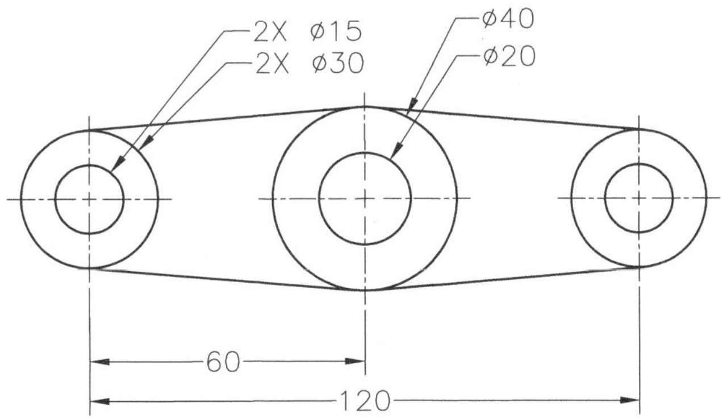

Figure 5-12 Drawing for Exercise 4

PASTING CONTENTS FROM THE CLIPBOARD

Ribbon: Home > Clipboard > Paste > Paste as Block **Command:** PASTEBLOCK

The **Paste as Block** tool is used to paste the contents of the Clipboard into a new drawing or in the same drawing at a new location. You can also invoke the **PASTEBLOCK** command from the shortcut menu by right-clicking in the drawing area and then choosing **Clipboard > Paste as Block**.

PASTING CONTENTS USING THE ORIGINAL COORDINATES

Ribbon: Home > Clipboard > Paste > Paste to Original Coordinates
Command: PASTEORIG

The **Paste to Original Coordinates** tool is used to paste the contents of the Clipboard into a new drawing by using coordinates from the original drawing. You can invoke the **PASTEORIG** command from the shortcut menu by right-clicking in the drawing area and then choosing **Clipboard > Paste to Original Coordinates**. Note that this command will be available only when the Clipboard contains AutoCAD data from a drawing other than the current drawing.

OFFSETTING SKETCHED OBJECTS

Ribbon: Home > Modify > Offset **Toolbar:** Modify > Offset
Command: OFFSET/O

You can use the **Offset** tool to draw parallel lines, polylines, concentric circles, arcs, curves, and so on, refer to Figure 5-13. However, you can offset only one entity at a time. While offsetting an object, you need to specify the offset distance and the side to offset, or specify the distance through which the selected object has to be offset. Depending on the side to offset, the resulting object will be smaller or larger than the original object. For example, while offsetting a circle if the offset side is toward the inner side of the perimeter, the resulting circle will be smaller than the original one.

The prompt sequence that will follow when you choose the **Offset** tool from the **Modify** panel is given next.

Current settings: Erase source=No Layer=Source OFFSETGAPTYPE=0
Specify offset distance or [Through/Erase/Layer] <Through>: *Specify the offset distance*
Select object to offset or [Exit/Undo]<Exit>: *Select the object to offset*
Specify point on side to offset or [Exit/Multiple/Undo] <Exit>: *Specify a point on the side to offset*
Select object to offset or [Exit/Undo]<Exit>: *Select another object to offset or press* ENTER

Through Option

While offsetting the entities, the offset distance can be specified by entering a value or by specifying two points. The distance between these two points will be used as the offset distance. The **Through** option is generally used to create orthographic views. In this case, you do not need to specify a distance; you need to specify an offset point, refer to Figure 5-14. The offset distance is stored in the **OFFSETDIST** system variable. A negative value indicates that the offset value is set to the **Through** option. Using this option, you can offset lines, arcs, 2D polylines, xlines, circles, ellipses, elliptical arcs, polygons, rays, and planar splines. If you try to offset other objects; the message **Cannot offset that object** is displayed.

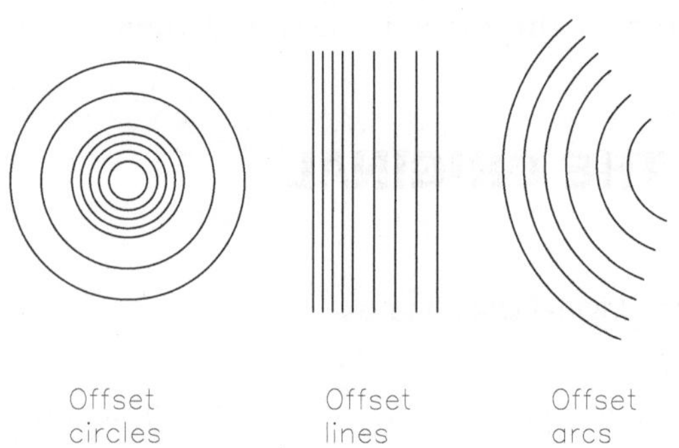

***Figure 5-13** Using the **Offset** tool multiple times to create multiple offset entities*

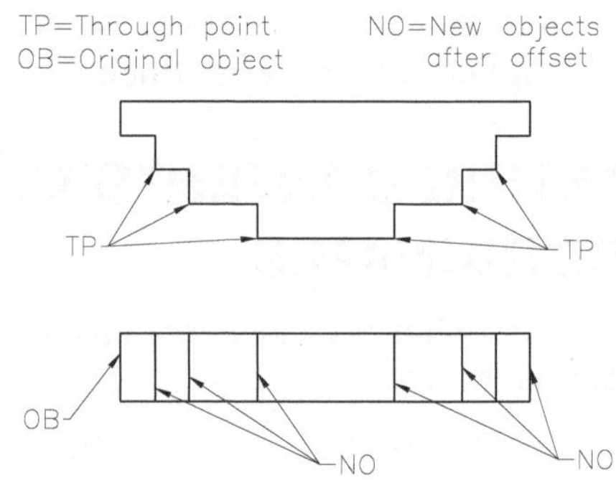

***Figure 5-14** Using the **Through** option*

Erase Option

The **Erase** option is used to specify whether the source object has to be deleted or not. Enter **Yes** at the **Erase source object after offsetting** prompt to delete the source object after creating the offset. The prompt sequence that will follow when you choose the **Erase** option is given next.

Current settings: Erase source=No Layer=Source OFFSETGAPTYPE=0
Specify offset distance or [Through/Erase/Layer] <current>: **E**
Erase source object after offsetting? [Yes/No] <No>: **Y**
Specify offset distance or [Through/Erase/Layer] <current>:

Layer Option

The **Layer** option is used to specify whether the offset entity will be placed in the current layer or the layer of the source object. The prompt sequence to offset the entity in the **Source** layer is given next.

Current settings: Erase source=No Layer=Source OFFSETGAPTYPE=0
Specify offset distance or [Through/Erase/Layer] <current>: **L**
Enter layer option for offset objects [Current/Source] <Source>: **S**
Specify offset distance or [Through/Erase/Layer] <current>:

Exercise 5 **Offset**

Use the **Offset** tool to draw the drawings for the Exercise 5(a) and Exercise 5(b) shown in Figure 5-15 and Figure 5-16, respectively.

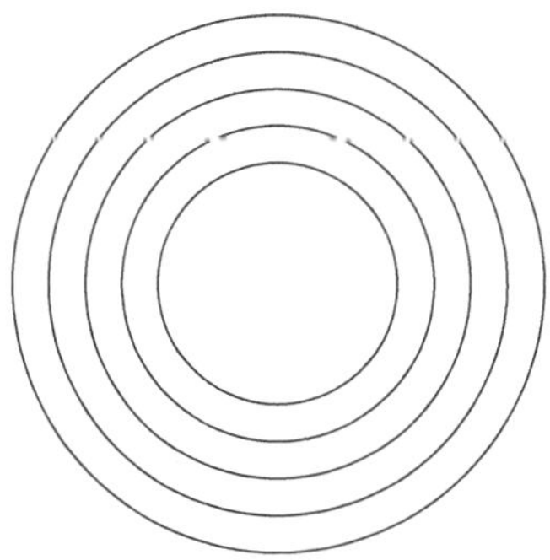

Figure 5-15 *Drawing for Exercise 5 (a)*

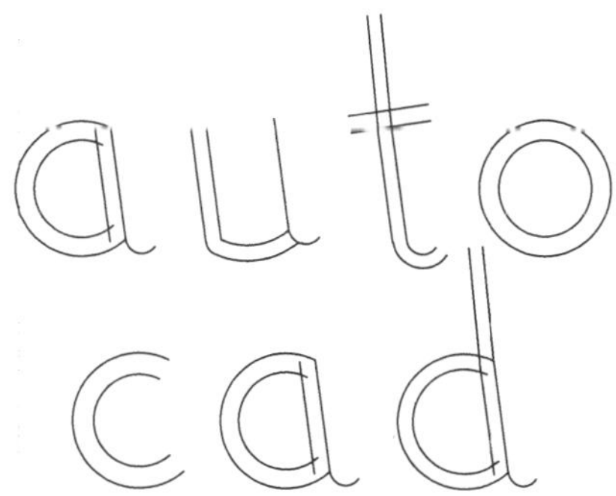

Figure 5-16 *Drawing for Exercise 5 (b)*

ROTATING SKETCHED OBJECTS

Ribbon: Home > Modify > Rotate **Toolbar:** Modify > Rotate
Command: ROTATE/RO

While creating designs, sometimes you have to rotate an object or a group of objects. You can accomplish this by using the **Rotate** tool. On invoking this tool, you will be prompted to select the objects and the base point about which the selected objects will be rotated. You should be careful in selecting the base point if the base point is not located on the known object. After you specify the base point, you need to enter the rotation angle. By default, a positive angle results in a counterclockwise rotation, whereas a negative angle results in a clockwise rotation, refer to Figure 5-17. The **Rotate** tool can also be invoked from the shortcut menu by selecting an object and right-clicking in the drawing area and choosing the **Rotate** tool from the shortcut menu.

If you need to rotate objects with respect to a known angle, you can do so by using the **Reference** option in two different ways. The first way is to specify the known angle as the reference angle, followed by the proposed angle by which the objects will be rotated, refer to Figure 5-18. Here the object is first rotated clockwise from the *X* axis, through the reference angle. Then the object is rotated through the new angle from this reference position in a counterclockwise direction.

The prompt sequence on choosing **Rotate** tool is given next.

Current positive angle in UCS: ANGDIR=*current* ANGBASE=*current*
Select objects: *Select the objects for rotation* Enter
Specify base point: *Specify the base point*
Specify rotation angle or [Copy/Reference]<current>: **R** Enter
Specify the reference angle <0>: *Enter reference angle* Enter
Specify the new angle or [Points] <0>: *Enter new angle or enter **P** to select two points for specifying the angle value* Enter

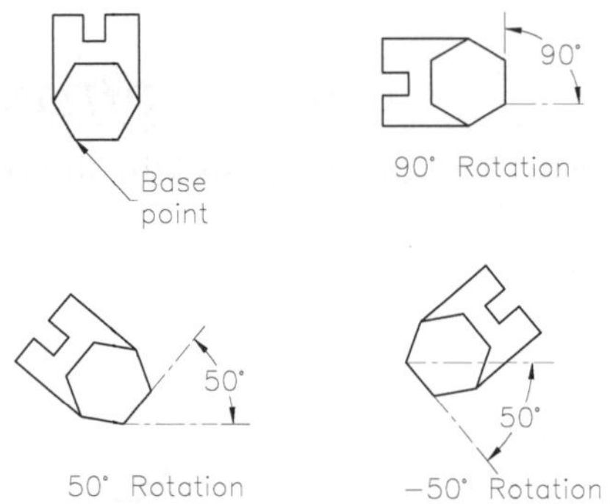

Figure 5-17 *Rotation of objects in different rotation angles*

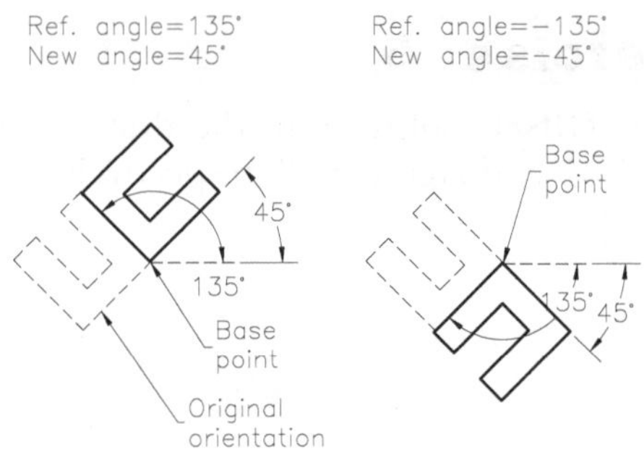

Figure 5-18 *Rotation using the **Reference** option*

The other method is used when the reference angle and the new angle are not known. In this case, you can use the edges of the original object and the reference object to specify the original object and the reference angle, respectively. Figure 5-19 shows a model and a line created at an unknown angle. In this case, this line will be used as a reference object for rotating the object. In such cases, the base point should be taken on the reference object. This is because you cannot define two points for specifying the new angle. You have to directly enter the angle value or specify only one point. Therefore, the base point will be taken as the first point and the second point can be defined for a new angle. Figure 5-20 shows the model after rotating it with reference to the line such that the line and the model are inclined at similar angles. The prompt sequence to rotate the model shown in Figure 5-19 is given next.

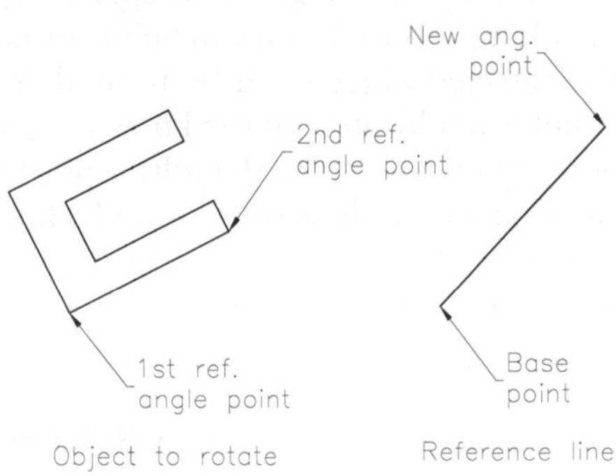

Figure 5-19 *Rotating the model using a reference line*

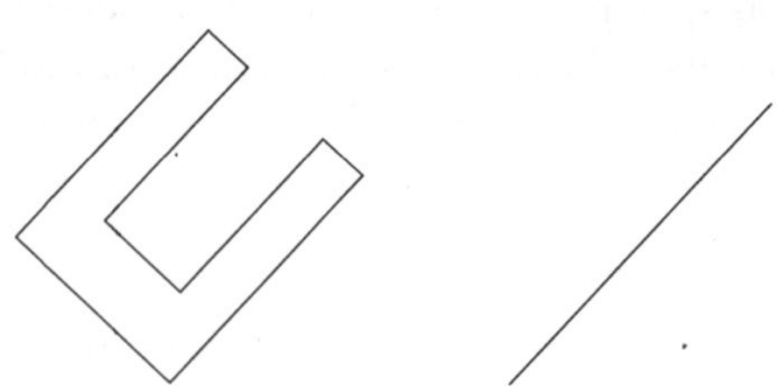

Figure 5-20 *The model after rotating with reference to the line*

Current positive angle in UCS: ANGDIR=*current* ANGBASE=*current*
Select objects: *Select the object for rotation* Enter
Specify base point: *Specify the base point as the lower endpoint of the line, refer to Figure 5-19*
Specify rotation angle or [Copy/Reference]<current>: **R** Enter
Specify the reference angle <current>: *Specify the first point on the edge of the model, refer to Figure 5-19*
Specify the reference angle <current>: Specify second point: *Specify the second point on the same edge of the model, see Figure 5-19*
Specify the new angle or [Points]<current>: *Select the other endpoint of the reference line, refer to Figure 5-19*

You can also specify a new angle by entering a numeric value at the **Specify the new angle or [Points]<current>** prompt.

If you want to retain the original object and create a copy while rotating, use the **Copy** option of the **Rotate** tool. The source entity is retained in its original orientation and a new instance is created and rotated through the specified angle. The prompt sequence for the **Copy** option is given next.

Current positive angle in UCS: ANGDIR=counterclockwise ANGBASE=0
Select objects: *Select the object for rotation* Enter
Specify base point: *Specify a base point about which the selected objects will be rotated*
Specify rotation angle or [Copy/Reference] <current>: **C** Enter
Rotating a copy of the selected objects
Specify rotation angle or [Copy/Reference] <current>: *Enter a positive or negative rotation angle, or specify a point*

SCALING THE SKETCHED OBJECTS

Ribbon: Home > Modify > Scale **Toolbar:** Modify > Scale
Command: SCALE/SC

Sometimes you need to change the size of objects in a drawing. You can do so by using the **Scale** tool. This tool dynamically enlarges or shrinks a selected object about a base point keeping the aspect ratio of the object constant. This means that the size of the object will be increased or reduced equally in the X, Y, and Z directions. The dynamic scaling property allows you to view the object as it is being scaled. Another advantage of this tool is that if you have dimensioned the drawing, they will also change accordingly. You can also invoke the **Scale** tool from the shortcut menu by right-clicking in the drawing area after selecting an object and choosing the **Scale** tool. The prompt sequence that will follow when you choose the **Scale** tool is given next.

Select objects: *Select the objects to be scaled* Enter
Specify base point: *Specify the base point, preferably a known point*
Specify scale factor or [Copy/Reference]: *Specify the scale factor*

The base point will not move from its position and the selected object(s) will be scaled with respect to the base point, refer to Figure 5-21 and Figure 5-22. To reduce the size of an object, the scale factor should be less than 1 and to increase its size, the scale factor should be greater than 1. You can enter a scale factor or select two points to specify a distance as a factor. When you select two points to specify a distance as a factor, the first point should be on the referenced object.

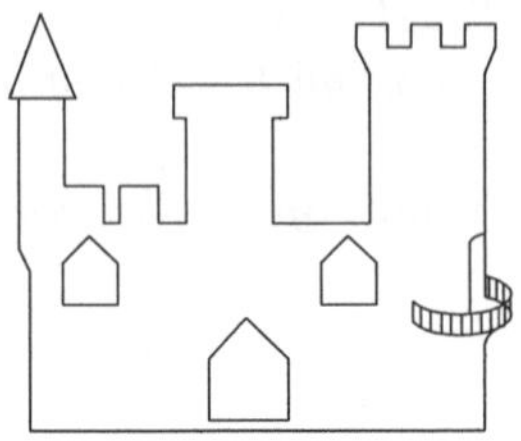

Figure 5-21 *Original object*

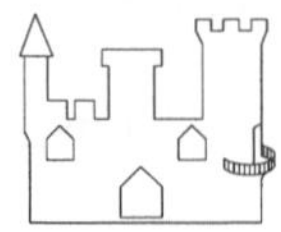

Figure 5-22 *Objects after scaling to 0.5 of the actual size*

Sometimes, it is time-consuming to calculate the relative scale factor. In such cases, you can scale the object by specifying a desired size in relation to the existing size (a known dimension). In other words, you can use a reference length. This can be done by entering **R** at the **Specify scale factor or [Copy/Reference]** prompt. Then, you can either specify two points to specify the length or enter a length. At the next prompt, enter the length relative to the reference length. For example, if a line is 2.5 units long and you want its length to be 1.00 unit, then instead of calculating the relative scale factor, you can use the **Reference** option. The prompt sequence for using the **Reference** option is given next.

Select objects: *Select the object to scale* Enter
Specify base point: *Specify the base point*
Specify scale factor or [Copy/Reference]: **R** Enter
Specify reference length <current>: *Specify the reference length*
Specify new length or [Points]: *Specify the new length or enter **P** to select two points for specifying the angle value*

Similar to the **Rotate** tool, you can also scale one object by using the reference of another object. Again, in this case also, the base point has to be taken on the reference object as you can define only one point for the new length.

You can use the **Copy** option to retain the source object and scale the copied instance of the source object. The prompt sequence for using the **Copy** option is given next.

Select objects: *Select the object to scale* Enter
Specify base point: *Specify the base point*
Specify scale factor or [Copy/Reference]: **C** Enter
Scaling a copy of the selected objects
Specify scale factor or [Copy/Reference]: *Specify the scale factor*

Tip

*If you need to change the dimensions of all the objects with respect to other units, you can use the **Reference** option of the **Scale** tool to correct the error. To do so, select the entire drawing by using the **ALL** selection option. Next, specify the **Reference** option, and then select the endpoints of the object whose desired length is known. Specify the new length; all the objects in the drawing will be scaled automatically to the desired size.*

FILLETING THE SKETCHES

Ribbon: Home > Modify > Fillet drop-down > Fillet **Toolbar:** Modify > Fillet
Command: FILLET/F

The edges in a model are generally filleted to reduce the area of stress concentration. The **Fillet** tool helps you form round corners between two entities that form a sharp vertex. As a result, a smooth round arc is created that connects the two objects. A fillet can also be created between two intersecting or parallel lines as well as non-intersecting and nonparallel lines, arcs, polylines, xlines, rays, splines, circles, and true ellipses. The fillet arc created will be tangent to both the selected entities. The default fillet radius is 0.0000. Therefore, after invoking this tool, you first need to specify the radius value. The prompt sequence displayed on choosing the **Fillet** tool from the **Fillet** drop-down in the **Modify** panel (Figure 5-23) is given next.

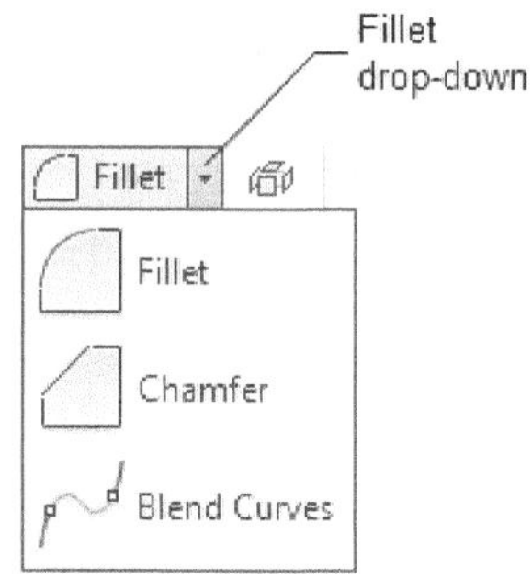

Figure 5-23 *Tools in the* ***Fillet*** *drop-down*

Current Settings: Mode= TRIM, Radius= 0.0000
Select first object or [Undo/Polyline/Radius/Trim/Multiple]:

Creating Fillets Using the Radius Option

The fillet you create depends on the radius distance specified. The default radius is 0.0000. You can enter a distance or specify two points. The new radius you enter becomes the default radius and remains in effect until changed. Note that the **FILLETRAD** system variable controls and stores the current fillet radius. The default value of this variable is 0.0000. The prompt sequence that is displayed on invoking the **Fillet** tool is given next.

Select first object or [Undo/Polyline/Radius/Trim/Multiple]: **R** Enter
Specify fillet radius <current>: *Enter a value or press ENTER to accept the current value*

Tip
A fillet with a zero radius has sharp corners and is used to clean up lines at corners if they overlap or have a gap.

Creating Fillets Using the Select First Object Option

This is the default method to fillet two objects. As the name implies, it prompts for the first object required for filleting. The prompt sequence to use this option is given next.

Current Settings: Mode= TRIM, Radius= current value
Select first object or [Undo/Polyline/Radius/Trim/Multiple]: *Specify the first object*
Select second object or shift-select to apply corner or [Radius]: *Select the second object or press the SHIFT key while selecting the object to create sharp corner*

The **Fillet** tool can also be used to cap the ends of two parallel as well as non-parallel lines, refer to Figure 5-24. The cap is a semicircle whose radius is equal to half the distance between the two parallel lines. The cap distance is calculated automatically when you select the two parallel lines for filleting. You can select lines by using the **Window**, **Crossing**, or **Last** option, but to avoid unexpected results, select the objects by picking them individually. Also, selection by picking objects is necessary in the case of arcs and circles that have the possibility of more than one fillet. They are filleted closest to the selected points, as shown in Figure 5-25.

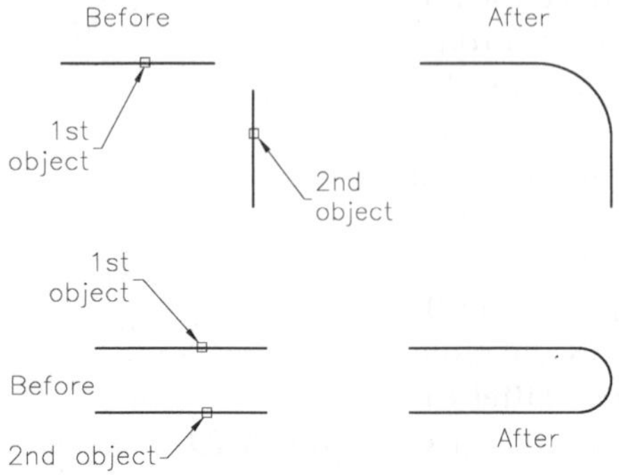

Figure 5-24 Filleting the parallel and non-parallel lines

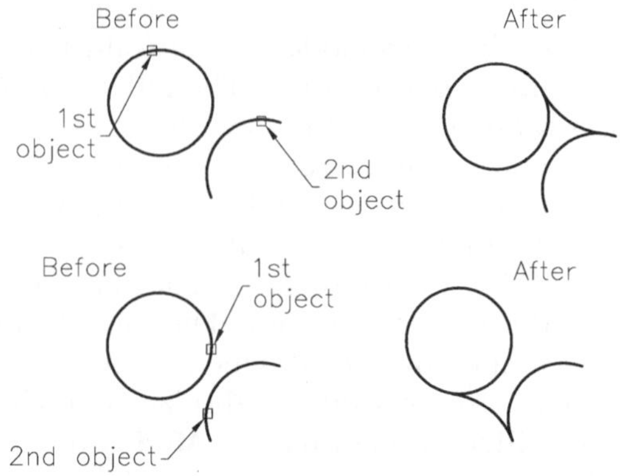

Figure 5-25 *Using the **Fillet** tool on circles and arcs*

Creating Fillets Using the Trim Option

When you create a fillet, an arc is created and the selected objects are either trimmed or extended at the fillet endpoint. This is because the **Trim** mode is set to **Trim**. If it is set to **No trim**, then the objects are left intact. Figure 5-26 shows a model filleted with the **Trim** mode set to **Trim** and **No trim**. The prompt sequence is given next.

Select first object or [Undo/Polyline/Radius/Trim/Multiple]: **T** Enter
Enter Trim mode option [Trim/No trim] <current>: *Enter **T** to trim edges, **N** to leave them intact. You can also choose the required option from the dynamic preview*

Creating Fillets Using the Polyline Option

If an object is created by using the **Polyline** or **Rectangle** tool, then the object will be a polyline. You can fillet all the sharp corners in a polyline by using the **Polyline** option of the **Fillet** tool, as shown in Figure 5-27. On selecting this option after specifying the fillet radius, you will be prompted to select a polyline. Select the polyline; all vertices of the polyline will be filleted with the same fillet radius. The prompt sequence for using this option is given next.

Current Settings: Mode= *current*, Radius= *current*
Select first object or [Undo/Polyline/Radius/Trim/Multiple]: **P** Enter
Select 2D polyline or [Radius]: *Select the polyline*

In AutoCAD, you can close a polyline using the **Fillet** tool. To do so, choose the **Fillet** tool from the **Fillet** drop-down in the **Modify** panel of the **Home** tab and select the two open ends of the polyline; the selected polyline will be closed and form a corner. Figure 5-28 shows an open polyline and Figure 5-29 shows a closed polyline after selecting the open entities.

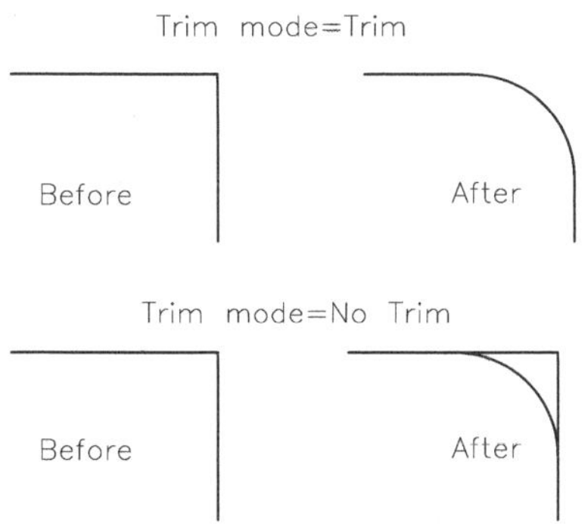

Figure 5-26 *Filleting the lines with the **Trim** mode set to **Trim** and **No trim***

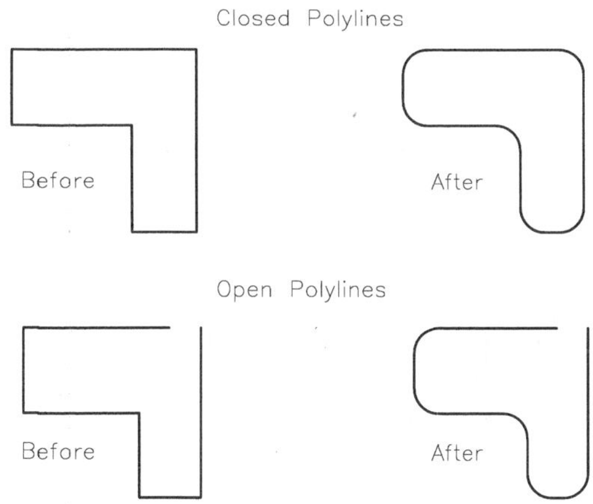

Figure 5-27 *Filleting closed and open polylines*

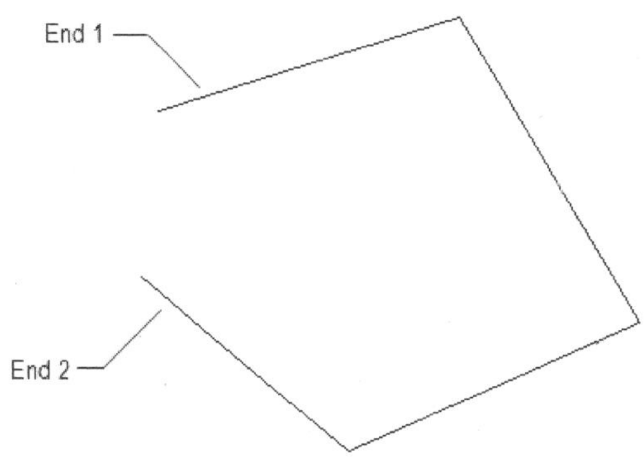

Figure 5-28 *Open polyline with two ends*

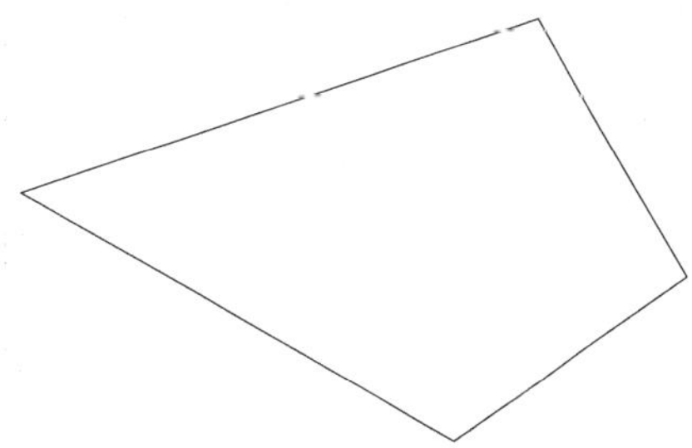

Figure 5-29 *Final closed polyline*

Creating Fillets Using the Multiple Option

When you invoke the **Fillet** tool, by default, a fillet is created between a pair of entities only. However, with the help of the **Multiple** option, you can add fillets to more than a pair of entities. On selecting this option, you will be prompted to select the first object and then the second object. On selecting two objects, a fillet will be created between the two entities and again you will be prompted to select the first object and then the second object. This prompt will continue until you press ENTER to terminate the **Fillet** tool. Note that you can use the **Undo** option to undo the fillet created. The prompt sequence to use this option is given next.

Current Settings: Mode= TRIM, Radius= current
Select first object or [Undo/Polyline/Radius/Trim/Multiple]: **M** [Enter]
Select first object or [Undo/Polyline/Radius/Trim/Multiple]: *Specify the first object of one set*
Select second object or shift-select to apply corner or [Radius]: *Select the second object or press down the SHIFT key while selecting the object to create sharp corner*
Select first object or [Undo/Polyline/Radius/Trim/Multiple]: *Specify the first object of the other set*
Select second object or shift-select to apply corner or [Radius]: *Select the second object or press down the SHIFT key while selecting the object to create sharp corner*

Select first object or [Undo/Polyline/Radius/Trim/Multiple]: *Specify the first object of the other set or press* Enter

Filleting Objects with a Different UCS

The **Fillet** tool also fillets the objects that are not in the current UCS plane. To create a fillet for these objects, AutoCAD automatically changes the UCS transparently so that it can generate a fillet between the selected objects.

Setting the TRIMMODE System Variable

The **TRIMMODE** system variable eliminates any size restriction on the **Fillet** tool. By setting **TRIMMODE** to **0**, you can create a fillet of any size without actually cutting the existing geometry. Also, there is no restriction on the fillet radius. This means that the fillet radius can be larger than one or both objects that are being filleted. The default value of this variable is 1.

Note

TRIMMODE = 0 *Fillet or chamfer without cutting the existing geometry.*
TRIMMODE = 1 *Extend or trim the geometry.*

CHAMFERING THE SKETCHES

Ribbon: Home > Modify > Fillet drop-down > Chamfer
Toolbar: Modify > Chamfer **Command:** CHAMFER/CHA

Chamfering the sharp corners is another method of reducing the areas of stress concentration in a model. Chamfering is defined as the process by which the sharp edges or corners are beveled. The size of a chamfer depends on its distance from the corner. If a chamfer is equidistant from the corner in both directions, it is a 45-degree chamfer. A chamfer can be drawn between two lines that may or may not intersect. This tool also works on a single polyline. In AutoCAD, the chamfers are created by defining two distances or by defining one distance and the chamfer angle.

The prompt sequence that will follow when you choose the **Chamfer** tool from the **Fillet** drop-down of the **Modify** panel is given next.

(TRIM mode) Current chamfer Dist1 = 0.0000, Dist2 = 0.0000
Select first line or [Undo/Polyline/Distance/Angle/Trim/mEthod/Multiple]:

The different options to create chamfers are discussed next.

Creating Chamfers Using the Distance Option

To create a chamfer by entering the distances, enter **D** at the **Select first line or [Undo/Polyline/Distance/Angle/Trim/mEthod/Multiple]** prompt. Next, enter the first and second chamfer distances. The first distance is the distance of the corner calculated along the edge selected first. Similarly, the second distance is calculated along the edge that is selected last. The new chamfer distances remain in effect until you change them. Instead of entering the distance values, you can specify two points to indicate each distance, refer to Figure 5-30. The prompt sequence is given next.

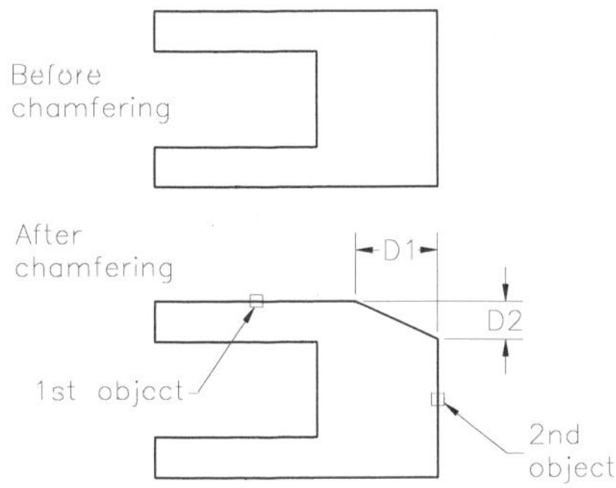

Figure 5-30 *Chamfering the model using the* ***Distance*** *option*

Select first line or [Undo/Polyline/Distance/Angle/Trim/mEthod/Multiple]: **D** Enter
Specify first chamfer distance <0.0000>: *Enter a distance value or specify two points*
Specify second chamfer distance <0.0000>: *Enter a distance value or specify two points*

Note

1. If Dist 1 and Dist 2 are set to zero, the ***Chamfer*** *tool will extend or trim the selected lines such that they end at the same point.*

2. The first and second chamfer distances are stored in the ***CHAMFERA*** *and* ***CHAMFERB*** *system variables. The default value of these variables is 0.0000.*

Creating Chamfers Using the Select First Line Option

In this option, you need to select two nonparallel objects so that they are joined with a beveled line. The size of a chamfer depends on the values of the two distances. The prompt sequence to do so is given next.

(TRIM mode) Current chamfer Dist1 = current, Dist2 = current
Select first line or [Undo/Polyline/Distance/Angle/Trim/mEthod/Multiple]: *Specify the first line*
Select second line or shift-select to apply corner or [Distance/Angle/Method]: *Select the second object or press down the SHIFT key while selecting the object to create sharp corner*

Creating Chamfer Using the Polyline Option

Similar to the **Fillet** tool, you can chamfer all the sharp corners in a polyline by using the **Polyline** option of the **Chamfer** tool, as shown in Figure 5-31. The prompt sequence to chamfer the polylines is given next.

(TRIM mode) Current chamfer Dist1 = current, Dist2 = current
Select first line or [Undo/Polyline/Distance/Angle/Trim/mEthod/Multiple]: **P** Enter
Select 2D polyline or [Distance/Angle/Method]: *Select the polyline*

Creating Chamfer Using the Angle Option

The other method of creating a chamfer is by specifying the distance and the chamfer angle, as shown in Figure 5-32. The prompt sequence to do so is given next.

(TRIM mode) Current chamfer Dist1 = current, Dist2 = current
Select first line or [Undo/Polyline/Distance/Angle/Trim/mEthod/Multiple]: *A* Enter
Specify chamfer length on the first line <0.0000>: *Enter a distance value or specify two points*
Specify chamfer angle from the first line <0>: *Enter an angle value*
Select first line or [Undo/Polyline/Distance/Angle/Trim/mEthod/Multiple]: *P* Enter
Select 2D polyline or [Distance/Angle/Method]: *Select the polyline*

Creating Chamfer Using the Trim Option

On selecting the **Trim** option, the selected objects are either trimmed or extended to the endpoints of the chamfer line or left intact. The prompt sequence to invoke this option is given next.

Select first line or [Undo/Polyline/Distance/Angle/Trim/mEthod/Multiple]: *T* Enter
Enter Trim mode option [Trim/No trim] <current>: *Enter **T** to trim edges, **N** to leave them intact.*

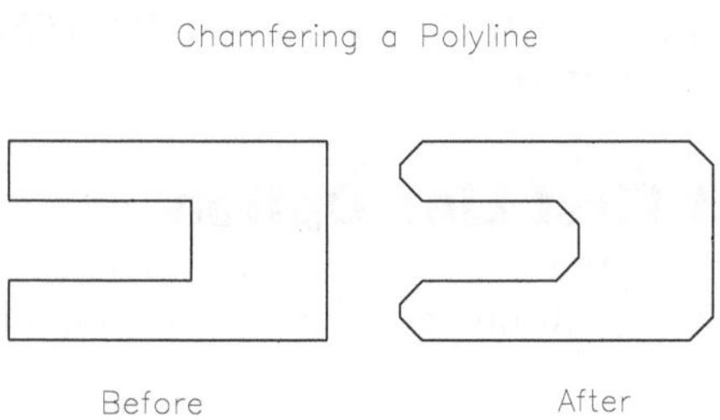

***Figure 5-31** Chamfering a polyline*

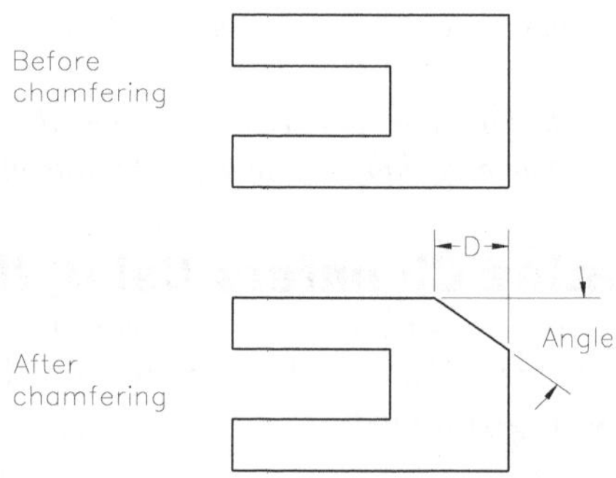

***Figure 5-32** Chamfering using the **Angle** option*

Creating Chamfer Using the Method Option

On using this option, you can toggle between the **Distance** method and the **Angle** method for creating a chamfer. The current settings of the selected method will be used for creating the chamfer. The prompt sequence to create the chamfer is given next.

Select first line or [Undo/Polyline/Distance/Angle/Trim/mEthod/Multiple]: **E** Enter
Enter trim method [Distance/Angle] <current>: *Enter **D** for the **Distance** option, **A** for the **Angle** option*

Creating Chamfers Using the Multiple Option

When you invoke the **Chamfer** tool, by default, a chamfer is created only between one pair of entities. However, with the help of the **Multiple** option, you can add chamfers to multiple pairs. On selecting this option, you will be prompted to select first line and then second line. On selecting the two lines, the chamfer will be created. Next, you will again be prompted to select first line and then second line. This prompt will continue until you press ENTER to terminate the **Chamfer** tool. The prompt sequence that follows to create multiple chamfers is given next.

(TRIM mode) Current chamfer Dist1 = current, Dist2= current
Select first line or [Undo/Polyline/Distance/Angle/Trim/mEthod/Multiple]: **M** Enter
Select first line or [Undo/Polyline/Distance/Angle/Trim/mEthod/Multiple]: *Specify the first line of one set*
Select second line or shift-select to apply corner or [Distance Angle Method]: *Select the second object or press the SHIFT key while selecting the object to create sharp corner*
Select first line or [Undo/Polyline/Distance/Angle/Trim/mEthod/Multiple]: *Specify the first line of the other set*
Select second line or shift-select to apply corner or [Distance/Angle/Method]: *Select the second object or press the SHIFT key while selecting the object to create sharp corner*
Select first line or [Undo/Polyline/Distance/Angle/Trim/mEthod/Multiple]: *Specify the first line of the other set or press **ENTER** to terminate the **Chamfer** tool*

Setting the Chamfering System Variables

The chamfer modes, distances, length, and angle can also be set by using the following variables:

CHAMMODE = 0	Distance/Distance (default)
CHAMMODE = 1	Length/Angle
CHAMFERA	Sets first chamfer distance on the first selected line (default = 0.0000)
CHAMFERB	Sets second chamfer distance on the second selected line (default = 0.0000)
CHAMFERC	Sets the chamfer length (default = 0.0000)
CHAMFERD	Sets the chamfer angle from the first line (default = 0)

BLENDING THE CURVES

Ribbon: Home > Modify > Fillet drop-down > Blend Curves
Command: BLEND

In AutoCAD, you can create a smooth or tangent continuous spline between the endpoints of two existing curves. The existing curves can be arcs, lines, helixes, open polylines, or open splines. To create a smooth curve between two open curves, choose the **Blend Curves** tool from the **Fillet** drop-down in the **Modify** panel, refer to Figure 5-33; you will be prompted to select the curves one after the other. Select two curves; a blend curve will be created between the selected curves. The length of the selected curves does not change. The prompt sequence to use this tool is given next.

*Choose the **Blend Curves** tool*
Select first object or [CONtinuity]: *Select the first object*
Select second object: *Select the second object*

This tool provides two options to specify the continuity of the blend curve with the two selected curves: **Tangent** and **Smooth**. By default, the **Tangent** option is chosen. As a result, a tangent continuous curve will be created between the two selected curves. The prompt sequence to use this option has been given earlier in this topic.

You can also blend two curves with a smooth continuity between them. To do so, first enter **CON** at the **Select first object or [CONtinuity]:** command prompt. Next, enter **S** at the command prompt and then select the two curves; a smooth curve will be created between the two selected curves. The prompt sequence to use this option is given next.

*Choose the **Blend Curves** tool*
Select first object or [CONtinuity]: **CON** Enter
Enter continuity [Tangent/Smooth] <Tangent>: **S** Enter
Select first object or [CONtinuity]: *Select the first object*
Select second object: *Select the second object*

Figure 5-33 shows the two curves selected and Figure 5-34 shows the resulting tangent and smooth curves as the blend curves.

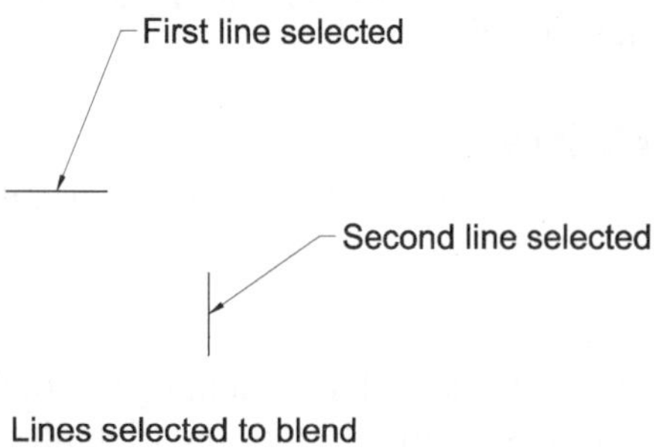

Figure 5-33 *Curves selected to be blended*

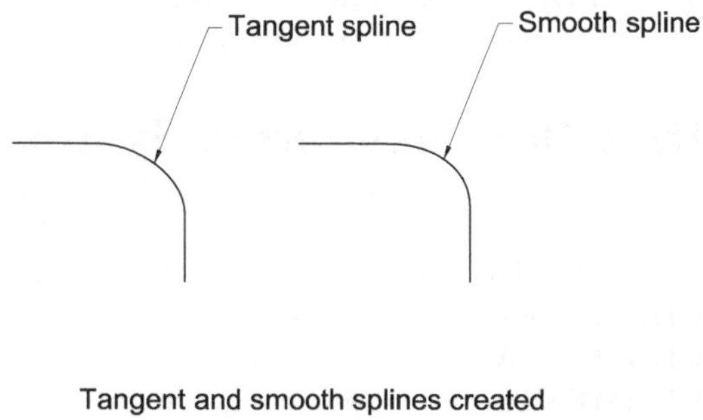

Figure 5-34 *Tangent and smooth blend curves created*

To view the continuity of the spline (blend curve) with the selected curves, select the spline; the control points will be displayed in the form of control vertices. You can change the display of control points from control vertices to fit points. To do so, click on the down-arrow on the spline; a shortcut menu will be displayed. Choose the **Fit** option from the shortcut menu to change the control vertices to fit points. Figure 5-35 shows the control vertices of a tangent continuous spline and a smooth spline created between two open lines. You can change the shape of the splines by dragging its control vertices.

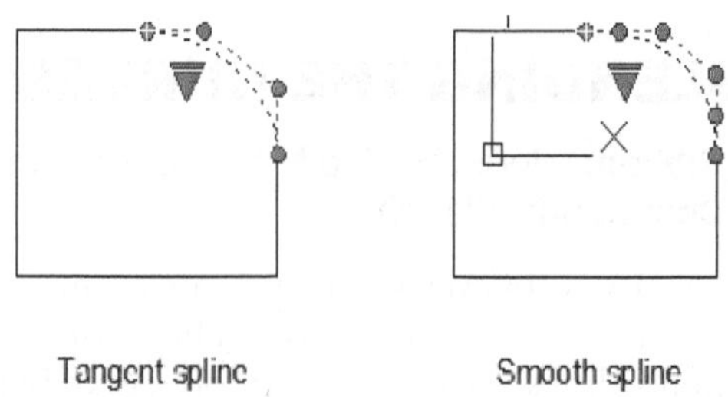

Figure 5-35 *Control vertices of tangent and smooth splines*

TRIMMING THE SKETCHED OBJECTS

Ribbon: Home > Modify > Trim drop-down > Trim **Toolbar:** Modify > Trim
Command: TRIM/TR

While creating a design, you may need to remove the unwanted and extended edges. Breaking individual objects takes time if you are working on a complex design with many objects. In such cases, you can use the **Trim** tool. This tool is used to trim the objects that extend beyond a required point of intersection. When you invoke this tool from the **Trim** drop-down in the **Modify** panel (Figure 5-36), you will be prompted to select the cutting edges or boundaries. These edges can be lines, polylines, circles, arcs, ellipses, xlines, rays, splines, text, blocks, or even viewports. There can be more than one cutting edge and you can use any selection method to select them. After the cutting edge or edges are selected, you must select each object to be trimmed. An object can be both a cutting edge and an object to be trimmed. You can trim lines, circles, arcs, polylines, splines, ellipses, xlines, and rays. The prompt sequence to trim objects is given next.

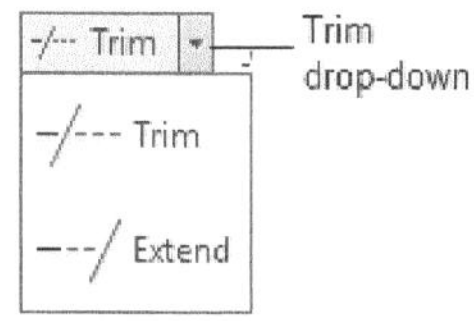

***Figure 5-36** Tools in the **Trim** drop-down*

Current settings: Projection=UCS, Edge=None
Select cutting edges...
Select objects or <select all>: *Select the cutting edges* Enter
Select object to trim or shift-select to extend or **TRIM** [Fence/Crossing/Project/Edge/eRase/Undo]:

Various options used to trim objects are discussed next.

Select object to trim Option

On selecting this option, you have to specify the objects you want to trim and the side from which the objects will be trimmed. This prompt is repeated until you press ENTER. This way you can trim several objects on invoking this tool once. The prompt sequence to use this option is given next.

Current settings: Projection= UCS, Edge= None
Select cutting edges...
Select objects or <select all>: *Select the cutting edges* Enter
Select object to trim or shift-select to extend or **TRIM** [Fence/Crossing/Project/Edge/eRase/Undo]: *Select the first object*
Select object to trim or shift-select to extend or **TRIM** [Fence/Crossing/Project/Edge/eRase/Undo]: *Select the second object. Refer to Figure 5-37*
Select object to trim or shift-select to extend or **TRIM** [Fence/Crossing/Project/Edge/eRase/Undo]: Enter

Shift-select to extend Option

This option is used to switch from trim mode to the extend mode. It is used to extend an object instead of trimming. In case the object to be extended does not intersect with the cutting edge, you can press the SHIFT key and then select the object to be extended; the selected edge will be extended taking the cutting edge as the boundary for extension. Note that you need to click near the endpoint that is closest to the cutting edge.

Edge Option

This option is used to trim those objects that do not intersect the cutting edges, but they intersect if the cutting edges were extended, refer to Figure 5-38. The prompt sequence is given next.

Current settings: Projection= UCS Edge= None
Select cutting edges...

Select objects: *Select the cutting edge*
Select objects: Enter
Select object to trim or shift-select to extend or **TRIM** [Fence/Crossing/Project/Edge/eRase/Undo]: **E** Enter
Enter an implied edge extension mode [Extend/No extend] <current>: **E** Enter
Select object to trim or shift-select to extend or **TRIM** [Fence/Crossing/Project/Edge/eRase/Undo]: *Select object to trim*

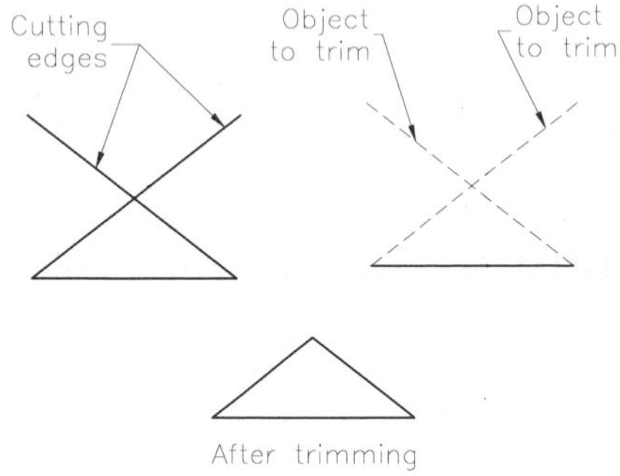

Figure 5-37 *Using the* ***Trim*** *Tool*

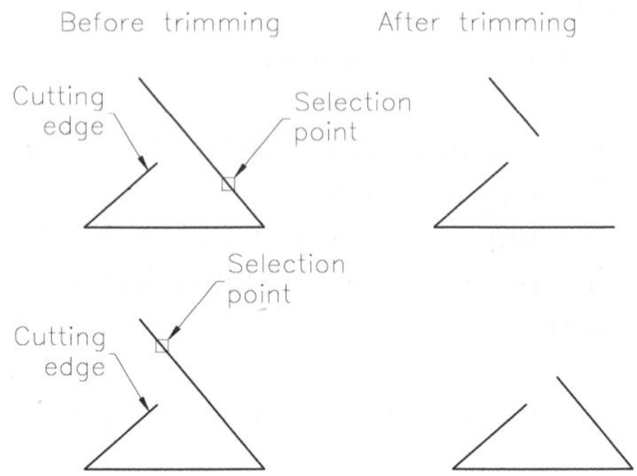

Figure 5-38 *Trimming an object using the* ***Edge*** *option* ***(Extend)***

Project Option

The **Project** option is used to trim those objects that do not intersect the cutting edges in 3D space, but do visually appear to intersect in a particular UCS or the current view. The prompt sequence to invoke this option is given next.

Select object to trim or shift-select to extend or [Fence/Crossing/Project/Edge/eRase/Undo]: **P** Enter
Enter a projection option [None/Ucs/View] <current>:

The **None** option is used whenever the objects to be trimmed intersects the cutting edges in 3D space. The **UCS** option is used to project the objects to the *XY* plane of the current UCS, while the **View** option is used to project the objects to the current view direction (trims to their apparent visual intersections).

Fence Option

As discussed in earlier chapters, the **Fence** option is used for the selection purpose. Using the **Fence** option, all the objects crossing the selection fence are selected. The prompt sequence for the **Fence** option is given next.

Select object to trim or shift-select to extend or [Fence/Crossing/Project/Edge/eRase/Undo]: **F** Enter
Specify first fence point: *Specify the first point of the fence*
Specify next fence point or [Undo]: *Specify the second point of the fence*
Specify next fence point or [Undo]: *Specify the third point of the fence*
Specify next fence point or [Undo]: Enter

Crossing Option

The **Crossing** option is used to select the entities by using a crossing window. On using this option, the objects touching the window boundaries are selected. The prompt sequence to trim objects using this option is given next.

Select object to trim or shift-select to extend or [Fence/Crossing/Project/Edge/eRase/Undo]: **C** Enter
Specify first corner: *Select the first corner of the crossing window*
Specify opposite corner: *Select the opposite corner of the crossing window*

Erase Option

The **Erase** option in the **Trim** tool is used to erase the entities without terminating the **Trim** tool.

Select object to trim or shift-select to extend or [Fence/Crossing/Project/Edge/eRase/Undo]: **R** Enter
Select objects to erase or <exit>: *Select object to erase*
Select objects to erase: *Select object to erase or* Enter
Select objects to erase: Enter

Undo Option

If you want to undo the previous change made by the **Trim** tool, enter **U** at the **Select object to trim or [Fence/Crossing/Project/Edge/eRase/Undo]** prompt.

Note

You can see the preview of the result in the drawing area. To do so, you need to select the ***Command preview*** *check box available in the* ***Selection*** *tab of the* ***Options*** *dialog box.*

Exercise 6 — Fillet, Chamfer, and Trim

Draw the top illustration shown in Figure 5-39 and then use the **Fillet**, **Chamfer**, and **Trim** tools to obtain the next illustration given in the same figure.

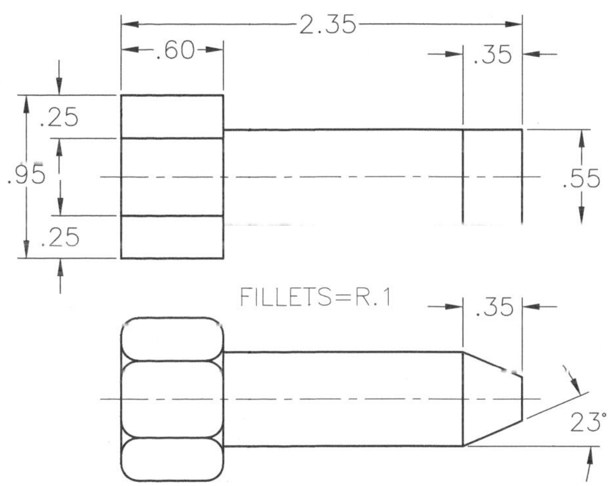

Figure 5-39 *Drawing for Exercise 6*

EXTENDING THE SKETCHED OBJECTS

Ribbon: Home > Modify > Trim drop-down > Extend
Toolbar: Modify > Extend **Command:** EXTEND/EX

The **Extend** tool may be considered as the opposite of the **Trim** tool. You can extend lines, polylines, rays, and arcs to connect to other objects by using the **Extend** tool. However, you cannot extend closed loops. The command prompt of the **Extend** tool is similar to that of the **Trim** tool. You are required to select the boundary edges first. The boundary edges are those objects that the selected lines or arcs extend to meet. These edges can be lines, polylines, circles, arcs, ellipses, xlines, rays, splines, text, blocks, or even viewports. The prompt sequence that will follow when you choose the **Extend** tool is given next.

Current settings: Projection=UCS, Edge=Extend
Select boundary edges ...
Select objects or <select all>: *Select boundary edges* Enter
Select object to extend or shift-select to trim or **EXTEND** [Fence/Crossing/Project/Edge/Undo]:

The options used to extend the objects are discussed next.

Select object to extend Option

In this option, you have to specify the object that you want to extend to the selected boundary, refer to Figure 5-40. This prompt is repeated until you press ENTER. Note that you can select a number of objects in a single **Extend** tool.

Shift-select to trim Option

This option is used to switch to the trim mode in the **Extend** tool, if two entities are intersecting. You can press the SHIFT key and then select the object to be trimmed. In this case, the boundary edges are taken as the cutting edges.

Project Option

The **Project** option is used to extend objects in the 3D space. The prompt sequence that will follow when you choose the **Extend** tool is given next.

Current settings: Projection=UCS, Edge=Extend
Select boundary edges ...
Select objects or <select all>: *Select boundary edges* Enter
Select object to extend or shift-select to trim or **EXTEND** [Fence/Crossing/Project/Edge/Undo]: **P** Enter
Enter a projection option [None/UCS/View] <current>:

The **None** option is used whenever the objects to be extended intersect with the boundary edge in 3D space. If you want to extend those objects that do not intersect the boundary edge in 3D space, use the **UCS** or **View** option. The **UCS** option is used to project the objects to the *XY* plane of the current UCS, while the **View** option is used to project the objects to the current view.

Edge Option

You can use this option for extending the objects that do not actually intersect the boundary edge, but would intersect its edge if the boundary edges were extended, refer to Figure 5-41. If you enter **E** at the prompt, the selected object is extended to the implied boundary edge. If you enter **N** at the prompt, only those objects that would actually intersect the real boundary edge are extended (the default). The prompt sequence to use this option is given next.

Current settings: Projection= UCS, Edge= Extend
Select boundary edges...
Select objects or <select all>: *Select the boundary edge* Enter
Select object to extend or shift-select to trim or **EXTEND** [Fence/Crossing/Project/Edge/Undo]: **E** Enter
Enter an implied extension mode [Extend/No extend] <current>: **E** Enter
Select object to extend or shift-select to trim or **EXTEND** [Fence/Crossing/Project/Edge/Undo]: *Select the line to extend.*

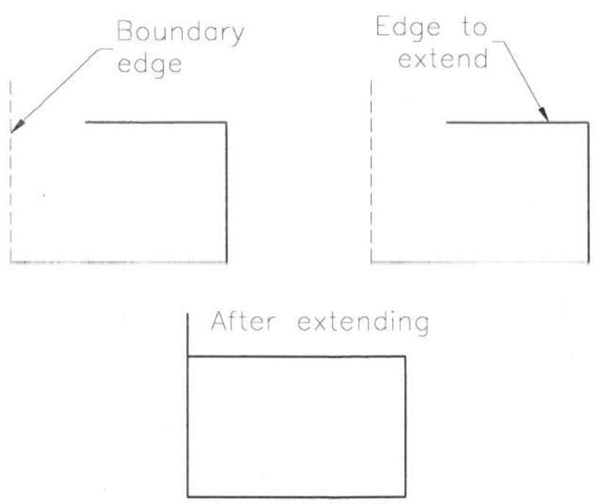

Figure 5-40 *Extending an edge*

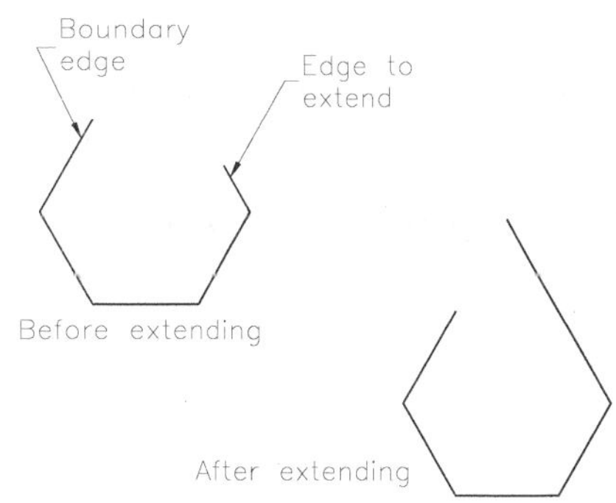

Figure 5-41 *Extending an edge using the **Edge** option (**Extend**)*

Note

*The function of the **Fence** and **Crossing** options in the **Extend** tool is same as that in the **Trim** tool.*

Undo Option

If you want to remove the previous change created by the **Extend** tool, enter **U** at the **Select object to extend or shift-select to trim or EXTEND [Fence/Crossing/Project/Edge/Undo]:** prompt.

Trimming and Extending with Text, Region, or Spline

The **Trim** and **Extend** tools can be used with text, regions, or splines as edges, refer to Figure 5-42. This makes the **Trim** and **Extend** tools the most useful editing tools. The **Trim** and **Extend** tools can also be used with arcs, elliptical arcs, splines, ellipses, 3D Polyline, rays, and lines. The system variables **PROJMODE** and **EDGEMODE** determine how the **Trim** and **Extend** tools are executed, refer to Figure 5-43. The values that can be assigned to these variables are discussed next.

Value	PROJMODE	EDGEMODE
0	True 3D mode	Use regular edge without extension (default)

1	Project to current UCS *XY* plane (default)	Extend or trim the selected object to an imaginary extension of the cutting or boundry edge
2	Project to current view plane	

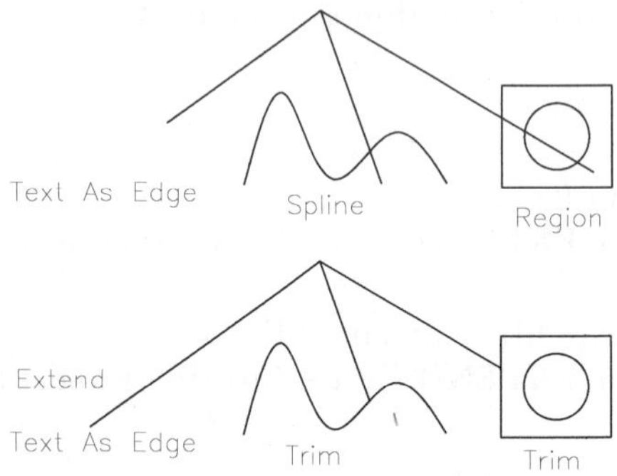

Figure 5-42 *Using the* ***Trim*** *and* ***Extend*** *tools with text, spline, and region*

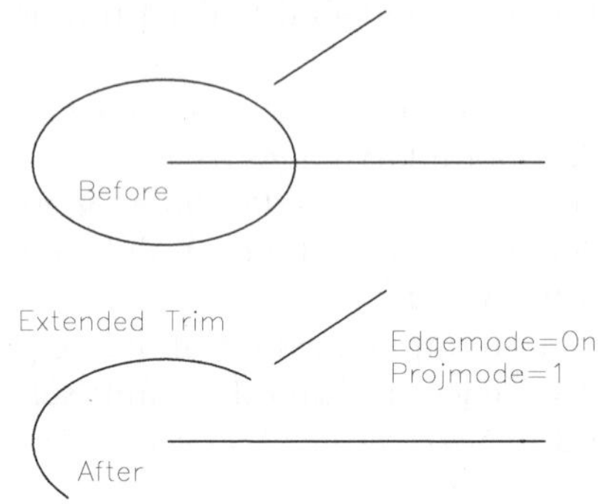

Figure 5-43 *Using the* ***PROJMODE*** *and* ***EDGEMODE*** *options to trim*

STRETCHING THE SKETCHED OBJECTS

Ribbon: Home > Modify > Stretch **Toolbar:** Modify > Stretch
Command: STRETCH/S

This tool is used to lengthen objects, shorten them, and alter their shapes, refer to Figure 5-44. To invoke this tool, choose the **Stretch** tool from the **Modify** panel; you will be prompted to select objects. Use the **Crossing** or **CPolygon** selection method to select the objects to be stretched. After selecting the objects, you will be prompted to specify the base point of displacement. Select the portion of the object that needs to be stretched; you will be prompted to specify the base point; after specifying the base point you will be prompted to specify the second point of displacement. Specify the new location; the object will lengthen or shorten. Figure 5-44 illustrates the usage of a crossing selection to simultaneously select two angled lines and then stretch their right ends.

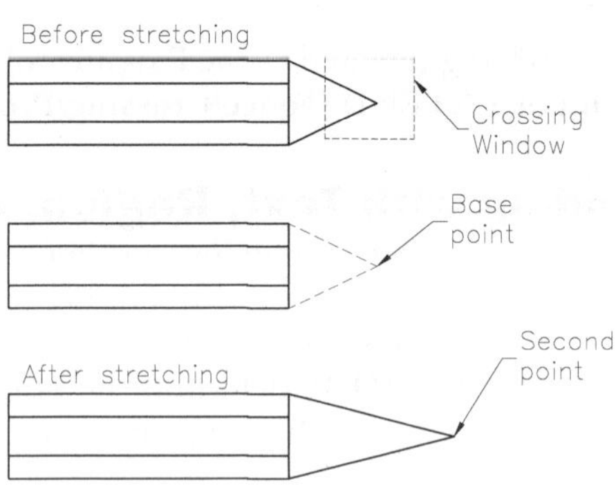

Figure 5-44 *Stretching the entities*

Note

The regions and solids cannot be stretched. If you select them, they will move instead of getting stretched.

LENGTHENING THE SKETCHED OBJECTS

Ribbon: Home > Modify > Lengthen **Command:** LENGTHEN/LEN

Like the **Trim** and **Extend** tools, the **Lengthen** tool can also be used to extend or shorten lines, polylines, elliptical arcs, and arcs. This tool has several options that allow you to change the length of objects by dynamically dragging the object endpoint, entering the delta value, entering the percentage value, or entering the total length of the object. This tool also allows the repeated selection of the objects for editing. The prompt that will follow when you invoke the **Lengthen** tool is given next.

Select an object to measure or [DElta/Percent/Total/DYnamic] <current>:

Select an object Option

This is the default selected option. It returns the current length or the included angle of the selected object. If the object is a line, AutoCAD returns only the length. However, if the selected object is an arc, AutoCAD returns the length and the angle. The same prompt sequence will be displayed, after you select the object.

DElta Option

The **DElta** option is used to increase or decrease the length or angle of an object by defining the distance or angle by which the object will be extended. The delta value can be entered by entering a numerical value or by specifying two points. A positive value will increase (Extend) the length of the selected object, whereas a negative value will decrease it (Trim), refer to Figure 5-45. The prompt sequence to change the length of the object after choosing the **Lengthen** tool is given next.

Select an object to measure or [DElta/Percent/Total/DYnamic] <current>: **DE** Enter
Enter delta length or [Angle] <current>: *Specify the delta length*
Select an object to change or [Undo]: *Select the object to be extended* Enter

Percent Option

The **Percent** option is used to extend or trim an object by defining the change as a percentage of the original length or the angle, see Figure 5-45. The current length of the line is taken as 100 percent. If you enter a value more than 100, the length will increase by that amount. Similarly, if you enter a value less than 100, then the length will decrease by that amount. For example, the numerical value 150 will increase the length by 50 percent and the numerical value 75 will decrease the length by 25 percent of the original value (negative and zero values are not allowed).

Total Option

The **Total** option is used to extend or trim an object by total length or angle, refer to Figure 5-45. For example, if you enter a total length of 1.25, AutoCAD will automatically increase or decrease the length of the object so that the new length is 1.25. The value can be entered by entering a numerical value or by specifying two points. The object is shortened or lengthened with respect to the endpoint that is closest to the selection point. The selection point is determined from where the object was selected.

Tip

*By default, the **Lengthen** tool is not available in the **Modify** toolbar. To add the **Lengthen** tool in the **Modify** toolbar, right-click on any toolbar to display the shortcut menu. Next, choose **Customize** from the shortcut menu to display the **Customize User Interface** dialog box. Select the **Modify** option in the **Filter the command list by category** drop-down list; all the tools that can be added or are currently available in the **Modify** toolbar will be displayed. Drag the **Lengthen** button from the **Command** area to the **Modify** toolbar in the drawing area. Choose the **OK** button from the **Customize User Interface** dialog box.*

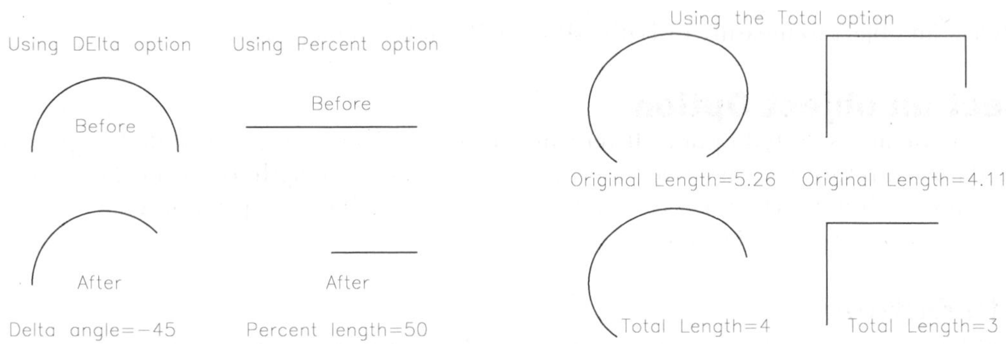

Figure 5-45 *Using the **DElta**, **Percent**, and **Total** options*

DYnamic

The **DYnamic** option allows you to dynamically change the length or angle of an object by specifying one of the endpoints and dragging it to a new location. The other end of the object remains fixed and unaffected by dragging. The angle of lines, radius of arcs, and shape of elliptical arcs remain unaffected on using this option.

ARRAYING THE SKETCHED OBJECTS

Ribbon: Home > Modify > Array **Command:** ARRAY/AR

In some drawings, you may need to create an object multiple times in a rectangular or circular arrangement. This type of arrangement can be obtained by creating an array of objects. An array is defined as the method of creating multiple copies of a selected object and arranging them in a rectangular or circular fashion. This method is more efficient and less time-consuming. In this type of arrangement, each resulting element of the array can be controlled separately. The arrays can be created by using the **Array** drop-down, refer to Figure 5-46. You can use this drop-down to create a rectangular, path, or polar array. The prompt sequence to be followed to create an array of an object after choosing the **Array** drop-down is given next.

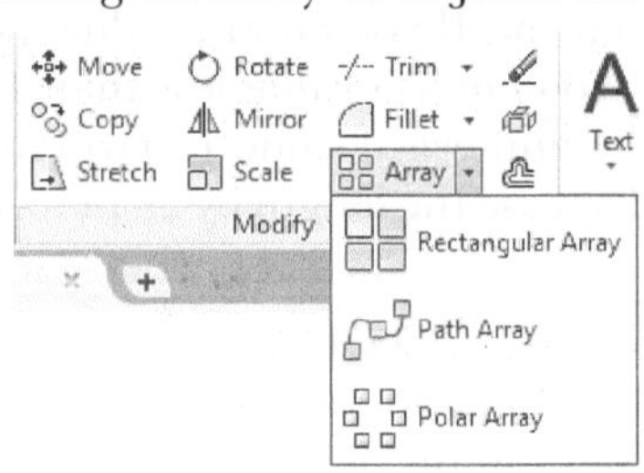

Figure 5-46 *Tools in the **Array** drop-down*

Select objects: *Select the object*
Select Objects: 1 found

Select Objects: Enter
Enter array type [Rectangular/PAth/POlar] <Rectangular>:

At the last prompt, you can specify the type of array to be created. The different types of arrays that can be created using the **Array** drop-down are discussed next.

Rectangular Array

Ribbon: Home > Modify > Array drop-down > Rectangular Array
Toolbar: Modify > Array drop-down > Rectangular Array **Command:** ARRAYRECT

A rectangular array is formed by making copies of the selected object along the *X* and *Y* directions of an imaginary rectangle (along rows and columns). To create a rectangular array, choose the **Rectangular Array** tool from the **Modify** panel; you will be prompted to select objects. Select the objects to be arrayed and press ENTER; you will be prompted to select the grip to edit the array. Select the grip and click to specify the spacing for the array, as required. Also, you can enter the value of spacing. Next, press ENTER or X; the array of the selected object will be created, refer to Figure 5-47. This figure also shows the location of the cursor while specifying the opposite corner. The prompt sequence to create the rectangular array of an object after choosing the **Rectangular Array** tool from the **Array** drop-down is given next.

Select objects: *Select the object*
Select objects: 1 found
Select objects: Enter
Type = Rectangular Associative = Yes
Select grip to edit array or [ASsociative/Base point/COUnt/Spacing/COLumns/Rows/Levels/eXit]<eXit>: *Press* Enter *or* ***X***

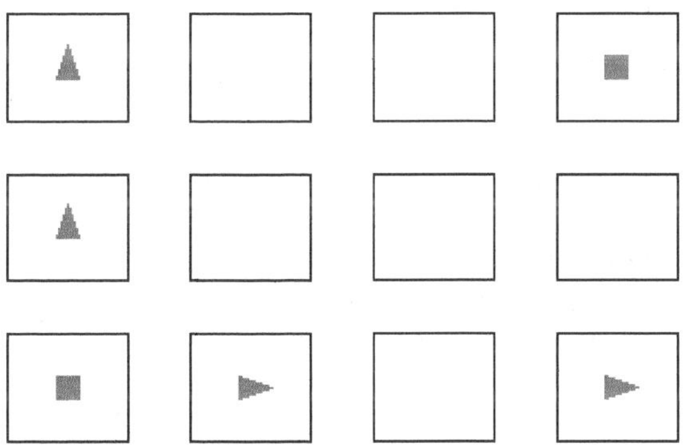

Figure 5-47 *Rectangular array created*

While specifying the opposite corner, if you move the cursor along the vertical or horizontal direction, the array will be created in the specified direction. Figure 5-48 and Figure 5-49 show the array created in the vertical and horizontal directions, respectively.

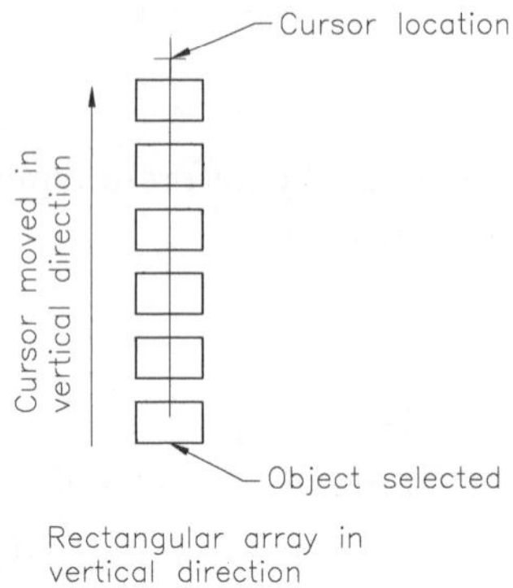

Figure 5-48 A vertical rectangular array created

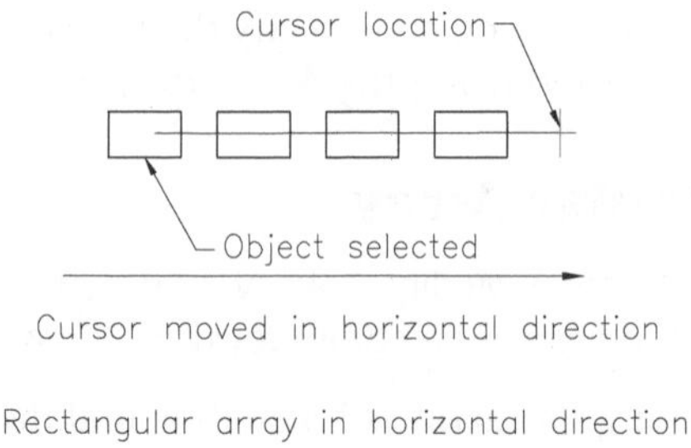

Figure 5-49 A horizontal rectangular array created

Rectangular Array Options

To create a rectangular array, you need to specify the options displayed at the **Select grip to edit array or [ASsociative/Base point/COUnt/Spacing/COLumns/Rows/Levels/eXit]<eXit>:** command prompt. Some of these options are discussed next.

Base point: This option is used to specify the base point of the array to be created. You can specify the base point by selecting a keypoint on the selected object. By default, the centroid is used as the base point for the array. However, you can specify any other point than the centroid of the object as the base point of the array. The prompt sequence that will follow when you invoke the **Base point** option is given next. In this prompt, the **Key point** option has been used.

Select grip to edit the array or [ASsociative/Base point/COUnt/Spacing/COLumns/Rows/Levels/eXit] <eXit>: **B** Enter
Specify base point or [Key point] <centroid> : **K** Enter
Specify a key point on a source object as the base point: *Select any keypoint on the object*

Levels: This option is used to specify the levels in the array, refer to Figure 5-50. If you enter **L** at the **Select grip to edit array or [ASsociative/Base point/COUnt/Spacings/COLumns/Rows/Levels/eXit]<eXit>** command prompt, you will be prompted to enter the number of levels. Enter the required level value and then specify the distance between levels. The prompt sequence that will follow when you invoke the **Level** option is given next.

Select grip to edit array or [ASsociative/Base point/COUnt/Spacings/COLumns/Rows/Levels/eXit]<eXit>: L Enter
Enter number of levels or [Expression] <1>: *Enter the level value* Enter
Specify the distance between levels or [Total/Expression] <1>: *Specify the distance between levels*

COUnt: This option is used to specify the number of rows and columns in the array. If you enter **COU** at the **Select grip to edit array or [ASsociative/Base point/COUnt/Spacings/COLumns/Rows/Levels/eXit]<eXit>:** command prompt, you will be prompted to specify the number of columns. Enter the number of columns in the array and press ENTER; you will be prompted to specify the number of rows in the array. Enter the number of rows and press ENTER.

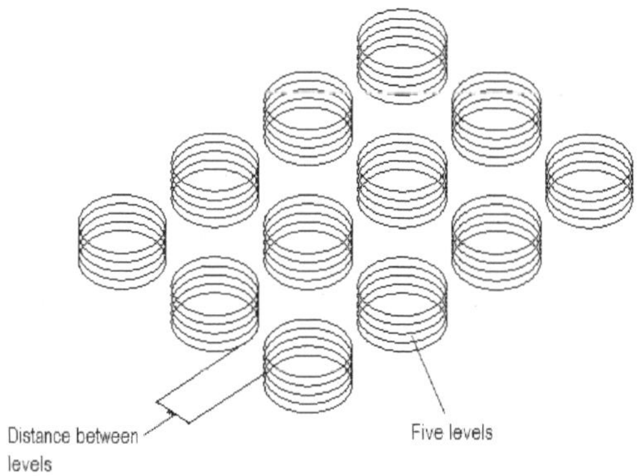

Figure 5-50 *Leveled rectangular array*

Select grip to edit array or [ASsociative/Base point/COUnt/Spacings/COLumns/Rows/Levels/eXit]<eXit>: **COU** Enter
Enter number of columns or [Expression] <current>: *Specify the number of columns* Enter
Enter number of rows or [Expression] <current>: *Specify the number of rows* Enter

You can also specify the number of columns and rows by using expressions or mathematical formulae. Figure 5-51 shows a rectangular array of three rows and six columns.

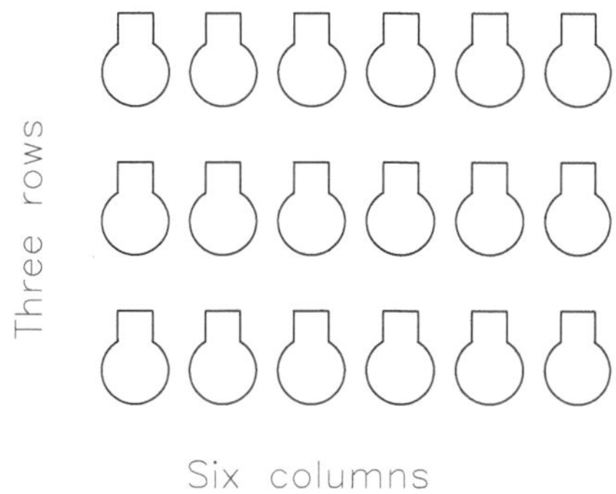

Figure 5-51 *Rectangular array of three rows and six columns*

You can also specify the associativity of the objects in the array. Associativity determines whether the objects of the array are dependent upon each other or not. To specify the associativity, enter **AS** or **ASSOCIATIVE** at the command prompt; you will be prompted to specify whether the objects of the resultant array will be associative or non-associative. Enter **Yes** at the command prompt to make the objects of the array associative. The associative array behaves as a single block. If you enter **No** at the command prompt, the objects of the resultant array will be non-associative. If you edit one of the objects in the non-associative array, the other objects in the array will not be affected. After creating the array, press ENTER or X to exit the **Rectangular Array** tool.

All aforementioned options for creating a rectangular array are also available at the Dynamic Input, refer to Figure 5-52, provided you have chosen the **Dynamic Input** button from the Status Bar.

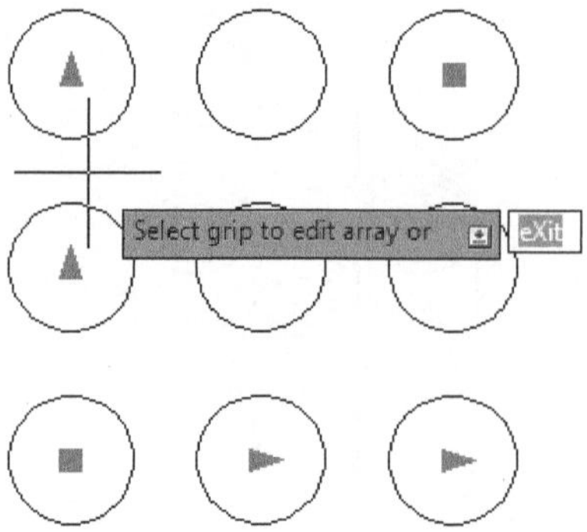

Figure 5-52 Dynamic input options for rectangular array

Editing the Associative Rectangular Array with Grips

You can change the number of rows, columns, and the distance between the objects in the associative array dynamically. To do so, select an object from the array; grips will be displayed on it, refer to Figure 5-53. If you hover the cursor over the parent grip of a multiple row and column array, a tooltip with two options, **Move** and **Level Count**, will be displayed, as shown in Figure 5-54. Choose the **Move** option from the tooltip to move the array. If you choose the **Level Count** option from the tooltip, you will be prompted to specify the number of levels. Levels allow you to create a 3D array. Specify the number of levels at the command prompt or in the **Dynamic Input**; the 3D array will be created. You can view the 3D array in any of the isometric views. The isometric views can be invoked by using the ViewCube or by using the options in the **Views** panel of the **View** tab in the **Ribbon**.

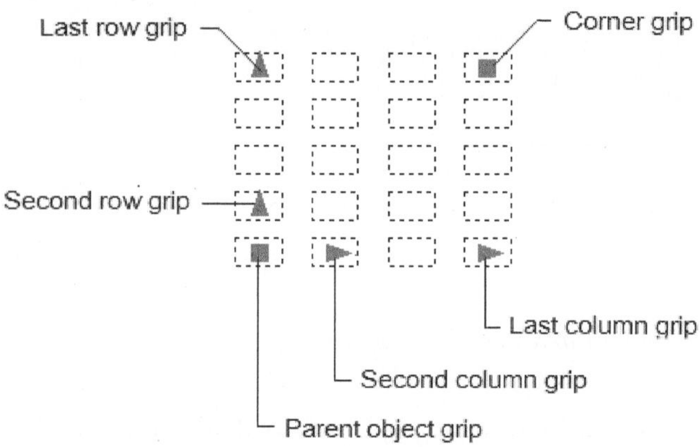

Figure 5-53 Grips of a rectangular array

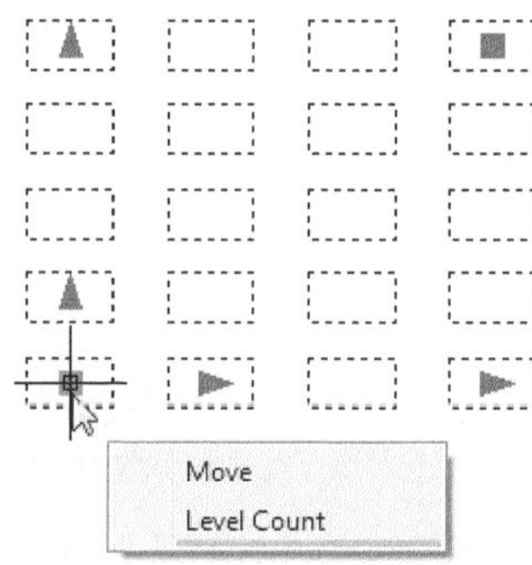

Figure 5-54 The parent grip tooltip

You can also click on the corner grip of the rectangular array to specify the number of rows and columns. Specify the number of rows and columns by dragging the cursor on the screen, preview of the array will be displayed accordingly, as shown in Figure 5-55.

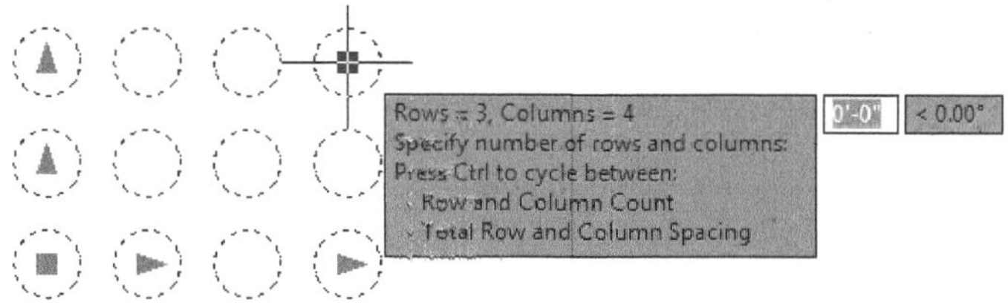

Figure 5-55 *Dynamic prompt displayed on clicking on the corner grip of the rectangular array*

You can change the distance between columns of the rectangular array by clicking on second column grip and then dragging the cursor. In this case, if the **Dynamic Input** button is chosen, the value between the two columns will be displayed in the edit box, refer to Figure 5-56. You can also specify the distance between columns in this edit box displayed.

If you want to increase the number of columns, click on the last column grip; you will be prompted to specify the number of columns, as shown in Figure 5-57. Specify the number of columns and press ENTER.

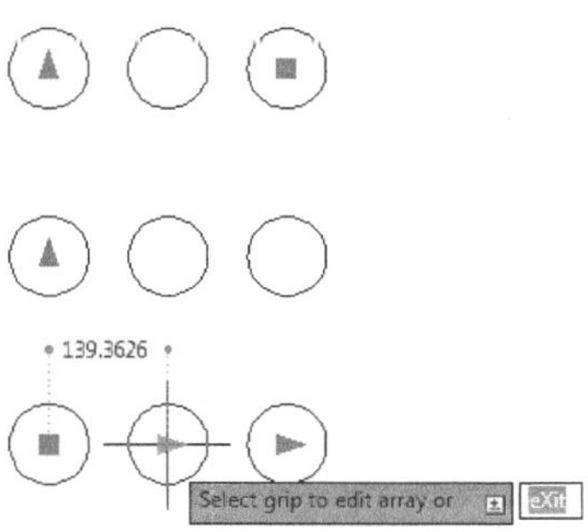

Figure 5-56 *Distance between two columns*

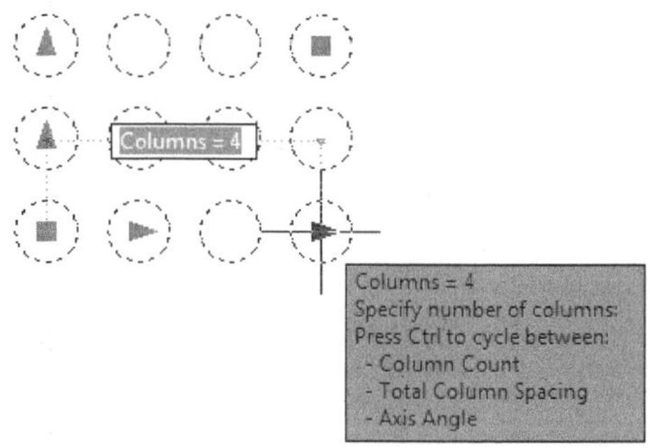

Figure 5-57 *The last column grip tooltip*

Similarly, if you click on the grip on the second row or the last row of the rectangular array, the prompt related to row count will be displayed. Specify the parameters for the rows of the array. Figure 5-58 shows a rectangular array with rows and columns at specified distance.

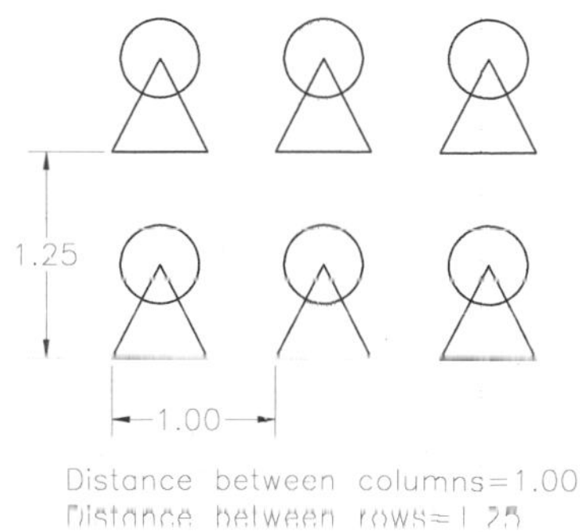

Figure 5-58 *A rectangular array with rows and columns at specified distance*

Editing the Associative Rectangular Array by Using the Array Contextual Tab

You can also edit the associative rectangular array by using the **Array** contextual tab that will be displayed when you select the rectangular array. The **Array** (Rectangular) contextual tab is shown in Figure 5-59.

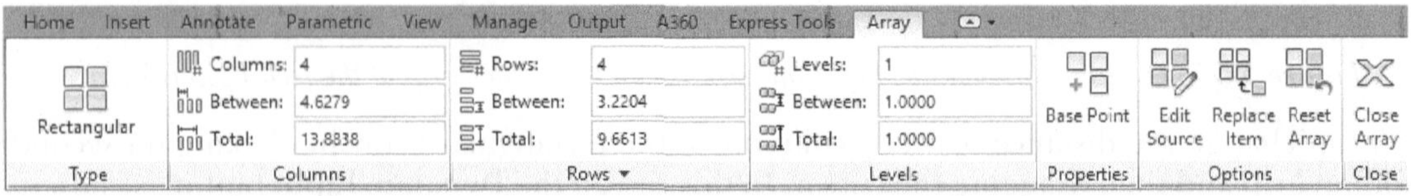

*Figure 5-59 The **Array** (Rectangular) contextual tab*

The different panels and their corresponding options in this tab are discussed next.

Type

This panel displays the type of array to be modified.

Columns

This panel displays three options which are used for changing the number of columns, the distance between two columns, and the total distance between the first and last columns. The description of these options is the same as those discussed in the previous topic.

Rows

This panel displays the options for changing the number of rows, the distance between two rows, and the total distance between the first and last rows. You can also specify the incremental elevation between the rows.

Levels

This panel displays three options for changing the number of levels, the distance between two levels, and the total distance between the first and last levels. The levels allow you to create a 3D array.

Properties

The **Base Point** tool in the **Properties** panel allows you to change the base point of the array.

Options

There are three tools in the **Options** panel: **Edit Source**, **Replace Item**, and **Reset Array**. These options are discussed next.

Edit Source: The **Edit Source** tool is used to edit the source of the array. On choosing this tool, you will be prompted to select an item in the array. Select any object in the array that will act as the source of the array. On selecting an item, the **Array Editing State** message box will be displayed, as shown in Figure 5-60, prompting you either to edit the source object or exit the editing state. Choose **OK** button in this message box; the **Edit Array** panel will be added to the **Home** tab of the **Ribbon**, indicating that you are now in the editing mode. Next, modify the source object geometry. On modifying the source object geometry, you will notice that the other items of the array are also modified. Next, choose the **Save Changes** button from the **Edit Array** panel; the changes made in the array will be saved.

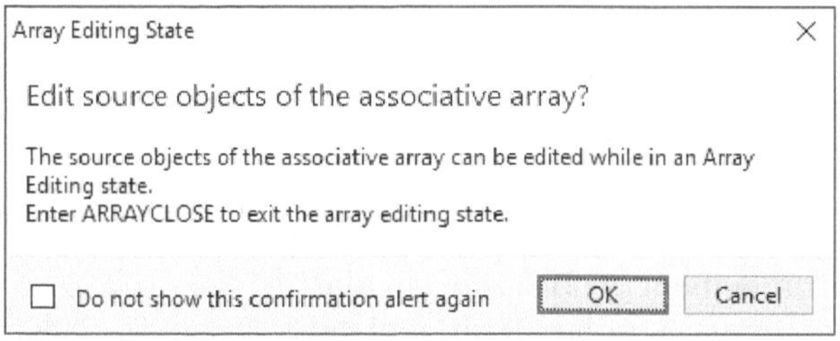

Figure 5-60 *The **Array Editing State** message box*

Figure 5-61 shows the rectangular array of a triangle and Figure 5-62 shows the source of the array being edited.

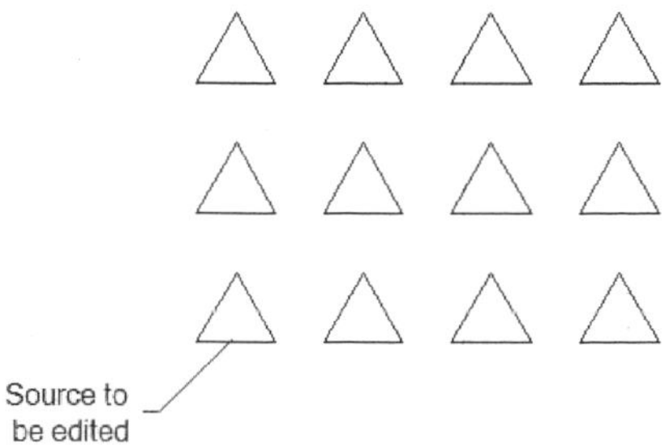

Figure 5-61 *A rectangular array*

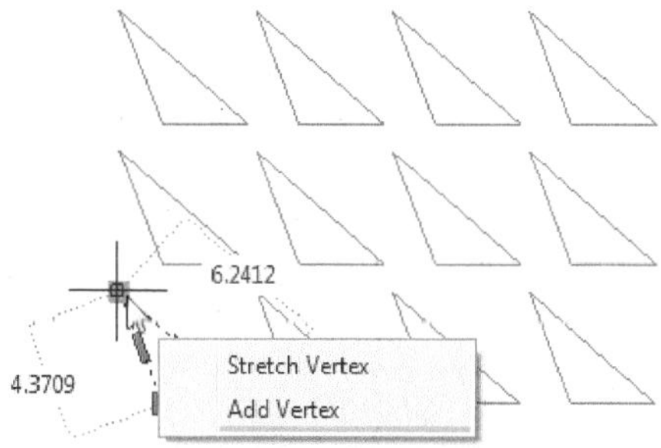

Figure 5-62 *Source of the array being edited*

Replace Item: This tool is used to replace an item in the array with another item. On choosing this tool, you will be prompted to select the replacement object. Select the replacement object and press ENTER; you will be prompted to specify the base point of the replacement object. Click to specify the base point of the replacement object. You can also specify a keypoint as the base point of the replacement object. To do so, enter **K** at the command prompt and then select any keypoint from the array. After specifying the base point, you will be prompted to specify the item to be replaced. Select an item from the array; the selected item will be replaced with the replacement item. You can continue replacing rest of the items in the array by selecting them. Figure 5-63 shows a rectangular array and the replacement object. Figure 5-64 shows the objects of the array after replacing with the selected object.

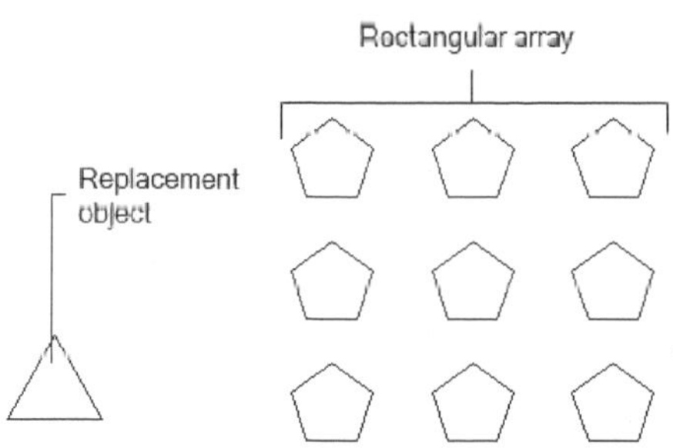

Figure 5-63 *Array with the replacement object*

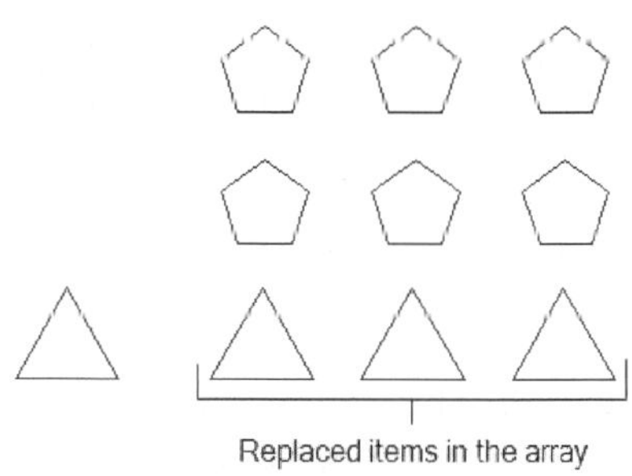

Figure 5-64 *Replaced items in the first row of the array*

Reset Array. This tool is used to restore the objects that have been deleted from the array. If you have made any replacements in the array, those replacements can also be reverted by using this tool.

Polar Array

Ribbon: Home > Modify > Array drop-down > Polar Array
Toolbar: Modify > Array drop-down > Polar Array **Command:** ARRAYPOLAR

Polar array is an arrangement of objects in circular pattern around a point. A polar array can be created by choosing the **Polar Array** tool from the **Array** drop-down of the **Modify** panel, refer to Figure 5-46. When you choose this tool, you will be prompted to select objects. Select objects to be arrayed; you will be prompted to specify the center point of the array. Select the center point of the array; you will be prompted to select grip to edit array. Press ENTER or X to exit the tool. Figure 5-65 shows a polar array with its center.

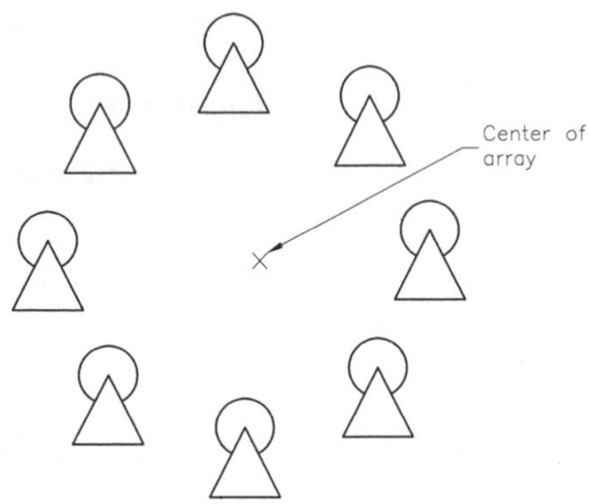

Figure 5-65 *Polar array created*

The prompt sequence to create the polar array of an object after choosing the **Polar Array** tool is given next.

Select objects: *Select the object(s)* Enter
Type = Polar Associative = Yes
Specify center point of array or [Base point/Axis of rotation]: *Click to specify the center point of array*
Select grip to edit array or [ASsociative/Base point/Items/Angle between/Fill angle/ROWs/Levels/ROTate items/eXit] <eXit>: **X** Enter

Polar Array Options

To create a polar array, you need to specify the options displayed at the **Specify center point of array or [Base point/Axis of rotation]:** command prompt. These options are discussed next.

Base point: This option is used to specify the base point of the polar array. You can specify the base point by clicking in the graphics window or by selecting a keypoint on the selected object. By default, the centroid is used as the base point for the array. You can also click in the drawing window to specify the base point of the array. The prompt sequence followed while using the **Base point** option is given next. In this prompt, the **Key point** option has been used.

Specify center point of array or [Base point/Axis of rotation]: **B** Enter
Specify base point or [Key point] <centroid> : **K** Enter
Specify a key point on a source object as the base point: *Select any keypoint on the object*

Axis of rotation: This option is used to specify the rotation angle of the array, refer to Figure 5-66. If you enter **A** at the **Specify center point of array or [Base point/Axis of rotation]:** command prompt, you will be prompted to specify the first point on the axis of rotation. Click to specify the first point; you will be prompted to specify the second point on the axis of rotation. Click to specify the second point; the preview of the polar array depending upon the axis of rotation will be displayed. You can also specify the first and second points of the axis of rotation by using the **Dynamic Input**.

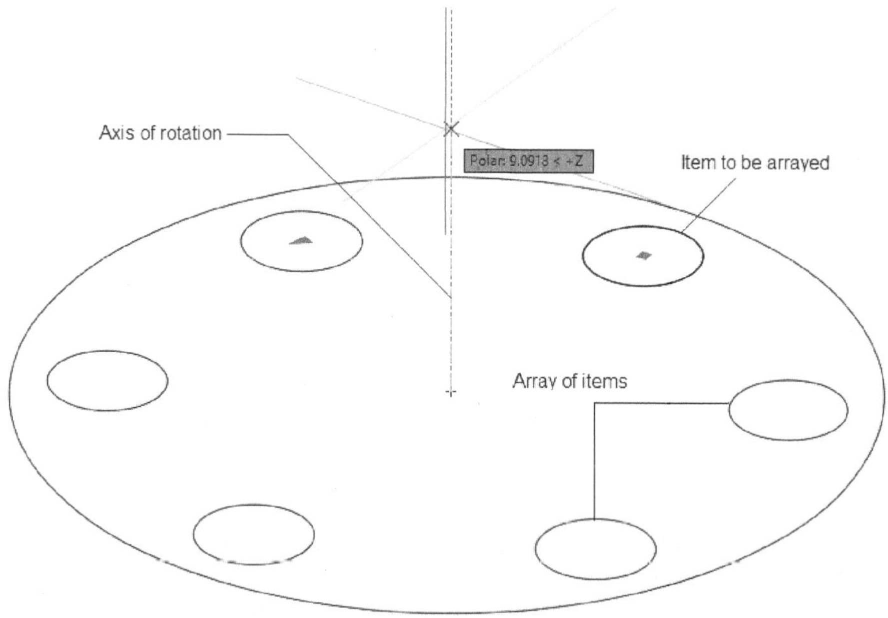

Figure 5-66 *Polar array created around the axis of rotation*

The prompt sequence followed while using the **Axis of rotation** option is given next.

Specify center point of array or [Base point/Axis of rotation]: **A** [Enter]
Specify first point on axis of rotation: *Click to specify the first point*
Specify second point on axis of rotation: *Click to specify the second point*

After specifying the required polar array option, you will be prompted to select grip to edit array. The prompt sequence to enter the number of items in the polar array is given next.

Select grip to edit array or [ASsociative/Base point/Items/Angle between/Fill angle/ROWs/Levels/ROTate items/eXit] <eXit>: **I** [Enter]
Enter number of items in array or [Expression] <current>:

As evident from the command prompt, you can specify the number of items in various ways. The first way is that you can enter the number of items directly at the command prompt. The second way to specify the number of items is by entering the number of items directly in the **Array Creation** contextual tab in the **Items** area. You can also change the angle between the items in the polar array. If you enter **ANGLE** or **A** at the command prompt, you will be prompted to enter the angle between the items. Specify the angle value at the command prompt and press ENTER. You can also specify the angle by using expressions or mathematical formulae. Another way of specifying the angle between the items of the polar array is by specifying the fill angle at the **Select grip to edit array or [ASsociative/Base point/Items/Angle between/Fill angle/ROWs/**

Levels/ROTate items/eXit]<eXit>: command prompt. This command prompt is displayed when you enter the angle between the items in the polar array. The prompt sequence to specify the angle between the items in the polar array of an object after choosing the **Polar Array** tool is given next. In this prompt sequence, the **Angle between** option is used.

Select objects: *Select the objects to be arrayed*
Select objects: Enter
Type = Polar Associative = Yes
Specify center point of array or [Base point/Axis of rotation]: *Click to specify the center point of the array*
Select grip to edit array or [ASsociative/Base point/Items/Angle between/Fill angle/ROWs/Levels/ROTate items/eXit] <eXit>: **A** Enter
Specify angle between items or [EXpression] <current>: *Enter the angle value*
Select grip to edit array or [ASsociative/Base point/Items/Angle between/Fill angle/ROWs/Levels/ROTate items/eXit] <eXit>: **F** Enter
Specify the angle to fill (+=ccw, -=cw) or EXpression <current>: *Enter the fill angle*
Select grip to edit array or [ASsociative/Base point/Items/Angle between/Fill angle/ROWs/Levels/ROTate items/eXit]<eXit>: **X** Enter

After specifying all the options for the polar array, enter X at the **Select grip to edit array or [ASsociative/Base point/Items/Angle between/Fill angle/ROWs/Levels/ROTate items/eXit]<eXit>:** command prompt to exit the **Polar Array** tool. The **ROWs** option is used to specify the number of items in the radially outward direction, whereas the **Levels** option is used to create a 3D polar array. You can view the 3D polar array in any of the isometric views.

Figure 5-67 shows a polar array created by specifying the number or items and the angle between the items. Figure 5-68 shows a polar array created by specifying the number of items and the fill angle.

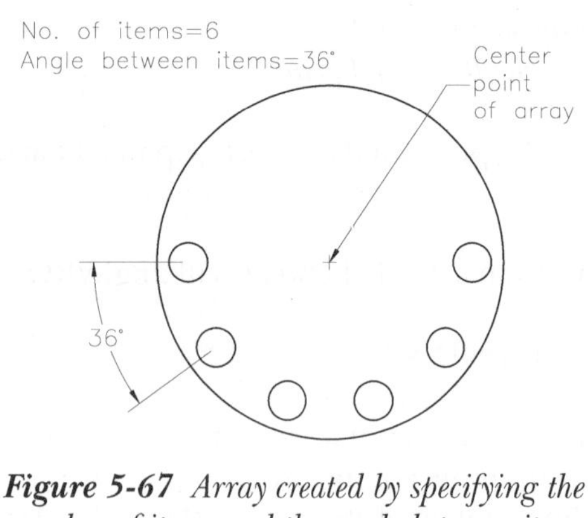

Figure 5-67 *Array created by specifying the number of items and the angle between items*

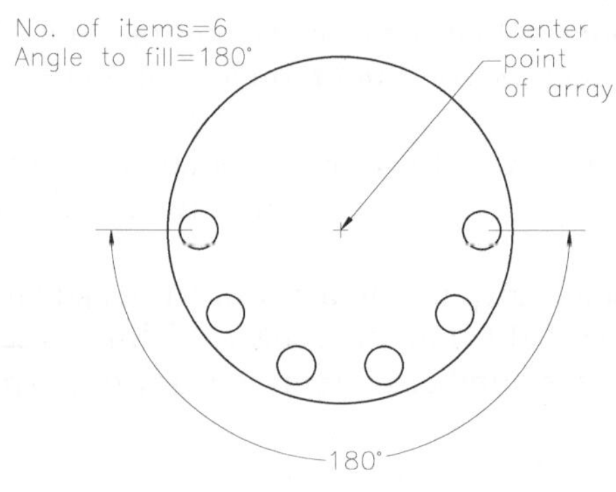

Figure 5-68 *Array created by specifying the number of items and the fill angle*

In an array, you can also make the objects associative. Associativity determines whether the objects of the array will be dependent upon each other or not. To specify the associativity, enter **ASSOCIATIVE** or **AS** at the **Select grip to edit array or [ASsociative/Base point/Items/Angle between/Fill angle/ROWs/Levels/ROTate items/eXit]<eXit>:** command prompt. On doing so, you will be prompted to specify whether the objects of the array created will be associative or non-associative. Enter **Yes** at the Command prompt to make the objects of the array associative. An associative array behaves as a single block. If you enter **No** at the command prompt, the objects of the array created will be non-associative. If you edit one of the objects in the non-associative array, the other objects in the array will not be affected. After creating the array, press ENTER or X to exit the **Polar Array** tool.

All above mentioned options for creating the polar array will also be available at the **Dynamic Input**, refer to Figure 5-69, provided the **Dynamic Input** button is chosen in the Status Bar.

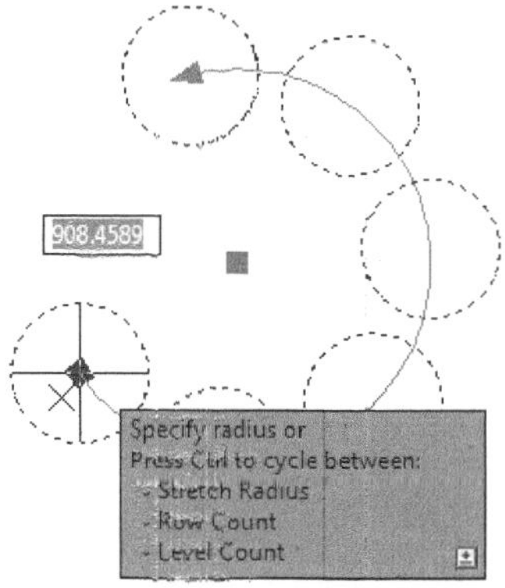

***Figure 5-69** Dynamic input options for polar array*

Editing the Associative Polar Array with Grips

You can change the number of rows, levels, and the fill angle between the objects in the associative array dynamically. To do so, select an object from the array; the grips will be displayed on the array, as shown in Figure 5-70. If you hover the cursor over the parent grip of a multiple row array, a tooltip with two options, **Stretch Radius** and **Level Count**, will be displayed, as shown in Figure 5-71. Choose the **Stretch Radius** option from the tooltip to change the radius of the array. If you choose the **Level Count** option from the tooltip, you will be prompted to specify the number of levels. Specify the number of levels at the command prompt or at the **Dynamic Input**; the 3D array will be created. You can view the 3D array in any of the isometric views. The isometric views can be invoked by using the ViewCube or by using the options in the **Views** panel of the **View** tab in the **Ribbon**.

If you hover the cursor over the second radial grip of the polar array, the angle between the parent item and the second items of the array will be displayed, as shown in Figure 5-72. If you click at this time, an edit box will be displayed and you will be prompted to specify the angle between the items. Enter the desired angle value in this edit box.

If you hover the cursor over the last radial grip of the polar array, a tooltip with two options, **Item Count** and **Fill Angle**, will be displayed, as shown in Figure 5-73. If you choose **Item Count** from the tooltip, an edit box will be displayed and you will be prompted to specify the number of items. Enter the number of items in this edit box. If you choose **Fill Angle** from the tooltip, an edit box will be displayed and you will be prompted to specify the fill angle. Enter the fill angle in this edit box.

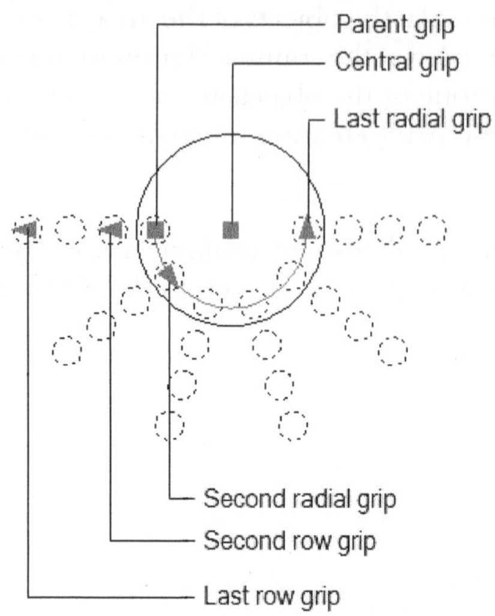

Figure 5-70 Grips of a polar array

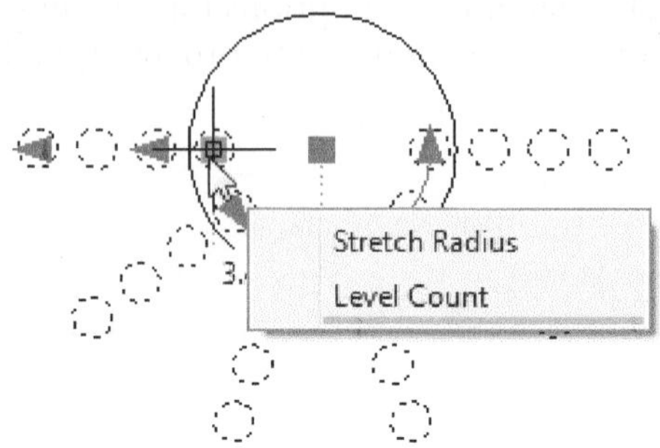

Figure 5-71 The parent grip tooltip

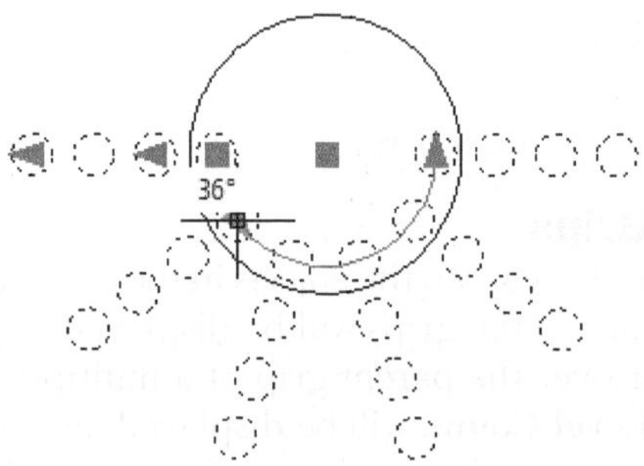

Figure 5-72 Angle displayed between the parent and second radial grips

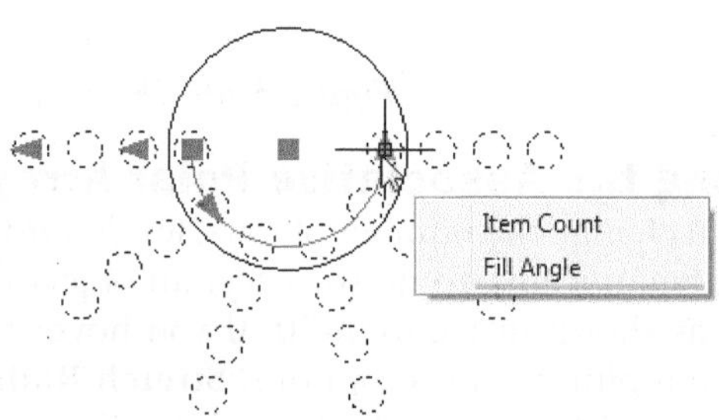

Figure 5-73 Tooltip displayed on the last radial grip

If you hover the cursor over the second row grip of the polar array, the current distance between two rows will be displayed, as shown in Figure 5-74. Click on this grip; an edit box will be displayed and you will be prompted to specify the distance between the two rows. Enter the new value in this edit box to specify the distance between the two rows.

If you hover the cursor over the last row grip of the polar array, a tooltip with two options, **Row Count** and **Total Row Spacing**, will be displayed, as shown in Figure 5-75. If you choose **Row Count** from the tooltip, an edit box will be displayed and you will be prompted to specify the number of rows. Specify the number of rows in the edit box to determine the number of rows in the array. If you choose **Total Row Spacing** from the tooltip, an edit box will be displayed and you will be prompted to specify the distance between the first and last row. Enter the desired value in this edit box.

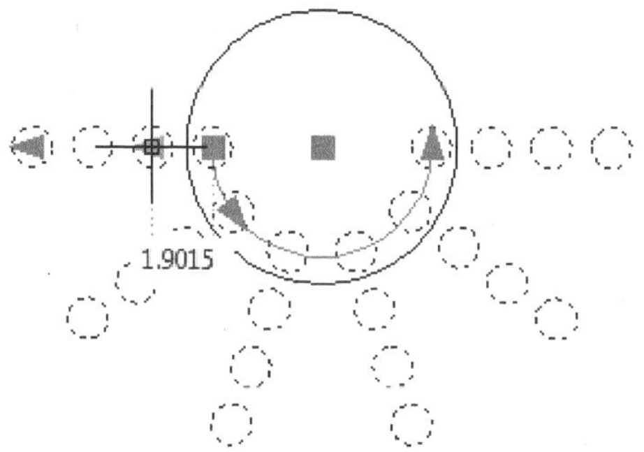

Figure 5-74 Distance displayed between parent and second row grips

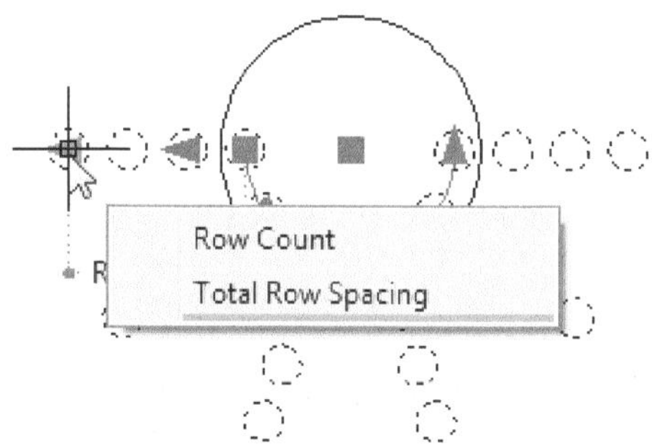

Figure 5-75 Tooltip displayed on the last row grip

In case of single row polar array, if you hover the cursor over the parent object, a tooltip with three options, **Stretch Radius**, **Row Count**, and **Level Count**, will be displayed. You can specify the radius, number of rows, and the number of levels with these options.

Editing the Associative Polar Array Using the Array Contextual Tab

You can also edit the associative polar array by using the **Array** contextual tab that will be displayed when you select the polar array. The **Array** contextual tab is shown in Figure 5-76. Most of the options in the **Array** contextual tab function the same way as those in the rectangular array. The options that are not similar are discussed next.

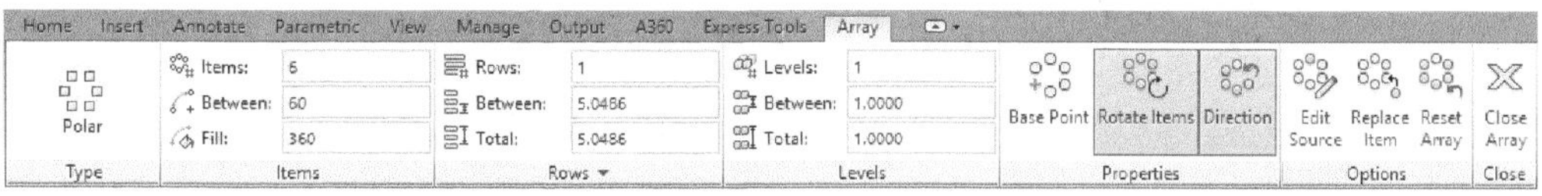

*Figure 5-76 The **Array** (Polar) contextual tab*

Items

This panel displays three options that are used for changing the number of items, angle between two items, and total fill angle between the first and last items. These options are the same as those discussed in the previous topic.

Properties

By default, the **Rotate Items** button is chosen in this panel. As a result, the polar array will be created on rotating the items. Choose the **Base Point** tool if you want to change the base point of the array.

Path Array

Ribbon: Home > Modify > Array drop-down > Path Array
Toolbar: Modify > Array drop-down > Path Array **Command:** ARRAYPATH

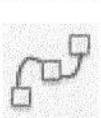

In AutoCAD, you can create an array of objects along a path called path arrays. The path can be a line, polyline, circle, helix, and so on. To create a path array, choose the **Path Array** tool from the **Modify** panel, refer to Figure 5-46. On doing so, you will be prompted to select objects. Select the objects to be arrayed and press ENTER; you will be prompted to select the path curve along which the object will be arrayed. Select the path curve; the preview of the path array will be displayed and you will be prompted to select the grip to edit array. Choose the desired option at the command prompt and press ENTER to accept or X to exit the tool. Figure 5-77 shows the item and the path curve and Figure 5-78 shows the path array created.

The prompt sequence to create the path array of an object after choosing the **Path Array** tool is given next.

> Select objects: *Select the object* Enter
> Type = Path Associative = Yes
> Select path curve: *Select the path*
> Select grip to edit array or [ASsociative/Method/Base point/Tangent direction/Items/Rows/Levels/Align items/Z direction/eXit] <eXit>: **I** Enter
> Specify the distance between items along path or [Expression] <current>: *Enter the distance value between the items*
> Specify number of items or [Fill entire path / Expression] <current>: Enter
> Select grip to edit array or [ASsociative/Method/Base point/Tangent direction/Items/Rows/Levels/Align items/Z direction/eXit] <eXit>:X Enter

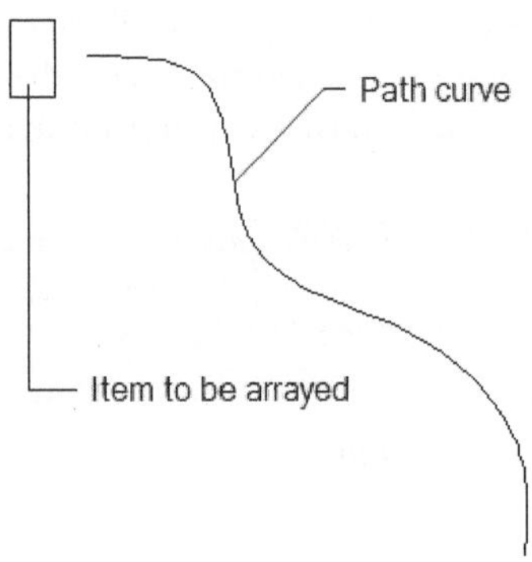

Figure 5-77 *Item and the path curve*

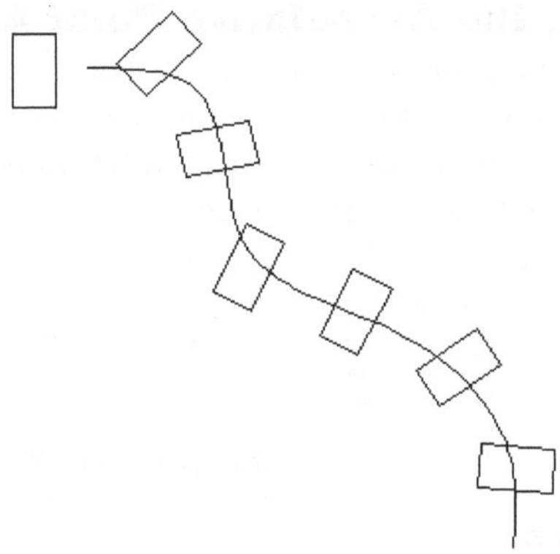

Figure 5-78 *Path array created*

For creating a path array, you need to specify the alignment of the items along the path curve. If you enter **A** at the **Select grip to edit array or [ASsociative/Method/Base point/Tangent direction/Items/Rows/Levels/Align items/Z direction/eXit] <eXit>:** command prompt, you will be prompted to specify whether to align arrayed items to path or not. Enter Y or N; the path array will be created. Figure 5-79 and Figure 5-80 show the path arrays created with the aligned direction and non-aligned (normal to the path curve) orientation of items, respectively.

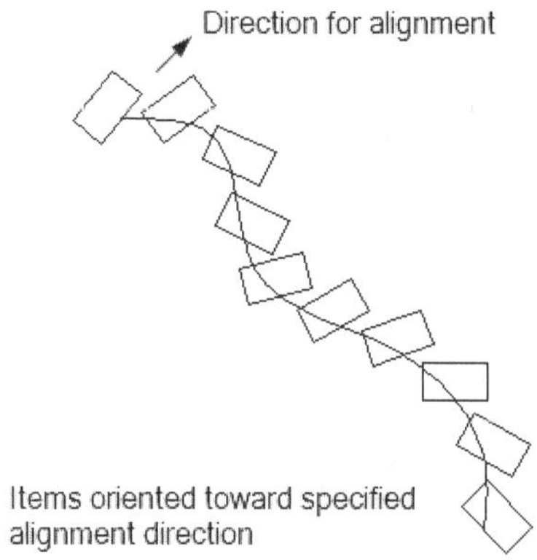

Figure 5-79 Path array created with aligned direction orientation

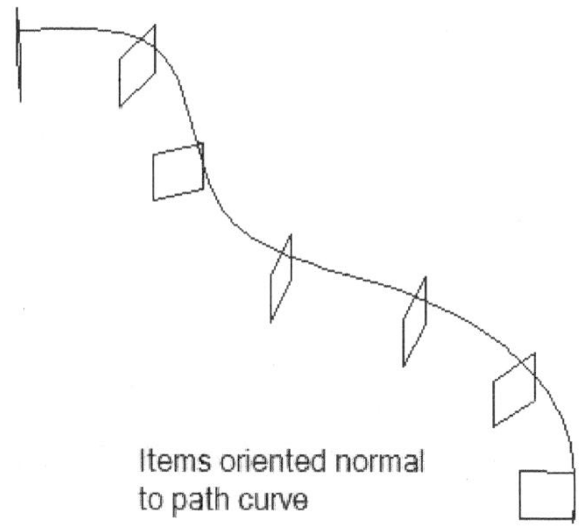

Figure 5-80 Path array created with non-aligned (normal to the path curve) direction orientation

After you have specified the number of items to be created, you need to specify the distance between the items. You can specify the number of items in two ways: **Divide** and **Measure**. Select the **Divide** option in the **Measure Method** drop-down of the **Properties** panel and put the values in the edit boxes available in the **Items** panel. Similarly, select the **Measure Method** option of the **Measure** drop-down in the **Properties** panel and put the values in the edit boxes. Figure 5-81 and Figure 5-82 shows the path array created by using the **Divide** and **Measure** options, respectively.

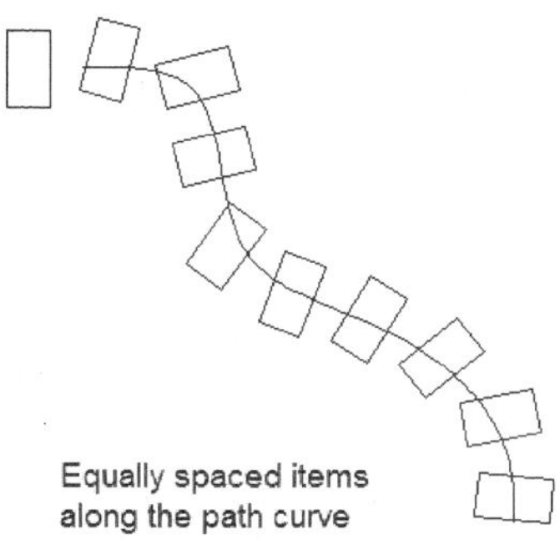

*Figure 5-81 Path array created using the **Divide** option*

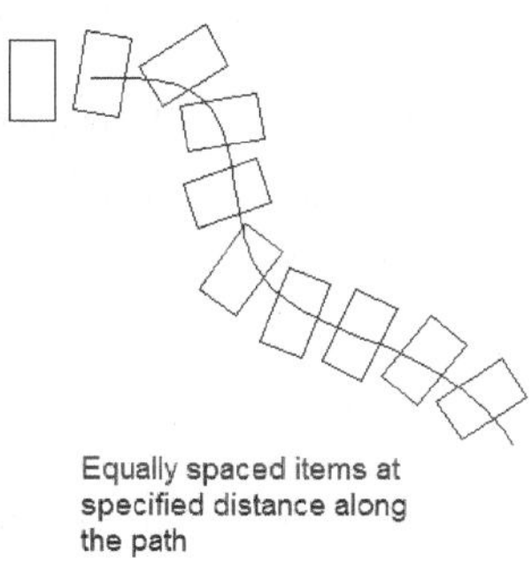

*Figure 5-82 Path array created using the **Measure** option*

All the options discussed here for creating the path array are also available at Dynamic Input, refer to Figure 5-83, which will be available only if the Dynamic Input option is selected from the Status Bar.

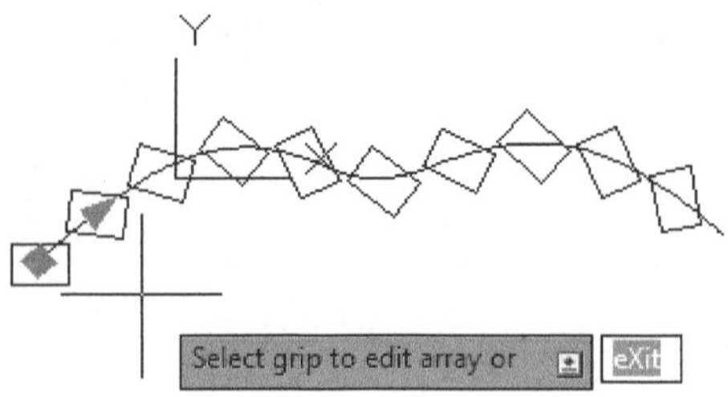

Figure 5-83 Dynamic input options for path array

Editing the Associative Path Array

Like rectangular and polar arrays, you can edit the associative path array by using either the grips or the **Array** contextual tab. The **Array**(Path) contextual tab, as shown in Figure 5-84, will be displayed when you select the path array. Most of the options in the **Array** contextual tab function the same way as those in the rectangular and polar arrays except the options of the **Properties** panel. By default, the **Align Items** and **Z Direction** tools are chosen in this panel. As a result, the path array will be aligned tangent to the path. Also, the original Z direction of the objects will be maintained in case the path is 3-dimensional. You can also use the **Measure** tool to specify the distance between the items of the path array.

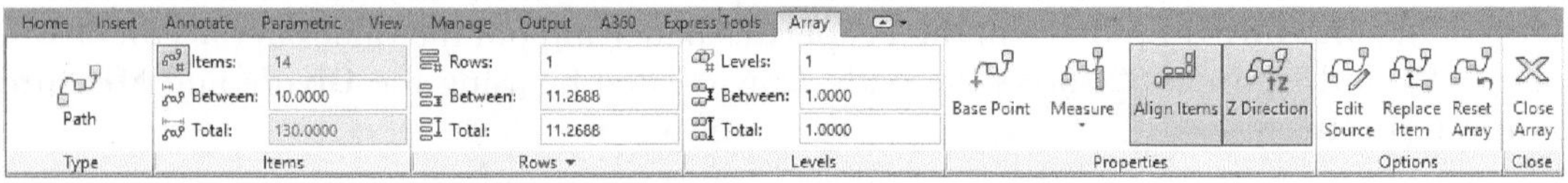

*Figure 5-84 The **Array** (Path) contextual tab*

MIRRORING THE SKETCHED OBJECTS

Ribbon: Home > Modify > Mirror **Toolbar:** Modify > Mirror
Command: MIRROR/MI

The **Mirror** tool is used to create a mirrored copy of the selected objects. The objects can be mirrored at any angle. This tool is helpful in drawing symmetrical figures. On invoking this tool, you will be prompted to select objects. On selecting the objects to be mirrored, you will be prompted to enter the first point of the mirror line and the second point of the mirror line. A mirror line is an imaginary line about which the objects are mirrored. You can specify the endpoints of the mirror line by specifying the points in the drawing area or by entering their coordinates. The mirror line can be specified at any angle. On selecting the first point of the mirror line, a preview of the mirrored objects will be displayed. Next, you need to specify the second endpoint of the mirror line, as shown in Figure 5-85. On selecting the second endpoint, you will be prompted to specify whether you want to delete the source object or not. Enter **Yes** to delete the source object and **No** to retain the source object, refer to Figure 5-86.

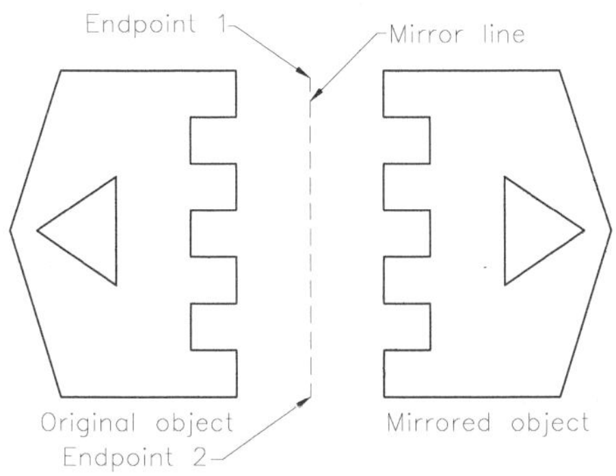

Figure 5-85 *Creating a mirror image of an object by using the **Mirror** tool*

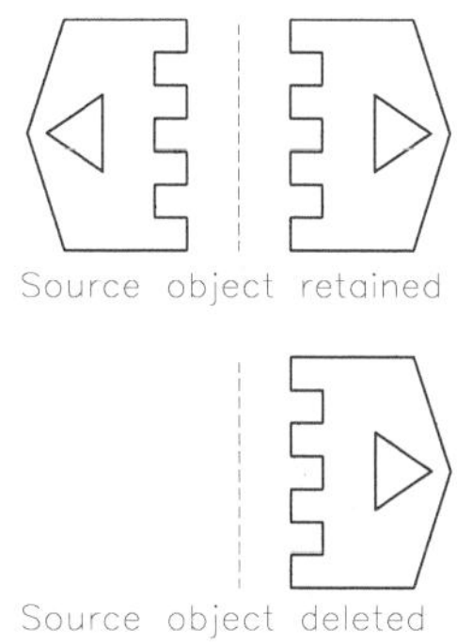

Figure 5-86 *Retaining and deleting source objects after mirroring*

The prompt sequence that will follow when you choose this tool is given next.

Select objects: *Select the objects to be mirrored* Enter
Specify first point of mirror line: *Specify the first endpoint*
Specify second point of mirror line: *Specify the second endpoint*
Erase source objects? [Yes/No] <No>: *Enter **Y** to delete the source object and **N** to retain the source object*

To mirror the objects at some angle, define the mirror line accordingly. For example, to mirror an object such that the mirrored object is placed at an angle of 90 degrees from the original object, define the mirror line at an angle of 45 degrees, refer to Figure 5-87.

Text Mirroring

By default, the **Mirror** tool reverses all the objects, except the text. But, if you want the text to be mirrored (written backward) then you need to modify the value of the **MIRRTEXT** system variable. This variable has two values that are given next, refer to Figure 5-88.

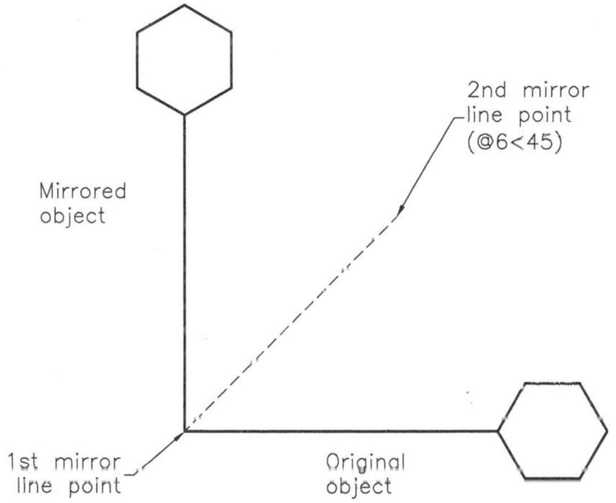

Figure 5-87 *Mirroring the object at an angle*

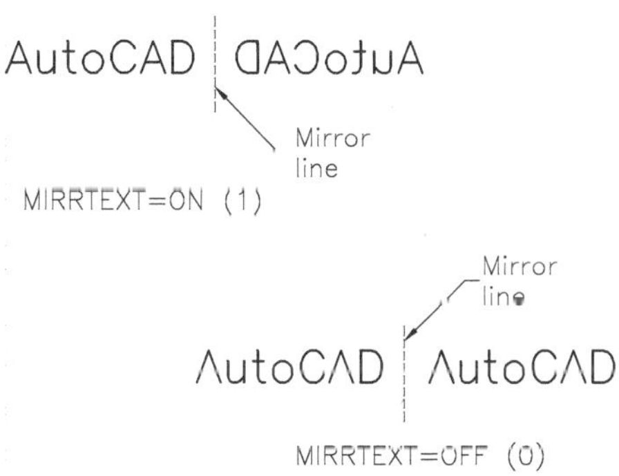

Figure 5-88 *Using the **MIRRTEXT** system variable for mirroring the text*

1 = Text is reversed in relation to the original object.
0 = Restricts the text from being reversed with respect to the original object. This is the default value.

BREAKING THE SKETCHED OBJECTS

Ribbon: Home > Modify > Break at Point, Break **Command:** BREAK/BR
Toolbar: Modify > Break at Point, Break

The **Break** tool breaks an existing object into two parts or erases a portion of an object. This tool can be used to remove a part of the selected objects or to break objects such as lines, arcs, circles, ellipses, xlines, rays, splines, and polylines. You can break the objects using the methods discussed next.

Break at Point

Choose the **Break at Point** tool from the **Modify** panel to break an object into two parts by specifying a breakpoint. On choosing this tool, you will be prompted to select the object to be broken. Once you have selected the object, you will be prompted to specify the first break point. Specify the first break point on the object; the object will be broken.

Break

To break an object by removing a portion of the object between two selected points, choose the **Break** tool from the **Modify** panel; you will be prompted to select the object. Select the object; you will be prompted to select the second break point. Select a point on the object; the portion of the object between the two selected points will be removed. Note that the point at which you select an object becomes the first break point.

The prompt sequence that will follow when you choose this tool is given next.

Select object: *Select the object to be broken*
Specify second break point or [First point]: *Specify the second break point on the object*

The object is broken and the portion in between the broken objects is removed, refer to Figure 5-89.

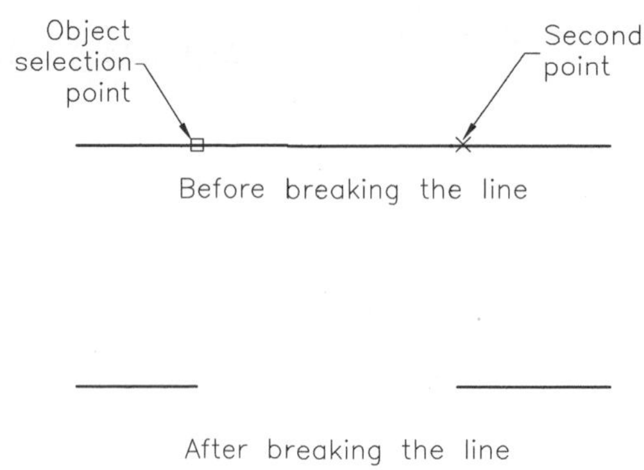

Figure 5-89 *Using the **Break** option for breaking the line*

You can also specify first break point after selecting the object. To do so, enter **F** at the **Specify second point or [First point]:** command prompt, refer to Figure 5-90. The prompt sequence that will follow when you choose the **Break** tool is given next.

Select object: *Select the object to be broken*
Specify second break point or [First point]: **F** Enter
Specify first break point: *Specify a new starting break point*
Specify second break point: *Specify the second break point on the object*

If you need to work on arcs or circles, make sure that you work in the counterclockwise direction, or you may end up cutting the wrong part. In this case, the second point should be selected in the counterclockwise direction with respect to the first one, refer to Figure 5-91.

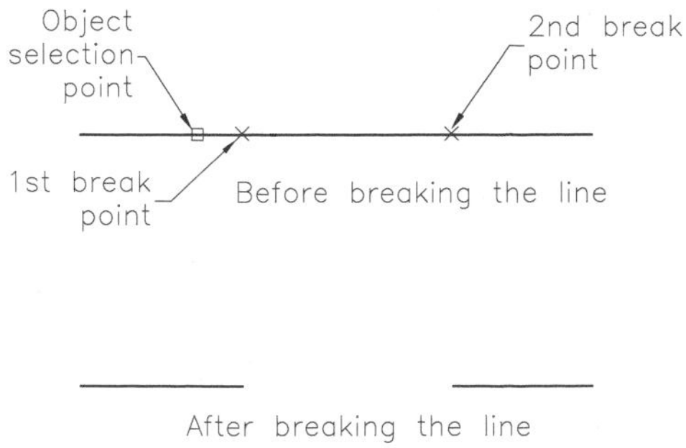

***Figure 5-90** Re-specifying the first break point for breaking the line*

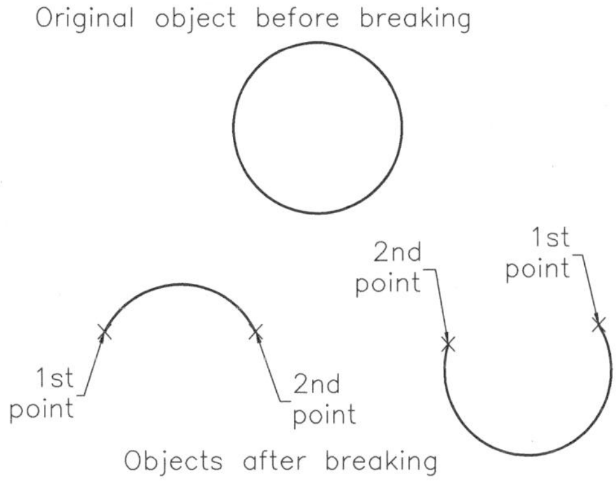

***Figure 5-91** Breaking a circle*

You can use the **Break** tool to break an object into two without removing a portion in between. This can be done by specifying the same point on the object as the first and second break points. If you specify the first break point on a line and the second break point beyond the end of the line, one complete end starting from the first break point will be removed.

Exercise 7 — Break

Break a line at five different places and then erase the alternate segments.

PLACING POINTS AT SPECIFIED INTERVALS

Ribbon: Home > Draw > Measure **Command:** MEASURE/ME

While drawing, you may need to segment an object at fixed distances without actually dividing it. You can use the **Measure** tool to accomplish this task. This tool places points or blocks (nodes) on a given object at a specified distance. The shape of these points is determined by the **PDMODE** system variable and the size is determined by the **PDSIZE** system variable. Alternatively, you can also determine the point size and point style by using the **Point Style** tool from the **Utilities** panel of the **Home** tab.

To measure an object, invoke the **Measure** tool from the **Draw** panel and select the object to be measured; you will be prompted to specify the length. Enter the length; the points will be placed at regular intervals of the specified length. Instead of entering a value, you can also select two points that will be taken as distance. The **Measure** tool starts measuring the object from the endpoint that is closest to the object selection point. Note that markers are placed at equal intervals of the specified distance without considering whether the last segment is at the same distance or not.

When a circle is to be measured, an angle from the center is formed that is equal to the Snap rotation angle. This angle becomes the start point of measurement, and markers are placed at equal intervals in the counterclockwise direction.

In Figure 5-92, a line and a circle are measured. The Snap rotation angle is 0 degree. The **PDMODE** variable is set to 3 so that X marks are placed as markers. The prompt sequence that will follow when you invoke this option from the **Draw** menu is given next.

Select object to measure: *Select the object to be measured*
Specify length of segment or [Block]: *Specify the length for measuring the object*

You can also place blocks as markers (Figure 5-93), but the block must already be defined within the drawing. You can align these blocks with the object to be measured. The prompt sequence is given next.

Select object to measure: *Select the object to be measured*
Specify length of segment or [Block]: **B** Enter
Enter name of block to insert: *Enter the name of the block*
Align block with object? [Yes/No] <Y>: *Enter **Y** to align, **N** to not align*
Specify length of segment: *Enter the measuring distance*

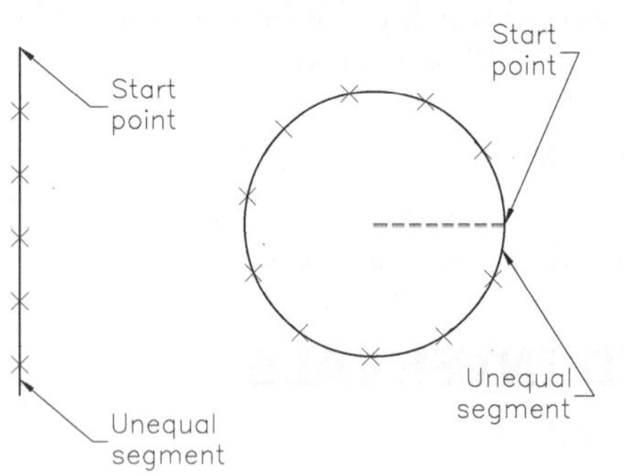

Figure 5-92 *Measuring a line and a circle*

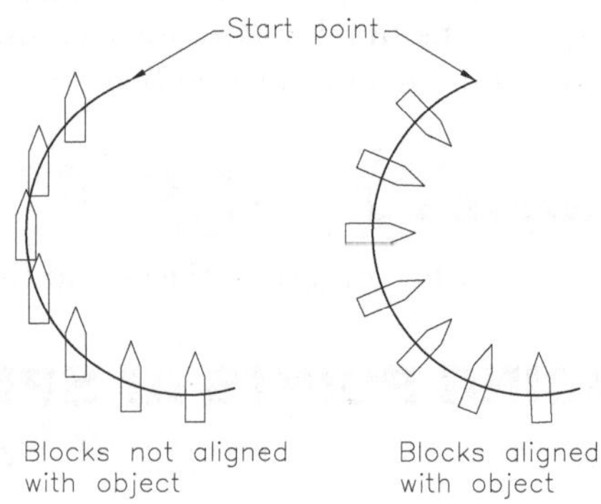

Figure 5-93 *Blocks placed as markers*

Note
You will learn more about creating and inserting blocks in Chapter 16 (Working with Blocks).

DIVIDING THE SKETCHED OBJECTS

Ribbon: Home > Draw > Divide **Command:** DIVIDE/DIV

The **Divide** tool is used to divide an object into a specified number of equal length segments without actually breaking it. This tool is similar to the **Measure** tool except that here you do not need to specify the distance. The **Divide** tool is used to calculate the total length of an object and place markers at equal intervals. This makes the last interval equal to the rest of the intervals. If you want to divide a line, invoke this tool and select the line, Then, enter the number of divisions or segments. The prompt sequence that will follow when you invoke this tool is given next.

Select object to divide: *Select the object you want to divide*
Enter number of segments or [Block]: *Specify the number of segments*

You can also place blocks as markers, but the blocks must be defined within the drawing. You can then align these blocks with the object to be measured. The prompt sequence to place a block as a marker after choosing the **Divide** tool is given next.

Select object to divide: *Select the object to be measured*
Enter number of segments or [Block]: **B** Enter
Enter name of block to insert: *Enter the name of the block*
Align block with object? [Yes/No] <Y>: *Enter **Y** to align, **N** to not align*
Enter number of segments: *Enter the number of segments*

Figure 5-94 shows a line and a circle divided by using this tool and Figure 5-95 shows the use of blocks for dividing the selected segment.

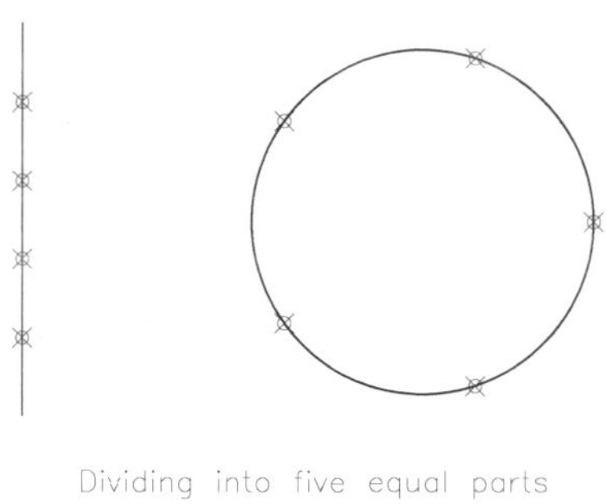

Figure 5-94 *Dividing a line and a circle*

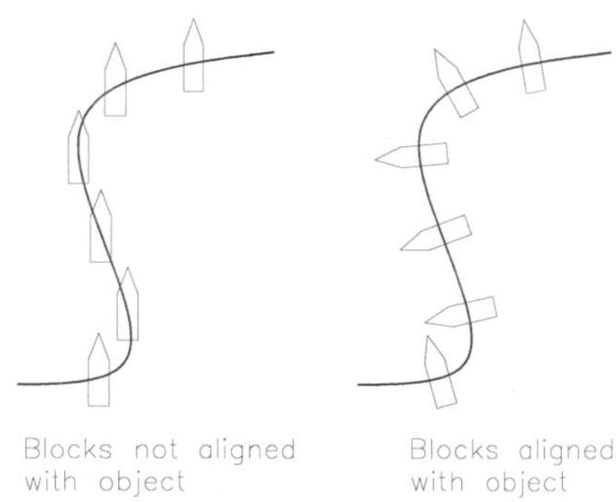

Figure 5-95 *Using blocks for dividing the segments*

Note

*The size and shape of the points placed by using the **Divide** and **Measure** tools are controlled by the **PDSIZE** and **PDMODE** system variables.*

JOINING THE SKETCHED OBJECTS

Ribbon: Home > Modify > Join **Command:** JOIN/J

The **Join** tool is used to join two or more collinear lines or arcs lying on the same imaginary circle. The lines or arcs can have gap between them. This tool can also be used to join two or more polylines or splines, but they should be on the same plane and should not have any gap between them. Note that this tool can also be used to join the two endpoints of an arc to convert it into a circle. On invoking this tool, you will be prompted to select the source object. The source object is the one with which other objects will be joined. The prompt sequence depends on the type of source object selected. The following prompt sequence is displayed when you invoke this tool:

Select source object or multiple objects to join at once: *Select a sketched entity (line, polyline, arc, elliptical arc, or spline)*
Select object to join: Enter

Joining Collinear Lines

If you have selected a line as the source object, you will be prompted to select lines to join to source. Remember that the lines will be joined only if they are collinear. If there is any gap between the endpoints of lines, the gap will be filled. The prompt sequence for joining two lines with a source line is given next.

Select lines to join to source: *Select the first line to join to the source*
Select lines to join to source: *Select the second line to join to the source*
Select lines to join to source: Enter
2 lines joined to source

Joining Arcs

Disjointed arcs can be joined by using the **Join** tool only if all of them lie on the same imaginary circle. The prompt sequence that follows when you select an arc as the source object is given next.

Select arcs to join to source or [cLose]: *Select the first arc to join to the source*
Select arcs to join to source: *Select the second arc to join to the source or* Enter

After selecting the first arc, enter **L** at the **Select arcs to join to source or [cLose]** prompt to close the arc and convert it into a circle.

Joining Elliptical Arcs

Elliptical arcs can be joined by using the **Join** tool only if they lie on the same imaginary ellipse on which the source elliptical arc lies. The prompt sequence that follows when you select an elliptical arc as the source object is given next.

Select elliptical arcs to join to source or [cLose]: *Select the first elliptical arc to join to the source*
Select elliptical arcs to join to source: *Select the second elliptical arc to join to the source or* Enter

After selecting an elliptical arc, enter **L** at the **Select arcs to join to source or [cLose]** prompt to close the arc and convert it into an ellipse.

Joining Splines

In this case, you need to select a spline as the source object. On doing so, you will be prompted to select splines to join to the source. The splines will be joined only if they are coplanar and are connected at their ends. The prompt sequence that follows when you select **Spline** as the source object is given next.

Select any open curves to join to source: *Select the first spline to join to the source*
Select any open curves to join to source: *Select the second spline to join to the source or* Enter

Joining Polylines

Only the end-connected polylines can be joined using this tool. The prompt sequence when you select a polyline as the source object is given next.

Select objects to join to source: *Select a polyline/arc/line to join to the source*
Select objects to join to source: *Select a polyline/arc/line to join to the source or* Enter

Example 1 — Rectangular and Polar Arrays

In this example, you will create the drawing of an end plate. The dimensions of the end plate are shown in Figure 5-96.

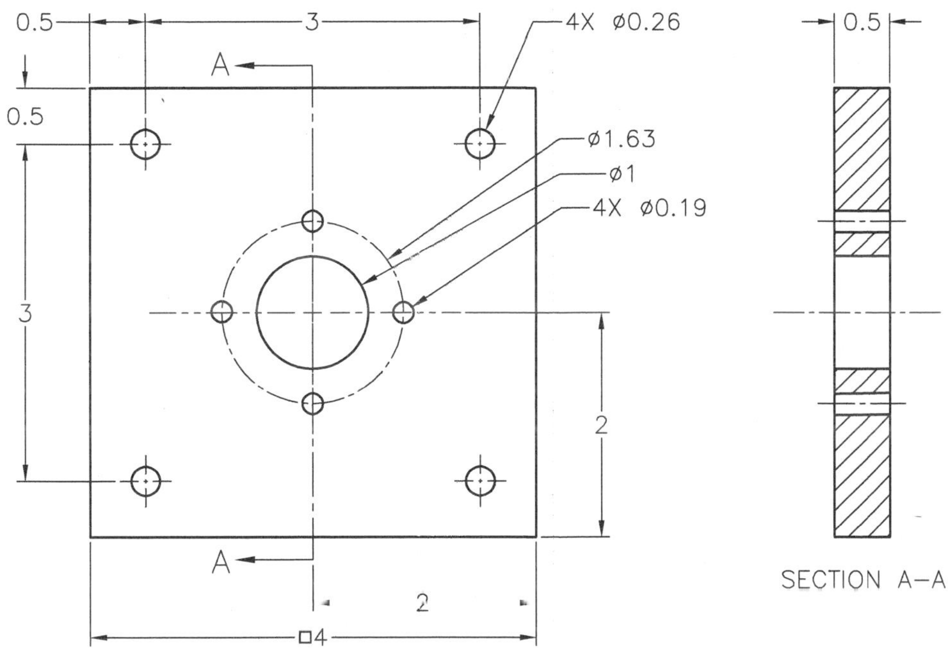

Figure 5-96 *Drawing for Example 1*

First, you need to create a rectangle by using the **Rectangle** tool.

1. Start a new drawing file in the **Drafting & Annotation** workspace.

2. Choose the **Rectangle** tool from **Home > Draw > Rectangle** drop-down and draw a rectangle of **4** units in length and breadth each. The prompt sequence to draw the rectangle is:

Choose the ***Rectangle*** *tool from the* ***Draw*** *panel*
Specify first corner point or [Chamfer/Elevation/Fillet/Thickness/Width]: **0,0** Enter
Specify other corner point or [Area/Dimensions/Rotation]: **@4,4** Enter

After creating the rectangle, you need to create three circles of different radii. These circles can be created by using the **Center, Radius** tool. You need to use the **From** object snap mode to create the third circle.

3. Choose the **Center, Radius** tool from **Home > Draw > Circle** drop-down and draw a circle of diameter **1** unit, as shown in Figure 5-97. The prompt sequence to draw the circle is:

   Choose the ***Center, Radius*** *tool from the* ***Draw*** *panel*
   Specify center point for circle or [3P/2P/Ttr (tan tan radius)]: **2,2** Enter
   Specify radius of circle or [Diameter] <current>: **D** Enter
   Specify diameter of circle <current>: **1** Enter

4. Press ENTER to invoke the **Center, Radius** tool again and draw a circle of diameter **0.26** unit, as shown in Figure 5-98. You can also invoke the **Center, Radius** tool from the **Ribbon**. The prompt sequence to draw the circle is:

   Choose the ***Center, Radius*** *tool from the* ***Draw*** *panel*
   Specify center point for circle or [3P/2P/Ttr (tan tan radius)]: **0.5, 0.5** Enter
   Specify radius of circle or [Diameter] <current>: **D** Enter
   Specify diameter of circle <current>: **0.26** Enter

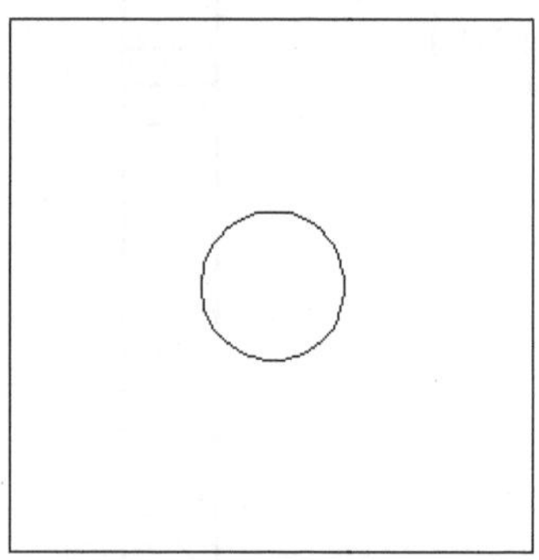

Figure 5-97 *Rectangle and circle created*

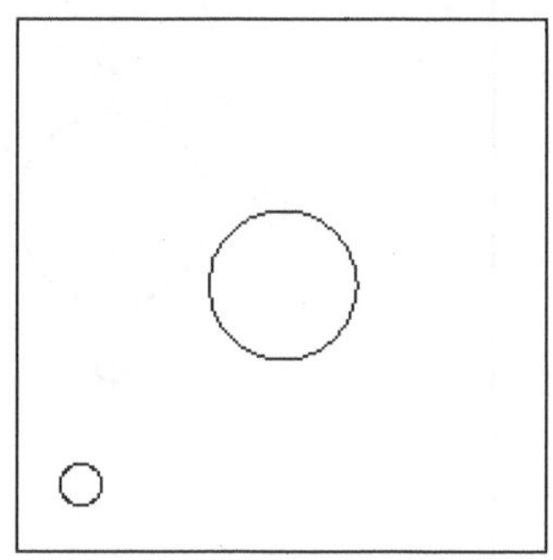

Figure 5-98 *Circle of diameter* ***0.26*** *unit created*

5. Again, press ENTER to invoke the **Center, Radius** tool. You can also invoke this tool from the **Draw** panel. Next, press SHIFT and then right-click to invoke a shortcut menu.

6. Choose the **From** option from the shortcut menu and then draw the circle, as shown in Figure 5-99 by following the prompt given next.

   Choose the ***Center, Radius*** *tool from the* ***Draw*** *panel*
   Specify center point for circle or [3P/2P/Ttr (tan tan radius)]: _from Base point: *Click the center of the circle of diameter 1 unit*
   _from Base point: <Offset>: **@-0.8125,0** Enter

Specify radius of circle or [Diameter] <current>: **D** Enter
Specify diameter of circle <current>: **0.19** Enter

After creating all circles, you need to create the pattern of two circles created last. The first array will be a rectangular array and second array will be a polar array. These arrays will be created by using the **Rectangular Array** and **Polar Array** tools.

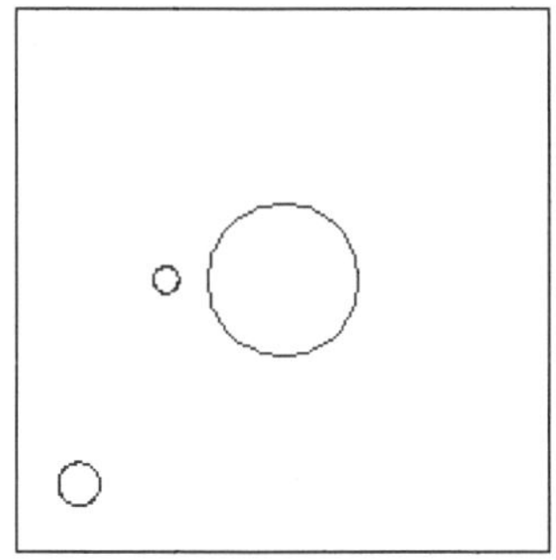

Figure 5-99 *Top view of the model*

7. Choose the **Rectangular Array** tool from **Home > Modify > Array** drop-down and follow the command prompt given next to create a rectangular array of the circle of diameter **0.26** unit shown in Figure 5-100.

*Choose the **Rectangular Array** tool from the **Modify** panel*
Select objects: *Select the circle of diameter 0.26 units and press ENTER*
Type = Rectangular Associative = Yes
Select grip to edit array or [ASsociative/Base point/COUnt/Spacing/COLumns/Rows/Levels/eXit]<eXit>: COU Enter
Enter the number of columns or [Expression] <4>: 2 Enter
Enter the number of rows or [Expression] <3>: 2 Enter
Select grip to edit array or [ASsociative/Base point/COUnt/Spacing/COLumns/Rows/Levels/eXit]<eXit>: S Enter
Specify the distance between columns or [Unit cell]<current>: 3 Enter
Specify the distance between rows <current>: 3 Enter
Select grip to edit array or [ASsociative/Base point/COUnt/Spacing/COLumns/Rows/Levels/eXit]<eXit>: X Enter

8. Next, choose the **Polar Array** tool from **Draw > Modify > Array** drop-down and follow the prompt given next to create a polar array of the circle of diameter **0.19** unit shown in Figure 5-101.

*Choose the **Polar Array** tool from the **Modify** panel*
Select objects: *Select the circle of diameter **0.19** unit and press ENTER*
Type = Polar Associative = Yes
Specify center point of array or [Base point/Axis of rotation]: *Click at the center point of circle of diameter 1 unit*
Select grip to edit array or [ASsociative/Base point/Items/Angle between/Fill angle/ROWs/Levels/ROTate items/eXit]<eXit>: I Enter
Enter number of items in array or [Expression] <current>: **4** Enter
Select grip to edit array or [ASsociative/Base point/Items/Angle between/Fill angle/ROWs/Levels/ROTate items/eXit]<eXit>: F Enter
Specify the angle to fill (+=ccw, -=cw) or [EXpression] <360>: **360** Enter
Press Enter to accept or [ASsociative/Base point/Items/Angle between/Fill angle/ROWs/Levels/ROTate items/eXit]<eXit>: **X** Enter

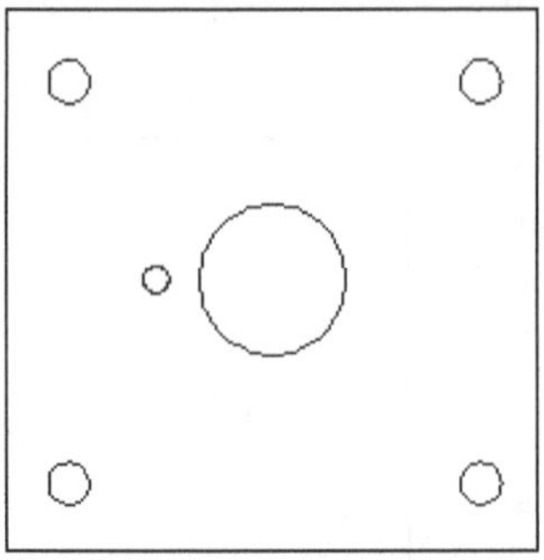

Figure 5-100 *Rectangular array created*

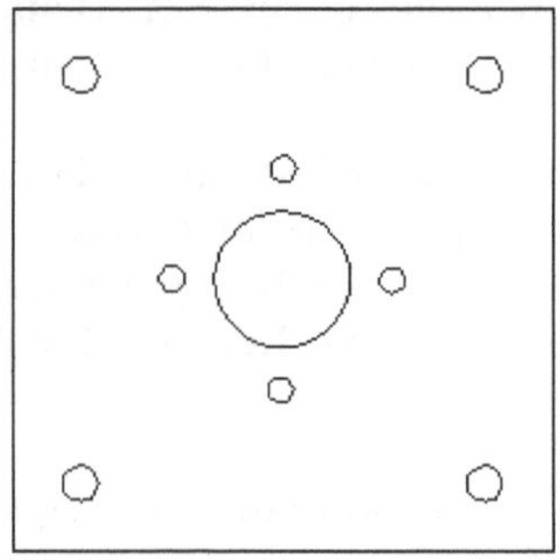

Figure 5-101 *Polar array created*

Self-Evaluation Test

Answer the following questions and then compare them to those given at the end of this chapter:

1. You can create small or large circles, ellipses, and arcs by using the __________ tool, depending on the side to be offset.

2. The __________ tool prunes the objects that extend beyond the required point of intersection.

3. The offset distance is stored in the __________ system variable.

4. Instead of specifying the scale factor, you can use the __________ option to scale an object with reference to another object.

5. If the __________ system variable is set to 1, the mirrored text is reversed with respect to the original object.

6. There are three types of arrays: __________, __________, and __________.

7. When you shift a group of objects by using the **Move** tool, the size and orientation of those objects change. (T/F)

8. The **Copy** tool is used to make copies of the selected object, leaving the original object intact. (T/F)

9. A fillet cannot be created between two parallel and non-intersecting lines. (T/F)

10. On selecting an object after invoking the **Break** tool, the selection point becomes the first break point. (T/F)

Review Questions

Answer the following questions:

1. Which of the following object selection methods is used to create a polygon that selects all the objects, touching or lying inside it?

   (a) **Last** (b) **WPolygon**
   (c) **CPolygon** (d) **Fence**

2. Which of the following tools is not used to enlarge the size of an object?

   (a) **Trim** (b) **Scaling**
   (c) **Stretch** (d) None of these

3. Which of the following tools is used to change the size of an existing object with respect to an existing entity?

   (a) **Rotate** (b) **Scale**
   (c) **Move** (d) None of these

4. Which of these options of the **Lengthen** tool is used to modify the length of the selected entity such that irrespective of the original length, the entity acquires the specified length?

   (a) **DElta** (b) **DYnamic**
   (c) **Percent** (d) **Total**

5. Which of the following selection options is used to select the most recently drawn entity?

   (a) **Last** (b) **Previous**
   (c) **Add** (d) None of these

6. If a selected object is within a window or crossing specification, the __________ tool works like the **Move** tool.

7. The __________ option of the **Extend** tool is used to extend objects to the implied boundary.

8. If a polyline is not closed then while creating a fillet by using the **Fillet** tool with the **Polyline** option selected, the __________ corner is not filleted.

9. When the chamfer distance is zero, the chamfer created is in the form of a __________.

10. AutoCAD saves the previous selection set and allows you to select it again by using the __________ selection option.

11. The __________ selection option is used to select objects by creating a section line touching the objects to be selected.

12. In the case of the **Through** option of the **Offset** tool, you do not need to specify a distance; you simply have to specify an offset point. (T/F)

13. Using the **Break** tool, you cannot break an object into two parts without removing a portion in between the two selected points. (T/F)

14. While creating a fillet by using the **Fillet** tool, the extrusion direction of the selected object must be parallel to the *Z* axis of the UCS. (T/F)

15. In AutoCAD, you can rotate a rectangular array. (T/F)

Exercise 8 *Divide*

Create the drawing shown in Figure 5-102. Use the **Divide** tool to divide the circle and use the **NODE** object snap to select the points. Assume the dimensions of the drawing.

Figure 5-102 *Drawing for Exercise 8*

Exercise 9

Create the drawing shown in Figure 5-103 and save it.

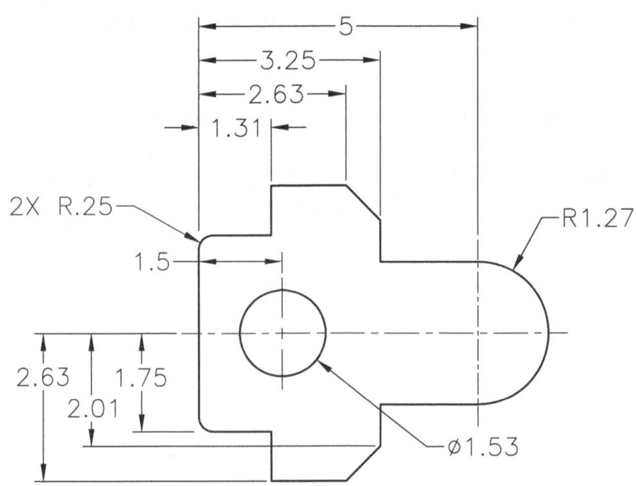

Figure 5-103 *Drawing for Exercise 9*

Exercise 10

Create the drawing shown in Figure 5-104 and save it.

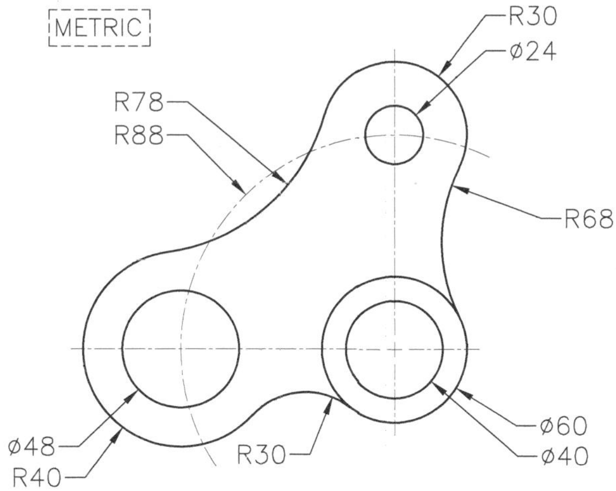

Figure 5-104 Drawing for Exercise 10

Exercise 11

Create the drawing shown in Figure 5-105 and save it.

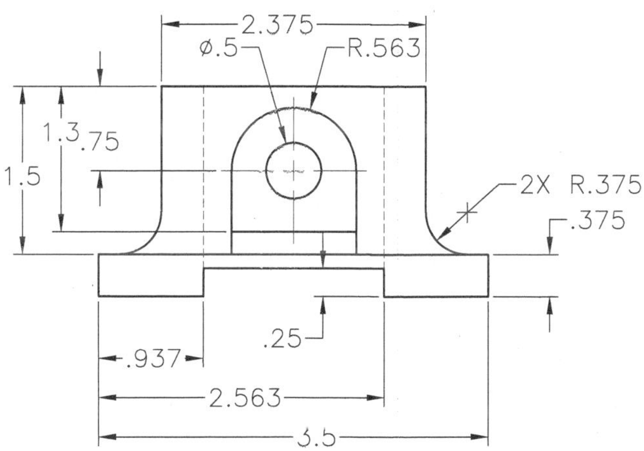

Figure 5-105 Drawing for Exercise 11

Problem-Solving Exercise 1

Create the drawing shown in Figure 5-106 and save it.

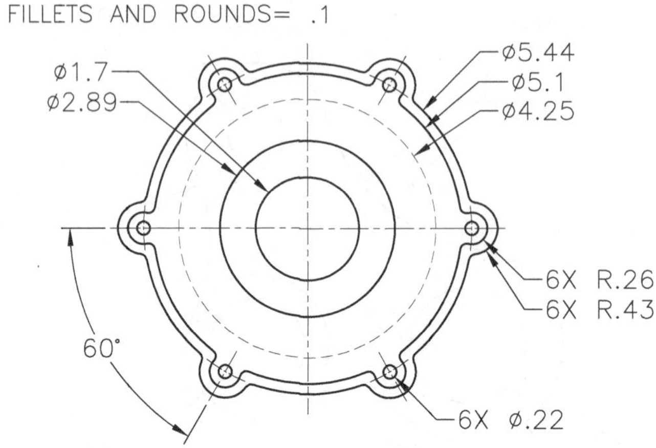

Figure 5-106 *Drawing for Problem-Solving Exercise 1*

Problem-Solving Exercise 2

Create the drawing shown in Figure 5-107 and save it.

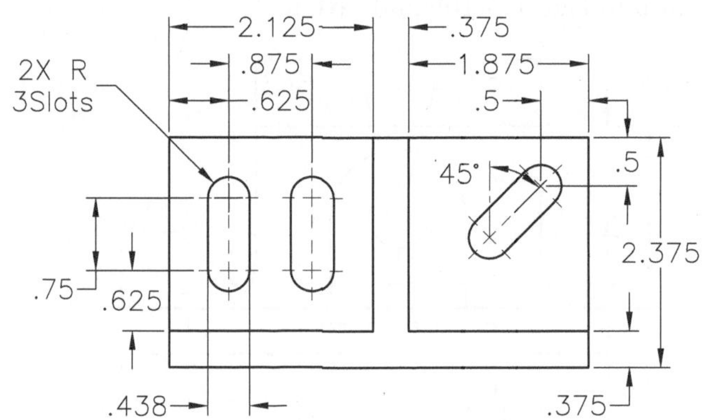

Figure 5-107 *Drawing for Problem-Solving Exercise 2*

Problem-Solving Exercise 3

Draw the dining table with chairs, as shown in Figure 5-108 and save the drawing.

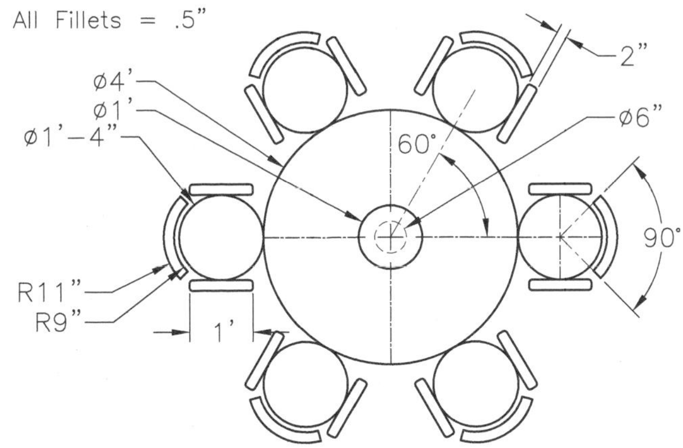

Figure 5-108 Drawing for Problem-Solving Exercise 3

Problem-Solving Exercise 4

Draw a reception table with chairs, as shown in Figure 5-109 and save the drawing. The dimensions of the chairs are the same as those used in Problem-Solving Exercise 3.

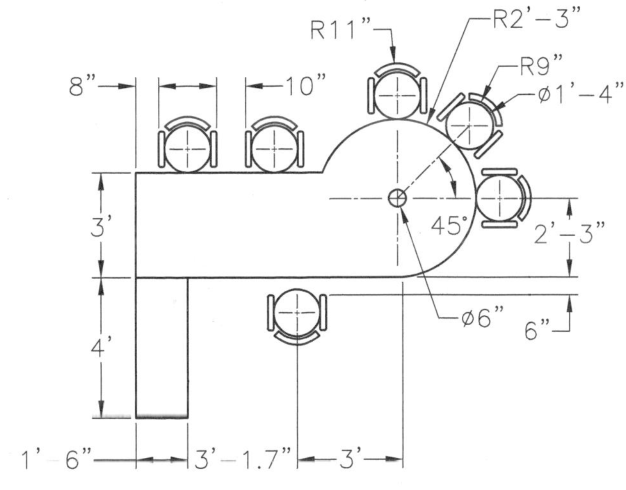

Figure 5-109 Drawing for Problem-Solving Exercise 4

Problem-Solving Exercise 5

Draw a center table with chairs, as shown in Figure 5-110, and save the drawing. The dimensions of the chairs are the same as those used in Problem-Solving Exercise 3.

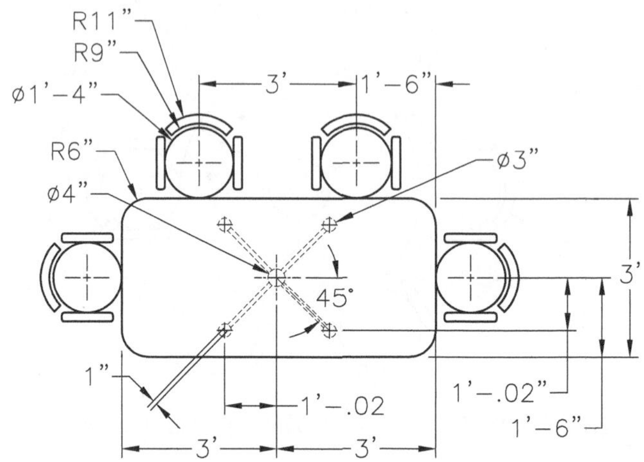

Figure 5-110 Drawing for Problem-Solving Exercise 5

Problem-Solving Exercise 6

Create the drawing shown in Figure 5-111 and save it. Refer to the note given in the drawing to create an arc of radius 30.

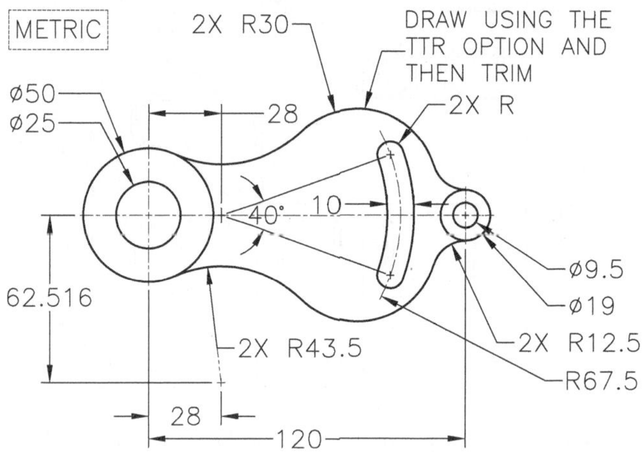

Figure 5-111 Drawing for Problem-Solving Exercise 6

Problem-Solving Exercise 7

Create the drawing shown in Figure 5-112 and save it.

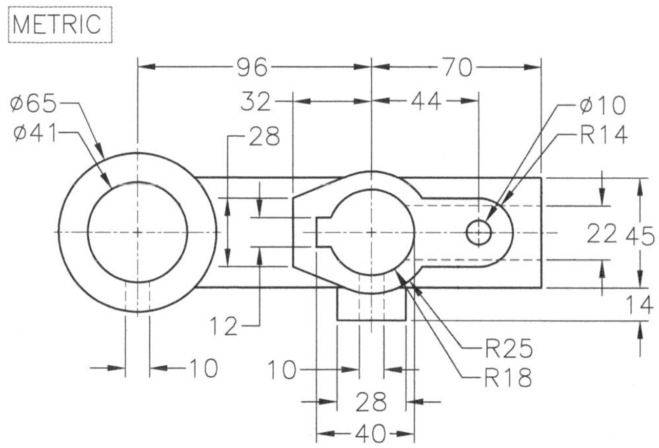

Figure 5-112 *Drawing for Problem-Solving Exercise 7*

Problem-Solving Exercise 8

Create the drawing shown in Figure 5-113 and save it.

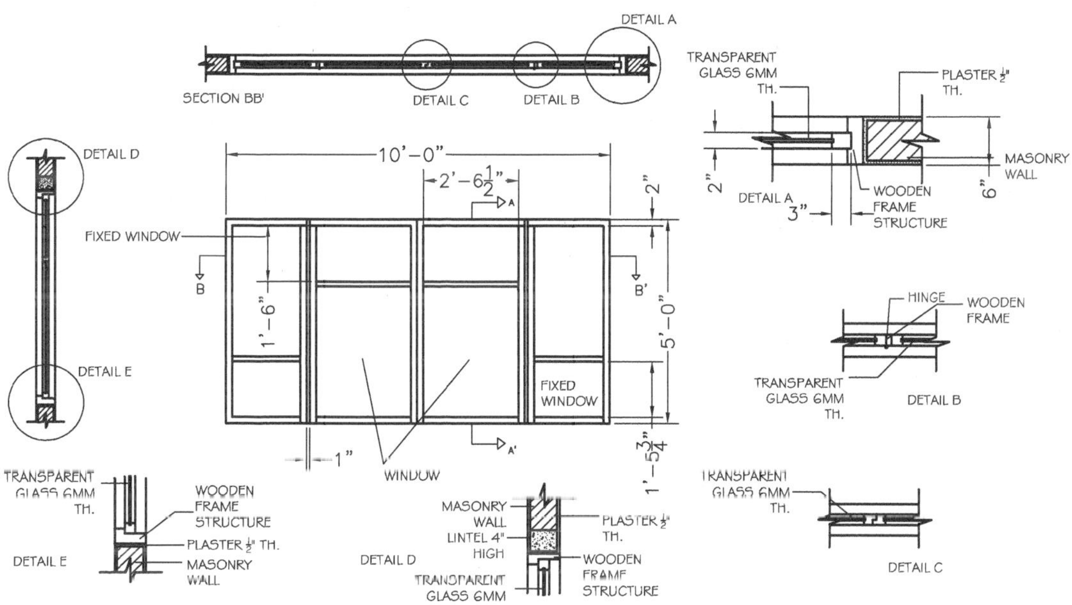

Figure 5-113 *Drawing for Problem-Solving Exercise 8*

Problem-Solving Exercise 9

Create the drawing shown in Figure 5-114 in the paper space area of the **Manufacturing Metric** template and save it.

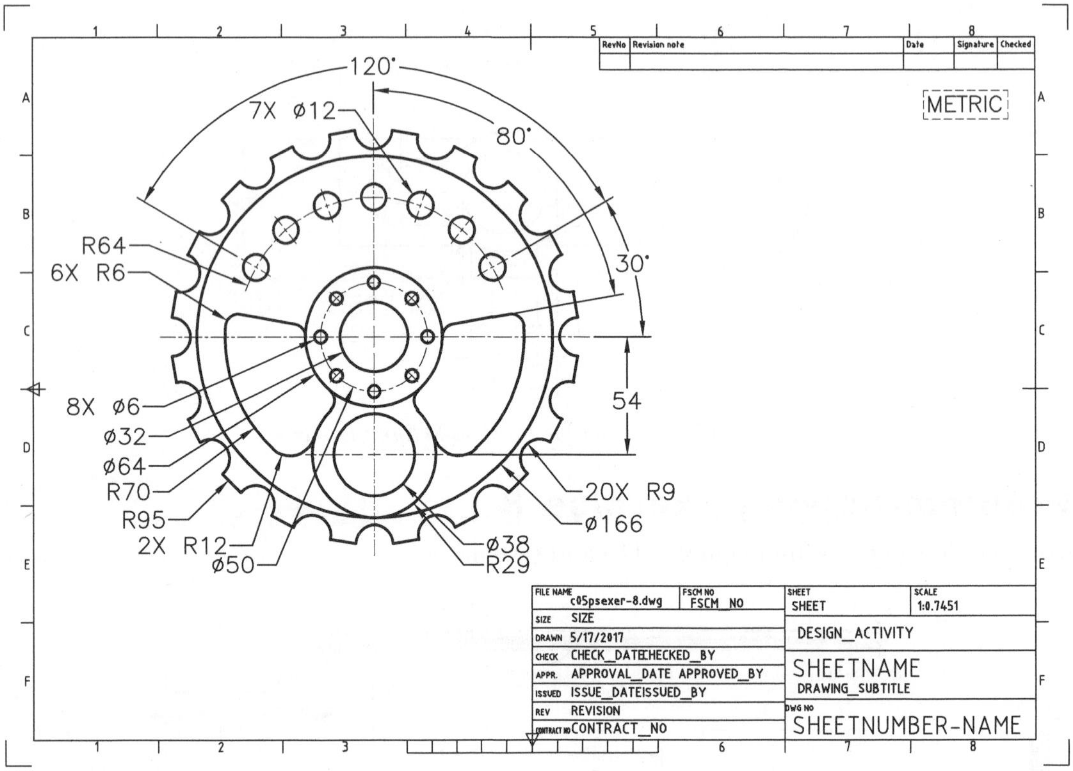

Figure 5-114 Drawing for Problem-Solving Exercise 9

Answers to Self-Evaluation Test

1. OFFSET, **2.** TRIM, **3.** OFFSETDIST, **4.** Reference, **5.** MIRRTEXT, **6.** Rectangular, Polar, Path, **7.** F, **8.** T, **9.** F, **10.** T

Chapter 6

Editing Sketched Objects-II

Learning Objectives

After completing this chapter, you will be able to:

- *Use grips and adjust their settings*
- *Stretch, move, rotate, scale, and mirror objects with grips*
- *Use the Match Properties tool to match properties of the selected objects*
- *Use the Quick Select tool to select objects*
- *Manage contents using the DesignCenter*
- *Use the Inquiry tools*
- *Use the REDRAW and REGEN commands*
- *Use the Zoom tools and its options*
- *Use the PAN and VIEW commands*
- *Use SHEET SET MANAGER*

Key Terms

- *Grips*
- *Properties Panel*
- *Quick Select*
- *DesignCenter*
- *Area*
- *Distance*
- *Locate Point*
- *List*
- *Time*
- *Status*
- *Regen*
- *Redraw*
- *Zoom*
- *SHEET SET MANAGER*

INTRODUCTION TO GRIPS

Grips provide a convenient and quick means of editing objects. Grips are small squares that are displayed on the key points of an object on selecting the object, as shown in Figure 6-1. If the grips are not displayed on selecting an object, invoke the **Options** dialog box, choose the **Selection** tab, and select the **Show grips** check box from the **Grips** area. Using grips you can stretch, move, rotate, scale, and mirror objects, change base point and also copy and load the Web browser. The number of grips depends on the selected object. For example, a line has three grip points and an arc has four grips. Similarly, a circle has five grip points and a dimension (vertical, horizontal, or inclined) has five grips.

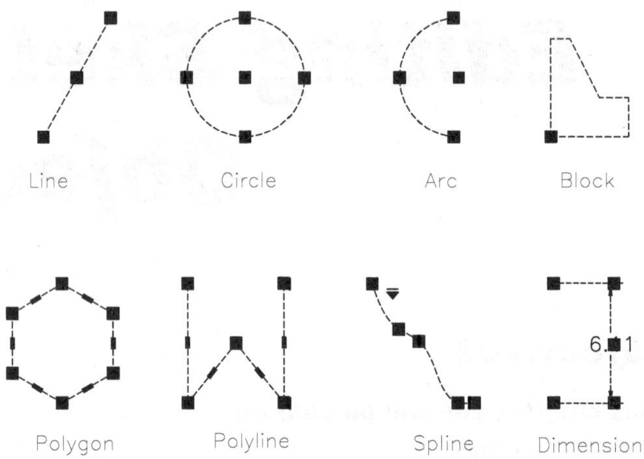

***Figure 6-1** Grips displayed on various objects*

Note

*If grips are not displayed after selecting the objects, refer to Figure 6-1, select the **Show grip tips**, **Show single grip on groups**, and **Show bounding box on groups** check boxes available in the **Grips** area of the **Selection** tab in the **Options** dialog box.*

TYPES OF GRIPS

Grips are classified into three types: unselected grips, hover grips, and selected grips. The selected grips are also called hot grips. When you select an object, the grips are displayed at the definition points of the object and the object is displayed as Neon blue line. These grips are called unselected grips and are displayed in blue. When the cursor is moved over an unselected grip, and paused for a second, the grip will be displayed in orange. These grips are called hover grips. Dimensions corresponding to a hover grip are displayed when you place the cursor on the grip, as shown in Figure 6-2.

If you select a grip, it is displayed in red color and is called as hot grip. Once the grip is hot, the object can be edited. To cancel the grip, press ESC twice. If you press ESC once, the hot grip is converted into an unselected grip.

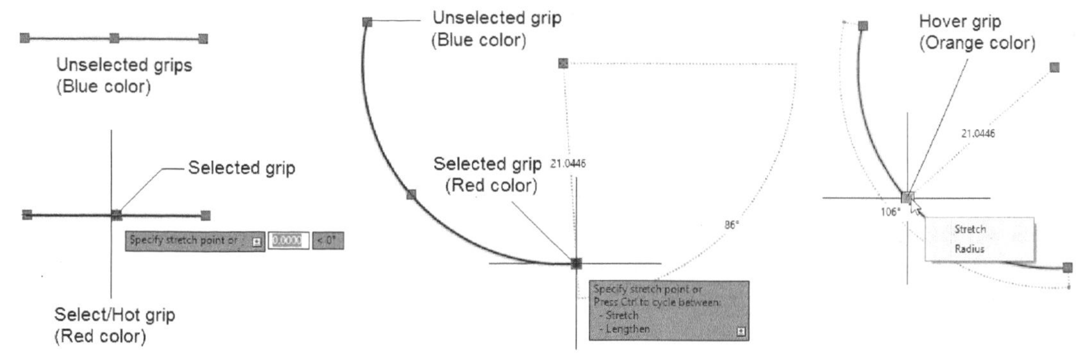

Figure 6-2 Hover Grip Types for different objects

ADJUSTING GRIP SETTINGS

Application Menu: Options **Command:** OPTIONS/OP

The grip settings can be adjusted by using the options in the **Selection** tab of the **Options** dialog box. This dialog box can also be invoked by choosing **Options** from the shortcut menu displayed upon right-clicking in the drawing area or by choosing the **Options** button from the **Application Menu**.

The options in the **Selection** tab of the **Options** dialog box, as shown in Figure 6-3, are discussed next.

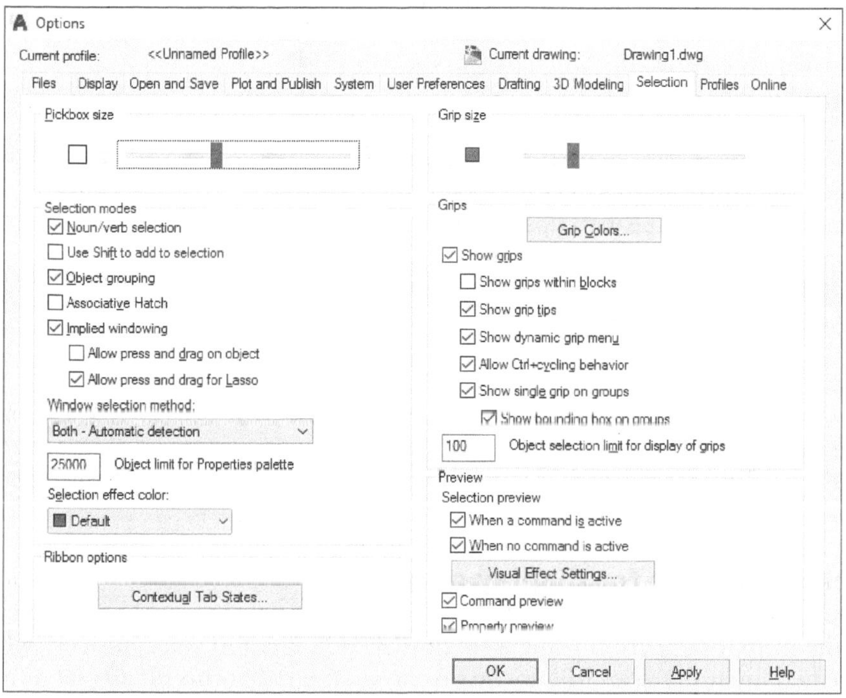

*Figure 6-3 The **Selection** tab of the **Options** dialog box*

Grip size Area

The **Grip size** area of the **Selection** tab of the **Options** dialog box consists of a slider bar and a rectangular box that displays the size of the grip. To adjust the size, move the slider bar left or right. The size can also be adjusted by using the **GRIPSIZE** system variable. The **GRIPSIZE** variable is defined in pixels, and its value can range from 1 to 255 pixels.

Grips Area

To assign the color to the unselected grip, selected grip, hover grip, and grip contour, choose the **Grip Colors** button; the **Grip Colors** dialog box will be displayed. Specify the colors in this dialog box. Grip contour is the color applied on the outline of the grip. You can also set the grip colors by using the following system variables:

Unselected grip color: GRIPCOLOR
Selected grip color: GRIPHOT
Hover grip color: GRIPHOVER
Grip contour color: GRIPCONTOUR

The **Grips** area has various check boxes such as **Show grips**, **Show grips within blocks**, and **Show grip tips**. Grips are displayed on selecting an object only if the **Show Grips** check box is selected. They can also be enabled by setting the **GRIPS** system variable to 1. On selecting the **Show grips within blocks** check box, all the grips in the blocks are displayed. You can also enable the grips within a block by setting the value of the **GRIPBLOCK** system variable to 1 (On). If you clear the **Show grips within blocks** check box, only one grip will be displayed at the insertion point of the block. Alternatively, set the **GRIPBLOCK** system variable to 0 (Off), refer to Figure 6-4. To display the grip tips when the cursor moves over the custom object that supports grip tips, select the **Show grip tips** check box. If you disable this check box, the grip tips are not displayed when the cursor moves over the custom object. You can also disable the grip tips by setting the value of the **GRIPTIPS** system variable to 0 (Off). If **GRIPTIPS** is set to 1 (On), the grip tips for the custom object will be displayed.

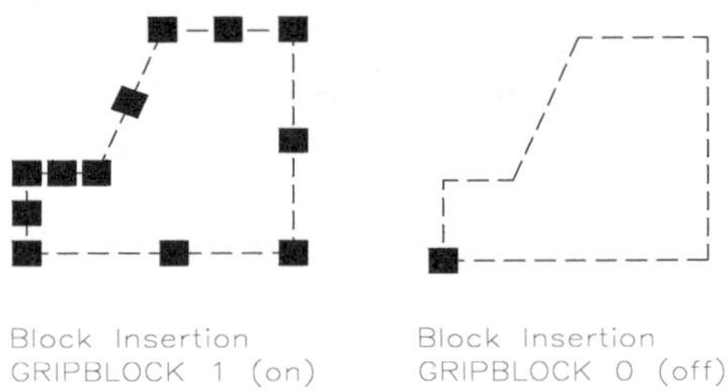

***Figure 6-4** Block insertion with GRIPBLOCK set to 1 and 0*

Note

*If a block has a large number of objects, and if **GRIPBLOCK** is set to 1 (On), AutoCAD will display grips for every object in the block. Therefore, it is recommended that you set the system variable **GRIPBLOCK** to 0 or clear the **Show grips within blocks** check box in the **Selection** tab of the **Options** dialog box.*

Object selection limit for display of grips

This text box is used to specify the maximum number of objects that can be selected in a single attempt for the display of grips. If using a single selection method you can select more objects than the specified limit, the grips will not be displayed. Note that this limit is set only for those objects that are selected at a single attempt using any of the crossing, window, fence, all, or multiple objects selection options.

EDITING OBJECTS BY USING GRIPS

As mentioned earlier, you can perform different kinds of editing operations using the selected grip. The editing operations are discussed next.

Stretching the Objects by Using Grips (Stretch Mode)

If you select an object, the unselected grips are displayed at the definition points of the object. If you select a grip for editing, you are automatically in the **Stretch** mode. The **Stretch** mode has a function similar to that of the **Stretch** tool. When you select a grip, it acts as a base point and is called a base grip. To select several grips, press and hold the SHIFT key and then select the grips. Now, release the SHIFT key and select one of the hot grips and stretch it; all selected grips will be stretched. The geometry between the selected base grips will not be altered. You can also make copies of the selected objects or define a new base point. When selecting grips on text objects, blocks, midpoints of lines, centers of circles and ellipses, and point objects in the stretch mode, the selected objects are moved to a new location. The following example illustrates the use of the **Stretch** mode and other associated options.

1. Use the **Polyline** tool to draw a W-shaped figure and select the object; grips will be displayed at the endpoints and midpoints of each line, as shown in Figure 6-5(a).

2. Hold the SHIFT key and select the grips on the lower endpoints of the two vertical lines, refer to Figure 6-5(b). The selected grips will become hot grips and their color will change from blue to red.

3. Release the SHIFT key and select one of the hot grips, and drag downwards; the profile will be stretched, refer to Figure 6-5(c). When you select a grip, the following prompt is displayed in the command prompt area.

   STRETCH
   Specify stretch point or [Base point/Copy/Undo/eXit]:

Note
To select multiple grips, you need to press and hold the SHIFT key before selecting the first grip.

Tip
To stretch a line to some desired length, enter a numerical value in the dimensional input box that will be displayed on selecting a grip of the line.

The Stretch mode has several options: **Base point**, **Copy**, **Undo**, and **eXit**. The **Base Point** and **Copy** options can also be invoked from the shortcut menu, as shown in Figure 6-6. The **Base point** option is used to move an object with respect to a base point and the **Copy** option is used to make copies.

4. Select the grip where the two inclined lines intersect, as shown in Figure 6-7(a), and right-click to display a shortcut menu. Choose the **Copy** option and specify a new stretch point; the two inclined lines will be copied, as shown in Figure 6-7(b). You can also select a grip, press the CTRL key and specify the point to make multiple copies of the selected object.

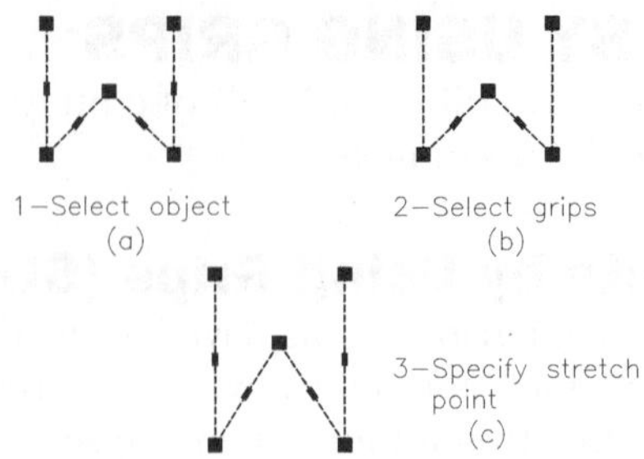

Figure 6-5 *Using the* ***Stretch*** *mode to stretch the lines*

5. To move a grip with respect to a base point, select the grip, refer to Figure 6-7(c).Next, choose the **Base Point** option from the shortcut menu and select the base point and then specify the displacement point, as shown in Figure 6-7(d).

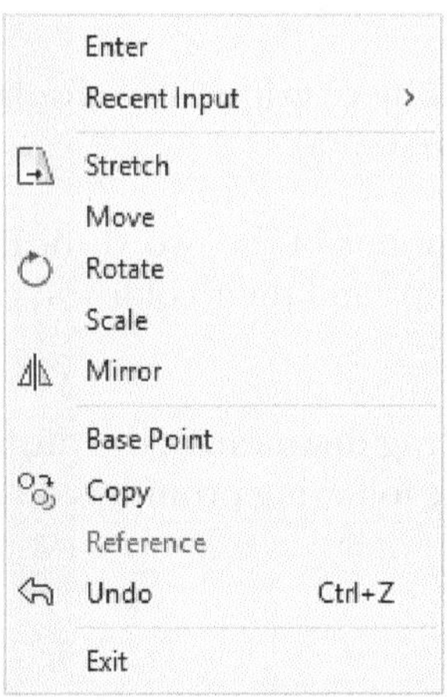

Figure 6-6 *Shortcut menu with editing options*

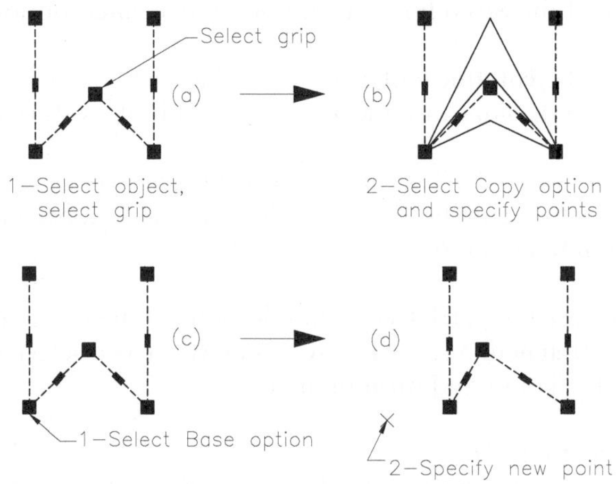

Figure 6-7 *Using the* ***Copy*** *and* ***Base point*** *options of the* ***Stretch*** *mode*

6. To terminate the grip editing mode, right-click when the grip is hot to display the shortcut menu and then choose the **Exit** option. You can also enter **X** at the command prompt or press ESC to exit.

Note

*You can choose an option (**Copy** or **Base Point**) from the shortcut menu that can be invoked by right-clicking your pointing device after selecting a grip. The different modes can also be selected from the shortcut menu. You can also cycle through all the different modes by selecting a grip and pressing the ENTER key or the SPACEBAR.*

Moving the Objects by Using Grips (Move Mode)

The **Move** mode allows you move the selected objects to a new location. When you move objects, their size and angles do not change. You can also use this mode to make the copies of the selected objects or to redefine the base point. The following example illustrates the use of the **Move** mode:

1. Invoke the **Line** tool and draw the shape, as shown in Figure 6-8(a). When you select the objects, grips will be displayed at the definition points and the objects will be highlighted.

2. Select the grip located at the lower left corner, as shown in Figure 6-8(b) and then choose **Move** from the shortcut menu. You can also select a grip and give a null response by pressing the SPACEBAR or ENTER key to invoke the **Move** mode; the following prompt will be displayed at the command prompt:

   MOVE
   Specify move point or [Base point/Copy/Undo/eXit]:

3. Specify the displacement point. You can also enter coordinates to specify the displacement. If you hold down the CTRL key and then specify the displacement point, the objects will be copied. Also, the distance between the first and the second object defines the snap offset for subsequent copies, refer to Figure 6-8(c).

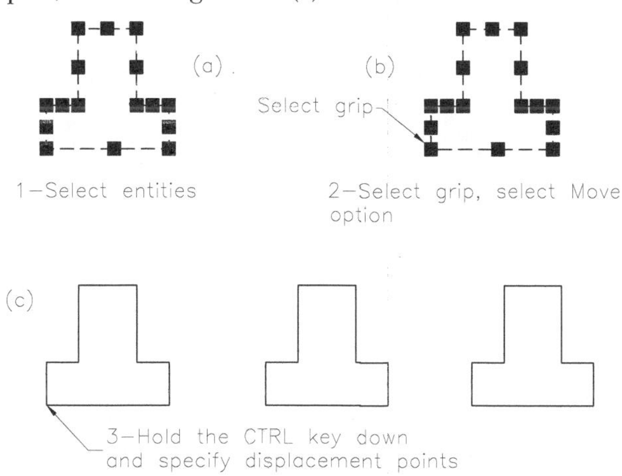

Figure 6-8 *Using the **Move** mode to move and make copies of the selected objects*

Rotating the Objects by Using Grips (Rotate Mode)

The **Rotate** mode allows you to rotate objects around the base point without changing their size. The options of the **Rotate** mode can be used to redefine the base point, specify a reference angle, or make multiple copies that are rotated about the specified base point. You can access the **Rotate** mode by selecting the grip and then choosing **Rotate** from the shortcut menu, or by giving a null response twice by pressing the SPACEBAR or the ENTER key. The following example illustrates the use of the **Rotate** mode:

1. Use the **Line** tool to draw the shape, as shown in Figure 6-9(a). When you select the objects, grips will be displayed at the definition points and the shape will be highlighted.

2. Select the grip located at the lower left corner and then invoke the **Rotate** mode. AutoCAD will display the following prompt.

   ROTATE
   Specify a rotation angle or [Base point/Copy/Undo/Reference/eXit]:

3. At this prompt, enter the rotation angle. By default, the rotation angle will be entered through the dimensional input below the cursor in the drawing area. AutoCAD will rotate the selected objects by the specified angle, as shown in Figure 6-9(b).

4. To make a copy of the original drawing, as shown in Figure 6-9(c), select the objects, and then select the grip located at its lower left corner. Invoke the **Rotate** mode and then choose the **Copy** option from the shortcut menu or enter **C** (Copy) at the command prompt or the **Copy** option from the dynamic preview. Enter the rotation angle. AutoCAD will rotate the copy of the object through the specified angle, refer to Figure 6-9(d).

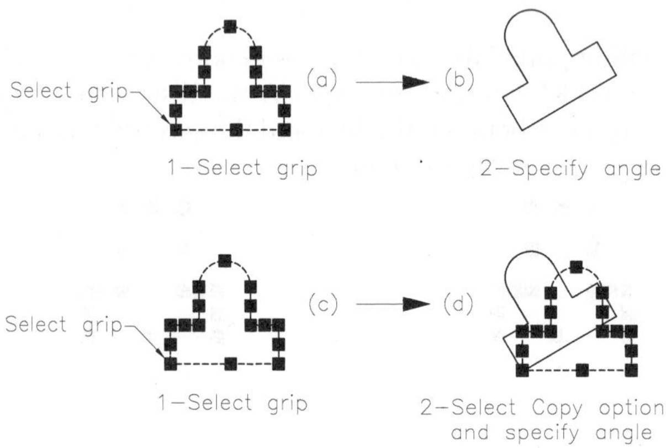

Figure 6-9 *Using the **Rotate** mode to rotate and make the copies of the selected objects*

5. To make another copy of the object, as shown in Figure 6-10(a), select it, and then select the grip at point (P0). Access the **Rotate** mode and the copy option as described earlier. Choose the **Reference** option from the shortcut menu, enter **R** at the prompt sequence, or select the **Reference** option from the dynamic preview, as shown in Figure 6-10(b). The prompt sequence is given next.

   **ROTATE (multiple) **
   Specify Base point: **R**
   Specify reference angle <0>: *Select the grip at (P1).*
   Specify second point: *Select the grip at (P2).*
   Specify new angle or [Base point/Copy/Undo/Reference/eXit]: **45**

In response to the **Specify reference angle <0>:** prompt, select the grips at points (P1) and (P2) to define the reference angle. When you enter a new angle, AutoCAD will rotate and insert a copy at the specified angle [Figure 6-10(c)]. For example, if the new angle is 45 degree, the selected objects will be rotated about the base point (P0) so that the line P1P2 makes a 45 degree angle with respect to the positive *X* axis.

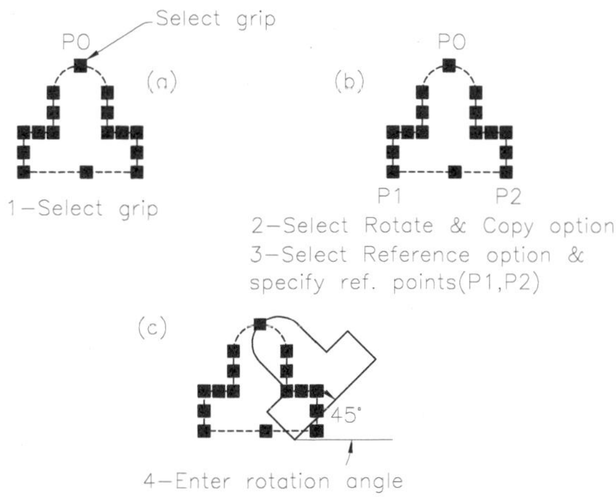

Figure 6-10 *Using the **Rotate** mode to rotate the selected objects by giving a reference angle*

Scaling the Objects by Using Grips (Scale Mode)

The **Scale** mode allows you to scale objects with respect to the base point without changing their orientation. The options of **Scale** mode can be used to redefine the base point, specify a reference length, or make multiple copies that are scaled with respect to the specified base point. You can access the **Scale** mode by selecting the grip and then choosing **Scale** from the shortcut menu, or giving a null response three times by pressing the SPACEBAR or the ENTER key. The following example illustrates the use of the **Scale** mode:

1. Use the **Polyline** tool to draw the shape shown in Figure 6-11(a). Then, select the objects; the grips will be displayed at the definition points.

2. Select the grip located at the lower left corner as the base grip, and then invoke the **Scale** mode. AutoCAD will display the following prompt in the command prompt area.

   SCALE
   Specify scale factor or [Base point/Copy/Undo/Reference/eXit]:

3. At this prompt, enter the scale factor or move the cursor and select a point to specify a new size. AutoCAD will scale the selected objects by the specified scale factor, refer to Figure 6-11(a). If the scale factor is less than 1 (<1), the objects will be scaled down by the specified factor. If the scale factor is greater than 1 (>1), the objects will be scaled up.

4. To make a copy of the original drawing, as shown in Figure 6-11(b), select the objects, and then select the grip located at their lower left corner. Invoke the **Scale** mode. At the following prompt, enter **C** (Copy), and then enter **B** for the base point.

   **SCALE (multiple) **
   Specify scale factor or [Base point/Copy/Undo/Reference/eXit]: **B**

5. At the **Specify base point** prompt, select the point (P0) as the new base point, and then enter **R** at the following prompt:

**SCALE (multiple) **
Specify scale factor or [Base point/Copy/Undo/Reference/eXit]: **R**
Specify reference length <1.000>: *Select grips at (P1) and (P2).*

After specifying the reference length at the **Specify new length or [Base point/Copy/Undo/Reference/eXit]** prompt, enter the actual length of the line. AutoCAD will scale the objects so that the length of the bottom edge is equal to the specified value, refer to Figure 6-11(c).

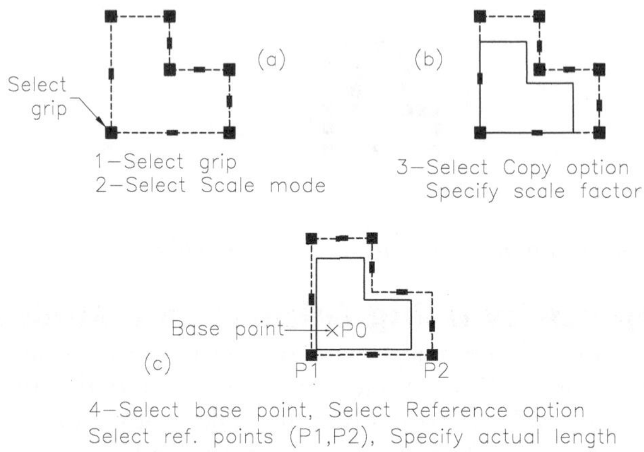

Figure 6-11 *Using the **Scale** mode to scale and make the copies of the selected objects*

Mirroring the Objects by Using Grips (Mirror Mode)

The **Mirror** mode allows you to mirror the objects across the mirror axis without changing their size. The mirror axis is defined by specifying two points. The first point is the base point, and the second point is the point that you select when AutoCAD prompts for the second point. The options of the **Mirror** mode can be used to redefine the base point and make a mirror copy of the objects. You can access the **Mirror** mode by selecting a grip and then choosing **Mirror** from the shortcut menu, or giving a null response four times by pressing the SPACEBAR or the ENTER key. The following is the example for the **Mirror** mode.

1. Use the **Polyline** tool to draw the shape shown in Figure 6-12(a). Select the objects; grips will be displayed at the definition points.

2. Select the grip located at the lower right corner (P1), and then invoke the **Mirror** mode. The following prompt will be displayed:

   MIRROR
   Specify second point or [Base point/Copy/Undo/eXit]:

3. At this prompt, specify the second point (P2); the selected objects will be mirrored, with line P1P2 as the mirror axis, as shown in Figure 6-12(b).

4. To make a copy of the original figure, as shown in Figure 6-12(c), select the object, and then select the grip located at its lower right corner (P1). Invoke the **Mirror** mode and then choose the **Copy** option to make a mirror image while retaining the original object.

Alternatively, you can also hold down the CTRL key and make several mirror copies by specifying the second point.

5. Select point (P2) in response to the prompt **Specify second point or [Base point/Copy/Undo/eXit]**. AutoCAD will create a mirror image, and the original object will be retained.

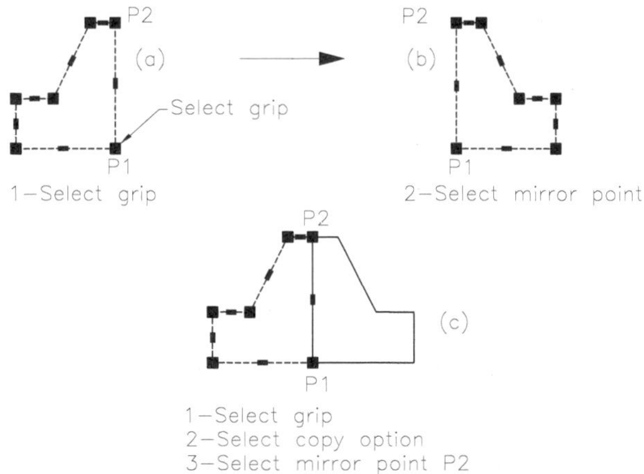

Figure 6-12 *Using the **Mirror** mode to create a mirror image of the selected objects*

Note

*1. You can use some editing tools such as **Erase**, **Move**, **Rotate**, **Scale**, **Mirror**, and **Copy** on an object with unselected grips. However, this is possible only if the **PICKFIRST** system variable is set to **1** (On).*

2. To remove an object from the selection set displaying grips, press the SHIFT key and then select that object. The object, which is removed from the selection set, will no longer be highlighted.

Editing a Polyline by Using Grips

In AutoCAD, when you select a polyline, three grips are displayed in each segment of the polyline. You can edit the polyline by using these grips. To do so, move the cursor on one of the grips and pause for a while; a tooltip will be displayed, as shown in Figure 6-13. To stretch the polyline, choose the **Stretch Vertex** option and specify a new point; the polyline will be stretched. After choosing the **Stretch Vertex** option, you can also invoke the **Base Point** or **Copy** option from the shortcut menu, as discussed earlier.

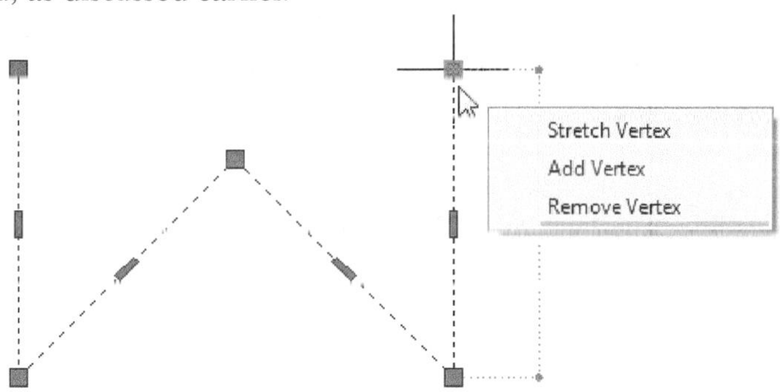

Figure 6-13 *Tooltip displayed near the grip*

To add a new vertex, choose the **Add Vertex** option from the tooltip, as shown in Figure 6-14; you will be prompted to specify a new vertex point. Specify a point; a new vertex will be added between the selected vertex and the next vertex, as shown in Figure 6-15. However, if the selected vertex is the last vertex, then a new segment will be added to the last vertex.

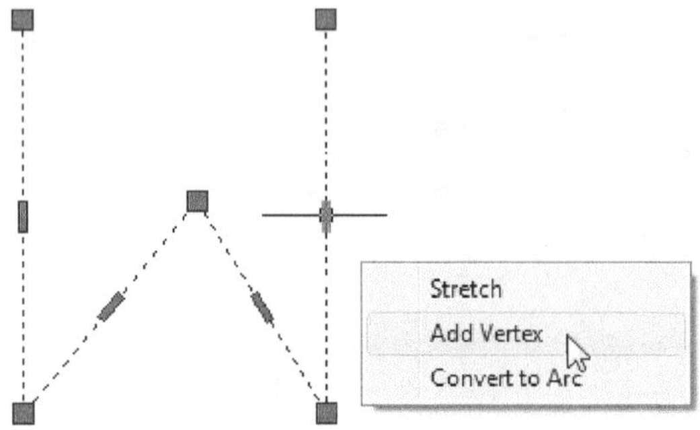

Figure 6-14 *Choosing the* ***Add Vertex*** *option from the tooltip*

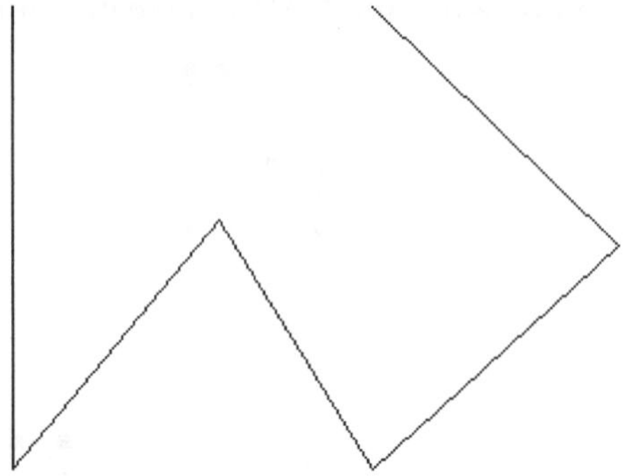

Figure 6-15 *Polyline after adding a new vertex*

To remove a vertex, move the cursor over the vertex to be removed and choose the **Remove Vertex** option from the tooltip displayed.

If you place the cursor on the middle grip, the tooltip will display the **Convert to Arc** option instead of the **Remove Vertex** option. Choose this option to convert (see Figure 6-16) the selected line to an arc. On choosing this option, you will be prompted to specify the midpoint of the arc. Specify a point on the periphery of the arc; the line will be converted into an arc, as shown in Figure 6-17. If you have drawn an arc using the **Polyline** tool or converted a polyline to an arc, you can convert the arc back to the line by choosing the **Convert to Line** option from the tool tip that is displayed on placing the cursor on the middle grip of the arc.

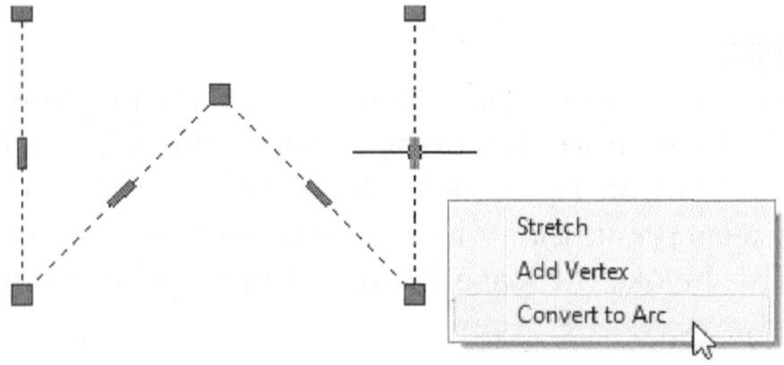

Figure 6-16 *Selecting the* ***Convert to Arc*** *option from the tooltip*

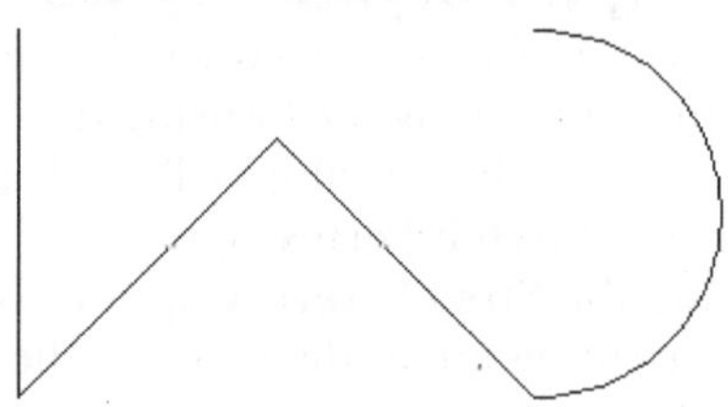

Figure 6-17 *Polyline after converting a line into an arc*

Tip

After choosing an option from the tooltip, you can cycle through the options in the tooltip by pressing the CTRL key.

LOADING HYPERLINKS

If you have already added a hyperlink to an object, you can also use the grips to open a file associated with it. For example, the hyperlink could start a word processor or activate the Web browser and load a Web page that is embedded in the selected object. To launch the Web browser that provides hyperlinks to other Web pages, select the URL-embedded object and then right-click to display the shortcut menu. In the shortcut menu, choose the **Hyperlink > Open** "web page" option and AutoCAD will automatically load the Web browser. When you move the cursor over or near the object that contains a hyperlink, AutoCAD displays the hyperlink information with the cursor.

Note

The process of working with hyperlinks is discussed in the later chapters.

EDITING GRIPPED OBJECTS

You can also edit the properties of the gripped objects by using the **Properties** panel in the **Home** tab, refer to Figure 6-18. When you select objects without invoking a tool, the grips (rectangular boxes) will be displayed on the selected objects. For example, to change the color of the gripped objects, select the **Object Color** drop-down list in the **Properties** panel and then select a color from it. The color of the gripped objects will change to the selected color. Similarly, to change the layer, lineweight, or linetype of the gripped objects, select the required linetype, lineweight, or layer from the corresponding drop-down lists. If the gripped objects have different colors, linetypes, or lineweights, the **Object Color**, **Linetype**, and **Lineweight** drop-down lists will appear blank. You can also change the plot style of the selected objects using this panel.

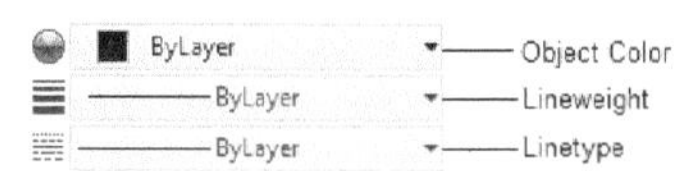

*Figure 6-18 The **Properties** panel*

CHANGING THE PROPERTIES USING THE PROPERTIES PALETTE

Ribbon: View > Palettes > Properties **Toolbar:** Quick Access > Properties
Command: PROPERTIES/PR/MO/CH

As mentioned earlier, each object has properties associated with it such as the color, layer, linetype, line weight, and so on. You can modify these properties by using the **PROPERTIES** palette. To view this palette, choose the **Properties** tool from the **Palettes** panel in the **View** tab; the **PROPERTIES** palette will be displayed, as shown in Figure 6-19. The **Properties** palette can also be displayed when you double-click on the object to be edited. The contents of the **PROPERTIES** palette change depending upon the objects selected. For example, if you select a text entity, the related properties such as its height, justification, style, rotation angle, and so on, will be displayed.

The **PROPERTIES** palette can also be invoked from the shortcut menu. To do so, select an entity and right-click in the drawing area. Choose the **Properties** option from the shortcut menu. If you select more than one entity, the common properties of the selected entities will be displayed in the **PROPERTIES** palette. To change the properties of the selected entities, click in the cell next to the name of the property and change the values manually. Alternatively, you can choose an option from the drop-down list, if available. You can cycle through the options by double-clicking in the property cell.

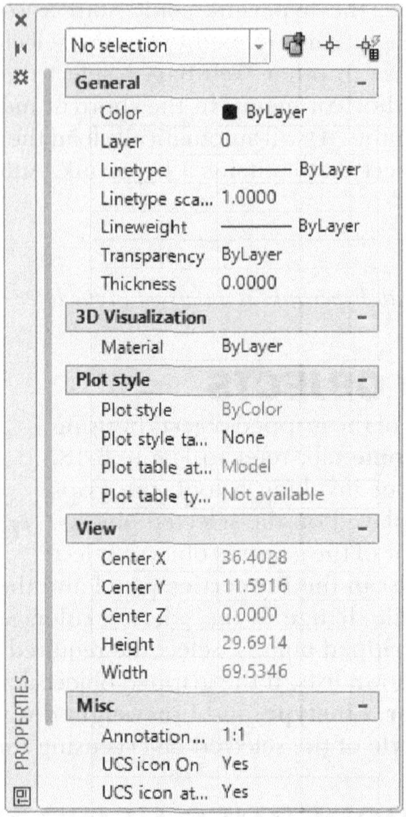

*Figure 6-19 The **PROPERTIES** palette for editing the properties of an entity*

Note

*Some of the options in the **PROPERTIES** palette have been explained in Chapter 4. Other options are explained in detail in the later chapters.*

MATCHING THE PROPERTIES OF SKETCHED OBJECTS

Ribbon: Home > Properties > Match Properties **Command:** MATCHPROP/MA
Quick Access Toolbar: Match Properties (Customize to Add)

The **Match Properties** tool is used to apply properties like color, layer, linetype, and linetype scale of a source object to the selected objects. On invoking this tool, you will be prompted to select the source object and then the destination objects. The properties of the destination objects will be replaced with the properties of the source object. This is a transparent tool and can be used when another tool is active. The prompt sequence that will follow when you choose the **Match Properties** tool is given next.

Select source object: *Select the source object.*
Current active settings: Color Layer Ltype Ltscale Lineweight Transparency Thickness PlotStyle Dim Text Hatch Polyline Viewport Table Material Multileader Center object
Select destination object(s) or [Settings]:

If you select the destination object in the **Select destination object(s) or [Settings]** prompt, the properties of the source object will be forced on it. If you select the **Settings** option, the **Property Settings** dialog box will be displayed, as shown in Figure 6-20. The properties displayed are those of the source object. You can use this dialog box to edit the properties that are copied from the source to destination objects.

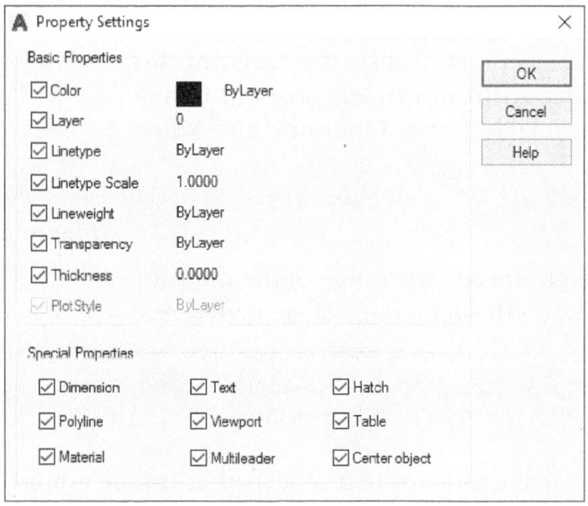

Figure 6-20 The ***Property Settings*** *dialog box*

QUICK SELECTION OF SKETCHED OBJECTS

Ribbon: Home > Utilities > Quick Select **Command:** QSELECT

The **Quick Select** tool is used to create a new selection set that will either include or exclude all objects whose object type and property criteria match as specified for the selection set. The **Quick Select** tool can be used to select the entities in the entire drawing or in the existing selection set. If a drawing is partially opened, the **Quick Select** tool does not consider the objects that are not loaded. The **Quick Select** tool can be invoked from the **Utilities** panel. You can also choose the **Quick Select** option from the shortcut menu displayed by right clicking in the drawing area. On invoking this tool, the **Quick Select** dialog box will be displayed, as shown in Figure 6-21. The **Quick Select** dialog box is used to specify the object filtering criteria and create a selection set from it.

Apply to

The **Apply to** drop-down list specifies whether to apply the filtering criteria to the entire drawing or to the current selection set. If there is an existing selection set, the **Current selection** is the default value. Otherwise, the **Entire drawing** is the default value. You can select the objects to create a selection set by choosing the **Select objects** button on the right side of this drop-down list. The **Quick Select** dialog box is temporarily closed when you choose this button and you will be prompted to select the objects. The dialog box will be displayed again once the selection set is made.

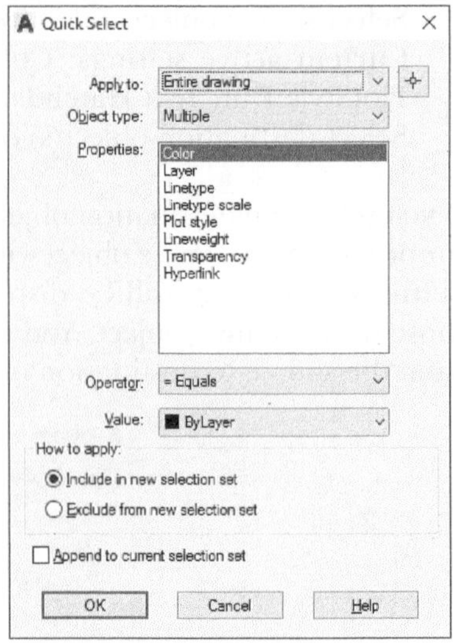

*Figure 6-21 The **Quick Select** dialog box*

Object type

This drop-down list specifies the type of object to be filtered. It lists all the available object types and if some objects are selected, it lists all the selected object types. **Multiple** is the default option selected in this drop-down list.

Properties

This list box displays the properties to be filtered. All the properties related to the object type will be displayed in this list box. The property selected from this list box will define the options that will be available in the **Operator** and **Value** drop-down lists.

Operator

This drop-down list is used to specify the range of the filter for the chosen property. The filters that are available are given next.

- Equals =
- Not Equal <>
- Greater than >
- Less than <
- Select All
- Wildcard Match (Available only for text objects that can be edited and if you select the **Hyperlink** option from the **Properties** list.)

Note

*The **Value** drop-down list will not be available when you select **Select All** from the **Operator** drop-down list.*

Value

This drop-down list is used to specify the property value of the filter. If the values are known, you can select a value. Otherwise, you can enter a value.

How to apply Area

The options under this area are used to specify whether the filtered entities will be included or excluded from the new selection set. This area provides the following two radio buttons.

Include in new selection set

If this radio button is selected, the filtered entities will be included in the new selection set. If selected, this radio button creates a new selection set composed only of those objects that conform to the filtering criteria.

Exclude from new selection set

If this radio button is selected, the filtered entities will be excluded from the new selection set. This radio button creates a new selection set of objects that do not conform to the filtering criteria.

Append to current selection set

On selecting this check box, a cumulative selection set is created by using multiple uses of Quick Select. It specifies whether the objects selected using the **Quick Select** tool replace the current selection set or append the current selection set. If you select this check box, then the **Select objects** button available next to **Apply to** drop-down list will be deactivated.

> **Tip**
> *Quick Select supports objects and their properties that are created by some other applications. If the objects have properties other than AutoCAD then the source application of the object should be running for the properties to be available in the QSELECT.*

CYCLING THROUGH SELECTION

In AutoCAD, you can cycle through the objects to be selected if they are overlapping or close to other entities. This feature helps in selecting the entities easily and quickly. To enable this feature, choose the **Selection Cycling** button in the Status Bar. Now, if you move the cursor near an entity that has other entities nearby it then the selection cycling symbol will be displayed, as shown in Figure 6-22. If you select any one of the entities when the selection cycling symbol is displayed, the **Selection** list box with a list of the entities that can be selected will be displayed, as shown in Figure 6-23. You can select the entities from the **Selection** list box.

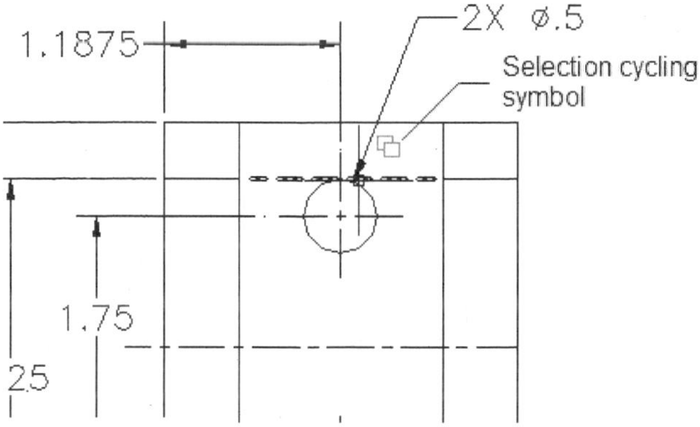

Figure 6-22 *The selection cycling symbol displayed*

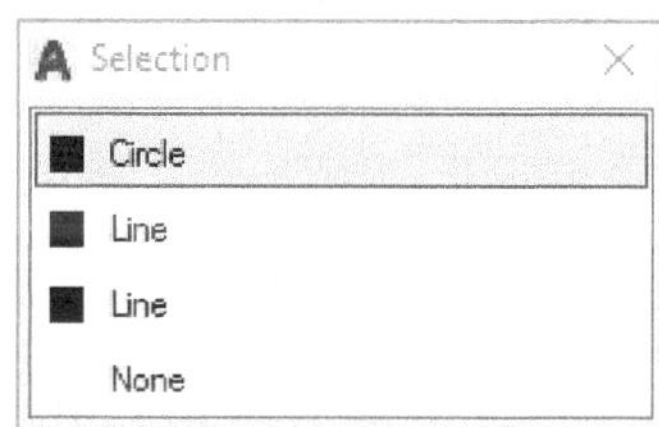

Figure 6-23 *The **Selection** list box*

MANAGING CONTENTS USING THE DesignCenter

Ribbon: View > Palettes > DesignCenter **Command:** ADCENTER/ADC
Menu Bar: Tools > Palettes > DesignCenter

The **DESIGNCENTER** palette is used to locate and organize drawing data, and to insert blocks, layers, external references, and other customized drawing content. These contents can be selected from either your own files, local drives, a network, or the Internet. You can even access and use the contents between the files or from the Internet. You can use the **DesignCenter** to conveniently drag and drop any information that has been previously created into the current drawing. This powerful tool reduces the repetitive tasks of creating information that already exists. To invoke the **DESIGNCENTER** palette, choose the **DesignCenter** tool from the **Palettes** panel of the **View** tab; the **DESIGNCENTER** palette will be displayed, refer to Figure 6-24.

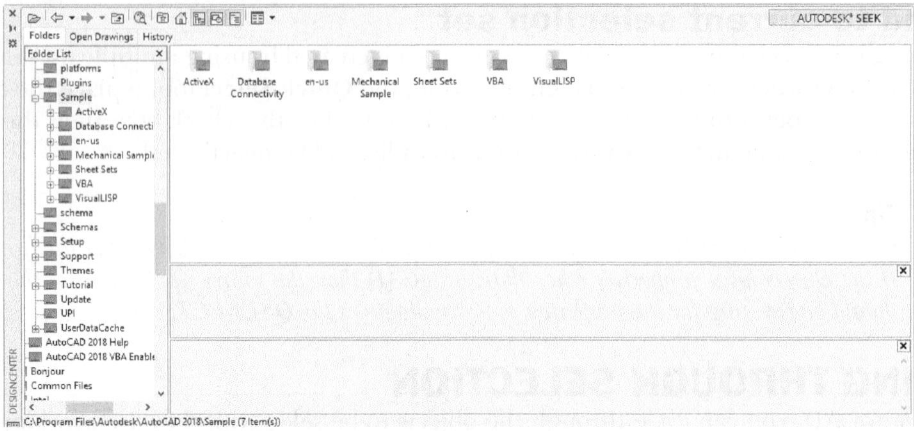

***Figure 6-24** The **DESIGNCENTER** palette*

To move the **DesignCenter**, drag the title bar located on the left of the window. To resize it, click on the borders and drag them to the right or left. Right-clicking on the title bar of the window displays a shortcut menu to move, resize, close, allow docking, anchor left, anchor right, and auto-hide the **DESIGNCENTER** palette. The **Auto-Hide** button on the title bar acts as a toggle button for hiding and displaying the **DesignCenter**. Also, double-clicking on the title bar of the window docks the **DESIGNCENTER** palette. To use this option, make sure that the **Allow Docking** option is selected from the shortcut menu that is displayed on right-clicking on the title bar.

Note

*The **DesignCenter** can be turned on and off by pressing the CTRL+2 keys.*

Figure 6-25 shows the buttons in the **DesignCenter** toolbar. When you choose the Tree View **Toggle** button on the **DesignCenter** toolbar, it displays the Tree View (Left Pane) with a tree view of the contents of the drives. If the tree view is not displayed, you can also right-click in the window and choose **Tree** from the shortcut menu displayed. Now, the window is divided into two parts, the Tree View (left pane) and the Palette (right pane). The Palette displays folders, files, objects in a drawing, images, Web-based content, and custom content. You can also resize both the Tree View and the Palette by clicking and dragging the bar between them to the right or the left.

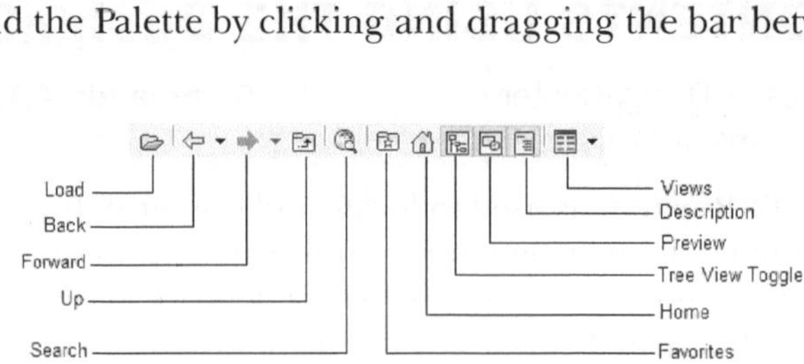

***Figure 6-25** The **DesignCenter** toolbar*

The **DesignCenter** has three tabs below the **DesignCenter** toolbar buttons. They are **Folders**, **Open Drawings**, and **History**. The description of these tabs is given next.

Folders Tab

The **Folders** tab lists all the folders and files in the local and network drives. When this tab is chosen, the Tree View displays the tree view of the contents of the drives and the Palette displays various folders and files in a drawing, images, and the Web-based content in the selected drive.

In the Tree View, you can browse the contents of any folder by clicking on the plus sign (+) adjacent to it to expand the view. Further, expanding the contents of a file displays the categories such as **Blocks**, **Dimstyles**, **Layers**, **Layouts**, **Linetypes**, **Textstyles**, **Xrefs**, and so on. Clicking on any one of these categories in the **Tree View** displays the listing under the selected category in the Palette, refer to Figure 6-26.

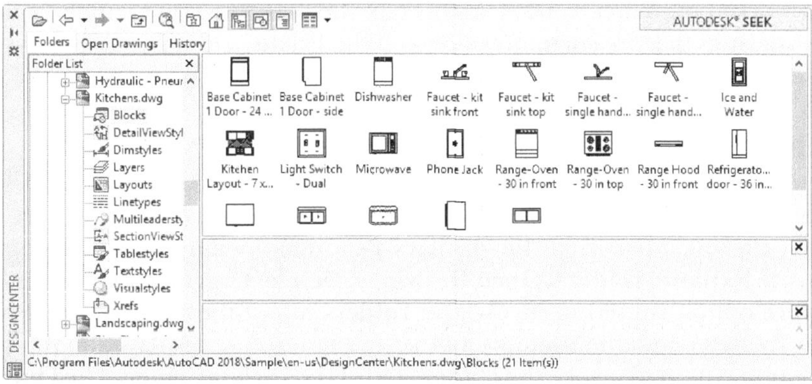

***Figure 6-26** The **DesignCenter** displaying the Tree pane, Palette, Preview pane, and Description box*

You can drag and drop any of the contents into the current drawing, or add them by double-clicking on them. These are then reused as part of the current drawing. When you double-click on specific Xrefs and blocks, AutoCAD displays the **Attach External Reference** dialog box and the **Insert** dialog box, respectively. The **Attach External Reference** dialog box helps in attaching the external reference and the **Insert** dialog box helps in inserting the block. Right-clicking a block displays the options of **Insert Block**, **Insert and Redifine**, **Redifine only**, **Block editor**, **Copy**, and **Create Tool Palette** and right-clicking an Xref displays the options of **Attach Xref** and **Copy** in the shortcut menus. Similarly, when you double-click on a layer, text style, dimstyle, layout, or linetype style, they also get added to the current drawing.

If any of these named objects already exist in the current drawing, duplicate definition is ignored and it is not added again. When you right-click on a specific linetype, layer, textstyle, layout, or dimstyle in the palette, a shortcut menu is displayed that gives you an option to **Add** or **Copy**. The **Add** option directly adds the selected named object to the current drawing. The **Copy** option copies the specific named object to the clipboard from where you can paste it into a particular drawing.

Note

You will learn more about inserting blocks in Chapter 16, Working with Blocks.

Right-clicking a particular folder or file in the Tree View displays a shortcut menu. The various options in the shortcut menu are **Explore**, **Search**, **Add to Favorites**, **Organize Favorites**, **Create**

Tool Palette, and **Set as Home**. **Add to Favorites** adds the selected file or folder to the **Favorites** folder, which contains the most often accessed files and folders. **Organize Favorites** allows you to reorganize the contents of the **Favorites** folder. When you select **Organize Favorites** from the shortcut menu, the **Autodesk** folder is opened in a window. **Create Tool Palette** adds the blocks of the selected file or folder to the **Tool Palettes** window, which contains the predefined blocks. **Set as Home** sets the selected file or folder as the **Home** folder. You will notice that when the **Design Center** tool is invoked the next time, the file that was last set as the **Home** folder is displayed selected in the **DesignCenter**.

Open Drawings Tab

The **Open Drawings** tab lists all the drawings that are open, including the current drawing which is being worked on. When you select this tab, the Tree View (left pane) displays the tree view of all the drawings that are currently open and the Palette (right pane) displays the various contents in the selected drawing.

History Tab

The **History** tab lists the locations of the most recently accessed files through the **DesignCenter**. When you choose this tab, the Tree View (left pane) and the Palette (right pane) are replaced by a list box. Right-clicking a particular file displays a shortcut menu. The various options in the shortcut menu are **Explore**, **Folders**, **Open Drawings**, **Delete**, **Organize Favourites**, and **Search** etc. The **Explore** option is used to invoke the **Folders** tab of the **DesignCenter** with the file selected in the Tree View and the contents of the selected file are displayed in the Palette View. The **Folders** option is used to invoke the **Folders** tab of the **DesignCenter**. The **Open Drawings** option is used to invoke the **Open Drawings** tab of the **DesignCenter**. The **Delete** option deletes the selected drawing from the **History** list. The **Search** option allows you to search for drawings or named objects such as blocks, textstyles, dimstyles, layers, layouts, external references, or linetypes. The **Organize Favourites** option is used to open **Autodesk** folder in a window.

Autodesk Seek design content Link

The **Autodesk Seek design content** link allows you to download the *.dwg*, *.dwf*, *.pdf*, *.dgn*, *.gsm*, *.skp*, *.rfa* and all other files of various products from the Autodesk online source for product specification and design files. To access the online source, click on the **Autodesk seek design content** located at upper right corner of the **DesignCenter**; a new web page will be displayed. In this page, you can search for the required file type using the **Search** option. Once you get the required files, you can download them to your system.

Choosing the **Back** button in the **DesignCenter** toolbar displays the last item selected in the **DesignCenter**. If you pick the down arrow on the **Back** button, a list of the recently visited items is displayed. You can view the desired item in the **DesignCenter** by selecting it from the list. The **Forward** button is available only if you have chosen the **Back** button once. This button displays the same page as the current page before you choose the **Back** button. The **Up** button moves one level up in the tree structure from the current location. Choosing the **Favorites** button displays shortcuts to files and folders that are accessed frequently by you and are stored in the **Favorites** folder. This reduces the time you take to access these files or folders from their normal location. Choosing the **Tree View Toggle** button in the **DesignCenter** toolbar displays or hides the tree pane with the tree view of the contents displayed in a hierarchical form. Choosing the **Load** button displays the **Load** dialog box, whose options are similar to those of the standard

Select File dialog box. When you select a file from this dialog box and choose the **Open** button, AutoCAD displays the selected file and its contents in the **DesignCenter**.

The **Views** button gives four display format options for the contents of the palette: **Large icons**, **Small icons**, **List**, and **Details**. The **List** option lists the contents in the palette while the **Details** option gives a detailed list of the contents in the palette with the name, file size, and type. Right-clicking in the palette displays a shortcut menu with all the options provided in the **DesignCenter** in addition to the **Add to Favorites**, **Organize favorites**, and **Create Tool Palette of Blocks** options. The **Create Tool Palette of Blocks** option adds the drawings of the selected file or folder to the **Tool Palettes**, which contains the predefined blocks. The following example will illustrate how to use the **DesignCenter** to locate a drawing and then use its contents in the current drawing.

Example 1 — DesignCenter

Use the **DesignCenter** to locate and view the contents of the drawing *Kitchens.dwg*. Also, use the **DesignCenter** to insert a block from this drawing and import a layer and a textstyle from the *Blocks and Tables - Imperial.dwg* file located in the **Sample** folder. Use these to make a drawing of a Kitchen plan (*MyKitchen.dwg*) and then add text to it, as shown in Figure 6-27.

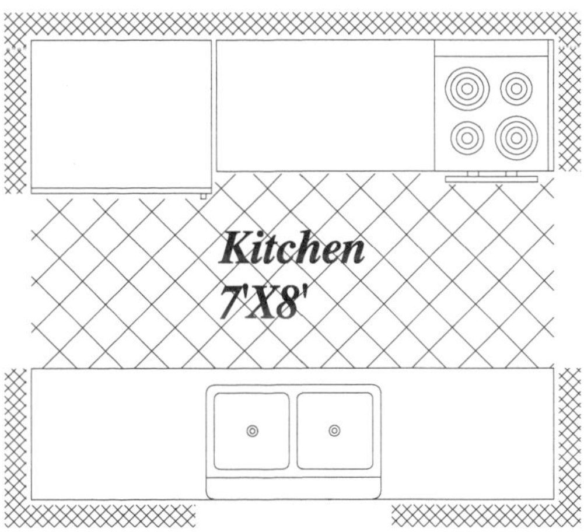

Figure 6-27 *Drawing for Example 1*

1. Open a new drawing using the **Start from Scratch** option. Make sure the **Imperial (feet and inches)** radio button is selected in the **Create New Drawing** dialog box.

2. Change the units to **Architectural** using the **Drawing Units** dialog box. Increase the limits to **10',10'**. Use the **Zoom All** tool to increase the drawing display area.

3. Choose the **DesignCenter** tool from the **Palettes** panel in the **View** tab; the **DesignCenter** window is displayed at its default location.

4. In the **DesignCenter** toolbar, choose the **Tree View Toggle** button to display the Tree View and the Palette (if is not already displayed). Also, choose the **Preview** button, if it is not

displayed already. You can resize the window, if needed, to view both the Tree View and the Palette, conveniently.

5. Choose the **Search** button in the **DesignCenter** to display the **Search** dialog box. Here, select **Drawings** from the **Look for** drop-down list and **C:** (or the drive in which AutoCAD 2018 is installed) from the **In** drop-down list. Select the **Search subfolders** check box. In the **Drawings** tab, type **Kitchens** in the **Search for the word(s)** edit box and select **File Name** from the **In the field(s)** drop-down list. Now, choose the **Search Now** button to commence the search. After the drawing has been located, its details and path are displayed in a list box at the bottom of the dialog box.

6. Now, right-click on *Kitchens.dwg* in the list box of the **Search** dialog box and choose **Load into Content Area** from the shortcut menu. You will notice that the drawing and its contents are displayed in the Tree view.

7. Close the **Search** dialog box, if it is still open.

8. Double-click on *Kitchens.dwg* in the Tree View to expand the tree view and display its contents, in case they are not displayed. You can also expand the contents by clicking on the + sign located on the left of the file name in the Tree view.

9. Select **Blocks** in the Tree View to display the list of blocks in the drawing in the **Palette**. Using the left mouse button, drag and drop the block **Kitchen Layout-7x8 ft** in the current drawing.

10. Now, double-click on the *AutoCAD Textstyles and Linetypes.dwg* file located in the **DesignCenter** folder in the same directory to display its contents in the Palette.

11. Double-click on **Textstyles** to display the list of text styles in the Palette. Select **Dutch Bold Italic** in the **Palette** and drag and drop it in the current drawing. You can use this textstyle for adding text to the current drawing.

12. Invoke the **Multiline Text** tool and use the imported textstyle to add the text to the current drawing and complete it, refer to Figure 6-27.

13. Save the current drawing with the name *MyKitchen.dwg*.

Note

1. To create text, refer to Figure 6-27, you need to change the text height.

2. You can import Blocks, Dimstyles, Layers, and so on to the current drawing from any existing drawing.

MAKING INQUIRIES ABOUT OBJECTS AND DRAWINGS

When you create a drawing or examine an existing one, you often need some information about the entities in your drawing. The information can be regarding the distance from one location to another, the area of an object like a polygon or circle, coordinates of a location on the drawing, and so on. In manual drafting, you need to measure and calculate manually to get the required information. In AutoCAD, you need to use the inquiry tools or commands to obtain information about the selected objects. However, these tools and commands do not affect the drawings in any way. The following is the list of inquiry tools and commands:

Area	**Distance**	**ID**	**List**	**DBLIST**
STATUS	**TIME**	**DWGPROPS**	**MASSPROP**	

For most of the inquiry tools and commands, you are prompted to select objects. Once the selection is complete, AutoCAD switches from the graphics mode to the text mode, and all relevant information about the selected objects is displayed. For some tools and commands, information is displayed in the **AutoCAD Text Window**. The display of the text screen can be tailored to your requirements using a pointing device. Therefore, by moving the text screen to one side, you can view the drawing screen and the text screen, simultaneously. If you choose the **Minimize** button or the **Close** button, you will return to the graphics screen. You can also return to the graphics screen by entering the **GRAPHSCR** command at the command prompt. Similarly, you can return to the AutoCAD Text Window by entering **TEXTSCR** at the command prompt.

Measuring Area of Objects

Ribbon: Home > Utilities > Measure drop-down > Area **Menu Bar:** Tools > Inquiry > Area
Toolbar: Inquiry > Distance drop-down > Area **Command:** AREA/AA

Calculating the area of an object manually is time consuming. In AutoCAD, the **Area** tool is used to automatically calculate the area of an object in square units. This tool saves time when calculating the area of complicated or irregular shapes. You can use the default option of the **Area** tool to calculate the area and perimeter or circumference of the space enclosed by the sequence of specified points.

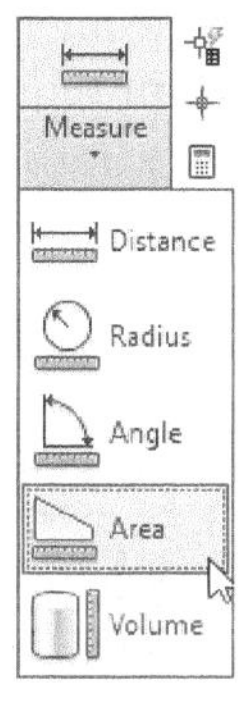

Figure 6-28 *Tools in the* ***Measure*** *drop-down*

For example, to find the area of a pentagon created with the help of the **Line** tool, invoke the **Area** tool, refer to Figure 6-28 and select all the vertices of the polygon to define the shape whose area is to be calculated. This is the default method for determining the area of an object. Note that all the points you specify should be in a plane parallel to the *XY* plane of the current UCS. You can use object snaps such as the Endpoint, Intersect, and Tangent, or running Osnaps, to select the vertices quickly and accurately. The prompt sequence that will be displayed on choosing the **Area** tool from the **Utilities** panel is given next.

Specify first corner point or [Object/Add area/Subtract area] <Object>: *Specify first point.*
Specify next point or [Arc/Length/Undo] : *Specify the second point.*
Specify next point or [Arc/Length/Undo] : *Continue selecting until all points enclosing the area have been selected.*
Specify next point or [Arc/Length/Undo/Total] <Total>: Enter
Area = X, Perimeter = Y

Here, X represents the numerical value of the area and Y represents the circumference/ perimeter.

It is not possible to determine the area of a curved object accurately with the default option of the **Area** tool. However, the approximate area of a curved object can be calculated by specifying several points on the curved entity. If the object whose area you want to find is not closed (formed of independent segments) and has curved lines, you should use the following steps to determine the accurate area of such an object:

1. Convert all the segments in that object into polylines using the **Edit Polyline** tool.

2. Join all the individual polylines into a single polyline. Once you have performed these operations, the object becomes closed and you can then use the **Object** option of the **Area** tool to determine the area.

Object Option

The **Object** option is used to find the area of objects such as polygons, circles, polylines, regions, solids, and splines. If the selected object is a polyline or polygon, the area and perimeter of the polyline will be displayed. In case of open polylines, the area is calculated assuming that the last point is joined to the first point. Additionally, the length of this segment is calculated not the perimeter. If the selected object is a circle, ellipse, or planar closed spline curve, information about its area and circumference will be displayed. For a solid, the surface area is displayed. For a 3D polyline, all vertices must lie in a plane parallel to the *XY* plane of the current UCS. The extrusion direction of a 2D polyline whose area you want to determine should be parallel to the *Z* axis of the current UCS. In case of polylines that have a width, the area and length of the polyline are calculated using the centerline. If any of these conditions is violated, an error message is displayed. The prompt sequence for using the **Object** option of the **Area** tool is given below.

Specify first corner point or [Object/Add area/Subtract area] <Object>: **O** Enter
Select objects: *Select an object.*
Area = (X), Perimeter = (Y)

Here X represents the numerical value of the area and Y represents the circumference/perimeter.

Tip
*The easiest and most accurate way to find the area of a region enclosed by multiple objects is to use the **Boundary** tool to create a polyline, and then use the **Object** option. (You will learn about the **Boundary** tool in Chapter 12)*

Add area Option

Sometimes you want to add areas of different objects to determine the total area. For example, while drawing the plan of a house, you need to add the areas of all the rooms to get the total floor area. In such cases, you can use the **Add area** option of the **Area** tool. The **Object** option adds the areas and perimeters of selected objects. After choosing this option, specify the first corner point at the **Specify first corner point or [Object/Subtract area]** prompt. Then continue specifying other corner points and press ENTER; the selected region will be displayed in green color and its area and perimeter will be displayed at the command prompt. As the **Add area** option is on, you will be prompted to select next corner point again. Keep selecting all corner points to define the area and press ENTER twice to exit the tool; the total area will be displayed. After invoking the **Add area** option, you can also invoke the **Object** option, at the **Specify first corner point or [Object/Subtract area]** prompt, to select the objects. On selecting the objects, the regions are displayed in green color, and the area and length of the selected object as well as the combined area will be displayed at the command prompt. In this manner, you can add areas of different objects. Until the **Add area** mode is active, the string **ADD mode** is displayed along with all subsequent object selection prompts to remind you that the **Add** mode is active.

If the polygon whose area is to be added is not closed, the area and perimeter are calculated assuming that there exists a line that connects the first point to the last point. The length of this imaginary line is added to the perimeter.

Subtract area Option

The **Subtract area** option is used along with the **Add area** option to subtract an area from the previously added area. For example, to calculate the area of the closed profile after subtracting the areas of the circles in Figure 6-29, you need to use the **Subtract area** option. First, invoke the **Area** tool and calculate the area of the closed profile using the **Add area** option; the region will be enclosed in green color area and the total area and the perimeter will be displayed. Give a single null response to exit the **Add area** option. Then, choose the **Subtract area** option and invoke the **Object** option. Now, select both the circles; the circles will be displayed in different colors and their areas will be displayed. Also, the total area will be displayed.

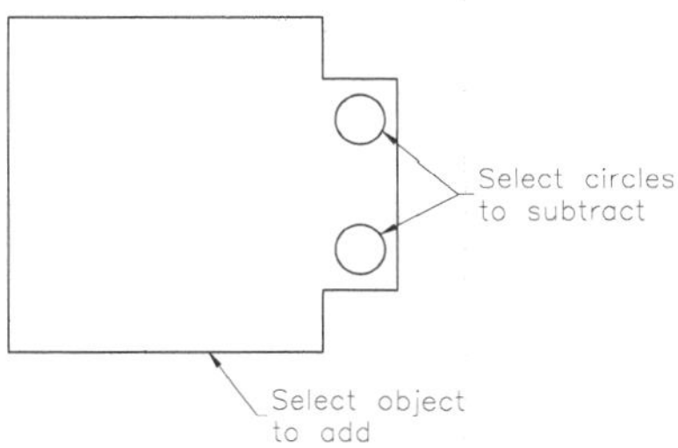

***Figure 6-29** Measuring the area of a sketch using the **Add** and **Subtract area** options*

The prompt sequence for these two modes is given next.

Specify first corner point or [Object/Add area/Subtract area]<Object>: **A** Enter
Specify first corner point or [Object/Subtract area]: **O** Enter
(ADD mode) Select objects: *Select the polyline.*
Area = 2.4438, Length = 6.4999
Total area = 2.4438
(ADD mode) Select objects: Enter
Specify first corner point or [Object/Subtract area]: **S** Enter
Specify first corner point or [Object/Add area]: **O** Enter
(SUBTRACT mode) Select objects: *Select the circle.*
Area = 0.0495, Circumference = 0.7890
Total area = 2.3943
(SUBTRACT mode) Select objects: *Select the second circle.*
Area = 0.0495, Circumference = 0.7890
Total area = 2.3448
(SUBTRACT mode) Select objects: Enter
Specify first corner point or [Object/Add area]: Enter

The **AREA** and **PERIMETER** system variables hold the area and perimeter (or circumference in the case of circles) of the previously selected polyline (or circle). Whenever you use the **Area** tool, the **AREA** variable is reset to zero.

Tip

*If an architect wants to calculate the area of flooring and skirting in a room, the **Area** tool provides you with its area and perimeter. You can use these parameters to calculate the skirting.*

Measuring the Distance Between Two Points

Ribbon: Home > Utilities > Measure drop-down > Distance
Toolbar: Inquiry > Distance drop-down
Menu Bar: Tools > Inquiry > Distance **Command:** DIST/DI

The **Distance** tool is used to measure the distance between two selected points, as shown in Figure 6-30. The angles that the selected points make with the *X* axis and the *XY* plane are also displayed. The measurements are displayed in the current units. Additionally, the Delta X (horizontal displacement), Delta Y (vertical displacement), and Delta Z values are displayed. The distance computed by the **Distance** tool is saved in the **DISTANCE** variable.

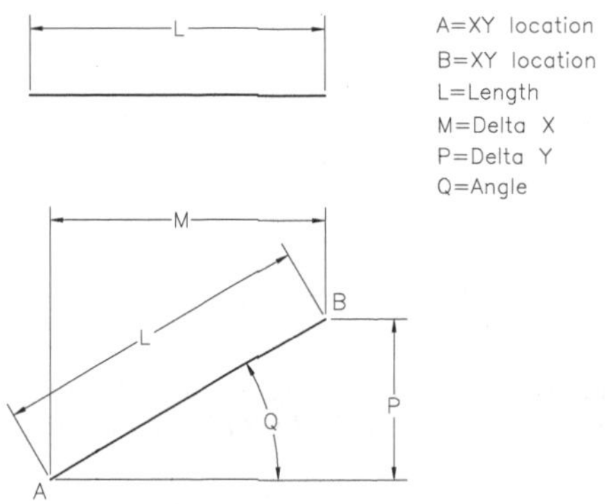

Figure 6-30 *Using the **Distance** tool to measure distance*

The prompt sequence that will follow when you choose the **Distance** tool is given next.

Specify first point: *Specify a point.*
Specify second point or [Multiple points]: *Specify a point.*

AutoCAD returns the following information.
Distance = *Calculated distance between the two points.*
Angle in XY plane = *Angle between the two points in the XY plane.*
Angle from XY plane = *The angle which the specified point makes with the XY plane.*
Delta X = *Change in X,* Delta Y = *Change in Y,* Delta Z = *Change in Z.*

If you give a null response at the **Specify first point** prompt and enter a single number or fraction at the **Specify second point or [Multiple points]** prompt, AutoCAD will convert it into the current unit of measurement and display in the command line. Also, the other values will be calculated with respect to the last used point.

Note

The Z coordinate is used in 3D distances. If you do not specify the Z coordinates of the two points between which you want to know the distance, AutoCAD takes the current elevation as the Z coordinate value.

Identifying the Location of a Point

Ribbon: Home > Utilities > ID Point	**Toolbar:** Inquiry > Locate Point
Menu Bar: Tools > Inquiry > ID Point	**Command:** ID

The **ID Point** tool is used to identify the position of a point in terms of its *X*, *Y*, and *Z* coordinates. The prompt sequence that will follow when you choose the **ID Point** tool from the **Utilities** panel is given next.

Specify point: *Specify the point to be identified.*
X = X coordinate Y = Y coordinate Z = Z coordinate

The current elevation is taken as the *Z* coordinate value. If an **Osnap** mode is used to snap to a 3D object in response to the **Specify point** prompt, the *Z* coordinate displayed will be that of the selected feature of the 3D object.

The coordinates of the point specified in the **ID Point** tool are saved in the **LASTPOINT** system variable. You can locate a point with respect to the **ID** point by using the relative or polar coordinate system.

Listing Information about Objects

Ribbon: Home > Properties > List	**Toolbar:** Inquiry > List
Menu Bar: Tools > Inquiry > List	**Command:** LIST/LI

The **List** tool displays all the information pertaining to the selected objects. The information is displayed in the **AutoCAD Text Window**. The prompt sequence that follows when you invoke the **List** tool from the **Properties** panel is given next.

Select objects: *Select objects whose data you want to list.*
Select objects: Enter

Once you select the objects to be listed, a new **AutoCAD Text Window** window will be displayed. The information displayed (listed) varies from object to object. The information about the type of the object, its coordinate position with respect to the current UCS (user coordinate system), the name of the layer on which it is drawn, and whether the object is in model space or paper space is listed for all types of objects. If the color, lineweight, and the linetype are not BYLAYER, they are also listed. Also, if the thickness of the object is greater than 0, that is also displayed. The elevation value is displayed in the form of a *Z* coordinate (in the case of 3D objects). If an object has an extrusion direction different from the *Z* axis of the current UCS, the object's extrusion direction is also provided.

More information based on the objects in the drawing is also provided. For example, the following information is displayed for a line.

1. The coordinates of the endpoints of the line.
2. Its length (in 3D).
3. The angle made by the line with respect to the *X* axis of the current UCS.
4. The angle made by the line with respect to the *XY* plane of the current UCS.
5. Delta X, Delta Y, and Delta Z: this is the change in each of the three coordinates from the start point to the endpoint.
6. The name of the layer in which the line was created.
7. Whether the line is drawn in Paper space or Model space.

For a circle, the center point, radius, true area, and circumference are displayed. For polylines, this tool displays the coordinates. In addition, for a closed polyline, its true area and perimeter are also given. If the polyline is open, AutoCAD lists its length and also calculates the area by assuming a segment connecting the start point and endpoint of the polyline. In the case of wide polylines, whole computation is done based on the centerlines of the wide segments. For a selected viewport, the **List** tool displays whether the viewport is on and active, on and inactive, or off. Information is also displayed about the scale relative to paper space. If you use the **List** tool on a polygon mesh, the size of the mesh, the coordinate values of all the vertices in the mesh, and whether the mesh is closed or open, are all displayed. As mentioned before, if all the information does not fit on a single screen, AutoCAD pauses to allow you to press ENTER to continue the listing.

Listing Information about all Objects in a Drawing

Command: DBLIST

The **DBLIST** command displays information pertaining to all the objects in a drawing. Once you invoke this command, information is displayed at the command prompt. If you want to display the drawing information in the AutoCAD Text Window, press the F2 key. If the information does not fit on a single screen, AutoCAD pauses to allow you to press ENTER to continue the listing. To terminate the command, press ESC. To return to the graphics screen, close the AutoCAD Text Window.

Checking Time-Related Information

Menu Bar: Tools > Inquiry > Time **Command:** TIME

The time and date set in your system are used by AutoCAD to provide information about several time factors related to the drawings. Hence, you should be careful about setting the current date and time in your computer. The **TIME** command is used to display information pertaining to time related to a drawing and the drawing session. The display obtained by invoking the **TIME** command is similar to the following:

Command: **TIME**
Current time: Wednesday, April 5, 2017 3:32:04:007 PM
Times for this drawing:
Created: Wednesday, April 5, 2017 3:29:59:962 PM
Last updated: Wednesday, April 5, 2017 3:30:27:354 PM
Total editing time: 0 days 00:02:04:057

```
Elapsed timer (on):          0 days 00:02:04:055
Next automatic save in:      0 days 00:08:34:178
```

Enter option [Display/ON/OFF/Reset]: *Enter the required option.*

Obtaining Drawing Status Information

Menu Bar: Tools > Inquiry > Status **Command:** STATUS

The **STATUS** command displays information about the prevalent settings of various drawing parameters, such as snap spacing, grid spacing, limits, current space, current layer, current color, and various memory parameters. Once you enter this command, AutoCAD displays information similar to the following.

```
106 objects in Drawing.dwg
Model space limits are         X: 0.0000      Y: 0.0000(On)
                               X: 6.0000      Y: 4.4000
Model space uses               X:0.6335       Y:-0.2459     **Over
                               X:8.0497       Y: 4.9710     **Over
Display shows                  X: 0.0000      Y:-0.2459
                               X: 8.0088      Y: 5.5266
Insertion base is              X: 0.0000      Y: 0.0000      Z: 0.0000
Snap resolution is             X: 0.2500      Y: 0.2500
Grid spacing is                X: 0.2500      Y: 0.2500
Current space:        Model space
Current layout:       Model
Current layer:        "OBJ"
Current color:        BYLAYER -- 7 (white)
Current linetype:     BYLAYER -- "Continuous"
Current material:     BYLAYER -- "Global"
Current lineweight:   BYLAYER
Current elevation:    0.0000   thickness:   0.0000
Fill on  Grid on  Ortho off  Qtext off  Snap off  Tablet  on
Press ENTER to continue:
Object snap modes: None
Free dwg disk space (C:) space: 2047.7 MBytes
Free temp disk (C:) space: 2047.7 MBytes
Free physical memory: 15.0 MBytes (out of 6029.6M).
Free swap file space: 1987.5 MBytes (out of 6029.6M).
```

All the values (coordinates and distances) on this screen are given in the format declared in the **Units** tool in the **Format** menu bar. This signifies that the drawing is not confined within the drawing limits. The amount of memory on the disk is given in the **Free dwg disk space** line. Information on the name of the current layer, current color, current space, current linetype, current lineweight, current elevation, snap spacing (snap resolution), grid spacing, various tools that are on or off (such as Ortho, Snap, Fill, Tablet, Qtext), and which object snap modes are active is also provided by the display obtained by invoking the **STATUS** command.

Displaying Drawing Properties

Application Menu: Drawing Utilities > Drawing Properties	**Command:** DWGPROPS

The **DWGPROPS** command is used to display information about drawing properties. Choose **Drawing Utilities > Drawing Properties** from the **Application Menu**; the **Drawing Properties** dialog box will be displayed, as shown in Figure 6-31. This dialog box has four tabs under which information about the drawing is displayed. This information helps you look for the drawing more easily. These tabs are discussed next.

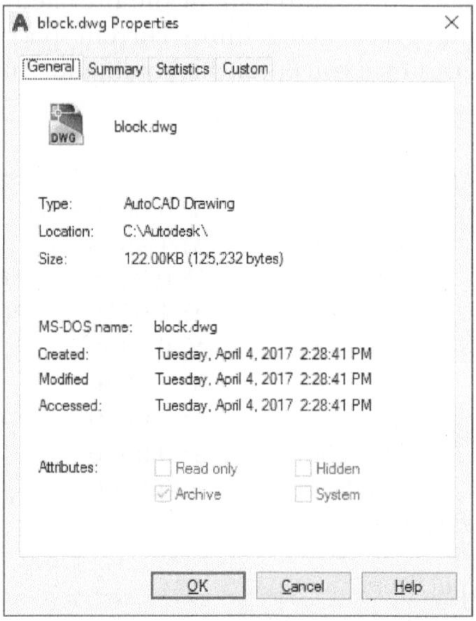

*Figure 6-31 The **Drawing Properties** dialog box*

General

This tab displays general properties about a drawing like the **Type**, **Size**, and **Location**.

Summary

The **Summary** tab displays predefined properties like the Author, title, and subject. Also this tab is displayed at the last that allows you to specify the information related to the drawing.

Statistics

This tab stores and displays data such as dates about the drawing when it was created, last saved or modified.

Custom

This tab displays custom file properties including values assigned by you.

BASIC DISPLAY OPTIONS

Drawing in AutoCAD is much simpler than manual drafting in many ways. Sometimes while drawing manually, it is very difficult to see and alter minute details. In AutoCAD, you can overcome this problem by viewing only a specific portion of the drawing. For example, to display a part of the drawing on a larger area, use the Zoom tools to enlarge or reduce the size of the drawing displayed. Similarly, use the **REGEN** command to regenerate the drawing and **REDRAW** to refresh the screen. In this chapter, you will learn some of the drawing display commands, such as **REDRAW**, **REGEN**, **PAN**, **ZOOM**, and **VIEW**. These commands can also be used in the transparent mode. It means you can use these commands while another command is in progress.

REDRAWING THE SCREEN

Menu Bar: View > Redraw **Command:** REDRAW

The **REDRAW** command is used to redraw the drawing area. It is used to remove the temporary graphics from the drawing area which are left after using the **VSLIDE** command and some other operations. The **REDRAW** command also redraws the objects that are not displayed on the screen as a result of editing some other object. In AutoCAD, several commands redraw the screen automatically (for example, when a grid is turned off), but sometimes it is useful to redraw the screen explicitly.

To use the **REDRAW** command in transparent mode, add apostrophe as a prefix. For example, if you are drawing a line after specifying few points, type **'REDRAW** at the command prompt as given below.

Specify next point or [Close/Undo]: *Specify a point.*
Specify next point or [Close/Undo]: ***'REDRAW***
Resuming LINE command.
Specify next point or [Close/Undo]: *Specify a point.*

In this case, the redrawing process takes place without any prompt for information. The **REDRAW** command affects only the current viewport. If you have more than one viewport, use the **REDRAWALL** command to redraw all the viewports.

REGENERATING DRAWINGS

Menu Bar: View > Regen **Command:** REGEN/RE

The **REGEN** command is used to regenerate the modified drawing. The need for regeneration usually occurs when you change certain aspects of the drawing. All the objects in the drawing are recalculated and redrawn in the current viewport. One of the advantages of this command is that the drawing is refined by smoothening out circles and arcs. To use this command, type **REGEN** at the command prompt and press ENTER; the message **Regenerating model** will be displayed while the system regenerates the drawing. The **REGEN** command affects only the current viewport. If you have more than one viewport, use the **REGENALL** command to regenerate all of them. The **REGEN** command can be aborted by pressing ESC. This saves time if you are going to use another command that causes automatic regeneration.

Note

*Under certain conditions, the **Zoom** and **Pan** tools automatically regenerate the drawing. Some other commands also perform regenerations under certain conditions.*

ZOOMING DRAWINGS

Ribbon: View > Navigate > Extents	**Toolbar:** Navigation Bar > Zoom Extents
Menu bar: View > Zoom > Extents	**Command:** ZOOM > E

Creating drawings in AutoCAD would not be of much use if you cannot magnify the drawing view to work on the minute details. The ability to zoom in or magnify has been helpful in creating the minuscule circuits used in the electronics and computer industries. This is performed using the Zoom tools in the **Zoom** drop-down. These are the most frequently used tools. Getting close to or away from the drawing is the function of the Zoom tools. In other words, these tools enlarge or reduce the view of the drawing on the screen, but it does not affect the actual size of the objects. In this way, the Zoom tools function like the zoom lens of a camera. When you magnify the apparent size of a section of the drawing, you see that area in greater detail. On the other hand, if you reduce the apparent size of the drawing, you see a larger area.

The Zoom tools can also be used in transparent mode. This means that these tools can be used while working with other tools. Various tools in the **Zoom** drop-down are shown in Figure 6-32. You can also invoke these tools by right-clicking in the drawing area and then choosing the **Zoom** tool from the shortcut menu even when you are working with some other tool, refer to Figure 6-33. Various tools of the **Zoom** drop-down have been made available in the **Navigation Bar** in the drawing area, as shown in Figure 6-34. The various zoom tools available in the **Navigation Bar** are discussed next.

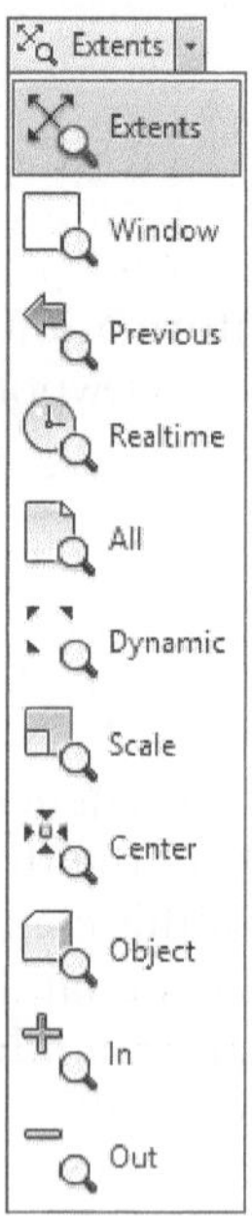

*Figure 6-32 Tools in the **Zoom** drop-down*

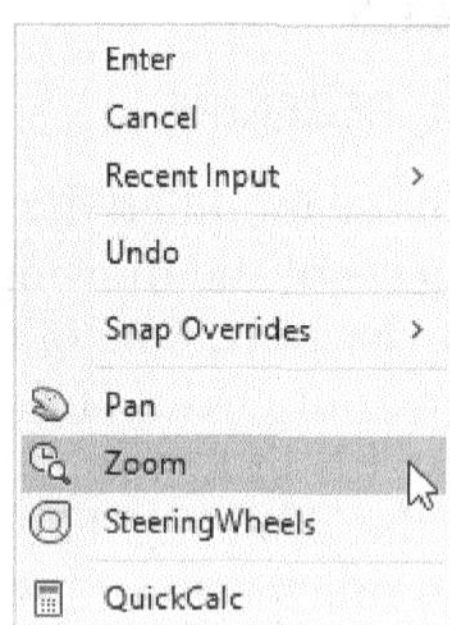

*Figure 6-33 The **Zoom** option in the shortcut menu*

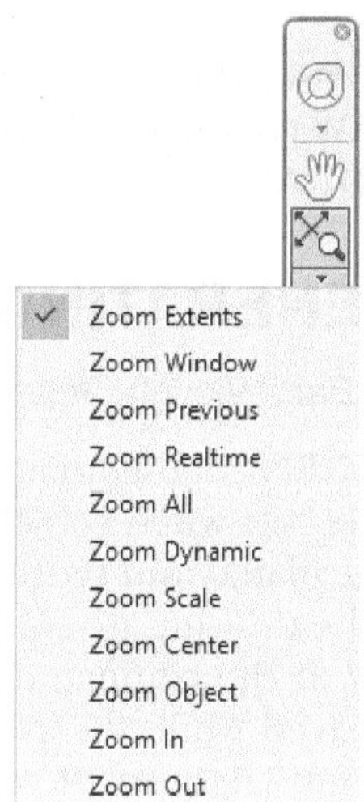

*Figure 6-34 The Zoom tools in the **Navigation Bar***

Zoom Realtime

You can zoom in or zoom out the drawing by using the **Zoom Realtime** tool available in the **Navigation Bar**. To zoom in, invoke this tool and then hold the pick button down and move the cursor up. If you want to zoom in further, release the pick button and bring the cursor down. Specify a point and move the cursor up again. Similarly, to zoom out, hold the pick button down and move the cursor down. If you move the cursor vertically up from the midpoint of the screen to the top of the window, the drawing will be magnified by 100% (zoom in 2x magnification). Similarly, if you move the cursor vertically down from the midpoint of the screen to the bottom of the window, the drawing display will be reduced to 100% (zoom out 0.5x magnification). Realtime zoom is the default setting for the **Zoom** tool. Alternatively, you can invoke the **Zoom Realtime** tool by choosing the **Zoom** tool from the shortcut menu displayed by right-clicking in the drawing area.

When you use the realtime zoom, the cursor turns into a magnifying glass and displays a plus sign (+) and a minus sign (–). To exit the realtime zoom, press ENTER or ESC, or choose the **Exit** option from the shortcut menu.

Zoom All

This tool is used to adjust the display area on the basis of the drawing limits, as shown in Figure 6-35 or extents of an object, whichever is greater. Even if the objects are not within the limits, they are still included in the display. Therefore, with the **Zoom All** option, you can view the entire drawing in the current viewport, as shown in Figure 6-36.

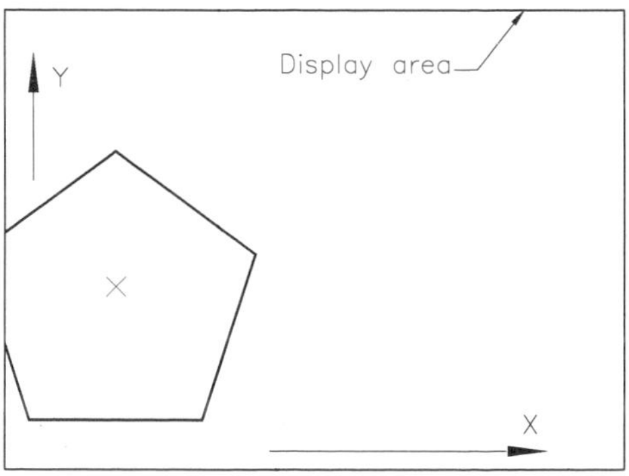

Figure 6-35 *Drawing showing the limits*

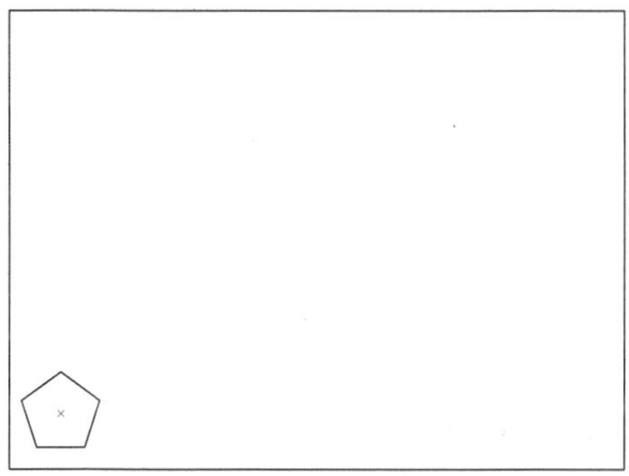

Figure 6-36 *Using the **Zoom All** option*

Zoom Center

This tool is used to define a new display window by specifying the center point and magnification or height of the window. Here, you are required to enter the center and the height of the subsequent screen display. If you press ENTER instead of entering a new center point, the center of the view will remain unchanged. Instead of entering a height, you can enter the magnification factor by typing a number. If you press ENTER at the height prompt, or if the height you enter is the same as the current height, magnification does not take place. For example, if the current height is 2.7645 and you press ENTER at the **Enter magnification or height <current>** prompt, magnification will not take place. The smaller the value, the greater is the enlargement of the image. You can also enter a number followed by **X**. This indicates the change in magnification, not as an absolute value, but as a value relative to the current screen, refer to Figure 6-37 and Figure 6-38.

The prompt sequence displayed on invoking the **Zoom Center** tool is given next.

Choose the ***Zoom Center*** *tool from the* ***Navigation Bar***
Specify center point: *Specify a center point.*
Enter magnification or height <current>: **5X**

In Figure 6-38, the current magnification height is 5X, which magnifies the display five times. If you enter the value **2**, the size (height and width) of the zoom area changes to 2 X 2 around the specified center. In Figure 6-39, if you enter 0.12 as the height after specifying the center point as the circle's center, the circle will zoom to fit in the display area since its diameter is 0.12. The prompt sequence is given next.

Choose the ***Zoom Center*** *tool from the* ***Navigation Bar***
Specify center point: *Select the center of the circle.*
Enter magnification or height <current>: **0.12**

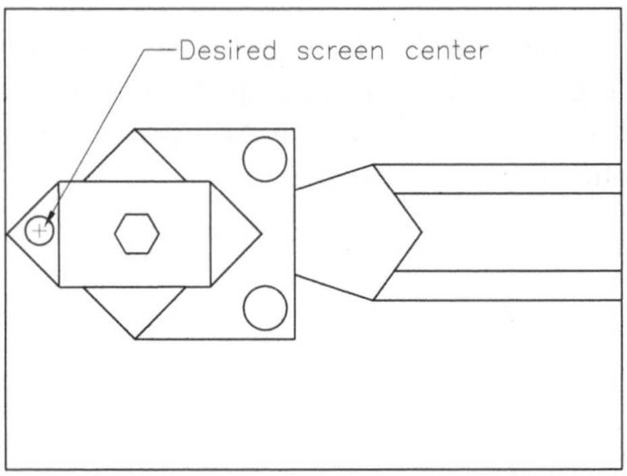

Figure 6-37 *Drawing before using the* ***Zoom Center*** *tool*

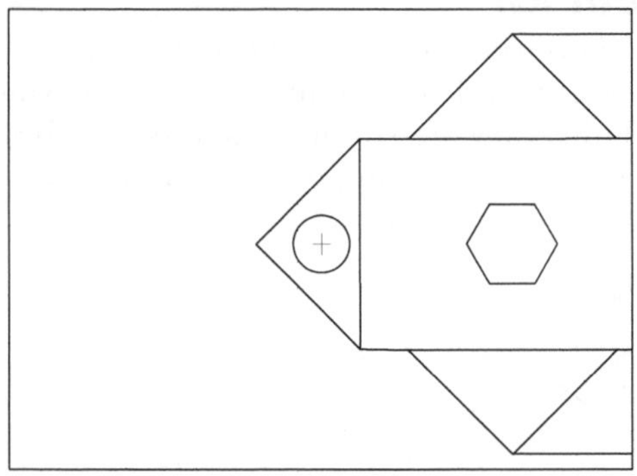

Figure 6-38 *Drawing after using the* ***Zoom Center*** *tool*

Zoom Extents

As the name indicates, this tool is used to zoom to the extents of the biggest object in the drawing. The extents of the drawing comprise the area that has the drawings in it. The rest of the empty area is neglected. On invoking this tool, all the objects in the drawing are magnified to the largest possible display, refer to Figure 6-40.

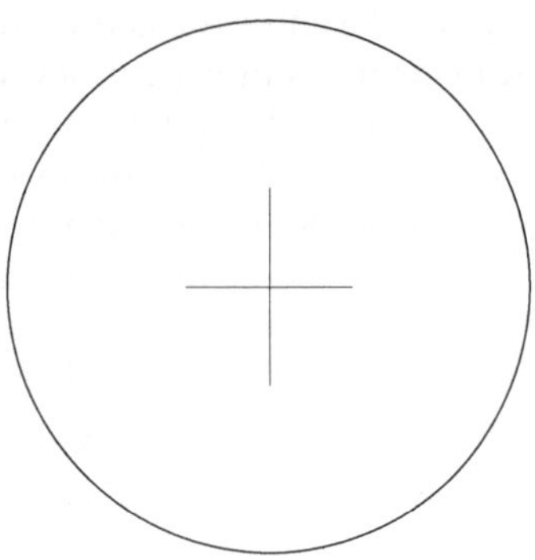

Figure 6-39 *Drawing after using the* ***Zoom Center*** *tool*

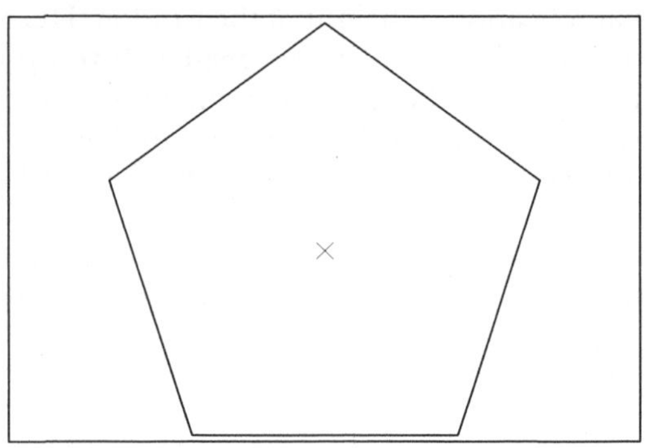

Figure 6-40 *Drawing after using the* ***Zoom Extents*** *tool*

Zoom Dynamic

This tool is used to display the portion of a drawing by specifying the area using the view box. To do so, choose this tool from the **Navigation Bar**; a view box will be attached to the cursor and you will be prompted to specify the area to zoom.

Blue dashed box representing drawing extents

Drawing extents are represented by a dashed blue box, which constitutes the drawing limits or the actual area occupied by the drawing, refer to Figure 6-41.

Green dashed box representing the current view

A green dashed box is formed to represent the area of the current viewport, refer to Figure 6-42.

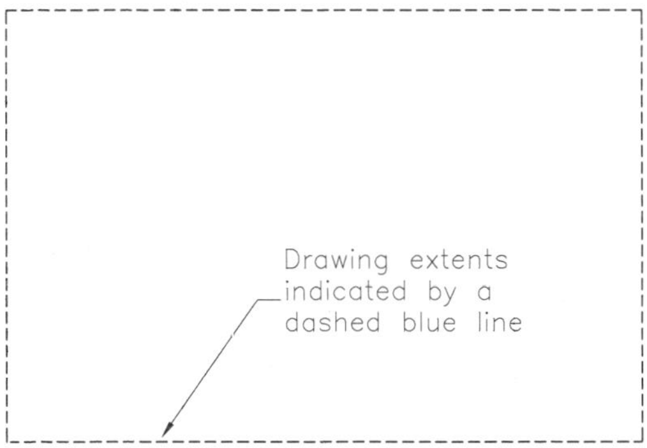

Figure 6-41 Box representing drawing extents

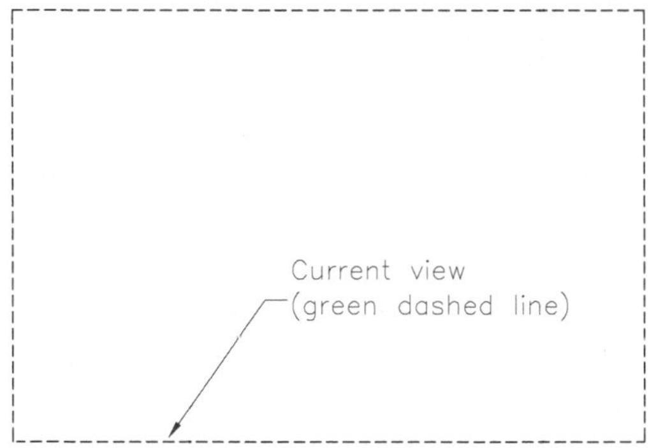

Figure 6-42 Representation of the current view

Panning view box (X in the center)

A view box initially of the same size as the current view box is displayed with an X at the center. You can move this box with the help of your pointing device. This box is known as the panning view box and it helps you to find the center point of the zoomed display you want. When you have found the center, press the pick button to display the zooming view box, refer to Figure 6-43.

Zooming view box (arrow on the right side)

On pressing the pick button at the center of the panning view box, the X at the center of the view box is replaced by an arrow pointing at the right edge of the box. This zooming view box indicates the ZOOM mode. You can now increase or decrease the area of this box according to the area you want to zoom into. To shrink the box, move the pointer to the left; to increase it, move the pointer to the right. The top, right, and bottom sides of the zooming view box move as you move the pointer, but the left side remains fixed, with the zoom base pointing at the midpoint of the left side. You can slide it up or down along the left side. When you have the zooming view box in the desired size for your zoom display, press ENTER to complete the command and zoom into the desired area of the drawing. Before pressing ENTER, if you want to change the position of the zooming view box, click the pick button of your pointing device to redisplay the panning view box. After repositioning, press ENTER, refer to Figure 6-44.

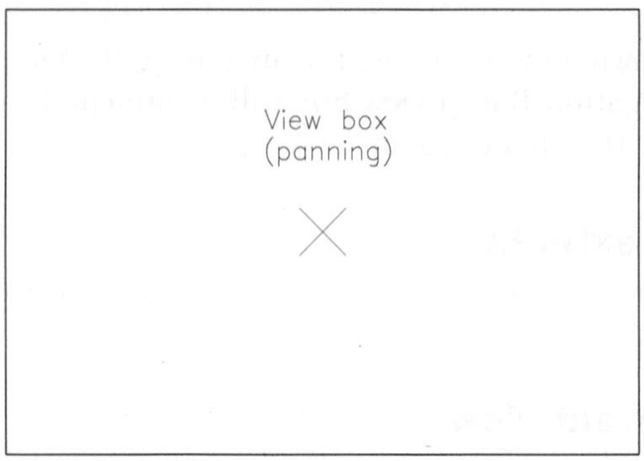

Figure 6-43 *The panning view box*

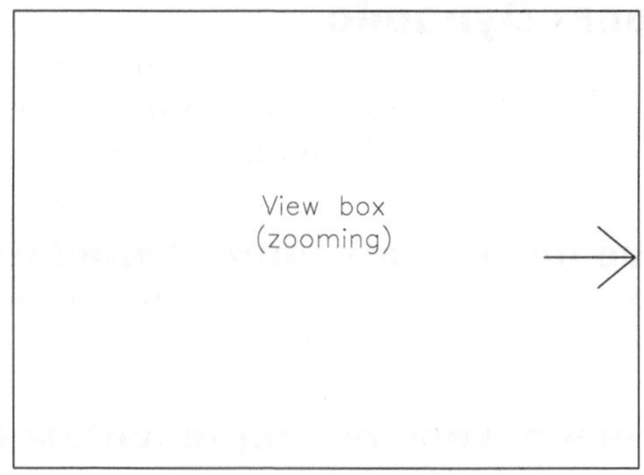

Figure 6-44 *The zooming view box*

Zoom Previous

While working on a complex drawing, you may need to zoom in on a portion of the drawing to edit some minute details. Once the editing is over, you may want to return to the previous view. This can be done by choosing the **Zoom Previous** tool from the **Zoom** drop-down in the **Navigation Bar**. Without this tool, it would be very tedious to zoom back to the previous views. AutoCAD saves the view specification of the current viewport whenever it is being altered by any of the **Zoom** tools. Up to ten views are saved for each viewport. To zoom back the last view, choose the **Zoom Previous** tool from the **Navigation Bar**; the view will switch back to the previous view.

If you erase some objects and then choose the **Zoom Previous** tool, the previous view is restored, but the erased objects are not.

Zoom Window

This is the most commonly used tool of the **Zoom** drop-down. After invoking this tool, you need to specify the area you want to zoom in by specifying two opposite corners of a rectangular window. The center of the specified window becomes the center of the zoomed area. The area inside the window is magnified or reduced in size to fill the display as completely as possible. The points can be specified either by selecting them with the help of the pointing device or by entering their coordinates. The prompt sequence is given next.

*Choose the **Zoom Window** tool from the **Navigation Bar***
Specify first corner: *Specify first point.*
Specify first corner: Specify opposite corner: *Specify another point.*

Whenever the **Zoom** drop-down is invoked, the window method is one of two default options. This is illustrated by the previous prompt sequence where you can specify the two corner points of the window without invoking any tool of the **Zoom** drop-down. The **Window** option can also be used by entering **W**. The prompt sequence for using this option is given next.

Zoom Scale

The **Zoom Scale** tool of the **Zoom** drop-down is a very versatile option. It can be used in the following ways:

Scale: Zoom Scale: Relative to full view

This option of the **Zoom Scale** tool is used to magnify or reduce the size of a drawing according to a scale factor, refer to Figure 6-45. A scale factor equal to 1 displays an area equal in size to the area defined by the established limits. This may not display the entire drawing if the previous view was not centered on the limits or if you have drawn outside the limits. To get a magnification relative to the full view, you can enter any other number. For example, you can type 4 if you want the displayed image to be enlarged four times. If you want to decrease the magnification relative to the full view, you need to enter a number that is less than 1. In Figure 6-46, the image size is decreased because the scale factor is less than 1. In other words, the image size is half of the full view because the scale factor is 0.5.

The prompt sequence after choosing the **Zoom Scale** tool is given next.

Enter a scale factor (nX or nXP): **0.5** Enter

*Figure 6-45 Drawing before using the **Zoom Scale** tool*

*Figure 6-46 Drawing after using the **Zoom Scale** tool*

Scale: Zoom Scale: Relative to current view

The second way to scale is with respect to the current view, refer to Figure 6-47. In this case, instead of entering only a number, enter a number followed by an **X**. The scale is calculated with reference to the current view. For example, if you enter **0.25X**, each object in the drawing will be displayed at one-fourth (¼) of its current size. The following example shows how to increase the display magnification by a factor of **0.25** relative to its current value, refer to Figure 6-48.

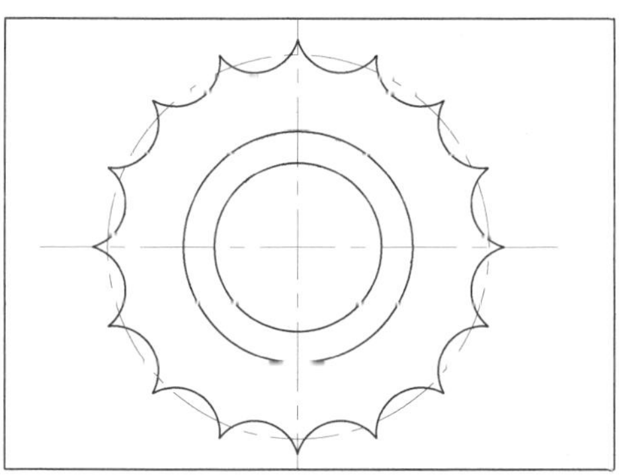

Figure 6-47 Current view of the drawing

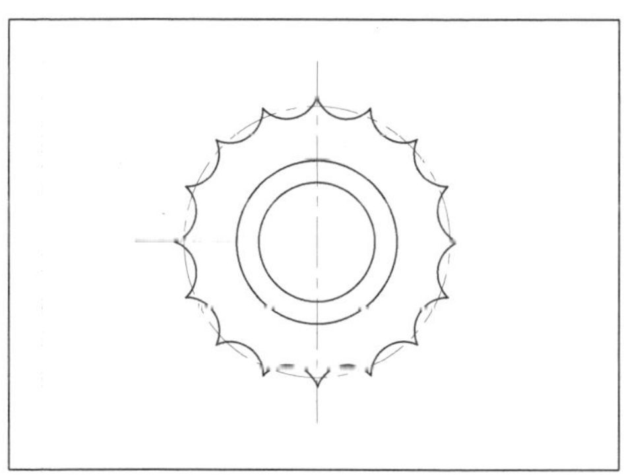

Figure 6-48 Drawing after applying magnification factor of 0.25X

*Choose the **Zoom Scale** tool from the **Navigation Bar***
Enter a scale factor (nX or nXP) : **0.25X** Enter

Scale: Zoom Scale: Relative to paper space units

The third method of scaling is with respect to paper space. You can use paper space in a variety of ways and for various reasons. For example, you can array and plot various views of your model in the paper space. To scale each view relative to paper space units, you can use the **ZOOM XP** option. Each view can have an individual scale. The drawing view can be at any scale of your choice in a model space viewport. For example, to display a model space at one-fourth (¼) the size of the paper space units, the prompt sequence is given next.

*Choose the **Zoom Scale** tool from the **Navigation Bar***
Enter a scale factor (nX or nXP) : **1/4XP** Enter

Note

For better understanding of this topic, refer to "Model Space Viewports, Paper Space Viewports, and Layouts" in Chapter 13.

Zoom Object

This tool is used to select one or more than one objects and display them at the center of the screen in the largest possible size.

Zoom In

This tool is used to zoom in the drawing, which doubles the drawing view size. In this case, the center of the screen is taken as the reference point for enlarging the view of a drawing.

Zoom Out

This tool is used to decrease the size of the drawing view by half. In this case, the center of the screen is taken as the reference point for reducing the view of a drawing.

Exercise 1 — Zoom

Draw the profile shown in Figure 6-49 based on the given dimensions. Use the **Zoom** tools to get a bigger view of the drawing. Do not dimension the drawing.

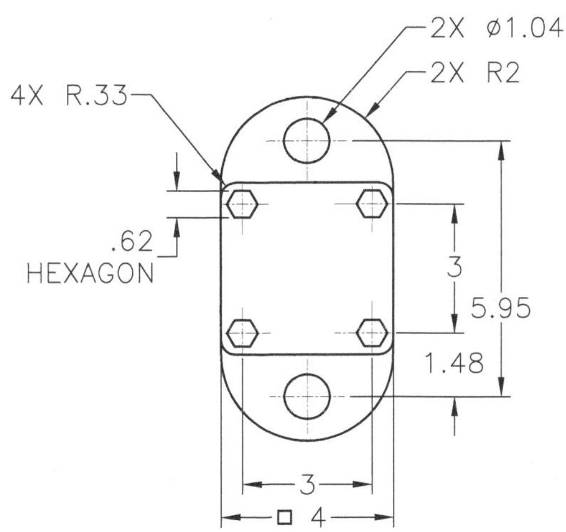

Figure 6-49 Drawing for Exercise 1

PANNING DRAWINGS

Ribbon: View > Navigate > Pan **Command:** PAN/P
Menu Bar: View > Pan > Realtime

You may want to view or draw on a particular area outside the current display. You can do this using the **Pan** tool. If done manually, this would be like holding one corner of the drawing and dragging it across the screen. The **Pan** tool allows you to bring into view the portion of the drawing that is outside the current display area. This is done without changing the magnification of the drawing. The effect of this command can be illustrated by imagining that you are looking at a big drawing through a window (display window) that allows you to slide the drawing right, left, up, and down to bring the part you want to view inside this window. You can invoke the **Pan** tool from the shortcut menu also.

Panning in Realtime

You can use the **Realtime** option of the **Pan** tool to pan the drawing interactively. To pan a drawing, invoke the tool and then hold the left mouse button or hold the middle mouse button and move the cursor in any direction. When you select the realtime pan, an image of a hand will be displayed indicating that you are in the **Realtime** option of the **Pan** tool. This is the default setting for the **Pan** tool. Choosing the **Realtime** option of the **Pan** tool in the toolbar or entering **PAN** at the command prompt automatically invokes the realtime pan. To exit the realtime pan, press ENTER or ESC, or choose **Exit** from the shortcut menu.

The **Pan** tool has various options to pan a drawing in a particular direction. These options can be invoked only from the menu bar, as shown in Figure 6-50. These options are discussed next.

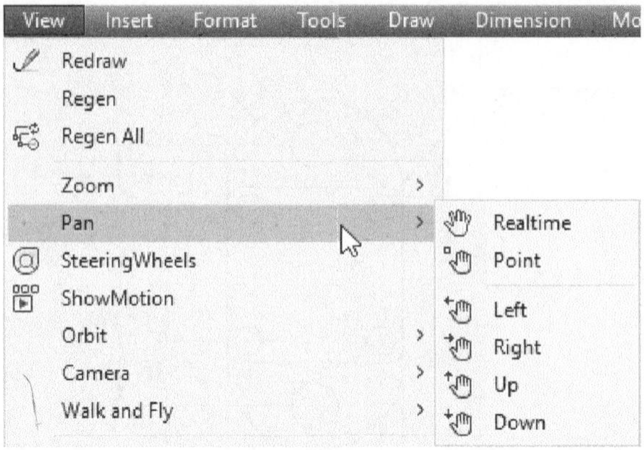

*Figure 6-50 Invoking the **Pan** options from the **View** menu*

Point

This option is used to specify the actual displacement. To do this, you need to specify in what direction you want to move the drawing and by what distance. You can give the displacement either by entering the coordinates of the points or by specifying the coordinates by using a pointing device. The coordinates can be entered in two ways. One way is to specify a single coordinate pair. In this case, AutoCAD takes it as a relative displacement of the drawing with respect to the screen. For example, in the following case, the **Pan** tool would shift the displayed portion of the drawing 2 units to the right and 2 units up.

*Select the **Point** option from the **View** menu.*
Specify base point or displacement: **2,2** [Enter]
Specify second point: [Enter]

In the second case, you can specify two coordinate pairs. AutoCAD computes the displacement from the first point to the second. Here, the displacement is calculated between point (3,3) and point (5,5).

*Select the **Point** option from the **View** menu.*
Specify base point or displacement: **3,3** [Enter] *(Or specify a point.)*
Specify second point: **5,5** [Enter] *(Or specify a point.)*

Left

Moves the drawing to the left so that some of the right portion of the drawing is brought into view.

Right

Moves the drawing to the right so that some of the left portion of the drawing is brought into view.

Up

Moves the drawing up so that some of the bottom portion of the drawing is brought into view.

Down

Moves the drawing down so that some of the top portion of the drawing is brought into view.

> **Tip**
> *You can use the scroll bars to pan the drawing vertically or horizontally. The scroll bars are located at the right side of the drawing area. You can control the display of the scroll bars in the **Display** tab of the **Options** dialog box.*

CREATING VIEWS

Ribbon: View > Views (Customize to add) > View Manager **Command:** VIEW
Menu Bar: View > Named Views

While working on a drawing, you may frequently be working with the **Zoom** and **Pan** tools, and you may need to work on a particular drawing view (some portion of the drawing) more often than others. Instead of wasting time by recalling your zooms and pans and selecting the same area from the screen over and over again, you can store the view under a name and restore it using the name you have given. To do so, choose the **View Manager** tool from the **Views** panel of the **View** tab; the **View Manager** dialog box will be displayed, as shown in Figure 6-51. This dialog box is used to save the current view with a name so that you can restore (display) it later. It does not save any drawing object data. It stores only the view parameters needed to redisplay that portion of the drawing.

This dialog box is very useful when you are saving and restoring many views. The **Views** area lists the current view and all the existing named views in the model space and layouts. This area also lists all the preset views such as orthographic and isometric views. As soon as you select a view from the list box, the information about it will be displayed in the **Information** area provided on the middle of the **View Manager** dialog box.

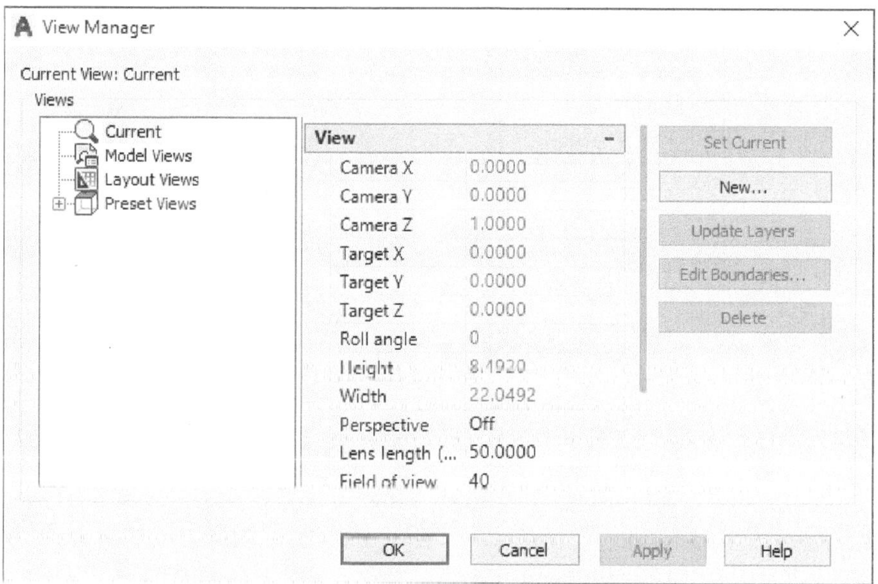

***Figure 6-51** The **View Manager** dialog box*

Other options in the **Views** area of the **View Manager** dialog box are discussed next.

Set Current

The **Set Current** button is used to replace the current view by the view you select from the list box in the **Views** area. You can select any predefined view or any preset view to be made current. AutoCAD uses the center point and magnification of each saved view and executes a **Zoom Center** with this information when a view is restored.

New

The **New** button is used to create and save a new view by giving it a name. When you choose the **New** button, the **New View / Shot Properties** dialog box is displayed, as shown in Figure 6-52. The options in this dialog box are discussed next.

View name

You can enter the name for the view in the **View name** edit box.

View category

You can specify the category of the view in the **View category** edit box. The categories include the front view, top view, and so on. If there are some existing categories, you can select them from this drop-down list also.

View type

You can specify the type of view by selecting option from this drop-down list.

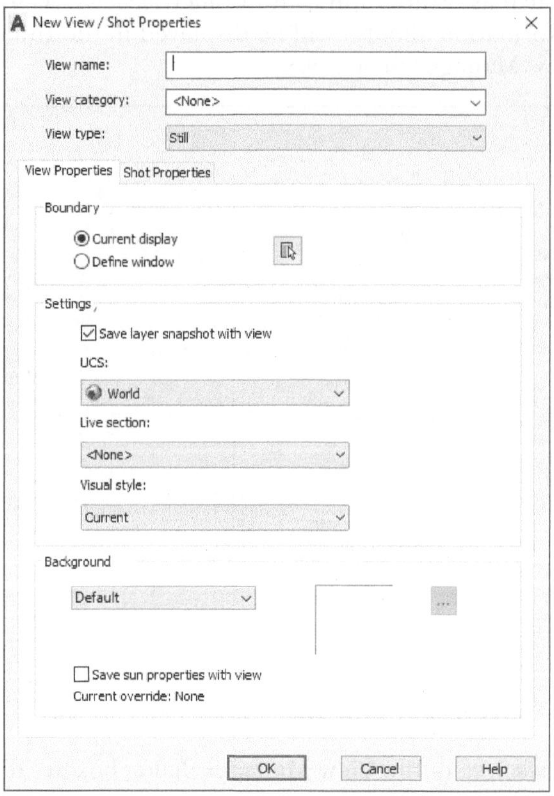

*Figure 6-52 The **New View / Shot Properties** dialog box*

Boundary Area

This area is used to specify the boundary of the view. To save the current display as the view, select the **Current display** radio button. To define a window that will specify the new view (without first zooming in on that area), select the **Define window** radio button. As soon as you select this radio button, the dialog boxes will be temporarily closed and you will be prompted to define two corners of the window. You can modify the window by choosing the **Define view window** button. You can also enter the *X* and *Y* coordinates in the **Specify first corner** and **Specify other corner** in the command line.

Settings Area

This area allows you to save the layer visibility, UCS, Live section, and Visual style in which you want to visualize the object with the new view. To save the settings of the visibility of the current layers with the view, select the **Save layer snapshot with view** check box. You can select the WCS or the UCS to be saved with the view from the **UCS** drop-down list. If you have created a live section in model space for 3D objects, you can select it from the **Live section** drop-down list, in order to save it with the view. You can also select the visual style to view the object from the **Visual style** drop-down list.

Note

The concept of WCS, UCS, live section, and visual style will be discussed in later chapters.

Background Area

This area allows you to save a view in different background types. To do so, select the type of background from the drop-down list in the **Background** area; the **Background** dialog box will be displayed. You can select the background type from the **Type** drop-down list. Alternatively, you can select these options directly from the drop-down list in the **Background** area of the **New View/Shot Properties** dialog box. On selecting the **Solid** type background, you can select any one color to be displayed in the background. To change the color, click on the **Color** area and select the type of color from the **Select Color** dialog box. On selecting the **Gradient** type background, you can apply two or three colors to the background. On selecting the **Image** type background, you can insert an image in the background. To select an image file, choose the **Browse** button from the **Image options** area of the **Background** dialog box. You can also set sun and sky in the background of a view. To do so, select the **Sun & Sky** option from the drop-down list in the **Background** area of the **New View / Shot Properties** dialog box; the **Adjust Sun & Sky Background** dialog box will be displayed. Specify the settings of the sun and sky background in this dialog box and choose the **OK** button. To save the specified sun and sky properties with the view, select the **Save sun properties with view** check box from the **New View / Shot Properties** dialog box if not selected by default.

Note

The effect of background can be visualized only if you have saved the view in the model space with a visual style other than the 2D Wireframe.

Update Layers

The **Update Layers** button is chosen to update the layer information saved with an existing view.

Edit Boundaries

The **Edit Boundaries** button is chosen to edit the boundary that was defined using the **View Manager** dialog box while creating the new view.

> **Tip**
>
> *1. You can use the shortcut menu to rename or delete any named view in the dialog box. You can also update the layer information or edit the boundary of a view using this shortcut menu.*
>
> *2. The options of the **VIEW** command can be used in the transparent mode by entering **-VIEW** at the command prompt.*

UNDERSTANDING THE CONCEPT OF SHEET SETS

The sheet sets feature allows you to logically organize a set of multiple drawings as a single unit, called the sheet set. For example, consider a setup in which there are a number of drawings in different folders in the hard drive of a computer. Organizing or archiving these drawings is tedious and time consuming. However, this can be easily and efficiently done by creating sheet sets. In a sheet set, you can import the layouts from an existing drawing or create a new sheet with a new layout and place the views in the new sheet. You can easily plot and publish all the drawings in the sheet set. You can also manage and create sheet sets using the **SHEET SET MANAGER**. To do so, choose the **Sheet Set Manager** tool from the **Palettes** panel in the **View** tab or press the CTRL+4 keys.

Creating a Sheet Set

AutoCAD allows you to create two different types of sheet sets. The first one is an example sheet set that uses a well organized structure of settings. The second one is used to organize existing drawings. The procedure for creating both these types of sheet sets is discussed next.

Creating an Example Sheet Set

To create an example sheet set, select **New Sheet Set** from the **Open** drop-down list in the **SHEET SET MANAGER** or choose **New > Sheet Set** from the **Application Menu**. You can also enter **NEWSHEETSET** at the command prompt. When you invoke this command, the **Create Sheet Set** wizard will be displayed with the **Begin** page, as shown in Figure 6-53. In this page, select the **An example sheet set** radio button, if it is not selected by default. Choose the **Next** button; the **Sheet Set Example** page will be displayed, as shown in Figure 6-54.

By default, the **Select a sheet set to use as an example** radio button is selected in this page. The list box below this radio button displays the list of sheet sets that you can use as an example. Each of these sheet sets has structurally organized settings for the sheets. You can select the required sheet set from this list box. The title and the description related to the selected sheet set are displayed in the lower portion of the dialog box.

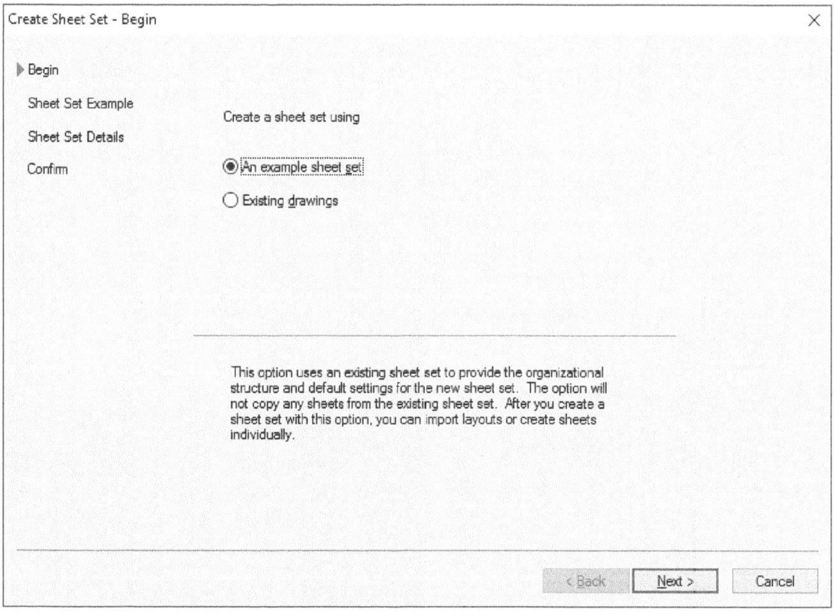

*Figure 6-53 The **Begin** page of the **Create Sheet Set** wizard*

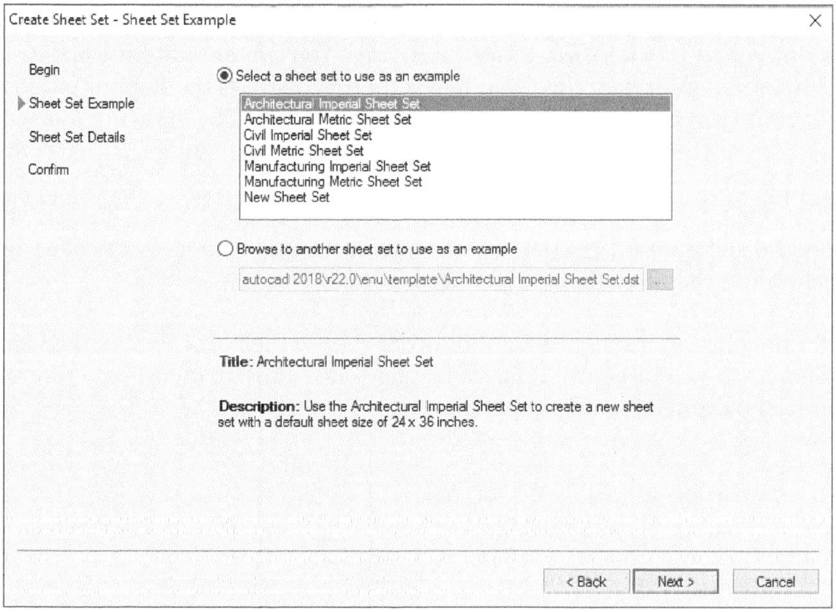

*Figure 6-54 The **Sheet Set Example** page of the **Create Sheet Set** wizard*

You can also select the **Browse to another sheet set to use as an example** radio button to select another sheet set located at a different location. You can enter the location of the sheet set in the edit box below this radio button or choose the **[...]** button to display the **Browse for Sheet Set** dialog box. Using this dialog box, you can locate the sheet set file, which is saved with the *.dst* extension. After selecting the sheet set to use as an example, choose the **Next** button; the **Sheet Set Details** page will be displayed, as shown in Figure 6-55.

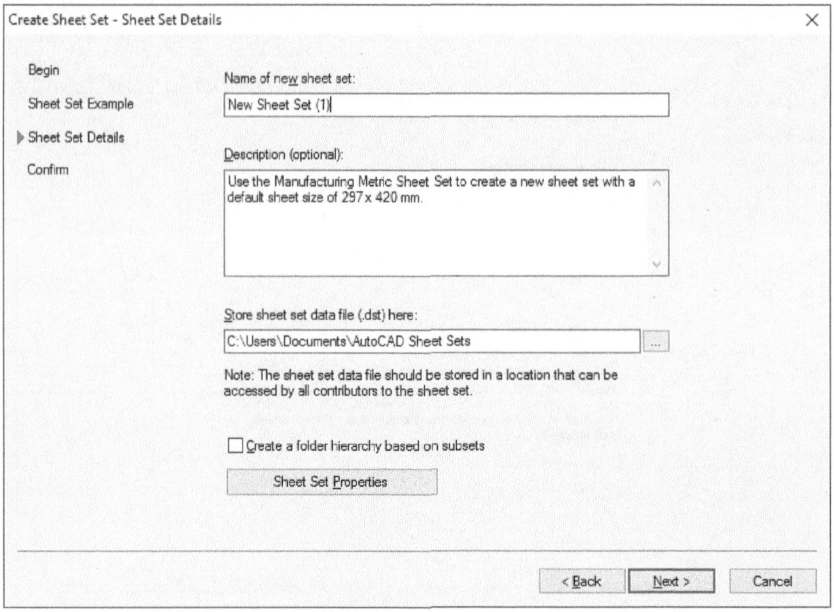

***Figure 6-55** The **Sheet Set Details** page of the **Create Sheet Set** wizard*

Enter the name of the new sheet set in the **Name of new sheet set** edit box. By default, some description is added in the **Description (optional)** area. You can enter additional description in this area. The **Store sheet set data file (.dst) here** edit box displays the default location in which the sheet set data file will be stored. You can modify this location by entering a new location or by selecting the folder using the **Browse for Sheet Set Folder** dialog box, which is displayed by choosing the **[...]** button.

You can modify the sheet set properties such as name, storage location, template, description, and so on by choosing the **Sheet Set Properties** button.

Once all the parameters on this page are configured, choose the **Next** button; the **Confirm** page will be displayed, as shown in Figure 6-56. This page shows the detailed structure of the sheet set and also lists its parameters and properties.

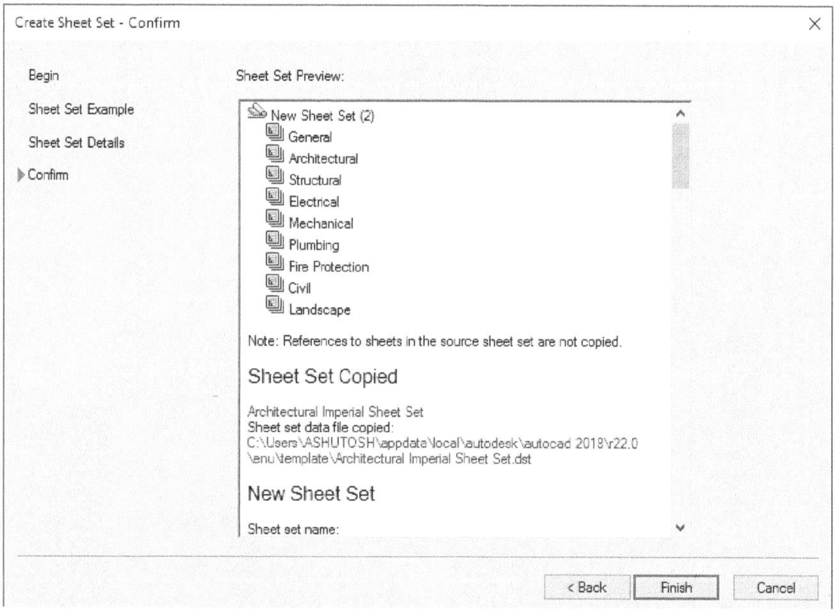

Figure 6-56 *The **Confirm** page of the **Create Sheet Set** wizard*

After checking all the parameters and properties, choose the **Finish** button; the **SHEET SET MANAGER** will be displayed with the sheet structure in the **Sheets** area and the details of that sheet set in the **Details** area, as shown in Figure 6-57. If the **Details** area is not displayed, right-click in the **SHEET SET MANAGER** and select the **Preview/Details Pane** option from the shortcut menu.

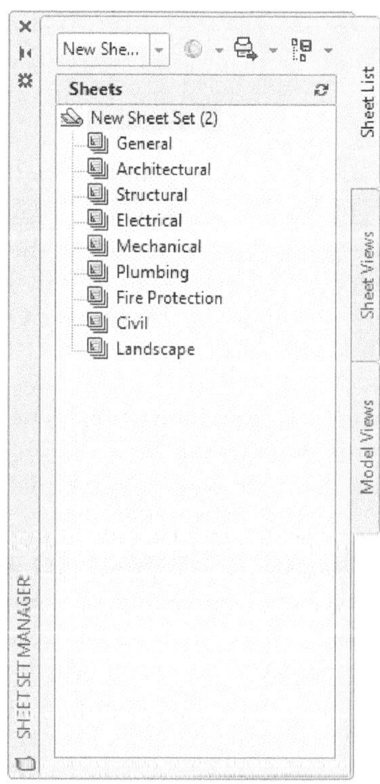

Figure 6-57 *The **SHEET SET MANAGER***

Creating a Sheet Set Using Existing Drawings

As mentioned earlier, this sheet set is used to organize and archive an existing set of drawings. To create this type of sheet set, select the **Existing drawings** radio button from the **Begin** page of the **Create a Sheet Set** wizard and then choose the **Next** button. The **Sheet Set Details** page will be displayed, which is similar to the one shown in Figure 6-55. Enter the name of the sheet set and the description on this page. Note that by default, there will be no description given about the new sheet set. After setting the parameters on this page, choose the **Next** button; the **Choose Layouts** page will be displayed, as shown in Figure 6-58.

Choose the **Browse** button from this page and browse for the folder in which the files to be included in the sheet set are saved. All the drawing files, along with their initialized layouts, are displayed in the list box available below the **Browse** button. You can select as many folders as you want by choosing the **Browse** button.

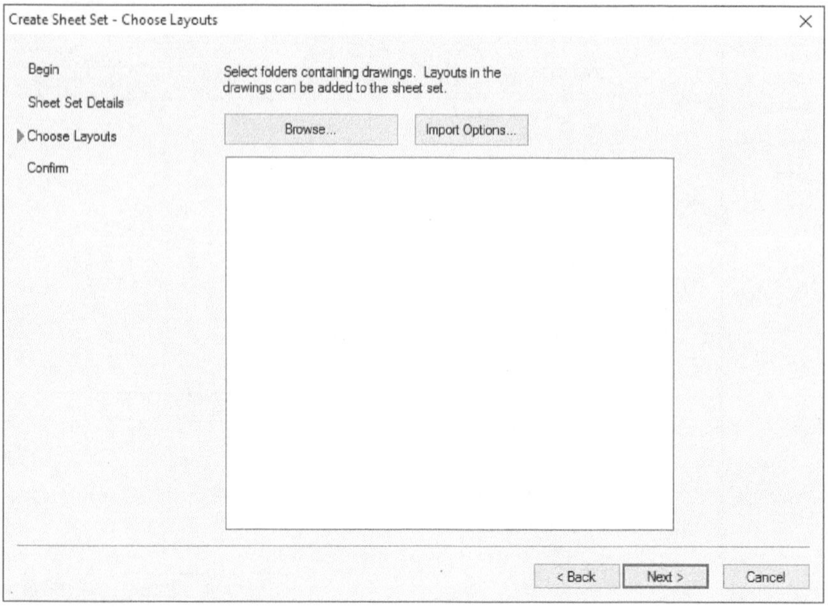

Figure 6-58 The ***Choose Layouts*** *page of the* ***Create Sheet Set*** *wizard*

Tip
You can remove the folders from the list box in the ***Choose Layouts*** *page by selecting them and pressing the DELETE key.*

When you select a folder, all the drawings in it and all the initialized layouts in the drawings have a check mark on their left. This suggests that all these drawings and layouts will be included in the sheet set. You can clear the check box of the folder to clear all the check boxes and then select the check boxes of only the required drawings and layouts. You can modify the import options by using the **Import Options** dialog box, which is displayed by choosing the **Import Options** button.

After selecting the layouts to be included, choose the **Next** button to display the **Confirm** page similar to the one shown in Figure 6-56. This page lists all the layouts that will be included in the sheet set. Choose the **Finish** button to complete the process of creating the sheet set.

Adding a Subset to a Sheet Set

For a better and more efficient organization of a sheet set, it is recommended that you add subsets to the sheet set. For example, consider a case where you have created a sheet set called Mechanical Drawings in which you want to store all the mechanical drawings. In this sheet set, you can create subsets such as Bolts, Nuts, Washers, and so on and place the sheets of bolts, nuts, and washers for a more logical organization of the sheet set.

To add a subset to a sheet set, right-click on the sheet set or subset and choose the **New Subset** option from the shortcut menu. The **Subset Properties** dialog box is displayed, as shown in Figure 6-59.

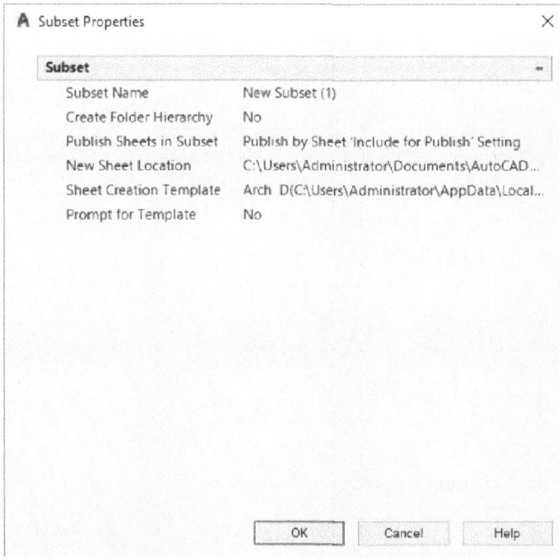

***Figure 6-59** The **Subset Properties** dialog box*

Enter the name of the subset in the **Subset name** field. Also, specify the location for saving the DWG file and the template for creating the sheets using this dialog box. If you specify **Yes** in the **Create Folder Hierarchy** field, a new folder will be created under the sheet set. If you specify **Yes** in the **Prompt for Template** field, which will prompt you to select the template for the drawings. Choose **OK** after configuring all the parameters. A new subset will be added to the sheet set or the subset that you selected.

Adding Sheets to a Sheet Set or a Subset

To add a new sheet to a sheet set or a subset, right-click on it in the **SHEET SET MANAGER** palette and choose **New Sheet** from the shortcut menu; the **New Sheet** dialog box is displayed. In this dialog box, enter the number and the title of the sheet, along with the file name. You can also set the path of the folder and the sheet template to be used, using this dialog box. Choose the **OK** button after configuring all the parameters. A new sheet will be added to the sheet set or the subset that you selected.

Archiving a Sheet Set

AutoCAD allows you to archive a sheet set as a zip file or a file folder. All files related to the sheet set are automatically included in the zip file. To archive a sheet set, right-click on its name in the **SHEET SET MANAGER** and choose the **Archive** option from the shortcut menu. After AutoCAD gathers the archive information, the **Archive a Sheet Set** dialog box will be displayed, as shown in Figure 6-60.

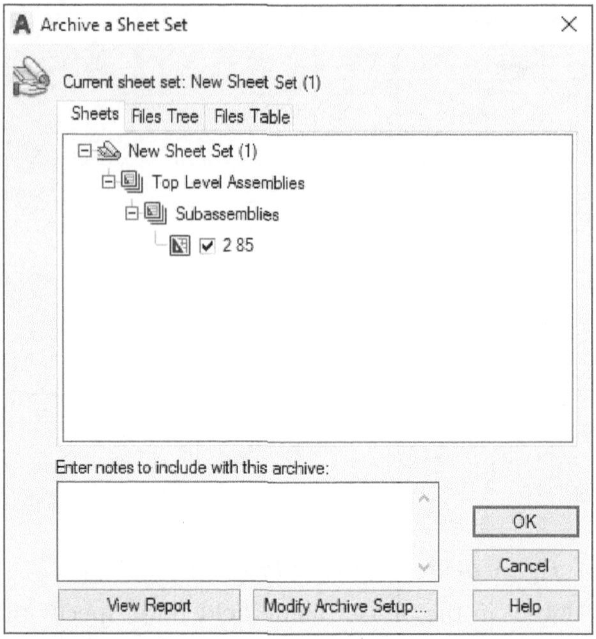

***Figure 6-60** The **Archive a Sheet Set** dialog box*

Before archiving the sheet set, you can modify the archiving options by using the **Modify Archive Setup** dialog box, as shown in Figure 6-61. This dialog box is displayed when you choose the **Modify Archive Setup** button. Using the **Archive package type** drop-down list, you can specify whether the archived file is a zip file or a file folder. You can also specify the format, in which you want to save the files. You can select the current release format, keep existing drawing file formats, AutoCAD 2018/LT 2018, AutoCAD 2013/LT 2013, AutoCAD 2010/LT 2010, AutoCAD 2007/LT 2007, AutoCAD 2004/LT 2004, or AutoCAD 2000/LT 2000 formats for archiving the files.

After setting the parameters, choose the **OK** button from the **Archive a Sheet Set** dialog box. The **Specify Zip File** dialog box will be displayed, which can be used to specify the name and the location of the resultant file.

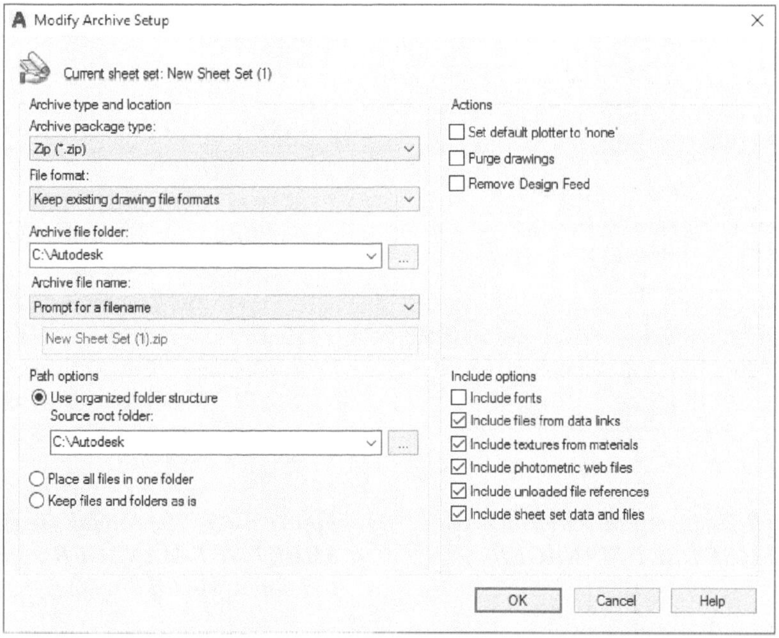

*Figure 6-61 The **Modify Archive Setup** dialog box*

Resaving all Sheets in a Sheet Set

The **SHEET SET MANAGER** allows you to easily resave all the sheets in a sheet set. To save all the sheets in a sheet set again, right-click on the name of the sheet set in the **SHEET SET MANAGER** and choose the **Resave All Sheets** option from the shortcut menu, as shown in Figure 6-62. All the sheets in the sheet set will be saved once again.

PLACING VIEWS ON A SHEET OF A SHEET SET

You can place views in the sheets of a sheet set. To place a view on a sheet, open the sheet by double-clicking on it in the **SHEET SET MANAGER**. Next, you need to locate the file from which you want to copy the view. To locate this file, choose the **Model Views** tab. If the location of the file is not already listed in this tab, double-click on **Add New Location** to display the **Browse for Folder** dialog box. Using this dialog box, select the folder in which you have saved the file. All the files of that folder are listed. Click on the plus sign (+) located on the left of the file to display all the views created in that file.

Now, right-click on the view and choose **Place on Sheet** from the shortcut menu, as shown in Figure 6-63; the preview of the view will be attached to the cursor and you will be prompted to specify the insertion point. By default, the view will be placed with 1:1 scale. But, you can change the view scale before placing the view. To change the scale, right-click to display the shortcut menu that has various preset view scales. Choose the desired view scale from this shortcut menu and then place the view. The view will be placed inside the paper space viewport in the layout. Also, the name of the view is displayed below the view in the layout where you placed the view. You can view the list of all the views in the current sheet set by choosing the **View List** tab.

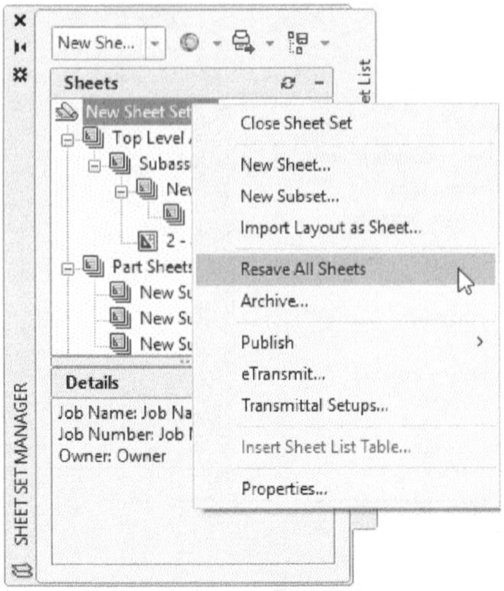

Figure 6-62** Resaving all the sheets in a sheet set using the **SHEET SET MANAGER

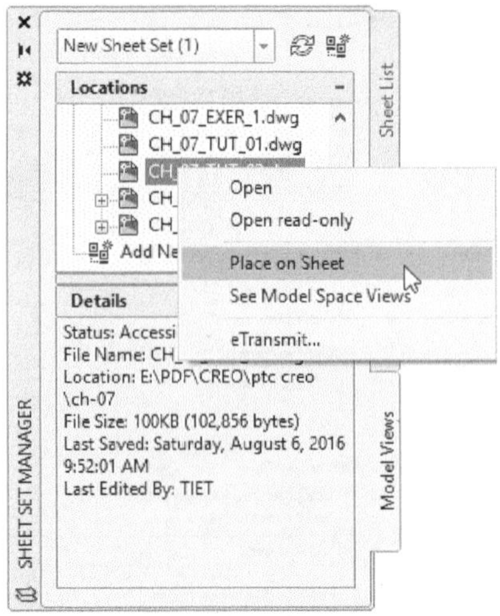

***Figure 6-63** The **Model Views** tab of the **SHEET SET MANAGER** displaying the views in a selected drawing*

Self-Evaluation Test

Answer the following questions and then compare them to those given at the end of this chapter:

1. After selecting a polyline, if you place the cursor on the _________ of the grip, the **Convert to Arc** option will be displayed in the tooltip.

2. The color of the unselected grips can also be changed by using the _________ system variable.

3. You can access the **Mirror** mode by selecting a grip and then using the _________ tool or giving a null response by pressing the SPACEBAR four times.

4. The _________ drop-down list will not be available if you select **Select All** from the **Operator** drop-down list of the **Quick Select** dialog box.

5. While using the **Zoom Scale** tool with respect to the current view, you need to enter a number followed by **X**. (T/F)

6. The number of grips that will be displayed on an object depends on the object itself. (T/F)

7. You can use the **Options** dialog box to modify grip parameters. (T/F)

8. You need at least one source object while using the **Match Properties** tool. (T/F)

9. You cannot drag and drop entities from the **DesignCenter** window. (T/F)

10. The **Zoom All** tool displays drawing limits or extents, whichever is greater. (T/F)

Review Questions

Answer the following questions:

1. Which of these system variables is used to modify the color of a selected grip?

   (a) **GRIPCOLOR** (b) **GRIPHOT**
   (c) **GRIPCOLD** (d) **GRIPBLOCK**

2. Which of these system variables is used to enable the display of grips inside blocks?

   (a) **GRIPCOLOR** (b) **GRIPHOT**
   (c) **GRIPCOLD** (d) **GRIPBLOCK**

3. Which of the following system variables is used to modify the size of grips?

   (a) **GRIPCOLOR** (b) **GRIPSIZE**
   (c) **GRIPCOLD** (d) **GRIPBLOCK**

4. How many views are saved using the **Previous** tool?

   (a) 6 (b) 8
   (c) 10 (d) 12

5. Which of the following commands recalculates all the objects in a drawing and redraws the current viewport only?

   (a) **REDRAW** (b) **REDRAWALL**
   (c) **REGEN** (d) **REGENALL**

6. You can view the entire drawing (even if it is beyond limits) with the help of the __________ option.

7. The **GRIPSIZE** is defined in pixels and its value can range from __________ to __________ pixels.

8. The **View Manager** tool does not save any drawing object data. Only the __________ parameters required to redisplay that portion of the drawing are saved.

9. The __________ mode is used to move the selected objects to a new location.

10. The __________ mode allows you to scale objects with respect to the base point without changing their orientation.

11. The **Mirror** tool allows you to mirror objects about the __________ without changing the size of the objects.

12. If you select a grip of an object, the grip becomes a hot grip. (T/F)

13. The **Rotate** mode is used to rotate objects around the base point without affecting their size. (T/F)

14. If you have already added a hyperlink to an object, you can also use the grips to open a file associated with it. (T/F)

15. When you zoom an object using the Zoom tools, the actual size of the object is changed. (T/F)

16. The **REDRAW** command can be used as a transparent command. (T/F)

Exercise 2

1. Use the **Line** tool to draw the shape shown in Figure 6-64(a).

2. Use grips (**Stretch** mode) to get the shape shown in Figure 6-64(b).

3. Use the **Rotate** and **Stretch** modes to get the copies shown in Figure 6-64(c).

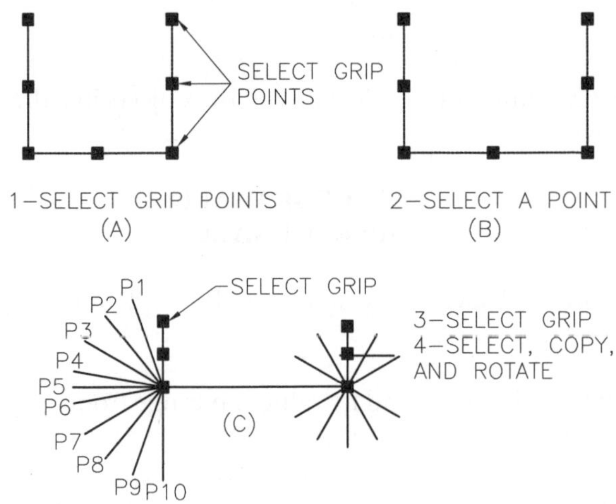

Figure 6-64 Drawing for Exercise 2

Exercise 3

Use the drawing and editing tools to create the sketch shown in Figure 6-65. Use the display tools to facilitate the process.

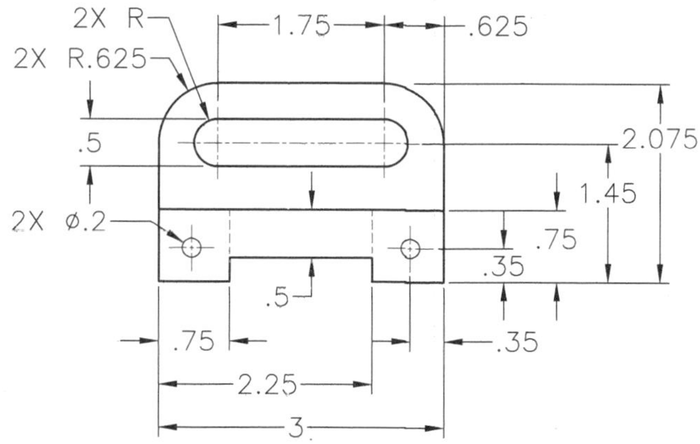

Figure 6-65 Drawing for Exercise 3

Exercise 4

Use the drawing and editing tools to create the sketch shown in Figure 6-66. Use the display tools to facilitate the process.

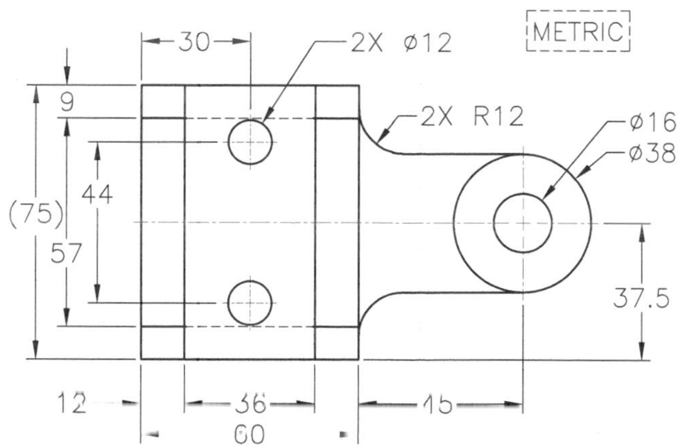

Figure 6-66 Drawing for Exercise 4

Problem-Solving Exercise 1

Draw the sketch shown in Figure 6-67 using the draw and edit tools. Use the **Mirror** tool to mirror the shape 15 units across the *Y* axis so that the distance between the two center points is 15 units. Mirror the shape across the *X* axis and then reduce the mirrored shape by 75 percent. Join the two ends to complete the shape of the open end spanner. Save the file. Assume the missing dimensions. Note that this is not a standard size spanner.

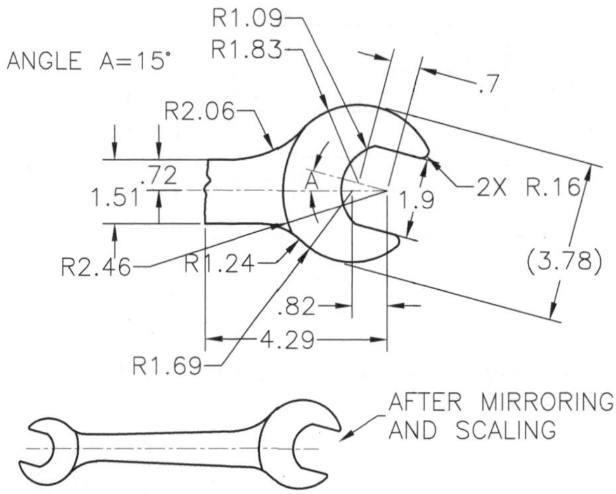

***Figure 6-67** Drawing for Problem-Solving Exercise 1*

Problem-Solving Exercise 2

Use the drawing and editing tools to create the drawing shown in Figure 6-68. Use the display tools to facilitate the process.

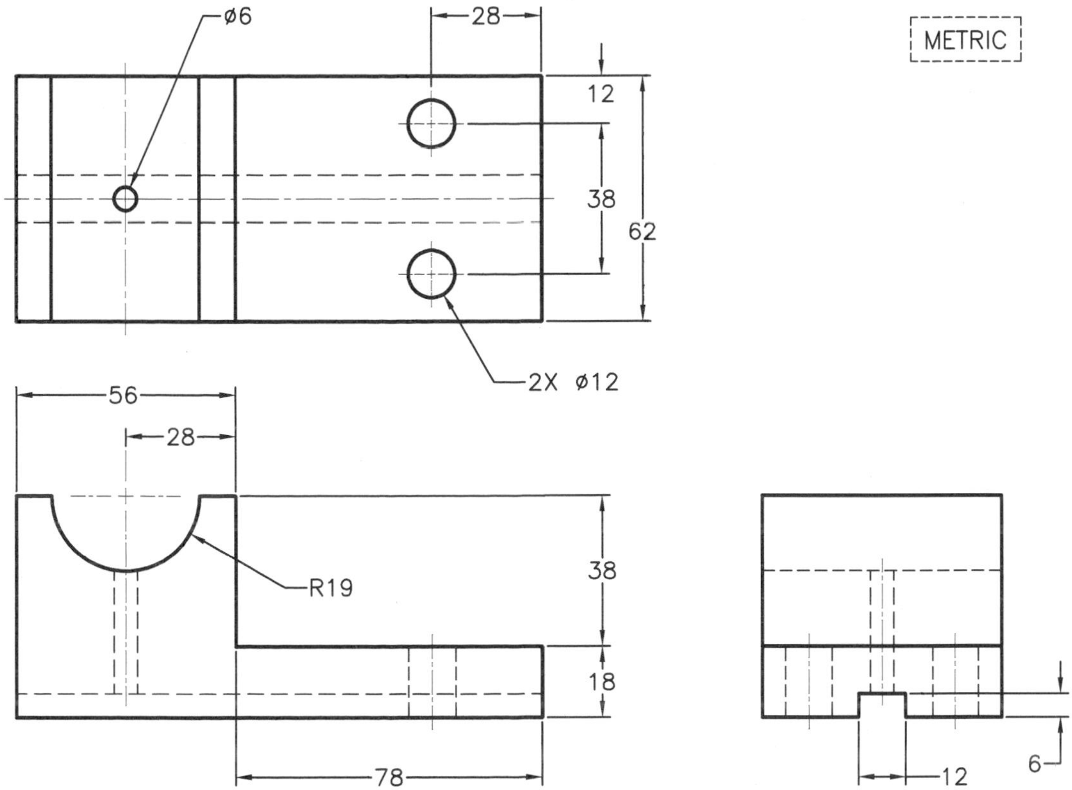

Figure 6-68 *Drawing for Problem-Solving Exercise 2*

Problem-Solving Exercise 3

Use the drawing and editing tools to create the drawing shown in Figure 6-69. Use the display tools to facilitate the process.

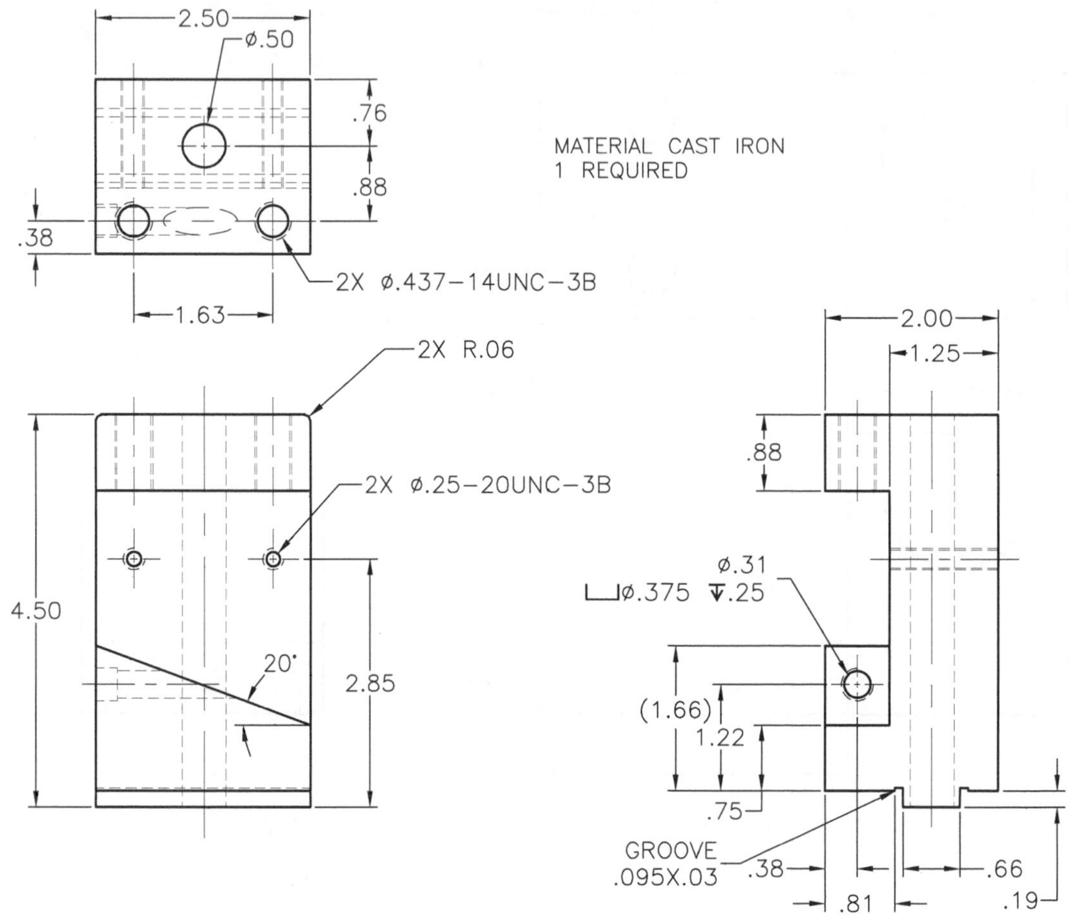

Figure 6-69 Drawing for Problem-Solving Exercise 3

Problem-Solving Exercise 4

Draw the reception desk shown in Figure 6-70.

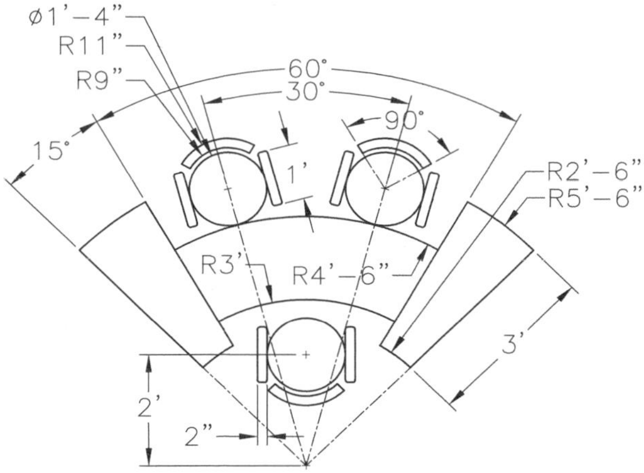

Figure 6-70 *Drawing of reception desk for Problem-Solving Exercise 4*

Problem-Solving Exercise 5

Draw the views of Vice Body shown in Figure 6-71. The dimensions given in the figure are only for your reference.

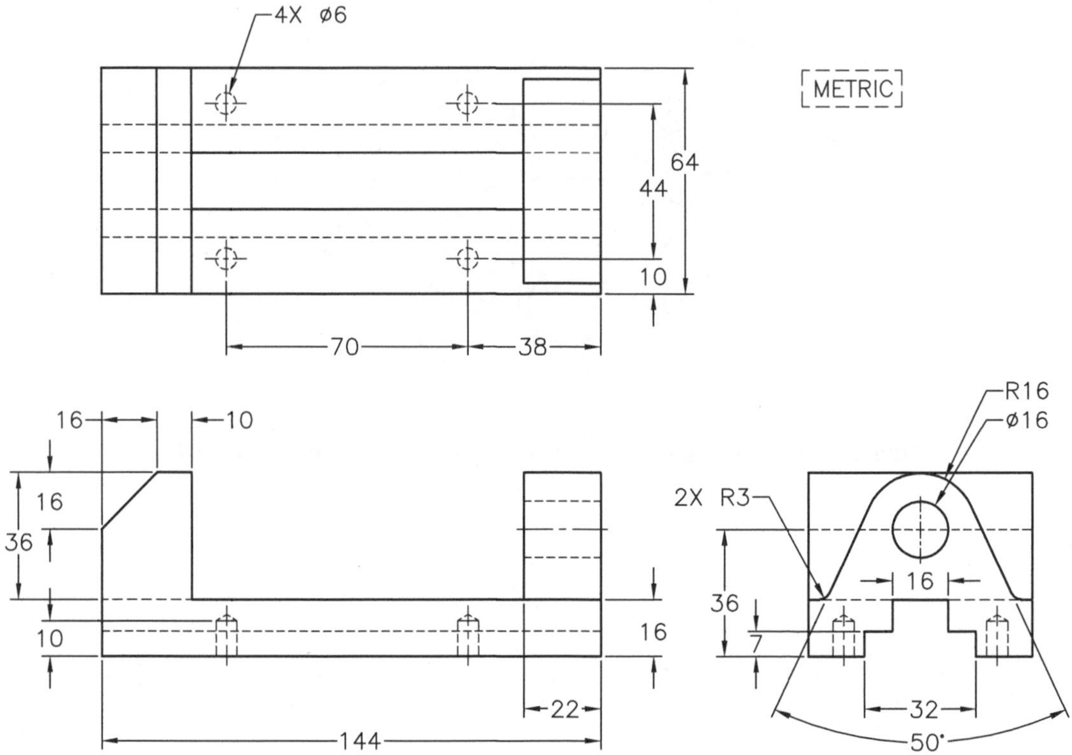

Figure 6-71 Views and dimensions of the Vice Body

Problem-Solving Exercise 6

Use the drawing and editing tools to create the drawing shown in Figure 6-72 in the **Manufacturing Metric** template. Use the display tools to facilitate the process.

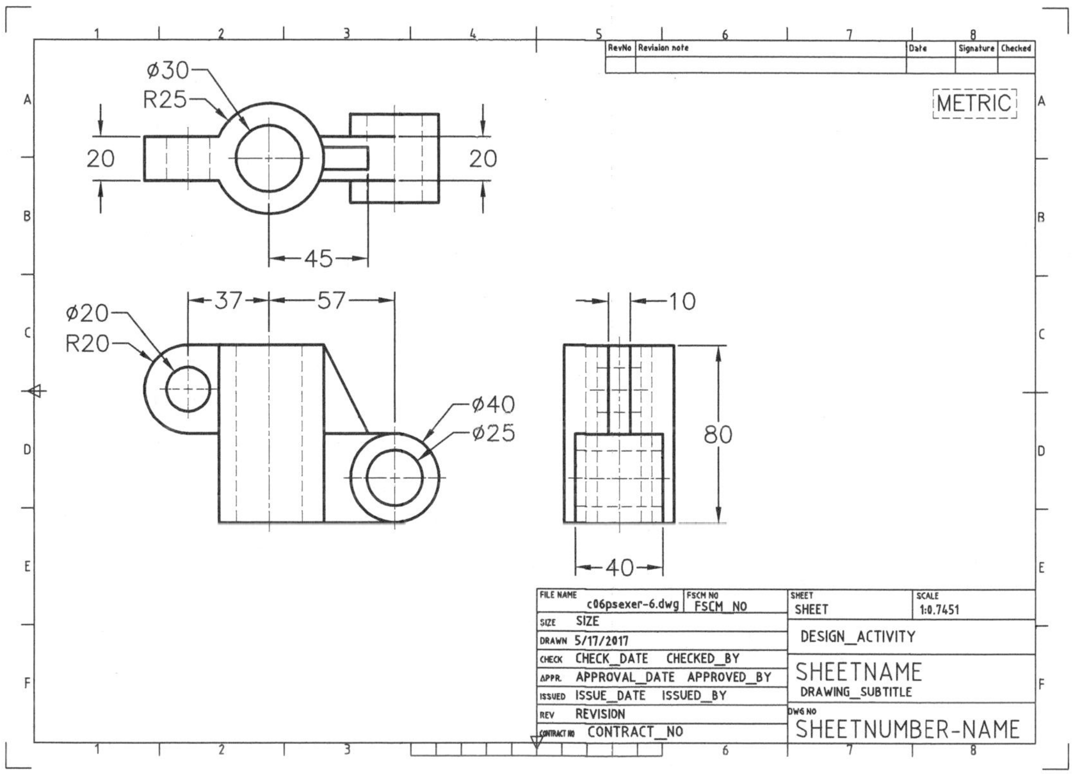

Figure 6-72 Drawing for Problem-Solving Exercise 6

Problem-Solving Exercise 7

Use the drawing and editing tools to create the drawing shown in Figure 6-73. Use the display tools to facilitate the process.

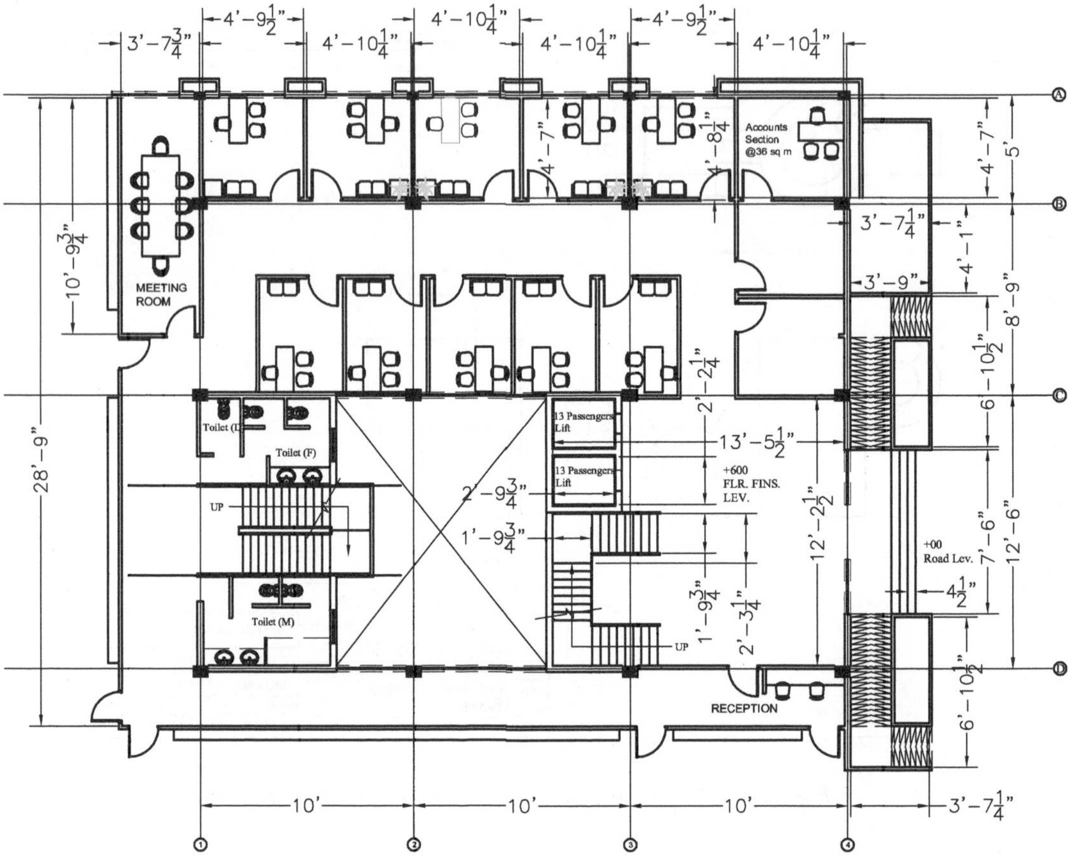

Figure 6-73 Drawing for Problem-Solving Exercise 7

Answers to Self-Evaluation Test

1. middle, 2. **GRIPCOLOR**, 3. **MIRROR**, 4. **Value**, 5. T, 6. T, 7. T, 8. F, 9. F, 10. T

Chapter 7

Creating Texts and Tables

Learning Objectives

After completing this chapter, you will be able to:

- *Understand the use of annotative objects*
- *Write text using the Single Line and Multi Line Text tools*
- *Edit text using the Edit tool*
- *Create text styles*
- *Combine Text*
- *Draw tables using the Table tool*
- *Create and modify the table style*
- *Use the PROPERTIES palette to change properties*

Key Terms

- *Annotative Objects*
- *Annotation Scale*
- *Text*
- *TEXTEDIT*
- *Table*
- *Data Link*
- *Text Style*
- *Annotative Text*
- *TEXTALIGN*
- *Sheet Set Table*

ANNOTATIVE OBJECTS

AutoCAD provid7es improved functionality of the drawing annotation that enables you to annotate your drawing easily and efficiently. Annotations are the notes and objects that are inserted into a drawing to add important information to it. The list of annotative objects is given next.

Text	Mtext	Dimensions	Leaders	Blocks
Multileaders	Hatches	Tolerances	Attributes	

All the above mentioned annotative objects have an annotative property. This annotative property allows you to automate the process of display of the drawings at the desired scale on the paper.

ANNOTATION SCALE

Annotation Scale is a feature that allows you to control the size of the annotative objects in model space.

Generally, the formula used to calculate the height of the annotative objects in model space is:

Height of the annotative object in model space = Annotation scale X Height of the annotative object in paper space.

For example, if you need to create an annotative object with a height of 1/4" on paper, and assume that annotation scale is set to 1/2" = 1' (implies 1" = 2', or 1' = 24"). Then, the height of the object in model space will be 1/4" X 24"= 6" and the object will be displayed in model space with its height equal to 6".

Note

The above calculation is performed automatically by AutoCAD and has been explained to make the concept clear.

Assigning Annotative Property and Annotation Scales

You can assign the annotative properties to objects in many ways. The objects (Mtext, Hatches, Blocks, and Attributes) that are drawn with the help of dialog boxes have the **Annotative** check boxes in their respective dialog box. You can also create the annotative styles, and all the objects created using that style will have the annotative property automatically. The objects that are created using the command prompt can be converted into annotative after creating them through the **PROPERTIES** palette. You can also override the annotative property of an individual object through the **PROPERTIES** palette, refer to Figure 7-1.

All annotative objects are indicated with an annotative symbol attached to the cursor. When you move the cursor over an annotative object, the annotative symbol starts rolling on, refer to Figure 7-2. All annotative styles are indicated with the same annotative symbol displayed next to the cursor.

To assign the annotation scale while working in model space, choose the **Annotation scale of the current view** button displayed on the right of the Status Bar; a flyout will be displayed. Select the desired annotation scale from the flyout. This flyout displays 33 commonly used imperial and metric scales, and this list can also be customized. Among these scales, 1:1 annotation scale is selected by default. To change the default annotation scale, enter **CANNOSCALE** in the command prompt and specify the new annotation scale. To assign the annotation scale while working in viewport, select a viewport first and then assign the annotation scale.

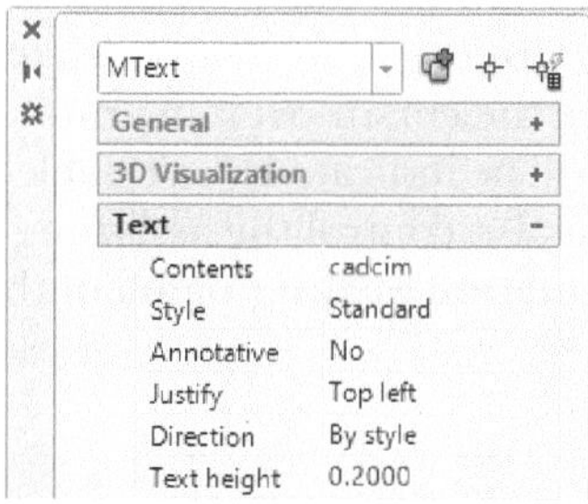

***Figure 7-1** Assigning annotative property through the **PROPERTIES** palette*

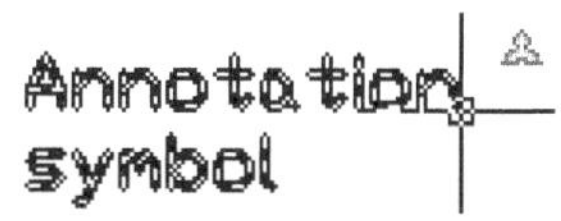

***Figure 7-2** Annotation symbol attached to the cursor*

Customizing Annotation Scale

In any drawing, only few annotation scales are used. Therefore, you can delete the unwanted scales from the list according to your requirement. To customize the Annotation scale list, choose the **Custom** option from the flyout that is displayed when you click on the **Annotation scale of the current view** button in the Status Bar; the **Edit Drawing Scales** dialog box will be displayed, as shown in Figure 7-3. With this dialog box, you can add, modify, delete, change the sequence of scales displayed, and restore the default list of scales.

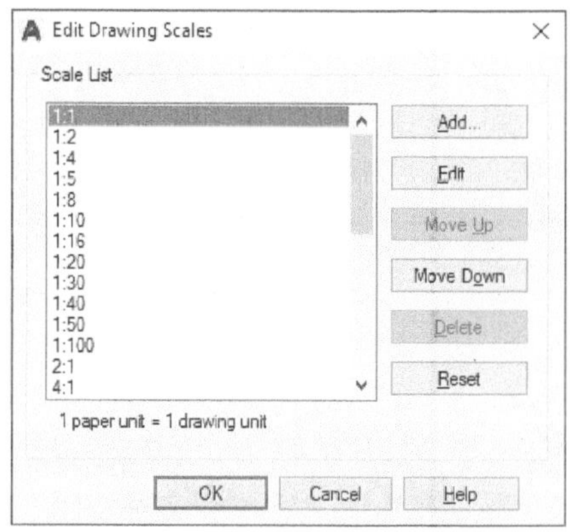

***Figure 7-3** The **Edit Drawing Scales** dialog box*

Note

You cannot delete the annotation scales that have been used to draw annotative object in the drawing.

MULTIPLE ANNOTATION SCALES

Ribbon: Annotate > Annotation Scaling > Add/Delete Scales **Command:** OBJECTSCALE
Menu Bar: Modify > Annotative Object Scale > Add/Delete Scales

You can assign multiple annotation scales to an annotative object. This enables you to display or print the same annotative object in different sizes. The annotative object is displayed or printed based on the current annotation scale. Assigning multiple annotation scales to annotative objects saves a considerable amount of time that is lost while creating a set of objects with different scales in different layers. You can add multiple annotation scales to objects manually and automatically. Both these methods are discussed next.

Assigning Multiple Annotation Scales Manually

To assign multiple annotation scales manually to an annotative object, invoke the **Add/Delete Scales** tool; you will be prompted to select an annotative object to which you want to add another annotation scale. Select one or more annotation objects and then press ENTER; the **Annotation Object Scale** dialog box will be displayed, as shown in Figure 7-4. Alternatively, select an annotative object and right-click to display the shortcut menu. Now, choose **Annotative Object Scale > Add / Delete Scales** from the shortcut menu to display the **Annotation Object Scale** dialog box. Using this dialog box, you can add annotation scale to an annotative object or delete the annotation scale assigned to the selected annotative object. However, you cannot delete the current annotation scale by using this dialog box. When you place the cursor over an annotative object, all the annotative objects with multiple annotation scales will be indicated by a double-annotation symbol attached to the cursor, refer to Figure 7-5. You can also control the assigning of multiple annotation scales to annotative objects by using the **Annotation Scaling** panel of the **Annotate** tab, refer to Figure 7-6.

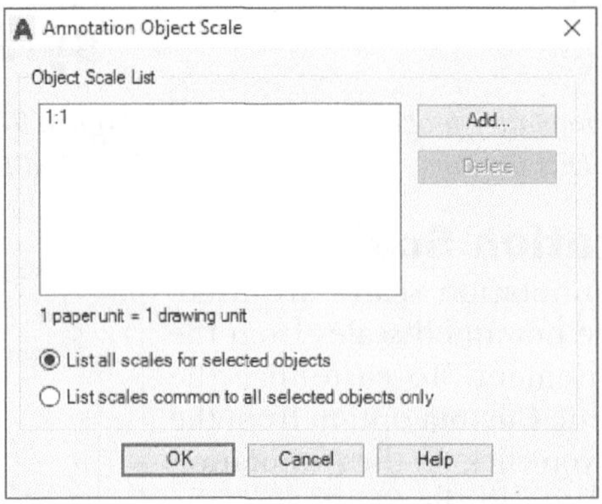

*Figure 7-4 The **Annotation Object Scale** dialog box*

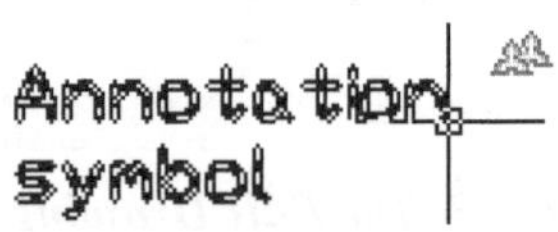

Figure 7-5 Multiple annotation scale symbol attached to the cursor

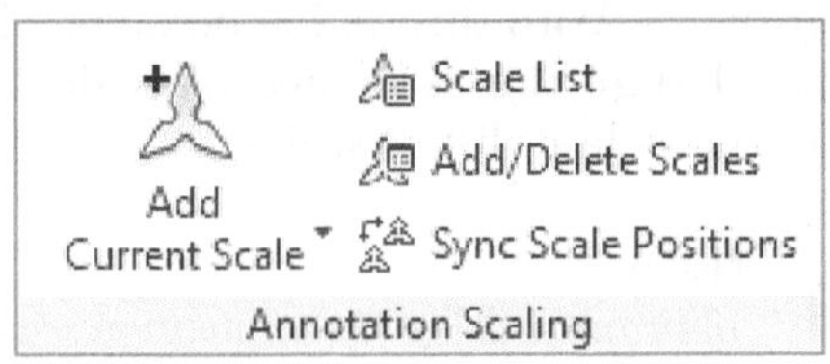

*Figure 7-6 The **Annotation Scaling** panel in the **Ribbon***

Assigning Multiple Annotation Scales Automatically

The annotation scales that have been set as current can be assigned to annotative objects without invoking the **Annotation Object Scale** dialog box. To do so, choose the **Add scales to annotative objects when the annotation scale changes** button located at the bottom of the Status Bar to activate it. Now onward, all annotation scales that are set as current will be automatically added to the annotation objects.

By default, the annotation scale will be applied to all objects irrespective of their layers. However, you can control the assignment of annotation scale depending upon the layer of the object by using the **ANNOAUTOSCALE** system variable. This system variable can have values ranging from -4 to 4. The description of these values is given next.

0 = This value does not assigns any annotation scale to any annotative object.

1 = This value assigns the current annotation scale to all annotative objects, except the annotative objects that are in the locked, turned off, frozen, and viewport frozen layers.
2 = This value assigns the current annotation scale to all annotative objects, except the annotative objects that are in the turned off, frozen, and viewport frozen layers.
3 = This value assigns the current annotation scale to all annotative objects, except the ones that are in the locked layers.
4 = This value assigns the current annotation scale to all objects.
-1 = On assigning this value, the **ANNOAUTOSCALE** gets turned off, but when it is turned on again, it regains the value 1.
-2 = On assigning this value, the **ANNOAUTOSCALE** gets turned off, but when it is turned on again, it regains the value 2.
-3 = On assigning this value, the **ANNOAUTOSCALE** gets turned off, but when it is turned on again, it regains the value 3.
-4 = On assigning this value, the **ANNOAUTOSCALE** gets turned off, but when it is turned on again, it regains the value 4.

CONTROLLING THE DISPLAY OF ANNOTATIVE OBJECTS

After assigning annotation scale to objects, the paper height display scale (in case of plotting) or the viewport scale (in case of viewports) is automatically applied to annotative objects and they are displayed accordingly in the model space or viewport. The annotative objects that do not support the current annotation scale will not be scaled and will be displayed according to the previous annotation scale applied to them.

You can control the display of annotative objects by using the **Show annotation objects** button in the Status Bar. If this button is turned on, all annotative objects will be displayed in the model space or viewport regardless of the current annotation scale. If this button is turned off, only the annotative objects that have annotation scale equal to that of the current annotation scale will be displayed. Note that the **Show annotation objects** buttons in the model and layout tabs are independent of each other.

When you select an annotative object, you can observe that the selected annotative object is displayed in all annotative scales assigned to it. The annotation scale that is equal to the current scale is displayed in dark lines, whereas the other scales of the object are displayed in faded lines. You can position the annotation object of different scales at different locations with the help of grips. However, if you need to synchronize the start point of annotative objects of different scale factors with current annotative objects, select the annotative object and then right-click in the drawing area; a shortcut menu will be displayed. Choose **Annotative Object Scale > Synchronize Multiple-scale Positions** from the shortcut menu; the start point of annotative objects will be synchronized. Alternatively, you can also use the **ANNORESET** command to synchronize the start point.

SELECTIONANNODISPLAY system variable is used to control the display of the supported scale representations. If you assign 0 to the system variable, it will stop displaying all the supported scale representations selected; only the representations with the current annotation scale will be displayed. If you assign 1 to this system variable, it will display all the supported scale representations selected.

Note

*Whenever you create a drawing that involves annotative objects in it, use the **Drafting & Annotation** workspace. This workspace displays the **Ribbon** with drafting and annotation panels visible by default and hides many of the tools. This workspace makes the drawing and annotating work much easier. For all examples and exercises given onward and involving annotative objects, you can use this workspace.*

CREATING TEXT

In manual drafting, lettering is accomplished by hand using a lettering device, pen, or pencil. This is a very time-consuming and tedious job. Computer-aided drafting has made this process extremely easy. Engineering drawings invoke certain standards to be followed in connection with the placement of a text in a drawing. In this section, you will learn how a text can be added in a drawing by using the **Single Line** and **Multiline Text** tools.

Writing Single Line Text

Ribbon: Home > Annotation > Text drop-down > Single Line Or Annotate > Text > Text drop-down > Single Line
Toolbar: Text > Single Line Text
Menu Bar: Draw > Text > Single Line Text
Command: TEXT/DTEXT/DT

The **Single Line** tool is used to write text on a drawing. While writing, you can delete the typed text by using the BACKSPACE key. On invoking the **Single Line** tool, you will be prompted to specify the start point. The default and the most commonly used option in the **Single Line** tool is the **start point** option. By specifying a start point, the text is left-justified along its baseline. Baseline refers to the line along which its base lies. After specifying the start point, you need to set the height and the rotation angle of the text.

The **Specify height <current>:** prompt determines the distance by which the text extends above the baseline, measured by the capital letters. This distance is specified in drawing units. You can specify the text height by specifying two points or by entering a value. In the case of a null response, the default height, that is, the height used for the previous text drawn in the same style will be used.

The **Specify rotation angle of text <current>:** prompt determines the angle at which the text line will be drawn. The default value of the rotation angle is 0-degree (along east); and in this case, the text is drawn horizontally from the specified start point. The rotation angle is measured in counterclockwise direction. The last angle specified becomes the current rotation angle and if you give a null response, the last angle specified will be used as default rotation angle. You can also specify the rotation angle by specifying two points. The text will be drawn upside down if a point is specified at a location to the left of the start point.

You can now enter the text in the text window. The characters will be displayed as you type them. After entering the text, click outside the text window and press ESC. The prompt sequence displayed on choosing this tool is given next.

Specify start point of text or [Justify/Style]: *Specify the start point.*
Specify height <0.2000>: **0.15** Enter
Specify rotation angle of text <0>: Enter; *the textbox will be displayed. Start typing in it.*

After completing a line, press ENTER; the cursor will automatically be placed at the start of the next line and you can enter the next line of the text. However, if you place the cursor at a new location, a new textbox will be displayed, and you can start typing text at this location with a new start point and the same text parameters. You can enter multiple lines of text at any desired location in the drawing area on invoking the **Single Line** tool once. By pressing BACKSPACE, you can delete one character to the left of the current position of the cursor box. Even if you have entered several lines of text, you can use BACKSPACE to delete the text, until you reach the start point of the first line. To exit the tool, click outside the text box and press the ESC key.

This tool can be used with most of the text alignment modes, although it is most useful in the case of left-justified texts. In the case of aligned texts, this tool is used to assign a height appropriate for the width of the first line to every line of the text. Even if you select the **Justify** option, the text is first left-aligned at the selected point.

Justify Option

AutoCAD offers various options to align text. Alignment refers to the layout of a text. The main text alignment modes are left, center, and right. You can align a text by using a combination of modes, for example, top/middle/bottom and left/center/right, refer to Figure 7-7. Top refers to a line along which lie the top points of the capital letters. Letters with descenders (such as p, g, and y) dip below the baseline to the bottom. When the **Justify** option is invoked, the user can place the text in one of the fifteen alignment types by selecting the desired alignment option using the command prompt or the selection preview, refer to Figure 7-8. Note that the selection preview will only be displayed if the **Enable Pointer Input** check box is selected in the **Drafting Settings** dialog box. (Text styles and fonts are discussed later in this chapter). For now, assume that the text style orientation is horizontal.

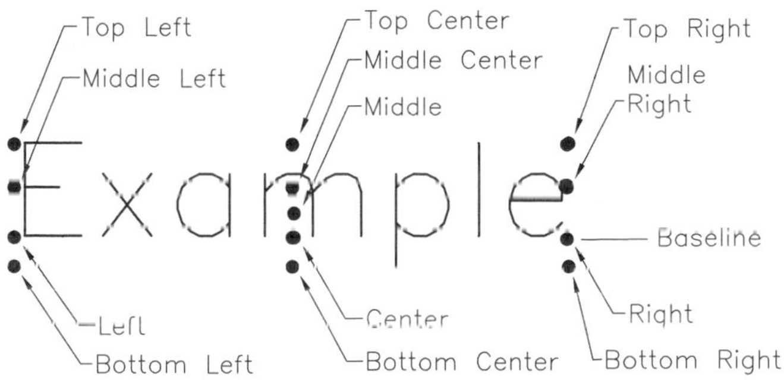

Figure 7-7 Text alignment positions

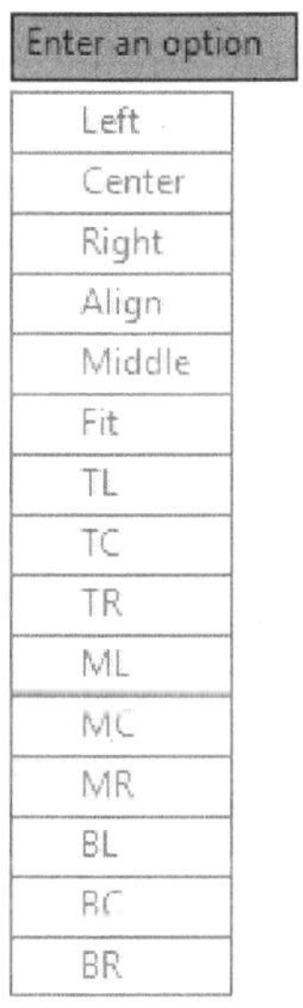

*Figure 7-8 Selection preview for the **Justify** option*

The prompt sequence that will follow when you choose the **Single Line** tool to use this option is given next.

Specify start point of text or [Justify/Style]: **J** Enter
Enter an option [Left/Center/Right/Align/Middle/Fit/TL/TC/TR/ML/MC/MR/BL/BC/BR]: *Select any of these options.*

If the text style is vertically oriented (refer to the "Creating Text Styles" section later in this chapter), only four alignment options are available. The prompt sequence is given next.

Specify start point of text or [Justify/Style]: **J** Enter
Enter an option [Align/Center/Middle/Right]: *You can select the desired alignment option.*

If you know what justification you want, you can enter it directly at the **Specify start point of text or [Justify/Style]** prompt instead of first entering **J** to display the justification prompt. If you need to specify a style as well as a justification, you must specify the style first. The various alignment options are as follows:

Left Option: This option is used to specify the start point as lower left corner of the text, that means, the text is **Left** justified. The prompt sequence that will follow when you choose this button is given next.

Specify start point of text or [Justify/Style]: **J** Enter
Enter an option [Left/Center/Right/Align/Middle/Fit/TL/TC/TR/ML/MC/MR/BL/BC/BR]: **L** Enter
Specify start point of text: *Specify a point.*
Specify height<current>: *Enter the height.*
Specify rotation angle of text<0>: Enter

Align Option: In this option, the text string is written between two points, refer to Figure 7-9. You must specify the two points that act as the endpoints of the baseline. The two points may be specified horizontally or at an angle. AutoCAD adjusts the text width (compresses or expands) so that it fits between the two points. The text height is also changed, depending on the distance between points and the number of letters.

Specify start point of text or [Justify/Style]: **J** Enter
Enter an option [Left/Center/Right/Align/Middle/Fit/TL/TC/TR/ML/MC/MR/BL/BC/BR]: **A** Enter
Specify first endpoint of text baseline: *Specify a point.*
Specify second endpoint of text baseline: *Specify a point.*

Fit Option: This option is very similar to the previous one. The only difference is that in this case, you select the text height, and it does not vary according to the distance between the two points. AutoCAD adjusts the letter width to fit the text between the two given points, but the height remains constant, refer to Figure 7-9. The **Fit** option is not accessible for vertically oriented text styles. If you try the **Fit** option on the vertical text style, you will notice that the text string does not appear in the prompt. The prompt sequence is given next.

Enter an option [Left/Center/Right/Align/Middle/Fit/TL/TC/TR/ML/MC/MR/BL/BC/BR]: **F** Enter

Specify first endpoint of text baseline: *Specify a point.*
Specify second endpoint of text baseline: *Specify a point.*
Specify height<current>: *Enter the height.*

Note
Instead of selecting the ***Justify*** *option (J) for selecting the text justification. You can enter the text justification by directly by entering justification when AutoCAD prompts "Specify start point of text or [Justify/Style]:"*

Center Option: You can use this option to select the midpoint of the baseline for the text. This option can be invoked by entering **Justify** and then **Center** or **C** at the command prompt. After you select or specify the center point, you must enter the text height and the rotation angle, refer to Figure 7-9.

Specify start point of text or [Justify/Style]: **C** Enter
Specify center point of text: *Specify a point.*
Specify height<current>: **0.15** Enter
Specify rotation angle of text<0>: Enter

Middle Option: Using this option, you can center text not only horizontally, as in the previous option, but also vertically. In other words, you can specify the middle point of the text string, refer to Figure 7-9. You can alter the text height and the angle of rotation to meet your requirement. The prompt sequence that follows is given next.

Specify start point of text or [Justify/Style]: **M** Enter
Specify middle point of text: *Specify a point.*
Specify height<current>: **0.15** Enter
Specify rotation angle of text<0>: Enter

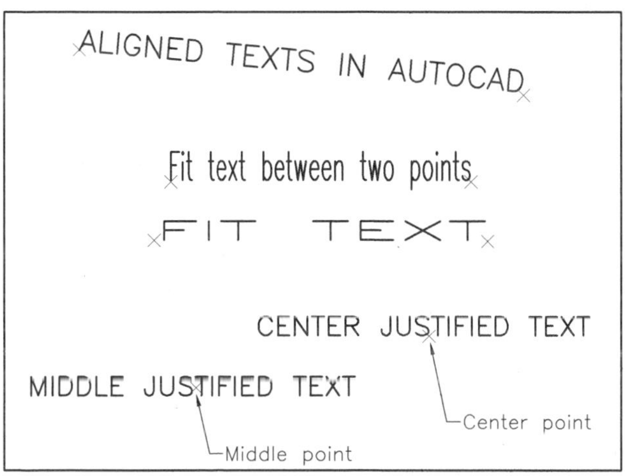

Figure 7-9 *Writing the text using the* ***Align***, ***Fit***, ***Center***, *and* ***Middle*** *options*

Right Option: This option is similar to the default left-justified start point option. The only difference is that the text string is aligned to the lower right corner (the endpoint you specify), that is, the text is **Right** justified, refer to Figure 7-10. The prompt sequence that will follow when you choose this button is given next.

Specify start point of text or [Justify/Style]: **R** Enter
Specify right endpoint of text baseline: *Specify a point.*
Specify height<current>: **0.15** Enter
Specify rotation angle of text<0>: Enter

TL Option: In this option, the text string is justified from top left, refer to Figure 7-10. The prompt sequence is given next.

Specify start point of text or [Justify/Style]: **TL** Enter
Specify top-left point of text: *Specify a point.*
Specify height<current>: **0.15** Enter
Specify rotation angle of text <0>: Enter

Note
The rest of the text alignment options are similar to those already discussed, and you can try them on your own. The prompt sequence is almost the same as those given for the previous examples.

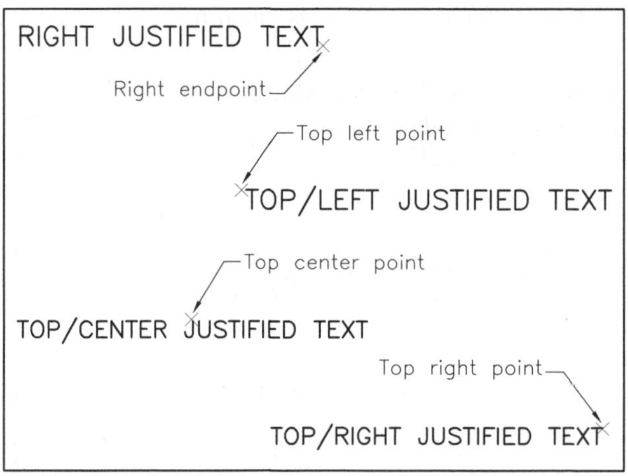

***Figure 7-10** Writing the text using the **Right**, **Top-Left**, **Top-Center**, and **Top-Right** option*

Style Option

With this option, you can specify another existing text style. Different text styles can have different text fonts, heights, oblique angles, and other features. This option can be invoked by entering **TEXT** and then **S** at the next prompt. The prompt sequence that will follow when you choose the **Single Line** text tool for using this option is given next.

Specify start point of text or [Justify/Style]: **S** Enter
Enter style name or [?] <current>: *Specify the desired style or enter* **?** *to list all styles.*

If you want to work in the previous text style, just press ENTER at the last prompt. If you want to activate another text style, enter the name of the style at the last prompt. You can also choose from a list of available text styles, which can be displayed by entering **?**. After you enter **?**, the next prompt is given next.

Enter text style(s) to list <*>: *Specify the text styles to list or enter * to list all styles.*

As you press ENTER, the available text style names and the details of the current styles and commands are displayed in the **AutoCAD Text Window**.

Note
*With the help of the **Style** option of the **Single line** text tool, you can select a text style from an existing list. If you want to create a new style, use the **STYLE** command which is explained later in this chapter.*

ENTERING SPECIAL CHARACTERS

In almost all drafting applications, you need to use special characters (symbols) in the normal text and in the dimension text. For example, you may want to use the degree symbol (°) or the diameter symbol (ø), or you may want to underscore or overscore some text. This can be achieved with the appropriate sequence of control characters (control code). For each symbol, the control sequence starts with a percent sign written twice (%%). The character immediately following the double percent sign depicts the symbol. The control sequences for some of the symbols are given next.

Control sequence	Special character
%%c	Diameter symbol (ø)
%%d	Degree symbol (°)
%%p	Plus/minus tolerance symbol (±)

For example, if you want to write 25° Celsius, you need to enter **25%%dCelsius**. If you want to write 43.0ø, you need to enter **43.0%%c**.

To insert a euro symbol, press and hold the ALT key and enter any numeric value from the numeric keypad and then release the ALT key. Before entering the numbers, make sure that the NUM LOCK is on.

You can also insert symbols by using the **Symbol** drop-down in the **Insert** panel of the **Text Editor** tab. You will learn more about the **Text Editor** tab later in this chapter.

CREATING MULTILINE TEXT

Ribbon: Home > Annotation > Text drop-down > Multiline Text **Command:** MTEXT
Menu Bar: Draw > Text > Multiline Text **Tool Palette:** Draw > MText
Toolbar: Draw > Multiline Text Or Text > Multiline Text

The **Multiline Text** tool in the **Text** drop-down of the **Text** panel (Figure 7-11) is used to write a multiline text whose width is specified by defining two corners of the text boundary or by entering a width using the coordinate entry. The text created by using the **Multiline Text** tool is a single object regardless of the number of lines it contains. On invoking the **Multiline Text** tool, a sample text "abc" is attached to the cursor and you are prompted to specify the first corner. Specify the first corner and move the pointing device so that a box that shows the location and size of the paragraph text is formed. An arrow is displayed within the boundary indicating the direction of the text flow. Specify the other corner to define the boundary. When you define the text boundary, it does not mean that the text paragraph will fit within the defined boundary. AutoCAD only uses the width of the defined boundary as the width of the text paragraph. The height of the text boundary has no effect on the text paragraph.

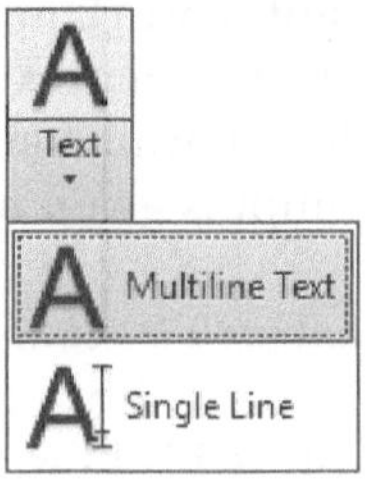

***Figure 7-11** The **Multiline Text** tool in the **Text** drop-down*

Note

*On invoking the **Multiline Text** tool, a sample text "abc" is attached to the cursor. The **MTJIGSTRING** system variable stores the default contents of the sample text. You can specify a string of ten alphanumeric characters as the default sample text.*

The prompt sequence that will be displayed after choosing the **Multiline Text** tool is given next.

Specify first corner: *Select a point to specify first corner.*
Specify opposite corner or [Height/Justify/Line spacing/Rotation/Style/Width/Columns]: *Select an option or select a point to specify other corner. Now, you can write text in this boundary.*

Note

Although the specified box boundary controls the width of a paragraph but if the width of a word is more than than the box boundary specified, AutoCAD will write the word irrespective of the box width and therefore, will exceed the boundary limits.

Once you have defined the boundary of the paragraph text, AutoCAD displays the **Text Editor** tab along with the text window, as shown in Figure 7-12. The text window and the **Text Editor** tab are discussed next.

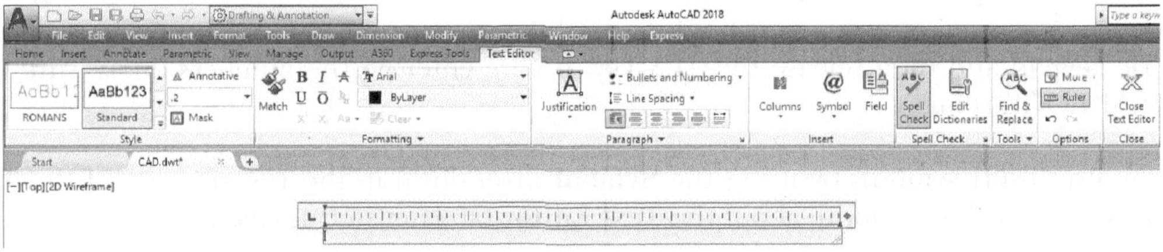

***Figure 7-12** The **Text Editor** tab and the text window*

Text Window

The text window is used to enter the multiline text. The width of the active text area is determined by the width of the window that you specify when you invoke the **Multiline Text** tool. You can increase or decrease the size of the text window by dragging the double-headed arrow. You can also move the scroll bar up or down to display the text.

The ruler on the top of the text window is used to specify the indentation of the current paragraph. The top slider of the ruler specifies the indentation of the first line of the paragraph while the bottom slider specifies the indentation of the other lines of the paragraph.

Text Editor Tab

On creating the text window a contextual tab will be added to the **Ribbon**. The options in this tab are discussed next.

Text Style

The list of available text styles are grouped on the left of the **Style** panel in the **Text Editor** tab. Click the down arrow to scroll down the list of text styles. If you choose the double arrow, a flyout containing text styles created in the current drawing will be displayed. You can select the desired text style from this flyout.

Annotative

The **Annotative** button is used to write the annotative text. The annotative text scales itself according to the current annotative setting. The annotative text also keeps on scaling according to the change in the annotative scale. The annotative texts are defined in the drawing area in terms of the paper height and the current annotation scale setting.

Note

*1. While editing the text, the **Annotative** button is used to convert a non-annotative multiline text into an annotative multiline text and vice-versa.*

*2. You can also change a non-annotative text to an annotative by setting the text's **Annotative** property to **Yes** in the **PROPERTIES** palette. This applies to both single line and multiline text.*

Text Height

The **Text Height** drop-down list is used to specify the text height of the multiline text. The default value in this drop-down list is 0.2000. Once you modify the height, AutoCAD retains that value till you change it. Remember that the multiline text height does not affect the height specified for the **TEXT** command.

Bold, Italic, Underline, Overline

You can use the appropriate buttons in the **Formatting** panel to make the selected text bold, italic, underlined, or create overlined text. Bold and italics are not supported by SHX fonts and hence, they will not be available for the particular fonts. These four buttons toggle between on and off.

Font

The **Font** drop-down list in the **Formatting** panel displays all the fonts available in AutoCAD. You can select the desired font from this drop-down list, as shown in Figure 7-13. Irrespective of the font assigned to a text style, you can assign a different font to that style for the current multiline text by using the **Font** drop-down list.

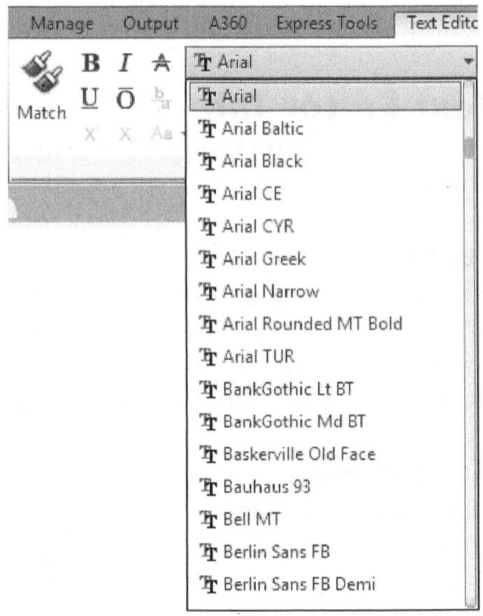

*Figure 7-13 The **Font** drop-down list*

Match

The **Match** tool is used to copy the formatting of a text and then apply it to the other text.

UPPERCASE

When you select text in the text window and choose this button, the alphabets written in the lowercase are converted to the uppercase.

lowercase

When you choose this button, the uppercase text is changed to lowercase text.

Superscript

The **Superscript** button is used to superscribe a text. To do so, select the text and choose the **Superscript** button from the **Formatting** panel of the **Text Editor** contextual tab; the selected text will become a superscript.

Subscript

The **Subscript** button is used to subscribe a text. To subscribe a text, select the text and choose the **Subscript** button from the **Formatting** panel of the **Text Editor** contextual tab; the selected text will become a subscript.

Color

The **Color** drop-down list is used to set the color for the multiline text. You can also select the color from the **Select Color** dialog box that is displayed by selecting **More Colors** in the drop-down list.

Mask

The **Mask** option is used for defining background color for multiline text. When you choose this option, the **Background Mask** dialog box will be displayed, as shown in Figure 7-14. To add background mask, select the **Use background mask** check box and select the required color from the drop-down list in the **Fill Color** area. You can set the size of the colored background behind the text using the **Border offset factor** edit box. The previous value of the offset factor is automatically selected in the edit box. The box that

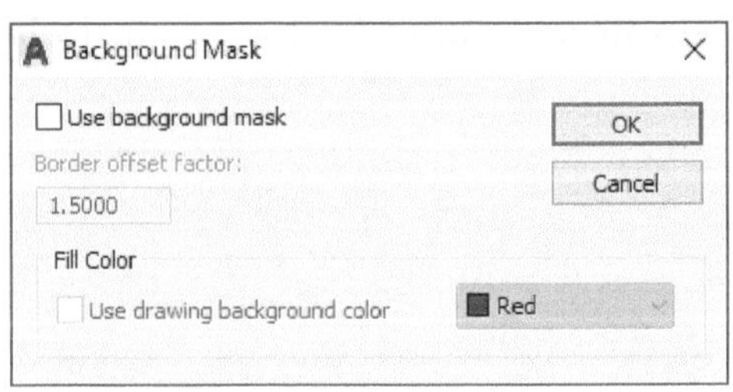

*Figure 7-14 The **Background Mask** dialog box*

defines the background color will be offset from the text by the value you define in this edit box. The value in this edit box is based on the height of the text. If you enter **1** as the value, the height of the colored background will be equal to the height of the text and will extend through the length of the window defined to write the multiline text. Similarly, if you enter **2** as the value, the height of the colored box will be twice the height of the text and will be equally offset above and below the text. However, the length of the colored box will still be equal to the length of the window defined to write the multiline text. You can select the **Use drawing background color** check box in the **Fill Color** area to use the color of the background of the drawing area to add the background mask. The previous color used is automatically selected.

Oblique Angle

Expand the **Formatting** panel to view this option. This option is used to specify the slant angle for the text. Enter the angle in the **Oblique Angle** edit box or use spinner to specify the slant angle.

Tracking

Expand the **Formatting** panel to view this option. This option is used to control the spacing between the selected characters. Select the characters and enter the value of the spacing in the **Tracking** edit box. You can also use the **Tracking** spinner to specify this value. The default tracking value is 1.000. You can specify values ranging from 0.7500 to 4.0000.

Width Factor

Expand the **Formatting** panel to view this option. This option is used to control the width of characters. By default, the value is set to 1.000. Select the characters and use the **Width Factor** edit box or the **Width Factor** spinner to specify the width of characters.

Justification

In large complicated technical drawings, the **Justification** option is used to fit the text matter with a specified justification and alignment. For example, if the text justification is bottom-right (BR), the text paragraph will spill to the left and above the insertion point, regardless of how you define the width of the paragraph. When you choose the **Justification** button in the **Paragraph** panel of the **Text Editor** contextual tab in the **Ribbon**, a cascading menu appears that displays the predefined text justifications. By default, the text is **Top Left** justified. You can choose the new justification from the cascading menu. The various justifications are TL, ML, BL, TC, MC, BC, TR, MR, and BR. Figure 7-15 shows various text justifications for multiline text.

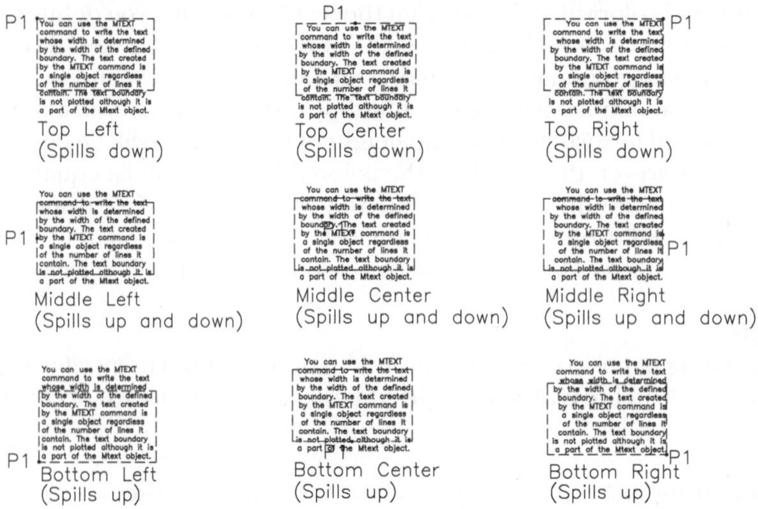

Figure 7-15 Text justifications for multiline text (P1 is the text insertion point)

Paragraph

You can control the settings such as tab, indent, alignment, paragraph spacing and line spacing, of a paragraph by using the options in the **Paragraph** dialog box, as shown in Figure 7-16. When you click on the small inclined arrow at the bottom right of the **Paragraph** panel, the **Paragraph** dialog box is displayed. The options in the **Paragraph** dialog box are discussed next.

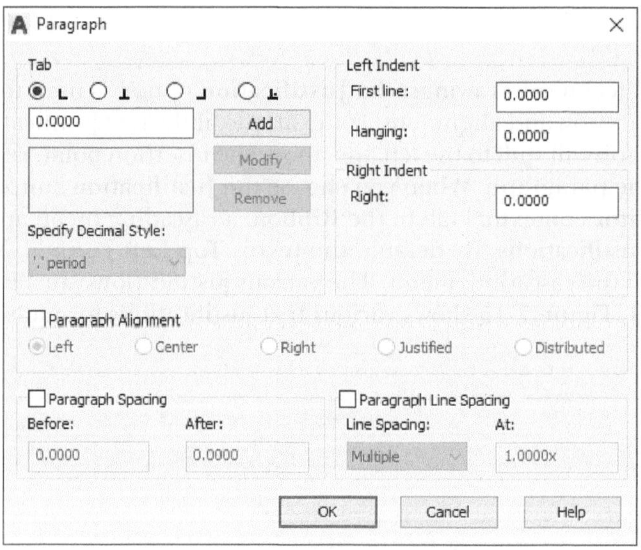

*Figure 7-16 The **Paragraph** dialog box*

Tab: This area is used to specify the tab type by selecting the required radio button. This area is also used to add or remove the additional tab positions up to which the cursor is moved while pressing the TAB key once at the start of a new paragraph for the left, center, right, and decimal justification. This option can also be set by clicking on the ruler of the text window.

Left Indent: In this area, you can set the indent of the first line and the following lines of multiline text by entering the values in the **First line** and the **Hanging** edit boxes.

Right Indent: In this area, you can set the right indent of the paragraph of the multiline text by entering the value in the **Right** edit box.

Paragraph Alignment: Select the **Paragraph Alignment** check box to set the alignment for the current or the selected paragraph in the text window. As you select this check box, the radio buttons available below this check box will be activated. The **Left** radio button is used to left align the text written. The **Center** radio button is used to center align the text. The **Right** radio button is used to right align the text. The **Justified** radio button is used to adjust horizontal spacing so that the text is aligned evenly in between the left and right margins. Justifying the text creates a smooth edge on both sides. The **Distributed** radio button is used to adjust the text evenly throughout the width of the column in the text window.

Paragraph Spacing: Select the **Paragraph Spacing** check box (if not selected by default) to set the gap before the start of the paragraph and after the end of the paragraph. According to the gap set by you, AutoCAD calculates the gap between two consecutive paragraphs. This gap is equal to the sum of after paragraph gap for the upper paragraph and the before paragraph gap for the lower paragraph.

Paragraph Line Spacing: Select the **Paragraph Line Spacing** check box to set the gap between the two consecutive lines. Select the **Exactly** option from the **Line Spacing** drop-down list to maintain the gap exactly specified by you in the **At** edit box, irrespective of the text height. On selecting the **At least** option, both the user specified arbitrary value as well as the text height will be considered to determine the gap. If the text height is smaller than the specified value, the line space will be determined by the user specified value. If the text height is larger, the line spacing will be equal to the text height value. By selecting the **Multiple** option, you can specify the spacing according to the text height. When the text height is not equal in a line, the line space will be determined by the largest text height value of that line.

Note

The spaces entered at the end of a line are also considered while justifying a text.

Line Spacing

Line spacing is the distance between two consecutive lines in a multiline text. Choose **Paragraph > Line Spacing** from the **Text Editor** contextual tab to display a flyout containing options to select some predefined line spacing or for opening the **Paragraph** dialog box, refer to Figure 7-17. The **1.0x**, **1.5x**, **2x**, **2.5x** options set the line spacing in the multiples of the largest text height value in the same line. The **More** option is chosen to open the **Paragraph** dialog box that has been discussed earlier. The **Clear Line Space** option removes the space setting for the lines of the selected or the current paragraph. As a result, the line spacing will retrieve the default mtext line space setting.

Bullets and Numbering

This option is used to control the settings to display the bullets and numbering in a multiline text. Choose the **Bullets and Numbering** option; a flyout will be displayed, as shown in Figure 7-18. The options in this flyout are discussed next.

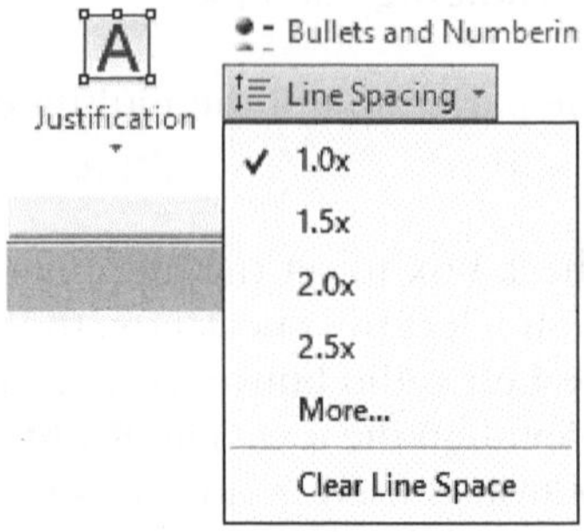

Figure 7-17 Options in the ***Line Spacing*** *flyout*

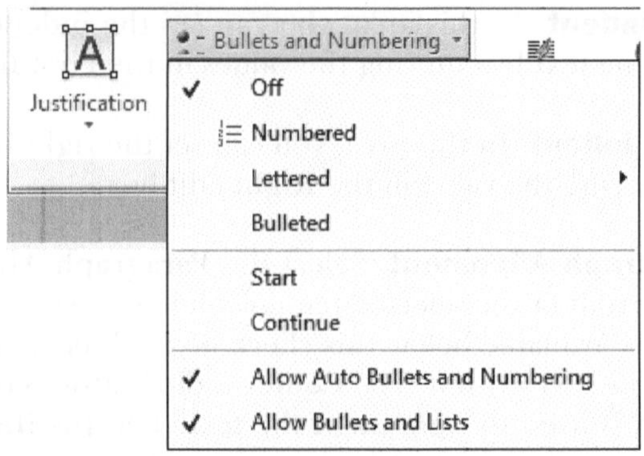

Figure 7-18 Flyout displayed on choosing the ***Bullets and Numbering*** *option*

Off: Select this option to remove letters, numbers, and bullets from the selected text.

Numbered: This option inserts numbers for the list formatting.

Lettered: This option inserts the letters for list formatting. You can choose the uppercase letters and lower case letters to be used for the list formatting.

Note

If the number of items exceed the number of alphabets, the numbering continues again from the start but by using the double alphabet.

Bulleted: This option inserts bullets for the list formatting.

Start: This option restarts a new letter or a numbering sequence for the list formatting.

Continue: This option adds the selected paragraphs to the last list and continues the sequence.

Allow Auto Bullets and Numbering: Select this option and follow the procedure given below to automatically start the formatting of list.

1. Start a line of text by entering a number.
2. Use period (.), comma (,), close angle bracket (>), close square bracket (]), close parenthesis ()), or close curly bracket (}) as punctuation after the number.
3. Provide space by pressing the TAB key.
4. Enter the required text.
5. Press the ENTER key to move to the next line; the new line will be automatically listed.
6. Press the SHIFT+ENTER key to add a plain paragraph.
7. To end auto-listing, press the ENTER key twice.

Allow Bullets and Lists: If this option is checked, the list formatting will be applied to the whole text lines in the multiline text area. If you clear this option, any list formatting in the multiline text object will be removed and the items will be converted into the plain text. And, all the bullets and lists options, including the allow auto-list available on the contextual tab will become unavailable. To make these options available, again right-click in the text window and choose the **Allow Bullets and Lists** sub-option from the **Bullets and Lists** option.

Columns

This button is chosen to create columns in the multiline text. On choosing this button from the **Insert** panel, a flyout will be displayed that has the options to control the number, height, and gap between the columns. These options are shown in Figure 7-19 and are discussed next.

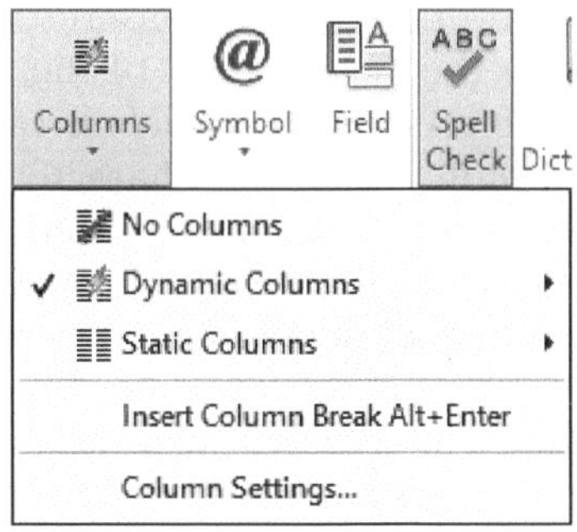

***Figure 7-19** The options in the **Column** flyout*

No Columns: This option does not create any column. The whole of the multiline text is written in a single column. When you start a multiline text, this option is selected by default.

Dynamic Columns: The dynamic columns are the text driven columns that change according to the quantity of the text. According to the quantity of text written, the columns are added or removed automatically. The **Auto height** and **Manual height** options in the **Column Settings** dialog box are used to control the height of the dynamic columns. The **Column Settings** dialog box is available on choosing the **Column Settings** option of the flyout. The **Auto Height** option automatically starts a new column when the text exceeds the range that the preset column can accommodate. The default height of the first column is decided by the height of the window that you create while starting the multiline text. All the other new columns generated are equal in height to the first column. If you change the height of the first column, the height of the remaining columns changes accordingly, in order to be in level with the first one. The **Manual Height** option, on the other hand, provides the flexibility to control the height of each column individually. A new column will not start if the text exceeds the range that the present column can accommodate. The text will keep on adding to the same column by increasing the height of that column. Later on, you can add extra columns by adjusting the height of the present column. When you decrease the height of the column in which you have entered the text that does not fit the height of the new column, a new column will start automatically. Similarly, you can add more columns by adjusting the height of the last column.

Static Columns: The **Static Columns** option allows you to specify the number of columns before writing the text. All the generated columns are of the same height and width. You can also change the number of columns after writing the text.

Insert Column Break Alt+Enter: This option is used to start writing text in a new column manually. When you insert a column break, the cursor automatically moves to the start of the next column. You can also press the ALT+ENTER key to insert a column break.

Column Settings: This option controls the settings to create a column. Choose this option to invoke the **Column Settings** dialog box, refer to Figure 7-20. The **Column Settings** dialog box has four areas: **Column Type**, **Column Number**, **Height**, and **Width**. The **Column Type** area specifies the type of column you want to create. All options in this area are similar to the options discussed above. In the **Column Number** area, you can specify the number of columns to be generated when you create the manual type of columns. In the **Height** area, you can specify the height of the columns to be generated for Auto Height Dynamic Columns and Static Column type. The **Width** area controls the width of the columns and the gap between two consecutive columns.

Symbol

This option is used to insert special characters in the text. When you choose the **Symbol** option from the **Insert** panel of the **Text Editor** tab in the **Ribbon**, a flyout will be displayed with some predefined special characters, refer to Figure 7-21. You can also choose **Other** from the flyout to display the **Character Map** dialog box. This dialog box has a number of other special characters that you can insert in the multiline text. To insert characters from the dialog box, select the character that you want to copy and then choose the **Select** button. Once you have selected all the required special characters, choose the **Copy** button and then close the dialog box. Now in the text window, position the cursor where you want to insert the special characters and right-click to display the shortcut menu. Choose **Paste** to insert the selected special character in the text window.

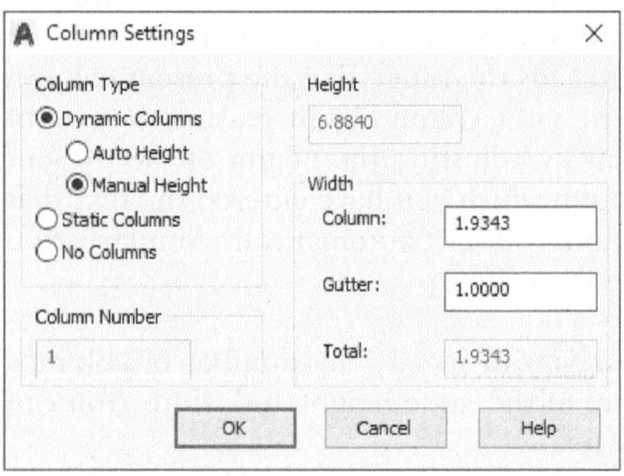

*Figure 7-20 The **Column Settings** dialog box*

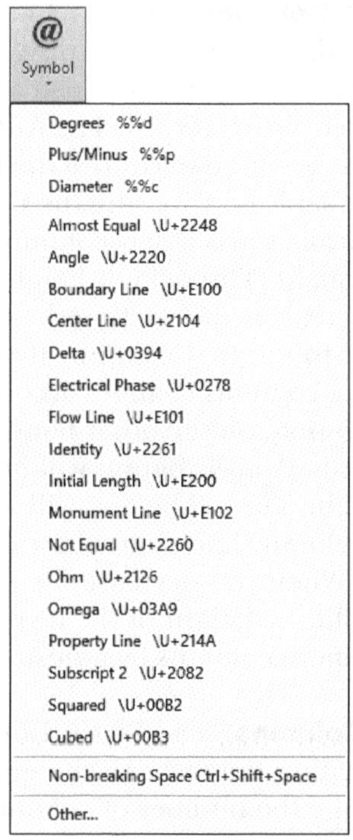

*Figure 7-21 Flyout displayed on choosing the **Symbol** button from the **Insert** panel*

Field

AutoCAD allows you to insert a field in the multiline text. A field contains data that is associated with the property that defines the field. For example, you can insert a field having the author's name on the current drawing. If you have already defined the author of the current drawing in the **Drawing Properties** dialog box, it will automatically be displayed in the field. If you modify the author and update the field, the changes will automatically be made in the text. When you choose this option, the **Field** dialog box will be displayed, as shown in Figure 7-22. You can select the field to be added to the **Field names** list box and define the format of the field using the

Format list box. Choose **OK** after selecting the field and format. If the data in the selected field is already defined, it will be displayed in the text window. If not, the field will display dashes (----).

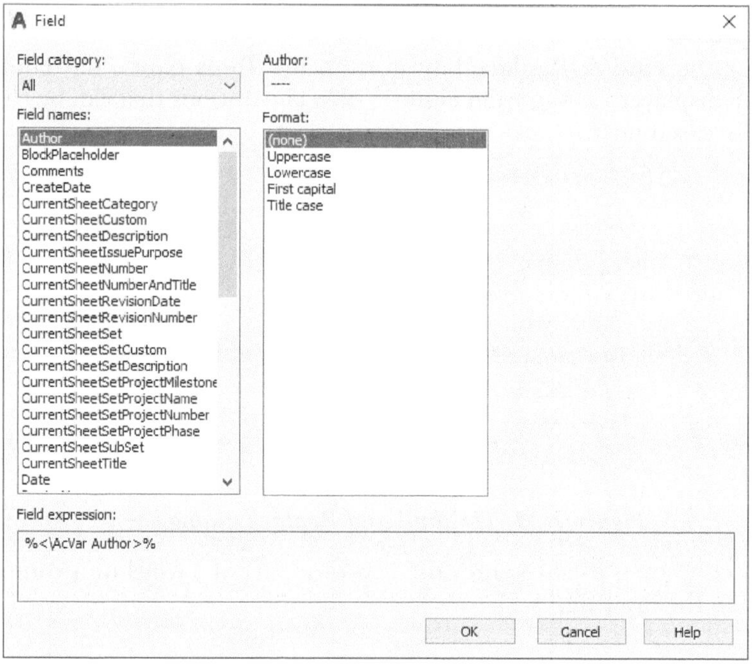

*Figure 7-22 The **Field** dialog box*

Note

*To update a field after the text of that field is modified, double-click on the multiline text to display the text window. Click and select the field in the text window and then right-click to display the shortcut menu. Choose **Update Field** from this menu; the field will be updated. You can also edit the field or convert it into text using the same shortcut menu.*

Spell Check

To check spelling errors, choose the **Spell Check** button; the misspelt words will appear with a red underline. You can specify settings to check spelling errors as per your requirement. To do so, left-click on the inclined arrow in the **Spell Check** panel; the **Check Spelling Settings** dialog box will be displayed. This dialog box is used to specify what to include for spell check such as the dimension text, block attributes, sub option, and text in external references.

You can also specify what not to include like capitalized words, mixed cases, uppercase, and words with numbers or punctuation.

Edit Dictionaries

By using this option the words in the drawing are matched to the words in the current, main and current custom dictionaries, during a spelling check. On choosing this option, the **Dictionaries** dialog box will be displayed. This dialog box has two areas, **Main dictionary** and **Custom dictionaries**. In the **Main dictionary** area, you can select the required dictionary from a list of different language dictionaries. And in the **Custom dictionaries** area, you can add the commonly used words to a *.cus* file. You can also import the words from other dictionaries to the current customized *.cus* file.

Find and Replace

When you choose the **Find & Replace** button from the **Tools** panel, the **Find and Replace** dialog box will be displayed, as shown in Figure 7-23. The options that can be chosen from this dialog box are discussed next.

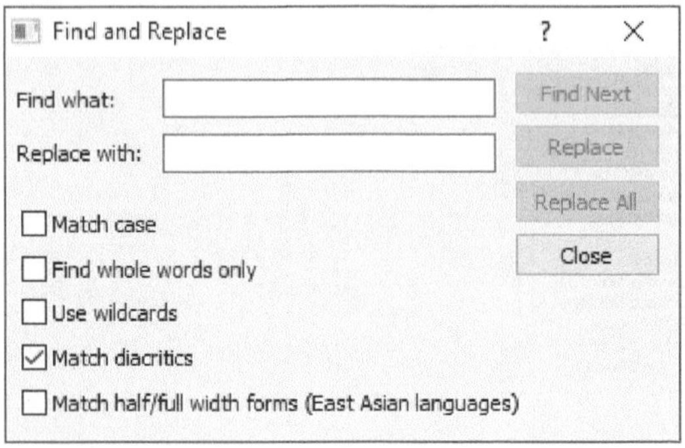

*Figure 7-23 The **Find and Replace dialog** box*

Find what: This edit box is used to enter the text or a part of a word or a complete word that you need to find in the drawing.

Replace with: If you want some text to be replaced, enter new text for replacement in this text box.

Match case: If this check box is selected, AutoCAD will find out the word only if the case of all characters in the word are identical to the word mentioned in the **Find what** edit box.

Find whole words only: If this check box is selected, AutoCAD will match the word in the text only if it is a single word, identical to the one mentioned in the **Find what** text box. For example, if you enter **and** in the **Find what** edit box and select the **Find whole words only** check box, AutoCAD will not match the string **and** in words like sand, land, band, and so on.

Use wildcards: This check box is selected to use the wildcard characters such as * , ?, and so on in the **Find what** edit box and then replace the selected text.

Match diacritics: This check box is selected to match the Latin characters, diacritical marks, or assent in your search.

Match half/full width forms (East Asian languages): If this check box is selected, you can match half or full width characters in your search.

Find Next: Choose this button to continue the search for the text entered in the **Find what** box.

Replace: Choose this button to replace the highlighted text with the text entered in the **Replace with** text box.

Replace All: If you choose this button, all the words in the current multiline text that match the word specified in the **Find what** text box will be replaced with the word entered in the **Replace with** text box.

Import Text

Expand the **Tools** panel to view this option. When you choose this option, AutoCAD displays the **Select File** dialog box. In this dialog box, select any text file that you want to import as the multiline text; the imported text will be displayed in the text area. Note that only the ASCII or RTF file is interpreted properly.

ALL CAPS

Expand the **Tools** panel to view this option. If you choose this option, the case of all the text written or imported after choosing this option will be changed to uppercase. However, the case of the text written before choosing this option is not changed.

More

To edit a text, select it and then choose the **More** button from the **Options** panel in the **Text Editor** tab; a flyout will be displayed. The options in the **More** flyout are discussed next.

Character Set: This option is used to define the character set for the current font. You can select the desired character set from the cascading menu that is displayed when you choose this option.

Editor Settings: The **Editor Settings** option has the sub-options to control the display of the **Text Formatting** toolbar. These sub-options are shown in Figure 7-24 and are discussed next.

Always Display as WYSIWYG (What you see is what you get). This option controls the display size and orientation of the text in the **Text Editor** tab. If you choose this sub-option, the text in the **Text Editor** tab will be displayed in the text window with its original size, position, and orientation. But, if the text is very small, or very large or rotated, then you can deselect this sub-option so that the displayed text is oriented horizontally and is displayed in readable size.

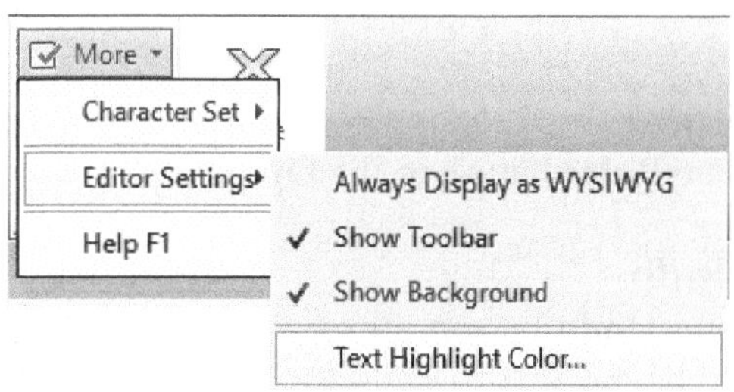

*Figure 7-24 The sub-options of the **Editor Settings** option*

Show Toolbar: This sub-option is used to show or hide the **Text Formatting** toolbar.

Show Background: Choose this sub-option to make the background of the text window opaque. By default, the background is transparent. Invoke the text window over the existing objects/entities in the drawing window to see the effect of the opaque background sub-option.

Text Highlight Color

This sub-option is used to change the highlighted color of the text that appears when you select the text for editing. When you choose this sub-option, the **Select Color** dialog box will be displayed, as shown in Figure 7-25. There are three tabs available in the dialog box:

Index Color, **True Color**, and **Color Books**. By default, the **True Color** tab is selected. You can set the colors by using the options available in these tabs.

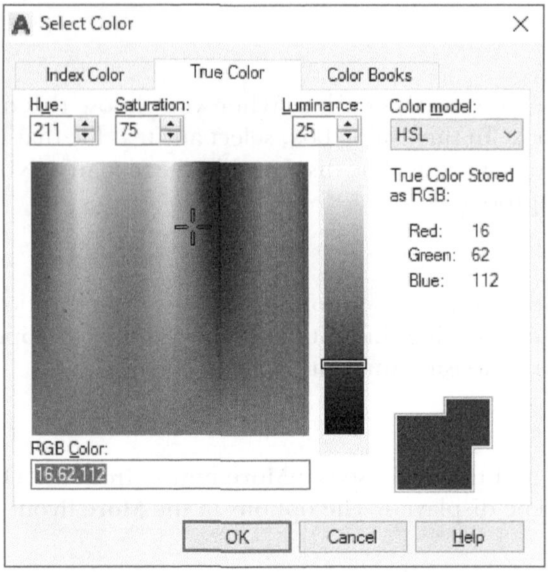

*Figure 7-25 The **Select Color** dialog box*

Note

*You can also remove formatting such as bold, italics, or underline from the selected text. To do so, select the text whose formatting you need to change and then right-click to display a shortcut menu. From the menu, choose the **Remove Formatting** option. Under the sub-headings, you can choose between the Character, Paragraph or All; the formatting of the selected text will be removed.*

Ruler

The **Ruler** button in the **Options** panel is used to toggle the display of ruler in the text window.

Undo

The **Undo** button allows you to undo the actions in the text window. You can also press the CTRL+Z keys to undo the previous actions.

Redo

The **Redo** button allows you to redo the actions in the text window. You can also press the CTRL+Y keys to redo the previous actions.

The options discussed next are not available in the **Text Editor** tab. However, in the **Text Formatting** toolbar, these options will be displayed on choosing **More > Editor Settings > Show Toolbar** from the **Text Editor** tab.

Stack

To create a fraction text, you must use the stack option with the specialcharacters /, ^, and #. In AutoCAD, this option is available in sleep mode in the **Text Editor** tab. When you enter two numbers separated by / or ^ , the stack option becomes active. Alternatively, press ENTER or

SPACEBAR after entering two characters; a small yellow icon will be displayed. Click on that icon; a flyout will be displayed, as shown in Figure 7-26. Choose **Stack Properties**; the **Stack Properties** dialog box will be displayed, as shown in Figure 7-27. You can use this dialog box to control the Stack properties. The character/stacks the text vertically with a line, and the character ^ stacks the text vertically without a line (tolerance stack). The character # stacks the text with a diagonal line. The stacked text is displayed equal to 70 percent of the actual height. The Stack options available in the flyout are discussed next.

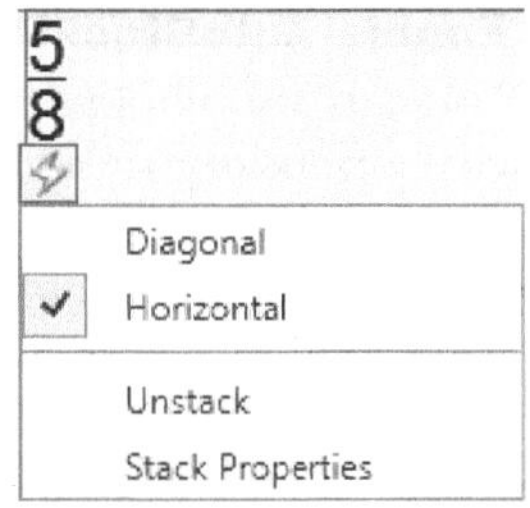

Figure 7-26 Flyout with the Stack options

Diagonal: This option stacks the selected text with the first number on top of the second number separated by a diagonal line.

Horizontal: This option stacks the selected text with the first number on top of the second number separated by a horizontal line.

Unstack: This option is used to unstack the selected stacked text.

Stack Properties

When you choose this option, the **Stack Properties** dialog box will be displayed, as shown in Figure 7-27. This dialog box is used to edit the text and the appearance of the selected stacked text. The options in this dialog box are discussed next.

Text Area: You can change the upper and the lower values of the stacked text by entering their values in the **Upper** and **Lower** text boxes, respectively.

Appearance Area: You can change the style, position, and size of the stacked text by entering their values in the **Style**, **Position**, and **Text size** text boxes, respectively.

Defaults: This drop-down list allows you to restore the default values or save the new settings as the default settings for the selected stacked text.

AutoStack: When you choose this button, the **AutoStack Properties** dialog box will be displayed, as shown in Figure 7-28. The options in this dialog box are discussed next.

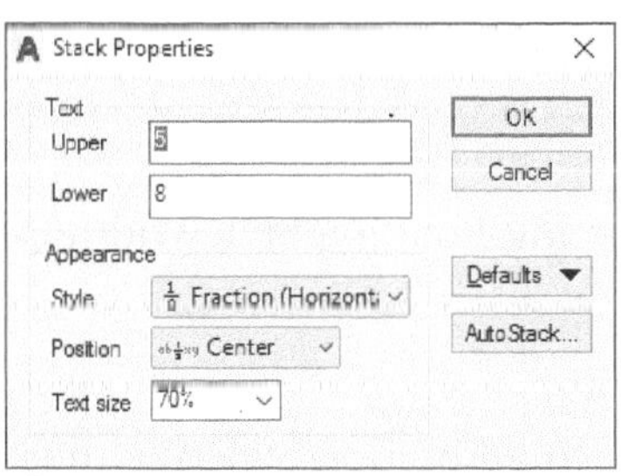

*Figure 7-27 The **Stack Properties** dialog box*

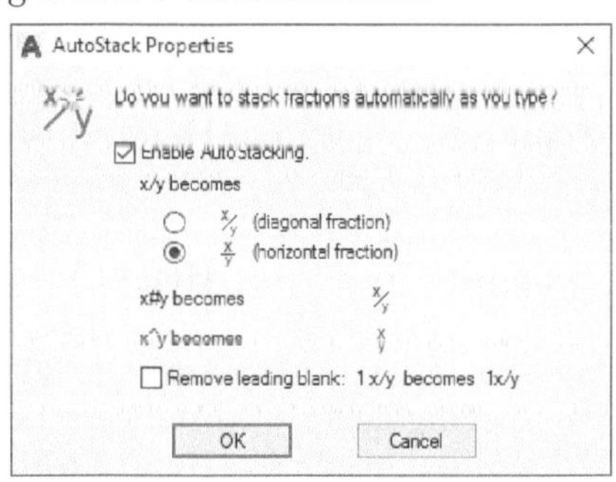

*Figure 7-28 The **AutoStack Properties** dialog box*

Enable AutoStacking: You can enable or disable autostacking by using this check box. You can also choose between the diagonal and horizontal fraction display by selecting the corresponding radio button.

If you clear the **Enable AutoStacking** check box, then the flyout showing the stack options, refer to Figure 7-26, will not be displayed. For invoking the flyout, select the fractional text. Next, right-click and choose **Stack** from the shortcut menu, then click on the small yellow icon.

Remove leading blank: This option removes the gap between a number and a fractional text. For example 1 x/y becomes 1x/y.

Note

*The **Cut** and **Copy** sub-options of the **Edit** option can be used to move or copy the text from the text window to any other application. Similarly, using the **Paste** sub-option, you can paste text from any windows text-based application to the text window.*

Example 1 — *Multiline Text*

In this example, you will use the **Multiline Text** tool to write the following text.

For long, complex entries, create multiline text using the MTEXT option. The angle is 10°, dia = 1/2", and length = 32 1/2".

The font of the text is **Swis721 BT**, text height is 0.20, color is red, and written at an angle of 10-degree with Middle-Left justification. Make the word "multiline" bold, underline the text "multiline text", and make the word "angle" italic. The line spacing type and line spacing between the lines are **At least** and **1.5x**, respectively. Use the symbol for degrees. After writing the text in the text window, replace the word "option" with "command".

1. Choose the **Multiline Text** tool from the **Annotation** panel in the **Home** tab in the **Drafting & Annotation** workspace. After invoking this tool, specify the first corner on the screen to define the first corner of the paragraph text boundary. You need to specify the rotation angle of the text before specifying the second corner of the paragraph text boundary. The prompt sequence is given next.

   Current text style: "Standard" Text height: 0.2000 Annotative: No
   Specify first corner: *Select a point to specify the first corner.*
   Specify opposite corner or [Height/Justify/Line spacing/Rotation/Style/Width/Columns]: **R** Enter
   Specify rotation angle <0>: 10 Enter
   Specify opposite corner or [Height/Justify/Line spacing/Rotation/Style/Width/Columns]: **L** Enter
   Enter line spacing type [At least/Exactly] <At least>: Enter
   Enter line spacing factor or distance <1x>: **1.5x**
   Specify opposite corner or [Height/Justify/Line spacing/Rotation/Style/Width/Columns]: *Select another point to specify the other corner.*

The text window and the **Text Editor** tab are displayed.

2. Select the **Swis721 BT** font from the **Font** drop-down list of the **Formatting** panel in the **Text Editor** tab.

3. Enter **0.20** in the **Text Height** edit box of the **Style** panel, if the value in this edit box is not 0.2.

4. Select **Red** from the **Color** drop-down list in the **Formatting** panel.

5. Now, enter the text in the text window, as shown in Figure 7-29. To add the degree symbol, choose the **Symbol** button from the **Insert** panel of the **Text Editor** tab in the **Ribbon**; a flyout is displayed. Choose **Degrees** from the flyout. When you type 1/2 after dia = and then press the " key, AutoCAD displays a small yellow icon. Click on the icon; a flyout will appear. Choose the **Diagonal** option from the flyout.

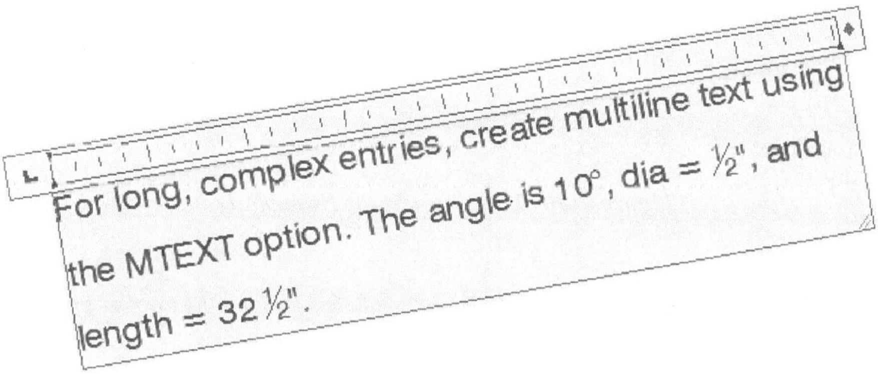

Figure 7-29 *Text entered in the text window*

Similarly, when you type 1/2 after length = 32 and then press the " key, AutoCAD displays a small yellow icon. Click on the icon; a flyout will appear. Choose the **Diagonal** option from the flyout.

6. Double-click on the word "multiline" to select it (or click and drag to select the text) and then choose the **B** button to make it boldface and underline the words "multiline text" by using the **U** button from the **Formatting** panel.

7. Highlight the word "angle" by double-clicking on it and then choose the **Italic** button from the **Formatting** panel.

8. Choose the **Middle Left ML** option from the **Justification** drop-down in the **Paragraph** panel.

9. Choose the **Find & Replace** button from the **Tools** panel in the **Text Editor** tab. Alternatively, right-click on the text window and choose **Find and Replace** from the shortcut menu. You can also use CTRL+R keys. On doing so, the **Find and Replace** dialog box is displayed.

10. In the **Find what** edit box, enter **option** and in the **Replace with** edit box, enter **command**.

11. Choose the **Find Next** button. AutoCAD finds the word "option" and highlights it. Choose the **Replace** button to replace **option** by **command**. The **AutoCAD** information box is displayed informing you that AutoCAD has finished searching for the word. Choose **OK** to close the information box.

Note
To set the width of the multiline text objects, hold and drag the arrowhead on the right side of the ruler. In this example, the text has been accommodated into three lines.

12. Now, choose **Close** to exit the **Find and Replace** dialog box. To exit the editor mode, click outside the text window; a text is displayed on the screen, as shown in Figure 7-30.

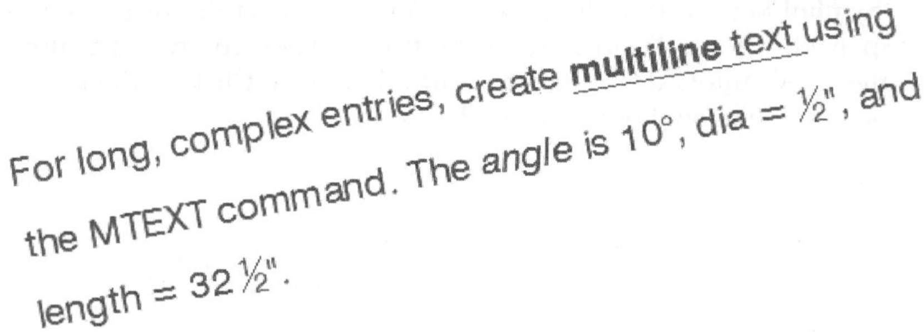

***Figure 7-30** Multiline text for Example 1*

Tip
The text in the text window can be selected by double-clicking on the word or by triple-clicking on the text to select the entire line or paragraph.

Exercise 1 — Single Line & Multiline Text

Write the text using the **Single Line** and **Multiline Text** tools, as shown in Figure 7-31 and Figure 7-32. Use the special characters and the text justification options shown in the drawing. The text height is 0.1 and 0.15 respectively in Figure 7-31 and Figure 7-32.

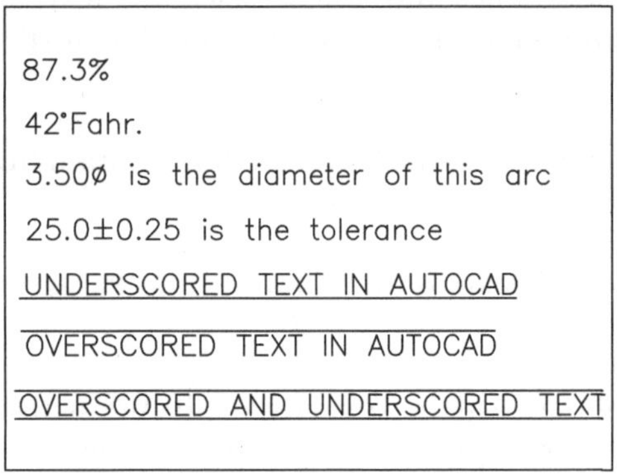

***Figure 7-31** Drawing for Exercise 1*

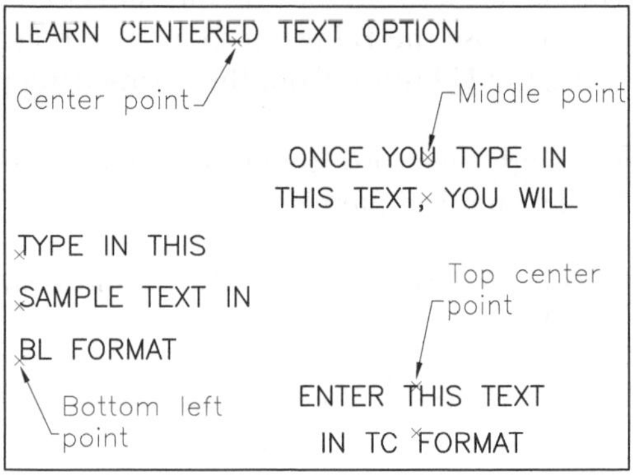

***Figure 7-32** Drawing for Exercise 1*

EDITING TEXT

The contents of a Multiline Text object or a Single Line text object, or the text in a dimension object can be edited by using the **TEXTEDIT** command or the **PROPERTIES** palette. You can also use the AutoCAD editing tools such as **Move**, **Erase**, **Rotate**, **Copy**, and **Mirror** upon any text object.

In addition to editing, you can also modify the text in AutoCAD. The modification that you can perform on the text include changing its scale and justification. The various editing and modifying operations are discussed next.

Editing Text Using the TEXTEDIT Command

Menu Bar: Modify > Object > Text > Edit
Toolbar: Text > Edit **Command:** TEXTEDIT/TEDIT

You can use the **TEXTEDIT** command to edit a text object. The most convenient way of invoking this command is by double-clicking on the text object. If you double-click on a single line text written by using the **Single Line** tool, AutoCAD creates an edit box around the text and highlights it. You can modify the text string in this edit box. The size of the bounding box increases or decreases as you add more text or remove the existing text. Note that for the text object, you cannot modify any of its properties in the bounding box. However, if you double-click on a multiline text written by using the **Multiline Text** tool, the text will be displayed in the text window. You can make changes using various options in the **Text Editor** tab. Apart from changing the text string, you can also change the properties of a paragraph text.

You can also select the text for editing and then right-click in the drawing area; a shortcut menu is displayed. Depending on the text object you have selected, the **Edit** or **Mtext Edit** options will be available in the shortcut menu. On choosing an appropriate option, the text window and the **Text Editor** tab will be displayed.

The prompt sequence to edit a text object using the **TEXTEDIT** command is given next.

Select an annotation object or [Undo/Mode]: **M** Enter
Enter a text edit mode option [Single/Multiple] <Multiple>: **M** Enter
Edit mode = Multiple
Select an annotation object or [Undo/Mode]: *Select a text object to edit.*

By choosing the **Multiple** option, you can edit multiple text objects at a time without restarting the command.

Editing Text Using the PROPERTIES Palette

Using the **TEXTEDIT** command with the Single Line text, you can only change the text string, and not its properties such as height, angle, and so on. In this case, you can use the **PROPERTIES** palette for changing the properties. Select the text, right click to invoke the shortcut menu, and choose the **Properties** option from the shortcut menu; the **PROPERTIES** palette with all properties of the selected text will be displayed, refer to Figure 7-33. In this palette, you can change any value and the text string.

You can edit a single line text in the **Contents** edit box. However, to edit a multiline text, you must choose the swatch button in the **Contents** edit box. On doing so, the text window will be displayed and you can make the changes.

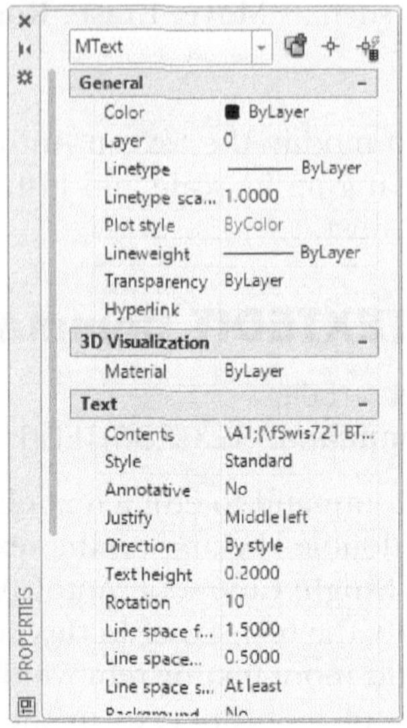

*Figure 7-33 The **PROPERTIES** palette*

Modifying the Scale of the Text

Ribbon: Annotate > Text > Scale	**Toolbar:** Text > Scale
Menu Bar: Modify > Object > Text > Scale	**Command:** SCALETEXT

You can modify the scale factor of a text by using the **Scale** tool in the extended options of the **Text** panel of the **Annotate** tab. On invoking this tool, you can select the text and specify the base point for scaling the text. AutoCAD lists the justification options as the base point to scale the text. Specify the appropriate base point and press ENTER; you will be prompted to specify the new model height or select one of the options. All these options are discussed next.

Paper Height

It scales the text height depending on the annotative properties of a drawing. The **Paper height** option can only be applied to the annotative objects.

Match object

You can use the **Match object** option to select an existing text whose height is used to scale the selected text.

Scale factor

You can use the **Scale factor** option to specify a scale factor to scale the text. You can also use the **Reference** option to specify the scale factor for the text.

Modifying the Justification of the Text

Ribbon: Annotate > Text > Justify **Toolbar:** Text > Justify
Menu Bar: Modify > Object > Text > Justify **Command:** JUSTIFYTEXT

You can modify the justification of a text by choosing the **Justify** tool of the **Text** panel in the **Annotate** tab; you will be prompted to select the objects. Select the text and press ENTER; AutoCAD lists the justification options and you will be prompted to specify the justification. Specify the justification; the justification will be modified. Note that even after modifying the justification using this tool, the location of the text will not be changed. However, you can notice the changed justification location on selecting the text.

Aligning Text

Ribbon: Annotate > Text > Text Align **Command:** TEXTALIGN

In AutoCAD, you can align single, multiple, and attribute texts. To align text, you need to enter **TEXTALIGN** command at the command prompt. On entering the command, you will be prompted to select the text object to be aligned. Select the text objects and press ENTER; then select the object which will act as a reference for the text object to align; you will be prompted to specify the second point for positioning the text to be aligned. While specifying the second point, you can specify spacing and positioning. To do so, enter **O** in the command prompt; the options will be displayed in the command prompt and in a flyout. These options are discussed next.

Distribute

The **Distribute** option is used to place the text dynamically.

Set spacing

The **Set spacing** option is used to set uniform spacing around the reference object. After specifying the spacing, the text object can be placed around the reference object with fixed spacing value.

current Vertical

The **current Vertical** option is used to specify the deflection value vertically from the insertion point of the other text.

current Horizontal

The **current Horizontal** option is used to specify the deflection value horizontally from the insertion point of the other text.

Select the required options and specify the second point; the text will get aligned with specified values.

COMBINE TEXT

Ribbon: Insert > Import > Combine Text **Command:** TXT2MTXT

In AutoCAD 2018, you can convert a single line text into multiline text or combine different text strings to form a single multiline text. To do so, choose the **Combine Text** tool from **Import** panel of the **Insert** tab; you will be prompted to select objects. Select all the text strings that you want to combine together to form a multiline text by using any selection method. The prompt sequence for combining text is given below:

Choose the ***Combine Text*** *tool*
Select objects or [SEttings]: *Select the text strings to combine and press ENTER.*

You can also set the order of the combined text using the **Text to Mtext Settings** dialog box. To do so, choose the **SEttings** option from the **Select objects or [SEttings]:** prompt; the **Text to Mtext Settings** dialog box is displayed, as shown in Figure 7-34. Next, select the **Sort top-down** radio button from the **Text ordering** area (if not selected by default) to combine the text in top to bottom order. The **Select order of text** radio button is used to set the order of combined text by arranging the text strings in selected order.

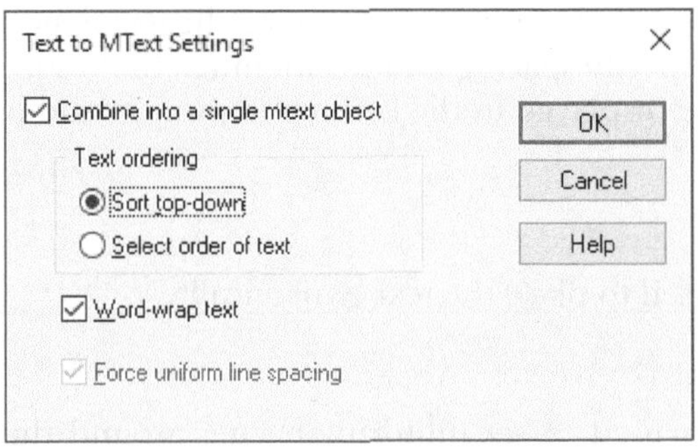

Figure 7-34 *The* ***Text to Mtext Settings*** *dialog box*

INSERTING TABLE IN THE DRAWING

Ribbon: Home > Annotation > Table Or Annotate > Tables > Table
Menu Bar: Draw > Table **Toolbar:** Draw > Table
Tool Palette: Draw > Table **Command:** TABLE

A number of mechanical, architectural, electric, or civil drawings require a table in which some information about the drawing is displayed. For example, the drawing of an assembly needs the Bill of Material, which is a table that provides details such as the number of parts in the drawing, their names, their material, and so on. To enter these information, AutoCAD allows you to create tables using the **Table** tool, refer to Figure 7-35. When you invoke this tool, the **Insert Table** dialog box is displayed, as shown in Figure 7-36. The options in this dialog box are discussed next.

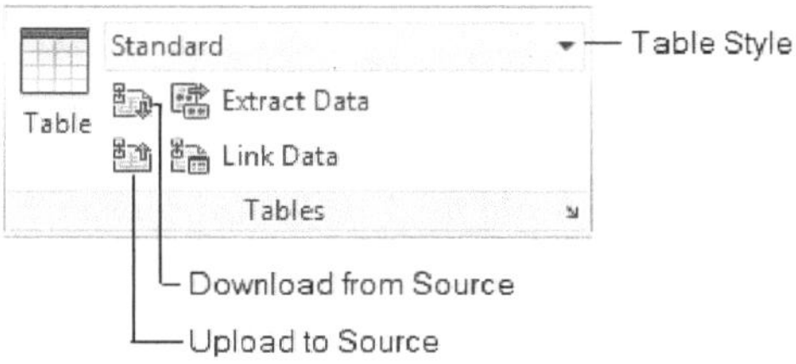

*Figure 7-35 Tools in the **Tables** panel of the **Annotate** tab*

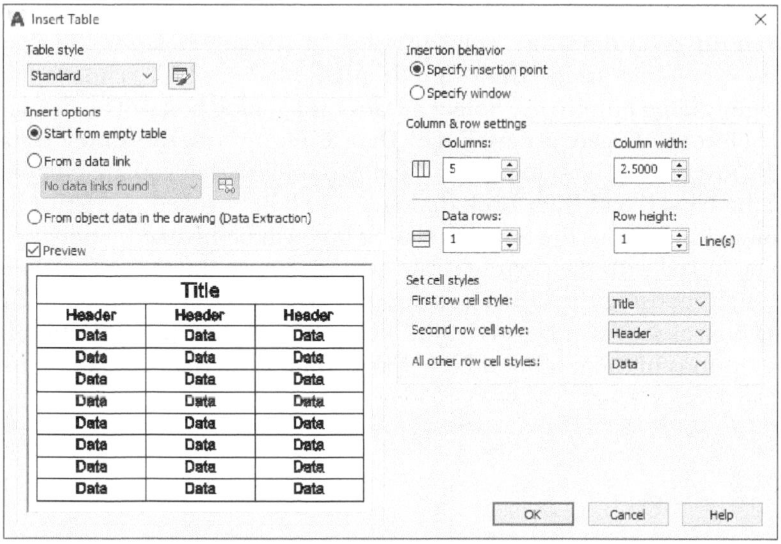

*Figure 7-36 The **Insert Table** dialog box*

Table style Area

The drop-down list in this area displays the names of the various table styles in the current drawing. By default, the **Standard** table style is displayed in the drop-down list. Choose the **Launch the Table Style dialog** button on the right of this drop-down list to display the **Table Style** dialog box. This dialog box can be used to create a new table style, modify, or delete an existing table style. You can also set the selected table style as the current table style. You will learn more about creating a new table style in the next section.

Insert options Area

The options in this area enable you to create tables with different types of data. You can add static data, externally-linked data, or object data to a table. The options in this area are discussed next.

Start from empty table

This option enables you to enter the data manually in the table. On invoking this option, an empty table is created in which you have to enter the values manually. This type of table data is known as the static data. This is the default option selected for creating a table.

Tip

You can copy an existing excel spreadsheet and paste it on an existing drawing as a table with the static data. To do so, choose the ***Paste Special*** *tool from the* ***Paste*** *drop-down in the* ***Clipboard*** *panel of the* ***Home*** *tab and paste the copied data as AutoCAD entity. The resulting table will be similar to the table created using the* ***Start from empty table*** *option.*

From a data link

This option enables you to create a table automatically in AutoCAD from an excel sheet. This excel sheet remains linked with the drawing and any changes made in the excel sheet will reflect in the table. From the drop-down list, you can select an already linked excel sheet or you can also attach a new excel sheet to the drawing. To link a new excel file, choose the **Launch the Data Link Manager dialog** button; the **Select a Data Link** dialog box will be displayed, as shown in Figure 7-37. Select the **Create a new Excel Data Link** option; the **Enter Data Link Name** dialog box will be invoked. Enter a name for the new data link that you are creating and choose the **OK** button; the **New Excel Data Link** dialog box will be invoked, as shown in Figure 7-38. Choose the **Browse [...]** button; the **Save As** dialog box will be invoked. Specify the location of the excel file to be linked with the current drawing and choose the **Open** button from the **Save As** dialog box. After choosing the **Open** button, more options will be added to the **New Excel Data Link** dialog box, as shown in Figure 7-39. Click on the **More Options** button to expand this dialog box. The options in the modified **New Excel Data Link** dialog box are discussed next.

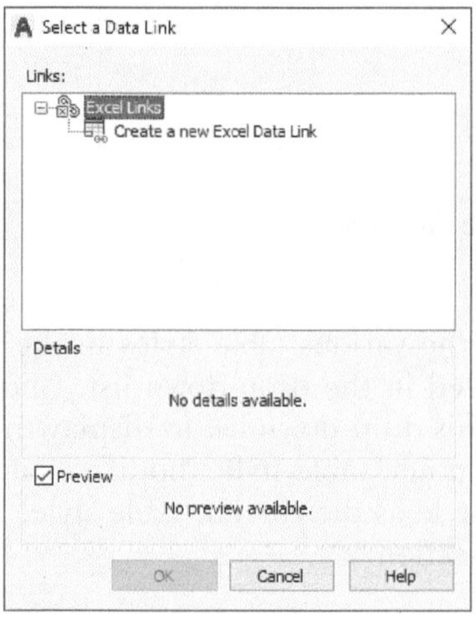

Figure 7-37 The ***Select a Data Link*** *dialog box*

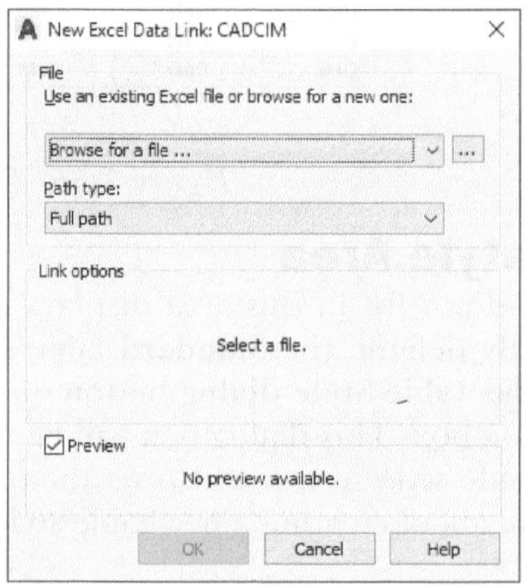

Figure 7-38 The ***New Excel Data Link*** *dialog box*

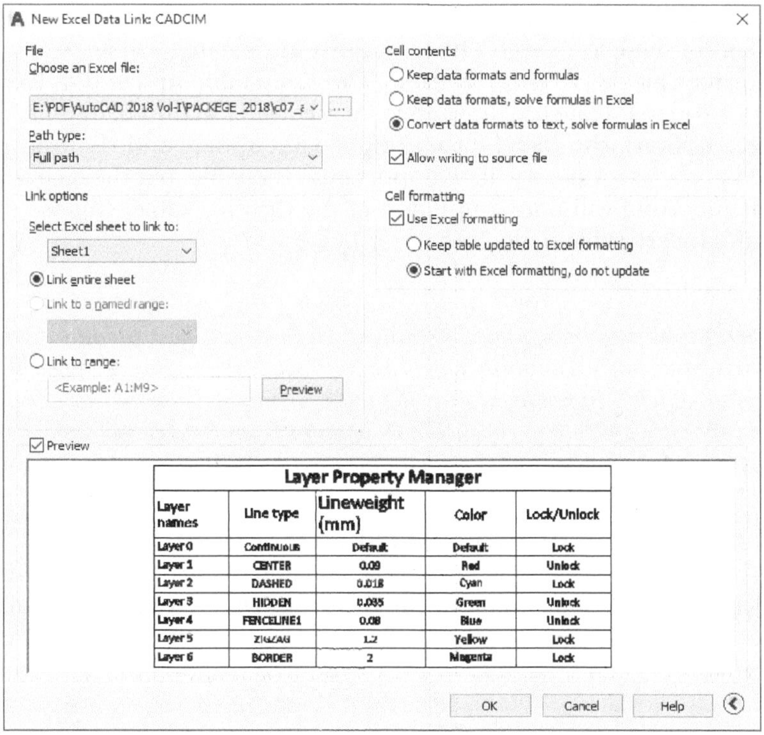

*Figure 7-39 The modified **New Excel Data Link** dialog box*

Choose an Excel file: This drop-down list displays the excel file attached to the current drawing. Choose the **Browse [...]** button to change the excel file to be linked with the current drawing.

Link options Area: In this area, you can specify the part of the excel file to be linked with the drawing. Select the **Link entire sheet** radio button to link the entire worksheet in the form of a table to the drawing. Select the **Link to a named range** radio button to link the already defined name ranges from the excel sheet to the drawing. Select the **Link to range** radio button to enter the range of cells to be included in the data link. Choose the **Preview** button; the preview of the range of cells included in the data link will be displayed. The preview of the attached data from the excel sheet will be displayed in the preview area. Clear the **Preview** check box to disable the preview of the table.

Cell contents Area: The **Keep data formats and formulas** radio button in this area allows you to link the excel file data along with the supported formulas. The **Keep data formats, solve formulas in Excel** radio button allows you to import data from the excel file, but the calculations made using the formulas are done in Excel. The **Convert data formats to text, solve formulas in Excel** radio button in this area is selected by default and lets you import the data of the excel file as text, and the calculations are done in Excel. The **Allow writing to source file** check box is selected by default. This check box enables you to choose the **Download from Source** button from the **Tables** panel of the **Annotate** tab in the **Ribbon** to update the changes made in the drawing table that is linked to the excel sheet.

Cell formatting Area: Select the **Use Excel formatting** check box to import any formatting settings if specified in the excel sheet. Other options in this area will be available only when the **Use Excel formatting** check box is selected. The **Keep table updated to Excel formatting** radio button allows you to update the drawing table according to the changes made in the excel sheet. If you select the **Start with Excel formatting, do not update** radio button, any formatting changes specified in the excel sheet will be imported to the table, but the changes made in the excel sheet after importing will not be updated in the drawing table. Choose the **OK** button twice to display the **Insert Table** dialog box.

Tip

If you have made any changes in the drawing table, choose the ***Upload to Source*** *tool from the* ***Tables*** *panel in the* ***Annotate*** *tab; the changes made in the drawing file will be reflected in the excel sheet that is linked to the drawing table. Similarly, if you have made any changes in the excel file after uploading, choose the* ***Download from Source*** *tool from the* ***Tables*** *panel in the* ***Annotate*** *tab; the changes made in the excel file will be reflected in the drawing file.*

From object data in the drawing (Data Extraction)

To create a table by automatically extracting the data related to the objects created in the current drawing file, select the **From object data in the drawing (Data Extraction)** radio button from the **Insert Table** dialog box and choose the **OK** button; AutoCAD will start the **Data Extraction** wizard that will guide you step-by-step to insert the desired data into the current drawing.

Note

For more information regarding the ***Data Extraction*** *wizard, refer to Chapter 17 (Defining Block Attributes).*

Insertion behavior Area

The options in this area are used to specify the method of placing the table in the drawing. These options are discussed next.

Specify insertion point

This radio button is selected to place the table using the upper left corner of the table. If this radio button is selected and you choose the **OK** button from the **Insert Table** dialog box, you will be prompted to select the insertion point, which is by default the upper left corner of the table. By creating a different table style, you can change the point using which the table is inserted.

Specify window

If this radio button is selected and you choose the **OK** button from the **Insert Table** dialog box, you will be prompted to specify two corners for placing the table. The number of rows and columns in the table will depend on the size of the window you define.

Column and row settings Area

The options in this area are used to specify the number and size of rows and columns. The availability of these options depends on the option selected from the **Insert options** and **Insertion behavior** area. These options are discussed next.

Columns
This spinner is used to specify the number of columns in the table.

Column width
This spinner is used to specify the width of columns in the table.

Data rows
This spinner is used to specify the number of rows in the table.

Row height
This spinner is used to specify the height of rows in the table. The height is defined in terms of lines and the minimum value is one line.

Set cell styles Area
The options in this area are used to assign different cell styles for the rows in the new table. You can assign different cell styles to all the rows of a table. The options in this area are discussed next.

First row cell style
This drop-down list is used to specify a cell style for the first row of the table. By default, the **Title** cell style is selected for the first row of the table.

Second row cell style
This drop-down list is used to specify a cell style for the second row of the table. By default, the **Header** cell style is selected for the second row of the table.

All other row cell styles
This drop-down list is used to specify a cell style for all the other rows of the table. By default, the **Data** cell style is selected for the remaining rows of the table.

After setting the parameters in the **Insert Table** dialog box, choose the **OK** button. Depending on the type of insertion behavior selected, you will be prompted to insert the table. As soon as you complete the insertion procedure, the text window is displayed and you are allowed to enter the parameters in the first row of the table. By default, the first row is the title of the table. After entering the data, press ENTER. The first field of the first column is highlighted, which is the column head, and you are allowed to enter the data in it.

AutoCAD allows you to use the arrow keys on the keyboard to move to the other cells in the table. You can enter the data in the field and then press the arrow key to move to the other cells in the table. After entering the data in all the fields, press ENTER to exit the **Text Formatting** toolbar.

Tip
You can also right-click while entering the data in the table to display the shortcut menu. This shortcut menu is similar to that shown in the ***In-Place Text Editor*** *and can be used to insert field, symbols, text, and so on.*

CREATING A NEW TABLE STYLE

Ribbon: Home > Annotation > Table Style	**Toolbar:** Styles > Table Style
Menu Bar: Format > Table Style	**Command:** TABLESTYLE

To create a new table style, choose the **Table Style** tool from the extended options of the **Annotation** panel in the **Home** tab; the **Table Style** dialog box will be displayed, as shown in Figure 7-40. You can also invoke this dialog box by choosing the inclined arrow of the **Tables** panel in the **Annotate** tab.

To create a new table style, choose the **New** button from the **Table Style** dialog box; the **Create New Table Style** dialog box will be displayed, as shown in Figure 7-41.

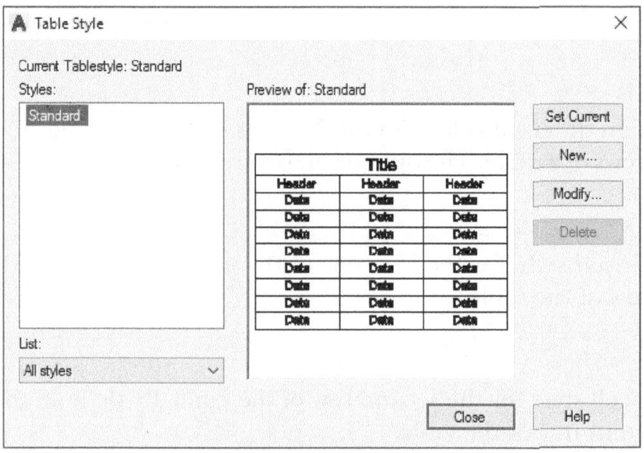

*Figure 7-40 The **Table Style** dialog box*

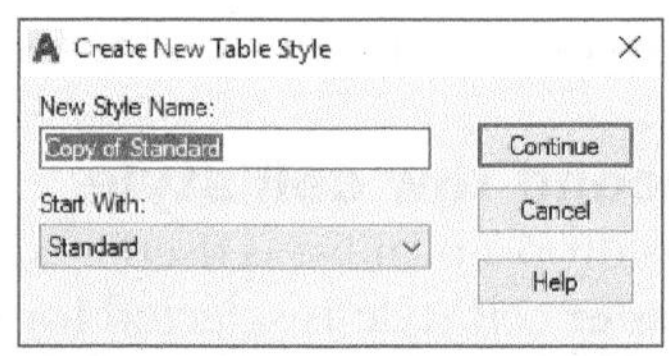

*Figure 7-41 The **Create New Table Style** dialog box*

Enter the name of the table style in the **New Style Name** edit box. Select the style on which you want to base the new style from the **Start With** drop-down list. By default, this drop-down list shows only the **Standard** table style. After specifying the settings, choose the **Continue** button from the **Create New Table Style** dialog box; the **New Table Style** dialog box will be displayed, as shown in Figure 7-42. The options in this dialog box are discussed next.

Starting table Area

The options in this area enable you to select a table in your drawing to be used as reference for formatting the current table style. Once the table is selected, the table style associated with that table gets copied to the current table style and then you can modify it according to your requirement. The **Remove the starting table from this table style** button allows you to remove the initial table style from the current table style. This button is highlighted only when a table style is attached to the current one.

General Area

The **Table direction** drop-down list from the **General** area is used to specify the direction of the table. By default, this direction is **Down**. As a result, the title and headers will be at the top and the data fields will be below them. If you select **Up** from the **Table direction** drop-down list, the title and headers will be at the bottom of this table and the data fields will be on the top of the table.

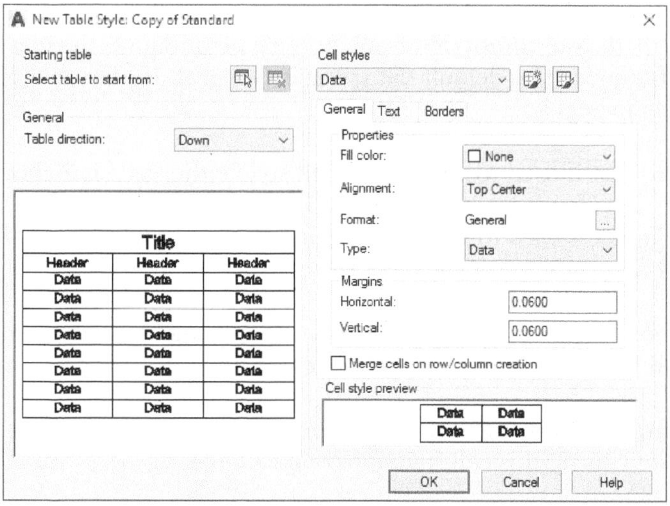

*Figure 7-42 The **New Table Style** dialog box*

Cell styles Area

This area has the options to define a new cell style or to modify the existing ones. The **Cell styles** drop-down list displays the existing cell styles within the table. It also displays the options to create a new cell style or to manage the existing ones. These options are discussed next.

Create new cell style

To create a new cell style, select this option from the **Cell styles** drop-down list. Alternatively, you can choose the **Create a new cell style** button on the right of the **Cell styles** drop-down list. On choosing this button, the **Create New Cell Style** dialog box will be invoked. Next, enter a style name for the new cell style. Select the existing cell style from the **Start With** drop-down list; the settings from the existing style will be used as a reference for the new one to be created. Next, choose the **Continue** button; the new cell style will get added to the **Cell styles** drop-down list. Next, you can modify this new cell style by modifying the options in the **General**, **Text**, and **Borders** tab of the **New Table Style** dialog box.

General Tab

The options in this tab are used to control the general appearance, alignment, and formatting of the table cells. These options are shown in Figure 7-43 and are discussed next.

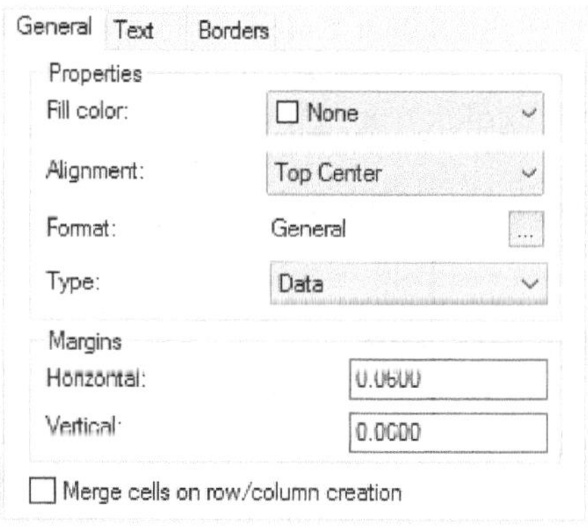

*Figure 7-43 The **General** tab of the **New Table Style** dialog box*

Fill color: This drop-down list is used to specify the fill color for the cells.

Alignment: This drop-down list is used to specify the alignment of the text entered in the cells. The default alignment is top center.

Format: If you choose the **Browse** [...] button available on the right of **Format** option, the **Table Cell Format** dialog box will be displayed. This dialog box is used to specify the data type and format of the data type to be entered in the table. While creating the table, once the data type and format are specified, you cannot enter any other type of data or format without changing or modifying the table style. The default data type is **General**. In this data type, you can enter any alphanumeric characters.

Type: This drop-down list is used to specify the cell style either as a **Label** or **Data**.

Horizontal: This edit box is used to specify the minimum spacing between the data entered in the cells and the left and right border lines of the cells.

Vertical: This edit box is used to specify the minimum spacing between the data entered in the cells and the top and bottom border lines of the cells.

Merge cells on row/column creation: This check box is selected to merge all the new rows and columns created by using this cell style into one cell.

Text Tab

The options in this tab are used to control the display of the text to be written in the cells. These options are shown in Figure 7-44 and are discussed next.

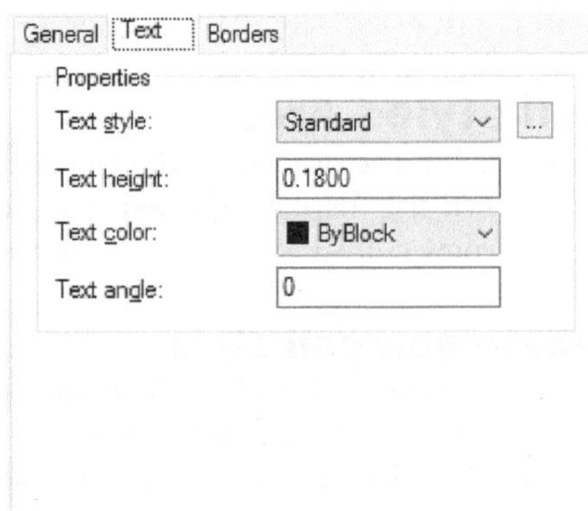

*Figure 7-44 The **Text** tab of the **New Table Style** dialog box*

Text style: This drop-down list is used to select the text style that is used for entering the text in the cells. By default, it shows only **Standard**, which is the default text style. You will learn to create more text styles later in this chapter.

Text height: This edit box is used to specify the height of the text to be entered in the cells.

Text color: This drop-down list is used to specify the color of the text that will be entered in the cells. If you select the **Select Color** option, the **Select Color** dialog box will be displayed, which can be used to select from index color, true color, or from the color book.

Text angle: This edit box is used to specify the slant angle of the text to be entered in the cell.

Borders Tab

The options in this tab are used to set the properties of the border of the table, as shown in Figure 7-45. The line weight and color settings that you specify using this tab will be applied to all borders, outside borders, inside borders, bottom border, left border, top border,

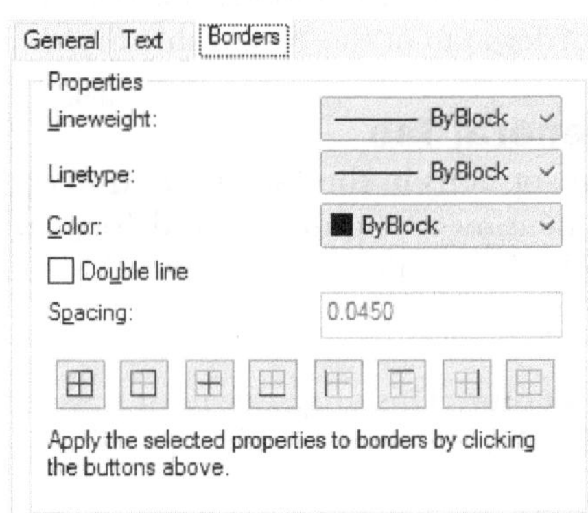

*Figure 7-45 The **Borders** tab of the **New Table Style** dialog box*

right border, or without border depending on which button is chosen from this tab. Select the **Double line** check box to display the borders with double lines. You can also control the spacing between the double lines by entering the gap value in the **Spacing** edit box.

Manage cell styles

To manage cell styles, select this option from the **Cell styles** drop-down list. Alternatively, choose the **Manage Cell Styles** button on the right of the **Cell styles** drop-down list; the **Manage Cell Styles** dialog box will be invoked, as shown in Figure 7-46. This dialog box displays all cell styles in the current table. You can also create a new cell style, delete, or rename an existing cell style. Note that the cell styles; **Title**, **Header**, and **Data** are the default table styles provided in AutoCAD, and they cannot be deleted or renamed.

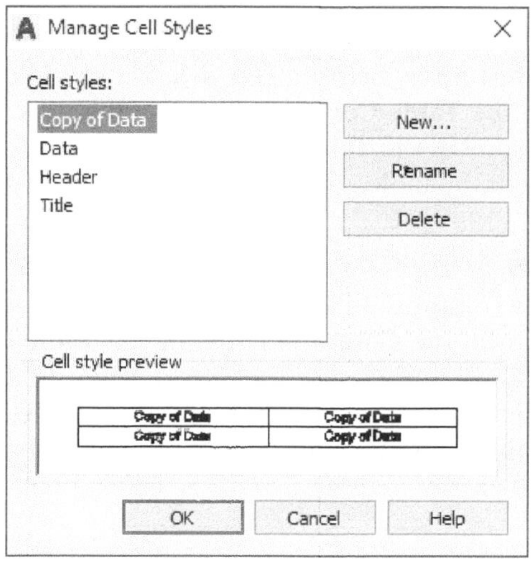

*Figure 7-46 The **Manage Cell Styles** dialog box*

SETTING A TABLE STYLE AS CURRENT

To set a table style as the current style for creating all the new tables, invoke the **Table Style** dialog box by choosing **Table Style** from the extended options of the **Annotation** panel in the **Home** tab. Next, select the table style from the **Styles** list box in the **Table Style** dialog box and choose the **Set Current** button. You can also set a table style current by selecting it from the **Table Style** drop-down list in the **Tables** panel in the **Annotate** tab. This is a convenient method of setting a table style current.

MODIFYING A TABLE STYLE

To modify a table style, choose the **Table Style** tool in the extended options of the **Annotation** panel in the **Home** tab; the **Table Style** dialog box will be displayed. Select the table style from the **Styles** list box in the **Table Style** dialog box and choose the **Modify** button; the **Modify Table Style** dialog box is displayed. This dialog box is similar to the **New Table Style** dialog box. Modify the options in the various tabs and areas of this dialog box and then choose the **OK** button to exit the **Modify Table Style** dialog box.

MODIFYING TABLES

Select any cell in the table; the **Table Cell** tab will be added to the **Ribbon**, as shown in Figure 7-47. The options in the **Table Cell** tab are used to modify the table, insert block, add formulas, and perform other operations.

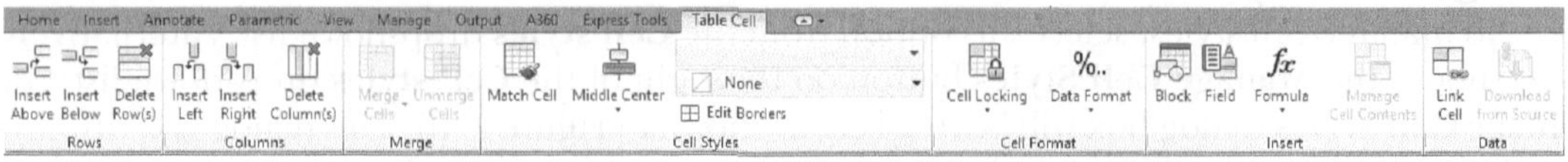

*Figure 7-47 The **Table Cell** tab added to the **Ribbon***

Modifying Rows

To insert a row above a cell, select a cell and choose the **Insert Above** tool from the **Rows** panel in the **Table Cell** tab. To insert a row below a cell, select a cell and choose the **Insert Below** tool from the **Rows** panel in the **Table Cell** tab. To delete the selected row, choose the **Delete Row(s)** tool from the **Rows** panel in the **Table Cell** tab. You can also add more than one row by selecting more than one row in the table.

Modifying Columns

This option is used to modify columns. To add a column to the left of a cell, select the cell and choose the **Insert Left** tool from the **Columns** panel in the **Table Cell** tab. To add a column to the right of a cell, select a cell and choose the **Insert Right** tool from the **Columns** panel in the **Table Cell** tab. To delete the selected column, choose the **Delete Column(s)** tool from the **Columns** panel in the **Table Cell** tab. You can also add more than one column by selecting more than one row in the table.

Merge Cells

This button is used to merge cells. Choose this button; the **Merge Cells** drop-down is displayed. There are three tools available in the drop-down. Select multiple cells using the **SHIFT** key and then choose the **Merge All** tool from the drop-down to merge all the selected cells. To merge all the cells in the row of the selected cell, choose the **Merge By Row** button from the drop-down. Similarly, to merge all cells in the column of the selected cell, choose the **Merge By Column** tool from the drop-down. You can also divide the merged cells by choosing the **Unmerge Cells** button from the **Merge** panel.

Match Cell

This button is used to inherit the properties of one cell into the other. For example, if you have specified **Top Left** cell alignment in the source cell, then using the **Match Cells** button, you can inherit this property to the destination cell. This option is useful if you have assigned a number of properties to one cell, and you want to inherit these properties in some specified number of cells. Choose the **Match Cell** tool from the **Cell Styles** panel in the **Table Cell** tab; the cursor is changed to the match properties cursor and you are prompted to choose the destination cell. Choose the cells to which you want the properties to be inherited and then press ENTER.

Table Cell Styles

This drop-down list displays the pre-existing cell styles or options to modify the existing ones. Select the desired cell style to be assigned to the selected cell. The **Cell Styles** drop-down list also has the options to create a new cell style or manage the existing ones. These options have been discussed earlier in the **Creating a New Table Style** topic.

Edit Borders

Choose the **Edit Borders** button from the **Table Cell** tab; the **Cell Border Properties** dialog box will be displayed, as shown in Figure 7-48. The options in this dialog box are similar to those in the **Border** tab of the **New Table Style** dialog box.

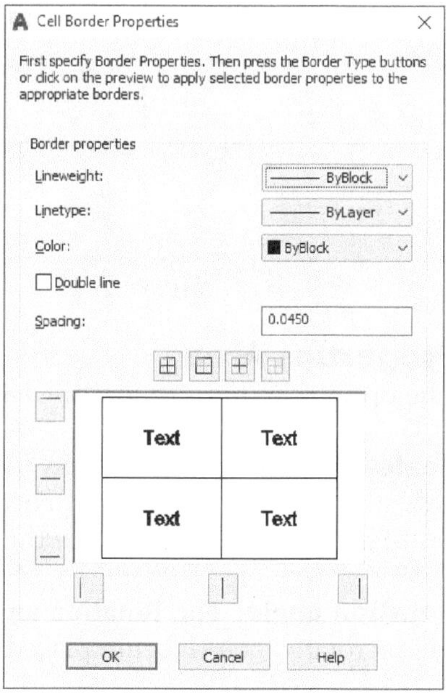

*Figure 7-48 The **Cell Border Properties** dialog box*

Text Alignment

The down arrow with the **Middle-Center** button of the **Cell Styles** panel in the **Ribbon** is used to align the text written in cells with respect to the cell boundary. Choose this button; the **Text Alignment** drop-down will be displayed. Select the desired text alignment from this drop-down; the text of the selected cell will get aligned accordingly.

Cell Locking

This button is used to lock the cells so that they cannot be edited by accident. Select a cell and choose **Cell Locking** from the **Cell Format** panel in the **Table Cell** tab; the **Cell Locking** drop-down list will be displayed. Four options are available in the drop-down list. The **Unlocked** option is chosen by default. Choose the **Content Locked** option to prevent the modification in the selected content of the text, but you can modify the formatting of the text. Choose the **Format Locked** option to prevent the modification in the formatting of the text, but in this case, you can modify the content of the text. Select the **Content and Format Locked** option to prevent the modification of both formatting and content of the text.

Data Format

The display of the text in the cell depends on the format type selected. Choose the **Data Format** to change the format of the text in the cell. On doing so, the **Data Format** drop-down list is displayed. Choose the required format from it. You can also select the **Custom Table Cell Format** option and choose the required format from the **Data type** list box in the **Table Cell Format** dialog box and then choose the **OK** button.

Block

The **Block** tool is used to insert a block inside a selected cell. Choose the **Block** tool from the **Insert** panel; the **Insert a Block in a Table Cell** dialog box will be displayed, refer to Figure 7-49. Enter the name of the block in the **Name** edit box or choose the **Browse** button to locate the destination file of the block. If you have browsed the file path, it will be displayed in the **Path** area. The options available in the **Insert a Block in a Table Cell** dialog box are discussed next.

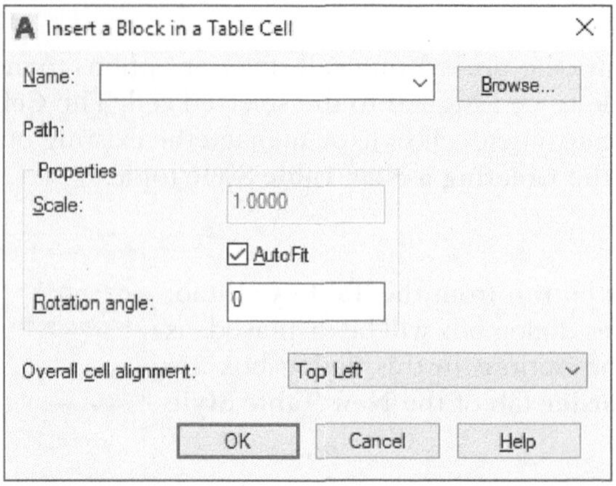

*Figure 7-49 The **Insert a Block in a Table Cell** dialog box*

Properties Area

The options in this area are discussed next.

Scale: This edit box is used to specify the scale of the block. By default, this edit box is not available because the **AutoFit** check box is selected below this drop-down list. Selecting the **AutoFit** check box ensures that the block is scaled such that it fits in the selected cell.

Rotation angle: The **Rotation angle** edit box is used to specify the angle by which the block will be rotated before being placed in the cell.

Overall cell alignment: This drop-down list is used to define the block alignment in the selected cell.

Field

You can also insert a field in the cell. The field contains the data that is associative to the property that defines the field. For example, you can insert a field that has the name of the author of the current drawing. If you have already defined the author of the current drawing in the **Drawing Properties** dialog box, it will automatically be displayed in the field. If you modify the author name and update the field, the changes will automatically be made in the text. When you choose the **Field** button from the **Insert** panel, the **Field** dialog box will be displayed. You can select the field to be added from the **Field names** list box and select the format of the field from the **Format** list box. Choose **OK** after selecting the field and format. If the data in the selected field is already defined, it will be displayed in the text window. If not, the field will display dashes (----).

Formula

Choose the **Formula** tool from the **Insert** panel; a drop-down list is displayed. This drop-down list contains the formulas that can be applied to a given cell. The formula calculates the values for that cell using the values of other cell. In a table, the columns are named with letters (like A, B, C, ...) and rows are named with numbers (like 1, 2, 3, ...). The **TABLEINDICATOR** system variable controls the display of column letters and row numbers. By default, the **TABLEINDICATOR** system variable is set to 1, which means the row numbers and column letters will be displayed when **Text Editor** tab is invoked. Set the system variable to zero to turn off the visibility of row numbers and column letters. The nomenclature of cells is done using the column letters and row numbers. For example, the cell corresponding to column A and row 2 is A2. For better understanding, some of the cells have been labeled accordingly in Figure 7-50.

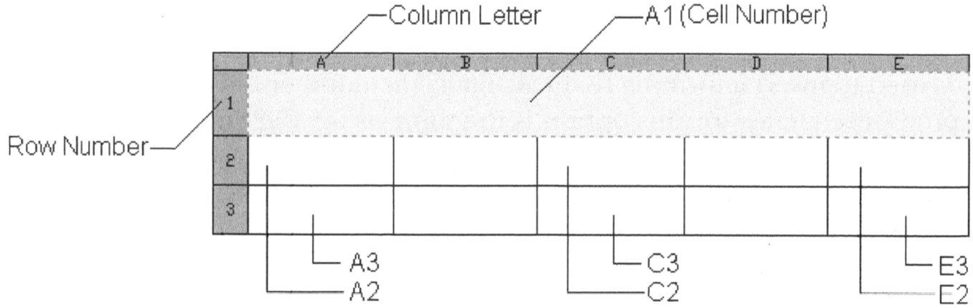

***Figure 7-50** The Table showing nomenclature for Columns, Rows, and Cells*

Formulas are defined by the range of cells. The range of cells is specified by specifying the name of first and the last cell of the range, separated by a colon (:). The range takes all the cells falling between specified cells. For example, if you write A2 : C3, this means all the cells falling in 2nd and 3rd rows, Column A and B will be taken into account. To insert a formula, double click on the cell; **Text Editor** is invoked. You can now write the syntax of the formula in the cell. The syntax for different formulas are discussed later while explaining different formulas. Formulas can also be inserted by using the **Formula** drop-down list. Different formulas available in the **Formula** drop-down list are discussed next.

Sum

The **Sum** option gives output for a given cell as the sum of the numerical values entered in a specified range of cells. Choose the **Sum** option from the **Table Cell > Insert > Formula** drop-down; you will be prompted to select the first corner of the table cell range and then the second corner. The sum of values of all the cells that fall between the selected range will be displayed as the output. As soon as you specify the second corner, the **Text Editor** is displayed and also the formula is displayed in the cell. In addition to the formula, you can also write multiline text in the cell. Choose the **Close Text Editor** tool from the **Close** panel to exit the editor. When you exit the text editor, the formula is replaced by a hash (#). Now, if you enter numerical values in the cells included in the range, the hash (#) is replaced according to the addition of those numerical values. The prompt sequence, when you select the **Sum** option, is given next.

Select first corner of table cell range: *Specify a point in the first cell of the cell range.*
Select second corner of table cell range: *Specify a point in the last cell of the cell range.*

Note

*The syntax for the **Sum** option is: =Sum{Number of the first cell of cell range (for example: A2): Number of the last cell of the cell range (for example: C5)}*

Average

This option is used to insert a formula that calculates the average of values of the cells falling in the cell range. The prompt sequence for this option is the same as for the **Sum** option.

Note

The syntax for the ***Average*** *option is: =Average{Number of the first cell of the cell range (for example: A2): Number of the last cell of the cell range (for example: C5)}*

Count

This option is used to insert a formula that calculates the number of cells falling under the cell range. The prompt sequence for this option is the same as for the **Sum** option.

Note

The syntax for the ***Count*** *option is: =Count{Number of the first cell of cell range (for example: A2): Number of the last cell of cell range (for example: C5)}*

Cell

This option equates the current cell with a selected cell. Whenever there is a change in the value of the selected cell, the change is automatically updated in the other cell. To do so, choose the **Cell** option from **Table Cell > Insert > Formula** drop-down; you will be prompted to select a table cell. Select the cell with which you want to equate the current cell. The prompt sequence for the **Cell** option is given next.

Select table cell: *Select a cell to equate with the current cell.*

Note

The syntax for the ***Cell*** *option is: =Number of the cell.*

Equation

Using this option, you can manually write equations. The syntax for writing the equations should be the same as explained earlier.

Manage Cell Content

The **Manage Cell Content** tool is used to control the sequence of the display of blocks in the cell, if there are more than one block in a cell. Choose the **Manage Cell Contents** tool from the **Insert** panel; the **Manage Cell Content** dialog box will be displayed, as shown in Figure 7-51. The options in the **Manage Cell Content** dialog box are discussed next.

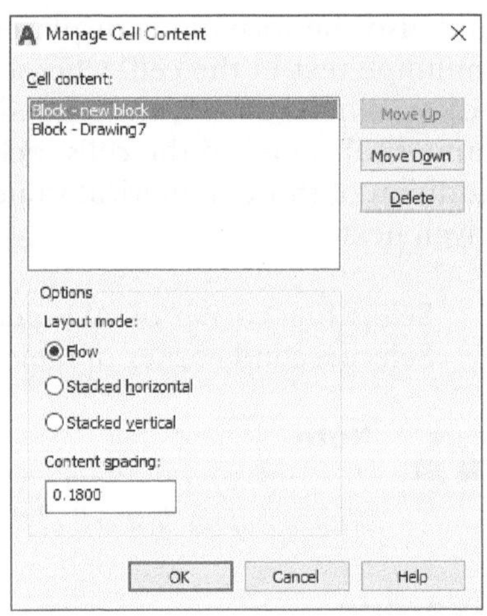

Figure 7-51 The ***Manage Cell Content*** *dialog box*

Cell content Area

This area lists all blocks entered in the cell according to the order of their insertion sequence.

Move Up

This button is used to move the selected block one level up in the display order.

Move Down

This button is used to move the selected block one level down in the display order.

Delete

This button is used to delete the selected block from the table cell.

Options Area

The options in this area are used to control the direction in which the inserted block is placed in the cell. If you select the **Flow** radio button, the direction of placement of the blocks in the cell will depend on the width of the cell. Select the **Stacked horizontal** radio button to place the inserted blocks horizontally. Similarly, select the **Stacked vertical** radio button to place the inserted blocks vertically. You can also specify the gap to be maintained between the two consecutive blocks by entering the desired gap value in the **Content spacing** edit box.

Link Cell

To insert data from an excel sheet into the selected table, choose **Data > Link Cell** from the **Table Cell** tab; the **Select a Data Link** dialog box will be displayed. The options in this dialog box are similar to the **Select a Data Link** dialog box that has been discussed earlier in the "**Inserting Table in the Drawing**" topic of this chapter.

Download from source

If the contents of the attached excel spreadsheet are changed after linking it to a cell, you can update these changes in the table by choosing this button. AutoCAD will inform you about the changes in the content of the attached excel sheet by displaying an information bubble at the lower-right corner of the screen.

Tip

*The **Cut** and **Copy** options can be used to move or copy the content from one cell to another. Using the **Paste** option, you can paste the content that you have cut or copied from one cell to another. Place the cursor on the **Recent Input** option; a flyout containing the recent command inputs will be displayed. Choose the **Remove All Property Overrides** option to restore all the default properties of the table.*

Note

*The options in the **Table Cell** tab are also available in the shortcut menu that is displayed when you select any cell in the table and then right-click on it.*

CREATING TEXT STYLES

Ribbon: Annotate > Text > Text Style (Inclined arrow)
Toolbar: Text > Text Style or Styles > Text Style
Menu Bar: Format > Text Style **Command:** STYLE/ST

By default, the text in AutoCAD is written using the **Standard** text style. This text style is assigned a default text font (*txt.shx*). Another text style that is available is **Annotative**. This text style is also assigned a default text font (*txt.shx*). If you need to write a text using some other fonts and other parameters, you need to use the **Text Editor** tab.

However, it is a tedious job to use the **Text Editor** tab every time to write the text and change its properties. That is why, AutoCAD provides you with an option for modifying the default text style or creating a new text style. After creating a new text, you can make it current. All the texts written after making the new style current will use this style. To create a new text style or modify the default style, left click on the inclined arrow in the **Text** panel of the **Annotate** tab; the **Text Style** dialog box will be displayed, as shown in Figure 7-52.

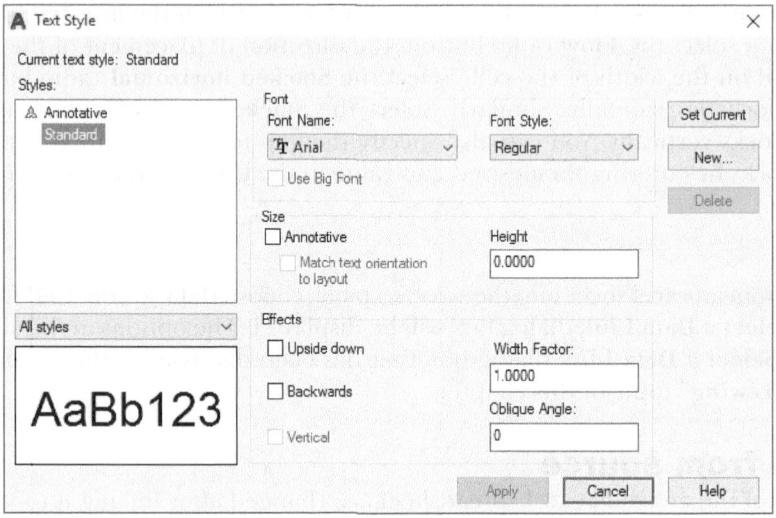

***Figure 7-52** The **Text Style** dialog box*

The **Styles** area displays the styles present in the drawing along with the current style highlighted in blue. An annotative symbol is displayed in front of the annotative text styles. The Style List Filter drop-down list below the **Styles** area is used to specify whether all styles will be displayed or only the styles that have been used in the drawing will be displayed. To create a new style, choose the **New** button from the **Text Style** dialog box; the **New Text Style** dialog box will be displayed, as shown in Figure 7-53. Choose the **OK** button from the dialog box; a new text style with the name and the properties entered in the **Text Style** dialog box will be created. To modify a style, select the style name from the list box and then change the settings by entering new values in the appropriate boxes. You can change the font by selecting a new font from the **Font Name** drop-down list. Similarly, you can change the text height, width, and oblique angle.

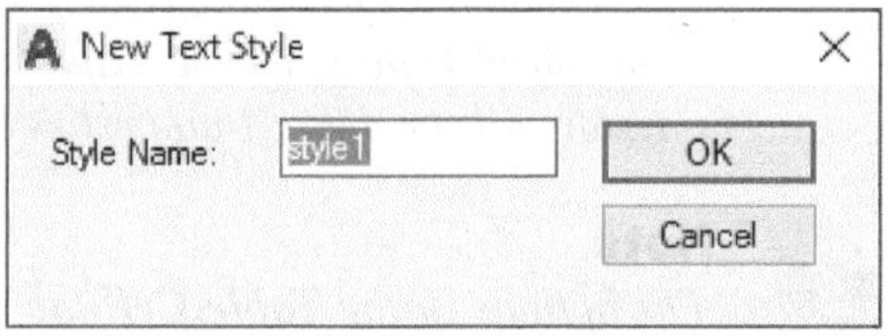

***Figure 7-53** The **New Text Style** dialog box*

Remember that if you have already specified the height of the text in the **Text Style** dialog box, AutoCAD will not prompt you to enter the text height while writing the text using the **Single Line** tool. The text will be created using the height specified in the text style. If you want AutoCAD to prompt you for the text height, specify 0 text height in the dialog box. Select the **Annotative** check box to automate the process of scaling the text height. Annotative texts are defined according to the height of the text to be displayed on the paper. According to the annotation scale set for the spaces, the text will be displayed in the viewports and the model space. Select the **Match text orientation to layout** check box to match the orientation of the text in the paper space viewport with the orientation of the layout.

For **Width Factor**, 1 is the default value. If you want the letters expanded, enter a width factor greater than 1. For compressed letters, enter a width factor less than 1. Similarly, for the **Oblique Angle**, 0 is the default value. If you want the slant of the letters toward the right, the value should be greater than 0; to slant the letters toward the left, the value should be less than 0. You can also force the text to be written upside down, backwards, and vertically by checking their respective check boxes. As you make the changes, you can see their effect in the **Preview** box. After making the desired changes, choose the **Apply** button and then the **Close** button to exit the dialog box. Figure 7-54 shows the text objects with all these settings.

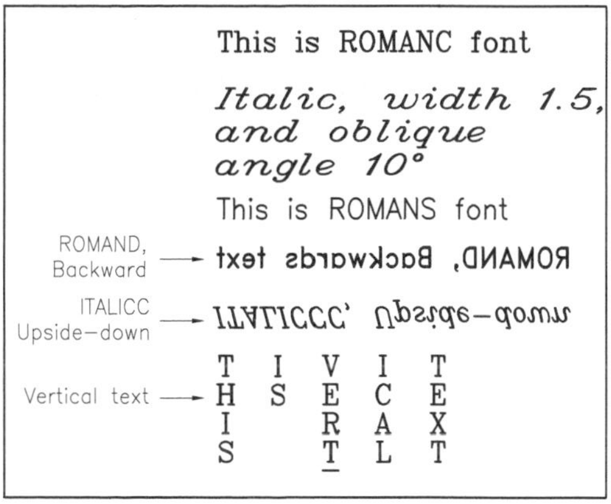

Figure 7-54 *Specifying different features to text style files*

CREATING ANNOTATIVE TEXT

In AutoCAD, you do not need to calculate the text height in advance. While creating the annotative text, if you decide the text height to be displayed on the paper, the current annotation scale will automatically decide the display size of the text in the model space or the paper space viewport. For example, if you want the text to be displayed at a height of 1/4" on the paper, you can define a text style having a Paper Text Height of 1/4". When you add text to a viewport having a scale of 1/4"=1'0", the current annotation scale, which is set as the same scale as of the viewport, automatically scales the text to display appropriately at 12". You can create annotative text by assigning the annotative text style that has been explained earlier.

To write a single line annotative text, choose an annotative type text style from the **Text Style** dialog box and set it as the current text style. The annotative type text style will be displayed with an annotative symbol on its side. Next, enter the text in the drawing using the **Single Line** tool in the command prompt. To write multiline annotative text, enter the **Multiline Text** tool at the command prompt and specify the two opposite corners of the box denoting the width of the multiline text; the text window will be displayed on the screen. You can also select an existing annotative text style from **Text Style** option in the **Text Editor** tab or choose **Annotative** button in the **Style** panel of the **Text Editor** tab to create the annotative multiline text.

The existing non-annotative texts whether it is single line or multiline can also be converted into the annotative text. To do so, select the text object and right-click on it to choose the **Properties** option from the shortcut menu. In the **PROPERTIES** palette below the **Text** area, click on the **Annotative** edit box and select the **Yes** option from the drop-down list.

CHECKING SPELLING

Ribbon: Annotate > Text > Check Spelling	**Toolbar:** Text > Spell Check
Menu Bar: Tools > Spelling	**Command:** SPELL/SP

You can check the spelling of the text in a drawing. The text that can be checked for spelling by using the **Check Spelling** tool are: single line or multiline text, dimension text, text in external references, and block attribute text. To check the spelling in a given text, choose the **Check Spelling** tool from the **Text** panel in the **Annotate** tab; the **Check Spelling** dialog box will be displayed, as shown in Figure 7-55. To start the spell check, choose the **Start** button from the **Check Spelling** dialog box. If there is no spelling mistake in the drawing, the **AutoCAD Message** dialog box with the message '**Spelling check complete**' will be displayed. Choose the **OK** button from the **AutoCAD Message** dialog box to close it. If any spelling error is found in the drawing, AutoCAD will highlight the word and zoom it according to the size of the window so that it is easily visible. The options in the **Check Spelling** dialog box are discussed next.

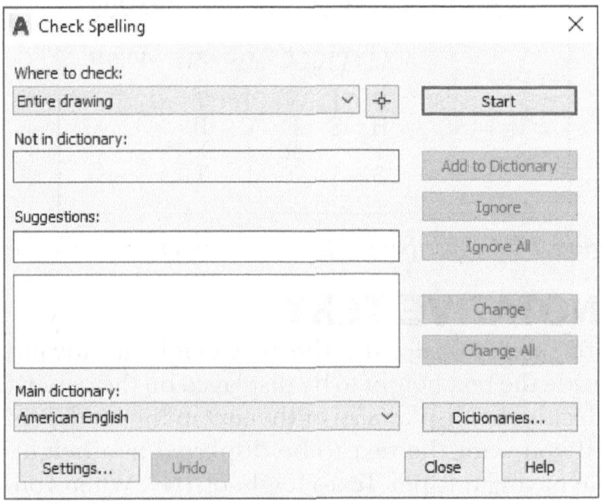

***Figure 7-55** The **Check Spelling** dialog box*

The **Where to check** drop-down list displays three options to specify the portion of the drawing to be spell checked during the spelling check. These options are: **Entire drawing**, **Current space/layout**, and **Selected objects**. You can choose the **Select objects** button to select the text in the drawing to be checked. The **Not in dictionary** box displays the text that is found to be misspelled. The correct spelled alternate words are listed in the **Suggestions** box. The **Main dictionary** drop-down list displays the language options in which you want to check the text.

The **Add to Dictionary** button is used to add the identified misspelled word to the dictionary. The **Ignore** button leaves the identified misspelled words intact. The **Ignore All** button leaves all the identified misspelled words intact. The **Change** button substitutes the present word with the word suggested in the **Suggestions** box. The **Change All** button substitutes all the words that are similar to the currently selected word with the word suggested in the **Suggestions** box. You can also use the MS Word dictionary or any other dictionary for checking spellings. Choose the **Dictionaries** button; the **Dictionaries** dialog box will be displayed, as shown in Figure 7-56. Next, select the **Manage custom dictionaries** option from the **Current custom dictionary** drop-down list; the **Manage Custom Dictionaries** dialog box will be displayed, as shown in Figure 7-57. From this dialog box, you can create a new dictionary, add an existing dictionary, or delete a dictionary from the **Custom dictionaries list**. To add the words listed in the custom dictionary, choose the **Add** button from the **Dictionaries** dialog box. The **Settings** button in the **Check Spelling** dialog box is used to specify the type of text to be checked for spelling in your drawing.

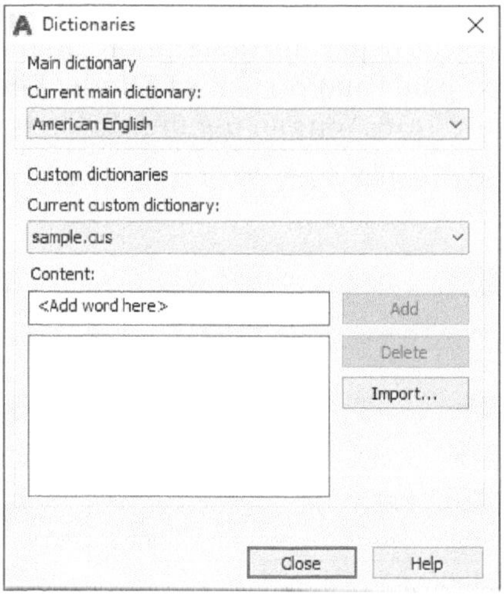

***Figure 7-56** The **Dictionaries** dialog box*

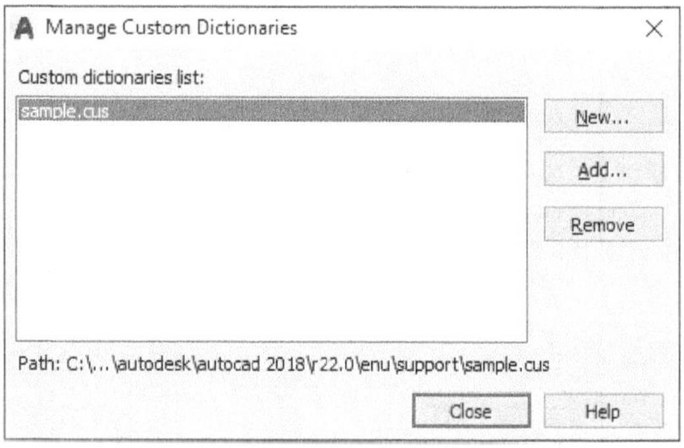

***Figure 7-57** The **Manage Custom Dictionaries** dialog box*

Note

*The dictionaries can also be changed by specifying the name in the **DCTMAIN** or **DCTCUST** system variable.*

TEXT QUALITY AND TEXT FILL

AutoCAD supports **TrueType fonts**. You can use your own TrueType fonts by adding them to the fonts directory. You can also keep your fonts in a separate directory. In such a case, you must specify the location of your fonts directory in the AutoCAD search path.

The resolution and text fill of the TrueType font text is controlled by the **TEXTFILL** and **TEXTQLTY** system variables. If **TEXTFILL** is set to 1, the text will be filled. If the value is set to 0, the text will not be filled. On the screen the text will appear filled, but when it is plotted the text will not be filled. The **TEXTQLTY** variable controls the quality of the TrueType font text. The value of this variable can range from 0 to 100. The default value is 50, which gives a resolution of 300 dpi (dots per inch). If the value is set to 100, the text will be drawn at 600 dpi. The higher the resolution, the more time it takes to regenerate or plot the drawing.

FINDING AND REPLACING TEXT

Ribbon: Annotate > Text > Find Text	**Toolbar:** Text > Find
Menu Bar: Edit > Find	**Command:** FIND

You can use the **Find Text** search box to find and replace a text. The text can be a line text created by the **Single Line** tool, paragraph text created by the **Multiline Text** tool, dimension annotation text, block attribute value, hyperlinks, or hyperlink description. To find a text, enter the text in the **Find Text** search box in the **Text** panel and press ENTER; the **Find and Replace** dialog box will be displayed, as shown in Figure 7-58. You can use this dialog box to perform the following functions:

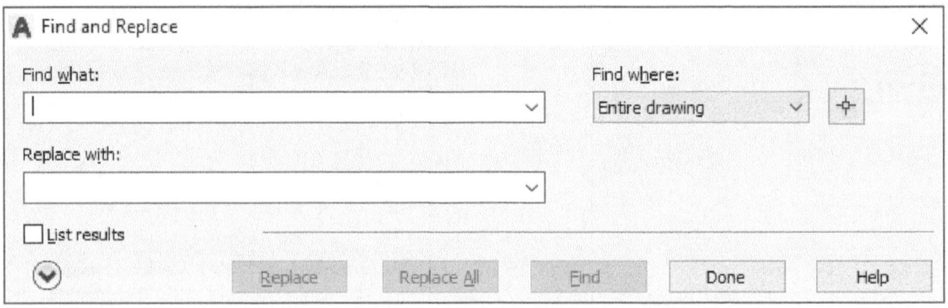

*Figure 7-58 The **Find and Replace** dialog box*

Finding Text

To find a text, enter the text that you want to find in the **Find what** edit box. You can search the entire drawing or confine your search to the selected text. To select the text, choose the **Select objects** button available to the right of the **Find where** drop-down list. The **Find and Replace** dialog box will temporarily be closed and AutoCAD switches to the drawing window. Once you have selected the text, the **Find and Replace** dialog box is displayed again. In the **Find where** drop-down list, you can specify if you need to search the entire drawing or the current selection. Choose the **More Options (Alt+ Shift +>)** button available at the bottom left corner of the **Find and Replace** dialog box; the **Find and Replace** dialog box gets expanded, as shown in Figure 7-59. In this dialog box, you can specify whether to find the whole word and whether to match the case of the specified text. To find the text, choose the **Find** button. The text found along with the surrounding text will be displayed in the **Text** column of the **List results** area, provided the **List results** check box is selected. To find the next occurrence of the text, choose the **Find** button again.

Replacing Text

If you want to replace the specified text with the new text, enter the new text in the **Replace with** edit box. Now, if you choose the **Replace** button, only the found text will be replaced. If you choose the **Replace All** button, all occurrences of the specified text will be replaced by the new text.

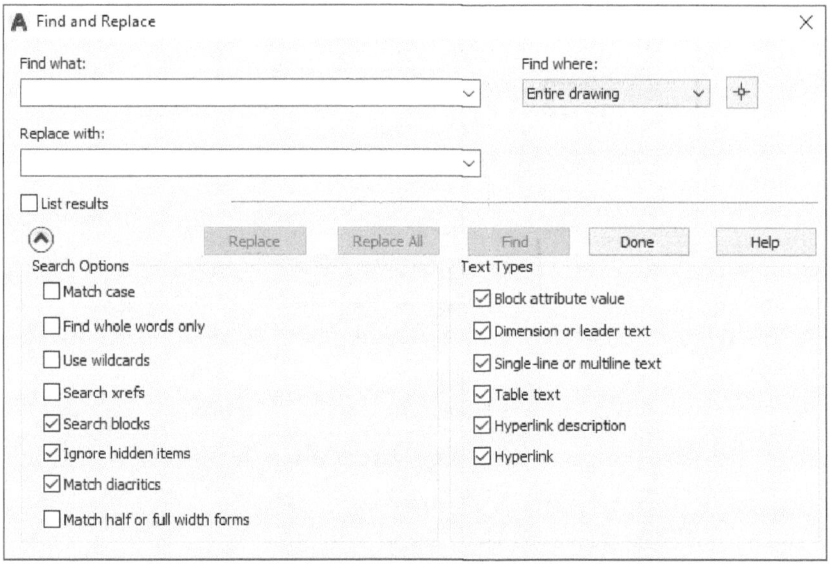

Figure 7-59 *The expanded* ***Find and Replace*** *dialog box*

CREATING TITLE SHEET TABLE IN A SHEET SET

While working with a sheet set, it is recommended that you create a title sheet that has the details about the sheets in the sheet set. You can enter the details about the sheets in the table. The advantage of using a table is that the information in it can be automatically updated if there is a change in the sheet number or name. Also, if a sheet is removed from the current sheet set, you can easily update the table to reflect the change in the sheet set.

To create a table in a sheet set, double-click on any one of the layouts added to the sheet set. Remember that this layout will be the title sheet.

Tip

If the title sheet is displayed at the bottom of the list in the ***SHEET SET MANAGER****, you can drag and move it to the top, below the name of the sheet set. Hold the left mouse button down on the title sheet and drag the cursor upward. Next, release the left mouse button below the name of the sheet set.*

When the title sheet is opened, right-click on the name of the sheet set in the **SHEET SET MANAGER**, and then choose the **Insert Sheet List Table** option from the shortcut menu, as shown in Figure 7-60. Note that this option will not be available, if the model tab is active or if the layout is not from the current sheet set. On choosing the **Insert Sheet List Table** option, the **Sheet List Table** dialog box will be displayed, as shown in Figure 7-61.

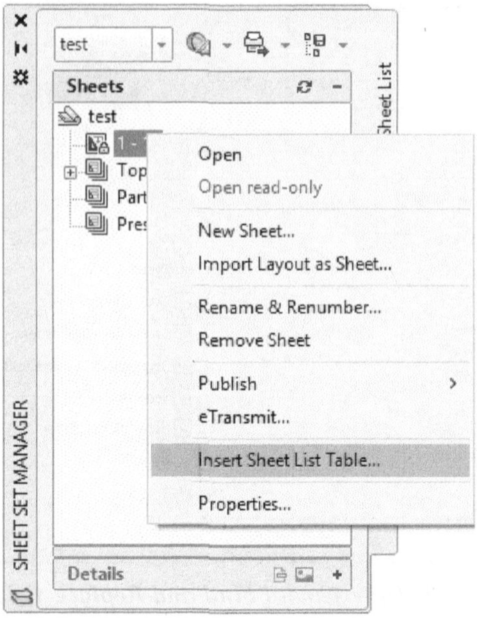

Figure 7-60 *Inserting table in the title sheet using the* ***SHEET SET MANAGER***

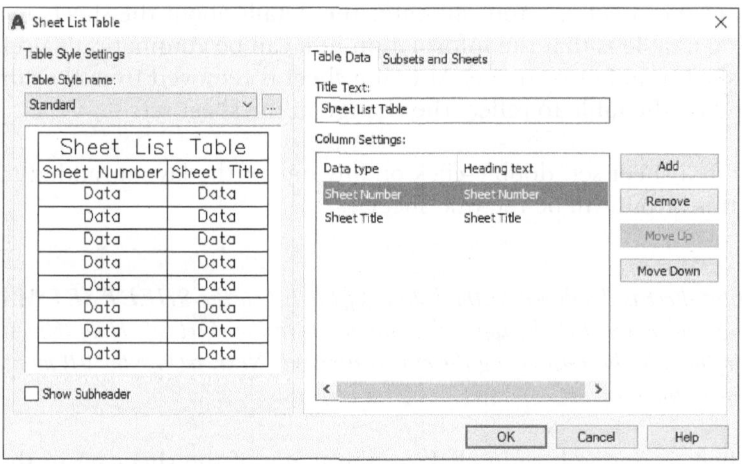

Figure 7-61 *The* ***Sheet List Table*** *dialog box*

Enter the title of the table in the **Title Text** text box in the **Table Data** tab. By default, two rows will be displayed for each subset in the table. This is because there are only two rows displayed in the **Column Settings** area. You can add additional rows by choosing the **Add** button. To change the data type of a row, click on the field in the **Data type** column. The field will be changed into a drop-down list. Select the required data type from this drop-down list. After specifying all the parameters, choose **OK** from the **Insert Sheet List Table** dialog box. The table will be attached to the cursor and you will be prompted to specify the insertion point. Specify the insertion point for the table, the table will be inserted and based on the parameters selected, the sheets are displayed in the table. Figure 7-62 shows a sheet list table inserted in a title sheet.

Sheet List Table	
1	Title Sheet
Main Parts	
2	Base Part
3	Brasses
4	Cap
Fastners	
5	Bolt
6	Nut
7	Washer

Figure 7-62 *Sheet list table*

If any changes are made in the sheet set numbering or any other property of the sheets in the sheet set, you can easily highlight those changes in the sheet list table by updating it. To update the sheet list table, right-click on it, and then choose **Update Table Data Links** from the shortcut menu. The sheet list table is automatically updated.

Self-Evaluation Test

Answer the following questions and then compare them to those given at the end of this chapter:

1. Multiple lines of text can be entered at any desired location in the drawing area by using the __________ tool.

2. Using the __________ justification option of the **Single Line** tool, AutoCAD fits the text width between two given points while keeping the height constant.

3. While writing a text by using the **Multiline Text** tool, the height specified in the **Text Editor** tab does not affect the __________ system variable.

4. You can change the text string in the edit box by using the __________ tool to edit a single line text.

5. You can use the __________ system variable to specify the new font mapping file.

6. You can change single line text to multiline text by using the __________ tool.

7. Tables in AutoCAD are created using the **Tablet** tool. (T/F)

8. An annotative text automatically gets scaled according to the viewport's scale. (T/F)

9. You can insert a block into a table cell. (T/F)

10. The **Standard** text style cannot be used for creating annotative text. (T/F)

11. You can control the height of an individual column separately by choosing the **Manual height** sub-option from **Text Editor > Insert > Columns > Dynamic Columns** of the **Ribbon**. (T/F)

Review Questions

Answer the following questions:

1. Which of the following tools in the **Table Cell** contextual tab is used to inherit the properties from one cell to another?

   (a) **Table Cell Styles** (b) **Match Cell**
   (c) **Link Cell** (d) **Manage Cell Contents**

2. Which of the following text styles is not a default text style in AutoCAD?

   (a) **Standard** (b) **Annotative**
   (c) **Auto text** (d) None of these

3. If you want the text to be displayed at a height of 1/4" on the paper, you can define a text style having a paper height of 1/4". When you add a text to a viewport having a scale of 1/4"=1'0", the current annotation scale, which is set to the same scale as the viewport, automatically scales the text to display approximately at __________.

   (a) 0.1875" (b) 0.375"
   (c) 2.66" (d) 4.8"

4. Which of the following characters in the text window is used to stack the text with a diagonal line without using the **Autostack Properties** dialog box?

   (a) ^ (b) /
   (c) # (d) @

5. Which of the following commands can be used to create a new text style and modify the existing ones?

   (a) **TEXT** (b) **MTEXT**
   (c) **STYLE** (d) **SPELL**

6. The __________ sub-option in the **Formula** flyout of the **Insert** panel in the **Table Cell** contextual tab is used to equate the current cell with the selected cell.

7. The four main text alignment modes are __________, __________, and __________.

8. You can use the __________ tool to write a paragraph text whose width can be specified by defining the __________ of the text boundary.

9. When the **Justify** option is invoked, the user can place the text in one of the __________ types of alignment by choosing the desired alignment option.

10. A text created by using the __________ tool is a single object irrespective of the number of lines it contains.

11. Using the **Multiline Text** tool, the character __________ stacks a text vertically without a line (tolerance stack).

12. If you want to edit text, select it and then right-click such that various editing options __________ in the menu are available.

13. The __________ tool is used to check the spelling of all the texts written in the current drawing.

14. You cannot insert a field by using the **Multiline Text** tool. (T/F)

15. You can add or delete rows and columns from a table by using the **Table Cell** contextual tab. (T/F)

16. The **Single Line** tool does not allow you to see the text on the screen as you type it. (T/F)

17. The columns created by the **Insert > Columns > Dynamic Columns > Auto height** of the **Text Editor** tab are equal in size. (T/F)

Exercise 2 — Text

Write the text, shown in Figure 7-63, on the screen. Use the text justification that will produce the text as shown in the drawing. Assume a value for text height. Use the **PROPERTIES** palette to change the text, as shown in Figure 7-64.

Figure 7-63 *Drawing for Exercise 2*

Figure 7-64 *Drawing after changing the text*

Exercise 3 *Text Style*

Write the text on the screen, as shown in Figure 7-65. First, you must define new text styles by using the **STYLE** command with the attributes shown in the figure. The text height is 0.25 units.

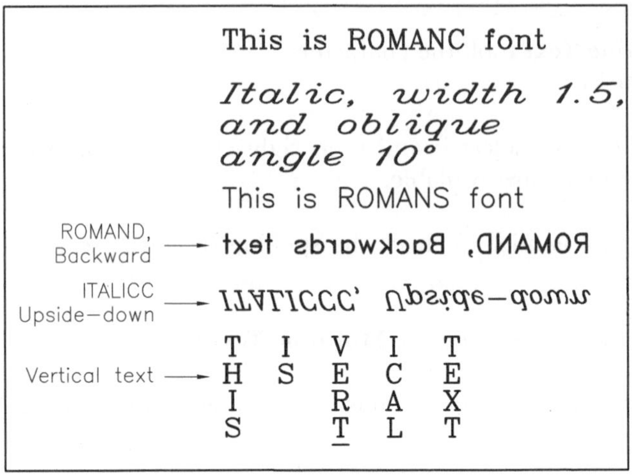

Figure 7-65 *Drawing for Exercise 3*

Exercise 4

Draw the sketch shown in Figure 7-66 using the draw, edit, and display commands. Do not dimension the drawing.

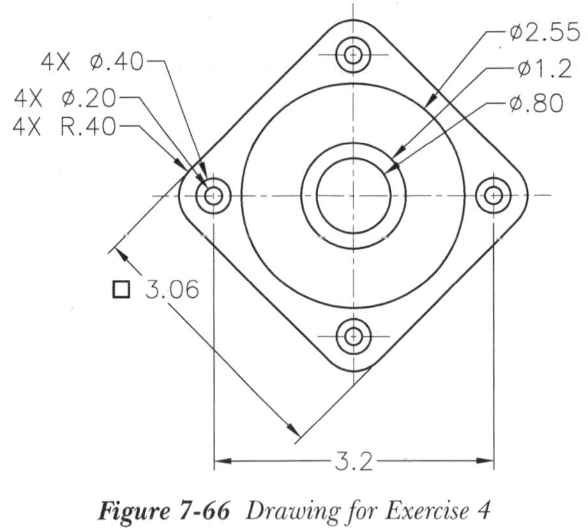

Figure 7-66 *Drawing for Exercise 4*

Exercise 5 Mirror

Draw the sketches shown in Figure 7-67 and Figure 7-68. Use the **Mirror** tool to duplicate the features that are identical. Do not dimension the drawing.

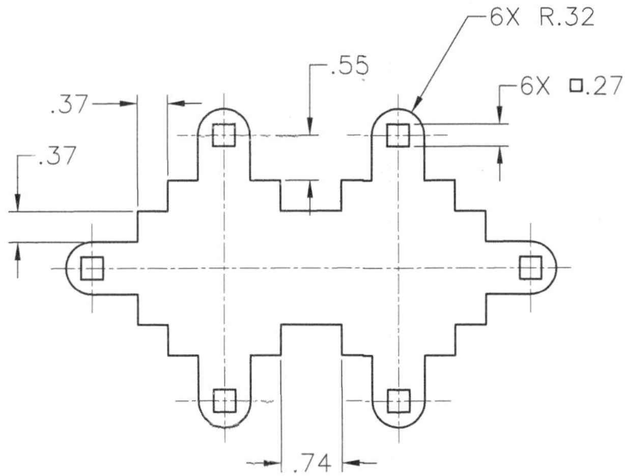

Figure 7-67 *Drawing for Exercise 5*

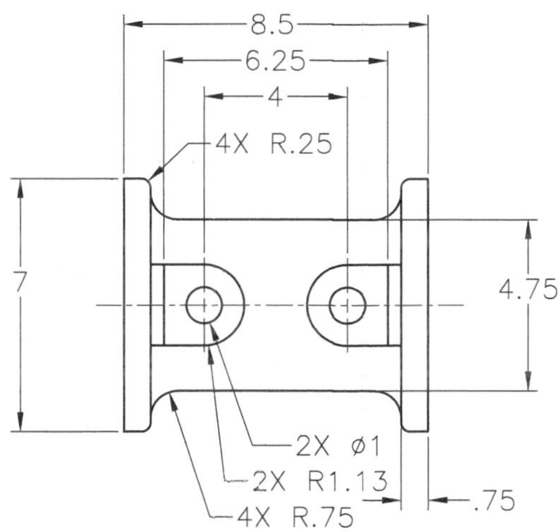

Figure 7-68 *Drawing for Exercise*

Exercise 6

Draw Figure 7-69. Do not dimension the drawing.

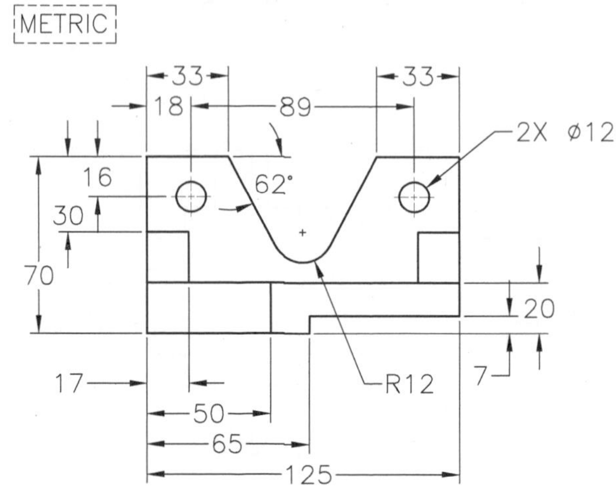

Figure 7-69 *Drawing for Exercise 6*

Problem-Solving Exercise 1

Draw the sketch shown in Figure 7-70 using the draw, edit, and display commands. Assume the missing dimensions. Do not dimension the drawing.

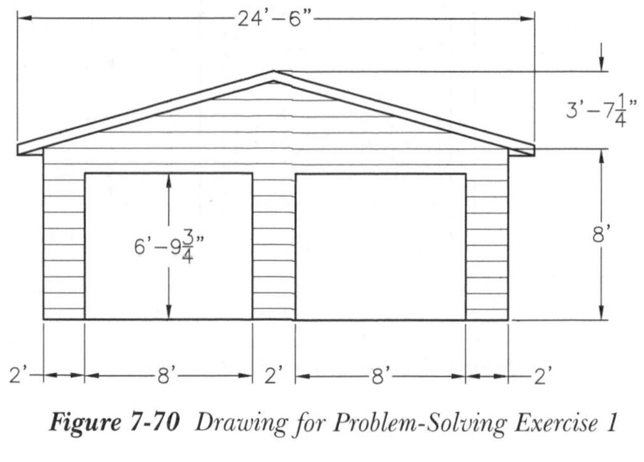

Figure 7-70 *Drawing for Problem-Solving Exercise 1*

Problem-Solving Exercise 2

Draw Figure 7-71 using the drawing, editing, and displaying tools of AutoCAD. Also, add text to the drawing. Assume the missing dimensions. Do not dimension the drawing.

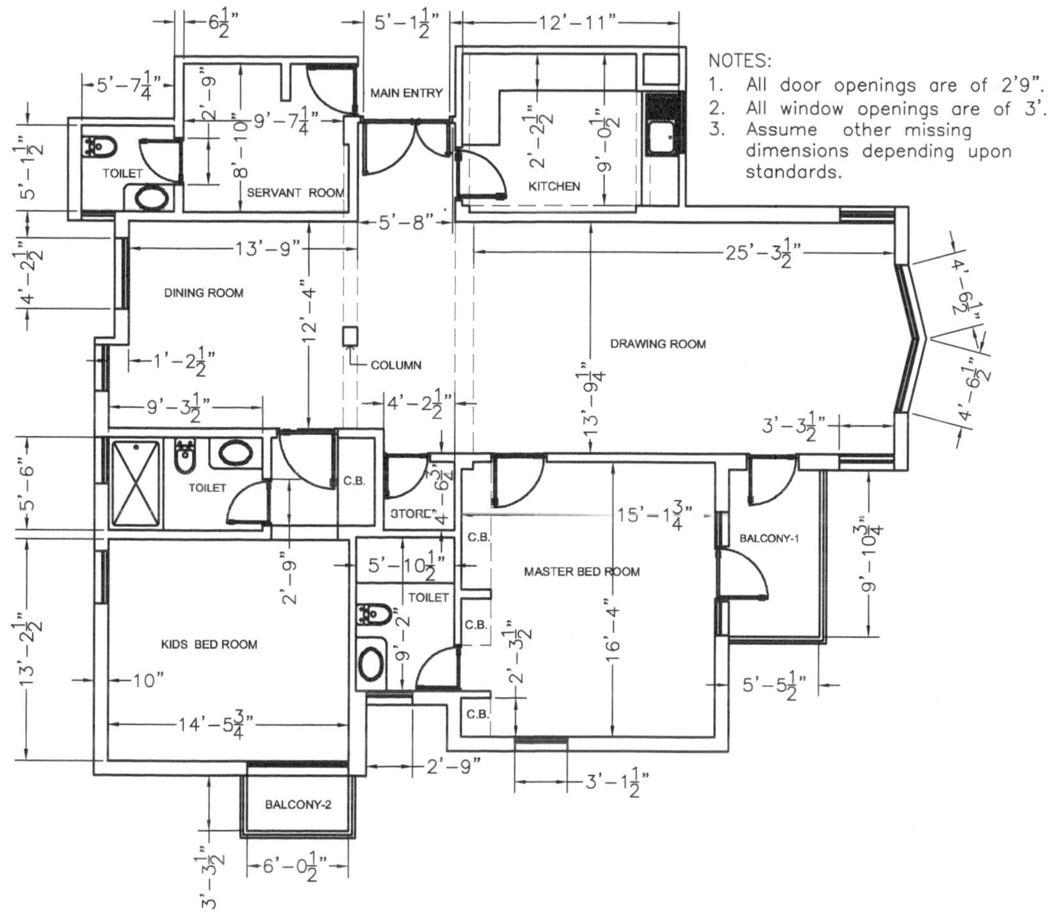

Figure 7-71 Drawing for Problem-Solving Exercise 2

Problem-Solving Exercise 3

Draw Figure 7-72 by using the **Manufacturing Metric** template. Do not dimension the drawing.

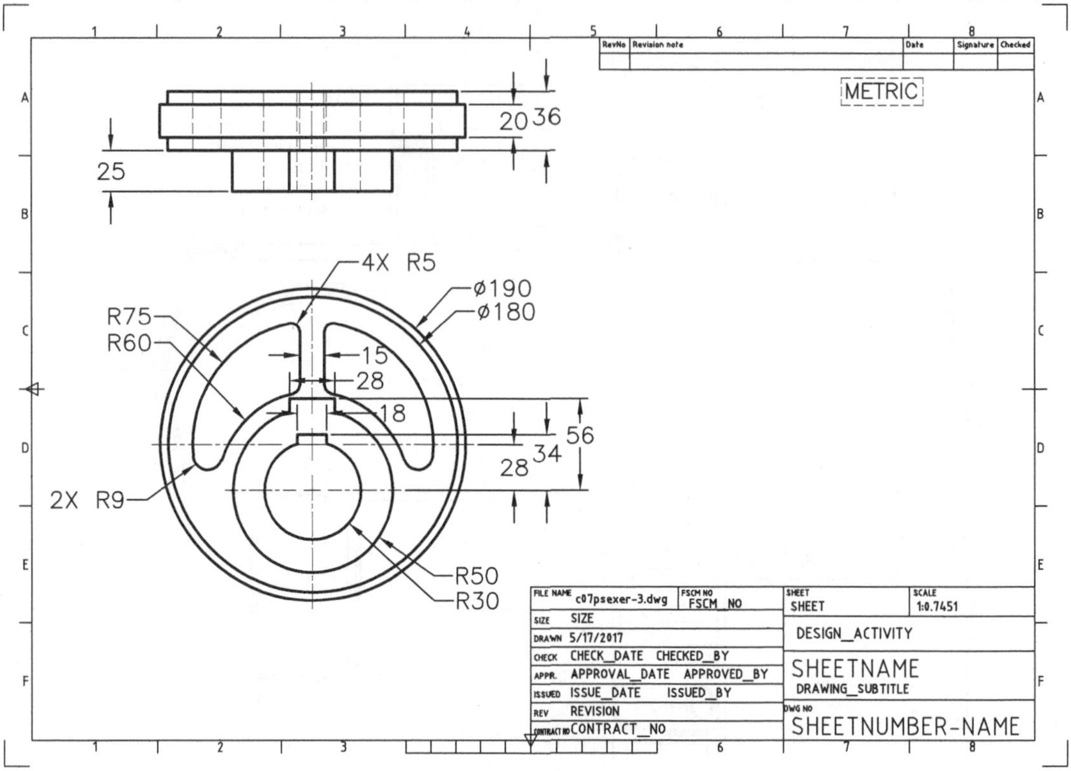

Figure 7-72 Drawing for Problem-Solving Exercise 3

Answers to Self-Evaluation Test

1. **Single Line**, **2.** **Fit**, **3.** **TEXTSIZE**, **4.** **Edit**, **5.** **FONTMAP**, **6.** **Combine Text**, **7.** F, **8.** T, **9.** T, **10.** F, **11.** T

Chapter 8

Basic Dimensioning, Geometric Dimensioning, and Tolerancing

Learning Objectives

After completing this chapter, you will be able to:

- *Understand the need of dimensioning in drawings*
- *Understand fundamental dimensioning terms*
- *Apply the associative and annotative dimensioning*
- *Use the Quick Dimension option for quick dimensioning*
- *Create various types of dimensions in a drawing*
- *Create center marks and centerlines*
- *Attach leaders to objects*
- *Attach and modify multileaders*
- *Use geometric tolerancing, feature control frames, and characteristic symbols*
- *Combine geometric characteristics and create composite position tolerancing*
- *Use the projected tolerance zone*
- *Use feature control frames with leaders*

Key Terms

- *Associative Dimensions*
- *Definition Points*
- *Annotative Dimensions*
- *Dimension Break*
- *Center Marks and Centerlines*
- *Inspection Dimensions*
- *Leaders*
- *Multileaders*
- *Geometric Tolerance*
- *Complex Feature Control Frames*
- *Projected Tolerance Zone*

NEED FOR DIMENSIONING

To make designs more informative and practical, a drawing must convey more than just the graphic picture of a product. To manufacture an object, the drawing of that object must contain size descriptions such as the length, width, height, angle, radius, diameter, and location of features. These informations are added to the drawing by dimensioning. Some drawings also require information about tolerances with the size of features. The information conveyed through dimensioning are vital and often as important as the drawing itself. With the advancement in computer-aided design/drafting and computer-aided manufacturing, it has become mandatory to draw part to actual size so that dimensions reflect the actual size of features. At times, it may not be necessary to draw the object of the same size as the actual object would be, but it is absolutely essential that the dimensions be accurate. Incorrect dimensions will lead to manufacturing errors.

By dimensioning, you not only give the size of a part, but also give a series of instructions to a machinist, an engineer, or an architect. The way the part is positioned in a machine, the sequence of machining operations, and the location of various features of the part depend on how you dimension the part. For example, the number of decimal places in a dimension (2.000) determines the type of machine that will be used to do that machining operation. The machining cost of such an operation is significantly higher than for a dimension that has only one digit after the decimal (2.0). Similarly, whether a part is to be forged or cast, the radii of the edges, and the tolerance you provide to these dimensions determine the cost of the product, the number of defective parts, and the number of parts you get from a single die.

DIMENSIONING IN AutoCAD

The objects that can be dimensioned in AutoCAD range from straight lines to arcs. The dimensioning tools provided by AutoCAD can be classified into four categories:

Dimension Drawing tools
Dimension Style tools
Dimension Editing tools
Dimension Utility tools

While dimensioning an object, AutoCAD automatically calculates the length of the object or the distance between two specified points. Also, settings such as the gap between the dimension text and the dimension line, the space between two consecutive dimension lines, arrow size, and text size are maintained and used when the dimensions are being generated for a particular drawing. The generation of arrows, lines (dimension lines, extension lines), and other objects that form a dimension is automatically performed by AutoCAD to save the user's time. This also results in uniform drawings. However, you can override the default measurements computed by AutoCAD and change the settings of various standard values. The modification of dimensioning standards can be achieved through the dimension variables.

The dimensioning functions offered by AutoCAD provide you with extreme flexibility in dimensioning by letting you dimension various objects in a variety of ways. This is of great help because different industries, such as architectural, mechanical, civil, or electrical have different standards for the placement of dimensions.

FUNDAMENTAL DIMENSIONING TERMS

Before studying AutoCAD's dimensioning tools, it is important to know and understand various dimensioning terms that are common to linear, angular, radius, diameter, and ordinate dimensioning. Figure 8-1 and Figure 8-2 show various dimensioning parameters.

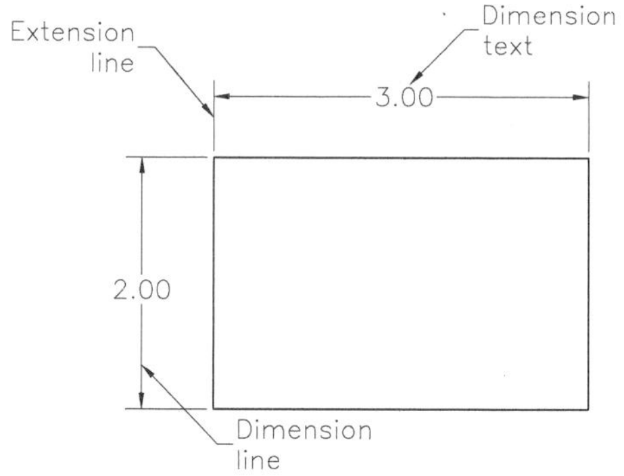

Figure 8-1 *Various dimensioning parameters*

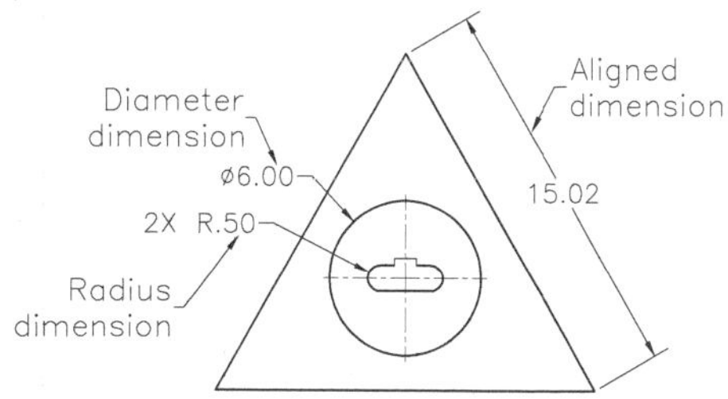

Figure 8-2 *Various dimensioning parameters*

Dimension Line

The dimension line indicates the distance or the angle being measured. Usually, this line has arrows at both ends, and the dimension text is placed along the dimension line. By default, the dimension line is drawn between the extension lines, refer to Figure 8-1 and Figure 8-2. If the dimension line does not fit inside, two short lines with arrows pointing inward are drawn outside the extension lines. The dimension line for angular dimensions (which are used to dimension angles) is an arc. You can control the positioning and various other features of the dimension lines by setting the parameters in the dimension styles. (The dimension styles are discussed in Chapter 10.)

Dimension Text

The dimension text is a text string that reflects the actual measurement (dimension value) between the selected points as calculated by AutoCAD. You can accept the value that AutoCAD returns or enter your own value. In case you use the default text, AutoCAD can be supplied with instructions to append the tolerances to it. Also, you can attach prefixes or suffixes of your choice to the dimension text.

Arrowheads

An arrowhead is a symbol used at the end of a dimension line (where dimension lines meet the extension lines). Arrowheads are also called terminators because they signify the end of the dimension line. Since drafting standards differ from company to company, AutoCAD allows you to draw arrows, oblique, closed arrows, open arrows, dots, right angle arrows, or user-defined blocks, refer to Figure 8-3. The user-defined blocks at the two ends of the dimension line can be customized to your requirements. The size of the arrows, tick oblique marks, user blocks, and so on can be regulated by using the dimension variables.

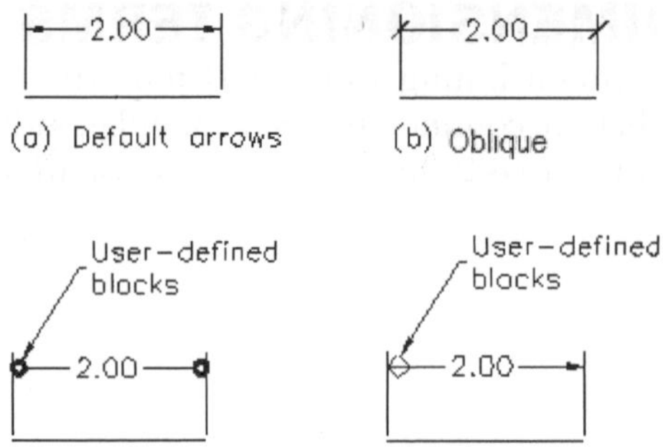

Figure 8-3 *Using arrows, oblique marks, and user-defined blocks*

Extension Lines

Extension lines are drawn from the object measured to the dimension line, as shown in Figure 8-4. These lines are also called witness lines. Extension lines are used in linear and angular dimensioning. Generally, extension lines are drawn perpendicular to the dimension line. However, you can make extension lines inclined at an angle by choosing the **Oblique** tool from the **Dimensions** panel of the **Annotate** tab. Alternatively, you can choose the **Dimension Edit** tool from the **Dimension** toolbar. AutoCAD also allows you to suppress either one or both extension lines in a dimension, refer to Figure 8-5. You can insert breaks in a dimension or an extension line if they intersect other geometric objects or dimension entities. You can also control various other features of the extension lines by setting parameters in dimension styles. (Dimension styles are discussed in Chapter 10.)

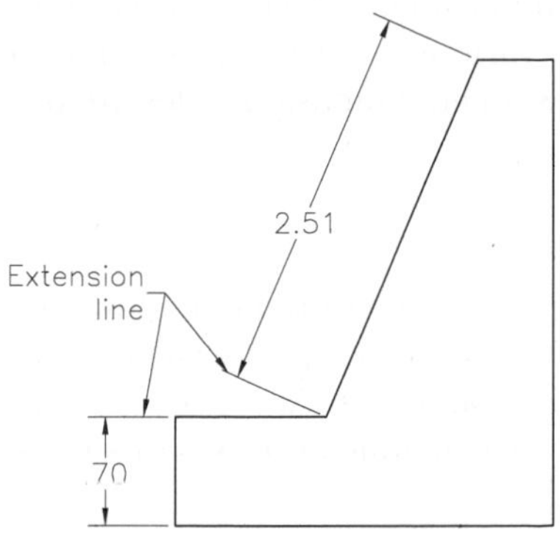

Figure 8-4 *Extension lines*

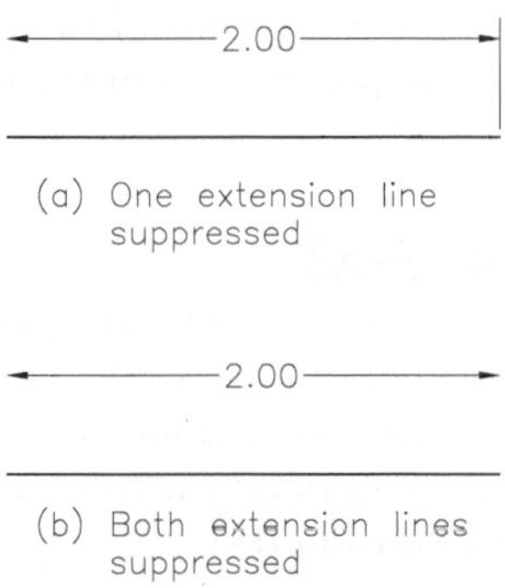

Figure 8-5 *Extension line suppressed*

Leader

A leader is a line that stretches from the dimension text to the object being dimensioned. Sometimes the text for dimensioning and other annotations do not adjust properly near the object. In such cases, you can use a leader and place the text at the end of the leader line. For example, the circle shown in Figure 8-6 has a keyway slot that is too small to be dimensioned. In this situation, a leader can be drawn from the text to the keyway feature. Also, a leader can be used to attach annotations such as part numbers, notes, and instructions to an object. You can also draw multileaders that are used to connect one note to different places or many notes to one place.

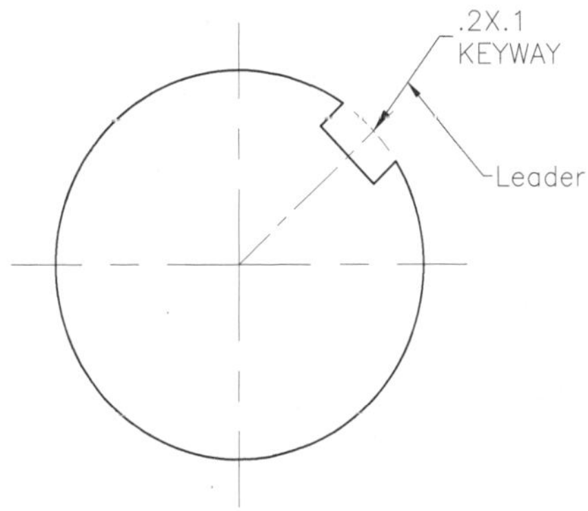

Figure 8-6 *Leader used to attach annotation*

Center Mark and Centerlines

The center mark is a cross mark that represents the center point of a circle or an arc. Centerlines are mutually perpendicular lines that pass through the center of a circle/arc and intersect the circumference of the circle/arc. A center mark or a centerline is automatically drawn when you dimension a circle or an arc, refer to Figure 8-7. The length of center mark and the extension of centerline beyond the circumference of circle are determined by the value assigned to the **DIMCEN** dimension variable. You can toggle between the center mark and the centerlines by entering a positive and a negative value respectively for the **DIMCEN** variable. Alternatively, you can use the **Dimension Style Manager** dialog box to toggle between the center mark and the centerlines. This will be discussed in detail in Chapter 10.

Alternate Units

With the help of alternate units, you can generate dimensions for two systems of measurement at the same time, as shown in Figure 8-8. For example, if the dimensions are in inches, you can use the alternate units dimensioning facility to append metric dimensions to the dimensions (the process of controlling the alternate units through the dimension variables is discussed in Chapter 10).

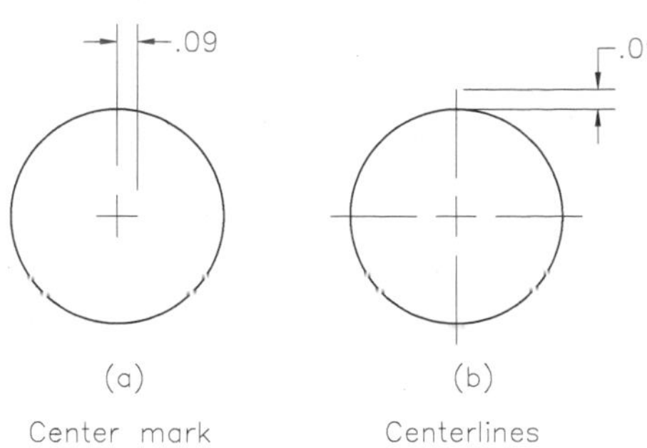

Figure 8-7 *Center mark and centerlines*

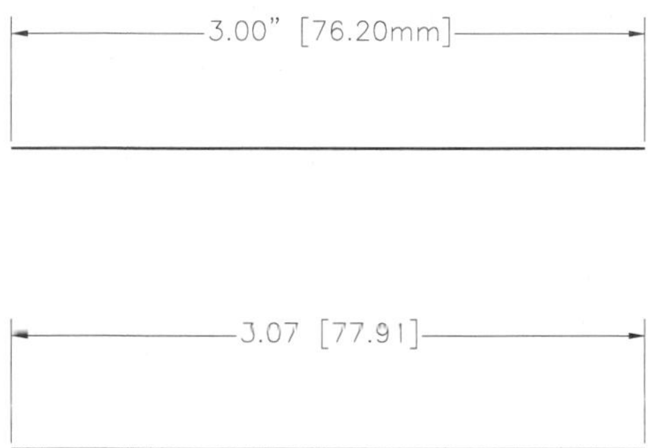

Figure 8-8 *Using alternate units for dimensioning*

Tolerances

Tolerance is the amount by which the actual dimension can vary, refer to Figure 8-9. AutoCAD can attach the plus/minus tolerances to the dimension text (actual measurement computed by AutoCAD). This is also known as deviation tolerance. The plus and minus tolerances that you specify can be same or different. You can use the dimension variables to control the tolerance feature (these variables are discussed in Chapter 10).

Limits

Instead of appending tolerances to dimension text, you can apply tolerances to the measurement itself, refer to Figure 8-10. Once you define tolerances, AutoCAD automatically calculates the upper and lower limit values of the dimension. These values are then displayed as a dimension text.

For example, if the actual dimension as computed by AutoCAD is 2.6105 units and the tolerance values are +0.025 and -0.015, the upper and lower limits will be 2.6355 and 2.5955. After calculating the limits, AutoCAD will display them as a dimension text, as shown in Figure 8-10. The dimension variables that control the limits are discussed in Chapter 10.

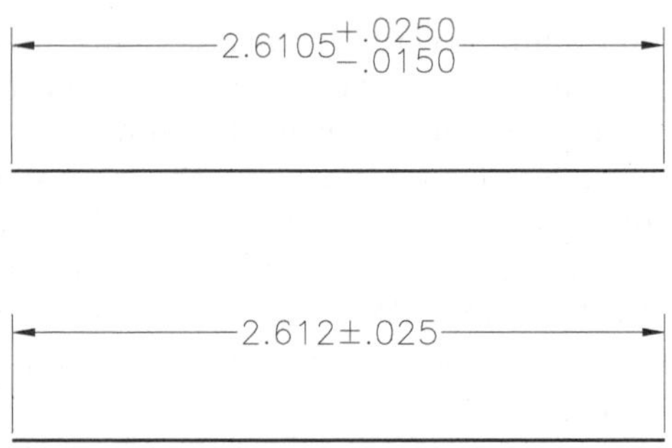

Figure 8-9 Using tolerances with dimensions

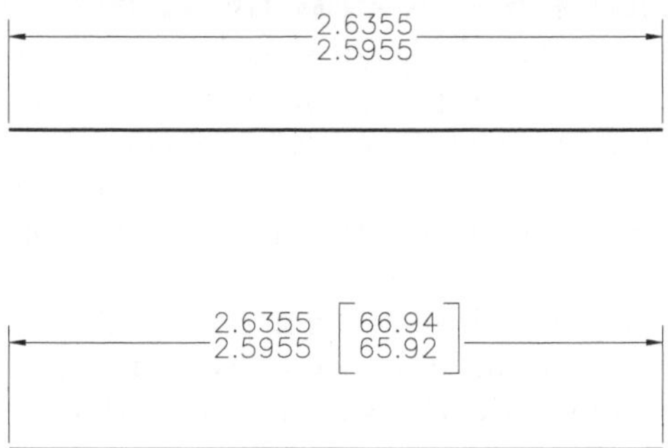

Figure 8-10 Using limits with dimensions

ASSOCIATIVE DIMENSIONS

The Associative dimensioning is a method of dimensioning in which the dimension is associated with the object that is dimensioned. In other words, the dimension is influenced by the changes in the size of the object. In the earlier releases of AutoCAD, the dimensions were not truly associative but were related to the objects being dimensioned by definition points on the DEFPOINTS layer. To cause the dimension to be associatively modified, these definition points had to be adjusted along with the object being changed. If, for example, you use the **Scale** tool to change an object's size and select the object, the dimensions will not be modified. If you select the object and its defpoints (using the Crossing selection method), then the dimension will be modified. If the dimensions are associated to the object and the object changes its size, the dimensions will also change automatically. With the introduction of the true associative dimensions, there is no need to select the definition points along with the object. This eliminates the use of definition points for updating the dimensions.

The values and location of the associative dimensions are updated automatically if the value or location of the object is modified. For example, if you edit an object using simple editing operations such as breaking an object using the **Break** tool, then the true associative dimension will be modified automatically. The dimensions can be converted into the true associative dimensions using the **Reassociate** tool in the **Dimensions** panel of the **Annotate** tab to reassociate the dimension. The association of the dimensions with the objects can be removed using the **DIMDISASSOCIATE** command. Both these commands will be discussed later in this chapter.

The dimensioning variable **DIMASSOC** controls the associativity of dimensions. The default value of this variable is **2** which means the dimensions are associative. When the value is **1**, the dimensions placed are non-associative. When the **DIMASSOC** is turned off (value of this variable is **0**), then the dimension will be placed in the exploded format. This means that the dimensions will now be placed as a combination of individual arrowheads, dimension lines, extension lines, and text. Also note that the exploded dimensions cannot be associated to any object.

DEFINITION POINTS

Definition points are the points drawn at the positions used to generate a dimension object. The definition points are used by the dimensions to control their updating and rescaling. AutoCAD draws these points on a special layer called **Defpoints**. These points are not plotted by the plotter because AutoCAD does not plot any object on the **Defpoints** layer. If you explode a dimension (which is as good as turning **DIMASSOC** off), the definition points are converted to point objects on the **Defpoints** layer. In Figure 8-11, the small circles indicate the definition points for different objects.

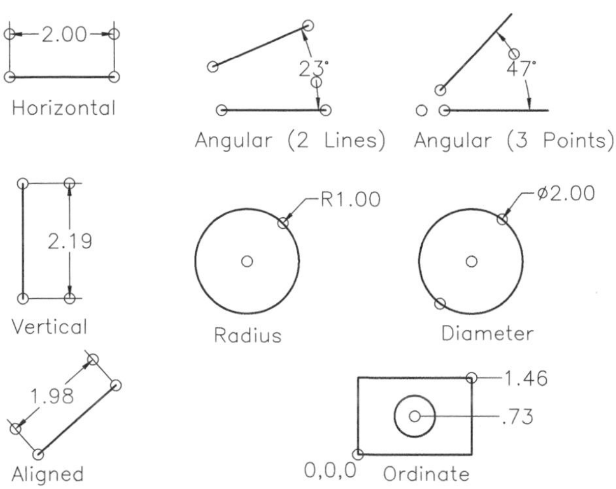

Figure 8-11 *Definition points of linear, radial, angular, and ordinate dimensions*

The definition points for linear dimensions are the points used to specify the extension lines and the point of intersection of the first extension line and the dimension line. The definition points for the angular dimension are the endpoints of the lines used to specify the dimension and the point used to specify the dimension line arc. For example, for a three-point angular dimension, the definition points are the extension line endpoints, angle vertex, and the point used to specify the dimension line arc.

The definition points for the radius dimension are the center point of the circle or arc, and the point where the arrow touches the object. The definition points for the diameter dimension are the points where the arrows touch the circle. The definition points for the ordinate dimension are the UCS origin, feature location, and leader endpoint.

Note

In addition to the definition points just mentioned, the middle point of the dimension text serves as the definition point for all types of dimensions.

ANNOTATIVE DIMENSIONS

When all the elements of a dimension such as text, spacing, and arrows get scaled according to the specified annotation scale, it is known as Annotative Dimension. They are created in the drawing by assigning annotative dimension styles to them. You can also change the non-annotative dimensions to annotative by changing their **Annotative** property to **Yes** in the **PROPERTIES** palette.

SELECTING DIMENSIONING TOOLS

AutoCAD provides the following fundamental dimensioning types:

Quick dimensioning	Linear dimensioning	Diameter dimensioning
Radius dimensioning	Angular dimensioning	Ordinate dimensioning
Arc Length dimensioning	Aligned dimensioning	Jogged dimensioning

Figure 8-12 and Figure 8-13 show various fundamental dimension types.

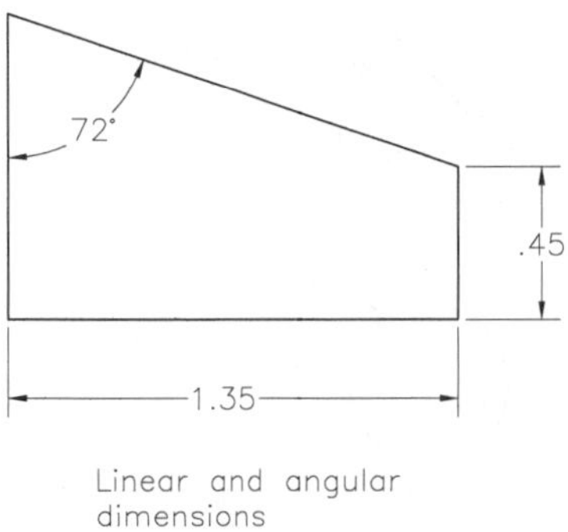

Figure 8-12 Linear and angular dimensions

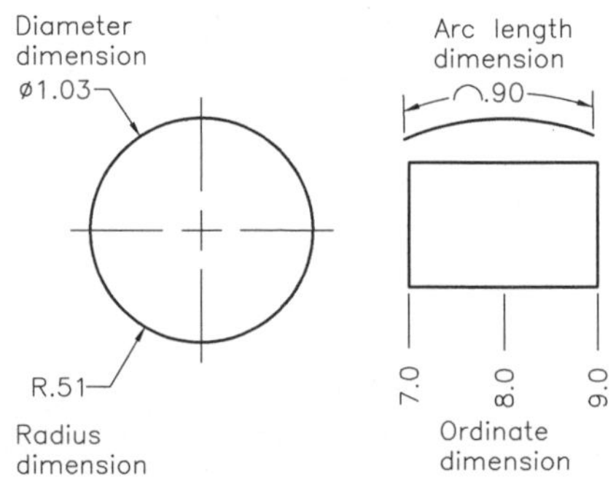

Figure 8-13 Radius, diameter, and ordinate dimensions

You can select the requisite tool from the menu bar, toolbar, and Ribbon to apply dimensions. You can also use the command prompt to work with the dimensions. The procedure to select the dimensioning tool is discussed next.

Using the Ribbon and the Toolbar

You can select the dimensioning tools from the **Dimensions** panel of the **Annotate** tab, as shown in Figure 8-14 or from the **Dimension** toolbar, as shown in Figure 8-15. The **Dimension** toolbar can be displayed by choosing **Tools > Toolbars > AutoCAD > Dimension** from the menu bar, if the menu bar is displayed.

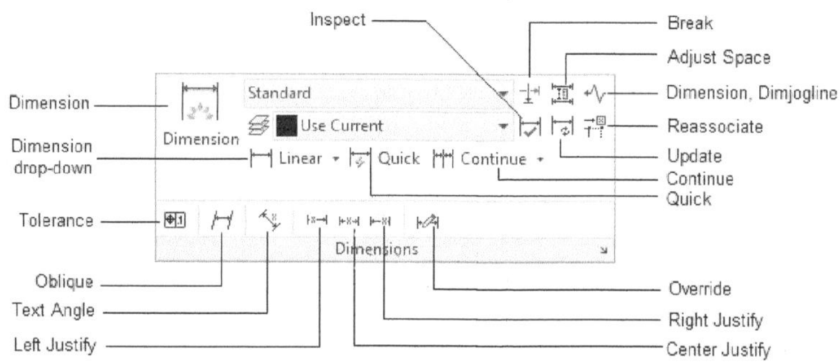

Figure 8-14 The updated view of the ***Dimensions*** *panel*

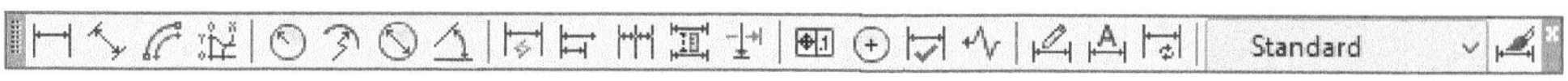

Figure 8-15 The ***Dimension*** *toolbar*

Note

The ***DIMDEC*** *variable sets the number of decimal places for the value of primary dimension and the* ***DIMADEC*** *variable for angular dimensions. For example, if* ***DIMDEC*** *is set to* ***3****, AutoCAD will display the decimal dimension up to three decimal places (2.037).*

DIMENSIONING A NUMBER OF OBJECTS TOGETHER

Ribbon: Annotate > Dimensions > Quick	**Command:** QDIM
Menu Bar: Dimension > Quick Dimension	**Toolbar:** Dimension > Quick Dimension

The **Quick Dimension** tool is used to dimension a number of objects at the same time. It also helps you to quickly edit dimension arrangements already existing in drawing and also creates new dimension arrangements. It is especially useful while creating a series of baseline or continuous dimensions. It also allows you to dimension multiple arcs and circles at the same time. When you are using the **Quick Dimension** tool, you can relocate the datum base point for baseline and ordinate dimensions. The prompt sequence that will follow when you choose this tool is given next.

Select geometry to dimension: *Select the objects to be dimensioned and press ENTER.*
Specify dimension line position, or [Continuous/Staggered/Baseline/Ordinate/Radius/Diameter/datumPoint/Edit/seTtings] <Continuous>: *Press ENTER to accept the default dimension arrangement and specify dimension line location or enter new dimension arrangement or edit the existing dimension arrangement.*

For example, you can dimension all circles in a drawing (Figure 8-16) by using the quick dimensioning as follows:

Associative dimension priority = Endpoint.
Select geometry to dimension: *Select all circles* Enter
Specify dimension line position, or [Continuous/Staggered/Baseline/Ordinate/Radius/Diameter/datumPoint/Edit/seTtings] <Continuous>: *Press D for diameter dimensioning and select a point where you want to position the diametric dimension.*

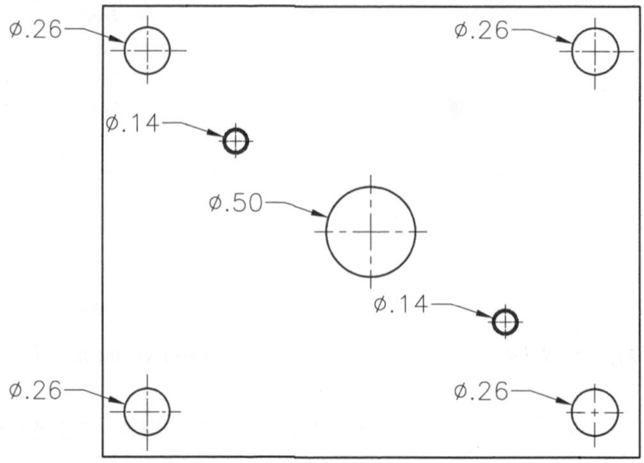

Figure 8-16 *Using the* ***Quick Dimension*** *tool to dimension multiple circles*

CREATING LINEAR DIMENSIONS

Ribbon: Annotate > Dimensions > Dimension drop-down > Linear
Menu Bar: Dimension > Linear **Toolbar:** Dimension > Linear
Command: DIMLIN or DIMLINEAR

Linear dimensioning is used to measure the horizontal or vertical distance between two points. You can directly select the object to dimension or select two points. The points can be any two points in the space, endpoints of an arc or line, or any set of points that can be identified. To achieve accuracy, points must be selected with the help of object snaps or by selecting an object to dimension. In case the object selected is aligned, then the linear dimensions will add the Horizontal or Vertical dimension to the object. The prompt sequence that will follow when you choose the **Linear** tool is given next.

Specify first extension line origin or <select object>: Enter
Select object to dimension: *Select the object.*
Specify dimension line location or
[Mtext/Text/Angle/Horizontal/Vertical/Rotated]: *Select a point to locate the position of the dimension.*

Instead of selecting the object, you can also select the two endpoints of the line that you want to dimension, refer to Figure 8-17. Usually the points on the object are selected by using the object snaps (endpoints, intersection, center, and so on). The prompt sequence is as follows.

Specify first extension line origin or <select object>: *Select a point.*
Specify second extension line origin: *Select second point.*

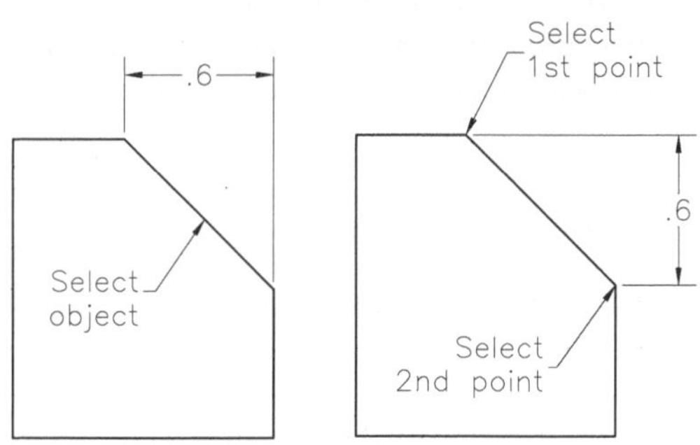

Figure 8-17 *Drawing linear dimensions*

Specify dimension line location or
[Mtext/Text/Angle/Horizontal/Vertical/Rotated]: *Select a point to locate the position of the dimension.*

Using the **Linear** tool, you can obtain the horizontal or vertical dimension by simply defining the appropriate dimension location point. If you select a point above or below the dimension, AutoCAD creates a horizontal dimension. If you select a point that is on the left or right of the dimension, AutoCAD creates a vertical dimension through that point.

Linear Tool Options

The options displayed after choosing the **Linear** tool are discussed next.

Mtext Option

The **Mtext** option is used to override the default dimension text and also change the font, height, and so on by using the **Text Editor**. When you enter **M** at the **Specify dimension line location or [Mtext/Text/Angle/Horizontal/Vertical/Rotated]** prompt, the **Text Editor** is displayed. You can change the text by entering a new text. You can also use various options of the **Text Editor** (explained in Chapter 7). However, if you override the default dimensions, the dimensional associativity of the dimension text is lost. This means that if you modify the object using the definition points, AutoCAD will not recalculate the dimension text. Even if the dimension is a true associative dimension, the text will not be recalculated when the object is modified. The prompt sequence to invoke this option is given next.

Specify first extension line origin or <select object>: *Specify a point.*
Specify second extension line origin: *Specify the second point.*
Specify dimension line location or
[Mtext/Text/Angle/Horizontal/Vertical/Rotated]: **M** Enter *(Enter the dimension text in the text window and then click outside the text window to accept the changes.)*
Specify dimension line location or
[Mtext/Text/Angle/Horizontal/Vertical/Rotated]: *Specify the dimension location.*

Text Option

This option also allows you to override the default dimension. However, this option will prompt you to specify the new text value in the command prompt itself, refer to Figure 8-18. The prompt sequence to invoke this option is given next.

Specify first extension line origin or <select object>: *Select a point.*
Specify second extension line origin: *Select second point.*
Specify dimension line location or
[Mtext/Text/Angle/Horizontal/Vertical/Rotated]: **T** Enter
Enter dimension text <Current>: *Enter new text.* Enter
Specify dimension line location or
[Mtext/Text/Angle/Horizontal/Vertical/Rotated]: *Specify the dimension location.*

Angle Option

This option allows you to change the angle of the dimension text, refer to Figure 8-18.

Rotated Option
This option allows you to create a dimension that is rotated at a specified angle, refer to Figure 8-18.

Horizontal Option
This option allows you to create a horizontal dimension regardless of where you specify the dimension location, refer to Figure 8-19.

Vertical Option
This option allows you to create a vertical dimension regardless of where you specify the dimension location, refer to Figure 8-19.

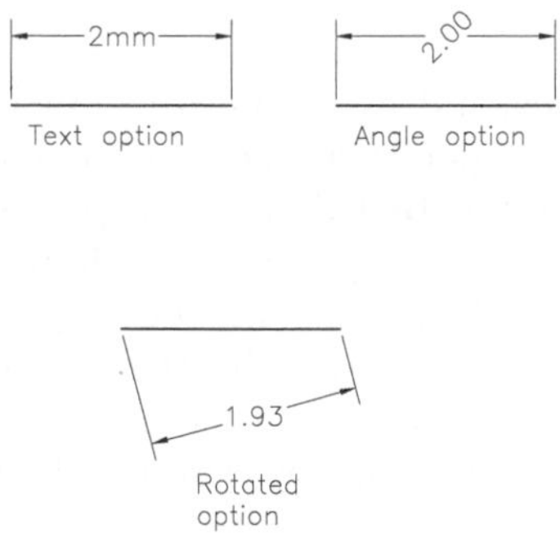

***Figure 8-18** The **Text**, **Angle**, and **Rotated** options*

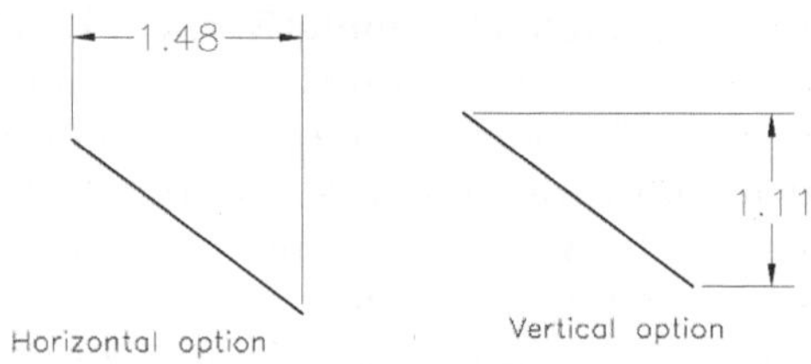

***Figure 8-19** The **Horizontal** and **Vertical** options*

Note

If you override the default dimensions, the dimensional associativity of the dimension text is lost and AutoCAD will not recalculate the dimension when the object is scaled.

Example 1 — Horizontal Dimension

In this example, you will use linear dimensioning to dimension a horizontal line of 4 units length. The dimensioning will be done first by selecting the object and later on by specifying the first and second extension line origins. Using the **Text Editor** tab, modify the default text such that the dimension is underlined.

Selecting the Object

1. Start a new file in the **Drafting & Annotation** workspace and draw a line of 4 units length.

2. Choose the **Linear** tool from **Annotate > Dimensions > Dimension** drop-down; you will be prompted to specify the extension line origin or the object. The prompt sequence to apply the linear dimension is as follows:

   Specify first extension line origin or <select object>: Enter
   Select object to dimension: *Select the line.*
   Specify dimension line location or
   [Mtext/Text/Angle/Horizontal/Vertical/Rotated]: **M** Enter

*The **Text Editor** tab will be displayed, as shown in Figure 8-20. Select the default dimension value and then choose the **Underline** button from the **Formatting** panel of the **Text Editor** tab of the **Ribbon** to underline the text. Click anywhere in the drawing area to exit the **Text Editor** tab.*

Specify dimension line location or
[Mtext/Text/Angle/Horizontal/Vertical/Rotated]: *Place the dimension.*
Dimension text = 4.0000

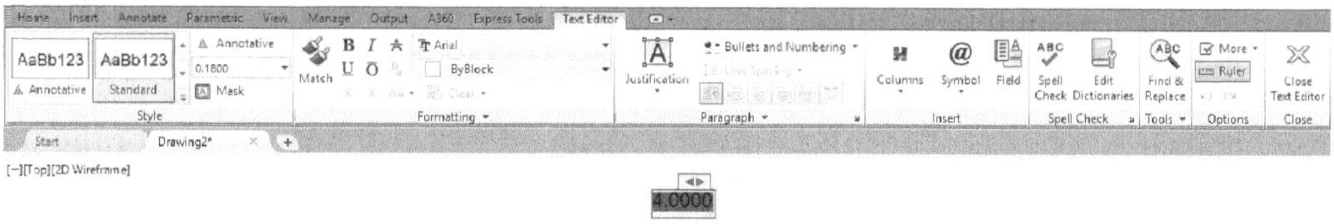

Figure 8-20 *The **Text Editor** tab*

Specifying Extension Line Origins

1. Choose the **Linear** tool from **Annotate** > **Dimensions** > **Dimension** drop-down. The prompt sequence is as follows:

Specify first extension line origin or <select object>: *Select the first endpoint of the line using the **Endpoint** object snap, refer to Figure 8-21.*

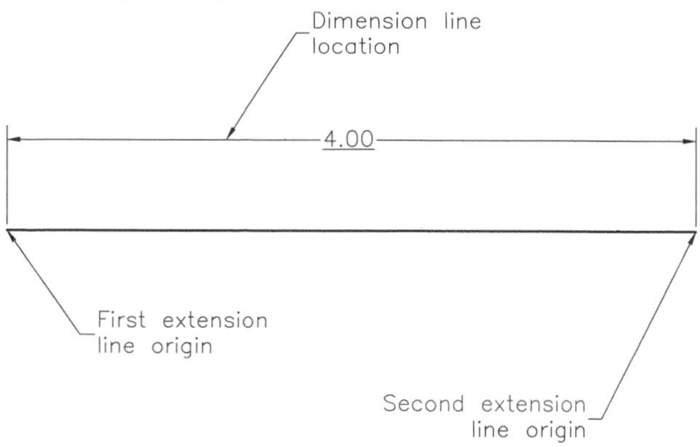

Figure 8-21 *Line for Example 1*

Specify second extension line origin: *Select the second endpoint of the line using the **Endpoint** object snap, refer to Figure 8-21.*
Specify dimension line location or
[Mtext/Text/Angle/Horizontal/Vertical/Rotated]: **M** Enter
*Select the text and then choose the **Underline** button from the **Ribbon** to underline the text in the **Text Editor**. Click anywhere in the drawing area.*
Specify dimension line location or
[Mtext/Text/Angle/Horizontal/Vertical/Rotated]: *Place the dimension.*
Dimension text = 4.00

CREATING ALIGNED DIMENSIONS

Ribbon: Annotate > Dimensions > Dimension drop-down > Aligned
Menu Bar: Dimension > Aligned **Toolbar:** Dimension > Aligned
Command: DIMALI or DIMALIGNED

Generally, the drawing consists of various objects that are neither parallel to the *X* axis nor to the *Y* axis. Dimensioning of such objects can be done using aligned dimensioning. In horizontal or vertical dimensioning, you can only measure the shortest distance from the first extension line origin to the second extension line origin along the horizontal or vertical axis, respectively whereas with the help of aligned dimensioning, you can measure the true aligned distance between two points. The function of the **Aligned** tool is similar to that of the other linear dimensioning tools. The dimension created with the **Aligned** tool is parallel to the object being dimensioned. The prompt sequence that will follow when you choose this tool is given next.

Specify first extension line origin or <select object>: *Specify the first point or press ENTER.*
Specify second extension line origin: *Specify second point.*
Specify dimension line location or [Mtext/Text/Angle]: *Specify the location for the dimension line.*

The options in this tool are similar to those of the **Linear** tool. Figure 8-22 illustrates the aligned dimensioning.

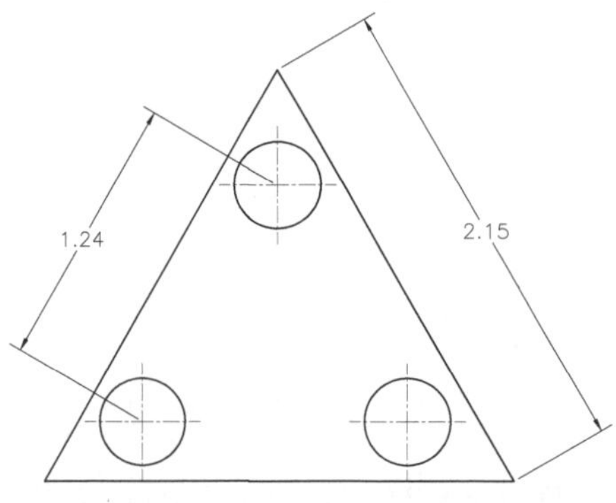

Figure 8-22 *The aligned dimensioning*

Exercise 1 — *Aligned Dimension*

Draw the object shown in Figure 8-23 and then use linear and aligned dimensioning to dimension the part. The distance between the dotted lines is 0.5 units. The dimensions should be up to 2 decimal places. To get dimensions up to 2 decimal places, enter DIMDEC at the command prompt and then enter 2. (There will be more information about dimension variable in Chapter 10.)

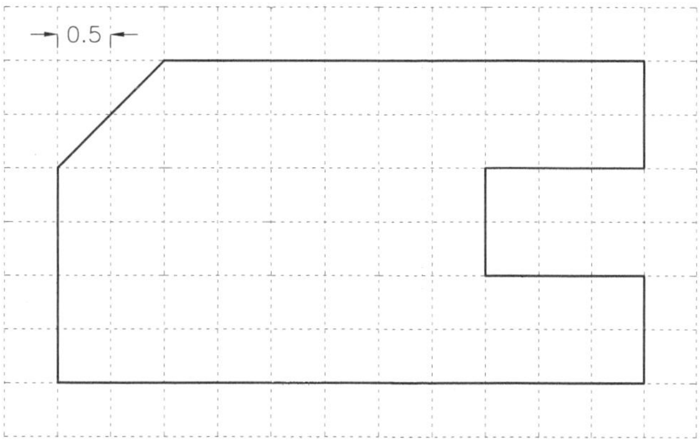

Figure 8-23 Drawing for Exercise 1

CREATING ARC LENGTH DIMENSIONS

Ribbon: Annotate > Dimensions > Dimension drop-down > Arc Length
Menu Bar: Dimension > Arc Length **Toolbar:** Dimension > Arc Length
Command: DIMARC

The Arc Length dimensioning is used to dimension the length of an arc or the polyline arc segment. You are required to select an arc or a polyline arc segment and the dimension location. Figure 8-24 shows the Arc Length dimensioning of an arc. Choose the **Arc Length** tool in the **Dimensions** panel. The prompt sequence that will follow after choosing this tool is given next.

Select arc or polyline arc segment: *Select arc or polyline arc segment to dimension.*
Specify arc length dimension location, or [Mtext/Text/Angle/Partial/Leader]: *Specify the location for the dimension line.*

Using the **Partial** option, you can dimension a selected portion of the arc, as shown in Figure 8-25. The prompt sequence for the **Partial** option is given next.

Select arc or polyline arc segment: *Select arc or polyline arc segment to dimension.*
Specify arc length dimension location, or [Mtext/Text/Angle/Partial/Leader]: **P** Enter
Specify first point for arc length dimension: *Specify the first point on arc.*
Specify second point for arc length dimension: *Specify the second point on arc.*
Specify arc length dimension location, or [Mtext/Text/Angle/Partial/Leader]: *Specify the location for the dimension line.*

Using the **Leader** option, you can attach a leader to the dimension text, starting from its circumference. This leader is drawn radial to the arc, as shown in Figure 8-26.

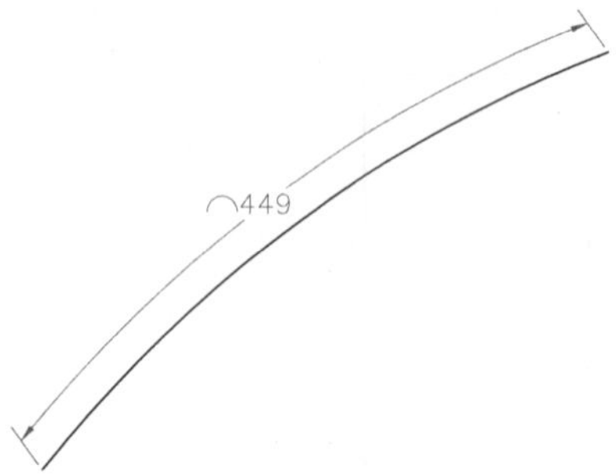

Figure 8-24 Arc Length dimensioning

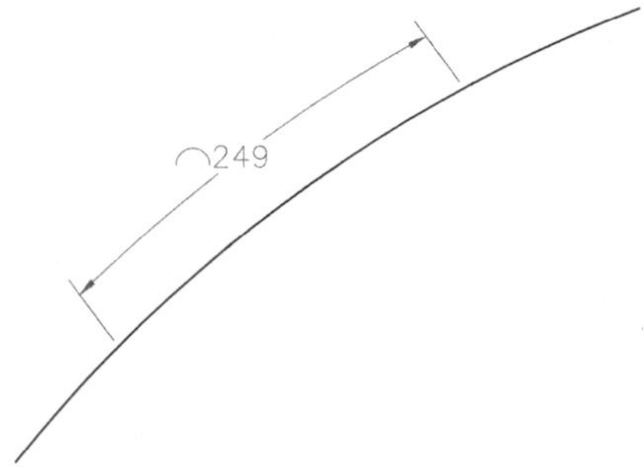

Figure 8-25 Partial Arc Length dimensioning

Note

*The **Leader** option is displayed only when the arc subtends an included angle greater than 90 degrees at its centre.*

CREATING ROTATED DIMENSIONS

Rotated dimensioning is used when you want to place the dimension line at an angle (if you do not want to align the dimension line with the selected extension line origins), as shown in Figure 8-27. You can invoke this option by entering **Rotated** at the command line after choosing the **Linear** tool from the **Dimensions** panel. The **Rotated** dimension option will prompt you to specify the dimension line angle. The prompt sequence is given next.

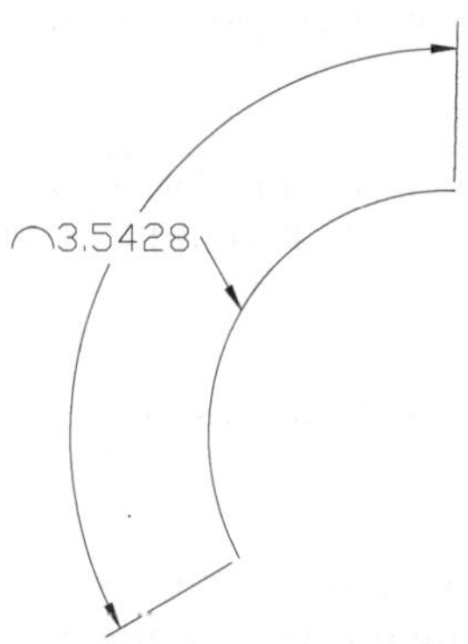

Figure 8-26 Leader Arc Length dimensioning

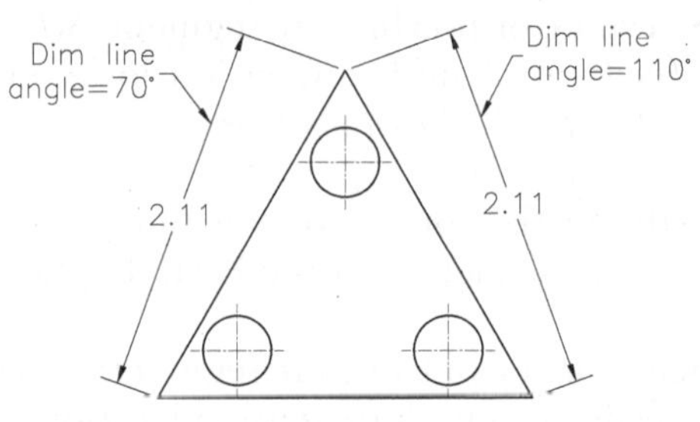

Figure 8-27 Rotated dimensioning

Specify first extension line origin or <select object>: *Select the origin of the first extension line.*
Specify second extension line origin: *Select the origin of the second extension line.*
Specify dimension line location or
[Mtext/Text/Angle/Horizontal/Vertical/Rotated]: **R** Enter
Specify angle of dimension line <current>: **110** Enter
Specify dimension line location or [Mtext/Text/Angle/Horizontal/Vertical/Rotated]: *Select the location for the dimension line.*

Note

You can draw horizontal and vertical dimensioning by specifying the rotation angle of 0-degree for horizontal dimensioning and 90 degree for vertical dimensioning.

CREATING BASELINE DIMENSIONS

Ribbon: Annotate > Dimensions > Continue drop-down > Baseline
Menu Bar: Dimension > Baseline **Toolbar:** Dimension > Baseline
Command: DIMBASE or DIMBASELINE

Sometimes in manufacturing, you may want to locate different points and features of a part with reference to a fixed point (base point or reference point). This can be accomplished by using the Baseline dimensioning, refer to Figure 8-28. To invoke the Baseline dimension, choose the **Baseline** tool from the **Continue** drop-down of the **Dimensions** panel. Using this tool, you can continue a linear dimension from the first extension line origin of the first dimension to the dimension point. The new dimension line is automatically offset by a fixed amount to avoid overlapping of the dimension lines. This has to be kept in mind that there must be already existing a linear, ordinate, or angular associative dimension to use the Baseline dimensions. When you choose the **Baseline** tool, the last linear, ordinate, or angular dimension created will be selected and used as the baseline. The prompt sequence that will follow when you choose this tool is given next.

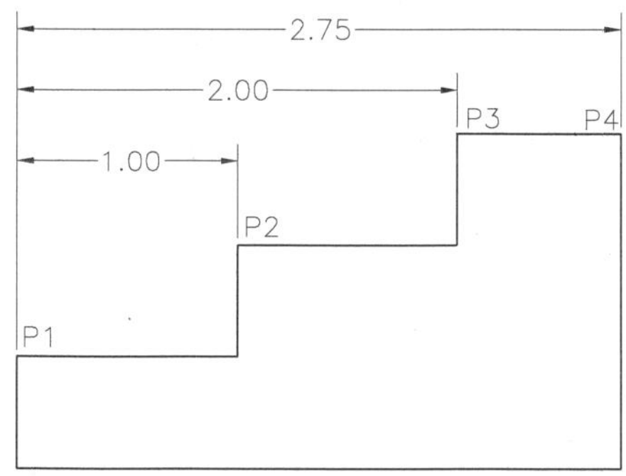

***Figure 8-28 Baseline** dimensioning*

Specify second extension line origin or [Select/Undo] <Select>: *Select the origin of the second extension line.*
Specify second extension line origin or [Select/Undo] <Select>: *Select the origin of the second extension line.*
Specify second extension line origin or [Select/Undo] <Select>: *Select the origin of the second extension line or press ENTER.*
Select base dimension: Enter

When you use the **Baseline** tool, you cannot change the default dimension text. However, the **DIM** command allows you to override the default dimension text.

Command: **DIM**
Select objects or specify first extension line origin or [Angular/Baseline/Continue/Ordinate/aliGn/Distribute/Layer/Undo]:*Specify the first point.*
Specify second extension line origin or [Undo]:*Select the second point.*
Specify dimension line location or second line for angle [Mtext/Text/text aNgle/Undo]:T Enter
Enter dimension text < Current >: 1 Enter
Specify dimension line location or second line for angle [Mtext/Text/text aNgle/Undo]: *Select the location for the dimension line.*
Select objects or specify first extension line origin or [Angular/Baseline/Continue/Ordinate/aliGn/Distribute/Layer/Undo]:B Enter
Specify first extension line origin as baseline or [Offset]: *Select the second extension line.*
Specify second extension line origin or [Select/Offset/Undo] <Select>: *Specify the second point of dimension line* Enter Enter

Select objects or specify first extension line origin or [Angular/Baseline/Continue/Ordinate/aliGn/Distribute/Layer/Undo]: Enter Enter Enter

The next dimension line is automatically spaced and drawn by AutoCAD. Note that in AutoCAD if the value of **DIMCONTINUEMODE** system variable is set to 0, the dimensions created by using the **Baseline** tool will be based on the current dimension style. Whereas, if you set the value to 1 then the dimensions will be created based upon the selected dimension.

CREATING CONTINUED DIMENSIONS

Ribbon: Annotate > Dimensions > Continue drop-down > Continue
Menu Bar: Dimension > Continue **Toolbar:** Dimension > Continue
Command: DIMCONT or DIMCONTINUE

Using the **Continue** tool, you can continue a linear dimension from the second extension line of the previous dimension. This is also called as Chained or Incremental dimensioning. Note that there must be existing linear, ordinate, or angular associative dimension to use the Continue dimensions. The prompt sequence that will follow when you choose this tool is given next.

Specify second extension line origin or [Select/Undo] <Select>: *Specify the point on the origin of the second extension line.*
Specify second extension line origin or [Select/Undo] <Select>: *Specify the point on the origin of the second extension line.* Enter
Select continued dimension:

Also, in this case, the **DIM** command should be used if you want to change the default dimension text.

Command: **DIM**
Select objects or specify first extension line origin or [Angular/Baseline/Continue/Ordinate/aliGn/Distribute/Layer/Undo]:(P1, refer to Figure 8-29). *Specify the first point.*
Specify second extension line origin or [Undo]::*Select the second point.*
Specify dimension line location or second line for angle [Mtext/Text/text aNgle/Undo]:T Enter
Enter dimension text <8478.5>: 0.75 Enter
Specify dimension line location or second line for angle [Mtext/Text/text aNgle/Undo]: *Select the location for the dimension line.*
Select objects or specify first extension line origin or [Angular/Baseline/Continue/Ordinate/aliGn/Distribute/Layer/Undo]:C
Specify first extension line origin to continue:*Select the second extension line.*
Specify second extension line origin or [Select/Undo] <Select>: *Select the second point.*
Specify second extension line origin or [Select/Undo] <Select>: Enter Enter Enter

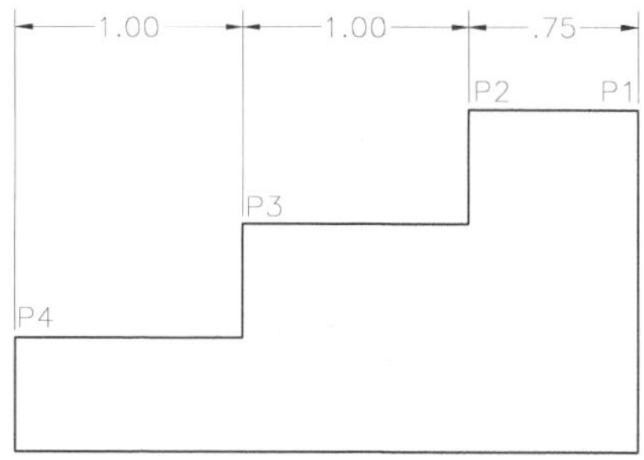

Figure 8-29 *Continue dimensioning*

> **Tip**
> *You can use the **Select** option of the **Baseline** and **Continue** tools to select any other existing dimension to be used as the baseline or continuous dimension.*

Exercise 2 — Baseline Dimension

Draw the object shown in Figure 8-30 and then use baseline dimensioning to dimension the top half and continue dimensioning to dimension the bottom half. The distance between the dotted lines is 0.5 unit.

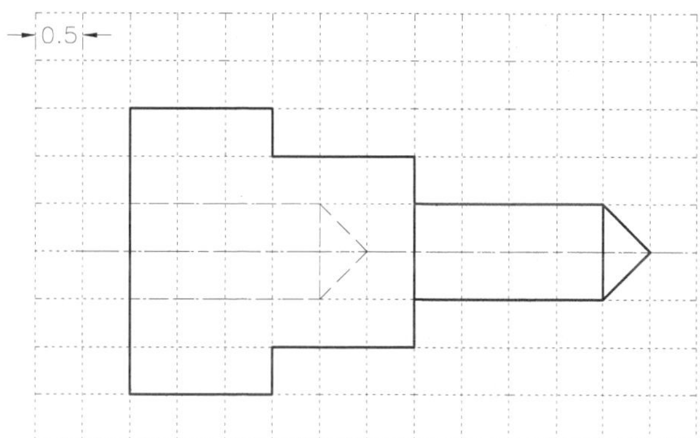

Figure 8-30 *Drawing for Exercise 2*

CREATING ANGULAR DIMENSIONS

Ribbon: Annotate > Dimensions > Dimension drop down > Angular
Menu Bar: Dimension > Angular **Toolbar:** Dimension > Angular
Command: DIMANG or DIMANGULAR

The Angular dimensioning is used for applying angular dimension to an entity. The **Angular** tool is used to generate a dimension arc (dimension line in the shape of an arc with arrowheads at both ends) to indicate the angle between two nonparallel lines. This tool can also be used to dimension the vertex and two other points, a circle with another point, or the angle of an arc. For every set of points, there exists one acute angle and one obtuse angle (inner and outer angles). If you specify the dimension arc location between the two points, you will get the acute angle; if you specify it outside the two points, you will get the obtuse angle. Figure 8-31 shows the four ways to dimension two nonparallel lines. The prompt sequence that will follow when you choose this tool is given next:

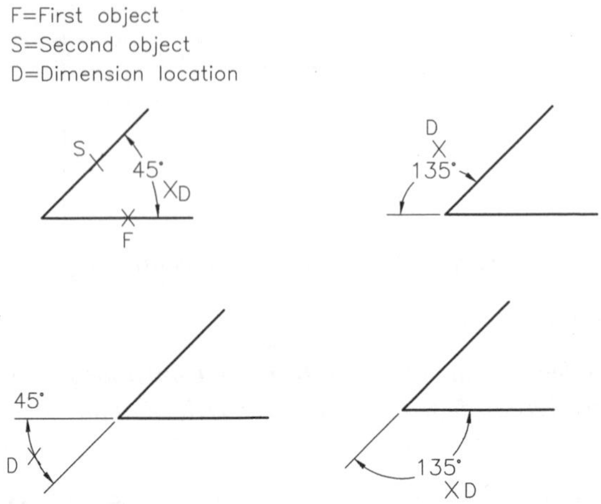

Figure 8-31 *Angular dimensioning between two nonparallel lines*

> Select arc, circle, line, or <specify vertex>: *Select the object.*
> Select second line: *Select the second object.*
> Specify dimension arc line location or [Mtext/Text/Angle/Quadrant]: *Place the dimension or select an option.*

If you want to override the default angular value, use the **Mtext** or **Text** option. Use the %%d control sequence after the number at the text prompt. For example, for 45°, type 45%%d and then press ENTER.

The methods of dimensioning various entities using this tool are discussed next.

Dimensioning the Angle between Two Nonparallel Lines

The angle between two nonparallel lines or two straight line segments of a polyline can be dimensioned using the **Angular** tool.

The following example illustrates the dimensioning of two nonparallel lines by choosing the **Angular** tool from the **Dimension** drop-down in the **Dimensions** panel. You can also apply the angular dimension by using the **DIMANGULAR** command.

> Select arc, circle, line, or <specify vertex>: *Select the first line.*
> Select second line: *Select the second line.*
> Specify dimension arc line location or [Mtext/Text/Angle/Quadrant]: **M** Enter *(Enter the new value in the **Text Editor** and click anywhere in the drawing area.*
> Specify dimension arc line location or [Mtext/Text/Angle/Quadrant]: *Specify the dimension arc location or select an option.*

The location of the extension lines and the dimension arc is determined by the placement of the dimension arc. In AutoCAD, you can place the dimension text outside the quadrant in which you measure the angle by extending the dimension arc. Choose the **Quadrant** option from the shortcut menu or from the **Specify dimension arc line location or [Mtext/Text/Angle/Quadrant]** prompt. Next, you will be prompted to specify the quadrant in which you want to measure the angle. Then, specify the quadrant with mouse. If the dimension arc line is lying outside the quadrant that is being measured, the dimension arc will be extended up to that location with the help of extension line. Figure 8-32(a) shows a dimension created without using the **Quadrant** option and Figure 8-32(b) shows the same dimension created by using the **Quadrant** option.

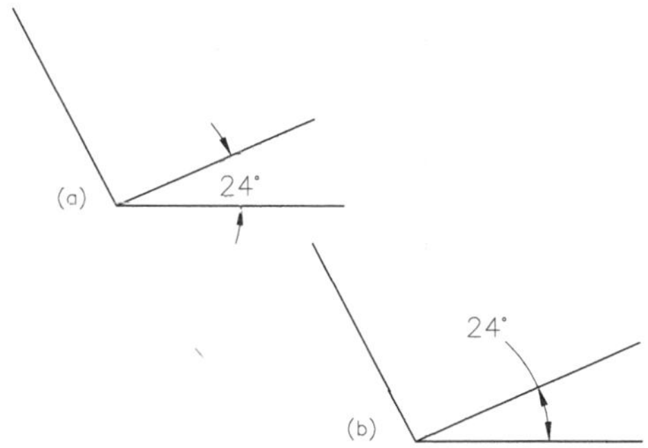

Figure 8-32 *The angular dimension created without and with choosing the* ***Quadrant*** *option*

Dimensioning the Angle of an Arc

Angular dimensioning can also be used to dimension the angle of an arc. In this case, the center point of the arc is taken as the vertex and the two endpoints of the arc are used as the extension line origin points for the extension lines, refer to Figure 8-33. The following is the prompt sequence for dimensioning of an arc by using the **Angular** tool:

Select arc, circle, line, or <specify vertex>: *Select the arc.*
Specify dimension arc line location or [Mtext/Text/Angle/Quadrant]: *Specify a location for the arc line or select an option.*

Angular Dimensioning of Circles

The angular feature associated with the circle can be dimensioned by selecting a circle object at the **Select arc, circle, line, or <specify vertex>** prompt. The center of the selected circle is used as the vertex of the angle. The first point selected (when the circle is selected for angular dimensioning) is used as the origin of the first extension line. In a similar manner, the second point selected is taken as the origin of the second extension line, refer to Figure 8-34. The following is the prompt sequence for dimensioning a circle:

Select arc, circle, line, or <specify vertex>: *Select the circle at the point where you want the first extension line.*
Specify second angle endpoint: *Select the second point on or away from the circle.*
Specify dimension arc line location or [Mtext/Text/Angle/Quadrant]: *Select the location for the dimension line.*

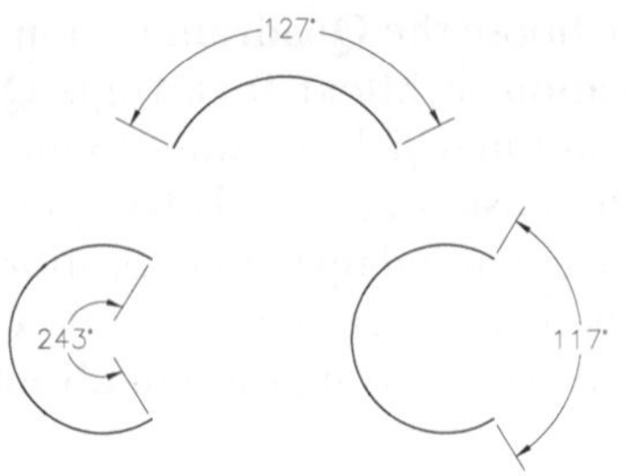

Figure 8-33 *Angular dimensioning of arcs*

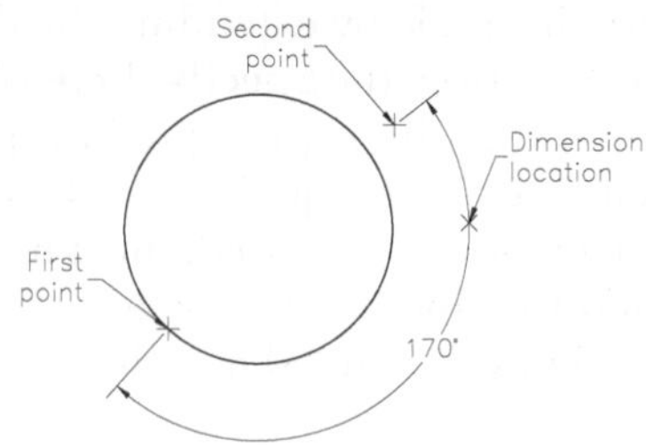

Figure 8-34 *Angular dimensioning of a circle*

Angular Dimensioning based on Three Points

If you press ENTER at the **Select arc, circle, line, or <specify vertex>** prompt, AutoCAD allows you to select three points to create an angular dimension. The first point is the vertex point, and the other two points are the first and second angle endpoints of the angle, refer to Figure 8-35. The coordinate specifications of the first and the second angle endpoints must not be identical. However, the angle vertex coordinates and one of the angle endpoint coordinates can be identical. The following is the prompt sequence for angular dimensioning by defining three points:

Select arc, circle, line, or <specify vertex>: Enter
Specify angle vertex: *Specify the first point vertex. This is the point where two segments meet. If the two segments do not meet, use the **Apparent Intersection** object snap.*
Specify first angle endpoint: *Specify the second point. This point will be the origin of the first extension line.*
Specify second angle endpoint: *Specify the third point. This point will be the origin of the second extension line.*
Specify dimension arc line location or [Mtext/Text/Angle/Quadrant]: *Select the location for the dimension line.*

Exercise 3 — Angular Dimension

Draw the profile, as shown in Figure 8-36 and then use angular dimensioning to dimension all angles of the part. The distance between the dotted lines is 0.5 unit.

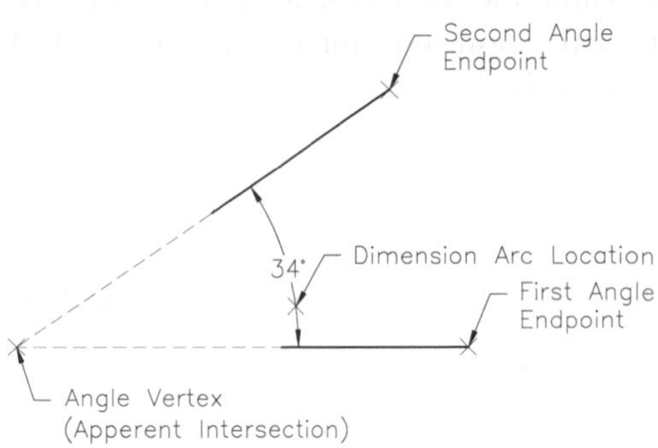

Figure 8-35 *Angular dimensioning using 3 points*

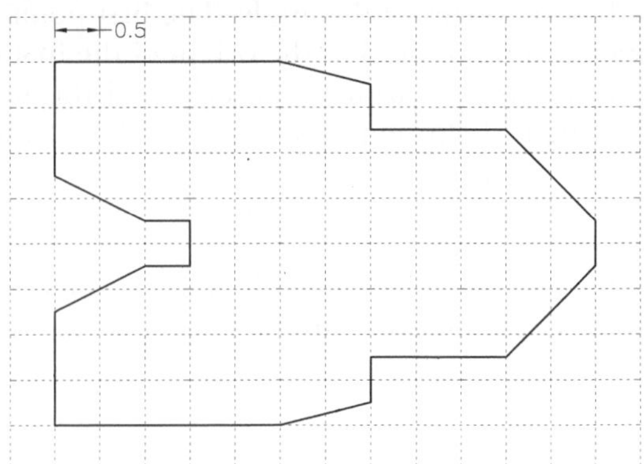

Figure 8-36 *Drawing for Exercise 3*

CREATING DIAMETER DIMENSIONS

Ribbon: Annotate > Dimensions > Dimension drop-down > Diameter
Menu Bar: Dimension > Diameter **Toolbar:** Dimension > Diameter
Command: DIMDIA or DIMDIAMETER

Diameter dimensioning is used to dimension a circle or an arc. Here, the measurement is done between two diametrically opposite points on the circumference of the circle or the arc, refer to Figure 8-37. The dimension text generated by AutoCAD begins with the ø symbol to indicate a diameter dimension. The prompt sequence that will follow when you choose the **Diameter** tool in the **Dimensions** panel is given next.

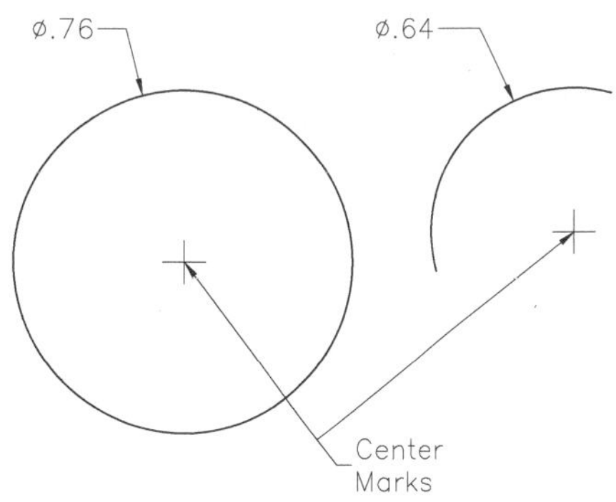

***Figure 8-37** Diameter dimensioning*

Select arc or circle: *Select an arc or circle by selecting a point anywhere on its circumference.*
Dimension text = Current
Specify dimension line location or [Mtext/Text/Angle]: *Specify a point to position the dimension.*

If you want to override the default value of the dimension text, use the **Mtext** or the **Text** option. The control sequence %%C is used to obtain the diameter symbol ø. It is followed by the dimension text that should appear in the diameter dimension. For example, if you want to write a text that displays a value ø20, then enter %%c20 at the text prompt.

CREATING JOGGED DIMENSIONS

Ribbon: Annotate > Dimensions > Dimension drop-down > Jogged
Menu Bar: Dimension > Jogged **Toolbar:** Dimension > Jogged
Command: DIMJOGGED

The necessity of the Jogged dimension arises because of the space constraint. Also, the Jogged dimension is used when you want to avoid the merging of the dimension line with other dimensions. Also, there are instances when it is not possible to show the center of the circle in the sheet. In such situations, the jogged dimensions are used, as shown in Figure 8-38. The jogged dimensions can be added using the **Jogged** tool. Note that with this tool, you can add only jogged radius dimensions. To add jogged dimensions, invoke the **Jogged** tool from the **Dimensions** panel and select an arc or a circle from the drawing area; you will be prompted to select the center location override. Specify a new location to override the existing center. This point will also become the start point of the dimension line. Next, specify the location of the dimension line and the jog. The command prompt that will follow when you invoke the **Jogged** tool is given next.

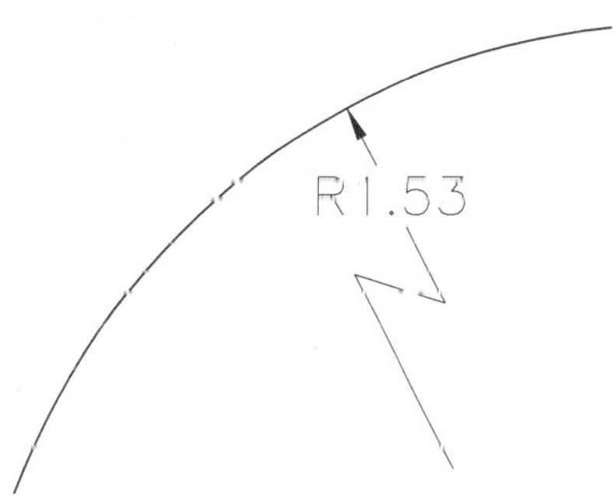

***Figure 8-38** Jogged dimensioning*

Select arc or circle: *Select arc or circle to be dimensioned.*
Specify center location override: *Specify a point which will currently override the actual center point location.*
Dimension text = *Current*
Specify dimension line location or [Mtext/Text/Angle]: *Specify a point to position dimension line.*
Specify jog location: *Specify a point for the positioning of jog.*

CREATING RADIUS DIMENSIONS

Ribbon: Annotate > Dimensions > Dimension drop-down > Radius
Menu Bar: Dimension > Radius **Toolbar**: Dimension > Radius
Command: DIMRAD or DIMRADIUS

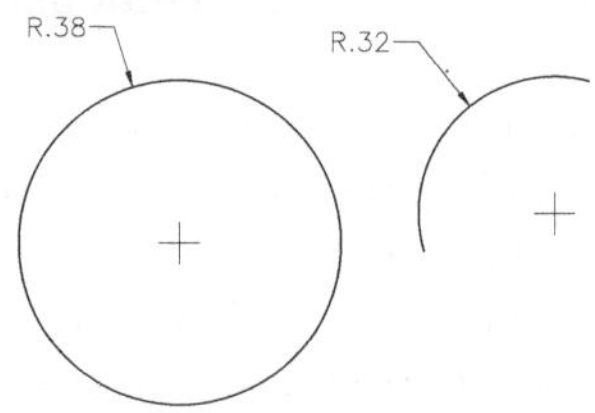

Figure 8-39 Radius dimensioning

The Radius dimensioning is used to dimension a circle or an arc as shown in Figure 8-39. Radius and diameter dimensioning are similar; the only difference is that instead of the diameter line, a radius line is drawn (half of the diameter line), which is measured from the center to any point on the circumference. The dimension text generated by AutoCAD is preceded by the letter R to indicate a radius dimension. If you want to use the default dimension text (dimension text generated automatically by AutoCAD), simply specify a point to position the dimension at the **Specify dimension line location or [Mtext/Text/Angle]** prompt. You can also enter a new value or specify a prefix or suffix, or suppress the entire text by entering a blank space following the **Enter dimension text <current>** prompt. A center mark for the circle/arc is drawn automatically, provided the center mark value controlled by the DIMCEN variable is not 0. The prompt sequence that will follow when you choose this button is given next.

Select arc or circle: *Select the object that you want to dimension.*
Dimension text = Current
Specify dimension line location or [Mtext/Text/Angle]: Specify the dimension location.

If you want to override the default value of the dimension text, use the **Text** or the **Mtext** option. You can also enter the required value at the text prompt.

Note

*In case of diametric, radial, and jogged radial dimensions, you can extend the dimension line beyond the endpoints of the arc by creating the arc extension line beyond the endpoints. These arc extension lines are similar to the other extension lines. The system variables **DIMSE1** and **DIMSE2** allow the display of the first and the second extension lines, respectively. These variables should be **ON** in order to suppress the respective extension line.*

CREATING JOGGED LINEAR DIMENSIONS

Ribbon: Annotate > Dimensions > Dimension, Dimjogline
Menu Bar: Dimension > Jogged Linear
Toolbar: Dimension > Jogged Linear **Command:** DIMJOGLINE

The **Dimension, Dimjogline** tool is used to add or remove a jog in the existing dimensions. This kind of dimensioning technique is generally used to dimension the components that have a high length to width ratio, refer to Figure 8-40. To add a jog to a linear dimension, choose the **Dimension, Dimjogline** tool from the **Dimensions** panel and select the dimension to which you want to add a jog. Next, pick a point along the dimension line to specify the location of the jog placement. Alternatively, you can press the ENTER key to place the jog automatically. To remove a jog, invoke the **Dimension, Dimjogline** tool and choose **Remove** from the shortcut menu. Next, specify the dimension line from which you want to remove the jog. You can modify the location of the jog symbol with the help of grips. Note that you can add a jog only to the linear or aligned dimensions with this tool.

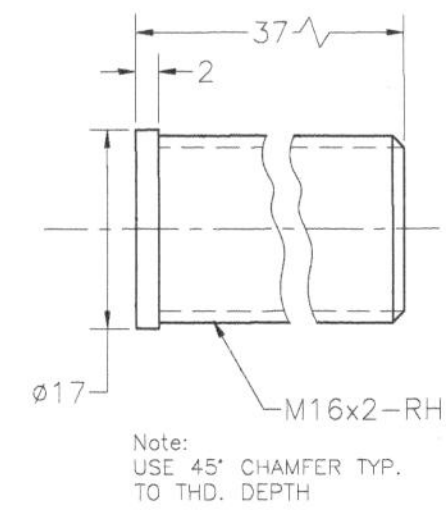

Figure 8-40 *Jogged linear dimensioning*

Note

The height of jog symbol can be changed by varying the ***Jog height factor*** *in the* ***Lines & Arrows*** *rollout of the* ***PROPERTIES*** *palette.*

GENERATING CENTER MARKS AND CENTERLINES

Toolbar: Dimension > Center Mark **Command:** DIMCENTER
Menu bar: Dimension > Center Mark

When circles or arcs are dimensioned with the **Radius** or **Diameter** tool, a small mark known as center mark, or a line known as centerline may be drawn at the center of the circle/arc. Sometimes, you need to mark the center of a circle or an arc without using these dimensioning tools. This can be achieved with the help of the **Center Mark** tool. You can invoke this tool from the **Dimension** toolbar or by entering **DIMCENTER** in the command line. When you invoke this tool, you are prompted to select the arc or the circle. The result of this tool will depend upon the value of the **DIMCEN** variable. If the value of this variable is positive, center marks are drawn, refer to Figure 8-41 and if the value is negative, centerlines are drawn, refer to Figure 8-42.

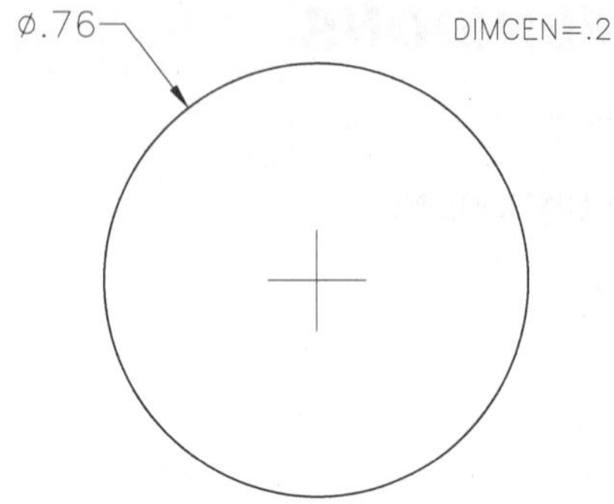

Figure 8-41 *Using a positive value for the **DIMCEN** variable*

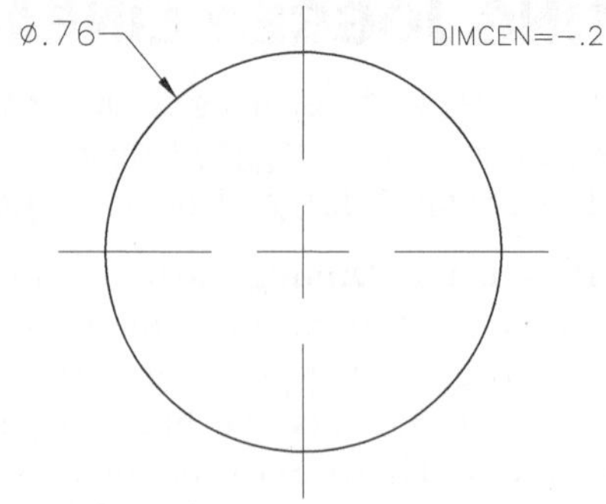

Figure 8-42 *Using a negative value for the **DIMCEN** variable*

Note

*The center marks created by using the **Center Mark** tool are lines and not associative dimensioning objects. These center marks have an explicit linetype.*

CREATING ASSOCIATIVE CENTER MARKS

Ribbon: Annotate > Centerlines > Center Mark **Command:** CENTERMARK

The **Center Mark** tool is used to create an associative center mark at the center of a selected circle, arc, or polygonal arc. A center mark is a combination of two elements, center cross and extension lines. The center marks created using the **Center Mark** tool are associated with the selected object. If the dimension or position of the object is updated, the center mark also gets updated automatically. On invoking this tool, you are prompted to select a circle or an arc to add the center mark. Select a circle or an arc to create an associative center mark, refer to Figure 8-43. You can add a center mark to one or more circles at a time as the **CENTER MARK** command automatically repeats after selecting a circle or an arc. You can change the properties of the center mark by using the **PROPERTIES** palette, as shown in Figure 8-44. The appearance of the centermark can be controlled by using the system variables like CENTEREXE, CENTERMARKEXE, CENTERLAYER, CENTERLTYPE, CENTERLTSCALE, CENTERCROSSSIZE, and CENTERCROSSGAP.

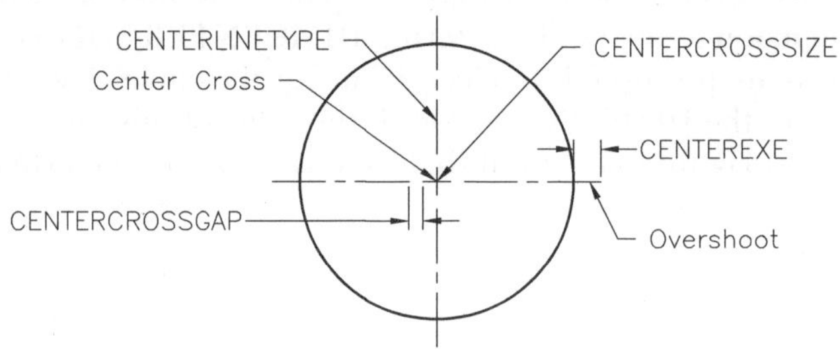

Figure 8-43 *Circle with the associative center mark*

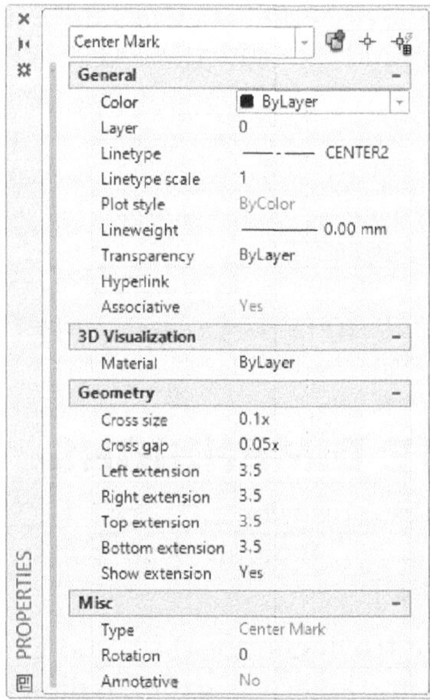

Figure 8-44 The Centre Mark ***PROPERTIES*** *palette*

CREATING ASSOCIATIVE CENTERLINES

Ribbon: Annotate > Centerlines > Centerline **Command:** CENTERLINE

The **Centerline** tool is used to create centerline geometry of a specified linetype associated with selected lines and polylines. The **Centerline** tool creates a centerline between the apparent midpoint of the start and endpoints of the selected two lines. If the lines are nonparallel lines, the centerline will be drawn between the imaginary intersection point and the endpoints of the selected lines. To create a centre line between two lines or polylines, choose the **Centerline** tool from the **Centerlines** panel in the **Annotate** tab and you will be prompted to select the first line. Select the first line, and you will be prompted to select the second line. After selecting the second line, the centre line will be created, as shown in Figure 8-45 and Figure 8-46.

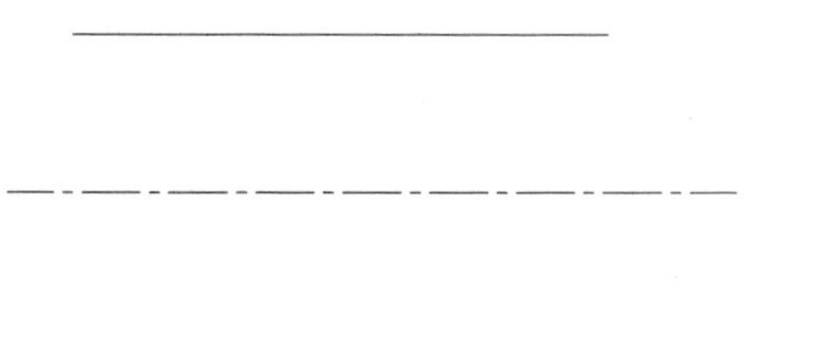

Figure 8-45 Centerline created between two parallel lines

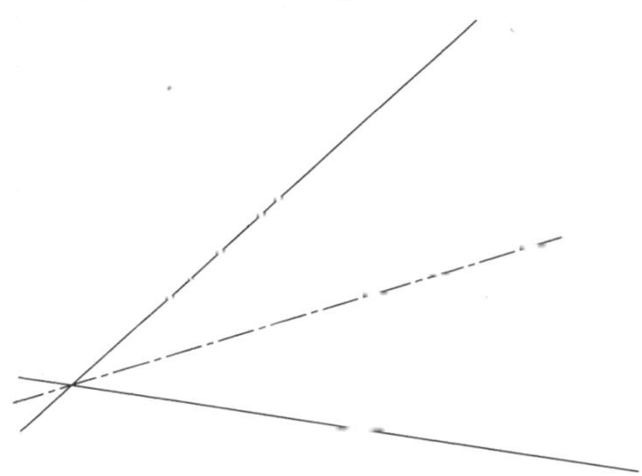

Figure 8-46 Centerline created between two nonparallel lines

You can change the appearance of the centerlines by using the system variables like CENTEREXE, CENTERLAYER, CENTERLTYPE, and CENTERLTSCALE, as they are valid for both centerlines and center marks.

Note

*1. You can disassociate centerlines and center marks from objects using the **CENTERDISASSOCIATE** command.*

*2. You can reassociate centerlines and center marks with selected objects using the **CENTERREASSOCIATE** command.*

CREATING ORDINATE DIMENSIONS

Ribbon: Annotate > Dimensions > Dimension drop-down > Ordinate
Menu Bar: Dimension > Ordinate **Toolbar:** Dimension > Ordinate
Command: DIMORD or DIMORDINATE

Ordinate dimensioning is used to dimension the X and Y coordinates of the selected point. This type of dimensioning is also known as arrowless dimensioning because no arrowheads are drawn in it. Ordinate dimensioning is also called datum dimensioning because all dimensions are related to a common base point. The current UCS (user coordinate system) origin becomes the reference or the base point for ordinate dimensioning. With ordinate dimensioning, you can determine the X or Y displacement of a selected point from the current UCS origin.

Dimension text (*X* or *Y* coordinate value) and the leader line along the *X* or *Y* axis are automatically placed using Ordinate dimensioning, refer to Figure 8-47. Since ordinate dimensioning pertains to either the *X* coordinate or the *Y* coordinate, you should keep ORTHO on. When ORTHO is off, the leader line is automatically given a bend when you select the second leader line point that is offset from the first point. This allows you to generate offsets and avoid overlapping text on closely spaced dimensions. In ordinate dimensioning, only one extension line (leader line) is drawn.

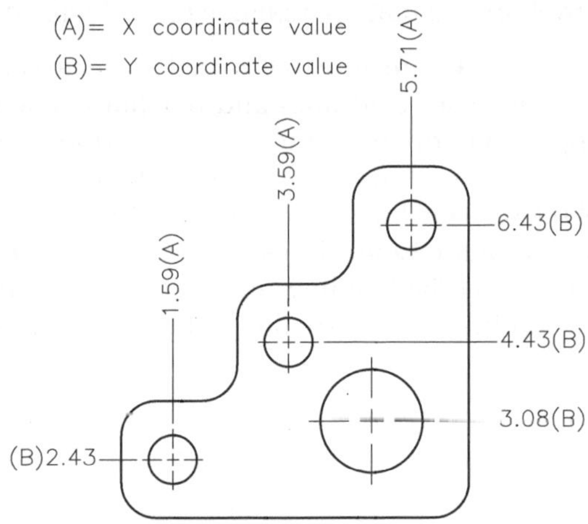

***Figure 8-47** Ordinate dimensioning*

The leader line for an *X* coordinate value will be drawn perpendicular to the *X* axis, and the leader line for a *Y* coordinate value will be drawn perpendicular to the *Y* axis. Since you cannot override this, the leader line drawn perpendicular to the *X* axis will have the dimension text aligned with the leader line. The dimension text is the X datum of the selected point. The leader line drawn perpendicular to the *Y* axis will have the dimension text, which is the Y datum of the selected point, aligned with the leader line. Any other alignment specification for the dimension text is nullified. Hence, changes in the Text Alignment in the **Dimension Style Manager** dialog box (**DIMTIH** and **DIMTOH** variables) have no effect on the alignment of the dimension text. You can specify the coordinate value that you want to dimension at the **Specify leader endpoint or [Xdatum/Ydatum/MText/Text/Angle]** prompt.

If you select or enter a point, AutoCAD checks the difference between the feature location and the leader endpoint. If the difference between the *X* coordinates is greater, the dimension measures the *Y* coordinate; otherwise, the *X* coordinate is measured. In this manner, AutoCAD determines whether it is an X or Y type of ordinate dimension. However, if you enter Y instead of specifying a point, AutoCAD will dimension the *Y* coordinate of the selected feature. Similarly, if you enter X, AutoCAD will dimension the *X* coordinate of the selected point. The prompt sequence that follows when you choose this tool is given next.

Specify feature location: *Select a point on an object.*
Specify leader endpoint or [Xdatum/Ydatum/Mtext/Text/Angle]: *Enter the endpoint of the leader.*

You can override the default text with the help of the **Mtext** or **Text** option. If you use the **Mtext** option, the **Text Editor** will be displayed. If you use the **Text** option, you will be prompted to specify the new text in the command line itself.

Exercise 4 — Ordinate Dimension

Draw the model shown in Figure 8-48 and then use ordinate dimensioning to dimension the part. The distance between the dotted lines is 0.5 unit.

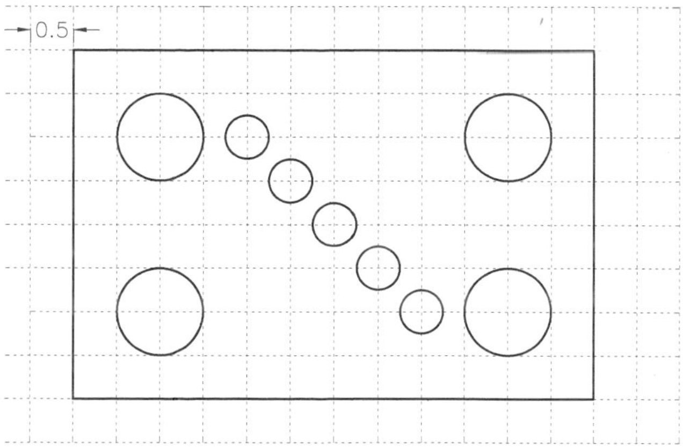

Figure 8-48 *Drawing for Exercise 4*

MAINTAINING EQUAL SPACING BETWEEN DIMENSIONS

Ribbon: Annotate > Dimensions > Adjust Space **Toolbar:** Dimension > Dimension Space
Menu Bar: Dimension > Dimension Space **Command:** DIMSPACE

The **Adjust Space** tool is used to equally space the overlapped or the unequally spaced linear and angular dimensions. Maintaining equal spacing between the dimension lines increases the clarity of the drawing display. Figure 8-49 shows a drawing with unequally spaced dimensions, and Figure 8-50 shows the same drawing with equally spaced dimensions after the use of the **Adjust Space** tool. Figure 8-51 shows a drawing with its angular dimensions equally spaced.

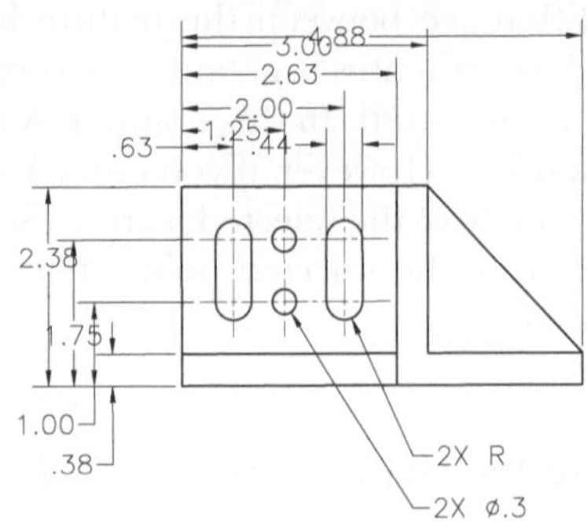

Figure 8-49 Drawing with its linear dimensions unequally spaced

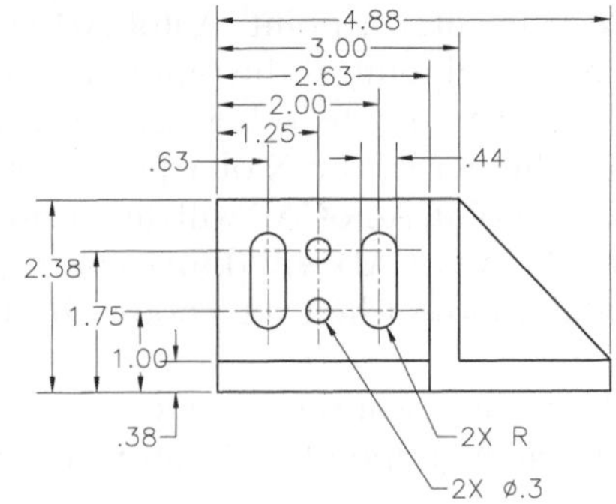

Figure 8-50 Drawing with its linear dimensions equally spaced

The prompt sequence that will follow when you choose the **Adjust Space** tool is given next.

Select base dimension: *Select a linear or an angular dimension with respect to which all other dimensions will get spaced.*
Select dimensions to space: *Select the dimensions that you want to be equally spaced from the specified base dimension.*
Select dimensions to space: *Select more similar dimensions or press* Enter
Enter value or [Auto] <Auto>: *Enter a value to specify the spacing between the selected dimensions or enter A to automatically calculate the gap between the dimensions.*

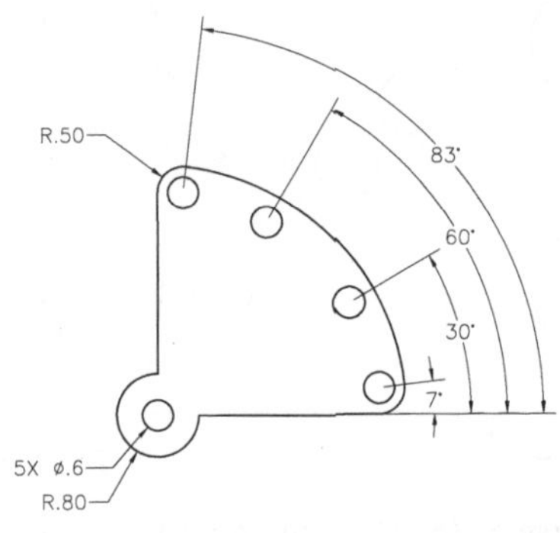

Figure 8-51 Drawing with its angular dimensions equally spaced

Enter **0** in the above prompt to align all the selected dimensions in a single line. With the **Auto** option selected, AutoCAD will calculate the space value on the basis of the dimension text height. The spacing is automatically maintained to a value that is double of the dimension text height.

CREATING DIMENSION BREAKS

Ribbon: Annotate > Dimensions > Break	**Toolbar:** Dimension > Dimension Break
Menu Bar: Dimension > Dimension Break	**Command:** DIMBREAK

The **Break** tool is used to create a break in the dimension line, extension line, or multileaders at the point where they intersect with other drawing entities or annotations. Inserting dimension breaks will keep annotative objects separate from the main drawing, which increases the clarity of the drawing, refer to Figure 8-52. The prompt sequence that will follow when you choose this tool is given next.

> Select dimension to add/remove break or [Multiple]: *Select a dimension in which you want to insert a break.*
> Select object to break dimension or [Auto/Manual/Remove] <Auto>: *Select objects or dimensions that intersect the above selected dimension, enter an option or press* Enter *to choose the* ***Auto*** *option.*

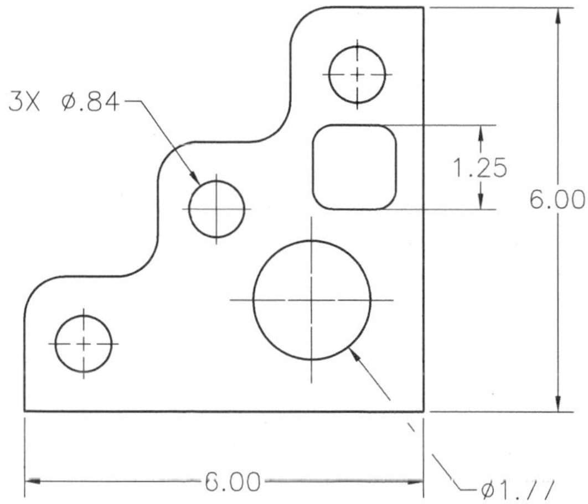

Figure 8-52 *Drawing with dimension breaks*

The options in the **Break** tool are discussed next.

Multiple

This option allows you to select more than one dimension for adding or removing a break. The prompt sequence that will follow is given next.

> Select dimensions: *Select the dimensions by any object selection method and press* Enter
> Select object to break dimensions or [Auto/Remove] <Auto>: *Enter an option or press* Enter

The **Auto** option available in the above prompt creates breaks automatically at the intersections of the selected dimensions with the other drawing and annotation entities. Also, if the selected dimensions are self-intersecting, then the **Auto** option, if chosen, creates a break at the point of intersection. The **Remove** option removes all the dimension breaks that exist in the selected dimensions.

Auto

This option automatically creates the break at the intersection of the selected dimension with the other drawing objects and annotation entities.

Note

*All dimension breaks created by using the **Multiple** and **Auto** options update automatically when you modify the broken dimension or the intersecting objects. However, the new objects that are created over the broken dimension do not have any effect on the display of the broken dimension. For example, the dimension that has already been broken will not be further broken with respect to newly created objects even if the object(s) interfere with the dimension. To break the newly created dimension, you need to use the **Break** tool again.*

Remove

This option removes all the dimension breaks from the selected dimension.

Manual

This option is used to manually create a break in a dimension. You have to specify two points between which you want to break the dimension or the extension line. You can create dimension break at only one location with this option.

Note

*1. The dimension breaks created by the **Manual** option do not update automatically when you modify the broken dimension or the intersecting objects. For updating the dimension break, you need to remove the dimension and then again add the dimension break.*

2. You cannot add dimension breaks to straight leaders, spline leaders, and spline multileaders.

CREATING INSPECTION DIMENSIONS

Ribbon: Annotate > Dimensions > Inspect	**Toolbar:** Dimensions > Inspection
Menu Bar: Dimension > Inspection	**Command:** DIMINSPECT

A drawing sheet provides every minute information about the dimension of the product, including the inspection rate. The **Inspect** tool in AutoCAD is used to describe inspection rate of critical dimension of the product to ensure its quality. The inspection rate is used to specify how frequently the dimensions are to be checked to ensure that the variations in the dimensions are within the range. Select a dimension from the drawing and choose the **Inspect** tool from the **Dimensions** panel; the **Inspection Dimension** dialog box will be displayed, as shown in Figure 8-53. Choose the **OK** button; the selected dimension will change into the inspection dimension that consists of three fields, which are discussed next.

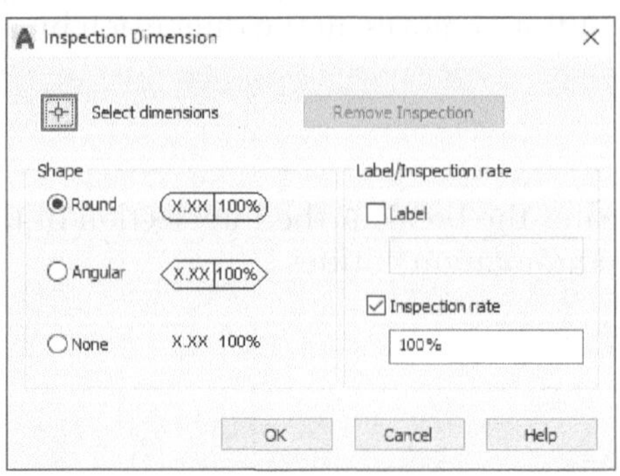

*Figure 8-53 The **Inspection Dimension** dialog box*

Inspection Label

The inspection label is located at the extreme left of the inspection dimension and is used to specify the particular inspection dimension, refer to Figure 8-54.

Dimension Value

The dimension value is located in the middle of the inspection dimension and is used to display the value of the dimension to be maintained, refer to Figure 8-54.

Inspection Rate

The inspection rate is located at the right-end of the inspection dimension. It is used to specify the frequency of carrying out inspections, refer to Figure 8-54. The frequency of inspection is specified in terms of percentage value. The value 100% signifies that you need to check the dimension each time you inspect a component. Similarly, if the value is 50 % then you need to check the dimension for every second component.

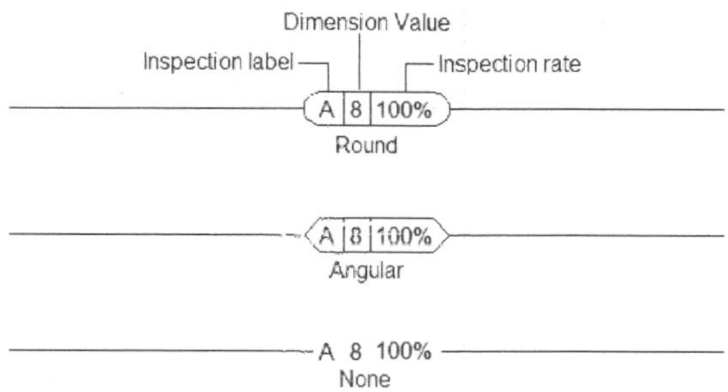

Figure 8-54 *Shapes and components of inspection dimension*

If you have not selected the dimension before invoking the **Inspect** tool, choose the **Select dimensions** button from the **Inspection Dimension** dialog box, refer to Figure 8-53; the dialog box will temporarily disappear from the screen, thereby enabling you to select the dimension that you want to convert into the inspection dimension. Select the dimensions and press the ENTER key; the **Inspection Dimension** dialog box will be displayed again. All the selected dimensions will display the same value of the label and inspection rate. Next, specify the shape of the boundary around the inspection dimension from the **Shape** area. Figure 8-54 displays the shapes available in the **Inspection Dimension** dialog box. Next, enter the values for the label and inspection rate in their respective edit boxes in the **Label/Inspection rate** area and choose the **OK** button. You can also control the display of label and inspection rate in the inspection dimension by clearing or selecting the **Label** and **Inspection rate** check boxes respectively. To remove the inspection dimension of the selected dimension, choose the **Remove Inspection** button from the **Inspection Dimension** dialog box and then choose the **OK** button.

WORKING WITH TRUE ASSOCIATIVE DIMENSIONS

The true associative dimensions are the dimensions that are automatically modified when the objects to which they are associated are modified. By default, all dimensions in AutoCAD are true associative dimensions. If the dimension attached to the object is true associative, then it will be modified automatically when the object is modified. In this case, you do not have to select the definition points of the dimensions. Any dimension in AutoCAD can be converted into a disassociated dimension and then converted back to the true associative dimension. The procedure to do so is discussed next.

Removing the Dimension Associativity

Command: DIMDISASSOCIATE

The **DIMDISASSOCIATE** command is used to remove the associativity of the dimensions from the object to which they are associated. When you invoke this command, you will be prompted to select the dimensions to be disassociated. The true association of the selected dimensions is automatically removed once you exit this command. The number of dimensions disassociated is displayed in the command prompt.

Converting a Dimension into a True Associative Dimension

Ribbon: Annotate > Dimensions > Reassociate **Command:** DIMREASSOCIATE
Menu Bar: Dimension > Reassociate Dimensions

The **Reassociate** tool is used to create a true associative dimension by associating the selected dimension to the specified object. When you invoke this tool, you will be prompted to select the objects. These objects are the dimensions to be associated. Select the dimensions to be associated and press ENTER; a cross is displayed and you are prompted to select the feature location. This cross implies that the dimension is not associated. You can define a new association point for the dimensions by selecting the objects or by using the object snaps. If you select a dimension that has already been associated to an object, the cross will be displayed inside a box. The prompt sequence that is displayed varies depending upon the type of dimension selected. In case of linear, aligned, radius, and diameter dimensions, you can directly select the object to associate the dimension. If the arcs or circles are assigned angular dimensions using three points, then also you can select these arcs or circles directly for associating the dimensions. For rest of the dimension types, you can use the object snaps to specify the point to associate the dimensions.

Note

*If you have edited a dimension by using the **Mtext** or **Text** option, then on using the **Reassociate** tool, the overridden value will be replaced by the original value.*

Exercise 5

Draw and dimension the object, as shown in Figure 8-55.

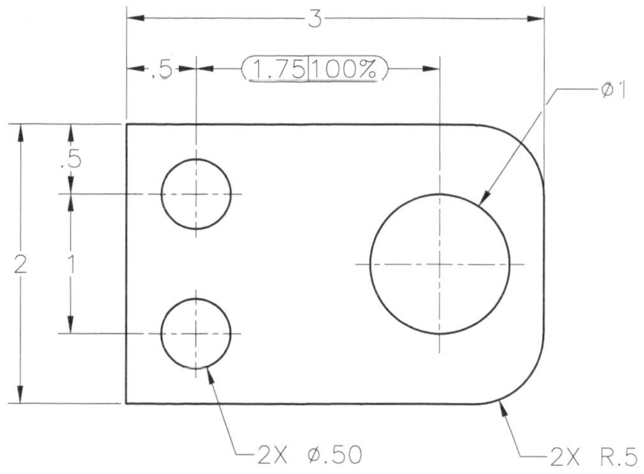

Figure 8-55 *Drawing for Exercise 5*

DRAWING LEADERS

Command: QLEADER

The leader line is used to attach annotations to an object or when the user wants to show a dimension without using another dimensioning tool. Sometimes, leaders of the dimensions of circles or arcs are so complicated that you need to construct a leader of your own. The leaders can be created using the **QLEADER** command. The leaders drawn by using this command create the arrow and the leader lines as a single object. The text is created as a separate object. This command can create multiline annotations and offer several options such as copying existing annotations and so on. You can customize the leader and annotation by selecting the **Settings** option at the **Specify first leader point, or [Settings] <Settings>** prompt. The prompt sequence that will follow when you use this command is given next.

Specify first leader point, or [Settings] <Settings>: *Specify the start point of the leader.*
Specify next point: *Specify the endpoint of the leader.*
Specify next point: *Specify the next point.*
Specify text width <current>: *Enter the text width of multiline text.* Enter
Enter first line of annotation text <Mtext>: *Press ENTER; AutoCAD displays the **Text Editor**. Enter text in text window and then choose the **Close Text Editor** button from the **Ribbon** to exit the tool.*

If you press ENTER at the **Specify first leader point, or [Settings] <Settings>** prompt, then the **Leader Settings** dialog box is displayed, refer to Figure 8-56. The **Leader Settings** dialog box gives you a number of options for the leader line and the text attached to it. It has the following tabs.

Annotation Tab

This tab provides you with various options to control annotation features, as shown in Figure 8-56.

Annotation Type Area

The options in the **Annotation Type** area and their usage are discussed next.

MText: When this radio button is selected, AutoCAD uses the **Text Editor** to create an annotation. Therefore, on selecting this radio button, the options in the **MText options** area become available.

Copy an Object: This radio button allows you to copy an existing annotation object (like multiline text, single line text, tolerance, or block) and attach it at the end of the leader. For example, if you have a text string in the drawing that you want to place at the end of the leader, you can use the **Copy an Object** radio button to place it at the end of the leader.

Tolerance: Select the **Tolerance** radio button and choose the **OK** button to exit from the **Leader Settings** dialog box. Then, complete the leader line; AutoCAD will display the **Geometric Tolerance** dialog box. In this dialog box, specify the tolerance and choose the **OK** button to exit it. AutoCAD will place the specified geometric tolerance with the feature control frame at the end of the leader, refer to Figure 8-57.

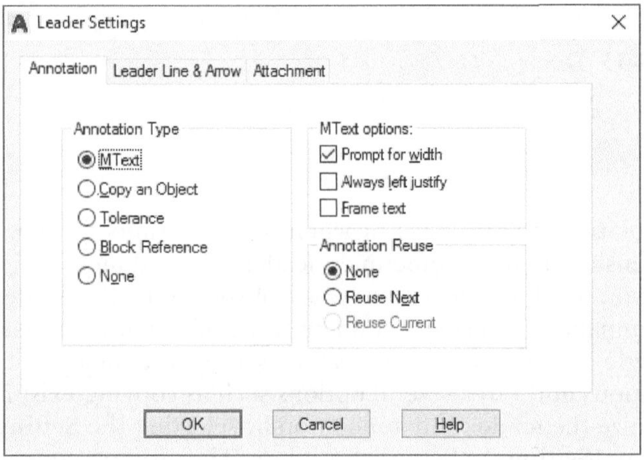

*Figure 8-56 The **Annotation** tab of the **Leader Settings** dialog box*

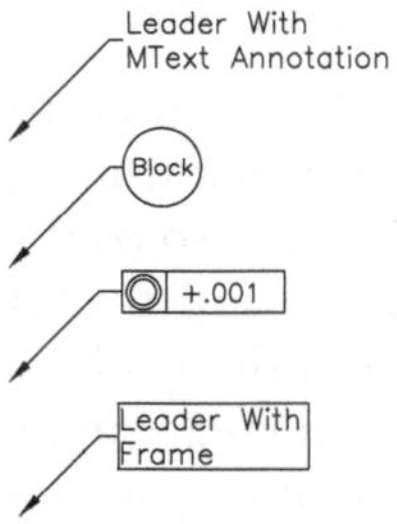

Figure 8-57 Leaders with different annotation types

Block Reference: The **Block Reference** radio button allows you to insert a predefined block at the end of the leader. When you select this option, AutoCAD will prompt you to enter the block name and insertion point.

None: This radio button creates a leader without placing any annotation at the end of the leader.

MText options Area

The options under this area will be available only if the **MText** radio button is selected from the **Annotation Type** area. This area provides you with the following options.

Prompt for width: Selecting this check box allows you to specify the width of the multiline text annotation.

Always left justify: Select this check box to left justify the multiline text annotation in all situations. Selecting this check box makes the prompt for the width option unavailable.

Frame text: Selecting this check box draws a box around the multiline text annotation.

Annotation Reuse Area
The options under this area allow you to reuse the annotation.

None: When this radio button is selected, AutoCAD cannot reuse the leader annotation.

Reuse Next: This radio button is used to reuse the annotation that you are going to create next for all subsequent leaders.

Reuse Current: This radio button allows you to reuse the current annotation for all subsequent leaders.

Leader Line & Arrow Tab
The options in the **Leader Line & Arrow** tab are related to the leader parameters, as shown in Figure 8-58.

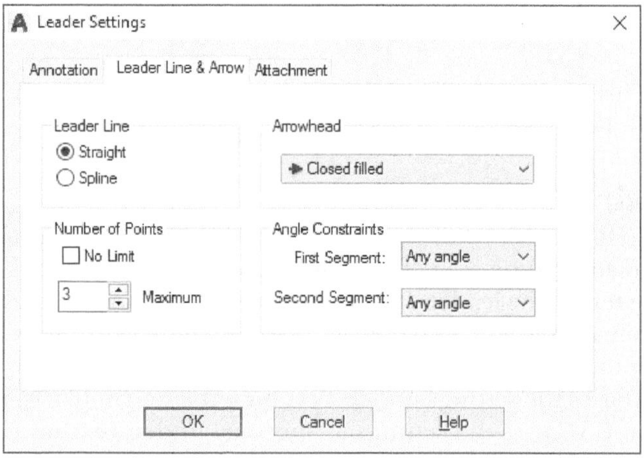

***Figure 8-58** The **Leader Line & Arrow** tab of the **Leader Settings** dialog box*

Leader Line Area
This area has the options for the leader line type such as straight or spline. The **Spline** option draws a spline through the specified leader points and the **Straight** option draws straight lines. Figure 8-59 shows the straight and splined leader lines.

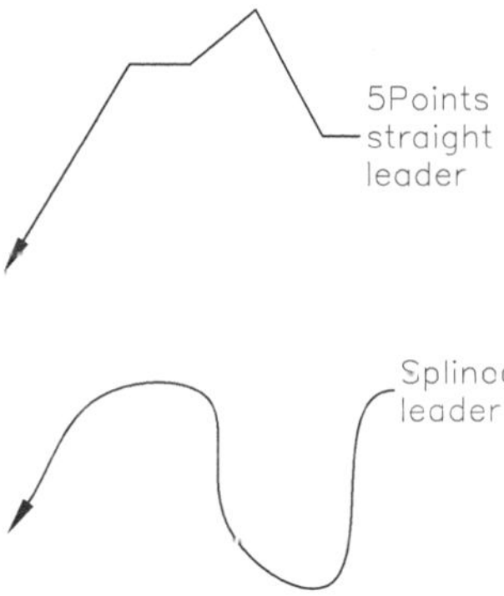

***Figure 8-59** Straight and splined leader lines*

Number of Points Area
The options provided under this area are used to specify the number of points in the leader.

No Limit: If this check box is selected, you can define as many numbers of points as you want in the leader line. AutoCAD will keep prompting you for the next point, until you press ENTER at this prompt.

Maximum: This spinner is used to specify the maximum number of points on the leader line. The default value in this spinner is 3; as a result, there will be only three points in the leader line. You can specify the number of points by using this spinner to control the shape of the leader. This has to be kept in mind that the start point of the leader is the first leader point. This spinner will be available only if the **No Limit** check box is clear. Figure 8-59 shows a leader line with five points.

Arrowhead Area

The options in the drop-down list under this area allow you to define a leader arrowhead. The arrowhead is the same as the one for dimensioning. You can also use the user-defined arrows by selecting the **User Arrow** button from the drop-down list.

Angle Constraints Area

The options provided under this area are used to define the angle for the segments of the leader lines.

First Segment: This drop-down list is used to specify the angle at which the first leader line segment will be drawn. You can select the predefined values from this drop-down list.

Second Segment: This drop-down list is used to specify the angle at which the second leader line segment will be drawn.

Attachment Tab

The **Attachment** tab (Figure 8-60) will be available only if you have selected the **MText** radio button from the **Annotation Type** area of the **Annotation** tab. The options in this tab are used to attach the multiline text to the leader. It has two columns: **Text on left side** and **Text on right side**. Both these columns have five radio buttons below them. You can select the required radio button corresponding to the options for attaching the multiline text. If you draw a leader from right to left, AutoCAD uses the settings under **Text on left side**. Similarly, if you draw a leader from left to right, AutoCAD uses the settings as specified under **Text on right side**. This area also provides you with the **Underline bottom line** check box. If this check box is selected, then the last line of the multiline text will be underlined.

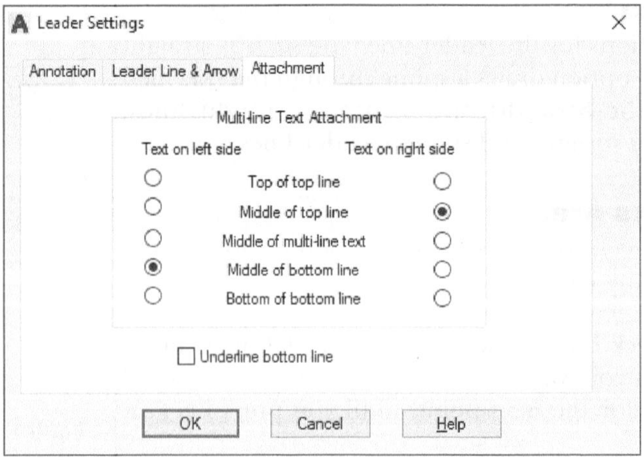

***Figure 8-60** The **Attachment** tab of the **Leader Settings** dialog box*

Note

*You can use the command line to create leaders with the help of the **LEADER** command. The options under this command are similar to those under the **QLEADER** command. The only difference is that the **LEADER** command uses the command line.*

Exercise 6 — Qleader

Make the drawing shown in Figure 8-61 and then use the **QLEADER** command to dimension the part accordingly. The distance between the dotted lines is 0.5 units.

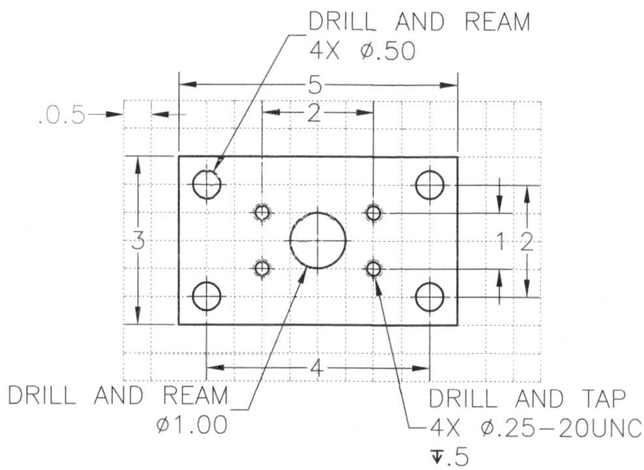

Figure 8-61 *Drawing for Exercise 6*

MULTILEADERS

Ribbon: Annotate > Leaders > Multileader **Toolbar:** Multileader > Multileader
Command: MLEADER/MLD

Multileaders are the enhanced leaders, wherein the leader and its content is part of the same object. A Multileader provides you enough flexibility so that you can create either the arrowhead or the tail end first. Alternatively, you can specify the content of the leader first and then draw the leader. Multileaders can have more than one leader so that a single comment can be pointed at more than one location. Besides this, multiple notes can be attached to a single leader so that more than one comment can be pointed at a single location. You can add or remove leaders from the previously created multileaders. You can also control and modify the appearance of the multileaders.

DRAWING MULTILEADERS

To draw a multileader, choose the **Multileader** tool from the **Leaders** panel of the **Annotate** tab. The prompt sequence after choosing this tool is given next.

Specify leader arrowhead location or [leader Landing first/Content first/Options] <Options>: *Specify the location for the arrowhead from where the leader will start.*
Specify leader landing location: *Specify the leader landing location, refer to Figure 8-62.*

The ***Text Editor*** tab is added to the ribbon. Enter the text in text window and click outside the editor to accept and exit the tool. If you click outside the editor without entering any text and exit the tool, no text will be attached to the multileader.

The other options in the **Multileader** tool are discussed next.

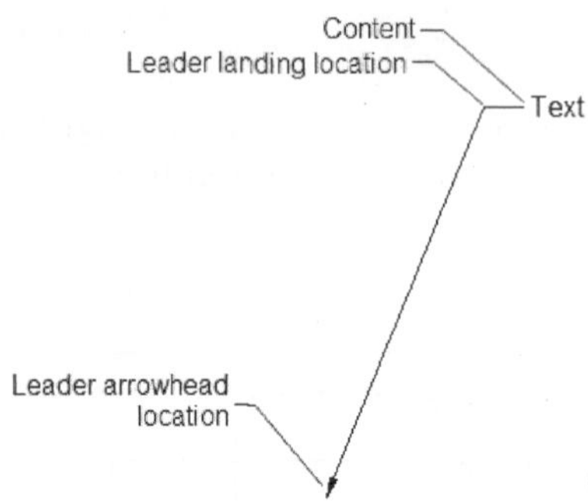

Figure 8-62 *Image displaying the options to locate the leader start point*

leader Landing first

This option is used to locate the leader landing line first. Choose the **leader Landing first** option from the shortcut menu at the **Specify leader arrowhead location or [leader Landing first/Content first/Options] <Options>** prompt to invoke this option. Alternatively, if the **Dynamic Input** button is turned on in the Status Bar, then you can choose this option from the dynamic input box associated with the cursor. On doing so, you will be prompted to specify a point where the leader landing should be placed. Specify the leader landing location; you will be prompted to specify the leader arrowhead location. The leader landing will automatically adjust itself to the leader landing point depending upon the direction in which you create the leader. For example, if you create the leader on the left of the leader landing location, a landing will automatically be created at the right of the leader landing location.

Content first

This option is used to specify the content (multiline text or block) of the leader first. Choose the **Content first** option from the shortcut menu or from the **Specify leader arrowhead location or [leader Landing first/Content first/Options] <Options>** prompt to invoke this option. Alternatively, if the **Dynamic Input** button is turned on in the Status Bar, you can choose this option from the dynamic input box associated with the cursor. After specifying the content to be attached with the leader, a horizontal leader landing will automatically be attached to the content and then you can specify the leader arrowhead location.

Note

If you have previously drawn a multileader by using any one of the above-mentioned options, then the succeeding multileaders will be created by using that option only until otherwise modified.

Options

The sub options within this option are used to control the leader type, content to be attached with the leader, size of the leader landing, and so on. These suboptions are discussed next.

Leader type

This option provides the suboptions for the leader line type such as straight, spline, or none. The **Spline** suboption draws a spline through the specified leader points and the **Straight** option draws straight lines. Figure 8-59 shows straight and spline leader lines. The **None** option enables you to draw the content of the leader without drawing the leader itself.

leader landing

This option provides you the suboptions to control the display of the horizontal landing line. The **No** suboption will create a leader with no horizontal landing and the **Yes** suboption will create a leader with the horizontal landing. If you choose the **Yes** suboption, then you will be prompted to specify the length of the horizontal landing. The new leader will be created with the specified landing length. Figure 8-63 shows the leaders created by using various suboptions of the **leader landing**.

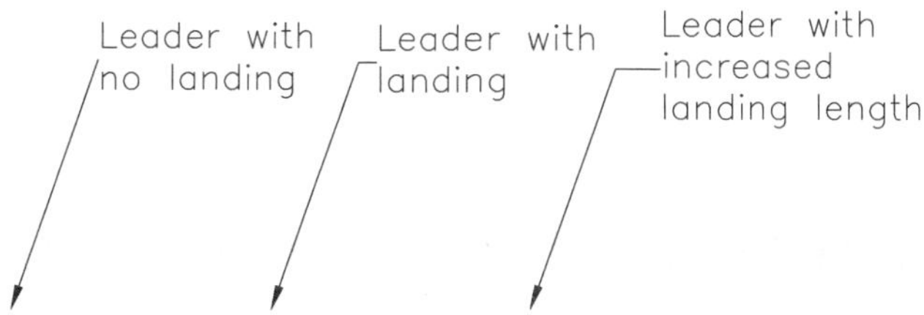

Figure 8-63 *Leaders drawn by using various types of landing suboptions*

Content type

This option is used to specify the type of content to be attached with the leader. The **Mtext** suboption uses the AutoCAD **Text Editor** to create the content. The **Block** suboption allows you to insert a predefined block at the end of the leader. When you select this option, AutoCAD will prompt you to enter the block name and the specified block will be attached to the new leader. The **None** suboption creates a leader without placing any content at the end of the leader.

Maxpoints

This option is used to specify the maximum number of points on the leader line. The default value is 2 which means there will be only two points on the leader line. You can specify the maximum number of points by entering the new value. This has to be kept in mind that the start point of the leader is the first leader point.

First angle

This option is used to constrain the angle of the first leader line to a fixed value. You can only specify a value which is the natural number multiple of 15-degree.

Second angle

This option is used to constrain the angle of the second leader line with respect to the end point of the first leader line. You can only specify a value which is the natural number multiple of 15-degree.

eXit options

This option will return you back to the main options of the multileader.

Note

All settings specified in the ***Options*** *heading of the multileader will last only for that particular leader, and the next leader will be created with the default settings. You can also change the default settings of the multileader from the* ***Multileader Style Manager*** *dialog box that will be discussed in detail in Chapter 10.*

ADDING LEADERS TO EXISTING MULTILEADER

Ribbon: Annotate > Leaders > Add Leader **Toolbar:** Multileaders > Add Leader
Command: MLEADEREDIT

The **Add Leader** tool is used to add leaders to an existing multileader so that you can point a single content to more than one location. To do so, choose the **Add Leader** tool in the **Leaders** panel; you will be prompted to select the multileader to which you want to attach the new leader. After selecting the desired multileader, a new leader will branch out from the landing location of the existing multileader. Next, you will be prompted to specify the location of the arrowhead of the new leader. Next, you can attach any number of leaders to the selected multileader. To exit this tool, press the ENTER key.

REMOVING LEADERS FROM EXISTING MULTILEADER

Ribbon: Annotate > Leaders > Remove Leader **Toolbar:** Multileaders > Remove Leader
Command: MLEADEREDIT

The **Remove Leader** tool is used to remove leaders from an existing multileader. To remove a leader, choose the **Remove Leader** tool from the **Leaders** panel; you will be prompted to select the multileader from which you want to remove leaders. Select the multileader; you will be prompted to select the leaders to be removed from the selected multileader. Select the leaders and then press the ENTER key. You can also select all the leaders of the specified multileader. But, in such cases, all multileaders will get deleted from the drawing area.

ALIGNING MULTILEADERS

Ribbon: Annotate > Leaders > Align **Toolbar:** Multileaders > Align Multileaders
Command: MLEADERALIGN/MLA

The **Align** tool is used to arrange the selected multileaders by aligning them about a line or making them parallel or by maintaining the spacing between the horizontal landing of the leaders. To do so, choose the **Align** tool from the **Leaders** panel; you will be prompted to select the multileaders to be aligned. After selecting the multileaders, press the ENTER key. Next, you will be prompted to select one of the multileaders with respect to which all other multileaders will get aligned. Also, you can choose the alignment type from the different options available at the command prompt. The prompt sequence after choosing the **Align** tool is given next.

Select multileaders: *Select the multileaders to be aligned and press* Enter.
Current mode: *Use current spacing.*
All further prompt sequences will vary with the alignment type used in aligning the leaders. The alignment type used previously will become the default alignment type for the current tool.

Select multileader to align to or [Options]: *Enter **O** to choose the type of alignment.*
Enter an option [Distribute/make leader segments Parallel/specify Spacing/Use current spacing] <Use current spacing>: *Specify an option and press* Enter.

The options in the above prompt sequence are discussed next.

Distribute

This option is used to accommodate all the selected multileaders at constant spacing between two specified points. The prompt sequence that will be followed is given next.

Enter an option [Distribute/make leader segments Parallel/specify Spacing/Use current spacing] <current>: **D** Enter.
Specify first point or [Options]: *Specify the location of the first point.*
Specify second point: *Specify the location of the second point and its orientation with respect to the first point.*

The tail end of all the selected leaders landing will get aligned with equal spacing along the line joining the first and the second specified point. Figure 8-64 shows a drawing with its multileaders nonaligned. Figure 8-65 displays the same drawing with its multileaders aligned along an imaginary vertical line by using the **Distribute** option.

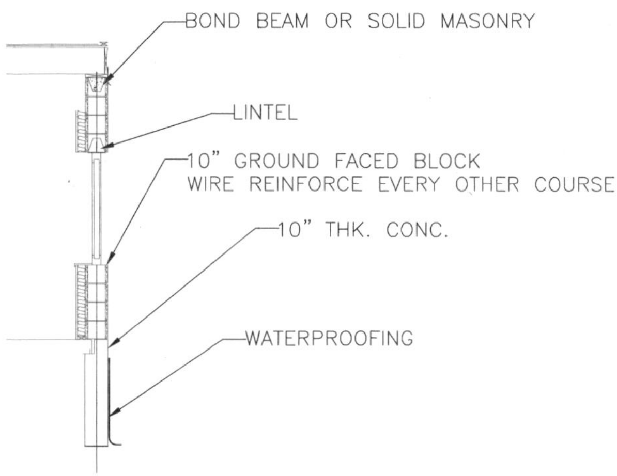

Figure 8-64 *Drawing with non- aligned multileaders*

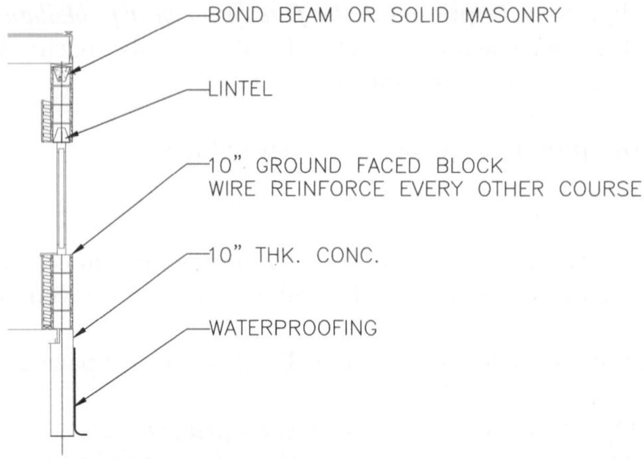

Figure 8-65 *Drawing with multileaders aligned using the **Distribute** option*

make leader segments Parallel

This option is used to make all the selected multileaders parallel to one of the leaders selected as reference. The prompt sequence that will be followed is given next.

Enter an option [Distribute/make leader segments Parallel/specify Spacing/Use current spacing] <current>: **P** Enter.
Select multileader to align to or [Options]: *Select the leader with which you want to make all other selected multileaders parallel.*

Figure 8-66 shows the drawing with its leader aligned parallel to the lowest leader of the drawing.

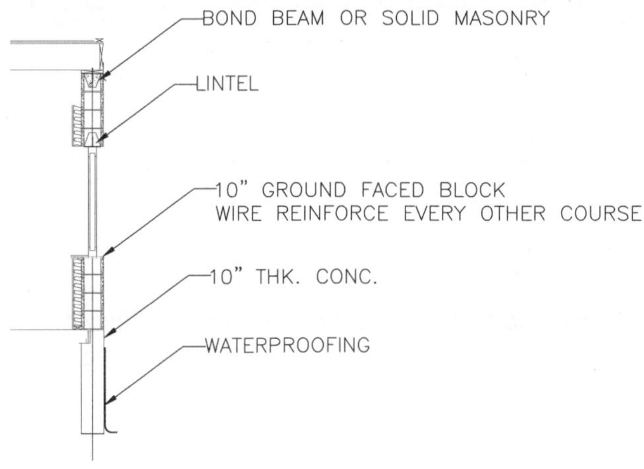

Figure 8-66 *Drawing with multileaders aligned using the **make leader segments Parallel** option*

Specify Spacing

This option is used to align the selected multileaders in the specified direction and also to maintain a constant spacing between the landing lines. You need to specify one reference leader, with respect to which the specified interval and direction will be measured. The prompt sequence that will be followed is given next.

Enter an option [Distribute/make leader segments Parallel/specify Spacing/Use current spacing] <current>: **S** Enter.
Specify spacing <current>: *Enter the distance value to be maintained between the two consecutive leader landing lines.*
Select multileader to align to or [Options]: *Select one of the leaders with respect to which the specified distance will be measured.*
Specify direction: *Specify the desired direction in the drawing area for the alignment of multileaders.*

When you select a multileader to align with other multileaders, an imaginary line will be displayed in the drawing area. This line allows you to specify the direction of alignment. All the multileaders will get aligned to the selected multileader at the specified distance and direction. Figure 8-67 shows the drawing with its multileaders aligned vertical using the **specify Spacing** option.

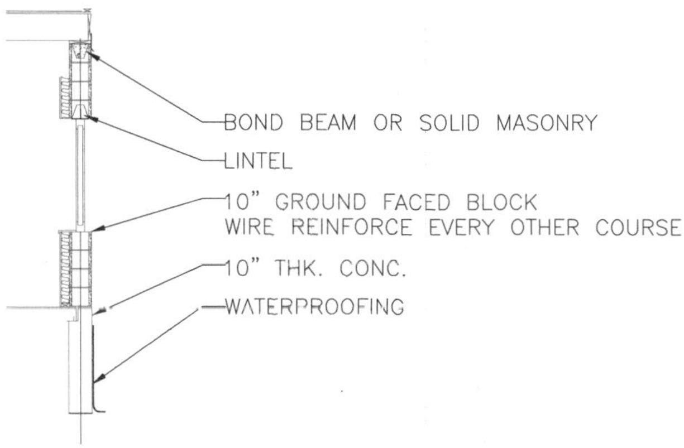

Figure 8-67 *Drawing with multileaders aligned using the **specify Spacing** option*

Use current spacing

This option is used to align the selected multileaders in the specified direction and also to retain the distance between the landing lines intact. You need to specify one reference leader with respect to which the distance will be measured in the specified direction. The prompt sequence that will be followed is given next.

Enter an option [Distribute/make leader segments Parallel/specify Spacing/Use current spacing] <specify Spacing>: **U** Enter.
Select multileader to align to or [Options]: *Select one of the leaders with respect to which the direction to be specified is maintained.*
Specify direction: *Specify the desired direction in the drawing area for the alignment of the multileaders.*

COLLECTING MULTIPLE LEADERS

Ribbon: Annotate > Leaders > Collect	**Toolbar:** Multileader > Collect Multileaders
Command: MLEADERCOLLECT/MLC	

The **Collect** tool is used to collect the content of the selected multileaders and attach them to a single leader landing. Note that only the multileaders having predefined blocks as content can be collected by this tool. To collect the multileaders, choose the **Collect** tool from the **Leaders** panel. Select the multileaders in the order in which you want them to be collected and press ENTER. The content of the last selected multileader will be retained to its landing position and the content of all other multileaders will move to the last multileader. Next, specify a point in the drawing area where the upper left-corner of the collected content of the multileaders will be placed. You can collect the content horizontally or vertically by placing the content one after another, or by specifying the space between which the contents will be placed, and the content exceeding the specified distance will be sent to the next row. The prompt sequence after choosing the **Collect** tool is given next.

> Select multileaders: *Select the multileaders in the order in which you want to collect the content of these multileaders and press* Enter.
> Specify collected multileader location or [Vertical/Horizontal/Wrap] <current>: *Specify a point in the drawing area where the upper left-corner of the collected content will be placed or choose an option.*

If you choose the **Horizontal** option from the shortcut menu or from the **Specify collected multileader location or [Vertical/Horizontal/Wrap] <current>** prompt sequence, the contents of the selected multileaders will get collected horizontally. Figure 8-68 shows the multileaders prior to the collection and Figure 8-69(a) shows the same leaders after the horizontal alignment. If you choose the **Vertical** option from the shortcut menu or from the **Specify collected multileader location or [Vertical/Horizontal/Wrap] <current>** prompt sequence, the contents of the selected multileaders will get collected vertically, refer to Figure 8-69(b).

If you choose the **Wrap** option from the shortcut menu or from the **Specify collected multileader location or [Vertical/Horizontal/Wrap] <current>** prompt sequence, you will be prompted to enter a value for the wrap width. The contents of the selected multileaders will be placed side by side and the contents that could not be accommodated into the specified wrap width will be sent to the next row. In Figure 8-69(c), three blocks get accommodated into the specified wrap width and the remaining one is sent to the next row. Alternatively, you can also enter the number of blocks to be accommodated into one row and the remaining content will automatically be sent to the next row. Choose **Number** from the shortcut menu displayed by right-clicking or from the **Specify wrap width or [Number]** prompt sequence. Next, enter the number of blocks to be accommodated into each row. In Figure 8-69(d), only two blocks are specified to be accommodated into each row, so the remaining two blocks have been sent to the second row.

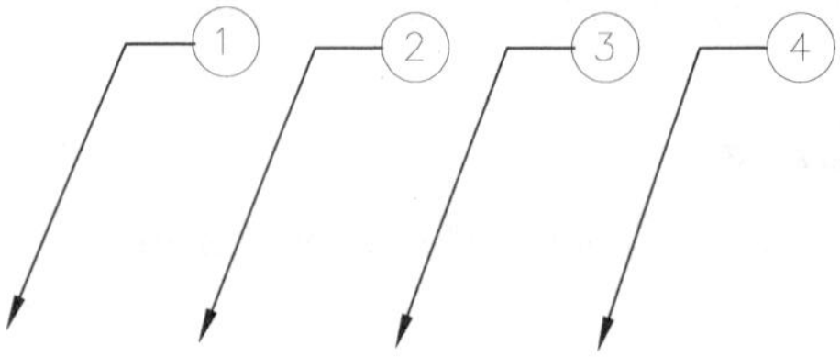

Figure 8-68 *Multileaders prior to the collection*

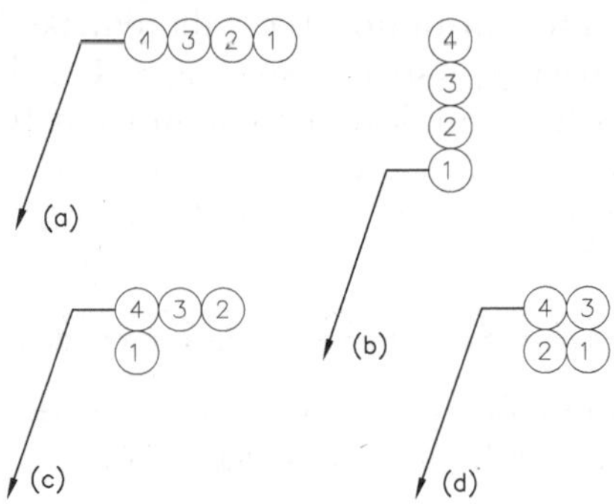

Figure 8-69 *Contents of the multileaders after being collected*

GEOMETRIC DIMENSIONING AND TOLERANCING

One of the most important parts of the design process is assigning the dimensions and tolerances to parts, since every part is manufactured from the dimensions given in the drawing. Therefore, every designer must understand and have a thorough knowledge of the standard practices used in the industry to make sure that the information given on the drawing is correct and can be understood by other people. Tolerancing is equally important, especially in the assembled parts. Tolerances and fits determine how the parts will fit. Incorrect tolerances could result in a product that is not usable. In addition to dimensioning and tolerancing, the function and the relationship that exists between the mating parts is important if the part is to perform the way it was designed. This aspect of the design process is addressed by geometric dimensioning and tolerancing, generally known as GD & T.

Geometric dimensioning and tolerancing is a means to design and manufacture parts with respect to the actual function and relationship that exists between different features of the same part or the features of the mating parts. Therefore, a good design is not achieved by just giving dimensions and tolerances. The designer has to go beyond dimensioning and think of the intended function of the part and how the features of the part are going to affect its function. For example, Figure 8-70 shows a part with the required dimensions and tolerances. In this drawing, there is no mention of the relationship between the pin and the plate. Is the pin perpendicular to the plate? If it is, to what degree should it be perpendicular? Also, it does not mention on which surface the perpendicularity of the pin is to be measured. A design like this is open to individual interpretation based on intuition and experience. This is where geometric dimensioning and tolerancing play an important part in the product design process.

Figure 8-71 has been dimensioned using geometric dimensioning and tolerancing. The feature symbols define the datum (reference plane) and the permissible deviation in the perpendicularity of the pin with respect to the bottom surface. From a drawing like this, chances of making a mistake are minimized.

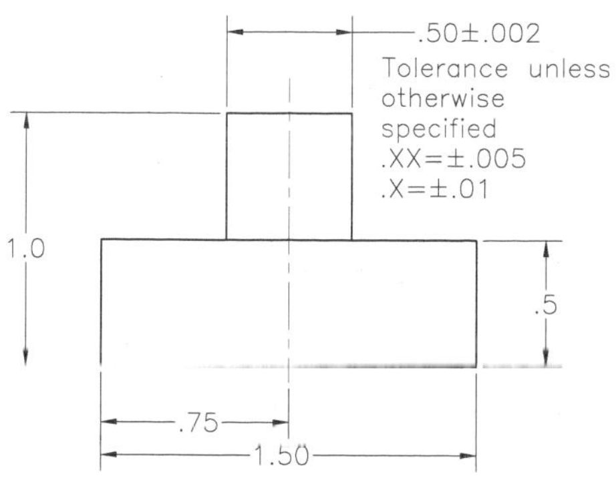

Figure 8-70 Traditional dimensioning and tolerancing technique

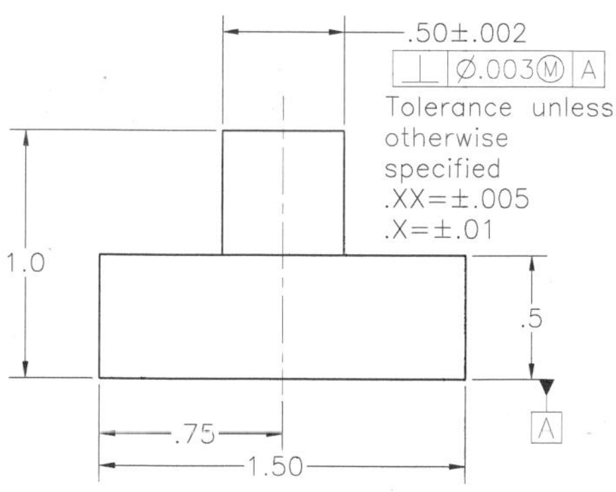

Figure 8-71 Geometric dimensioning and tolerancing

Geometric Characteristics and Symbols

Before discussing the application of AutoCAD tools in geometric dimensioning and tolerancing, you need to understand the following feature symbols and tolerancing components. Figure 8-72 shows the geometric characteristics and symbols used in geometric dimensioning and tolerancing.

Note

Symbols used in geometric dimensioning and tolerancing are the building blocks of geometric dimensioning and tolerancing.

Kind of feature	Type of feature	Characteristics	
Related	Location	Position	⌖
		Concentricity or Coaxiality	◎
		Symmetry	⌯
	Orientation	Parallelism	//
		Perpendicularity	⊥
		Angularity	∠
Individual	Form	Cylindricity	⌭
		Flatness	▱
		Circularity or Roundness	○
		Straightness	—
Individual or related	Profile	Surface Profile	⌓
		Line Profile	⌒
Related	Runout	Circular Runout	↗
		Total Runout	⌰

Figure 8-72 *Characteristics and symbols used in Geometric Tolerancing*

ADDING GEOMETRIC TOLERANCE

Ribbon: Annotate > Dimensions > Tolerance **Toolbar:** Dimension > Tolerance
Menu Bar: Dimension > Tolerance **Command:** TOLERANCE/TOL

Geometric tolerance displays the deviations of profile, orientation, form, location, and runout of a feature. In AutoCAD, geometrical tolerancing is displayed by feature control frames. The frames contain all information about tolerances for a single dimension. To display feature control frames with various tolerancing parameters, you need to enter specifications in the **Geometric Tolerance** dialog box, as shown in Figure 8-73. You can invoke the **Geometric Tolerance** dialog box by choosing the **Tolerance** tool from the extended **Dimensions** panel.

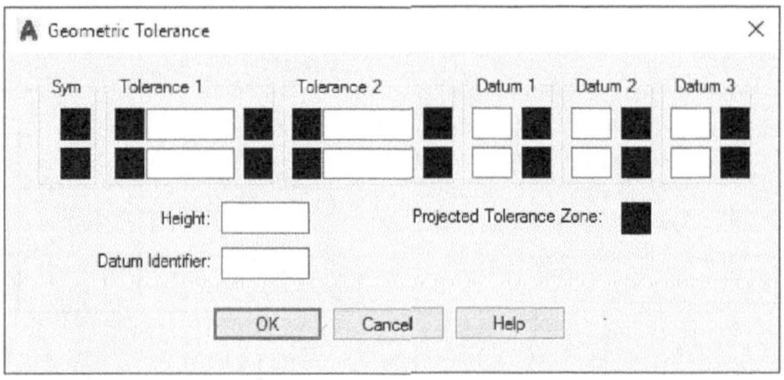

Figure 8-73 *The* ***Geometric Tolerance*** *dialog box*

Various components that constitute geometric tolerancing (GTOL) are shown in Figure 8-74 and Figure 8-75.

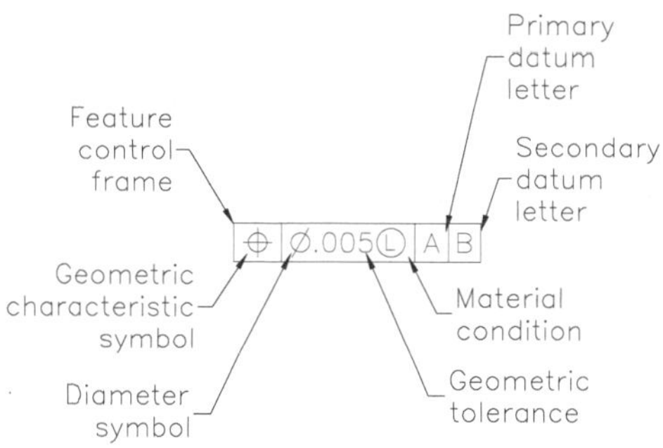

Figure 8-74 *Components of GTOL*

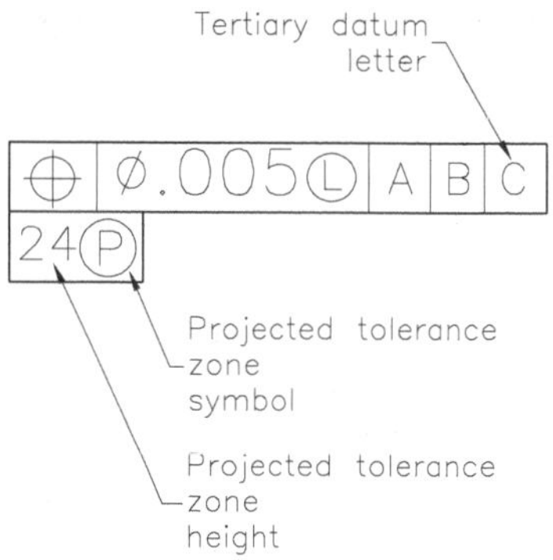

Figure 8-75 *Components of GTOL*

Feature Control Frame

The feature control frame is a rectangular box that contains the geometric characteristics symbols and tolerance definition. The box is automatically drawn to standard specifications, you do not need to specify its size. You can copy, move, erase, rotate, and scale the feature control frame. You can also snap to them using various Object snap modes. You can edit feature control frames using the **TEXTEDIT** command or you can also edit them using **GRIPS**. The system variable **DIMCLRD** controls the color of the feature control frame. The system variable **DIMGAP** controls the gap between the feature control frame and the text.

Geometric Characteristics Symbol

The geometric characteristics symbols indicate the characteristics such as straightness, flatness, perpendicularity, and so on of a feature. You can select the required symbol from the **Symbol** dialog box, as shown in Figure 8-76. This dialog box is displayed by selecting the box provided in the **Sym** area of the **Geometric Tolerance** dialog box. To select the required symbol, just pick the symbol using the left mouse button. The symbol will now be displayed in the box under the **Sym** area.

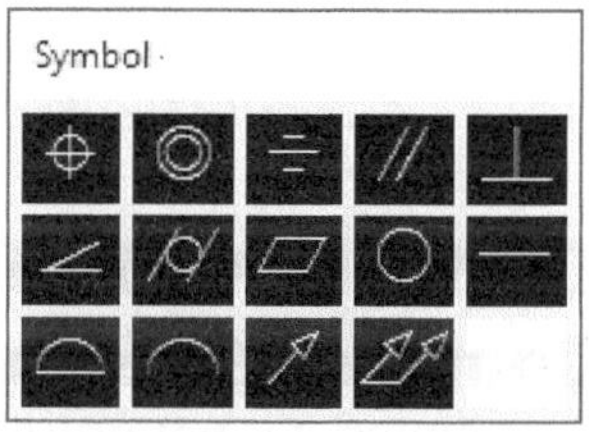

Figure 8-76 *The* ***Symbol*** *dialog box*

Tolerance Value and Tolerance Zone Descriptor

The tolerance value specifies the tolerance on the feature as indicated by the tolerance zone descriptor. For example, a value of .003 indicates that the feature must be within a 0.003 tolerance zone. Similarly, .003 indicates that this feature must be located at a true position within a 0.003 diameter. The tolerance value can be entered in the edit box provided under the **Tolerance 1** or the **Tolerance 2** area of the **Geometric Tolerance** dialog box. The tolerance zone descriptor can be invoked by selecting the box located to the left of the edit box. The system variable **DIMCLRT** controls the color of the tolerance text, variable **DIMTXT** controls the tolerance text size, and variable **DIMTXSTY** controls the style of the tolerance text. On using the **Projected Tolerance Zone**, the projected tolerance zone symbol, which is an encircled P will be inserted after the projected tolerance zone value.

Material Condition Modifier

The material condition modifier specifies the material condition when the tolerance value takes effect. For example, .003(M) indicates that this feature must be located at a true position within a 0.003 diameter at maximum material condition (MMC). The material condition modifier symbol can be selected from the **Material Condition** dialog box, as shown in Figure 8-77. This dialog box can be invoked by selecting the boxes located on the right side of the edit boxes under the **Tolerance 1**, **Tolerance 2**, **Datum 1**, **Datum 2**, and **Datum 3** areas of the **Geometric Tolerance** dialog box.

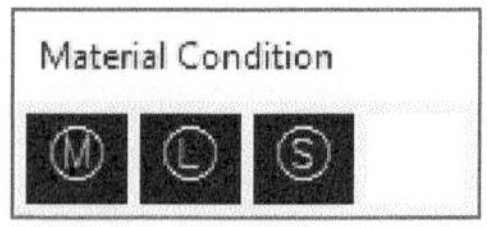

***Figure 8-77** The **Material Condition** dialog box*

Datum

The datum is the origin, surface, or feature from which the measurements are made. The datum is also used to establish the geometric characteristics of a feature. The datum feature symbol consists of a reference character enclosed in a feature control frame. You can create the datum feature symbol by entering characters (like -A-) in the **Datum Identifier** edit box in the **Geometric Tolerance** dialog box and then selecting a point where you want to establish this datum.

You can also combine datum references with geometric characteristics. AutoCAD automatically positions the datum references on the right end of the feature control frame.

Note

*In AutoCAD, you can change the specifications of GTOL. To change the specifications, double-click on GTOL; the **Geometric Tolerance** dialog box will be displayed. In the dialog box, you can change the specifications as required.*

COMPLEX FEATURE CONTROL FRAMES

Combining Geometric Characteristics

Sometimes, it is not possible to specify all geometric characteristics in one frame. For example, Figure 8-78 shows the drawing of a plate with a hole in the center.

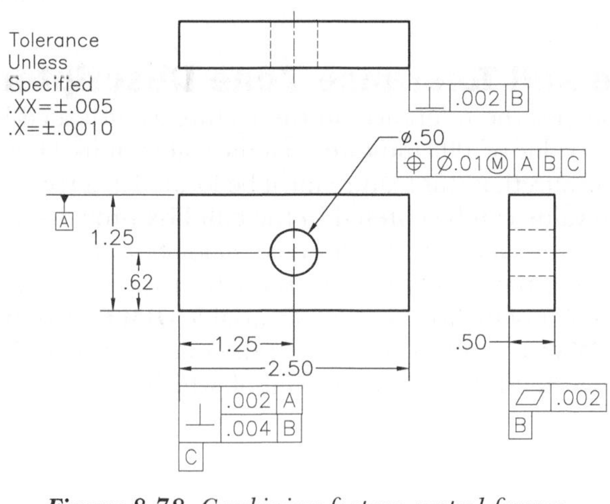

***Figure 8-78** Combining feature control frames*

In this part, it is determined that surface C must be perpendicular to surfaces A and B within 0.002 and 0.004, respectively. Therefore, we need two frames to specify the geometric characteristics of surface C. The first frame specifies the allowable deviation in perpendicularity of surface C with respect to surface A. The second frame specifies the allowable deviation in perpendicularity of surface C with respect to surface B. In addition to these two frames, we need a third frame that identifies datum surface C.

All the three feature control frames can be defined in one instance of the **Tolerance** tool.

1. Choose the **Tolerance** tool to invoke the **Geometric Tolerance** dialog box. Select the box under the **Sym** area to display the **Symbol** dialog box. Select the **perpendicular** symbol. AutoCAD will display the selected symbol in the first row of the **Sym** area.

2. Enter **.002** in the edit box under the **Tolerance 1** area of the first row and enter **A** in the first row edit box under the **Datum 1** area.

3. Select the second row box under the **Sym** area to display the **Symbol** dialog box. Select the **perpendicular** symbol. AutoCAD will display the selected symbol in the second row box of the **Sym** area.

4. Enter **.004** in the second row edit box under the **Tolerance 1** area and enter **B** in the second row edit box under the **Datum 1** area.

5. In the **Datum Identifier** edit box, enter **C** and then choose the **OK** button to exit the dialog box.

6. In the graphics screen, select the position to place the frame. Similarly, create the remaining feature control frames.

Composite Position Tolerancing

Sometimes the accuracy required within a pattern is more important than the location of the pattern with respect to the datum surfaces. To specify such a condition, composite position tolerancing may be used. For example, Figure 8-79 shows four holes (pattern) of diameter 0.15. The design allows a maximum tolerance of 0.025 with respect to datum A, B, and C at the maximum material condition (holes are smallest). The designer wants to maintain a closer positional tolerance (0.010 at MMC) between the holes within the pattern. To specify this requirement, the designer must insert the second frame. This is generally known as composite position tolerancing. AutoCAD provides the facility to create two composite position tolerance frames by means of the **Geometric Tolerance** dialog box. The composite tolerance frames can be created as follows:

1. Invoke the **Tolerance** tool to display the **Geometric Tolerance** dialog box. Select the box under the **Sym** area to display the **Symbol** dialog box. Select the **position** symbol. AutoCAD will display the selected symbol in the first row of the **Sym** area.

2. In the first row of the **Geometric Tolerance** dialog box, enter the geometric characteristics and the datum references required for the first position tolerance frame.

3. Next, select the box under the **Sym** area from the second row to display the **Symbol** dialog box. Select the position symbol; AutoCAD will display the selected symbol in the second row of the **Sym** area.

4. In the second row of the **Geometric Tolerance** dialog box, enter the geometric characteristics and the datum references required for the second position tolerance frame.

5. When you have finished entering the values, choose the **OK** button in the **Geometric Tolerance** dialog box, and then select the point where you want to insert the frames. AutoCAD will create two frames and automatically align them with the common position symbol, as shown in Figure 8-79.

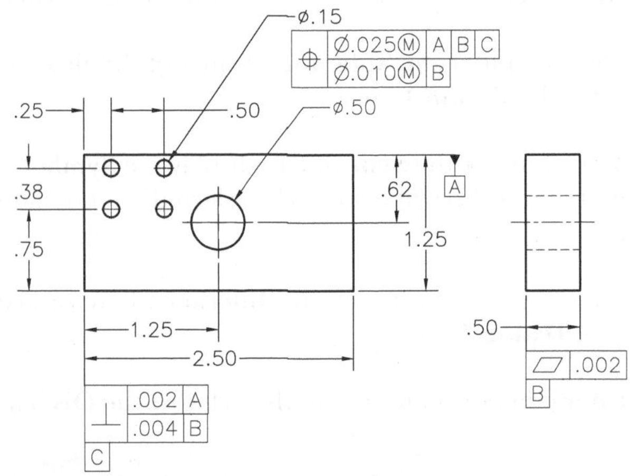

***Figure 8-79** Composite position tolerancing*

USING FEATURE CONTROL FRAMES WITH LEADERS

The **Leader Settings** dialog box that is invoked by using the **QLEADER** command has the **Tolerance** option which allows you to create feature control frame and attach it to the end of the leader extension line, refer to Figure 8-80. The following is the prompt sequence for using the **QLEADER** command with the **Tolerance** option:

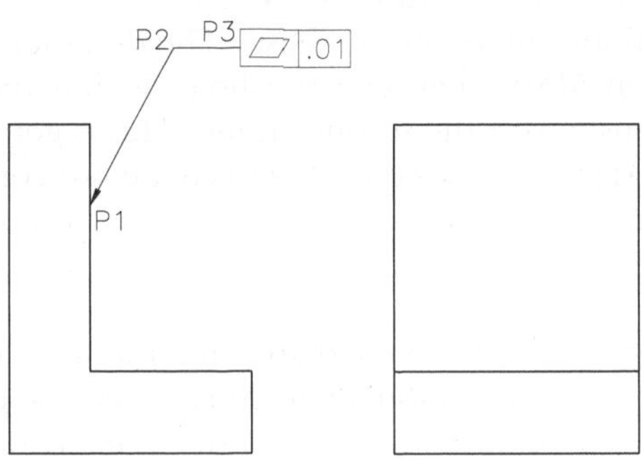

***Figure 8-80** Using the feature control frame with leader*

Specify first leader point, or [Settings] <Settings>: *Press ENTER to display the **Leader Settings** dialog box. Choose the **Annotation** tab. Now, select the **Tolerance** radio button from the **Annotation Type** area. Choose the **OK** button.*
Specify first leader point, or [Settings] <Settings>: *Specify the start point of the leader line.*
Specify next point: *Specify the second point.*
Specify next point: *Specify the third point to display the **Geometric Tolerance** dialog box.*

Now, specify the tolerance value and choose the **OK** button; the **Feature Control Frame** will be displayed with leader.

PROJECTED TOLERANCE ZONE

Figure 8-81 shows two parts joined with a bolt. The lower part is threaded, and the top part has a drilled hole. When these two parts are joined, the bolt that is threaded in the lower part will have the orientation error that exists in the threaded hole. In other words, the error in the threaded hole will extend beyond the part thickness, which might cause interference, and the parts may not assemble. To avoid this problem, projected tolerance is used. The projected tolerance establishes a tolerance zone that extends above the surface. In Figure 8-81, the position tolerance for the threaded hole is 0.010, which extends 0.1 above the surface (datum A). By using the projected tolerance, you can ensure that the bolt is within the tolerance zone up to the specified distance, refer to Figure 8-81.

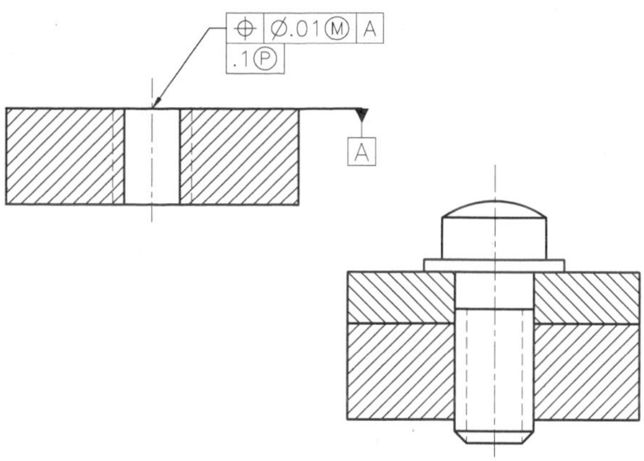

Figure 8-81 *Projected tolerance zone*

You can use the AutoCAD GD & T feature to create feature control frames for the projected tolerance zone as discussed next.

1. Invoke the **QLEADER** command and then press ENTER at the **Specify first leader point, or [Settings] <Settings>** prompt to display the **Leader Settings** dialog box.

2. Choose the **Annotation** tab and then select the **Tolerance** radio button from the **Annotation Type** area. Choose **OK** to return to the command line. Specify the first, the second, and the third leader points, refer to Figure 8-81. On specifying the third point, the **Geometric Tolerance** dialog box will be displayed. Click once in the **Sym** area in the first row; the **Symbol** dialog box will be displayed. Choose the position symbol from the **Symbol** dialog box.

3. In the first row of the **Geometric Tolerance** dialog box, enter the geometric characteristics and the datum references required for the first position tolerance frame.

4. In the **Height** edit box, enter the height of the tolerance zone (.1 for the given drawing) and select the box on the right of **Projected Tolerance Zone**. The projected tolerance zone symbol will be displayed in the box.

5. Choose the **OK** button in the **Geometric Tolerance** dialog box. AutoCAD will create two frames and automatically align them, refer to Figure 8-81.

Example 2 *Tolerance*

In this example, you will create a feature control frame to define the perpendicularity specification, as shown in Figure 8-82.

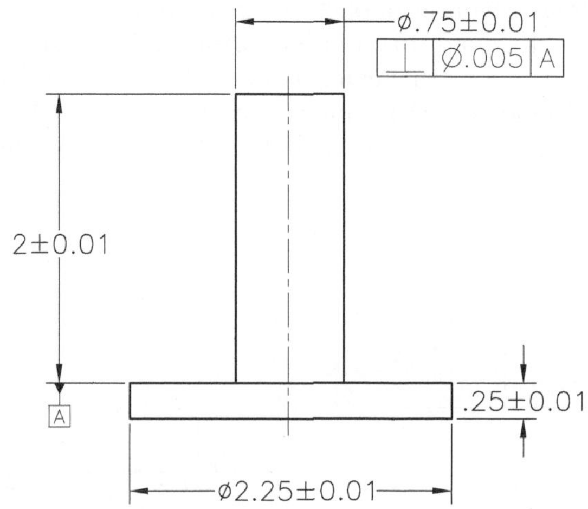

Figure 8-82 *Drawing for Example 2*

1. Choose the **Tolerance** tool from the **Dimensions** panel of the **Annotate** tab to display the **Geometric Tolerance** dialog box. Choose the upper box from the **Sym** area to display the **Symbol** dialog box. Select the perpendicularity symbol. This symbol will be displayed in the **Sym** area.

2. Select the box on the left of the upper edit box under the **Tolerance 1** area; the diameter symbol will appear to denote a cylindrical tolerance zone.

3. Enter **.005** in the upper edit box under the **Tolerance 1** area in the **Geometric Tolerance** dialog box.

4. Enter **A** in the edit box under the **Datum 1** area. Choose the **OK** button to accept the changes made in the **Geometric Tolerance** dialog box.

5. The **Enter tolerance location** prompt is displayed in the command line area and the feature control frame is attached to the cursor at its middle left point. Select a point to insert the frame.

6. To attach the datum symbol, invoke the **Leader Settings** dialog box and select the **Tolerance** radio button as explained in step 1.

7. Choose the **Leader Line & Arrow** tab and select the **Datum triangle filled** option from the drop-down list in the **Arrowhead** area.

8. Set the number of points in the leader to **2** in the **Maximum** spinner of **Number of Points** area.

9. Choose the **OK** button to return to the command line. Specify the first and second leader points, refer to Figure 8-82. On specifying the second point, the **Geometric Tolerance** dialog box will be displayed.

10. Enter **A** in the **Datum Identifier** edit box. Choose the **OK** button to exit the **Geometric Tolerance** dialog box. On doing so, the datum symbol will be displayed, refer to Figure 8-82.

Example 3 — Tolerance

In this example, you will create a leader with combination feature control frames to control runout and cylindricity, as shown in Figure 8-83.

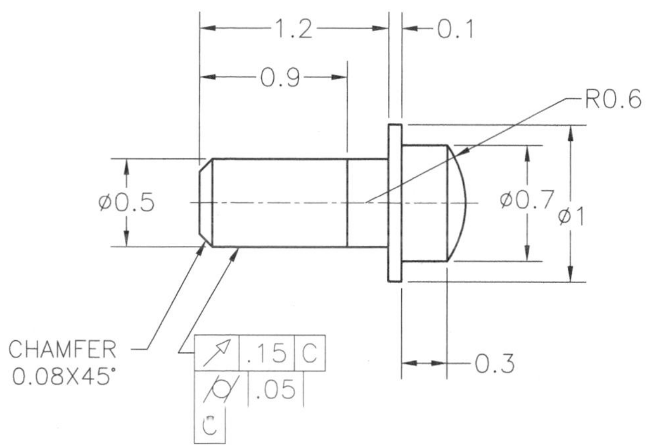

Figure 8-83 *Drawing for Example 3*

1. Enter the **QLEADER** command and follow the prompt sequence given below.

Specify first leader point, or [Settings] <Settings>: *Press ENTER to display the* ***Leader Settings*** *dialog box. Choose the* ***Annotation*** *tab. Select the* ***Tolerance*** *radio button from the* ***Annotation Type*** *area. Next, choose the* ***OK*** *button to exit the dialog box.*
Specify first leader point, or [Settings] <Settings>: *Specify the leader start point, as shown in Figure 8-83.*

Specify next point: *Specify the second point of the leader.*
Specify next point: *Specify the third point of the leader line to display the* ***Geometric Tolerance*** *dialog box.*

2. Choose the runout symbol from the **Symbol** dialog box; the runout symbol will be displayed on the first row of the **Sym** area. Enter **.15** in the first row edit box under the **Tolerance 1** area.

3. Enter **C** in the edit box under the **Datum 1** area.

4. Select the edit box on the second row of the **Sym** area and select the cylindricity symbol; the cylindricity symbol will be displayed in the second row of the **Sym** area.

5. Enter **.05** in the second row edit box of the **Tolerance 1** area.

6. Enter **C** in the **Datum Identifier** edit box.

7. Choose the **OK** button to accept the changes in the **Geometric Tolerance** dialog box; the control frames will be automatically attached at the end of the leader.

CREATING ANNOTATIVE DIMENSIONS, TOLERANCES, LEADERS, AND MULTILEADERS

Annotative dimensions are drawn in the drawing by assigning annotative dimension style to the current drawing. To assign annotative dimension, select the **Dimension**, **Dimension Style** (inclined arrow) from the **Dimensions** panel or from the **Dimension** toolbar. Note that the dimension style selected should have an annotative symbol next to it. You can also change the non-annotative dimensions to annotative by changing the dimension's **Annotative** property to **Yes** in the **PROPERTIES** palette.

For drawing the annotative geometric tolerances and leaders, you first need to add the simple tolerances to the drawing and then select all tolerances. Next, you need to modify the **Annotative** property under the **Misc** area of the **PROPERTIES** palette to **Yes**.

The annotative leaders are drawn by assigning annotative dimension style, whereas the annotative multileaders are drawn by assigning annotative multileader style. The leaders are created with two components: the leader and its content. Therefore, drawing annotative leaders does not ensure that the content attached to the leader will also be annotative. But, the multileaders are drawn as a single component, so the multileaders drawn with annotative style will have annotative content also.

Note

The procedure of creating and modifying dimension styles and multileader styles will be discussed in detail in Chapter 10.

Self-Evaluation Test

Answer the following questions and then compare them to those given at the end of this chapter:

1. The __________ tool is used to dimension the *X* coordinate of a selected object.

2. The __________ symbols are the building blocks of geometric dimensioning and tolerances.

3. In thc __________ dimensioning, the dimension text is aligned by default with the object being dimensioned.

4. The __________ dimensions are automatically updated when the object to which they are assigned is modified.

5. The __________ point is taken as the vertex point of the angular dimensions while dimensioning an arc or a circle.

6. Extra leaders can be added or removed from existing multileaders by using the __________ tool.

7. You can specify dimension text or accept the measured value computed by AutoCAD. (T/F)

8. The **Adjust Space** tool is used to maintain equal spacing between linear dimensions or angular dimensions. (T/F)

9. The leaders drawn by using the **Leader** tool create arrow, leader lines, and text as a single object. (T/F)

10. You cannot combine GTOL with leaders. (T/F)

Review Questions

Answer the following questions:

1. Which of the following tools can be used to convert dimensions into true associative dimensions?

   (a) **Reassociate** (b) **Associate**
   (c) **Disassociate** (d) None of the above

2. Which of the following tools can be used to dimension more than one object in a single effort?

   (a) **Linear** (b) **Angular**
   (c) **Quick Dimension** (d) None of these

3. Which of the following tools is used to dimension different points and features of a part with reference to a fixed point?

   (a) **Baseline** (b) **Angular**
   (c) **Radius** (d) **Aligned**

4. Which of the following tools can be used to add geometric dimensions and tolerance to the current drawing?

   (a) **GTOL** (b) **Tolerance**
   (c) **Single Line** (d) None of these

5. Which of the following options of the **Align** tool can be used to maintain a constant spacing between the selected multileader landing lines?

   (a) **Distribute** (b) **make leader segments Parallel**
   (c) **Specify Spacing** (d) **Use current spacing**

6. Geometric dimensioning and tolerancing is generally known as _________.

7. Give three examples of geometric characteristics that indicate the characteristics of a feature _________, __________, and _________.

8. The three ways to return to the command prompt from the **Dim:** prompt (dimensioning mode) are _________, __________, and _________.

9. The six fundamental dimensioning types which are provided by AutoCAD to dimension an object are ________.

10. Horizontal dimensions measure displacement along the _________.

11. Only inner angles (acute angles) can be dimensioned with angular dimensioning. (T/F)

12. In addition to the most recently drawn dimension (the default base dimension), you can use any other linear dimension as the base dimension. (T/F)

13. In the continued dimensions, the base point for the successive continued dimensions is the base dimension's first extension line. (T/F)

14. You cannot add dimension break to straight multileaders. (T/F)

15. Using the **Multileader** tool, you can specify the content of a multileader before drawing the leader itself. (T/F)

Exercise 7

Draw the object shown in Figure 8-84 and then dimension it. Save the drawing as *DIMEXR7*.

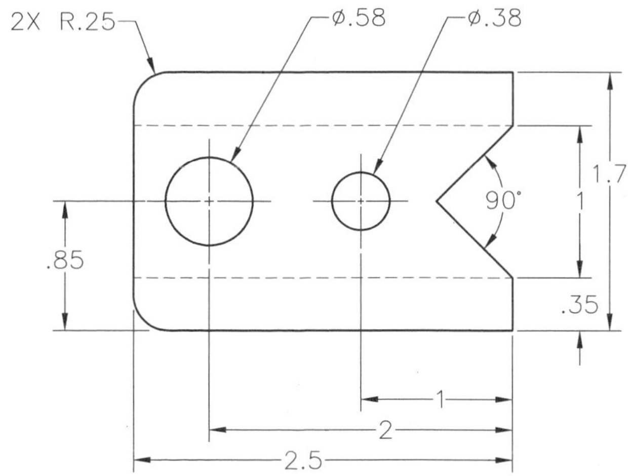

Figure 8-84 *Drawing for Exercise 7*

Exercise 8

Draw and dimension the object shown in Figure 8-85. Save the drawing as *DIMEXR8*.

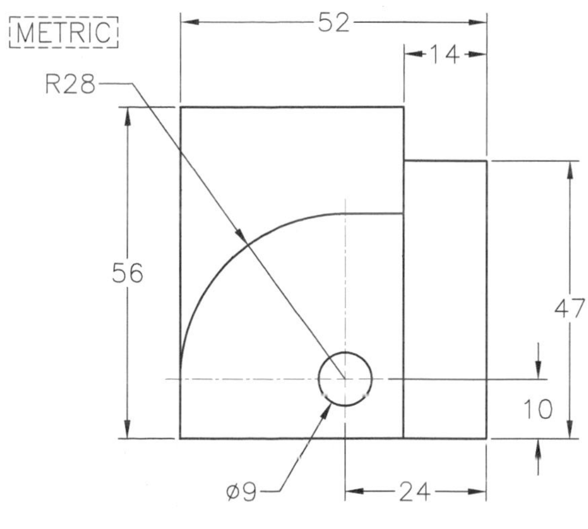

Figure 8-85 *Drawing for Exercise 8*

Exercise 9

Draw the object shown in Figure 8-86 and then dimension it. Save the drawing as *DIMEXR9*.

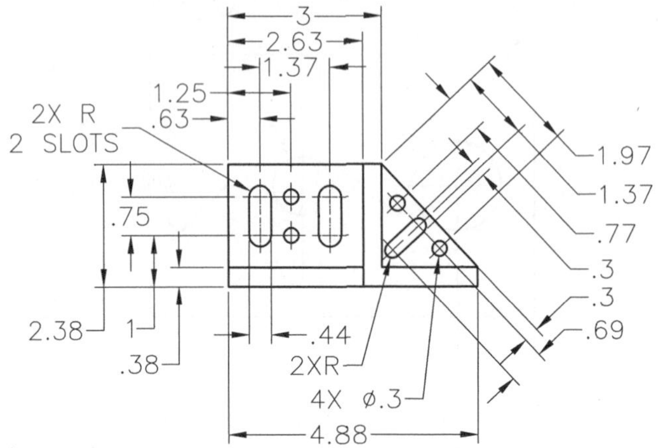

Figure 8-86 Drawing for Exercise 9

Exercise 10

Draw the object shown in Figure 8-87 and then dimension it. Save the drawing as *DIMEXR10*.

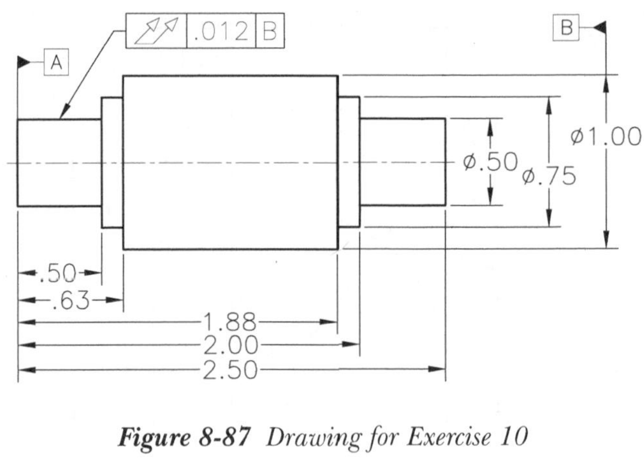

Figure 8-87 Drawing for Exercise 10

Exercise 11

Draw the object shown in Figure 8-88 and then dimension it. Save the drawing as *DIMEXR11*.

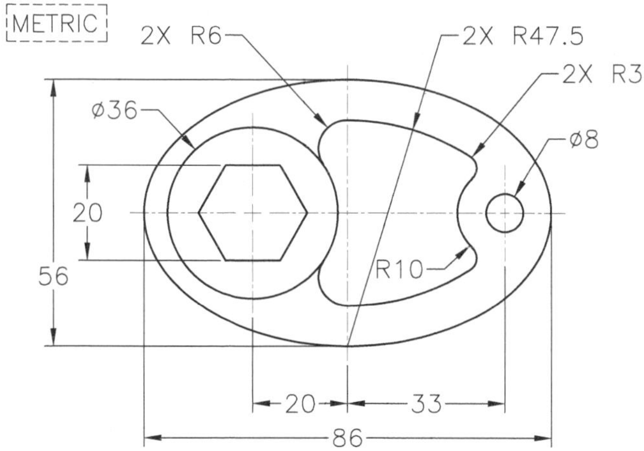

Figure 8-88 *Drawing for Exercise 11*

Exercise 12

Draw the object shown in Figure 8-89 and then dimension it. Save the drawing as *DIMEXR12*.

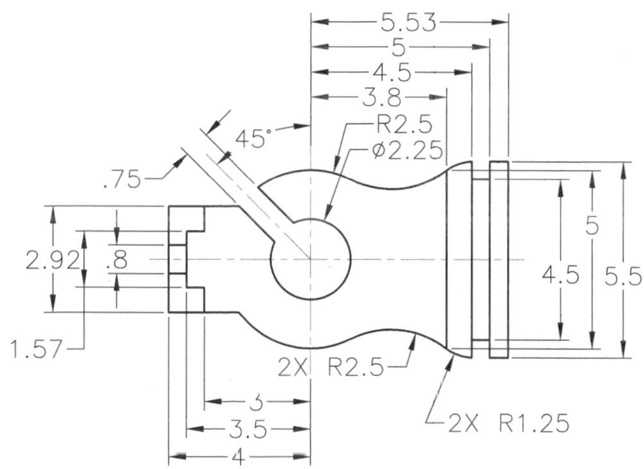

Figure 8-89 *Drawing for Exercise 12*

Exercise 13

Draw the object shown in Figure 8-90 and then dimension it. Save the drawing as *DIMEXR13*.

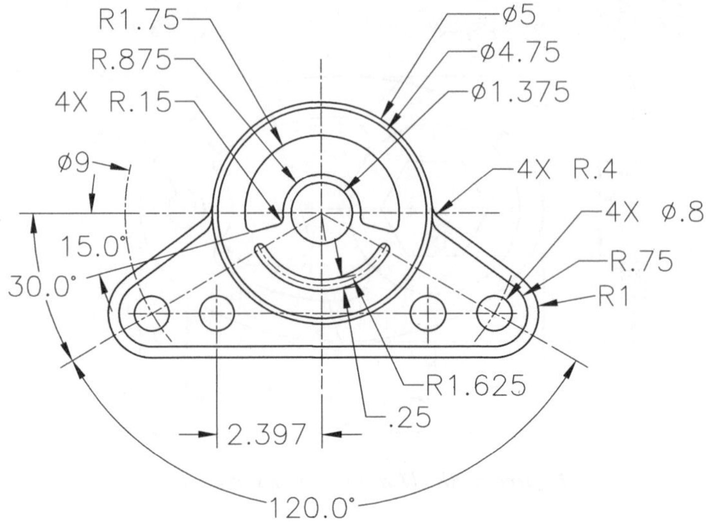

Figure 8-90 Drawing for Exercise 13

Problem-Solving Exercise 1

Draw the object shown in Figure 8-91 and dimension it, as shown in the drawing. Save the drawing as *DIMPSE1*.

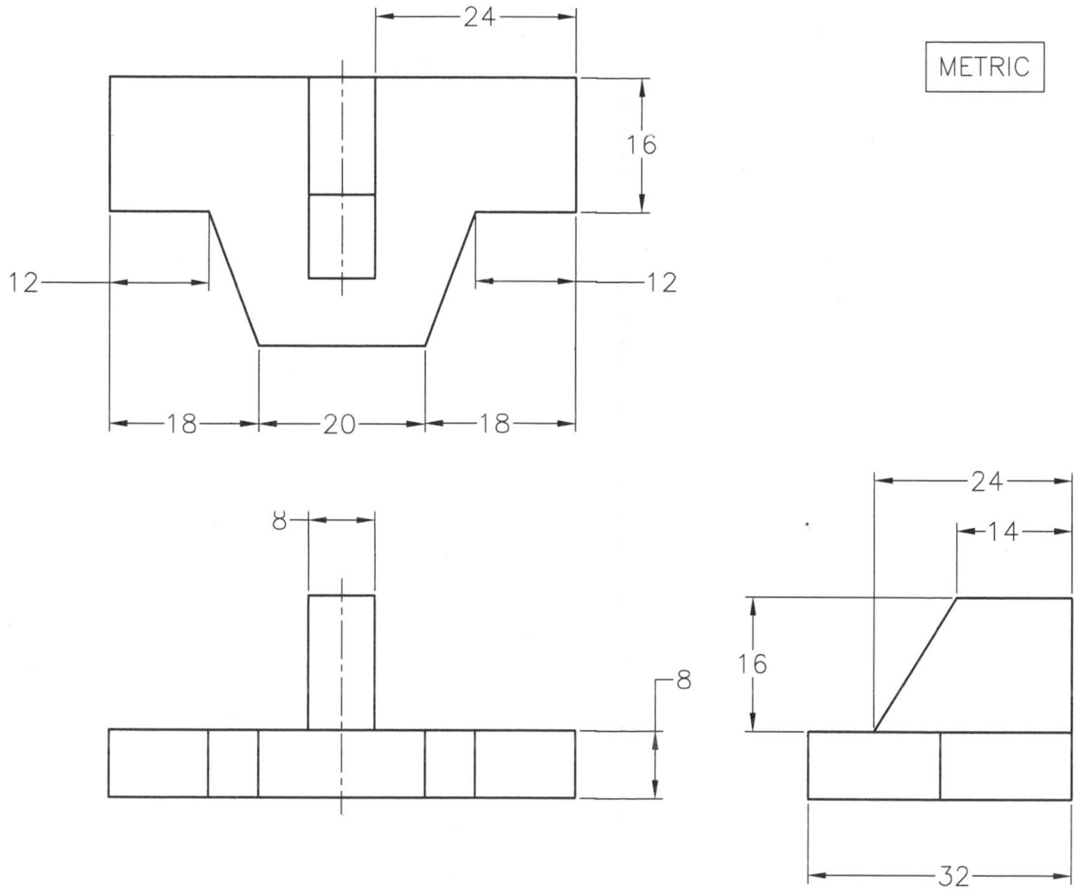

Figure 8-91 *Drawing for Problem-Solving Exercise 1*

Problem-Solving Exercise 2

Draw Figure 8-92 and then dimension it, as shown in the drawing. Save the drawing as *DIMPSE2*.

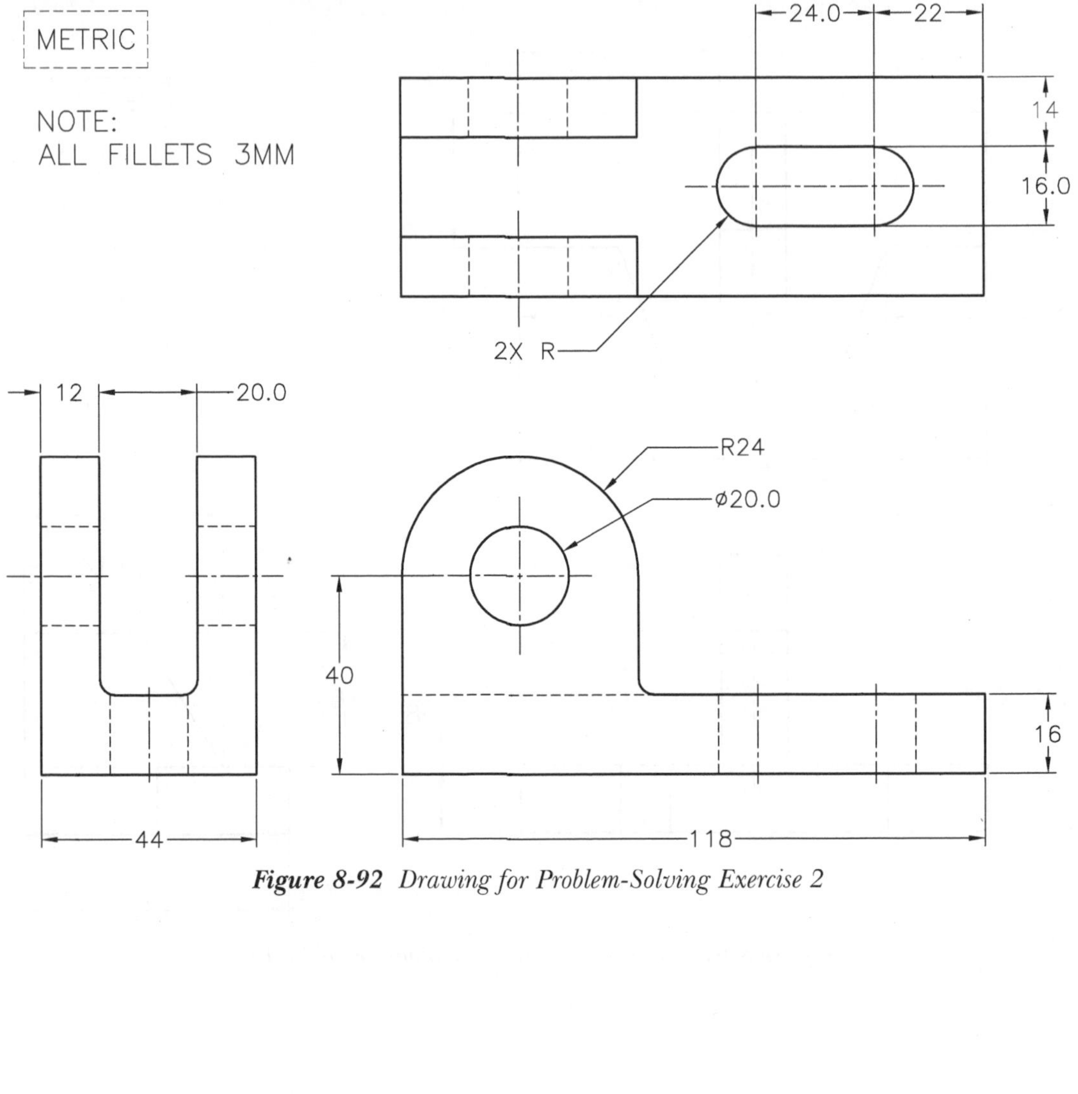

Figure 8-92 *Drawing for Problem-Solving Exercise 2*

Problem-Solving Exercise 3

Draw Figure 8-93 and then dimension it, as shown in the drawing. Save the drawing as *DIMPSE3*.

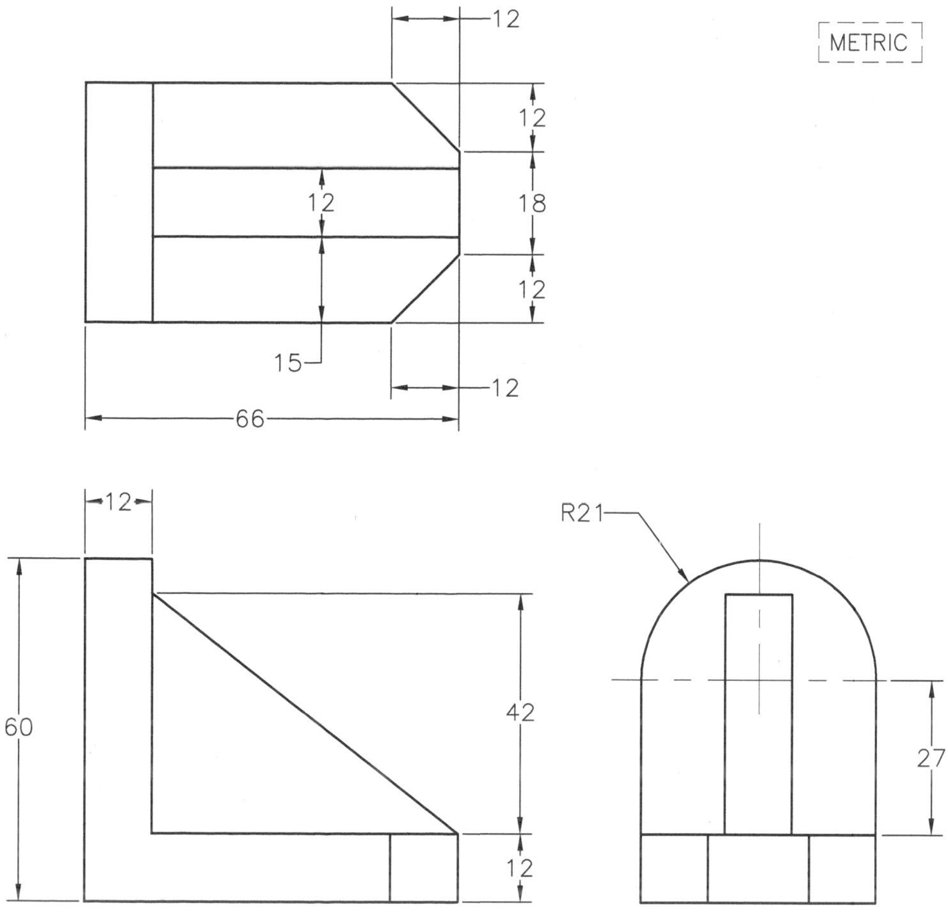

Figure 8-93 *Drawing for Problem-Solving Exercise 3*

Problem-Solving Exercise 4

Draw Figure 8-94 and then dimension it, as shown in the drawing.

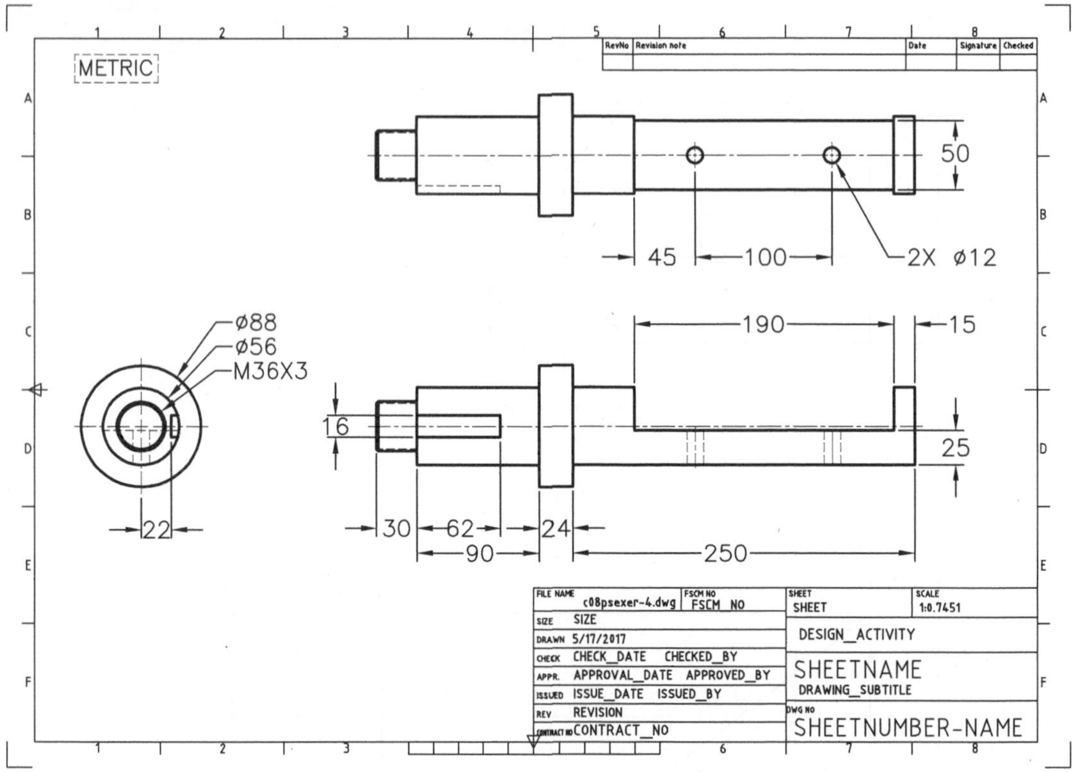

Figure 8-94 Drawing for Problem-Solving Exercise 4

Problem-Solving Exercise 5

Draw Figure 8-95 and then dimension it, as shown in the drawing.

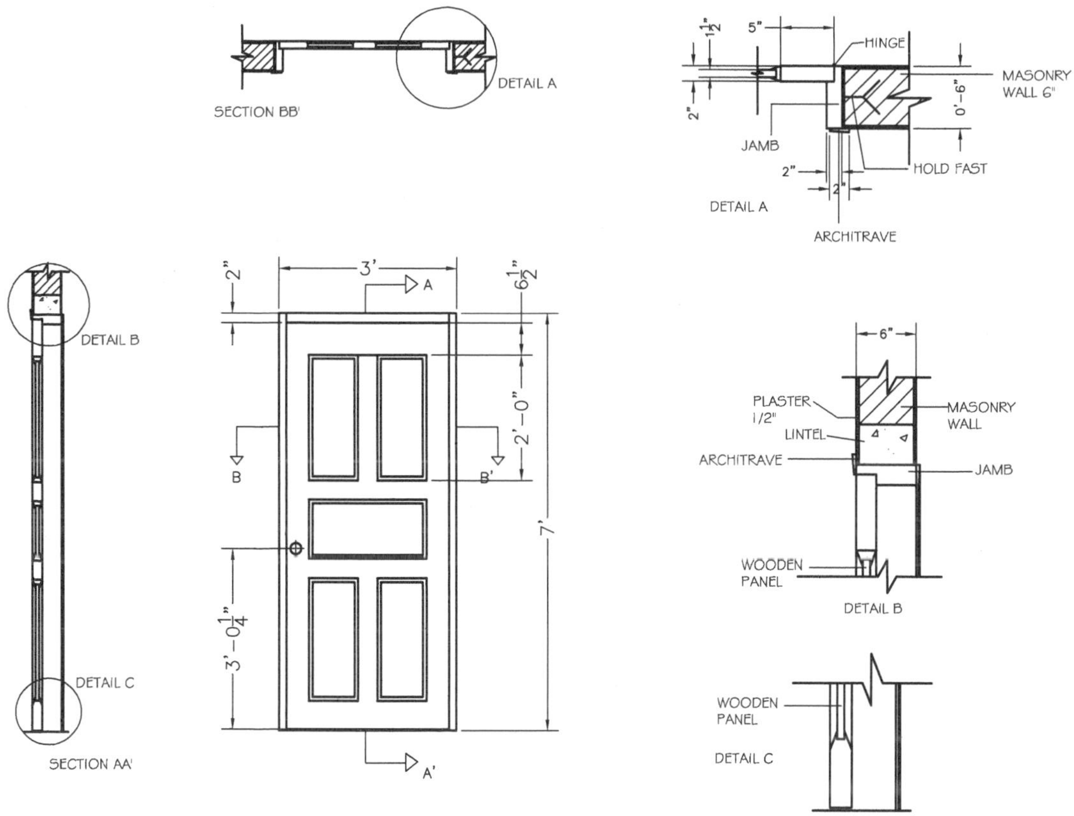

Figure 8-95 Drawing for Problem-Solving Exercise 5

Answers to Self-Evaluation Test

1. **Ordinate**, 2. geometric characteristics, 3. aligned, 4. true associative, 5. center, 6. **Remove Leader** or **Add Leader**, 7. T, 8. T, 9. F, 10. F

Chapter 9

Editing Dimensions

Learning Objectives

After completing this chapter, you will be able to:

- *Edit dimensions*
- *Stretch, extend, and trim dimensions*
- *Use the Oblique and Text Angle command options to edit dimensions*
- *Update dimensions using the Update command*
- *Use the PROPERTIES palette to edit dimensions*
- *Dimension in model space and paper space*

Key Terms

- *Dimension editing tools*
- *Stretch*
- *Trim*
- *Extend*
- *Edit Dimension Text*
- *Update*
- *Dimension PROPERTIES Palette*
- *Multileader PROPERTIES Palette*
- *Model Space Dimension*
- *Paper Space Dimension*

EDITING DIMENSIONS USING EDITING TOOLS

For editing dimensions, AutoCAD has provided some special editing tools that work with dimensions. These editing tools can be used to define a new dimension text, return to the home text, create oblique dimensions, and rotate and update the dimension text. You can also use the **Trim**, **Stretch**, and **Extend** tools to edit the dimensions. In case the dimension assigned to the object is a true associative dimension, it will be automatically updated if the object is modified. However, if the dimension is not true associative dimension, you will have to include the dimension along with the object in the edit selection set. The properties of the dimensioned objects can also be changed using the **PROPERTIES** palette or the **Dimension Style Manager**.

Editing Dimensions by Stretching

You can edit a dimension by stretching it. However, to stretch a dimension, appropriate definition points must be selected by using the crossing or window method. As the middle point of the dimension text is a definition point for all types of dimensions, you can easily stretch and move the dimension text to any location you want. When you stretch the dimension text, the gap in the dimension line gets filled automatically. While editing, the definition points of the dimension being edited must be included in the selection crossing box. The dimension is automatically calculated when you stretch the dimension.

Note

The dimension type remains the same after stretching. For example, the vertical dimension maintains itself as a vertical dimension and measures only the vertical distance even after the line it dimensions is modified or converted into an inclined line. The following example illustrates the stretching of object lines and dimensions.

Example 1 — *Edit by Stretching*

In this example, you will stretch the objects and dimensions shown in Figure 9-1 using grips. The new location of the lines and dimensions is at a distance of 0.5 units in the positive *Y* axis direction, as shown in Figure 9-2.

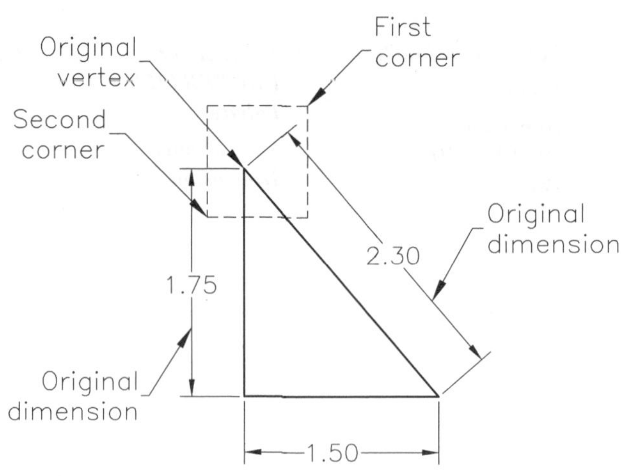

Figure 9-1 *Original location of lines and dimensions*

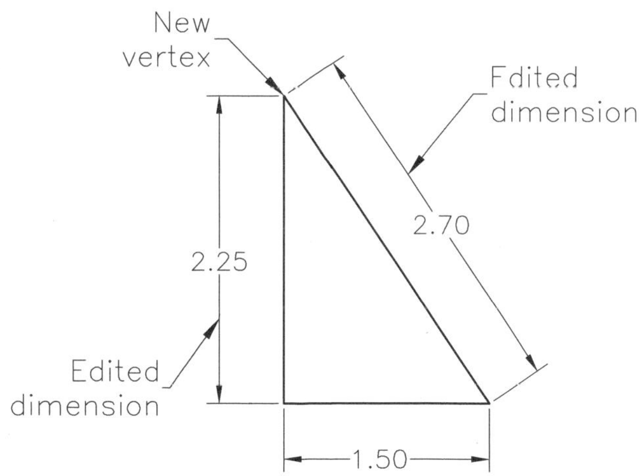

Figure 9-2 *New location of lines and dimensions*

1. Choose the **Stretch** tool from the **Modify** panel of the **Home** tab. The prompt sequence after choosing this tool is given below:

   Select objects to stretch by crossing-window or crossing-polygon
   Select objects: *Define a crossing window using the first and second corners, as shown in Figure 9-1.*
   Select objects: Enter
   Specify base point or [Displacement]<Displacement>: *Select original vertex using the osnap as the base point.*
   Specify second point or <use first point as displacement>: **@0.5<90**

2. The selected entities will be stretched to the new location. The dimension that was initially 1.75 will become 2.25 and the dimension that was initially 2.30 will become 2.70, refer to Figure 9-2.

Exercise 1

The two dimensions given in Figure 9-3(a) are too close. Fix the drawing by stretching the dimension, as shown in Figure 9-3(b).

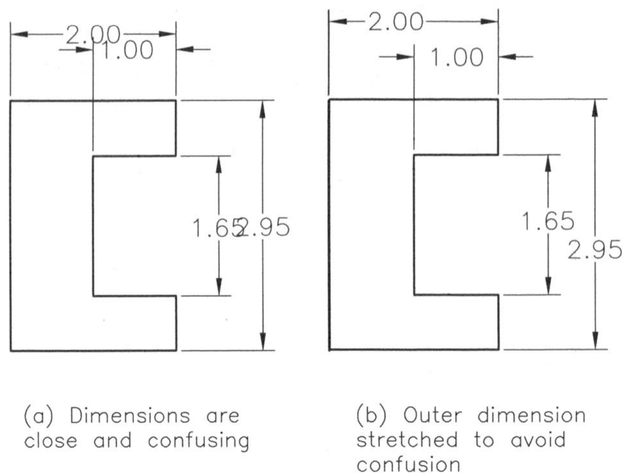

Figure 9-3 Drawing for Exercise 1, stretching dimensions

1. Stretch the outer dimension to the right so that there is some distance between the two dimensions.
2. Stretch the dimension text of the outer dimension so that the dimension text is staggered (lower than the first dimension).

Editing Dimensions by Trimming and Extending

Trimming and extending operations can be carried out with all types of linear dimensions (horizontal, vertical, aligned, and rotated) and the ordinate dimension. Even if the dimensions are true associative, you can extend and trim them, refer to Figures 9-4 and 9-5. AutoCAD trims or extends a linear dimension between the extension line definition points and the object used as a boundary or trimming edge. To extend or trim an ordinate dimension, AutoCAD moves the feature location (location of the dimensioned coordinate) to the boundary edge. To retain the original ordinate value, the boundary edge to which the feature location point is moved should be orthogonal to the measured ordinate. In both cases, the imaginary line drawn between the two extension line definition points is trimmed or extended by AutoCAD, and the dimension is adjusted automatically.

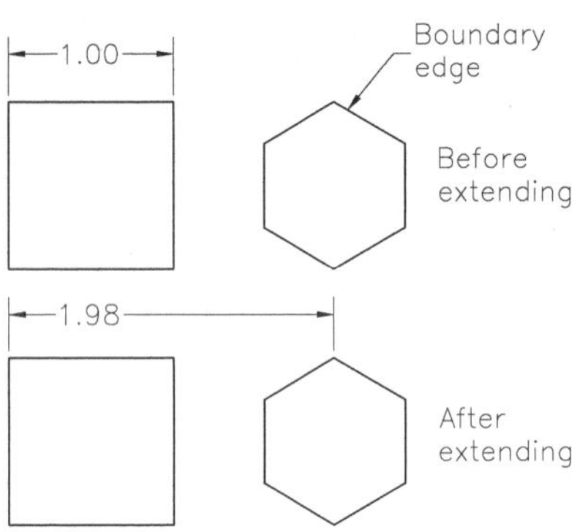

Figure 9-4 Dimensions edited by extending

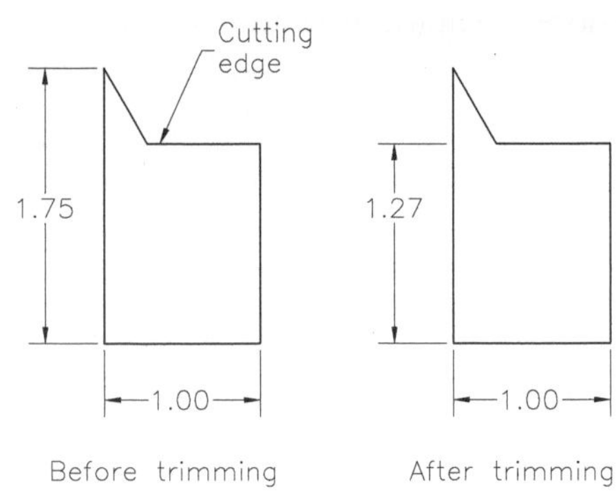

Figure 9-5 Edgemode extended trimming

Exercise 2

Use the **Edge > Extend** option of the **Trim** tool to trim the dimension given in Figure 9-6(a), so that it looks like Figure 9-6(b).

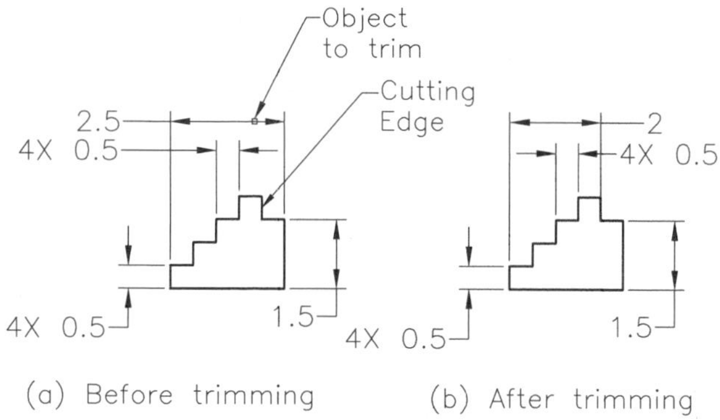

***Figure 9-6** Drawing for Exercise 2*

1. Make the drawing and dimension it, as shown in Figure 9-6(a). Assume the missing dimensions.
2. Trim the dimensions by using the **Edge > Extend** option of the **Trim** tool.

Flipping Dimension Arrow

You can flip the arrowheads individually. To flip the arrow, select the dimension. Place the cursor on the grip corresponding to the arrowhead that you want to flip. When the color of the grip turns pink, a shortcut menu will be invoked. Now, choose the **Flip Arrow** option from the shortcut menu.

MODIFYING THE DIMENSIONS

Toolbar: Dimension > Dimension Edit **Command:** DIMEDIT

The dimensions can be modified by choosing the **Dimension Edit** tool from the **Dimension** toolbar, refer to Figure 9-7. Alternatively, you can use the **DIMEDIT** command to modify the dimensions. This command has four options: **Home**, **New**, **Rotate**, and **Oblique**. The prompt sequence that will follow when you choose this tool is given below:

Enter type of dimension editing [Home/New/Rotate/Oblique] <Home>: *Enter an option.*

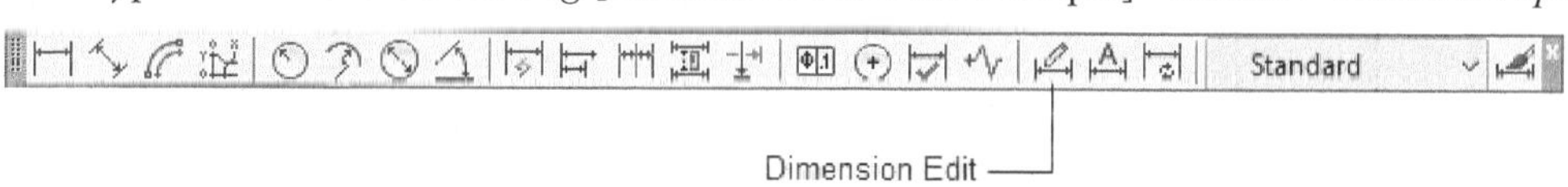

***Figure 9-7** Choosing the **Dimension Edit** tool from the **Dimension** toolbar*

Home

The **Home** option restores the text of a dimension to its original (home/default) location if the position of the text has been changed by stretching or editing, refer to Figure 9-8.

New

The **New** option is used to replace the existing dimension with a new text string. When you invoke this option, the **Text Editor** will be displayed. By default, 0.0000 will be displayed. Using the **Text Editor**, enter the dimension or write the text string with which you want to replace the existing dimension. Once you have entered a new dimension in the editor and exit the **Text Editor**, you will be prompted to select the dimension to be replaced. Select the dimension and press ENTER; it will be replaced with the new dimension, refer to Figure 9-8.

Rotate

The **Rotate** option is used to position the dimension text at the specified angle. With this option, you can change the orientation (angle) of the dimension text of any number of associative dimensions. The angle can be specified by entering a value at the **Specify angle for dimension text** prompt or by specifying two points at the required angle. Once you have specified the angle, you will be prompted to select the dimension text to be rotated. Select the dimension and press ENTER; the text will rotate about its middle point, refer to Figure 9-8. You can also invoke this option by choosing the **Text Angle** tool from the extended **Dimensions** panel of the **Annotate** tab.

Figure 9-8 *Using the **Dimension Edit** tool to edit dimensions*

Oblique

In linear dimensions, extension lines are drawn perpendicular to the dimension line. The **Oblique** option bends the linear dimensions. It draws extension lines at an oblique angle, refer to Figure 9-9. This option is particularly important to create isometric dimensions and can be used to resolve conflicting situations due to the overlapping of extension lines with other objects. Making an existing dimension oblique by specifying an angle oblique to it does not affect the generation of new linear dimensions. The oblique angle is maintained even after performing most editing operations. When you invoke this option, you will be prompted to select the dimension to be edited. After selecting it, you will be prompted to specify the oblique angle. The extensions lines will be bent at the angle specified. You can also invoke this option by choosing the **Oblique** tool from the extended **Dimensions** panel.

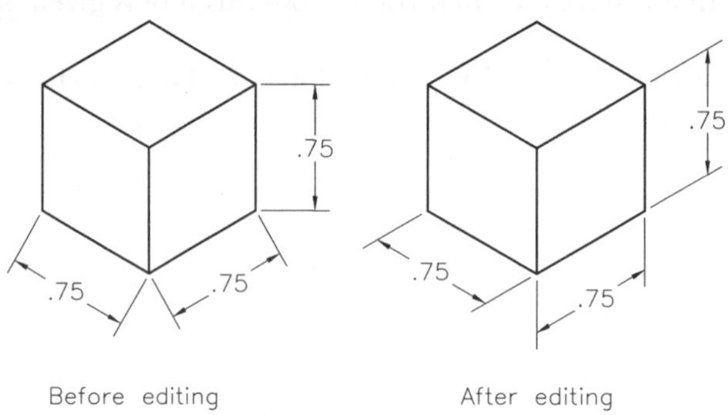

Figure 9-9 *Using the **Oblique** option to edit dimensions*

EDITING THE DIMENSION TEXT

Toolbar: Dimension > Dimension Text Edit **Menu Bar:** Dimension > Align Text	**Command:** DIMTED or DIMTEDIT

The dimension text can be edited by using the **Dimension Text Edit** tool from the **Dimension** toolbar. This tool is used to edit the placement and orientation of a single existing dimension. You can use this tool in cases where dimension texts of two or more dimensions are too close together. In such cases, the **Dimension Text Edit** tool is invoked to move the dimension text to some other location so that there is no confusion. The prompt sequence that will follow when you choose the **Dimension Text Edit** tool is given next.

Select dimension: *Select the dimension to modify.*
Specify new location for dimension text or [Left/Right/Center/Home/Angle]:

Left

Using this option, you can left justify the dimension text along the dimension line. The vertical placement setting determines the position of the dimension text. In this setting, the horizontally aligned text is moved to the left and the vertically aligned text is moved down, refer to Figure 9-10. This option can be used only with the linear, diameter, or radial dimensions. You can also invoke this option by choosing the **Left Justify** tool from the **Dimensions** panel.

Right

Using this option, you can right justify the dimension text along the dimension line. Similar to the Left option, the vertical placement setting determines the position of the dimension text. The horizontally aligned text is moved to the right, and the vertically aligned text is moved up, refer to Figure 9-10. This option can be used only with linear, diameter, and radial dimensions. You can also invoke this option by choosing the **Right Justify** tool from the **Dimensions** panel.

Center

Using this option, you can center justify the dimension text for linear and aligned dimensions, refer to Figure 9-10. The vertical setting controls the vertical position of the dimension text. You can also invoke this option by choosing the **Center Justify** tool from the **Dimensions** panel.

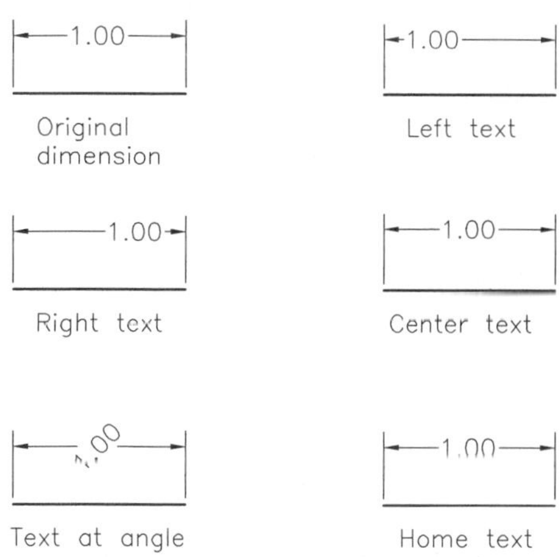

***Figure 9-10** Using the **Dimension Text Edit** tool to edit dimensions*

Home

The **Home** option is used to restore (move) the text of a dimension to its original (home/default) location, if the position of the text has changed, refer to Figure 9-10.

Angle

Using the **Angle** option, you can position the dimension text at the angle you specify, refer to Figure 9-10. The angle can be specified by entering its value at the **Specify angle for dimension text** prompt or by specifying two points at the required angle. You will notice that the text rotates around its middle point. If the information about the dimension style is available on the selected dimension, AutoCAD uses it to redraw the dimension, or the prevailing dimension variable settings are used for the redrawing process. Entering 0 degree angle changes the text to its default orientation.

UPDATING DIMENSIONS

Ribbon: Annotate > Dimensions > Update	**Toolbar:** Dimension > Dimension Update
Menu Bar: Dimension > Update	

The **Update** tool is used to regenerate and update the prevailing dimension entities (such as arrows heads and text height) using the current settings for the dimension variables, dimension style, text style, and units. On choosing this tool, you will be prompted to select the dimensions to be updated. You can select all the dimensions or specify those that should be updated.

EDITING DIMENSIONS WITH GRIPS

You can also edit dimensions by using the GRIP editing modes. GRIP editing is the easiest and quickest way to edit dimensions. You can perform the following operations with GRIPS.

1. Position the text anywhere along the dimension line. Note that you cannot move the text and position it above or below the dimension line.
2. Stretch a dimension to change the spacing between the dimension line and the object line.
3. Stretch the dimension along the length. When you stretch a dimension, the dimension text automatically changes.
4. Move, rotate, copy, erase or scale the dimensions.
5. Relocate the dimension origin.
6. Load Web browser (if any *Universal Resource Locator* is associated with the object).

EDITING DIMENSIONS USING THE PROPERTIES PALETTE

Ribbon: View > Palettes > Properties	**Toolbar:** Standard > Properties
Menu Bar: Modify > Properties	**Command:** PROPERTIES/PR/CH/MO

You can also modify a dimension or leader by using the **PROPERTIES** palette. The **PROPERTIES** palette is displayed when you choose the **Properties** button from the **Palettes** panel of the **View** tab. Alternatively, you can invoke the **PROPERTIES** palette by choosing the **Properties** option from the **Palettes** flyout from the **Tools** menu. All the **properties** of the selected object are displayed in the **PROPERTIES** palette, refer to Figure 9-11. Select the dimension before invoking the **PROPERTIES** palette, otherwise it would not give the description of the dimension.

PROPERTIES Palette (Dimension)

You can use the **PROPERTIES** palette to change the properties, the dimension text style, or geometry, format, and annotation-related features of the selected dimension. The changes take place dynamically in the drawing. The **PROPERTIES** palette provides the following categories for the modification of dimensions.

General

In the **General** category, the **Color**, **Layer**, **Linetype**, **Linetype scale**, **Plot style**, **Lineweight**, **Transperancy**, **Hyperlink**, and **Associative** parameters are available with their current values. To change the color of the selected object, select the **Color** property and then select the required color from the drop-down list. Similarly, the properties such as layer, plot style, linetype, and lineweight can be changed from the respective drop-down lists. The linetype scale can be changed manually in the corresponding cell.

Misc

This category displays the dimension style by name and also specifies whether the dimension text will be annotative or not. You can change the dimension style and the annotative property of the text from the respective drop-down lists of the selected dimension.

Lines & Arrows

The various parameters of the lines and arrows in the dimension such as arrowhead size, type, arrow lineweight, and so on can be changed in this category.

Text

The various parameters that control the text in the dimension object such as text color, text height, vertical position text offset, and so on can be changed in this category.

Fit

In the **Fit** category, the **Dim line forced**, **Dim line inside**, **Dim scale overall**, **Fit**, **Text inside**, and **Text movement** parameters are available. All parameters can be changed in the drop-down list, except **Dim scale overall** (which can be changed manually).

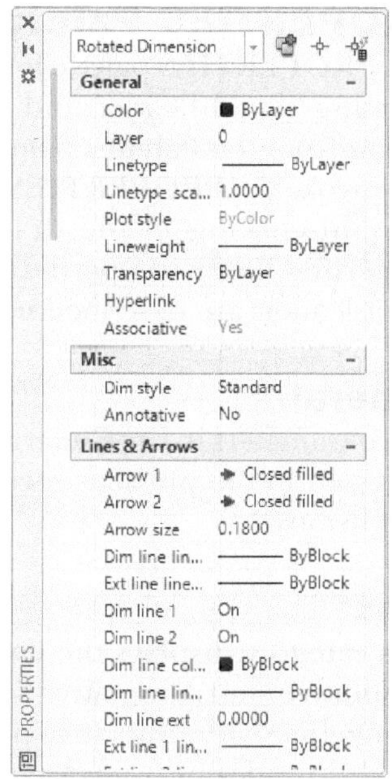

***Figure 9-11** The **PROPERTIES** palette for dimensions*

Primary Units

In the **Primary Units** category, the **Decimal separator**, **Dim prefix**, **Dim suffix**, **Dim roundoff**, **Dim sub-units suffix**, **Dim scale linear**, **Dim units**, **Dim sub-units scale**, **Suppress leading zeros**, **Suppress trailing zeros**, **Suppress zero feet**, **Suppress zero inches**, and **Precision** parameters are available. Among these parameters, **Dim units**, **Suppress leading zeros**, **Suppress trailing zeros**, **Suppress zero feet**, **Suppress zero inches**, and **Precision** can be changed with the help of corresponding drop-down lists. The other parameters can be changed manually.

Alternate Units

Alternate units are required when a drawing is to be read in two different units. For example, if an architectural drawing is to be read in both metric and imperial, you can turn the alternate units on. The primary units can be set to metric and the alternate units to engineering. As a result, the dimensions of the drawing will be displayed in metric units as well as in engineering. In the alternate unit category, there are various parameters for the alternate units. They can be changed only if the **Alt enabled** parameter is **On**. The parameters such as **Alt format**, **Alt precision**, **Alt suppress leading zeros**, **Alt suppress trailing zeros**, **Alt suppress zero feet**, and **Alt suppress zero inches** can be changed from the respective drop-down lists and others can be changed manually.

Tolerances

The parameters of this category can be changed only if the **Tolerances** display parameter has some mode of the tolerance selected. The parameters listed in this rollout depend on the mode of tolerance selected.

PROPERTIES Palette (Multileader)

The **PROPERTIES** palette for **Multileader** can be invoked by selecting a multileader and then choosing the **Properties** option from the **Palettes** panel, refer to Figure 9-12. You can also invoke the **PROPERTIES** palette from the shortcut menu by right-clicking in the drawing area and then choosing **Properties**. Various properties under the **PROPERTIES** palette (Multileader) are described next.

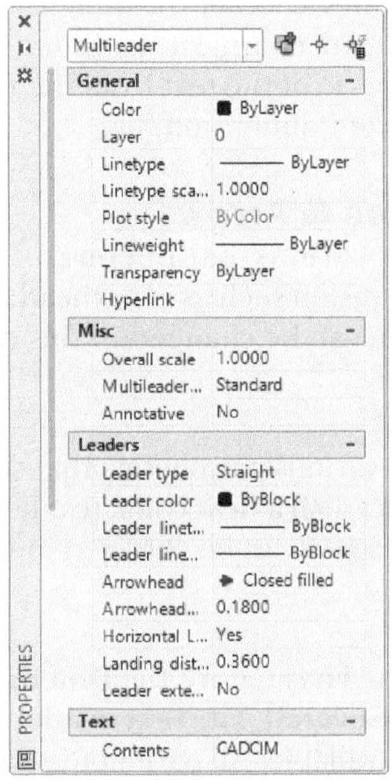

*Figure 9-12 The **PROPERTIES** palette for modifying multileaders*

General

The parameters in the **General** category are the same as those discussed in the previous section (**PROPERTIES** palette for dimensions).

Misc

This category displays the **Overall scale**, **Multileader style**, **Annotative**, and **Annotative scale** of the **Multileader**. You can change the style, annotative property, and annotation scale of the Multileader by using the respective drop-down lists.

Leaders

This category controls the display of certain elements such as lines, arrowheads, landing distance, and so on. The multileader is composed of these elements.

Text

This category displays the properties that are used to control the text appearance and location of the multileader text. These properties can be changed by selecting the desired option from the respective drop-down lists. Now, you can modify the dimension text by double-clicking on the required dimension.

Example 2 Modify Dimensions

In this example, you will modify the dimensions given in Figure 9-13 so that they match the dimensions given in Figure 9-14.

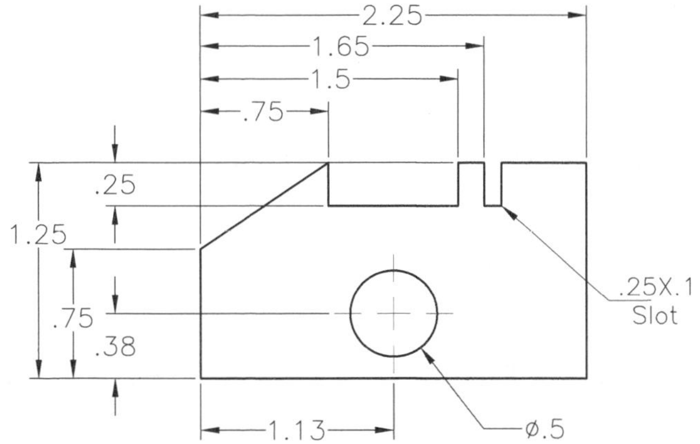

Figure 9-13 Drawing for Example 2

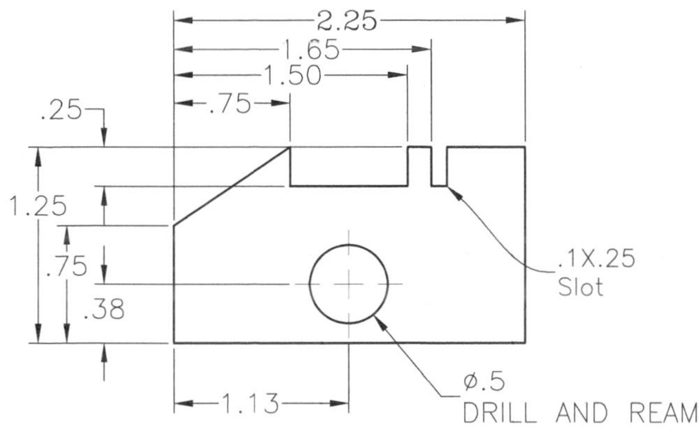

Figure 9-14 Drawing after editing the dimensions

1. Choose the **Text Style** (inclined arrow) tool from the **Text** panel of the **Annotate** tab and create a new text style with the name **ROMANC**. Select **romanc.shx** as the font for the style.

2. Select the dimension **2.25** and enter **PR** at the command prompt to display the **PROPERTIES** palette.

3. In the **Text** category, select the **Text style** drop down list and then select the **ROMANC** style from this drop-down list; the changes will take place dynamically.

4. Once all the required changes are made in the linear dimension, choose the **Select Objects** button in the **PROPERTIES** palette; you will be prompted to select the object. Select the leader line and then press ENTER.

5. The **PROPERTIES** palette will display the leader options. Select **Spline** from the **Leader type** drop-down list in the **Leaders** category; the straight line will be dynamically converted into a spline with an arrow.

6. Close the **PROPERTIES** palette.

7. Choose the **Dimension Edit** tool from the **Dimension** toolbar. Enter **N** in the prompt sequence to display the **Text Editor**.

8. Enter **%%C.5 DRILL AND REAM** in the **Text Editor** and then click outside it to accept the changes. You will be prompted to select the object to be changed.

9. Select the diameter dimension and then press ENTER; the diameter dimension will be modified to the new value.

MODEL SPACE AND PAPER SPACE DIMENSIONING

Objects can be drawn and dimensioned in the model space or paper space. If the drawings are in model space, associative dimensions should also be created in them. If the drawings are in the model space and the associative dimensions are in the paper space, the dimensions will not change when you perform any editing operations such as stretching, trimming, extending, zooming or paning in the model space. The definition points of a dimension are located in the space where the drawing is drawn. You can select the **Scale dimensions to layout** radio button in the **Fit** tab, refer to Figure 9-15. This tab is available when you choose the **Modify, New,** or **Override** buttons from the **Dimension Style Manager** dialog box, depending on whether you want to modify the present style or you want to create a new style. Choose **OK** and then **Close** to exit the dialog boxes. AutoCAD calculates a scale factor that is compatible with the model space and the paper space viewports. Now, choose the **Update** tool from the **Dimension** toolbar and select the dimension objects for updating.

The drawing shown in Figure 9-16 uses paper space scaling. The main drawing and detail drawings are located in different floating viewports (paper space). The zoom scale factors for these viewports are different: 0.3XP, 1.0XP, and 0.5XP. When you use paper scaling, AutoCAD automatically calculates the scale factor for dimensioning so that the dimensions are uniform in all the floating viewports (model space viewports).

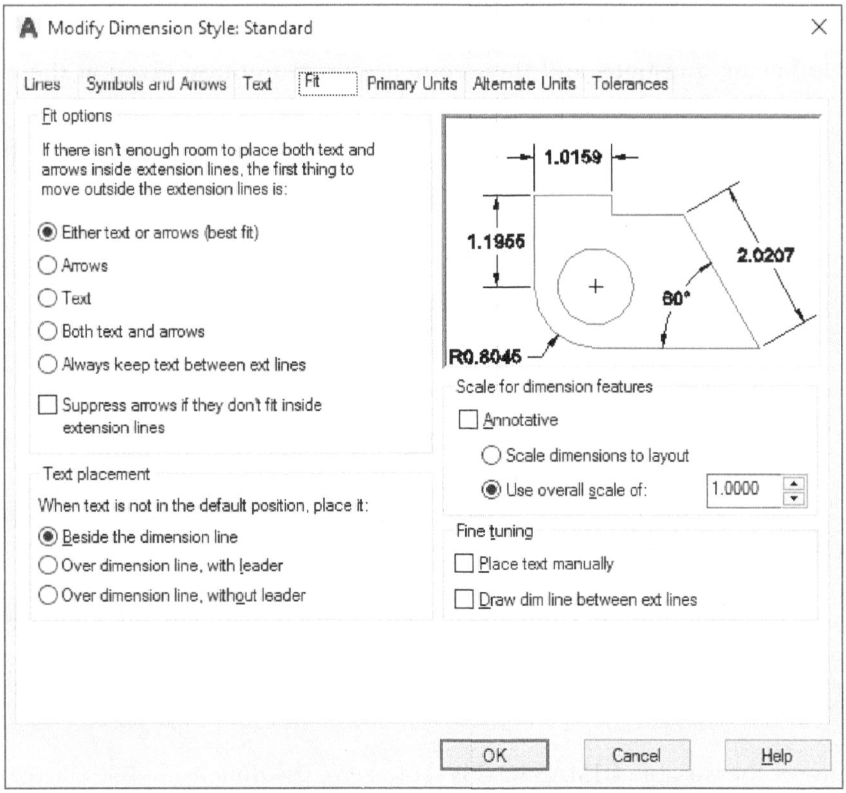

*Figure 9-15 Selecting paper space scaling in the **Modify Dimension Style** dialog box*

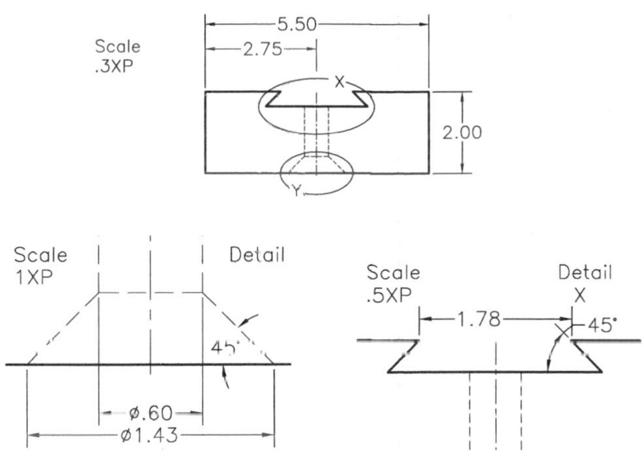

*Figure 9-16 Dimensioning in paper model space viewports using paper space scaling or setting **DIMSCALE** to 0*

Self-Evaluation Test

Answer the following questions and then compare them to those given at the end of this chapter:

1. The _________ option of the **Dimension Text Edit** tool is used to position the dimension text at the specified angle.

2. The _________ option of the **Dimension Text Edit** tool is used to justify the dimension text toward the left side.

3. The _________ option of the **Dimension Text Edit** tool is used to justify the dimension text to the center of the dimension.

4. The _________ option of the **Dimension Text Edit** tool is used to create a new text string.

5. The _________ option of the **Dimension Text Edit** tool is used to bend the extension lines through the specified angle.

6. The _________ tool from the **Dimensions** panel is used to update the dimensions.

7. In associative dimensioning, the items constituting a dimension (such as dimension lines, arrows, leaders, extension lines, and dimension text) are drawn as a single object. (T/F)

8. If the value of the variable **DIMASSOC** is set to zero, the dimension lines, arrows, leaders, extension lines, and dimension text are drawn as independent objects. (T/F)

9. You cannot edit dimensions using grips. (T/F)

10. The true associative dimensions cannot be trimmed or extended. (T/F)

Review Questions

Answer the following questions:

1. With the _________ command, you can edit the dimension text.

2. The _________ tool is particularly important for creating isometric dimensions and is applicable in resolving conflicting situations arose due to overlapping of extension lines with other objects.

3. The _________ command is used to edit the placement and orientation of a single existing dimension.

4. The _________ tool regenerates (updates) prevailing associative dimension objects (like arrows and text height) using the current settings for the dimension variables, dimension style, text style, and units.

5. The horizontal, vertical, aligned, and rotated dimensions cannot be edited using grips. (T/F)

6. Trimming and extending operations can be carried out with all types of linear (horizontal, vertical, aligned, and rotated) dimensions and with the ordinate dimension. (T/F)

7. To extend or trim an ordinate dimension, AutoCAD moves the feature location (location of the dimensioned coordinate) to the boundary edge. (T/F)

8. Once moved from the original location, the dimension text cannot be restored to its original position. (T/F)

Exercise 3 — Edit Dimensions

1. Create the drawing shown in Figure 9-17.
2. Dimension the drawing, as shown in Figure 9-17.
3. Edit the dimensions so that they match the dimensions shown in Figure 9-18.

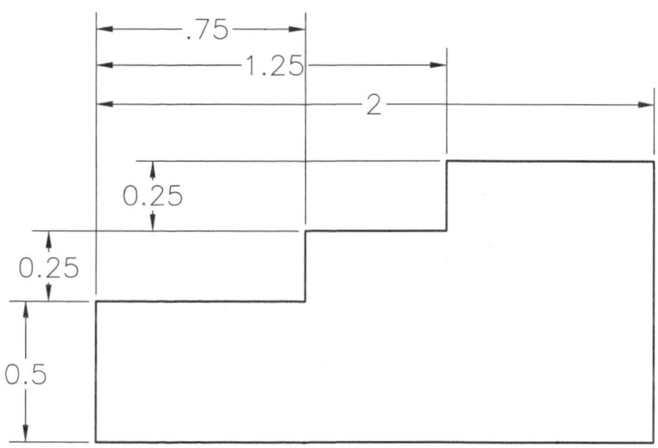

Figure 9-17 *Drawing for Exercise 3 before editing dimensions*

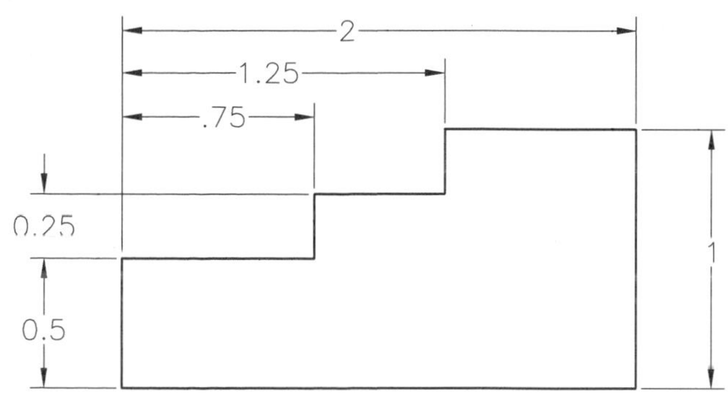

Figure 9-18 *Drawing for Exercise 3 after editing dimensions*

Exercise 4 — Edit Dimensions

1. Draw the object shown in Figure 9-19(a). Assume the dimensions where necessary.
2. Dimension the drawing, as shown in Figure 9-19(a).
3. Edit the dimensions so that they match the dimensions shown in Figure 9-19(b).

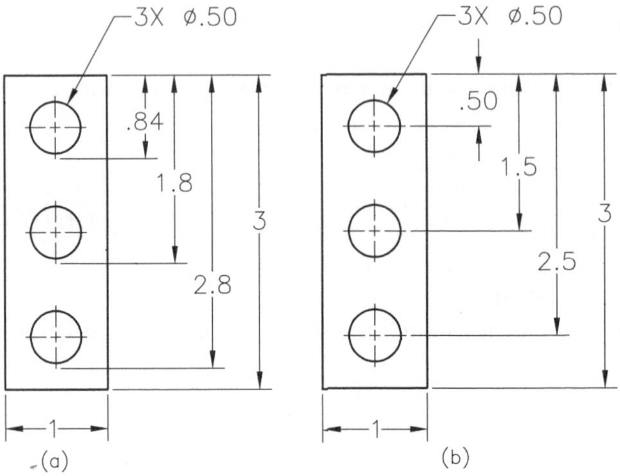

Figure 9-19 *Drawings for Exercise 4*

Problem-Solving Exercise 1

Create the drawing shown in Figure 9-20 and then dimension it. Edit the dimensions so that they are positioned as shown in the drawing. You can change the dimension text height and arrow size to 0.08 unit.

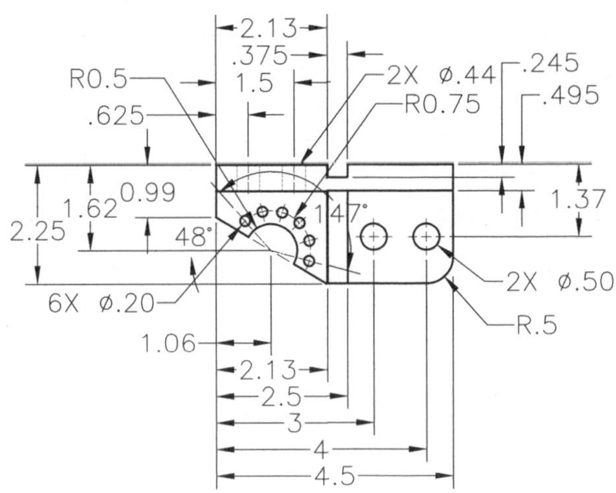

Figure 9-20 *Drawing for Problem-Solving Exercise 1*

Problem-Solving Exercise 2

Draw the front and side view of an object shown in Figure 9-21 and then dimension the two views. Edit the dimensions so that they are positioned as shown in the drawing. You can change the dimension text height and arrow size to 0.08 units.

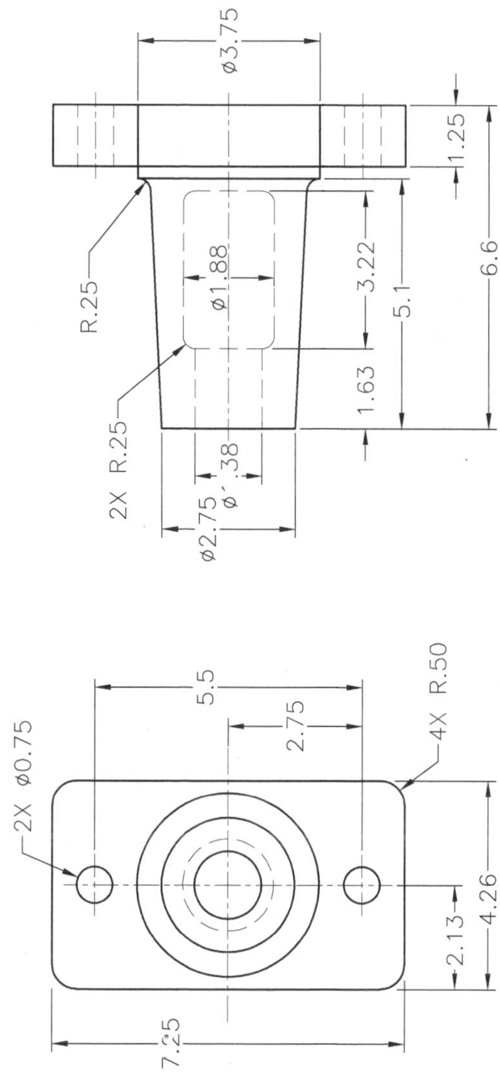

Figure 9-21 *Drawing for Problem-Solving Exercise 2*

Problem-Solving Exercise 3

Create the drawing of the floor plan shown in Figure 9-22 and then apply dimensions to it. Edit the dimensions, if needed, so that they are positioned as shown in the drawing.

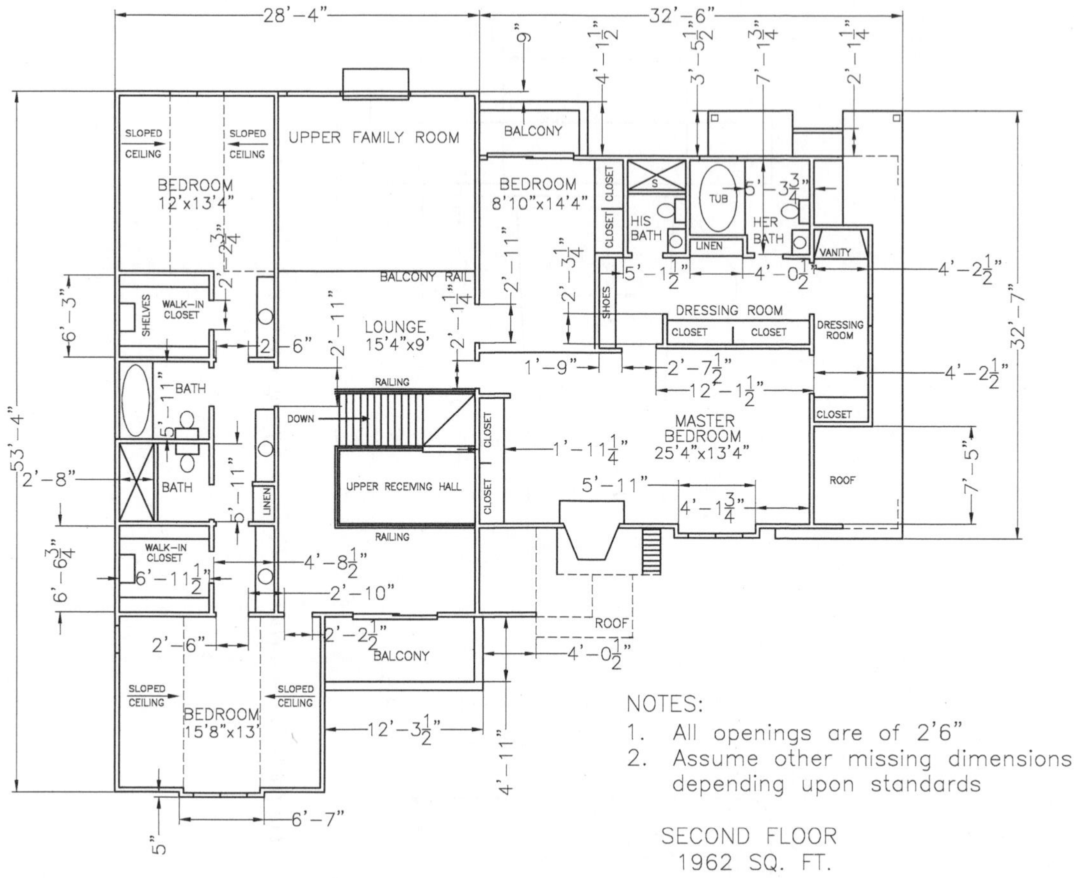

Figure 9-22 Drawing for Problem-Solving Exercise 3

Problem-Solving Exercise 4

Create the drawing shown in Figure 9-23 and then dimension it. Edit the dimensions so that they are positioned as shown in the drawing. You can change the dimension text height and arrow size to 0.08 unit.

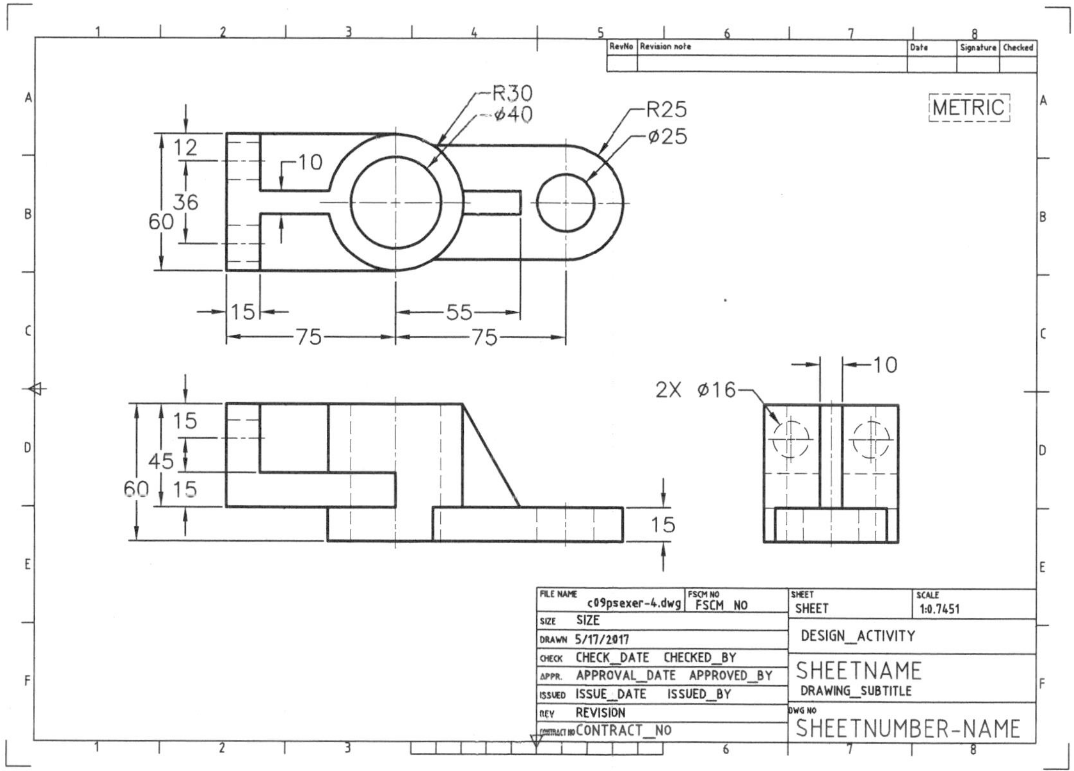

Figure 9-23 Drawing for Problem-Solving Exercise 4

Answers to Self-Evaluation Test

1. Angle, **2.** Left, **3.** Center, **4.** New, **5.** Oblique, **6.** Update, **7.** T, **8.** T, **9.** F, **10.** F

Chapter 10

Dimension Styles, Multileader Styles, and System Variables

Learning Objectives

After completing this chapter, you will be able to:

- *Use styles and variables to control dimensions*
- *Create dimension styles*
- *Set dimension variables*
- *Use dimension style overrides*
- *Compare and list dimension styles*
- *Import externally referenced dimension styles*
- *Create, restore, and modify multileader styles*

Key Terms

- *DIMSTYLE*
- *DIMCEN*
- *Dimension Style Families*
- *Dimension Styles Overrides*
- *MLEADERSTYLE*

USING STYLES AND VARIABLES TO CONTROL DIMENSIONS

In AutoCAD, the appearance of dimensions on the drawing area and the manner in which the dimensions are saved in the drawing database are controlled by a set of dimension variables. The dimensioning tools use these variables as arguments. The variables that control the appearance of dimensions can be managed using dimension styles. You can use the **Dimension Style Manager** dialog box to control the dimension styles and dimension variables through a set of dialog boxes.

CREATING AND RESTORING DIMENSION STYLES

Ribbon: Annotate > Dimensions > Dimension Style (The inclined arrow)
Toolbar: Dimension > Dimension Style or Styles > Dimension Style
Command: DIMSTYLE/D

The dimension styles control the appearance and positioning of dimensions and leaders in the drawing. If the default dimensioning style (Standard or Annotative) does not meet your requirements, you can select another existing dimensioning style or create a new one. The default names of the dimension style files are **Standard** and **Annotative**. Dimension styles can be created by using the **Dimension Style Manager** dialog box. Left-click on the inclined arrow in the **Dimensions** panel of the **Annotate** tab to invoke the **Dimension Style Manager** dialog box, as shown in Figure 10-1.

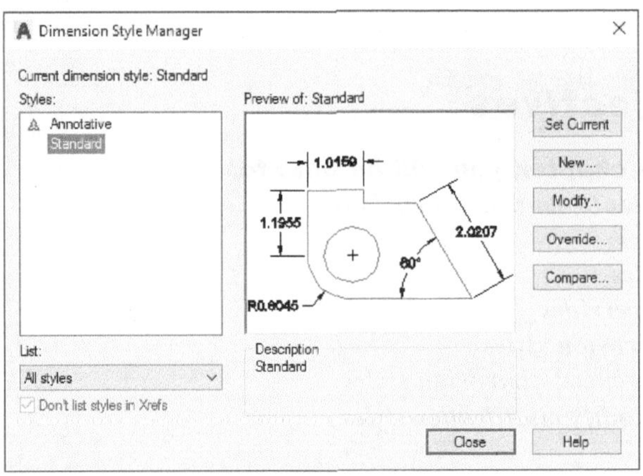

Figure 10-1 *The* ***Dimension Style Manager*** *dialog box*

In the **Dimension Style Manager** dialog box, choose the **New** button to display the **Create New Dimension Style** dialog box, as shown in Figure 10-2. Enter the dimension style name in the **New Style Name** text box and then select a style that you want to be the basis of your style from the **Start With** drop-down list. Select the **Annotative** check box to make the new dimension style annotative. Choose the **Help** button to get the help and information about all the options in this dialog box. The **Use for** drop-down list allows you to select the dimension type to which you want to apply the new dimension style. For example, if you wish to use the new style only for the diameter dimension, select **Diameter dimensions** from the **Use for** drop-down list. Choose the **Continue** button to display the **New Dimension Style** dialog box. The parameters of the **New Dimension Style** dialog box will be discussed later. After specifying the parameters of the new dimension style in the **New Dimension Style** dialog box, choose the **OK** button; the **Dimension Style Manager** dialog box will be displayed again. The options in this dialog box are discussed next.

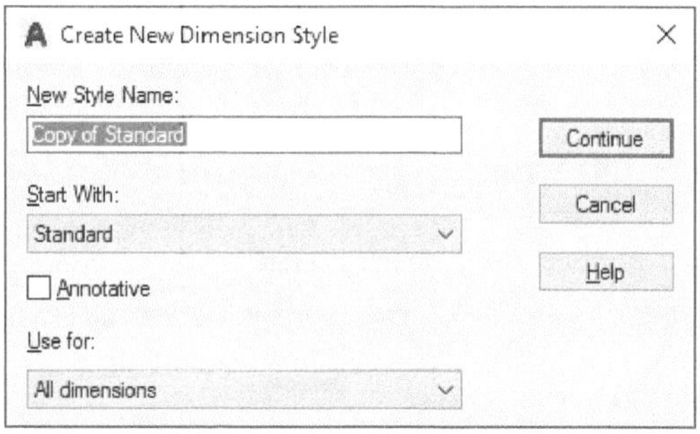

***Figure 10-2** The **Create New Dimension Style** dialog box*

In the **Dimension Style Manager** dialog box, the current dimension style name is shown in front of **Current dimension style** and is also shown highlighted in the **Styles** list box. A brief description of the current style (its differences from the default settings) is also displayed in the **Description** area. The **Dimension Style Manager** dialog box also has the **Preview of** window that displays the preview of the current dimension style. A style can be made current (restored) by selecting the name of the dimension style you want to make current from the list of defined dimension styles and choosing the **Set Current** button. You can also make a style current by double-clicking on the style name in the **Styles** list box. The list of dimension styles displayed in the **Styles** list box is dependent on the option selected from the **List** drop down-list. If you select the **Styles in use** option, only the dimension styles in use will be listed in the **Styles** list box. If you right-click on a style in the **Styles** list box, a shortcut menu is displayed that provides you with the options to **Set current**, **Rename**, or **Delete** a dimension style. Selecting the **Don't list styles in Xrefs** check box does not list the names of Xref styles in the **Styles** list box. Choosing the **Modify** button displays the **Modify Dimension Style** dialog box where you can modify an existing style. Choosing the **Override** button displays the **Override Current Style** dialog box where you can define overrides to an existing style (discussed later in this chapter). Both these dialog boxes along with the **New Dimension Style** dialog box have identical options. Choosing the **Compare** button displays the **Compare Dimension Styles** dialog box (also discussed later in this chapter) that allows you to compare two existing dimension styles.

Note

*The **Dimension Style** drop-down list in the **Dimensions** panel under the **Annotate** tab also displays the dimension styles. Selecting a dimension style from this list also sets it current.*

NEW DIMENSION STYLE DIALOG BOX

The **New Dimension Style** dialog box can be used to specify the dimensioning attributes (variables) that affect the various properties of the dimensions. The various tabs provided under the **New Dimension Style** dialog box are discussed next.

Lines Tab

The options in the **Lines** tab (Figure 10-3) of the **New Dimension Style** dialog box are used to specify the dimensioning attributes (variables) that affect the format of the dimension lines.

For example, the appearance and behavior of the dimension lines and extension lines can be changed in this tab. If the settings of the dimension variables have not been altered in the current editing session, the settings displayed in the dialog box are the default settings.

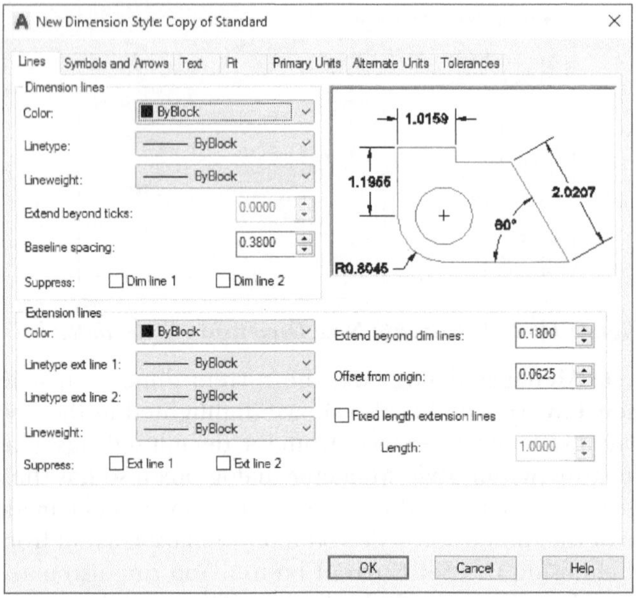

*Figure 10-3 The **Lines** tab of the **New Dimension Style** dialog box*

Dimension lines Area

This area provides you with the options for controlling the display of the dimension lines and leader lines. These options are discussed next.

Color: This drop-down list is used to set the colors for the dimension lines and arrowheads. Its dimension arrowheads have the same color as the dimension line because arrows constitute a part of the dimension line. The color you set here will also be assigned to the leader lines and arrows. The default color for the dimension lines and arrows is ByBlock. You can specify the color of the dimension line by selecting it from the **Color** drop-down list. You can also select the **Select Color** option from the **Color** drop-down list to display the **Select Color** dialog box where you can choose a specific color. The color number or the special color label is stored in the **DIMCLRD** variable, the default value is 0.

Linetype: This drop-down list is used to set the linetype for the dimension lines.

Lineweight: This drop-down list is used to specify the lineweight for the dimension line. You can select the required lineweight by selecting the corresponding option from this drop-down list. This value is also stored in the **DIMLWD** variable. The default value is ByBlock(-2). The other values for assigning lineweight to dimension lines are By Layer (-1). Remember that you cannot assign lineweight to the arrowheads using this drop-down list.

Extend beyond ticks: The **Extend beyond ticks** spinner will be available only when you select the Oblique, Architectural tick, or any such arrowhead type in the **First** and **Second** drop-down lists in the **Arrowheads** area from the **Symbols and Arrows** tab. This spinner is used to specify the distance by which the dimension line will extend beyond the extension line. The extension value entered in the **Extend beyond ticks** edit box gets stored in the **DIMDLE** variable.

Baseline spacing: The **Baseline spacing** (baseline increment) spinner is used to control the spacing between successive dimension lines drawn using the baseline dimensioning, refer to Figure 10-4. You can specify the dimension line increment as per your requirement by specifying the desired value using the **Baseline spacing** spinner. The default value displayed in the **Baseline spacing** spinner is 0.3800 units.

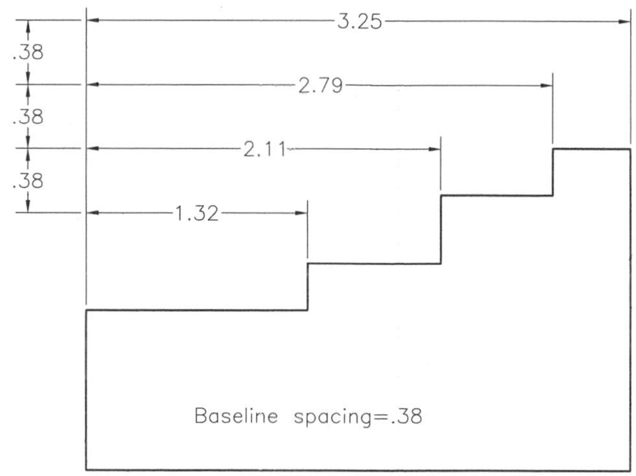

Figure 10-4 *Baseline spacing*

Suppress: The **Suppress** check boxes control the display of the first and second dimension lines. By default, both dimension lines will be drawn. You can suppress one or both the dimension lines by selecting their corresponding check boxes.

Note

The first and second dimension lines are determined by how you select the extension line origins. If the first extension line origin is on the right, the first dimension line will also be on the right.

Extension lines Area

The options in this area are discussed next.

Color: This drop-down list is used to control the color of the extension lines. The default extension line color is ByBlock. You can assign a new color to the extension lines by selecting it from this drop-down list.

Linetype ext line 1: The options in this drop-down list are used to specify the linetype of extension line 1. By default, the line type for the extension line 1 is set to ByBlock. You can change the linetype by selecting a new value of linetype from the drop down list.

Linetype ext line 2: The options in this drop-down list are same as for the Linetype ext line 1. These options are used to specify the line type of extension line 2.

Note

You can specify different linetypes for the dimension and extension lines. Use the ***Linetype*** *drop-down list in the* ***Dimension Lines*** *area to specify the linetype for dimensions. Use the* ***Linetype ext line 1*** *and* ***Linetype ext line 2*** *drop-down lists to specify the linetype for the extension lines.*

Lineweight: This drop-down list is used to modify the lineweight of the extension lines. The default value is ByBlock. You can change the lineweight value by selecting a new value from this drop-down list.

Extend beyond dim lines: It is the distance by which the extension lines extend past the dimension lines, refer to Figure 10-5. You can change the extension line offset using the **Extend beyond dim lines** spinner. The default value for the extension distance is 0.1800 units.

Offset from origin: It is the distance by which the extension line is offset from the point you specify as the origin of the extension line, refer to Figure 10-6. You may need to override this setting for specific dimensions while dimensioning curves and angled lines. You can specify an offset distance of your choice using this spinner. AutoCAD stores this value in the **DIMEXO** variable. The default value for this distance is 0.0625.

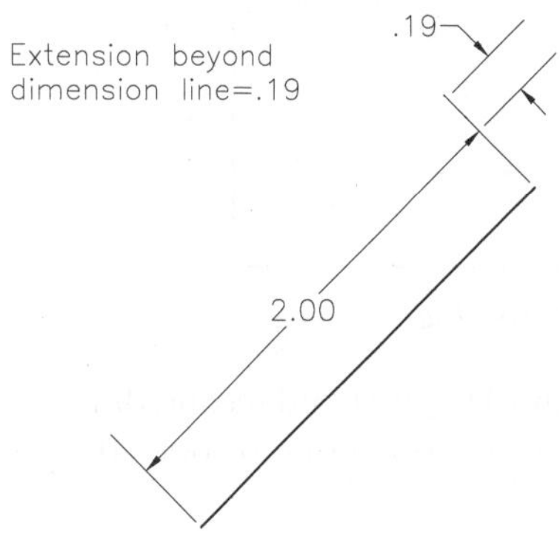

Figure 10-5 Extension beyond dimension lines

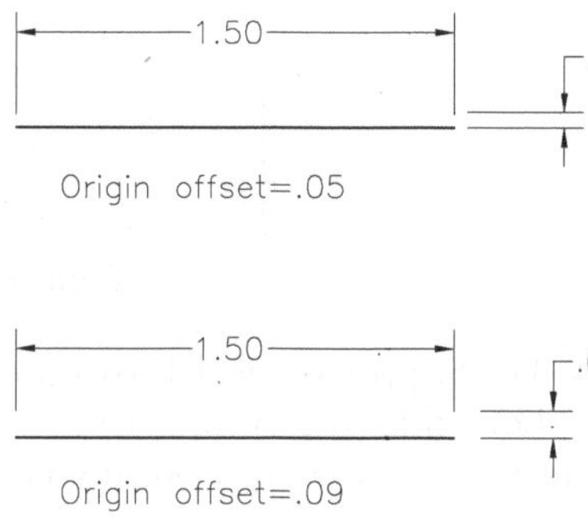

Figure 10-6 The offset from origin

Fixed length extension lines: With the selection of the **Fixed length extension lines** check box, you can specify a fixed length (starting from the dimension line to the origin) for the extension lines in the **Length** edit box. By default, the check box is cleared and the **Length** spinner is not available. Once the check box is selected, you can specify the length of the extension line either by entering a numerical value in the **Length** edit box or using the spinner. Figure 10-7 displays a drawing with full length extension lines and Figure 10-8 displays the same drawing with fixed length extension lines.

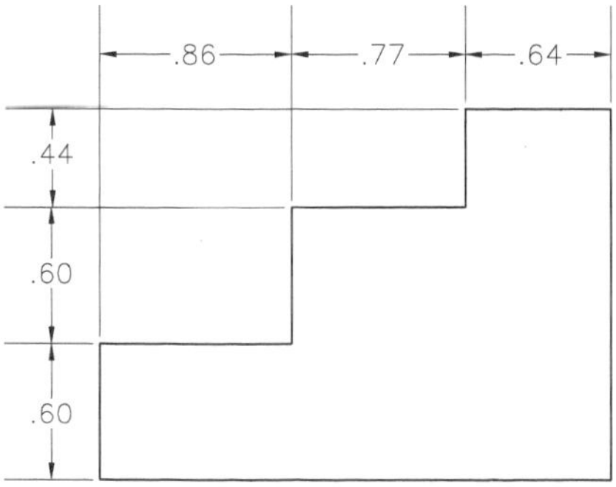

Figure 10-7 *Drawings with full length extension lines*

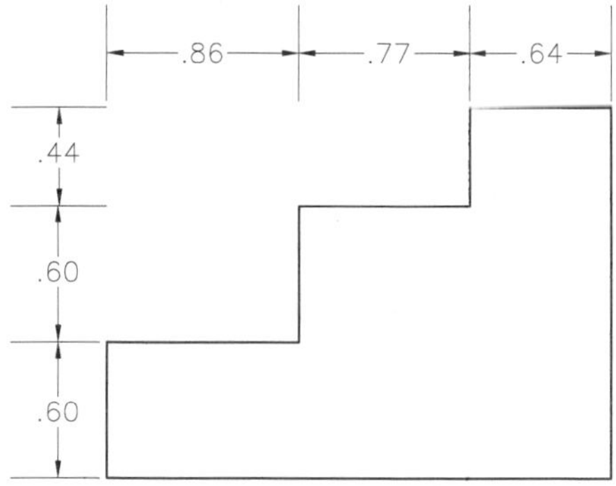

Figure 10-8 *Drawing with fixed length extension lines*

Suppress: The **Suppress** check boxes are used to control the display of the extension lines. By default, both extension lines will be drawn. You can suppress one or both of them by selecting the corresponding check boxes, refer to Figure 10-9.

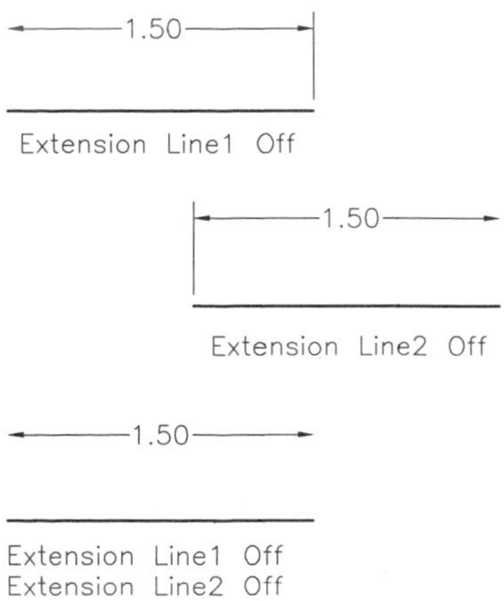

Figure 10-9 *Suppressing the extension lines*

Symbols and Arrows Tab

The options in the **Symbols and Arrows** tab (Figure 10-10) of the **New Dimension Style** dialog box are used to specify the variables and attributes that affect the format of the symbols and arrows. You can change the appearance of symbols and arrows.

Note

The first and second extension lines are determined by how you select the extension line origins. If the first extension line origin is on the right, the first extension line will also be on the right.

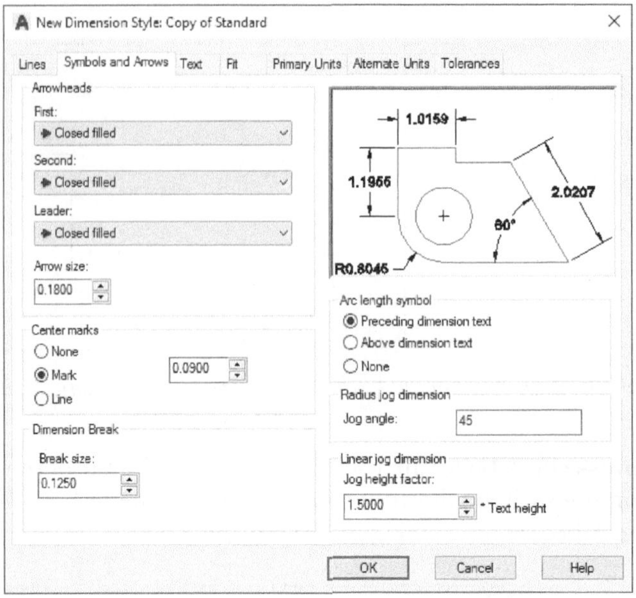

Figure 10-10 The ***Symbols and Arrows*** *tab of the* ***New Dimension Style*** *dialog box*

Arrowheads Area

The options in this area are used to specify the arrowheads and are discussed next.

First/Second: When you create a dimension, AutoCAD draws the terminator symbols at the two ends of the dimension line. These terminator symbols, generally referred to as **Arrowheads**, represent the beginning and the end of a dimension. AutoCAD has provided nineteen standard termination symbols that you can apply at each end of the dimension line. In addition to these, you can create your own arrows or terminator symbols. By default, the same arrowhead type is applied at both ends of the dimension line. If you select the first arrowhead, it is automatically applied to the second end by default. However, if you want to specify a different arrowhead at the second dimension line endpoint, you must select the desired arrowhead type from the **Second** drop-down list. The first endpoint of the dimension line is the intersection point of the first extension line and the dimension line. The first extension line is determined by the first extension line origin. However, in angular dimensioning, the second endpoint is located in a counterclockwise direction from the first point, regardless of how the points were selected while creating the angular dimension. The specified arrowhead types are selected from the **First** and **Second** drop-down lists.

AutoCAD provides you with an option of specifying a user-defined arrowhead. To define a user-defined arrow, you must create one as a block. (Refer to Chapter 16 for information regarding blocks.) Now, from the **First** or the **Second** drop-down list, select the **User Arrow** option; the **Select Custom Arrow Block** dialog box will be displayed, as shown in Figure 10-11.

All the blocks in the current drawing will be available in the **Select from Drawing Blocks** drop-down list. You can select the desired block and it will become the current arrowhead.

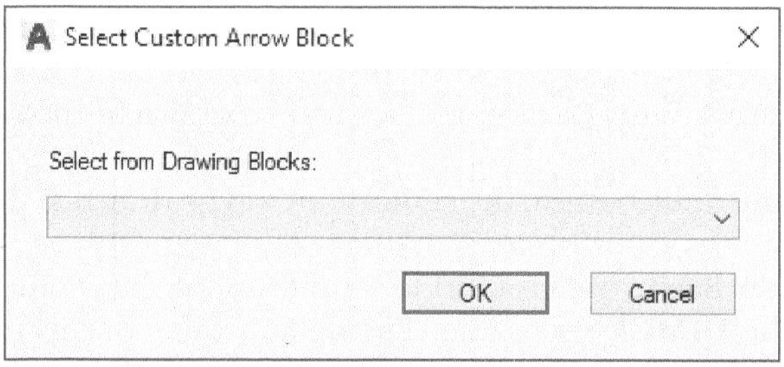

Figure 10-11 The ***Select Custom Arrow Block*** *dialog box*

Creating an Arrowhead Block

1. To create a block for an arrowhead, you will use a 0.60 X 1.00 box, refer to Figure 10-12. AutoCAD automatically scales the X and Y scale factors of the block to the arrowhead size multiplied by the overall scale. You can specify the arrow size in the **Arrow size** spinner. The **DIMASZ** variable controls the length of the arrowhead. For example, if **DIMASZ** is set to 0.25, the length of the arrow will be 0.25 units. Also, if the length of the arrow is not 1 unit, it will leave a gap between the dimension line and the arrowhead block.

2. The arrowhead must be drawn as it would appear on the right side of the dimension line. Choose the **Create block** tool from **Block** panel in the **Home** tab to convert it into a block.

3. The insertion point of the arrowhead block must be the point that will coincide with the extension line, refer to Figure 10-12.

Leader: The **Leader** drop-down list displays the arrowhead types for the Leader arrow. Here, also, you can either select the standard arrowheads from the drop-down list or select the **User Arrow** option that allows you to define and use a user-defined arrowhead type.

Arrow size: This spinner is used to define the size of the arrowhead, refer to Figure 10-13. The default value is 0.1800 unit which is stored in the **DIMASZ** system variable.

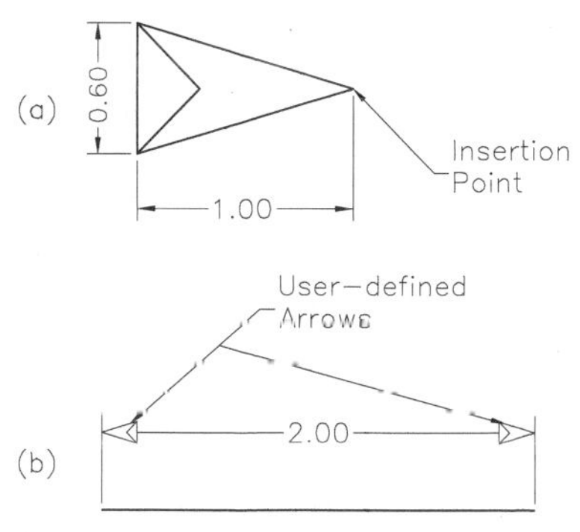

Figure 10-12 Creating user-defined arrows

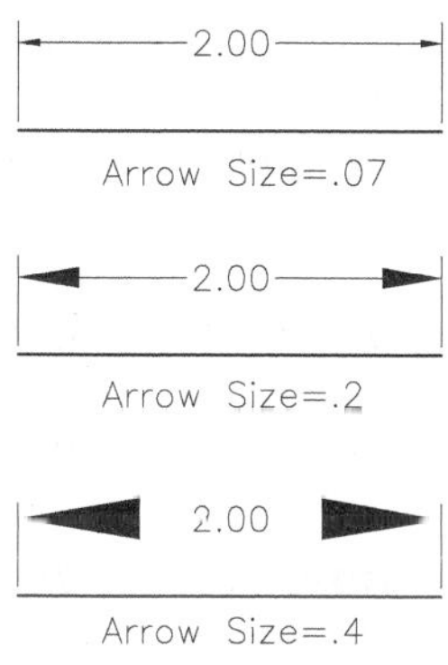

Figure 10-13 Defining arrow sizes

Center marks Area

This area deals with the options that control the appearance of the center marks and centerlines in the radius and diameter dimensioning. However, keep in mind that the center marks or the centerlines will be drawn only when dimensions are placed outside the circle.

None: If you select the **None** radio button, no mark or line will be drawn at the center of the circle.

Mark: If you select the **Mark** radio button, a mark will be drawn at the center of the circle.

Line: If you select the **Line** radio button, the centerlines will be drawn at the center of the circles.

The spinner in the **Center marks** area is used to set the size of the center marks or centerlines. This value is stored in the **DIMCEN** variable. The default value of this variable is 0.0900.

Note

*If you use the **DIMCEN** command, a positive value will create a center mark whereas a negative value will create a centerline. If the value is 0, AutoCAD does not create center marks or centerlines.*

Dimension Break Area

The **Break size** spinner in this area is used to control the default break length in the dimension while applying the break dimensions. The default value of this spinner is 0.1250. Figure 10-14 shows a drawing with dimensioning breaks.

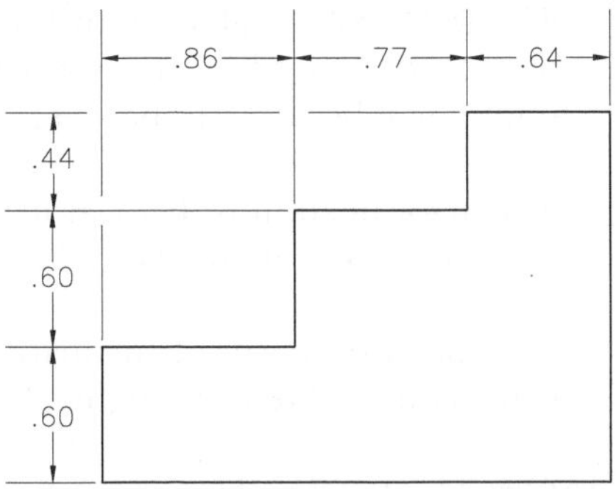

Figure 10-14 *Drawing with dimension breaks*

Arc length symbol Area

The radio buttons in this area are used to specify the position of arc when applying the arc length dimension.

Preceding dimension text: If you select the **Preceding dimension text** radio button, the arc symbol will appear before the dimension text while applying the arc length dimension.

Above dimension text: With the **Above dimension text** radio button selected, the arc symbol in the arc length dimension will appear above the dimension text.

None: Select the **None** radio button, if you do not want the arc symbol to appear with the arc length dimension.

Radius jog dimension Area

The **Jog angle** edit box in this area is used to specify the angle of jog that appears while applying the jogged radius dimension. By default, its value is 45-degrees.

Linear jog dimension Area

The option in this area is used to control the height of the jog (vertical height from the vertex of one jog angle to another) that appears while applying the jogged linear dimension. The jog height is always maintained with respect to the text height of the dimension. The **Jog height factor** spinner is used to change the factor that will be multiplied with the text height to calculate the linear jog height.

Note

*Unlike the **DIMCEN** variable, you cannot enter a negative value in the **Size** spinner. On selecting the **Line** radio button, the value in the **Size** spinner is automatically applied to the centerlines and the **DIMCEN** will be set to a value negative of the value shown in the spinner.*

Exercise 1

Draw and dimension the drawing, shown in Figure 10-15.

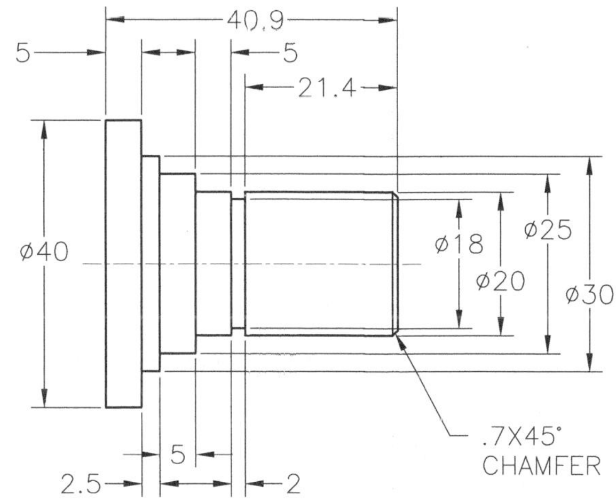

***Figure 10-15** Drawing for Exercise 1*

CONTROLLING THE DIMENSION TEXT FORMAT

Text Tab

You can control the dimension text format through the **Text** tab of the **New Dimension Style** dialog box, as shown in Figure 10-16. In the **Text** tab, you can control the parameters such as the placement, appearance, horizontal and vertical alignment of the dimension text, and so on. For example, you can force AutoCAD to align the dimension text along the dimension line. You can also force the dimension text to be displayed at the top of the dimension line. You can save the settings in a dimension style file for future use. The **New Dimension Style** dialog box has the **Preview** window that updates dynamically to display the text placement as the settings are changed. Individual items of the **Text** tab and the related dimension variables are described next.

Text appearance Area

The options in this area are discussed next.

Text style: The **Text style** drop-down list displays the names of the predefined text styles. From this list, you can select the style name that you want to use for dimensioning. You must define the text style before you can use it in dimensioning (refer to "Creating Text Styles" in Chapter 7). Choosing the **[...]** button displays the **Text Style** dialog box that allows you to create a new or modify an existing text style. The change in the dimension text style does not affect the text style you are using to draw the other text in the drawing.

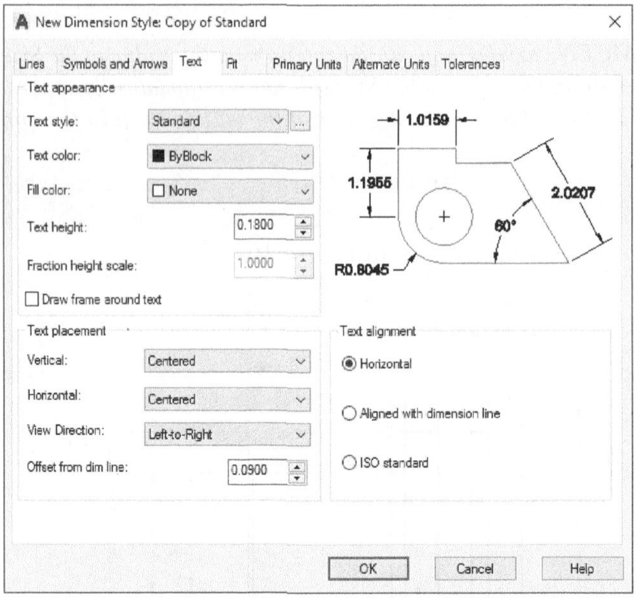

*Figure 10-16 The **Text** tab of the **New Dimension Style** dialog box*

Text color: This drop-down list is used to modify the color of the dimension text. The default color is **ByBlock**. If you select the **Select Color** option from the **Text color** drop-down list, the **Select Color** dialog box is displayed, where you can choose a specific color.

Fill color: This drop-down list is used to set the fill color of the dimension text. A box of the selected color will be placed around the dimension text.

Text height: This spinner is used to modify the height of the dimension text, refer to Figure 10-17. You can change the dimension text height only when the current text style does not have a fixed height. In other words, the text height specified in the **STYLE** command should be zero. This is because a predefined text height (specified in the **STYLE** command) overrides any other setting for the dimension text height. This value is stored in the **DIMTXT** variable. The default text height is 0.1800 units.

Fraction height scale: This spinner is used to set the scale of the fractional units in relation to the dimension text height. This spinner will be available only when you select a format for the primary units, in which you can define the values in fractions, such as architectural or fractional.

Draw frame around text: You can select this check box to draw a frame around the dimension text, refer to Figure 10-18.

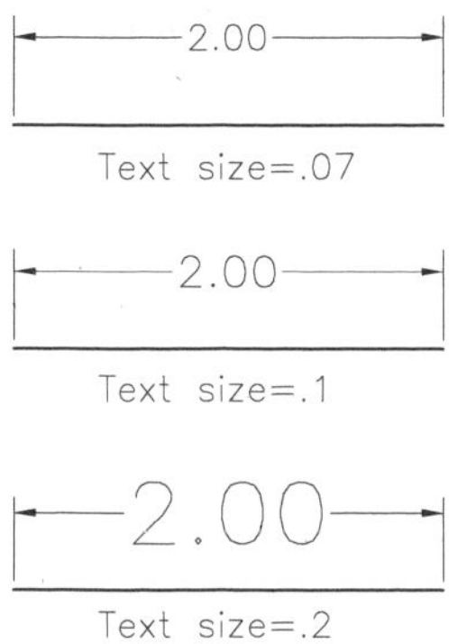

Figure 10-17 Changing the dimension height

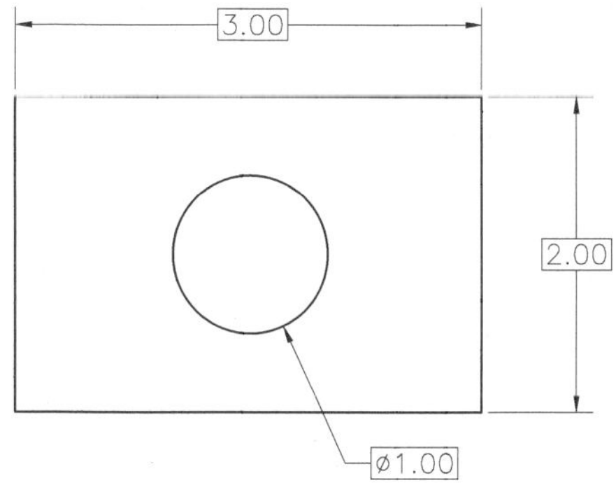

Figure 10-18 Dimension text inside the frame

Text placement Area

The options in this area are discussed next.

Vertical: The **Vertical** drop-down list displays the options that control the vertical placement of the dimension text. The current setting is highlighted. Controlling the vertical placement of the dimension text is possible only when the dimension text is drawn in its normal (default) location. This setting is stored in the **DIMTAD** system variable. The options in this drop-down list are discussed next.

Centered: If this option is selected, the dimension text gets positioned on the dimension line in such a way that the dimension line splits to allow the placement of the text, refer to Figure 10-19. If the 1st or 2nd Extension Line option is selected in the **Horizontal** drop-down list, then the text will be positioned on the extension line, not on the dimension line. The value stored in the **DIMTAD** system variable for **Center** is 0.

Above: If this option is selected, the dimension text is placed above the dimension line, except when the dimension line is not horizontal and the dimension text inside the extension lines is horizontal. The distance of the dimension text from the dimension line is controlled by the **DIMGAP** variable. This results in an unbroken solid dimension line under the dimension text, refer to Figure 10-19. The value stored in the **DIMTAD** system variable for **Above** is 1.

Outside: This option places the dimension text on the side of the dimension line. The value stored in the **DIMTAD** system variable for **Outside** is 2.

JIS: This option lets you place the dimension text to conform to the **JIS** (Japanese Industrial Standards) representation. The value stored in the **DIMTAD** system variable for **JIS** is 3.

Below: This option places the dimension text below the dimension line. The value stored in the **DIMTAD** system variable for **Below** is 4.

Note

*The horizontal and vertical placement options selected are reflected in the dimensions shown in the **Preview** window.*

Horizontal: This drop-down list is used to control the horizontal placement of the dimension text. You can select the required horizontal placement from this list. However, remember that these options will be useful only when the **Place text manually** check box in the **Fine Tuning** area of the **Fit** tab is cleared. The options in this drop-down list are discussed next.

Centered: This option is used to the dimension text between the extension lines. This is the default option.

At Ext Line 1: This option is used to place the text near the first extension line along the dimension line, refer to Figure 10-20.

At Ext Line 2: This option is selected to place the text near the second extension line along the dimension line, refer to Figure 10-20.

Over Ext Line 1: This option is selected to place the text over the first extension line and also along the first extension line, refer to Figure 10-20.

Over Ext Line 2: This option is selected to place the text over the second extension line and also along the second extension line, refer to Figure 10-20.

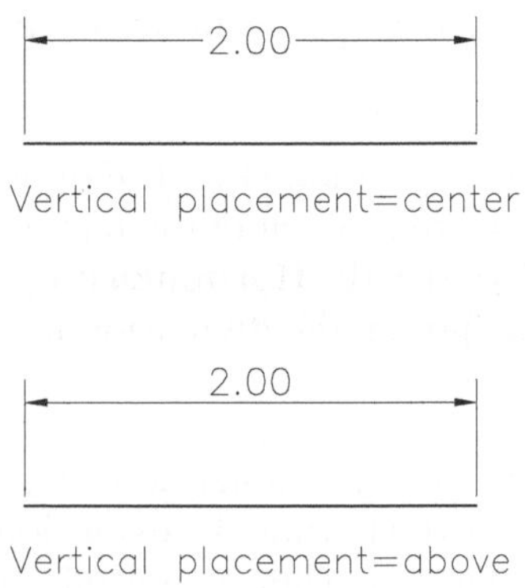

Figure 10-19 Vertical text placement

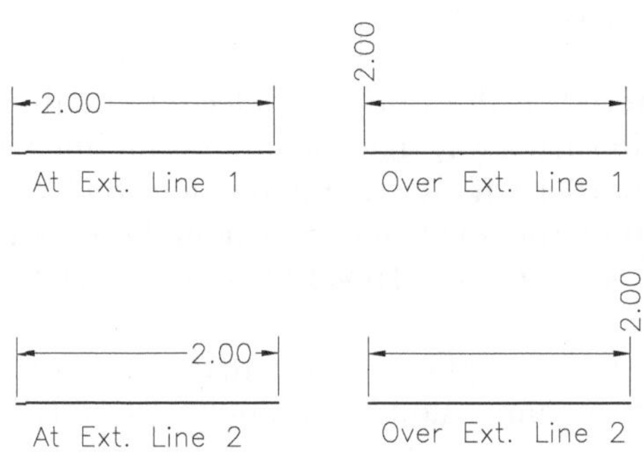

Figure 10-20 Horizontal text placement

View Direction: The options in this drop-down list are used to change the viewing direction of the dimensions either from Left-to-Right or Right-to-Left. Figure 10-21 and Figure 10-22 show the dimensions applied to the entities using the **Left-to-Right** and **Right-to-Left** options, respectively.

Offset from dim line: This spinner is used to specify the distance between the dimension line and the dimension text, refer to Figure 10-23. You can also set the text gap in this spinner. The text gap value is also used as the measure of minimum length for the segments of the dimension line and in basic tolerance. The default value specified in this box is 0.09 units. The value of this setting is stored in the **DIMGAP** system variable.

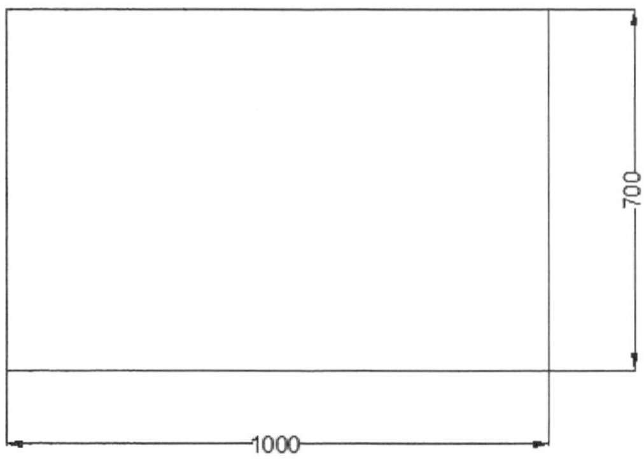

*Figure 10-21 Dimensioning the entity using the **Left-to-Right** option*

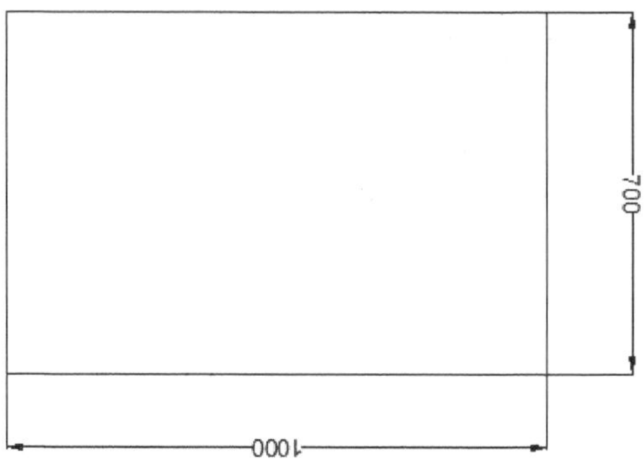

*Figure 10-22 Dimensioning the entity using the **Right-to-Left** option*

Text alignment Area

The options in this area are discussed next.

Horizontal: This is the default option and if selected, the dimension text is drawn horizontally with respect to the current UCS (user coordinate system). The alignment of the dimension line does not affect the text alignment. Selecting this radio button turns both the **DIMTIH** and **DIMTOH** system variables on. The text is drawn horizontally even if the dimension line is at an angle.

Aligned with dimension line: If this radio button is selected then the text aligns with the dimension line and both the system variables **DIMTIH** and **DIMTOH** are turned off, refer to Figure 10-24.

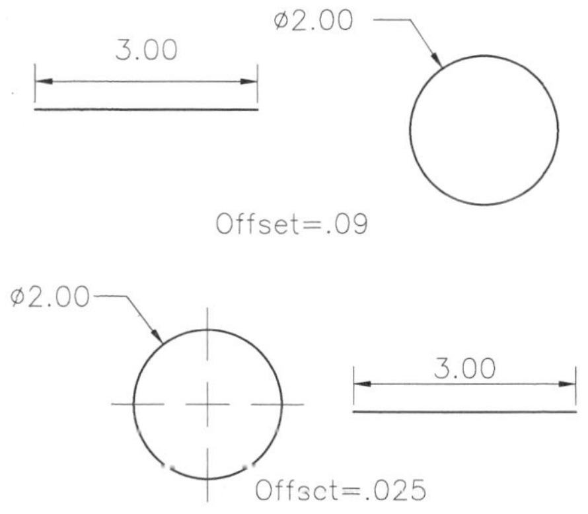

Figure 10-23 Offset from the dimension line

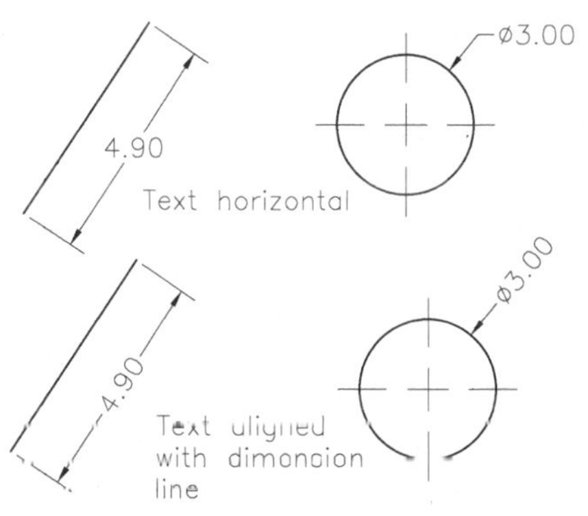

Figure 10-24 Specifying the text alignment

ISO standard: If you select the **ISO standard** radio button, the dimension text is aligned with the dimension line, only when the dimension text is inside the extension lines. Selecting this option turns the system variable **DIMTOH** on. This means the dimension text outside the extension line is horizontal regardless of the angle of the dimension line.

Exercise 2

Create the drawing shown in Figure 10-25 and then set the values in the **Lines**, **Symbols and Arrows**, and **Text** tabs of the **New Dimension Style** dialog box to dimension the drawing, as shown in the figure. (Baseline spacing = 0.25, Extension beyond dimension lines = 0.10, Offset from origin = 0.05, Arrow size = 0.09, Text height = 0.08.)

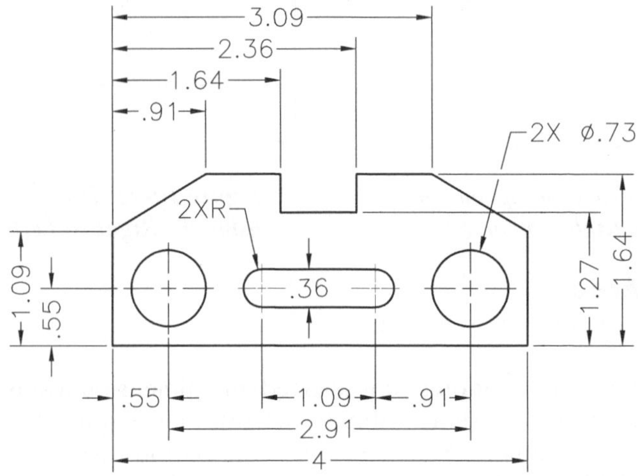

Figure 10-25 Drawing for Exercise 2

FITTING DIMENSION TEXT AND ARROWHEADS

Fit Tab

The **Fit** tab provides you with the options that are used to control the placement of dimension lines, arrowheads, leader lines, text, and the overall dimension scale, refer to Figure 10-26. The options in this tab are discussed next.

Fit options Area

These options are used to set the priorities for moving the text and arrowheads outside the extension lines if the space between the extension lines is not enough to fit both of them.

Either text or arrows (best fit): This is the default option. In this option, AutoCAD places the dimension where it fits best between the extension lines.

Arrows: When you select this radio button, AutoCAD places the text and arrowheads inside the extension lines if there is enough space to fit the both. If the space is not available, the arrows are moved outside the extension lines. If there is not enough space for text, both text and arrowheads are placed outside the extension lines.

Text: When you select this radio button, AutoCAD places the text and arrowheads inside the extension lines, if there is enough space to fit both. If there is enough space to fit the arrows, the arrows will be placed inside and the dimension text moves outside the extension lines. However, if there is not enough space for either the text or the arrowheads, both are placed outside the extension lines.

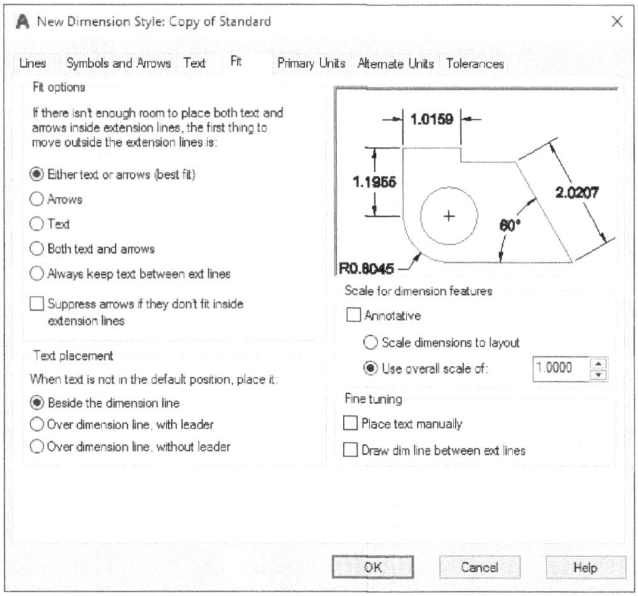

*Figure 10-26 The **Fit** tab of the **New Dimension Style** dialog box*

Both text and arrows: If you select this radio button, AutoCAD will place the arrows and dimension text between the extension lines, if there is enough space available to fit both. Otherwise, both the text and arrowheads are placed outside the extension lines.

Always keep text between ext lines: This option always keeps the text between the extension lines even in cases where AutoCAD would not do so. Selecting this radio button does not affect the radius and diameter dimensions.

Suppress arrows if they don't fit inside extension lines: If you select this check box, the arrowheads are suppressed if the space between the extension lines is not enough to adjust them.

Text placement Area

This area provides you with the options to position the dimension text when it is moved from the default position. The options in this area are as follows:

Beside the dimension line: This option places the dimension text beside the dimension line.

Over dimension line, with leader: Selecting this radio button places the dimension text away from the dimension line and a leader line is created, which connects the text to the dimension line. But if the dimension line is too close to the text, a leader is not drawn. The Horizontal placement decides whether the text is placed to the right or left of the leader.

Over dimension line, without leader: In this option, AutoCAD does not create a leader line, if there is insufficient space to fit the dimension text between the extension lines. The dimension text can be moved freely, independent of the dimension line.

Scale for dimension features Area

The options under this area are used to set the value for the overall dimension scale or scaling to the paper space.

Annotative: This check box is used to specify that the selected dimension style is annotative. With this option, you can also convert an existing non-annotative dimension style to annotative and vice-versa. If you select the **Annotative** check box from the **Create New Dimension Style** dialog box, then the **Annotative** check box will also be selected by default.

Use overall scale of: The current general scaling factor that pertains to all of the size-related dimension variables, such as text size, center mark size, and arrowhead size, is displayed in the **Use overall scale of** spinner. You can alter the scaling factor to your requirement by entering the scaling factor of your choice in this spinner. Altering the value in the **Use overall scale of** spinner alters the value of the **DIMSCALE** variable, as the current scaling factor is stored in it. The overall scale (**DIMSCALE**) is not applied to the measured lengths, coordinates, angles, or tolerance. The default value for this variable is 1.0. In this condition, the dimensioning variables assume their preset values and the drawing is plotted at full scale. The scale factor is the reciprocal of the drawing size and so the drawing is to be plotted at the half size. The overall scale factor (**DIMSCALE**) will be the reciprocal of ½, which is 2.

Note

*If you are in the middle of the dimensioning process and you change the **DIMSCALE** value and save the changed setting in a dimension style file, the dimensions with that style will be updated.*

Tip

*When you increase the limits of a drawing, you need to increase the overall scale of the drawing using the **Use overall scale of** spinner before dimensioning. This will save the time required in changing the individual scale factors of all the dimension parameters.*

Scale dimensions to layout: If you select the **Scale dimensions to layout** radio button, the scale factor between the current model space viewport and the floating viewport is computed automatically. Also, by selecting this radio button, you disable the **Use overall scale of** spinner (it is disabled in the dialog box) and the overall scale factor is set to 0. When the overall scale factor is assigned a value of 0, AutoCAD calculates an acceptable default value based on the scaling between the current model space viewport and the paper space. If you are in the paper space (**TILEMODE=0**), or are not using the **Scale dimensions to layout** feature, AutoCAD sets the overall scale factor to 1; otherwise, AutoCAD calculates a scale factor that makes it possible to plot text sizes, arrow sizes, and other scaled distances at the values, in which they have been previously set. (For further details regarding model space and layouts, refer to Chapter 13.)

Fine tuning Area

The **Fine tuning** area provides additional options governing placement of the dimension text. The options are as follows.

Place text manually: When you dimension, AutoCAD places the dimension text in the middle of the dimension line (if there is enough space). If you select the **Place text manually** check box, you can position the dimension text anywhere along the dimension line. You will also notice that when you select this check box, the horizontal justification is ignored. The default value of this variable is **off**. Selecting this check box enables you to position the dimension text anywhere along the dimension line.

Draw dim line between ext lines: This check box is selected when you want the dimension line to appear between the extension lines, even if the text and dimension lines are placed outside the extension lines. When you select this option in the radius and diameter dimensions (when default text placement is horizontal), the dimension line and arrows are drawn inside the circle or arc, and the text and leader are drawn outside.

FORMATTING PRIMARY DIMENSION UNITS

Primary Units Tab

You can use the **Primary Units** tab of the **New Dimension Style** dialog box to control the dimension text format and precision values, refer to Figure 10-27. You can use the options under this tab to control Unit format, Precision, and Zero suppression for dimension measurements. AutoCAD lets you attach a user-defined prefix or suffix to the dimension text. For example, you can define the diameter symbol as a prefix by entering %%C in the **Prefix** edit box; AutoCAD will automatically attach the diameter symbol in front of the dimension text. Similarly, you can define a unit type, such as **mm**, as a suffix; AutoCAD will then attach **mm** at the end of every dimension text. This tab also enables you to define zero suppression, precision, and dimension text format.

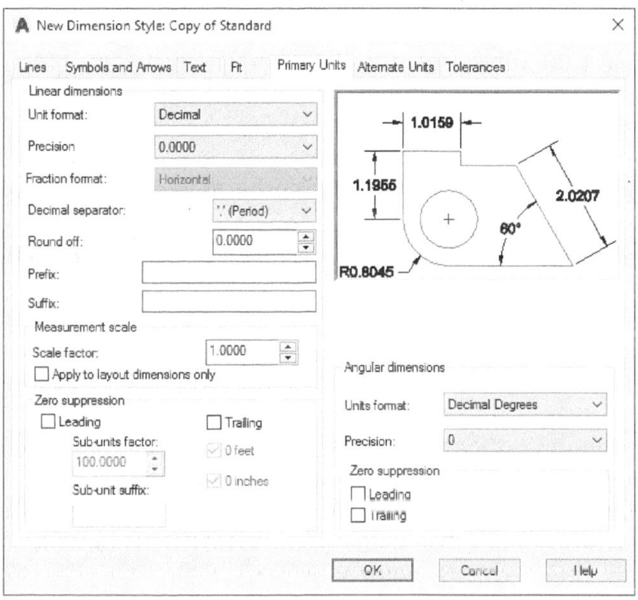

*Figure 10-27 The **Primary Units** tab of the **New Dimension Style** dialog box*

Linear dimensions Area

The options in this area are discussed next.

Unit format: This drop-down list provides you with the options of specifying the units for the primary dimensions. The formats include **Scientific, Decimal**, **Engineering**, **Architectural**,

Fractional and **Windows Desktop**. Remember that by selecting a dimension unit format, the drawing units (which you might have selected by using the **Units** command) are not affected. The unit setting for linear dimensions is stored in the **DIMLUNIT** system variable. The values for system variable stored for **Scientific**, **Decimal**, **Engineering**, **Architectural**, **Fractional**, and **Windows Desktop** are 1, 2, 3, 4, 5, and 6.

Precision: This drop-down list is used to control the number of decimal places for the primary units. The settings for precision (number of decimal places) are saved in the **DIMDEC** variable and depends upon the units and angle format you have selected.

Fraction format: This drop-down list is used to set the fraction format. The options are **Horizontal**, **Diagonal**, and **Not Stacked**. This drop-down list will be available only when you select **Architectural** or **Fractional** from the **Unit format** drop-down list. The value is stored in the **DIMFRAC** variable.

Decimal separator: This drop-down list is used to select an option that will be used as the decimal separator; for example, period [.], comma [,] or space [ ]. If you have selected **Windows Desktop** units in the **Unit format** drop-down list, AutoCAD uses the decimal symbol settings.

Round off: The **Round off** spinner is used to set the value for rounding off the dimension values. The number of decimal places of the round off value should always be less than or equal to the value in the **Precision** edit box. For example, if the **Round off** spinner is set to 0.05, all dimensions will be rounded off to the nearest 0.05 unit. Therefore, the value 1.06 will round off to 1.05 and the value 1.09 will round off to 1.10, see Figure 10-28. The value is stored in the **DIMRND** variable and the default value in the **Round off** edit box is 0.

Prefix: You can append a prefix to the dimension measurement by entering it in this edit box. The dimension text is converted into Prefix<dimension measurement> format. For example, if you enter the text "Abs" in the **Prefix** edit box, "Abs" will be placed in front of the dimension text, as shown in Figure 10-29. The prefix string is saved in the **DIMPOST** system variable.

Note

*Once you specify a prefix, default prefixes such as **R** in radius dimensioning and **ø** in diameter dimensioning are cancelled.*

Suffix: Just like appending a prefix, you can append a suffix to the dimension measurement by entering the desired suffix in this edit box. For example, if you enter the text **mm** in the **Suffix** edit box, the dimension text will have <dimension measurement>mm format, refer to Figure 10-29. AutoCAD stores the suffix string in the **DIMPOST** variable.

Tip

*The **DIMPOST** variable is used to append both prefix and suffix to the dimension text. This variable takes string value as its argument. For example, if you want to have a suffix for centimeters, set **DIMPOST** to **cm**. To establish a prefix to a dimension text, type the prefix text string and then "<>".*

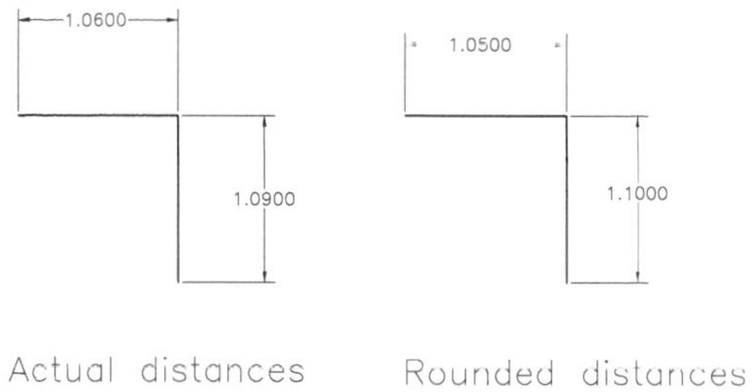

Figure 10-28 *Rounding off the dimension measurements*

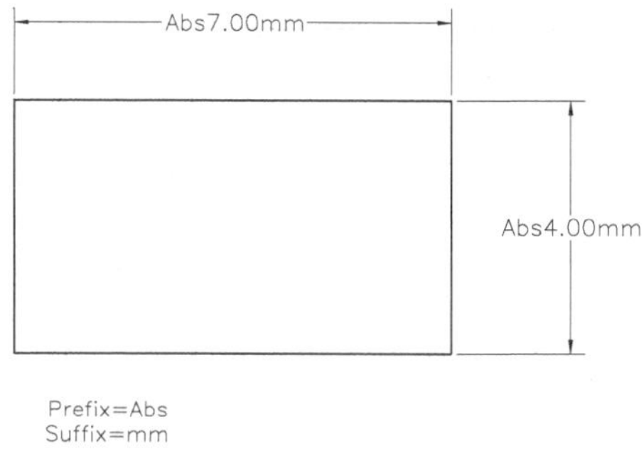

Figure 10-29 *Adding prefix and suffix to the dimensions*

Measurement scale Area

The options in this area are discussed next.

Scale factor: You can specify a global scale factor for the linear dimension measurements by setting the desired scale factor in the **Scale factor** spinner. All the linear distances measured by dimensions, which include radii, diameters, and coordinates, are multiplied by the existing value in this spinner. For example, if the value of the **Scale factor** spinner is set to 2, two unit segments will be dimensioned as 4 units (2 X 2). However, the angular dimensions are not affected. In this manner, the value of the linear scaling factor affects the contents of the default (original) dimension text (Figure 10-30). The default value for linear scaling is 1. With the default value, the dimension text generated is the actual measurement of the object being dimensioned. The linear scaling value is saved in the **DIMLFAC** variable.

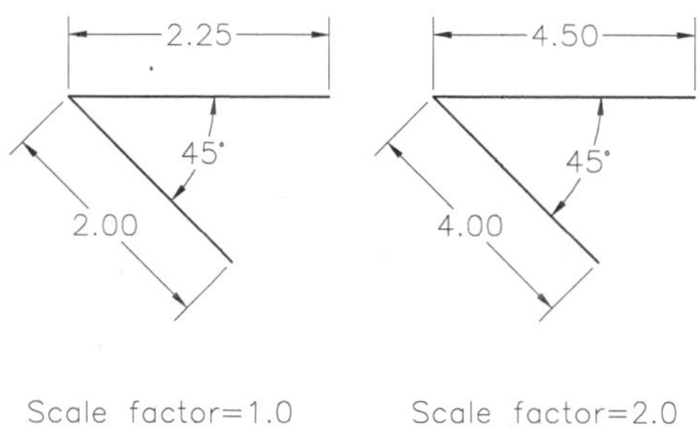

Figure 10-30 *Identical figures dimensioned using different scale factors*

Note

The linear scaling value is not exercised on rounding a value, or on plus or minus tolerance value. Therefore, changing the linear scaling factor will not affect the tolerance values.

Apply to layout dimensions only. When you select the **Apply to layout dimensions only** check box, the scale factor value is applied only to the dimensions in the layout. The value is stored as a negative value in the **DIMLFAC** variable.

Zero suppression Area

The options in this area are used to suppress the leading or trailing zeros in the dimensioning. This area provides you with four check boxes. These check boxes can be selected to suppress the leading or trailing zeros or zeros in the feet and inches. The **0 feet** and the **0 inches** check boxes will be available only when you select **Engineering** or **Architectural** from the **Unit format** drop-down list. When the Architectural units are being used, the **Leading** and **Trailing** check boxes are disabled. For example, if you select the **0 feet** check box, the dimension text 0'-8 ¾" becomes 8 ¾". By default, the 0 feet and 0 inches value is suppressed. If you want to suppress the inches part of a feet-and-inches dimension when the distance in the feet portion is an integer value and the inches portion is zero, select the **0 inches** check box. For example, if you select the **0 inches** check box, the dimension text 3'-0" becomes 3'. Similarly, if you select the **Leading** check box, the dimension that was initially 0.53 will become .53. If you select the **Trailing** check box, the dimension that was initially 2.0 will become 2.

Sub-units factor and Sub-unit suffix

The **Sub-units factor** option is used to set the value from sub-units into a single unit and the **Sub-unit suffix** option is used to add a suffix after the single unit. For example, assume an entity having dimension 0.05 unit. After selecting the **Leading** and **Trailing** check boxes from the **Zero suppression** area in the **Primary Units** tab of the **New Dimension Style** dialog box, refer to Figure 10-27, if you set **Sub-units factor** as 100 (by typing manually or using spinner) and enter "**m**" in **Sub-unit suffix** then AutoCAD will display dimension as **5m** on the screen.

Angular dimensions Area

This area provides you with the options to control the units format, precision, and zero suppression for the Angular units.

Units format: The **Units format** drop-down list displays a list of unit formats for the angular dimensions. The default value in which the angular dimensions are displayed is **Decimal Degrees**. The value for angular dimensions is stored in the **DIMAUNIT** variable.

Precision: You can select the number of decimal places for the angular dimensions from this drop-down list. This value is stored in the **DIMADEC** variable.

Zero suppression Area: Similar to the linear dimensions, you can suppress the **Leading** and **Trailing** or both zeros in the angular dimensions by selecting the respective check boxes in the area.

FORMATTING ALTERNATE DIMENSION UNITS

Alternate Units Tab

By default, the options in the **Alternate Units** tab of the **New Dimension Style** dialog box are disabled. If you want to perform alternate units dimensioning, select the **Display alternate units** check box. By doing so, AutoCAD activates various options in this area, as shown in Figure 10-31. This tab sets the format, precision, angles, placement, scale, and so on for the alternate units in use. In this tab, you can specify the values that will be applied to the alternate dimensions.

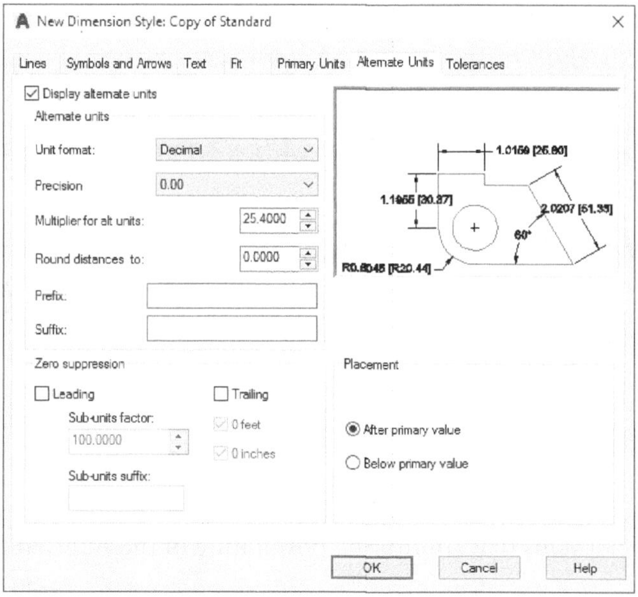

*Figure 10-31 The **Alternate Units** tab of the **New Dimension Style** dialog box*

Alternate units Area

The options in this area are identical to those under the **Linear dimensions** area of the **Primary Units** tab. This area provides you with the options to set the format for all dimension types.

Unit format: You can select a unit format from this drop-down list to apply to the alternate dimensions. The options under this drop-down list include **Scientific**, **Decimal**, **Engineering**, **Architectural Stacked**, **Fractional Stacked**, **Architectural**, **Fractional**, and **Windows Desktop**.

Precision: You can select the number of decimal places for the alternate units from the **Precision** drop-down list.

Multiplier for alt units: To generate a value in the alternate system of measurement, you need a factor with which all the linear dimensions will be multiplied. The value for this factor can be set using the **Multiplier for alt units** spinner. The default value of 25.4 is for dimensioning in inches with the alternate units in millimeters.

Round distances to: This spinner is used to set a value to which you want all your measurements (made in alternate units) to be rounded off. For example, if you set the value of the **Round distances to** spinner to 0.25, all the alternate dimensions get rounded off to the nearest .25 unit.

Prefix/Suffix: The **Prefix** and **Suffix** edit boxes are similar to the edit boxes in the **Linear dimensions** area of the **Primary Units** tab. You can enter the text or symbols that you want to precede or follow the alternate dimension text. You can also use control codes and special characters to display special symbols.

Zero suppression Area

This area allows you to suppress the leading or trailing zeros in decimal unit dimensions by selecting either both, or none of the **Trailing** and **Leading** check boxes. Similarly, selecting the **0 feet** check box suppresses the zeros in the feet area of the dimension, when the dimension value is less than a foot. Selecting the **0 inches** check box suppresses the zeros in the inches area of the dimension. For example, 1'-0" becomes 1'.

Sub-units factor and Sub-unit suffix

The **Sub-units factor** sets the value from sub-units into a single unit and **Sub-units suffix** adds a suffix after the single unit. For example, assume an entity having dimension 0.05 unit. After choosing the **Leading** and **Trailing** check boxes under the **Zero suppression** area in the **Alternate Units** tab of the **New Dimension Style** dialog box, refer to Figure 10-31, if you set **Sub-units factor** as 100 (by typing manually or using spinner) and enter **m** in **Sub-units suffix** then AutoCAD will display the dimension as **5m** on the screen.

Placement Area

This area provides the options that control the positioning of the Alternate units.

After primary value: Selecting the **After primary value** radio button places the alternate units dimension text after the primary units. This is the default option, refer to Figure 10-32.

Below primary value: Selecting the **Below primary value** radio button places the alternate units dimension text below the primary units, refer to Figure 10-32.

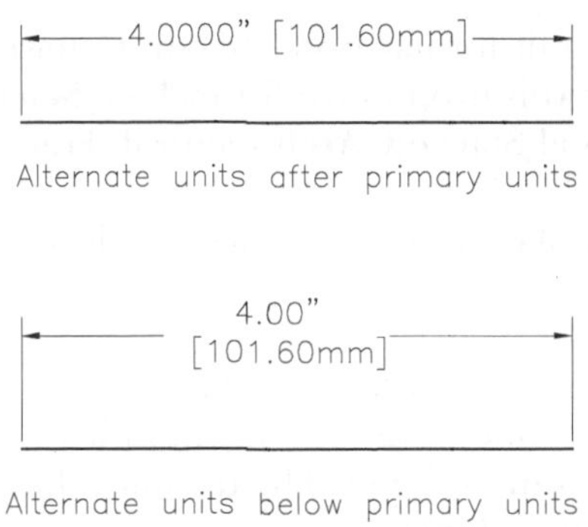

Figure 10-32 Placement of alternate units

FORMATTING THE TOLERANCES

Tolerances Tab

The **Tolerances** tab allows you to set the parameters for options that control the format and display of the tolerance dimension text, refer to Figure 10-33. These include the alternate unit tolerance dimension text.

Tolerance format Area

The **Tolerance format** area of the **Tolerances** tab is used to specify the tolerance method, tolerance value, position of tolerance text, and precision and height of the tolerance text. For example, if you do not want a dimension to deviate more than plus 0.01 and minus 0.02, you can specify this by selecting **Deviation** from the **Method** drop-down list and then specifying the plus and minus deviation in the **Upper value** and the **Lower value** edit boxes. When you dimension, AutoCAD will automatically append the tolerance to it. The **DIMTP** variable sets the maximum (or upper) tolerance limit for the dimension text and **DIMTM** variable sets the minimum (or lower) tolerance limit for the dimension text. Different settings and their effects on relevant dimension variables are explained in the following sections.

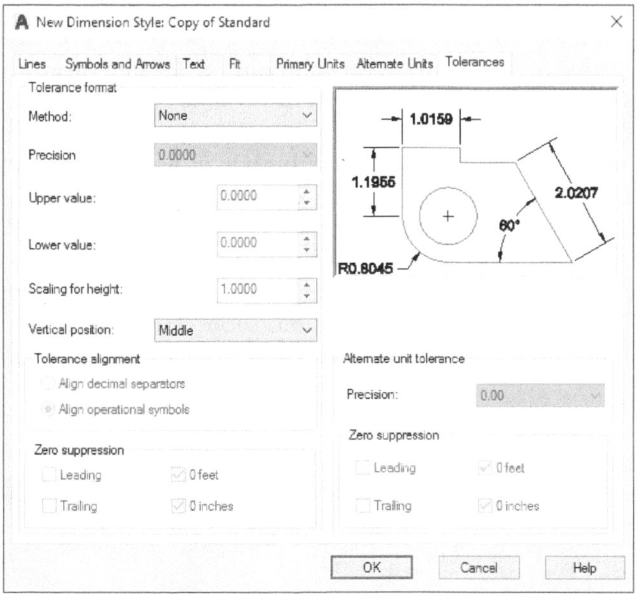

*Figure 10-33 The **Tolerances** tab of the **New Dimension Style** dialog box*

Method: The **Method** drop-down list lets you select the tolerance method. The tolerance methods supported by AutoCAD are **Symmetrical**, **Deviation**, **Limits**, and **Basic**. These tolerance methods are described next.

None: Selecting the **None** option sets the **DIMTOL** variable to 0 and does not add tolerance values to the dimension text, that is, the options in the **Tolerances** tab are disabled.

Symmetrical: This option is used to specify the symmetrical tolerances. When you select this option, the **Lower value** spinner is disabled and the value specified in the **Upper value** spinner is applied to both plus and minus tolerances. For example, if the value specified in the **Upper value** spinner is 0.01, the tolerance appended to the dimension text is ±0.01, refer to Figure 10-34. The value of **DIMTOL** is set to 1 and the value of **DIMLIM** is set to 0.

Deviation: If you select the **Deviation** tolerance method, the values in the **Upper value** and **Lower value** spinners will be displayed as plus and minus dimension tolerances. If you enter values for the plus and minus tolerances, AutoCAD appends a plus sign (+) to the positive values of the tolerance and a negative sign (–) to the negative values of the tolerance. For example, if the upper value of the tolerance is 0.05 and the lower value of the tolerance is 0.01, the resulting dimension text generated will have a positive tolerance of 0.05 and a negative tolerance of 0.01 (Figure 10-34). Even if one of the tolerance values is 0, a sign is appended to it. On specifying the deviation tolerance, AutoCAD sets the **DIMTOL** variable value to 1 and the **DIMLIM** variable value to 0. The values in the **Upper value** and **Lower value** edit boxes are saved in the **DIMTP** and **DIMTM** system variables, respectively.

Limits: If you select the **Limits** tolerance method from the **Method** drop-down list, AutoCAD adds the upper value (contents of the **Upper value** spinner) to the dimension text (actual measurement) and subtracts the lower value (contents of the **Lower value** spinner) from the dimension text. The resulting values are displayed as the dimension text, refer to Figure 10-34. Selecting the **Limits** tolerance method results in setting the **DIMLIM** variable value to 1 and the **DIMTOL** variable value to 0. The numeral values in the **Upper value** and **Lower value** edit boxes are saved in the **DIMTP** and **DIMTM** system variables, respectively.

Basic: A basic dimension text is a dimension text with a box drawn around it, refer to Figure 10-34. The basic dimension is also called a reference dimension. Reference dimensions are used primarily in geometric dimensioning and tolerances. The basic dimension can be realized by selecting the basic tolerance method. The distance provided around the dimension text (distance between dimension text and the rectangular box) is stored as a negative value in the **DIMGAP** variable. The negative value signifies the basic dimension. The default setting is off, resulting in the generation of dimensions without the box around the dimension text.

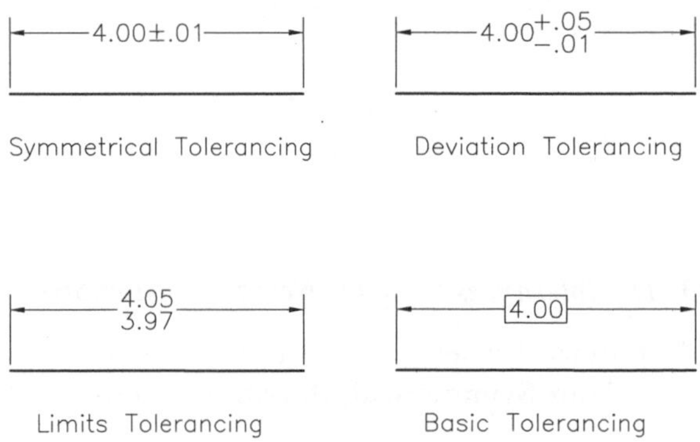

Figure 10-34 Specifying tolerance using various tolerancing methods

Precision: The **Precision** drop-down list is used to select the number of decimal places for the tolerance dimension text. The value is stored in **DIMTDEC** variable.

Upper value/Lower value: In the **Upper value** spinner, the positive upper or maximum value is specified. If the method of tolerances is symmetrical, the same value is used as the lower value also. The value is stored in the **DIMTP** variable. In the **Lower value** spinner, the lower or minimum value is specified. The value is stored in the **DIMTM** variable.

Scaling for height: The **Scaling for height** spinner is used to specify the height of the dimension tolerance text relative to the dimension text height. The default value is 1, which means the height of the tolerance text is the same as the dimension text height. If you want the tolerance text to be 75 percent of the dimension height text, enter 0.75 in the **Scaling for height** edit box. The ratio of the tolerance height to the dimension text height is calculated by AutoCAD and then stored in the **DIMTFAC** variable. **DIMTFAC = Tolerance Height/Text Height.**

Vertical position: This drop-down list allows you to specify the location of the tolerance text for deviation and symmetrical methods only. The three possible alignments are the **Bottom**, **Middle**, or **Top** of the main dimension text. The settings are saved in the **DIMTOLJ** system variable (Bottom=0, Middle=1, and Top=2).

Tolerance alignment Area

The options in this area are used to control the alignment of the tolerance value text when they are placed in stacked condition. These options get highlighted only when you select the **Deviation** or **Limits** option from the **Method** drop-down list. Select the **Align decimal separators** radio button to align the tolerance text vertically along the decimal point, refer to Figure 10-35. Select the **Align operational symbols** radio button to align the tolerance text vertically along the plus sign (+) and negative sign(-), refer to Figure 10-35.

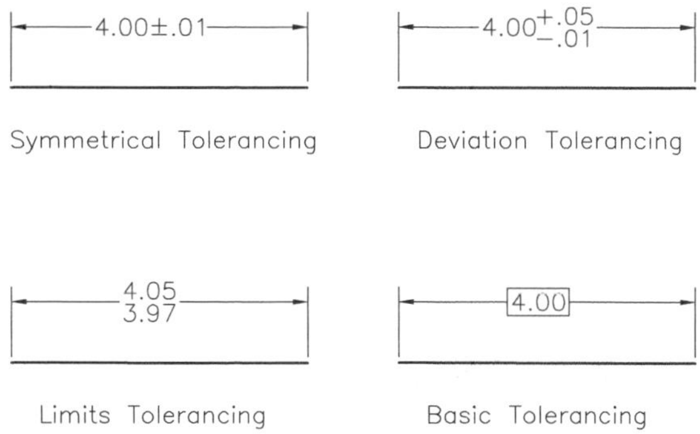

Figure 10-35 Various tolerance alignment options

Zero suppression Area

This area controls the zero suppression in the tolerance text depending on which one of the check boxes is selected. Selecting the **Leading** check box suppresses the leading zeros in all the decimal tolerance text. For example, 0.2000 becomes .2000. Selecting the **Trailing** check box suppresses the trailing zeros in all the decimal tolerance text. For example, 0.5000 becomes 0.5. Similarly, selecting both the boxes suppresses both the trailing and leading zeros and selecting none, suppresses none. If you select **0 feet** check box, the zeros in the feet portion of the tolerance dimension text are suppressed if the dimension value is less than one foot. Similarly, selecting the **0 inches** check box suppresses the zeros in the inches portion of the dimension text.

Alternate unit tolerance Area

The options in this area define the precision and zero suppression settings for the alternate unit tolerance values. The options under this area will be available only when you display the alternate units along with the primary units.

Precision: This drop-down list is used to set the number of decimal places to be displayed in the tolerance text of the alternate dimensions

Zero suppression Area

Selecting the respective check boxes controls the suppression of the **Leading** and **Trailing** zeros in decimal values and the suppression of zeros in the Feet and Inches portions for dimensions in the feet and inches format.

Exercise 3 — Dimension Style

Create the drawing as shown in Figure 10-36 and then dimension it by setting the values in various tabs of the **New Dimension Style** dialog box, as follows. (Baseline spacing = 0.25, Extension beyond dim lines = 0.10, Offset from origin = 0.05, Arrowhead size =0.07, Text height = 0.08.)

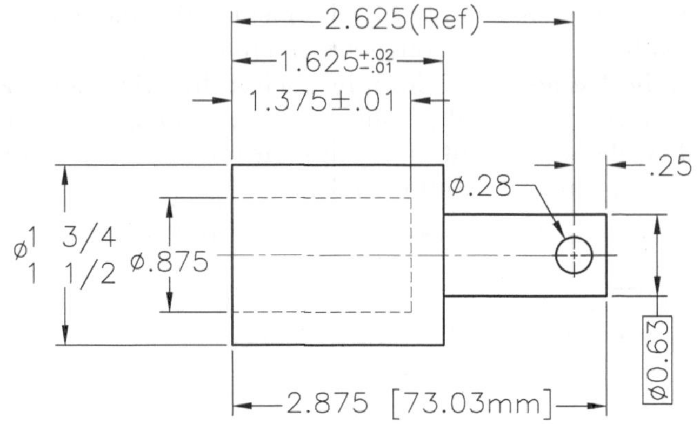

Figure 10-36 Drawing for Exercise 3

DIMENSION STYLE FAMILIES

The dimension style feature of AutoCAD lets the user define a dimension style with values that are common to all dimensions. For example, the arrow size, dimension text height, and color of the dimension line are generally same in all types of dimensioning such as linear, radial, diameter, and angular. These dimensioning types belong to the same family because they have some characteristics in common. In AutoCAD, this is called a dimension style family, and the values assigned to the family are called dimension style family values.

After you have defined the dimension style family values, you can specify variations on it for other types of dimensions such as radial and diameter. For example, if you want to limit the number of decimal places to two in radial dimensioning, you can specify that value for radial dimensioning. The other values will stay the same as the family values to which this dimension type belongs. When you use the radial dimension, AutoCAD automatically uses the style that was defined for radial dimensioning otherwise, it creates a radial dimension with the values as defined for the family. After you have created a dimension style family, any changes in the parent style are applied to family members, if the particular property is the same. Special suffix codes are appended to the dimension style family names that correspond to different dimension types. For example, if the dimension style family name is MYSTYLE and you define a diameter type of dimension, AutoCAD will append $4 at the end of the dimension style family name. The name of the diameter type of dimension will be MYSTYLE$4. The following are the suffix codes for different types of dimensioning.

Suffix Code	Dimension Type	Suffix Code	Dimension Type
0	Linear	2	Angular
3	Radius	4	Diameter
6	Ordinate	7	Leader

Example 1 Dimension Style Family

The following example illustrates the concepts of dimension style families, refer to Figure 10-37.

1. Specify the values for the dimension style family.
2. Specify the values for the linear dimensions.
3. Specify the values for the diameter and radius dimensions.
4. After creating the dimension style, use it to dimension the given drawing.

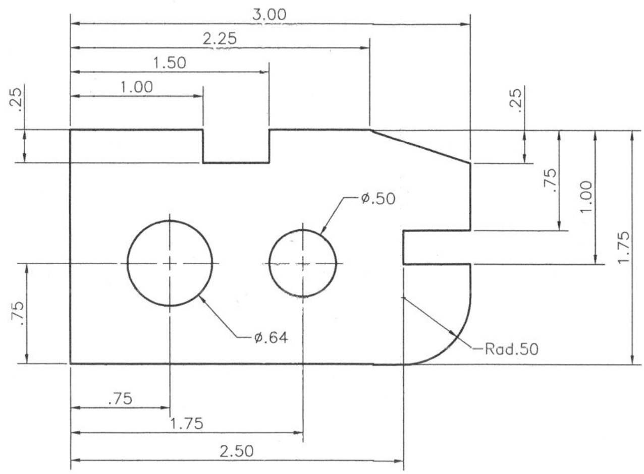

Figure 10-37 *Drawing for Example 1*

The steps for creating a dimension style family are given next:

1. Start a new file in the **Drafting & Annotation** workspace and draw an object, as shown in Figure 10-37.

2. Left-click on the inclined arrow in the **Dimensions** panel of the **Annotate** tab; the **Dimension Style Manager** dialog box is displayed.

3. Choose the **New** button to display the **Create New Dimension Style** dialog box. In this dialog box, enter **MyStyle** in the **New Style Name** edit box. Select **Annotative** from the **Start With** drop-down list. Also select **All dimensions** from the **Use for** drop-down list.

   Now, choose the **Continue** button to display the **New Dimension Style: MyStyle** dialog box. In this dialog box, Choose the **Lines** and **Symbols and Arrows** tab and then enter the following values in their respective options.

   Lines tab
   Baseline Spacing: 0.15
   Offset from origin: 0.03
   Extend beyond dim lines: 0.07

   Symbols and Arrows tab
   Arrow size: 0.09
   Center marks: Select the **Line** radio button
   Enter **0.05** in the spinner in the **Center marks** area

4. Choose the **Text** tab and change the following values:

   Text Height: 0.09 Offset from dim line: 0.03

5. Choose the **Fit** tab and make sure the **Annotative** check box is selected.

6. After entering the values, choose the **OK** button to return to the **Dimension Style Manager** dialog box. This dimension style contains the values that are common to all dimension types.

7. Now, choose the **New** button again in the **Dimension Style Manager** dialog box to display the **Create New Dimension Style** dialog box. AutoCAD displays **Copy of MyStyle** in the **New Style Name** edit box. Select **MyStyle** from the **Start With** drop-down list if it is not already selected. From the **Use for** drop-down list, select **Linear dimensions**. Choose the **Continue** button to display the **New Dimension Style: MyStyle: Linear** dialog box and set the following values in the **Text** tab:

   a. Select the **Aligned with dimension line** radio button in the **Text alignment** area.
   b. In the **Text placement** area, select **Above** from the **Vertical** drop-down list.

8. In the **Primary Units** tab, set the precision to two decimal places by selecting **0.00** from the **Precision** drop-down list. Select the **Leading** check box in the **Zero suppression** area. Next, choose the **OK** button to return to the **Dimension Style Manager** dialog box.

9. Choose the **New** button again to display the **Create New Dimension Style** dialog box. Select **MyStyle** from the **Start With** drop-down list and the **Diameter dimensions** type from the **Use for** drop-down list. Next, choose the **Continue** button; the **New dimension Style: MyStyle: Diameter** dialog box is displayed.

10. Choose the **Text** tab and select the **Centered** option from the **Vertical** drop-down list in the **Text placement** area, if it is not selected by default. Then select the **Horizontal** radio button from the **Text alignment** area, if it is not selected by default.

11. Choose the **Primary Units** tab and then set the precision to two decimal places. Select the **Leading** check box in the **Zero suppression** area. Next, choose the **OK** button to return to the **Dimension Style Manager** dialog box.

12. In this dialog box, again choose the **New** button to display the **Create New Dimension Style** dialog box. Select **MyStyle** from the **Start With** drop-down list and **Radius dimensions** from the **Use for** drop-down list. Choose the **Continue** button to display the **New Dimension Style: MyStyle: Radial** dialog box.

13. Choose the **Primary Units** tab and then set the precision to two decimal places. Select the **Leading** check box in the **Zero suppression** area. Next, enter **Rad** in the **Prefix** edit box.

14. In the **Fit** tab, select the **Text** radio button in the **Fit options** area. Next, choose the **OK** button to return to the **Dimension Style Manager** dialog box.

15. Select **MyStyle** from the **Styles** list box in the **Dimension Style Manager** dialog box and choose the **Set Current** button. Choose the **Close** button to exit the dialog box.

16. Choose the **Linear** tool from the **Dimensions** panel; the **Select Annotation Scale** dialog box is displayed. Select the **1:1** option from the drop-down list and choose the **OK** button.

17. Use the linear and baseline dimensions to draw the linear dimensions, refer to Figure 10-37. While entering linear dimensions, you will notice that AutoCAD automatically uses the values that were defined for the linear type of dimensioning.

18. Use the diameter dimensioning to dimension the circles, refer to Figure 10-37. Again, notice that the dimensions are drawn based on the values specified for the diameter type of dimensioning.

19. Now, use the radius dimensioning to dimension the fillet, refer to Figure 10-37.

USING DIMENSION STYLE OVERRIDES

Most of the dimension characteristics are common in a production drawing. The values that are common to different dimensioning types can be defined in the dimension style family. However, at times, you might have different dimensions. For example, you may need two types of linear dimensioning: one with tolerance and one without it. One way to draw these dimensions is to create two dimensioning styles. You can also use the dimension variable overrides to override the existing values. For example, you can define a dimension style (**MyStyle**) that draws dimensions without tolerance. Now, to draw a dimension with tolerance or update an existing dimension, you can override the previously defined value through the **Dimension Style Manager** dialog box or by setting the variable values at the command prompt. Now, you can remove style override of any selected dimension by choosing the **Remove Style Overrides** option from the shortcut menu displayed on right clicking. The following example illustrates how to use the dimension style overrides.

Example 2 — *Dimension Style Override*

In this example, you will update the overall dimension (3.00) so that the tolerance is displayed with the dimension. You will also add linear dimensions, as shown in Figure 10-38.

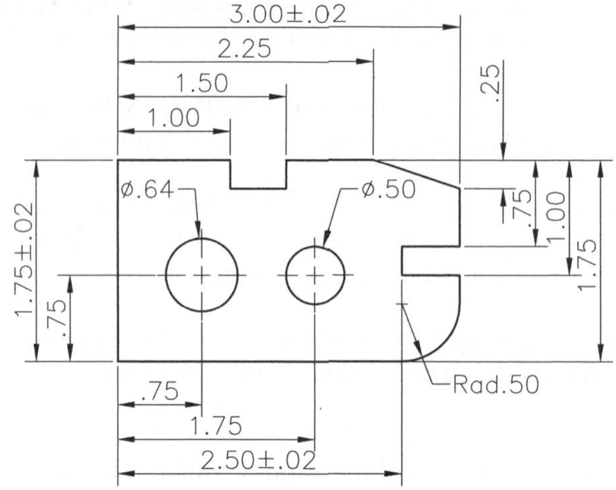

Figure 10-38 *Drawing for Example 2*

This problem can be solved by using dimension style overrides as well as by using the **PROPERTIES** palette. However, here only the dimension style overrides method is discussed.

1. Invoke the **Dimension Style Manager** dialog box. Select **MyStyle** from the **Styles** list box and choose the **Override** button to display the **Override Current Style: MyStyle** dialog box. The options in this dialog box are same to the **New Dimension Style** dialog box discussed earlier in this chapter.

2. Choose the **Tolerances** tab and select **Symmetrical** from the **Method** drop-down list.

3. Set the value of the **Precision** spinner to two decimal places. Set the value of the **Upper value** spinner to **0.02** and select the **Leading** check box in the **Zero suppression** area. Next, choose the **OK** button to exit the dialog box (this does not save the style). On doing so, you will notice that **<style overrides>** is displayed under **MyStyle** in the **Styles** list box, indicating that the style overrides the **MyStyle** dimension style.

4. The **<style overrides>** is displayed until you save it under a new name or under the style it is displayed in, or until you delete it. Select **<style overrides>** and right-click to display the shortcut menu. Choose the **Save to current style** option from the shortcut menu to save the overrides to the current style. Choosing the **Rename** option allows you to rename the style override and save it as a new style.

5. Choose the **Update** tool from the **Dimension** panel in the **Annotate** tab and select the dimension that measures **3.00**. The dimension now displays the symmetrical tolerance.

6. Draw the remaining two linear dimensions. They will automatically appear with the tolerances, refer to Figure 10-38.

Tip

*You can also use the **Override** tool from the **Dimensions** panel of the **Annotate** tab to apply the change to the existing dimensions.*

COMPARING AND LISTING DIMENSION STYLES

Choosing the **Compare** button in the **Dimension Style Manager** dialog box displays the **Compare Dimension Styles** dialog box where you can compare the settings of two dimensions styles or list all the settings of a single dimension style, refer to Figure 10-39.

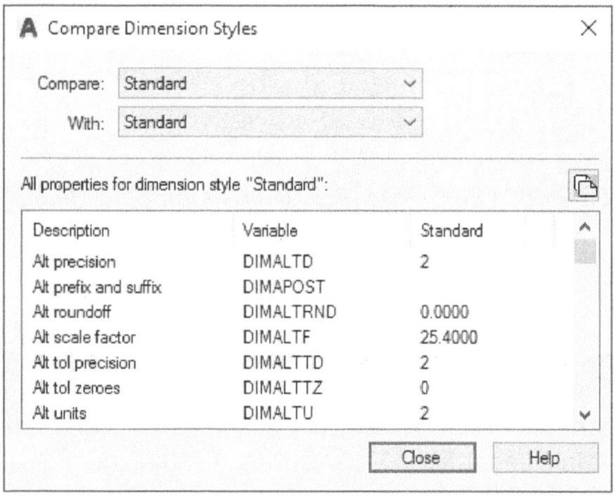

***Figure 10-39** The **Compare Dimension Styles** dialog box*

The **Compare** and the **With** drop-down lists display the dimension styles in the current drawing. Selecting the dimension style from the respective list compares the two styles. In the **With** drop-down list, if you select **<none>** or the same style as selected from the **Compare** drop-down list, all the properties of the selected style are displayed. The comparison results are displayed under different headings: **Description** of the Dimension Style property, the System **Variable** controlling a particular setting, and the values of the variable for both the dimension styles which differ in the two styles in comparison. The number of differences between the selected dimension styles are displayed below the **With** drop-down list. The button (at the right side in the middle) provided in this dialog box prints the comparison results to the Windows clipboard from where they can be pasted to other Windows applications.

USING EXTERNALLY REFERENCED DIMENSION STYLES

The externally referenced dimensions cannot be used directly in the current drawing. When you Xref a drawing, the drawing name is appended to the style name and the two are separated by a vertical bar (|) symbol. It uses the same syntax as the other externally dependent symbols. For example, if the drawing (FLOOR) has a dimension style called DIM1 and you Xref this drawing in the current drawing, AutoCAD will rename the dimension style to FLOOR|DIM1. You cannot make this dimension style current, nor can you modify or override it. However, you can use it as a template to create a new style. To accomplish this, invoke the **Dimension Style Manager** dialog box. If the **Don't list styles in Xrefs** check box is selected, the styles in the Xref are not displayed. Clear this check box to display the Xref dimension styles and choose the **New** button. In the **New Style Name** edit box of the **Create New Dimension Style** dialog box, as shown in Figure 10-40, enter the name of the dimension style. AutoCAD will create a new dimension style with the same values as those of the externally referenced dimension style (FLOOR|DIM1).

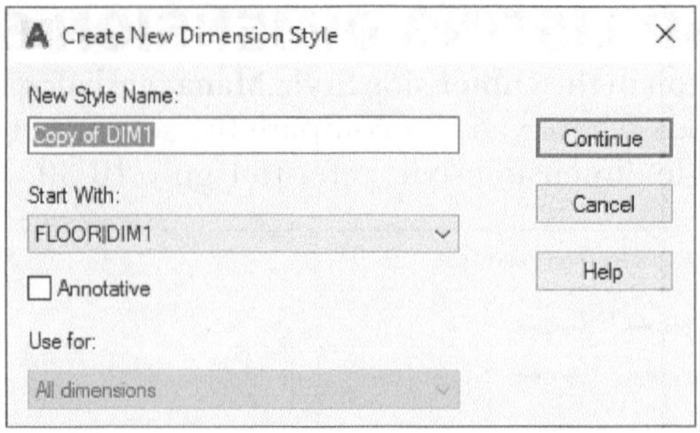

Figure 10-40 *The* ***Create New Dimension Style*** *dialog box*

Note

You will learn more about External References in Chapter 18.

CREATING AND RESTORING MULTILEADER STYLES

Ribbon: Annotate > Leaders > Multileader Style Manager (Inclined arrow)
Toolbar: Multileader > Multileader Style or Styles > Multileader Style
Command: MLEADERSTYLE/MLS

The multileader styles control the appearance and positioning of multileaders in the drawing. If the default multileader styles (**Standard** and **Annotative**) do not meet your requirement, you can edit the default multileader styles or create a new one as per your requirement. Left-click on the inclined arrow in the **Leaders** panel of the **Annotate** tab; the **Multileader Style Manager** dialog box will be displayed, as shown in Figure 10-41(a).

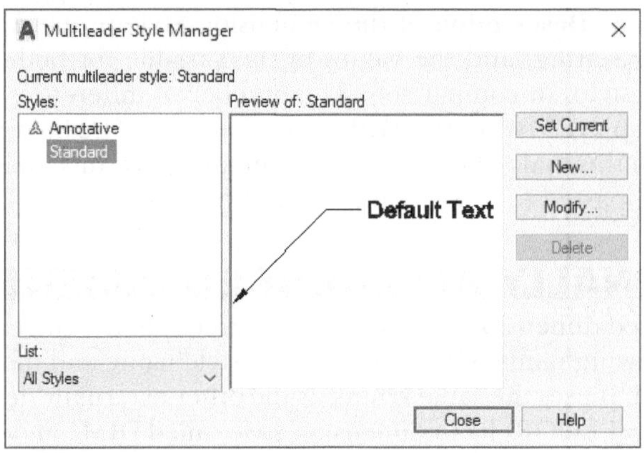

Figure 10-41(a) *The* ***Multileader Style Manager*** *dialog box*

From the **Multileader Style Manager** dialog box, choose the **New** button to display the **Create New Multileader Style** dialog box, as shown in Figure 10-41(b). Enter the multileader style name in the **New style name** text box and then select a style from the **Start with** drop-down list on which you want to base your current style. Select the **Annotative** check box to specify that the new dimension style should be annotative. Click on the **Help** button to get the help and information about the various options in this dialog box. Choose the **Continue** button to display the **Modify Multileader Style** dialog box in which you can define the new style. After defining the new style, choose the **OK** button. The parameters of the **New Multileader Style** dialog box are discussed in the next section.

In the **Multileader Style Manager** dialog box, the current multileader style name is shown in front of the **Current multileader style** area and is also highlighted in the **Styles** list box. The **Multileader Style Manager** dialog box also has a **Preview** window that displays a preview of the current multileader style. A style can be made current (restored) by selecting the name of the multileader style that you want to make current from the list of defined multileader styles and choosing the **Set Current** button. You can also make a style current by double-clicking on the style name in the **Styles** list box. The **Multileader Style** drop-down list in the **Leaders** panel also displays the multileader styles. Select the required multileader style from this list to set it as current. The list of multileader styles displayed in the **Styles** list box depends on the option selected from the **List** drop down-list. If you select the **Styles in use** option, only the multileader styles in use will be listed in the **Styles** list box. If you right-click on a style in the **Styles** list box, a shortcut menu will be displayed to provide you with the options such as **Set current**, **Modify, Rename**, and **Delete**. Choose the **Modify** button to display the **Modify Multileader Style** dialog box in which you can modify an existing style. Choose the **Delete** button to delete the selected multileader style that has not been used in the drawing.

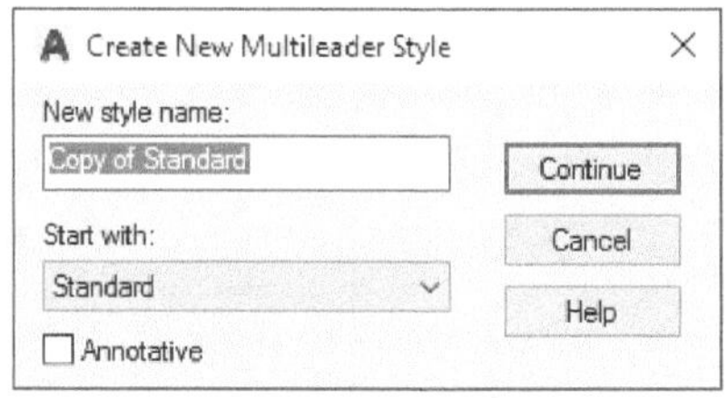

Figure 10-41(b) *The* ***Create New Multileader Style*** *dialog box*

MODIFY MULTILEADER STYLE DIALOG BOX

The **Modify Multileader Style** dialog box can be used to specify the multileader attributes (variables) that affect various properties of the multileader. The various tabs provided in the **Modify Multileader Style** dialog box are discussed next.

Leader Format Tab

The options in the **Leader Format** tab of the **Modify Multileader Style** dialog box are used to specify the multileader attributes that affect the format of the multileader lines, refer to Figure 10-42. For example, the appearance and behavior of the multileader lines and the arrow head can be changed with this tab.

General Area

This area provides you the options for controlling the display of the multileader lines. These options are discussed next.

Type: This option is used to specify the type of lines to be used for creating the multileaders. You can select the **Straight**, **Spline**, or **None** option from the **Type** drop-down list. Select the **None** option to create the multileader with no leader lines. You will only be able to draw the content of that multileader. The default line type for the multileaders is **Straight**.

Color: This drop-down list is used to set the colors for the leader lines and arrowheads. The multileader arrowheads have the same color as the multileader lines because the arrows are a part of the multileader lines. The default color for the multileader lines and arrows is **ByBlock**.

Select the **Select Color** option from the **Color** drop-down list to display the **Select Color** dialog box from where you can choose a specific color.

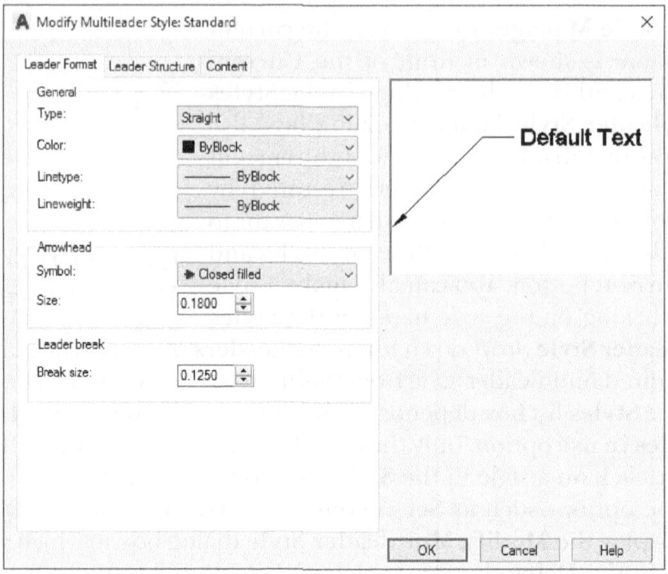

Figure 10-42 The ***Leader Format*** *tab of the* ***Modify Multileader Style*** *dialog box*

Linetype: This drop-down list is used to set the linetype for the multileader lines.

Lineweight: This drop-down list is used to specify the lineweight for the multileader lines. You can select the required lineweight from this drop-down list. The default value is **ByBlock**. Note that you cannot assign the lineweight to the arrowheads using this drop-down list.

Arrowhead Area

This area provides you the options for controlling the shape and size of the arrowhead. The options in this area are discussed next.

Symbol: When you create a multileader, AutoCAD draws the terminator symbol at the starting point of the multileader line. This terminator symbol is generally referred to as the arrowhead, and it represents the beginning of the multileader. AutoCAD provides you nineteen standard termination symbols that can be selected from the **Symbol** drop-down list of the **Arrowhead** area. In addition to this, you can create your own arrows or terminator symbols.

Size: This spinner is used to specify the size of the arrowhead.

Leader break Area

The **Break size** spinner in this area is used to specify the break length in the multileader while applying the dimension breaks. The default value of **Break size** is 0.1250.

Leader Structure Tab

The options in the **Leader Structure** tab of the **Modify Multileader Style** dialog box are used to specify the dimensioning attributes that affect the structure of the multileader lines, refer to Figure 10-43. The attributes that can be controlled by using the **Leader Structure** tab are the number of lines to be drawn before adding the content, adding landing before the content, length of the landing line, multileader to be annotative or not, and so on.

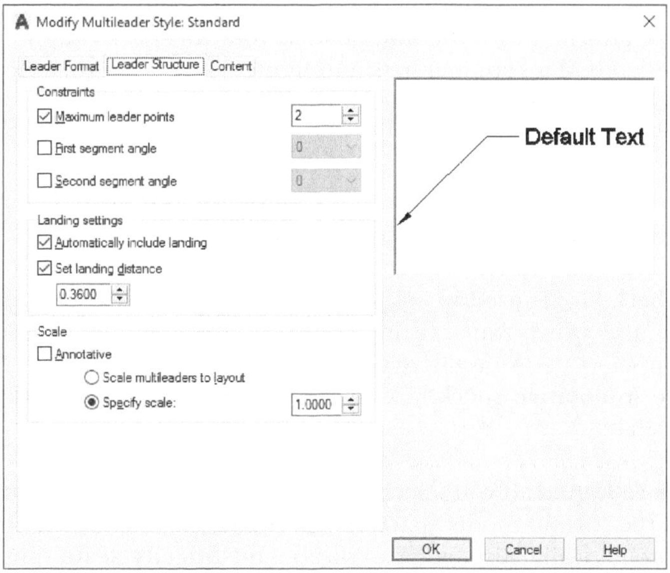

*Figure 10-43 The **Leader Structure** tab of the **Modify Multileader Style** dialog box*

Constraints Area

This area provides you the options to control the number of multileader points and the direction of the multileader.

Maximum leader points: This check box is used to specify the maximum number of points in the multileader line. The default value is 2, which means that there will be only two points in the leader line. Select the check box to specify the maximum number of points. You can change the value of the maximum leader points in the spinner in front of this option. Note that the start point of the multileader is the first multileader point and it should also be included in the counting.

First segment angle: This check box is used to specify the angle of the first multileader line from the horizontal. Select this check box to specify a value in the drop-down list displayed in front of it.

Second segment angle: This check box is used to specify the angle of the second multileader line from the horizontal. Select this check box to specify a value in the drop-down list displayed in front of it.

Note

The First and Second segment angle values can be in multiples of the angle value specified in the respective spinners.

Landing settings Area

This area provides you the options to control the inclusion of landing line and its length.

Automatically include landing: Select this check box to attach a landing line to the multileader. By default, this check box is selected and is used to attach the landing line to the multileaders.

Set landing distance: By default, this check box is selected and used to specify the length of the landing line to be attached with the multileader. You can specify the value in the spinner that is below this check box. This spinner gets highlighted only when you select the **Set landing distance** check box. The default value of the landing length is set to 0.36.

Scale Area

The options under this area are used to set the value for the overall multileader scale or the scale of the multileader in the paper space.

Annotative: This check box is used to set the selected multileader style to annotative. With this option, you can also convert an existing non-annotative multileader style to annotative and vice-versa. If you select the **Annotative** check box from the **Create New Multileader Style** dialog box, then the **Annotative** check box in the **Modify Multileader Style** dialog box will also be selected by default.

Scale multileaders to layout: If you select the **Scale multileaders to layout** radio button, the scale factor between the current model space viewport and the floating viewport (paper space) will be computed automatically. Also, you can disable the **Specify scale** spinner (it is disabled in the dialog box) and the overall scale factor is set to 0 by selecting this radio button. When the overall scale factor is assigned a value of 0, AutoCAD calculates an acceptable default value based on the scaling between the current model space viewport and the paper space. AutoCAD sets the overall scale factor to 1 if you are in the paper space or not using the **Scale multileaders to layout** feature. Otherwise, AutoCAD calculates a scale factor that makes it possible to plot the multileaders at the values in which they have been previously set. For further details regarding the model space and layouts, refer to Chapter 13.

Specify scale: All the current multileaders are scaled with a value specified in the **Specify scale** spinner. You can alter the scaling factor as per your requirement by entering the scaling factor of your choice in this spinner. The default value for this variable is **1.0**. With this value, AutoCAD assumes its preset value and the drawing is plotted in a full scale. The scale factor is the reciprocal of the drawing size. So, for plotting the drawing at the one-fourth size, the overall scale factor will be 4.

Content Tab

The options in the **Content** tab of the **Modify Multileader Style** dialog box are used to specify the multileader attributes that affect the content and the format of the text or block to be attached with the multileader.

You can attach the multiline text or block to the multileader. You can also attach nothing as a content to the multileader. Select the desired multileader type from the **Multileader type** drop-down list; the other options in the **Content** tab of the **Modify Multileader Style** dialog box will vary with the change in the multileader type. Figure 10-44 displays the options in the **Modify Multileader Style** dialog box for the **Mtext** multileader type and these options are discussed next.

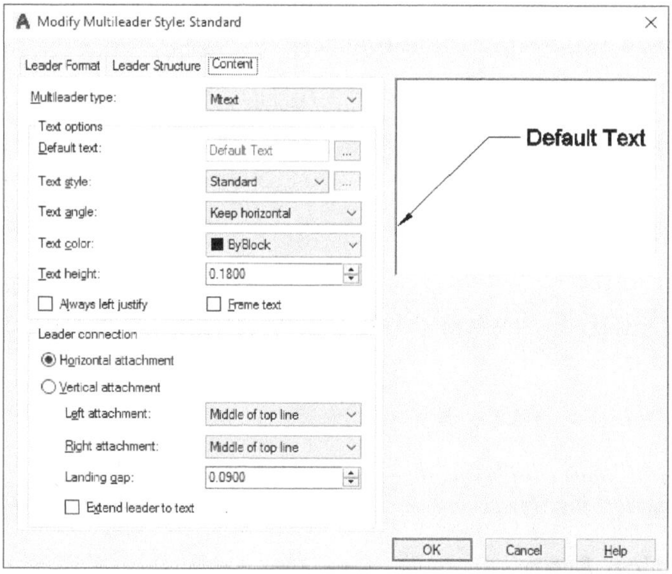

*Figure 10-44 The **Content** tab of the **Modify Multileader Style** dialog box*

Text options Area

The options in this area are discussed next.

Default text: This option is used to specify the default text to be attached with the multileader. Choose the **[...]** button; the **Text Editor** will be displayed. Enter the text that you want to display with the multileader by default and then click outside the text editor window; the preview window in the **Content** tab will display the multileader with the default text attached to it. While creating a new multileader, AutoCAD prompts you to specify whether you want to retain the default text or overwrite it with a new text.

Text style: This drop-down list is used to select the text style to be used for writing the content of the multileader. Only the predefined and default text styles are displayed in the drop-down list.

Text angle: This drop-down list is used to control the rotation of the multiline text with respect to the landing line.

Text color: This drop-down list is used to select the color to be used for writing the content of the multileader.

Text height: This spinner is used to specify the height of the multiline text to be attached with the multileader.

Always left justify: Select this check box to left justify the text attached to the multileader. On clearing the **Always left justify** check box, a multileader with the multileader style shown in Figure 10-45 (a) is displayed. On selecting this check box, a multileader with the multileader style as shown in Figure 10-45 (b) is displayed.

Frame text: Select this check box; you will be enabled to draw a rectangular frame around the multiline text to be attached with the multileader, as shown in Figure 10-46.

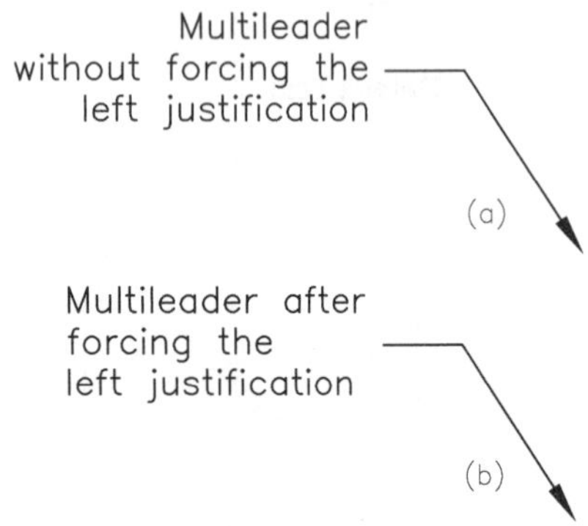

Figure 10-45 Multileaders displaying the effect of the ***Always left justify*** *option*

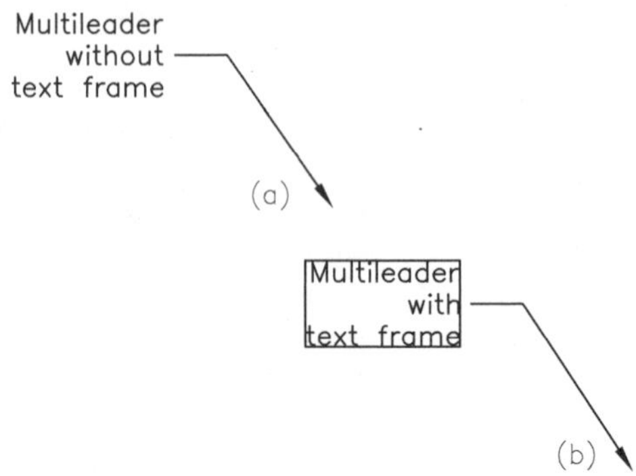

Figure 10-46 Multileaders displaying the effect of the ***Frame text*** *option*

Leader connection Area

The options provided in this area are used for controlling the attachment of the multiline text to the multileader.

Horizontal attachment: Select this radio button to place the leader at the right or left of the text. If you select this radio button, you need to select an appropriate option from the **Left attachment** and **Right attachment** drop-down lists to attach the multiline text to the landing line.

Vertical attachment: Select this radio button to place the leader at the top or bottom of the text. If you select this radio button, you need to select an appropriate option from the **Top attachment** and **Bottom attachment** drop-down lists to attach the multiline text with the landing line.

Landing gap: This spinner is used to specify the gap between the landing line and the multiline text at the point of attachment. It is available in both the cases; Horizontal attachment or Vertical attachment. The default value in the spinner is 0.09.

Extend leader to text: Select this check box to extend the leader line to text. If you deselect it then the leader can be extended upto the frame only.

If you select **Block** from the **Multileader type** drop-down list, the options will change accordingly. Figure 10-47 displays the options in the **Modify Multileader Style** dialog box for the **Block** option of the **Multileader type** drop-down list and these options are discussed next.

Block options Area

Source block: This drop-down list is used to select the block to be attached with the multileader as content. You can attach the standard block listed in the drop-down list or attach the user defined blocks to the multileader by selecting **User Block** from the drop-down list. Six standard shapes of block are available in this drop-down list with their previews on the side of the block name. While creating the multileader, if you select the **Detail Callout** option from the **Source block** drop-down list, you will be prompted to specify the **View number** and **Sheet number** to be displayed within the block in stacked form. For the other remaining standard blocks, you will be prompted to specify the **TAGNUMBER** only to be displayed within the block. To attach the user-defined block to the multileader, select **User Block** from the **Source block** drop-down list; the **Select Custom Content Block** dialog box will be displayed with the list of all the blocks defined in the current drawing under the **Select from Drawing Blocks** drop-down list. Select the desired block and choose the **OK** button; the selected block will be added to the **Source block** drop-down list for the current drawing. Also, it will be attached to the multileader as content.

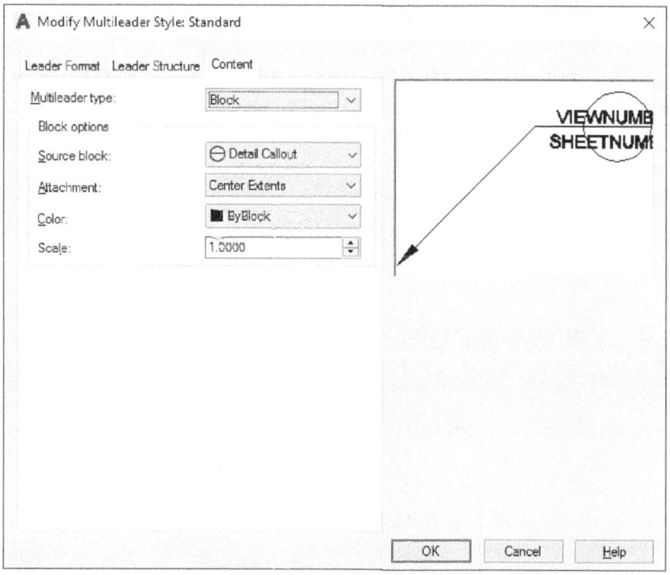

*Figure 10-47 The **Content** tab of the **Modify Multileader Style** dialog box for the **Block** option of the **Multileader type** drop-down list*

Attachment: This drop-down list is used to specify the point of attachment of the block to the leader. Select **Center Extents** from the drop-down list to attach the leader landing line in the middle of the outer boundary of the block, if it is not already selected by default. Select **Insertion point** to attach the leader landing line to the insertion point specified while defining the block.

Color: This drop-down list is used to specify the color of the block to be attached with the leader landing line.

Scale: This spinner is used to specify the scale of the block to be inserted. For example, if the block is 1 square inch and the scale specified is 0.5000, then the block inserted will be 1/2 inch square.

Self-Evaluation Test

Answer the following questions and then compare them to those given at the end of this chapter:

1. The **DIMTVP** variable is used to control the __________ position of the dimension text.

2. When you select the **Arrows** option from the **Fit** tab of the **Dimension Style** dialog box, AutoCAD places the text and arrowheads __________.

3. A basic dimension text is the dimension text with a __________ drawn around it.

4. The **Suppress** check boxes in the **Dimension Lines** area are used to control the display of __________ and __________.

5. You can specify the tolerance using __________ methods.

6. The __________ button in the **Dimension Style Manager** dialog box is used to override the current dimension style.

7. You can invoke the **Dimension Style Manager** dialog box using both the **Annotate** and **Home** tabs. (T/F)

8. The size of the arrow block is determined by the value specified in the **Arrow size** edit box. (T/F)

9. A block can be set as default content to be attached with the multileader. (T/F)

10. The size of the tolerance text with respect to dimensions can be defined. (T/F)

Review Questions

Answer the following questions:

1. Which of the following buttons can be used to make a dimension style active for dimensioning?

   (a) **Set Current** (b) **New**
   (c) **Override** (d) **Modify**

2. Which of the following tabs in the **New/Modify Dimension Style Manager** dialog box is used to add the suffix **mm** to dimensions?

   (a) **Fit** (b) **Text**
   (c) **Primary Units** (d) **Alternate Units**

3. Which tab of the **New/Modify Dimension Style Manager** dialog box will be used if you want to place the dimension text manually every time you create a dimension?

   (a) **Fit** (b) **Text**
   (c) **Primary Units** (d) **Alternate Units**

4. The size of the __________ is determined by the value stored in the **Arrow size** edit box.

5. When **DIMSCALE** is assigned the value __________, AutoCAD calculates an acceptable default value based on the scaling between the current model space viewport and the paper space.

6. If you use the **DIMCEN** command, a positive value will create a center mark, whereas a negative value will create a __________.

7. If you select the __________ check box, you can position the dimension text anywhere along the dimension line.

8. You can append a prefix to the dimension measurement by entering the desired prefix in the **Prefix** edit box of the __________ dialog box.

9. If you select the **Limits** option from the **Method** drop-down list, AutoCAD __________ the upper value to the dimension and __________ the lower value from the dimension text.

10. You can use the __________ tool to override a dimension value.

11. The named dimension style associated with the dimension being updated by overriding is not updated. (T/F)

12. You cannot replace the default arrowheads at the end of dimension lines. (T/F)

13. When the **DIMTVP** variable has a negative value, the dimension text is placed below the dimension line. (T/F)

14. The length of a multileader landing line cannot be changed. (T/F)

Exercises 4 Through 9

Create the drawings shown in Figure 10-48 through Figure 10-53. You must create dimension style and multileader style files and specify the values for the different dimension types such as linear, radial, diameter, and ordinate.

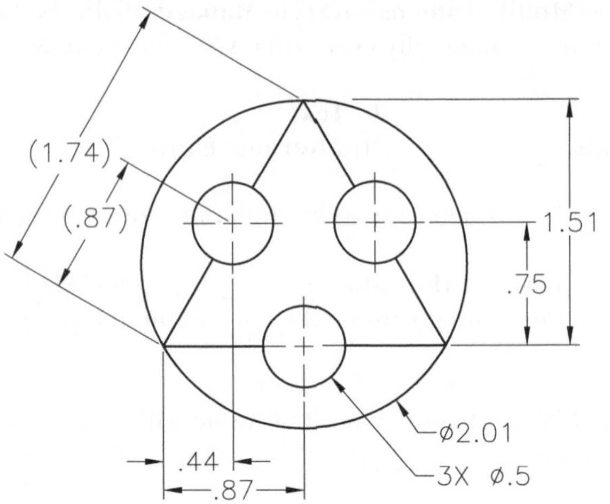

Figure 10-48 Drawing for Exercise 4

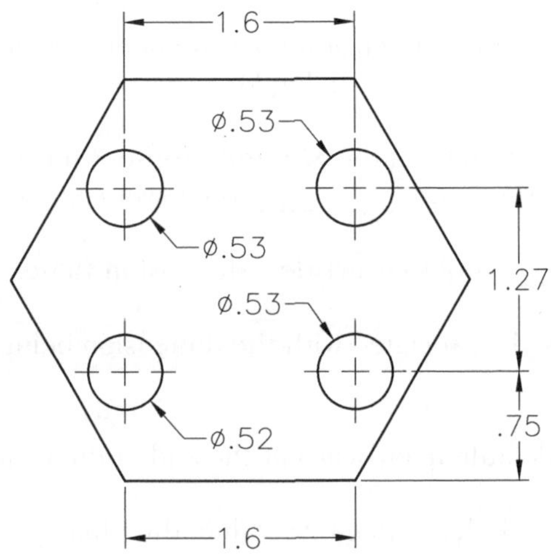

Figure 10-49 Drawing for Exercise 5

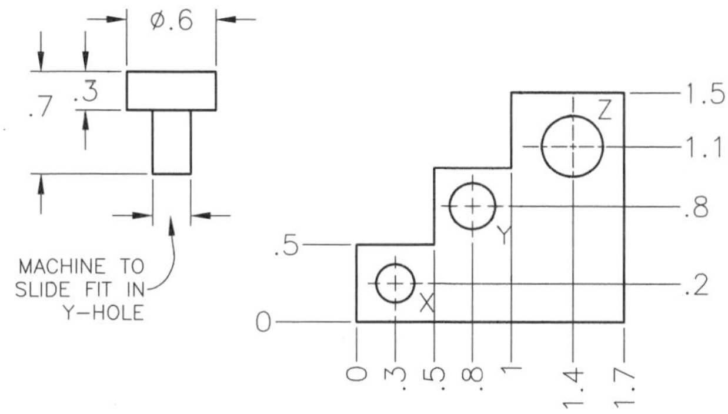

HOLE	X	Y	Z
DIA.	.25	.3H7	.40

***Figure 10-50** Drawing for Exercise 6*

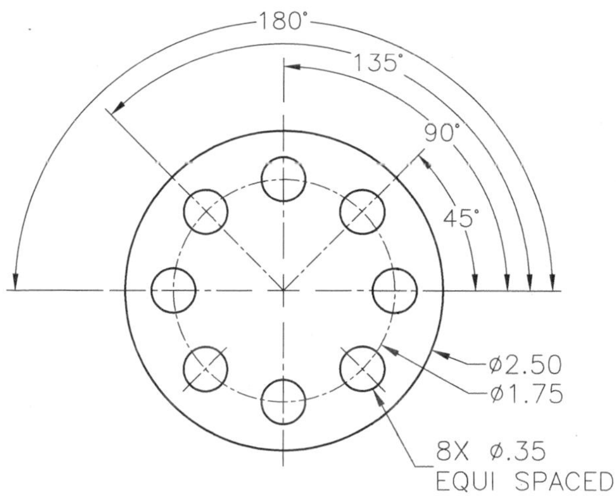

***Figure 10-51** Drawing for Exercise 7*

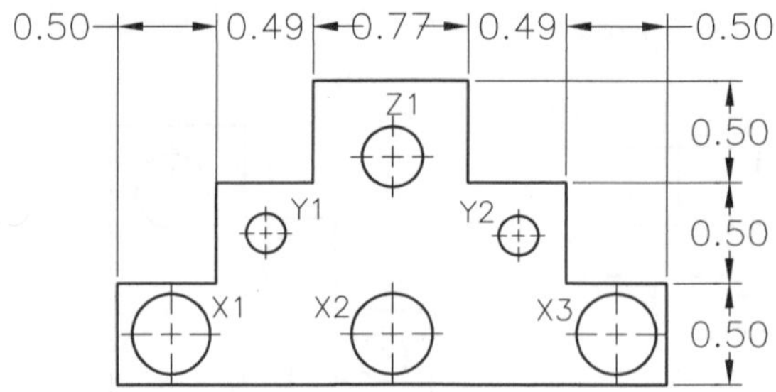

HOLE	X1	X2	X3	Y1	Y2	Z1
DIM.	R.2	R.2	R.2	R.1	R.1	R.15
QTY.	1	1	1	1	1	1
X	.25	1.375	2.50	.75	2.0	1.375
Y	.25	.25	.25	.75	.75	1.125
Z	THRU	THRU	THRU	1.0	1.0	THRU

Figure 10-52 *Drawing for Exercise 8*

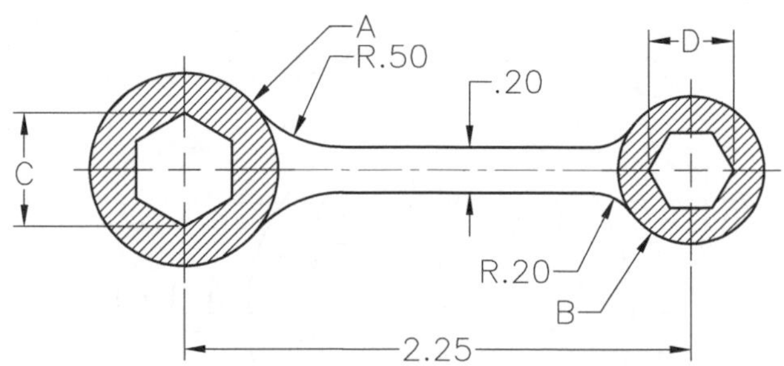

SPANNER NO.	A	B	C	D
S1	.85	.65	.50	.38
S2	1.00	.75	.59	.44
S3	1.15	.88	.67	.52
S4	1.25	.95	.74	.56

Figure 10-53 *Drawing for Exercise 9*

Exercise 10

Draw the sketch shown in Figure 10-54. You must create the dimension style and multileader style. Specify different dimensioning parameters. Also, suppress the leading and trailing zeros in the dimension style.

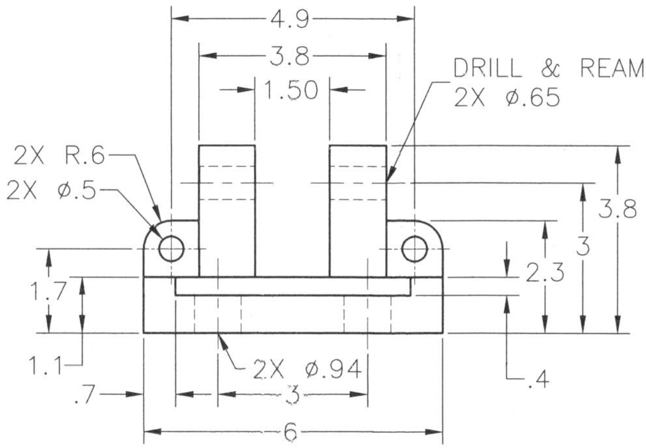

Figure 10-54 Drawing for Exercise 10

Exercise 11

Draw the sketch shown in Figure 10-55. You must create the dimension style and specify different dimensioning parameters in the dimension style.

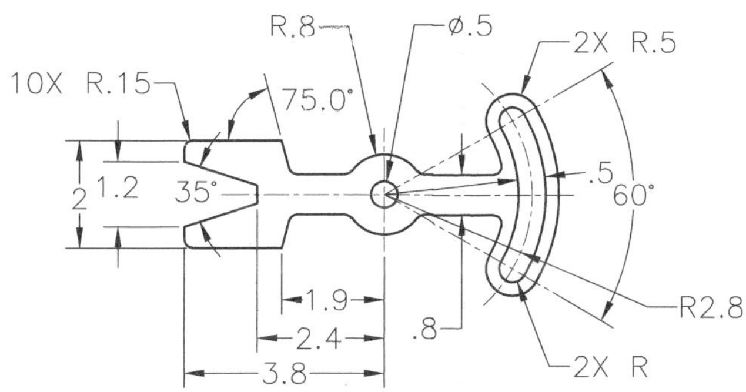

Figure 10-55 Drawing for Exercise 11

Exercise 12 — *Dimension Style*

Draw the sketch shown in Figure 10-56. You must create the dimension style and specify different dimensioning parameters in the dimension style.

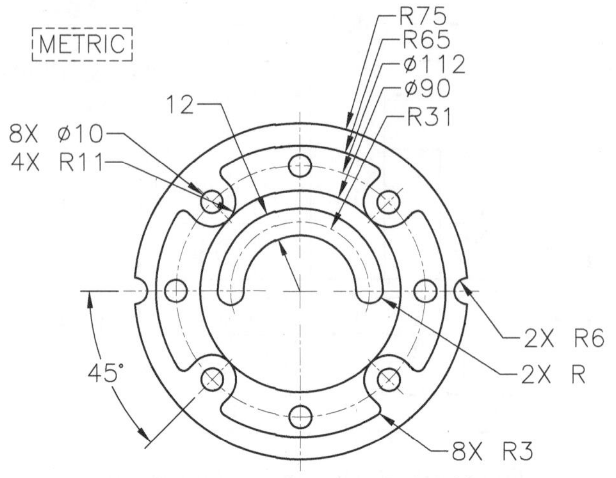

Figure 10-56 Drawing for Exercise 12

Problem-Solving Exercise 1 — Dimension Style

Create the drawing shown in Figure 10-57. You must create the dimension style and specify different dimensioning parameters in the dimension style. Also, suppress the leading and trailing zeros in the dimension style.

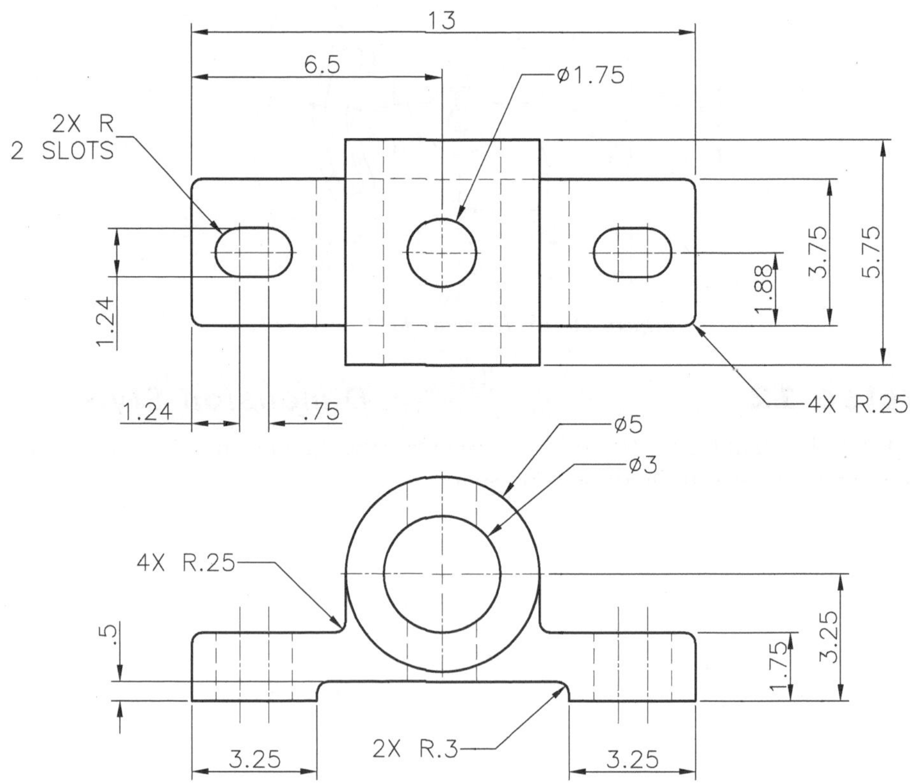

Figure 10-57 Drawing for Problem-Solving Exercise 1

Problem-Solving Exercise 2 Dimension Style

Draw the shaft shown in Figure 10-58. You must create the dimension style and specify the dimensioning parameters based on the given drawing.

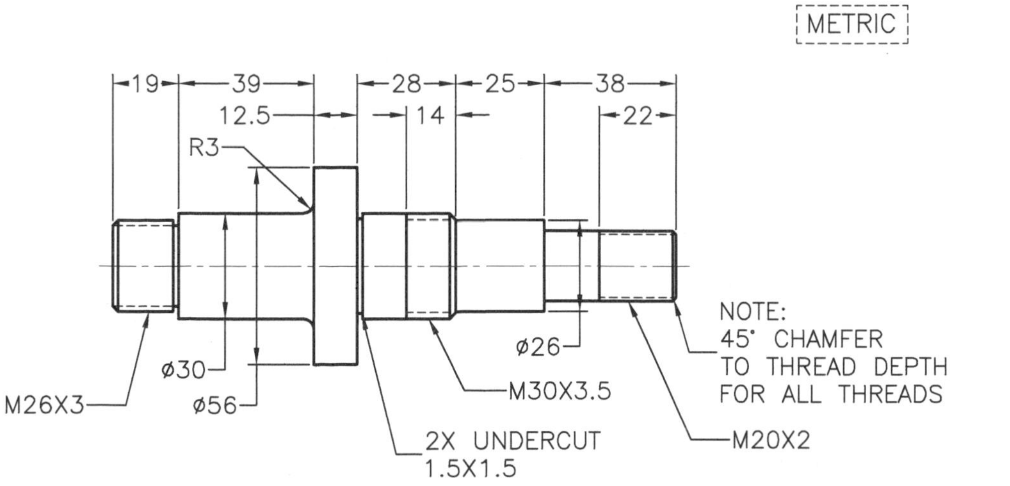

Figure 10-58 Drawing for Problem-Solving Exercise 2

Problem-Solving Exercise 3 Dimension Style

Draw the connecting rod shown in Figure 10-59. You must create the dimension style and specify the dimensioning parameters based on the given drawing.

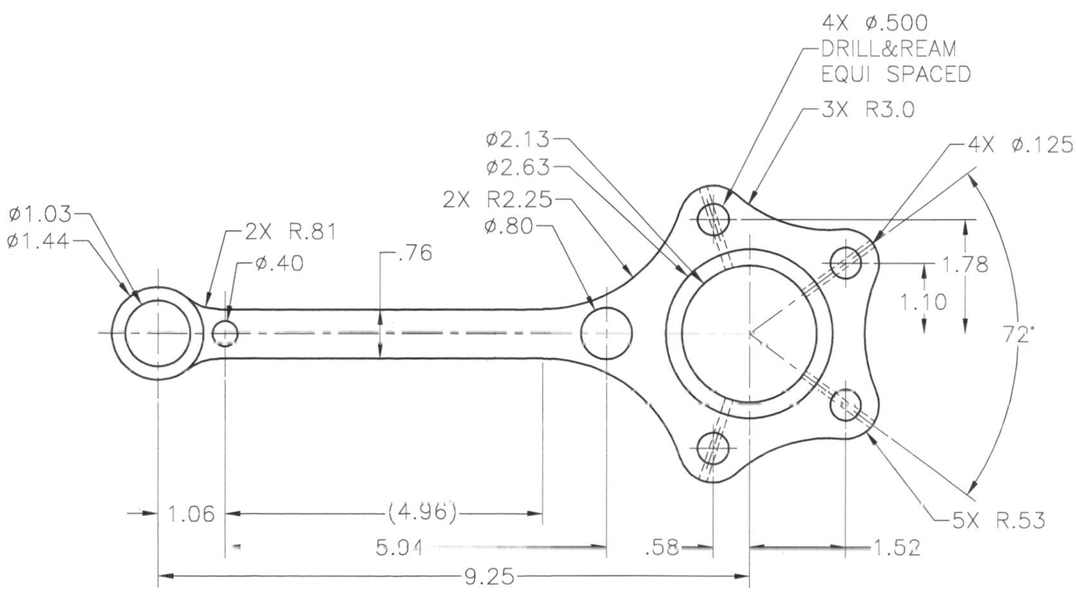

Figure 10-59 Drawing for Problem-Solving Exercise 3

Problem-Solving Exercise 4

Create the drawing shown in Figure 10-60.

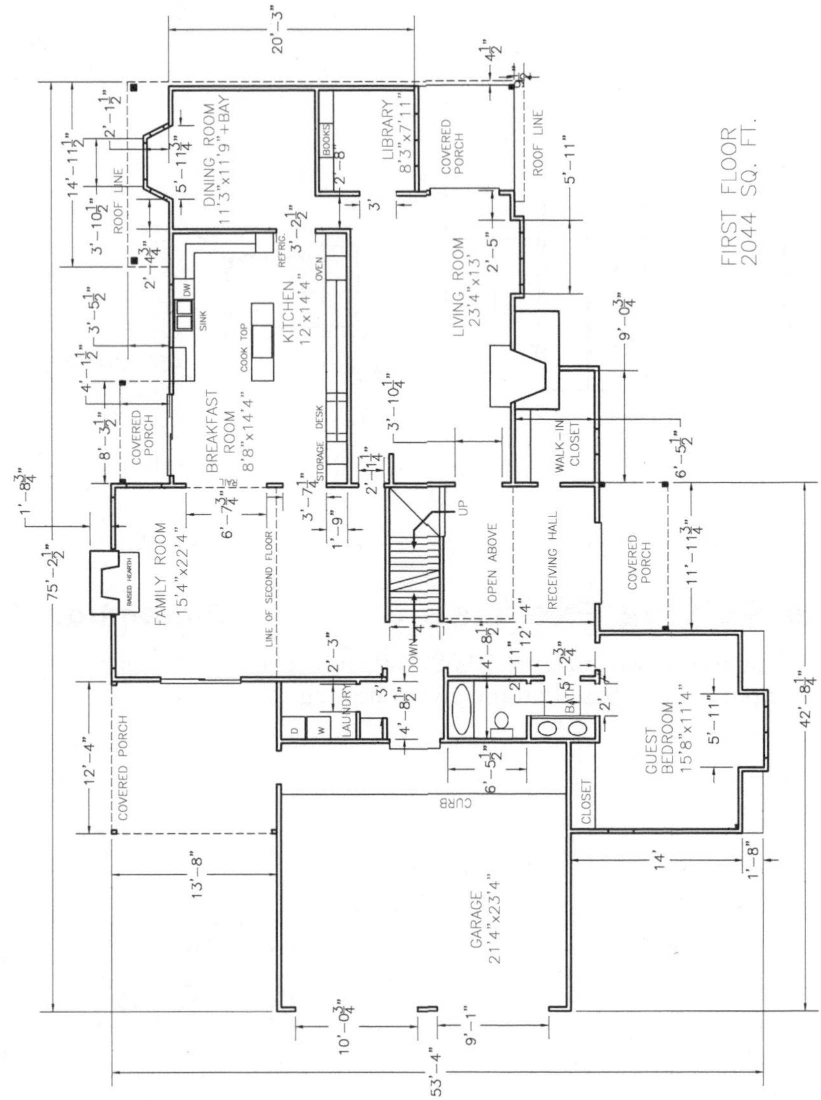

Figure 10-60 Drawing for Problem-Solving Exercise 4

Problem-Solving Exercise 5

Create the drawing shown in Figure 10-61.

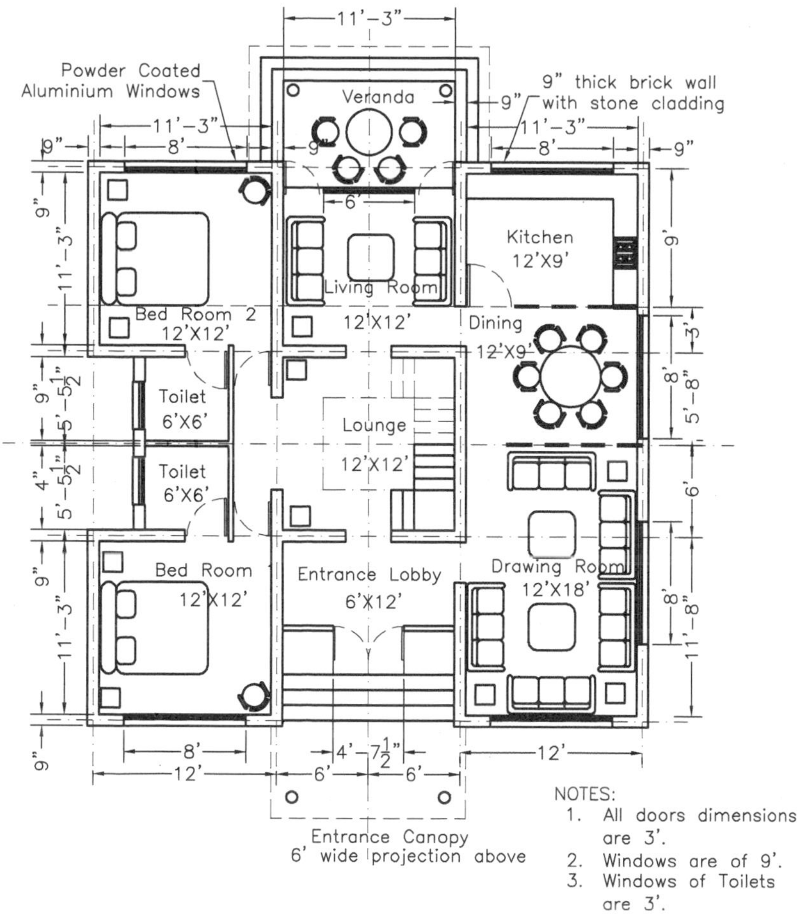

Figure 10-61 Drawing for Problem-Solving Exercise 5

Answers to Self-Evaluation Test

1. vertical, **2.** inside, **3.** frame, **4.** first, second dimension lines, **5.** four, **6. Override**, **7.** T, **8.** T, **9.** T, **10.** T

Chapter 11

Adding Constraints to Sketches

Learning Objectives

After completing this chapter, you will be able to:

- *Add geometric constraints to sketches*
- *Control the display of constraints*
- *Apply constraints automatically*
- *Apply dimensional constraints to sketches*
- *Convert a dimensional constraint into an annotational constraint*
- *Create expressions*

Key Terms

- *Horizontal*
- *Vertical*
- *Coincident*
- *Fix*
- *Collinear*
- *Parallel*
- *Concentric*
- *Tangent*
- *Symmetric*
- *Equal*
- *Smooth*
- *Infer Constraints*
- *Dimensional Constraints*
- *Annotational Constraints*
- *Dynamic Constraint Mode*
- *Annotational Constraint Mode*
- *Fully-Defined Sketch*
- *Under-Defined Sketch*
- *Over-Defined Sketch*
- *Parameters Manager*

INTRODUCTION

In AutoCAD, a wide set of tools are available that help you create parametric drawings. These tools are available in the **Parametric** tab of the **Ribbon** as well as in the **Parametric** toolbar. The parametric nature of a drawing implies that the shape and size of a geometry can be defined using standard properties or parameters. The main function of parametric property is to drive a new size or shape to the selected geometry without considering its original dimensions. Also, you can modify the shape and size of any entity of a sketch at any stage of the design process. This property makes the designing process very easy.

To make a drawing parametric, you need to apply constraints. When you apply constraints to sketches, it restricts their degrees of freedom, thereby making them stable. The stability ensures that the size, shape, and location of sketches do not change unexpectedly with respect to surroundings. You can apply two types of constraints to sketches, geometric and dimensional. Geometric constraints are applied between two entities in a sketch and they control the shape of a drawing, whereas dimensional constraints are applied to a single entity and they control the size of the object in a drawing. Remember that dimensions applied and dimensional constraints applied are two different things. You will learn about the difference in this chapter.

If you need to draw a sketch of parts such as bolt, nut, valves, and so on in which the size of one entity is driven by one basic dimension, then in AutoCAD, you can draw these parts quickly and easily using the **Parameters Manager**.

ADDING GEOMETRIC CONSTRAINTS

AutoCAD provides you with twelve types of geometric constraints. Usually, these constraints are applied between two entities in a sketch and control the shape of a drawing. However, there are constraints, such as Fix, that are applied to a single entity. Whenever you apply a geometric constraint between two entities, the entity that is selected last is affected. For example, if you apply the parallel constraint between two lines, the line selected second will orient toward the first line. It is recommended to first apply geometric constraints so that the shape of a sketched entity does not change on applying dimensional constraints. If the **Infer Constraints** button is chosen in the Status Bar, some of the geometric constraints are applied automatically while sketching or editing. For example, if you draw a horizontal line then the **Horizontal** constraint will be applied automatically and the corresponding constraint bar will be displayed above the line. In the following section, different geometric constraints and the procedure to apply them manually are discussed.

Applying the Horizontal Constraint

Ribbon: Parametric > Geometric > Horizontal **Command:** GEOMCONSTRAINT > H
Toolbar: Geometric Constraint > Horizontal or
Parametric > Constraint drop-down > Horizontal
Menu Bar: Parametric > Geometric Constraints > Horizontal

The **Horizontal** constraint forces a selected line, polyline, or two points to become horizontal. To apply this constraint, choose the **Horizontal** tool from the **Geometric** panel of the **Parametric** tab of the **Ribbon**. The prompt sequence after choosing this tool is given next.

Select an object or [2Points] <2Points>: *Select a line or polyline.*

Remember that if you apply this constraint to a line on which no other constraint is applied, then the line will orient such that the endpoint nearer to the location you clicked on will become the fixed point and the other endpoint will become horizontal, thereby making the line horizontal.

If you need to make two points horizontal, press ENTER when the **Select an object or [2Points] <2Points>** prompt is displayed. The following prompt sequence will be displayed:

Select an object or [2Points] <2Points>: [Enter]
Select first point: *Select the first point*
Select second point: *Select the second point*

Note
You can also apply constraints by entering ***GEOMCONSTRAINT*** *at the command prompt.*

Applying the Vertical Constraint

Ribbon: Parametric > Geometric > Vertical **Command:** GEOMCONSTRAINT > V
Toolbar: Geometric Constraint > Vertical or Parametric > Constraint drop-down > Vertical
Menu Bar: Parametric > Geometric Constraints > Vertical

The **Vertical** constraint forces a selected line, polyline, or two points to become vertical. To apply this constraint, choose the **Vertical** tool from the **Geometric** panel of the **Parametric** tab. The prompt sequence after choosing this tool is given next.

Select an object or [2Points] <2Points>: *Select a line or polyline*

Remember that if you apply this constraint to a line on which no other constraint is applied, then the line will orient such that the endpoint nearer to the location you clicked on will become the fixed point and the other endpoint will become vertical, thereby making the line vertical.

If you need to make two points vertical, press ENTER when the **Select an object or [2Points] <2Points>** prompt is displayed. The following prompt sequence will be displayed:

Select an object or [2Points] <2Points>: [Enter]
Select first point: *Select the first point*
Select second point: *Select the second point*

Note
On applying a constraint to an entity, the corresponding symbol is displayed near the entity, as shown in Figure 11-1. If you move the cursor over the symbol, the symbol will be highlighted and a cross mark (X) will be displayed. Click on the cross mark to hide the symbol. However, if you place the cursor on the entity on which a constraint has already been applied, a glyph will be displayed stating that a constraint is applied.

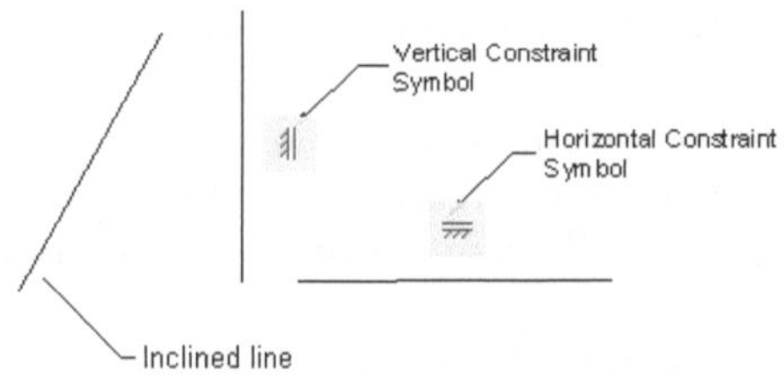

Figure 11-1 *The Vertical and Horizontal Constraint symbols*

Applying the Coincident Constraint

Ribbon: Parametric > Geometric > Coincident **Command:** GEOMCONSTRAINT > C
Toolbar: Geometric Constraint > Coincident or
Parametric > Constraint drop-down > Coincident
Menu Bar: Parametric > Geometric Constraints > Coincident

The **Coincident** constraint forces a selected point or keypoint of an entity to be coincident with the point or keypoint of another entity. The entity selected can be a line, polyline, circle, an arc or ellipse. Similarly, the selected point can be a point, or keypoints such as an endpoint or midpoint of a line, an arc or a polyline, or the centerpoint of an arc, ellipse, or a circle. To apply this constraint, choose the **Coincident** tool from the **Geometric** panel of the **Parametric** tab; the cursor will be replaced by a selection box along with the coincident symbol. Also, you will be prompted to select first point. Move the cursor over an entity; the keypoint that is close to the cursor will be highlighted in red. Next, click to select it; you will be prompted to select the second point to be coincident with the first object. Select the keypoint of the second entity; the keypoint of the second entity will move and coincide with that of the first entity.

Even if you have drawn the complete sketch by snapping keypoints, the coincident constraint will not be applied automatically. To apply the coincident constraints at all intersections at the same time, invoke the **Coincident** tool. The command prompt sequence to apply the **Autoconstrain** is given next.

Select first point or [Object/Autoconstrain] <Object>: *A* Enter
Select objects: *Select objects individually or by using the selection window:*
Select objects: *Select more objects or* Enter

Note
The options to change the default settings for the ***Autoconstrain*** *option will be discussed later in this chapter.*

Applying the Fix Constraint

Ribbon: Parametric > Geometric > Fix **Command:** GEOMCONSTRAINT > F
Toolbar: Geometric Constraint > Fix or Parametric > Constraint drop-down > Fix
Menu Bar: Parametric > Geometric Constraints > Fix

The **Fix** constraint forces the selected entity to become fixed at a position. If you apply this constraint to a line or to an arc, its location will be fixed with respect to the selected keypoint. But you can change the size of the entity by dragging its endpoints. To apply the **Fix** constraint, choose the **Fix** tool from the **Geometric** panel of the **Parametric** tab; you will be prompted to select a point or an object. Next, move the cursor over the entity; the point closer to the cursor will be highlighted. Click to fix the highlighted keypoint. Now, you cannot move the fixed keypoint. However, you can drag and relocate other keypoints.

To fix all keypoints of an object, invoke the **Fix** constraint and press ENTER when the **Select point or [Object] <Object>** command prompt is displayed; you will be prompted to select an object. Select the object; all its keypoints will be fixed.

Applying the Perpendicular Constraint

Ribbon: Parametric > Geometric > Perpendicular **Command:** GEOMCONSTRAINT > P
Toolbar: Geometric Constraint > Perpendicular or
Parametric > Constraint drop-down > Perpendicular
Menu Bar: Parametric > Geometric Constraints > Perpendicular

The **Perpendicular** constraint forces the selected lines to become perpendicular to each other. To apply this constraint, choose the **Perpendicular** tool from the **Geometric** panel; you will be prompted to select the first object. Select a line or a polyline; you will be prompted to select the second object. Select another line or a polyline. The object selected second will become perpendicular to the object selected first. Figure 11-2 shows two lines before and after applying the **Perpendicular** constraint.

Applying the Parallel Constraint

Ribbon: Parametric > Geometric > Parallel **Command:** GEOMCONSTRAINT > PA
Toolbar: Geometric Constraint > Parallel or Parametric > Constraint drop-down > Parallel
Menu Bar: Parametric > Geometric Constraints > Parallel

The **Parallel** constraint forces the selected lines to become parallel to each other. To apply this constraint, choose the **Parallel** tool from the **Geometric** panel; you will be prompted to select the first object. Select a line or a polyline; you will be prompted to select the second object. Select another line or a polyline; the object selected second will become parallel to the object selected first. Figure 11-3 shows two lines before and after applying the **Parallel** constraint.

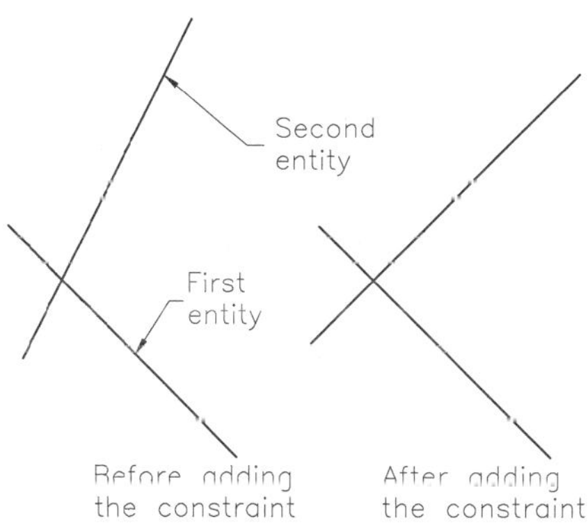

*Figure 11-2 Entities before and after applying the **Perpendicular** constraint*

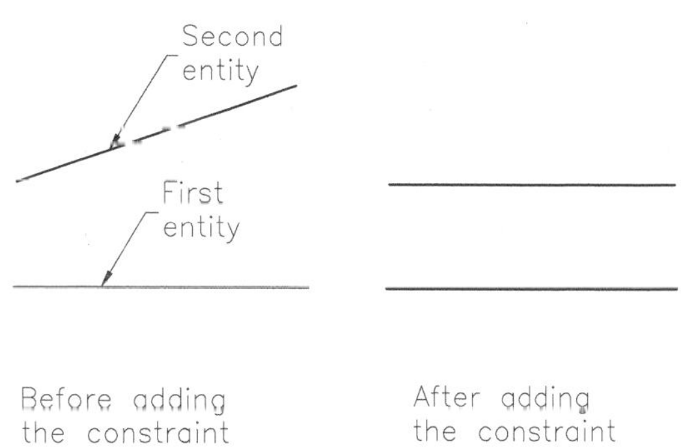

*Figure 11-3 Entities before and after applying the **Parallel** constraint*

Applying the Collinear Constraint

Ribbon: Parametric > Geometric > Collinear **Command:** GEOMCONSTRAINT > COL
Toolbar: Geometric Constraint > Collinear or Parametric > Constraint drop-down > Collinear
Menu Bar: Parametric > Geometric Constraints > Collinear

The **Collinear** constraint forces the selected lines to lie on the same infinite line. To apply this constraint, choose the **Collinear** tool from the **Geometric** panel; you will be prompted to select the first object. Select a line; you will be prompted to select the second object. Select another line; the line selected later will become collinear with the first line.

To apply the **Collinear** constraint to multiple lines, choose the **Collinear** tool; the **Select first object or [Multiple]** prompt will be displayed at the command prompt. Enter **M** and press ENTER; you will be prompted to select the first object. Select a line; you will be prompted to select the second object. Select the lines that need to be made collinear with the line selected first and then press ENTER; the selected lines will become collinear to the line selected first.

Applying the Concentric Constraint

Ribbon: Parametric > Geometric > Concentric **Command:** GEOMCONSTRAINT > CON
Toolbar: Geometric Constraint > Concentric or Parametric > Constraint drop-down > Concentric
Menu Bar: Parametric > Geometric Constraints > Concentric

The **Concentric** constraint forces the selected arc or circle to share the center point of another arc, circle, or ellipse. To apply this constraint, choose the **Concentric** tool from the **Geometric** panel; you will be prompted to select the first object. Select an arc, ellipse, or a circle; you will be prompted to select the second object. Select another arc, ellipse, or circle; the object selected second will become concentric to the object selected first.

Applying the Tangent Constraint

Ribbon: Parametric > Geometric > Tangent **Command:** GEOMCONSTRAINT > T
Toolbar: Geometric Constraint > Tangent or Parametric > Constraint drop-down > Tangent
Menu Bar: Parametric > Geometric Constraints > Tangent

The **Tangent** constraint forces the selected arc, circle, spline, or ellipse to become tangent to another arc, circle, spline, ellipse, or line. To apply this constraint, choose the **Tangent** tool from the **Geometric** panel; you will be prompted to select the first object. Select an arc, circle, spline, line, or an ellipse; you will be prompted to select the second object. Select another arc, circle, spline, ellipse, or line; the object selected second will become tangent to the object selected first. Figure 11-4 shows a line and a circle before and after applying the **Tangent** constraint. Figure 11-5 shows two arcs before and after applying the **Tangent** constraint.

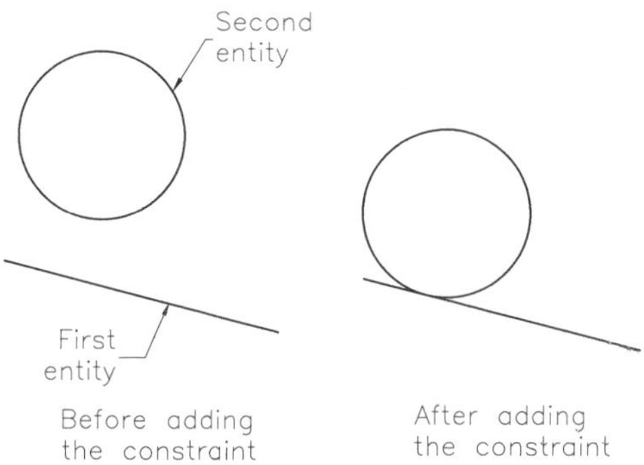

*Figure 11-4 A line and a circle before and after applying the **Tangent** constraint*

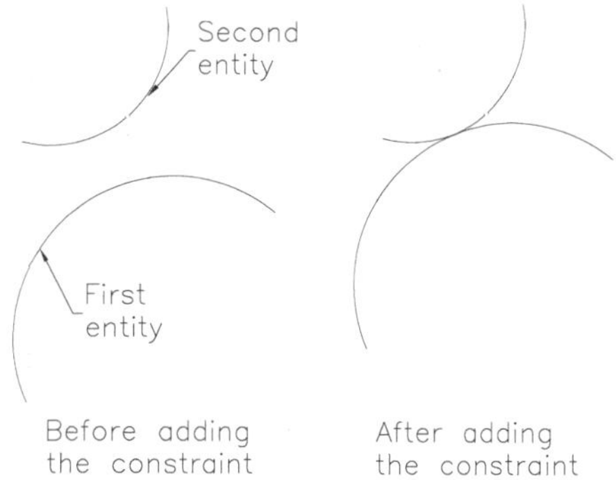

*Figure 11-5 Two arcs before and after applying the **Tangent** constraint*

Applying the Symmetric Constraint

Ribbon: Parametric > Geometric > Symmetric **Command:** GEOMCONSTRAINT > S
Toolbar: Geometric Constraint > Symmetric or
Parametric > Constraint drop-down > Symmetric
Menu Bar: Parametric > Geometric Constraints > Symmetric

The **Symmetric** constraint forces two selected lines, arcs, circles, or ellipses to remain equidistant from the centerline. To apply this constraint, choose the **Symmetric** tool from the **Geometric** panel; you will be prompted to select the first object or two points. Select an arc, an ellipse, a line, or a circle; you will be prompted to select the second object. Select another arc, ellipse, circle, or line; you will be prompted to select the symmetry line. Select a line; the selected objects will become symmetric with respect to the selected line. You can also make two points symmetric. To do so, press ENTER at the **Select first object or (2 points)** command prompt. Next, select two points and the symmetric line; the selected points will become symmetric to the selected line.

Applying the Equal Constraint

Ribbon: Parametric > Geometric > Equal **Command:** GEOMCONSTRAINT > E
Toolbar: Geometric Constraint > Equal or Parametric > Constraint drop-down > Equal
Menu Bar: Parametric > Geometric Constraints > Equal

The **Equal** constraint forces the selected lines or polylines to have equal length, or the selected circles, arcs, or an arc and a circle to have equal radii. To apply this constraint, choose the **Equal** tool from the **Geometric** panel; you will be prompted to select an object. Select the first object; you will be prompted to select the second object. Select another object; the size of the second object will become equal to that of the object selected first.

If you need to apply the equal constraint to multiple objects, choose the **Equal** tool from the **Geometric** panel; the **Select first object or [Multiple]** prompt will be displayed at the command prompt. Enter **M** and press ENTER, you will be prompted to select the first object. Select an object; you will be prompted to select other objects. Select the other objects that need to be equal and press ENTER; the size of the objects selected later will become equal to that of the object selected first.

Applying the Smooth Constraint

Ribbon: Parametric > Geometric > Smooth **Command:** GEOMCONSTRAINT > SM
Toolbar: Geometric Constraint > Smooth or Parametric > Constraint drop-down > Smooth
Menu Bar: Parametric > Geometric Constraints > Smooth

The **Smooth** constraint is used to apply curvature continuity between a spline and an entity connected together. The entities that can be connected to a spline include a line, spline, polyline, or an arc. To apply this constraint, choose the **Smooth** tool from the **Geometric** panel; you will be prompted to select the first object. Select a spline as the first object; you will be prompted to select the second object. Select another object; the smooth constraint will be applied between the selected objects.

CONTROLLING THE DISPLAY OF CONSTRAINTS

To control the display of the constraints, click on the inclined arrow in the **Geometric** panel of the **Parametric** tab; the **Constraint Settings** dialog box will be displayed, as shown in Figure 11-6. In this dialog box, the **Geometric** tab will be chosen and the check boxes of all constraints will be selected. Also, the **Show constraint bars after applying constraints to selected objects** check box will be selected by default. Therefore, on applying a constraint, a constraint bar will be displayed above the sketch and the symbol of that particular constraint will be displayed in the constraint bar by default. If you do not need any particular constraint symbol to be displayed then in the **Constraint bar display settings** area, clear the check box of the constraints that you do not want to be displayed. If you do not need the constraint bar to be displayed on applying the constraints, then clear the **Show constraint bars after applying constraints to selected objects** check box. However, if the **Show constraint bars when objects are selected** check box is selected, then the constraint bars will be displayed when you select an object. You can control the transparency of the constraint bars by setting the value in the **Constraint bar transparency** area of the **Constraint Settings** dialog box. In AutoCAD, you can apply the constraints while sketching or editing. To do so, select the **Infer geometric constraints** check box. You can also choose the **Infer Constraints** button from the Status Bar to apply constraints while sketching or editing. After specifying the parameters, choose the **OK** button to exit the dialog box.

On moving the cursor over a constraint bar, the constraint symbol and entities on which the constraint was applied will be highlighted. If multiple constraints are displayed in a sketch, it causes confusion. Therefore, you need to hide or display the constraint symbols. To hide a particular constraint, move the cursor over that constraint; the constraint bar will be highlighted and a cross-mark will be displayed on it. Click on the cross-mark to hide that constraint. To hide all constraints, choose the **Hide All** button in the **Geometric** panel. To display all hidden constraints, choose the **Show All** button from the **Geometric** panel. If you need to display constraints of a particular entity, choose the **Show/Hide** button from the **Geometric** panel; you will be prompted to select an entity. Select the entity from the drawing area and press ENTER; a menu will be displayed and you will be prompted to select an option. Select the **Show** option; the constraints of that particular entity will be displayed. Remember that hiding a constraint does not delete that constraint. To delete a constraint, move the cursor over the constraint bar and press the DELETE key. If you need to delete multiple applied constraints, choose the **Delete Constraints** button in the **Manage** panel of the **Parametric** tab of the **Ribbon**; you will be prompted to select entities. Select the entities individually or by using the selection box, and then press ENTER; the constraints applied on the selected entities will be deleted.

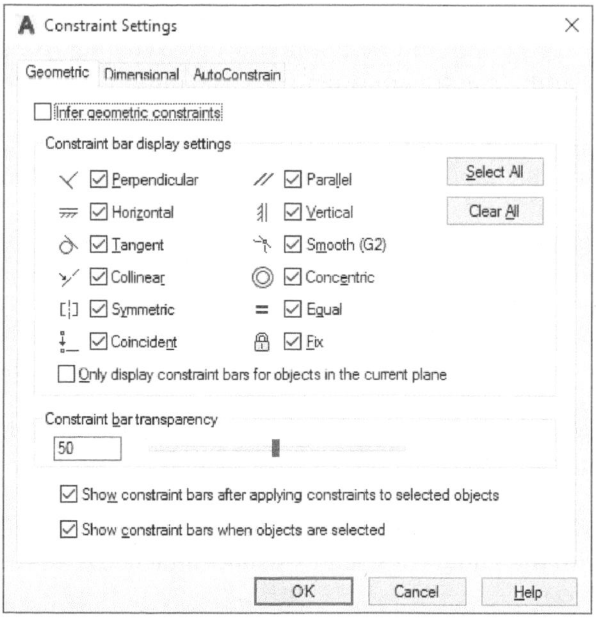

Figure 11-6 The ***Constraint Settings*** *dialog box with the* ***Geometric*** *tab chosen*

Tip

If you move the cursor over a constraint bar and right-click, a shortcut menu will be displayed. Choose the corresponding option to delete or hide a constraint. Also, you can choose the ***Constraint Bar Settings*** *option to display the* ***Constraint Settings*** *dialog box.*

Example 1

Draw the sketch shown in Figure 11-7 and apply appropriate constraints to it. Do not dimension the sketch.

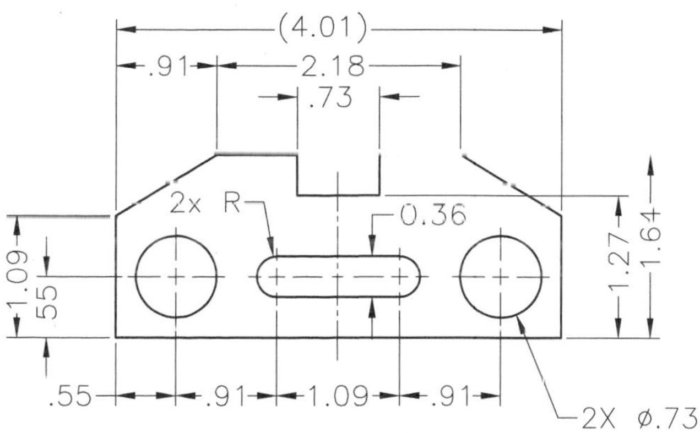

Figure 11-7 Sketch for Example 1

In this example, you will select the **Infer geometric constraints** check box and draw the sketch. Therefore, some of the constraints will be applied while sketching. Next, you will apply the constraints that are not applied automatically while sketching. First, you will create the outer loop of the sketch using the **Line** tool.

1. Start a new file with the *acad.dwt* template in the **Drafting & Annotation** workspace.

2. Ensure that the **Infer Constraints** button is chosen in the Status Bar. By using the **Line** tool, draw the outer profile similar to that shown in Figure 11-7. Make sure that the endpoints are snapped so that they form a closed sketch, as shown in Figure 11-8. Note that in your drawing, the constraints applied by default may be different from that shown in Figure 11-8, as it depends upon the start point and the procedure used to draw the lines.

   Next, you need to apply the constraints that are not applied by default. First, you will apply the **Equal** constraint.

3. Choose the **Equal** tool from the **Geometric** panel in the **Parametric** tab; the cursor changes to a selection box with the **Equal** constraint's symbol attached to it. Also, you are prompted to select the first object.

4. Select the vertical line on the left as the first object; you are prompted to select the second object.

5. Select the vertical line on the right as the second object; the equal constraint is applied and the constraint bar is displayed.

6. Similarly, apply the equal constraint between the two inclined lines, two small vertical lines, and two small horizontal lines. The sketch after applying all the constraints is shown in Figure 11-9.

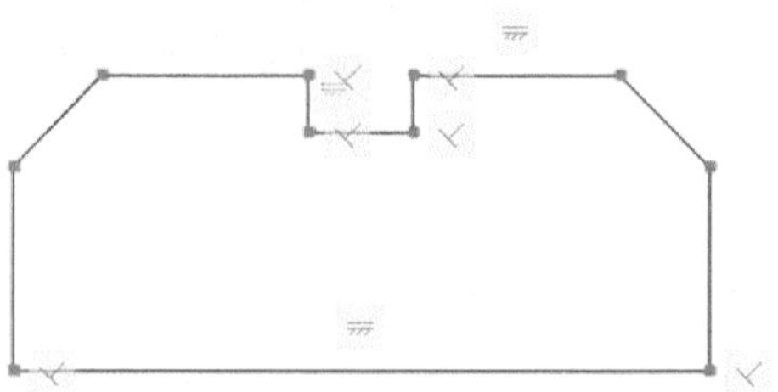

***Figure 11-8** Outer loop of the sketch*

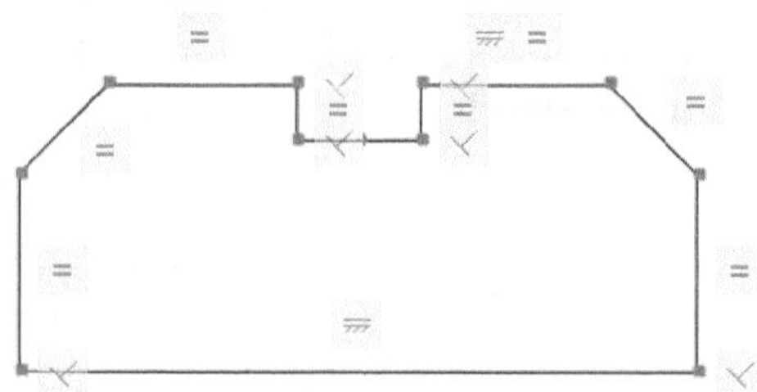

***Figure 11-9** Sketch after applying all constraints*

   Next, you need to apply the symmetric constraint between entities on either side of the centerline.

7. Choose the **Infer Constraints** button from the Status Bar to turn off the infer constraints.

8. Draw a vertical centerline that passes through the midpoint of the horizontal line at the bottom, as shown in Figure 11-10.

9. Choose the **Symmetric** tool from the **Geometric** panel; the cursor changes to a selection box with symmetric symbol attached to it. Also, you are prompted to select the first object.

10. Select the vertical line on the left as the first object; you are prompted to select the second object.

11. Select the vertical line on the right as the second object; you are prompted to select the symmetry line.

12. Select the centerline as the symmetry line; the vertical lines become symmetric to the centerline and the symmetric symbol is displayed, as shown in Figure 11-11. Note that in this figure, other constraints are hidden for clarity.

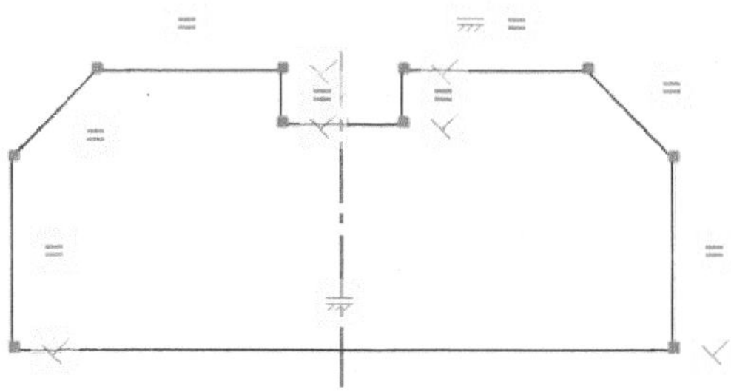

Figure 11-10 *Sketch after drawing the centerline*

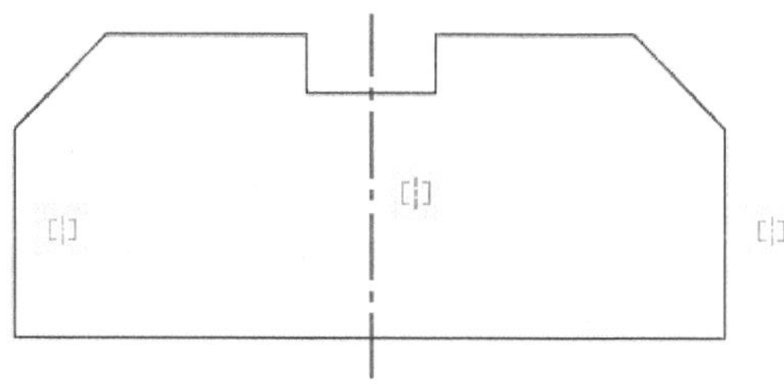

Figure 11-11 *The* ***Symmetric*** *constraint symbol*

13. Similarly, apply the symmetric constraints between the two inclined lines and then between the two small horizontal lines. The three symmetric constraints are applied as shown in Figure 11-12.

14. Choose the **Hide All** button from the **Parametric** tab of the **Geometric** panel to hide all constraint bars. Figure 11-13 shows the sketch after hiding all constraint bars.

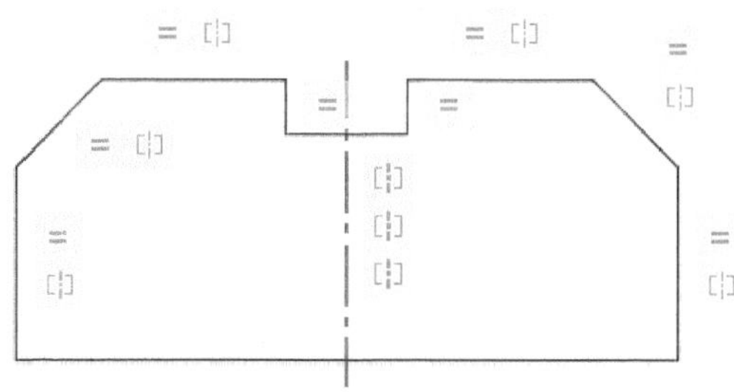

Figure 11-12 *Sketch with symmetric constraints*

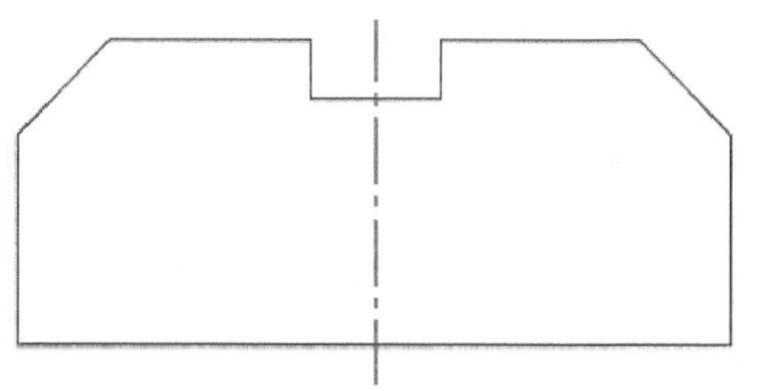

Figure 11-13 *Sketch after hiding all constraints*

Next, you need to create the inner loop using the **Arc**, **Circle**, and **Line** tools at an arbitrary location. But the profile should be similar to that given in Figure 11-7. Next, you need to apply the constraints.

15. Draw two circles of any radius inside the outer loop.

16. Choose the **Infer Constraints** button from the Status Bar to turn on the infer constraints.

17. Draw a slot using the **Center**, **Start**, **End** arc and **Line** tools. The sketch after drawing the circles and the slot is shown in Figure 11-14. You can also draw the profile of the slot using the **Polyline** tool. However, the sketch in this example has been drawn using the **Center**, **Start**, **End** arc and **Line** tools.

18. Apply the equal constraint first between two circles and then between two arcs.

19. Apply the symmetric constraint between the circles as well as between the arcs.

20. Choose the **Tangent** tool from the **Geometric** panel; the cursor changes to a selection box with the tangent symbol attached to it. Also, you are prompted to select the first object.

21. Select an arc; you are prompted to select the second object.

22. Select a line; the tangent constraint will be applied at one end of the line and the tangent symbol will be displayed.

23. Similarly, apply the tangent constraint at all other places in the slot, as shown in Figure 11-15. You need to choose the **Show/Hide** button to display all constraints.

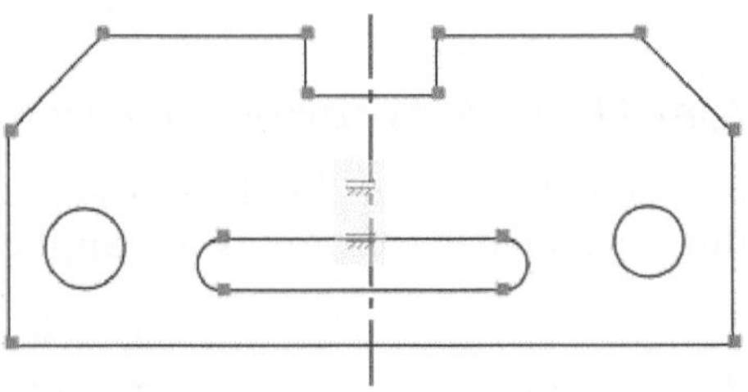

Figure 11-14 *Sketch after applying the* ***Coincident*** *constraint*

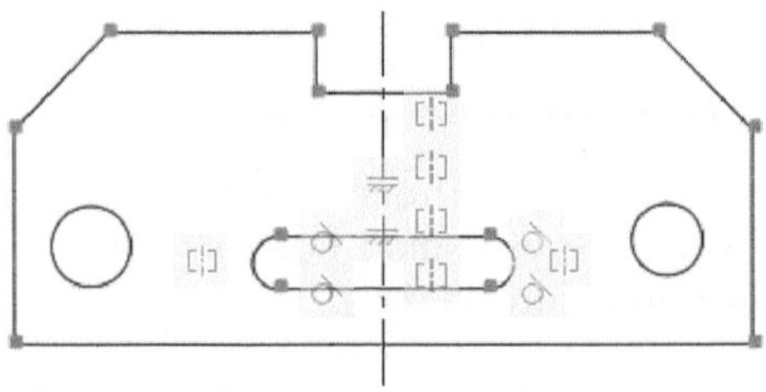

Figure 11-15 *Sketch after applying all* ***Tangent*** *constraints*

Next, you need to make the centerpoint of the circles and the slot to be in a straight line.

24. Choose the **Horizontal** tool from the **Geometric** panel; the prompt sequence that follows is given next.

    Select an object or [2Points] <2Points>: Enter
    Select first point: *Select the circle on the left side* Enter
    Select second point: *cen* Enter
    of: *Select the center of the arc on the left side* Enter

    The sketch after applying the **Horizontal** constraint is shown in Figure 11-16.

25. Similarly, apply the **Horizontal** constraint to the circle and arc on the right side.

26. Choose the **Show/Hide** button from the **Parametric** tab and hide the display of all constraint bars and save the drawing. The sketch after applying and hiding all constraints is shown in Figure 11-17.

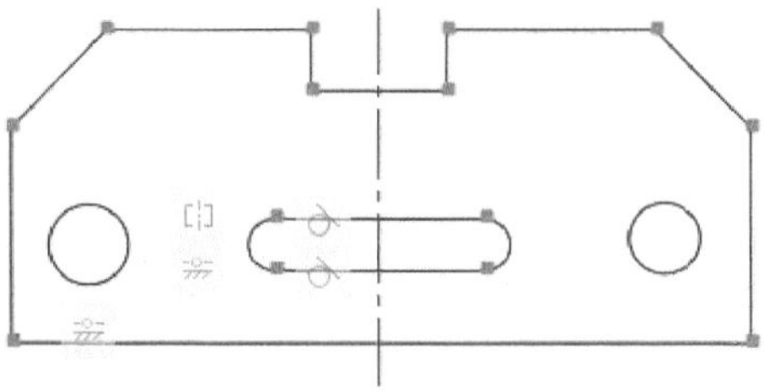

Figure 11-16 *Sketch after applying the* ***Horizontal*** *constraint between a circle and an arc*

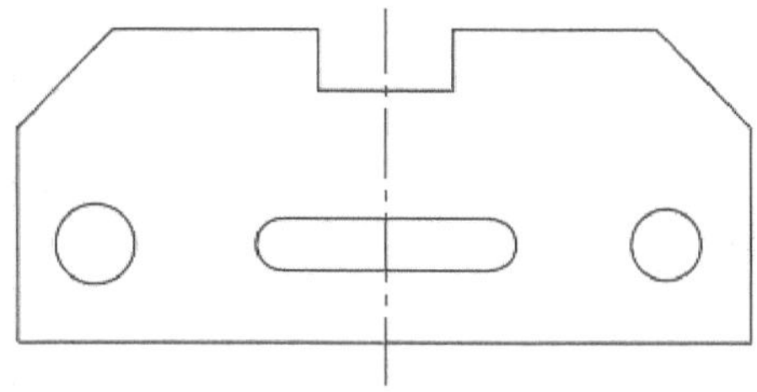

Figure 11-17 *Sketch after applying and hiding all constraints*

APPLYING CONSTRAINTS AUTOMATICALLY

In the previous section, twelve types of constraints are discussed. Nine of these constraints can be applied automatically, provided you have a closed sketch. To apply constraints automatically, choose the **AutoConstrain** tool in the **Geometric** panel of the **Parametric** tab of the **Ribbon**; you will be prompted to select an object. Select the entities individually or by using the selection box, and then press ENTER; all possible constraints will be applied automatically.

You can also specify the settings of the constraints that need to be applied automatically. To do so, choose the **AutoConstrain** button; the **Select objects or [Settings]** prompt will be displayed at the command prompt. Enter **S** at the command prompt and press the ENTER key; the **Constraint Settings** dialog box will be displayed, as shown in Figure 11-18.

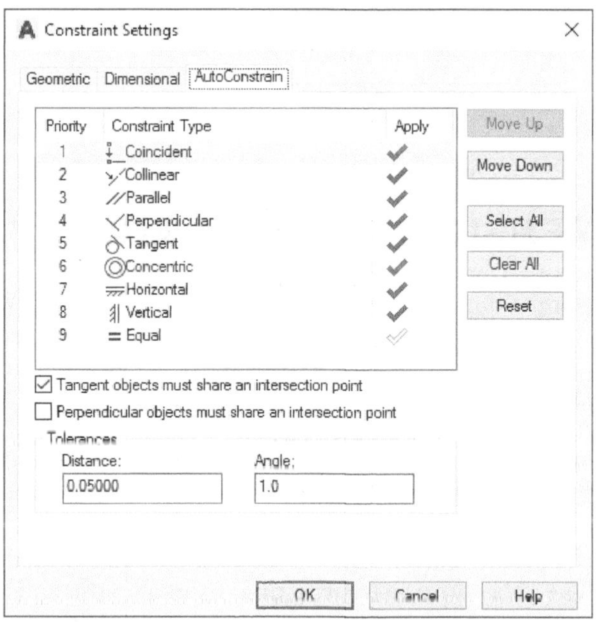

Figure 11-18 *The* ***Constraint Settings*** *dialog box with the* ***AutoConstrain*** *tab chosen*

In this dialog box, the **AutoConstrain** tab is chosen by default and the nine constraints that can be applied automatically are displayed. You can rearrange these constraints according to your priorities by choosing the **Move Up** or **Move Down** button. If you do not need a particular constraint to be applied automatically to the sketch, click on the green tick mark corresponding to the constraint; the tick mark will turn white indicating that the corresponding constraints will not be applied automatically. If the **Tangent objects must share an intersection point** check box is selected, the tangent constraint will be applied, only if the two entities intersect at a point. If you clear this check box, the tangent constraint will be applied, only if the distance between the endpoints satisfies the value specified in the **Tolerances** area. Similarly, if the **Perpendicular objects must share an intersection point** check box is selected, the **Perpendicular** constraint will be applied, only if the two entities intersect at a point. If you clear this check box, the **Perpendicular** constraint will be applied, only if the distance between the endpoints satisfies the tolerances value specified in the **Tolerances** area.

Exercise 1

Draw the sketch shown in Figure 11-19 and apply appropriate constraints to it. Do not dimension the sketch.

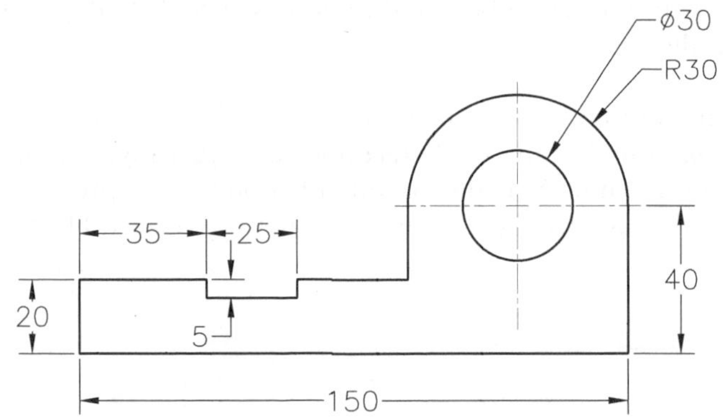

Figure 11-19 *Sketch for Exercise 1*

APPLYING DIMENSIONAL CONSTRAINTS

The older versions of AutoCAD were mainly used during the documentation stage of a design. However, the introduction of dimensional constraint has made AutoCAD a complete design package. In AutoCAD, you can apply dimensional constraint to an entity and change the size of the entity with ease. Therefore, now you can use AutoCAD at the initial design stage itself. Remember that the dimensions, which you apply using the tools in the **Dimensions** panel of the **Annotate** tab of the **Ribbon** do not change the size of the entity. However, because of their associative nature, if you change the size of an entity by dragging grips, the dimension will get changed.

You can apply the horizontal, vertical, aligned, angular, radius, and diameter dimensional constraint to a sketch. The procedure to apply a dimensional constraint to an entity is similar to that of applying dimension to an entity. For example, to apply the horizontal dimensional constraint, invoke the **Linear** tool from **Parametric > Dimensional > Dimensional Constraints** drop-down; you will be prompted to select the first constraint point. Move the cursor near one of the keypoints; it will be highlighted. Click to select the keypoint; you will be prompted to select the second constraint point. Move the cursor near the other keypoint and click, when it gets highlighted; the dimension will be attached to the cursor and you will be prompted to place the dimension. On placing the dimension, the dimension value will be displayed in a textbox. Press ENTER to accept the value. If you need to change the value, enter a new value in the dimension box and press ENTER. A lock symbol will be displayed next to the dimension value indicating that it is a dimensional constraint. In this way, you can apply other dimensional constraints as well.

Instead of selecting keypoints to apply the dimensional constraint, you can also select the entity to be dimensioned. To do so, invoke the **Linear** tool from **Parametric > Dimensional > Dimensional Constraints** drop-down and press ENTER when the **Specify first constraint point or [Object] <Object>** prompt is displayed; you will be prompted to select an object. Select the object; the dimension will be attached to the cursor. Place it at the required position.

Tip

*You can also enter the arithmetic functions directly in the text box that is displayed on placing a dimensional constraint. For example, if you have an arithmetic function such as (22 *5.5)-30+5, which is equal to 96, you do not need to calculate this function. Just enter the function in the text box and press ENTER; AutoCAD will automatically solve the mathematical expression. However, only the mathematical expression will be displayed in the text box and not the result.*

CONVERTING A DIMENSIONAL CONSTRAINT INTO AN ANNOTATIONAL CONSTRAINT

As discussed earlier, the dimensional constraint applied and the dimensions applied are different. The dimensional constraints are applied by using the tools available in the **Dimensional** panel of the **Parametric** tab. Whereas, dimensions are applied using the tools in the **Dimensions** panel of the **Annotate** tab. The dimensions that are applied using the tools from the **Dimensions** panel are called annotational constraints as they are used only for annotational purpose and cannot control the size of an entity.

If you have applied a dimension (annotational constraint) to an entity, you can convert it into a dimensional constraint. To do so, choose the **Convert** tool from the **Dimensional** panel of the **Parametric** tab; you will be prompted to select a dimension. Select the dimension and press ENTER; the dimension (annotational constraint) will be converted into the dimensional constraint.

You can also convert a dimensional constraint into an annotational constraint. To do so, select a dimensional constraint and invoke the **PROPERTIES** palette. Select **Annotational** from the **Constraint Form** field in the **Constraint** rollout; the dimensional constraint will change to the annotational constraint and the options in the **Properties** rollout will change accordingly.

A dimensional constraint will not be plotted when you plot the drawing using the **Plot** tool. Therefore, you need to convert a dimensional constraint into an annotational constraint, as discussed above. You can also place the dimensional constraint in the annotational constraint mode. To do so, expand the **Dimensional** panel in the **Parametric** tab. You will notice that the **Dynamic Constraint Mode** is chosen by default. Choose the **Annotational Constraint Mode**. Now, if you place the dimensional constraint, you can plot them.

You can also make a dimensional constraint as a reference constraint. A reference constraint is displayed in brackets and is driven by a dimensional or annotational constraint. To make a dimensional constraint as reference, invoke the **PROPERTIES** palette of a dimensional constraint and select **Yes** in the **Reference** field of the **Constraint** rollout. If you have changed a dimensional constraint to an annotational constraint, you can make this annotational constraint as a reference constraint using the **PROPERTIES** palette.

CONCEPT OF A FULLY-DEFINED SKETCH

It is important for you to understand the concept of fully-defined sketches. If you have created a sketch in the design stage, you need to add the required geometrical and dimensional constraints to the sketch to constrain its degrees of freedom with respect to the surrounding. After applying the required constraints, the sketch may exist in any of the following three states:

1. Under-defined
2. Fully-defined
3. Over-defined

Under-defined

An under-defined sketch is the one in which some of the geometrical constraints or dimensional constraints are not defined. As a result, the degrees of freedom of the sketch are not fully constrained, and therefore, the entities may move or change their size unexpectedly. So, you need to add some geometrical constraints or dimensional constraints to it to make it fully-defined.

Fully-defined

A fully-defined sketch is the one in which all entities and their positions are fully-defined by geometrical constraints, dimensional constraints, or both. In a fully-defined sketch, all degrees of freedom of a sketch are constrained, and therefore, the sketched entities cannot move or change their size and location unexpectedly.

Over-defined

An over-defined sketch is the one in which some of the geometrical constraints, dimensional constraints, or both are conflicting. Also, if the geometrical constraints or the dimensional constraints in a sketch exceed the required number, the sketch will be over-defined. If you try to apply more geometrical constraints or dimensional constraints to a fully-defined entity, a message box will be displayed with the message that applying this constraint will over define the entity, as shown in Figure 11-20 and Figure 11-21.

Note

*If you apply dimensional constraint to a fully-defined entity, the **Dimensional Constraints** message box will be displayed, refer to Figure 11-21. Choose the **Create a reference dimension** option from the message box to convert that particular dimension into a reference dimension.*

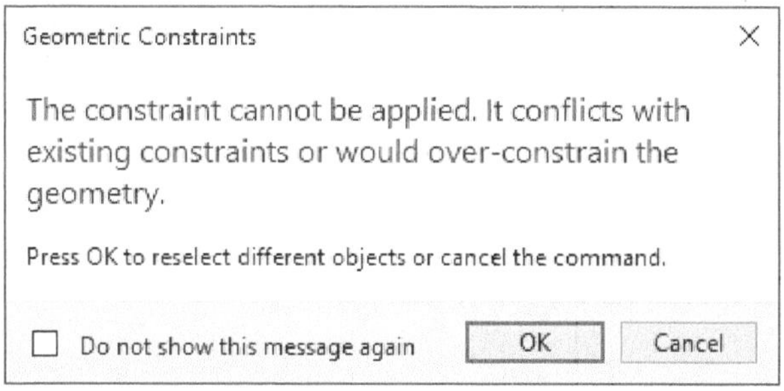

***Figure 11-20** The **Geometric Constraints** message box displayed on applying more than the required geometric constraints*

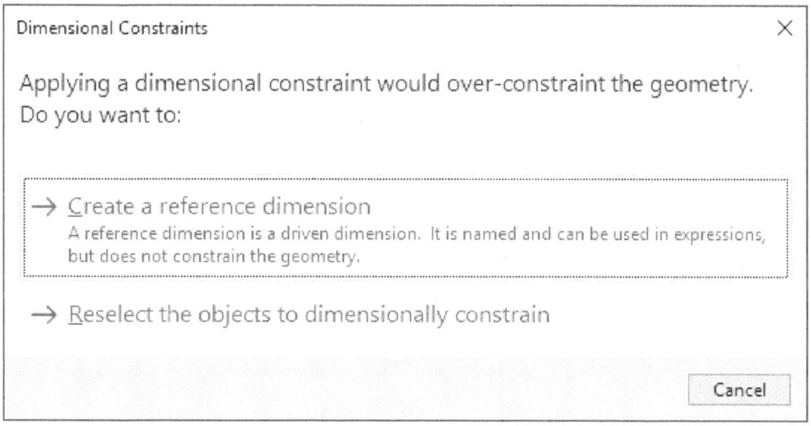

***Figure 11-21** The **Dimensional Constraints** message box displayed on applying more than the suggested dimensional constraints*

CONTROLLING THE DISPLAY OF THE DIMENSIONAL CONSTRAINT

On applying a dimensional constraint to an entity, a value will be displayed along with a name. If you have also applied annotational constraints to the sketch, then the sketch will be cluttered with dimensions. Therefore, you need to hide these constraints. To do so, choose the **Hide All** button from the **Dimensional** panel of the **Parametric** tab.

You can hide the selected dimensional constraints of an object by using the **Show/Hide** button. To do so, choose the **Show/Hide** button and select the respective constraint and press enter. Next, right-click in the drawing area; a shortcut menu will be displayed. Choose the **Hide** option from it; the selected constraint will be hidden.

To display all dimensional constraints in the drawing, choose the **Show All** button from the **Dimensional** panel of the **Parametric** tab. To hide the annotational constraint, turn off the corresponding layer from the **LAYER PROPERTIES MANAGER**.

When you apply a dimensional constraint to an entity, a default name and a lock symbol will be displayed along with the value. If you need to display only the value, click on the inclined arrow on the **Dimensional** panel of the **Parametric** tab; the **Constraint Settings** dialog box will be displayed with the **Dimensional** tab chosen, as shown in Figure 11-22. Specify the format of the dimensional constraint to be displayed in the **Dimension name format** drop-down list available in the **Dimensional constraint format** area of this dialog box.

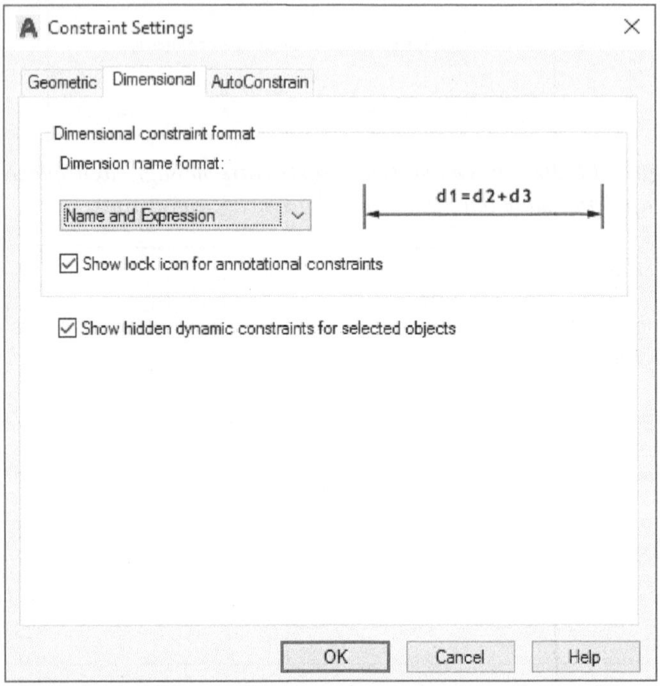

***Figure 11-22** The **Constraint Settings** dialog box with the **Dimensional** tab chosen*

If you convert a dimensional constraint into an annotational constraint, a lock symbol will be displayed. If you do not need the lock symbol to be displayed for an annotational constraint, clear the **Show lock icon for annotational constraints** check box from the **Constraint Settings** dialog box. In case, you want to view the dynamic constraints of an entity whose dimensional constraints are hidden by choosing the **Show lock icon for annotational constraints** button, select the **Show hidden dynamic constraints for selected objects** check box in the **Constraint Settings** dialog box. Now, if you select an entity whose dynamic constraints are hidden, the dynamic constraints will be displayed.

Example 2

In this example, you will draw the sketch shown in Figure 11-23, and then apply the geometric and dimensional constraints to it.

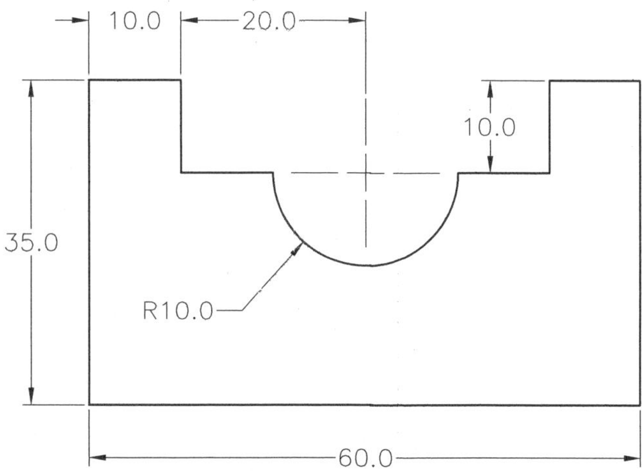

Figure 11-23 *Sketch for Example 2*

First, you will draw the profile and apply the geometrical constraints.

1. Start a new file with the *acad.dwt* template in the **Drafting & Annotation** workspace and draw the outer profile with dimensions close to that given in Figure 11-23. Make sure that the endpoints are snapped so that they form a closed sketch, as shown in Figure 11-24.

2. Choose the **AutoConstrain** button from the **Geometric** panel of the **Parametric** tab, enter **S** at the command prompt, and press ENTER; the **Constraint Settings** dialog box is displayed.

3. Make sure that all constraints are selected. As there is no need to apply the concentric or tangent constraints in this sketch, select the **Concentric** and **Tangent** constraints individually and move them down using the **Move Down** button.

4. Choose the **OK** button; you are prompted to select objects. Select all entities of the sketch by dragging a selection box. Next, press ENTER; all possible constraints are applied to the sketch, as shown in Figure 11-25.

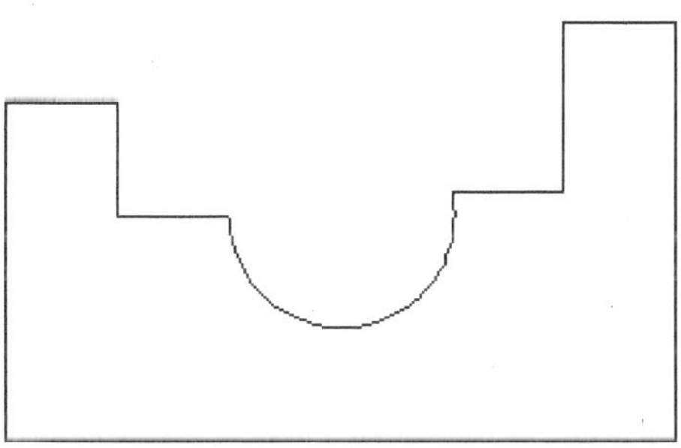

Figure 11-24 *Closed sketch drawn*

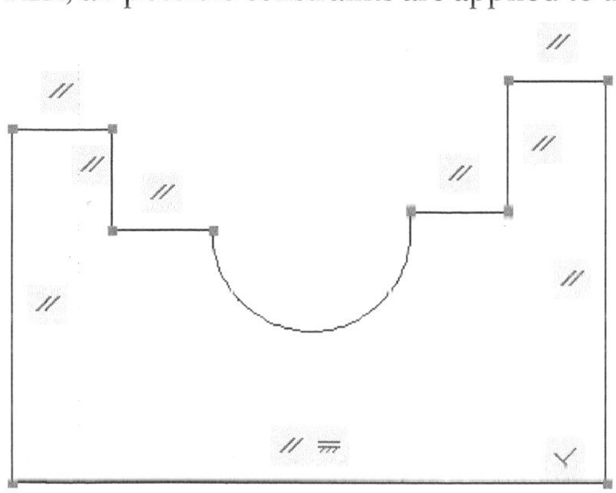

Figure 11-25 *Constraints applied automatically*

Note

*The constraints applied using the **AutoConstrain** tool may vary depending upon the profile. In your case, if the constraints are different from that shown in Figure 11-25, apply the missing constraints. Also, choose the **Show All** button from the **Geometric** panel if the constraints are not visible by default.*

5. Now, you need to apply the equal constraint. To do so, choose the **Equal** tool from the **Geometric** panel of the **Parametric** tab and apply the **Equal** constraint between the lines that are supposed to have equal dimensions. For dimensions, refer to Figure 11-23. The equal constraints need to be applied to the two pairs of horizontal and two pairs of vertical lines in the sketch. The sketch after applying the **Equal** constraint is shown in Figure 11-26.

Note

*If you do not want to apply the **Equal** constraint to vertical lines, you need to apply the **Collinear** constraint to the two pairs of horizontal lines. But after applying the **Equal** constraint if you apply the **Collinear** constraint, a message box will be displayed stating that this constraint cannot be applied and conflicts the existing constraints or is over-constraining the geometry.*

Next, you need to make the centerpoint of the circle and the horizontal line to be in a line.

6. Choose the **Horizontal** tool from the **Geometric** panel of the **Parametric** tab; the prompt sequence that will follow is given next.

Select an object or [2Points] <2Points>: Enter
Select first point: *Move the cursor over the horizontal line and click when the endpoint near the arc is highlighted*
Select second point: *cen* Enter *and select the arc on the left side*

The sketch after applying the **Horizontal** constraint is shown in Figure 11-27.

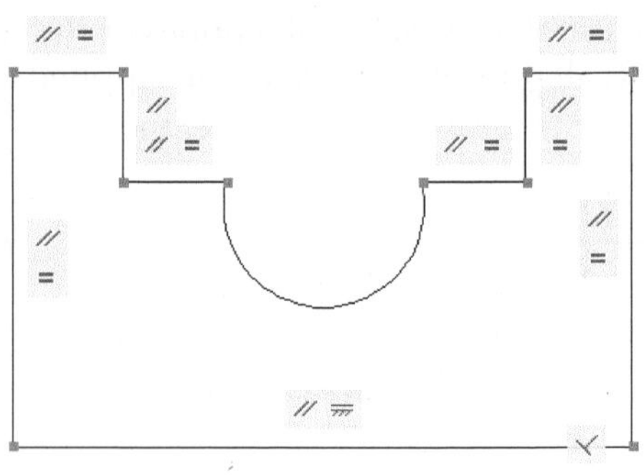

***Figure 11-26** Sketch after applying the **Equal** constraint*

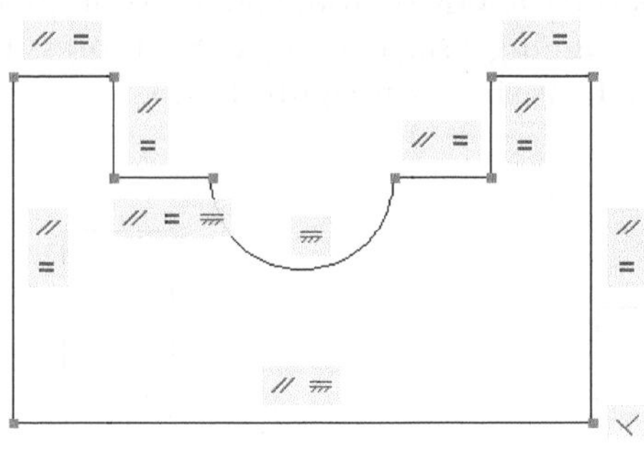

***Figure 11-27** Sketch after applying the **Horizontal** constraint*

7. Choose the **Hide All** button from the **Geometric** panel in the **Parametric** tab; all constraint bars disappear.

Now, you need to apply dimensional constraints. Before that, expand the **Dimensional** panel and ensure that the **Dynamic Constraint Mode** option is chosen.

8. Choose the **Linear** tool from **Parametric > Dimensional > Dimensional Constraint** drop-down and follow the prompt sequence given next.

   Specify first constraint point or [Object] <Object>: [Enter]
   Select object: *Select the horizontal line at the bottom.*
   Specify dimension line location: *Move the cursor down and place the horizontal dimension at the required location. Type **60** in the text box and press ENTER.*

9. Press the ENTER key again or choose the **Linear** tool from the **Dimensional** panel of the **Parametric** tab and follow the prompt sequence given next.

   Specify first constraint point or [Object] <Object>: [Enter]
   Select object: *Select the vertical line on the left*
   Specify dimension line location: *Move the cursor on the left and place the vertical dimension at the required location. Enter **35** in the textbox.*

10. Similarly, apply the dimension to the horizontal and vertical lines, refer to Figure 11-28 and change the value to **10**.

11. Choose the **Radius** tool from the **Dimensional** panel of the **Parametric** tab; you are prompted to select the arc or the circle.

12. Select the arc and enter **10** as radius.

Now, you need to apply the dimension between the center of the arc and the vertical line on the left, refer to Figure 11-23.

13. Invoke the **Linear** tool from the **Parametric > Dimensional > Dimensional Constraints** drop-down and follow the prompt sequence given next.

    Specify first constraint point or [Object] <Object>: *Select the keypoint at the top of the smaller vertical line on the left.*
    Specify second constraint point: *cen* [Enter] *and select the arc.*
    Specify dimension line location: *Place the dimension at the required location and enter **20**; the **Dimensional Constraints** message box is displayed.*

14. Choose the **Create a reference dimension** option from the message box. The value **20** is displayed in parenthesis stating that it is a reference dimension. The sketch after applying all dimensional constraints is shown in Figure 11-28.

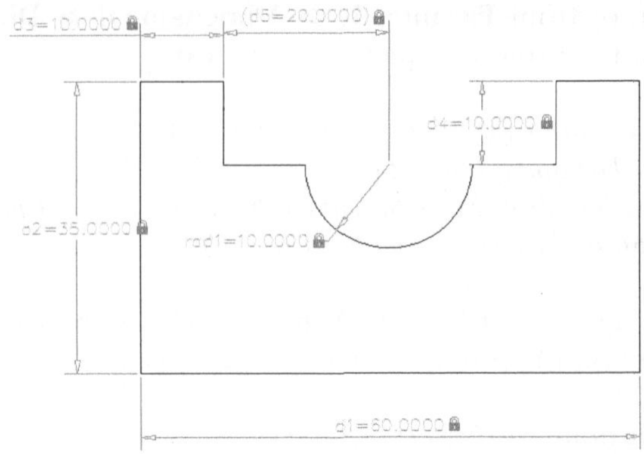

Figure 11-28 Sketch with all dimensional constraints

WORKING WITH EQUATIONS

Equations are mathematical relations between dimensions. Consider the sketch of a bolt. All the dimensions of a bolt are driven by the base diameter. In AutoCAD, if you need to draw the sketch of an object whose dimensions are driven by a base dimension, you can draw it easily by using equations in which all dimensions are equated with base dimensions. If you want to relate one or two dimensions with base dimension, you can do so by applying a dimensional constraint. But if most of the dimensions need to be represented as equations, then you need to use the **Parameters Manager**. Both these methods are discussed next.

Adding Equations while Applying Dimensional Constraints

When you apply the dimensional constraint using the tools from the **Dimensional** panel, the dimensions are displayed along with a default name. For the next dimensional constraint to be placed, you can represent it as an equation with the name of the first constraint. For example, to create a rectangle of length *l* units and width *w* units, which is half the length, you need to follow the steps given below.

1. Draw a rectangle and apply the required geometric constraints to it.
2. Choose the **Linear** tool from the **Dimensional** panel and select one of the lines representing the length and place the dimension; a text box will be displayed.
3. Enter **10** in the text box and press ENTER; a new dimension will be displayed with the default name d1=10.0000.
4. Choose the **Linear** tool from the **Dimensional** panel and select one of the lines representing the width and place the dimension; a text box will be displayed.
5. Enter **0.5*d1** in the text box and press ENTER; the rectangle will resize and a new dimension will be displayed with the default name fx: d2=0.5*d1.
6. Now, if you change the dimension of the length, the width will also change automatically.

Note that, if you change the default name, d1, the name in the expression d2 will also change.

Adding Equations Using the Parameters Manager

Adding equations to dimensions while applying constraints may look simpler, but in actual practice, when there are more dimensions, it is quite difficult. This problem can be solved by applying equations to dimensions using the **PARAMETERS MANAGER**. After applying dimensional constraints, choose the **Parameters Manager** button from the **Manage** panel of the **Parametric** tab; the **PARAMETERS MANAGER** palette will be displayed with all dimensions and expressions, as shown in Figure 11-29. The names of the dimensional constraints applied will be listed under the **Name** column in the **Dimensional Constraint Parameters** node. Also, the expression of the corresponding constraints will be listed in the **Expression** column.

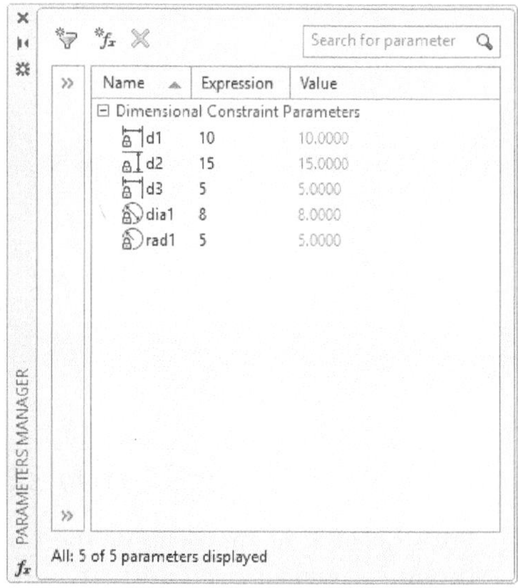

Figure 11-29 The ***PARAMETERS MANAGER*** *palette*

Now, you can change the existing expressions or add new expressions. To do so, double-click in the corresponding **Expression** field and add a new expression. If you want to add a list of new user-defined expressions, choose the **Creates a new user parameter** button from the **PARAMETERS MANAGER** palette; a new field will be added under the **User Parameters** node.

Example 3

In this example, you will open the sketch created in Exercise 1 of this chapter. You had applied geometrical constraints to this sketch. Now, you will apply dimensional constraints and then equate all the dimensions except the dimension 20 mm, with respect to the base length, 150 mm. For the dimension 20 mm, you will apply user-defined expressions as d150 = 20, d75 = 10, d300 = 40, and d100 = 13.3.

1. Choose the **Open** button from the **Quick Access Toolbar** and open the drawing created in Exercise 1 of this chapter.

2. Make sure that you have applied all the required geometrical constraints, as shown in Figure 11-30.

Note

If you have not applied all constraints to the sketch, it may get deformed while applying dimensional constraints.

3. Invoke the **Linear** tool from **Parametric > Dimensional > Dimensional Constraints** drop-down and follow the prompt sequence given next.

Specify first constraint point or [Object] <Object>: Enter
Select object: *Select the horizontal line at the bottom.*
Specify dimension line location: *Move the cursor down and place the horizontal dimension at the required location. Type* ***150*** *in the text box and press ENTER.*

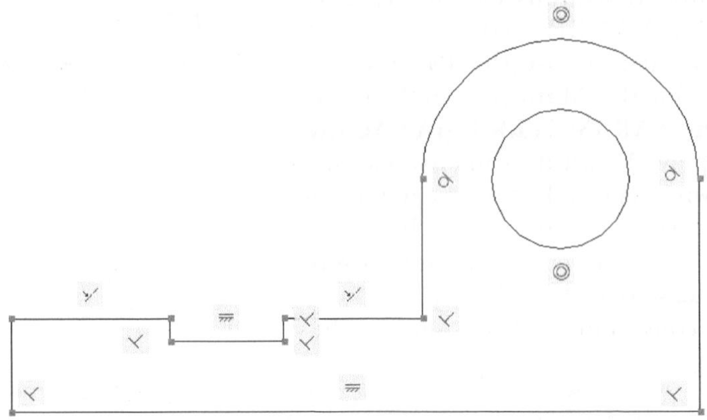

Figure 11-30 Sketch with all constraints applied

4. Press ENTER again or choose the **Linear** tool from the **Dimensional** panel and follow the prompt sequence given next.

   Specify first constraint point or [Object] <Object>: Enter
   Select object: *Select the vertical line on the left.*
   Specify dimension line location: *Move the cursor to left side and place the vertical dimension at the required location. Enter **20** in the text box and press ENTER.*

5. Similarly, apply dimensions to other horizontal and vertical lines.

6. Choose the **Radius** tool from the **Dimensional** panel of the **Parametric** tab; you are prompted to select an arc or a circle.

7. Select the arc and enter **30** as the value of radius.

8. Choose the **Diameter** tool from the **Dimensional** panel of the **Parametric** tab; you are prompted to select the circle.

9. Select the circle and enter **30** as diameter.

10. Choose the **Parameters Manager** button from the **Manage** panel; the **PARAMETERS MANAGER** palette will be displayed with the names of dimensional constraints and their values, as shown in Figure 11-31.

11. Double-click on **40** in the **Expression** column of the **PARAMETERS MANAGER** palette and enter **d1/3.75**.

12. Resize the palette. Double-click in the **Description** column corresponding to the value **40** and enter **Hole Location**.

13. Similarly, add the expression and description to all dimensions, except the vertical dimension **20**, as given next.

Value to be selected from the Expression column	Expression to be added	Description to be added
35	d1/30*7	Slot Location
25	d1/6	Slot Width
5	d1/30	Slot Depth
30 (Diameter value)	d1/5	Hole Diameter
30 (Radius value)	d1/5	Radius

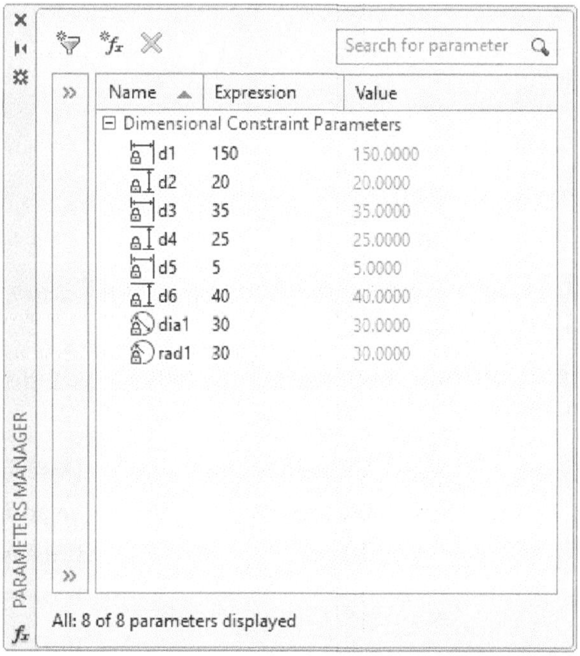

***Figure 11-31** The **PARAMETERS MANAGER** palette after applying all dimensions*

Note

*If the **Type** and **Description** columns are not added by default, right-click on the title of a column and choose appropriate options.*

The **PARAMETERS MANAGER** palette after you have changed all the expressions, is shown in Figure 11-32.

For the value 20, you need to create a user-defined expression as follows:

14. Choose the **Creates a new user parameter** button in the **PARAMETERS MANAGER** palette; the **User Parameters** node is added with the default name, **user1**.

15. Change the name user1 to **d150**, the corresponding expression to **20**, and the description to **If d1 = 150**.

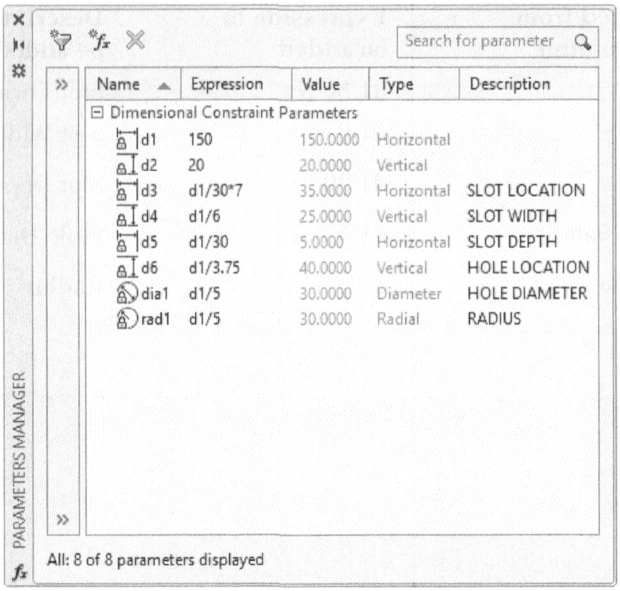

Figure 11-32 *The* ***PARAMETERS MANAGER*** *palette after adding all expressions*

16. Similarly, add three more user parameters and their corresponding expressions and descriptions as given below.

User parameter to be added	**Expression to be added**	**Description to be added**
d75	10	If d1 = 75
d300	40	If d1 = 300
d100	13.3	If d1 = 100

Note

You can also write a suitable expression for the dimension ***20*** *in the* ***Dimensional Constraints*** *node. For illustration, the expression for the dimension* ***20*** *is given as a user variable.*

17. If the dimensional constraints are displayed, choose the **Show/Hide** button from the **Dimensional** panel of the **Parametric** tab to hide the dimensional constraints.

18. Now, change the dimensional constraints **d1** and **d2**, as specified below in the **PARAMETERS MANAGER** palette. Observe the change in the sketch in the drawing area and the dimension value in the **Value** column of the **PARAMETERS MANAGER** palette.

d1 = 300, d2 = d300
d1 = 100, d2 = d100
d1 = 150, d2 = 20

Self-Evaluation Test

Answer the following questions and then compare them to those given at the end of this chapter:

1. Which of the following tools should be chosen in the **Dimensional** panel to apply both horizontal and linear dimensional constraints?

   (a) **Aligned** (b) **Linear**
   (c) **Lateral** (d) None of these

2. What will be the state of the sketch which does not have all its constraints defined?

   (a) Under-defined (b) Fully-defined
   (c) Over-defined (d) All of these

3. AutoCAD provides you __________ types of geometric constraints.

4. The __________ constraints are applied between two entities in a sketch and they control the shape of the drawing.

5. The __________ constraint forces the selected lines to lie on the same infinite line.

6. Invoke the __________ palette to add equations to dimensional constraints.

7. Whenever you apply a geometric constraint between two entities, the entity selected first will be affected. (T/F)

8. You cannot apply the coincident constraint to all the keypoints at a time. (T/F)

9. It is always recommended to first apply dimensional constraints so that the shape of the sketched entity does not change on applying geometric constraints. (T/F)

10. You can add equations while applying dimensional constraints. (T/F)

Review Questions

Answer the following questions:

1. How many geometric constraints can be applied automatically?

   (a) Nine (b) Ten
   (c) Eight (d) Twelve

2. Which of the following constraints forces two lines or polylines to have equal length and the selected circles, arcs, or an arc and circle to have equal radii?

   (a) **Concentric** (b) **Equal**
   (c) **Collinear** (d) **Lock**

3. The __________ makes you to change or modify the shape and size of an entity of a sketch at any stage of the design process.

4. The __________ constraint is used to apply curvature continuity between a spline and an entity connected together.

5. A __________ dimensional constraint is displayed in brackets and is driven by a dimensional or annotational constraint.

6. The dimensions that you apply using the tools in the __________ panel do not change the size of an entity.

7. The symmetric constraint forces two selected lines, arcs, circles, or splines to remain equidistant from the centerline. (T/F)

8. Using the fix constraint, you can only fix the points. (T/F)

9. You can also enter arithmetic symbols directly in the text box that is displayed on placing a dimensional constraint. (T/F)

10. If you hide the display of a constraint, the constraint applied gets deleted. (T/F)

Exercise 2

Draw the sketches shown in Figure 11-33 and Figure 11-34. Next, add geometric and dimensional constraints to them.

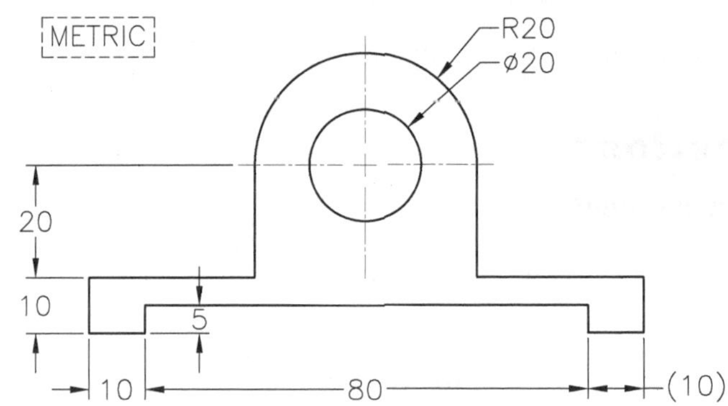

Figure 11-33 Sketch for Exercise 2

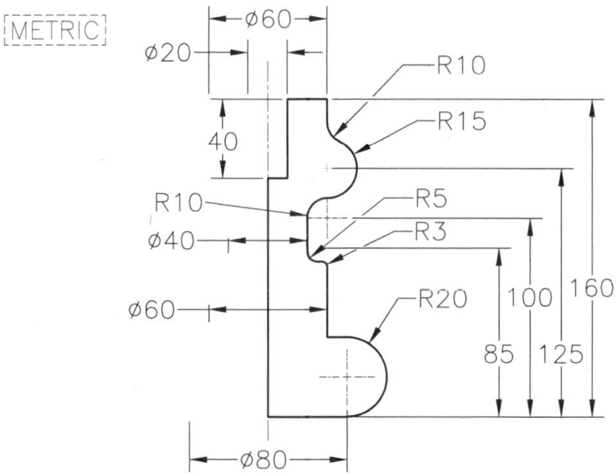

Figure 11-34 Sketch for Exercise 2

Answers to Self-Evaluation Test

1. b, **2.** a, **3.** twelve, **4. Geometric**, **5. Collinear**, **6. PARAMETERS MANAGER**, **7.** F, **8.** F, **9.** F, **10.** T

Chapter 12

Hatching Drawings

Learning Objectives

After completing this chapter, you will be able to:

- *Hatch an area by using the Hatch tool*
- *Use boundary hatch with Pre-defined, User-defined, and Custom hatch patterns as options*
- *Specify pattern properties*
- *Preview and apply hatching*
- *Create annotative hatching*
- *Edit associative hatch and hatch boundary*
- *Hatch inserted blocks*
- *Align hatch lines in adjacent hatch areas*

Key Terms

- *Hatching*
- *Pattern*
- *Gradient*
- *Boundaries*
- *Islands*
- *Edit Hatch*

HATCHING

In many drawings, such as sections of solids, the sectioned area needs to be filled with some pattern. Different filling patterns make it possible to distinguish between different parts or components of an object. Also, the material of which an object is made can be indicated by the filling pattern. You can also use these filling patterns in graphics for rendering architectural elevations of buildings, or indicating the different levels in terrain and contour maps. Filling objects with a pattern is known as hatching, refer to Figure 12-1. This hatching process can be accomplished by using the **Hatch** tool in the **Draw** panel of the **Home** tab or the **Tool Palettes**.

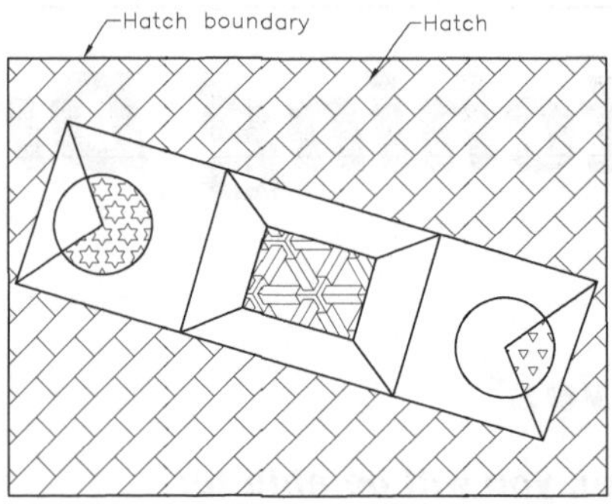

Figure 12-1 *Illustration of hatching*

Before using the **Hatch** tool, you need to understand the terminology related to hatching. Some of the terms are explained next.

Hatch Patterns

AutoCAD supports a variety of hatch patterns, refer to Figure 12-2. Every hatch pattern consists of one or more hatch lines or a solid fill. The lines are placed at specified angles and spacing. You can change the angle and the spacing between the hatch lines. These lines may be broken into dots and dashes, or may be continuous, as required. The hatch pattern is trimmed or repeated, as required, to fill the specified area exactly. The lines comprising the hatch are drawn in the current drawing plane. The basic mechanism behind hatching is that the line objects of the pattern you have specified are generated and incorporated in the desired area in the drawing. Although a hatch can contain many lines, AutoCAD normally groups them together into an internally generated object and uses them for all practical purposes. For example, if you want to perform an editing operation, such as erasing the hatch, all you need to do is select any point on the hatch and press ENTER; the entire pattern gets deleted. If you want to break a pattern into individual lines to edit them, you can use the **Explode** tool from the **Modify** panel of the **Home** tab.

Hatch Boundary

Hatching can be used on parts of a drawing enclosed by a boundary. This boundary may be lines, circles, arcs, polylines, 3D faces, or other objects, and at least part of each bounding object must be displayed within the active viewport.

Figure 12-2 Example of some hatch patterns

HATCHING DRAWINGS USING THE HATCH TOOL

Ribbon: Home >Draw > Hatch drop-down > Hatch **Toolbar:** Draw > Hatch
Menu Bar: Draw > Hatch **Command:** HATCH/H

The **Hatch** tool is used to hatch a region enclosed within a boundary (closed area) by selecting a point inside the boundary or by selecting the objects to be hatched. This tool automatically designates a boundary and ignores other objects (whole or partial) that may not be a part of this boundary. When you choose the **Hatch** tool, the **Hatch Creation** tab will be displayed, as shown in Figure 12-3. Also, you will be prompted to pick internal point. Select the type of hatch pattern from the **Pattern** panel of the **Hatch Creation** tab, set the properties of the hatch pattern in the **Properties** panel, and move the cursor inside a closed profile; the preview of the hatch pattern will be displayed. Now, pick the internal point; the hatch will be applied.

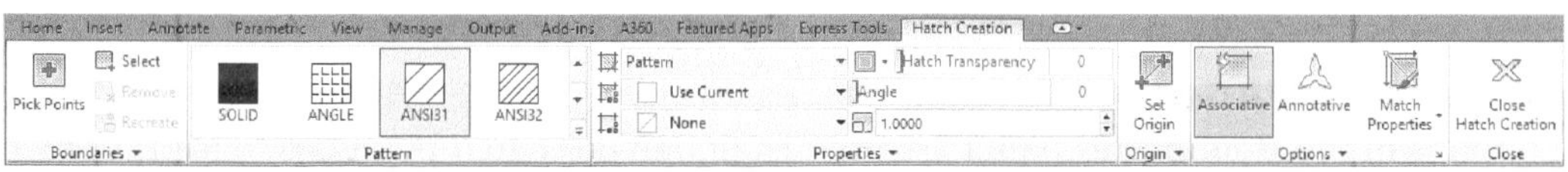

*Figure 12-3 The **Hatch Creation** tab*

Example 1 — Hatch

In this example, you will hatch a circle using the default hatch settings. Later, in the chapter, you will learn to change the settings to get the desired hatch pattern.

1. Create a circle and then choose the **Hatch** tool from the **Draw** panel; the **Hatch Creation** tab is displayed and you are prompted to **Pick internal point or [Select objects/Undo/seTtings]:** move the cursor inside the circular region; a preview of the hatch pattern is displayed.

2. Select a point inside the circle (P1) (Figure 12-4) and press ENTER; the hatch is applied, as shown in Figure 12-5.

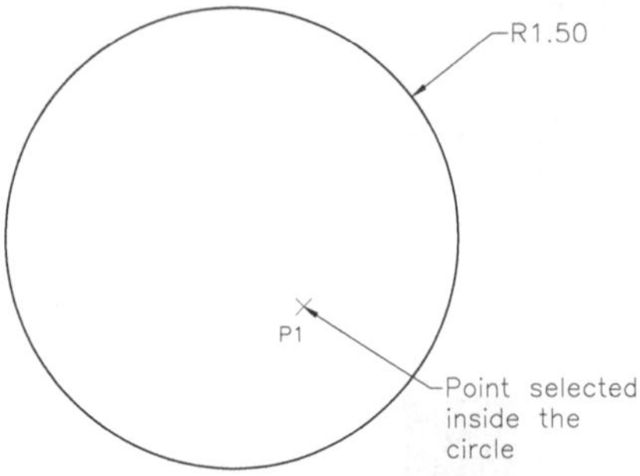

Figure 12-4 Specifying a point to hatch the circle

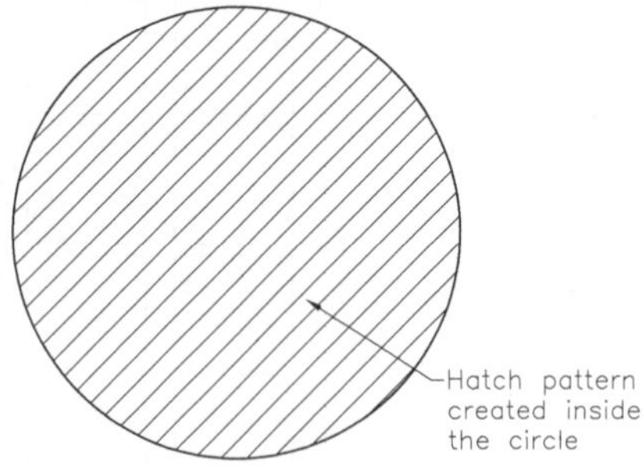

Figure 12-5 Drawing after hatching

Tip

*1. The **FILLMODE** system variable is set to On by default (value of the variable is 1) and hence the hatch patterns are displayed. In case of large hatching areas, you can set the **FILLMODE** to Off (value of the variable is 0) so that the hatch pattern is not displayed and the regeneration time is saved.*

2. You can also hatch the selected face of a solid model. However, to hatch a face of the solid model, you need to align the UCS at that face. You will learn more about this in later chapters.

PANELS IN THE HATCH CREATION TAB

Before or after specifying the pick points, you can change the parameters of a hatch pattern using various options in the panels of the **Hatch Creation** tab. These panels and their options are discussed next.

Boundaries Panel

The options in the **Boundaries** panel are used to define the hatch boundary. This is done by selecting a point inside a closed area to be hatched or by selecting the objects. You can also remove islands, create hatch boundary, and define the boundary set by using the options in this panel, as discussed next.

Pick Points

This option is chosen by default and used to define a boundary from the objects that form a closed area. After invoking the **Hatch** tool, move the cursor over a closed region; the preview of the hatch will be displayed. Click inside the closed object; a boundary will be defined around the selected point and the hatch will be applied, as shown in Figure 12-6. The following prompts appear when you click inside the closed object.

Pick internal point or [Select objects/Undo/seTtings]: *Select a point inside the object to hatch* Enter.

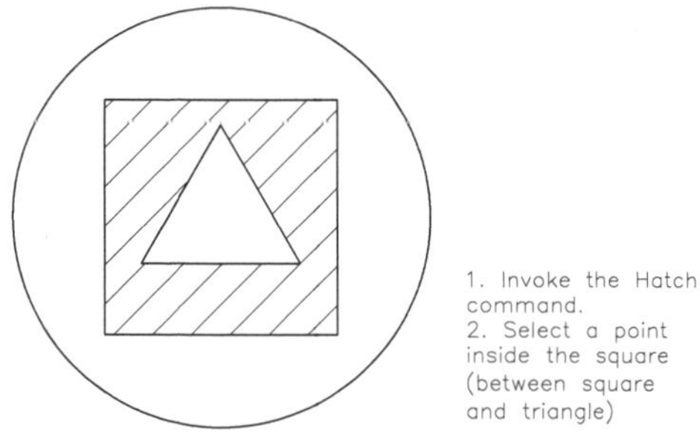

Figure 12-6 *Defining multiple hatch boundaries by selecting a point*

Tip

*Suppose, you have selected a point within an area for hatching and later you realized that you have selected a wrong area, in such a case, you can enter **U** or select **Undo** at the command prompt to undo the last selection. You can also undo a hatch pattern that you have already applied to an area by entering **Undo** at the command prompt.*

Hatch-Boundary Definition Error: Sometimes, while selecting the boundary to be hatched, AutoCAD displays an error. This error may occur due to various reasons. AutoCAD displays different types of **Boundary Definition Error** message boxes, depending on the kind of error occurred while selecting the boundary. For example, if you pick a point inside any boundary that is not closed, a message box will be displayed, as shown in Figure 12-7, informing that the hatch boundary is not valid. Choose the **Close** button and then create a closed sketch as boundary. You can also specify the gap tolerance value in the **Gap Tolerance** edit box in the **Options** panel so that hatch can be created if the gap is within the permissible limit. If the **Gap Tolerance** value is within the permissible limit, then while creating the hatch pattern, the **Hatch-Open Boundary** message box will be displayed informing that the hatch boundary is not closed. You can continue or stop hatching by choosing the corresponding option from the message box or you can close the message box by clicking on the **Close** button.

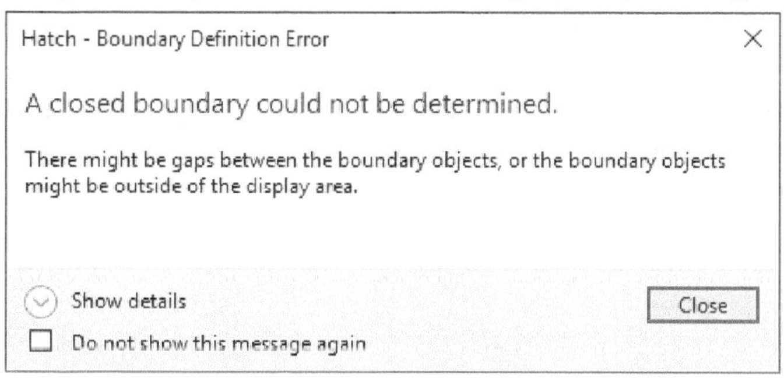

Figure 12-7 *The **Hatch-Boundary Definition Error** message box*

Select

This option allows you select objects that form the boundary for hatching. It is useful when you have to hatch an object and disregard objects that lie inside it or intersect with it. When you select this option, AutoCAD will prompt you to select objects. You can select the objects individually or use the other object selection methods. In Figure 12-8, the **Select** option is used to select the triangle. It uses the triangle as the hatch boundary, and everything inside it is hatched. The text inside the triangle, in this case, also gets hatched. To avoid hatching of such internal objects, select them at the next select objects prompt. In Figure 12-9, the text is selected to exclude from hatching. While using the **Pick Points** option, the text automatically gets selected to be excluded from the hatching.

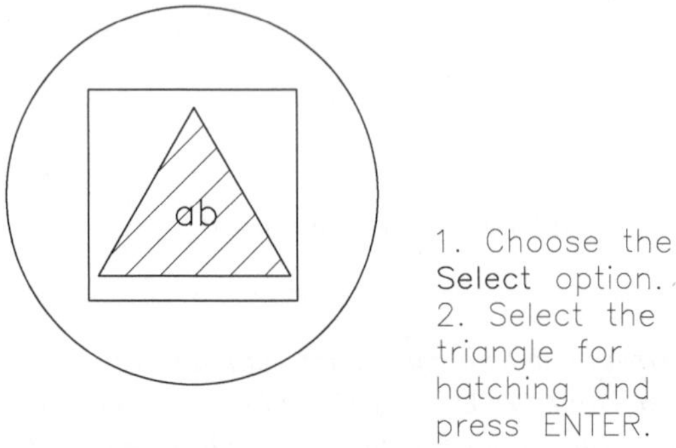

***Figure 12-8** Using the **Select** option to specify the hatching boundary*

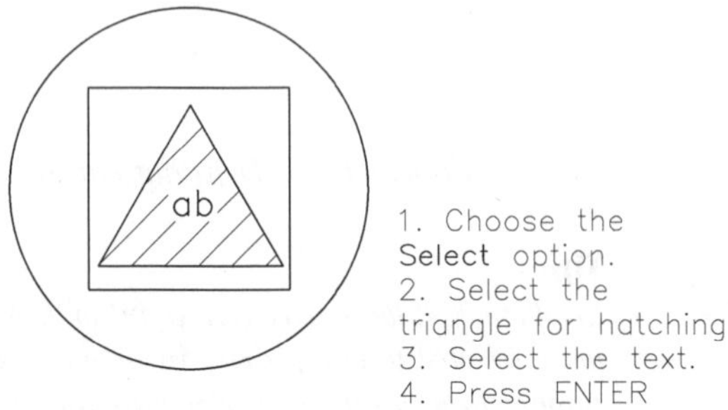

***Figure 12-9** Using the **Select** option to exclude the text from hatching*

Tip

1. If an area with many intersecting objects is to be hatched then select the entire object to be hatched rather than choosing the internal points within each of the smaller regions created by the intersection.

2. The layers containing text or lines that make the selection of hatch boundaries difficult can be turned off.

Remove

This option is used to remove boundaries and islands from the hatching area. Boundaries inside another boundary are known as islands. If you choose the **Pick Points** option to hatch an area, the inside boundaries, which are known as islands, will not be hatched by default. But if you want to hatch the islands, you can choose the **Select** option and then the **Remove** option in the **Boundaries** panel. For example, if you have a rectangle with circles in it, as shown in Figure 12-10, you can use the **Pick points** option to select a point inside the rectangle. On choosing this option, AutoCAD will select both the circles and the rectangle. To remove the circles (islands), you can use the **Remove** option. When you select this option, AutoCAD will prompt you to select the islands to be removed. Select the islands to be removed and press ENTER. Similarly, you can remove boundaries.

Tip

*If you want to remove islands from the hatching area, use the **Select Objects** option to select the object containing islands.*

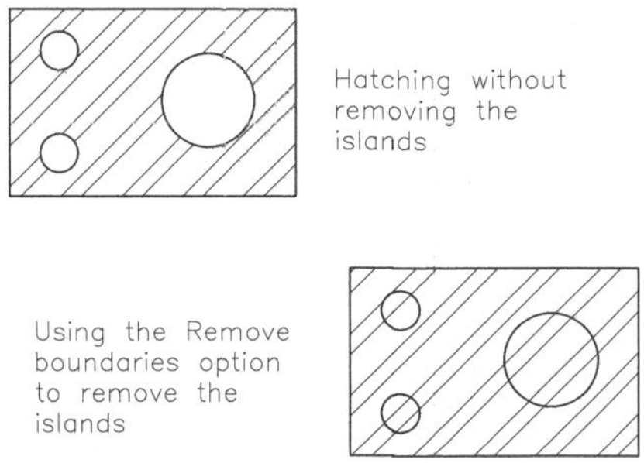

***Figure 12-10** Using the **Remove** tool to remove islands from the hatch area*

Recreate

This option gets available while editing a hatch and is used to recreate boundaries around the existing hatch pattern. On choosing this option, you will be prompted to specify whether you want to recreate boundaries as a region or as a polyline. You can also associate the hatch to the new boundary.

Retain Boundary Objects Drop-down List

When you select an internal point in a region to be hatched, a boundary is created around it. By default, this boundary will be removed as soon as the hatch pattern is applied. The **Retain Boundary Objects** drop-down list (refer to Figure 12-11) provides options to specify whether the boundary is to be retained as an object or not. You can also specify the type of object either as a polyline or a region.

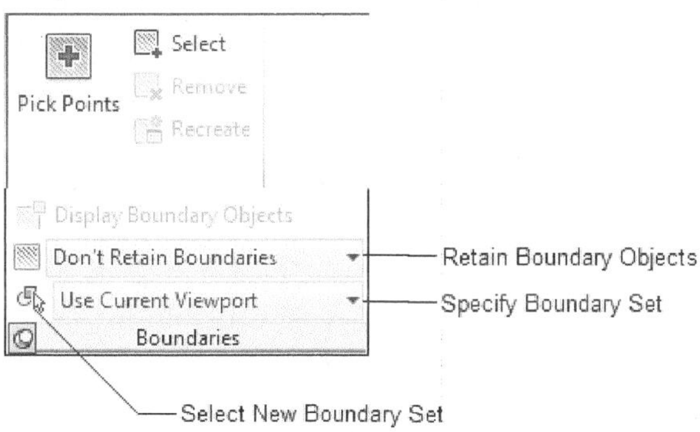

***Figure 12-11** Options in the expanded **Boundaries** panel*

Select the **Don't Retain Boundaries** option, if you do not need the boundary to be saved. In case, you need to retain the boundary, you can retain it as a polyline or region. If you select the **Retain Boundaries - Polyline** option the boundary created around the hatch area will be a polyline. Similarly, when you select the **Retain Boundaries - Region** option, the boundary of the hatch area will become a region. Region is a two-dimensional area that can be created from closed shapes or loops.

Display Boundary Objects

If you have chosen any one of the **Retain Boundaries** option then you can choose this option to display the resulting boundary, while editing. However, the boundary will merge with the profile of the drawing object. You can use the **Move** command to view the resulting hatch boundary.

Defining Boundary Set Area

When you invoke the **Hatch** tool and you have not formed a boundary set, there is only one option, **Use Current Viewport** available in the **Specify Boundary Set** drop-down list, refer to Figure 12-11. The benefit of creating a selection set is that when you select a point or select the objects to define the hatch boundary, AutoCAD will search only for the objects that are in the selection set.

The default boundary set is **Use Current Viewport**, which comprises everything that is visible in the current viewport. Hatching is made faster by specifying a boundary set because, in this case, AutoCAD does not have to examine everything on screen. This option allows you to define a boundary area so that only a specific portion of the drawing is considered for hatching. You use this option to create a new boundary set.

When you choose the **Select New Boundary Set** button, you are prompted to select the objects to be included in the new boundary set. While constructing the boundary set, AutoCAD uses only those objects that you select and that are hatchable. If a boundary set already exists, it is replaced by the new one. If you do not select any hatchable objects, no new boundary set is created. AutoCAD retains the current set, if there is any. Once you have selected the objects to form the boundary set, press ENTER; you will notice that **Use Boundary Set** gets added to the drop-down list.

Remember that by confining the search to the objects in the selection set, the hatching process becomes faster. If you select an object that is not a part of the selection set, AutoCAD will ignore it. When a boundary set is formed, it becomes the default for hatching until you exit the **Hatch** tool or select the **Use Current Viewport** option from the **Specify Boundary Set** drop-down list.

Tip

To improve the hatching speed and to define the boundary to be hatched easily in large drawings, you should zoom in the area to be hatched. Since AutoCAD does not have to search the entire drawing to find hatch boundaries, the hatch process gets faster.

Pattern Panel

The **Pattern** panel displays all predefined patterns available in AutoCAD. However, the list depends upon the option selected in the **Hatch Type** drop-down list in the **Properties** panel. By default, the **Pattern** option is selected in this drop-down list and the predefined patterns are listed in the **Pattern** panel. A predefined pattern consists of **ANSI**, **ISO**, and other pattern types. The hatch pattern selected in this panel will be applied to the object. The selected pattern will be stored in the **HPNAME** system variable. **ANSI31** is the default pattern in the **HPNAME** system variable. If you need to hatch a solid by using a solid color, then choose the **Solid** option and specify the color in the **Hatch Color** option in the **Properties** panel. Similarly, if you need to create a user-defined pattern, choose the **USER** option from the **Pattern** panel and set the properties.

Properties Panel

The options in this panel (refer to Figure 12-12) are used to set the properties of the pattern selected in the **Pattern** panel. The different options are discussed next.

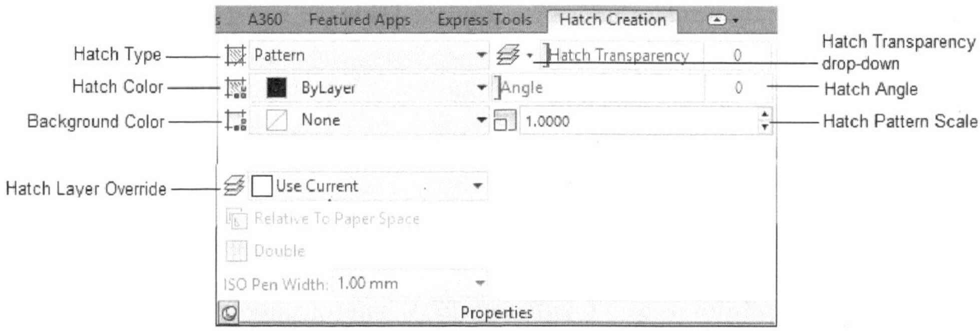

*Figure 12-12 Options in the **Properties** panel of the **Hatch Creation** tab*

Hatch Type

The **Hatch Type** drop-down list displays the types of patterns that can be used for hatching drawing objects. The four types of hatch patterns available are **Solid**, **Gradient**, **Pattern**, and **User defined**. The predefined types of patterns come with AutoCAD and are stored in the *acad.pat* and *acadiso.pat* files. The **Pattern** type of hatch pattern is the default type. If you select the **Gradient** option from this drop-down list, the corresponding options will be listed in the **Hatch Creation** tab. These options are discussed later.

Hatch Color

Specify the color of the hatch in this drop-down list. On selecting the **Use Current** option, the color set in the **Properties** panel of the **Home** tab will be applied to the hatch.

Background Color

If you need to apply a background color to a hatch, then choose a color from the **Background Color** drop-down list.

Hatch Transparency

If you need a hatch to be displayed in the transparent mode, set the transparency value in this edit box. You can also set the value by using the slider or by double-clicking in the edit box. By default, it uses the transparency value set in the **Properties** panel of the **Home** tab. If you need to change the value, then select the required option in the **Hatch Transparency** drop-down. The options available in this list are **Use Current**, **ByLayer Transparency**, **ByBlock Transparency**, and **Transparency Value**.

Hatch Angle

The **Hatch Angle** slider is used to set the angle by which you can rotate the hatch pattern with respect to the *X* axis of the current UCS. The angle value is stored in the **HPANG** system variable. The angle of hatch lines of a particular hatch pattern is governed by the values specified in the hatch definition. For example, in the **ANSI31** hatch pattern definition, the specified angle of hatch lines is 45-degree. If you select an angle of 0, the angle of hatch lines will be 45-degree. If you enter an angle of 45 degree, the angle of the hatch lines will be 90-degree.

Hatch Pattern Scale

The **Hatch Pattern Scale** edit box is used to set the scale factors by which you can expand or contract the selected hatch pattern. You can enter the scale factor of your choice in the edit box by double-clicking in it. The scale value is stored in the **HPSCALE** system variable. The value 1 does not mean that the distance between the hatch lines is 1 unit. The distance between the hatch lines and other parameters of a hatch pattern is governed by the values specified in the hatch definition. For example, in the **ANSI31** hatch pattern definition, the specified distance between the hatch lines is 0.125. If you select a scale factor of 1, the distance between the lines will be 0.125. If you enter a scale factor of 0.5, the distance between the hatch lines will be 0.5 X 0.125 = 0.0625.

Double

This option is available only for user-defined patterns. When you choose this option, AutoCAD doubles the original pattern by drawing a second set of lines at right angle to the original lines in the hatch pattern. For example, if you have a parallel set of lines as a user-defined pattern and if you select the **Double** option, the resulting pattern will have two sets of lines intersecting at 90-degree. You can notice the effect of selecting the **Double** option as various type of hatching in Figure 12-13. If the **Double** option is selected, the **HPDOUBLE** system variable is set to 1.

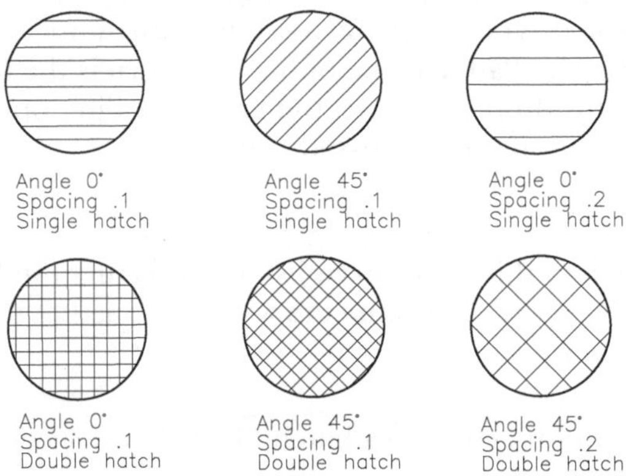

*Figure 12-13 Effect of selecting the **Double** option as various type of hatching*

Relative To Paper Space

This option is available only in a layout. If this option is selected, then AutoCAD will automatically scale the hatched pattern relative to the paper space units. This option can be used to display the hatch pattern at a scale that is appropriate for your layout.

ISO Pen Width

The **ISO Pen Width** drop-down list is available only for ISO hatch patterns. You can select the desired pen width value from the **ISO Pen Width** drop-down list. The value selected specifies the ISO-related pattern scaling.

Origin Panel

Hatch pattern alignment is an important feature of hatching, as on many occasions, you need to hatch adjacent areas with similar or sometimes identical hatch patterns while keeping the adjacent hatch patterns properly aligned. Proper alignment of hatch patterns is taken care of automatically by generating all lines of every hatch pattern from the same reference point. The reference point is normally at the origin point (0,0). Figure 12-14 shows two adjacent hatch areas. The area on the right is hatched using the pattern **ANSI32** at an angle of 0-degree and the area on the left is hatched using the same pattern at an angle of 90-degree. When you hatch these areas, the hatch lines may not be aligned, as shown in Figure 12-14(a). The options in the **Origin** panel allow you to specify the origin of hatch so that they get properly aligned, as shown in Figure 12-14(b). The options in this panel are discussed next.

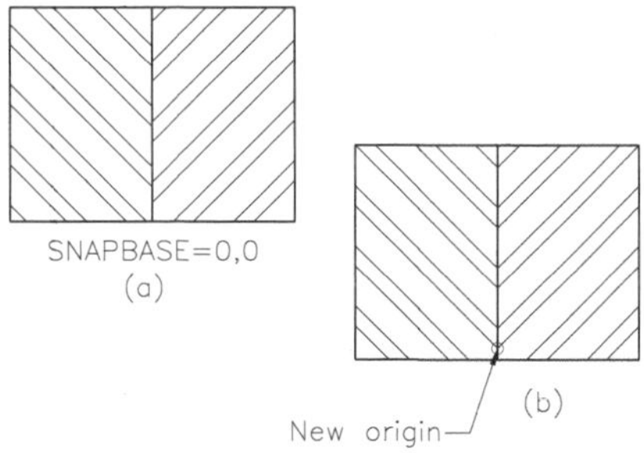

Figure 12-14 *Aligning hatch patterns using the* ***SNAPBASE*** *variable*

By default, the **Use Current Origin** button is chosen. This implies that the origin of the hatch pattern to be created is the origin of the current drawing. On choosing **Set Origin**, you need to specify the origin point for the hatch pattern in the drawing area.

You can also choose the other buttons to set the origin. For example, if you choose the **Bottom Left** button from this panel, the origin of the hatch pattern will be at the bottom left corner of the boundary. Choose the **Store as Default Origin** button to store the origin just selected as the default origin for all the hatch patterns to be created now onwards.

Note

The reference point for hatching can also be changed using the ***SNAPBASE*** *system variable.*

Options Panel

The options in this panel allow you to specify the draw order and some commonly used properties of the hatch pattern.

Associative

This button is chosen by default, therefore when you modify the boundary of a hatch object, the hatch patterns will be automatically updated to fill up the new area. But, if the hatch boundary is a region, you cannot edit the shape of the hatch boundary. One of the major advantages with the associative hatch feature is that you can edit the hatch pattern or edit the geometry that is hatched without having to modify the associated pattern or boundary separately. After editing, AutoCAD automatically regenerates the hatch and the hatch geometry to reflect the changes To edit the hatch boundary, select it and edit it by using grips.

Annotative

Choose this button to create an annotative hatch. An annotative hatch is defined relative to the paper space size. The scale of the annotative hatch objects changes in the viewport or layout according to the annotation scale assigned to the hatch objects and the annotation scale specified for that particular layout or viewport.

Gap Tolerance

The **Gap Tolerance** edit box is used to set the value up to which the open area will be considered closed when selected for hatching using the **Pick Points** method. The default value of the gap tolerance is 0. As a result, an open area will not be selected for hatching. You can set the value of the gap tolerance using the **Gap Tolerance** edit box. If the gap in the open area is less than the value specified in this edit box, the area will be considered closed and will be selected for hatching.

Create Separate Hatches

If you hatch multiple closed areas that are not nested, then on selecting this option, a separate hatch will be created for each closed area. As a result, you can edit the hatches separately. If this option is not selected, the hatch created in all the selected closed areas will be treated as a single entity.

Island Detection Style

The drop-down list below the **Create Separate Hatches** option is used to select the style of the island detection during hatching. There are four styles available in this drop-down list. The effect of using a particular style is displayed in the form of an illustration in the image tile placed before the name and is also shown in Figure 12-15. To set a particular style, select the corresponding option. The four styles available in this drop-down list are discussed next.

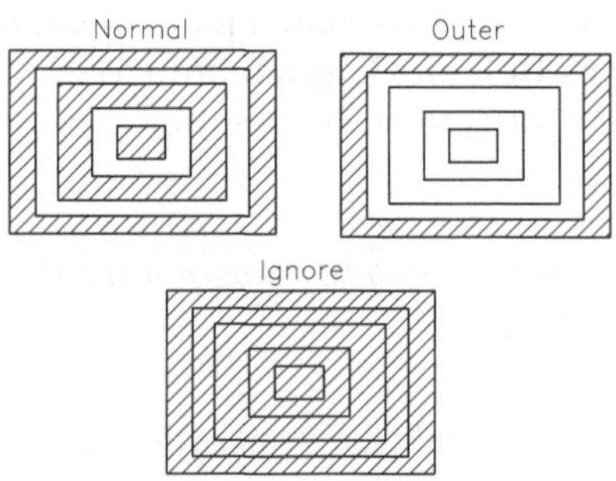

Figure 12-15 Using hatching styles

Note

The selection of an island detection style carries meaning only if the objects to be hatched are nested (that is, one or more selected boundaries are within another boundary).

Normal Island Detection: This style hatches inward starting at the outermost boundary. If it encounters an internal boundary, it turns off the hatching. An internal boundary causes the hatching to turn off until another boundary is encountered. In this manner, alternate areas of the selected object are hatched, starting with the outermost area. Thus, areas separated from the outside of the hatched area by an odd number of boundaries are hatched, while those separated by an even number of boundaries are not.

Outer Island Detection: This particular option also allows you hatch inward from an outermost boundary, but the hatching is turned off if an internal boundary is encountered. Unlike the previous case, it does not turn on the hatching again. The hatching process, in this case, starts from both ends of each hatch line; only the outermost level of the structure is hatched.

Ignore Island Detection: In this option, all areas bounded by the outermost boundary are hatched. The option ignores hatch boundaries that are within the outer boundary. All islands are completely ignored and everything within the selected boundary is hatched.

No Island Detection: In this option, even if the object is nested, the individual closed boundary is hatched separately.

Tip

*It is also possible to set the pattern and the island detection style at the same time by using the **HPNAME** system variable. AutoCAD stores the Normal style code by adding **N** to the pattern name. Similarly, **O** is added for the Outer style, and **I** for the Ignore style to the value of the **HPNAME** system variable. For example, if you want to apply the BOX pattern using the outer style of island detection, you should enter the **HPNAME** value to the **BOX, O**. Now, when you apply the hatch pattern, the BOX pattern is applied using the outer style of hatching.*

Match Properties

The **Match Properties** drop-down list is used to hatch the specified boundaries using the properties of an existing hatch. This drop-down list has two options. By default, the **Use current origin** option is selected. As a result, the current origin will be taken as the hatch origin. If you select the **Use source hatch origin** option, the hatch pattern will accept the origin of the source hatch as the origin of the current hatch pattern.

On selecting any one of the options, the following command sequence appears. Note that you must have applied hatch to an object before invoking this option.

Select hatch object: *Select the object from which you have to inherit the hatch pattern*
Pick internal point or [Select objects/Undo/seTtings]: *Pick a point inside the object to hatch.*
Pick internal point or [Select objects/Undo/seTtings]: Enter *(The selected pattern now becomes the current hatch pattern. If you then want to adjust the hatch properties, such as the angle or scale of the pattern, you can do so.)*

Specifying the Draw Order

The drop-down list below the **Island Detection** drop-down list in the expanded **Options** panel is used to assign a draw order to the hatch. If you want to send the hatch behind all the entities, select the **Send to Back** option. Similarly, if you want to place the hatch in front of all the entities, select the **Bring to Front** option. If you want to place the hatch behind the hatch boundary, select **Send Behind Boundary**. Similarly, if you want to place the hatch in front of the boundary, select **Bring in Front of Boundary**. You can also select the **Do Not Assign** option, if you do not want to assign the draw order to the hatch.

Hatch Settings

You can also set the parameters discussed above using the **Hatch and Gradient** dialog box, as shown in Figure 12-16. To invoke this dialog box, choose the inclined arrow in the **Options** panel of the **Hatch Creation** tab or after choosing the **Hatch** tool from the **Draw** panel of the **Home** tab, type **T** and press ENTER when you are prompted to pick internal point. The default appearance of the **Hatch and Gradient** dialog box is slightly different from the one shown in Figure 12-16. This is because options like **Islands** and **Boundary retention** are not visible by default. To make such options visible, choose the **More Options** button available at the lower right corner of the **Hatch and Gradient** dialog box.

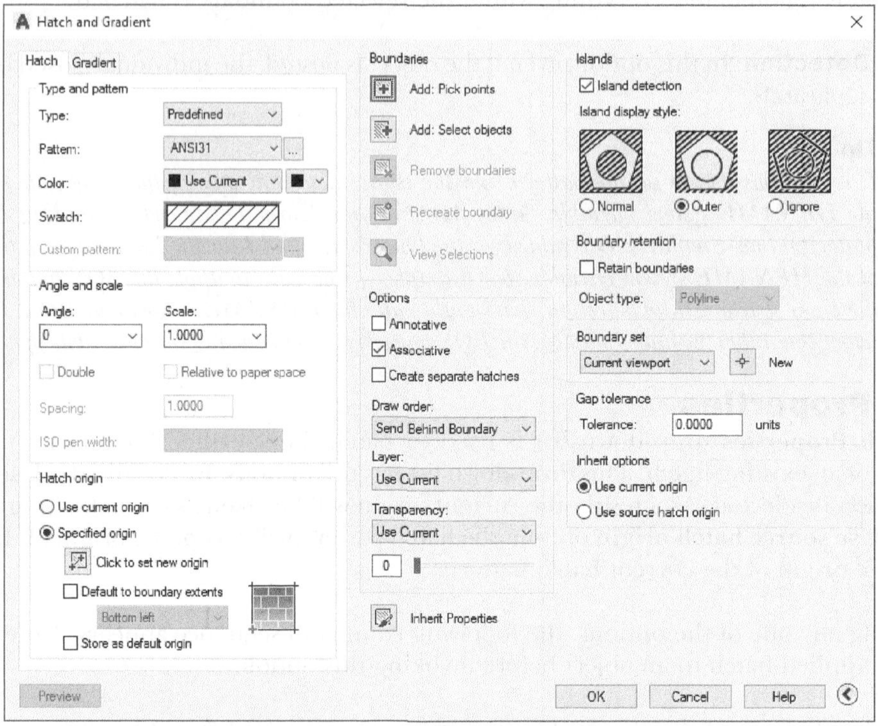

*Figure 12-16 The **Hatch and Gradient** dialog box*

Close

Choose the **Close Hatch Creation** button to close the **Hatch Creation** tab. You can also click once in the drawing area after completing the hatching process to exit the **Hatch Creation** tab.

Exercise 1 — Hatch Scale & Hatch Angle

In this exercise, you will hatch the given drawing using the hatch pattern named **STEEL**. Set the scale and the angle to match the drawing shown in Figure 12-17.

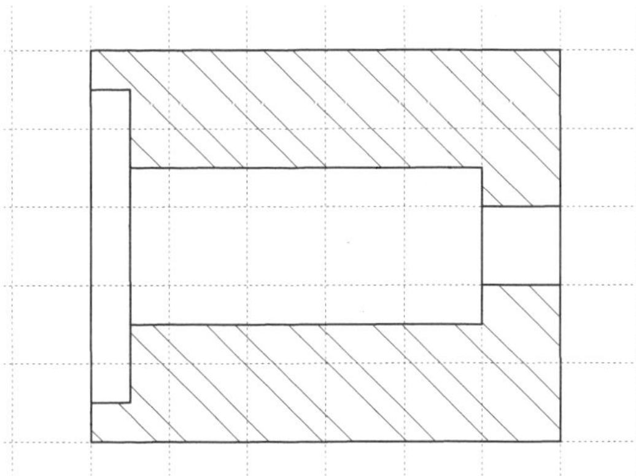

Figure 12-17 *Drawing for Exercise 1*

Exercise 2 Hatch Pattern

In this exercise, you will hatch the front section view of the drawing shown in Figure 12-18 using the hatch pattern for brass. Two views, top and front are shown. In the top view, the cutting plane indicates how the section is cut and the front view shows the full section view of the object. The section lines must be drawn only where the material is actually cut.

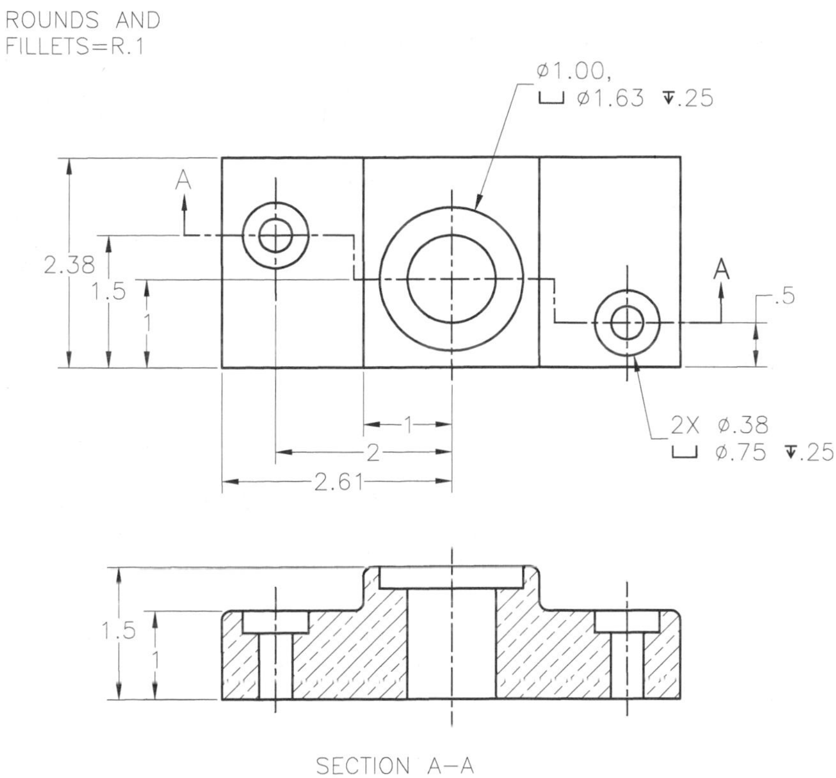

Figure 12-18 *Drawing for Exercise 2*

Exercise 3 — Align Hatch

In this exercise, you will hatch the given drawing using the hatch pattern **ANSI31**. Align the hatch lines as shown in the Figure 12-19.

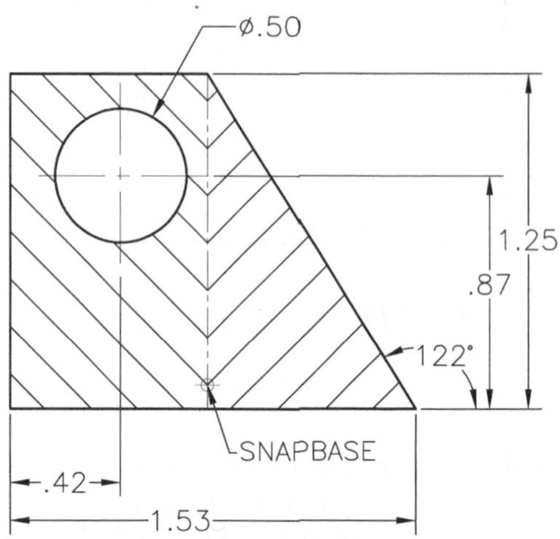

Figure 12-19 Drawing for Exercise 3

Setting the Parameters for Gradient Pattern

During the hatching, you can select the **Gradient** option in the **Hatch Type** drop-down list to fill the boundary in a set pattern of colors. On selecting the **Gradient** option from the **Hatch Type** drop-down list, nine fixed patterns will be listed in the **Pattern** panel and their corresponding option will be displayed in the **Hatch Creation** tab, as shown in Figure 12-20. You can select the required gradient or specify the gradient pattern by entering its value in the **GFNAME** system variable. The default value of this variable is 1. As a result, the first gradient pattern is selected.

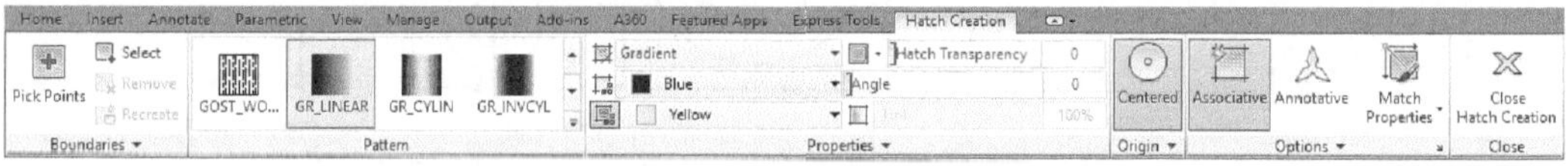

***Figure 12-20** The **Hatch Creation** tab with the options for the **Gradient** pattern*

You can set two colors for the gradient from the **Gradient Color 1** and **Gradient Color 2** drop-down lists available in the **Properties** panel of the **Hatch Creation** tab. By default, you can not set color tint for the gradient. If you need to set color tint then choose the **Gradient Colors** button available on the left of the **Gradient Color 2** drop-down list. On doing so, the **Gradient Color 2** drop-down list will be disabled. Now, you can set the color tint by using the **Gradient Tint and Shade** slider. You can set the angle of the color by using the **Gradient Angle** sliders.

The **Gradient Angle** slider displays the angles that you can rotate the gradient fill with respect to the *X* axis of the current UCS. You can select any angle from this slider or you can also double-click and enter an angle of your choice in the edit box. The angle value is stored in the **GFANG** system variable.

The symmetric condition of the gradient is set by choosing the **Centered** button in the **Origin** panel. If this button is not chosen, then the gradient fill will move up to the left direction.

The other options are same as discussed earlier.

Tip
*To snap the hatch objects, set the **OSOPTIONS** system variable to **1**. You can also invoke the **Options** dialog box and choose the **Drafting** tab. Then, clear the **Ignore hatch objects** check box from the **Object Snap Options** area.*

CREATING ANNOTATIVE HATCH

You can create annotative hatch having similar annotative properties like text and dimensions. The annotative hatch are defined relative to the viewport scaling, you only have to specify the hatch scale according to its display on the sheet. The display size of the hatch in the model space will be controlled by the current annotation scale multiplied by the paper space height. You can also control the annotative properties of the hatch pattern as discussed in Chapter 7.

To create an annotative hatch, choose the **Hatch** tool from the **Draw** panel; the **Hatch Creation** tab will be displayed. Choose the **Select** tool from the **Boundaries** panel, select the objects that you want to hatch, and enter **T** (for setting); the **Hatch and Gradient** dialog box will be displayed. In the **Options** area of this dialog box, select the **Annotative** check box and choose the **OK** button. You can also convert the existing non-annotative hatch into the annotative hatch. To do so, select the non-annotative hatch in the drawing and select **Yes** from the **Annotative** drop-down list in the **Pattern** list of the **PROPERTIES** palette or just select the **Annotative** option from the **Options** panel of the **Hatch Creation** tab.

Note
*While creating the annotative hatch, pattern will only be displayed in the drawing area for the annotative scale that is set current. To display that hatch pattern at any other annotative scale, you have to add that scale to the selected hatch using the **OBJECTSCALE** command.*

HATCHING THE DRAWING USING THE TOOL PALETTES

Ribbon: View > Palettes > Tool Palettes **Command:** TOOLPALETTES
Toolbar: Standard Annotation > Tool Palettes Window
Menu Bar: Tools > Palettes > Tool Palettes

You can use the **Tool Palettes** shown in Figure 12-21 to insert predefined hatch patterns and blocks in the drawings. A number of tabs such as **Command Tool Samples, Hatches and Fills**, **Civil, Structural, Electrical**, and so on are available in this palette. In this chapter, you will learn to insert **Imperial Hatches**, **ISO Hatches** and **Gradient Samples** in the **Hatches and Fills** tab of the **Tool Palettes** palette. The **Imperial Hatches** list provides the options to insert the hatch patterns that are created using the Imperial units. The **ISO Hatches** list provides the options to insert the hatch patterns that are created using the Metric units. You will notice that the hatch patterns provided in both these lists are similar. The basic difference between the two lists is their scale factor. The **Gradient Samples** list provides option to add color gradients to objects as hatch.

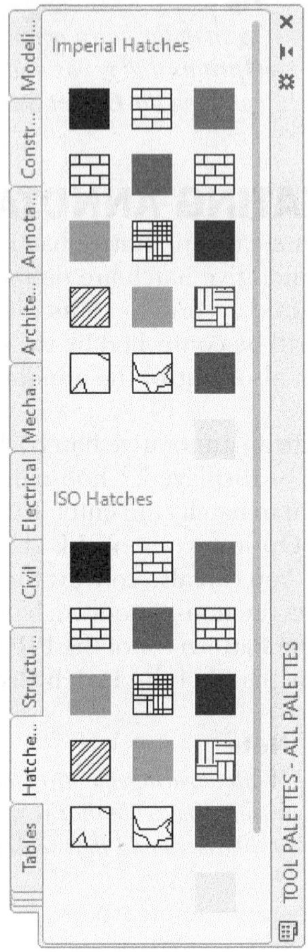

Figure 12-21 The ***Hatches and Fills*** *tab of the* ***TOOL PALETTES*** *window*

Tip
*The **Tool Palettes** can be turned on and off by pressing the CTRL+3 keys.*

AutoCAD provides two methods to insert the predefined hatch patterns from the **Tool Palettes**: **Drag and Drop** method and **Select and Place** method. Both these methods are discussed next.

Drag and Drop Method

To insert the predefined hatch pattern from the **TOOL PALETTES** using this method, move the cursor over the desired predefined pattern in the **TOOL PALETTES**. As you move the cursor over the hatch pattern, you will notice that a tool tip with the name of the hatch pattern is displayed. Press and hold the left mouse button and drag the cursor within the area to be hatched. Release the left mouse button, and you will notice that the selected predefined hatch pattern is added to the drawing.

Select and Place Method

You can also add the predefined hatch patterns to the drawings using this method. To add the hatch pattern, move the cursor over the desired pattern in the **TOOL PALETTES** and click the left mouse button; the selected hatch pattern will be attached to the cursor and you will be prompted to specify the insertion point of the hatch pattern. Now, move the cursor within the area to be hatched and click the left mouse button; the selected hatch pattern will be inserted at the specified location.

Modifying the Properties of the Predefined Patterns available in Tool Palettes

To modify the properties of the predefined hatch patterns, move the cursor over the hatch pattern in the **TOOL PALETTES** and right-click on it to display the shortcut menu. Using the options available in this shortcut menu, you can **Cut** or **Copy** the desired hatch pattern available in one tab of **TOOL PALETTES** and paste it on the other tab. You can also delete and rename a selected hatch pattern using the **Delete** and **Rename** options, respectively. To update and change the image displayed on the selected hatch pattern, choose the **Update tool image** or **Specify image** option. To modify the properties of the selected hatch pattern, choose **Properties** from the shortcut menu, as shown in Figure 12-22; the **Tool Properties** dialog box will be displayed, as shown in Figure 12-23.

*Figure 12-22 Choosing **Properties** from the shortcut menu*

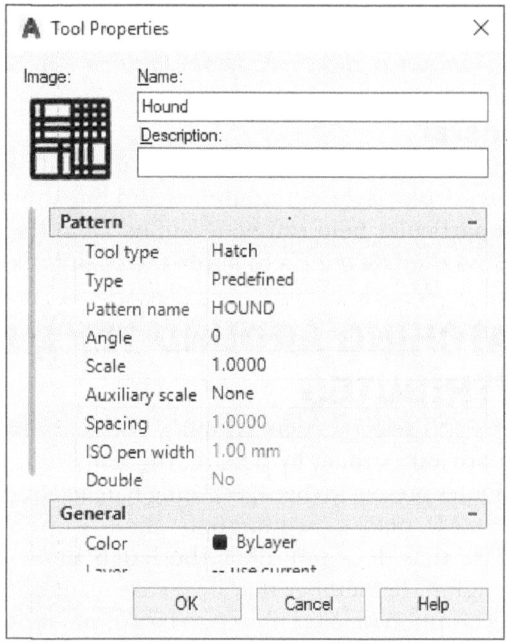

*Figure 12-23 The **Tool Properties** dialog box*

In the **Tool Properties** dialog box, the name of the selected hatch pattern is displayed in the **Name** edit box. You can also rename the hatch pattern by entering a new name in the **Name** edit box. The **Image** area available on the left of the **Name** edit box displays the image of the selected hatch pattern. You can change the displayed image by choosing the **Specify image** option from the shortcut menu that will be displayed when you right-click on the image. If you enter a description of the hatch pattern in the **Description** text box, it is stored with the hatch definition in the **TOOL PALETTES**. Now, when you move the cursor over the hatch pattern in **TOOL PALETTES** and pause for a second, the description of the hatch pattern appears along with its name in the tooltip. The **Tool Properties** dialog box displays the properties of the selected hatch pattern under the following categories.

Pattern

In this category, you can change the tool type, pattern type, pattern name, angle, and scale of the selected pattern. You can modify the spacing of the **User defined** patterns in the **Spacing** text box. Also, the ISO pen width of the ISO patterns can be redefined in the **ISO pen width** text box. The **Double** drop-down list is available only for the **User-defined** hatch patterns. You can select **Yes** or **No** from the **Double** drop-down list to determine the hatch pattern to be doubled at right angles to the original pattern or not. When you choose the button in the **Type** property field, AutoCAD displays the **Hatch Pattern Type** dialog box. You can select the type of hatch pattern from the **Pattern Type** drop-down list. If the **Predefined** pattern type is selected, you can specify the pattern name by either selecting it from the Pattern drop-down list or from the **Hatch Pattern Palette** dialog box displayed on choosing the **Pattern** button. Similarly, if you select the **Custom** pattern type, you can enter the name of the custom pattern in the **Custom Pattern** edit box. If you select the **User defined** pattern type, both the Pattern drop-down list and the **Custom Pattern** edit box are not available.

General

In this category, you can specify the general properties of the hatch pattern such as color, layer, linetype, plot style, transparency, and line weight for the selected hatch pattern. The properties of a particular field can be modified from the drop-down list available on selecting that field. Choose the **OK** button to apply the changes and close the dialog box.

HATCHING AROUND TEXT, DIMENSIONS, AND ATTRIBUTES

When you select a point within a boundary to be hatched and if it contains text, dimensions, and attributes then, by default, the hatch lines do not pass through the text, dimensions, and attributes present in the object being hatched by default. AutoCAD places an imaginary box around these objects that does not allow the hatch lines to pass through it. Remember that if you are using the select objects option to select objects to hatch, you must select the text/attribute/shape along with the object in which it is placed when defining the hatch boundary. If multiple line text is to be written, the **Multiline Text** tool is used. You can also select both the boundary and the text when using the window selection method. Figure 12-24 shows you how hatching takes place around multiline text, attributes, and dimensions.

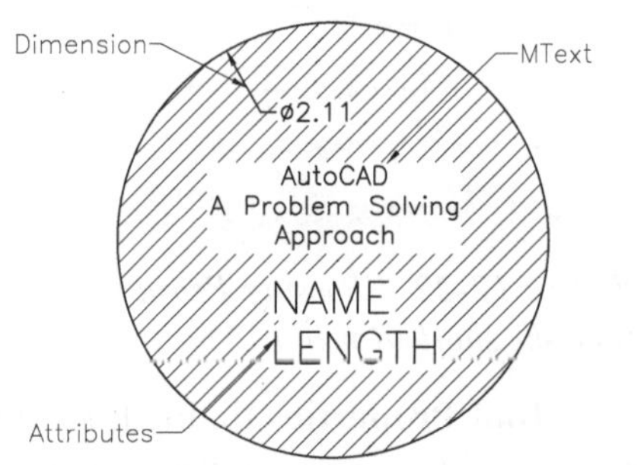

***Figure 12-24** Hatching around dimensions, multiline text, and attributes*

EDITING HATCH PATTERNS

Using the Hatch Editor Tab

On selecting a hatch pattern, the **Hatch Editor** tab will be displayed in the **Ribbon**, as shown in Figure 12-25. The panels and their options in this tab are similar to that of the **Hatch Creation** tab. Change the parameters of the hatch pattern in the corresponding panels; the hatch pattern will be modified instantaneously. Press ESC to exit the **Hatch Editor** tab.

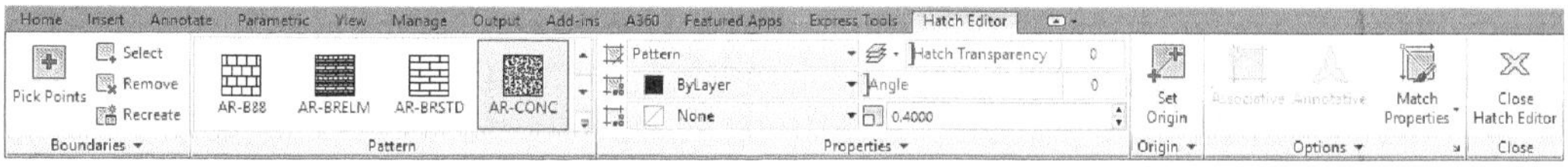

*Figure 12-25 The **Hatch Editor** tab with the options for the hatch pattern*

Using the Edit Hatch Tool

Ribbon: Home > Modify > Edit Hatch **Toolbar:** Modify II > Edit Hatch
Tool Palette: Modify (Customize to Add) > Edit Hatch **Command:** HATCHEDIT/HE

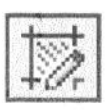

The **Edit Hatch** tool is used to edit a hatch pattern. When you invoke this tool and select the hatch for editing, the **Hatch Edit** dialog box will be displayed, as shown in Figure 12-26.

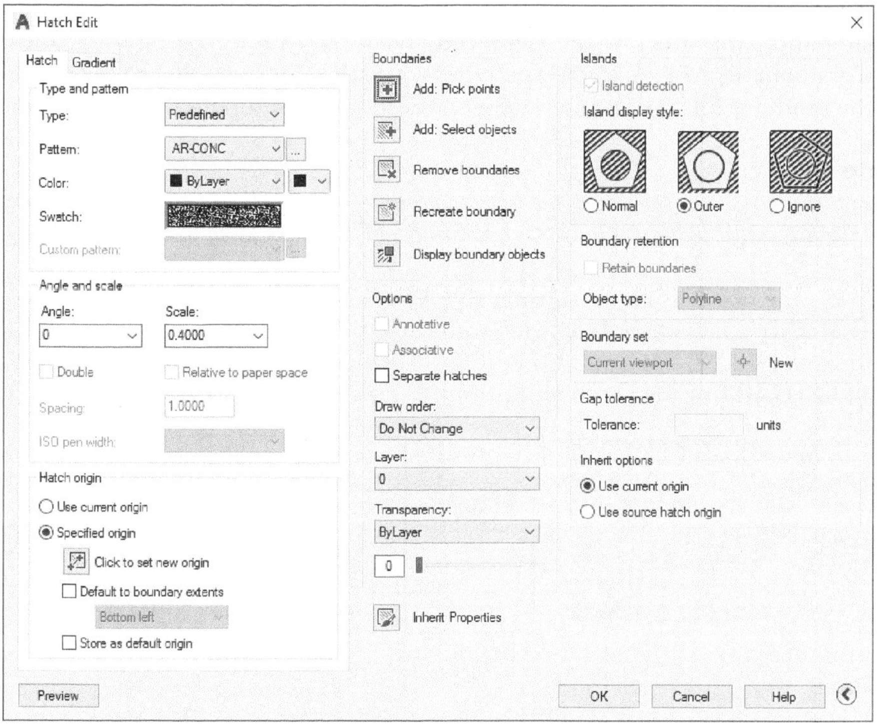

*Figure 12-26 The **Hatch** tab of the **Hatch Edit** dialog box*

The **Hatch Edit** dialog box is used to change or modify a hatch pattern. This dialog box is the same as the **Hatch and Gradient** dialog box, except that only the options that control the hatch pattern are available. The available options work in the same way as they do in the **Hatch and Gradient** dialog box.

The **Hatch Edit** dialog box has two tabs. They are **Hatch** and **Gradient**. In the **Hatch** tab, you can redefine the type of hatch pattern by selecting another type from the **Type** drop-down list. If you are using the **Predefined** pattern, you can select a new hatch pattern name from the **Pattern** drop-down list. You can also change the scale or angle by entering new values in the **Scale** or **Angle** edit box from the **Angle and scale** area. While using the **User defined** pattern, you can redefine the spacing between the lines in the hatch pattern by entering a new value in the

Spacing edit box. If you are using the **Custom** pattern type, you can select another pattern from the **Custom pattern** drop-down list. You can also redefine the island detection style by selecting either of the **Normal**, **Outer**, or **Ignore** styles from the **Islands** area of the dialog box. You can also convert a non-annotative hatch into an annotative hatch and vice-versa. If you want to copy the properties from an existing hatch pattern, choose the **Inherit Properties** button, and then select the hatch whose properties you want to be inherited. You can also change the draw order of the hatch pattern using the options available in the **Draw order** area. If the **Associative** radio button in the **Options** area of the dialog box is selected, the pattern is associative. This implies that whenever you modify the hatch boundary, the hatch pattern is automatically updated. The appearance of the gradient fill can be specified using the **Gradient** tab of the dialog box. You can specify the gradient fill comprising different shades and tints of a single color or double colors by selecting the **One color** and **Two color** radio buttons, respectively. You can also specify the color of the gradient fill or the shade and tint of a single color using the color swatch and the **Shade and Tint** Slider. If the **Centered** check box is selected, AutoCAD will apply a symmetrical gradient fill. Also, AutoCAD provides you with an option to select the desired display pattern of the gradient fill by selecting any one of the nine fixed patterns for the gradient fill.

Note

If a hatch pattern is associative, the hatch boundary can be edited using grips and editing tools and the associated pattern is modified accordingly. This is discussed later.

In Figure 12-27, the object is hatched using the **ANSI31** hatch pattern. Using the **Edit Hatch** tool from the **Modify** panel of the **Home** tab, you can edit the hatch using the **Hatch Edit** dialog box, refer to Figure 12-28. You can also edit an existing hatch through the command line by entering **-HATCHEDIT** at the command prompt.

***Figure 12-27** ANSI31 hatch pattern*

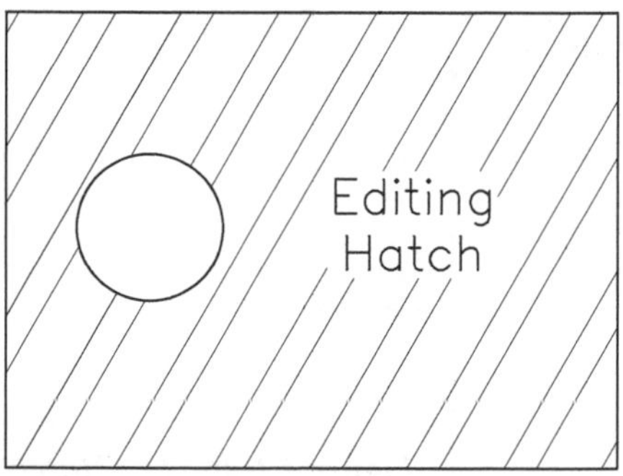

***Figure 12-28** The modified hatch pattern using the **Edit Hatch** tool*

Using the Properties Tool

Ribbon: View > Palettes > Properties **Command:** PROPERTIES/PR/CH/MO
Menu Bar: Modify > Properties
Quick Access Toolbar: Properties (*Customize to Add*)

You can use the **Properties** tool to edit a hatch pattern. When you select a hatch pattern for editing, and invoke the **Properties** tool, AutoCAD displays the **PROPERTIES** palette for the hatch, refer to Figure 12-29. You can also invoke the **PROPERTIES** palette by selecting and right-clicking the hatch pattern and choosing the **Properties** option from the shortcut menu displayed. This palette displays the properties of the selected pattern under the following categories.

General

In this category, you can change the general pattern properties like color, layer, linetype, linetype scale, lineweight, and so on. When you click on the field corresponding to a particular property, a drop-down list is displayed from where you can select an option or value. Whenever a drop-down list does not get displayed, you can enter a value in the field.

Pattern

In this category, you can change the pattern type, pattern name, annotative property, annotation scale (will be displayed when you choose **Yes** for annotative property), angle, scale, spacing, associativity, and island detection style properties of the pattern. In the case of ISO patterns, you can redefine the ISO pen width of the pattern modify the spacing of the **User defined** patterns. You can also determine whether you want to have a **User defined** pattern as double or not. When you choose the button in the **Type** property field, AutoCAD displays the **Hatch Pattern Type** dialog box, as shown in Figure 12-30. Here, you can select the type of hatch pattern from the **Pattern Type** drop-down list. If you have selected a **Predefined** pattern type, you can select a pattern name from the Pattern drop-down list or choose the **Pattern** button to display the **Hatch Pattern Palette** dialog box. You can then select a pattern here in one of the tabs and then choose the **OK** button to exit the dialog box. Now, choose the **OK** button from the **Hatch Pattern Type** dialog box to return to the **PROPERTIES** palette. You will notice that the pattern name you have selected is displayed in the **Pattern name** field.

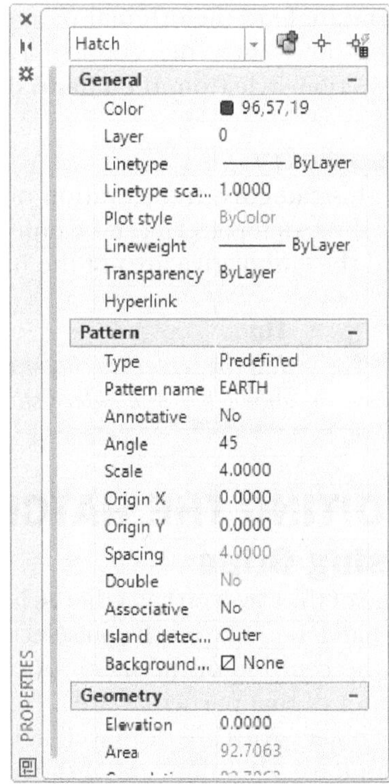

*Figure 12-29 The **PROPERTIES** palette (Hatch)*

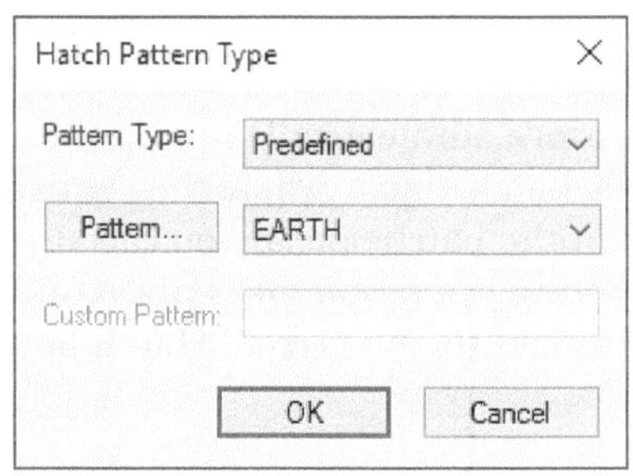

*Figure 12-30 The **Hatch Pattern Type** dialog box*

Similarly, if you select the **Custom** pattern type, you can enter the name of the custom pattern in the **Custom Pattern** edit box. If you select a **User defined** pattern type, both the **Pattern Type** drop-down list and the **Custom Pattern** edit box will not be available. When you click in the **Pattern name** property field, the button is displayed. When you choose the button, the **Hatch Pattern Palette** dialog box is displayed. Select the **Yes** or **No** option from the **Annotative** drop-down list to convert the existing hatch into annotative or non-annotative respectively. When you click on the **Annotation scale** property field, the button will be displayed. On choosing the button, the **Annotation Object Scale** dialog box will be invoked. You can add other annotation scales to the selected hatch with the help of this dialog box. The values of the angle, scale, and spacing properties can be entered in the corresponding fields. A value for the ISO pen width can be selected from the **ISO pen width** edit box. For the user-defined hatch patterns, you can select **Yes** or **No** from the **Double** drop-down list to specify if you want the hatch pattern to double at right angle to the original pattern or not. You can also select **Yes** or **No** from the **Associative** drop-down list to determine if a pattern is associative or not. Similarly, you can select an island detection style from the **Island detection style** drop-down list.

Geometry

In this category, the elevation of the hatch pattern can be changed. A new value of elevation for the hatch pattern can be entered in the **Elevation** field. This category also displays the area and the cumulative area of the hatch.

> **Tip**
> *It is convenient to choose the button in the **Type** edit box to display the **Hatch Pattern Type** dialog box and enter both the type and name of the pattern at the same time.*

EDITING THE HATCH BOUNDARY

Using Grips

One of the ways you can edit the hatch boundary is by using grips. You can select the hatch pattern or hatch boundaries. If you select the hatch pattern, the hatch highlights and a grip is displayed at the centroid of the hatch. A centroid for a region that is coplanar with the *XY* plane is the center of that particular area. However, if you select an object that defines the hatch boundary, the object grips are displayed at the defining points of the selected object. Once you change the boundary definition, and if the hatch pattern is associative, AutoCAD will re-evaluate the hatch boundary and then hatch the new area. When you edit the hatch boundary, make sure that there are no open spaces in it. AutoCAD will not create a hatch if the outer boundary is not closed. Figure 12-31 shows the result of moving the circle and text, and shortening the bottom edge of the hatch boundary of the object shown in Figure 12-28. The objects were edited by using grips and since the pattern is associative, when modifications are made to the boundary object, the pattern automatically fills up the new area. If you select the hatch pattern, AutoCAD will display the hatch object grip at the centroid of the hatch. You can select the grip to make it hot and then edit the hatch object. You can stretch, move, scale, mirror, or rotate the hatch pattern. Once an editing operation takes place on the hatch pattern then, the associativity is lost and AutoCAD displays the message: "**Hatch boundary associativity removed**" in the prompt window.

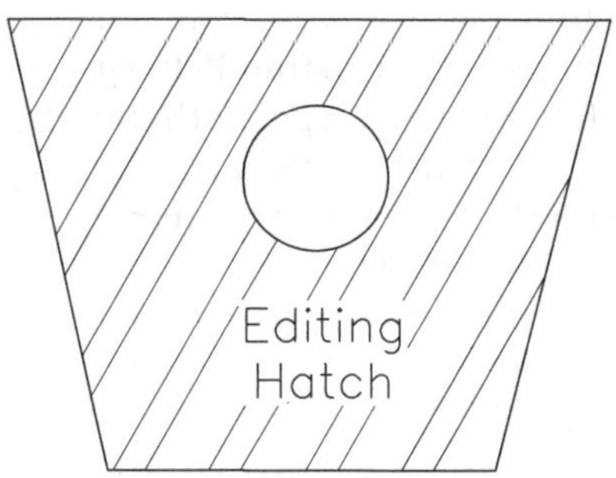

Figure 12-31 *The result of using grips to edit the hatch boundary of the object shown in Figure 12-28*

While creating the hatch, the **Don't Retain Boundaries** option is selected in the **Retain Boundary Objects** drop-down list of the **Hatch Creation** panel. Therefore, all objects selected or found by the selection or point selection processes during hatch creation are associated with the hatch as boundary objects. And, editing any of them may affect the hatch. If, however, the **Retain Boundaries - Polyline** or the **Retain Boundaries-Region** check boxes was selected when the hatch was created, only the retained polyline boundary created by **HATCH** is associated with the hatch as its boundary object. Editing it will affect the hatch, and editing the objects selected or found by selection or point selection processes during the hatch created will have no effect on the hatch. You can, of course, select and simultaneously edit the objects selected or found by the selection or point selection processes, as well as the retained polyline boundary created by the **Hatch** tool.

Trimming the Hatch Patterns

You can trim the hatch patterns by using a cutting edge. For example, Figure 12-32 shows a drawing before trimming the hatch. In this drawing, the outer loop was selected as the object to be hatched. This is the reason the space between the two vertical lines on the right is also hatched. Figure 12-33 shows the same drawing after trimming the hatch using the vertical lines as the cutting edge. You will notice that even after trimming some of the portions of the hatch, it remains a single entity.

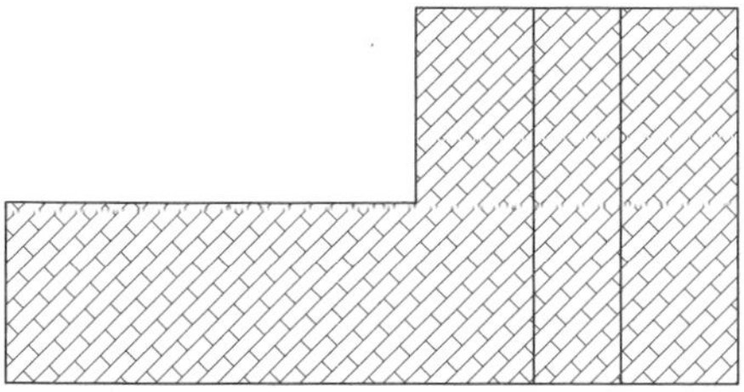

Figure 12-32 *Before trimming the hatch*

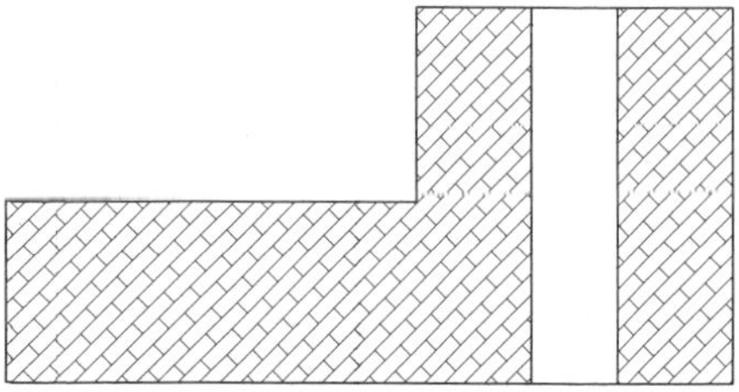

Figure 12-33 *After trimming the hatch by using the vertical lines as the cutting edge*

Example 2 Hatch

In this example, you will hatch the drawing, as shown in the Figure 12-34, using various hatch patterns.

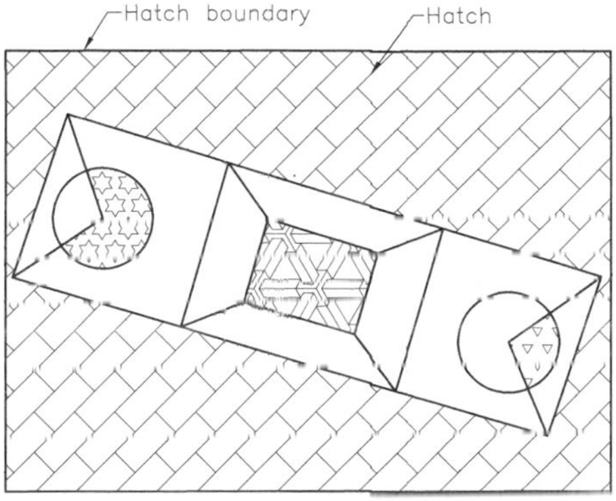

Figure 12-34 *Example 2 for Hatching*

1. Make a drawing, refer to Figure 12-34.

2. Choose the **Hatch** tool from the **Draw** panel in the **Home** tab; the **Hatch Creation** tab is displayed.

3. Select the **AR-BRSTD** pattern from the **Pattern** panel and click inside the outer rectangle's boundary to select the internal pick point.

4. Next, you need to change the angle of the hatch pattern to 45°. To do so, drag the **Angle** slider in the **Properties** panel. Also, adjust the **Hatch Pattern Scale** using the **Hatch Pattern Scale** spinner.

5. Select the **Outer Island Detection** option from the **Island Detection** drop-down list in the **Options** panel, if it is not selected by default.

6. Exit the **Hatch Creation** tab by pressing ENTER.

7. Again, choose the **Hatch** tool and select the **STARS** pattern from the **Pattern** panel; you are prompted to pick an internal point in the object. Select a point in the right section of the left circle, refer to Figure 12-34; preview of the pattern is displayed. You have to specify the values of the **Hatch Angle** and **Hatch Pattern Scale** options. After making the required changes, exit the **Hatch Creation** tab.

8. Choose the **Hatch** tool and select the **ESCHER** pattern from the **Pattern** panel; you are prompted to pick an internal point in the object. Select a point in the innermost rectangle in the middle, refer to Figure 12-34; a preview will be displayed. Adjust the scale of the hatch pattern, if required and then exit.

9. Invoke the **Hatch** tool once again and select **TRIANG** from the **Pattern** panel; you are prompted to pick an internal point in the object. Select a point in the right section of the right circle, refer to Figure 12-34; preview of the pattern is displayed. Set the desired values for **Hatch Angle** and **Hatch Pattern Scale** and then exit.

Example 3 — *Hatch*

In this example, you will hatch the drawing as shown in Figure 12-35. But, the hatching should be in two entities.

To create this kind of hatching, you have to follow the steps given below:

1. Make a drawing, refer to Figure 12-35.

2. Choose the **Hatch** tool from the **Draw** panel in the **Home** tab; the **Hatch Creation** tab is displayed. Make sure that the entities having different hatch patterns are drawn as different entities.

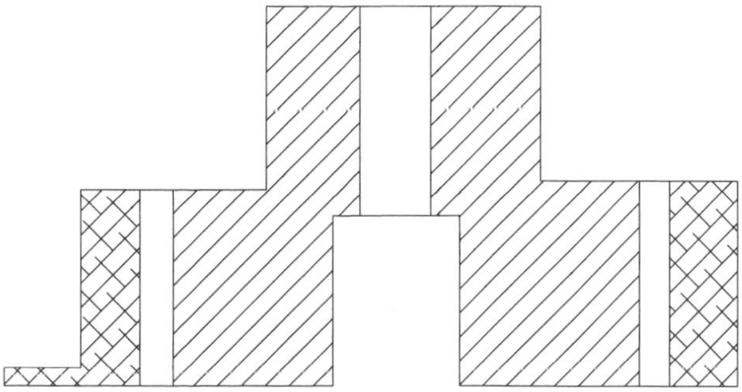

Figure 12-35 Example 3 for hatching

3. Select **ANSI38** from the **Pattern** panel; you will be prompted to pick an internal point. Select any internal point of the two outermost entities. Set the scale of the pattern, if required.

4. Press SPACEBAR to exit the tool.

5. Choose the **Hatch** tool and select the **ANSI31** pattern from the **Pattern** panel; you will be prompted to pick an internal point in the object.

6. Select the internal points of the remaining two entities; a preview is displayed. Set the scale of pattern, if required. After making the required adjustments, exit the tool by choosing the **Close Hatch Creation** button in the **Close** panel.

Using AutoCAD Editing Tools

When you use the editing tools such as **Move**, **Rotate**, **Scale**, and **Stretch**, associativity is maintained, provided all objects that define the selected boundary are selected for editing. If any of the boundary-defining objects is missing, the associativity will be lost and AutoCAD will display the message **Hatch boundary associativity removed**. When you rotate or scale an associative hatch, the new rotation angle and the scale factor are saved with the hatch object data. This data is then used to update the hatch. When using the **Array**, **Copy**, and **Mirror** tools, you can array, copy, or mirror just the hatch boundary, without the hatch pattern. Similarly, you can erase just the hatch boundary using the **Erase** tool and associativity is removed. If you explode an associative hatch pattern, the associativity between the hatch pattern and the defining boundary is removed. Also, when the hatch object is exploded, each line in the hatch pattern becomes a separate object.

When the original boundary objects are being edited, the associated hatch gets updated, but the new boundary objects do not have any effect. For example, when you have a square island within a circular boundary and then you erase the square, the hatch pattern is updated to fill up the entire circle. But, once the island is removed, another island cannot be added, since it was not calculated as a part of the original set of boundary objects.

HATCHING BLOCKS AND XREF DRAWINGS

When you apply hatching to inserted blocks and xref drawings, their internal structure is treated as if the block or xref drawing were composed of independent objects. This means that if you have inserted a block that consists of a circle within a rectangle and you want the internal circle to be hatched, you need to invoke the **Hatch** tool and then specify a point within the circle to generate the hatch, refer to Figure 12-36. However, if you choose the **Select** option from the **Boundaries** panel of the **Hatch Creation** tab, you will be prompted to select an object. Select an object; the entire block will be selected and a hatch will be created, as shown in Figure 12-36.

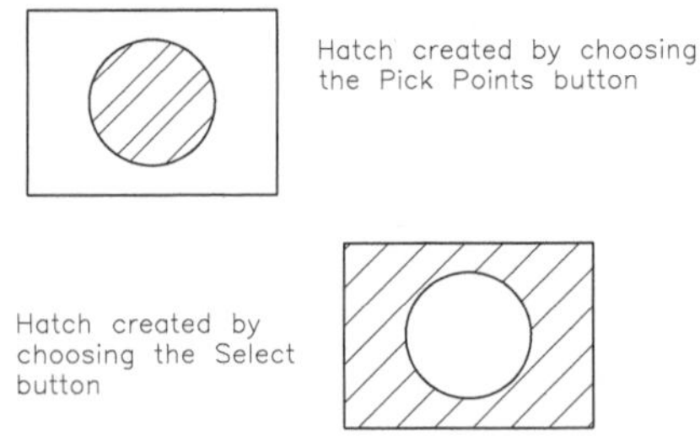

Figure 12-36 Hatching inserted blocks

When you xref a drawing, you can hatch any part of the drawing that is visible. Also, if you hatch an xref drawing and then use the **XCLIP** command to clip it, the hatch pattern is not clipped, although the hatch boundary associativity is removed. Similarly, when you detach the xref drawing, the hatch pattern and its boundaries are not detached, although the hatch boundary associativity is removed.

CREATING A BOUNDARY USING CLOSED LOOPS

Ribbon: Home > Draw > Hatch drop-down > Boundary
Menu Bar: Draw > Boundary **Command:** BOUNDARY/BO

The **Boundary** tool is used to create a polyline or region around a selected point within a closed area, in a manner similar to the one used for defining a hatch boundary. When this tool is invoked, AutoCAD displays the **Boundary Creation** dialog box, as shown in Figure 12-37.

The options in the **Boundary Creation** dialog box are similar to those in the **Boundaries** panel of the **Hatch Creation** tab discussed earlier. Although, only the options related to boundary selections are available, the **Pick Points** button in the **Boundary Creation** dialog box is used to create a boundary by selecting a point inside the object, whose boundary you want to create.

When you choose the **Pick Points** button, the dialog box disappears temporarily and you are prompted to select the internal point. Select a point that lies within the boundary of the object. Once you select an internal point, a polyline or a region will be formed around the boundary, refer to Figure 12-38. To end this process, press ENTER or right-click at the **Pick internal point** prompt. Whether the boundary created is a polyline or a region is determined by the option you have selected from the **Object type** drop-down list in the **Boundary retention** area. **Polyline** is the default option. You can edit the boundary that has been created with the editing tools. The boundary is selected by using the **Last** object selection option.

Similar to the **Hatch** tool, you can also define a boundary set here by choosing the **New** button in the **Boundary set** area of the dialog box. The dialog box will temporarily close to allow you to select objects to be used to create a boundary. The default boundary set is current viewport, which means everything visible in the current viewport consists of the boundary set. As discussed earlier, the boundary set option is especially useful when you are working with large and complex drawings, where examining everything on the screen becomes a time-consuming process.

The **Boundary Creation** dialog box also provides you the option of determining the island detection method. The **Island detection** check box is available below the **Pick Points** button and it is selected by default. As a result, the Island detection method is Flood type and islands are included as boundary objects. If you clear this check box, the Ray casting method of island detection is enabled, where rays shall be cast from the selected internal point in all directions (by default, using the dialog box). The nearest closed object it encounters is used for boundary creation. If the selected point does not lie within the encountered boundary, a **Boundary Definition Error** dialog box is displayed and you have to select another internal point.

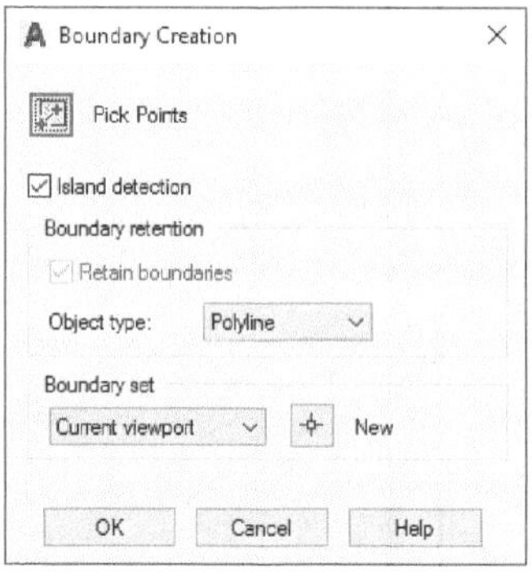

***Figure 12-37** The **Boundary Creation** dialog box*

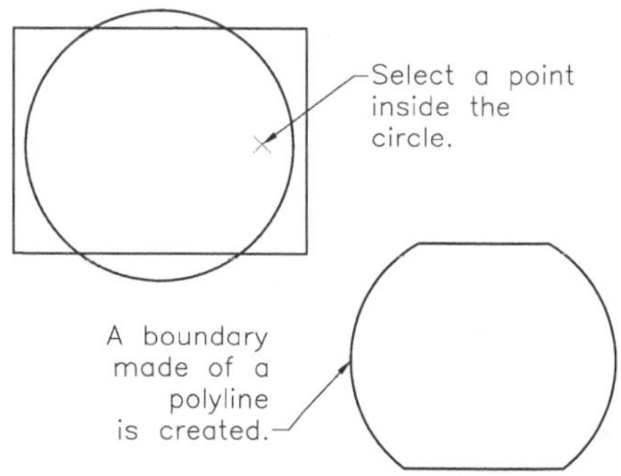

***Figure 12-38** Using the **Boundary** tool to create a polyline boundary*

Note

*The **HPBOUND** system variable controls the type of boundary object created using the **Boundary** tool. If its value is 1, the object created is a polyline, and if its value is 0, the object created is a region.*

OTHER FEATURES OF HATCHING

1. In AutoCAD, the hatch patterns are separate objects. The objects store the information about the hatch pattern boundary with reference to the geometry that defines the pattern for each hatch object.

2. When you save a drawing, the hatch patterns are stored with the drawing. Therefore, the hatch patterns can be updated even if the hatch pattern file that contains the definitions of hatch patterns is not available.

3. If the system variable **FILLMODE** is 0 (Off), the hatch patterns are not displayed. To see the effect of a changed **FILLMODE** value, you must use the **REGEN** command to regenerate the drawing after the value has been changed.

4. You can edit the boundary of a hatch pattern even when the hatch pattern is not visible (**FILLMODE**=0).

5. When you save an AutoCAD drawing in Release 12 format (DXF), the hatch objects are automatically converted to Release 12 hatch blocks.

6. You can use the **CONVERT** command to change the pre-Release hatch patterns to AutoCAD 2018 objects. You can also use this command to change the pre-Release 17 polylines to AutoCAD optimized format to save memory and disk space.

Exercise 4 — Boundary

Draw Figure 12-39 and then create the drawing shown in Figure 12-40 using the **Boundary** tool to create a hatch boundary. Move the boundary from the drawing shown in Figure 12-40, and then hatch.

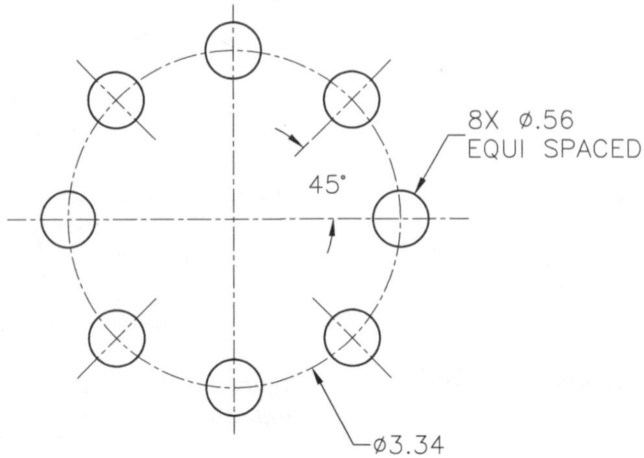

Figure 12-39 *Drawing for Exercise 4*

Figure 12-40 *Final drawing for Exercise 4*

Self-Evaluation Test

Answer the following questions and then compare them to those given at the end of this chapter:

1. If you need to hatch a drawing that has a gap, then specify the gap value in the __________ edit box in the **Hatch Creation** tab.

2. One of the ways to specify a hatch pattern from the group of stored hatch patterns is by selecting an option from the __________ drop-down list.

3. The value that you enter in the __________ edit box allows you rotate a hatch pattern with respect to the *X* axis of the current UCS.

4. The __________ option in the **Hatch Creation** tab allows you select the objects that form a boundary for hatching.

5. While hatching, you can select the __________ option from the **Hatch Type** drop-down list to fill the boundary in a set pattern of colors.

6. The **ISO Pen Width** drop-down list is available in the **Hatch Creation** tab only for the __________ patterns.

7. Different filling patterns make it possible to distinguish between different parts or components of an object. (T/F)

8. If AutoCAD does not find the entered pattern in the *acad.pat* file, it searches for it in a file with the same name as the pattern. (T/F)

9. When a boundary set is formed, it does not become the default boundary set for hatching. (T/F)

10. You can edit the hatch boundary and the associated hatch pattern by using grips. (T/F)

Review Questions

Answer the following questions:

1. Which of the following system variables has to be set to 1 if the **Double** hatch box is selected?

   (a) **HPSPACE** (b) **HPDOUBLE**
   (c) **HPANG** (d) **HPSCALE**

2. For which of the following hatch patterns the **ISO pen width** drop-down list will be available?

   (a) **ANSI** (b) **Predefined**
   (c) **Custom** (d) **ISO**

3. Which of the following options should be chosen if you want to have the same hatching pattern, style, and properties as that of the existing hatch?

   (a) **Match Properties** (b) **Select**
   (c) **Pick points** (d) **Inherit Properties**

4. Which of the following variables can be used to align the hatches in adjacent hatch areas?

   (a) **SNAPBASE** (b) **FILLMODE**
   (c) **SNAPANG** (d) **HPANG**

5. In which of the following system variables the specified hatch spacing value will be stored?

   (a) **HPDOUBLE** (b) **HPANG**
   (c) **HPSCALE** (d) **HPSPACE**

6. One of the advantages of using the __________ tool is that you don't have to select each object comprising the boundary of the area you want to hatch, as in the case of the __________ tool.

7. To select a custom hatch pattern, first select the **Custom** option from the **Type** drop-down list and then select the name of a previously stored hatch pattern from the __________ drop-down list.

8. There are three hatching styles available in AutoCAD. They are solid, __________, and __________.

9. If you select the __________ option from **Islands** area, all the areas bounded by the outermost boundary are hatched, ignoring hatch boundaries that lie within the outer boundary.

10. The **Hatch** tool does not allow you to hatch a region enclosed within a boundary (closed area) by selecting a point inside the boundary. (T/F)

11. The **Boundary Definition Error** message box is displayed if AutoCAD finds that the selected point is not inside the boundary or that the boundary is not closed. (T/F)

12. The **Tolerance** edit box is used to set the value up to which the open area will be considered closed when selected for hatching using the **Pick Points** method. (T/F)

13. When you use editing tools such as **Move**, **Scale**, **Stretch**, and **Rotate**, the associativity is lost even if all the boundary objects are selected. (T/F)

14. The hatching procedure in AutoCAD does not work on inserted blocks. (T/F)

15. Patterns drawn using the **Hatch** tool are associative. (T/F)

Exercise 5 — Hatch Pattern

Hatch the drawings shown in Figure 12-41 and Figure 12-42 using the hatch pattern to match.

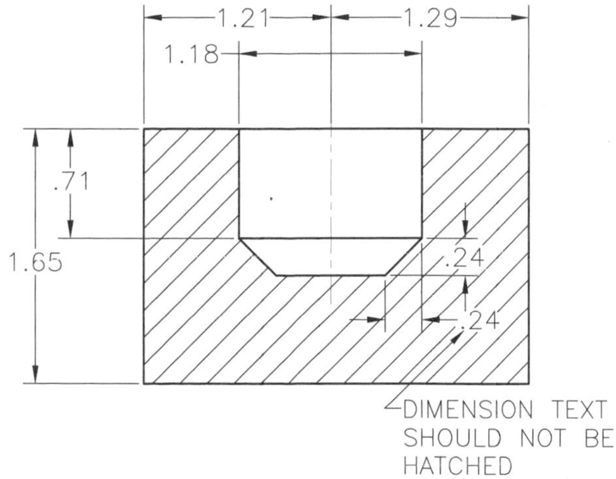

Figure 12-41 Drawing for Exercise 5

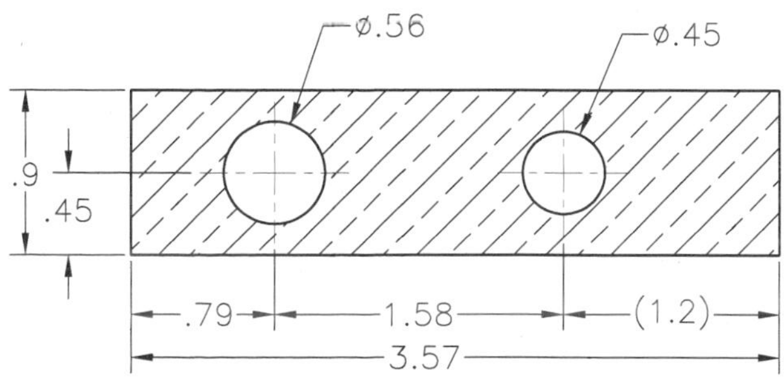

Figure 12-42 Drawing for Exercise 5

Exercise 6 — Hatch Align

Hatch the drawing, as shown in Figure 12-43, using the hatch pattern **ANSI31**. Use the **SNAPBASE** variable to align the hatch lines, as shown in the drawing.

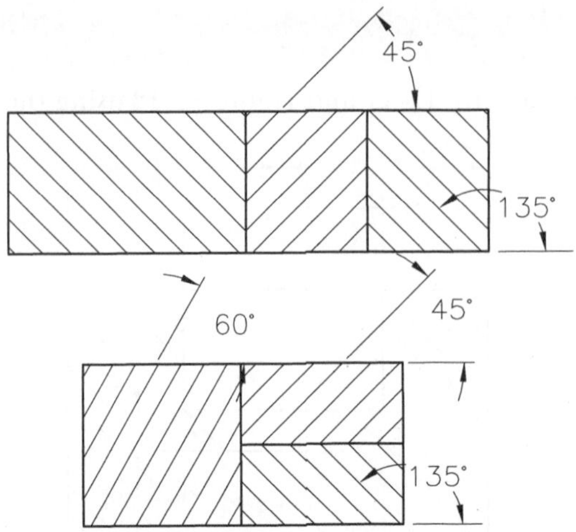

Figure 12-43 Drawing for Exercise 6

Exercise 7 — Hatch

Figure 12-44 shows the top and front views of an object. It also shows the cutting plane line. Based on the cutting plane line, hatch the front views in section. Use the hatch pattern of your choice.

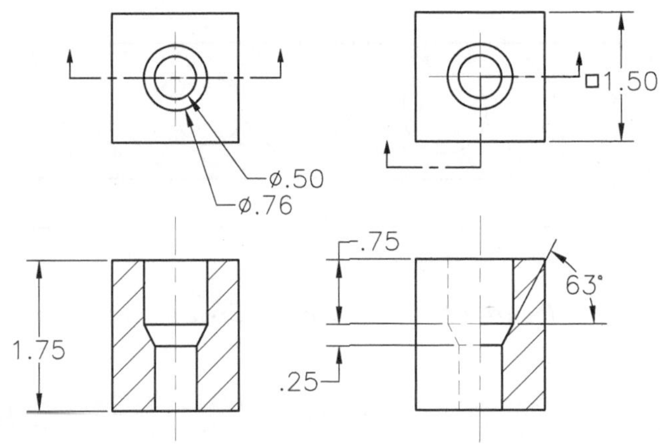

Figure 12-44 Drawing for Exercise 7

Exercise 8 *Hatch*

Figure 12-45 shows the top and front views of an object. Hatch the front view in full section. Use the hatch pattern of your choice.

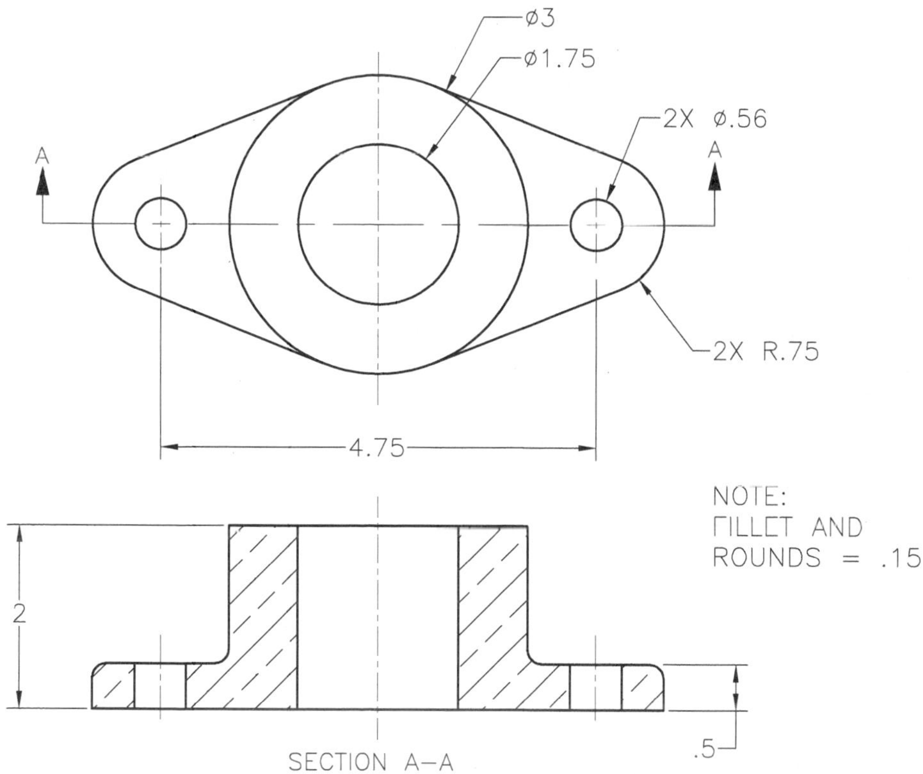

Figure 12-45 *Drawing for Exercise 8*

Exercise 9 — Hatch

Figure 12-46 shows the front and side views of an object. Hatch the side view in half section. Use the hatch pattern of your choice.

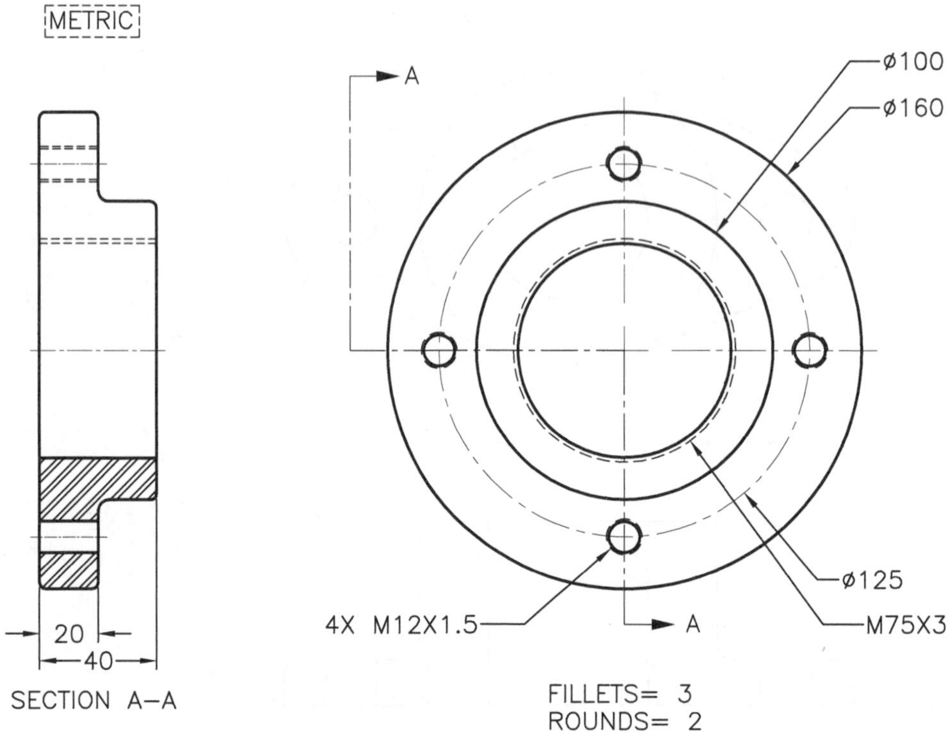

Figure 12-46 Drawing for Exercise 9

Exercise 10 Hatch

Figure 12-47 shows the front view with the broken section and top views of an object. Hatch the front view as shown. Use the hatch pattern of your choice.

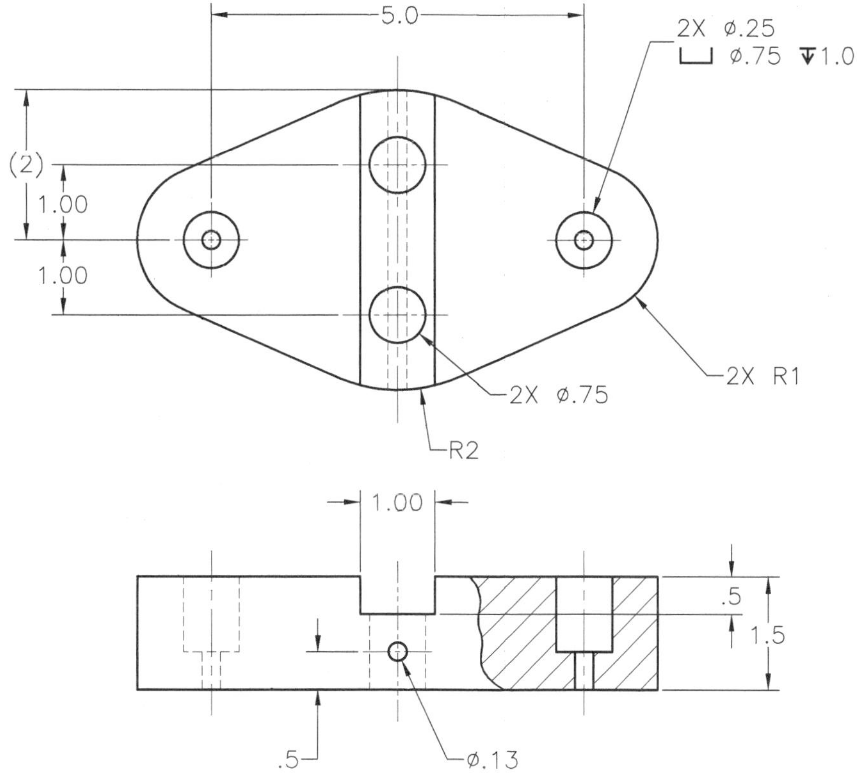

Figure 12-47 Drawing for Exercise 10

Exercise 11 *Hatch*

Figure 12-48 shows the front, top, and side views of an object. Hatch the side view in section using the hatch pattern of your choice.

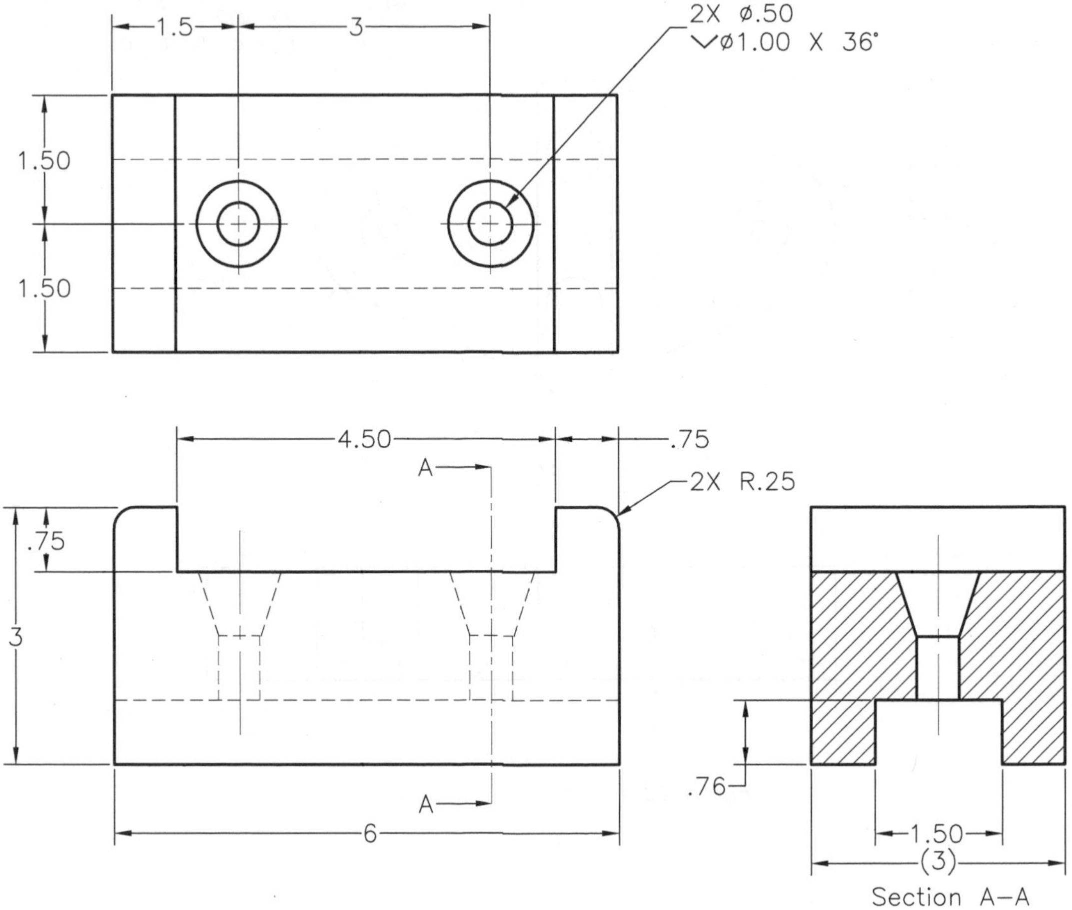

Figure 12-48 *Drawing for Exercise 11*

Problem-Solving Exercise 1

Figure 12-49 shows an object with front and side views with aligned section. Hatch the side view using the hatch pattern of your choice.

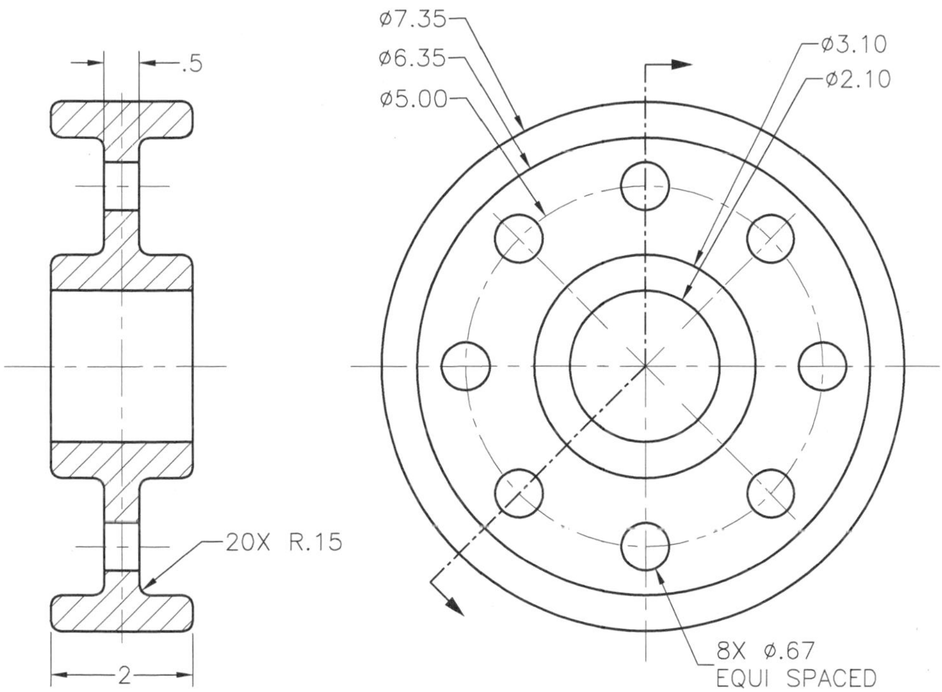

Figure 12-49 *Drawing for Problem-Solving Exercise 1*

Problem-Solving Exercise 2

Figure 12-50 shows the front view, side view, and the detail "A" of an object. Hatch the side view and draw the detailed drawing as shown.

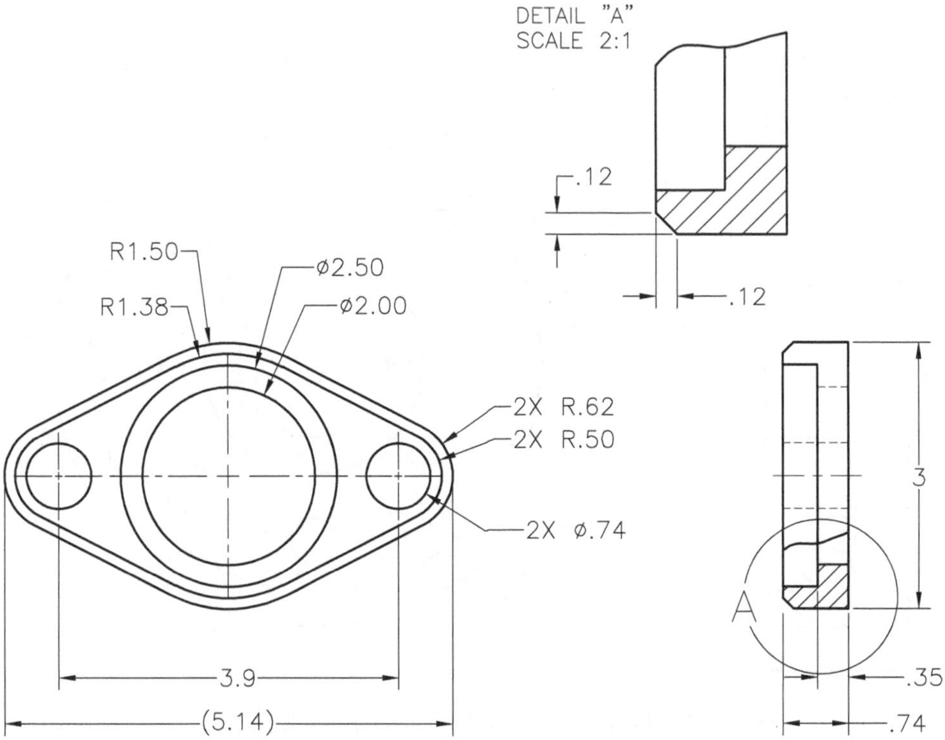

Figure 12-50 Drawing for Problem-Solving Exercise 2

Problem-Solving Exercise 3

Create the drawing shown in Figure 12-51.

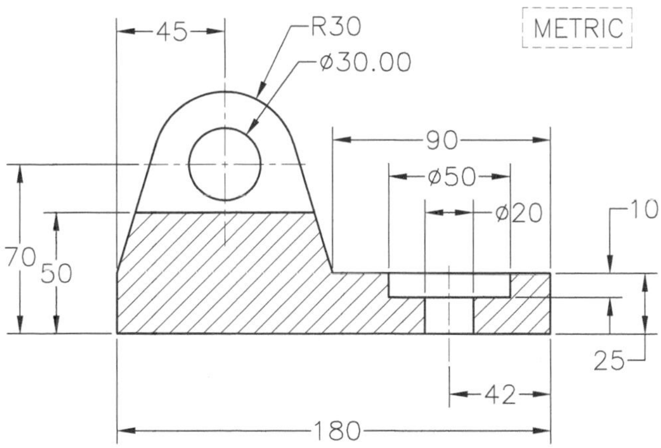

Figure 12-51 Drawing for Problem-Solving Exercise 3

Problem-Solving Exercise 4

Create the drawing shown in Figure 12-52.

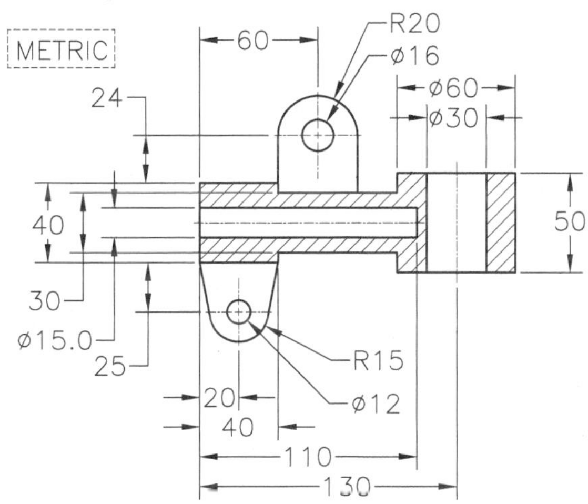

Figure 12-52 Drawing for Problem-Solving Exercise 4

Problem-Solving Exercise 5

Draw a detail drawing whose top, side, and section views are given in Figure 12-53. Then, hatch the section view.

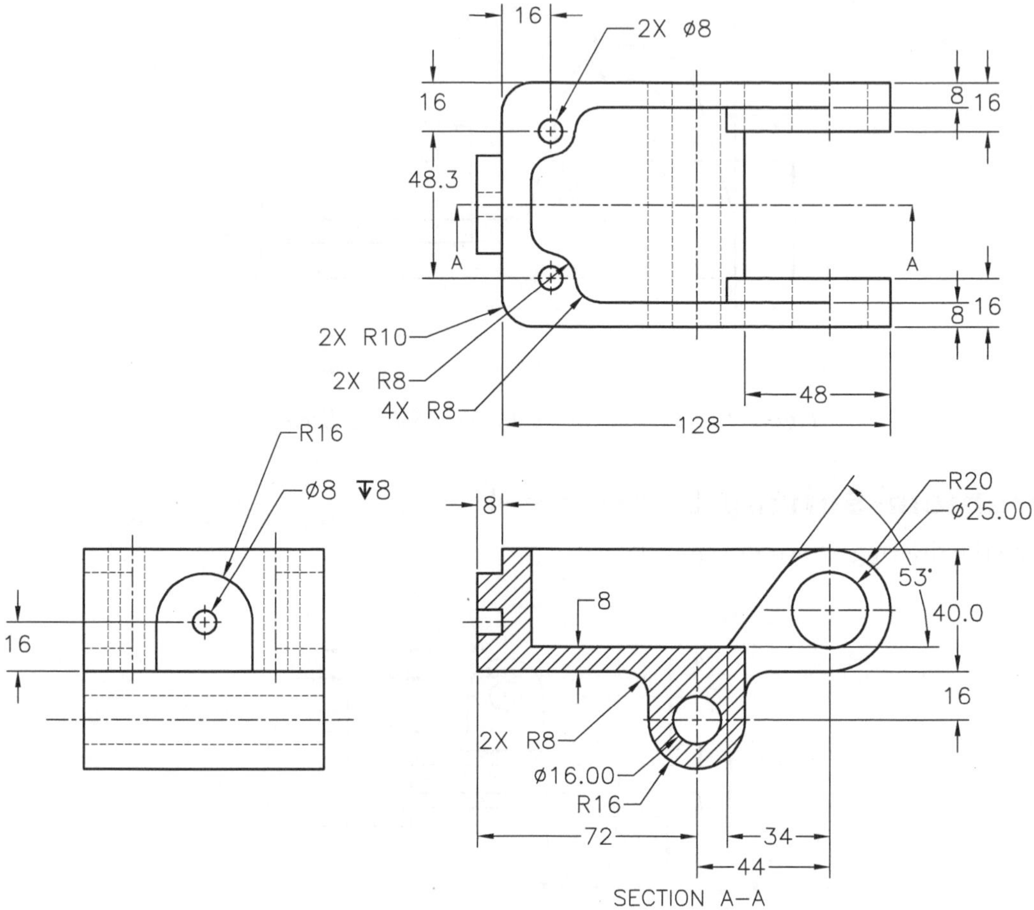

Figure 12-53 Views and dimensions of the drawing for Problem-Solving Exercise 5

Problem-Solving Exercise 6

Create the drawing shown in Figure 12-54.

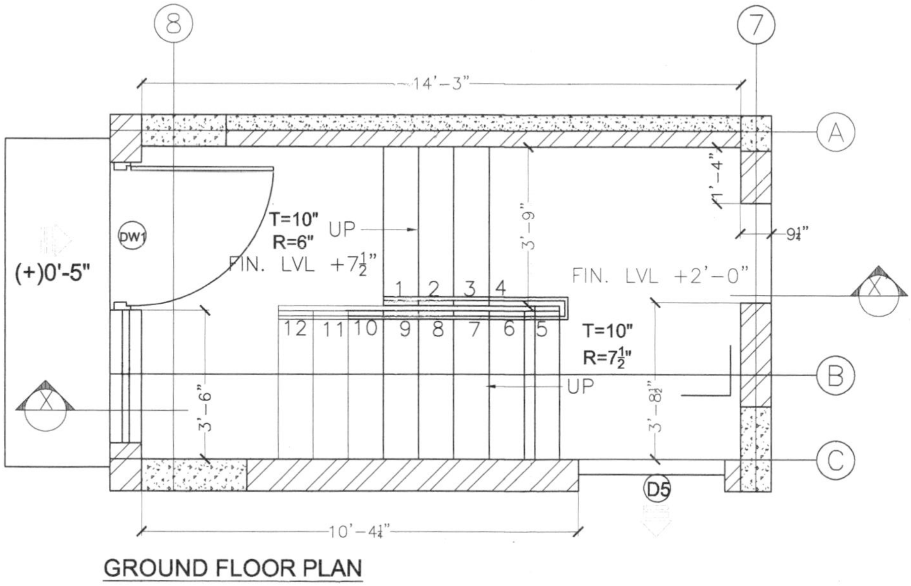

Figure 12-54 Drawing for Problem-Solving Exercise 6

Answers to Self-Evaluation Test

1. **Gap Tolerance**, **2.** **Pattern**, **3.** **Angle**, **4.** **Select Boundary Objects**, **5.** **Gradient**, **6.** ISO hatch, **7.** T, **8.** T, **9.** F, **10.** T

Chapter 13

Model Space Viewports, Paper Space Viewports, and Layouts

Learning Objectives

After completing this chapter, you will be able to:

- *Understand the concepts of model space and paper space*
- *Create tiled viewports in the model space*
- *Create floating viewports*
- *Control the visibility of viewport layers*
- *Set the linetype scaling in paper space*
- *Control the display of annotative objects in viewports*

Key Terms

- *Viewports*
- *Model Space*
- *Paper Space*
- *Tiled Viewport*
- *Temporary Model Space*
- *Rectangular Viewport*
- *Polygonal Viewport*
- *Maximize Viewport*
- *MVIEW*
- *VPLAYER*
- *PAGESETUP*
- *MVSETUP*
- *SPACETRANS*

MODEL SPACE AND PAPER SPACE/LAYOUTS

For ease in designing, AutoCAD provides two different types of environments, model space and paper space. The paper space is also called layout. The model space is basically used for designing or drafting work. This is the default environment that is active when you start AutoCAD. Almost the entire design is created in the model space. The paper space is used for plotting drawings or generating drawing views for the solid models. By default, the paper space provides you with two layouts. A layout can be considered a sheet of paper on which you can place the design created in the model space and then print it. You can also assign different plotting parameters to these layouts for plotting. Almost all the commands of the model space also work in the layouts. Note that you cannot select the drawing objects created in model space when they are displayed in the viewports in layouts. However, you can snap on to the different points of the drawing objects such as the endpoints, midpoints, center points, and so on using the **OSNAP** options.

You can shift from one environment to the other by choosing the **Model** tab or the **Layout1/ Layout2** tabs at the bottom of the drawing area. If these tabs are not available by default, then to display these tabs, select the **Layout Tabs** option from the **Interface** panel of the **View** tab of the **Ribbon**.

You can also shift from one environment to the other using the **TILEMODE** system variable. The default value of this variable is **1**. If the value of this system variable is set to **0**, you will be shifted to the layouts and if its value is set to **1**, you will be shifted to model space. The viewports created in the model space are called tiled viewports and viewports in layouts are called floating viewports.

MODEL SPACE VIEWPORTS (TILED VIEWPORTS)

Ribbon: View > Model Viewports > Viewport Configuration drop-down
Toolbar: Viewports > Display Viewports Dialog or Layouts > Display Viewports Dialog
Menu Bar: View > Viewports > New Viewports **Command:** VPORTS

A viewport in the model space is defined as a rectangular area of the drawing window in which you can create the design. When you start AutoCAD, only one viewport is displayed in the model space. You can create multiple non-overlapping viewports in the model space to display different views of the same object, refer to Figure 13-1. Each of these viewports will act as individual drawing area. This is generally used while creating solid models. You can view the same solid model from different positions by creating the tiled viewports and defining the distinct coordinate system configuration for each viewport. You can also use the **Pan** or **Zoom** tool to display different portions or different levels of the detail of the drawing in each viewport. The tiled viewports can be created using the **Named** tool available in the **Model Viewports** panel.

Creating Tiled Viewports

As mentioned earlier, the display screen in the model space can be divided into multiple non-overlapping tiled viewports. All these viewports are created only in rectangular shape. This number depends on the equipment and the operating system on which AutoCAD is running. Each tiled viewport contains a view of the drawing. The tiled viewports touch each other at the edges without overlapping. While using tiled viewports, you are not allowed to edit, rearrange, or turn individual viewports on or off. These viewports are created using the **Named** tool when the system variable **TILEMODE** is set to 1 or the **Model** tab is active. When you choose the **Named** tool from the **Model Viewports** panel of the **View** tab, the **Viewports** dialog box is displayed. You can use this dialog box to create new viewport configurations and save them. The options under both the tabs of the **Viewports** dialog box are discussed next.

Figure 13-1 *Screen display with multiple tiled viewports*

New Viewports Tab

The **New Viewports** tab of the **Viewports** dialog box, as shown in Figure 13-2, provides the options related to standard viewport configurations. You can also save a user-defined configuration using this tab. The name for the new viewport configuration can be specified in the **New name** edit box. If you do not enter a name in this edit box, the viewport configuration you create is not saved and, therefore, cannot be used later. A list of standard viewport configurations is listed in the **Standard viewports** list box. This list also contains the ***Active Model Configuration***, which is the current viewport configuration. From the **Standard viewports** list, you can select and apply any one of the listed standard viewport configurations. A preview image of the selected configuration is displayed in the **Preview** window. The **Apply to** drop-down list has the **Display** and **Current Viewport** options. Selecting the **Display** option applies the selected viewport configuration to the entire display and selecting the **Current Viewport** option applies the selected viewport configuration to only the current viewport. With this option, you can create more viewports inside the existing viewports. The changes will be applied to the current viewport and the new viewports will be created inside the current viewport.

From the **Setup** drop-down list, you can select **2D** or **3D**. When you select the **2D** option, it creates the new viewport configuration with the current view of the drawing in all the viewports initially. Using the **3D** option, you can apply the standard orthogonal and isometric views to the viewports. For example, if a configuration has four viewports, they are assigned the **Top**, **Front**, **Right**, and **SE Isometric** views, respectively. You can also modify these standard orthogonal and isometric views by selecting from the **Change view to** drop-down list and replacing the existing view in the selected viewport. For example, you can select the viewport that is assigned the **Top** view and then select the **Bottom** view from the **Change view to** drop-down list to replace it. The preview image in the **Preview** window reflects the changes you make. If you use the **2D** option, you can select a named viewport configuration to replace the selected one. From the **Visual Style** drop-down list, you can select the visualization mode of your model. For example, you can select a viewport and then select **Hidden** from the **Visual Style** drop-down list. Now, the model will be displayed with the hidden edges invisible in this viewport. Choose the **OK** button to exit the dialog box and apply the created or selected configuration to the current display in the drawing. When you save a new viewport configuration, it saves the information about the number and position of viewports, the viewing direction and zoom factor, and the grid, snap, coordinate system, and UCS icon settings.

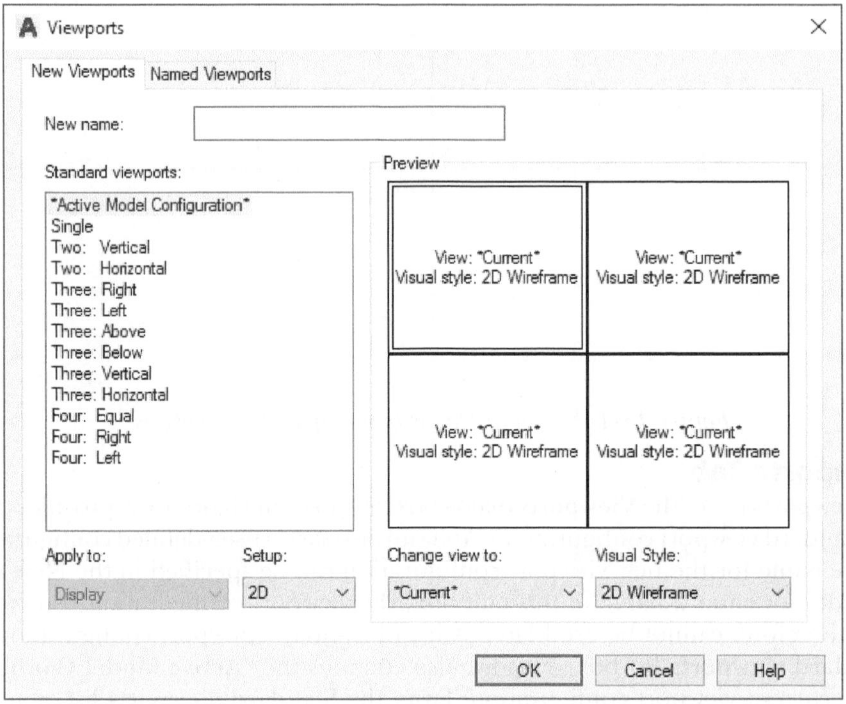

***Figure 13-2** The **New Viewports** tab of the **Viewports** dialog box*

Named Viewports Tab

The **Named Viewports** tab of the **Viewports** dialog box, as shown in Figure 13-3, displays the name of the current viewport in the **Current name** area. The names of all the saved viewport configurations in a drawing are displayed in the **Named viewports** list box. You can select any one of the named viewport configurations and apply it to the current display. A preview image of the selected configuration is displayed in the **Preview** window. In the **Named viewports** list box, you can select a name and right-click to display a shortcut menu. On choosing the **Delete** option, the selected viewport configuration will be deleted and on choosing the **Rename** option, you can rename the selected viewport configuration. Choose the **OK** button to exit the dialog box and apply the selected viewport configuration to the current display.

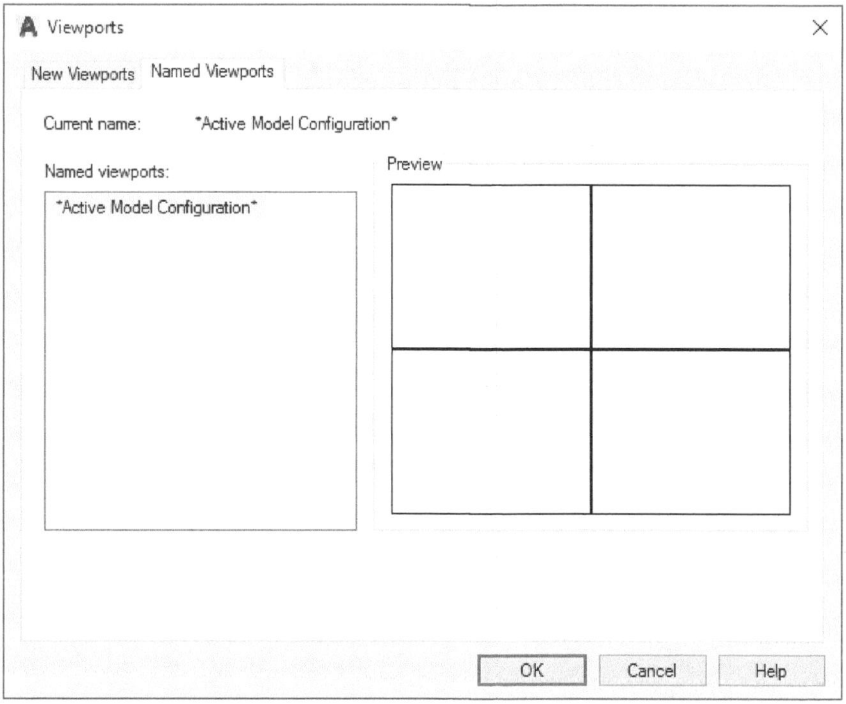

***Figure 13-3** The **Named Viewports** tab of the **Viewports** dialog box*

MAKING A VIEWPORT CURRENT

The viewport you are currently working in is called the current viewport. You can display several model space viewports on the screen, but you can work in only one of them at a time. You can switch from one viewport to another even when you are in the middle of a command. For example, you can specify the start point of the line in one viewport and the endpoint of the line in the other viewport. The current viewport is indicated by a border that is heavy compared to the borders of the other viewports. Also, the graphics cursor appears as a drawing cursor (screen crosshairs) only when it is within the current viewport. Outside the current viewport this cursor appears as an arrow cursor. You can enter points and select objects only from the current viewport. To make a viewport current, you can select it with the pointing device. Another method of making a viewport current is by assigning its identification number to the **CVPORT** system variable. The identification numbers of the named viewport configurations are not listed in the display.

JOINING TWO ADJACENT VIEWPORTS

Ribbon: View > Model Viewports > Join Viewports
Menu Bar: View > Viewports > Join **Command:** -VPORTS > J

AutoCAD provides you with an option of joining two adjacent viewports. However, remember that the viewports you wish to join should together form a rectangular-shaped viewport only. As mentioned earlier, the viewports in the model space can only be in rectangular shape. Therefore, you will not be able to join two viewports, in case they do not result in a rectangular shape. The viewports can be joined by using the **Join Viewports** tool available in the **Model Viewports** panel. On invoking this tool, you will be prompted to select the dominant viewport. A dominant viewport is the one whose display will be retained after joining. After selecting the dominant viewport, you will be prompted to select the viewport to be joined. Figure 13-4 shows the viewport configuration before joining and Figure 13-5 shows the viewport configuration after joining.

Figure 13-4 *Selecting the dominant viewport and the viewport to be joined*

Figure 13-5 *Viewports after joining*

Note

*You can also use the **-VPORTS** command to create, save, restore, delete, or join the viewport configurations.*

SPLITTING AND RESIZING VIEWPORTS IN MODEL SPACE

In AutoCAD, you can split the viewports in the model space. To do so enter the **-VPORTS** command; the **Enter an option [Save/Restore/Delete/Join/Single/?/2/3/4/Toggle/MOde] <3>:** prompt will be displayed. Next, enter **2**, **3**, or **4** at the command prompt to split a viewport in 2, 3, or 4 viewports, respectively.

Also, you can resize the viewports in model space using the horizontal and vertical splitting lines. To resize a viewport, hold down the left mouse button on the horizontal or vertical splitting line and drag the cursor in a direction; the viewport will be resized in the specified direction. You can also resize all the viewports at a time. To do so, hold down the cursor at the intersection point of horizontal and vertical splitting line and drag the cursor in a direction; all the viewports will be resized according to the specified direction.

PAPER SPACE VIEWPORTS (FLOATING VIEWPORTS)

As mentioned earlier, the viewports created in the layouts are called floating viewports. This is because unlike in model space, the viewports in the layouts can be overlapping and of any shape without any restriction. You can even convert a closed object into a viewport in the layouts. Figure 13-6 shows a layout with floating viewports. The methods of creating floating viewports are discussed next.

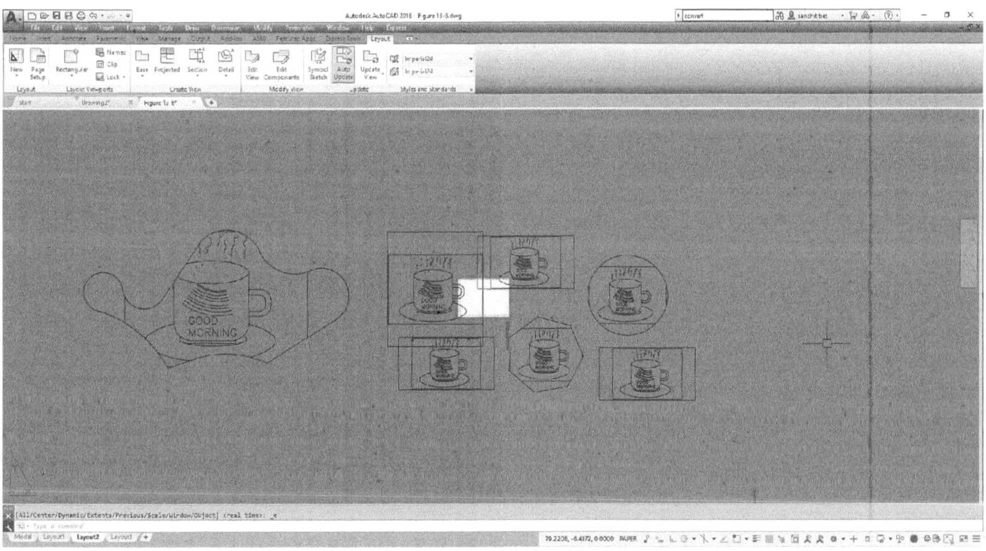

Figure 13-6 *Screen display with multiple floating viewports*

Creating Floating Viewports

Ribbon: Layout contextual tab > Layout Viewports > Named
Toolbar: Viewports > Display Viewports Dialog or Layouts > Display Viewports Dialog
Menu Bar: View > Viewports > New Viewports **Command:** VPORTS

This tool is used to create the floating viewports in layouts. However, when you invoke this tool in the layouts, the dialog box displayed is slightly modified. Instead of the **Apply to** drop-down list in the **New Viewports** tab, the **Viewport Spacing** spinner is displayed, refer to Figure 13-7. This spinner is used to set the spacing between the adjacent viewports. The rest of the options in both the **New Viewports** and the **Named Viewports** tabs of the **Viewports** dialog box are the same as those discussed under the tiled viewports. When you select a viewport configuration and choose the **OK** button, you will be prompted to specify the first and the second corner of a box that will act as a reference for placing the viewports. You will also be given an option of **Fit**. This option fits the configuration of viewports such that they fit exactly in the current display.

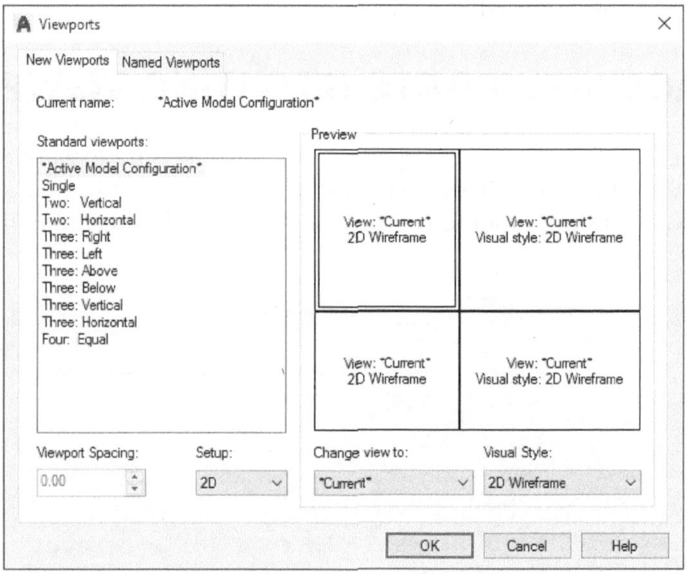

***Figure 13-7** The **New Viewports** tab of the **Viewports** dialog box displayed in layouts*

Note

*You can also use the **+VPORTS** command to display the **Viewports** dialog box. When you invoke this command, you will be prompted to specify the **Tab Index**. Enter **0** to display the **New Viewports** tab and enter **1** to display the **Named Viewports** tab.*

Creating Rectangular Viewports

Ribbon: Layout contextual tab > Layout Viewports > Viewports drop-down > Rectangular
Menu Bar: View > Viewports > New Viewports
Toolbar: Viewports > Single Viewport **Command:** -VPORTS

To create a rectangular viewport, choose the **Rectangular** tool from **Layout > Layout Viewports > Viewports** drop-down in the **Ribbon**, refer to Figure 13-8. The prompt sequence that will follow is given next.

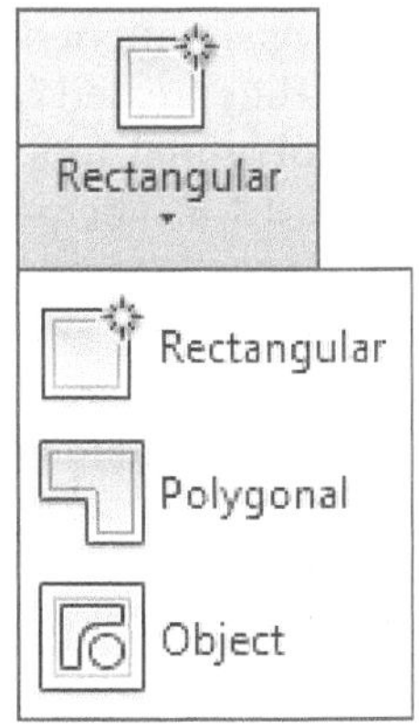

Figure 13-8 *Tools in the **Viewports** drop-down*

Specify corner of viewport or
[ON/OFF/Fit/Shadeplot/Lock/Object/Polygonal/Restore/LAyer/2/3/4] <Fit>:
Specify the start point of the viewport.
Specify opposite corner: *Specify the end point of the viewport.*

You can also create 2, 3, or 4 viewports in one go by entering 2, 3, or 4 at the prompt **Specify corner of viewport or [ON/OFF/Fit/Shadeplot/Lock/Object/Polygonal/Restore/LAyer/2/3/4] <Fit>**. The viewports automatically fit in the drawn rectangular area.

The prompt sequence for the 2 Viewports option is given next.

Command: **-VPORTS**
Specify corner of viewport or
[ON/OFF/Fit/Shadeplot/Lock/Object/Polygonal/Restore/LAyer/2/3/4] <Fit>: 2 Enter
Enter viewport arrangement [Horizontal/Vertical] <Vertical>: *Specify the orientation of the viewport.*
Specify first corner or [Fit] <Fit>: *Specify the start point of the viewport.*
Specify opposite corner: *Specify the end point of the viewport.*

The prompt sequence for creating 3 viewports is given next.

Command: **-VPORTS**
Specify corner of viewport or
[ON/OFF/Fit/Shadeplot/Lock/Object/Polygonal/Restore/LAyer/2/3/4] <Fit>: 3 Enter
Enter viewport arrangement
[Horizontal/Vertical/Above/Below/Left/Right] <Right>: *Specify the orientation of the viewport using Horizontal or Vertical option. You can also specify the position of the largest viewport among the three using Above, Below, Left, or Right option.*
Specify first corner or [Fit] <Fit>: *Specify the start point of the viewport.*
Specify opposite corner: *Specify the end point of the viewport.*

The prompt sequence for creating 4 viewports is given next.

Command: **-VPORTS**
Specify corner of viewport or
[ON/OFF/Fit/Shadeplot/Lock/Object/Polygonal/Restore/LAyer/2/3/4] <Fit>: 4 Enter
Specify first corner or [Fit] <Fit>: *Specify the start point of the viewport.*
Specify opposite corner: *Specify the end point of the viewport.*

Creating Polygonal Viewports

Ribbon: Layout contextual tab > Layout Viewports > Viewports drop-down > Polygonal
Menu Bar: View > Viewports > Polygonal Viewport
Toolbar: Viewports > Polygonal Viewports **Command:** -VPORTS > P

As mentioned earlier, you can create floating viewports of any closed shape. The viewports thus created can even be self-intersecting in shape. To create a polygonal viewport, choose the **Polygonal** tool from the **Layout > Layout Viewports > Viewports** drop-down, refer to Figure 13-8. The prompt sequence that will follow when you choose this tool is given next.

Command: **-VPORTS**
Specify corner of viewport or
[ON/OFF/Fit/Shadeplot/Lock/Object/Polygonal/Restore/LAyer/2/3/4] <Fit>: P Enter
Specify start point: *Specify the start point of the viewport.*
Specify next point or [Arc/Length/Undo]: *Specify the next point or select an option.*
Specify next point or [Arc/Close/Length/Undo]: *Specify the next point or select an option.*

Various options in the prompt sequence are discussed next.

Arc

This option is used to switch to the arc mode for creating the viewports. When you invoke this option, the options for creating the arcs will be displayed. You can switch back to the line mode by choosing the **Line** option.

Length

This option is used to specify the length of the next line of the viewport. The line will be drawn in the direction of the last drawn line segment. In case the last drawn segment was an arc, the line will be drawn tangent to it.

Undo

This option is used to undo the last drawn segment of the polygonal viewport.

Close

This option is used to close the polygon and create the viewport. The last entity that will be used to close the polygon will depend upon whether you were in the arc mode or in the line mode. If you were in the line mode, the last entity will be a line. If you were in the arc mode, the last entity will be an arc.

Figure 13-9 shows the polygonal viewport created using a combination of lines and arcs.

Figure 13-9 *An object viewport*

Converting an Existing Closed Object into a Viewport

Ribbon: Layout contextual tab > Layout Viewports > Viewports drop-down > Object
Menu Bar: View > Viewports > Object **Command:** -VPORTS > O
Toolbar: Viewports > Convert Object to Viewport

This tool allows you to convert an existing closed object into a viewport. However, remember that the object selected should be a single entity. The objects that can be converted into a viewport include polygons drawn using the **Polygon** tool, rectangles drawn using the **Rectangle** tool, polylines (last segment closed using the **Close** option), circles, ellipses, closed splines, or regions. To convert any of these objects into a viewport, choose the **Object** tool from the **Layout Viewports** panel. You will be prompted to select the object that needs to be converted into a viewport. Figure 13-10 shows a viewport created using a polygon of nine sides and Figure 13-11 shows a viewport created using a closed spline.

Figure 13-10 A viewport created using a polygon of nine sides

Figure 13-11 A viewport created using a closed spline

TEMPORARY MODEL SPACE

Sometimes when you create a floating viewport in the layout, the drawing is not displayed completely inside it, refer to Figure 13-10 and Figure 13-11. In such cases, you need to zoom or pan the drawings to fit them in the viewport. But when you invoke any of the **Zoom** or the **Pan** tools in the layouts, the display of the entire layout is modified instead of the display inside of the viewport. Now, to change the display of the viewports, you will have to switch to the temporary model space. The temporary model space is defined as a state when the model space is activated in the layouts. The temporary model space is exactly similar to the actual model space and you can make any kind of modifications in the drawing from temporary model space. Therefore, the main reason for invoking the temporary model space is that you can modify the display of the drawing. The temporary model space can be invoked by choosing the **PAPER** button from the Status Bar. You can also switch to the temporary model space by double-clicking inside the viewports. You will see that the model space UCS icon is automatically displayed when you switch to the temporary model space. Also, the extents of the viewport become the extents of the drawing. You can use the **Zoom** and **Pan** tools to fit the model inside the viewport. The temporary model space can also be invoked using the **MSPACE** command.

Once you have modified the display of the drawing in the temporary model space, you have to switch back to the paper space. This is done by choosing the **MODEL** button from the Status Bar. You can also switch back to the paper space by double-clicking anywhere in the layout outside the viewport, or by using the **PSPACE** command.

Example 1 — Create Viewports

In this example, you will draw the object shown in Figure 13-12 and then create a floating viewport of the shape shown in Figure 13-13 to display the object in the layout. The dimensions of the viewport are in the paper space. Do not dimension the object.

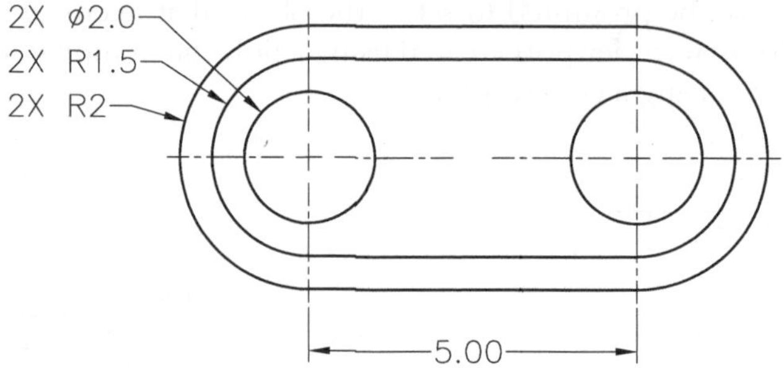

Figure 13-12 Model for Example 1

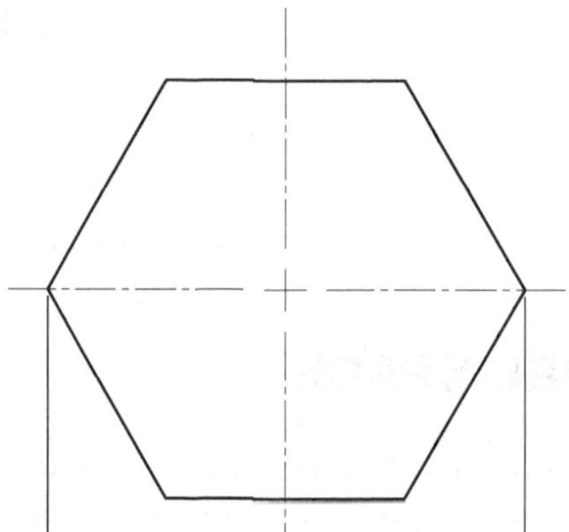

Figure 13-13 Shape of the floating viewport

1. Start a new drawing and then draw the object shown in Figure 13-12.

2. Choose the **Layout1** tab to switch to the layout; a rectangular viewport will be displayed in this layout.

3. Choose the **Erase** tool from the **Modify** panel of the **Home** tab; you will be prompted to select the object. Type **L** in this prompt to delete the last object. In this case, the last object is viewport so you need to delete it.

4. Choose the **Polygon** tool from the **Draw** panel of the **Home** tab and create the required hexagon, refer to Figure 13-13.

5. Choose the **Object** tool from **Layout > Layout Viewports > Viewports** drop-down; you will be prompted to select an object. Select the hexagon; it will be converted into a viewport. You will see that the complete object is not displayed inside the viewport. Therefore, you need to modify its display.

6. Double-click inside the viewport to switch to the temporary model space. The border of the viewport will become thick, indicating that you have switched to the temporary model space.

7. Now, using the **Zoom** and the **Pan** tools, fit the drawing inside the viewport.

8. Choose the **MODEL** button from the Status Bar to switch back to the paper space. The drawing will be displayed fully inside the viewport, refer to Figure 13-14.

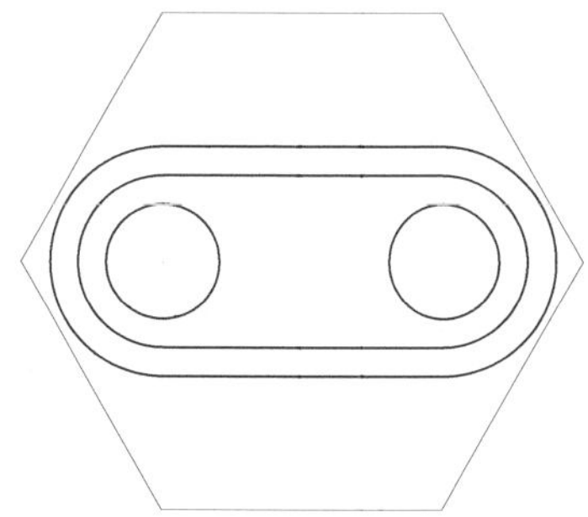

***Figure 13-14** Displaying the drawing inside the polygonal viewport*

EDITING VIEWPORTS

You can perform various editing operations on the viewports. For example, you can control the visibility of the objects in the viewports, lock their display, clip the existing viewports using an object, and so on. All these editing operations are discussed next.

Controlling the Display of Objects in Viewports

The display of the objects in the viewports can be turned on or off. If the display is turned off, the objects will not be displayed in the viewport. However, the object in the model space is not affected by this editing operation. To control the display of the objects, select the viewport entity in the layout and right-click to display the shortcut menu. In this menu, choose **Display Viewport Objects > No**. However, if there are more than one viewports, the visibility of the selected viewports will be automatically turned off when you choose **Display Viewport Objects > No** from the shortcut menu. Similarly, you can again turn on the display of the objects by choosing **Display Viewport Objects > Yes** from the shortcut menu. This shortcut menu is displayed on selecting the viewport and right-clicking. This editing operation can also be done using the **OFF** option of the **MVIEW** or the **-VPORTS** command.

Locking the Display of Objects in Viewports

To avoid accidental modification in the display of objects in the viewports, you can lock their display. If the display of a viewport is locked, the tools such as **Zoom** and **Pan** do not work in it. Also, you cannot modify the view in the locked viewport. For example, if the display of a viewport is locked, you cannot zoom or pan the display or change the view in that viewport even if you switch to the temporary model space. To lock the display of the viewports, select it and right-click on it to display the shortcut menu. In this menu, choose **Display Locked > Yes**. Now, the display of this viewport will not be modified. However, you can draw objects or delete objects in this viewport by switching to the temporary model space. Similarly, you can unlock the display of the objects in the viewports by choosing **Display Locked > No** from the shortcut menu. You can also lock or unlock the display of the viewports using the **Lock** option of the **MVIEW** command or the **-VPORTS** command.

Controlling the Display of Hidden Lines in Viewports

While working with three-dimensional solid or surface models, there are a number of occasions where you have to plot the solid models such that the hidden lines are not displayed. Plotting solid models in the model space (Tilemode=1) can be easily done by selecting the **Hidden** option from the **Shade plot** drop-down list. This drop-down list is available in the **Shaded viewport options** area in the **Plot** dialog box. If this area is not available by default, you need to choose the **More Options** button in the dialog box. This option is not available in layouts. In this case, you will have to control the display of the hidden lines in the viewports. To control the display of the hidden lines, select the viewport and right-click to display the shortcut menu. In this menu, choose **Shade plot > Hidden**. Although the hidden lines will be displayed in the viewports, now they will not be displayed in the printouts. The display of the hidden lines can also be controlled using the **Shadeplot** option of the **MVIEW** command or the **-VPORTS** command.

Note

*You can also use the other options in the **Shade plot** drop-down list. These options are explained in detail in Chapter 14 (Plotting Drawings).*

Tip

Apart from the previously mentioned editing operations, you can also move, copy, rotate, stretch, scale, or trim the viewports using the respective commands. You can also use the grips to edit the viewports.

Clipping Existing Viewports

Ribbon: Layout contextual tab > Layout Viewports > Clip
Menu Bar: Modify > Clip > Viewport
Toolbar: Viewports > Clip existing viewport **Command:** VPCLIP

You can modify the shape of any existing viewport by clipping it using an object or by defining the clipping boundary. The viewports can be clipped by choosing the **Clip** tool from the **Layout Viewports** panel in the **Layout** tab. This command can also be invoked by using the **VPCLIP** command. The prompt sequence that will follow when you invoke this tool is given next.

Select viewport to clip: *Select the viewport to be clipped.*
Select clipping object or [Polygonal/Delete] <Polygonal>: *Select an object for clipping the viewport or specify an option.*

Select Clipping Object Option

This option is used to clip the viewport using a selected closed loop. The objects that can be used for clipping the viewports include circles, ellipses, closed polylines, closed splines, and regions. As soon as you select the clipping object, the original viewport will be deleted and the selected object will be converted into a viewport. The portion of the display that was common to both the original viewport and the object selected will be displayed. You can, however, change the display of the viewport using the **Zoom** tool or the **Pan** tool. Figure 13-15 shows a viewport and an object that will be used to clip the viewport and Figure 13-16 shows the new viewport created after clipping.

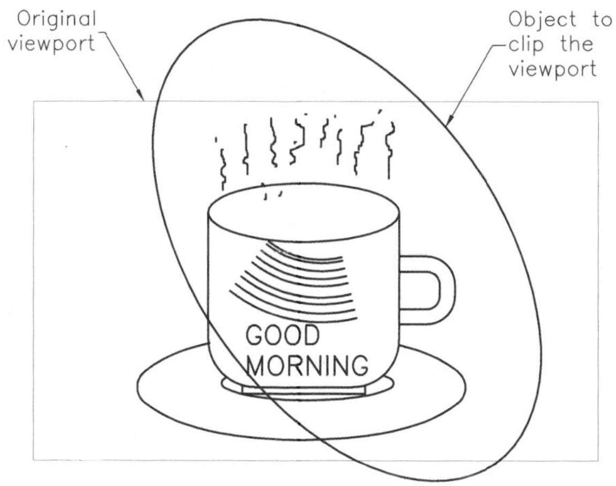

Figure 13-15 Selecting the object for clipping the viewport

Figure 13-16 New viewport created after clipping

Polygonal

This option is used to create a polygonal boundary for clipping the viewports. When you invoke this option, the options for creating a polygonal boundary will be displayed. You can draw a polygonal boundary for clipping the viewport using this option.

Delete

This option is used to delete the new clipping boundary created using an object or using the **Polygonal** option. The original viewport is restored when you invoke this option which will be available only if the viewport has been clipped at least once. If the viewport is clipped more than once, you can restore only the last viewport clipping boundary.

Maximizing Viewports

Status Bar: Maximize Viewport

While working with floating viewports, you may need to invoke the temporary model space to modify the drawing. One of the options is that you double-click inside the viewport to invoke the temporary model space and make the changes in the drawing. But in this case, the shape and size of the floating viewport will control the area of the temporary model space. If the viewport is polygonal and small in size, you may have to zoom and pan the drawing a number of times. To avoid this, AutoCAD allows you to maximize a viewport on the screen. This provides you all the space in the drawing area to make the changes in the drawing.

To maximize a floating viewport, choose the **Maximize Viewport** button from the Status Bar. The viewport is automatically maximized in the drawing area and the **Maximize Viewport** button is replaced by the **Minimize Viewport** button. These arrows can be used to switch the display in the other floating viewports. After making changes in the drawing, choose the **Minimize Viewport** button to restore the original display of the layout. When you do so, the view and the magnification in all the viewports is the same as that before maximizing them. Also, the visibility of the layers remains the same as that before maximizing the viewport.

CONTROLLING THE PROPERTIES OF VIEWPORT LAYERS

Command: VPLAYER

You can control the properties of layers inside a floating viewport using the **VPLAYER** command or by using the **LAYER PROPERTIES MANAGER**. The **VPLAYER** command is used to control the visibility of layers in individual floating viewports. For example, you can use the **VPLAYER** command to freeze a layer in the selected viewport. The contents of this layer will not be displayed in the selected viewport, although in the other viewports, they will be displayed. This command can be used from either temporary model space or paper space. The only restriction is that **TILEMODE** is set to 0 (Off); that is, you can use this command only in the **Layout** tab.

Command: **VPLAYER** Enter
Enter an option [?/Color/Ltype/LWeight/TRansparency/Freeze/Thaw/Reset/Newfrz/Vpvisdflt]:

? Option

You can use this option to obtain a listing of the frozen layers in the selected viewport. When you enter ?, you will be prompted to select the viewport. Select the viewport; **AutoCAD Text Window** will be displayed showing all the layers that are frozen in the current layer. On invoking this command in temporary model space, AutoCAD will temporarily shift you to the paper space to let you select the viewport.

Color Option

The **Color** option is used to assign a color to a layer (or layers) in the viewports. You can either use True colors or you can specify a Color book, if you have previously installed any. The changes can be applied on the current, selected, or all the viewports.

Ltype Option

You can use this option to specify any linetype to a layer (or layers) in the current, selected, or all the viewports.

LWeight Option

The **LWeight** option is used to specify a line width to a particular layer or layers. You can specify the width between 0.0mm to 2.11 mm. Then you are prompted to specify the name(s) of the layer(s) to assign the line width. In this case also, you can apply the changes to the current, selected, or all the viewports.

TRansparency Option

The **TRansparency** option is used to set the transparency level of a layer (or layers) in one or more viewports. When you select this option, you will be prompted to specify the transparency level. Specify the transparency level; you will be prompted to specify the layer for which you need to set the transparency level. If you want to specify more than one layer, the names of the layers must be separated by commas. If you are working on a temporary model space, you can also select an object whose layer you want to set the transparency level. On specifying the name of the layer(s), AutoCAD will prompt you to select the viewport(s) to change the transparency. Select one or all viewports; the transparency level will be applied to the specified layers in the viewport after you exit this command.

Freeze Option

The **Freeze** option is used to freeze a layer (or layers) in one or more viewports. When you select this option, you will be prompted to specify the name(s) of the layer(s) you want to freeze. If you want to specify more than one layer, the layer names must be separated by commas. You can also select an object whose layer you want to freeze. Once you have specified the name of the layer(s), AutoCAD prompts you to select the viewport(s), to freeze the specified layer(s). You can select one or all the viewports. The layers will be frozen after you exit this command.

Thaw Option

With this option, you can thaw the layers that have been frozen in the viewports. Layers that have been frozen, thawed, turned on, or turned off globally are not affected by VPLAYER Thaw. For example, if a layer has been frozen, the objects on it are not regenerated on any viewport, even if VPLAYER Thaw is used to thaw that layer in any viewport. If you want to thaw more than one layer, they must be separated by commas. You can thaw the specified layers in the current, selected, or all the viewports.

Reset Option

With the **Reset** option, you can set the visibility of the layer(s) in the specified viewports to their current default setting. The visibility defaults of a layer can be set by using the **Vpvisdflt** option of the **VPLAYER** command. When you invoke the **Reset** option, you will be prompted to specify the names of the layers to be reset. You can reset the layers in the current viewport, in selected viewports or in all the viewports.

Newfrz (New Freeze) Option

With this option, you can create new layers that are frozen in all the viewports. This option is used mainly where you need a layer that is visible only in one viewport. This can be accomplished by creating the layer with the **Newfrz** option and then thawing it in the viewport where you want to make the layer visible. On invoking this option, you will be prompted to specify the name(s) of the new layer(s) that will be frozen in all the viewports. To specify more than one layer, separate the layer names with commas. After you specify the name(s) of the layer(s), AutoCAD creates frozen layers in all viewports. Also, the default visibility setting of the new layer(s) is set to Frozen; therefore, if you create any new viewports, the layers created with VPLAYER Newfrz are also frozen in them

Vpvisdflt (Viewport Visibility Default) Option

With this option, you can define default settings for the visibility of the layer(s) in the subsequent new viewports. When a new viewport is created, the frozen/thawed status of any layer depends on the **Vpvisdflt** setting for that particular layer. When you invoke this option, you will be prompted to specify the names of the layer(s) whose visibility is to be changed. After specifying the name(s), you will be prompted to specify whether the layers should be frozen or thawed in the new viewports.

CONTROLLING THE LAYERS IN VIEWPORTS USING THE LAYER PROPERTIES MANAGER

You can use the **LAYER PROPERTIES MANAGER** to control the layer display properties in viewports. To invoke the **LAYER PROPERTIES MANAGER**, choose the **Layers Properties** tool from the **Layers** panel in the **Home** tab. When you invoke this palette, some additional properties are added to it, refer to Figure 13-17. These properties are used to override the global property of the layer in a particular viewport while retaining the global layer properties in other floating viewports and the model space. To set properties of a viewport, double-click inside it to activate the temporary model space and then set the properties. The properties are discussed next.

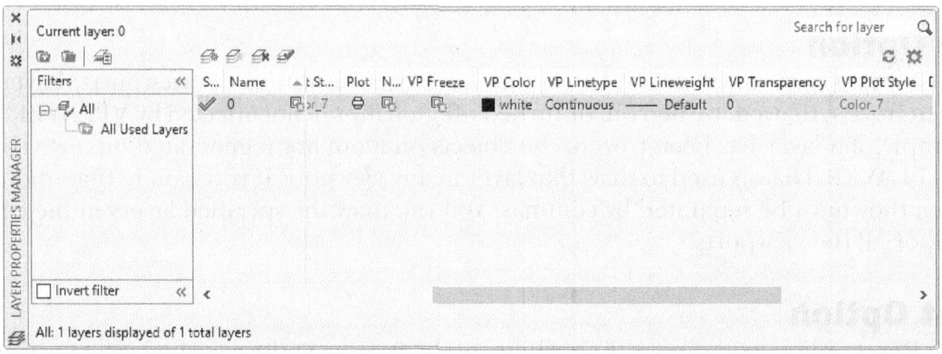

Figure 13-17** Controlling the visibility of layers in the viewports using the **LAYER PROPERTIES MANAGER

VP Freeze

When the **TILEMODE** option is turned off, you can freeze or thaw the selected layers in the current floating viewport by selecting the **VP Freeze** option. You can freeze a layer in the current floating viewport if it is thawed in the model space but you cannot thaw a layer in the current viewport if it is frozen in the model space. The frozen layers still remain visible in other viewports.

VP Color

The swatch under the **VP Color** column is used to change the display color of the objects in the selected layer in the current floating viewport. In all other floating viewports and model space, the color of the objects remains unaffected.

VP Linetype

The field under the **VP Linetype** column is used to change the linetype defined for the selected layer in the active floating viewport. In all other floating viewports and model space, the linetype remains unaffected.

VP Lineweight

The field under the **VP Lineweight** column is used to override the lineweight defined for the selected layer in the active floating viewport. In all other floating viewports and the model space, the lineweight remains unaffected.

VP Transparency

The field under the **VP Transparency** column is used to override the transparency defined for the layer selected in the active floating viewport. In all other floating viewports and the model space, the transparency remains unaffected.

VP Plot Style

The field under the **VP Plot Style** column is used to override the plot style settings assigned to the selected layer in the active floating viewport. The plot style for all other floating viewports and model space remains unaffected. You cannot override the plot styles for the color dependent plot styles. The override for the plot style also does not affect the plot if the visual style is set to **Realistic** or **Conceptual**.

Note

*By default, all the overrides that you have defined for the current active viewport will get highlighted in light blue color in the **LAYER PROPERTIES MANAGER**. Also, the icon of the selected layer under the **Status** column will change to inform you that some of the properties of the selected layer have been overridden by the new one.*

Removing Viewport Overrides

To remove the viewport overrides defined for the active viewports, open the **LAYER PROPERTIES MANAGER** in the active viewport and right-click on the layer property from which you want to remove the viewport override; a shortcut menu will be displayed. Next, choose the **Remove Viewport Overrides for** option from the shortcut menu to display the cascading menu. You can make a choice to remove the override for a single property / all properties of the selected layer / all layers in the current viewport / all viewports, refer to Figure 13-18. Choose the required option from the cascading menu to remove the viewport overrides. You can also remove the layer property overrides for all layers of the selected viewports from the paper space. To do so, make the paper space current; select the boundaries of the viewports for which you want to remove the override and choose the **Remove Viewport Overrides for All Layers** option from the shortcut menu.

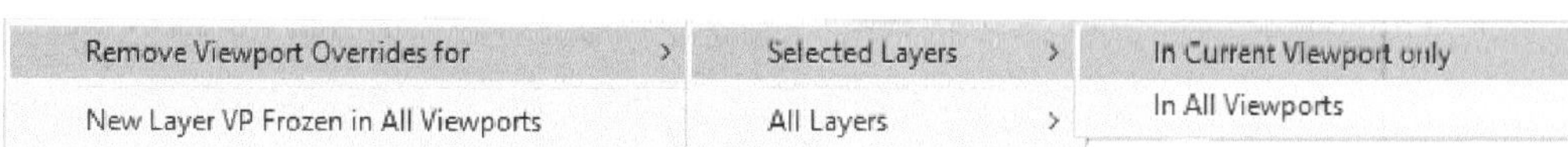

***Figure 13-18** Cascading menu displayed for the **Remove Viewport Overrides for** option in the **Layer** shortcut menu*

Note

*For more information about the **LAYER PROPERTIES MANAGER**, refer to Chapter 4.*

PAPER SPACE LINETYPE SCALING (PSLTSCALE SYSTEM VARIABLE)

By default, the linetype scaling is controlled by the **LTSCALE** system variable. Therefore, the display size of the dashes depends on the **LTSCALE** factor, on the drawing limits, or on the drawing units. If you have different viewports with different zoom (XP) factors, the size of the dashes will be different for these viewports. Figure 13-19 shows three viewports with different sizes and different zoom (XP) factors. You will notice that the dash length is different in each of these three viewports.

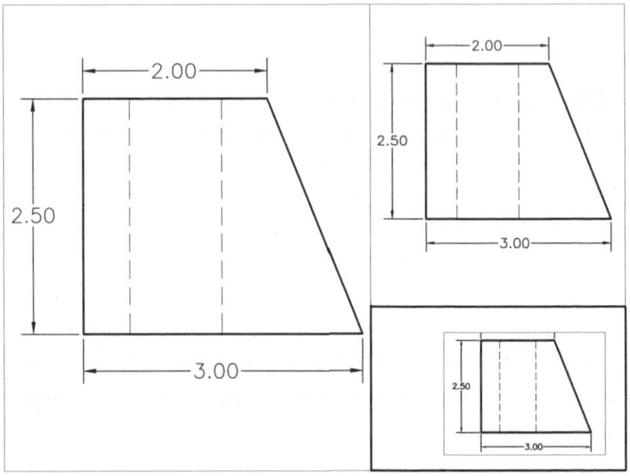

Figure 13-19 *Varying sizes of the dashed lines with* ***PSLTSCALE*** *= 0*

Generally, it is desirable to have identical line spacing in all viewports. This can be achieved with the **PSLTSCALE** system variable. If you set the **PSLTSCALE** is to 0, the size of the dashes will depend upon the **LTSCALE** system variable and on the zoom (XP) factor of the viewport where the objects have been drawn. If you set **PSLTSCALE** to **1** and **TILEMODE** to **0**, the size of the dashes for objects in the model space are scaled to match the **LTSCALE** of objects in the paper space viewport, regardless of their zoom scale. In other words, if **PSLTSCALE** is set to 1, even if the viewports are zoomed to different sizes, the length of the dashes will be identical in all viewports. Figure 13-20 shows three viewports with different sizes. Notice that the dash length is identical in all the three viewports.

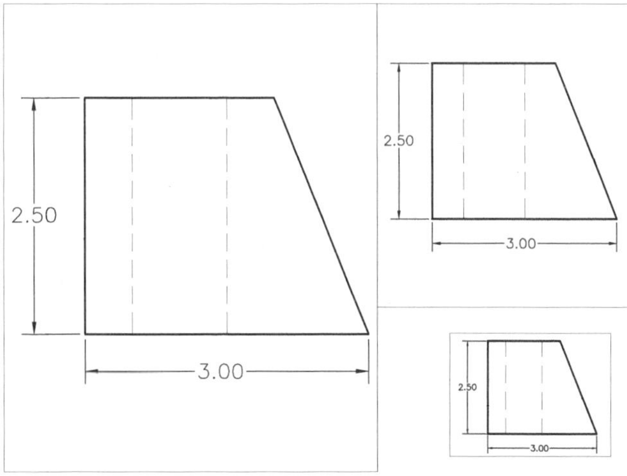

Figure 13-20 Identical sizes of the dashed lines with ***PSLTSCALE*** *= 1*

Tip

You can control the scale factor for displaying the objects in the viewports using the ***Viewport Scale Control*** *drop-down list. This drop-down list is available in the* ***Viewports*** *toolbar.*

INSERTING LAYOUTS

Ribbon: Layout contextual tab > Layout > Layout drop-down > New Layout
Toolbar: Layouts > New Layout **Menu Bar:** Insert > Layout > New Layout
Command: LAYOUT

The **New Layout** tool, available in the **Layout** drop-down of the **Layout** panel in the **Layout** contextual tab of the **Ribbon**, is used to create new layouts. The **LAYOUT** command can also be used to create a new layout. This command also allows you to rename, copy, saveas, and delete existing layouts. A drawing designed in the **Model** tab can be composed for plotting in the **Layout** tab. The prompt sequence is as follows.

Enter layout option [Copy/Delete/New/Template/Rename/SAveas/Set/?]<Set>:

The options in the prompt sequence are discussed next.

New Option

This option is used to create a new layout. On choosing this option, you will be prompted to specify the name of the new layout. A new tab with the new layout name will appear in the drawing. Alternatively, you can right-click on the **Model** or the **Layout** tab and choose **New Layout** from the shortcut menu to add a new layout. The new layout tab will be added at the end of the existing layout tabs with the default name **LayoutN**, where **N** is a natural number starting from one and acquires an ascending value that has not been used in the layout names of the current drawing.

Copy Option

This option is used to copy a layout. When you invoke this option, you will be prompted to specify the layout that has to be copied. On specifying the layout, you will be prompted to specify the name of the new layout. If you do not enter a name, the name of the copied layout is assumed with an incremental number in the brackets next to it. For example, Layout1 is copied as Layout1 (2). The name of the new layout appears as a new tab next to the copied layout tab. Alternatively, you can right-click on the **Model** or **Layout** tab and then choose the **Move or Copy** option from the shortcut menu to move or copy the selected layout; the **Move or Copy** dialog box will be displayed, as shown in Figure 13-21. Select the layout from the **Before layout** area to move it above the previous layout and then choose the **OK** button. For example, if you want to move the Layout 2 before Layout 1, then select Layout 2 from the **Move or Copy** dialog box; the Layout 2 will be moved before Layout 1. To create a copy of the selected layout, select the **Create a copy** check box.

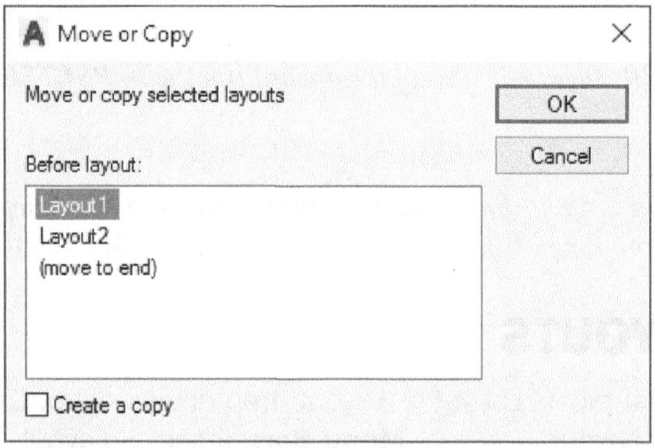

*Figure 13-21 The **Move or Copy** dialog box*

Tip

You can also drag and drop layouts to move them. To create copies of the selected layouts, press the CTRL key as you drag and drop the layouts.

Delete Option

This option is used to delete an existing layout. On invoking this option, you will be prompted to specify the name of the layout to be deleted. The current layout is the default layout for deleting. You can also right-click on the **Model** or the **Layout** tab and choose the **Delete** option from the shortcut menu; the AutoCAD alert window will be displayed. Choose the **OK** button to delete the selected layout. Note that the **Model** tab cannot be deleted.

Template Option

This option is used to create a new template based on the existing layout template in the *.dwg*, *.dwt*, or *.dxf* files. This option invokes the **Select Template From File** dialog box, as shown in Figure 13-22. You can also invoke this dialog box by right-clicking on the **Model** tab, the **Layout** tab, and then choosing the **From Template** option from the shortcut menu.

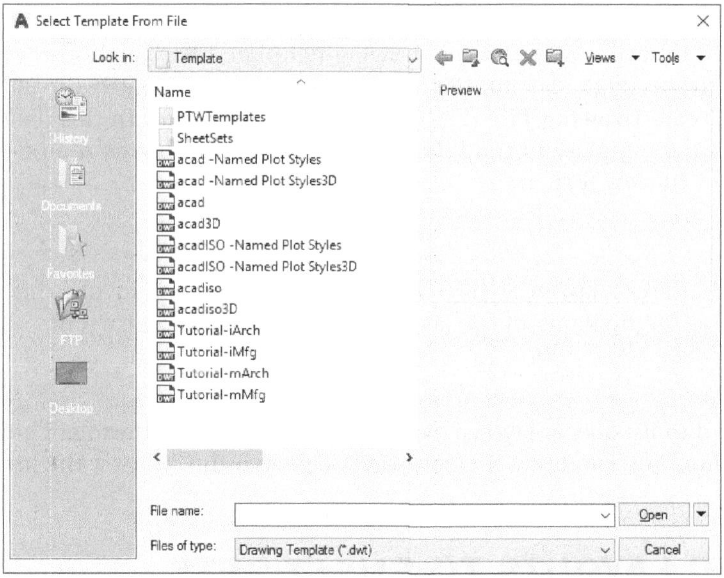

***Figure 13-22** The **Select Template From File** dialog box*

The layout and geometry from the specified template or drawing file is inserted into the current drawing. After the *dwt*, *dwg*, or *dxf* file is selected, the **Insert Layout(s)** dialog box is displayed, as shown in Figure 13-23.

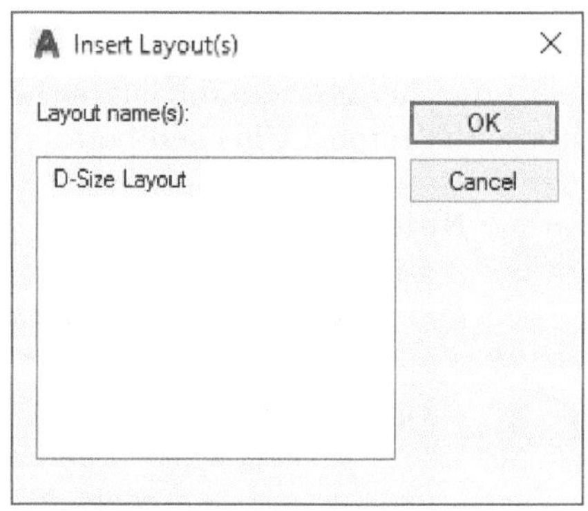

***Figure 13-23** The **Insert Layout(s)** dialog box*

You can also choose the **Layout from Template** button from the **Layouts** toolbar to create a layout using an existing template or a drawing file.

Note

If you insert a template that has a title block, it will be inserted as a block and all the text in the title block will be inserted as attributes. You will learn more about blocks and attributes in the later chapters.

Rename Option

This option allows you to rename a layout. On choosing this option, you will be prompted to specify the name of the layout to be renamed. On specifying the name, you will be prompted to specify the new name of the layout. The layout names have to be unique and can contain up to 255 characters out of which only 32 are displayed in the tab. The characters in the name are not case-sensitive. You can also right-click on the **Model** or the **Layout** tab and choose the **Rename** option from the shortcut menu to rename the selected layout.

Tip

*You can also double-click on the **Layout** tab to rename the layout.*

SAveas Option

This option is used to save a layout in the drawing template file. On choosing this option, you will be prompted to specify the layout that has to be saved. If you specify the name of the layout to be saved, the **Create Drawing File** dialog box will be displayed. In this dialog box, you can enter the name of the template in the **File name** edit box. The layout templates can be saved in the *.dwg*, *.dwt*, or the *.dxf* format.

Set Option

This option is used to set a layout as the current layout. When you invoke this option, you will be prompted to specify the name of the layout that has to be made current.

? Option

This option is used to list all the layouts available in the current drawing. The list is displayed in the command line. You can open the **AutoCAD Text Window** to view the list by pressing the F2 key.

IMPORTING LAYOUTS TO SHEET SETS

To add a layout to the current sheet set, right-click on the **Layout** tab and then choose the **Import Layout as Sheet** option from the shortcut menu; the **Import Layout as Sheet** dialog box will be invoked. This dialog box displays all the layouts available in the selected drawing. Select the check box on the left of the drawing file name under the **Drawing Name** column and choose the **Import Checked** button to import the selected layouts into the current sheet set.

Note

A layout can be imported to only one sheet set. If a layout already belongs to a sheet set, you have to create a copy of the drawing to import its layout to another sheet set.

Tip

You can also drag and drop the layout from a drawing to add it to the sheet set. But make sure that you save the drawing file before you drag and drop the layout.

INSERTING A LAYOUT USING THE WIZARD

Command: LAYOUTWIZARD

This command displays the **Create Layout Wizard** that guides you step-by-step through the process of creating a new layout.

DEFINING PAGE SETTINGS

Ribbon: Output > Plot > Page Setup Manager	**Command:** PAGESETUP
Toolbar: Layouts > Page Setup Manager	

The **Page Setup Manager** tool is used to specify the layout and plot device settings for each new layout. You can also right-click on the current **Layout** tab and choose the **Page Setup Manager** option from the shortcut menu to invoke this command. When you invoke this command, the **Page Setup Manager** dialog box is displayed, which will be discussed in Chapter 14.

Example 2

In this example, you will create a drawing in the model space and then use the paper space to plot the drawing. The drawing to be plotted is shown in Figure 13-24.

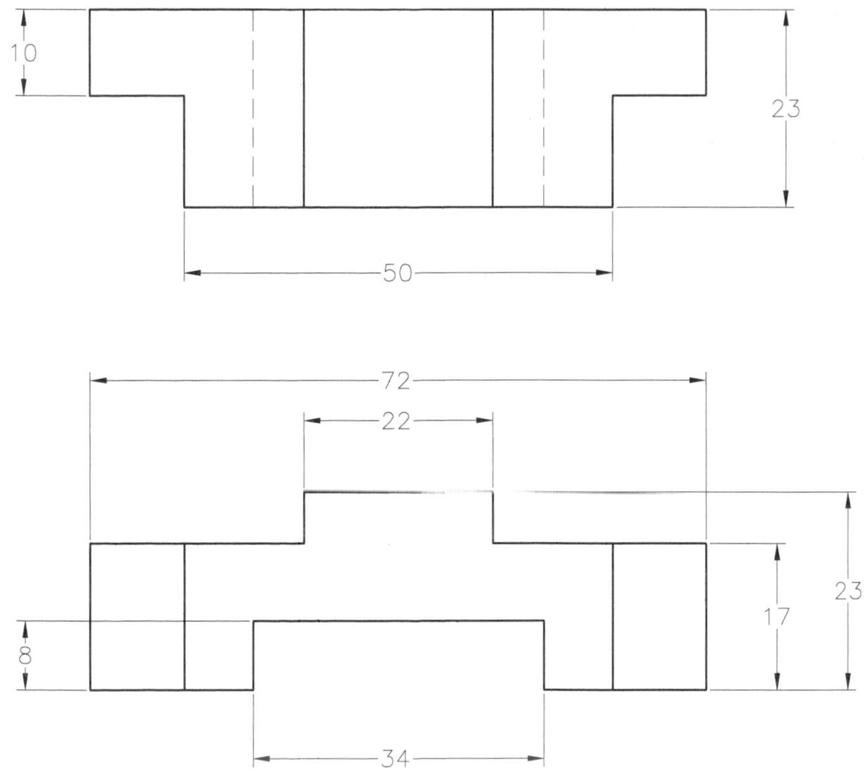

Figure 13-24 *Drawing for Example 2*

1. Increase the limits to 75, 75 and then draw the sketch shown in Figure 13-24.

2. Choose the **Layout1** tab; AutoCAD displays **Layout1** with the default viewport. Delete this viewport. Right-click on the **Layout1** tab and then choose the **Page Setup Manager** option from the shortcut menu to display the **Page Setup Manager** dialog box. **Layout1** is automatically selected in the **Current page setup** list box.

3. Choose the **Modify** button to display the **Page Setup - Layout1** dialog box. Select the printer or plotter from the **Name** drop-down list in the **Printer/plotter** area. In this example, **HP Lasejet4000** is used. From the drop-down list in the **Paper size** area, select the paper size that is supported by your plotting device. In this example, the paper size is **ISO full bleed A4 (210.00 x 297.00 MM)**. Choose the **OK** button to accept the settings and exit the dialog box. Close the **Page Setup Manager** dialog box by choosing the **Close** button.

4. Choose the **Rectangular** tool from the **Viewports** drop-down in the **Layout Viewports** panel of the **Layout** contextual tab in the **Ribbon**; you are prompted to specify the corner point of the viewport. The prompt sequence is as follows:

Specify corner of viewport or [ON/OFF/Fit/Shadeplot/Lock/Object/Polygonal/Restore/LAyer/2/3/4] <Fit>: **F** Enter
Regenerating model.

5. Choose the **Extents** tool from the **Zoom** drop-down in the **Navigate** panel of the **View** tab in the **Ribbon** to zoom to the extents of the viewport.

6. Double-click in the viewport to switch to the temporary model space and repeat the previous step.

7. Create the dimension style with the text height of 1.5 and the arrowhead height of 1.25. Define all the other parameters based on the text and arrowhead heights and then select the **Annotative** check box from the **Scale for dimension features** area of the **Fit** tab in the **New Dimension Style** dialog box.

8. Using the new dimension style, dimension the drawing. Repeat step 5.

9. Double-click in the paper space to switch back to the paper space. Choose the **Plot** tool from the **Quick Access Toolbar**, the **Batch Plot** message box is displayed. Select the **Continue to plot a single sheet** option from this message box to display the **Plot - Layout1** dialog box.

10. Choose the **Window** option from the **What to plot** drop-down list in the **Plot area**; the dialog box will be closed temporarily and you will be prompted to specify the first and second corners of the window. Define a window selecting the opposite corners of the boundary of the viewport.

11. As soon as you define both the corners of the window, the **Plot** dialog box will be redisplayed on the screen. Select the **Fit to paper** check box from the **Plot scale** area.

12. Select the **Center the plot** check box from the **Plot offset (origin set to printable area)** area.

13. Choose the **Preview** button to display the plot preview. You can make any adjustments, if required, by redefining the window.

14. After you are satisfied with the preview, right-click and choose the **Plot** option from the shortcut menu. The drawing will be printed. Save this drawing with the name *Example2.dwg*.

WORKING WITH THE MVSETUP COMMAND

The **MVSETUP** command is a very versatile command and can be used both in the **Model** tab and in the **Layout** tab. This means that this command can be used when the **Tilemode** is set to **1** or when it is set to **0**. The fuctions of this command in both the drawing environments are discussed next.

Using the MVSETUP Command in the Model Tab

On the **Model** tab, this command is used to set the units, scale factor for the drawing, and the size of the paper. On invoking this command, you will be prompted to specify whether or not you want to enable the paper space. Enter **N** at this prompt to use this command on the **Model** tab. When you enter **N** in the command prompt, the following prompt sequence will be displayed.

> Enter units type [Scientific/Decimal/Engineering/Architectural/Metric]: *Specify the unit. In this case,* ***Architectural*** *is selected.*
>
> Architectural Scales
> ======================
> (480) 1/40"=1'
> (240) 1/20"=1'
> (192) 1/16"=1'
> (96) 1/8"=1'
> (48) 1/4"=1'
> (24) 1/2"=1'
> (16) 3/4"=1'
> (12) 1"=1'
> (4) 3"=1'
> (2) 6"=1'
> (1) FULL
>
> Enter the scale factor: *Specify the scale factor for displaying the drawing.*
> Enter the paper width: *Specify the width of the paper.*
> Enter the paper height: *Specify the height of the paper.*

A box of the specified width and height will be drawn and the drawing will be displayed inside the box. The display of the drawing will depend upon the scale factor you have specified.

Using the MVSETUP Command in the Layout Tab

The way this command works in the **Layout** tab is entirely different from that in the **Model** tab. In the **Layout** tab, it is used to insert a title block, create an array of viewports, align the objects in the viewports, and so on. The prompt sequence that will follow when you invoke this command in the **Layout** tab is given next.

> Enter an option [Align/Create/Scale viewports/Options/Title block/Undo]: *Select an option.*

Align Option

This option is used to align the objects in one of the viewports with that of another viewport. You can specify horizontal, vertical, angled, or rotated alignment. After you have selected the option, you will be prompted to select the base point. The base point is the point which will be used as the reference point for moving the objects in the specified viewport. Once you have specified the base point, you will be prompted to specify the point in the viewport that will be panned. This point will be aligned with the base point and thus the objects in this viewport will be moved.

Create Option

This option is used to create the viewports in the layouts. On invoking this option, you will be prompted to specify whether you want to create a viewport, delete the objects in it, or undo the previous option. If the **Create viewports** option is selected, the **AutoCAD Text Window** is displayed. This window provides you with four options. These options are discussed next.

0:	**None**	**1:**	**Single**
2:	**Std. Engineering**	**3:**	**Array of Viewports**

If you enter **0**, the viewports will not be created and the previous prompt will be displayed again. If you enter **1**, you will be prompted to specify two points for the bounding box of the viewport. A new viewport will be created inside the specified bounding box. If you enter **2**, you will be prompted to specify two corners of the bounding box. Inside the specified bounding box, four standard engineering viewports will be created. The first viewport will display the model from the top view, the second will display the model from the SE isometric view, the third will display the front view of the model (*ZX* plane of the current UCS), and the fourth will display the right-side view of the model (*YZ* plane of the current UCS). This option is generally used while working with 3D models. You will also be prompted to specify the distances between the viewports in the X direction and in the Y direction.

If you enter **3**, you will be allowed to create an array of viewports along the *X* axis and the *Y* axis. You will be prompted to define a bounding box in which the viewports will be created. After you have defined the bounding box, you will be prompted to specify the number of viewports in the X and Y directions. Then you will be prompted to specify the distances between the viewports in the X and Y directions. Figure 13-25 shows an array of viewports in the layout with the distance between the viewports in the *X* axis and *Y* axis directions set to zero.

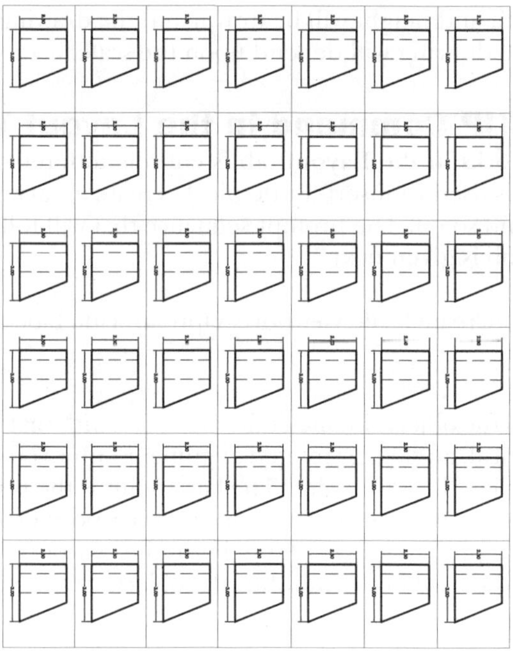

***Figure 13-25** Array of viewports*

Scale viewports Option

This option is used to modify the scale factors of the viewports. This scale factor is defined by the ratio of the paper space units to model space units. You can select one or more than one viewports to modify the scale factors. If you select more than one viewport, you will be prompted to specify whether you want to define a uniform scale factor for the viewports or define individual scale factors. You will be first prompted to specify the number of the paper space units in the viewport and then the model space units in it. The display in the viewports will be automatically modified once you have defined both the values.

Options Option

This option is used to set the parameters for inserting the title block. The parameters that can be set include layers, limits, units, and external reference options. Using the **Layers** option, you can predefine the layer into which the title block will be inserted. Using the **Limits** option, you can specify whether or not the limits should be reset to the extents of the title block after it is inserted. Using the **Units** option, you can set the units in which the size of the title block will be translated. Using the **Xref** option, you can set whether the title block, after inserting, will become the entity of the current drawing or remain as an Xref object.

Title block Option

This option is used to insert the title block of the desired size in the current layout, delete the entities from the current layout, or reset the origin of the current layout. The default option is used for inserting a title block. If you select this option, the **AutoCAD Text Window** will be invoked displaying different sizes and formats of the title blocks that can be inserted. The various options that will be displayed are given next.

0: None | **1: ISO A4 Size(mm)**
2: ISO A3 Size(mm) | **3: ISO A2 Size(mm)**
4: ISO A1 Size(mm) | **5: ISO A0 Size(mm)**
6: ANSI-V Size(in) | **7: ANSI-A Size(in)**
8: ANSI-B Size(in) | **9: ANSI-C Size(in)**
10: ANSI-D Size(in) | **11: ANSI-E Size(in)**
12: Arch/Engineering (24 x 36in)
13: Generic D size Sheet (24 x 36in)

You can enter the number corresponding to a title block to insert that title block in the current layout. The properties of this layout will depend on the parameters set using the **Options** option. You can also add or delete the title blocks in this default list. Figure 13-26 shows a layout with an A4 size title block and a viewport created in it.

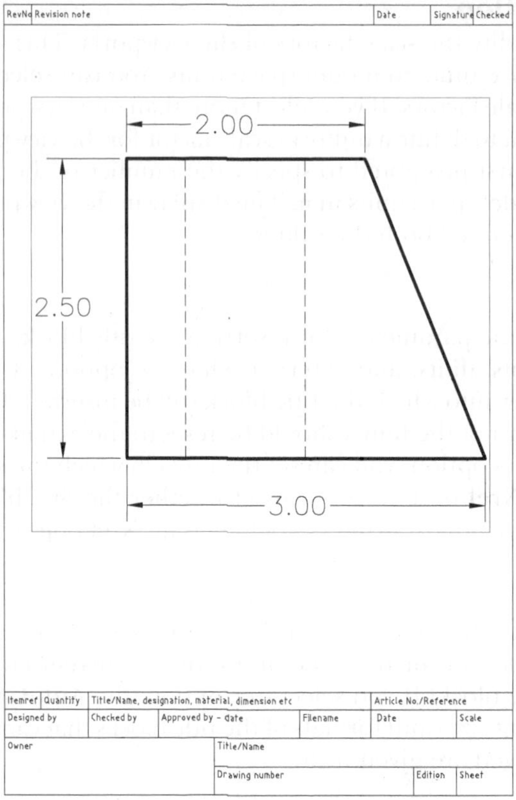

***Figure 13-26** Layout with the title block*

CONVERTING THE DISTANCE BETWEEN MODEL SPACE AND PAPER SPACE

Toolbar: Text > Convert distance between spaces | **Command:** SPACETRANS

While working with drawings in layouts, you may need to find a distance value that is equivalent to a specific distance in the model space. For example, you may need to write text whose height should be equal to a similar text written in the model space. To convert these distances between the model space and layouts, AutoCAD provides the **SPACETRANS** command. Note that this command does not work in the model space. This command works only in layouts or in the temporary model space invoked from the layouts, but there should be at least one viewport in the drawing. When you invoke this command in the paper space, AutoCAD prompts you to select the viewport. After selecting the viewport, AutoCAD prompts you to specify the model space distance. Enter the original distance value that was measured in the model space; AutoCAD displays the paper space equivalent to the specified distance.

Similarly, when you invoke this command in the temporary model space, AutoCAD prompts you to specify the paper space distance. Enter the distance value measured in the paper space. AutoCAD displays the model space equivalent to the specified distance.

CONTROLLING THE DISPLAY OF ANNOTATIVE OBJECTS IN VIEWPORTS

Some new buttons need to be added to the Status Bar to control the annotation scale in viewports and model space separately. When you activate a floating viewport, a new **Viewport Scale** button is added to the Status Bar. The **Viewport Scale** button lists the same set of scales as the **Annotation Scale**. You can set an annotation display scale either from the **Viewport Scale** button or the **Annotation Scale** button, and the other scales will be updated accordingly. The viewport will zoom to an appropriate scale so that the annotation objects can be displayed at the specified scale.

Also, when you activate a floating viewport, the **Viewport Lock** button is added to the Status Bar. With the help of this button, you can toggle between the lock and unlock states of the viewport. The **Viewport Scale** and **Annotation Scale** buttons are not accessible when the viewport is locked. If the viewport is unlocked and you zoom the drawing instead of specifying the viewport scale, the annotation scale will not be changed and the current scale representation will remain intact and visible. But, the viewport scale will be changed to display the actual scale of the viewport.

The example given next will explain various concepts related to creating and controlling the display of annotations in viewports.

Note

When the paper space is active, the annotation scale is always 1:1 and it cannot be modified.

Example 3 — Annotative Text

In this example, you will draw the object, as shown in Figure 13-27, and create the floating viewports, as shown in Figure 13-28. The left viewport has a scale of 3/8"=1'-0" and the right viewport has a scale of 1-1/2"=1'-0". All the annotations that are created in the model space should be displayed with a text height of 0.08" on the sheet even if the same annotation appears in multiple viewports.

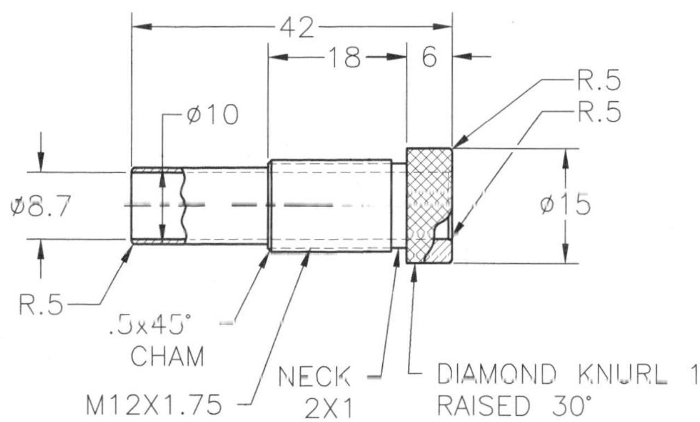

Figure 13-27 Model for Example 3

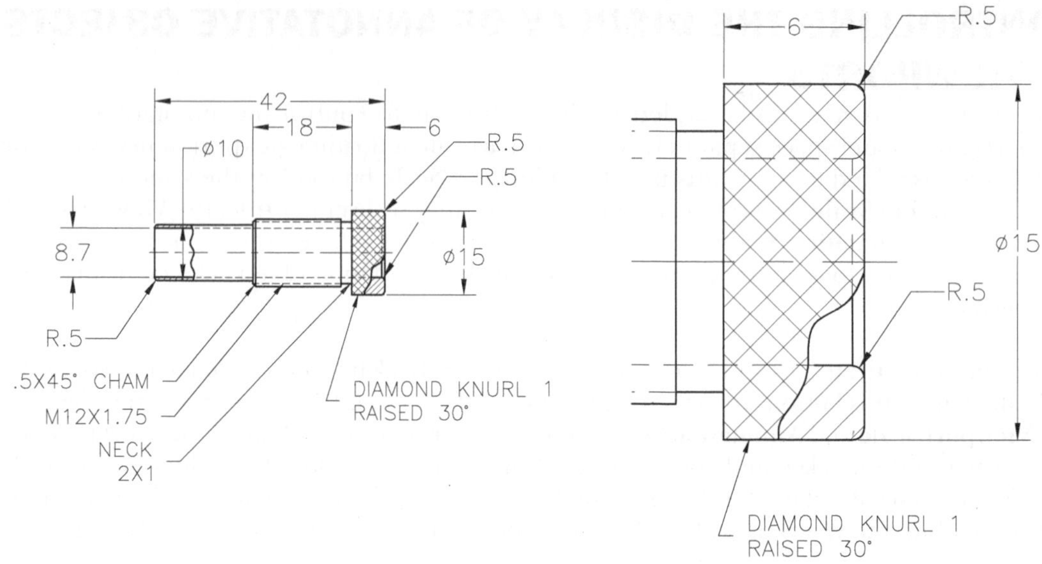

Figure 13-28 Displaying the drawing in two viewports

1. Start a new file in the **Drafting & Annotation** workspace and draw the object, as shown in Figure 13-27.

2. Set the **Annotation Scale** to 3/8"=1'-0" in the Status Bar.

3. Create an annotative text style with the **Paper Text Height** equal to **0.08**.

4. Create an annotative dimension style with the values given next and create the dimensions, refer to Figure 13-27.
   Arrow size = **0.07**
   Text height = **0.08**

5. Create an annotative multileader style with the values given next and draw the multileaders, refer to Figure 13-27.

   Landing distance = **0.075**
   Arrowhead size = **0.07**
   Text height = **0.08**

6. Change the annotation scale to 1-1/2"=1'-0", select all the dimensions from the right of the object, and then choose the **Add Current Scale** tool from the **Annotation Scaling** panel of the **Annotate** tab; the annotation scale of 1-1/2"=1'-0" is added to the selected dimensions. You will notice that the selected dimensions and multileaders appear smaller than the other annotations because they reflect the current annotation scale of 1-1/2"=1'-0".

7. Turn the **Annotation Visibility** button off. Now you can see the annotations that support a scale of 1-1/2"=1'-0". This helps you to find out the dimensions to which the scale of 1-1/2"=1'-0" has been assigned.

8. Select the annotations from the right of the object and adjust their locations with the help of grips such that the placement of dimensions remains similar to the one shown in Figure 13-27. Notice that when you select the annotation object, its different scale representations are displayed with faded dashed lines.

9. From the Status Bar, set the annotation scale to 3/8"=1'-0" and then change it back to 1-1/2"=1'-0". Now you will notice that the same annotation objects not only change the size but also change the location.

10. Choose the **Layout1** tab to switch to the layouts.

11. A rectangular viewport is automatically created in this layout. Choose the **Erase** tool from the **Modify** panel of the **Home** tab; you will be prompted to select the object. Enter **L** in this prompt to delete the last object which in this case is the viewport.

12. Draw two rectangles of dimensions **3'X3.5'** and **2.25'X3.5'** side-by-side, refer to Figure 13-28.

13. Choose the **Object** tool from **Layout > Layout Viewports > Object Viewports** drop-down of the **Ribbon**; you will be prompted to select the object. Select one of the rectangles; it will be converted into a viewport. Similarly, convert the second rectangle into a viewport.

14. Activate the viewport on the left and set its annotation scale to 3/8"=1'-0" in the Status Bar.

15. Similarly, activate the viewport on the right and set its annotation scale to 1-1/2"=1'-0". Pan the view so that it looks similar to Figure 13-28.

Self-Evaluation Test

Answer the following questions and then compare them to those given at the end of this chapter:

1. The __________ tool is used to create tiled viewports.

2. The viewports in layouts are called __________ viewports.

3. The two working environments provided by AutoCAD are __________ and __________.

4. The __________ command is used to insert a title block in the current layout.

5. When you join two adjacent viewports, the resultant viewport is __________ in shape.

6. The default viewport that is created in a new layout is __________ in shape.

7. Viewports in the model space can be of any shape. (T/F)

8. Viewports in the model space can overlap each other. (T/F)

9. You can join two different tiled viewports. (T/F)

10. You cannot insert any additional layout in the current drawing. (T/F)

Review Questions

Answer the following questions:

1. Which of the following commands can be used to control the display of objects in the viewports?

   (a) **MVIEW** (b) **DVIEW**
   (c) **LAYOUT** (d) **MSPACE**

2. Which of the following tools can be used to switch to the temporary model space?

   (a) **Quick View Drawings** (b) **Named**
   (c) **Quick View Layouts** (d) **Model or Paper space**

3. Which of the following options in the paper space can be used to hide the hidden lines of solid models in printing?

   (a) **Hide** (b) **Shadeplot**
   (c) **Create** (d) **None**

4. Which of the following tools can be used to clip an existing floating viewport?

   (a) **View Manager** (b) **Join**
   (c) **Clip** (d) **Restore**

5. Which of the following options of the **VPLAYER** command is used to create a layer that will be frozen in all viewports?

   (a) **Freeze** (b) **Thaw**
   (c) **Newfrz** (d) **Reset**

6. The __________ option of the **MVSETUP** command can be used to set the parameters related to inserting of the title blocks.

7. You can work only in the __________ tiled viewport.

8. The __________ tool can be used to set same linetype scale for all the viewports.

9. The __________ tool is used to switch back to the paper space from the temporary model space.

10. The __________ dialog box is used to save a viewport configuration in the model space.

11. Layers that have been frozen, thawed, switched on, or switched off globally are not affected by the _________ tool.

12. Viewports in the model space can be of any shape. (T/F)

13. Viewports in the model space can overlap each other. (T/F)

14. You can join two different tiled viewports. (T/F)

15. You cannot insert any additional layout in the current drawing. (T/F)

Exercise 1 — *Tiled Viewport*

In this exercise, you will perform the following operations:

a. In the model space, make the drawing of the shaft shown in Figure 13-29.
b. Create three tiled viewports in the model space and then display the drawing in all the three tiled viewports.
c. Create a new layout with the name **Title Block** and insert a title block of ANSI A size in this layout.
d. Create two viewports, one for the drawing and one for the detail "A". Refer to Figure 13-29 for the approximate size and location. The dimensions in detail "A" viewport must not be shown in the other viewport. Also, adjust the LTSCALE factor for hidden and center lines.
e. Plot the drawing.

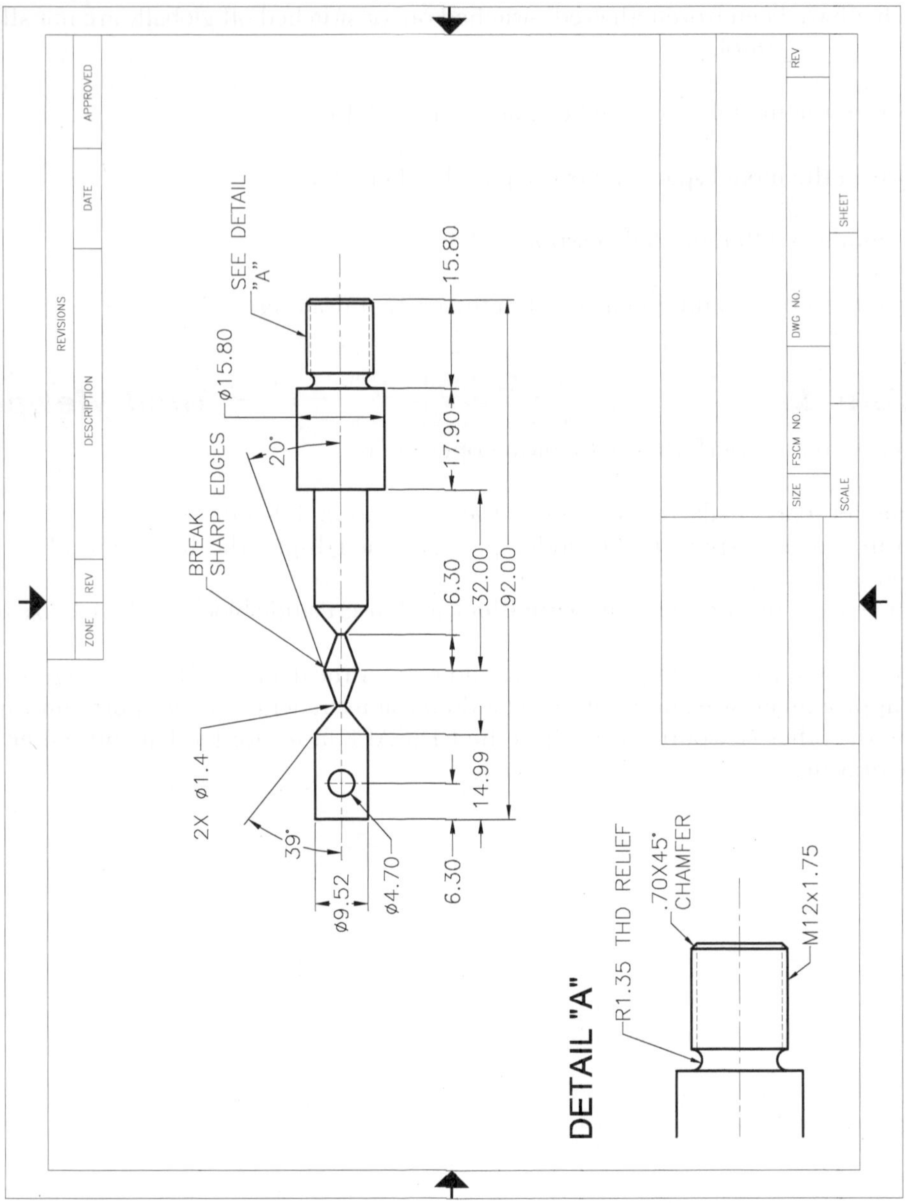

***Figure 13-29** Drawing for Exercise 1*

Answers to Self-Evaluation Test

1. VPORTS, **2.** floating, **3.** model space, paper space/layouts, **4. MVSETUP**, **5.** rectangular, **6.** rectangular, **7.** F, **8.** F, **9.** T, **10.** F

Chapter 14

Plotting Drawings

Learning Objectives

After completing this chapter, you will be able to:

- *Set plotter specifications and plot drawings*
- *Configure plotters and edit their configuration files*
- *Create, use, and modify plot styles and plot style tables*
- *Plot sheets in a sheet set*

Key Terms

- *Plot*
- *Page Setup*
- *Plot Style*
- *Plotter Manager*
- *Styles Manager*
- *Plot Style Table Editor*
- *Named Plot Style*
- *Color Dependent Plot Style*

PLOTTING DRAWINGS IN AutoCAD

After you have completed a drawing, you can store it on the computer storage device such as the hard drive or diskette. However, to get its hard copy, you should plot the drawing on a sheet of paper using a plotter or printer. A hard copy is a handy reference for professionals working on site. With pen plotters, you can obtain a high-resolution drawing. Basic plotting has already been discussed in Chapter 2, Getting Started with AutoCAD. You can plot drawings in the **Model** tab or any of the layout tabs. A drawing has a **Model** and two layout tabs (**Layout1**, **Layout2**) by default. Each of these tabs has its own settings and can be used to create different plots. You can also create new layout tabs using the **New Layout** tool. This is discussed in Chapter 13.

PLOTTING DRAWINGS USING THE PLOT DIALOG BOX

Ribbon: Output > Plot > Plot	**Application Menu:** Print > Plot
Toolbar: Standard > Plot	**Command:** Ctrl+P/PLOT
Quick Access Toolbar: Plot	

The **Plot** tool is used to plot a drawing. When you choose this tool, the **Plot** dialog box is displayed. This dialog box can also be invoked by right-clicking on the **Model** tab or any of the **Layout** tabs and then choosing the **Plot** option from the shortcut menu displayed. Figure 14-1 shows the expanded **Plot** dialog box.

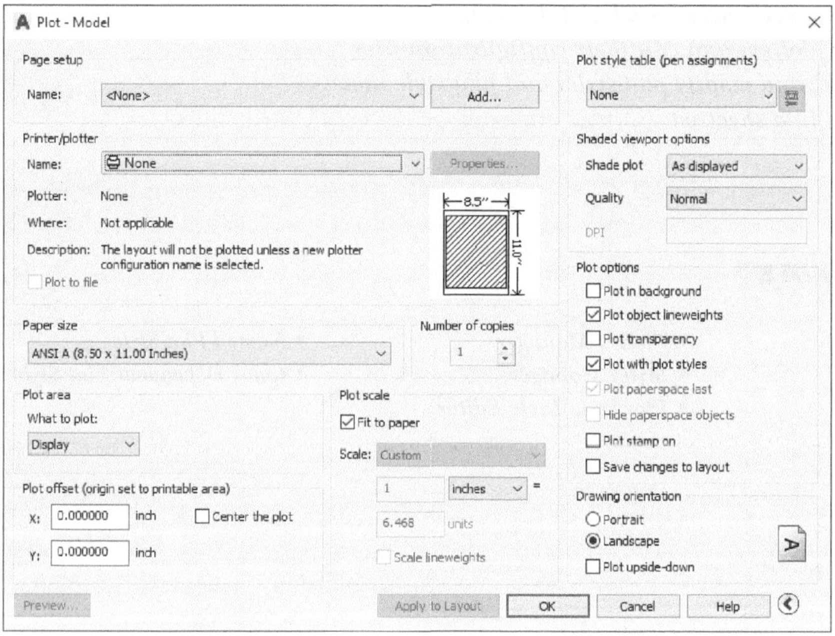

***Figure 14-1** The expanded **Plot** dialog box*

In this dialog box, some values were set when AutoCAD was first configured. You can examine these values and if they conform to your requirements, you can start plotting directly. Otherwise, you can alter these values to define plot specifications by using the options in the **Plot** dialog box. The available plot options are discussed next.

Page setup Area

The **Name** drop-down list in this area displays all the saved and named page setups. A page setup contains the settings required to plot a drawing on a sheet of paper to create a layout. It consists of all the settings related to the plotting of a drawing such as the scale, pen settings, and so on. These settings can be saved as a named page setup, which can be later selected from this drop-down list and used for plotting a drawing. If you select **Previous plot** from the drop-down list, the settings used for the last drawing plotted are applied to the current drawing. You can also import the existing page setup from the other files by selecting the **Import** option from the drop-down list. The page setup can be imported from any drawing file(*.dwg*), from a template file(*.dwt*), or from a drawing interchange format file(*.dxf*). You can choose the base for the page setup on a named page setup, or you can add a new named page setup by choosing the **Add** button, which is located next to the drop-down list. When you choose this button, AutoCAD displays the **Add Page Setup** dialog box, as shown in Figure 14-2.

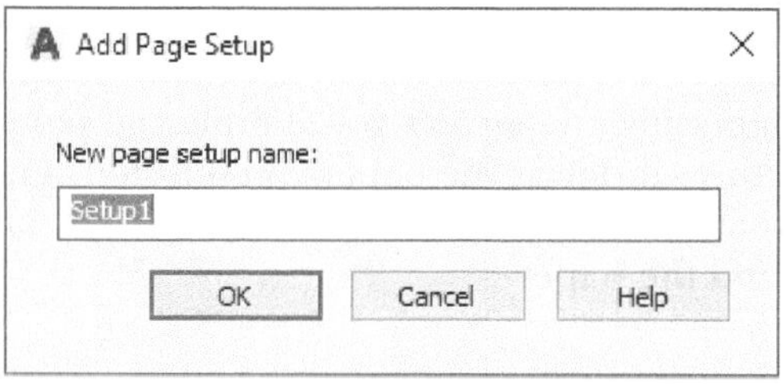

***Figure 14-2** The **Add Page Setup** dialog box*

Enter the name of the new page setup in this dialog box and choose the **OK** button. All the settings that you configure in the current **Plot** dialog box will be saved under this page setup.

Tip

*To create a new page setup based on the existing one, select the existing page setup from the **Name** drop-down list and make modifications in it. Next, choose the **Add** button; the modified page setup will be saved.*

Printer/plotter Area

This area displays all the information about the printer and plotter currently selected in the **Name** drop-down list. It displays information of the plotter driver and the printer port being used. It also displays the physical location and some description text about the selected plotter or printer. All the currently configured plotters are displayed in the **Name** drop-down list.

Note

*To add plotters and printers to the **Name** drop-down list, choose the **Plotter Manager** tool from the **Plot** panel in the **Output** tab; a window will be displayed. Double-click on the **Add-A-Plotter Wizard** icon in this window to display the **Add Plotter** wizard. You can use this wizard to add a plotter to the list of configured plotters. Once the plotter is added, the plotter configuration file (PC3) for the plotter will be created. This file consists of all the settings needed by the specific plotter to plot the drawing. (The **Plotters** window will be discussed later in this chapter in the section "Adding Plotters").*

Properties

To check information about a configured printer or plotter, choose the **Properties** button. When you choose this button, the **Plotter Configuration Editor** dialog box will be displayed. This dialog box lists all the details of the selected plotter under three tabs: **General**, **Ports**, and **Device and Document Settings**. The **Plotter Configuration Editor** dialog box will be discussed later in the "Editing the Plotter Configuration" section of this chapter.

Plot to file

If you select this check box, AutoCAD plots the output to a file rather than to the plotter. Depending on the plotter selected, the file can be plotted in the *.dwf*, *.plt*, *.jpg*, or *.png* format. On selecting this check box and choosing the **OK** button from the **Plot** dialog box, the **Browse for Plot File** dialog box will be displayed. Specify the file name and its location in this dialog box.

Partial Preview Window

The window displayed below the **Properties** button is called the Partial Preview window. The preview in this window dynamically changes as you modify the parameters in the **Plot** dialog box. The outer rectangle in this window is the paper you selected. The inner hatched rectangle is the section of the paper that is used by the image. If the image extends beyond the paper, a red border is displayed around the paper.

Paper size Area

The drop-down list in this area displays all standard paper sizes for the selected plotting device. You can select any size from the list to make it current. If **None** has been selected currently from the **Name** drop-down list in the **Printer/plotter** area, AutoCAD will display the list of all standard paper sizes.

Number of copies Area

You can use the spinner available in this area to specify the number of copies that you want to plot. If multiple layouts and copies are selected and some of the layouts are set for plotting to a file or AutoSpool, they will produce a single plot. AutoSpool allows you to send a file for plotting while you are working on another program.

Plot area Area

Using the **What to plot** drop-down list provided in this area, you can specify the portion of the drawing to be plotted. You can also control the way plotting will be carried out. The options in the **What to plot** drop-down list are described next.

Display

If you select this option, the portion of the drawing that is currently being displayed on the screen is plotted.

Extents

This option resembles the **Extents** tool of the **Zoom** drop-down and prints the drawing to the extents of the objects. If you add more objects to drawing, they are also included in the plot and the extents of the drawing are recalculated. If you reduce the drawing extents by erasing, moving, or scaling the objects, the extents of the drawing are again recalculated. You can use the **Extents** tool to determine which objects shall be plotted.

Limits

This option will be available only when you plot from the **Model** tab. When this option is selected, the complete area defined within the drawing limits is plotted.

Window

On selecting this option, you need to specify the section of the drawing to be plotted by defining a window. To define a window, select the **Window** option from the **What to plot** drop-down list; the **Plot** dialog box will be temporarily closed and you will be prompted to specify two points on the screen that define a window. Specify the points to define the window; the area within this window will be plotted. Once you have defined the window, the **Plot** dialog box is displayed again on the screen. Also you will notice that the **Window<** button is now displayed on the right of the **What to plot** drop-down list. To again select the area to be plotted, choose the **Window** button. If the **Model** tab is chosen, you will notice that the previously selected area is displayed in white and the remaining area is displayed in gray. After selecting the area to be plotted, you can choose the **OK** button in the dialog box to plot the drawing.

View

Selecting the **View** option enables you to plot a view that was created with the **View Manager** dialog box. The view must be defined in the current drawing. If no view has been created, the **View** option is not displayed. When you select this option, a drop-down list is displayed in this area. You can select a view for plotting from this drop-down list and then choose the **OK** button in the **Plot** dialog box. While using the **View** option, the specifications of the plot will depend upon the specifications of the named view.

Layout

This option will be available only when you are plotting from the layout. This option prints the entire content of the drawing that lies inside the printable area of the paper selected from the drop-down list in the **Paper size** area.

Plot offset (origin set to printable area) Area

This area allows you to specify an offset of the plotting area from the lower left corner of the paper. The lower left corner of the specified plot area is positioned at the lower left margin of the paper by default. If you select the **Center the plot** check box, AutoCAD automatically centers the plot on the paper by calculating the *X* and *Y* offset values. You can specify an offset from the origin by entering positive or negative values in the **X** and **Y** edit boxes. For example, if you want the drawing to be plotted 4 units to the right and 4 units above the origin point, enter **4** in both the **X** and **Y** edit boxes. Depending on the units you have specified in the **Paper size** area of the dialog box, the offset values are either in inches, in millimeters, or in pixels.

Plot scale Area

This area controls the drawing scale of the plot area. Apart from the **Custom** option, the **Scale** drop-down list has thirty-three architectural and decimal scales by default. The default scale setting is **1:1** when you are plotting a layout. However, if you are plotting in the **Model** tab, the

Fit to paper check box is selected. The **Fit to paper** option allows you to automatically fit the entire drawing on the paper. It is useful when you have to print a large drawing using a printer that uses a smaller size paper.

Whenever you select a standard scale from the drop-down list, the scale is displayed in the edit boxes as a ratio of the plotted units to the drawing units. You can also change the scale factor manually in these edit boxes. When you do so, the **Scale** edit box displays **Custom**. For example, for an architectural drawing, which is to be plotted at the scale 1/4"=1'-0", you can enter either 1/4"=1'-0" or 1=48 in the edit boxes.

Note

*The **PSLTSCALE** system variable controls the paper space linetype scaling and has a default value of 1. This implies that irrespective of the zoom scale of the viewports, the linetype scale of the objects in the viewports remains the same. If you want the linetype scale of the objects in different viewports with different magnification factors to appear different, you should set the value of the **PSLTSCALE** variable to 0. This has been discussed in detail in Chapter 13 (Model Space Viewports, Paper Space Viewports, and Layouts).*

The **Scale lineweights** check box will be available only when you are plotting in a layout. This option is not available in the **Model** tab. If you select the **Scale lineweights** check box, you can scale lineweights in proportion to the plot scale. Lineweights generally specify the linewidth of the printable objects and are plotted with the original lineweight size, regardless of the plot scale.

Note

*You can save the custom scales that you use during plotting or in layouts in the **Edit Drawing Scales** dialog box. To invoke the **Edit Drawing Scales** dialog box, choose the **Scale List** tool from the **Annotation Scaling** panel in the **Annotate** tab. The **Scale List** area lists the default scales in AutoCAD. Choose the **Add** button to invoke the **Add Scale** dialog box. Enter a name for the custom scale in the **Name appearing in the scale list** edit box. Next, enter the scale in the **Scale properties** area and choose the **OK** button; the name specified for the custom scale will be listed in the **Scale List** area. In this way, you can keep a track of the custom scales used.*

Plot style table (pen assignments) Area

This area will be available when you expand the **Plot** dialog box. This area allows you to view and select a plot style table, edit the current plot style table, or create a new plot style table. A plot style table is a collection of plot styles. A plot style is a group of pen settings that are assigned to an object or layer and that determines the color, linetype, thickness, line ending, line joining and the fill style of the drawing objects when they are plotted. It is a named file that allows you to control the pen settings for a plotted drawing.

You can select the required plot style from the drop-down list in this area. Whenever you select a plot style, AutoCAD displays the **Question** message box prompting you to specify whether the selected plot style should be assigned to all layouts or not. If you choose **Yes**, the selected plot style will be used to plot from all layouts. You can also select **None** from the drop-down list to plot a drawing without using any plot styles. You can assign different plot style tables to a drawing and plot the same drawing differently each time. The use of plot styles will be discussed later in this chapter.

You can also select the **New** option from the drop-down list to create a new plot style. When you select this option, a wizard will be started that will guide you through the process of creating a new plot style.

Edit

Using this button, you can edit the plot style table selected from the **Plot style table** drop-down list. This button is not available if you have selected **None** from the drop-down list. When you choose the **Edit** button, AutoCAD displays the **Plot Style Table Editor**, where you can edit the selected plot style table. This dialog box has three tabs: **General**, **Table View**, and **Form View**. The **Plot Style Table Editor** will be discussed later in the "Using Plot Styles" section of this chapter.

Shaded viewport options Area

The options in this area are used to print a shaded or a rendered image and are discussed next.

Shade plot

This drop-down list is used to select a technique that will be used for plotting the drawings. This drop-down list will be available only while plotting from the model space. If you select **As displayed** from this drop-down list, the drawing will be plotted as it is displayed on the screen. If you select the **Legacy wireframe** option, the model will be plotted in wireframe mode displaying all hidden geometries, even if it is shaded in the drawing. If you select the **Legacy hidden** option, then the model will be plotted with hidden lines suppressed. On selecting the **Hidden**, **Wireframe**, **Conceptual**, **Realistic**, **Shaded**, **Shaded with edges**, **Shades of Gray**, **Sketchy**, and **X-Ray** options, the drawing will be plotted in the corresponding visual style even if the model is displayed in some other visual styles. Similarly, selecting the **Rendered** option will plot the rendered image of the drawing. The other options in the drop-down list are used to specify the quality for plotting the shaded and rendered model. But if you are plotting a drawing from the paper space, the display settings of the viewport will be used for plotting it. To set the display settings of a viewport, select the viewport and right-click; a shortcut menu will be displayed. Choose the **Shade plot** option from the shortcut menu and then select the desired shading option.

Quality

This drop-down list is used to select printing quality in terms of dots per inch (dpi) for the printed drawing. The **Draft** option prints the drawing with 0 dpi, which results in the wireframe printout. The **Preview** option prints the drawing at 150 dpi, the **Normal** option prints the drawing at 300 dpi, the **Presentation** option prints the drawing at 600 dpi, the **Maximum** option prints the drawing at the selected plotting device's maximum dpi. You can also specify a custom dpi by selecting the **Custom** option from this drop down list. The custom value of dpi can be specified in the **DPI** edit box which is enabled below the **Quality** drop-down list on selecting the **Custom** option.

Plot options Area

This area displays various check boxes that can be selected as per the plot requirements. They are described next.

Plot in background

Select this check box to perform the printing and plotting operation in the background. While plotting in the background, you can return immediately to your drawing without waiting for the printing or plotting operation to finish. By default, the background plotting is turned off for plotting and it is turned on for publishing. The **BACKGROUNDPLOT** system variable is used to control the default settings for background plotting.

Plot object lineweights

Select this check box, if you need to plot the drawing with specified lineweights.

Plot transparency

When you select this check box, AutoCAD will plot drawing using the transparency applied to the objects.

Plot with plot styles

When you select the **Plot with plot styles** check box, AutoCAD plots using the plot styles applied to the objects in the drawing and defined in the plot style table. The different property characteristics associated with the different style definitions are stored in the plot style tables and can be easily attached to the geometry.

Plot paperspace last

This check box is not available when you are in the **Model** tab because no paper space objects are present in the **Model** tab. This option is available when you are working in the layout tab. By selecting the **Plot paperspace last** check box, you can plot the model space geometry before paper space objects. Usually the paper space geometry is plotted before the model space geometry. This option is also useful when there are multiple tabs selected for plotting and you want to plot the model space geometry before the layout tabs.

Hide paperspace objects

This check box is available in the **Layout** tab only and is used to specify whether or not the objects drawn in layouts will be hidden while plotting. If this check box is selected, the objects created in layouts will be hidden.

Plot stamp on

This check box is selected to turn the plot stamp on. The plot stamp is a user-defined information that will be displayed on the sheet while plotting. You can set the plot stamp information when you select this check box. When you select this check box, the **Plot Stamp Settings** button is displayed on the right of this check box. You can choose this button to display the **Plot Stamp** dialog box to set the parameters for the plot stamp.

Save changes to layout

This check box is selected to save the changes made using the **Plot** dialog box.

Drawing orientation Area

This area provides options to specify the orientation of the drawing on the paper. You can change the drawing orientation by selecting the **Portrait** or **Landscape** radio button with or without selecting the **Plot upside-down** check box. The paper icon displayed on the right side of this area indicates the orientation of the selected paper and the letter icon (A) on it indicates the orientation of the drawing on the page. The **Landscape** radio button is selected by default for AutoCAD drawings and orients the length of the paper along the *X* axis. Assume the orientation to be at a rotation angle of 0 degree, then while selecting the **Portrait** radio button, the plot is oriented with the width along the *X* axis, which is equivalent to the plot being rotated through a rotation angle of 90 degrees. Similarly, if you select both the **Landscape** radio button and the **Plot upside-down** check box at the same time, the plot gets rotated through a rotation angle of 180-degree and if you select both the **Portrait** radio button and the **Plot upside-down** check box at the same time, the plot gets rotated through a rotation angle of 270 degrees. The AutoCAD screen conforms to the landscape orientation by default.

Preview

When you choose the **Preview** button, AutoCAD displays the drawing on the screen just as it would be plotted on the paper. Once the regeneration is performed, the dialog boxes on the screen disappear, and an outline of the paper size is shown. In the plot preview, refer to Figure 14-3, the cursor is replaced by the **Zoom Realtime** icon. This icon can be used to zoom in and out interactively by pressing and moving the left mouse button. You can right-click to display a shortcut menu and then choose **Exit** to exit the preview or press the ENTER or ESC key to return to the dialog box. You can also choose **Plot** to plot the drawing right away or choose the other zooming options available.

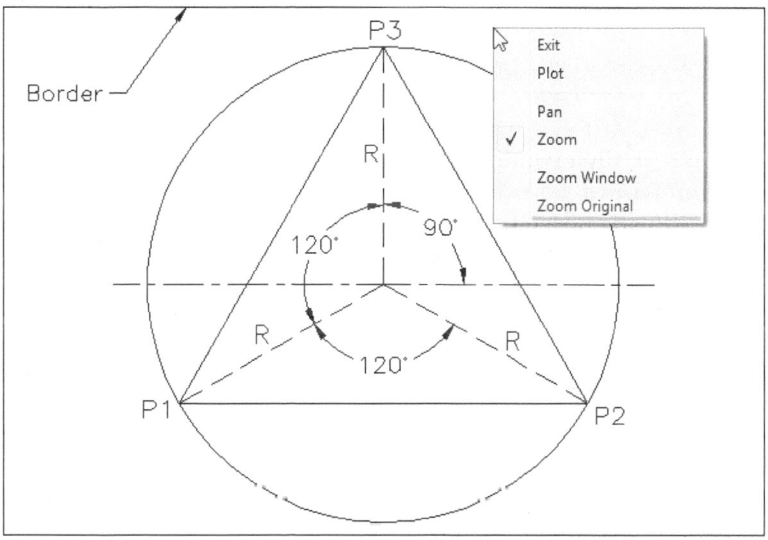

Figure 14-3 *Full plot preview with the shortcut menu*

After setting all the parameters, if you choose the **OK** button in the **Plot** dialog box, AutoCAD starts plotting the drawing in the file or plotters as specified. Also, the **Plot Job Progress** dialog box where you can view the progress of plotting will be displayed.

ADDING PLOTTERS

Ribbon: Output > Plot > Plotter Manager **Application Menu:** Print > Manage Plotters
Command: PLOTTERMANAGER

When you invoke the **Plotter Manager** tool, AutoCAD will display the **Plotters** window, refer to Figure 14-4.

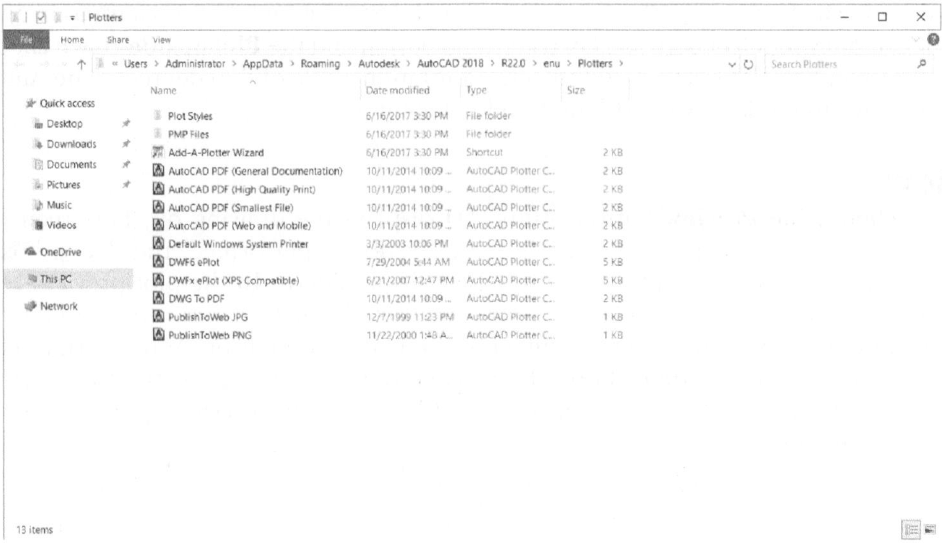

***Figure 14-4** The **Plotters** window*

The **Plotters** window is basically a Windows Explorer window. It displays all the configured plotters and the **Add-A-Plotter Wizard** icon. You can right-click on any one of the icons belonging to the plotters that have already been configured to display a shortcut menu. You can choose the **Delete** option from the shortcut menu to remove a plotter from the list. You can also choose the **Rename** option from the shortcut menu to rename the plotter configuration file or choose the **Properties** option to view the properties of the configured device.

Add-A-Plotter Wizard

If you double-click on the **Add-A-Plotter Wizard** icon in the **Plotters** window, AutoCAD guides you to configure a nonsystem plotter for plotting your drawing files. AutoCAD stores all the information of a configured plotter in configured plot (PC3) files. The PC3 files are stored at the location *C:\Users\<owner>\AppData\Roaming\Autodesk\AutoCAD 2018\R22.0\enu\Plotters* by default. You can add your own folder to store information of a configured plotter. To do so, add path of the folder in the **Support File Search Path** given in the **Files** tab of the **Options** dialog box. The steps for configuring a new plotter using the **Add-A-Plotter Wizard** are given next.

1. Open the **Plotters** window by choosing the **Plotter Manager** tool from the **Plot** panel and double-click on the **Add-A-Plotter Wizard** icon, the **Add Plotter - Introduction Page** will be displayed.

2. In the **Add Plotter - Introduction Page**, read the introduction carefully, and then choose the **Next** button to move to the **Add Plotter - Begin** page.

3. On the **Add Plotter - Begin** page, the **My Computer** radio button is selected by default. Choose the **Next** button; the **Add Plotter - Plotter Model** page is displayed.

4. On this page, select a manufacturer and model of required plotter from the **Manufacturers** and **Models** list boxes, respectively. If your plotter is not present in the list of available plotters, and you have a driver disk for your plotter, choose the **Have Disk** button to locate the *.hif* file from the driver disk, and install the driver supplied with your plotter. Now, choose the **Next** button; the **Add Plotter - Import Pcp or Pc2** page is displayed.

5. In the **Add Plotter - Import Pcp or Pc2** page, if you want to import configuring information from a PCP or a PC2 file created with a previous version of AutoCAD, you can choose the **Import File** button and select the file. Otherwise, simply choose the **Next** button to advance to the **Add Plotter - Ports** page.

6. On the **Add Plotter - Ports** page, select the port from the list to be used while plotting, and choose the **Next** button.

7. On the **Add Plotter - Plotter Name** page, you can specify the name of the currently configured plotter or the default name will be entered automatically. Next, choose the **Next** button.

8. When you reach the **Add Plotter - Finish** page, you can choose the **Finish** button to exit the **Add Plotter Wizard**.

   You can also choose the **Edit Plotter Configuration** button to display the **Plotter Configuration Editor** dialog box where you can edit the current plotter's configuration. Also, in this page, you can choose the **Calibrate Plotter** button to display the **Calibrate Plotter** wizard. This wizard allows you to calibrate your plotter by setting up a test measurement. After test plotting, it compares the plot measurements with the actual measurements and computes a correction factor.

Once you have chosen the **Finish** button to exit the wizard, a PC3 file for the newly configured plotter will be displayed in the **Plotters** window. This PC3 file contains all the settings needed by the plotter to plot. Also, the newly configured plotter name is added to the **Name** drop-down list in the **Printer/plotter** area in the **Plot** dialog box. You can now use the plotter for plotting.

EDITING THE PLOTTER CONFIGURATION

You can modify the properties of the selected plot device by using the **Plotter Configuration Editor** dialog box. This dialog box can be invoked in several ways. As discussed earlier, while using the **Plot** or **Page Setup** dialog box, you can choose the **Properties** button in the **Printer/plotter** area to display the **Plotter Configuration Editor** dialog box, refer to Figure 14-5. You can modify the default settings of a plotter while configuring it by choosing the **Edit Plotter Configuration** button on the **Add Plotter - Finish** page of the **Add Plotter** wizard. You can also select the PC3 file for editing in the **Plotters** window by using Windows Explorer (by default, PC3 files are stored in *C:\Users\<owner>\AppData\Roaming\Autodesk\AutoCAD 2018\R22.0\enu*

Plotters) and double-click on the file. The three tabs in the **Plotter Configuration Editor** dialog box are discussed next.

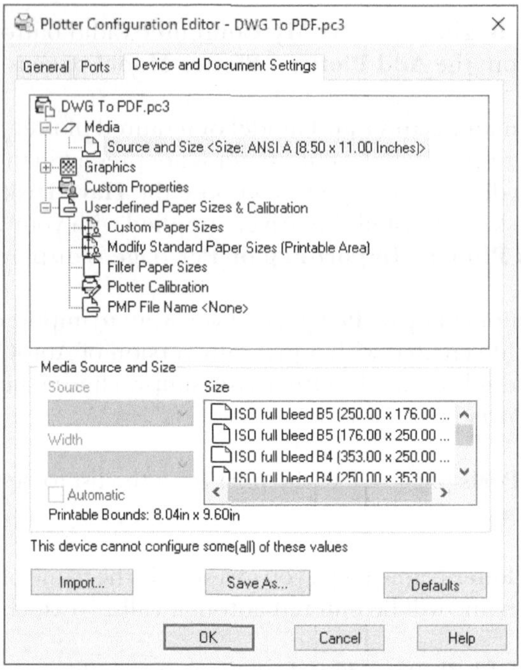

Figure 14-5 The ***Plotter Configuration Editor*** *dialog box*

General Tab

This tab contains basic information about the configured plotter or the PC3 file. You can make changes only in the **Description** area. The rest of the information in the tab is read only. This tab contains information on the configured plotter file name, plotter driver type, HDI driver file version number, name of the system printer (if any), and the location and name of the PMP file (if any calibration file is attached to the PC3 file).

Ports Tab

This tab contains information about the communication between the plotting device and your computer. You can choose between a serial (local), parallel (local), or network port. The default settings for parallel and serial ports are **LPT1** and **COM1**, respectively. You can also change the port name, if your device is connected to a different port. You can also select the **Plot to File** radio button, if you want to save the plot as a file. You can select the **AutoSpool** radio button, if you want plotting to occur automatically, while you continue to work on another application.

Device and Document Settings Tab

This tab contains the plotting options specific to the selected plotter. These options are displayed as a tree view in the window. For example, if you configure a plotter, you have the option to modify the pen characteristics. You can select any plotter properties from the tree view displayed in the window to change the values as required. Whenever you select an icon from the tree view in the window, the corresponding information is displayed in an area below it. For example, if you select **PMP File Name <None>** in the tree view of the window, the **PMP file** area is displayed below. This area contains the current settings and the options to modify it. The information that is displayed within brackets (< >) can be modified. By default, **Custom properties** is displayed as highlighted in the window because it contains the properties that are modified commonly. The **Access Custom Dialog** area is displayed below the window. On choosing the **Custom Properties** button in this area, a dialog box specific to the selected plotter will be displayed. This dialog box has several properties of the selected plotter grouped and displayed under various areas and can be modified here.

Once you have made the desired changes, choose the **Save As** button in the **Plotter Configuration Editor** dialog box to save the changes you just made to the PC3 file.

> **Tip**
> *It is better to create a new PC3 file for a plotter and keep the original file as it is so that you encounter no error while using the specific printer later. The PC3 files determine the proper function of a plotter and any modifications may lead to errors.*

IMPORTING PCP/PC2 CONFIGURATION FILES

If you want to import a PCP or PC2 configuration file or plot settings created by previous releases of AutoCAD into the **Model** tab or the current layout for the drawing, you can use the **PCINWIZARD** command to display the **Import PCP or PC2 Plot Settings** wizard. All information from a PCP or PC2 file regarding plot area, plot offset, paper size, plot scale, and plot origin can be imported. Read the **Introduction** page of the wizard that is displayed carefully and then choose the **Next** button. The **Browse File name** page is displayed. Here, you can either enter the name of the PCP or PC2 file directly in the **PC2 or PCP file name** edit box or choose the **Browse** button to display the **Import** dialog box, where you can select the file to be imported. After you specify the file for importing, choose **Open** to return to the wizard. Choose the **Next** button to display the **Finish** page. After importing the files, you can modify the rest of the plot settings for the current layout.

SETTING PLOT PARAMETERS

Before starting with the drawing, you can set various plotting parameters in the **Model** tab or in the layouts tab. The plot parameters that can be set include the plotter to be used, for example, plot style table, the paper size, units, and so on. All these parameters can be set using the **Page Setup Manager** tool as discussed next.

Working with Page Setups

Ribbon: Output > Plot > Page Setup Manager **Application Menu:** Print > Page Setup
Toolbar: Layouts > Page Setup Manager **Command:** PAGESETUP

As discussed earlier, a page setup contains the settings required to plot a drawing. Each layout as well as the **Model** tab can have a unique page setup attached to it. You can use the **Page Setup Manager** tool to create named page setups that can be used later. A page setup consists of specifications for the layout page, plotting device, paper size, and settings for the layouts to be plotted. This tool can also be invoked by choosing the **Page Setup Manager** option from the shortcut menu displayed on right-clicking on the current **Model** or **Layout** tab.

Remember that the **Page Setup Manager** option will be available in the shortcut menu only for the current **Model** or **Layout** tab.

When you invoke the **Page Setup Manager** tool, AutoCAD displays the **Page Setup Manager** dialog box. The names of the tabs displayed in the **Current page setup** list box of the **Page setups** area depend on the tab from which you invoke this dialog box. For example, if you invoke this dialog box from the **Model** tab, it displays only **Model** in this list box. However, if you invoke this dialog box from the **Layout** tab, it displays the list of all the layouts that are invoked at least once. Figure 14-6 shows the **Page Setup Manager** dialog box invoked from the **Layout1** tab. In this case, only the **Layout1** was activated at least once. You can use this dialog box to create a new page setup, modify the existing page setup, or import a page setup from an existing file.

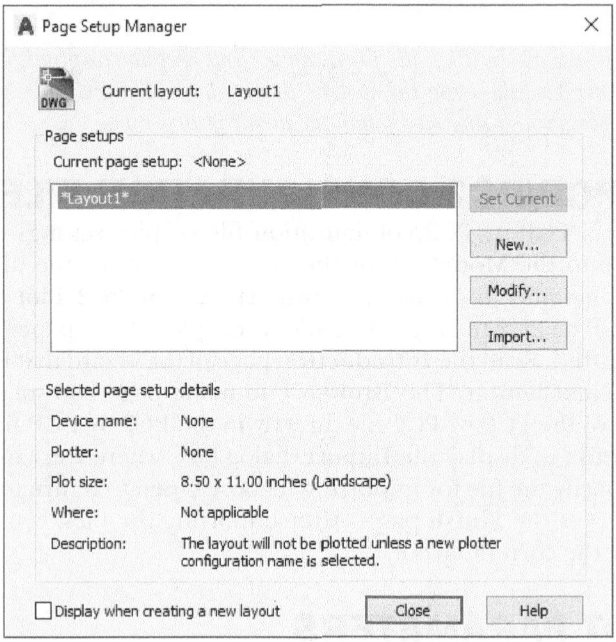

***Figure 14-6** The **Page Setup Manager** dialog box invoked from the **Layout1** tab*

Creating a New Page Setup

To create a new page setup, choose the **New** button from the **Page Setup Manager** dialog box. The **New Page Setup** dialog box will be displayed, as shown in Figure 14-7. Enter the name of the new page setup in the **New page setup name** text box. The existing page setups with which you can start working are shown in the **Start with** area. You can select any of the page setups listed in this area and choose the **OK** button to proceed.

When you choose the **OK** button, the **Page Setup** dialog box will be displayed, as shown in Figure 14-8. This dialog box is similar to the **Plot** dialog box, refer to Figure 14-1.

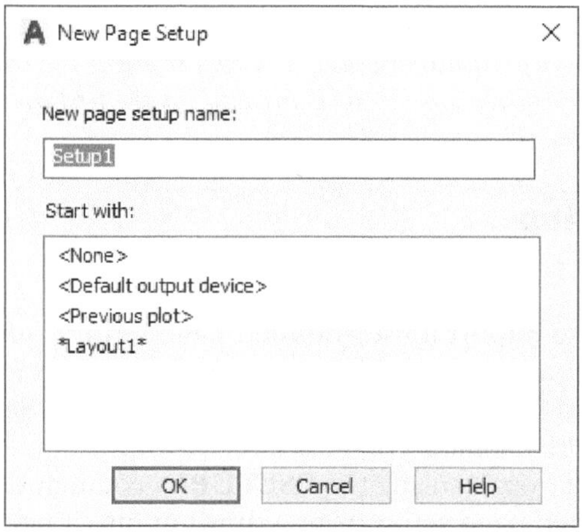

*Figure 14-7 The **New Page Setup** dialog box*

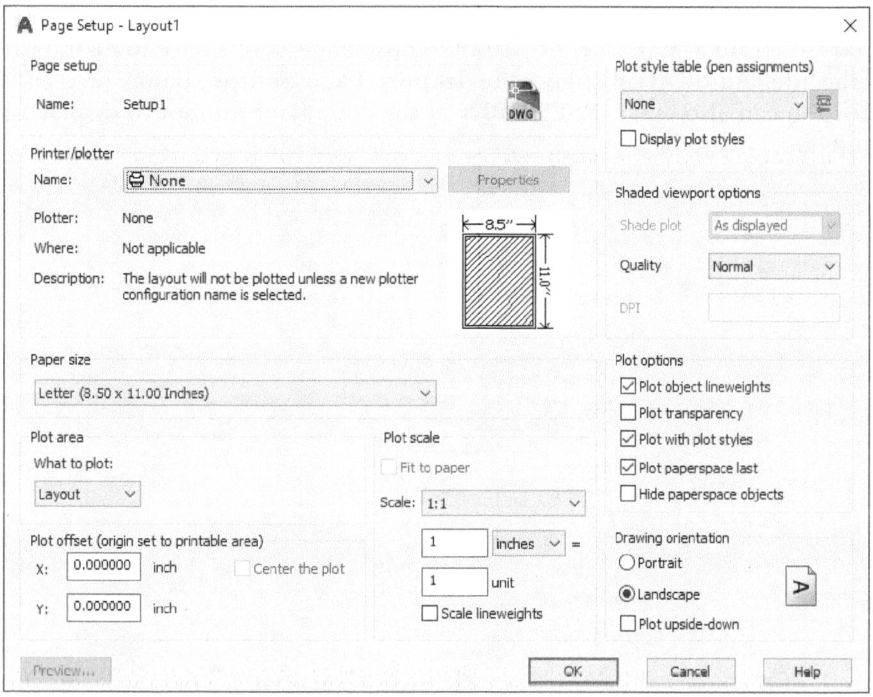

*Figure 14-8 The **Page Setup** dialog box*

Modifying the Page Setup

To modify the page setup, select the page setup from the **Current page setup** list box and choose the **Modify** button; the **Page Setup** dialog box will be displayed. Modify the parameters in this dialog box and exit.

Note

If you close the ***Page Setup Manager*** *dialog box after selecting the* ***Display when creating a new layout*** *check box then whenever a layout is invoked for the first time, the* ***Page Setup Manager*** *dialog box will be displayed.*

Importing a Page Setup

Command: PSETUPIN

AutoCAD allows you to import a user-defined page setup from an existing drawing and use it in the current drawing or base the current page setup for the drawing on it. This option is available on choosing the **Import** button from the **Page Setup Manager** dialog box. It is also possible to bypass this dialog box and directly import a page setup from an existing drawing into a new drawing layout by using the **PSETUPIN** command. This command facilitates importing a saved and named page setup from a drawing into a new drawing. The settings of the named page setup can be applied to layouts in the new drawing. When you choose the **Import** button from the **Page Setup Manager** dialog box or invoke the **PSETUPIN** command, the **Select Page Setup From File** dialog box is displayed, as shown in Figure 14-9. You can use this dialog box to locate a *.dwg*, *.dwt*, or *.dwf* file whose page setups have to be imported. After you select the file, AutoCAD displays the **Import Page Setups** dialog box, as shown in Figure 14-10. You can also enter **-PSETUPIN** at the command prompt to display prompts at the command line.

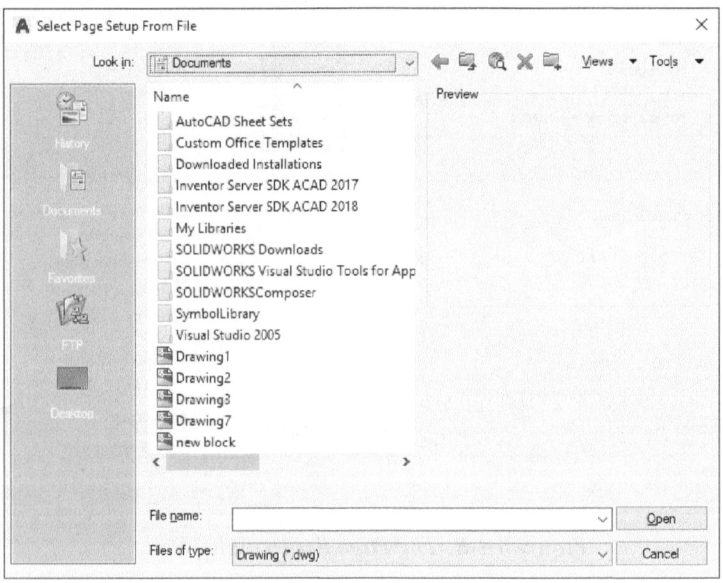

Figure 14-9 The ***Select Page Setup From File*** *dialog box*

Note

If a page setup with the same name already exists in the current file, the ***Question*** *message box will be displayed and you will be informed that " A layout page setup has already been defined. Would you like to redefine it?" If you choose* ***Yes*** *in this message box, the current page setup will be redefined.*

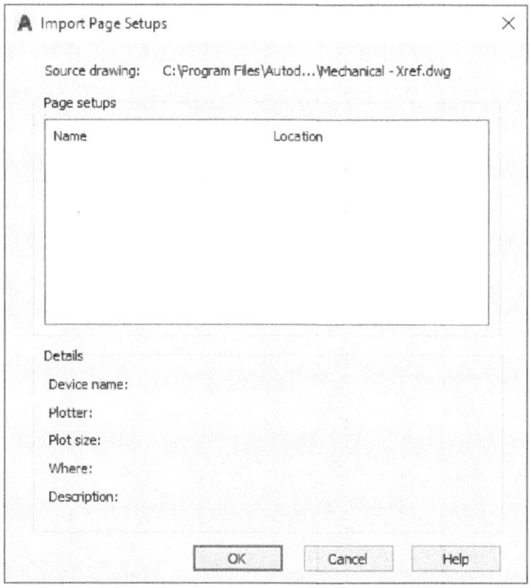

***Figure 14-10** The **Import Page Setups** dialog box*

USING PLOT STYLES

The plot styles can change the complete look of a plotted drawing. You can use this feature to override the color, linetype, and lineweight of the drawing object. For example, if an object is drawn on a layer that is assigned red color and no plot style is assigned to it, the object will be plotted as red. However, if you have assigned a plot style to the object with the color blue, the object will be plotted as blue irrespective of the layer color it was drawn on. Similarly, you can change the Linetype, Lineweight, end, join, and fill styles of the drawing, and also change the output effects such as dithering, grayscales, pen assignments, and screening. Basically, you can use Plot Styles effectively to plot the same drawing in various ways.

Every object and layer in the drawing has a plot style property. The plot style characteristics are defined in the plot style tables attached to the **Model** tab, layouts, and viewports within the layouts. You can attach and detach different plot style tables to get different looks for your plots. Generally, there are two plot style modes. They are **Color-dependent** and **Named**. The **Color-dependent** plot styles are based on object color and there are **255** color-dependent plot styles. It is possible to assign each color in the plot style a value for the different plotting properties and these settings are then saved in a color-dependent plot style table file that has a *.ctb* extension. Similarly, **Named** plot styles are independent of the object color and you can assign any plot style to any object regardless of that object's color. These settings are saved in a named plot style table file that has *.stb* extension. Every drawing in AutoCAD is in either of the plot style modes.

Adding a Plot Style

Application Menu: Print > Manage Plot Styles
Command: STYLESMANAGER

All plot styles are saved in the *C:\Users\<owner>\AppData\Roaming\Autodesk\AutoCAD 2018\R22.0\enu\Plotters\Plot Styles* folder. On choosing **Print > Manage Plot Styles** from the

Application Menu, the **Plot Styles** window will be displayed, as shown in Figure 14-11. This window displays icons for all the available plot styles in addition to the **Add-A-Plot Style Table Wizard** icon. You can double-click on any of the plot style icons to display the **Plot Style Table Editor** dialog box and edit the selected plot style. When you double-click on the **Add-A-Plot Style Table Wizard** icon, the **Add Plot Style Table** wizard is displayed and you can use it to create a new plot style.

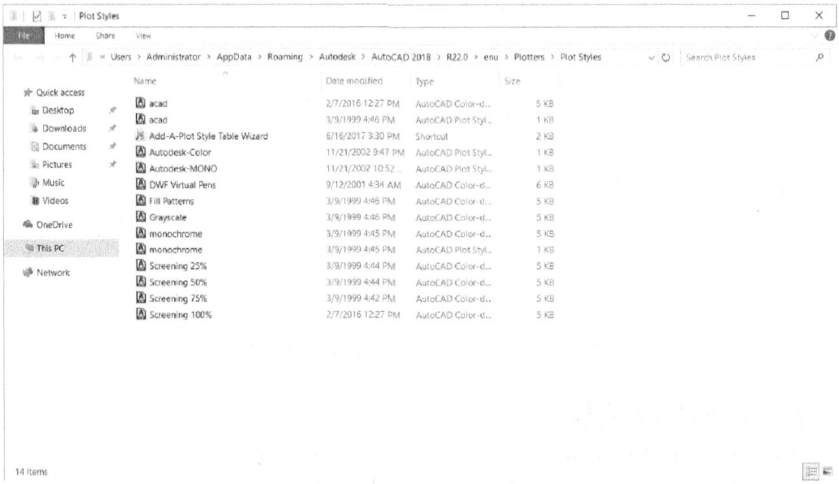

*Figure 14-11 The **Plot Styles** window*

Add-A-Plot Style Table Wizard

If you want to add a new plot style table to your drawing, double-click on the **Add-A-Plot Style Table Wizard** in the **Plot Styles** window to display the **Add Plot Style Table** wizard. The following steps are required for creating a new plot style table using the wizard.

1. Read the introduction page carefully and choose the **Next** button.

2. In the **Begin** page, select the **Start from scratch** radio button and choose the **Next** button. On selecting this option, a new plot style table is created. Therefore, the **Browse File** page is not available.

   In addition to the **Start from scratch** option, this page has three more options: **Use an existing plot style table**, **Use My R14 Plotter Configuration (CFG)**, and **Use a PCP or PC2 file**. When you use the **Use an existing plot style table** option, an existing plot style table is used as a base for the new plot style table you are creating. In such a situation, the **Table Type** page of the wizard is not available and is not displayed because the table type will be based on the existing plot style table you are using to create a new one. With the **Use My R14 Plotter Configuration (CFG)** option, the pen assignments from the Release 14 *acad.cfg* file are used as a base for the new table you are creating. If you are using the **Use a PCP or PC2 file** option, the pen assignments saved earlier in the Release 14 PCP or PC2 file are used to create the new plot style.

3. The **Pick Plot Style Table** page allows you to select the **Color-Dependent Plot Style Table** or the **Named Plot Style Table** according to your requirement. Select the **Color-Dependent Plot Style Table** radio button and then choose the **Next** button.

4. Since you have selected the **Start from scratch** radio button in the **Begin** page, the **Browse File** page is not available and the **File name** page is displayed. However, if you had selected any of the other three options on the **Begin** page, the **Browse File name** page would have been displayed. You can select an existing file from the drop-down list available in this page or choose the **Browse** button to display the **Select File** dialog box. You can then browse and select a file from a specific folder and choose the **Open** button to return to the wizard. You can also enter the name of the existing plot style table on which you want to base the new plot style table, directly in the edit box. After you have specified the file name, choose **Next** to display the **File name** page of the wizard. In the **File name** page, enter a file name for the new plot style table and choose the **Next** button. The **Finish** page is displayed.

Note

*If you are using the pen assignments from Release 14 acad.cfg file to define the new plot style table, you also have to specify the printer or plotter to use from the drop-down list available in the **Browse File** page of the wizard.*

5. The **Finish** page gives you the option of choosing the **Plot Style Table Editor** button to display the **Plot Style Table Editor** and then edit the plot style table you have created. If you select the **Use this plot style table for new and pre-AutoCAD 2018-English drawings** check box in this page of the wizard, the plot style table that you have created will become the default plot style table for all the drawings you create. This check box is available only if the plot style mode you have selected in the wizard is the same as the default plot style mode specified by you in the **Default plot style behavior for new drawings** area of the **Plot Style Table Settings** dialog box. This dialog box can be invoked by choosing the **Plot Style Table Settings** button from the **Plot and Publish** tab of the **Options** dialog box. Choose the **Finish** button in the **Finish** page of the wizard to exit the wizard. A new plot style table gets added to the **Plot Styles** window and can be used for plotting.

Note

*You can also choose **Add Color-Dependent Plot Style Table** from the **Tools > Wizards** menu to display wizards that are similar to the **Add Plot Style Table** wizard. However, in the **Begin** page, the **Use an existing plot style table** option is not available. Also, the **Table Type** page is not available and the **Finish** page has an additional option to use the new plot style table for the current drawing.*

Plot Style Table Editor

When you double-click on any of the plot style table icons in the **Plot Styles** window, the **Plot Style Table Editor** is displayed, where you can edit the particular plot style table. You can also choose the **Plot Style Table Editor** button in the **Finish** page to display the **Plot Style Table Editor**. Alternatively, expand the **Plot** dialog box and choose the **Edit** button adjacent to the drop-down list in the **Plot style table (pen assignments)** area to display the **Plot Style Table Editor** dialog box.

The **Plot Style Table Editor** dialog box has three tabs: **General**, **Table View**, and **Form View**. You can edit all properties of an existing plot style table using these tabs. The description of the tabs is as follows;

General Tab

This tab provides information about the file name, location of the file, version, and scale factor. All information except the description is read only. You can enter a description about the plot style table in the **Description** text box here. If you select the **Apply global scale factor to non-ISO linetypes** check box, all the non-ISO linetypes in a drawing are scaled by the scale factor specified in the **Scale factor** edit box below the check box. If this check box is cleared, the **Scale factor** edit box is not available.

Table View Tab

This tab displays all plot styles along with their properties in a tabular form and these plot styles can be edited individually in the table, refer to Figure 14-12.

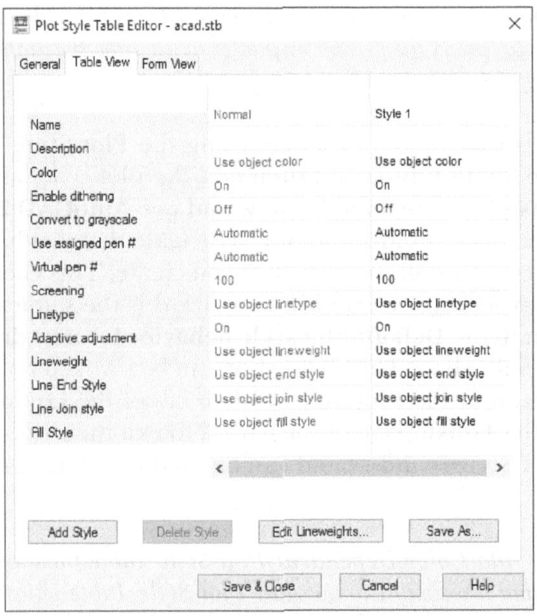

*Figure 14-12 The **Plot Style Table Editor** with the **Table View** tab chosen*

If you use **acad-Named Plot Style.dwt** template, then you can edit existing styles or add new styles by choosing the **Add Style** button. On doing so, a new column with the default style name **Style1** will be added to the table. You can change the style name if you want. To edit various properties in the table, select the particular value to be modified; the corresponding drop-down list will be displayed. You can select a value from this drop-down list. The **Normal** plot style table is not available, and therefore, it cannot be edited. This plot style is assigned to layers by default.

You can select a particular plot style by clicking on the white area above the column and the entire column gets highlighted. You can select several plot styles by pressing the SHIFT key and selecting more plot styles. All the plot styles that are selected are highlighted. If you choose the

Delete Style button now, the selected plot styles are removed from the table except the **Normal** style which can not be deleted.

On choosing the **Edit Lineweights** button, the **Edit Lineweights** dialog box will be displayed. You can select the units for specifying the lineweights from the **Units for Listing** area of the dialog box, and can use either **Millimeters (mm)** or **Inches (in)** for specifying units. You can also edit the value of a lineweight by selecting it in the **Lineweights** list box and choosing the **Edit Lineweight** button. After you have edited the lineweights, choose the **Sort Lineweights** button to rearrange the lineweight values in the list box. Choose the **OK** button to exit the **Edit Lineweights** dialog box and return to the **Plot Style Table Editor**.

With a color-dependent plot style table, the **Table View** tab displays all 255 plot styles, one for each color, and the properties can be edited in the table in the same way as discussed for named plot styles. The only difference is that you cannot add a new plot style or delete an existing one, and therefore, the **Delete Style** and **Add Style** buttons are not available. The properties that can be defined in a plot style are discussed next.

Name: This field displays the name of the color in the case of the color-dependent plot styles and the name of the style in the case of the named plot styles.

Description: You can enter the description about the plot style in this field.

Color: The color you assign to the plot style overrides the color of the object in the drawing. The default value is Use object color.

Enable dithering: Dithering is described as mixing of various colored dots to produce a new color. You can enable or disable this property by selecting from the drop-down list that is available in this field. Dithering is enabled by default and is independent of the color selected.

Convert to grayscale: If you are using a plotter that supports grayscaling, selecting **On** from the drop-down list in this field applies a grayscale to the objects color. By default, **Off** is selected and the object's color is used.

Use assigned pen #: This property is applied only to pen plotters. The pens range from 1 to 32. The default value is Automatic, which implies that the pen used will be based on the plotter configuration.

Virtual pen #: Other plotters can also behave like pen plotters using virtual pens. The value of this property lies between 1 and 255. The default value is Automatic. This implies that AutoCAD will assign a virtual pen automatically from the AutoCAD Color Index (ACI).

Screening: This property of a plot style indicates the amount of ink used while plotting. The value ranges between 0 and 100. The default value is 100, which creates the plot in its full intensity. Similarly, a value of 0 produces white color. This may be useful when plotting on a colored background.

Linetype: Like the property of color, the linetype assigned to a plotstyle overrides the object linetype on plotting. The default value is Use object linetype.

Adaptive adjustment: This property is applied by default and implies that the linetype scale of a linetype is applied such that on plotting, the linetype pattern will be completed.

Lineweight: The lineweight value assigned here overrides the value of the object lineweight on plotting. The default value is Use object lineweight.

Line End Style: This determines the manner in which a plotted line ends. The effect of this property is more noticeable when the thickness of the line is substantial. The line can end in a **Butt**, **Square**, **Round**, or **Diamond** shape. The default value is Use object end style.

Line Join style: You can select the manner in which two lines join in a plotted drawing. The available options are **Miter**, **Bevel**, **Round**, and **Diamond**. The default value is Use object join style.

Fill Style: The fill style assigned to a plot style overrides the objects fill style, when plotted. The available options are **Solid**, **Checkerboard**, **Crosshatch**, **Diamonds**, **Horizontal Bars**, **Slant Left**, **Slant Right**, **Square Dots**, and **Vertical Bars**.

Form View Tab

This tab displays all properties in one form, as shown in Figure 14-13. Also, it displays all available plot styles in the **Plot styles** list box. You can select any style from the list box and then edit its properties in the **Properties** area.

*Figure 14-13 The **Plot Style Table Editor** with the **Form View** tab chosen*

If you want to add a new plot style to the named plot style table, choose the **Add Style** button when the **Form View** tab is chosen; the **Add Plot Style** dialog box with the default plot style name **Style 2** will be displayed. You can change the name of a plot style in the **Plot style** edit box, refer to Figure 14-14. Now, when you choose the **OK** button, the new style will be added to the **Plot styles** list box and you can select it for editing. If you want to delete a style, select it and then choose the **Delete Style** button. With color-dependent plot styles, the **Form View** tab also does not provide options that allow you to add or delete plot styles.

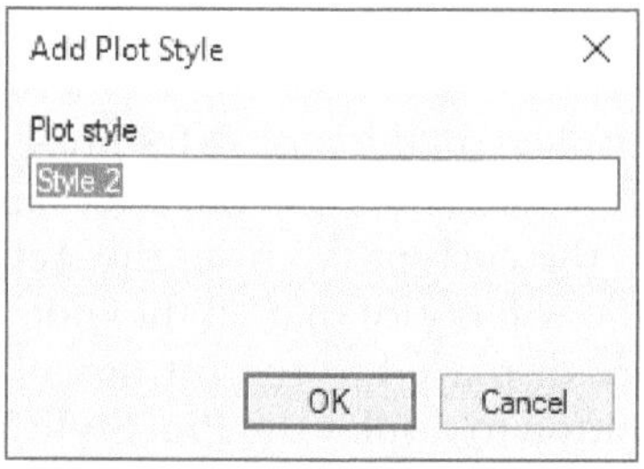

***Figure 14-14** The **Add Plot Style** dialog box*

After editing, choose the **Save & Close** button to save and return to the **Plot Styles** window. You can also choose the **Save As** button to display the **Save As** dialog box and save a plot style table with another name. To remove the changes you made to a plot style table, choose the **Cancel** button.

Applying Plot Styles

You can select a plot style table that you want to use as the default style for drawings from the **Current plot style table settings** area of the **Plot Style Table Settings** dialog box. To display the **Plot Style Table Settings** dialog box, choose the down arrow in the right of the **Plot** panel in the **Output** tab; the **Options** dialog box will be displayed with the **Plot and Publish** tab chosen. Choose the **Plot Style Table Settings** button; the **Plot Style Table Settings** dialog box will be displayed. If the **None** option is selected in the **Default plot style table** drop-down list, the drawing will be plotted with the object properties as displayed on the screen. When you select the **Use named plot styles** radio button from the **Default plot style behavior for new drawings** area of the **Plot Style Table Settings** dialog box, the **Default plot style for layer 0** and **Default plot style for objects** drop-down lists will be available. You can select the default plot styles that you want to assign to Layer 0 and to the objects in a drawing from these drop-down lists, respectively. If you choose the **Add or Edit Plot Style Tables** button from the **Plot Style Table Settings** dialog box, the **Plot Styles** window will be displayed. Here, you can double-click on any plot style table icon available and edit it using the **Plot Style Table Editor** that is displayed.

To change the plot style table for a current layout, you have to invoke the **Page Setup** or **Plot** dialog box and then select a plot style table from the **Plot styles** drop-down list in the **Plot style table (pen assignments)** area of the dialog box. A color-dependent plot style table can be selected and applied to a tab only if the default plot style mode has already been set to color dependent. Similarly, to apply a named plot style table to a tab, select the **Use named plot styles** radio button from the **Plot Style Table Settings** dialog box.

A color dependent plot style cannot be applied to objects or layers therefore the **Plot Style Control** drop-down list is not available in the **Properties** toolbar when a drawing has a color-dependent plot style mode. The plot styles also appear grayed out in the **LAYER PROPERTIES MANAGER** and cannot be selected and changed. However, named plot styles can be applied to objects and layers. A plot style applied to an object overrides the plot style applied to the layer on which the object is drawn. To apply a plot style to a layer, invoke the **LAYER PROPERTIES MANAGER** where all the layers in the selected tab are displayed. Select a layer to which you want to apply a plot style and select the default plot style (Normal) currently

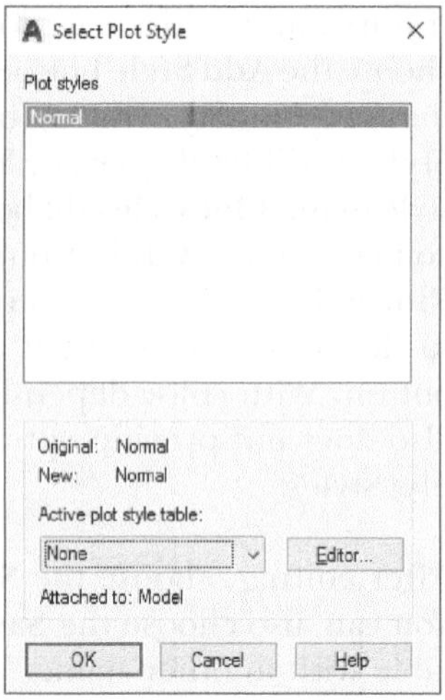

*Figure 14-15 The **Select Plot Style** dialog box*

applied to the layer; the **Select Plot Style** dialog box will be displayed, refer to Figure 14-15. The **Plot styles** list box in this dialog box displays all the plot styles present in the plot style table attached to the current tab. You can select another plot style table to be attached to the current tab from the **Active plot style table** drop-down list. You will notice that all the plot styles in the selected plot style table are displayed in the list box now. You can also choose the **Editor** button to display the **Plot Style Table Editor** to edit plot style tables, as discussed earlier. The **Select Plot Style** dialog box also displays the name of the original plot style assigned to the object adjacent to **Original**. Also, the new plot style to be assigned to the selected object is displayed next to **New**.

You can apply a named plot style to an object using the **Plot Style Control** drop-down list in the **Properties** toolbar or the **PROPERTIES** palette. The process is the same as that applied for layers, colors, linetypes, and lineweights. This named plot style is applied to an object irrespective of the tab on which it is drawn. If the plot style assigned to an object is present in the plot style table of the tab in which it is present, the object is plotted with the specified plot style. However, if the plot style assigned to the object is not present in the plot style table assigned to the tab on which it is drawn, the object will be plotted with the properties that are displayed on the screen. The default plot style assigned to an object is **Normal** and the default plot style assigned to a layer is **ByLayer**.

Setting the Current Plot Style

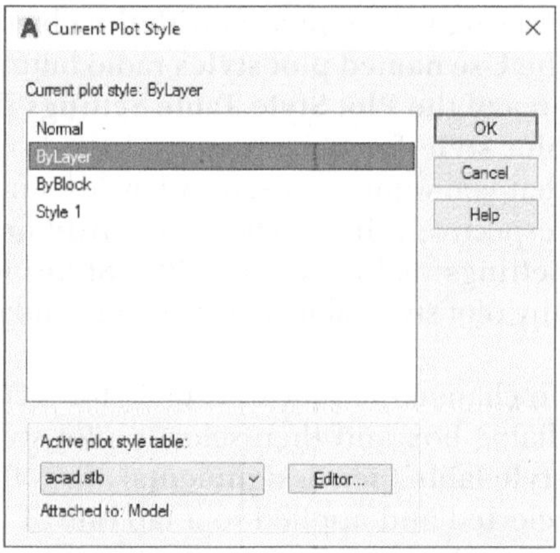

*Figure 14-16 The **Current Plot Style** dialog box*

You can use the **PLOTSTYLE** command to set the current plot style of new objects or of the selected object. You can set the current plot styles by choosing **Print > Edit Plot Style Tables** from the **Application Menu**, and if no object has been selected in the drawing, AutoCAD displays the **Current Plot Style** dialog box, as shown in Figure 14-16. You can select a plot style from the list box and choose **OK** to assign it to the selected objects in the drawing. All the plot styles present in the current plot style table that are assigned to the current tab are displayed in the list box in the **Current Plot Style** dialog box. You can select any one of these plot styles and choose **OK**. Now, if you create new objects, they will have the plot style that you had set current in the **Current Plot Style** dialog box. The parameters of this dialog box are described next.

Current plot style

The name of the current plot style is displayed adjacent to this label.

Plot style list box

This list box lists all the available plot styles that can be assigned to an object, including the default plot style, **Normal**.

Active plot style table

This drop-down list displays the names of all the available plot style tables. The current plot style table attached to the current layout or viewport is displayed in the edit box.

Editor

If you choose the **Editor** button adjacent to the **Active plot style table** drop-down list, AutoCAD displays the **Plot Style Table Editor** to edit the selected plot style table.

Attached to

The tab to which the selected plot style table is attached, such as **Model** or any one of the layout tabs, is displayed next to this label.

Example 1 — *Plot Style*

Create the drawing shown in Figure 14-17. Next, create a named plot style with the name *My First Table.stb* with a plot style having the following parameters:

1. Screening : 65%
2. Object line weight : 0.6000 mm
3. Line Type : ISO Dash
4. Object Color : Blue (5)

Additionally, plot the drawing using the **Date and Time** and **Paper size** stamps.

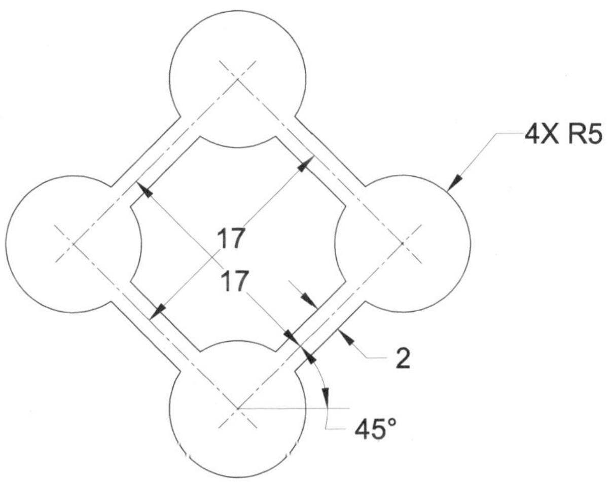

Figure 14-17 *Drawing for Example 1*

1. Select the **acad-Named Plot Styles.dwt** template from **Templates** drop-down list of the **Start** tab.

2. Create the drawing, as shown in Figure 14-17. You can create the drawing by making an octagon and then converting its alternate edge into an arc with the given radius.

3. Choose the **Print > Manage Plot Styles** from the **Application Menu**; a window is displayed with all the plot styles available. Double-click on the **Add-A-Plot Style Table Wizard** shortcut icon; the **Add Plot Style Table** wizard is displayed. Choose the **Next** button; the **Begin** page is displayed.

4. Select the **Start from scratch** radio button and choose the **Next** button; the **Pick Plot Style Table** page is displayed. Now, select the **Named Plot Style Table** radio button and then choose the **Next** button; a window is displayed prompting to enter the file name. Enter **My First Table** in the **File name** text box and then choose the **Next** button, the **Add Plot Style Table - Finish** window is displayed.

5. In the **Add Plot Style Table - Finish** window, select **Plot Style Table Editor** button; a window named **Plot Style Table Editor - My First Table.stb** is displayed with the **Table View** tab chosen by default.

6. Choose the **Add Style** button at the bottom left of the window; a new column named **Style 1** will be added. Now, enter the following values in the database:

Row	**Value**
• Screening	65
• Lineweight	0.6000 mm
• Linetype	ISO Dash
• Color	Blue

Next, choose the **Save & Close** button and then choose the **Finish** button in the displayed window.

7. Now, enter the PLOTSTYLE command to invoke the **Current Plot Style** dialog box. Next, select the **My First Table.stb** plot style from the drop-down list under the **Active plot style table** area of this dialog box. Choose the **OK** button.

8. Open the **LAYER PROPERTIES MANAGER** and click under the **Plot Style** coloumn to invoke the **Select Plot Style** dialog box. Select **Style 1** from the **Plot styles** area and choose the **OK** button.

9. Now, choose the **Plot** tool from the **Quick Access Toolbar**; the **Plot** dialog box is displayed. Next, select the **Plot stamp on** check box; the **Plot Stamp Settings** button will be displayed on the right of the check box. Choose this button; the **Plot Stamp** dialog box will be displayed. In this dialog box, select the **Date and Time** and **Paper size** check boxes. Next, clear all other check boxes. Choose the **OK** button to exit the dialog box, and then choose the **Preview** button from the **Plot-Model** dialog box to preview the plot. If the plot seems to be fine, right-click to invoke the shortcut menu. Choose the **Plot** option from the shortcut menu to take print.

Exercise 1 — *Plot Style*

Create the drawing shown in Figure 14-18. Create a named plot style table *My Named Table.stb* with three plot styles: Style 1, Style 2, and Style 3, in addition to the Normal plot style. The Normal plot style is used for plotting the object lines. These three styles have the following specifications:

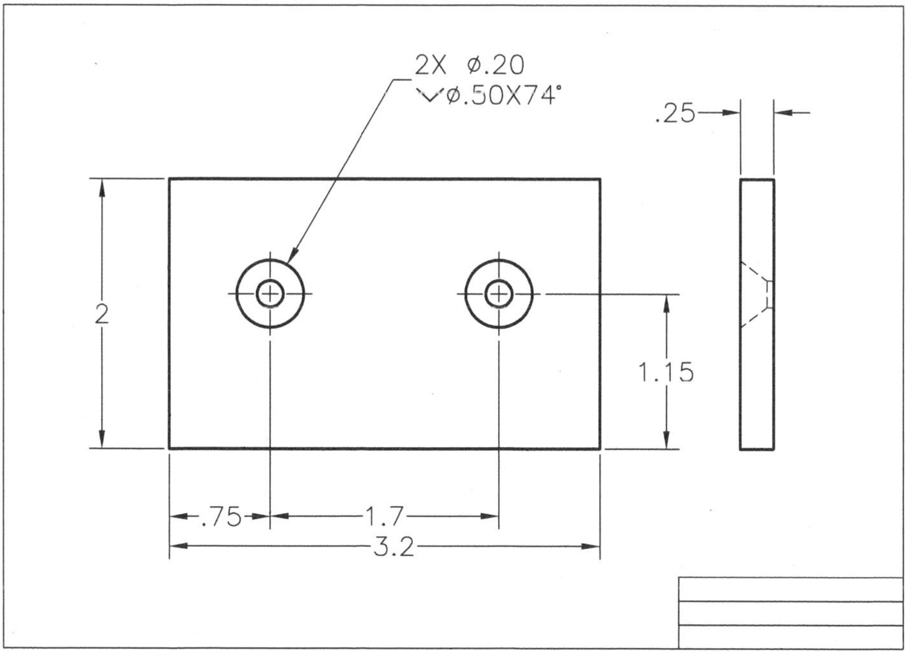

Figure 14-18 *Drawing for Exercise 1*

Style 1. This style has a value of Screening = 50. The dimensions, dimension lines, and the text in the drawing must be plotted with this style.

Style 2. This style has a value of Lineweight = 0.800. The border and title block must be plotted with this style.

Style 3. This style has a linetype of Medium Dash. The centerlines must be plotted with this plot style.

PLOTTING SHEETS IN A SHEET SET

Using the **Sheet Set Manager**, you can easily plot all the sheets available in a sheet set. However, before plotting the sheets in a sheet set, you need to make sure that you have selected the required printer in the page setup of all the sheets in the sheet set. This is because the printer set in the page setup of the sheet will be automatically selected to plot the sheet.

To print the sheets after setting the page setup, right-click on the name of the sheet set in the **Sheet Set Manager** and choose **Publish > Publish to Plotter** from the shortcut menu. If the value of the **BACKGROUNDPLOT** system variable is set to **2**, which is the default value, all the sheets will be automatically plotted in the background and you can continue working on the drawings.

Self-Evaluation Test

Answer the following questions and then compare them to those given at the end of this chapter:

1. The size of a plot can be specified by selecting any paper size from the drop-down list in the __________ area of the **Plot** dialog box.

2. If you want to store a plot in a file and not have it printed directly on a plotter, select the __________ check box in the **Printer/plotter** area.

3. The scale for a plot can be specified from the __________ area of the **Plot** dialog box.

4. If you select the __________ option from the **What to plot** drop-down list, the portion of the drawing that is in the current display is plotted.

5. Before you plot sheets in the sheet set, it is important that you set the __________ for the individual sheets in their page setups.

6. You can set the quality of a plot using the __________ drop-down list in the **Shaded viewport options** area.

7. All the settings of a plotter are saved in the *.PC3* file. (T/F)

8. Different objects in the same drawing can be plotted in different colors with different linetypes and line widths. (T/F)

9. You can partially or fully preview a drawing before plotting. (T/F)

10. The **PSLTSCALE** system variable controls the paper space linetype scaling and has a default value of 1. (T/F)

Review Questions

Answer the following questions:

1. Which of the following check boxes is not available in the **Plot options** area of the **Plot** dialog box while plotting in the **Layout** tab?

   (a) **Plot paperspace last** (b) **Hide objects**
   (c) **Plot with plot styles** (d) None of these

2. Which one of the following will be displayed in the **Plotters** window?

   (a) **Plot** (b) **Manage Plotters**
   (c) **Plot Style** (d) None of these

3. With which command is it possible to bypass the **Plot/Page Setup** dialog box and directly import a page setup from an existing drawing into a new drawing layout?

   (a) **PSETUPIN** (b) **PLOTTERMANAGER**
   (c) **PLOTSTYLE** (d) None of these

4. Which of the following tools is used to create a new plot style?

   (a) **Style** (b) **Manage Plot Styles**
   (c) **Plot Style** (d) None of these

5. Which of the following commands can be used to import a PCP or PC2 files?

   (a) **PCINWIZARD** (b) **PCIN**
   (c) **PLOTSTYLE** (d) None of these

6. You can view a plot on the specified paper size before actually plotting it by choosing the __________ button from the **Plot** dialog box.

7. The **Page Setup Manager** dialog box is displayed when you invoke the **Page Setup Manager** tool. (T/F)

8. By selecting the **View** option from the **What to plot** drop-down list in the **Plot** area, you can plot a view that was created by using the **View Manager** tool in the current drawing. (T/F)

9. If you do not want the hidden lines of a 3D object created in the **Model** tab, you can select the **Hidden** option from the **Shade plot** drop-down list in the **Shaded viewport options** area. (T/F)

10. The orientation of a drawing can be changed using the **Plot** dialog box. (T/F)

Exercise 2

Create the drawing shown in Figure 14-19 and plot it according to the following specifications. Also, create and use a plot style table with the specified plot styles.

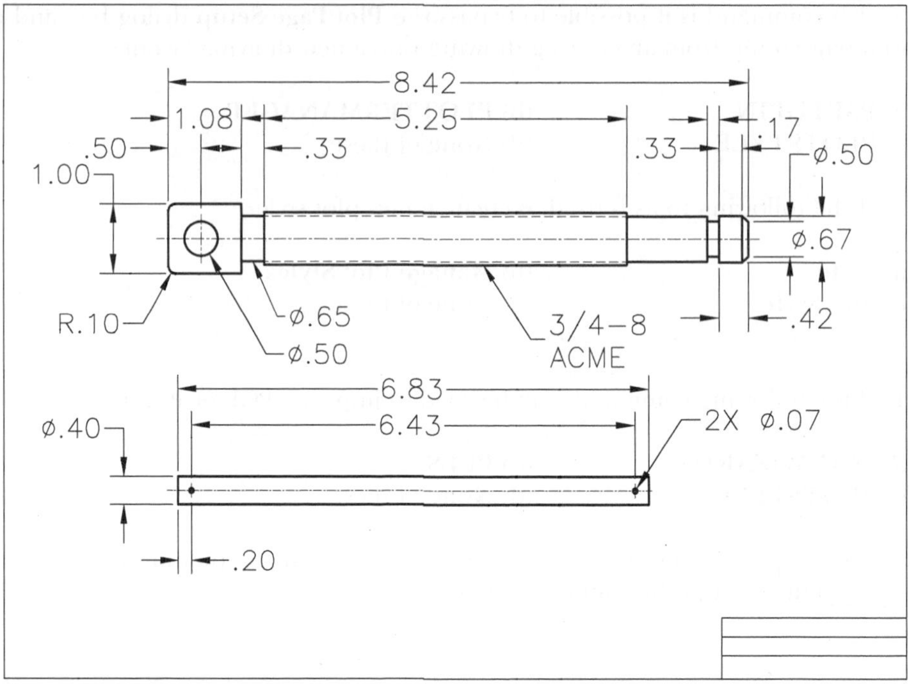

Figure 14-19 *Drawing for Exercise 2*

1. The drawing is to be plotted on 10 X 8 inch paper.
2. The object lines must be plotted with a plot style Style 1. Style 1 must have a lineweight = 0.800 mm.
3. The dimension lines must be plotted with plot style Style 2. Style 2 must have a value of screening = 50.
4. The centerlines must be plotted with plot style Style 3. Style 3 must have a linetype of Medium Dash and screening = 50.
5. The border and title block must be plotted with plot style Style 4. The value of the lineweight should be =0.25 mm.

Exercise 3

Create the drawing shown in Figure 14-20 and then plot it according to your specifications.

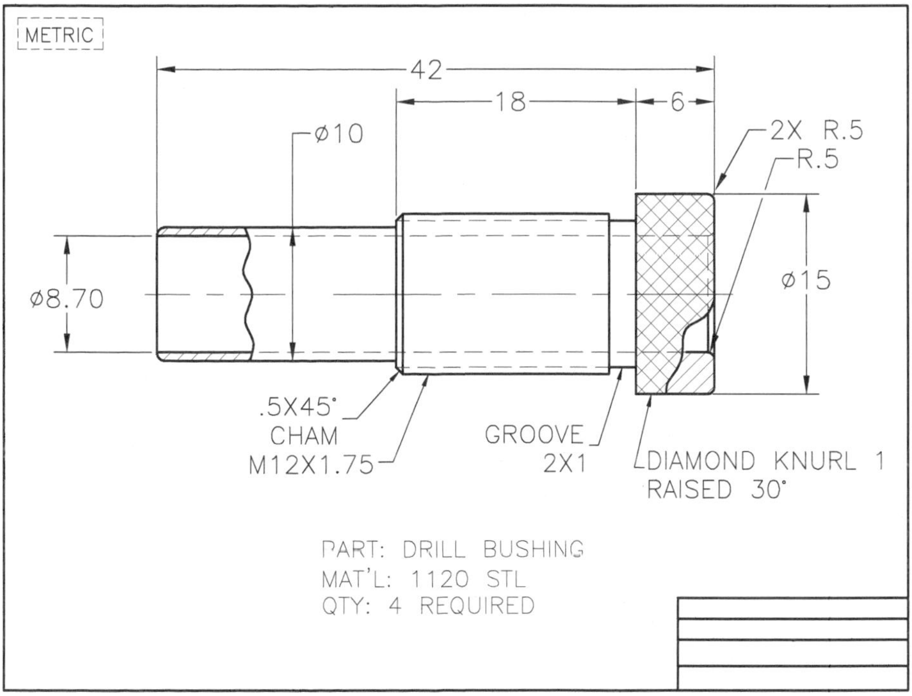

Figure 14-20 Drawing for Exercise 3

Problem-Solving Exercise 1

Make the drawing shown in Figure 14-21 and plot it according to your specifications.

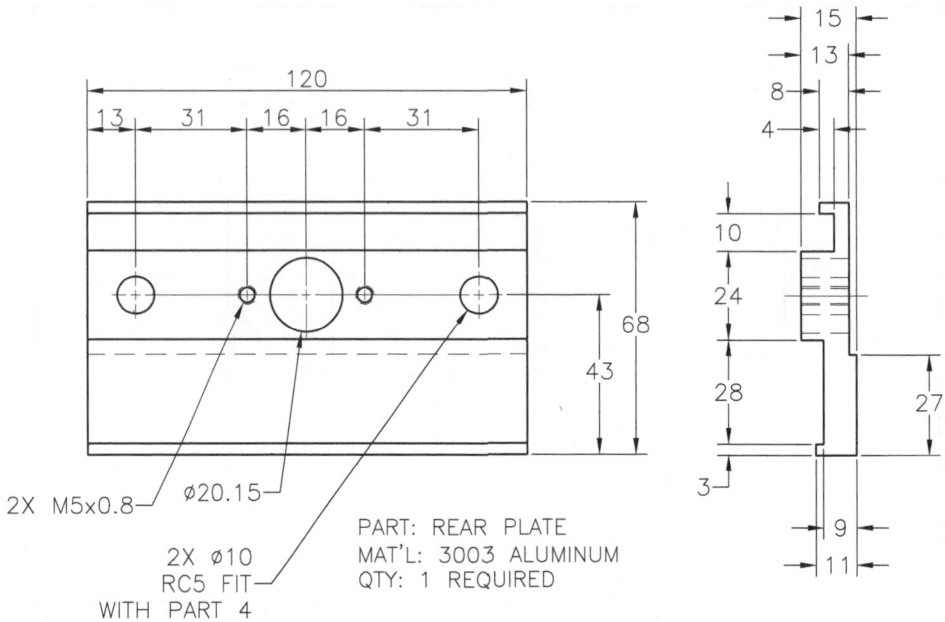

***Figure 14-21** Drawing for Problem-Solving Exercise 1*

Answers to Self-Evaluation Test

1. **Paper size**, **2.** **Plot to file**, **3.** **Plot scale**, **4.** **Display**, **5.** **Paper size**, **6.** **Quality**, **7.** T, **8.** T, **9.** F, **10.** T

Chapter 15

Template Drawings

Learning Objectives

After completing this chapter, you will be able to:

- *Create template drawings*
- *Load template drawings using dialog boxes and the command line*
- *Customize drawings with layers and dimensioning specifications*
- *Customize drawings with layouts, viewports, and paper space*

Key Terms

- *Template*
- *Plot Size*
- *Layout*
- *Template Files (*.dwt)*
- *LTSCALE*
- *Viewport*
- *Drawing Scale*
- *DIMSCALE*
- *STARTUP*
- *TEXTSIZE*

CREATING TEMPLATE DRAWINGS

One way to customize AutoCAD is to create template drawings that contain initial drawing setup information and if desired, visible objects and text. When the user starts a new drawing, the settings associated with the template drawing are automatically loaded. If you start a new drawing from the scratch, AutoCAD loads default setup values. For example, the default limits are (0.0,0.0), (12.0,9.0) and the default layer is 0 with white color and a continuous linetype. Generally, these default parameters need to be reset before generating a drawing on the computer using AutoCAD. A considerable amount of time is required to set up the layers, colors, linetypes, lineweights, limits, snaps, units, text height, dimensioning variables, and other parameters. Sometimes, border lines and a title block may also be needed.

In production drawings, most of the drawing setup values remain the same. For example, the company title block, border, layers, linetypes, dimension variables, text height, LTSCALE, and other drawing setup values do not change. You will save considerable time if you save these values and reload them when starting a new drawing. You can do this by creating template drawings that contain the initial drawing setup information configured according to the company specifications. They can also contain a border, title block, tolerance table, block definitions, floating viewports in the paper space, and perhaps some notes and instructions that are common to all drawings.

STANDARD TEMPLATE DRAWINGS

AutoCAD comes with standard template drawings like *Acad.dwt*, *Acadiso.dwt*, *Acad3d.dwt*, *Acadiso3D.dwt*, *Acad-named plot styles.dwt*, *Acadiso-named plot styles.dwt*, and so on. The iso template drawings are based on the drawing standards developed by ISO (International Organization for Standardization). When you start a new drawing with **STARTUP** system variable set to 1, the **Create New Drawing** dialog box will be displayed. To load the template drawing, choose the **Use a Template** button from this dialog box; the list of standard template drawings is displayed. From this list, you can select any template drawing according to your requirements. If you want to start a drawing with the default settings, choose the **Start from Scratch** button in the **Create New Drawing** dialog box and choose the **OK** button. The following are some of the system variables with the default values that are assigned to the new drawing.

System variable Name	Default Value
CHAMFERA	0.0000
CHAMFERB	0.0000
COLOR	Bylayer
DIMALT	OFF
DIMALTD	2
DIMALTF	25.4000
DIMPOST	None
DIMASO	ON
DIMASZ	0.1800
FILLETRAD	0.0000
GRID	0.5000
GRIDMODE	0
ISOPLANE	Top
LIMMIN	0.0000,0.0000
LIMMAX	12.0000,9.0000

LTSCALE 1.0000
MIRRTEXT 0 (Text not mirrored like other objects)
TILEMODE 1 (OFF)

Example 1 Advance Setup Wizard

Create a drawing template using the **Use a Wizard** button of the **Advanced Setup** wizard with the following specifications and save it with the name *proto1.dwt*.

Units Engineering with precision 0'-0.00"
Angle Decimal degrees with precision 0
Angle Direction Counterclockwise
Area 144'x96'

Step 1: Setting the STARTUP system variable

Set the value of the **STARTUP** system variable to 1. Choose the **New** tool from the **Quick Access Toolbar** to display the **Create New Drawing** dialog box, as shown in Figure 15-1. Choose the **Use a Wizard** button and then select the **Advanced Setup** option. Next, choose the **OK** button; the **Units** page of the **Advanced Setup** wizard is displayed, as shown in Figure 15-2.

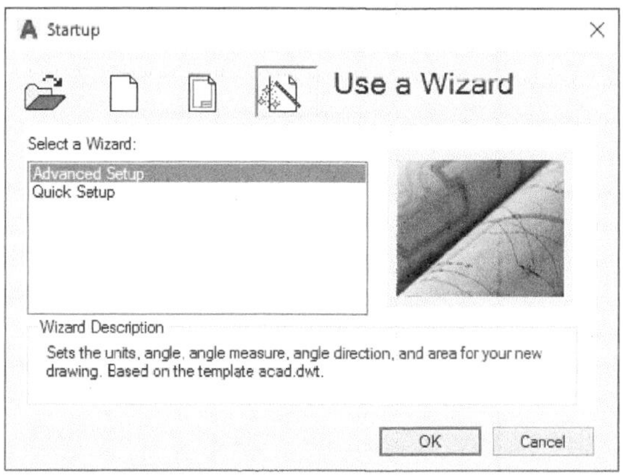

*Figure 15-1 The **Create New Drawing** dialog box*

Step 2: Setting the units of the drawing file

Select the **Engineering** radio button from the **Select the unit of measurement** area. Next, select **0'-0.00"** precision from the **Precision** drop-down list and then choose the **Next** button; the **Angle** page of the **Advanced Setup** wizard is displayed.

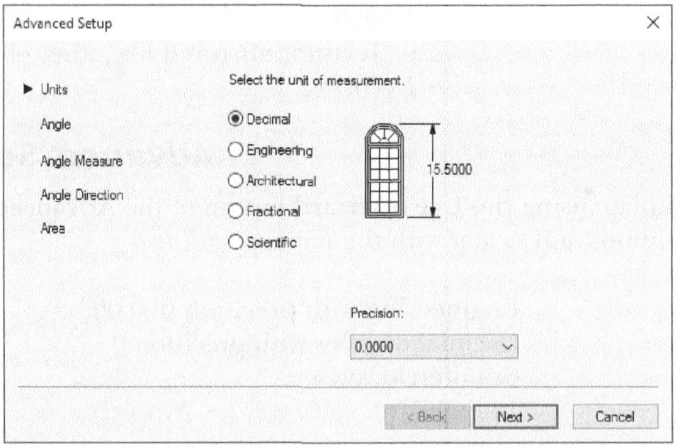

Figure 15-2 The ***Units*** *page of the* ***Advanced Setup*** wizard

Step 3: Setting the angle measurement system

In the **Angle** page, select the **Decimal Degrees** radio button, if not already selected and select **0** from the **Precision** drop-down list, as shown in Figure 15-3. Choose the **Next** button; the **Angle Measure** page of the **Advanced Setup** wizard is displayed.

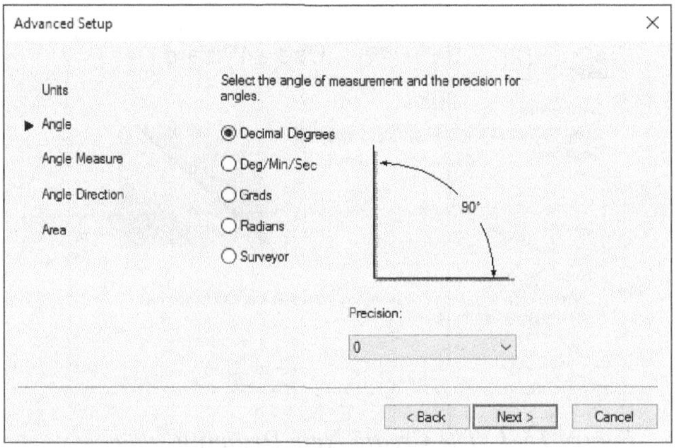

Figure 15-3 The ***Angle*** *page of the* ***Advanced Setup*** wizard

Step 4: Setting the horizontal axis for angle measurement

In the **Angle Measure** page, select the **East** radio button. Choose the **Next** button to display the **Angle Direction** page.

Step 5: Setting the angle measurement direction and drawing area

Select the **Counter-Clockwise** radio button and then choose the **Next** button; the **Area** page is displayed. Specify the area as 144' and 96' by entering the value of the width and length as **144'** and **96'** in the **Width** and **Length** edit boxes and then choose the **Finish** button. Use the **All** option from the **Zoom** drop-down list to display new limits on the screen.

Step 6: Saving the drawing as template file

Now, save the drawing as *proto1.dwt* using the **Save** tool from the **Quick Access Toolbar**. You need to select **AutoCAD Drawing Template (*.dwt)** from the **Files of type** drop-down list and enter **proto1** in the **File name** edit box in the **Save Drawing As** dialog box. Next, choose the **Save** button; the **Template Options** dialog box will be displayed on the screen, as shown in Figure 15-4. Enter the description about the template in the **Description** edit box and choose the **OK** button. Now, the drawing will be saved as *proto1.dwt* on the default drive.

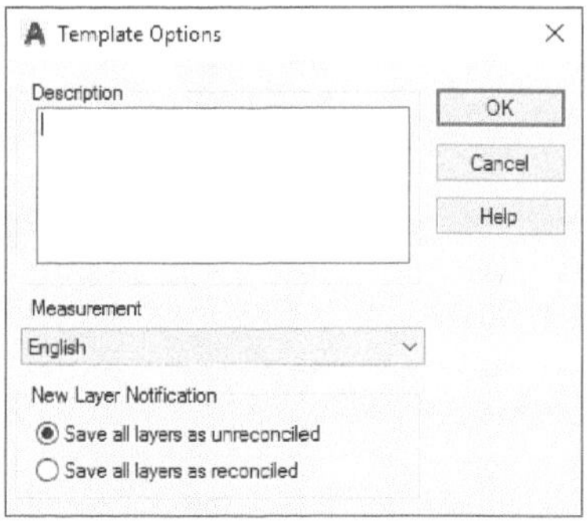

Figure 15-4 *The **Template Options** dialog box*

Note

*To customize only the units and area, you can use the **Quick Setup** option in the **Create New Drawing** dialog box.*

Example 2 Start from Scratch Option

Create a drawing template using the following specifications. The template should be saved with the name *proto2.dwt*.

Limits	18.0,12.0
Snap	0.25
Grid	0.50
Text height	0.125
Units	3 digits to the right of decimal point
	Decimal degrees
	2 digits to the right of decimal point
	0 angle along positive *X* axis (east)
	Angle positive if measured counterclockwise

Step 1: Starting a new drawing

Start AutoCAD and choose the **Start from Scratch** button from the **Create New Drawing** dialog box, as shown in Figure 15-5. From the **Default Settings** area, select the **Imperial (feet and inches)** radio button. Choose the **OK** button to open a new file.

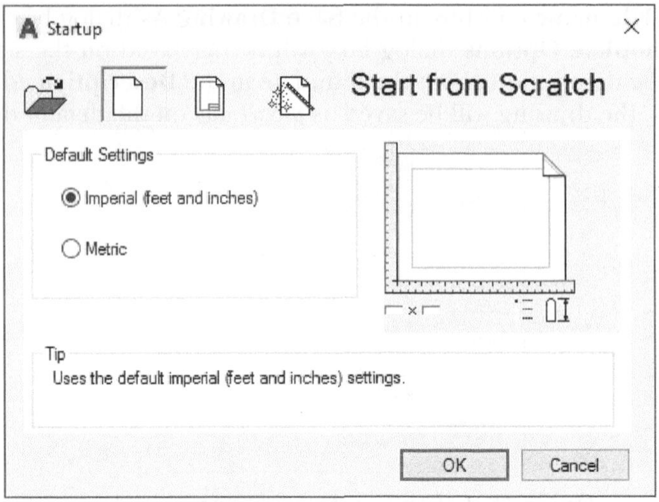

Figure 15-5 The ***Start from Scratch*** *button of the* ***Create New Drawing*** *dialog box*

Step 2: Setting limits, snap, grid, and text size

The **LIMITS** command can be invoked by entering **LIMITS** at the command prompt.

Command: **LIMITS**
Reset Model space limits:
Specify lower left corner or [ON/OFF] <0.0000,0.0000>: Enter
Specify upper right corner <12.0000,9.0000>: **18,12** Enter

After setting the limits, the next step is to expand the drawing display area. Select the **All** option from the **Zoom** drop-down list to display new limits on the screen.

Now, right-click on the **Grid Display** button in the Status Bar to display a shortcut menu. Choose the **Grid Settings** option from the shortcut menu to display the **Drafting Settings** dialog box. Choose the **Snap and Grid** tab. Enter **0.25** in the **Snap X spacing** and **Snap Y spacing** edit boxes in the **Snap spacing** area. Enter **0.5** in the **Grid X spacing** and **Grid Y spacing** edit boxes. Then, choose the **OK** button.

Note

You can also use the ***SNAP*** *and* ***GRID*** *commands to set these values.*

The size of the text can be changed by entering **TEXTSIZE** at the command prompt.

Command: **TEXTSIZE**
Enter new value for TEXTSIZE <0.2000>: **0.125** Enter

Step 3: Setting units

Choose the **Units** tool from the **Application Menu > Drawing Utilities** or enter **UNITS** at the command prompt to invoke the **Drawing Units** dialog box, as shown in Figure 15-6. In the **Length** area, select **0.000** from the **Precision** drop-down list. In the **Angle** area, select **Decimal**

Degrees from the **Type** drop-down list and **0.00** from the **Precision** drop-down list. Also, make sure the **Clockwise** check box in the **Angle** area is cleared.

Choose the **Direction** button from the **Drawing Units** dialog box to display the **Direction Control** dialog box, refer to Figure 15-7 and then select the **East** radio button. Exit both the dialog boxes.

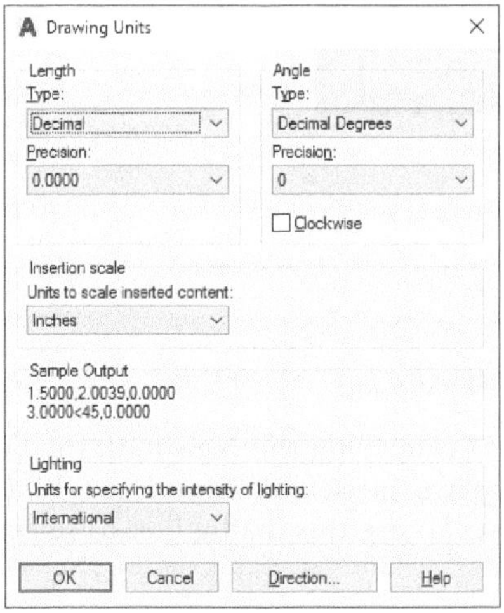

*Figure 15-6 The **Drawing Units** dialog box*

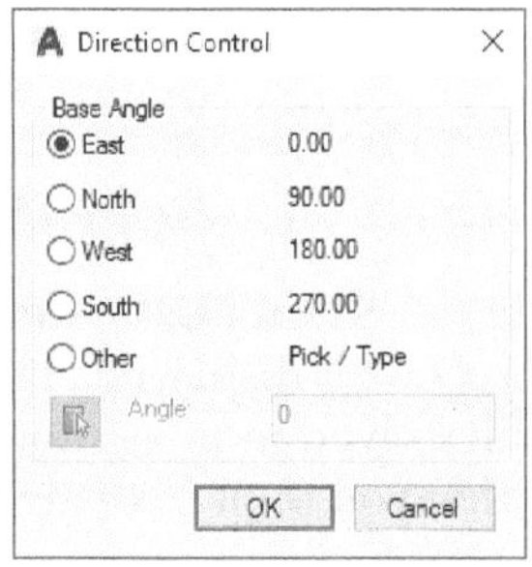

*Figure 15-7 The **Direction Control** dialog box*

Step 4: Saving the drawing as template file

Now, save the drawing as *proto2.dwt* using the **Save** tool from the **Quick Access** toolbar. You need to select **AutoCAD Drawing Template (*dwt)** from the **Files of type** drop-down list and enter **proto2** in the **File name** edit box in the **Save Drawing As** dialog box. Next, choose the **Save** button; the **Template Options** dialog box will be displayed on the screen. Enter the description about the template in the **Description** edit box and choose the **OK** button; the drawing will be saved as *proto2.dwt* on the default drive. You can also save this drawing to some other location by specifying other location from the **Save in** drop-down list of the **Save Drawing As** dialog box.

LOADING A TEMPLATE DRAWING

You can use the template drawing to start a new drawing file. To use the preset values of the template drawing, restart AutoCAD or choose the **New** tool from the **Quick Access Toolbar**. The dialog box that appears will depend on whether you have set the **STARTUP** system variable to **1** or **0**. If you have set this value as **1**, the **Create New Drawing** dialog box will appear. Choose the **Use a Template** button. All templates that are saved in the default **Template** directory will be shown in the **Select a Template** list box, as shown in Figure 15-8. If you have saved the template in any other location, choose the **Browse** button. On doing so, the **Select a template file** dialog box will be displayed. You can use this dialog box to browse the directory in which the template file is saved.

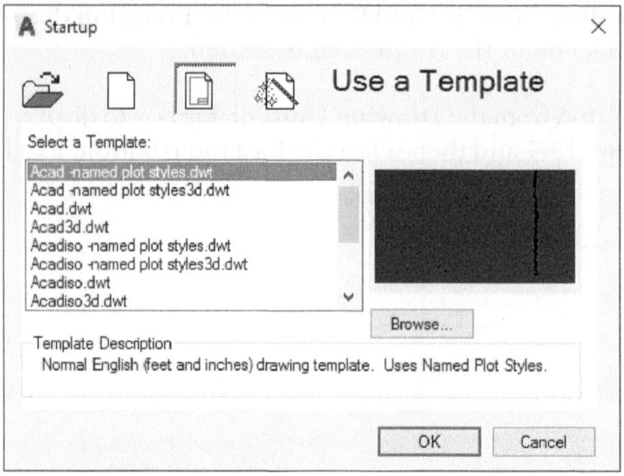

Figure 15-8 *The **Select a Template** list box*

If you have set the **STARTUP** system variable to 0, then on choosing the **New** tool, the **Select template** dialog box is displayed. This dialog box also displays the default **Template** folder and all template files saved in it, as shown in Figure 15-9. You can use this dialog box to select the template file that you want to open.

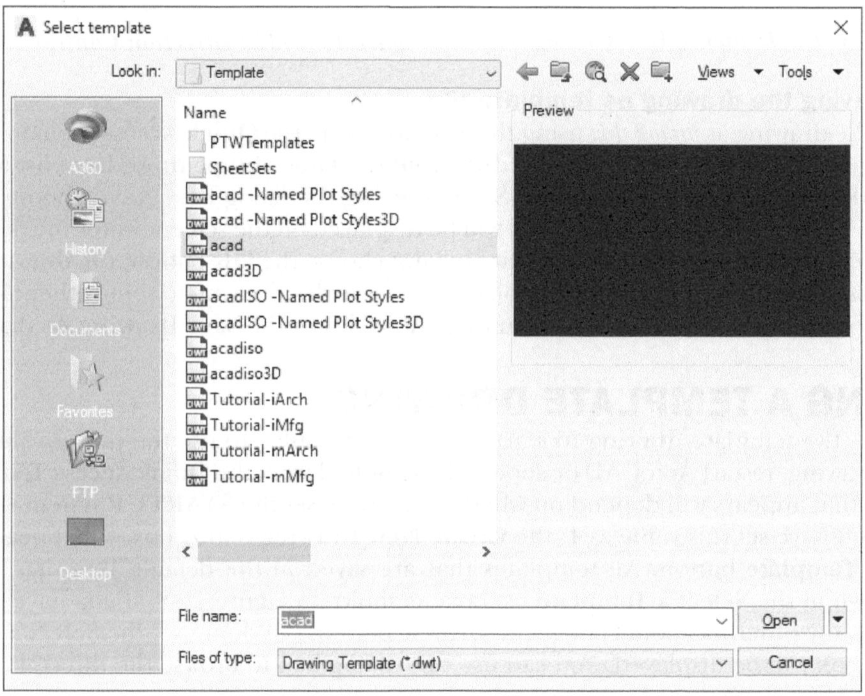

Figure 15-9 *The **Select template** dialog box that appears while starting a new drawing file, when the value of **STARTUP** variable is set to **0***

Using any of the previously mentioned dialog boxes, select the *proto1.dwt* template drawing. AutoCAD will start a new drawing that will have the same setup as that of the template drawing *proto1.dwt*.

You can have several template drawings, each with a different setup. For example, PROTOB for a 18" X 12" drawing, PROTOC for a 24" X 18" drawing. Each template drawing can be created according to user-defined specifications. You can then load any of these template drawings, as discussed previously.

CUSTOMIZING DRAWINGS WITH LAYERS AND DIMENSIONING SPECIFICATIONS

Most production drawings need multiple layers for different groups of objects. In addition to layers, it is a good practice to assign different colors to different layers to control the line width at the time of plotting. You can generate a template drawing that contains the desired number of layers with linetypes and colors according to your company specifications. You can then use this template drawing to make a new drawing. The next example illustrates the procedure used for customizing a drawing with layers, linetypes, and colors.

Example 3 Template with Title Block & Layers

Create a template drawing *proto3.dwt* that has a border and the company's title block, as shown in Figure 15-10.

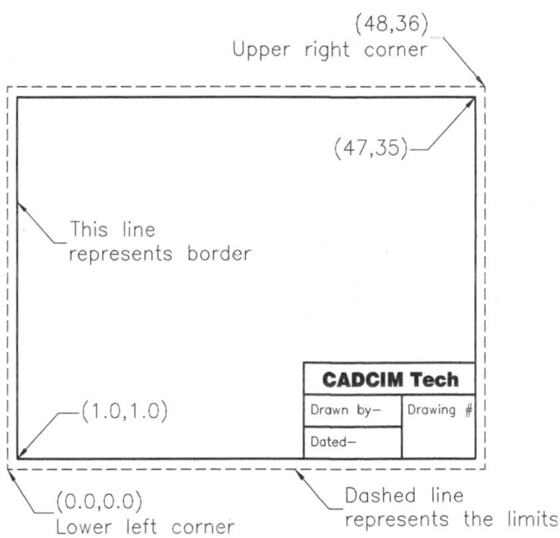

Figure 15-10 *The template drawing for Example 3*

This template drawing will have the following initial drawing setup:

Limits	48.0,36.0
Text height	0.25
Border line lineweight	0.012"
Ltscale	4.0

DIMENSIONS
Overall dimension scale factor 4.0

Dimension text above the extension line
Dimension text aligned with dimension line

LAYERS

Layer Name	Line Type	Color
0	Continuous	White
OBJ	Continuous	Red
CEN	Center	Yellow
HID	Hidden	Blue
DIM	Continuous	Green
BOR	Continuous	Magenta

Step 1: Setting limits, text size, polyline width, polyline, and linetype scaling

Start a new drawing with default parameters by selecting the **Start from Scratch** option in the **Create New Drawing** dialog box. In the new drawing file, use the AutoCAD tools to set up the values as given for this example. Also, draw a border and a title block, as shown in Figure 15-10. In this figure, the hidden lines indicate drawing limits. The border lines are 1.0 units inside the drawing limits. For border lines, increase the lineweight to a value of 0.012".

Use the following procedure to produce the prototype drawing for Example 3:

1. Invoke the **LIMITS** command by entering **LIMITS** at the command prompt. The prompt sequence is given next.

   Command: **LIMITS**
   Reset Model space limits:
   Specify lower left corner or [ON/OFF] <0.0000,0.0000>: Enter
   Specify upper right corner <current>: **48,36** Enter

2. Increase the drawing display area by selecting the **All** option from the **Zoom** drop-down list.

3. Enter **TEXTSIZE** at the command prompt to change the text size.

   Command: **TEXTSIZE**
   Enter new value for TEXTSIZE <0.2000>: **0.25** Enter

4. Next, draw the border using the **Rectangle** tool. The prompt sequence to draw the rectangle is:

   Command: **RECTANGLE**
   Specify first corner point or [Chamfer/Elevation/Fillet/Thickness/Width]: **1.0,1.0** Enter
   Specify other corner point or [Area/Dimensions/Rotation]: **47.0,35.0** Enter

5. Now, select the rectangle and change its lineweight to **0.012"**. Make sure that the **Show/Hide Lineweight** button is chosen in the Status Bar.

6. Enter **LTSCALE** at the command prompt to change the linetype scale.

Command: **LTSCALE**
Enter new linetype scale factor<Current>: **4.0** Enter

Step 2: Setting dimensioning parameters

You can use the **Dimension Style Manager** dialog box to set the dimension variables. Click the inclined arrow displayed on the **Dimensions** panel in the **Annotate** tab; the **Dimension Style Manager** dialog box is displayed, as shown in Figure 15-11.

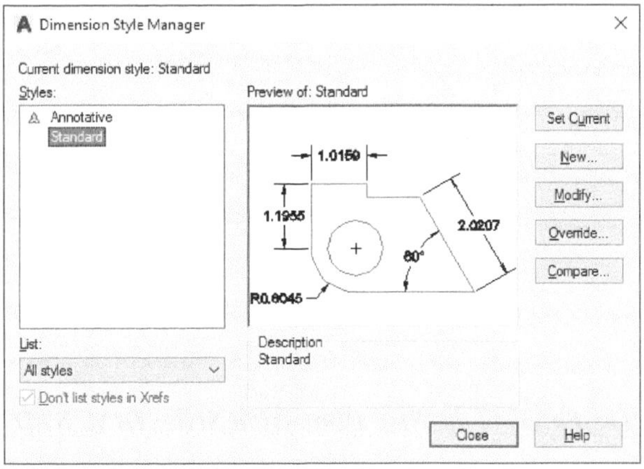

*Figure 15-11 The **Dimension Style Manager** dialog box*

You can also invoke this dialog box by entering **DIMSTYLE** at the command prompt. Choose the **New** button from the **Dimension Style Manager** dialog box; the **Create New Dimension Style** dialog box is displayed. Specify the new style name as **DIM_STD_1** in the **New Style Name** edit box, as shown in Figure 15-12, and then choose the **Continue** button; the **New Dimension Style:DIM_STD_1** dialog box is displayed.

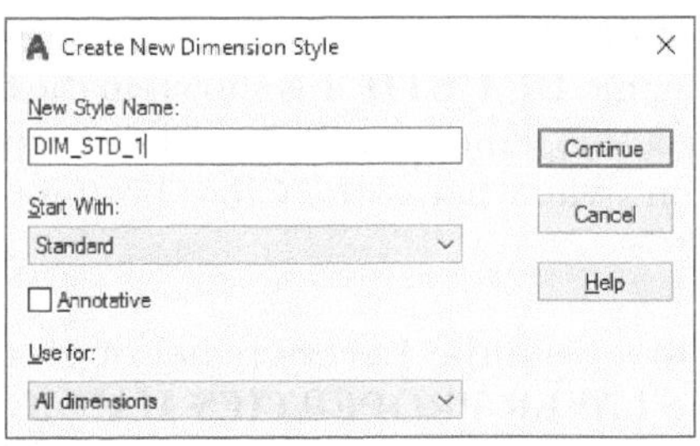

*Figure 15-12 The **Create New Dimension Style** dialog box*

Specifying overall dimension scale factor

To specify a dimension scale factor, choose the **Fit** tab in the **New Dimension Style: DIM_STD_1** dialog box. Next, select the **Use overall scale of** radio button in the **Scale for dimension features** area, as shown in Figure 15-13; the edit box corresponding to it is activated. Set the value in the edit box as **4**.

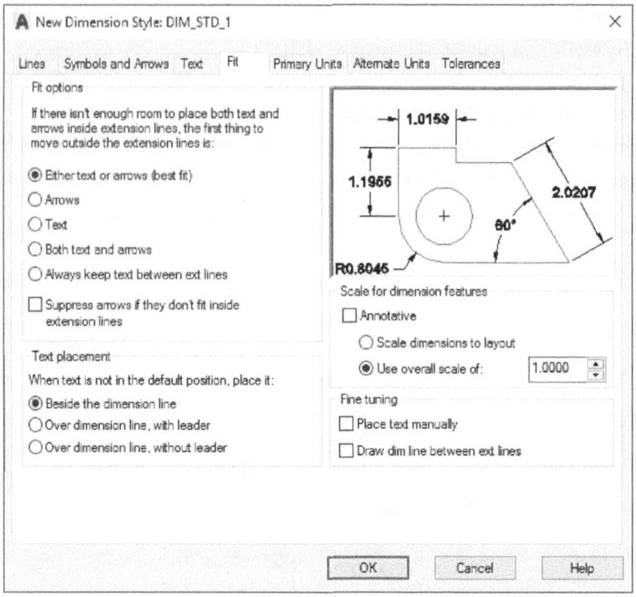

*Figure 15-13 The **Fit** tab of the **New Dimension Style: DIM_STD_1** dialog box*

Placing the dimension text over the dimension line

In the **Fit** tab of the **New Dimension Style: DIM_STD_1** dialog box, select the **Over dimension line, with leader** radio button from the **Text placement** area.

Dimensioning text aligned with the dimension line

In the **Text alignment** area of the **Text** tab of the **New Dimension Style: DIM_STD_1** dialog box, select the **Aligned with dimension line** radio button and then choose the **OK** button.

Setting the new dimension style to current

A new dimension style with the name **DIM_STD_1** is shown in the **Styles** area of the **Dimension Style Manager** dialog box. Select this dimension style and then choose the **Set Current** button to make it the current dimension style. Choose the **Close** button to exit this dialog box.

Step 3: Setting layers

Choose the **Layer Properties** tool from the **Layers** panel or choose the **Layer** tool from the **Format** menu bar to invoke the **LAYER PROPERTIES MANAGER**. Choose the **New Layer** button in the **LAYER PROPERTIES MANAGER** and rename **Layer1** as **OBJ**. Choose the color swatch of the OBJ layer to display the **Select Color** dialog box. Select the **Red** color and choose the **OK** button; the red color is assigned to the OBJ layer. Again, choose the **New Layer** button in the **LAYER PROPERTIES MANAGER** and rename the **Layer1** as **CEN**. Choose the linetype swatch to display the **Select Linetype** dialog box.

If different linetypes are not already loaded, choose the **Load** button to display the **Load or Reload Linetypes** dialog box. Select the **CENTER** linetype from the **Available Linetypes** area and then choose the **OK** button; the **Select Linetype** dialog box is displayed again. Select the **CENTER** linetype from the **Loaded linetypes** area and choose the **OK** button. Choose the color swatch to display the **Select Color** dialog box. Select the **yellow** color and choose the **OK** button; the color yellow and linetype center will be assigned to the layer CEN.

Similarly, different linetypes and different colors can be set for different layers mentioned in the statement of this example, as shown in Figure 15-14.

S...	Name	On	Freeze	Lock	Color	Linetype	Lineweight	Transparency	Plot
	0				white	Continuous	Defa...	0	Color
	BOR				magenta	Continuous	0.012"	0	Color
	CEN				yellow	CENTER	Defa...	0	Color
	DIM				green	Continuous	Defa...	0	Color
	HID				blue	HIDDEN	Defa...	0	Color
	OBJ				red	Continuous	Defa...	0	Color

Figure 15-14** Partial view of the **LAYER PROPERTIES MANAGER

Step 4: Adding title block

Next, add the tittle block and the text, as shown in Figure 15-0. After completing the drawing, save it as *proto3.dwt*. You have created a template drawing (proto3) that contains all the information given in Example 3.

CUSTOMIZING A DRAWING WITH LAYOUT

The Layout (paper space) provides a convenient way to plot multiple views of a three-dimensional (3D) drawing or multiple views of a regular two-dimensional (2D) drawing. It takes quite some time to set up the viewports in the model space with different vpoints and scale factors. You can create prototype drawings that contain predefined viewport settings, with vpoint and the other desired information. If you create a new drawing or insert a drawing, the views are automatically generated. The following example illustrates the procedure for generating a prototype drawing with paper space and model space viewports:

Example 4 — Template with Layouts

Create a drawing template, as shown in Figure 15-15, with four views in Layout3 (Paper space) that display front, top, side, and 3D views of the object. The plot size is 10.5 by 8 inches. The plot scale is 0.5 or 1/2" = 1". The paper space viewports should have the following vpoint settings:

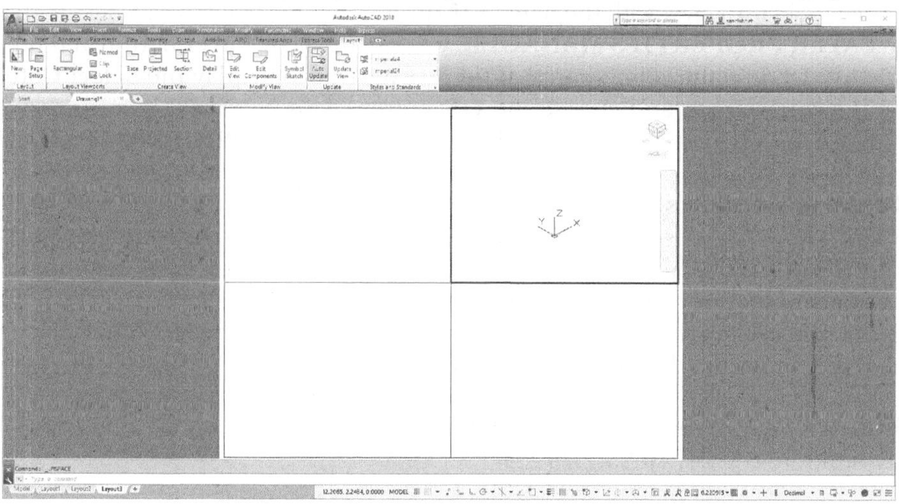

***Figure 15-15** Paper space with four viewports*

Viewports	Vpoint	View
Top right	1,-1,1	3D view
Top left	0,0,1	Top view
Lower right	1,0,0	Right side view
Lower left	0,-1,0	Front view

Start AutoCAD and create a new drawing. Use the following commands and options to set various parameters:

Step 1: Creating a new layout

First, choose the **New Layout** button Layout Tabs; a new layout is automatically added with the default name as Layout3.

Note

*You can also use the **LAYOUT** command to create a new layout.*

Step 2: Specifying the page setup for the new layout

Next, choose the new layout (Layout3) tab. The Layout3 will be displayed with the default viewport. Delete the existing viewport. Next, invoke the **Page Setup Manager** dialog box. To do so right-click on the layout in the Layout Tabs; a shortcut menu is displayed. Choose the **Page Setup Manager** option from the shortcut menu; the **Page Setup Manager** dialog box will be displayed. Choose the **Modify** button to modify the default page setup. In the **Page Setup - Layout3** dialog box, select the required printer from the **Printer/plotter** area. In this example, the **Microsoft XPS Document Writer** printer has been used.

Now, from the **Paper size** area, select the paper size that is supported by the selected plotting device. In this example, the paper size is A4. Choose the **OK** button to accept the settings and return to the **Page Setup Manager** dialog box. Choose the **Close** button to close the **Page Setup Manager** dialog box.

Step 3: Creating a new layer for the viewports object

Next, you need to set up a layer with the name VIEW for viewports object and assign it green color. Invoke the **LAYER PROPERTIES MANAGER**. Choose the **New Layer** button and rename the Layer1 as VIEW. Choose the color swatch of the VIEW layer to display the **Select Color** dialog box. Select the color **Green** and choose the **OK** button. This color will be assigned to VIEW layer. Also, make the VIEW layer current and then exit the **LAYER PROPERTIES MANAGER**.

Step 4: Creating viewports

To create four viewports, choose the **Named** tool from **Layout > Layout Viewports** in the **Ribbon**; the **Viewports** dialog box is displayed. Choose the **New Viewports** tab and then select the **Four: Equal** option from the **Standard viewports** list box. Next, choose the **OK** button from the dialog box; you will be prompted to specify the starting point of the viewports. The following is the prompt sequence that follows after choosing the **OK** button.

Specify first corner or [Fit] <Fit>: **0.25,0.25** Enter
Specify opposite corner: **10.25,7.75** Enter

Step 5: Setting the required viewpoint in all layers

Choose the **PAPER** button in the Status Bar to activate the model space or enter **MSPACE** at the command prompt.

Command: **MSPACE** (or **MS**)

Make the lower left viewport active by clicking on it. Next, you need to change the viewpoints of different paper space viewports by using the **Viewpoint** tool. To invoke this tool, choose the **Viewpoint** tool from **View > 3D Views** in the menu bar or enter **-VPOINT** at the command prompt. The viewpoint values for different viewports are given in the statement of Example 4. To set the view point for the lower left viewport, the command prompt sequence is given next.

*Choose the **Viewpoint** tool from **View > 3D Views** in the menu bar*
Current view direction: VIEWDIR= 0.0000,0.0000,1.0000 Enter
Specify a view point or [Rotate] <display compass and tripod>: **0,-1,0** Enter

Similarly, use the **Viewpoint** tool to set the viewpoint of the other viewports.

Note
You can also use the ViewCube or the SteeringWheel to orient the view in any viewport.

Make the top left viewport active by selecting a point in the viewport and then use the **Scale** tool to specify the paper space scale factor to 0.5. The **Scale** tool can be invoked by choosing **View > Zoom > Scale** from the menu bar or by entering **ZOOM** at the command prompt. The command prompt sequence is given next.

Command: **ZOOM**
Specify corner of window, enter a scale factor (nX or nXP), or [All/Center/Dynamic/Extents/Previous/Scale/Window/Object] <real time>: **0.5XP** Enter

Now, make the next viewport active and specify the zoom scale factor. Do the same for the remaining viewports.

Step 6: Creating border line

Use the **Model** button in the Status Bar to switch to model space environment and then set a new layer PBORDER with yellow color. Make the PBORDER layer current, draw a border, and if needed, a title block using the **Polyline** tool. You can also switch to paper space environment by entering **PSPACE** at the command prompt.

The **Polyline** tool can be invoked by choosing the **Polyline** tool from the **Draw** menu or by choosing the **Polyline** tool from the **Draw** panel. The **Polyline** tool can also be invoked by entering **PLINE** at the command prompt. While specifying the coordinate values for the **PLINE** command, make sure that the **Dynamic Input** button is turned off in the Status Bar.

Command: *Choose the **Polyline** tool from the **Draw** panel*
Specify start point: **0,0** Enter
Current line-width is 0.0000
Specify next point or [Arc/Halfwidth/Length/Undo/Width]: **0,8.0** Enter

Specify next point or [Arc/Close/Halfwidth/Length/Undo/Width]: **10.5,8.0** Enter
Specify next point or [Arc/Close/Halfwidth/Length/Undo/Width]: **10.5,0** Enter
Specify next point or [Arc/Close/Halfwidth/Length/Undo/Width]: **C** Enter

Step 7: Saving and testing the template file

The last step is to choose the **Model** tab (or change the **TILEMODE** to 1), if not already active and save the prototype drawing as template. To test the layout that you just created, make the 3D drawing, as shown in Figure 15-16, or make any 3D object. Switch to the **Layout 3** tab; you will find four different views of the object, as shown in Figure 15-17.

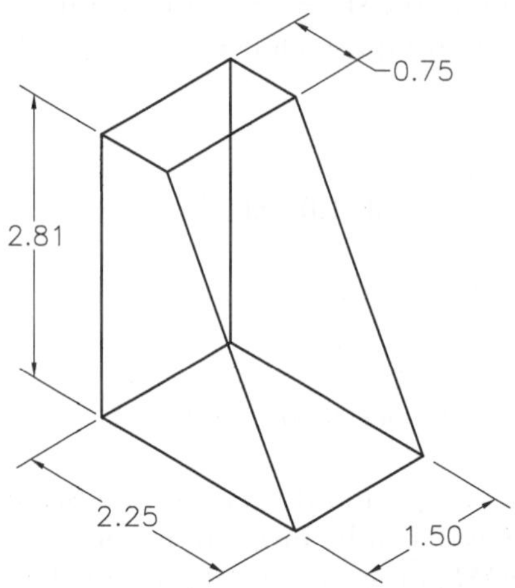

Figure 15-16 *3D tapered block*

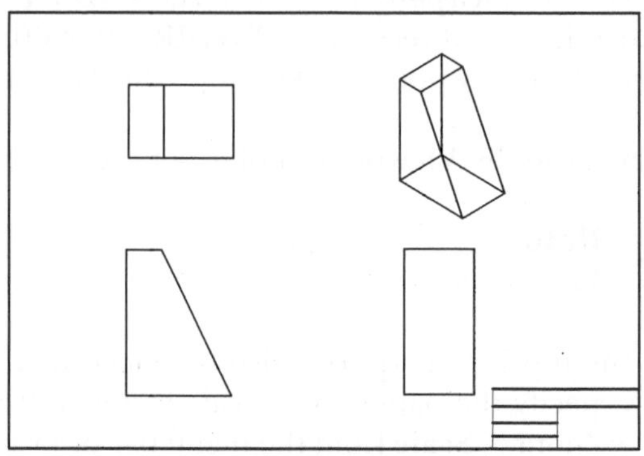

Figure 15-17 *Four views of a 3D object in paper space*

If the object views do not appear in the viewports, use the **PAN** command to position the views in the viewports. You can freeze the VIEW layer so that the viewports do not appear in the drawing. You can plot this drawing from the Layout3 with a plot scale factor of 1:1 and the size of the plot will be exactly as specified.

CUSTOMIZING DRAWINGS WITH VIEWPORTS

In certain applications, you may need multiple model space viewport configurations to display different views of an object. This involves setting up the desired viewports and then changing the viewpoint for different viewports. You can create a prototype drawing that contains a required number of viewports and the viewpoint information. If you insert a 3D object in one of the viewports of the prototype drawing, you will automatically get different views of the object without setting viewports or viewpoints. The following example illustrates the procedure for creating a prototype drawing with a standard number (four) of viewports and viewpoints.

Example 5 — *Template with Viewports*

Create a prototype drawing with four viewports, as shown in Figure 15-18. The viewports should have the following viewpoints:

Viewports	Vpoint	View
Top right	1,-1,1	3D view
Top left	0,0,1	Top view
Lower right	1,0,0	Right side view
Lower left	0,-1,0	Front view

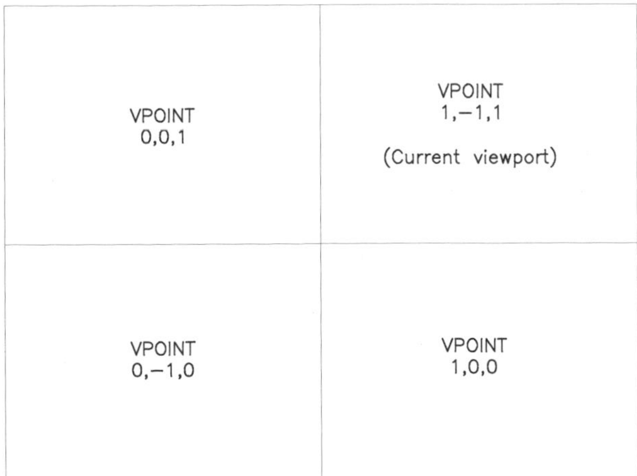

Figure 15-18 *Viewports with different viewpoints*

Step 1

Start AutoCAD and create a new drawing from scratch.

Step 2

Setting viewports in Model tab

Viewports and corresponding viewpoints can be set using the **VPORTS** command. You can also choose the **New Viewports** tool from **View > Viewports** in the menu bar, as shown in Figure 15-19. Select **Four: Equal** from the **Standard viewports** area. In the **Preview** area, four equal viewports are displayed. Select **3D** from the **Setup** drop-down list. The four viewports with the different viewpoints will be displayed in the **Preview** area as Top, Front, Right, and SE Isometric. **Top** represents the viewpoints as (0,0,1), **Front** represents the viewpoints as (0,-1,0), **Right** represents the viewpoints as (1,0,0) and **SE Isometric** represents the viewpoints as (1,-1,1) respectively. Choose the **OK** button. Save the drawing as *proto5.dwt*.

Viewports and viewpoints can also be set by entering **-VPORTS** and **VPOINT** at the command prompt, respectively.

Step 3

Start a new drawing and draw the 3D tapered block, as shown in Figure 15-16.

Step 4

Again, start a new drawing, TEST, using the prototype drawing *proto5.dwt*. Make the top right viewport current and then insert or create a drawing, refer to Figure 15-16. Four different views will be automatically displayed on the screen, as shown in Figure 15-20.

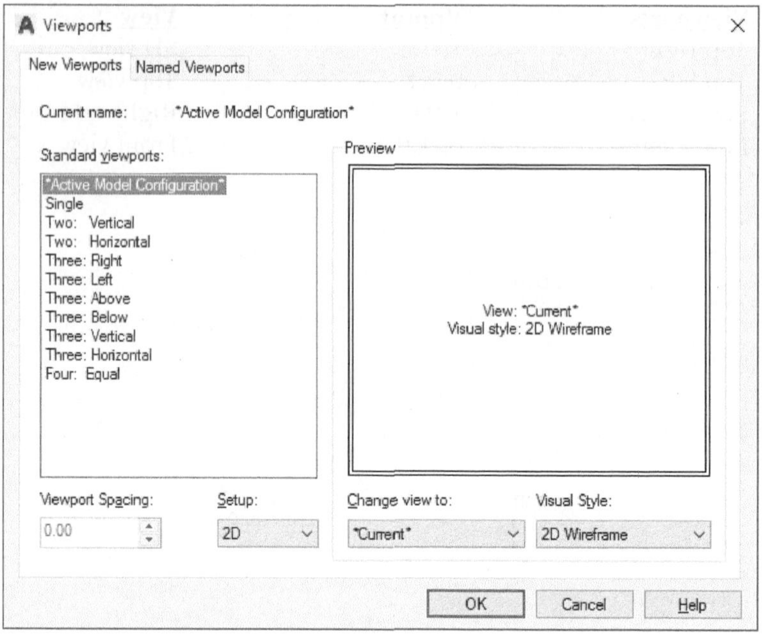

Figure 15-19 *The* ***Viewports*** *dialog box*

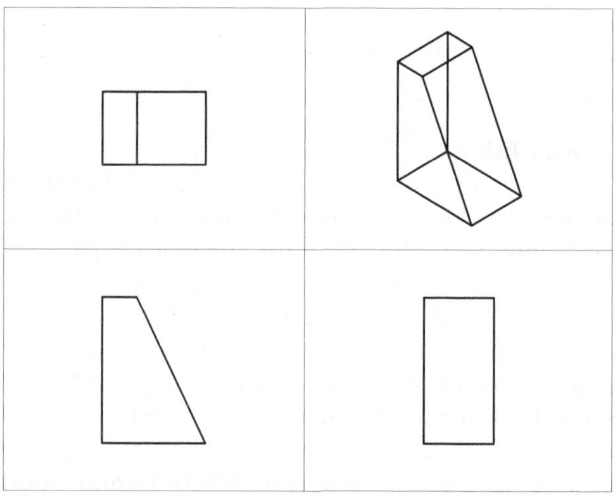

Figure 15-20 *Different views of a 3D tapered block*

CUSTOMIZING DRAWINGS ACCORDING TO PLOT SIZE AND DRAWING SCALE

For controlling the plot area, it is recommended to use layouts. You can make the drawing of any size, use the layout to specify the sheet size, and then draw the border and title block. However, you can also plot a drawing in the model space and set up the system variables so that the plotted drawing is according to your specifications. You can generate a template drawing according to plot size and scale. For example, if the scale is 1/16" = 1' and the drawing is to be plotted on a 36" by 24" area, you can calculate drawing parameters like limits, **DIMSCALE**, and **LTSCALE** and save them in a template drawing. This will save considerable time in the initial drawing setup and provide uniformity in the drawings. The next example explains the procedure involved in customizing a drawing according to a certain plot size and scale.

Example 6 Template with Plot Size and Drawing Scale

Create a drawing template (proto6.dwt) with the following specifications:

Plotted sheet size	36" by 24", refer to Figure 15-21.
Scale	1/8" = 1.0'
Snap	3'
Grid	6'
Text height	1/4" on plotted drawing
Linetype scale	Calculate
Dimscale factor	Calculate
Units	Architectural Precision, 16-denominator of the smallest fraction Angle in degrees/minutes/seconds Precision, 0d00' Direction control, base angle, east Angle positive, if measured counterclockwise
Border	Border should be 1" inside the edges of the plotted drawing sheet, using PLINE 1/32" wide when plotted, refer to Figure 15-21.

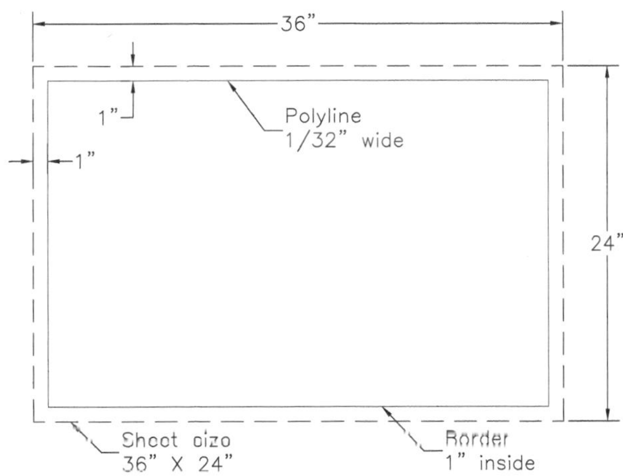

Figure 15-21 Border of the template drawing

Step 1: Calculating limits, text height, linetype scale, dimension scale, and polyline width

In this example, you need to calculate some values before you set the parameters. The limits of the drawing depend on the plotted size of the drawing and its scale. Similarly, **LTSCALE** and **DIMSCALE** depend on the plot scale of the drawing. The following calculations explain the procedure for finding the values of limits, ltscale, dimscale, and text height.

Limits

Given:
Sheet size 36" x 24"
Scale 1/8" = 1'
or 1" = 8'

Calculate:
X Limit
Y Limit
Since sheet size is 36" x 24" and scale is 1/8"=1'
Therefore, X Limit = 36 x 8' = 288'
Y Limit = 24 x 8' = 192'

Text height

Given:
Text height when plotted = 1/4"
Scale 1/8" = 1'

Calculate:
Text height
Since scale is 1/8" = 1'
or 1/8" = 12"
or 1" = 96"
Therefore, scale factor = 96
Text height = 1/4" x 96
= 24" = 2'

Linetype scale and dimension scale

Known:
Since scale is 1/8" = 1'
or 1/8" = 12"
or 1" = 96"

Calculate:
LTSCALE and DIMSCALE
Since scale factor = 96
Therefore, LTSCALE = Scale factor = 96
Similarly, DIMSCALE = 96
(All dimension variables, like DIMTXT and DIMASZ, will be multiplied by 96.)

Polyline Width

Given:
Scale is 1/8" = 1'

Calculate:
PLINE width
Since scale is 1/8" = 1'
or 1" = 8'
or 1" = 96"

Therefore,
PLINE width = 1/32 x 96
= 3"

After calculating the parameters, use the following AutoCAD commands to set up the drawing and save the drawing as *proto6.dwt*.

Step 2: Setting units

Start a new drawing and enter **UNITS** at the command prompt to display the **Drawing Units** dialog box. Select **Architectural** from the **Type** drop-down list in the **Length** area. Select **0'-01/16"** from the **Precision** drop-down list. Make sure the **Clockwise** check box in the **Angle** area is not selected. Select **Deg/Min/Sec** from the **Type** drop-down list and select **0d00'** from the **Precision** drop-down list in the **Angle** area. Now, choose the **Direction** button to display the **Direction Control** dialog box. Select the **East** radio button, if it is not selected, in the **Base Angle** area and then choose the **OK** button twice to close both the dialog boxes.

Step 3: Setting limits, snap and grid, textsize, linetype scale, dimension scale, dimension style and pline

To set limits, enter **LIMITS** at the command prompt.

Command: **LIMITS**
Specify lower left corner or [ON/OFF] <0'-0",0'-0">:**0,0** [Enter]
Specify upper right corner <1'-0",0'-9">: **288',192'** [Enter]

Choose the **All** option from the **Zoom** drop-down list to increase the drawing display area.

Right-click on the **Snap Mode** or **Grid Display** button in the Status Bar to invoke the shortcut menu. In the shortcut menu, choose **Settings** to display the **Drafting Settings** dialog box. In this dialog box, enter **3'** and **3'** in the **Snap X spacing** and **Snap Y spacing** edit boxes, respectively. Similarly, enter **6'** and **6'** in the **Grid X spacing** and **Grid Y spacing** edit boxes, respectively. Then, choose the **OK** button.

You can also set these values by entering **SNAP** and **GRID** at the command prompt.

The size of the text can be changed by entering **TEXTSIZE** at the command prompt.

Command: **TEXTSIZE**
Enter new value for TEXTSIZE <current>: **2'** [Enter]

To set the **LTSCALE**, choose the **Other** option from **Home > Properties > Linetype** drop-down list, or choose the **Linetype** option from the **Format** menu bar, or enter **LINETYPE** at the command prompt; the **Linetype Manager** dialog box will be invoked. Choose the **Show details** button; the **Linetype Manager** dialog box will be expanded. Now, specify the **Global scale factor** as **96** in the **Global scale factor** edit box. Choose the **OK** button to accept the changes and exit the **Linetype Manager** dialog box.

You can also change the scale of the linetype by entering **LTSCALE** at the command prompt.

Choose the inclined arrow displayed on the **Dimensions** panel in the **Annotate** tab to invoke the **Dimension Style Manager** dialog box, refer to Figure 15-11. Next, choose the **New** button from the **Dimension Style Manager** dialog box to invoke the **Create New Dimension Style** dialog box. Specify the new style name as **MYDIM2** in the **New Style Name** edit box and then choose the **Continue** button. The **New Dimension Style: MYDIM2** dialog box will be displayed. Choose the **Fit** tab and set the value in the **Use overall scale of** spinner to **96** in the **Scale for dimension features** area. Now, choose the **OK** button to display the **Dimension Style Manager** dialog box again. Next, choose the **Close** button to exit the dialog box.

You can invoke the **PLINE** command by choosing the **Polyline** tool from the **Draw** panel or entering **PLINE** at the command prompt. While specifying the coordinate values for the **PLINE** command, make sure that the **Dynamic Input** button is turned off in the Status Bar.

Command: *Choose the **Polyline** tool from the **Draw** panel*
Specify start point: **8',8'** Enter
Current line-width is 0'-0"
Specify next point or [Arc/Halfwidth/Length/Undo/Width]: **W** Enter
Specify starting width<0'-00">: **3** Enter
Specify ending width<0'-3">: Enter
Specify next point or [Arc/Halfwidth/Length/Undo/Width]: **@280,0** Enter
Specify next point or [Arc/Close/Halfwidth/Length/Undo/Width]: **@0,184** Enter
Specify next point or [Arc/Close/Halfwidth/Length/Undo/Width]: **@-280,0** Enter
Specify next point or [Arc/Close/Halfwidth/Length/Undo/Width]: **C** Enter

Now, save the drawing as *proto6.dwt*.

Self-Evaluation Test

Answer the following questions and then compare them to those given at the end of this chapter:

1. The template drawings are saved in the __________ format.

2. To use a template file, select the ________ option in the **Create New Drawing** dialog box.

3. To start a drawing with the default setup, select the __________ option in the **Create New Drawing** dialog box.

4. If the plot size is 36" x 24", and the scale is 1/2" = 1', then X Limit = __________ and Y Limit = __________.

5. You can use the __________ tool in AutoCAD to set up a viewport in the paper space.

6. You can use the __________ command in AutoCAD to switch to model space.

7. The values that can be assigned to **TILEMODE** are __________ and __________.

Review Questions

Answer the following questions:

1. The default value of **DIMSCALE** is __________.

2. The default value of **DIMTXT** is __________.

3. The default value of **SNAP** is __________.

4. Architectural units can be selected by using the __________ command or the __________ command.

5. Name any three standard template drawings that come with AutoCAD software __________, __________, and __________.

6. If the plot size is 24" x 18", and the scale is 1:20, the X Limit = __________ and Y Limit = __________.

7. If the plot size is 200 x 150 and limits are (0.00,0.00) and (600.00,450.00), the **LTSCALE** factor = __________.

8. __________ provides a convenient way to plot multiple views of a 3D drawing or multiple views of a regular 2D drawing.

9. You can use the __________ tool to switch to paper space.

10. In the model space, if you want to reduce the display size by half, the scale factor you enter for the **Scale** tool is __________.

Exercise 1 — *Template with Limits*

Create a drawing template (*protoe1.dwt*) with the following specifications:

Units	Architectural with precision 0'-0 1/16
Angle	Decimal Degrees with precision 0
Base angle	East
Angle direction	Counterclockwise
Limits	48' x 36'

Exercise 2 *Template with Limits, Text Height, & Units*

Create a drawing template (*protoe2.dwt*) with the following specifications:

Limits	36.0,24.0
Snap	0.5
Grid	1.0
Text height	0.25
Units	Decimal
	Precision 0.00
	Decimal degrees
	Precision 0
	Base angle, East
	Angle positive if measured counterclockwise

Exercise 3 *Template with Layers, LTSCALE, & DIMSCALE*

Create a drawing template (*protoe3.dwt*) with the following specifications:

Limits	48.0,36.0
Text height	0.25
PLINE width	0.03
LTSCALE	4.0
DIMSCALE	4.0
Plot size	10.5 x 8

LAYERS

Layer Name	Line Type	Color
0	Continuous	White
OBJECT	Continuous	Green
CENTER	Center	Magenta
HIDDEN	Hidden	Blue
DIM	Continuous	Red
BORDER	Continuous	Cyan

Exercise 4 *Relative Rectangular & Absolute Coordinates*

Create a prototype drawing (*protoe4.dwt*) with the following specifications:

Limits	36.0,24,0
Border	35.0,23.0
Grid	1.0
Snap	0.5
Text height	0.15
Units	Decimal (up to 2 places)
LTSCALE	1
Current layer	Object

LAYERS

Layer Name	Linetype	Color
0	Continuous	White
Object	Continuous	Red
Hidden	Hidden	Yellow
Center	Center	Green
Dim	Continuous	Blue
Border	Continuous	Magenta
Notes	Continuous	White

This prototype drawing should have a border line and a title block, as shown in Figure 15-22.

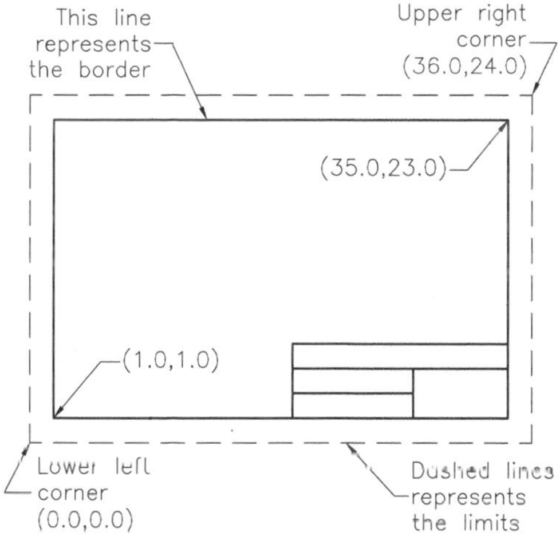

Figure 15-22 Prototype drawing

Exercise 5 *Template with Plot Sheet Size & Title Block*

Create a template drawing shown in Figure 15-23 with the following specifications and save it with the name *protoe5.dwt*:

Plotted sheet size	36" x 24" (Figure 15-23)
Scale	1/2" = 1.0'
Text height	1/4" on plotted drawing
LTSCALE	24
DIMSCALE	24
Units	Architectural
	32-denominator of smallest fraction to display
	Angle in degrees/minutes/seconds
	Precision 0d00"00"
	Angle positive if measured counterclockwise
Border	Border is 1-1/2" inside the edges of the plotted drawing sheet, using the PLINE 1/32" wide when plotted.

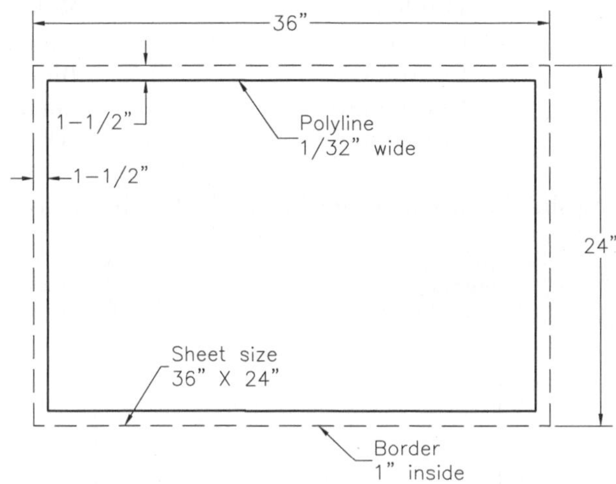

Figure 15-23 *Drawing for Exercise 5*

Exercise 6 *Template with Title Block & Dimension Style*

Create a prototype drawing, as shown in Figure 15-24, with the following specifications (the name of the drawing template is *protoe6.dwt*):

Plotted sheet size	24" x 18" (Figure 15-24)
Scale	1/2"=1.0'
Border	The border is 1" inside the edges of the plotted drawing sheet, using the PLINE 0.05" wide when plotted (Figure 15-24)

Dimension text over the dimension line
Dimensions aligned with the dimension line
Calculate overall dimension scale factor
Enable the display of alternate units
Dimensions to be associative

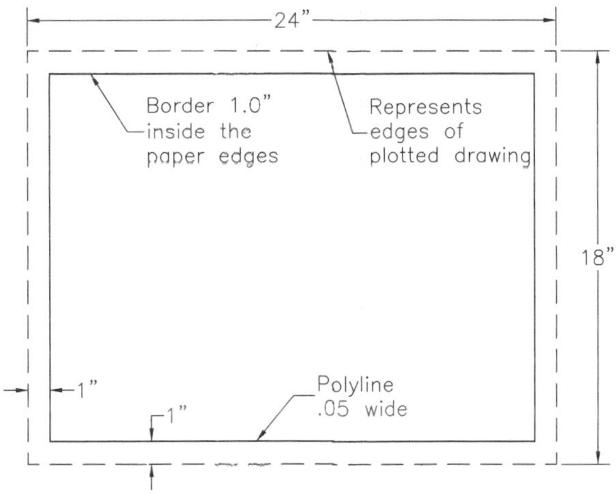

Figure 15-24 *Prototype drawing*

Exercise 7 *Creating & Using Template for Generating Drawing*

Create a template with the necessary specifications to draw the Articulated Rod shown in Figure 15-25, with the following specifications:

Limits	36.0,24,0
Border	35.0,23.0
Grid	1.0
Snap	0.5
Text height	0.15
Units	Decimal (up to 2 places)
LTSCALE	1
Current layer	Object

LAYERS

Layer Name	Linetype	Color
0	Continuous	White
Object	Continuous	Red
Hidden	Hidden	Yellow
Center	Center	Green
Dim	Continuous	Blue
Border	Continuous	Magenta
Notes	Continuous	White

Also, use this template and the layers created in it to draw the views of the Articulated Rod.

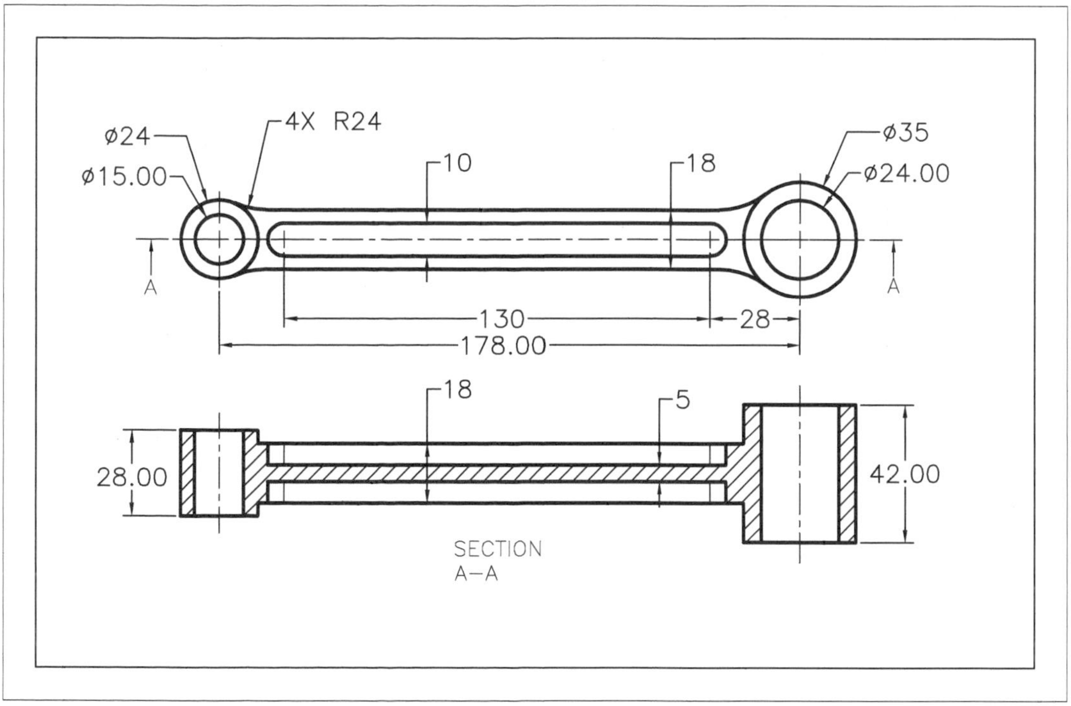

Figure 15-25 *Views and dimensions of the Articulated Rod*

Answers to Self-Evaluation Test

1. *.dwt*, **2. Use a Template**, **3. Start from Scratch**, **4.** 72',48', **5. Named**, **6. QVLAYOUT**, **7. 0, 1**

Chapter 16

Working with Blocks

Learning Objectives

After completing this chapter, you will be able to:

- *Create and insert blocks*
- *Add parameters and assign actions to the blocks to make them dynamic blocks*
- *Create drawing files by using the Write Block dialog box*
- *Use the DesignCenter to locate, preview, copy, or insert blocks and existing drawings*
- *Use the Tool Palettes to insert blocks*
- *Edit blocks*
- *Split a block*
- *Rename blocks and delete unused blocks*

Key Terms

- *Blocks*
- *Annotative Blocks*
- *Dynamic Blocks*
- *Parameters*
- *Actions*
- *Nesting of Blocks*
- *Write Block*
- *XPLODE*
- *Constraints to Blocks*

THE CONCEPT OF BLOCKS

The ability to store parts of a drawing, or the entire drawing, such that they need not be redrawn when required in the same drawing or another drawing is a great benefit to the user. These parts of a drawing, entire drawings, or symbols (also known as blocks) can be placed (inserted) in a drawing at the location of your choice, with the desired orientation, and scale factor. A block is given a name (block name) and is referenced (inserted) by its name. All objects within a block are treated as a single object. You can move, erase, or list the block as a single object, that is, you can select the entire block simply by clicking anywhere on it. As for the edit and inquiry commands, the internal structure of a block is immaterial, since a block is treated as a primitive object, like a polygon. If a block definition is changed, all references to the block in the drawing are updated to incorporate the changes.

A block is created by using the **Create Block** tool in the **Block Definition** panel of the **Insert** tab in the **Ribbon**. You can also save objects in a drawing, or an entire drawing as a block using the **Write Block** tool. The main difference between the two is that by using the **Insert** tool, a wblock can be inserted in any other drawing, but a block can be inserted only in the drawing file in which it was created.

One of the important features of AutoCAD is the annotative blocks that can be used as symbol to annotate your drawing. The annotative blocks are defined in terms of paper space height. The annotative blocks are displayed in floating viewports and their respective size in model space is calculated by multiplying the current annotation scale set for those spaces and the paper space height of the block.

Another feature of AutoCAD is that instead of inserting a symbol as a block (which results in the addition of the content of the referenced drawing to the drawing in which it is inserted), you can reference the other drawings (Xref) in the current file. This means that the contents of the referenced drawing are not added to the current drawing file, although they become part of that drawing on the screen. This is explained in detail in Chapter 18.

CONVERTING ENTITIES INTO A BLOCK

Ribbon: Insert > Block Definition > Block drop-down > Create Block or Home > Block > Create Block
Toolbar: Draw > Make Block **Command:** BLOCK/B

You can convert the entities in the drawing window into a block by using the **BLOCK** command or by choosing the **Create Block** tool from the **Block** panel of the **Home** tab. Alternatively, you can do so by choosing the **Make Block** tool from the **Draw** toolbar. When you invoke this tool, the **Block Definition** dialog box will be displayed, as shown in Figure 16-1. You can use the **Block Definition** dialog box to save any objects as a block.

In the **Name** edit box of the **Block Definition** dialog box, enter the name of the block you want to create. All the block names present in the current drawing are displayed in the **Name** drop-down list in an alphabetical and numerical order. This way you can verify whether a block you have defined has been saved or not. By default, the block name can have up to 255 characters. Also, it can contain letters, digits, blank spaces as well as any special characters including the

$ (dollar sign), - (hyphen), and _ (underscore), provided they are not being used for any other purpose by AutoCAD or Windows.

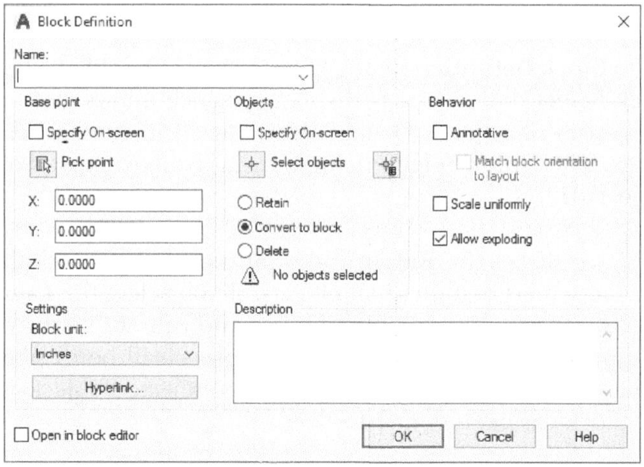

Figure 16-1 *The* ***Block Definition*** *dialog box*

Note

The block name is controlled by the ***EXTNAMES*** *system variable and its default value is 1. If the value is set to 0, the block name will be only thirty-one characters long and will not include spaces or any other special characters, apart from a $ (dollar sign), - (hyphen), or _ (underscore).*

If a block already exists, with the block name that you have specified in the **Name** edit box, and you choose the **OK** button in the **Block Definition** dialog box, the **Block - Redefine Block** message box will be displayed informing you that the block with this name is already defined. It will also prompt you to specify if you want to redefine the block or not. In this dialog box, you can either redefine the existing block by choosing the **Redefine block** option or you can exit it by choosing the **Don't redefine** option. You can then use another name for the block in the dialog box.

After you have specified a block name, you are required to specify the insertion base point, which will be used as a reference point to insert the block. Usually, either the center or the lower left corner of the block is defined as the insertion base point. Later on, when you insert the block, you will notice that it appears at the insertion point, and you can insert it with reference to this point. The point you specify as the insertion base point is taken as the origin point of the block's coordinate system. You can specify the insertion point by choosing the **Pick point** button in the **Base point** area of the dialog box. The dialog box is temporarily removed, and you can select a base point on the screen. Alternatively, you can also enter the coordinates in the **X**, **Y**, and **Z** edit boxes. Once the insertion base point is specified, the dialog box reappears and the *X*, *Y*, and *Z* coordinates of the insertion base point are displayed in the **X**, **Y**, and **Z** edit boxes respectively. If no insertion base point is selected, AutoCAD assumes the insertion point coordinates to be 0,0,0, which are the default coordinates.

After specifying the insertion base point, you are required to select the objects that will constitute the block. Until the objects are selected, AutoCAD displays a warning: **No objects selected**, at the bottom of the **Objects** area. Choose the **Select objects** button; the dialog box disappears. You can select the objects on the screen using any selection method. After completing the selection process, right-click or press the ENTER key to return to the dialog box. The number of objects selected is displayed at the bottom of the **Objects** area of the dialog box.

The **Objects** area of the **Block Definition** dialog box also has a **QuickSelect** button. On choosing this button, the **Quick Select** dialog box is displayed, which allows you to define a selection set based on the properties of objects. **QuickSelect** is used in cases where the drawings are very large and complex. The **Quick Select** dialog box has been discussed earlier in Chapter 6, Editing Sketched Objects-II.

In the **Objects** area, if you select the **Retain** radio button, the selected objects that form the block are retained on the screen as individual objects. If you select the **Convert to block** radio button, the selected objects are converted into a block and will not be displayed on the screen after the block has been defined. Rather, the created block will be displayed in place of the original objects. If you select the **Delete** radio button, the selected objects will be deleted from the drawing after the block has been defined.

If you select the **Annotative** check box in the **Behavior** area, the block created will become annotative. The block will now acquire annotative properties like text, dimension, hatch, and so on. On selecting the **Annotative** check box, the **Match block orientation to layout** check box will get highlighted. If you select the **Match block orientation to layout** check box, the orientation of the block in paper space viewport will always remain aligned to the orientation of the layout, while inserting the block. If you select the **Scale uniformly** check box, the block can only be scaled uniformly in all directions, while inserting the block in drawing area. In such cases, if you create an annotative block, you can scale it only uniformly while inserting the block in drawing area. The **Scale uniformly** check box is selected by default and will remain unavailable for modification when you select the **Annotative** check box. If you select the **Allow exploding** check box, the block can be exploded into separate entities using the **Explode** tool, whenever required.

In the **Settings** area, the **Block unit** drop-down list displays the units that will be used while inserting the current block. For example, if the block is created with inches as the units and you select **Feet** from the **Block unit** drop-down list, the block will be scaled to feet. You can also invoke the **Insert Hyperlink** dialog box by choosing the **Hyperlink** button in the **Settings** area. This dialog box allows you to link any specific files, websites, or named views with the current drawing. You can also link the drawing to a default e-mail address or you can select one from the recently used e-mail addresses.

The **Open in block editor** check box is available at the bottom of the **Block Definition** dialog box. If this check box is selected, the **Block Editor** will open as soon as you close the **Block Definition** dialog box. Also, the entities of the block will be displayed in the authoring area of the block editor. You will learn more about the **Block Editor** in the next section.

After setting all parameters in the **Block Definition** dialog box, choose the **OK** button to complete defining the block.

Exercise 1 — Block

Draw a circle of 1 unit radius and then draw multiple circles inside it, as shown in Figure 16-2. Next, convert them into a block and name the entity as CIRCLE. Refer to the following figure for details.

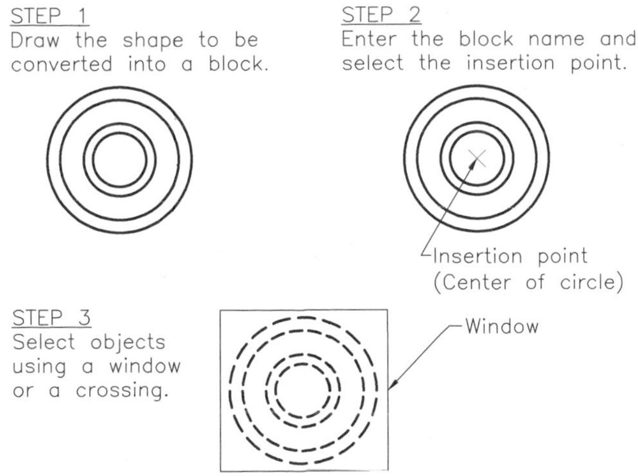

Figure 16-2 Block created from multiple circles

INSERTING BLOCKS

Ribbon: Home/Insert > Block > Insert Block	**Command:** INSERT/I
Toolbar: Insert > Insert Block or Draw > Insert drop-down > Insert Block	

The blocks created in the current drawing are inserted using the **Insert Block** tool. An inserted block is called a block reference. You should determine the layer and location to insert the block, and also the angle by which you want the block to be rotated prior to its insertion. If the layer on which you want to insert the block is not the current layer, select the appropriate option from the **Layer** drop-down list in the **Layers** panel of the **Home** tab or choose the **Set Current** button in the **LAYER PROPERTIES MANAGER** to make it current.

To insert a block, choose the **Insert Block** tool; a flyout will be displayed. In the flyout, the blocks available in the drawing are displayed. Click on the required block; the selected block will be attached to the cursor. Specify the required location to insert the block; the block will be inserted in the drawing. Note that if block is not available in the drawing and you choose the **Insert** tool, the **Insert** dialog box will be displayed, as shown in Figure 16-3. You can specify different parameters of the block or external file to be inserted in the **Insert** dialog box.

Name

This drop-down list is used to specify the name of the block to be inserted. Click on the down arrow to display the list of names. Select the name from this drop-down list. You can also enter a name for it. All blocks, created in the current drawing, are available in the **Name** drop-down list. The **Browse** button is used to insert external files. When you choose this button, the **Select Drawing File** dialog box is displayed, as shown in Figure 16-4.

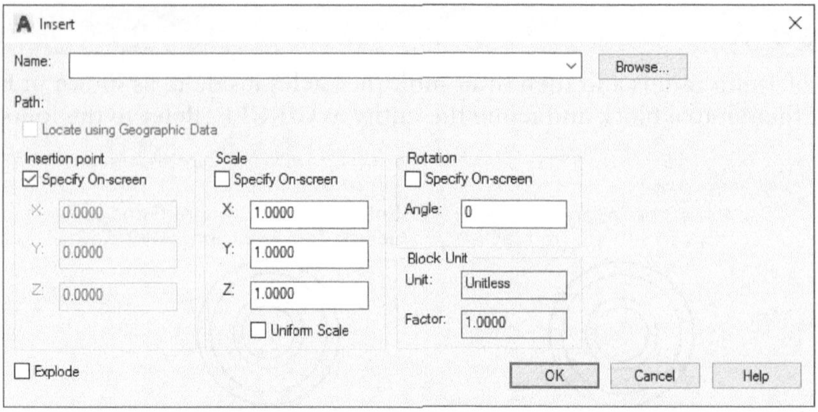

*Figure 16-3 The **Insert** dialog box*

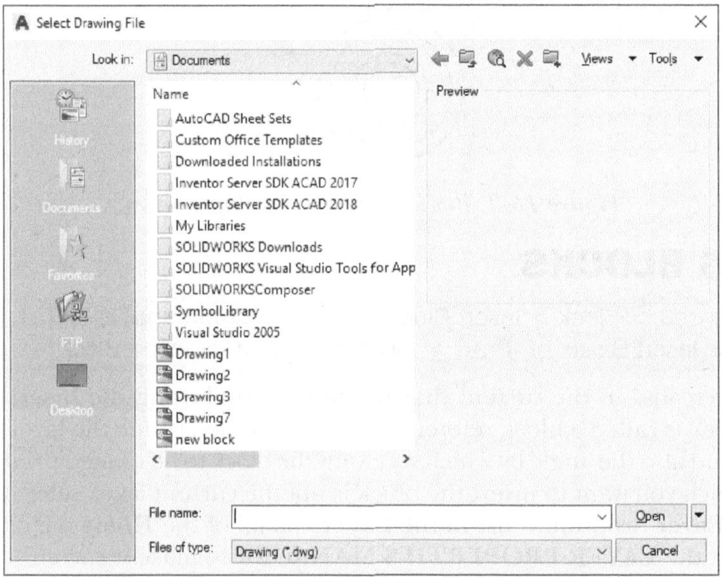

*Figure 16-4 The **Select Drawing File** dialog box*

This dialog box is similar to the standard **Select File** dialog box, which has been discussed earlier in Chapter 1. You can select a drawing file from the files listed in the current directory. You can also change the directory by selecting the desired directory from the **Look in** drop-down list. Once you select the drawing file, choose the **Open** button; the drawing file name is displayed next to the **Name** drop-down list of the **Insert** dialog box. The **Path** option displays the path of the external file selected to be inserted. Now, if you want to change the block name, just change the name in the **Name** drop-down list. In this manner, the drawing can be inserted with a different name. Changing the original drawing does not affect the inserted drawing.

Note

*1. If the name you have specified in the **Name** edit box does not exist as a block in the current drawing, AutoCAD will search the drives and directories on the path (specified in the **Options** dialog box) for a drawing of the same name. If the block is found, it will be inserted.*

*2. Also, suppose you have inserted a block in a drawing and then you want to insert a drawing with the same name as the block, AutoCAD will display a message with the information that XX is already defined as a block and prompts you to define the action you want to perform. If you choose **Redefine Block**, the block in the drawing will get replaced by the drawing with the same name, that is, the block gets redefined.*

Tip

*You can create a block in the current drawing from an existing drawing file. This saves the time by avoiding redrawing the object as a block. Locate and select an existing drawing file using the **Browse** button in the **Insert** dialog box. Next, choose the **Open** button after selecting the existing drawing. Next, choose the **OK** button; the **Insert** dialog box will be closed, prompting you to specify the insertion point. Now, instead of specifying the insertion point, press the ESC key; the selected file will be converted into a block, but will not be inserted into the drawing.*

Insertion point Area

When a block is inserted, its coordinate system is aligned parallel to the current UCS. In the **Insertion point** area, you can specify the *X*, *Y*, and *Z* coordinate locations of the block insertion point in the **X**, **Y**, and **Z** edit boxes, respectively. If you select the **Specify On-screen** check box, the **X**, **Y**, and **Z** edit boxes will not be available. You can specify the insertion point on the screen. By default, the **Specify On-screen** check box is selected, and hence, you can specify the insertion point on the screen.

Scale Area

In this area, you can specify the X, Y, and Z scale factors of the block to be inserted in the **X**, **Y**, and **Z** edit boxes, respectively. By selecting the **Specify On-screen** check box, you can specify the scale of the block at which it has to be inserted on the screen. The **Specify On-screen** check box is cleared by default and the block is inserted with the scale factors of 1 along the three axes. Also, if the **Uniform Scale** check box is selected, the X scale factor value is assumed for the Y and Z scale factors also. This means that if this check box is selected, you need to specify only the X scale factor. All dimensions in the block are multiplied by the same scale factors that you specify. These scale factors allow you to stretch or compress a block along the *X* and *Y* axes, respectively. You can also insert 3D objects into a drawing by specifying the third scale factor (since 3D objects have three dimensions), the Z scale factor. Figure 16-5 shows a block inserted with different X and Y scale factors.

Tip

1. By specifying negative scale factors, you can insert a mirror image of a block along a particular axis. A negative scale factor for both the X and Y axes is the same as rotating the block reference through 180 degrees, since it mirrors the block reference in the opposite quadrant of the coordinate system. The effect of the negative scale factor on the block (DOOR) can be marked by a change in position of the insertion point marked with an (X), as shown in Figure 16-6.

2. Also, on specifying a scale factor of less than 1, you can insert the block reference smaller than the original size. On specifying a scale factor greater than 1, you can insert the block reference larger than its original size.

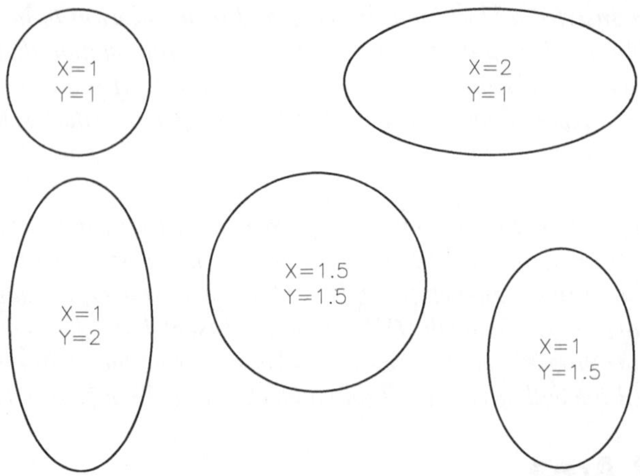

Figure 16-5 Block inserted with different scale factors

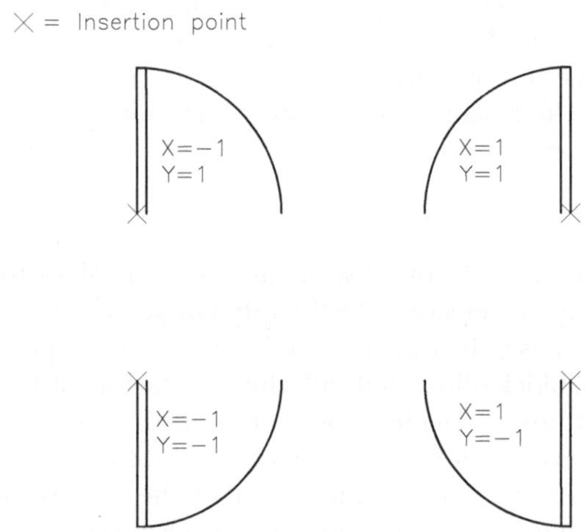

Figure 16-6 Block inserted using negative scale factors

Rotation Area

You can enter the angle of rotation for the block to be inserted in the **Angle** edit box. The insertion point is taken as the location about which the rotation takes place. Selecting the **Specify On-screen** check box enables you to specify the angle of rotation on the screen. This check box is cleared by default and the block is inserted at an angle of zero-degree.

Block Unit Area

This area displays the information related to the block unit specified in the **Block Definition** dialog box and the scale factor used for the unit to insert the block. For example, if you have defined a block with the block unit as feet and you insert the same block in a drawing whose unit is inches, the **Block Unit** area will display **Unit** as feet and **Factor** as 12. The information displayed in this area is read-only.

Note

You can control the units for the insertion of the block through the ***INSUNITS*** *system variable. While doing so, the* ***Factor*** *information displayed in the* ***Block Unit*** *area will change accordingly.*

Explode Check Box

By selecting this check box, the block is inserted as a collection of individual objects. The function of the **Explode** check box is identical to that of the **Explode** tool. Once a block is exploded, the X, Y, and Z scale factors become identical. Therefore, you are provided access to only one scale factor edit box (**X** edit box), the **Y** and **Z** edit boxes are not available, and the **Uniform Scale** check box also gets selected. The X scale factor is assigned to the Y and Z scale factors too. You must enter a positive scale factor value.

Note

If you select the ***Explode*** *check box before insertion, the block reference will be exploded and the objects will be inserted with their original properties such as layer, color, and linetype.*

Once you have entered the relevant information in the dialog box, choose the **OK** button to exit the **Insert** dialog box. If you have selected the **Specify On-Screen** check boxes, you can specify the insertion point, scale, and angle of rotation with a pointing device. Whenever the insertion point is to be specified on the screen (by default), you can specify the scale factors and rotation angle values. These values will override the values specified in the dialog box using the command line. Before specifying the insertion point on the screen, you can right-click to display the shortcut menu, which has all the options available through the command line. You can choose the options for insertion from the dynamic preview. On being prompted to specify the insertion point, press the down arrow key to see the options in the dynamic preview. However, if you have already specified an insertion point in the dialog box and have selected the **Specify On-screen** check boxes in the **Scale** or **Rotation** area of the **Insert** dialog box, you are allowed to specify only the scale factors or the rotation angle at the command line. The following command prompt will be displayed when all three **Specify On-screen** check boxes are selected:

Specify insertion point or [Basepoint/Scale/X/Y/Z/Rotate]: *Specify an insertion point on the screen.*
Enter X scale factor, specify opposite corner, or [Corner/XYZ] <1>: *Specify scale factor in X- axis or select an option or press ENTER to accept the default scale factor of 1.*
Enter Y scale factor <use X scale factor>: *Specify Y scale factor.*
Specify rotation angle <0>: *Specify the angle of rotation of the inserted block.*

The command prompt options are discussed next.

Basepoint

If you enter **B** at the **Specify insertion point or [Basepoint/Scale/X/Y/Z/Rotate]** prompt, or select the option from the dynamic preview, you are again prompted to specify the base point. Specify the base point by clicking the cursor at the desired location. This point will now act as the insertion point. All prompts are also displayed at the cursor input so there is no need to always take a look on the command prompt. The prompt sequence for this option is given next.

Specify insertion point or [Basepoint/X/Y/Z/Scale/Rotate]: **B** Enter
Specify base point: *Specify base point.*

Specify base point: Specify insertion point or [Basepoint/Scale/X/Y/Z/Rotate]: *Specify insertion point.*

Scale

On entering **S** at the **Specify insertion point or [Basepoint/Scale/X/Y/Z/Rotate]** prompt, you are prompted to enter the scale factor. After entering it, the block assumes the specified scale factor, and AutoCAD lets you drag the block until you locate the insertion point on the screen. The *X*, *Y*, and *Z* axes are uniformly scaled by the specified scale factor. The prompt sequence for this option is given next.

Specify insertion point or [Basepoint/Scale/X/Y/Z/Rotate]: **S** Enter
Specify scale factor for XYZ axes<1>: *Enter a value to preset general scale factor.*
Specify insertion point or [Basepoint/Scale/X/Y/Z/Rotate]: *Specify insertion point.*

X, Y, Z

After entering X, Y, or Z at the **Specify insertion point or [Basepoint/Scale/X/Y/Z/Rotate]** prompt, you can specify the scale factor along that axis. These options are only available when the **Uniform Scale** check box is cleared from the **Insert** dialog box. The prompt sequence when you use the **X** option is given next.

Specify insertion point or [Basepoint/Scale/X/Y/Z/Rotate]: **X** Enter
Specify X scale factor<1>: *Enter a value for the X scale factor.*
Specify insertion point or [Basepoint/Scale/X/Y/Z/Rotate]: *Select the insertion point.*

Rotate

On entering **R** at the **Specify insertion point or [Basepoint/Scale/X/Y/Z/Rotate]** prompt, you are prompted to specify the rotation angle. You can enter the angle of rotation or specify it by specifying two points on the screen. Dragging is resumed only when you specify the angle. Also, the block assumes the specified rotation angle. The prompt sequence for this option is given next.

Specify insertion point or [Basepoint/Scale/X/Y/Z/Rotate]: **R** Enter
Specify rotation angle<0>: *Enter a value for the rotation angle.*
Specify insertion point or [Basepoint/Scale/X/Y/Z/Rotate]: *Select the insertion point.*

The XYZ and Corner Options

Select the **Specify On-screen** check boxes from the **Insertion point** and **Scale** areas of the **Insert** dialog box and choose the **OK** button. Next, specify the insertion point on the screen; the following prompt will appear.

Enter X scale factor, specify opposite corner, or [Corner/XYZ] <1>: *Enter X scale factor, specify opposite corner or select an option.*

Here, the **XYZ** option can be used to enter a 3D block reference and the successive prompts allow you to specify the X, Y, and Z scale factors individually.

With the **Corner** option, you can specify both X and Y scale factors at the same time. When you invoke this option, and **DRAGMODE** is turned off, you will be prompted to specify the other corner (the first corner of the box is the insertion point). You can also enter a coordinate value, instead of moving the cursor. The length and breadth of the box are taken as the X and Y scale factors for the block. For example, if the X and Y dimensions (length and width) of the box are the same as that of the block, the block will be drawn without any change. The points selected should be above and to the right of the insertion block. Mirror images will be produced if points selected are below or to the left of the insertion point. The prompt sequence is given next.

Enter X scale factor, specify opposite corner, or [Corner/XYZ] <1>: **C** Enter
Specify opposite corner: *Select a point as the corner.*

The **Corner** option also allows you to use a dynamic scaling technique when **DRAGMODE** is turned to **Auto (default)**. You can also move the cursor at the **Enter X scale factor, specify opposite corner, or [Corner/XYZ] <1>** prompt to change the block size dynamically and, when the size meets your requirements, select a point.

Note

*1. You should avoid the use of the **Corner** option, if you want to have the same X and Y scale factors because it is difficult to select a point whose X distance equals its Y distance, unless the **SNAP** mode is on. If you use the **Corner** option, it is better to specify the X and Y scale factors explicitly or select the corner by entering coordinates.*

*2. If the **Uniform Scale** check box is selected in the **Insert** dialog box, then the **X/Y/Z** options will not be available at the command prompt.*

*3. You can also insert blocks using the command window either by entering the **-INSERT** command or by simply writing **-I**.*

Exercise 2 — Basepoint Insertion

Create a block with the name SQUARE at the insertion base point 1,2. Insert this block in the drawing. The X scale factor is 2 units, the Y scale factor is 2 units, and the angle of rotation is 35-degree. It is assumed that the block SQUARE is already defined in the current drawing.

Exercise 3 — Scaled Insertion

a. Insert the block CIRCLE created in Exercise 1. Use different X and Y scale factors to get different shapes after inserting this block.
b. Insert the block CIRCLE created in Exercise 1. Use the **Corner** option to specify the scale factor.

Exercise 4 — Scaled Insertion

a. Construct a triangle and form a block of it. Name the block as TRIANGLE. Now, set the Y scale factor of the inserted block as 2.
b. Insert the block TRIANGLE with a rotation angle of 45 degrees. After defining the insertion point, enter the X and Y scale factor of 2.

CREATING AND INSERTING ANNOTATIVE BLOCKS

You can create an annotative block by selecting the **Annotative** check box from the **Behavior** area of the **Block Definition** dialog box. The annotative block acquires the annotative properties like text, dimension, hatch, and so on. To convert an existing non-annotative block into an annotative one, choose the **Create Block** tool from the **Create Block** drop-down from the **Block Definition** panel of the **Insert** tab; the **Block Definition** dialog box will be displayed. Select the block to be converted to annotative from the **Name** drop-down list of the **Block Definition** dialog box. Select the **Annotative** check box from the **Behavior** area and then choose the **OK** button. AutoCAD will display a message box stating that the block definition has changed. Do you want to redefine it? If you want to redefine the block, choose the **Redefine block** button; the specified block will be converted to annotative.

The annotative blocks are indicated by an annotative symbol attached to the block in the preview displayed in the **Insert** dialog box. While inserting the annotative block in the AutoCAD session for the first time, the **Select Annotation Scale** dialog box will be displayed on the screen, as shown in Figure 16-7. Select the annotation scale from the drop-down list and then choose the **OK** button; the block will be inserted at the specified annotation scale. The Annotative blocks are inserted at a scale value decided by the multiplication of the current annotation scale and the block scale specified in the **Scale** area of the **Insert** dialog box.

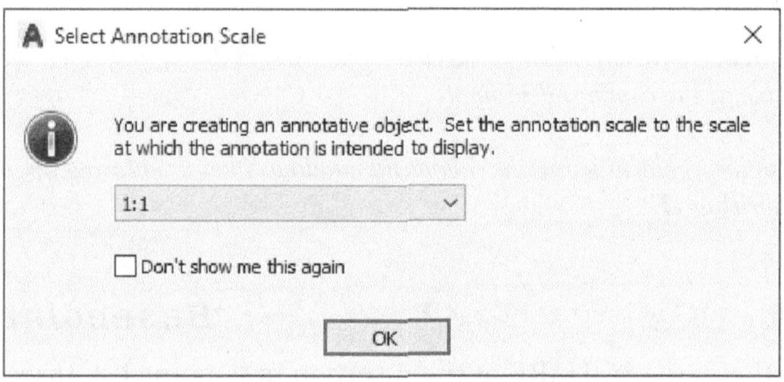

***Figure 16-7** The **Select Annotation Scale** dialog box*

Note

*While inserting the annotative blocks, the settings specified for the **INSUNITS** system variable are ignored. Also, the **Block Unit** area of the **Insert** dialog box will display no change in the factor value.*

Example 1 — *Annotative Block*

In this example, you will draw the object shown in Figure 16-8, and convert it into an annotative block, named NOR Gate. Next, you will insert the NOR Gate block into the drawing at the annotation scales of 1:1, 1:2, and 1:8 and notice the changes in the size of the annotative blocks inserted in the drawing.

1. Start a new file in the **Drafting & Annotation** workspace and draw the object, refer to Figure 16-8.

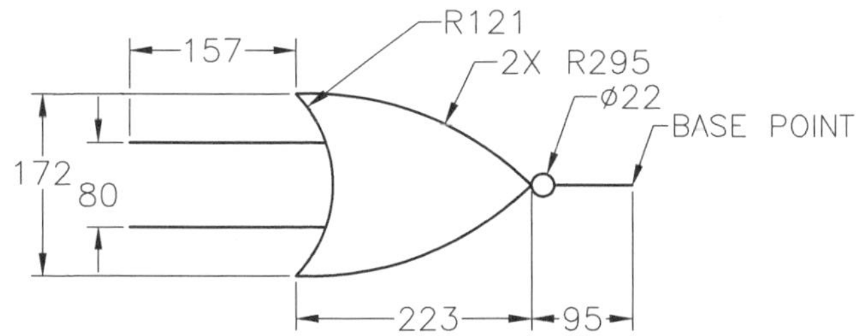

Figure 16-8 Drawing of block for Example 1

2. Invoke the **Block Definition** dialog box by choosing the **Create Block** tool from the **Create Block** drop-down of the **Block Definition** panel in the **Insert** tab.

3. Enter **NOR Gate** as the name of the block in the **Name** edit box. Next, choose the **Select Objects** button from the **Objects** area; the **Block Definition** dialog box is disappear. Select the object drawn and press the ENTER key; the **Block Definition** dialog box is appear. Next, select the **Delete** radio button from the **Objects** area.

4. Choose the **Pick point** button from the **Base point** area; the **Block Definition** dialog box will disappear from the screen. Specify the base point, as shown in Figure 16-8.

5. Select the **Annotative** check box from the **Behavior** area. Next, choose the **OK** button from the **Block Definition** dialog box; the selected objects disappear from the screen and an annotative block is defined with the name **NOR Gate**.

Before proceeding further, ensure that the **Add scales to annotative objects when the annotation scale changes** button is chosen in the Status Bar. Now, you need to change the annotation scale of the drawing to 1:8.

6. Click on the down-arrow on the right of the **Annotation Scale** button in the Status Bar, and choose the scale **1:8** from the flyout displayed.

7. To insert the block into the drawing at the annotation scale of 1:8, choose the **Insert Block** tool from the **Block** panel in the **Insert** tab and then choose **More Options** from the drop-down; the **Insert** dialog box is displayed.

8. Select the **NOR Gate** block from the **Name** drop-down list. Select the **Specify On-screen** check box from the **Insertion point** area and choose the **OK** button.

9. Specify the insertion point for the block by clicking on the screen; the block is inserted into the drawing at an annotation scale of 1:8.

10. Similarly, set the annotation scale to **1:2** in the Status Bar and insert the block. Next, set the annotation scale to **1:1** and insert the block.

11. Turn off the **Add scales to annotative objects when the annotation scale changes** button from the status bar. Next, change the scale to 1:8, 1:2, and 1:1 and you will notice the

difference in the sizes of the inserted blocks, refer to Figure 16-9. This automated variation in the size occurs due to annotative blocks.

12. Select the block to which you had added the annotation scales; the preview of the block with all annotation scales associated to the block is displayed, as shown in Figure 16-10. The bigger block with the current annotation (1:8) scale and the smaller blocks with other annotation scales (1:1, 1:2) are displayed with the faded dashed lines.

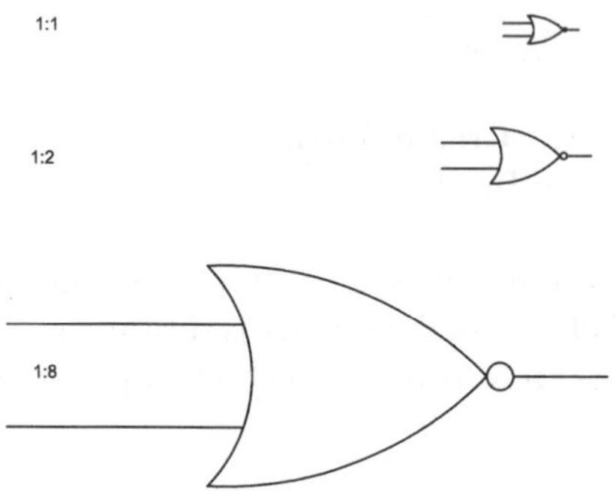

Figure 16-9 *Annotative blocks inserted at different annotation scales*

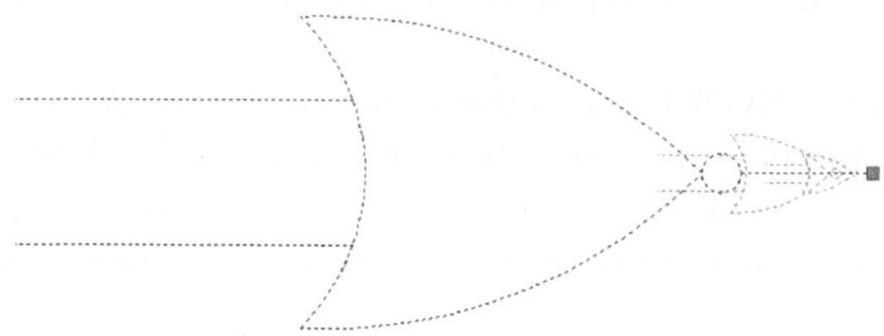

Figure 16-10 *Different annotation scales associated to a single block*

13. To move the block with the current annotation scale (1:8) to the other locations, select the blue grip displayed at the insertion point and move the block to the desired location. In this way, you can place the block with different annotation scales to any desired location.

Block Editor

Ribbon: Insert > Block Definition > Block Editor or Home > Block > Block Editor
Toolbar: Standard > Block Editor **Command:** BEDIT/BE

The **Block Editor** tool is used to edit existing blocks or create new blocks. To invoke the **Block Editor**, choose the **Block Editor** tool from the **Block Definition** panel of the **Insert** tab or enter **BE** (shortcut for the **BEDIT** command) at the command line. You can also double-click on the existing block to edit the block. On doing so, the **Edit Block Definition** dialog box will be displayed, as shown in Figure 16-11.

If you want to create a new block, enter its name in the **Block to create or edit** text box and choose the **OK** button; the **Block Editor** will be invoked where you can draw the entities in the new block. Similarly, if you want to edit a block, select it from the list box provided in this dialog box; its preview will be displayed in the **Preview** area. Also, its related description, if any, will be displayed in the **Description** area. Choose the **OK** button; the **Block Editor** is invoked.

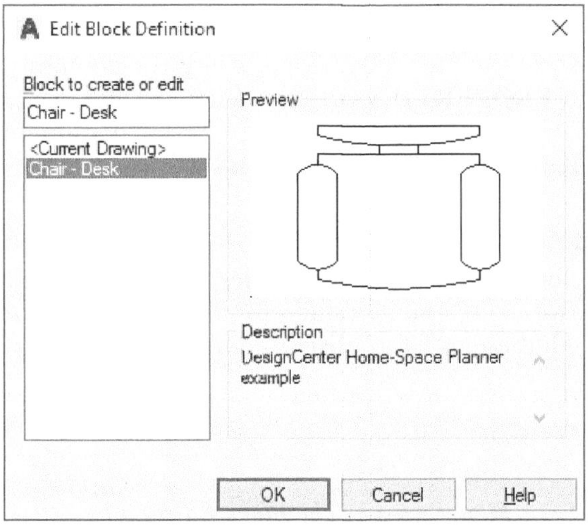

***Figure 16-11** The **Edit Block Definition** dialog box*

The default appearance of the **Block Editor** is shown in Figure 16-12. The drawing area of the **Block Editor** has a dull background and is known as the authoring area. You can edit existing entities or add new ones to the block in the authoring area.

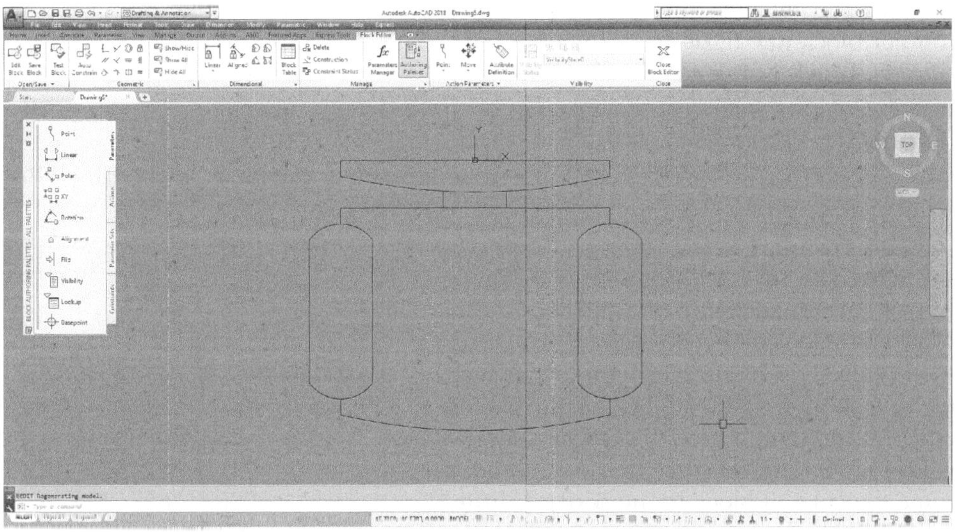

Figure 16-12** Default appearance of the **Block Editor

In addition to the authoring area, the **Block Editor** tab and **BLOCK AUTHORING PALETTES** are provided in the **Block Editor** that contain tools to create dynamic blocks. This will be discussed in detail later in this chapter. Now, you can edit a block using any tool as you did in the drawing. When you are finished with the editing, choose the **Save Block** tool in the **Open/Save** panel of the **Block Editor** tab to save the changes. Choose the **Close Block Editor** button from the **Close** panel to return to the drawing again. In this way, you can edit the block at any time of your design process.

DYNAMIC BLOCKS

Dynamic blocks provides you the flexibility of modifying the geometry of the inserted blocks dynamically or using the **PROPERTIES** palette. You can create dynamic blocks by adding Parameters and Actions to existing blocks using the **Action Parameters** panel in the **Block Editor** tab or the **BLOCK AUTHORING PALETTES**.

Block Editor Tab

The **Block Editor** tab, refer to Figure 16-13, provides the tools to create and modify dynamic blocks. Additionally, you can create visibility states for dynamic blocks using the **Visibility** panel of the **Block Editor** tab. All these tools are discussed next.

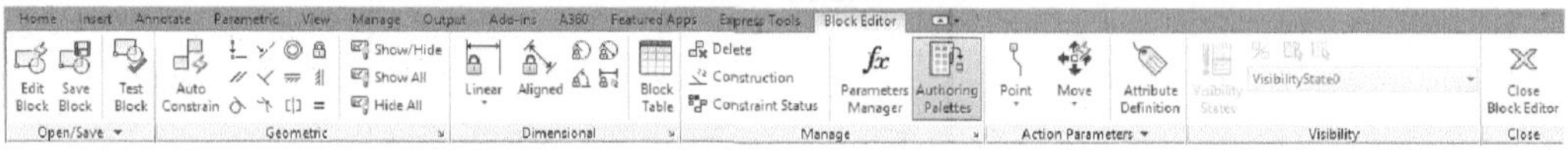

*Figure 16-13 The **Block Editor** tab*

Edit Block

If there are multiple blocks to be edited, choose this tool to display the **Edit Block Definition** dialog box. Note that if you have modified the current block using the tools in the **Block Editor**, you will be prompted to specify whether you want to save the changes in the current block or not. On saving the changes, the **Edit Block Definition** dialog box will be displayed. You can select another block to edit or enter the name of the new block that you want to create. Next, proceed to the **Block Editor** to edit the block.

Save Block

This tool is chosen to save the changes that you have made to the block in the **Block Editor**.

Save Block As

This tool is used to save a block with a different name. Expand the **Open/Save** panel and choose this tool; the **Save Block As** dialog box will be displayed, as shown in Figure 16-14. Enter the name with which you want to save the current block in the **Block Name** edit box and then choose the **OK** button; the block will be saved with the specified name and it will become the current block in the **Block Editor**.

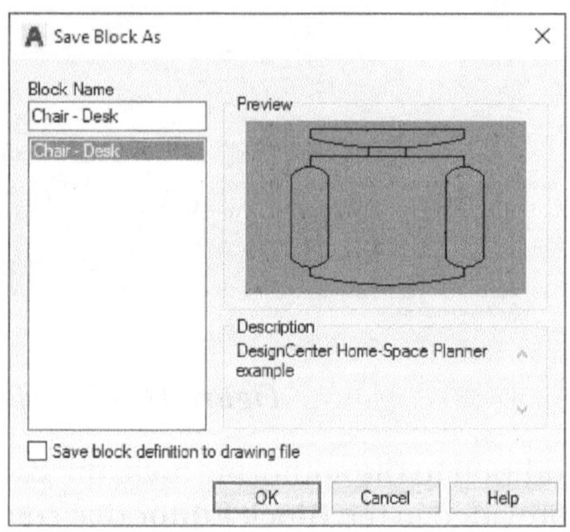

*Figure 16-14 The **Save Block As** dialog box*

Test Block

On choosing this button, the **Test Block Window** will be displayed. If you have made any changes to the block in the **Block Editor**, you can check them in this window without saving the block. After testing the block, choose the **Close Test Block** button to close the **Test Block Window**.

Authoring Palettes

The **Authoring Palettes** button is chosen from the **Manage** panel to toggle on/off the display of the **BLOCK AUTHORING PALETTES** in the authoring area. The **BLOCK AUTHORING PALETTES** contain the tools for creating dynamic blocks.

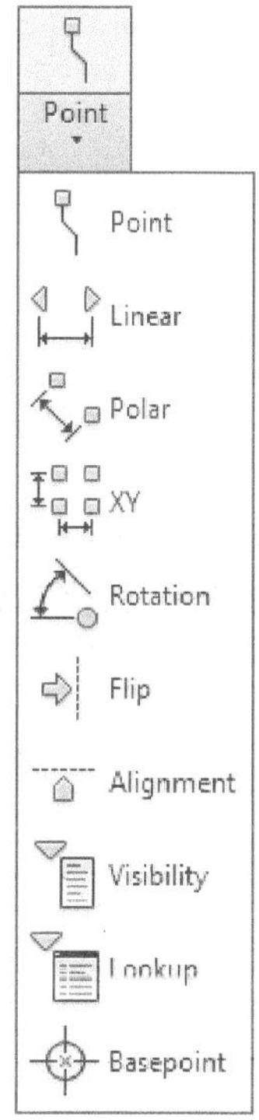

***Figure 16-15** Tools in the **Parameter** drop-down*

Parameters

You can set parameters for the blocks to enable them react dynamically. To add parameters to the existing blocks, choose a tool from the Parameter drop-down in the **Action Parameters** panel of the **Block Editor** tab and then choose one of the tools from the drop-down displayed, as shown in Figure 16-15. You can also enter **BPARAMETER** at the command prompt when the **Dynamic Input** button is chosen; all parameters will be listed in the dynamic preview. These parameters are discussed later in this chapter.

Actions

You can choose a tool from the Actions drop-down to assign actions to the parameters added to the dynamic blocks. Depending on the type of parameter selected, the possible actions are displayed in the dynamic preview. The types of actions in the **Block Editor** are discussed later in this chapter.

Attribute Definition

Choose the **Attribute Definition** tool from the **Action Parameters** panel of the **Block Editor** tab to invoke the **Attribute Definition** dialog box to assign attributes to the block. Attributes are discussed in detail in Chapter 17.

Note

*Choose the **Update Fields** tool from the **Data** panel in the **Insert** tab to regenerate the dynamic block such that the text size of the parameters and actions are updated.*

Close Block Editor

When you choose this button, the **Block Editor** tab is closed and you return to the drawing environment. If this button is chosen before saving the changes in the current block, the **Block - Changes Not Saved** message box will be displayed, as shown in Figure 16-16, and you will be prompted to specify whether or not you want to save changes in the current block.

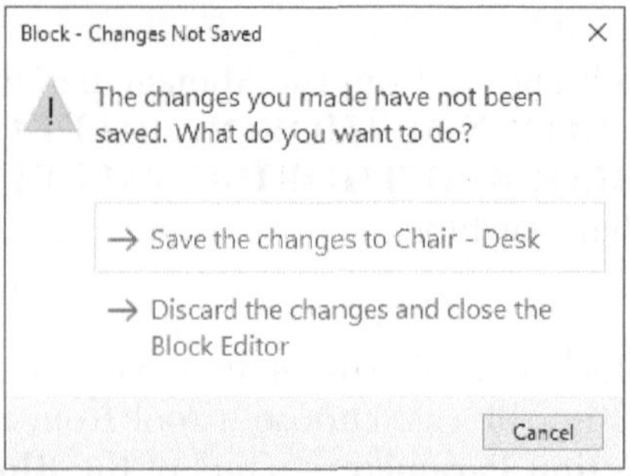

*Figure 16-16 The **Block - Changes Not Saved** message box*

Adding Parameters and Assigning Actions to Dynamic Blocks (BLOCK AUTHORING PALETTES)

The **BLOCK AUTHORING PALETTES**, shown in Figure 16-17, contains the tools to add parameters and actions to the dynamic blocks. You can also invoke these tools from the **Parameters** drop-down in the **Action Parameters** panel of the **Block Editor** tab, refer to Figure 16-15. On doing so, different types of parameters and actions will be displayed at the pointer input or the command prompt. The command sequence will be the same in both the cases. The types of parameters and actions that can be added to dynamic blocks are discussed next.

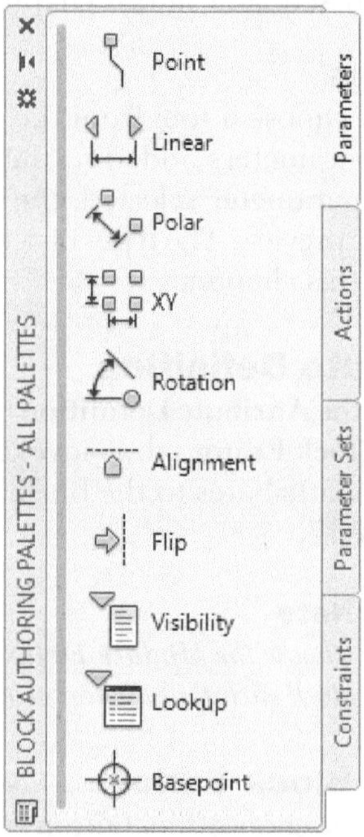

*Figure 16-17 The **Parameters** tab of the **BLOCK AUTHORING PALETTES***

Point Parameter

The **Point** parameter is used to assign the **Stretch** or **Move** action to a dynamic block. A grip point will be displayed at the location where you place the **Point** parameter. This grip point will be used as the base point when you assign an action to the **Point** parameter.

To assign a **Point** parameter, invoke the **Point** tool from the **Parameters** tab of the **BLOCK AUTHORING PALETTES**. The following prompt sequence will be displayed when you invoke this parameter from the **Parameters** tab:

Specify parameter location or [Name/Label/Chain/Description/Palette]: *Select a keypoint on the block to add the **Point** parameter.*
Specify label location: *Specify a point to place the label.*

The options available at the command prompt are discussed next.

Name: The type of a parameter is displayed in the **PROPERTIES** palette when you select the **Point** parameter in the **Block Editor**. The default type for the point parameter is Point. However, you can change the type of the parameter using this option. The prompt sequence to modify the type of a parameter is given next.

Specify parameter location or [Name/Label/Chain/Description/Palette]: **N** Enter
Enter parameter name <Point>: *Enter new name for the parameter* Enter.
Specify parameter location or [Name/Label/Chain/Description/Palette]: *Specify a location for the parameter.*

> **Tip**
> *You can double-click on the label to find out the actions that are assigned to that parameter. For example, if you double-click on the* ***Point*** *parameter, you can perform the move and stretch actions.*

Label: Labels of a parameter are displayed in the authoring area, as shown in Figure 16-18. The default label of a point parameter is Position(n). Using the **Label** option, you can modify the label of the point parameter. The prompt sequence for modifying the label is as follows:

Specify parameter location or [Name/Label/Chain/Description/Palette]: **L** Enter
Enter position property label <Position(n)>: *Enter the new label for the* ***Point*** *parameter*
Specify parameter location or [Name/Label/Chain/Description/Palette]: *Specify a location for the parameter*

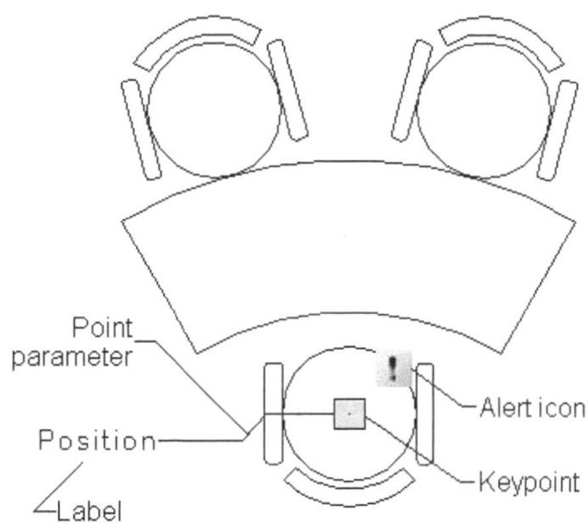

Figure 16-18 *Labels of the* ***Point*** *parameter*

Chain: This option is used when the current point parameter is assigned an action, which is also associated with other parameters. In this case, if the **Chain** option is set to **Yes** and the other parameters are edited, the point parameter is also edited with them. If this option is set to **No**, the point parameter is not edited, when the other parameters are edited.

Description: This option allows you to enter the description about a parameter. This description is displayed in the **PROPERTIES** palette in the **Block Editor**.

Palette. This option is used to specify whether or not the base X and base Y coordinate values of the keypoint where the parameter label is placed will be displayed in the **PROPERTIES** palette when you select the block outside the **Block Editor**.

Assigning the Move Action to the Point Parameter

To assign the move action to the **Point** parameter, double-click on the label and select the **Move** option from the dynamic preview or from the command line. You can also choose the **Move** action from the **Action Parameters** panel. Alternatively, you can choose the **Move** action from the **Actions** tab of the **BLOCK AUTHORING PALETTES**. The prompt sequence that will follow when you invoke it from the **BLOCK AUTHORING PALETTES** is given next.

Select parameter: *Select the point parameter.*
Specify selection set for action
Select objects: *Select objects on which action will be applied.*
Select objects: Enter

You need to specify the distance multiplier and angle offset properties to the actions using the **PROPERTIES** palette. The **Move** action will not work until these options are set.

Distance multiplier: This option is used for dynamic modification of the blocks by using grips of the parameters. Using this option, you can specify the distance by which the selected entities of the dynamic block will move with respect to the one unit movement of the cursor, while dragging it using the grips. To set the distance multiplier, select the action parameter and invoke the **PROPERTIES** palette. Now, enter the required multiplier value in the **Distance multiplier** field in the **Overrides** rollout of the **PROPERTIES** palette. By default, the value of the distance multiplier factor is 1. As a result, the entities will move by the same distance as moved by the cursor. If you set this value to 0.5, the entities will move half the distance moved by the cursor, refer to Figure 16-19.

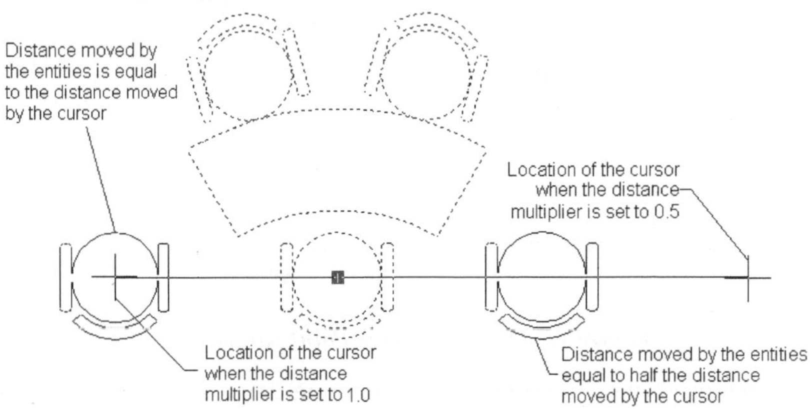

Figure 16-19 Results of different values of the distance multiplier

Note

*You can test the action parameters by invoking the **Test Block Window** and moving the block.*

Angle offset: This option is used to specify the angular offset for the selected entities of the dynamic block. The angle offset works when the entities are dragged using the parameter grip. To set the angle offset, select the action parameter and invoke the **PROPERTIES** palette. Now, enter the required value in the **Angle offset** field in the **Overrides** rollout of the **PROPERTIES** palette. By setting this value, you can ensure that the entities move at an angle from the trace line. For example, if you set the value of the angle offset to 30, the entities will be moved at an angle of 30 degrees with respect to the trace line, which is displayed while dragging the entities using the parameter grips. Figure 16-20 shows the manipulation of entities in the drawing with the default angle offset of 0 degree and an angle offset of 30 degrees.

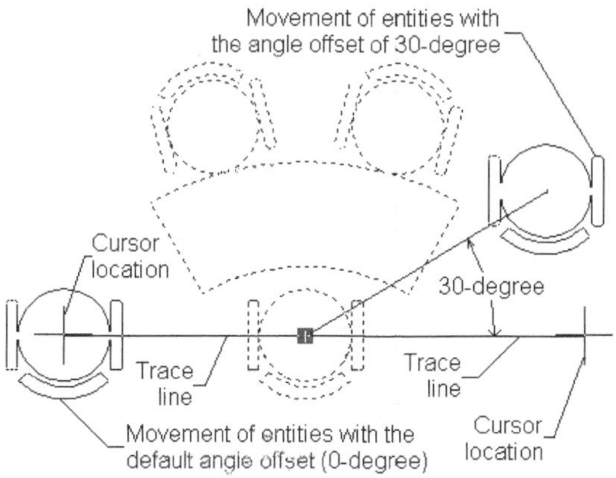

Figure 16-20 *Result of the angle offset during the dynamic manipulation*

Assigning the Stretch Action to the Point Parameter

You can invoke the **Stretch** action by double-clicking on the parameter or by choosing it from the **Actions** tab of the **BLOCK AUTHORING PALETTES**. On invoking this action and selecting the parameter, you are prompted to specify the stretch frame. The entities lying inside the stretch frame will be moved during the dynamic manipulation. The entities that are crossed by the stretch frame will be stretched. The following prompt sequence will be displayed on invoking this action:

Select parameter: *Select the parameter to associate the action.*
Specify first corner of stretch frame or [CPolygon]: *Specify the first corner of stretch frame or enter CP to define a crossing polygon for specifying the stretch frame.*
Specify opposite corner: *Specify opposite corner of stretch frame.*
Specify objects to stretch
Select objects: *Select objects for stretching.*
Select objects: Enter

Figure 16-21(a) shows the stretch frame and the entities selected for the stretch action and Figure 16-21(b) shows the preview of the entities during dynamic manipulation.

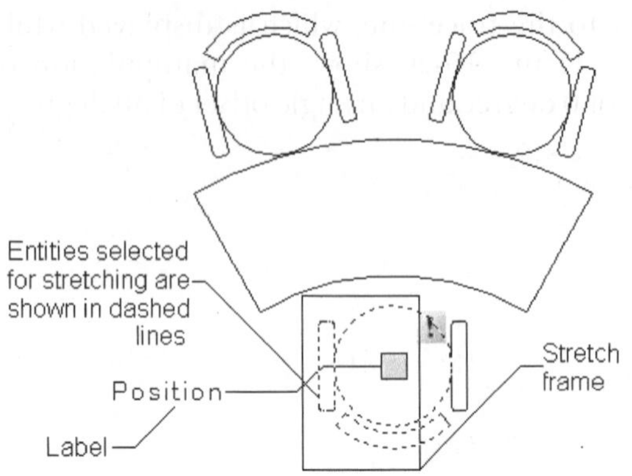

Figure 16-21 (a) Selecting entities for the ***Stretch*** *action*

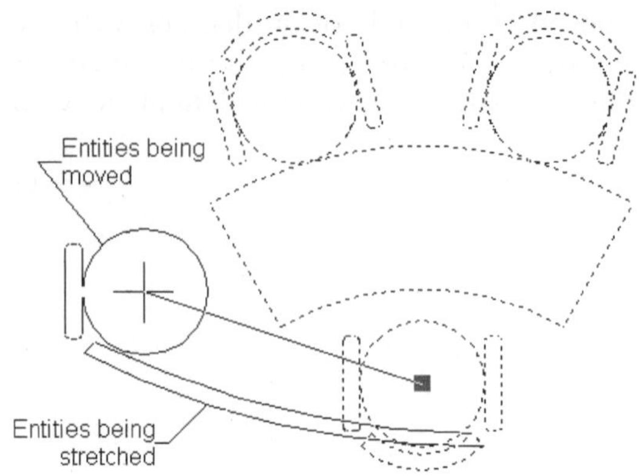

Figure 16-21 (b) Dynamically stretching the entities of a block

Linear Parameter

The linear parameter is displayed as the distance between two keypoints and is similar to a linear or an aligned dimension. This parameter can be associated with the Array, Move, Stretch, or Scale actions. Figure 16-22 shows a block with a linear parameter added to it. To add this parameter, choose the **Linear** parameter from the **Parameters** tab of the **BLOCK AUTHORING PALETTES**; the following prompt sequence will be displayed:

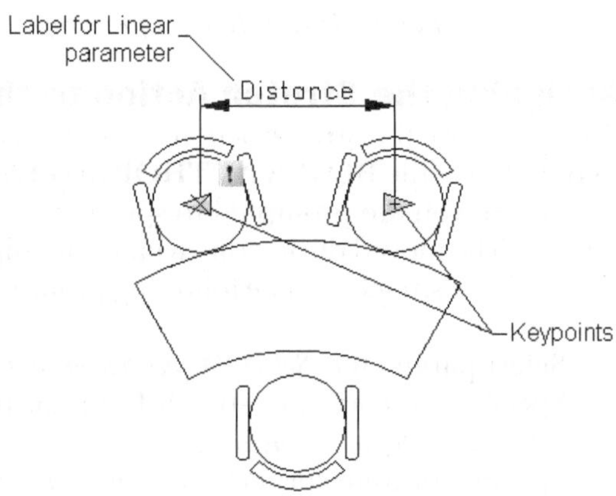

Figure 16-22 The ***Linear*** *parameter added to a block*

> Specify start point or [Name/Label/Chain/Description/Base/Palette/Value set]: *Specify start point for the parameter.*
> Specify endpoint: *Specify endpoint for the parameter.*
> Specify label location: *Specify a point where the label will be placed.*

You can specify the base of the parameter and the distance within which the entities are to be moved at the command prompt when you are prompted to specify the start point. Some of the options that will be available when you invoke the **Linear** Parameter tool have already been discussed in the **Point** parameter. The remaining options are discussed next.

Base: This option lets you to specify the base of the parameter. This base point will be stationary while editing the endpoint of the block. You can specify the option of keeping the start point or the midpoint stationary while using the **Base** option.

Value set: This option allows you specify a set of values for parameters such that the manipulation will be in accordance with these specified values. The values for the parameter can be specified by providing a list or by specifying the increment and range. If there is a specified value set for a parameter, small vertical grey lines are displayed at those values in the **Block Editor**. These vertical grey lines are also displayed in the drawing when you select the parameter grip to manipulate the block.

Note

You can also set the ***Base*** *and* ***Value Set*** *options in the* ***Misc*** *and* ***Value Set*** *rollouts of the* ***PROPERTIES*** *palette of the* ***Linear*** *Parameter, respectively.*

After adding the **Linear** parameter, you can perform the array, move, scale, and stretch actions. Assign the **Move** or **Stretch** action as discussed earlier.

Assigning the Scale Action to the Linear Parameter

Invoke the **Scale** action tool from the **Actions** tab of **BLOCK AUTHORING PALETTES**, or double-click on the linear parameter and select the **Scale** option. The prompt sequence that follows when you assign the **Scale** action is as follows:

Select parameter: *Select the linear parameter to associate the action.*
Specify selection set for action
Select objects: *Select the objects for scaling.*
Select objects: Enter

You can scale the blocks by using a property called **Base type**. To specify the **Base type** property, invoke the **PROPERTIES** palette for the **Scale** action. Next, specify the base type in the **Overrides** rollout. There are two types of base type, **Dependent** and **Independent**. The base type can be dependent on the original base point of the parameter to which the scale action is assigned. You can also make the base type independent so that the entities can be scaled based on the specified base point and the second point.

To test the action, choose the **Test Block** tool from the **Open/Save** panel and then select the block; the **Linear** parameter grips will be displayed. Click on a grip to select it; the **Specify point location or [Base Point/Undo/eXit]** prompt will be displayed. Specify the new base point, if needed. Moving the cursor in the second or third quadrant scales the entities by a factor more than 1, as shown in Figure 16-23. If you move the cursor in the first or fourth quadrant, the entities will be scaled by a factor less than 1.

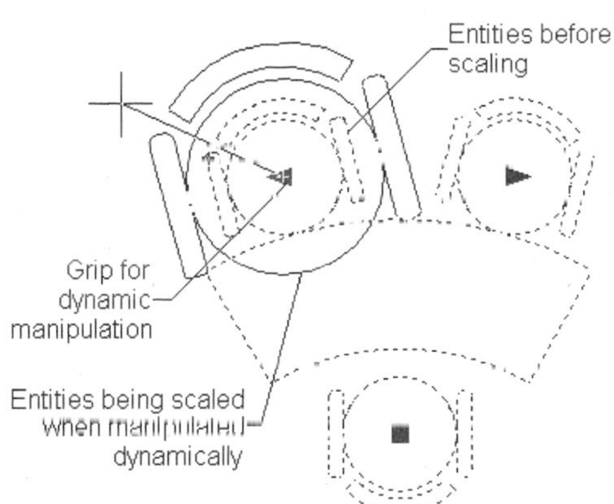

Figure 16-23 *Entities being scaled by using dynamic manipulation*

Assigning the Array Action to the Linear Parameter

By adding array action to the entities in the block, you can create the array dynamically by using grips. Invoke the **Array** action tool from **BLOCK AUTHORING PALETTES** or double-click on the linear parameter and select the **Array** option; you will be prompted to select the objects to create the array. Next, select the object and press ENTER; you will be prompted to enter the distance between the columns. The number of instances in the array will depend on the distance by which you move the cursor after selecting the parameter grip. Figure 16-24 shows the preview of an array being created dynamically using the **Array** action.

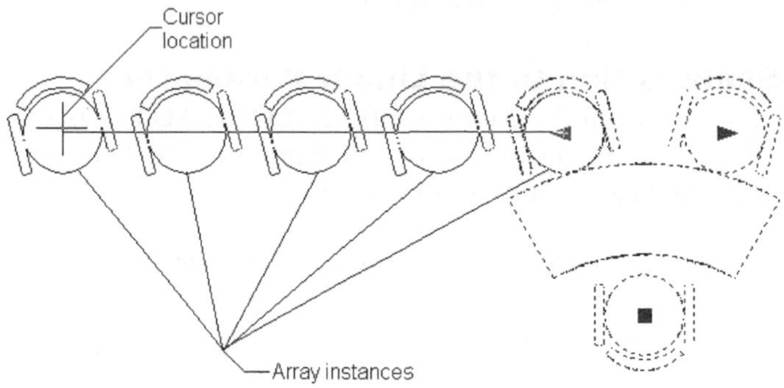

***Figure 16-24** Creating an array dynamically using the **Array** action*

Polar Parameter

The **Polar** parameter is defined by the distance between the two keypoints and an angle. The **Move**, **Scale**, **Stretch**, **Polar Stretch**, or **Array** actions can be associated with the **Polar** parameter. To add a polar parameter, choose **Polar** parameter from the Parameter drop-down of the **Action Parameters** panel of the **Block Editor**. The following prompt sequence will be displayed:

Specify base point or [Name/Label/Chain/Description/Palette/Value set]: *Specify start point for the parameter.*
Specify endpoint: *Specify endpoint for the parameter.*
Specify label location: *Specify a point where Label will be placed.*

Note that the working of the **Value set** option is different in case of the **Polar** parameter. You can invoke the **PROPERTIES** palette for the **Polar** parameter and change the value sets in the **Value Set** rollout, or specify them when you are prompted to specify the base point. The prompt sequence for this option is given next.

Specify base point or [Name/Label/Chain/Description/Palette/Value set]: **V** Enter
Enter distance value set type [None/List/Increment] <None>: **L** Enter
Enter list of distance values (separated by commas): *Specify list of values for the Distance* Enter
Enter angle value set type [None/List/Increment] <None>: **L** Enter
Enter list of angle values (separated by commas): *Specify list of values for the **Angle** parameter.*
Specify base point or [Name/Label/Chain/Description/Palette/Value set]:

Similarly, you can use the **Increment** option to specify the increment and range for the distance and angle parameters.

Assigning the Polar Stretch Action to the Polar Parameter

By specifying the polar stretch action, you can stretch the entities and at the same time, rotate them. As you move the cursor, the entities specified for rotation will rotate by the same angle that has been moved by the cursor. Remember that the polar stretch action can only be applied to the polar parameter. To add this action, choose the **Polar Stretch** action from the **BLOCK AUTHORING PALETTES** or double-click on the parameter and then select the polar stretch option. The following is the prompt sequence:

Select parameter: *Select the parameter to associate the action.*
Specify parameter point to associate with action or enter [sTart point/Second point] <Start>: *Specify the point that will be associated with the action.*
Specify first corner of stretch frame or [CPolygon]: *Specify the first corner of stretch frame.*
Specify opposite corner: *Specify opposite corner of stretch frame.*
Specify objects to stretch
Select objects: *Select the object to stretch, refer to Figure 16-25.*
Select objects: Enter
Specify objects to rotate only
Select objects: *Select only the object that needs to be rotated, refer to Figure 16-25.*
Select objects: Enter

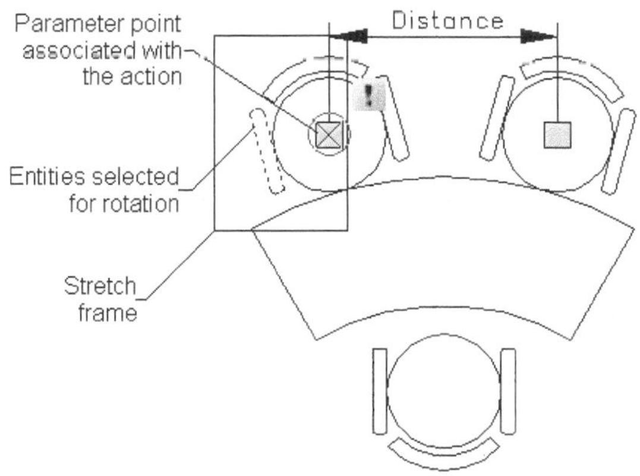

Figure 16-25 *Selecting the entities to assign the polar stretch action*

Set the **Distance multiplier** and **Angle offset** in the **PROPERTIES** palette, as discussed earlier. Next, invoke the **Test Block Window** and select the block; the polar parameter grips will be displayed.

Click on the grip to select it; you will be prompted to specify the point location. Specify the new point; some of the entities will stretch, whereas the others will rotate, as shown in Figure 16-26. Exit the **Test Block Window** by choosing the **Close Test Block** button.

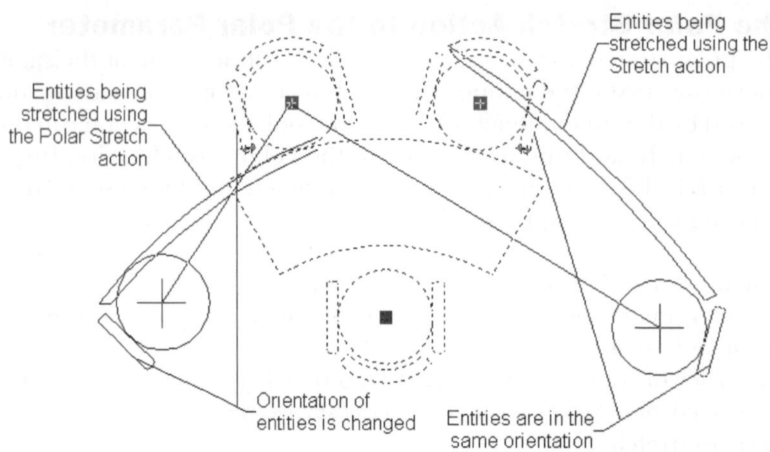

***Figure 16-26** Difference between the stretch action and the polar stretch action*

Tip

*While assigning different actions and parameters to the block entities in the **Block Editor**, there is no need to exit the block editor and check the actions. Choose the **Test Block** tool in the **Open/Save** panel in the **Block Editor**; a new test window will be displayed. In this window, you can check the changes applied to the block. To exit this window, choose the **Close Test Block** button from the **Close** panel.*

XY Parameter

The XY parameter is used to define the X and Y distances between a specified base point and an endpoint in the dynamic block. You can assign the array, move, scale, and stretch actions to the XY parameter. To add this parameter, choose the **XY** parameters tool from the **Parameters** tab of the **BLOCK AUTHORING PALETTES**. The prompt sequence that will be displayed is given next.

Specify base point or [Name/Label/Chain/Description/Palette/Value set]: *Specify the base point from where the X and Y distance will be measured.*
Specify endpoint: *Specify endpoint up to which the distances will be measured.*

Figure 16-27 shows the XY parameter. Double-click on the parameter to display the dynamic preview. The dynamic preview lists the actions that can be assigned to this parameter.

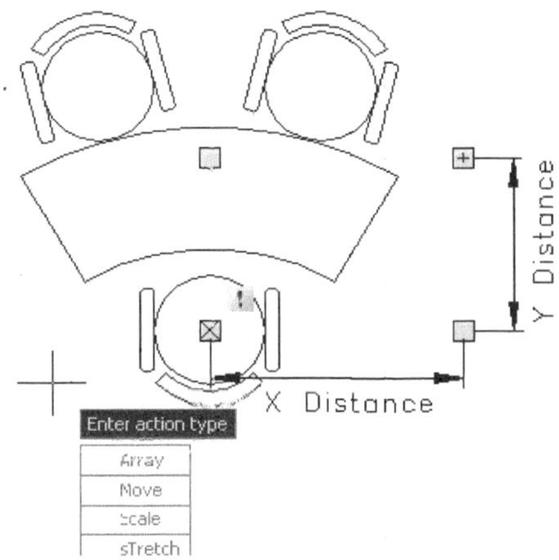

Figure 16-27 XY parameter assigned to a point and the actions that can be assigned to this parameter

Rotation Parameter

The rotation parameter is used to define an angular variation for the selected entities of the dynamic block. You can assign the rotate action to this parameter, which ensures that the selected entities of the dynamic block can be rotated around a predefined base point. To add this parameter, choose the **Rotation** parameter from the **Parameters** tab of the **BLOCK AUTHORING PALETTES**. The prompt sequence that will be displayed is as follows:

Specify base point or [Name/Label/Chain/Description/Palette/Value set]: *Specify base point around which the selected entities of the dynamic block will be rotated.*
Specify radius of parameter: *Specify the radius, which defines the imaginary circle along the circumference of which the entities will be rotated.*
Specify default rotation angle or [Base angle] <0>: *Specify default rotation angle at which the grip point will be placed for rotating the entities dynamically.*
Specify label location: *Specify a point where the label will be placed.*

When you specify the radius of the parameter, you will be prompted to specify the default rotation angle or base angle. The base angle defines the datum for measuring the rotation angle. By default, this value is 0-degree, which means that the angles will be measured from the positive X-axis. You can also modify the base angle to any other value, such that the angles are measured from the new base angle. For example, if you modify the base angle value to 30-degree, the default rotation angle will be measured from an axis defined at 30-degree from the X-axis, as shown in Figure 16-28.

Assigning the Rotate Action to the Rotation Parameter

The **Rotate** action can only be assigned to the **Rotation** parameter. This action allows you to rotate the selected components of the dynamic block using grips, as shown in Figure 16-29. To add the **Rotate** action, double-click on the **Rotation** parameter. The following prompt sequence will be displayed:

Specify selection set for action
Select objects: *Select the entities to be rotated.*
Select objects: Enter

Next, invoke the **Test Block Window** and select the block; the **Rotation** parameter grips will be displayed on the block. Click on a grip to select it; you will be prompted to specify the rotation angle. Specify the angle; the entities will rotate as specified. Exit the **Test Block Window** by choosing the **Close Test Block** button.

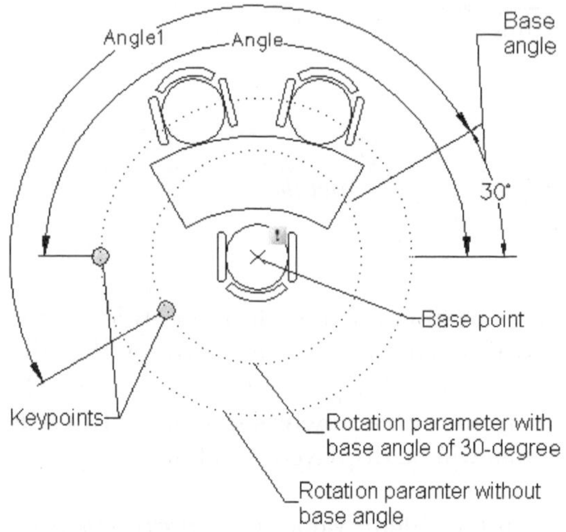

*Figure 16-28 The **Rotation** parameters with and without the base angle*

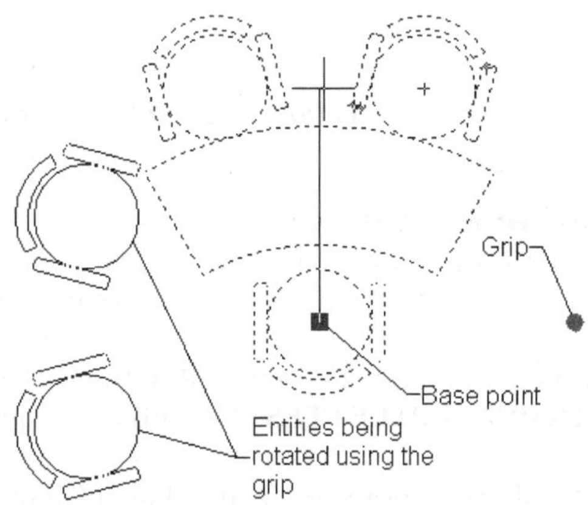

*Figure 16-29 The **Dynamic** manipulation of entities after adding the **Rotate** action*

Alignment Parameter

The **Alignment** parameter is used to align the entire dynamic block with the other entities in the drawing. The alignment is defined using the base point of alignment, at which the dynamic block grip is created. The block is rotated and moved while aligning. Remember that because the entire block is aligned using this parameter, you do not need to assign any action to this parameter. When you invoke this parameter, the following prompt sequence is displayed:

Specify base point of alignment or [Name]: *Specify the base point to align the dynamic block.*
Alignment type = Perpendicular
Specify alignment direction or alignment type [Type] <Type>: *Specify the alignment direction by defining another point in the drawing window.*

Remember that the dynamic block will be aligned at the angle that is defined while defining the alignment direction in the **Specify alignment direction or alignment type [Type] <Type>** prompt.

Type: Enter **T** at the **Specify alignment direction or alignment type [Type] <Type>** prompt to specify the type of alignment. The types of alignment are discussed next.

Perpendicular: This alignment type ensures that the dynamic block is aligned perpendicular to the entities in the drawing.

Tangent: This alignment type ensures that the dynamic block is aligned tangent to the entities in the drawing.

After adding the alignment parameter, invoke the **Test Block Window** and select the block; the dynamic block grip is displayed at the base point of the alignment parameter. Select the grip and then move the dynamic block close to an existing entity in the drawing. The dynamic block aligns itself to the entity and the alignment angle depends on the alignment direction that you defined. Exit the **Test Block Window** by choosing the **Close Test Block** button.

Flip Parameter

The **Flip** parameter is used to add a flip action to the dynamic block. The flip action reverses the orientation of the dynamic block. Thus in simple terms, the flip parameter is used to create a mirrored image of the dynamic block and remove the original block. The mirror line is defined by the reflection line, which you specify while defining the flip parameter, refer to Figure 16-30. Remember that depending on the location of the reflection axis, the location of the flipped entities also changes. When you add the flip action, an arrow is displayed at the base point. You can click on this arrow to flip the orientation of the selected entities of the dynamic block. The following prompt sequence will be displayed when you invoke the **Flip** parameter tool from the **Parameters** tab of the **BLOCK AUTHORING PALETTES**:

Specify base point of reflection line or [Name/Label/Description/Palette]: *Specify the base point from where the reflection line will start.*
Specify endpoint of reflection line: *Specify the endpoint of the reflection line, thus defining its orientation.*
Specify label location: *Specify location for label of the parameter.*

Assigning the Flip Action to the Flip Parameter

As mentioned earlier, you can assign the **Flip** action to the **Flip** parameter so as to reverse the orientation of the selected entities of the block. To assign the **Flip** action, double-click on the **Flip** parameter; you will be prompted to select the objects to be flipped. Select the objects and press ENTER; the flip action will be applied. Figure 16-31 shows the orientation and location of the selected entities before and after flipping.

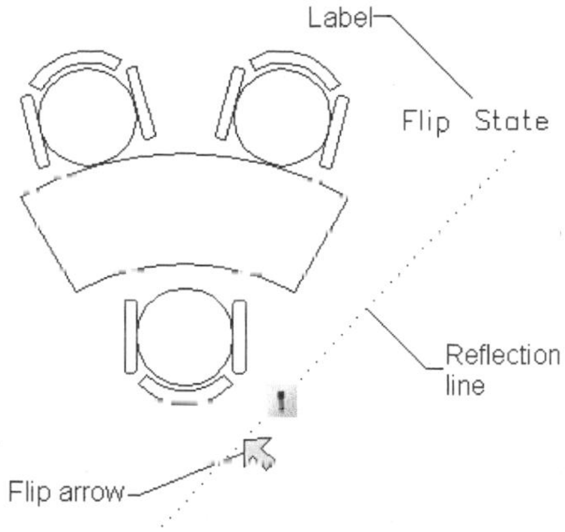

Figure 16-30 *Defining the* ***Flip*** *parameter*

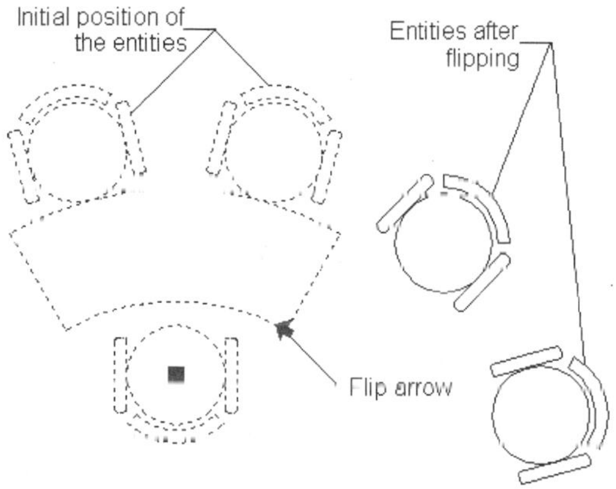

Figure 16-31 *Dynamically flipping the entities of the dynamic block*

Visibility Parameter

The visibility parameter is used to create visibility states of a dynamic block. Using the visibility states, you can control the display of entities in the dynamic block and specify whether they would be visible or hidden. When you invoke this tool, you will be prompted to specify the location of the parameter. As soon as the visibility parameter is added, the following options will be available in the **Visibility** panel of the **Block Editor**.

Visibility Mode: This button toggles the value of the **Visibility Mode** in between 0 and 1. The default value of this mode is set to 0 and therefore, the entities that have been made invisible will not be shown in the authoring area. If the value of this mode is set to 1, the entities that you make invisible will also be displayed in gray color in the authoring area.

Make Invisible: This tool is used to make some of the entities invisible in the current visibility state. When you choose this tool, you are prompted to select the entities to be hidden.

Make Visible: This tool is chosen to make the entities visible that were made invisible in the current visibility state using the **Make Invisible** tool. When you choose this tool, all the entities that were hidden are displayed in the authoring area, even if the **Visibility Mode** is set to 0. Select the entities that you want to make visible; the selected entities will be made visible after you exit the **Make Visible** tool.

Visibility States: This tool is used to create an additional visibility state. On choosing this tool, the **Visibility States** dialog box will be displayed, as shown in Figure 16-32. By default, **VisibilityState0** is available and listed in the **Visibility states** area. To create a new visibility state, choose the **New** button; the **New Visibility State** dialog box will be displayed, as shown in Figure 16-33. The options in this dialog box are discussed next.

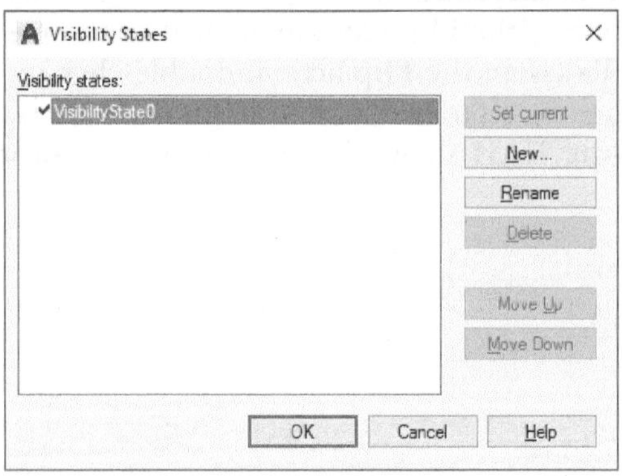

*Figure 16-32 The **Visibility States** dialog box*

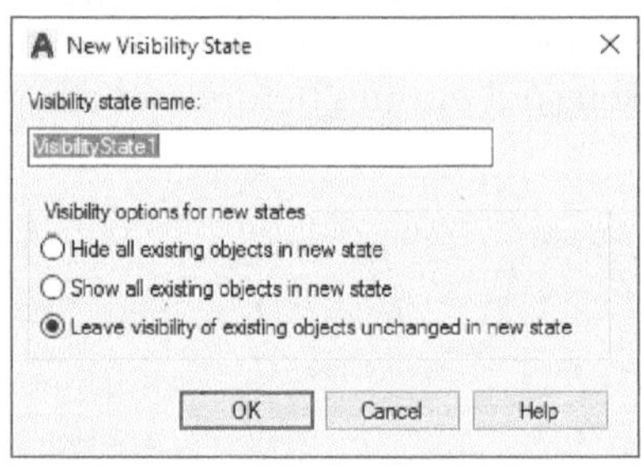

*Figure 16-33 The **New Visibility State** dialog box*

Visibility state name: Specify the name of the new visibility state in this edit box.

Visibility options for new states: The options in this area are used to control the visibility of the new visibility state. By default, the **Leave visibility of existing objects unchanged in new state** radio button is selected, implying that the visibility of entities in the new state will be similar to the visibility of the objects in the current state. If you select the **Hide all existing objects in new**

state radio button, all entities will be hidden in the new visibility state. If you select the **Show all existing objects in new state** radio button, all objects will be visible in the new visibility state.

The current visibility state is displayed in the drop-down list in the **Visibility** panel of the **Block Editor** tab. To make any other visibility state as the current visibility state, select it from the drop-down list. To rename an existing visibility state, select its name from the **Visibility states** list box available in the **Visibility States** dialog box and choose the **Rename** button.

After defining the visibility states, exit the **Block Editor**. Now, you can hide or show the entities as per the requirements of the drawing. When you select the dynamic block for which the visibility state has been defined, the lookup grip will be displayed, which resembles an arrow head. If you click on the lookup grip, a shortcut menu will be displayed, listing all available visibility states. In the list, the current visibility state is displayed with a check mark on its left. In Figure 16-34, **Visibility State0** is the current visibility state. Figure 16-35 shows the drawing in which the **Visibility State2** has been made as the current visibility state and therefore, the chair is hidden in it.

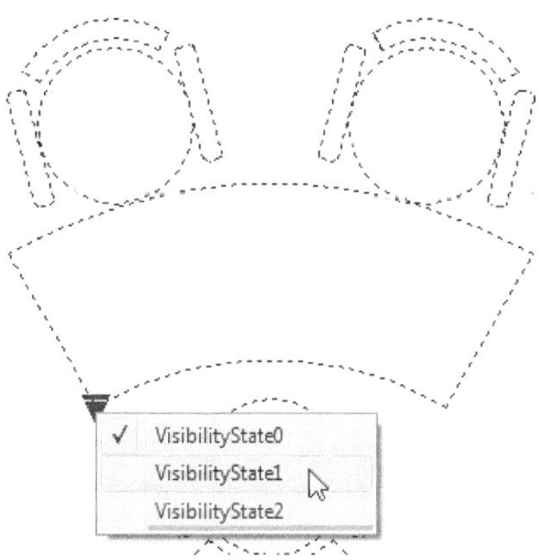

***Figure 16-34** Shortcut menu displayed on clicking the lookup grip*

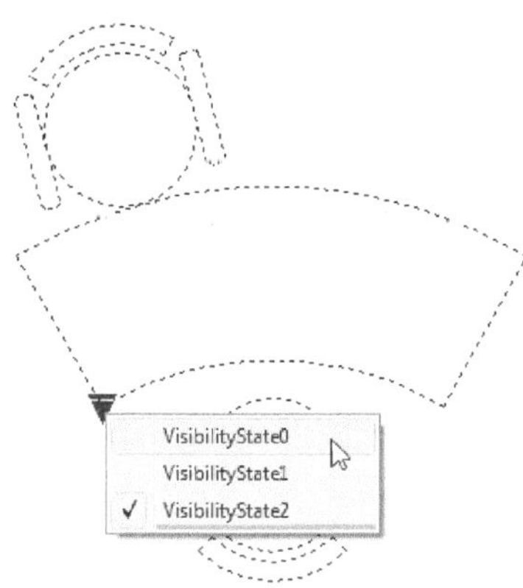

***Figure 16-35** Changing the visibility state using the shortcut menu*

Lookup Parameter

The **Lookup** parameter is added to assign a lookup action to the dynamic block. Using the lookup action, you can control the values of the parameters assigned to the dynamic block. To add this parameter, choose the **Lookup** tool from the **BLOCK AUTHORING PALETTES** and specify the location of the parameter.

Assigning the Lookup Action to the Lookup Parameter

To assign the lookup action to the lookup parameter, double-click on it; the **Property Lookup Table** dialog box will be displayed, as shown in Figure 16-36.

To add a lookup property, choose the **Add Properties** button; the **Add Parameter Properties** dialog box will be displayed, as shown in Figure 16-37. This dialog box displays the parameters assigned to the current dynamic block. Select single or multiple properties and choose the **OK** button; all properties will be added as rows in the **Input Properties** area of the

Property Lookup Table dialog box and choose the **OK** button from this dialog box. Save the changes and close the **Block Editor**.

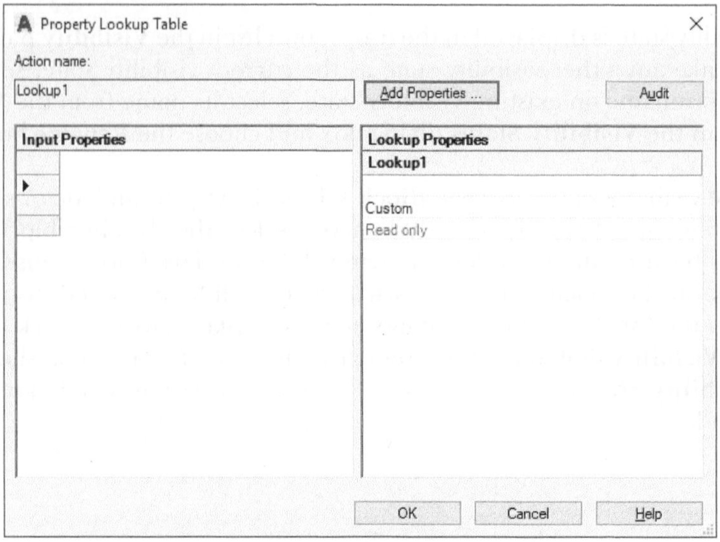

Figure 16-36 The ***Property Lookup Table*** *dialog box*

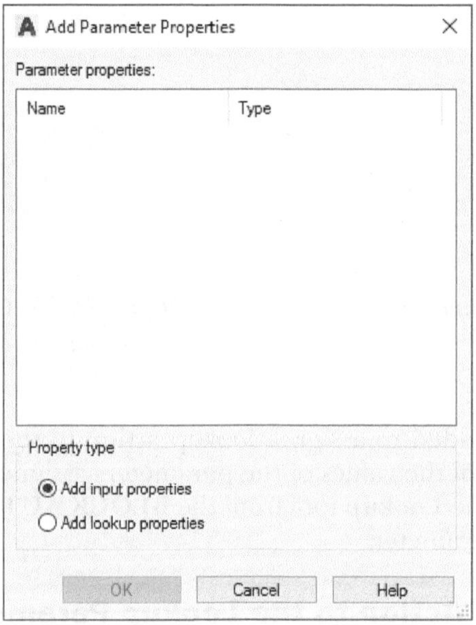

Figure 16-37 The ***Add Parameter Properties*** *dialog box*

Basepoint Parameter

The **Basepoint** parameter is used to create a base point for the block, which will be used as the insertion base point while inserting this block. Note that the blocks that are inserted are also modified, depending on the new base point that you specify using this parameter. To add this parameter, choose the **Basepoint** parameter from the **Parameters** tab of the **BLOCK AUTHORING PALETTES** and select the point that you want to use as the base point.

ADDING PARAMETER AND ACTION SIMULTANEOUSLY USING PARAMETER SETS

In the previous section, you learned how to add a parameter and then assign an action to it. AutoCAD also allows you to add parameters and actions simultaneously using the **Parameter Sets** tab of the **BLOCK AUTHORING PALETTES**, as shown in Figure 16-38. Various parameter-action combinations that can be defined for a dynamic block are available in this tab as individual sets. However, note that the entities that will be affected by the specified action are not automatically defined using the parameter sets. You need to double-click on the action to select the objects. For example, instead of first applying the **Point** parameter and then adding the **Move** action to it, you can directly apply the **Point Move** set. After you specify the parameter and the action, right-click on **Move** action in the authoring area to display the shortcut menu. Next, choose the **New Selection Set** option from the **Action Selection Set** flyout. Select the entities of the dynamic block that need to be moved using this action.

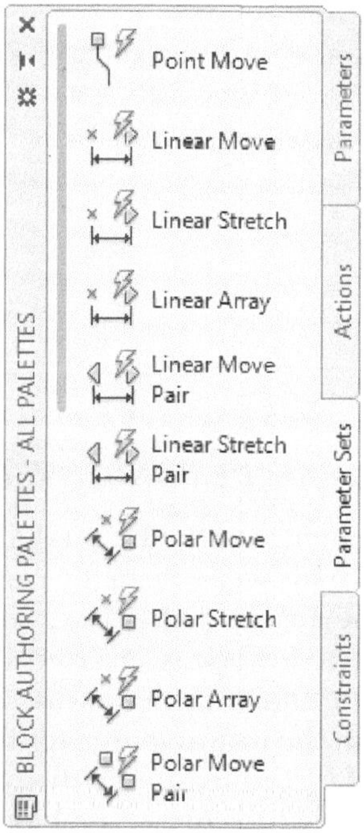

*Figure 16-38 The **Parameter Sets** tab of the **BLOCK AUTHORING PALETTES***

Tip

*To delete any action applied to a parameter, right-click on the action bar displayed on the parameter. Next, choose the **Delete** option from the shortcut menu displayed. You can also create a new selection set or modify the existing selection set by choosing the **Action Selection Set** option. To rename an action, choose the **Rename Action** option from the shortcut menu.*

INSERTING BLOCKS USING THE DESIGNCENTER

You can use the **DESIGNCENTER** to locate, preview, copy, or insert blocks from existing drawings into the current drawing. To insert a block, choose the **DesignCenter** tool from the **Palettes** panel in the **View** tab to display the **DESIGNCENTER** palette. By default, the tree pane is displayed. Choose the **Tree View Toggle** button to display the tree pane on the left side, if it is not already displayed. Expand **Computer** to display *C:/Program Files/Autodesk/AutoCAD 2018/Sample/en-us/DesignCenter* folder by clicking on the plus (+) signs on the left of the respective folders. Click on the plus sign adjacent to the folder to display its contents. Select a drawing file you wish to use to insert blocks from and then click on the plus sign adjacent to the drawing again. All the icons depicting the components such as blocks, dimension styles, layers, linetypes, text styles, and so on, in the selected drawing are displayed. Select **Blocks** by clicking on it in the tree pane; the blocks in the drawing are displayed in the palette. Select the block you wish to insert and drag and drop it into the current drawing. Later, you can move it in the drawing to the desired location. You can also right-click on the block name to display the shortcut menu, as shown in Figure 16-39.

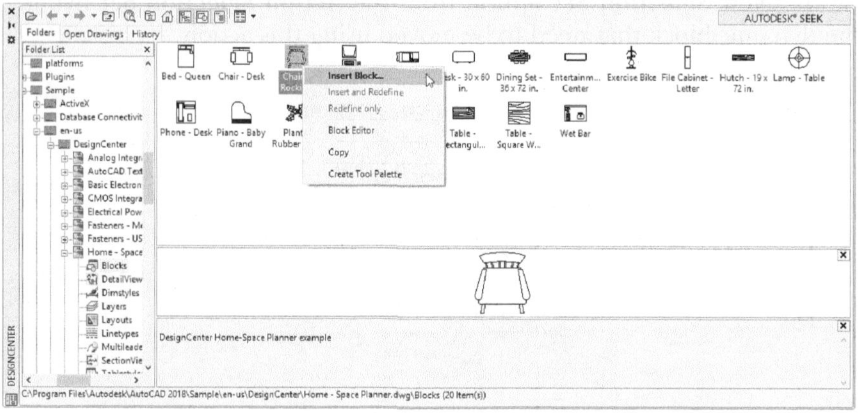

Figure 16-39 Using the DESIGNCENTER to insert blocks

Choose **Insert Block** from the shortcut menu; the **Insert** dialog box is displayed. Here, you can specify the insertion point, scale, and rotation angle in the respective edit boxes. On selecting the **Specify On-screen** check box in the **Insert** dialog box, you will be allowed to specify these parameters on the screen. The selected block is inserted into the current drawing. You can also choose the **Copy** option from the shortcut menu; the selected block will be copied to the clipboard. Now, you can right-click in the drawing area to display a shortcut menu and choose the **Paste** option from the **Clipboard** cascading menu; the preview of the selected block will be attached to the cursor and as you move the cursor, the block also moves with it. You can now select a point to paste the block. The advantage of this option over drag and drop is that you can select an insertion point at the time of pasting. In the case of drag and drop operation, you need to move the inserted block to a specific point after it has been dropped on the screen.

USING TOOL PALETTES TO INSERT BLOCKS

You can use the **TOOL PALETTES** to insert predefined blocks in the current drawing. The **TOOL PALETTES** has many tabs. You can view the complete list of tabs by clicking on stacks of the tabs available at the end of the list of tabs. In this chapter, you will learn how to insert blocks using the tabs of the **TOOL PALETTES**, refer to Figure 16-40.

Inserting Blocks in the Drawing

AutoCAD provides two methods to insert blocks from the **TOOL PALETTES**: Drag and Drop method and Select and Place method. Both methods of inserting blocks using the **TOOL PALETTES** are discussed next.

Drag and Drop Method

To insert blocks from the **TOOL PALETTES** in the drawing using this method, move the cursor over the desired predefined block in the **TOOL PALETTES**. You will notice that as you move the cursor over the block, a tooltip is displayed that shows the name and description of the block. Press and hold the left mouse button and drag the cursor to the drawing area. Release the left mouse button and you will notice that the selected block is inserted in the drawing. You may need to modify the drawing display area to view the block. Remember that when a block is inserted from the **TOOL PALETTES** using the drag and drop method, you are not prompted to specify its rotation angle or scale. The blocks are automatically inserted with their default scale factor and rotation angle.

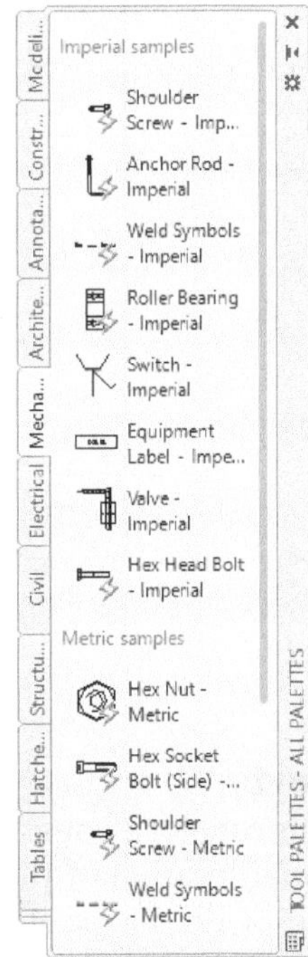

Figure 16-40 The TOOL PALETTES

Select and Place Method

You can also insert the desired block in the drawings using the select and place method. To insert the block using this method, move the cursor over the desired block in the **TOOL PALETTES**; a tooltip is displayed that shows the name and description of the block. Press the left mouse button; the selected block is attached to the cursor and the **Specify insertion point or [Basepoint/Scale/X/Y/Z/Rotate]** prompt is displayed. Modify any parameter using the prompt sequence and then move the cursor to the required location in the drawing area. Click the left mouse button; the selected block is inserted at the specified location.

Modifying Properties of the Blocks in the Tool Palettes

To modify the properties of a block, move the cursor over it in the **TOOL PALETTES** and right-click to display the shortcut menu. Using the options in this shortcut menu, you can cut or copy the desired block available in one tab of **TOOL PALETTES** and paste it on the other tab. You can also delete and rename the selected block using the **Delete** and **Rename** options, respectively. To modify the properties of the block, choose **Properties** from the shortcut menu; the **Tool Properties** dialog box is displayed, as shown in Figure 16-41.

In the **Tool Properties** dialog box, the name of the selected block is displayed in the **Name** edit box. You can rename the block by entering a new name in the **Name** edit box. The **Image** area on the left of the **Name** edit box displays the image of the selected block. If you enter a description of the block in the **Description** text box, it is stored with the block definition in the **TOOL PALETTES**. Now, when you move the cursor over the block in **TOOL PALETTES** and pause for a second, the description along with its name appears in the tooltip. The **Tool Properties** dialog box displays the properties of the selected block under the following categories.

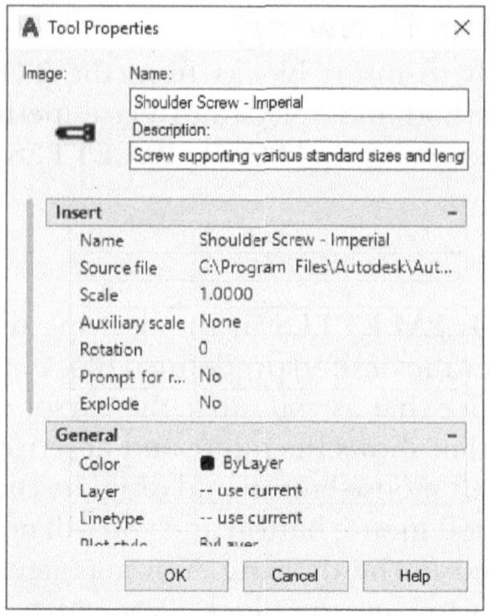

*Figure 16-41 The **Tool Properties** dialog box*

Insert

In this category, you can specify the insertion properties of the selected block such as its name, original location of the block file, scale, and rotation angle. The **Name** edit box specifies the name of the block. The **Source file** edit box displays the location of the file, in which the selected block is created. When you choose the button in the **Source file** edit box, AutoCAD displays the location of the file in the **Select Linked Drawing** dialog box. The **Scale** edit box is used to specify the scale factor of the block. The block will be inserted in the drawing according to the scale factor specified in this edit box. You can enter the angle of rotation in the **Rotation** edit box. The **Explode** edit box is used to specify whether the block will be exploded while inserting or will be inserted as a single entity.

General

In this category, you can specify the general properties of the block such as the **Color**, **Layer**, **Linetype**, **Plot style**, **Lineweight**, and **Transparency** for the selected block. The properties of a particular field can be modified from the drop-down list available on selecting that field.

Custom

In this category, you can specify the custom properties of the block, such as the dimensions and related parameters.

ADDING BLOCKS IN TOOL PALETTES

By default, the **TOOL PALETTES** displays the predefined blocks in AutoCAD. You can also add the desired block and the drawing file to the **TOOL PALETTES**. This is done using the **DESIGNCENTER**. AutoCAD provides two methods for adding blocks from the **DESIGNCENTER** to the **TOOL PALETTES**; Drag and Drop method and shortcut menu. These two methods are discussed next.

Drag and Drop Method

To add blocks from the **DESIGNCENTER** in the **TOOL PALETTES**, move the cursor over the desired block in the **DESIGNCENTER**. Press and hold the left mouse button on the block and drag the cursor to the **TOOL PALETTES**. You will notice that a box with a + sign is attached to the cursor and a black line appears on the **TOOL PALETTES**, as shown in Figure 16-42. If you move the cursor up and down in the **TOOL PALETTES**, the black line also moves between the two consecutive blocks. This line is used to define the position of the block to be inserted in the **TOOL PALETTES**. Release the left mouse button and you will notice that the selected block is added to the location specified by the black line in the **TOOL PALETTES**.

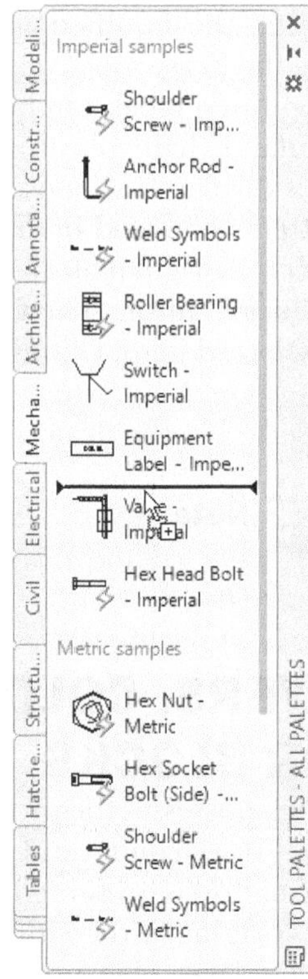

Figure 16-42 Specifying the location for inserting a block in the ***TOOL PALETTES*** *window*

Shortcut Menu

You can also add the desired block from the **DESIGNCENTER** to the **TOOL PALETTES** using the shortcut menu. To add the block, move the cursor over the desired block in the **DESIGNCENTER** and right-click on it to display a shortcut menu. Choose **Create Tool Palette** from it. You will notice that a new tab with the name **New Palette** is added to the **TOOL PALETTES**. And, the block is added in the new tab of the **TOOL PALETTES**. Also, a text box appears that displays the current name of the tab. You can change its name by entering a new one in this text box.

You can also add a number of blocks in a drawing to the **Tool Palettes** using the following two methods:

Select the **Blocks** folder of any drawing in the **DESIGNCENTER** and right-click in the Tree View area of the **DESIGNCENTER**; a shortcut menu will be displayed. Choose **Create Tool Palette** from the shortcut menu; a new tab will be added to the **TOOL PALETTES** with the same name as that of the drawing file selected in the **DESIGNCENTER**. This new tab contains all blocks which were in the folder that you selected from the **DESIGNCENTER**.

You can also add all the blocks in a drawing by right-clicking on the drawing in the tree view of the **DESIGNCENTER**; a shortcut menu is displayed. Choose **Create Tool Palette** from it; you will notice that a new tab is added to the **TOOL PALETTES**, which contains all the blocks that were available in the selected drawing. You will also notice that the new tab has the same name as that of the selected drawing

MODIFYING EXISTING BLOCKS IN THE TOOL PALETTES

If you modify an existing block that was added to the **TOOL PALETTES** and then insert it using the **TOOL PALETTES** in the same or a new drawing, you will notice that the modified block is inserted and not the original block. However, if you insert the modified block from the **TOOL PALETTES** in the drawing in which the original block was already inserted, AutoCAD inserts the original block and not the modified one. This is because the file already has a block of the same name in its memory.

To insert the modified block, you first need to delete the original block from the current drawing using the **Erase** tool. Next, you need to delete the block from the memory of the current drawing. The unused block can be deleted from the memory of the current drawing using the **PURGE** command. To invoke this command, enter **PURGE** at the command prompt. The **Purge** dialog box is displayed. Choose the (+) sign located on the left of **Blocks** in the tree view available in the **Items not used in drawing** area. You will notice that a list of blocks in the drawing is shown. Select the original block to be deleted from the memory of the current drawing and then choose the **Purge** button. The **Confirm Purge** dialog box is displayed, which confirms the purging of the selected item. Choose **Purge this item** and then choose the **Close** button to exit the **Purge** dialog box. Next, when you insert the block using the **TOOL PALETTES**, the modified block is inserted in the drawing.

Note

*You will learn more about **Purge** in Chapter 20, Grouping and Advanced Editing of Sketched Objects.*

LAYERS, COLORS, LINETYPES, AND LINEWEIGHTS FOR BLOCKS

A block possesses the properties of the layer on which it is drawn. The block may be composed of objects drawn on several different layers, with different colors, linetypes, and lineweights. All this information is preserved in the block. At the time of insertion, each object in the block is drawn on its original layer with the original linetype, lineweight, and color, irrespective of the current drawing layer, object color, object linetype, and object lineweights. You may want all instances of a block to have identical layers, linetype properties, lineweight, and color. This can be achieved by allocating all the properties explicitly to the objects forming the block. On the other hand, if you want the linetype and color of each instance of a block to be set according to the linetype and color of the layer on which it is inserted, draw all the objects forming the block on layer 0 and set the color, lineweight, and linetype to **By Layer**. Objects with the **By Layer** color, linetype, and lineweight can have their colors, linetypes, and lineweights changed after insertion by changing the layer settings. If you want the linetype, lineweight, and color of each instance of a block to be set according to the current explicit linetype, lineweight, and color at the time of insertion, set the color, lineweight, and linetype of its objects to **By Block**. You can use the **PROPERTIES** palette to change some of the characteristics associated with a block (such as layer).

For example, assume block B1 includes a square and a triangle that were originally drawn on layer X and layer Y, respectively. Let the color assigned to the layer X be red and to layer Y be green. Also, let the linetype assigned to layer X be continuous and for layer Y be hidden. Now, if you insert B1 on layer L1 with color yellow and linetype dot, block B1 will be on layer L1, but the square will be drawn on layer X with color red and linetype continuous. The triangle will be drawn on layer Y with the color green and the linetype hidden.

The **By Layer** option instructs AutoCAD to assign objects within the block the color and linetype of the layers on which they were created. There are three exceptions:

1. If objects are drawn on a special layer (layer 0), they are inserted on the current layer. These objects assume the characteristics of the current layer (the layer on which the block

is inserted) at the time of insertion, and can be modified after insertion by changing that layer's settings.

2. Objects created with the special color **By Block** are generated with the color that is current at the time of insertion of the block. This color may be explicit or **By Layer**. You are thus allowed to construct blocks that assume the current object color.

3. Objects created with the special linetype **By Block** are generated with the linetype that is prevalent at the time the block is inserted. Blocks are thus constructed with the current object linetype, which may be **By Layer** or explicit.

Note

If a block is created on a layer that is frozen at the time of insertion, it is not shown on the screen.

Tip

*If you provide drawing files to others for their use, then **BYLAYER** settings applied on the drawing files provide the greatest compatibility with varying office standards for layer/color/linetype/lineweight. This is because they can be changed more easily after insertion.*

NESTING OF BLOCKS

The concept of having one block within another block is known as the nesting of blocks. For example, you can insert several blocks by selecting them, and then with the **Create Block** tool, create another block. Similarly, if you use the **Insert** tool to insert a drawing containing several blocks into the current drawing, it creates a block containing nested blocks in the current drawing. There is no limit to the degree of nesting. The only limitation in nesting of blocks is that blocks that reference themselves cannot be inserted. The nested blocks must have different block names. Nesting of blocks affects layers, colors, and linetypes. The general rule is given next.

If an inner block has objects on layer 0, or objects with linetype or color **By Block**, these objects may be said to behave like fluids. They "float up" through the nested block structure until they find an outer block with fixed color, layer, or linetype. These objects then assume the characteristics of the fixed layer. If a fixed layer is not found in the outer blocks then the objects with color or linetype **By Block** are formed, which means the objects will assume the color white and linetype **CONTINUOUS**.

Example 2 — Nested Blocks

To clarify the concept of nested blocks, let us do the following example.

1. Draw a rectangle on layer 0, and form a block named X.
2. Change the current layer to OBJ, set its color to red, and linetype to hidden.
3. Draw a circle on OBJ layer.
4. Insert the block X in the OBJ layer.
5. Combine the circle with the block X (rectangle) to form a block Y.
6. Now, insert block Y in any layer (say, layer CEN) with the color green and linetype continuous.

You will notice that block Y is generated in red and its linetype is hidden. However, the block X, which is nested in block Y and created on layer 0, is not generated in the color (green) and linetype (continuous) of the layer CEN. This is because the object (rectangle) on layer 0 floated up through the nested block structure and assumed the color and linetype of the first outer block (Y) with a fixed color (red), layer (OBJ), and linetype (hidden). If both the blocks (X and Y) were on layer 0, the objects in the block Y would assume the color and linetype of the layer on which the block was inserted.

Example 3 — Nested Block

1. Change the color of layer 0 to red.
2. Draw a circle with color **By Block** and then form its block, B1. It appears white because its color is set to **By Block**, refer to Figure 16-43.
3. Set the color to **By Layer** and draw a square. The color of the square is red.
4. Insert block B1. Notice that the block B1 (circle) assumes red color.
5. Create another block B2 consisting of the Block B1 (circle) and square.
6. Create a layer L1 with green color and hidden linetype. Make it current. Insert block B2 in layer L1.
7. Explode block B2. Notice the change.
8. Explode block B1, circle. You will notice that the color of the circle changes to white because it was drawn with the color set to **By Block**.

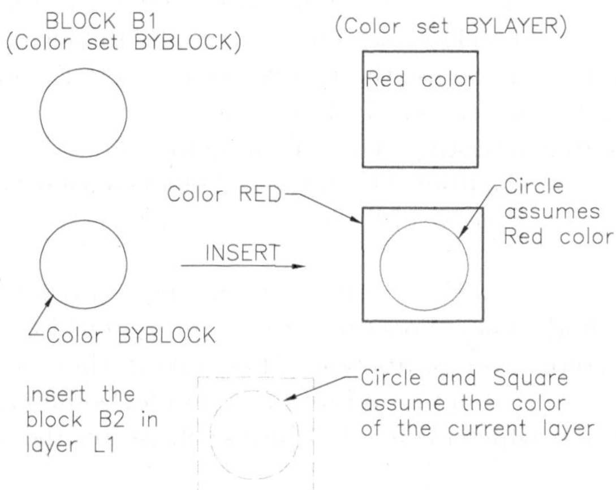

***Figure 16-43** Blocks with different layers and colors*

Example 4 — Nested Block

Part A

1. Draw a unit square on layer 0 and make it a block named B1.
2. Draw a circle of radius 0.5 and change it into a block named B2.
3. Insert block B1 into the drawing with an X scale factor of 3 and a Y scale factor of 4.
4. Now, insert the block B2 in the drawing and position it at the top of B1.
5. Make a block of the entire drawing and name it Plate.
6. Insert the block **Plate** in the current layer.

7. Create a new layer with different colors and linetypes and insert blocks B1, B2, and Plate. Keep in mind the layers on which the individual blocks and the inserted block were made.

Part B

Try nesting the blocks drawn on different layers and with different linetypes.

Part C

Change the layers and colors of the different blocks you have drawn so far.

INSERTING MULTIPLE BLOCKS

Command: MINSERT

The **MINSERT** (multiple insert) command is used for the multiple insertion of a block. Also, blocks inserted by using **MINSERT** cannot be exploded. With the **MINSERT** command, only one block reference is created. But, in addition to the standard features of a block definition (insert point, X/Y scaling, rotation angle, and so on), this block has repeated row and column counts. In this manner, using this command saves time and disk space. The prompt sequence is very similar to that of the **-INSERT** and **-ARRAY** commands. Consider an example in which you have to array a block named BENCH, with the following specifications: number of rows = 4, number of columns = 3, unit cell distance between rows = 0.50, and unit cell distance between columns = 2.0, refer to Figure 16-44. The prompt sequence for creating the arrangement of benches in an auditorium is given next.

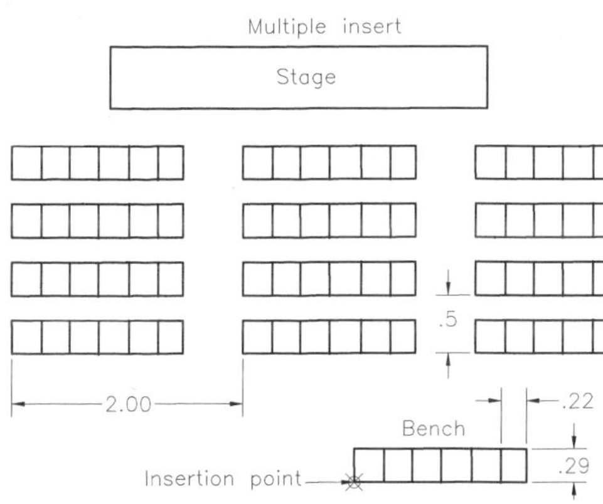

Figure 16-44 *Arrangement of benches in an auditorium*

Command: **MINSERT**
Enter block name or [?] <current>: **BENCH**
Units: Inches Conversion: 1.0000
Specify insertion point or [Basepoint/Scale/X/Y/Z/Rotate]. *Specify a base point and press ENTER*
Specify insertion point or [Basepoint/Scale/Rotate]: Specify scale factor <1>: *Press ENTER or specify a value and then press ENTER*
Specify rotation angle <0>: *Press ENTER or specify a value and then press ENTER*
Enter number of rows (---)<1>: **4**
Enter number of columns (|||) <1>: **3**
Enter distance between rows or specify unit cell (---): **0.50**
Specify distance between columns (|||): **2.0**

Note

*You cannot use an annotative block for the **MINSERT** command.*

All options of the **MINSERT** command are similar to the ones discussed earlier in the **-INSERT** command. The **?** option of the **Enter block name or [?]:** prompt lists the names of the blocks. When you specify the insertion point, AutoCAD prompts you to specify the scale factor. Once you specify the scale factor, you will be prompted to specify the rotation angle. If you need to insert the block at an angle, specify the angle and press ENTER. Next, you need to specify the number of rows, columns, distance between the rows, and distance between the columns in succession. The array of blocks will be created.

The prompts pertaining to the number of rows and columns require a positive nonzero integer. For the number of rows exceeding 1, you are prompted to specify the distance between the rows. Similarly, if the number of columns exceeds 1, you need to specify the distance between columns. The distance between rows and columns can be a positive or negative value. While specifying the distance between the rows and columns, you can also specify a unit cell by selecting two points on the screen that form a box whose width and height represent the distance between columns and rows respectively. While inserting a block, if you specify the block rotation, each copy of the inserted block is rotated through that angle. If you specify the rotation angle in the **MINSERT** command, the whole **MINSERT** block (array) is rotated by the specified rotation angle. If both the block and the **MINSERT** block (array) are rotated through the same angle, the block does not seem rotated in the **MINSERT** pattern. This is the same as an array with the rotation angle equal to 0-degree. If you want to rotate individual blocks within the array, you should first generate a rotated block and then **MINSERT** it.

Note

*1. In the array of blocks generated with the use of the **MINSERT** command, you can alter the number of rows or columns or the spacing between them. This is done using the **Misc** rollout of the **PROPERTIES** palette.*

2. When you right-click while specifying the insertion point at the Specify insertion point prompt, a shortcut menu is displayed where all the command line options are available.

Exercise 5 — *MINSERT*

1. Create a triangle with each side equal to 3 units.
2. Generate a block of the triangle.
3. Use the **MINSERT** command to insert the block to create a 3 by 3 array. The distance between the rows is 1 unit, and the distance between columns is 2 units.
4. Again, use the **MINSERT** command to insert the block to create a 3 by 3 array. The distance between the rows is 2 units and between the columns is 3 units. The array is rotated through 15 degrees.

CREATING DRAWING FILES USING THE WRITE BLOCK DIALOG BOX

Ribbon: Insert > Block Definition > Create Block drop-down > Write Block
Command: WBLOCK/W

The blocks are symbols created by the **Create Block** tool and can be used only in the drawing in which they were created. This is a shortcoming because you may need to use a particular block in different drawings. The **Write Block** tool is used to export symbols by writing them to new drawing files that can be inserted in any drawing. With the **Write Block** tool, you can create a drawing file (*.dwg* extension) of the specified blocks, selected objects in the current drawing, or the entire drawing. All the used named objects (linetypes, layers, styles, and system variables) of the current drawing are inherited by the new drawing created with the **Write Block** tool. This block can then be inserted in any drawing.

When you invoke the **Write Block** tool, the **Write Block** dialog box is displayed, as shown in Figure 16-45. This dialog box converts the blocks into drawing files and also saves objects as drawing files. You can also save the entire current drawing as a new drawing file.

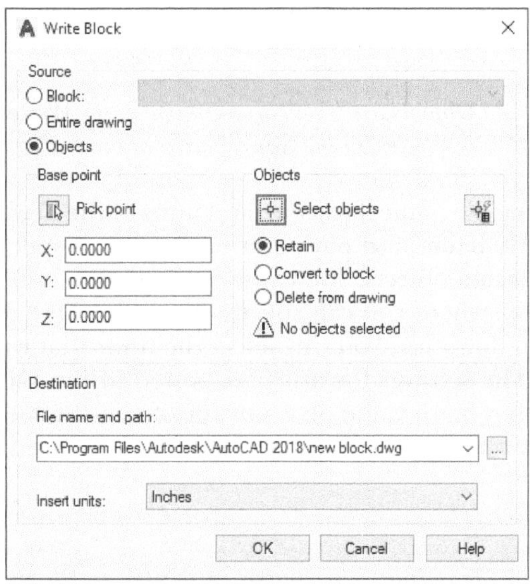

***Figure 16-45** The **Write Block** dialog box*

The **Write Block** dialog box has two main areas: **Source** and **Destination**. The **Source** area allows you to select objects and blocks, specify insertion base points, and convert them into drawing files. In this area of the dialog box, different default settings are displayed, depending upon the selection you make. By default, the **Objects** radio button is selected. In the **Destination** area, the **File name and path** edit box displays *new block.dwg* as the new file name and its location. The **Block** drop-down list is also not available. Now, you can select objects in a drawing and save them as a wblock, and can enter a name and a path for the file. Sometimes the current drawing consists of blocks. To save a block as a wblock, you can select the **Block** radio button. When the **Block** radio button is selected, the **Block** drop-down list is available. The **Block** drop-down list displays all the block names in the current drawing and you can select a block name to convert it into a wblock. The **Base point** and **Objects** areas are not available, since the insertion points and objects have already been saved with the block definition. Also, you will notice that in the **Destination** area, by default, the **File name and path** edit box displays the name of the selected block. This means that you can keep the name of the wblock the same as the selected block or you can change it. On selecting the **Entire drawing** radio button, the current drawing is selected as a block and saved as a new file. When you use this option, the **Base point** and **Objects** areas are not available.

The **Base point** area allows you to specify the base point of a wblock, which is used as an insertion point. You can either enter values in the **X**, **Y**, and **Z** edit boxes or choose the **Pick point** button to select it on the screen. The default value is 0, 0, 0. The **Objects** area allows you to select objects to save as a file. You can use the **Select objects** button to select objects or use the **QuickSelect** button to set parameters in the **Quick Select** dialog box to select objects in the current drawing. The number of objects selected is displayed at the bottom of the **Objects** area. If the **Retain** radio button is selected in the **Objects** area, the selected objects in the current drawing are kept as such, after they have been saved as a new file. If the **Convert to block** radio button is selected, the selected objects in the current drawing will be converted into a block with the same name as the new file, after being saved as a new file. Selecting the **Delete from drawing** radio button deletes the selected objects from the current drawing after they have been saved as a file.

Note

*Both the **Base point** and **Objects** areas will be available in the **Write Block** dialog box only when the **Objects** radio button is selected in the **Source** area of the dialog box.*

The **Destination** area sets the file name, location, and units of the new file, in which the selected objects are saved. In the **File name and path** edit box, you can specify the file name and the path of the block or the selected objects. You can choose the **[...]** button to display the **Browse for Drawing File** dialog box, where you can specify the path where the new file will be saved. From the **Insert units** drop-down list, you can select the units that will be used in the new file when inserted as a block. The settings for units are stored in the **INSUNITS** system variable and the default option Inches has a value of 1. On specifying the required information in the dialog box, choose the **OK** button. The objects or the block is saved as a new file in the path specified by you.

Tip

*By using the **Entire drawing** radio button in the **Write Block** dialog box, you can save the current drawing as a new drawing. It is a recommended method to reduce the file size of the drawing. This is because all unused blocks, layers, linetypes, text styles, dimension styles, multiline styles, shapes, and so on are removed from the drawing. The new drawing does not contain any information that is no longer needed. This **Entire drawing** option is faster than the **-PURGE** command (which also removes unused named objects from a drawing file) and can be used whenever you have completed a drawing and want to save it. The **-PURGE** command has been discussed later in this chapter.*

Note

Whenever a drawing is inserted into the current drawing, it acts as a single object. It cannot be edited unless exploded.

DEFINING THE INSERTION BASE POINT

Ribbon: Insert > Block Definition > Set Base Point or Home > Block > Set Base Point
Command: BASE

The **Set Base Point** tool lets you set the insertion base point for a drawing, just as you set the base insertion point using the **Create Block** tool. This base point is defined when you insert a drawing into some other drawings, the specified base point will be placed on the insertion point. By default, the base point is at the origin (0,0,0). When a drawing is inserted on a current layer, it does not inherit the color, linetype, or thickness properties of the current layer. On invoking the **Set Base Point** tool, following prompt sequence is displayed.

Enter base point <0.0000,0.0000,0.0000>: *Specify a base point or press ENTER to accept the default value.*

Exercise 6 — *WBLOCK*

1. Create a drawing file named CHAIR using the **Write Block** tool. Make a listing of your *.dwg* files and make sure that *CHAIR.dwg* is listed. Quit the drawing editor.
2. Begin a new drawing and insert the drawing file into it. Save the drawing.

EDITING BLOCKS

Ribbon: Insert > Reference > Edit Reference **Command:** REFEDIT
Toolbar: Refedit > Edit Reference In-Place

You can edit blocks by breaking them into parts and then making modifications and redefining them or by editing them in place. Both these methods have been discussed here.

Note
*The blocks inserted using the **MINSERT** command can be edited by reference. However, the non-uniformly scaled blocks cannot be edited by reference.*

Editing Blocks in Place

You can edit blocks in the current drawing by using the **Edit Reference** tool, referred to as the in-place reference editing. This feature of AutoCAD allows you to make minor changes to blocks, wblocks, or drawings that have been inserted in the current drawing without breaking them up into component parts or opening the original drawing and redefining them. This command saves valuable time of going back and forth between drawings and redefining blocks.

After selecting a reference object, choose the **Edit Reference** tool from the **Reference** panel in the **Insert** tab or by enter **REFEDIT** at the command prompt. On doing so, the **Reference Edit** dialog box will be displayed, as shown in Figure 16-46. Alternatively, select the block, right-click on any block reference and then choose the **Edit Block In-place** option from the shortcut menu displayed. When you invoke the **REFEDIT** command, the following prompt is displayed.

Select reference: *Select the block to edit.*

Once you have selected the block reference to be edited, the **Reference Edit** dialog box is displayed. The **Reference Edit** dialog box has two tabs: **Identify Reference** and **Settings**. The description of these tabs is as follows.

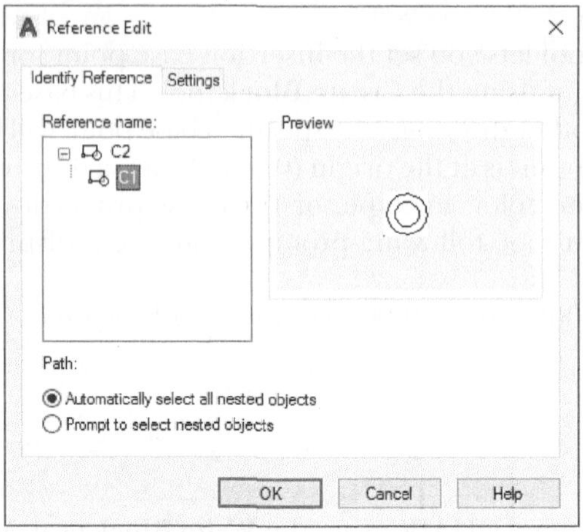

Figure 16-46 *The **Identify Reference** tab of the **Reference Edit** dialog box*

Identify Reference Tab

The **Identify Reference** tab, refer to Figure 16-46, provides information for identifying the reference edit, and selecting and editing the references.

Reference name: The **Reference name** list box displays the name of the selected reference. A plus sign (+) next to the name implies that the selected block reference contains nested references. When you click on the plus sign, the nested reference is displayed in a tree view. If a block does not contain any nested blocks, this plus sign is not displayed next to the reference name in the list box. In the figure, the block C1 contains a nested block C2. An image of the selected block is displayed in the **Preview** box. If you want to see a preview of the nested block, select its name in the list box; the corresponding preview image is displayed in the **Preview** area.

Path: It displays the location of the selected reference. Note that if the selected reference is a block, no path is displayed.

The **Automatically select all nested objects** radio button is selected by default and allows you to automatically include all the selected objects in the reference editing session. The selected objects also include the nested objects.

The **Prompt to select nested objects** radio button, when selected, allows you to individually select the nested objects in the reference editing session. If this radio button is selected and you choose the **OK** button, the **Reference Edit** dialog box is closed. You are prompted to select the nested objects in the reference that you want to edit.

Settings Tab

The **Settings** tab, as shown in Figure 16-47, provides options for editing references. The **Create unique layer, style, and block names** check box is selected by default and allows you to control the layer and symbol names of the objects that are extracted from the selected reference. If you clear this check box, the names of the layers remain the same as in the reference drawing. Similarly, the **Display attribute definitions for editing** check box, when selected, allows you to edit attributes and attribute definitions associated with the block references. The modified attribute definitions are effective for future insertions, and no changes are made in the current insertions. Attributes are explained in detail in the next chapter. The **Lock objects not in working set** check box allows you to lock all the objects that are not in the working set.

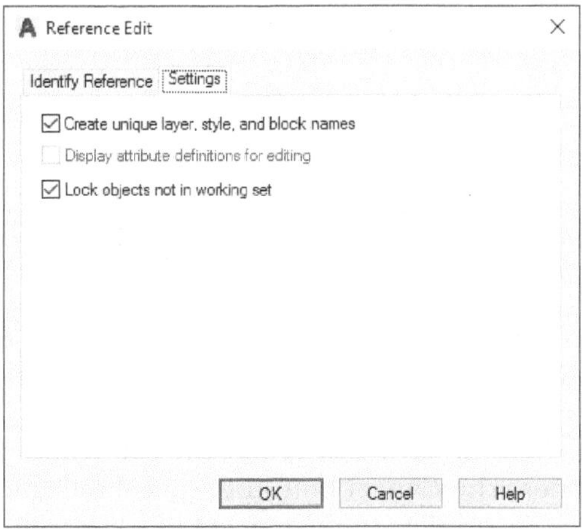

Figure 16-47 *The **Settings** tab of the **Reference Edit** dialog box*

After selecting the required block to edit, choose the **OK** button to exit the dialog box. If you have selected the **Prompt to select nested objects** radio button, the following prompt sequence will be displayed:

Select nested objects: *Select objects within the block that you want to modify.*
n entities added
Select nested objects: Enter
n items selected
Use **REFCLOSE** or the **Refedit** toolbar to end reference editing session.

Once you have selected the objects to be edited and pressed ENTER, the total number of selected objects will be displayed. Also, you will notice that the **Edit Reference** panel has been added to the **Ribbon** and the objects, except the selected ones have faded out. You can control the fading intensity of the objects by using the options from the **Fade control** area of the **Display** tab in the **Options** dialog box, refer to Figure 16-48. In this area, you can use the slider bar to increase or decrease the fading intensity or you can enter a value in the edit box. You can also control the fading intensity of other objects at the time of editing by using the **XFADECTL** variable. By default, the fading intensity value is set at 70.

The objects that have been selected for editing are referred to as the working set. You can use any drawing and editing command to modify this working set. Sometimes, you may need to add an external object from the current drawing to the block. To do so, choose the **Add to Working Set** tool in the **Edit Reference** panel, as shown in Figure 16-49. Next, select the objects to be added to the working set and press ENTER; these objects will then get deleted from the current drawing and added to the current working set. Similarly, to remove objects from a working set, choose the **Remove from Working Set** tool from the **Edit Reference** panel. You are prompted to select the objects from the working set that you want to remove. On completing the selection, press ENTER. The objects that have been removed from the working set appear faded and are added back to the current drawing. You can also use the **REFSET** command to add or remove objects from a working set. But this command can be used only when a reference has already been selected using the **REFEDIT** command.

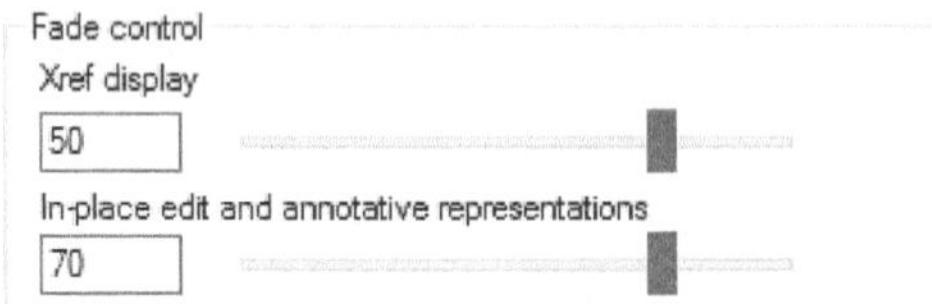

*Figure 16-48 The **Fade control** area in the **Display** tab of the **Options** dialog box*

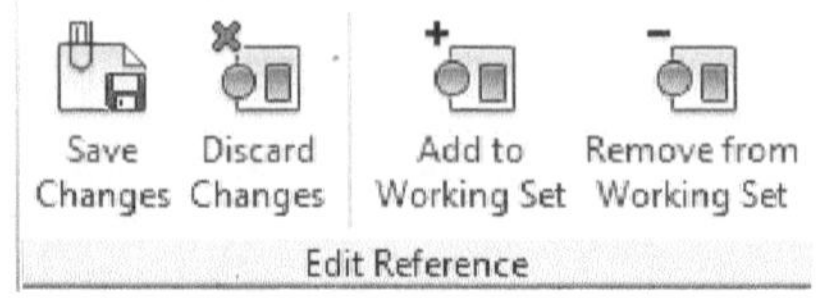

*Figure 16-49 The **Edit Reference** panel*

After adding or removing objects from the existing set, choose the **Save Changes** tool in the **Edit Reference** panel to save the changes; the **AutoCAD** information box will be displayed informing that all reference edits will be saved. This information box also prompts you to specify whether you want to continue saving or cancel the command. Choose the **OK** button to save the modifications or choose the **Cancel** button to cancel the command. If you choose the **OK** button, the modifications are applied to the current block as well as to all future insertions.

Note

The Automatic Save feature of AutoCAD is disabled during reference editing.

To exit reference editing without saving any changes in the block reference, choose the **Discard Changes** tool from the **Edit Reference** panel; the **AutoCAD** information box will be displayed, as shown in Figure 16-50, informing that all changes that have been made in the object will be discarded. To continue, choose the **OK** button, and to get back to reference editing, choose the **Cancel** button.

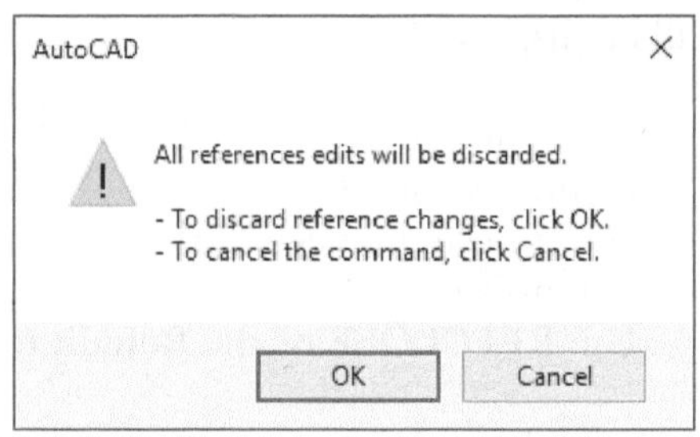

*Figure 16-50 The **AutoCAD** information box*

Note

*You can also use the **-REFEDIT** command to display prompts on the command line.*

Exploding Blocks Using the XPLODE Command

Command: XPLODE

With the **XPLODE** command, you can explode a block or blocks into component objects and simultaneously control their properties such as layer, linetype, color, and lineweight. The scale factor of the object to be exploded should be equal. Note that if the scale factor of the objects to be exploded is not equal, you need to change the value of the **EXPLMODE** system variable to 1. Note that if the **Allow exploding** check box in the **Behavior** area of the **Block Definition** dialog box was cleared while creating the block, you will not be able to explode the block. The command prompts for this command are as follows:

Command: **XPLODE**
Select objects: *Using any object selection method, select objects, and then press ENTER.*

On pressing ENTER, AutoCAD reports the total number of objects selected and also the number of objects that cannot be exploded. If you select multiple objects to explode, AutoCAD further prompts you to specify whether the changes in the properties of the component objects should be made individually or globally. The prompt is given next.

XPlode Individually/<Globally>: *Enter I, G, or press ENTER to accept the default option.*

If you enter **I** at the above prompt, AutoCAD will modify each object individually, one at a time. The next prompt is given below.

Enter an option [All/Color/LAyer/LType/LWeight/Inherit from parent block/Explode] <Explode>: *Select an option.*

The options available at the command line are discussed next.

All

This option sets all the properties such as color, layer, linetype, and lineweight of the selected objects, after exploding them. AutoCAD prompts you to enter new color, linetype, lineweight, and layer name for the exploded component objects.

Color

This option sets the color of the exploded objects. The prompt is given next.

New color [Truecolor/COlorbook] <BYLAYER>: *Enter a color option or press ENTER.*

When you enter **BYLAYER**, the component objects take on the color of the exploded object's layer and when you enter **BYBLOCK**, they take on the color of the exploded object.

Layer

This option sets the layer of the exploded objects. The default option inherit's the properties of the current layer. The command prompt is as follows.

Enter new layer name for exploded objects <current>: *Enter an existing layer name or press ENTER.*

LType

This option sets the linetype of the components of the exploded object. The command prompt is given next.

Enter new linetype name for exploded objects <ByLayer>: *Enter a linetype name or press ENTER to accept the default options.*

LWeight

This option sets the lineweight of the components of the exploded object. The command prompt is given next.

Enter new lineweight <ByLayer>: *Enter a lineweight or press ENTER to accept the default option.*

Inherit from parent block

This option sets the properties of the component objects to that of the exploded parent object, provided the component objects are drawn on layer 0 and the color, lineweight, and linetype are **BYBLOCK**.

Explode

This option explodes the selected object exactly as in the **EXPLODE** command.

On selecting the **Globally** option, changes will be applied to all the selected objects at the same time. The options are similar to the ones discussed in the **Individually** option.

RENAMING BLOCKS

Command: RENAME

Blocks can be renamed using the **RENAME** command. To rename a block, enter **RENAME** at the command prompt and press ENTER; the **Rename** dialog box will be displayed, as shown in Figure 16-51. In this dialog box, the **Named Objects** list box displays the categories of object types that can be renamed, such as blocks, layers, dimension styles, linetypes, Multileader styles, material, table styles and text styles, UCSs, views, and viewports. You can rename all of these object except layer 0 and continuous linetype. When you select **Blocks** from the **Named Objects** list, the **Items** list box displays all the block names in the current drawing. When you select a block name to rename from the **Items** list box, it is displayed in the **Old Name** edit box. Enter the new name to be assigned to the block in the **Rename To** edit box. Choosing the **Rename To** button applies the change in name to the old name. Choose the **OK** button to exit the dialog box. For example, to rename a block named **Bracket** to **Valve-3**, select **Bracket** from the **Items** list box; it is displayed in the **Old Name** edit box. Enter **Valve-3** in the **Rename To** edit box and choose the **Rename To** button; the **Valve-3** block appears in the **Items** list box. Now, choose the **OK** button to exit the dialog box.

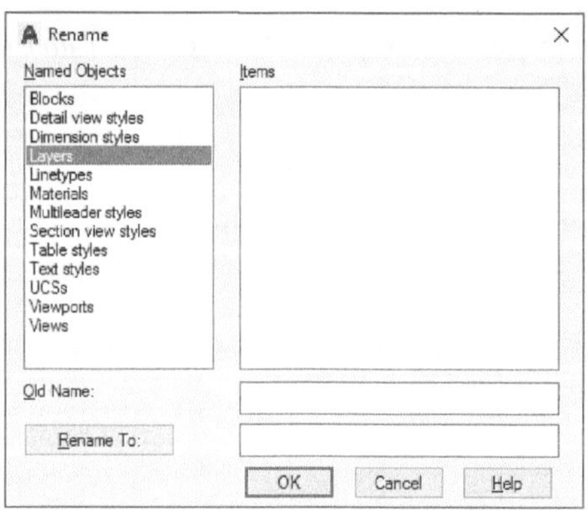

*Figure 16-51 The **Rename** dialog box*

Note

*1. The layer 0 and Continuous linetype cannot be renamed and therefore, they do not appear in the **Items** list box, when **Layers** and **Linetypes** are selected in the **Named Objects** list box.*

*2. To rename a block, enter **-RENAME** or **-REN** at the command window.*

DELETING UNUSED BLOCKS

Sometimes after completing a drawing, you may notice that the drawing contains several named objects, such as dimstyles, textstyles, layers, blocks, and so on that are not being used. Since these unused named objects unnecessarily occupy disk space, you may want to remove them. Unused blocks can be deleted with the **-PURGE** command. For example, to delete an unused block named Drawing2, the prompt sequence is given next.

Command: **-PURGE**
Enter type of unused objects to purge [Blocks/DEtailviewstyles/Dimstyles/Groups/LAyers/LTypes/MAterials/MUltileaderstyles/Plotstyles/SHapes/textSTyles/Mlinestyles/SEctionviewstyles/Tablestyles/Visualstyles/Regapps/Zero-length geometry/Empty text objects/orphaned data/All]: **B**
Enter name(s) to purge <*>: **Drawing2**
Verify each name to be purged? [Yes/No] <Y>: Enter
Purge block "Drawing2"? <N>: **Y**

If there are no objects to be removed, AutoCAD displays a message "No unreferenced blocks found.".

Note

*1. The unused blocks can also be deleted using the **PURGE** command discussed in Chapter 20 (Object Grouping and Editing Commands).*

*2. Preceding the name of the wblock with an (*) asterisk when entering the name of the wblock while using the **-WBLOCK** command has the same effect as while using the **-PURGE** command. Also, you can select the **Entire drawing** radio button in the **Write Block** dialog box when creating a block using the **Write Block** tool to get the same effect. But the **Write Block** tool is faster and deletes the unused named objects automatically, while the **-PURGE** command allows you to select the type of named objects you want to delete, and it also gives you an option to verify the objects before the deletion occurs.*

APPLYING CONSTRAINTS TO BLOCKS

While creating assembly drawings, you may need some parts that have same geometry but different sizes. AutoCAD allows you to create the drawings of these parts by using geometric and dynamic constraints, if you could control these constraints in a block table. Note that you need to apply the geometric and dynamic constraints to blocks in the **Block Editor**.

To create the parts having same geometry but different sizes, draw the sketch of the parts and then convert them into a block. Next, invoke the **Block Editor** to edit the block. In the **Block Editor**, apply the necessary geometric and dimensional constraints and make the sketch a fully-defined sketch. Now, choose the **Block Table** tool from the **Dimensional** panel of the **Block Editor** tab;

you will be prompted to specify the location of the parameter. Specify a suitable location; you will be prompted to specify the number of grips. If you enter **0**, no grip will be displayed in the drawing area. It is recommended to have atleast one grip. After specifying the number of grips, the **Block Properties Table** dialog box will be displayed, as shown in Figure 16-52.

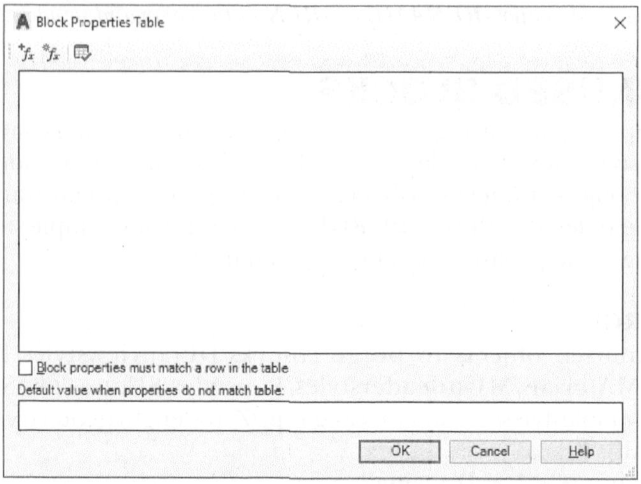

Figure 16-52 *The* ***Block Properties Table*** *dialog box*

In the **Block Properties Table** dialog box, choose the **Adds properties which appear as columns in the table** button to add all or some of the dimensional constraints added to the block. On choosing this button, the **Add Parameter Properties** dialog box will be displayed, as shown in Figure 16-53. Next, select the parameter properties to be added to the **Block Properties Table** dialog box by pressing and holding the CTRL key and then choose the **OK** button; the selected properties will be listed in the **Block Properties Table** dialog box. If you need to add any new parameter to the table, choose the **Creates a new user parameter and adds it to the table** button from the **Block Properties Table** dialog box; the **New Parameter** dialog box will be displayed, as shown in Figure 16-54. Specify the parameters and choose the **OK** button; the new parameter will be added to the **Block Properties Table** dialog box. You can also check the errors in the table. To do so, choose the **Audits the block property table for errors** button from the **Block Properties Table** dialog box. After specifying all parameters, choose the **OK** button from the **Block Properties Table** dialog box. Next, save the changes and exit the **Block Editor**. Now, if you select the block, the lookup grip will be displayed. Click on the grip; different values will be displayed in a shortcut menu, as shown in Figure 16-55. Next, choose the required value; the block will change accordingly. Note that if you have selected the **Block properties must match a row in the table** check box in the **Block Properties Table** dialog box, then the lookup grip will not be displayed and you cannot change the block sizes dynamically.

*Figure 16-53 The **Add Parameter Properties** dialog box*

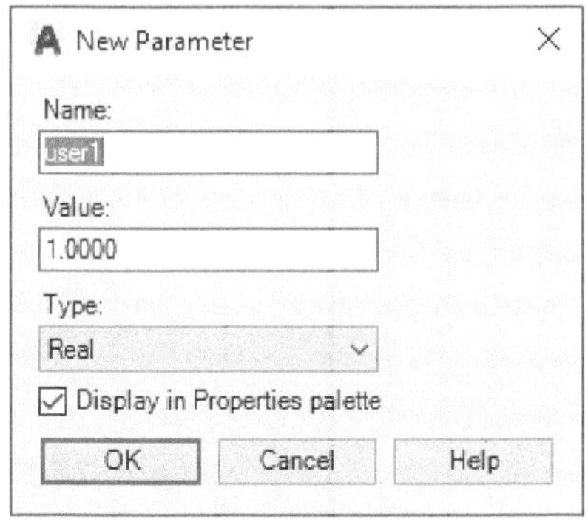

*Figure 16-54 The **New Parameter** dialog box*

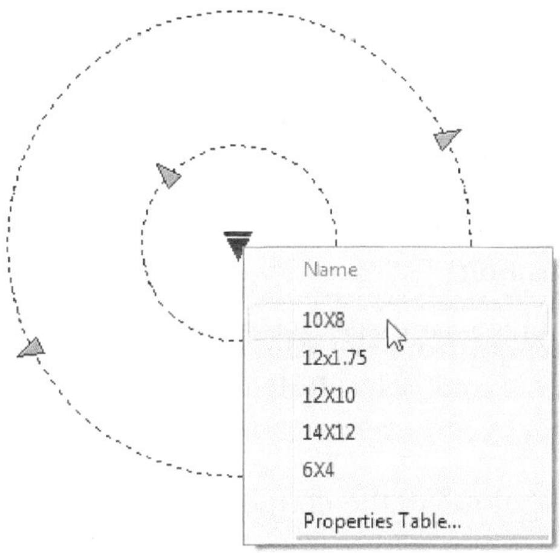

Figure 16-55 Shortcut menu displayed on selecting the lookup grip

Example 5 Constraints to Blocks

In this example, you will create the sketch of a bolt, as shown in Figure 16-56. Next, you will convert it to a block and then apply constraints such that the bolts of diameter 6, 10, 12.5, 15, 18, 24, and 25 are created.

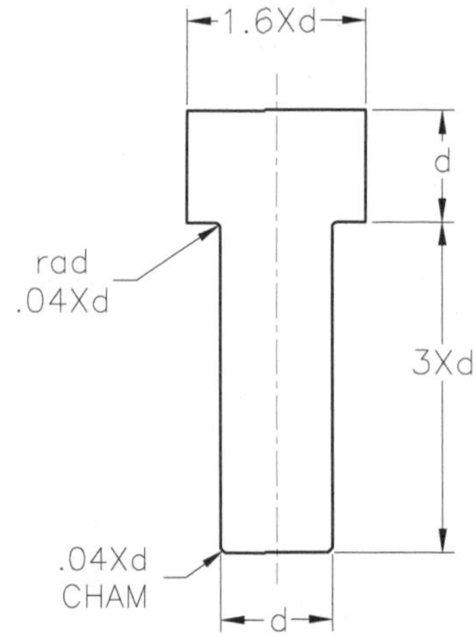

***Figure 16-56** Sketch for Example 5*

Note

The bolt shown in Figure 16-56 does not have any standard dimension or annotation. It is given for the purpose of example. However, you can follow the procedure given next to design a standard bolt.

1. Start a new file with the *acad.dwt* template in the **Drafting & Annotation** workspace. Draw the sketch assuming that the value of d=10 and it satisfies other relations that are shown in Figure 16-56. Make sure that the **Infer Constraints** button is chosen in the Status Bar and the endpoints are snapped so that it becomes a closed sketch, as shown in Figure 16-57.

2. Choose the **Create** tool from the **Block** panel of the **Home** tab and convert the sketch into a block. Name the block as **Bolt**.

3. Choose the **Block Editor** tool from the **Block** panel of the **Home** tab; the **Edit Block Definition** dialog box is displayed. Select **Bolt** and choose the **OK** button; the **Block Editor** environment is displayed.

4. Draw a vertical line passing through the midpoint of the bottom horizontal line.

5. Choose the **Construction Geometry** tool from the **Manage** panel of the **Block Editor** tab, select the vertical line drawn in the previous step, and press ENTER; you will be prompted to enter an option.

6. Enter **C** and press ENTER; the vertical line is converted into a construction line, as shown in Figure 16-58. Note that you can also create a centerline in the drawing mode but here this method is given for illustration purpose.

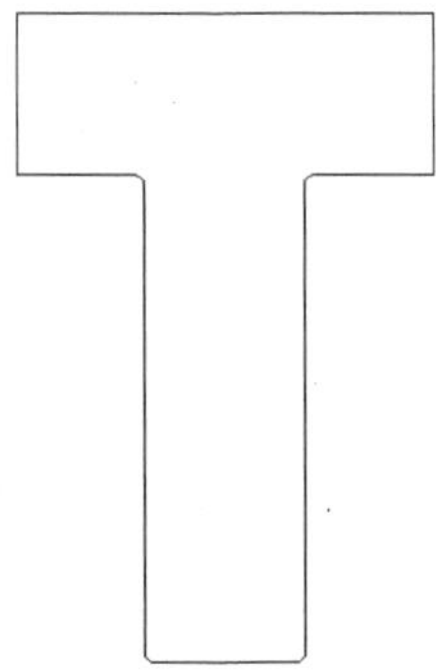

Figure 16-57 The closed sketch of the bolt

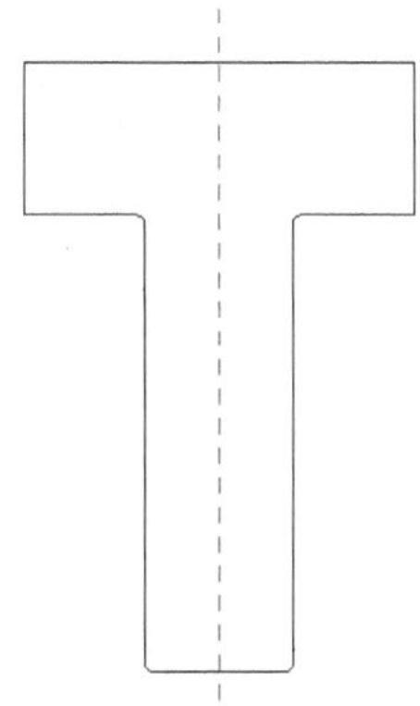

Figure 16-58 Block after converting the vertical line into a construction line

7. Choose the **Equal** tool from the **Geometric** panel and apply the equal constraints between fillets, chamfers, vertical lines tangential to fillets, horizontal lines tangential to fillets, and vertical lines at the top.

8. Choose the **Symmetric** tool from the **Geometric** panel and apply the symmetric constraints between all entities on either side of the construction line.

9. Hide all geometric constraints by choosing the **Hide All** button from the **Geometric** panel of the **Block Editor**.

10. Apply the dimensional constraints by using the tools in the **Dimensional** panel of the **Block Editor**. Figure 16-59 shows the sketch with all dimensional constraints applied. Also, make sure that you snap the end points of the vertical line while applying constraints to the base diameter and to the length of the bolt.

You can observe the grips (arrow) for every dimensional constraint. You need to hide them.

11. Select all dimensional constraints and invoke the **PROPERTIES** palette. In the **Misc** rollout, change the **Number of Grips** to 0.

12. Choose the **Parameters Manager** button from the **Manage** panel; the **PARAMETERS MANAGER** palette is displayed.

Next, you need to rename the constraints in the **Name** column of the **PROPERTIES MANAGER** palette, as shown in Figure 16-60.

13. To rename a constraint, select it in the **Name** column and press the F2 key or double-click on the respective field; an edit box will be displayed. Change the name of the constraint.

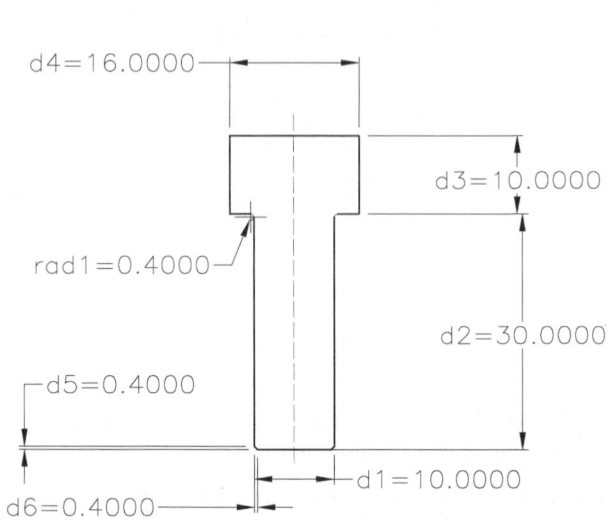

Figure 16-59 Sketch with all dimensional constraints

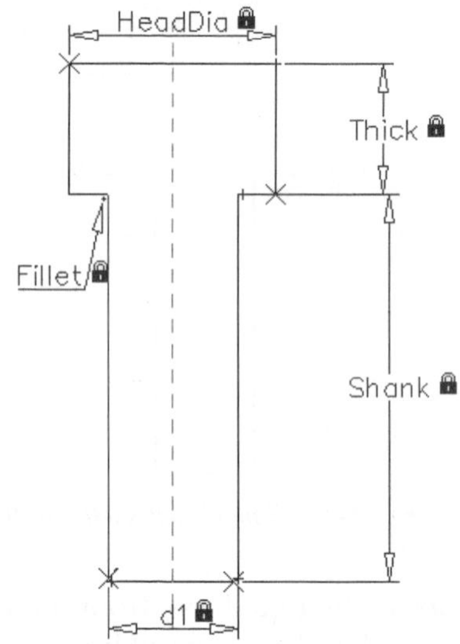

Figure 16-60 New name of the constraints

14. Apply a new expression to each renamed constraint, as shown in Figure 16-61. The **PARAMETERS MANAGER** palette after renaming the constraints and applying appropriate expressions is shown in Figure 16-61.

15. Choose the **Block Table** tool from the **Dimensional** panel of the **Block Editor**; you are prompted to specify the parameter location.

16. Select the midpoint of the horizontal line at the bottom; you are prompted to specify the number of grips.

17. Enter **1** and press ENTER; the **Block Properties Table** dialog box is displayed.

18. Choose the **Creates a new user parameter and adds it to the table** button; the **New Parameter** dialog box is displayed.

19. Enter **Size** in the **Name** edit box. Next, select the **String** option from the **Type** drop-down list and choose the **OK** button; a new column named **Size** is added to the **Block Properties Table** dialog box.

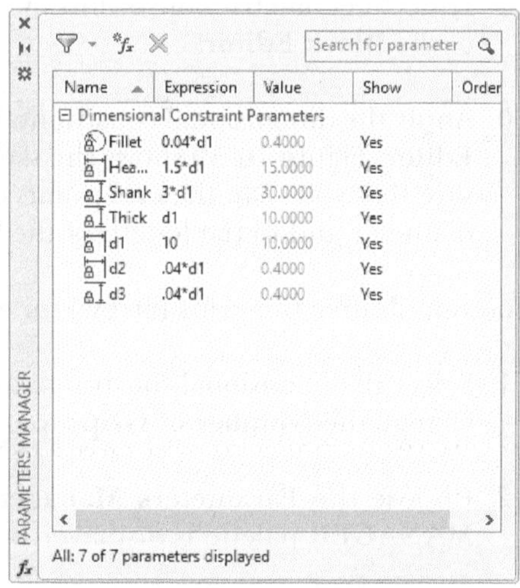

*Figure 16-61 The **PARAMETERS MANAGER** palette*

20. Choose the **Adds properties which appear as columns in the table** button from the **Block Properties Table** dialog box; the **Add Parameter Properties** dialog box is displayed.

21. Select the **d1** parameter and choose the **OK** button; the selected parameter is added to the **Block Properties Table** dialog box.

22. Clear the **Block properties must match a row in the table** check box, if not cleared already.

23. Enter the following values in the **Size** and **d1** columns:

Size	d1
M6	6
M10	10
M12.5	12.5
M15	15
M18	18
M24	24
M25	25

24. Choose the **Audits the block property table for errors** button; a message box is displayed stating that no errors have been found.

25. Close the message box and choose the **OK** button from the **Block Properties Table** dialog box; the **Size** parameter is added to the **PARAMETERS MANAGER** palette under the **User Parameters** node.

26. Now, you need to test the block by invoking the **Test Block Window**. To do so, choose the **Test Block** tool from the **Open/Save** panel of the **Block Editor**; the **Test Block Window** is opened. You can view the name of the new window at the title bar.

27. Select the block; the block is displayed in dashed lines and two grips are also displayed, one at the insertion point of the block and other at the midpoint of the horizontal line at the bottom. The triangular grip at the midpoint is known as lookup grip.

28. Click on the lookup grip; a shortcut menu is displayed.

29. Choose different sizes and check whether the block resizes without any error.

30. After checking the block, choose the **Close Test Block** button from the **Close** panel; the **Block Editor** is displayed.

31. Choose the **Close Block Editor** button to close the block editor; a message box is displayed.

32. Choose the **Save changes and exit the Block Editor** option from the message box.

33. Select the block and click on the lookup grip; different possible sizes are displayed. Select the required size.

34. Save the drawing and exit.

Note

In this example, the block has been created without creating a fully-defined sketch. But it is recommended to create a fully-defined sketch while working with dynamic blocks.

Self-Evaluation Test

Answer the following questions and then compare them to those given at the end of this chapter:

1. The __________ command lets you create a drawing file (*.dwg* extension) of a block defined in the current drawing.

2. The __________ command can be used to change the name of a block.

3. The __________ tool is used to place an existing block in a drawing.

4. You can delete the unreferenced blocks using the __________ command.

5. You can use the __________ to locate, preview, copy, and insert blocks or existing drawings into the current drawing.

6. The __________ command is used for in-place reference editing.

7. Individual objects in a block cannot be erased using the **Block Editor**. (T/F)

8. A block can be mirrored by providing a scale factor of -1 for X. (T/F)

9. You cannot redefine any existing block. (T/F)

10. An entire drawing can be converted into a block. (T/F)

Review Questions

Answer the following questions:

1. Which one of the following actions cannot be assigned to the **Point** parameter?

   (a) **Move** (b) **Array**
   (c) **Stretch** (d) None of these

2. Which of the following commands is used to get back the objects that consist of a block and have been removed from the drawing?

   (a) **OOPS** (b) **BLIPS**
   (c) **BLOCK** (d) **UNDO**

3. By what amount is a block rotated, if the value of both the X and Y scale factors is -1?

   (a) 90 (b) 180
   (c) 270 (d) 360

4. When you insert a drawing into the current drawing, how many blocks belonging to the inserted drawing are brought into the current drawing?

   (a) 1 (b) 2
   (c) All (d) None

5. The _________ command is used to create a rectangular array of a block.

6. The _________ tab of the **BLOCK AUTHORING PALETTES** allows you to insert a parameter set.

7. The automatic save feature is _________ during in-place reference editing.

8. You cannot use the **REFEDIT** command on blocks inserted using the _________ command.

9. The Layer 0 and the Continuous linetype _________ be renamed using the **RENAME** command.

10. The **Entire drawing** option of the **Write Block** tool has the same effect as the **PURGE** command. (T/F)

11. The objects in a block inherit the properties of the layer on which they are drawn, such as color and linetype. (T/F)

12. If the objects forming a block are drawn with linetype **BYLAYER**, then at the time of the insertion, each object that makes up a block is drawn with the linetype **BYLAYER**. (T/F)

13. Objects created with the special color **BYBLOCK** are generated with the color that was current at the time the block was inserted. (T/F)

14. In the array generated with the **MINSERT** command, there is no way to change the number of rows or columns or the spacing between them after insertion. (T/F)

Exercise 7 — *Block*

Draw part (a) of Figure 16-62 and define it as a block named B. Next, using the relevant insertion method, generate the pattern as shown in the same figure. Note that the pattern is rotated at 30 degrees.

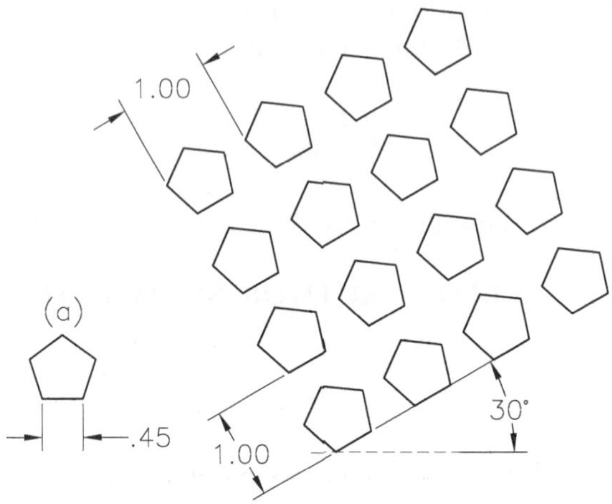

Figure 16-62 Drawing for Exercise 7

Exercise 8 — *Block*

Draw Block A given in Figure 16-63 and define it as a block named Chair. The dimensions of the chair can be referred from the Problem Solving Exercise 4 of Chapter 5. Next, using the block insert command, insert the chair around the table as shown in the same figure.

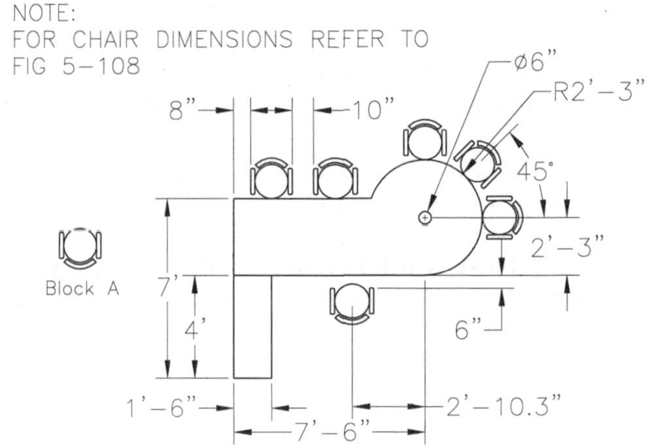

Figure 16-63 Drawing for Exercise 8

Exercise 9 Constraints to Block

Create the sketch of a bolt as shown in Figure 16-64. Next, convert it to a block and apply constraints such that you can create bolts of diameter 6, 10, 12.5, 15, 18, 24, and 25.

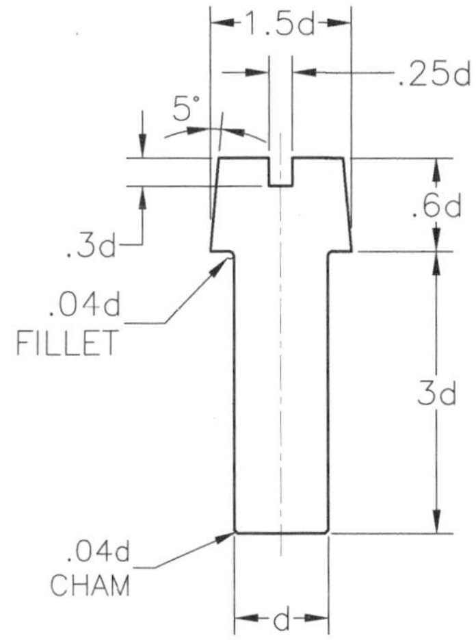

Figure 16-64 Drawing for Exercise 9

Problem-Solving Exercise 1

Create the drawing shown in Figure 16-65.

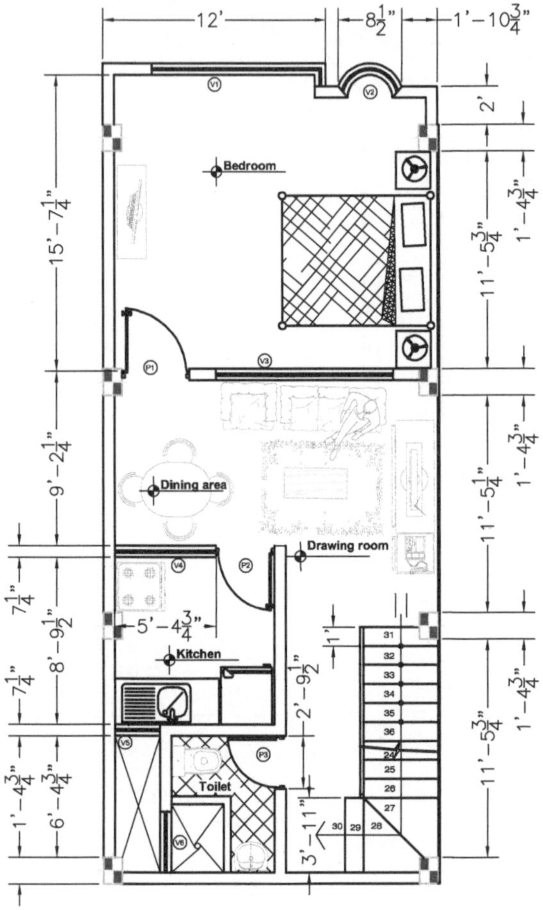

NOTES:
1. All door openings are of 3'.
2. All windows openings are of 5'.
3. All walls measures 9".
4. Assume other missing dimensions depending upon standards.

Figure 16-65 Drawing for Problem-Solving Exercise 1

Answers to Self-Evaluation Test

1. **WBLOCK**, **2.** **RENAME**, **3.** **Insert**, **4.** **PURGE**, **5.** **DESIGNCENTER**, **6.** REFEDIT, **7.** F, **8.** T, **9.** F, **10.** T

Chapter 17

Defining Block Attributes

Learning Objectives

After completing this chapter, you will be able to:

- *Understand block attributes*
- *Create annotative block attributes*
- *Edit attribute tag names*
- *Insert blocks with attributes and assign values to attributes*
- *Extract attribute values from inserted blocks*
- *Control attribute visibility*
- *Perform editing of attributes*
- *Insert a text file in a drawing to create Bill Of Materials*

Key Terms

- *Attribute Definition*
- *Block Attribute Manager*
- *Data Extraction*
- *ATTDISP*
- *EATTEDIT*
- *-ATTEDIT*
- *REFEDIT*

UNDERSTANDING ATTRIBUTES

AutoCAD has provided a facility that allows the user to attach information to blocks. This information can then be retrieved and processed by other programs for various purposes. For example, you can use this information to create a bill of material for a project, find the total number of computers in a building, or determine the location of each block in a drawing. Attributes can also be used to create blocks (such as title blocks) with prompted or preformatted text, to control text placement. The information associated with a block is known as attribute value or attribute. AutoCAD references the attributes with a block through tag names.

Before assigning attributes to a block, you must create an attribute definition by using the **Define Attributes** tool. The attribute definition describes the characteristics of the attribute. You can define several attribute definitions (tags) and include them in the block definition. Each time you insert a block, AutoCAD will prompt you to enter the value of the attribute. The attribute value automatically replaces the attribute tag name. The information (attribute values) assigned to a block can be extracted and written to a file by using **Extract Data** tool. This file can then be inserted in the drawing as a table or processed by other programs to analyze the data. The attribute values can be edited by using the tools in the **Edit Attribute** drop-down.

DEFINING ATTRIBUTES

Ribbon: Insert > Block Definition > Define Attributes	**Command:** ATTDEF/ATT

When you invoke the **Define Attributes** tool, the **Attribute Definition** dialog box will be displayed, as shown in Figure 17-1. The block attributes can be defined using this dialog box. When creating an attribute definition, you must define the Mode, Attribute, Insertion Point, and Text Settings for each attribute. All these information can be entered in the dialog box. The following is the description of each area of the **Attribute Definition** dialog box:

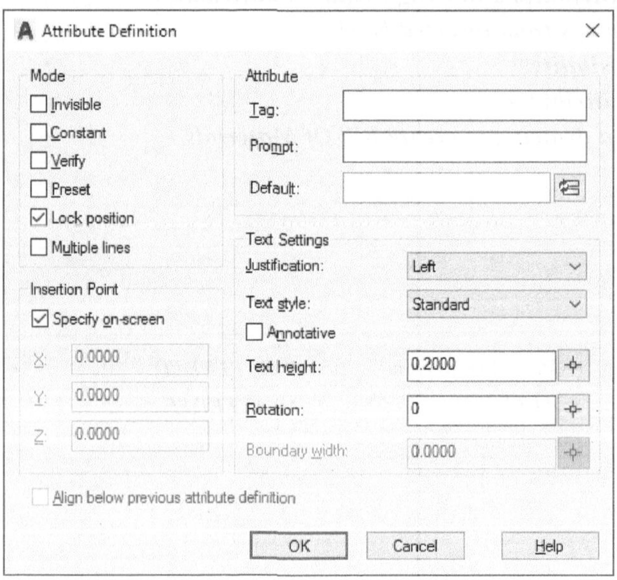

Figure 17-1 *The* ***Attribute Definition*** *dialog box*

Mode Area

The **Mode** area of the **Attribute Definition** dialog box has six check boxes: **Invisible**, **Constant**, **Verify**, **Preset**, **Lock position**, and **Multiple lines**. These check boxes determine the display and edit features of the block attributes. For example, if you select the **Invisible** check box, the attribute becomes invisible which means, it is not displayed on the screen. Similarly, if the **Constant** check box is selected, the attribute becomes constant. This means that its value is predefined and cannot be changed. These options are described next.

Invisible

This option allows you to create an attribute that is not visible on the screen. Select this check box if you want the attribute to be invisible.

Constant

This option allows you to create an attribute that has a fixed value and cannot be changed after block insertion.

Verify

This option allows you to verify the attribute value you have entered when inserting a block by asking you twice for the data.

Preset

This option allows you to create an attribute that is automatically set to the default value. The attribute values are not requested when you insert a block and the default values are used. But unlike a constant attribute, the preset attribute value can be edited later.

Lock position

This check box is selected by default. As a result, the position of the attributes with respect to the block object is locked. In case of non-dynamic blocks, if the attributes are created with the **Lock position** check box cleared, then a separate grip will be displayed on that attribute. This grip can be used to modify the location of the attribute. When the dynamic blocks are created with the **Lock position** check box cleared, the separate grip does not get displayed on the attribute. Besides this, the attribute cannot be manipulated by the parameters and action.

Multiple lines

Select this check box to specify that the default value of the attribute may be a single-line or multiple line text.

Attribute Area

The **Attribute** area, refer to Figure 17-2, of the **Attribute Definition** dialog box has three edit boxes: **Tag**, **Prompt**, and **Default**, where you can enter values. The three edit boxes have been described next.

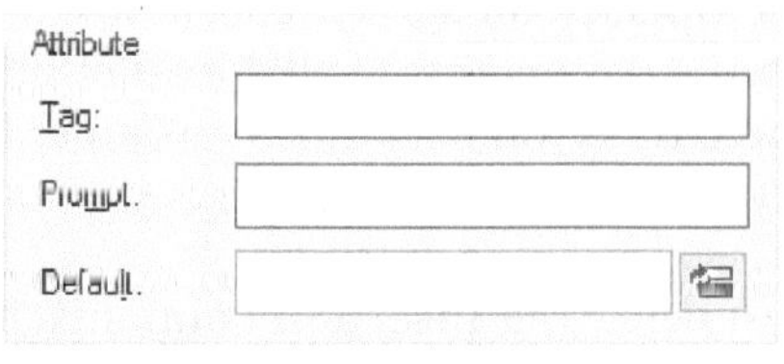

*Figure 17-2 The **Attribute** area of the **Attribute Definition** dialog box*

Tag

This is like a label that is used to identify an attribute. For example, the tag name COMPUTER can be used to identify an item. The tag names specified in lowercase letters are automatically converted into uppercase when displayed. The tag name cannot be null. Also, it must not contain any blank spaces.

Prompt

The text that you enter in the **Prompt** edit box is used as a prompt when you insert a block that contains the defined attribute. For example, if COMPUTER is the tag, you can enter WHAT IS THE MEMORY? or ENTER MEMORY: in the **Prompt** edit box. AutoCAD will then prompt you with this same statement when you insert the block with which the attribute is defined. If you have selected the **Constant** check box in the **Mode** area, the **Prompt** edit box is not available because no prompt is required if the attribute is constant. If you do not enter anything in the **Prompt** edit box, the entry made in the **Tag** edit box is used as the prompt.

Default

The entry in the **Default** edit box defines the default value of the specified attribute. If you do not enter a value, the attribute takes the value entered in the **Tag** edit box. The entry of a value is optional.

Insert Field

This button is used to insert a field as the value of the attribute. When you choose this button, the **Field** dialog box is displayed that can be used to insert the required field.

Multiline Editor

This button is displayed in place of the **Insert Field** button when the **Multiple lines** check box is selected from the **Mode** area. Choose this button to invoke the **Text Formatting** toolbar on the screen. You can enter the text that you want to assign as the default value of the attribute in the text window.

Note

*The **Text Formatting** toolbar displayed here has some commonly used options only. The full **Text Formatting** toolbar can be displayed by changing the value of the **ATTIPE** system variable to 1.*

Insertion Point Area

The **Insertion Point** area, refer to Figure 17-3, of the **Attribute Definition** dialog box allows you to define the insertion point of the block attribute text. You can define the insertion point by entering the values in the **X**, **Y**, and **Z** edit boxes or by specifying it on the screen. To specify the insertion point on the screen, select the **Specify on-screen** check box if not selected by default. Now, set the parameters in all the other fields and areas and then choose the **OK** button; you will be prompted to select the start point of the attribute.

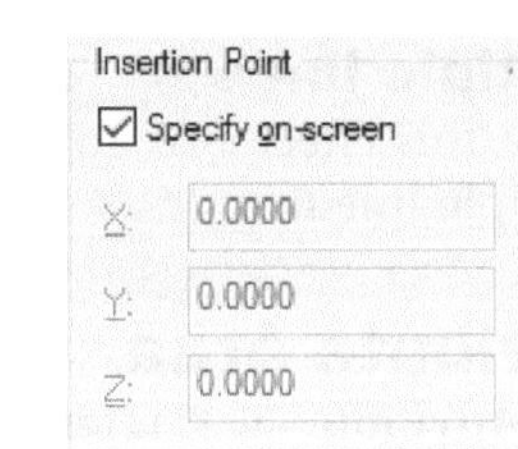

***Figure 17-3** The **Insertion Point** area*

Just below the **Insertion Point** area of the dialog box, their is a check box labeled **Align below previous attribute definition**. This check box is not available when you use the **Attribute Definition** dialog box for the first time. After you have defined an attribute and when you press ENTER to display the **Attribute Definition** dialog box again, this check box is available.

You can select this check box to place the subsequent attribute text just below the previously defined attribute automatically. When you select this check box, the **Insertion Point** area and the **Text Settings** areas of the dialog box are not available and AutoCAD assumes previously defined values for text such as text height, text style, text justification, and text rotation. The text is automatically placed on the following line.

Text Settings Area

The **Text Settings** area of the **Attribute Definition** dialog box allows you to control the justification, text style, annotation property, height, rotation, and boundary width of the attribute text, refer to Figure 17-4. To set the text justification, select a justification type from the **Justification** drop-down list. The default option is **Left** for the single line text and **Top left** for the multiline text. Similarly, you can use the **Text style** drop-down list to select a text style. All the text styles defined in the current drawing are displayed in the **Text style** drop-down list. The default text style is **Standard**. To write annotative attributes, select the **Annotative** text style from the **Text style** drop-down list. Select the **Annotative** check box to assign the annotative property to the attribute text. The annotative attributes can be attached to both the annotative or non-annotative blocks. You can specify the text height and text rotation in the **Text height** and **Rotation** edit boxes, respectively. You can also define the text height by choosing the **Text Height** button. When you choose this button, AutoCAD temporarily exits the **Attribute Definition** dialog box and allows you to enter the height value by selecting points on the screen or from the command prompt. Once the height on the screen is defined, the **Attribute Definition** dialog box will reappear and the defined text height will be displayed in the edit box. Similarly, you can define the text rotation by choosing the **Rotation** button and then selecting points on the screen or by entering the rotation angle at the command prompt. The **Boundary width** edit box is used to specify the maximum width for the multiline text. If the width of the text line is more than this value, the text will automatically go to the second line. This edit box will be available only when you select the **Multiple lines** check box from the **Mode** area.

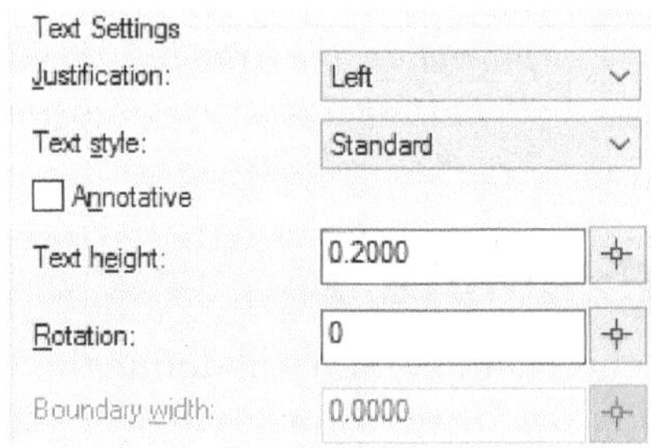

*Figure 17-4 The **Text Settings** area of the **Attribute Definition** dialog box*

Note

1. *The text style must be defined before it can be used to specify the text.*

2. *If you select a style that has a predefined height, AutoCAD automatically disables the **Text height** edit box.*

3. *If you have selected the **Align** option from the **Justification** drop-down list, the **Insertion Point** area, the **Text height**, and the **Rotation** edit boxes in the **Text Settings** area will be disabled.*

4. *If you have selected the **Fit** option from the **Justification** drop-down list, the **Insertion Point** area and the **Rotation** edit box are disabled. To specify the location of the attribute, choose the **OK** button from the dialog box; you will be prompted to specify the first and second endpoints of the text baseline. Specify the point; the text will fit between the two endpoints that you specify.*

After you complete the settings in the **Attribute Definition** dialog box and choose the **OK** button, the attribute tag text is inserted in the drawing at the specified insertion point. Now, you can use the **Create Block** tool to select all the objects and attributes to define a block.

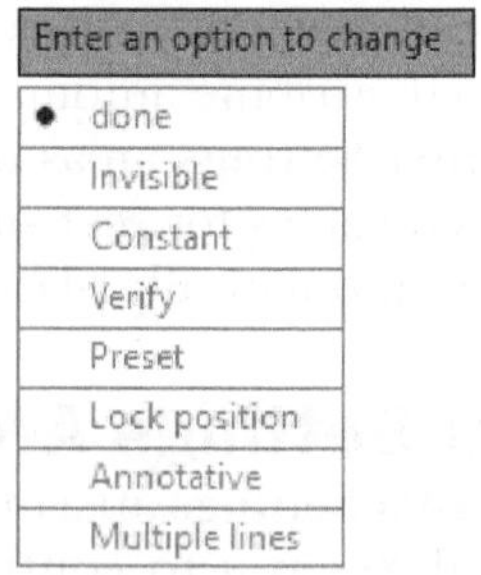

***Figure 17-5** Dynamic prompt for the **-ATTDEF** command*

Note

*You can use the **-ATTDEF** command to display the dynamic prompt in the drawing area. The options in the **Attribute Definition** dialog box are available through the dynamic prompt too, refer to Figure 17-5.*

Example 1 — Attribute Definition

In this example, you will define the following attributes for a computer and then create a block using the **Create Block** tool. The name of the block is COMP.

Mode	Tag name	Prompt	Default value
Constant	ITEM		Computer
Preset, Verify	MAKE	Enter make:	CAD-CIM
Verify	PROCESSOR	Enter processor type:	Unknown
Verify	HD	Enter Hard-Drive size:	40 GB
Invisible, Verify	RAM	Enter RAM:	256 MB

1. Draw the sketch of a computer and convert it into a block, as shown in Figure 17-6. Assume the dimensions, or measure the dimensions of the computer you are using for AutoCAD.

2. Choose the **Define Attributes** tool from the **Block Definition** panel in the **Insert** tab; the **Attribute Definition** dialog box is displayed.

3. Define the first attribute shown in the preceding table. Select the **Constant** check box in the **Mode** area. In the **Tag** edit box, enter the tag name, **ITEM**. Similarly, enter **COMPUTER** in the **Default** edit box. Note that the **Prompt** edit box is not available because the mode is constant.

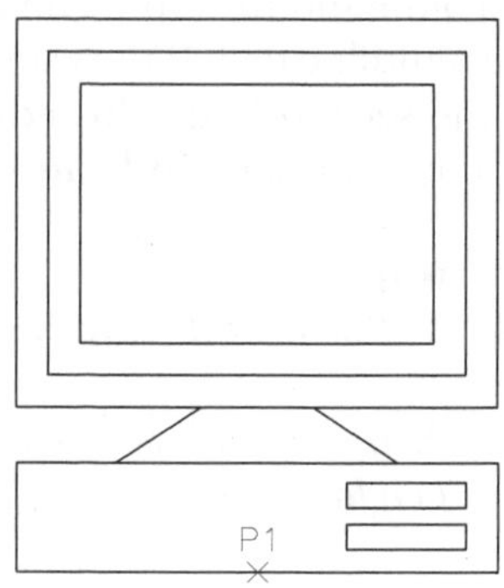

***Figure 17-6** Drawing for Example 1*

4. In the **Insertion Point** area, select the **Specify on-screen** check box to define the text insertion point, if not selected by default.

5. In the **Text Settings** area, specify the justification, style, annotative property, height, and rotation of the text.

6. Choose the **OK** button once you have entered information in the **Attribute Definition** dialog box. Select a point below the insertion base point (P1) of the computer to place the text.

7. Press ENTER to invoke the **Attribute Definition** dialog box again. Enter the mode and attribute information for the second attribute as shown in the table at the beginning of Example 1. You need not define the insertion point and text options again. Select the **Align below previous attribute definition** check box that is located just below the **Insertion Point** area. Now, choose the **OK** button. AutoCAD places the attribute text just below the previous attribute text.

8. Similarly, define the remaining attributes also, refer to Figure 17-7.

9. Now, use the **Create Block** tool to create a block. Make sure that the **Retain** radio button is selected in the **Objects** area. The name of the block is **COMP**, and the insertion point of the block is P1, midpoint of the base. When you select objects for the block, make sure you also select attributes.

10. Insert the block created. You will notice that the order of prompts is the same as the order of attributes selection.

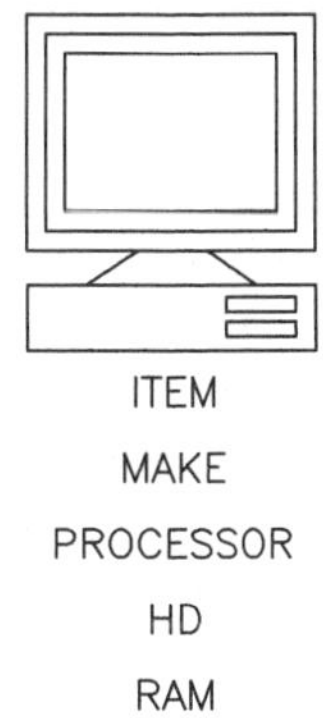

Figure 17-7 *Attributes defined below the computer drawing*

EDITING ATTRIBUTE DEFINITION

Menu Bar: Modify > Object > Text > Edit **Command:** TEXTEDIT

You can edit the text and attribute definitions before you define a block, using the **Edit** tool from the **Modify > Object > Text** menu. After invoking this tool, AutoCAD will prompt you to **Select an annotation object or [Undo/Mode]**. If you select an attribute, then the **Edit Attribute Definition** dialog box is displayed, as shown in Figure 17-8.

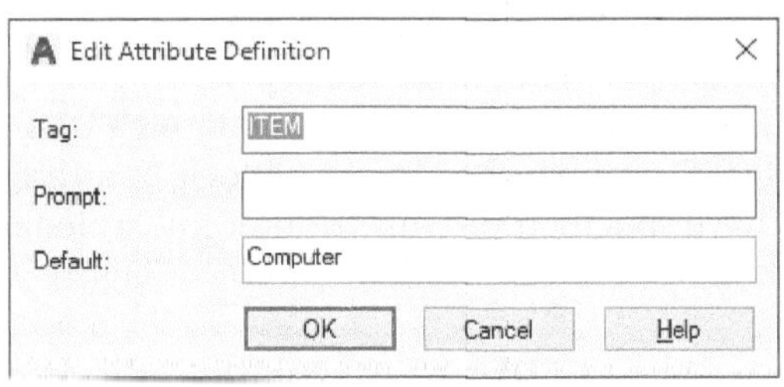

Figure 17-8 *The* ***Edit Attribute Definition*** *dialog box*

You can also invoke the **Edit Attribute Definition** dialog box by double-clicking on the attribute definition. You can enter the new values in the respective edit boxes. Once you have entered the changed values, choose the **OK** button in the dialog box. If you have selected the **Multiple** option in the mode of **TEXTEDIT** command, AutoCAD will continue to prompt you to select an annotation object. If you have finished editing and do not want to select another attribute object to edit, press ENTER to exit the command.

Using the PROPERTIES Palette

The **Properties** tool has already been discussed in Chapter 4. It can also be used to edit defined attributes. Select the attribute to be modified and right-click to display a shortcut menu. Next, choose the **Properties** option from the shortcut menu; the **PROPERTIES** palette will be displayed, as shown in Figure 17-9. You will notice that **Attribute Definition** is displayed in the drop-down located at the top of the palette. Also, you will find that all properties of the selected attribute are displayed under four headings. They are **General**, **3D Visualization**, **Text**, and **Misc**. You can change these values in their corresponding fields. For example, you can modify the color, layer, linetype, thickness, linetype scale, and so on, of the selected attribute under the **General** head. Similarly, you can modify the tag name, prompt, and value of the selected attribute in the **Tag**, **Prompt**, and **Value** fields under the **Text** heading. Under the **Text** head, you can also modify the text style, justification, annotation scale, text height, rotation angle, width factor, and make the angle values of the selected attribute oblique.

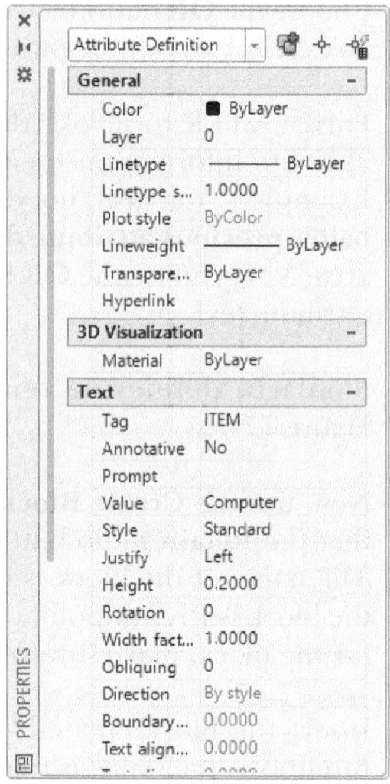

Figure 17-9 The PROPERTIES palette to modify attributes

You can also determine if you want the attribute text to appear upside down or backwards or not under the **Misc** heading. Here, you can also modify the attribute modes, which have been already defined. When you select a particular mode, for example **Invisible**, a drop-down list is available in the corresponding field. This list displays two options, **Yes** and **No**. If you select **Yes**, the attribute becomes invisible and if you select **No**, the attribute becomes visible. To select a particular mode, you should choose **Yes** from their corresponding drop-down lists.

INSERTING BLOCKS WITH ATTRIBUTES

The value of the attributes can be specified during block insertion, either at the command prompt or in the **Edit Attributes** dialog box, if the system variable **ATTDIA** is set to **1**. When you use the **Insert** tool or the **-INSERT** command to insert a block in a drawing (discussed earlier in Chapter 16), and after you have specified the insertion point, scale factors, and rotation angle, the **Edit Attributes** dialog box will be displayed, as shown in Figure 17-10.

If the value of the system variable **ATTDIA** is set to **0,** the **Edit Attributes** dialog box will be disabled and the prompts and their default values, which you had specified with the attribute definition, are then displayed at the command prompt after you have specified the insertion point, scale, and rotation angle for the block to be inserted.

In the **Edit Attributes** dialog box, the prompts that were entered at the time of attribute definition in the dialog box are displayed with their default values in the corresponding fields. If an attribute has been defined with the **Constant** mode, it is not displayed in the dialog box because a constant attribute value cannot be edited. You can enter the attribute values in the fields located next to the attribute prompt. If no new values are specified, the default values are displayed. If there are more attributes, they can be accessed by using the **Next** or **Previous** button. The block name is displayed at the top of the dialog box. After entering the new attribute values, choose the **OK** button. AutoCAD will place these attribute values at the specified location.

Figure 17-10 *The* ***Edit Attributes*** *dialog box*

Tip

1. It is convenient to use the ***Edit Attributes*** *dialog box because you can view all the attribute values at a glance and can correct them before placing. Therefore, it is a good idea to set the* ***ATTDIA*** *value to 1 (if not already set as 1), before you insert a block with attributes.*

2. Attributes can also be defined from the command prompt by setting the system variable ***ATTDIA*** *to 0. Now, when you choose the* ***Insert*** *tool, AutoCAD does not display the* ***Edit Attributes*** *dialog box. Instead, AutoCAD prompts you to enter the attribute values for various attributes that have been defined in the block at the pointer input.*

Example 2

In this example, you will insert the block (COMP) that was defined in Example 1. The following is the list of the attribute values for computers:

ITEM	MAKE	PROCESSOR	HD	RAM
Computer	Gateway	486-60	150 MB	16 MB
Computer	Zenith	486-30	100 MB	32 MB

Computer	IBM	386-30	80 MB	8 MB
Computer	Dell	586-60	450 MB	64 MB
Computer	CAD-CIM	Pentium-90	100 Min	32 MB
Computer	CAD-CIM	Unknown	600 MB	Standard

1. Draw the floor plan shown in Figure 17-11 (assume the dimensions).

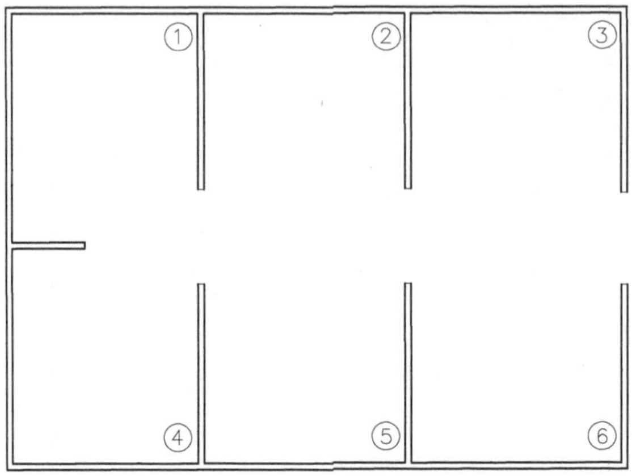

Figure 17-11 *Floor plan drawing for Example 2*

2. Choose the **Insert** tool available in the **Blocks** panel in the **Insert** tab to insert the blocks. When you invoke the **Insert** tool, the **Insert** dialog box is displayed. Enter **COMP** in the **Name** edit box and choose the **OK** button to exit the dialog box. Select an insertion point on screen to insert the block. After you specify the insertion point, the **Edit Attributes** dialog box is displayed. In this dialog box, you can specify the attribute values, if you need to, in the different edit boxes.

3. Choose the **Insert** tool again to insert other blocks and define their attribute values, as shown in Figure 17-12.

4. Save the drawing for further use.

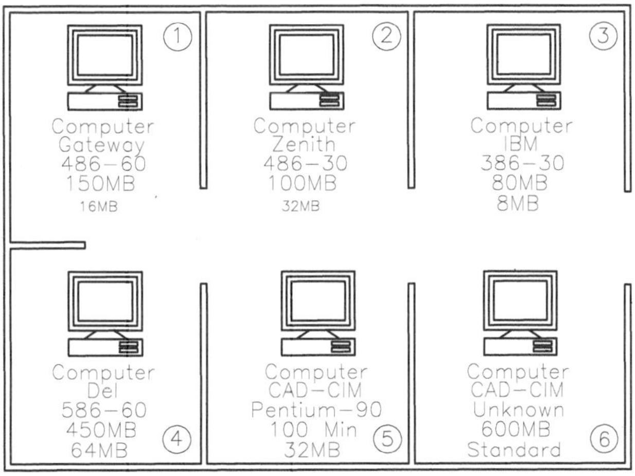

***Figure 17-12** The floor plan after inserting blocks and defining their attributes*

MANAGING ATTRIBUTES

Ribbon: Insert > Block Definition > Manage Attributes **Command:** BATTMAN
Menu Bar: Modify > Object > Attribute > Block Attribute Manager

The **Manage Attributes** tool allows you to manage attribute definitions for blocks in the current drawing through the **Block Attribute Manager** dialog box. This dialog box is shown in Figure 17-13. If the attribute that is edited in the **Constant** mode, then changes in the default value of the attribute in the existing drawing can be seen. If the mode is other than **Constant**, the changes in the attribute can only be seen for new block insertions.

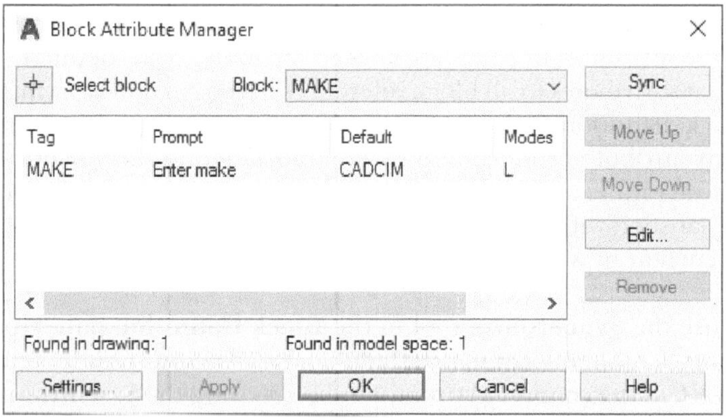

***Figure 17-13** The **Block Attribute Manager** dialog box*

When you invoke this tool, AutoCAD displays the number of blocks that exist in the current drawing below the list box in the dialog box. The block can be in the model space or in the layout. The names of the existing blocks in the current drawing are displayed in the **Block** drop-down list. Attributes of the selected block are displayed in the attribute list. By default, the **Tag**, **Prompt**, **Default**, **Modes**, and **Annotative** attribute properties are displayed in the attribute list. You can edit the attribute definitions in blocks, remove attributes from blocks, and change the order in which you were prompted for attribute values while inserting the block.

Select block

This button allows you to select a block from the drawing area whose attributes you want to edit. When you choose the **Select block** button, the dialog box closes temporarily until you select block from the drawing or cancel by pressing ESC. Once you have selected the block, the dialog box is displayed again. The name of the block you have selected is displayed in the **Block** drop-down list. If you modify the attributes of a block and then select a new block before saving the attribute changes, you will be prompted to save the changes before selecting another block through an alert message box, as shown in Figure 17-14.

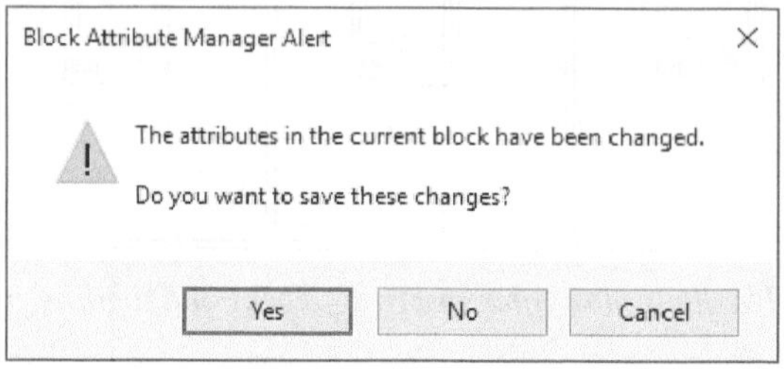

Figure 17-14 *The* ***Block Attribute Manager Alert*** *message box*

Block Drop-down List

This drop-down list in the **Block Attribute Manager** dialog box allows you to choose the block whose attributes you want to modify. It lists all the blocks in the current drawing that have attributes.

Sync

This button of the **Block Attribute Manager** dialog box allows you to update all instances of the selected block with the attribute properties currently defined. This does not affect any of the values assigned to attributes in each block when attributes were defined. On choosing this button, you can update attributes in all block references in the current drawing with the changes you made to the block definition. For example, you may have used the **Block Attribute Manager** dialog box to modify attribute properties of several block definitions in your drawing. But you do not want it to automatically update the existing block references when you made the changes. Now, when you are satisfied with the attribute changes you made, you can apply those changes to all blocks in the current drawing by using the **Sync** button.

You can also use the **Synchronize** tool in the **Block Definition** panel to update attribute properties in block references to match their block definition. This tool can also be invoked by entering **ATTSYNC** at the command prompt or by choosing the **Synchronize Attributes** tool from the **Modify II** toolbar.

Note

Changing the attribute properties of an existing block does not affect the values assigned to the block. For example, in a block containing an attribute whose Tag is Cost and default value is 200, the default value 200 remains unaffected, if the Tag is changed to UnitCost.

Move Up

This button moves the selected attribute tag earlier in the prompt sequence. Now, when you insert the block, the attribute you have just moved up will appear earlier in the prompt sequence. The **Move Up** button is not available when a constant attribute is selected and if the attribute is at the top most position in the attribute list.

Move Down

This button moves the selected attribute tag later in the prompt sequence. The **Move Down** button is not available when a constant attribute is selected and when the attribute is at the bottom position in the attribute list.

Edit

This button allows you to modify the attribute properties. To edit the attribute definition in blocks, select the attribute and then choose **Edit** from the dialog box; the **Edit Attribute** dialog box will be displayed.

Note

*To edit an attribute, you can also double-click on the attribute or choose the **Single** tool from **Home > Block > Edit Attributes** drop-down. Then, select the attribute to display the **Enhanced Attribute Editor** dialog box.*

The options in the **Edit Attribute** dialog box are discussed next.

Attribute Tab

The options under the **Attribute** tab of the **Edit Attribute** dialog box are used to modify the mode and data of attributes, refer to Figure 17-15. The options under the **Mode** area can be selected for the block. The **Data** area of the dialog box has three edit boxes: **Tag**, **Prompt**, and **Default**, where you can enter the data to be changed.

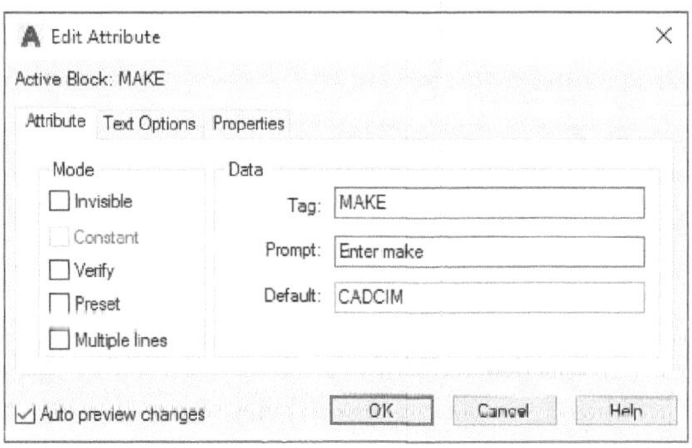

*Figure 17-15 The **Attribute** tab of the **Edit Attribute** dialog box*

Text Options Tab

The options under this tab are used to set the properties that define the way an attribute's text is displayed in the drawing, refer to Figure 17-16. The options in this tab are discussed next.

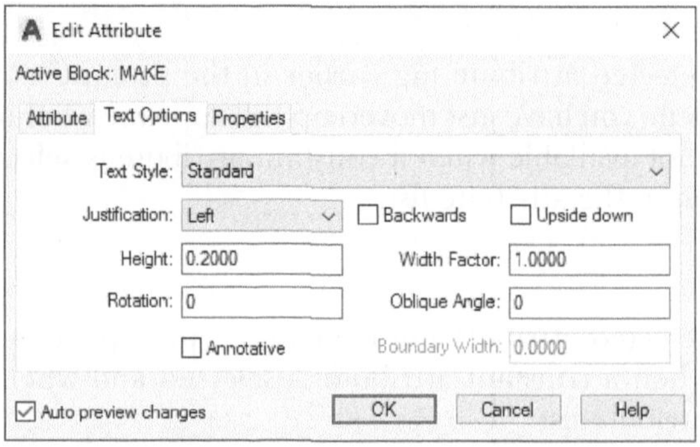

*Figure 17-16 The **Text Options** tab of the **Edit Attribute** dialog box*

Text Style: The options in this drop-down list are used to specify the text style for attribute text.

Justification: The options in this drop-down list are used to specify how attribute text is justified.

Height: This edit box is used to specify the height of the attribute text. If the height is defined in the current text style, this edit box is not available.

Rotation: This edit box is used to specify the rotation angle of the attribute text.

Backwards: This check box is used to specify whether or not the text is displayed backwards. Select this box to display the text backwards.

Upside down: This check box is used to specify whether or not the text is displayed upside down. Select this check box to display the text upside down.

Width Factor: This edit box is used to set the character spacing for attribute text. Entering a value less than 1.0 condenses the text and a value greater than 1.0 expands it.

Oblique Angle: This edit box is used to specify the angle at which the attribute text is slanted away from its vertical axis.

Annotative: This check box is used to convert the non-annotative attribute to the annotative attribute and vice-versa.

Boundary Width: This edit box sets the width of the boundary that will be displayed while writing the multiline text for the attributes' default value. The value specified here is the relative scale value. If you specify a value less than 1, it will decrease the boundary width. Whereas, if you specify a value more than 1, it will increase the boundary width. Accordingly, the paragraph width for the multiline text will increase or decrease. You can modify the value of the boundary width only when you select the **Multiple lines** check box from the **Mode** area of the **Attribute Definition** dialog box.

Properties Tab

The options under this tab of the **Edit Attribute** dialog box are used to define the layer, color, lineweight, and linetype of the attributes, refer to Figure 17-17. Also, if the drawing uses plot styles, you can assign a plot style to the attribute. The options of the **Properties** tab are discussed next.

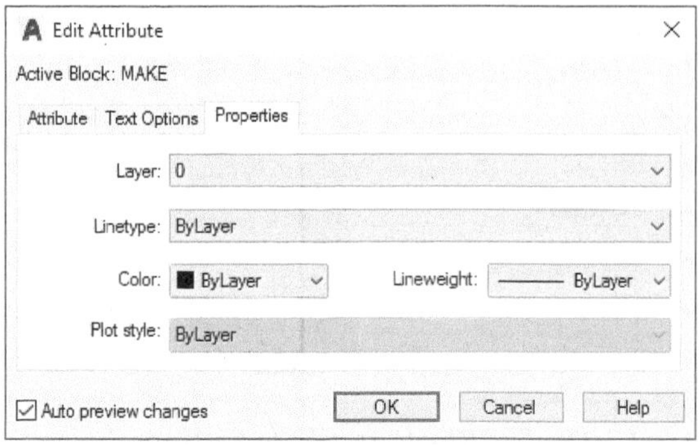

Figure 17-17 The ***Properties*** *tab of the* ***Edit Attribute*** *dialog box*

Layer: The layer(s) on which the attribute is defined is displayed in this drop-down list. You can also change the layer of the selected attribute using this drop-down list.

Linetype: The options in this drop-down list are used to specify the linetype of attribute text.

Color: The options in this drop-down list are used to specify the attribute's text color.

Lineweight: The options in this drop-down list are used to specify the lineweight of attribute text. The changes you make to this option do not come into effect if the **LWDISPLAY** system variable is off.

Plot Style: The options in this drop-down list are used to specify the plot style of the attribute. If the current drawing uses color-dependent plot styles, the **Plot style** list in this dialog box is not available.

Auto preview changes

This check box controls whether or not the drawing area is immediately updated to display any visible attribute changes you make. If the **Auto preview changes** check box is selected, changes are immediately visible. If this check box is cleared, changes are not immediately visible.

> **Tip**
> *The buttons such as* ***Move Up, Move Down, Edit, Remove,*** *and* ***Settings*** *can also be invoked by using the shortcut menu which appears by right-clicking on the attributes in the attribute list in the* ***Block Attribute Manager*** *dialog box.*

Settings

Choosing this button from the **Block Attribute Manager** opens the **Block Attribute Settings** dialog box, as shown in Figure 17-18, where you can customize how attribute information is listed in the **Block Attribute Manager**.

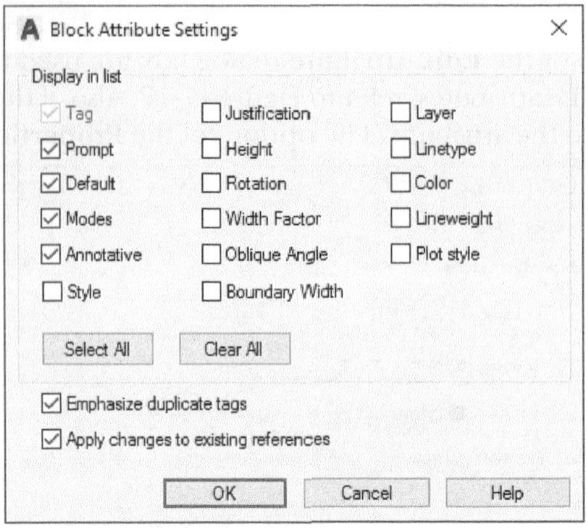

*Figure 17-18 The **Block Attribute Settings** dialog box*

Display in list

You can specify the attribute properties you want to be displayed in the list by selecting the check boxes available in this area of the **Block Attribute Settings** dialog box. This area shows the check boxes of all the properties that are displayed in the attribute list. Only the check boxes of the properties selected are displayed in the attribute list. These properties can be viewed in the attribute list by scrolling it. The **Tag** check box is always selected by default.

This area of the dialog box has two buttons, **Select All** and **Clear All**, which select and clear all the check boxes, respectively.

Emphasize duplicate tags

This check box turns duplicate tag emphasis on and off. If this check box is selected, duplicate attribute tags are displayed in red type in the attribute list. For example, if a block has PRICE as a tag more than once, the attribute PRICE will be displayed in red in the attribute list. If this check box is cleared, duplicate tags are not emphasized in the attribute list.

Apply changes to existing references

This check box is used to specify whether or not to update all existing instances of the block whose attributes you are modifying. Therefore, if this check box is selected, all instances of the block with the new attribute definitions are updated. If this check box is cleared, only new insertions of the block with the new attribute definitions are displayed.

Use **Sync** in the **Block Attribute Manager** to apply changes immediately to existing block instances. This temporarily overrides the **Apply changes to existing references** option.

Tip

*If constant attributes or nested attribute blocks are affected by your changes, use the **REGEN** command to update the display of those blocks in the drawing area.*

Remove

This button removes the selected attribute from the block definition. If the **Apply changes to existing references** check box is selected in the **Block Attribute Settings** dialog box before you choose the **Remove** button, the attribute is removed from all instances of the block in the current drawing. If this check box is cleared before choosing the **Remove** button, the attribute is removed only from the attribute list and the blocks that will be inserted henceforth. You can remove attributes from block definitions and from all existing block references in the current drawing. Attributes removed from existing block references do not disappear in the drawing area until you regenerate the drawing using the **REGEN** command. You cannot remove all attributes from the block, at least one attribute should remain. However, if you want to remove all the attributes, you have to redefine the block.

Note that the **Remove** button is not available for blocks with only one attribute.

EXTRACTING ATTRIBUTES

Ribbon: Insert > Linking & Extraction > Data Extraction
Command: EATTEXT or DATAEXTRACTION

The **Extract Data** tool allows you to extract the block attribute information and property information such as drawing summary from single or multiple drawings. When this tool is invoked, the **Data Extraction** wizard is displayed, as shown in Figure 17-19. This wizard includes the following pages:

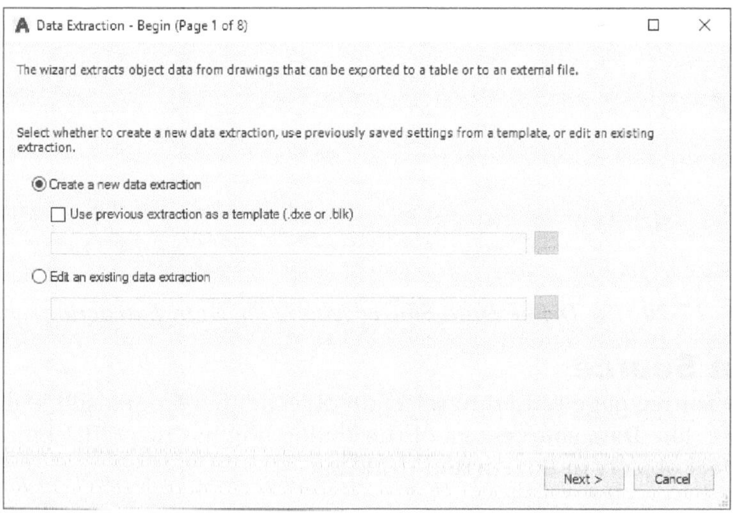

***Figure 17-19** The **Begin** page of the **Data Extraction** wizard*

Begin

The **Begin** page, refer to Figure 17-19, allows you to save extracted data to a new *.dxe* file or to modify an existing *.dxe* file. You can also use the saved *.dxe* or *.blk* file as the template for extracting data.

This wizard page has two radio buttons: **Create a new data extraction** and **Edit an existing data extraction**. If you select the **Use previous extraction as a template (.dxe or .blk)** check box, you will be allowed to select an existing template file. To select a template file, choose the Browse[...] button available on the right of the template name edit box. A .blk template file is a text file that allows you to specify the attribute and property values that you want to extract and the information about the drawing that you want to retrieve. The file can be created by using any text editor such as Notepad or WordPad. While using a *.blk* template file, you will be prompted to save the data extraction to a *.dxe* file to extract the information. Select the **Edit an existing data extraction** check box to modify an existing *.dxe* file. Now, you will be allowed to select the existing data file. To select a template file, choose the Browse[...] button available on the right of the template name edit box.

Choose the **Next** button from the **Begin** page of the **Data Extraction** wizard; the **Save Data Extraction As** dialog box will be invoked. Next, specify the desired name and location in this dialog box and choose the **Save** button; the **Define Data Source** page will be displayed, as shown in Figure 17-20.

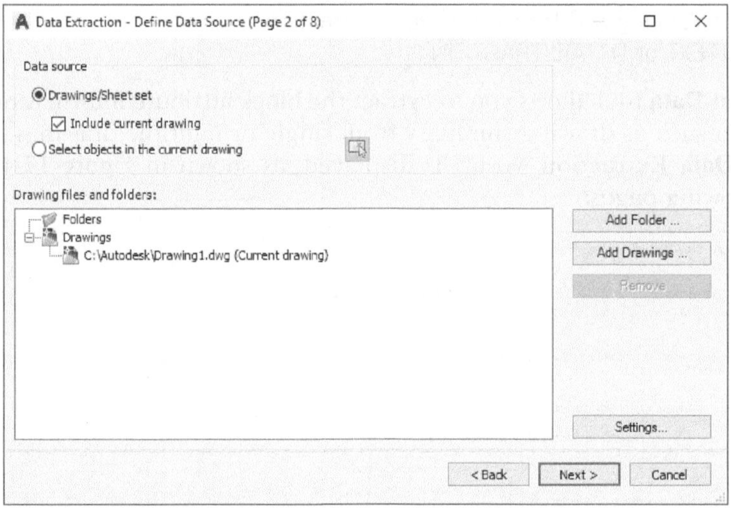

***Figure 17-20** The **Define Data Source** page of the **Data Extraction** wizard*

Define Data Source

The **Define Data Source** page is used to select an object either from a single drawing or from multiple drawings. The **Data source** area of this dialog box has two radio buttons: **Drawings/Sheet set** and **Select objects in the current drawing**.

Drawings/Sheet set

This radio button enables you to specify the drawings and folder from which you can extract the data. If this radio button is selected, the **Add Folder** and **Add Drawings** buttons will be enabled. The name of the drawings selected will be displayed with full path in the **Drawing files and folders** area.

Next, choose the **Add Folder** button; the **Add Folder Options** dialog box will be displayed, as shown in Figure 17-21. All drawings within the added folder will be considered for extracting data. To add a folder, choose the Browse[...] button available on the right of the **Folder** edit box. Select the **Automatically include new drawings added in this folder to the data extraction** check box in the **Options** area to automatically consider the new drawing added to this folder for data extraction. Select the **Include subfolders** check box to include the drawings within the sub-folders of the folder selected to be added. Select the **Utilize wild-card characters to select drawings** check box to include only the files matching the specified wild-card characters for data extraction. By default, *.dwg is used as the wild-card character and that is why, all the files with extension *.dwg* (all the drawing files) are considered for the data extraction. For example, if you want AutoCAD to consider all the drawing files having "computer" in their name, enter the wild-card character ***computer*.dwg**. Next, specify the desired settings and choose the **OK** button.

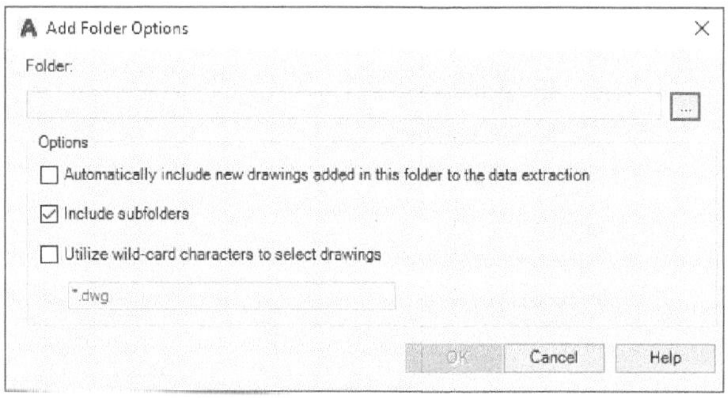

***Figure 17-21** The **Add Folder Options** dialog box*

Similarly, you can add a single drawing for the data extraction by choosing the **Add Drawings** button of the **Define Data Source** page of the **Data Extraction** wizard.

Select the **Include current drawing** check box in the **Define Data Source** page to add the current drawing for the data extraction including the folders and drawings.

Select objects in the current drawing

This radio button enables you to add the selected object from the current drawing for the data extraction. If you select this radio button, the **Select objects in the current drawing** button will be enabled. Choose this button to select the objects from the drawing.

Drawing files and folders

This area of the dialog box displays the tree view of all the drawing and folder names with their locations that are selected for the data extraction. All the drawing and folders are displayed under the **Folders** and **Drawings** heads respectively. Only the checked drawings under the folder are included for the data extraction. You can also remove the selected drawing or folder from the list of drawing to be used for data extraction. To remove the file or folder from the list of files and folders to be used for the data extraction, select them from the **Drawing files and folders** area and choose the **Remove** button.

Settings

Choose the **Settings** button from the **Define Data Source** page to invoke the **Data Extraction - Additional Settings** dialog box, as shown in Figure 17-22. This dialog box has two areas: **Extraction settings** and **Extract from**. By default, the **Extract objects from blocks** and **Extract objects from xrefs** check boxes are selected in the **Extraction settings** area. The first two check boxes allow you to specify whether you want to extract the block attribute information from the external reference drawings or the nested blocks, or both. If you select the **Include xrefs in block counts** check box, then the xrefs will automatically be included while counting the blocks. The two radio buttons available in the **Extract from** area allow you to control the settings for counting the blocks. If you select the **Objects in model space** radio button, only the blocks currently inserted into the model space will be counted. If you select the **All objects in drawing** radio button, all the blocks from the current drawing will be counted. Choose the **OK** button to exit the **Data Extraction - Additional Settings** dialog box. Choose the **Next** button from the **Define Data Source** page; the **Select Objects** page of the **Data Extraction** wizard will be displayed.

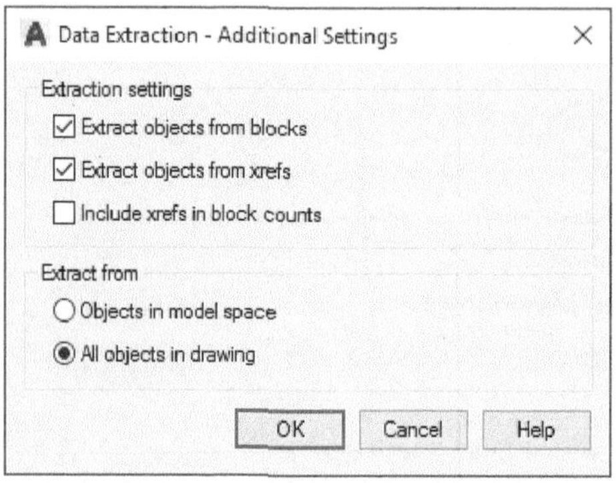

Figure 17-22 The ***Data Extraction - Additional Settings*** *dialog box*

Select Objects

The **Select Objects** page, as shown in Figure 17-23, allows you to filter out the objects to be included for data extraction. The objects that are checked in the **Objects** list box will only be considered for data extraction. The objects that are present in the current drawing are checked by default. Apart from the check box column, three more columns namely, **Object**, **Display Name**, and **Type** are displayed in the **Objects** list box. These columns display the information about the objects that are available to be selected and their type based on blocks and non-blocks.

The **Display options** area is used to control the objects to be displayed in the **Objects** list box. You can sort out the display from the blocks and non-blocks, blocks having attributes, and objects used in the current drawing. After specifying the objects to be displayed, choose the **Next** button from the **Select Objects** page to move to the **Select Properties** page.

Tip

You can reverse the display order of the entities by clicking on the respective column head in the ***Objects*** *list box. The direction of the arrow displayed at the column head of the selected column represents whether the data is arranged in the ascending or descending order.*

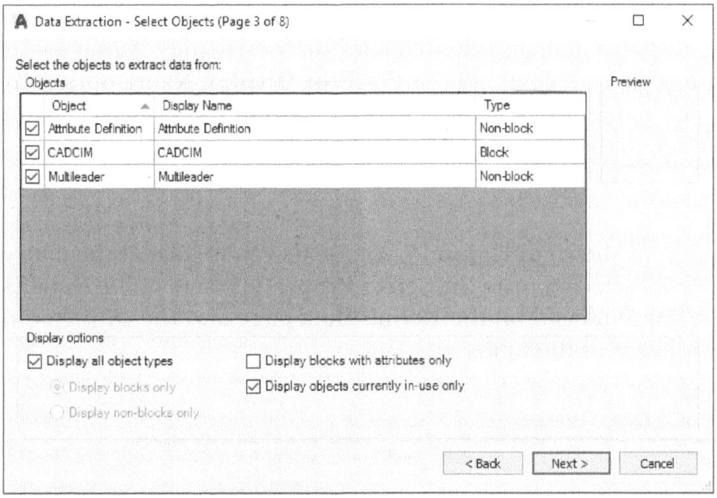

*Figure 17-23 The **Select Objects** page of the **Data Extraction** wizard*

Select Properties

The **Select Properties** page, as shown in Figure 17-24, allows you to select the properties of the objects to be included for data extraction. Only the properties that are checked in the **Properties** list box are considered for data extraction. Apart from the check box column, three more columns namely, **Property**, **Display Name**, and **Category** are displayed in the **Properties** list box. These columns display the information about the available properties and their category.

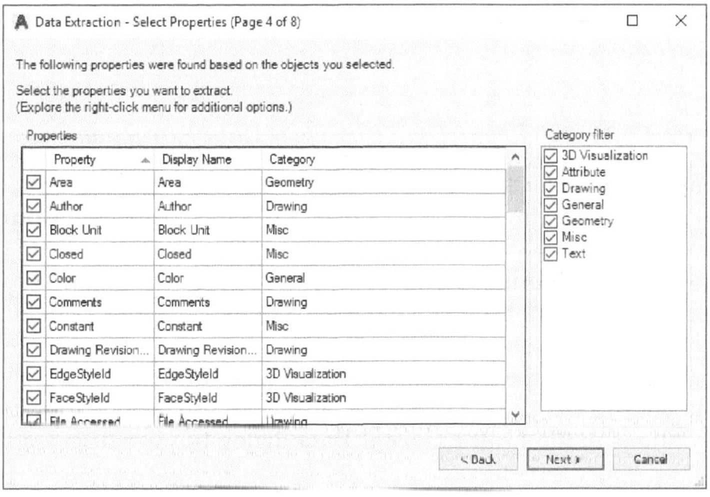

*Figure 17-24 The **Select Properties** page of the **Data Extraction** wizard*

The **Category filter** area is used to control the properties further to be displayed in the **Properties** list box. To do so, select the categories of the properties to be included in the **Properties** list box. For example, if you select the **Attribute** check box in the **Category filter** area, only the information about the attributes defined for the drawing will be extracted and displayed in the **Properties** list box. All the properties and categories displayed here are similar to the one displayed in the **PROPERTIES** palette.

You can also edit the names below the **Display Name** column. Select the row for which you want to change the display name and double-click on the **Display Name** column or right-click to display the shortcut menu. Next, choose the **Edit Display Name** option from the shortcut menu and enter a new name. After specifying the properties, choose the **Next** button from the **Select Properties** page to display the **Refine Data** page.

Refine Data

The **Refine Data** page, as shown in Figure 17-25, allows you to format the data extracted from a drawing. The properties selected from the **Select Properties** page of the **Data Extraction** wizard are displayed as the column head on the **Refine Data** page and the extracted data is displayed under these column heads of the table.

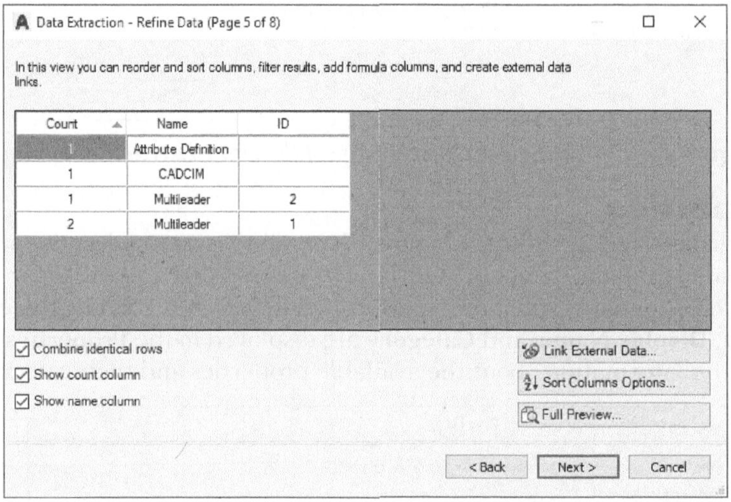

***Figure 17-25** The **Refine Data** page of the **Data Extraction** wizard*

The **Combine identical rows** check box is used to merge the rows having the same data. The sum of the merged rows having the same data will be displayed below the **Count** column head. The **Show count column** check box is used to display the **Count** column head on the extracted data table. The **Show name column** check box is used to display the **Name** column head on the extracted data table. All the check boxes explained above are selected by default.

You can also add columns from an excel sheet to the data extracted from a drawing. Choose the **Link External Data** button; the **Link External Data** dialog box will be displayed, as shown in Figure 17-26. The options in the **Link External Data** dialog box are discussed next.

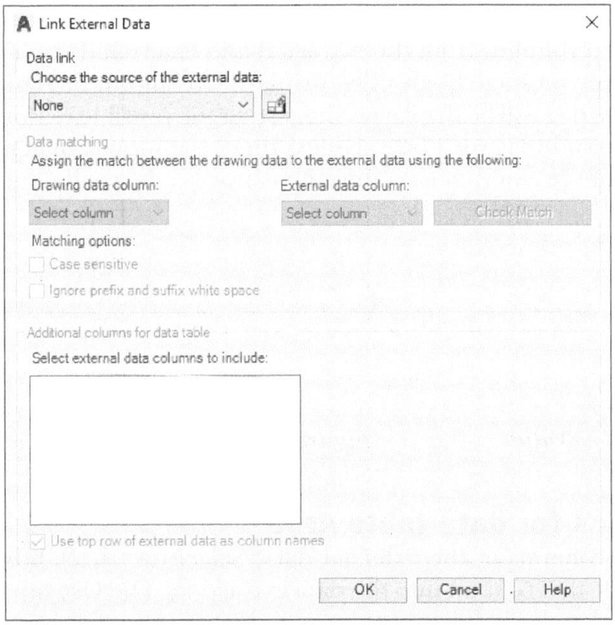

*Figure 17-26 The **Link External Data** dialog box*

Data link Area

This area is used to specify the Excel sheet to be attached with the drawing. The **Choose the source of the external data** drop-down list displays all the external data links that are attached to the current drawing. Select the external data link from which you want to include the columns. To attach a new Excel file to the drawing, choose the **Launch Data Link Manager** button; the **Data Link Manager** dialog box will be displayed on the screen. The other options in the **Data Link Manager** dialog box have been discussed earlier in Chapter 7 (Creating Texts and Tables). The rest of the options in the **Link External Data** dialog box will be available as soon as you specify the external data to be linked with the drawing.

Data matching Area

The options in this area are used to establish a relationship between the data extracted from the drawing and the attached external Excel sheet. There must be at least one cell with the matching data in the selected column of the drawing data and the external data column respectively. This matching data in the external and internal data acts as a key cell to specify the proper insertion of the external data into the extracted data.

The **Drawing data column** drop-down list displays all the property column heads of the data extracted by the drawing. Select the column head from this drop-down list that is to be used for matching. The **External data column** displays the column names from the external data. Select the column name from where you want to insert data into the extracted data. Select the **Case sensitive** check box to check the case of the alphabets while matching the data of the selected columns from the extracted and external data. Select the **Ignore prefix and suffix white space** check box to ignore the blank spaces in the front and back of the entries in the columns that are used for matching.

Specify preferences for matching the data and choose the **Check Match** button to compare the data of the specified columns from the extracted and external data. If the data matching is successful, the **Valid Key** message box will be displayed, as shown in Figure 17-27. Otherwise, the **Check Key** message box will be displayed suggesting the possible reasons of conflict between the two datums, as shown in Figure 17-28. Unless there is a proper matching between the two datums, the merging of the external data into the extracted data will not take place.

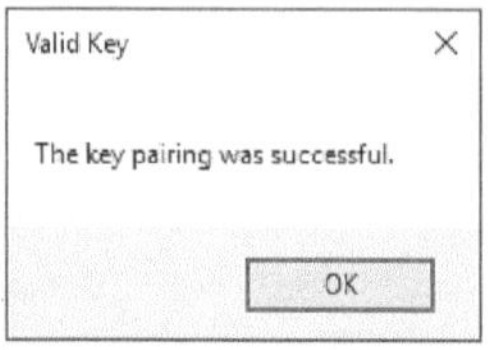

*Figure 17-27 The **Valid Key** message box*

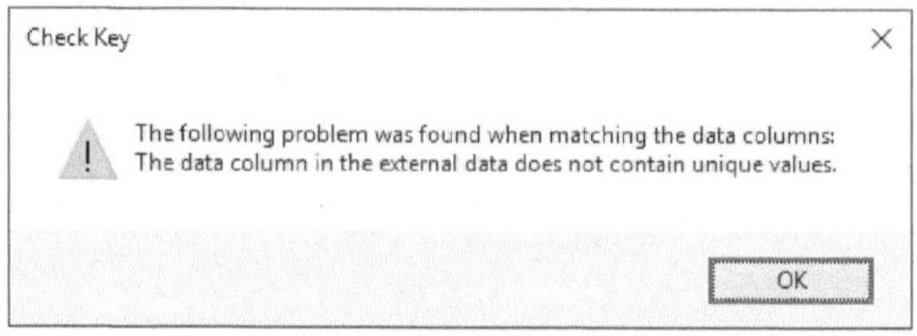

*Figure 17-28 The **Check Key** message box*

Additional columns for data table Area

This area displays all columns of the external data. Select the check box on the left of each column entry to include that column into the data extraction. The **Use top row of external data as column names** check box will be used to specify the first row of the selected columns as the column head for the extracted data. Otherwise, the column heads are displayed as **Column 1**, **Column 2**, and so on. By default, this check box is selected.

Specify the preferences for the external data to be included in the current data extraction in the **Link External Data** dialog box and choose the **OK** button. The specified columns of the external data will be added to the extracted data and displayed in the **Refine Data** page of the **Data Extraction** wizard. The drawing data column used for matching and the external data column included in the extracted data will be represented with an external data link symbol. This symbol will be displayed on the side of the column head in the **Refine Data** page, as shown in Figure 17-29.

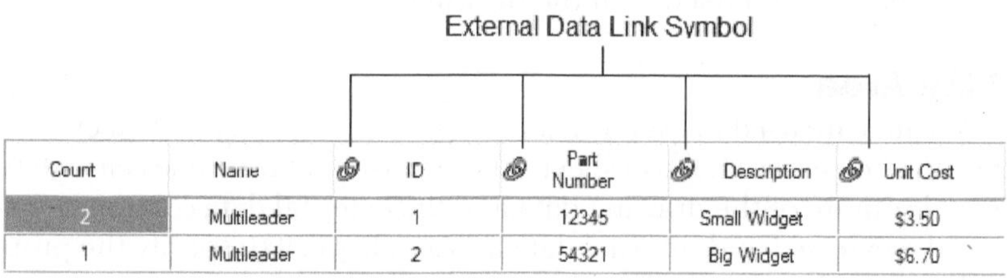

Figure 17-29 The external data link symbol

You can also change the display order of rows in the extracted data. To do so, choose the **Sort Columns Options** button from the **Refine Data** page; the **Sort Columns** dialog box will be displayed, refer to Figure 17-30. You can define the sort order for a single column or a group of columns at a time with this dialog box. The options in the **Sort Columns** dialog box are discussed next.

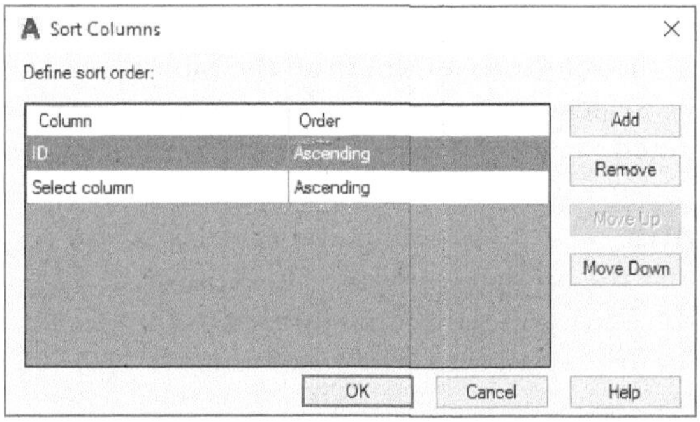

*Figure 17-30 The **Sort Columns** dialog box*

The **Define sort order** list box has two columns with the **Column** and **Order** column heads. Click on the drop-down arrow below the **Column** head to display all the column head entries for the extracted data. Select the column for which you want to change the display order of the rows. Choose the **Ascending** or **Descending** option from the **Order** drop-down list to specify the display order. Choose the **Add** button to add more rows in the **Define sort order** list box so as to specify the display order for other columns of the extracted data. The **Remove** button enables you to remove the selected sort order from the **Define sort order** list box. Choose the **Move Up** or **Move Down** button to move the selected row in the sort order, one level up or one level down respectively in the **Define sort order** list box.

Choose the **Full Preview** button; the preview will be displayed in the **Full Preview** window. Partial view of the **Full Preview** window is shown in Figure 17-31.

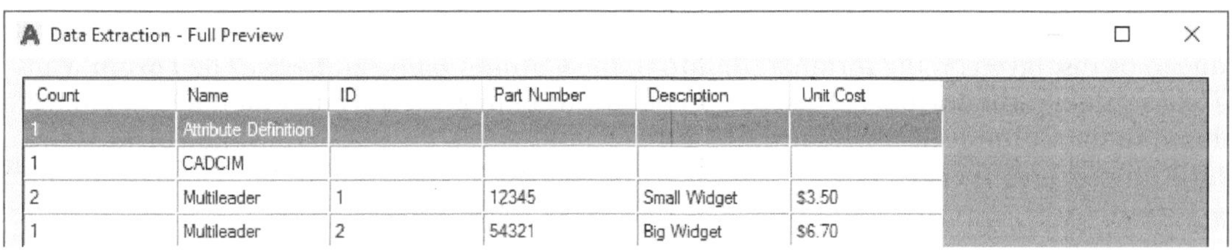

*Figure 17-31 Partial view of the **Full Preview** window*

When you right-click on the table displayed on the **Refine Data** page, a shortcut menu will be displayed, as shown in Figure 17-32. The options in the shortcut menu are discussed next.

Sort Descending/Sort Ascending

These options sort the data of the selected column in the descending/ ascending order.

Sort Columns Options

This option is used to invoke the **Sort Columns** dialog box which has been discussed earlier.

Rename Column

This option is used to rename the column head of the selected column.

Hide Column

This option is used to hide the selected column from the table of the extracted data. The selected column is only removed from the view, it is not deleted.

Show Hidden Columns

This option is used to display the hidden columns. This option becomes available only when atleast one column is hidden from the view. You can choose to display all the hidden columns or only the selected one.

Set Column Data Format

This option is used to invoke the **Set Cell Format** dialog box. You can set the data format for the selected row through this dialog box.

Insert Formula Column

This option is used to insert a formula column in the extracted data. Choose the **Insert Formula Column** option to invoke the **Insert Formula Column** dialog box, as shown in Figure 17-33. You can define and insert a formula column using this dialog box. The entries in the **Formula** column are governed by the mathematical formula defined by using one or more columns. The entry in a particular cell of the formula column can be calculated by using the formula and taking the value from the same row under the column that has been used to define the formula. Enter the column head name to be displayed on the formula column in the **Column name** edit box. The **Formula** area is used to define the formula. To select a column to define the formula, double click on the column in the **Columns** list box, or drag and drop the selected column into the **Formula** area. To use an operator such as +,-,*,or / in the formula, choose the desired operator button from the **Formula** area.

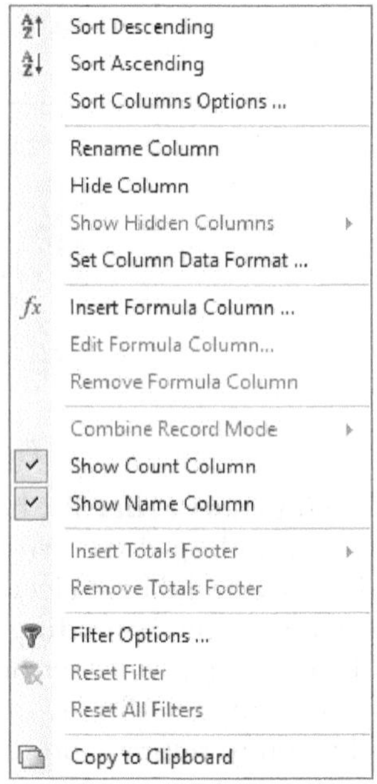

***Figure 17-32** The shortcut menu for the **Refine Data** page*

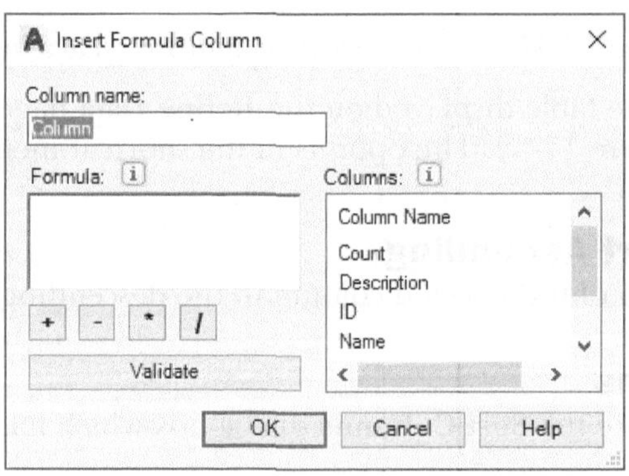

***Figure 17-33** The **Insert Formula Column** dialog box*

You can also make entry in the **Formula** area through the keyboard. Choose the **Validate** button to check the validity of the formula. If the defined formula is valid, AutoCAD will display the **Valid Equation** message box, as shown in Figure 17-34, and if the formula defined is invalid, the **Invalid Equation** message box will be displayed, as shown in Figure 17-35. The **Formula** column is always inserted on the right of the selected column and is indicated by a formula symbol, refer to Figure 17-36.

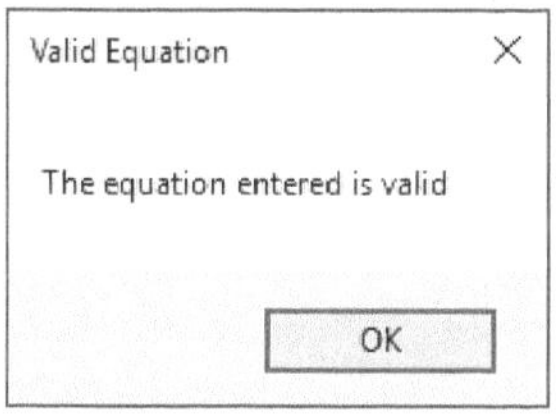

*Figure 17-34 The **Valid Equation** message box*

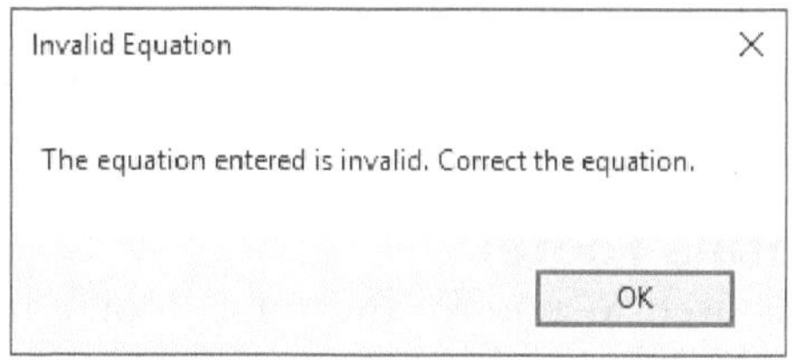

*Figure 17-35 The **Invalid Equation** message box*

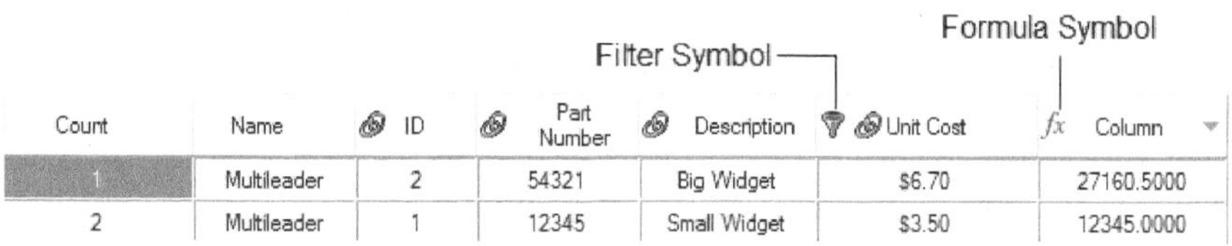

*Figure 17-36 The **Formula** and **Filter** symbols*

Edit Formula Column

This option is used to edit the pre-defined formula. Choose this option to invoke the **Edit Formula Column** dialog box.

Remove Formula Column

This option is used to delete the formula column from the extracted data. The **Edit Formula Column** and the **Remove Formula Column** options are available in the shortcut menu only when you right-click on the formula column.

Combine Record Mode

This option is used to control the display of the numeric data into the selected columns by displaying them either as separate values or collapsing the identical property rows into one and displaying their total sum. If any formula column is added and you apply the **Combine Record Mode** option to the formula column, then in case of the **Separate Values** sub-option, the formula will be applied after combining the identical rows. But in case of **Sum Values** sub-option, the formula will be applied to the individual rows and then the identical rows will be combined together and the resultant value will be displayed as the sum of those individual columns. This option will be available only when the selected columns have numerical data and the **Combine identical rows** check box is selected.

Show Count Column/Show Name Column

These options are used to display the **Count** column and the **Name** column, respectively. These options are selected by default.

Insert Totals Footer

This option is used to add a footer row under the selected column. This row can display the sum, maximum or minimum value in the selected column, and the average of all values above the footer row in that column. This option is only available for the columns that have numerical data.

Remove Totals Footer

This option is used to remove the totals footer from the selected row.

Filter Options

This option is used to decide the filter criterion for the selected column. Choose this option to invoke the **Filter <column name>** dialog box, refer to Figure 17-37. Only the entries that fulfill the specified filter criterion will be displayed on the table. The column on which the filter is applied is represented by a Filter symbol on the side of the column name, refer to Figure 17-36.

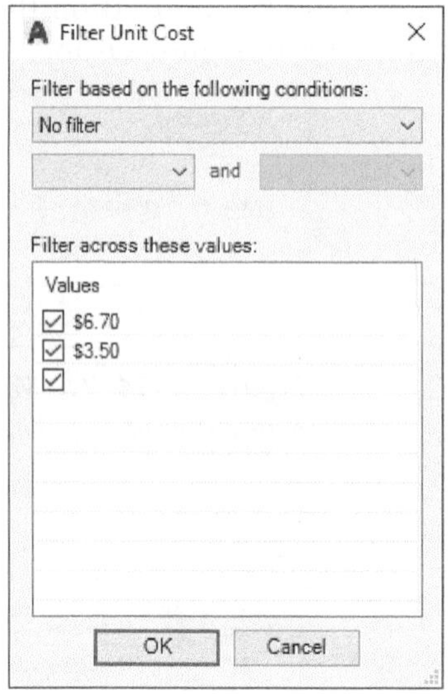

Figure 17-37 The ***Filter <column name>*** *dialog box*

Reset Filter/Reset All Filters

These options are used to remove the applied filters from the selected columns or from all the columns of the table at a time respectively.

Copy to Clipboard

This option is used to copy the selected table to the clipboard.

After formatting the data from the extracted files, choose the **Next** button to display the **Choose Output** page.

Choose Output

The **Choose Output** page, as shown in Figure 17-38, allows you to specify the format of the output file and the location to save it. Select the **Insert data extraction table into drawing** check box to insert the extracted data into the drawing as a table. Select the **Output data to external file (.xls .csv .mdb .txt)** check box to save the extracted data to a separate file at the end of the wizard. Select the Browse [...] button to specify the location to save this file. Choose the **Next** button from the **Choose Output** page to move to the **Table Style** page.

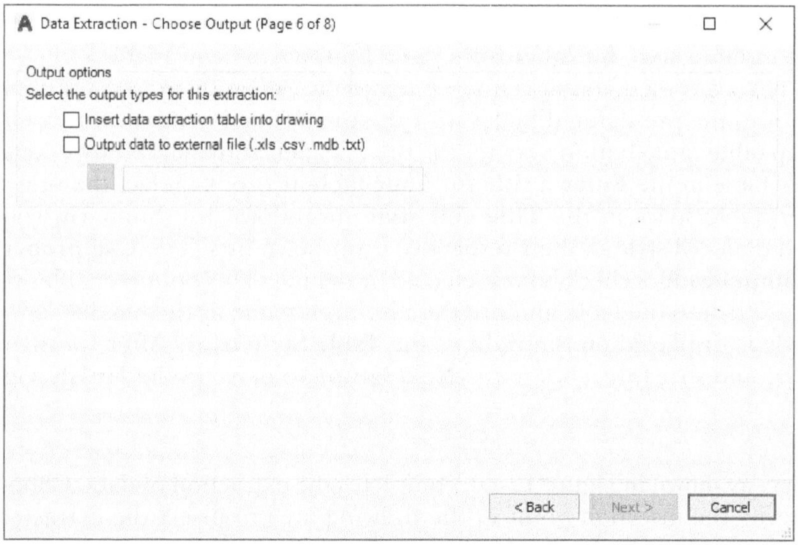

Figure 17-38 The ***Choose Output*** *page of the* ***Data Extraction*** *wizard*

Table Style

The **Table Style** page, as shown in Figure 17-39, will be available only if the **Insert data extraction table into drawing** check box is selected in the **Choose Output** page. The options in the **Table Style** page are discussed next.

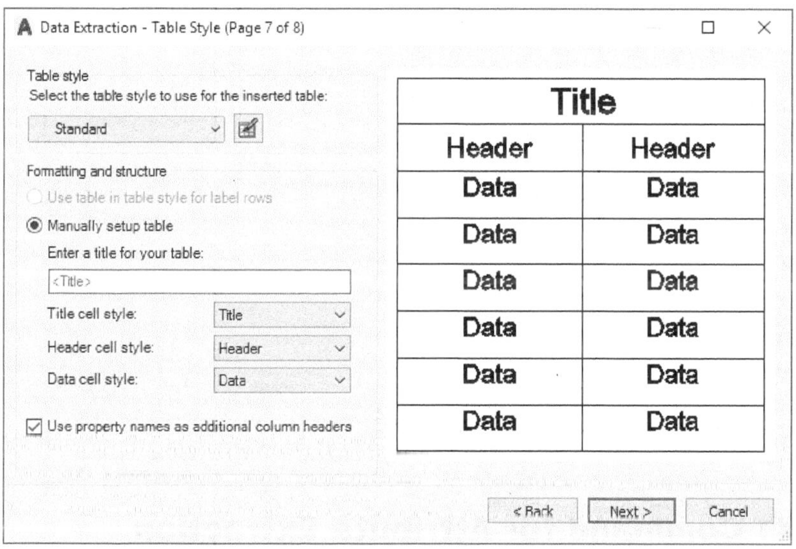

Figure 17-39 The ***Table Style*** *page of the* ***Data Extraction*** *wizard*

Table style Area

You can select the table style from the **Select the table style to use for the inserted table** drop-down list. By default, only the **Standard** table style is available. To create a new table style, choose the **Table Style** button on the right of the **Select the table style to use for the inserted table** drop-down list; the **Table Style** dialog box will be displayed. You can use this dialog box to create a new table style or modify an existing table style to be used for the extracted attributes.

Formatting and structure Area

The **Use table in table style for label rows** radio button will be available only when the table style that you have specified contains a table template. Select this radio button to insert the extracted data into the pre-defined tables with the pre-defined header and footers. Select the **Manually setup table** radio button to enter the title, header, and data cell styles manually. Enter the title for the table in the **Enter a title for your table** text box. Select the title style defined in the specified table styles in the **Title cell style** drop-down list. Similarly, you can specify the header and data cell style in their respective drop-down lists. The **Use property names as additional column headers** check box is selected by default. This option enables you to include the column headers into the table and use the displayed name as the header row. The preview of the table style is displayed on the right of the **Table Style** page. After specifying the **Table Style** formatting and structure, choose the **Next** button to move to the **Finish** page.

Finish

The **Finish** page, as shown in Figure 17-40, completes the extraction of data. Choose the **Finish** button and specify the insertion point in the drawing area to insert the extracted data. Note that this is possible only if the **Insert data extraction table into drawing** check box is selected on the **Choose Output** page of the **Data Extraction** wizard.

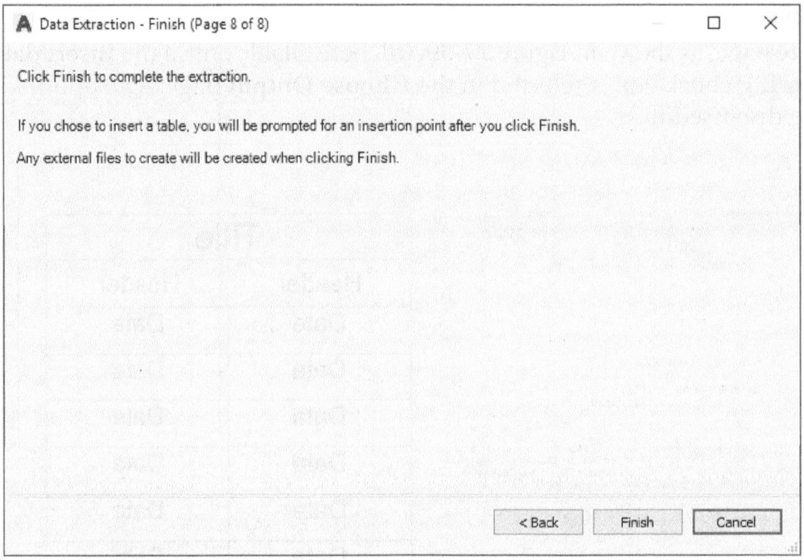

*Figure 17-40 The **Finish** page of the **Data Extraction** wizard*

The ATTEXT Command for Attribute Extraction

Command: ATTEXT

The **ATTEXT** command allows you to use the **Attribute Extraction** dialog box, as shown in Figure 17-41, for extracting attributes. The information about the **File Format**, **Template File**, and **Output File** must be entered in the dialog box to extract the defined attribute. Also, you must select the blocks whose attribute values you want to extract. If you do not specify a particular block, all the blocks in the drawing are used.

File Format Area

This area of the dialog box allows you to select the file format. You can select either of the three radio buttons available in this area, as per your requirement. The format selection is determined by the application that you plan to use to process data. Both CDF and SDF formats can be used with the database software. All of these formats are printable.

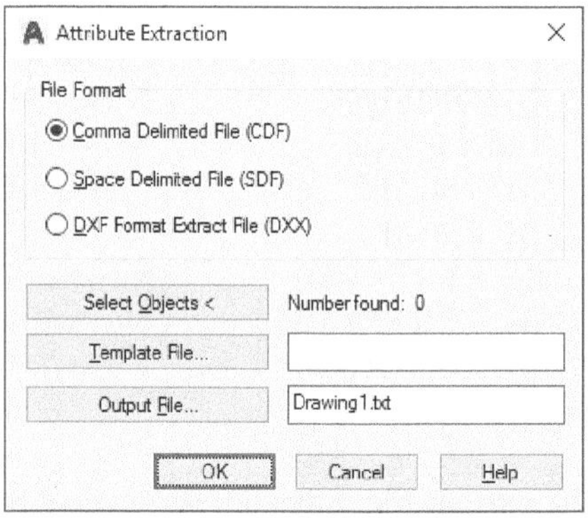

*Figure 17-41 The **Attribute Extraction** dialog box*

Comma Delimited File (CDF). When you select this radio button, the extracted attribute information is displayed in a CDF format. Here, each character field is enclosed in single quotes, and the records are separated by a delimiter (comma by default). A CDF file is a text file with the extension *.txt*. Of the three formats available, this is the most cumbersome.

Space Delimited File (SDF). In SDF format, the records are of fixed width as specified in the template file. The records are separated by spaces and the character fields are not enclosed in single quotes. The SDF file is a text file with the extension *.txt*. This file format is the most convenient and easy to use.

DXF Format Extract File (DXX). If you select this file format, you will notice that the **Template File** button and edit box in the **Attribute Extraction** dialog box are not available. This is because extraction in this file format does not require any template. The file created by this option contains only block references, attribute values, and end-of-sequence objects. The extension of these files is *.dxx*.

Select Objects

Select the blocks with attributes whose attribute information you want to extract. You can use any object selection method. Once you have selected the blocks that you want to use for attribute extraction, right-click or press ENTER. The **Attribute Extraction** dialog box is redisplayed and the number of objects you have selected is displayed adjacent to **Number found**.

Template File

When you choose the **Template File** button, the **Template File** dialog box is displayed, where you are allowed to select a template file that has been defined already. After you have selected a template file, choose the **Open** button to return to the **Attribute Extraction** dialog box. The name of the selected file is displayed in the **Template File** edit box. The template file is saved with the extension of the file as *.txt*. The following are the fields that you can specify in a template file (the comments given on the right are for explanation only; they must not be entered with the field description):

```
BL:LEVEL     Nwww000     (Block nesting level)
BL:NAME      Cwww000     (Block name)
BL:X         Nwwwddd     (X coordinate of block insertion point)
BL:Y         Nwwwddd     (Y coordinate of block insertion point)
BL:Z         Nwwwddd     (Z coordinate of block insertion point)
```

BL:NUMBER	Nwww000	(Block counter)
BL:HANDLE	Cwww000	(Block's handle)
BL:LAYER	Cwww000	(Block insertion layer name)
BL:ORIENT	Nwwwddd	(Block rotation angle)
BL:XSCALE	Nwwwddd	(X scale factor of block)
BL:YSCALE	Nwwwddd	(Y scale factor of block)
BL:ZSCALE	Nwwwddd	(Z scale factor of block)
BL:XEXTRUDE	Nwwwddd	(X component of block's extrusion direction)
BL:YEXTRUDE	Nwwwddd	(Y component of block's extrusion direction)
BL:ZEXTRUDE	Nwwwddd	(Z component of block's extrusion direction)
Attribute tag		(The tag name of the block attribute)

The extract file may contain several fields. For example, the first field might be the item name and the second field might be the price of the item. Each line in the template file specifies one field in the extract file. A line in a template file consists of the name of the field, the width of the field in characters, and its numerical precision (if applicable). For example, consider the case given next.

```
ITEM       N015002
BL:NAME    C015000
```

Where **BL:NAME** --Field name
Blankspaces ---Blank spaces (must not include the tab character)
C -----------------Designates a character field
N -----------------Designates a numerical field
015 ---------------Width of field in characters
002 ---------------Numerical precision

BL:NAME
or ITEM Indicates the field names; can be of any length.

C Designates a character field; that is, the field contains characters or it starts with characters. If the file contains numbers or starts with numbers, then C will be replaced by N. For example, **N015002**.

015 Designates a field that is fifteen characters long.

002 Designates the numerical precision. In this example, the numerical precision is 2, or two places following the decimal. The decimal point and the two digits following the decimal are **included in the field width**. In the next example, (000), the numerical precision, is not applicable because the field does not have any numerical value (the field contains letters only).

After creating a template file, when you choose the **Template File** button, the **Template File** dialog box is displayed. You can browse and select a template file from this dialog box, as shown in Figure 17-42.

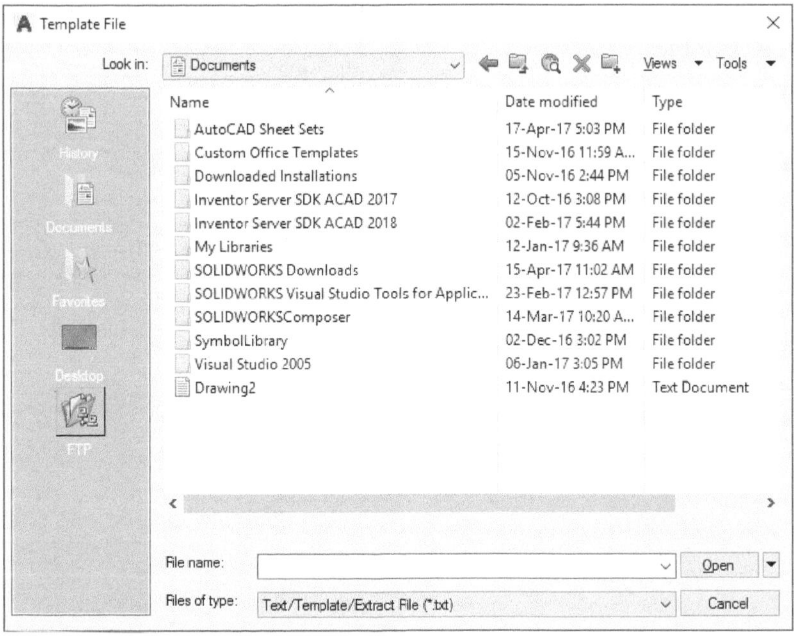

Figure 17-42 The ***Template File*** *dialog box to select a template file*

Note

1. You can put any number of spaces between the field name and the character C or N (ITEM N015002). However, you must not use the tab characters. Any alignment in the fields must be done by inserting spaces after the field name.

2. In the template file, a field name must not appear more than once. The template file name and the output file name must be different.

The template file must contain at least one field with an attribute tag name because the tag names determine which attribute values are to be extracted and from which blocks. If several blocks have different block names but the same attribute tag, AutoCAD will extract attribute values from all the selected blocks. For example, if there are two blocks in the drawing with the attribute tag PRICE, then when you extract the attribute values, AutoCAD will extract the value from both blocks (if both blocks were selected). To extract the value of an attribute, the tag name must match the field name specified in the template file. AutoCAD automatically converts the tag names and the field names to uppercase letters before making a comparison.

Output File

When you choose the **Output File** button, the **Output File** dialog box is displayed. You can select an existing file from the dialog box, if you want the extracted or output file to be saved as an existing file. You can enter a name in the **File name** edit box in the **Output File** dialog box, as shown in Figure 17-43 and then choose the **Save** button, if you want to save the output file as a new file. By default, the output file has the same name as the drawing name. For example, a drawing named *Drawing1.dwg* will have an output file by the name *Drawing1.txt* by default. Once a name for the output file is specified, it is displayed in the **Output File** edit box in the **Attribute Extraction** dialog box. You can also enter the file name in this edit box. As discussed earlier, AutoCAD appends *.txt* file extension for CDF or SDF files and *.dxx* file extension for DXF files.

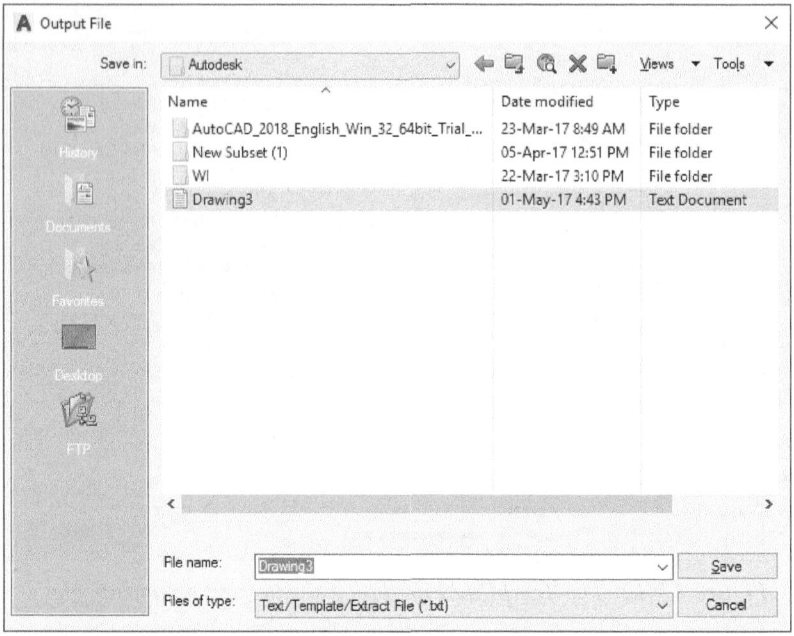

***Figure 17-43** The **Output File** dialog box to save an output file*

Note

*You can also use the **-ATTEXT** command to extract attributes using the command prompt. Here, you are prompted to specify a file format for the extracted information and you can also select specific blocks to extract their attribute information. You can specify a template file using the **Select Template File** dialog box and an extract file using the **Create extract file** dialog box.*

Example 3

In this example, you will extract the attribute values defined in Example 2. Extract the values of NAME, COUNT, MAKE, PROCESSOR, HD, RAM, and ITEM. These attribute values must be saved in a *.txt* format named TEST and arranged, as shown in the table given next.

COMP	1	Dell	586-60	450 MB	64 MB	Computer
COMP	1	CAD-CIM	Pentium-90	100 Min	32 MB	Computer
COMP	1	CAD-CIM	Unknown	600 MB	Standard	Computer
COMP	1	Gateway	486-60	150 MB	16 MB	Computer
COMP	1	Zenith	486-30	100 MB	32 MB	Computer
COMP	1	IBM	386-30	80 MB	8 MB	Computer

1. Open the drawing that you saved in Example 2.

2. Choose the **Data Extraction** tool from the **Link & Extraction** panel of the **Insert** tab; the **Data Extraction** wizard is displayed. Select the **Create a new data extraction** radio button from the **Begin** page and choose the **Next** button; the **Save Data Extraction As** dialog box is displayed.

3. Enter **TEST** in the **File name** edit box of the **Save Data Extraction As** dialog box and choose the **Save** button; the **Define Data Source** page is displayed.

4. Select the **Drawings/Sheet set** radio button and make sure that the **Include current drawing** check box is selected on the **Define Data Source** page. Choose the **Next** button; the **Select Objects** page is displayed.

5. Clear all check boxes in the **Object** column except the **COMP** object from the **Select Objects** page and choose the **Next** button; the **Select Properties** page is displayed.

6. Clear all check boxes except the **Attribute** check box from the **Category filter** area of the **Select Properties** page of the **Data Extraction** wizard. Also, make sure that the check box on the left of the **HD**, **ITEM**, **MAKE**, **PROCESSOR**, and **RAM** properties under the **Property** column are selected. Choose the **Next** button; the **Refine Data** page is displayed.

7. Arrange the display order of the columns according to the table displayed above, by dragging and dropping the column heads to the desired position in the **Refine Data** page of the **Data Extraction** wizard. Make sure that the **Show count column** and **Show name column** check boxes are selected. Choose the **Full Preview** button and check the data displayed in the **Data Extraction - Full Preview** window and match it with the table displayed above. Close the window and choose the **Next** button from the **Refine Data** page of the **Data Extraction** wizard; the **Choose Output** page is displayed.

8. Select the **Output data to external file (.xls .csv .mdb .txt)** check box and choose the Browse [...] button; the **Save As** dialog box is displayed. Specify the location to save the file, select the **Text/Template/Extract File (*.txt)** option from the **Files of type** drop-down list, enter **TEST** in the **File name** edit box, and choose the **Save** button. Choose the **Next** button from the **Choose Output** page; the **Finish** page is displayed.

9. Choose the **Finish** button from the **Finish** page of the **Data Extraction** wizard.

CONTROLLING THE ATTRIBUTE VISIBILITY

Ribbon: Home > Block > Retain Attribute Display drop-down **Command:** ATTDISP

The options to change the display of attributes are available in **Retain Attribute Display** drop-down of the **Block** panel in the **Home** tab of the **Ribbon**. Generally, the attributes are visible, unless they are defined invisible by using the **Invisible** mode. The invisible attributes are not displayed, but they are the part of the block definition. The tools to toggle the display of attributes **Retain Attribute Display**, **Display All Attributes**, and **Hide All Attributes** are available in the **Retain Attribute Display** drop-down.

The **Retain Attribute Display** tool is used to display the attributes as they were set while they were created. For example, the attributes created using the **Invisible** mode will not be displayed.

If you choose the **Hide All Attributes** tool, all attributes will become invisible.

If you choose the **Display All Attributes** tool, all attributes will be displayed in the drawing area.

In Example 2 of this chapter, the RAM attribute was defined with the **Invisible** mode. If you choose the **Retain Attribute Display** tool, the RAM values will not be displayed with the block, refer to Figure 17-44. If you want to make the RAM attribute values visible, choose the **Display All Attributes** tool from the **Block** panel.

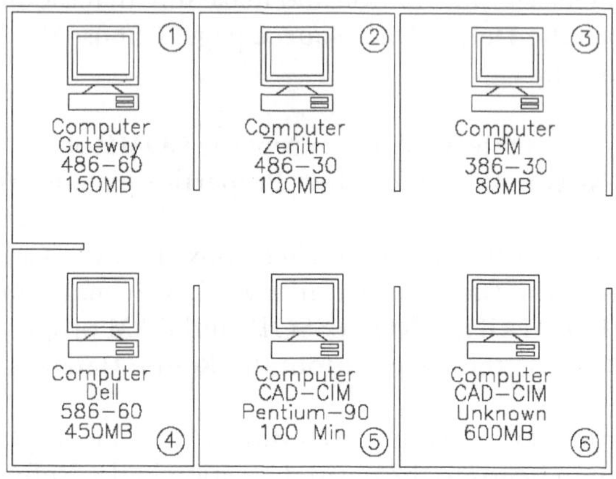

***Figure 17-44** The drawing of Example 2 after choosing the **Retain Attribute Display** tool*

Tip

After you have defined the attribute values and saved them with the block definition, it may be a good idea to hide all the attributes. By doing this, the drawing is simplified and also the regeneration time is reduced.

EDITING BLOCK ATTRIBUTES

The block attributes can be edited by using several methods. These methods are discussed next.

Editing Attributes Using the Enhanced Attribute Editor

Ribbon: Insert > Block > Edit Attribute drop-down > Single
Command: EATTEDIT **Toolbar:** Modify II > Edit Attribute

Choose the **Single** tool from the **Edit Attribute** drop-down from the **Block** panel to edit the block attribute values. When you invoke this tool, AutoCAD prompts you to select the block whose values you want to edit. After selecting the block, the **Enhanced Attribute Editor** dialog box is displayed, as shown in Figure 17-45. This dialog box allows you to change the **Attribute**, **Text Options**, and **Properties** of the block attribute. This dialog box can also be invoked by double-clicking on the block or the attribute in the current drawing. The **Enhanced Attribute Editor** dialog box displays all the attributes of the selected block and their properties. You can change the properties of the attribute you want. If an attribute has been defined with the **Constant** mode, it is not displayed in the dialog box because a constant attribute value cannot be edited. The dialog box displays the following tabs.

Attribute Tab

The options under this tab are used to change the value of the attribute. Also, here the **Mode** of the attribute is not displayed. The other attributes of the block such as **Tag**, **Prompt**, and **Value** are displayed, as shown in Figure 17-45.

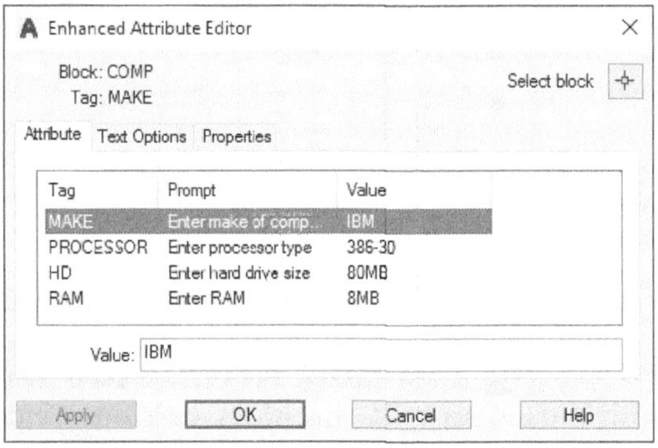

*Figure 17-45 The **Attribute** tab of the **Enhanced Attribute Editor** dialog box*

Text Options Tab

Under this tab, the options related to the text of attributes can be modified. This includes **Text Style**, **Justification**, **Height**, **Rotation**, **Backwards**, **Upside down**, **Width Factor**, **Oblique Angle**, **Annotative**, and **Boundary width**, as shown in Figure 17-46.

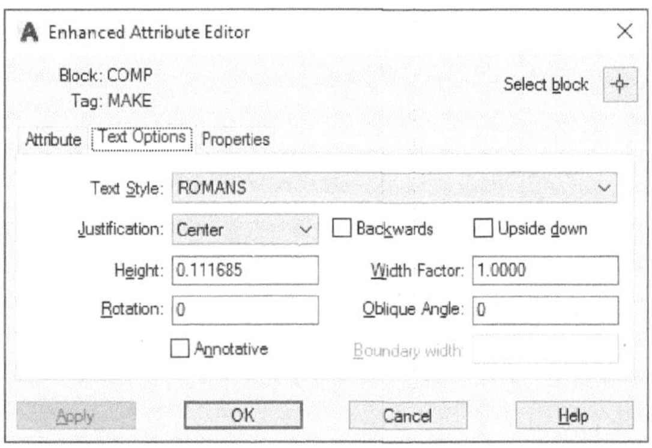

*Figure 17-46 The **Text Options** tab of the **Enhanced Attribute Editor** dialog box*

Properties Tab

This tab is used to edit the properties of attributes such as **Layer**, **Linetype**, **Color**, **Lineweight**, and **Plot style**. Choose the **Properties** tab of the **Enhanced Attribute Editor** dialog box to display the options in this tab, as shown in Figure 17-47.

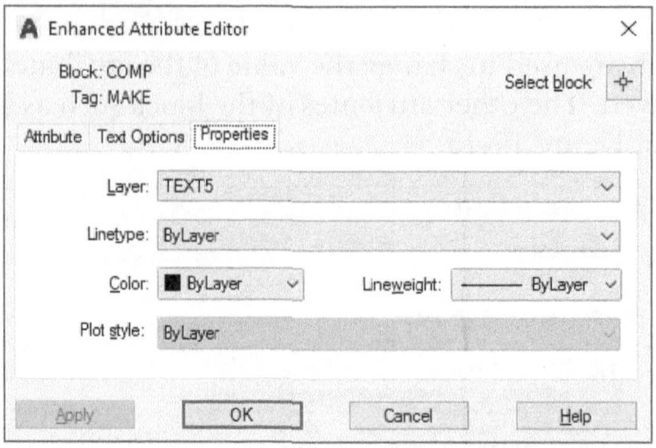

***Figure 17-47** The **Properties** tab of the **Enhanced Attribute Editor** dialog box*

Editing Attributes Using the Edit Attributes Dialog Box

The **ATTEDIT** command is used to edit the block attribute values through the **Edit Attributes** dialog box. Invoke this command; AutoCAD prompts you to select the block whose values are to be edited. After selecting the block, the **Edit Attributes** dialog box is displayed, as shown in Figure 17-48.

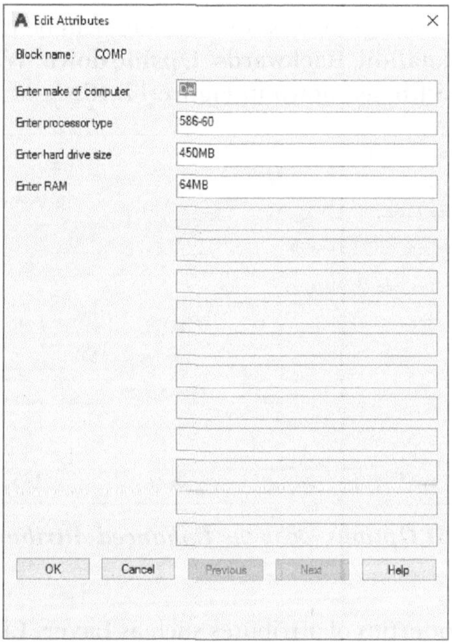

***Figure 17-48** The **Edit Attributes** dialog box*

The dialog box is similar to the **Enter Attributes** dialog box and shows the prompts and the attribute values of the selected block. If an attribute has been defined with the **Constant** mode, it is not displayed in the dialog box because a constant attribute value cannot be edited. To make any changes, select the existing value and enter a new value in the corresponding edit box. After you have made the modifications, choose the **OK** button. The attribute values are updated in the selected block.

If a selected block has no attributes, AutoCAD will display the alert message **That block has no editable attributes**. Similarly, if the selected object is not a block, AutoCAD again displays the alert message **That object is not a block**.

Note

*You cannot use the **ATTEDIT** command to perform the global editing of attribute values or to modify the position, height, or style of the attribute value. The global editing can be performed using the **-ATTEDIT** command which is discussed in the next section.*

Example 4

In this example, you will choose the **Single** tool from the **Edit Attribute** drop-down in the **Attributes** panel to change the attribute of the first computer (150 MB to 2.1 GB) which is located in Room-1.

1. Open the drawing created in Example 2. The drawing has six blocks with attributes. The name of the block is **COMP** and has five defined attributes. One of the attributes is invisible. Zoom in the drawing so that the first computer is displayed on the screen, refer to Figure 17-49.

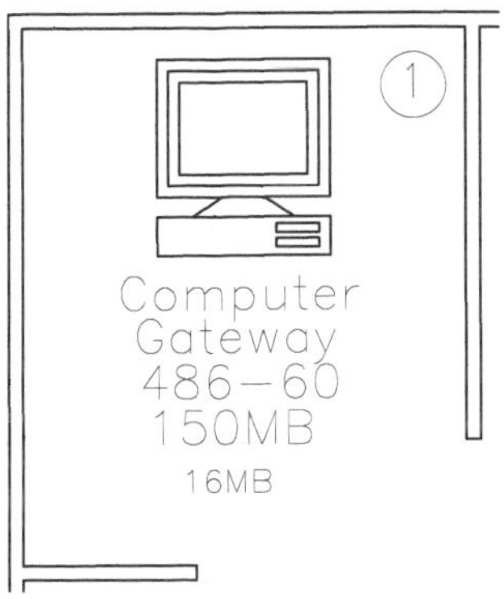

Figure 17-49 *Zoomed view of the first computer*

2. Choose the **Single** tool from **Insert > Block > Edit Attribute** drop-down; you are prompted to select a block. Select the computer located in Room-1. The **Enhanced Attribute Editor** dialog box showing the attribute prompts and values will be displayed, refer to Figure 17-45.

3. Edit the values, choose **Apply**, and then the **OK** button in the dialog box. When you exit the dialog box, the attribute values are updated.

Tip

*You can also replace the attributes with the **FIND** command. This command can be invoked by entering **FIND** at the pointer input. When you invoke this command, the **Find and Replace** dialog box is displayed.*

Global Editing of Attributes

Ribbon: Insert > Block > Edit Attribute drop-down > Multiple **Command:** -ATTEDIT

Choose the **Multiple** tool from the **Edit Attribute** drop-down in the **Block** panel to edit the attribute values independently of the blocks that contain the attribute reference. For example, if there are two blocks, COMPUTER and TABLE, with the attribute value PRICE, you can globally edit this value (PRICE) independently of the block that references these values. You can also edit the attribute values one at a time. For example, you can edit the attribute value (PRICE) of the block TABLE without affecting the value of the other block, COMPUTER. On choosing the **Multiple** tool from the **Edit Attribute** drop-down, AutoCAD displays the following prompt:

Edit attributes one at a time? [Yes/No]<Y>: **N** Enter

If you enter **N** at this prompt, it means that you want to do the global editing of the attributes. However, you can restrict the editing of attributes by block names, tag names, attribute values, and visibility of attributes on the screen.

Editing Visible Attributes Only

After you select global editing, AutoCAD will display the following prompt:

Edit only attributes visible on screen? [Yes/No] <Y>: **Y** Enter

If you enter **Y** at this prompt, AutoCAD will edit only those attributes that are visible and displayed on the screen. The attributes might not have been defined with the **Invisible** mode, but if they are not displayed on the screen, they are not visible for editing. For example, if you zoom in, some of the attributes may not be displayed on the screen. Since the attributes are not displayed on the screen, they are invisible and cannot be selected for editing.

Editing All Attributes

If you enter **N** at the previously mentioned prompt, AutoCAD flips from graphics to text screen and displays the message stating: '**Drawing must be regenerated afterwards**'.

Now, AutoCAD will edit all attributes even if they are not visible or displayed on the screen. Also, changes that you make in the attribute values are not reflected immediately. Instead, the attribute values are updated and the drawing is regenerated after you are done with the command.

Editing Specific Blocks

Although you have selected global editing, you can confine the editing of attributes to specific blocks by entering the block name at the prompt. For example,

Enter block name specification <*>: **COMP** Enter

When you enter the name of the block, AutoCAD will edit the attributes that have the given block (COMP) reference. You can also use the wild-card characters to specify the block names. If you want to edit attributes in all blocks that have attributes defined, press ENTER.

Editing Attributes with Specific Attribute Tag Names

Like blocks, you can confine attribute editing to those attribute values that have the specified tag name. For example, if you want to edit the attribute values that have the tag name MAKE, enter the tag name at the following AutoCAD prompt:

Enter attribute tag specification <*>: **MAKE** Enter

When you specify the tag name, AutoCAD will not edit attributes that have a different tag name, even if the values being edited are the same. You can also use the wild-card characters to specify the tag names. If you want to edit attributes with any tag name, press ENTER.

Editing Attributes with a Specific Attribute Value

Like blocks and attribute tag names, you can confine attribute editing to a specified attribute value. For example, if you want to edit the attribute values that have the value 100 MB, enter the value at the following AutoCAD prompt:

Enter attribute value specification <*>: **100MB** Enter

When you specify the attribute value, AutoCAD will not edit attributes that have a different value, even if the tag name and block specification are the same. You can also use the wild-card characters to specify the attribute value. If you want to edit attributes with any value, press ENTER.

Sometimes the value of an attribute is null, and these values are not visible. If you want to select the null values for editing, make sure you have not restricted the global editing to visible attributes. To edit the null attributes, enter \ at the following prompt:

Enter attribute value specification <*>: \ Enter

After you enter this information, AutoCAD will prompt you to select the attributes. You can select the attributes by selecting individual attributes or by using one of the object selection options (Window, Crossing, or individually).

Select Attributes: *Select the attribute values parallel to the current UCS only* Enter.

After you select the attributes, AutoCAD will prompt you to enter the string you want to change and the new string. A string is a sequence of consecutive characters. It could also be a portion of the text. AutoCAD will retrieve the attribute information, edit it, and then update the attribute values.

Enter string to change: *Enter the value to be modified* Enter.
Enter new string: *Enter the new value* Enter.

The following is the complete command prompt sequence after choosing the **Multiple** tool. It is assumed that the editing is global and for visible attributes only.

Edit attributes one at a time? [Yes/No] <Y>: **N** Enter
Edit only attributes visible on screen? [Yes/No] <Y>: **N** Enter
Drawing must be regenerated afterwards.

Enter block name specification <*>: Enter
Enter attribute tag specification <*>: Enter
Enter attribute value specification <*>: Enter
n attributes selected.
Enter string to change: *Enter the value to be modified* Enter.
Enter new string: *Enter the new value* Enter.

Note

1. AutoCAD regenerates the drawing at the end of the command automatically unless the system variable ***REGENAUTO*** *is off which controls automatic regeneration of the drawing.*

2. If you select an attribute defined with the ***Constant*** *mode using the* ***Multiple*** *tool, the prompt displays* ***0 found*** *since attributes with the* ***Constant*** *mode are not editable.*

Example 5

In this example, you will use the drawing from Example 2 to edit the attribute values that are highlighted in the following table. The tag names are given at the top of the table (ITEM, MAKE, PROCESSOR, HD, RAM). The RAM values are invisible in the drawing.

	ITEM	MAKE	PROCESSOR	HD	RAM
COMP	Computer	Gateway	486-60	150 MB	**16 MB**
COMP	Computer	Zenith	486-30	100 MB	**32 MB**
COMP	Computer	IBM	386-30	80 MB	**8 MB**
COMP	Computer	Dell	586-60	450 MB	**64 MB**
COMP	Computer	**CAD-CIM**	Pentium-90	100 Min	**32 MB**
COMP	Computer	**CAD-CIM**	**Unknown**	600 MB	Standard

Make the following changes in the highlighted attribute values shown in the above table.

1. Change Unknown to Pentium.
2. Change CAD-CIM to Compaq.
3. Change MB to Meg for all attribute values that have the tag name RAM. (No changes should be made to the values that have the tag name HD.)

The following steps are required to change the attribute value from **Unknown** to **Pentium**.

1. Choose the **Multiple** tool from **Insert > Block > Edit Attribute** drop-down and enter **N** at the next prompt and press ENTER as given below.

   Edit attributes one at a time? [Yes/No] <Y>: **N** Enter

2. You need to edit only those attributes that are visible on the screen, so press ENTER at the following prompt:

   Edit only attributes visible on screen? [Yes/No] <Y>: Enter

3. As shown in the table, the attributes belong to a single block, COMP. A drawing may have more blocks. To confine the attribute editing to the COMP block only, enter the name of the block (COMP) at the next prompt.

   Enter block name specification <*>: **COMP** Enter

4. At the next two prompts, enter the attribute tag name and the attribute value specification. When you enter these two values, only those attributes that have the specified tag name and attribute value will be edited.

   Enter attribute tag specification<*>: **Processor** Enter
   Enter attribute value specification<*>: **Unknown** Enter

   On entering these values, AutoCAD will prompt you to select attributes. Use any object selection option to select all the blocks. AutoCAD will search for the attributes that satisfy the given criteria (attributes belong to the block COMP, the attributes have the tag name Processor, and the attribute value is Unknown). Once AutoCAD locates such attributes, they are highlighted.

5. At the next two prompts, enter the string that you want to change, and then enter the new string.

   Enter string to change: **Unknown** Enter
   Enter new string: **Pentium** Enter

6. The following is the command prompt sequence to change the make of the computer from **CAD-CIM** to **Compaq**:

   *Choose the **Multiple** tool.*
   Edit attributes one at a time? [Yes/No] <Y>: **N** Enter
   Performing global editing of attribute values.
   Edit only attributes visible on screen? [Yes/No] <Y>: Enter
   Enter block name specification <*>: **COMP** Enter
   Enter attribute tag specification <*>: **MAKE** Enter
   Enter attribute value specification <*>: Enter
   Select Attributes: *Use any selection method to select the attributes* Enter.
   n attributes selected.
   Select Attributes: Enter
   Enter string to change: **CAD-CIM** Enter
   Enter new string: **Compaq** Enter

7. The following is the command prompt sequence to change **MB** to **Meg**:

   *Choose the **Multiple** tool.*
   Edit attributes one at a time? [Yes/No] <Y>: **N** Enter
   Performing global editing of attribute values.
   At the next prompt, you must enter **N** because the attributes you want to edit (tag name, RAM) are not visible on the screen.

Edit only attributes visible on screen? [Yes/No] <Y>: **N** [Enter]
Drawing must be regenerated afterwards.
Enter block name specification <*>: **COMP** [Enter]

At the next prompt, about the tag specification, you must specify the tag name because the text string MB also appears in the hard drive size (tag name, HD). If you do not enter the tag name, AutoCAD will change all MB attribute values to Meg.

Enter attribute tag specification <*>: **RAM** [Enter]
Enter attribute value specification <*>: [Enter]
n Attributes selected
Enter string to change: **MB** [Enter]
Enter new string: **Meg** [Enter]

8. Choose the **Display All Attributes** tool from the **Block** panel to display the invisible attributes.

Note

You can also use the ***-ATTEDIT*** *command to edit the attribute values individually. Attribute value, position, height, angle, style, layer, and color can be changed using this command.*

Example 6

In this example, you will use the drawing of Example 5 to edit attributes individually, refer to Figure 17-50. Make the following changes in the attribute values:

a. Change the attribute value 100 Min to 100 MB.

b. Change the height of all attributes with the tag name RAM to 0.075 units.

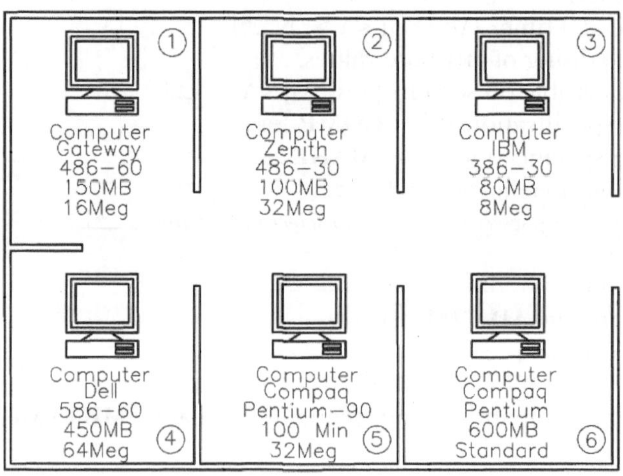

Figure 17-50 *The attribute values to be changed individually*

1. Load the drawing that you have saved in Example 5.

2. Double-click on the **100Min** attribute value in the drawing; the **Enhanced Attribute Editor** dialog box is displayed.

3. In the **Value** edit box, change **100 Min** to **100MB**. Choose **Apply** and then choose **OK**.

4. To change the height of attribute text, double-click on the value of **RAM** in the drawing; the **Enhanced Attribute Editor** dialog box is displayed.

5. In the dialog box, choose the **Text Options** tab and change the height to **0.075** in the **Height** edit box.

6. Choose **Apply** and then **OK**.

7. Change the height of the other attribute values using the process followed in Steps 5 and 6.

REDEFINING A BLOCK WITH ATTRIBUTES

If a block with attributes has been inserted a number of times in a drawing and you wish to edit the block geometry, or add or delete attributes from them, it may take a lot of time. You can use the **ATTREDEF** command to redefine an existing block with attributes, and once redefined, all the copies of the block with attributes get updated automatically. But before using this command, you need to explode a copy of the block containing the attributes and make the changes or you may use the new geometry. If you do not explode a block and try to use this command, an error message will be displayed: **New block has no attributes**. The prompt sequence is as follows:

Command: **ATTREDEF**
Enter name of the block you wish to redefine: *Enter the name of the block to be redefined and press ENTER.*
Select objects: *Select the new block geometry with attributes and press ENTER.*
Specify insertion base point of new Block: *Specify an insertion base point.*

After you select an insertion base point, the block is redefined and all the copies of the block in the drawing are updated. If you do not include an existing attribute when selecting objects for the new block, it will not be a part of the new block definition.

Note
*The **ATTREDEF** command removes all the formatting changes incorporated into the property by using the **ATTEDIT** or **EATTEDIT** command.*

In-place Editing of Blocks with Attributes

Ribbon: Insert > Reference > Edit Reference **Command:** REFEDIT
Toolbar: Refedit > Edit Reference In-Place

The **Edit Reference** tool has already been discussed in Chapter 16, Working with Blocks. This tool can also be used for in-place editing of blocks with attributes. After invoking the **Edit Reference** tool, select a block with attributes that you want to edit. The **Reference Edit** dialog box is displayed with the name of the block in the **Reference name** list box. To be able to edit attributes, you should select the **Display attribute definitions for editing** check box from the **Settings** tab of the dialog box and then choose the **OK** button to exit. When you select this check box, it displays the attributes and makes them available for editing. Next, you can select any part of the block with attributes that need to be edited and press ENTER. If you want to edit some other objects that are part of the block, you can select them too. All the selected objects become a part of the working set. You will notice that when you select the block with attributes, the tags replace the assigned attribute values and objects in the drawing that were not selected appear faded.

You can now edit the block geometry or edit only the attributes. To edit an attribute, double-click on it; the respective **Edit Attribute Definition** dialog box will be displayed, refer to Figure 17-51. Using the options in this dialog box, you can change the value of the attribute.

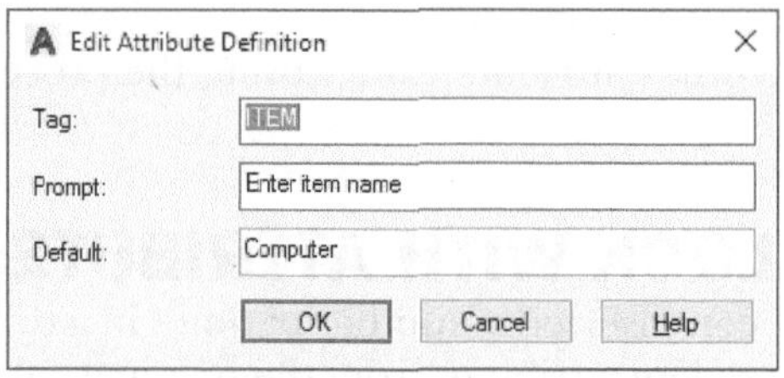

*Figure 17-51 The **Edit Attribute Definition** dialog box*

INSERTING TEXT FILES IN THE DRAWING

Ribbon: Annotate > Text > Text drop-down > Multiline Text **Command:** MTEXT
Menu Bar: Draw > Text > Multiline Text

You can insert a text file in a drawing by using the **Import Text** option that is displayed when you right-click in the text window.

On invoking the **Multiline Text** tool, AutoCAD prompts you to enter the insertion point and the other corner of the paragraph text box within which the text file will be placed. After you specify these points, the text window is displayed. To insert the text file *TEST.txt* (created in Example 3), right-click in the text window to display the shortcut menu. In this shortcut menu, choose the **Import Text** option. AutoCAD displays the **Select File** dialog box.

In the **Select File** dialog box, you can select the **TEST** text file from the list box and then choose the **Open** button. The imported text is displayed in the text window, refer to Figure 17-52. Note that only the ASCII files are properly interpreted. Now, click on the screen outside the text window to get the imported text in the selected area on the screen, refer to Figure 17-53.

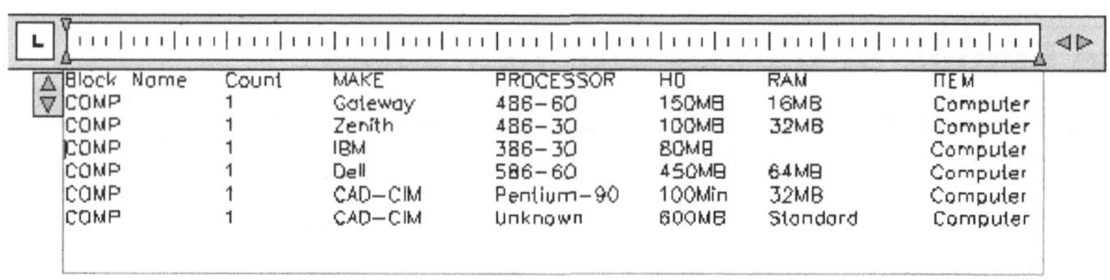

*Figure 17-52 The **Text Editor** displaying the imported text*

You can also use the **Multiline Text** tool to change the text style, height, direction, width, rotation, line spacing, and attachment.

Block Name	Count	MAKE	PROCESSOR	HD	RAM	ITEM
COMP	1	Gateway	486-60	150MB	16MB	Computer
COMP	1	Zenith	486-30	100MB	32MB	Computer
COMP	1	IBM	386-30	80MB8MB		Computer
COMP	1	Dell	586-60	450MB	64MB	Computer
COMP	1	CAD-CIM	Pentium-90	100Min	32MB	Computer
COMP	1	CAD-CIM	Unknown	600MB	Standard	Computer

Figure 17-53 *The imported text file on the screen*

Self-Evaluation Test

Answer the following questions and then compare them to those given at the end of this chapter:

1. If you have selected the **Align** option from the **Justification** drop-down list in the **Text Options** tab of the **Enhanced Attribute Editor** dialog box, the **Height** and **Rotation** edit boxes will be _________.

2. You can use the _________ tool of the **Edit Attribute** drop-down in the _________ panel of the **Insert** tab to edit attribute definitions.

3. If the value of the **ATTDIA** variable is _________, it disables the **Edit Attribute** dialog box.

4. In the _________ file, the records are not separated by a comma and the character fields are not enclosed in single quotes.

5. The _________ tool is used to redefine an existing block with attributes in a drawing.

6. Like the **Constant** attribute, the **Preset** attribute cannot be edited. (T/F)

7. In case of tag names, any lowercase letter is automatically converted into an uppercase letter. (T/F)

8. You can choose the **Single** tool from the **Edit Attribute** drop-down in the **Block** panel to modify the justification, height, or style of an attribute value. (T/F)

9. If you select the **Display All Attributes** option in the **Attribute Display** drop-down list of the **Block** panel, then even the attributes defined with the **Invisible** mode are displayed. (T/F)

Review Questions

Answer the following questions:

1. Which of the following buttons of the **Block Attribute Manager** is used to update all instances of the selected block?

   (a) **Settings** (b) **Edit**
   (c) **Sync** (d) None of these

2. Which of the following system variables when set to 0 will suppress the display of prompts for the new values?

   (a) **ATTDIA** (b) **ATTREQ**
   (c) **ATTMODE** (d) **ATTDEF**

3. Which of the following tools is used to invoke the **Block Attribute Manager** dialog box?

   (a) **Define Attributes** (b) **Manage Attributes**
   (c) **Block Editor** (d) **Edit Reference**

4. Which of the following tools is used to update the selected block after making changes in the block?

   (a) **Create Block** (b) **Edit Reference**
   (c) **Synchronize** (d) **Edit Attribute**

5. You can insert the text file in the drawing by choosing the _________ tool in the **Tools** panel of the **Text Editor** contextual tab displayed when using the **Multiline Text** tool.

6. The function of the **Preset** option is ______________.

7. If you select the _________ check box in the **Mode** area of the **Attribute Definition** dialog box, the **Prompt** edit box will be disabled.

8. You should select the _________ check box in the **Attribute Definition** dialog box to automatically place the subsequent attribute text just below the previously defined attribute.

9. The attribute extract file is saved as a _________ file.

10. If you do not enter anything in the **Prompt** edit box, the entry made in the **Tag** edit box will be displayed as prompt. (T/F)

11. You can also use the **Find and Replace** dialog box to modify attribute values. (T/F)

12. When using the **Edit Reference** tool for in-place editing of attributes, the existing blocks in a drawing do not get updated. Only the subsequent insertions display the modified block. (T/F)

13. You can use ? and * in the string value. When these characters are used in string value, AutoCAD does not interpret them as wild-card characters. (T/F)

14. The template file name and the output file name can be the same. (T/F)

Exercise 1 — Attribute Definition

In this exercise, you will define the following attributes for a resistor and then create a block using the **Create Block** tool. The name of the block is **RESIS**. The distance between the dotted lines is 0.5 units.

Mode	**Tag name**	**Prompt**	**Default value**
Verify	RNAME	Enter name	RX
Verify	RVALUE	Enter resistance	XX
Verify, Invisible	RPRICE	Enter price	00

1. Draw the resistor, as shown in Figure 17-54.

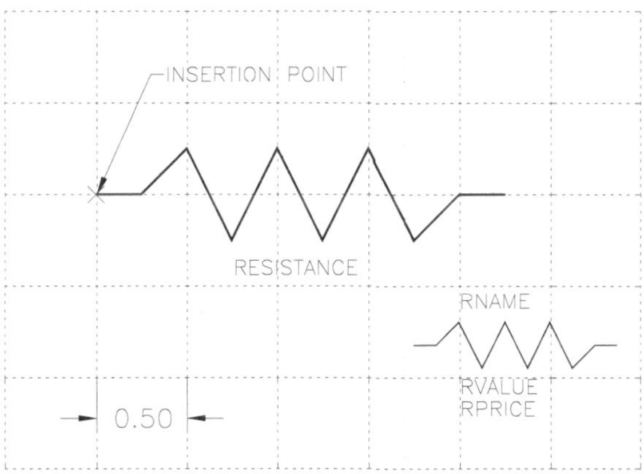

Figure 17-54 Drawing of a resistor for Exercise 1

2. Choose the **Define Attributes** tool to invoke the **Attribute Definition** dialog box.

3. Define the attributes, as shown in the preceding table, and position the attribute text as shown in Figure 17-54.

4. Use the **BLOCK** command to create a block. The name of the block is **RESIS**, and the insertion point of the block is at the left end of the resistor. When you select the objects for the block, make sure you also select the attributes.

Exercise 2

In this exercise, you will use the **Insert** tool to insert the block that was defined in Exercise 1 (RESIS). The following is the list of the attribute values for the resistances in the electric circuit:

RNAME	RVALUE	RPRICE
R1	35	.32
R2	27	.25
R3	52	.40
R4	8	.21
RX	10	.21

1. Draw the electric circuit diagram, as shown in Figure 17-55 (assume the dimensions).

2. Set the system variable **ATTDIA** to **1**. Use the **Insert** tool to insert the blocks and define the attribute values in the **Attribute Definition** dialog box.

3. Repeat the **Insert** tool to insert other blocks, and define their attribute values as given in the table. Save the drawing as *attexr2.dwg*, refer to Figure 17-56.

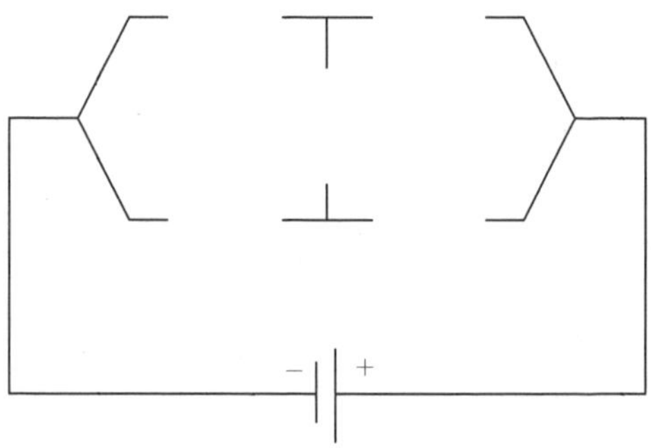

Figure 17-55 *Electric circuit diagram without resistors for Exercise 2*

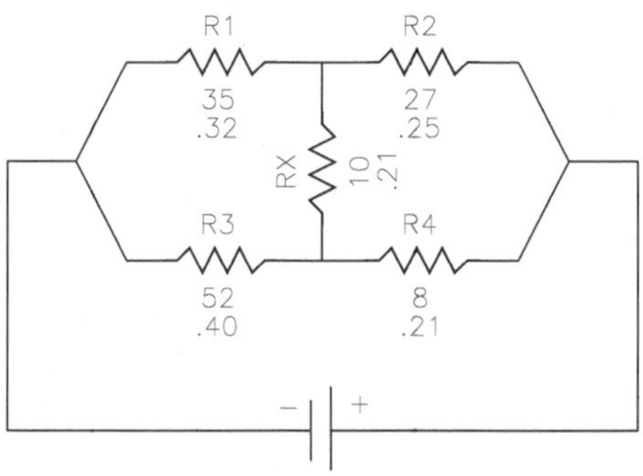

Figure 17-56 *Electric circuit diagram with resistors for Exercise 2*

Exercise 3 — Data Extraction

In this exercise, you will extract the attribute values that were defined in Exercise 2. Extract the values of RNAME, RVALUE, and RPRICE. These attribute values must be saved in a *.txt* file format named **RESISLST** and arranged, as shown in the following table.

RESIS	1	R1	35	.32
RESIS	1	R2	27	.25
RESIS	1	R3	52	.40
RESIS	1	R4	8	.21
RESIS	1	RX	10	.21

1. Load the drawing **ATTEXR2** that you saved in Exercise 2.

2. Use the **Data Extraction** tool to invoke the **Data Extraction** wizard and create a new data extraction. Next, select the **Select objects in the current drawing** radio button. Now, select the objects in the current drawing, whose attributes have to be extracted.

3. Choose the **Settings** button to invoke the **Additional Settings** dialog box. On the **Additional Settings** page, clear both the check boxes, of the **Extract objects from blocks** and **Extract objects from xrefs** and choose **OK** and then the **Next** button.

4. In the **Select Objects** page, under the object name heading, select the check box named **RESIS** if not selected by default. Choose **Next**; the **Select Properties** page is displayed.

5. In the **Select Properties** page, the list of properties that you want to extract is displayed. Clear all the check boxes, in the **Category filter** area except the **Attribute**. In the **Properties** area, clear all the check boxes and select the **RNAME**, **RVALUE**, and **RPRICE** check boxes. Choose **Next**; the **Refine Data** page is displayed, showing the preview of the data to be extracted.

6. In the **Refine Data** page you can reorder and sort columns, filter results, add formula columns, and create external data links. Choose the **Next** button; the **Choose Output** page is displayed.

7. Select **Insert data extraction table into drawing** and **Output data to external file .xls .csv .mdb .txt** check box and click on the browse button to invoke the **Save As** dialog box. Select **Text/Template/Extract file (* .txt)** in the **Files of type** drop-down. Enter *RESISLST* in the **File name** edit box and click **Save** and then the **Next** button.

8. On the **Table style** page, click **Next** and then choose the **Finish** button. You can use Notepad to open the output file, *RESISLST*. The table in the output file will be similar to the table shown at the beginning of Exercise 3.

Exercise 4 — *Edit Attribute*

In this exercise, you will use the **EATTEDIT** command to change the attributes of the resistances that are highlighted in the following table. You will also extract the attribute values and insert the text file in the drawing.

1. Load the drawing **ATTEXR2** that was created in Exercise 2. The drawing has five resistances with attributes. The name of the block is RESIS, and it has three defined attributes, one of them is invisible.

2. Double click on the block to edit the values that are highlighted in the following table.

RESIS	R1	**40**	.32
RESIS	R2	**29**	.25
RESIS	R3	52	**.45**

RESIS	R4	8	**.25**
RESIS	**R5**	10	.21

3. Extract the attribute values and write the values to a text file.

4. Use the **Multiline Text** tool to insert the text file in the drawing.

Exercise 5 *Attribute Data Extraction*

Use the information given in Exercise 3 to extract the attribute values, and write the data to the output file. The data in the output file should be Comma Delimited CDF. Use the **ATTEXT** or **-ATTEXT** commands to extract the attribute values.

Exercise 6 *Attribute Data Extraction*

In this exercise, you will create the blocks with the required attributes. Next, draw the circuit diagram shown in Figure 17-57 and then extract the attributes to create the Bill of Materials.

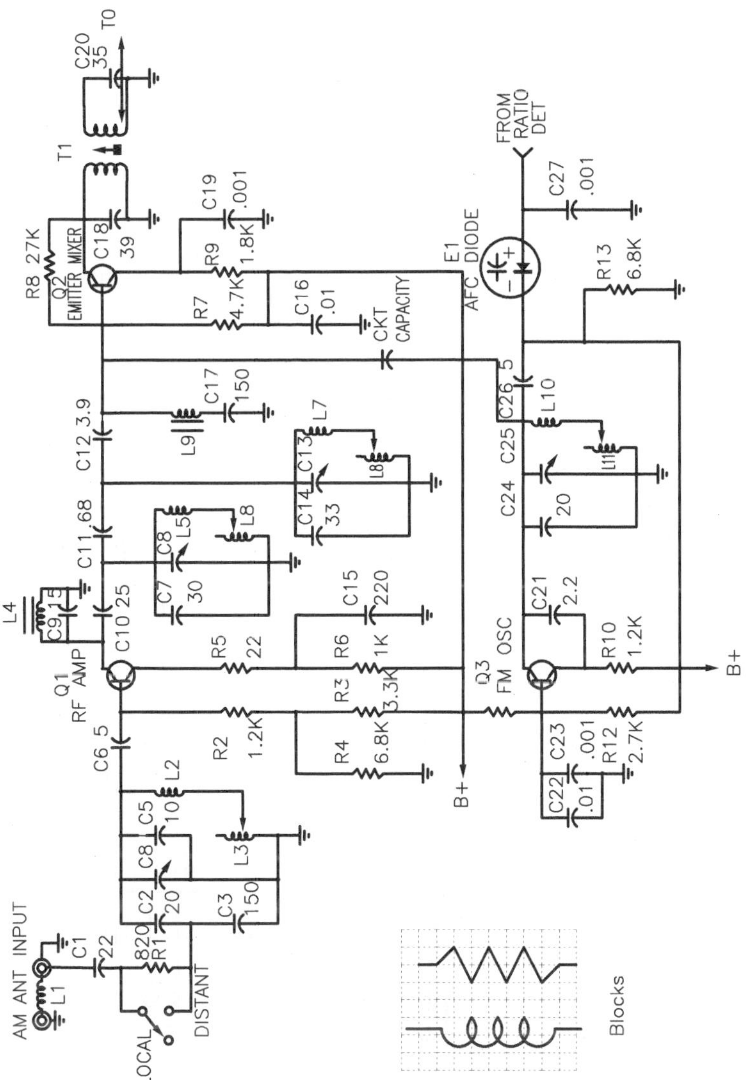

Figure 17-57 Drawing of the circuit diagram for Exercise 6

Exercise 7 — Data Extraction

In this exercise, you will create the blocks with the required attributes. Next, draw the circuit diagram shown in Figure 17-58 and then extract the attributes to create the Bill Of Materials.

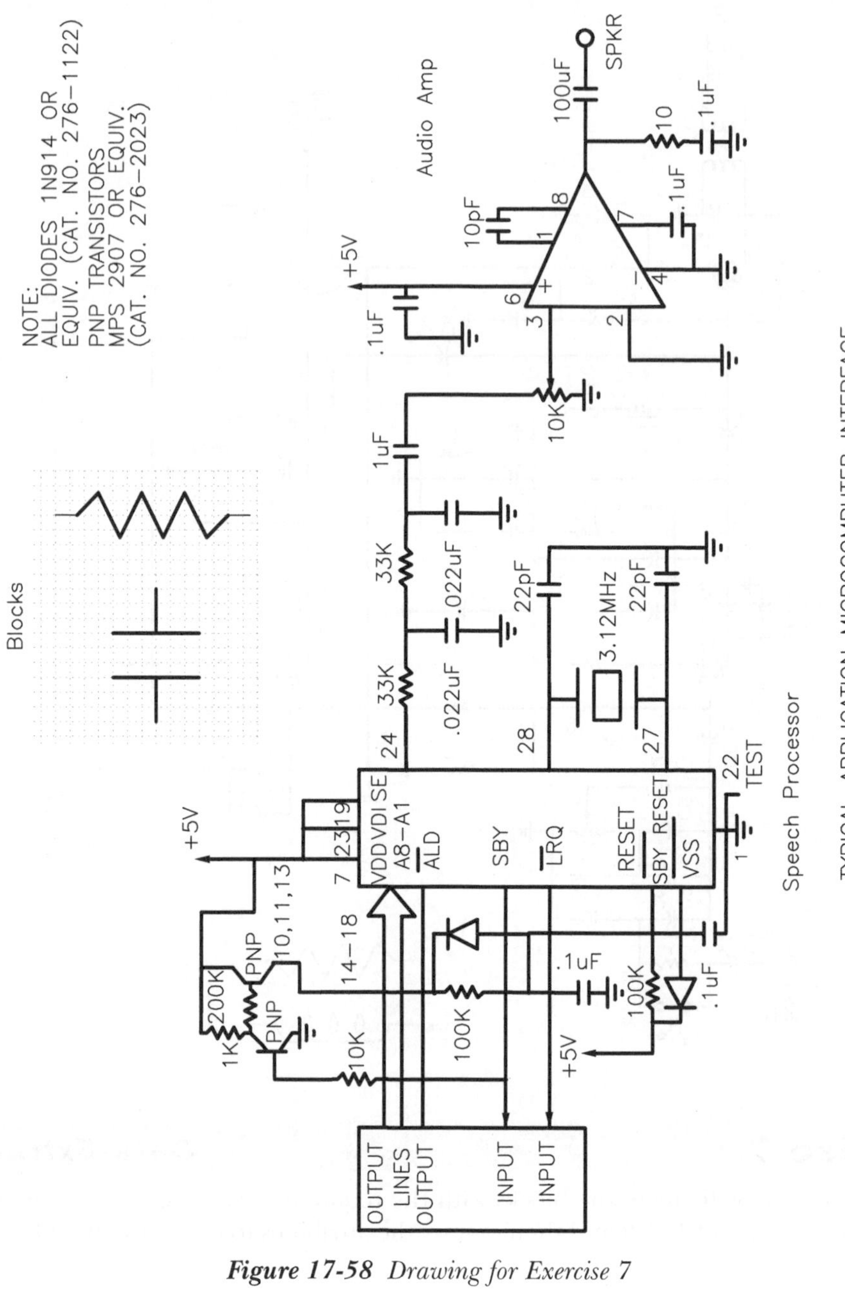

Figure 17-58 *Drawing for Exercise 7*

Answers to Self-Evaluation Test

1. disabled, 2. **Single**, **Block**, 3. 0, 4. Space Delimited, 5. **Edit Reference**, 6. F, 7. T, 8. T, 9. T

Chapter 18

Understanding External References

Learning Objectives

After completing this chapter, you will be able to:

- *Understand external references and their applications*
- *Understand dependent symbols*
- *Use the External References Palette*
- *Use the Attach, Unload, Reload, Detach, and Bind options*
- *Edit the path of an xref*
- *Understand the difference between the Overlay and Attachment options*
- *Use of the Attach tool*
- *Work with Underlays*
- *Use the DesignCenter to attach a drawing as an xref*
- *Use the Bind tool to add dependent symbols*
- *Use the Clip tool to clip xref drawings*
- *Use the Edit Reference tool for in-place editing*

Key Terms

- *XRef*
- *Attach*
- *Reload*
- *Detach*
- *Unload*
- *Bind*
- *Overlay*
- *Underlay*
- *Frame*
- *Clip*

EXTERNAL REFERENCES

The external reference feature allows you to reference an external drawing without making that drawing a permanent part of the existing drawing. For example, assume that you have an assembly drawing ASSEM1 that consists of two parts, SHAFT and BEARING. The SHAFT and BEARING are separate drawings created by two CAD operators or provided by two different vendors. You want to create an assembly drawing from these two parts. One way to create an assembly drawing is to insert these two drawings as blocks by using the **Insert** tool in the **Block** panel. Now assume that the design of BEARING has changed due to customer or product requirements. To update the assembly drawing, you have to make sure that you insert the BEARING drawing after the changes have been made. If you forget to update the assembly drawing, then the assembly drawing will not reflect the changes made in the piece part drawing. In a production environment, this could have serious consequences.

You can solve this problem by using the external reference facility, which lets you link the piece part drawings with the assembly drawing. If the xref drawings (piece part) get updated, the changes are automatically reflected in the assembly drawing. This way the assembly drawing stays updated, no matter when the changes were made in the piece part drawings. There is no limit to the number of drawings that you can reference. You can also have nested references. For example, the piece part drawing BEARING could be referenced in the SHAFT drawing, and the SHAFT drawing could be referenced in the assembly drawing ASSEM1. When you open or plot the assembly drawing, AutoCAD automatically loads the referenced drawing SHAFT and the nested drawing BEARING. While using external references, several people working on the same project can reference the same drawing and all the changes made are displayed everywhere the particular drawing is being used.

If you use the **Insert** tool to insert the piece parts, the piece parts become a permanent part of the drawing, and therefore, the drawing file size increases. However, if you use the external reference feature to link the drawings, the piece part drawings are not saved with the assembly drawing. AutoCAD only saves the reference information with the assembly drawing; therefore, the size of the drawing is minimized. Like blocks, the xref drawings can be scaled, rotated, or positioned at any desired location, but they cannot be exploded. You can also use only a part of the xref by making clipped boundary of xrefs.

Tip

External referenced drawings are useful for creating parts or subassemblies and then putting them together in one drawing to create the main assembly. You can also use it for laying out the contents of a drawing with multiple views before plotting.

DEPENDENT SYMBOLS

When you use the **Insert** tool to insert a drawing, the information about the named objects is lost, if names are duplicated. However, if they are unique, they are imported. The named objects are entries such as blocks, text styles and layers. For example, if the assembly drawing has a layer Hidden of green color and HIDDEN linetype and the piece part Bearing has also a layer Hidden of blue color and HIDDEN2 linetype, the values set in the assembly drawing will override the values of the inserted drawing when the Bearing drawing is inserted in the assembly drawing, refer to Figure 18-1. As a result, in the assembly drawing, the layer Hidden will retain green color and HIDDEN linetype, ignoring the layer settings of the inserted drawing. Only those layers that have the same names are affected. The remaining layers that have different layer names are added to the current drawing.

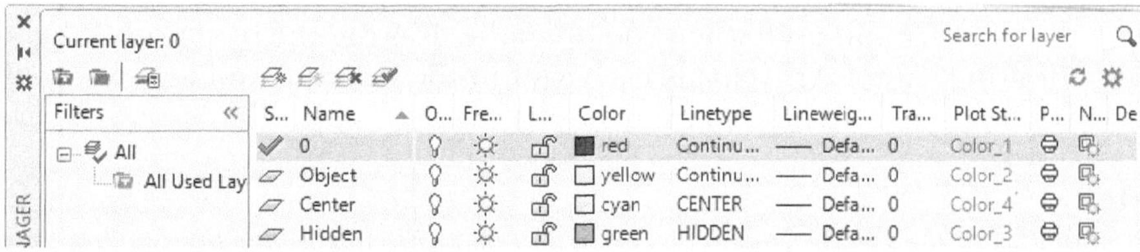

Figure 18-1** Partial view of the layer settings of the current drawing in the **LAYER PROPERTIES MANAGER

In the xref drawings, the information about the named objects is not lost because AutoCAD will create additional named objects such as specified layer settings, as shown in Figure 18-2. For xref drawings, these named objects become dependent symbols (features such as layers, linetypes, object color, text style, and so on).

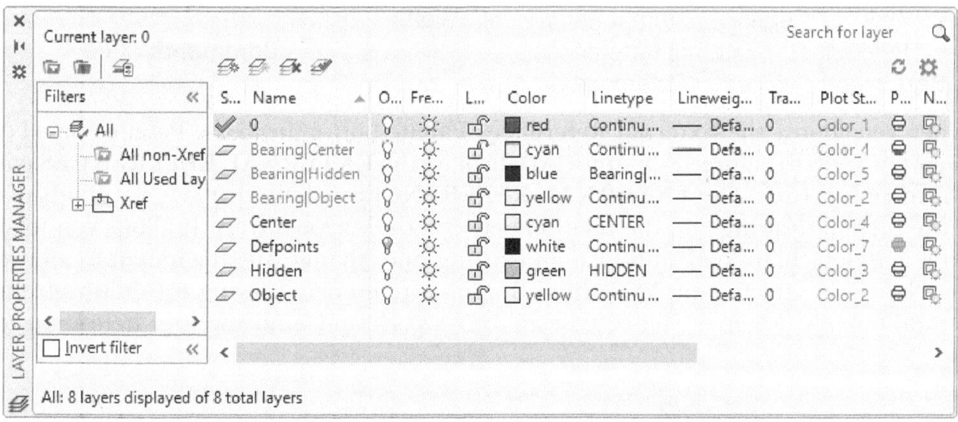

***Figure 18-2** Additional layers created by xref*

The layer Hidden of the xref drawing (Bearing) is appended with the name of the xref drawing Bearing, and the two are separated by the vertical bar symbol (|). The names of these layers appear in light gray color in the **LAYER PROPERTIES MANAGER** or **Layer** drop-down list of the **Layers** panel in the **Home** tab. These layers can neither be selected nor be made current. The layer name Object changes to Bearing|Object. Similarly, Center is renamed as Bearing|Center, refer to Figure 18-2. The information added to the current drawing is not permanent. It is added only when the xref drawing is loaded. If you detach the xref drawing, the dependent symbols are automatically erased from the current drawing.

When you xref a drawing, AutoCAD does not let you reference the symbols directly. For example, you cannot make the dependent layer, Bearing|Object, as current layer. Therefore, you cannot add any objects to that layer. However, you can change the color, linetype, lineweight, plotstyle, or visibility (on/off, freeze/thaw) of the layer in the current drawing. If the **Retain changes to Xref layers** check box in the **External References (Xrefs)** area of the **Open and Save** tab of the **Options** dialog box is cleared, which also implies that the system variable **VISRETAIN** is set to 0, the settings are retained only for the current drawing session. This means that when you save and exit the drawing, the changes are discarded and the layer settings return to their default status. If this check box is selected (default), which also implies that the **VISRETAIN** variable is set to 1, layer settings such as color, linetype, on/off, and freeze/thaw are retained, and they are saved with the drawing and used when you open the drawing the next time. Whenever you open or plot a drawing, AutoCAD reloads each xref in the drawing and as a result, the latest version of the drawing is loaded automatically.

Note

You cannot make the xref-dependent layers current in a drawing. When the xref drawing is bound to the current drawing by using the ***XBIND*** *command, only then you can make the xref-dependent layers a permanent part of the current drawing and use them. The* ***XBIND*** *command will be discussed later in this chapter.*

MANAGING EXTERNAL REFERENCES IN A DRAWING

Ribbon: View > Palettes > External References Palette
Toolbar: Reference > External References **Command:** XREF
Menu Bar: Insert > External References

When you choose the **External References Palette** button from the **Palettes** panel of the **View** tab, refer to Figure 18-3, AutoCAD displays the **EXTERNAL REFERENCES** palette, as shown in Figure 18-4. The **EXTERNAL REFERENCES** palette displays the status of each Xref in the current drawing and the relation between the various Xrefs. It allows you to attach a new xref and detach, unload, and load an existing one, change an attachment to an overlay, or an overlay to an attachment. You can also open a reference drawing for editing from this palette. Additionally, it allows you to edit an xref's path and bind the xref definition to the drawing.

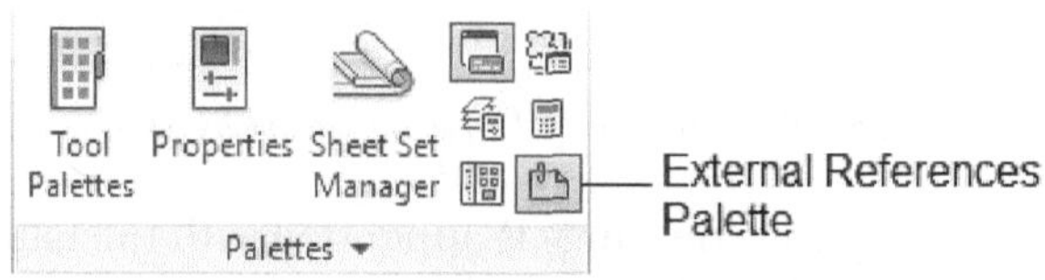

Figure 18-3 The ***Palettes*** *panel*

Apart from the methods mentioned in the command box, you can also invoke the **EXTERNAL REFERENCES** palette by selecting an xref in the current drawing and then right-clicking in the drawing area to display a shortcut menu. Next, choose **External References** from the shortcut menu; the **EXTERNAL REFERENCES** palette will be displayed.

The upper right corner of the palette has two buttons: **List View** and **Tree View**.

List View

When you choose the **List View** button, the xrefs present in the drawing are displayed in alphabetical order. This is the default view. The list view displays information about xrefs in the current drawing under the following headings:

Reference Name
This column lists the name of all existing references in the current drawing.

Status
This column lists the current status of each xref in the drawing. It lists whether an xref is loaded, unloaded, unreferenced, not found, orphaned, unresolved, or marked to be reloaded. A loaded xref implies that the xref is attached to the current drawing. You can then unload it and then reload it using the options in the dialog box (this will be discussed later). An xref selected to be unloaded or reloaded displays **Unload** and **Needs reloading** respectively, under the **Status** column. If the xref has nested references that cannot be found, the status is **Unreferenced**, and if the parent of the nested reference gets unloaded, or cannot be found, its status is described as **Orphaned**. An unreferenced xref will not be displayed. If the xref is not found in the search paths defined, its status is **Not Found**. A missing xref or one that cannot be found is **Unresolved**.

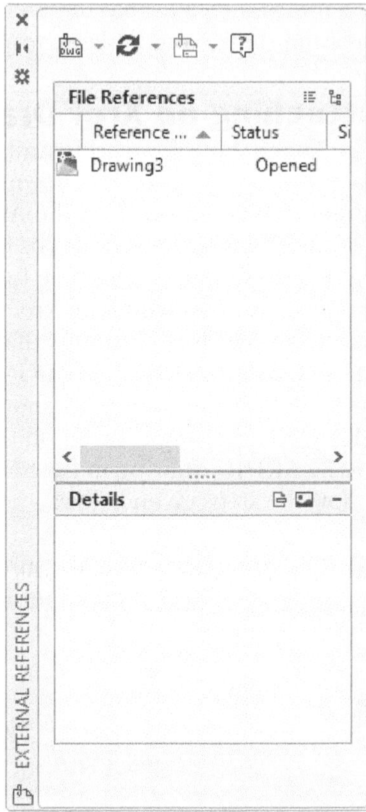

Figure 18-4 *The* ***EXTERNAL REFERENCES*** *palette*

Size
The file size of each xref is listed here.

Type
This column lists whether the xref is an attachment or overlay.

Date
This column lists the date on which the xref drawing was last saved.

Saved Path
This column lists the path of the xref, that is, the route taken to locate the particular referenced drawing.

Choose any of these headings; AutoCAD sorts and lists the Xrefs in the current drawing according to that particular title. For example, on choosing **Reference Name**, the xrefs are sorted and listed as per the name. The column widths can be increased or decreased as per your requirements. When you place your cursor at the edge of a column title button, the cursor changes to a horizontal resizing cursor. Now, press the pick button of your mouse and drag the column edge to increase or decrease its width. After you increase the column widths, it is possible that the width of the columns extend beyond the list box width. In such a case, a horizontal scroll bar appears at the bottom of the list box. You can use the scroll bar to view the columns that extend beyond the width of the list box.

Tree View
On choosing the **Tree View** button available in the right side of the **File References** title bar, the xrefs are displayed in a hierarchical tree view in the **EXTERNAL REFERENCES** palette. It

displays information on nested xrefs and their relationship with one another. Xrefs are indicated by an icon of a paper with a paper clip. This icon appears with a cross mark when the xref gets unloaded, and if there is a missing xref, the "!" sign appears. Similarly, the arrow pointing downward indicates that the xref is unloaded. You can also choose **List View** and **Tree View** by pressing the F3 and F4 keys, respectively.

Attaching an Xref Drawing (Attach Option)

The **Attach** drop-down list is available at the upper left corner of the **EXTERNAL REFERENCES** palette. If you choose the down arrow on this button, a flyout will be displayed. Choose the **Attach DWG** option from the **Attach** drop-down list to attach an xref drawing to the current drawing. This option can also be invoked by right-clicking on the **File References** area. The following examples illustrate the process of attaching an xref to the current drawing. In this example, it is assumed that there are two drawings, SHAFT and BEARING. SHAFT is the current drawing that is loaded on the screen, as shown in Figure 18-5 and the BEARING drawing is saved on the disk. If you want to xref the BEARING drawing in the SHAFT drawing, you need to follow the steps given below:

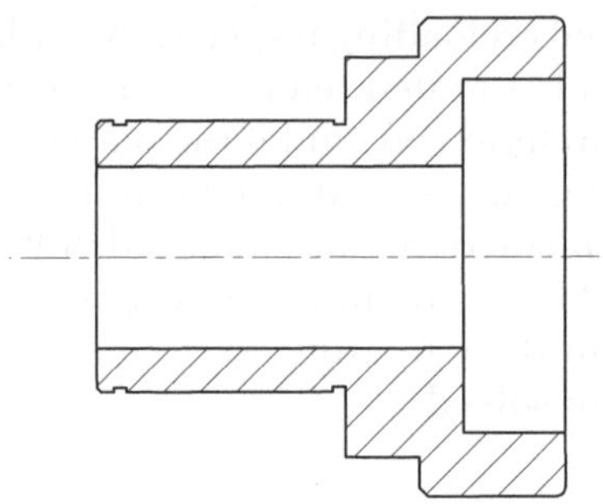

Figure 18-5 *Drawing of SHAFT*

1. The first step is to make sure that the SHAFT drawing is on the screen (draw the shaft drawing with assumed dimensions).

> **Tip**
> *No drawing needs to be on the screen. You could attach both drawings, BEARING and SHAFT to an existing drawing, even if it is a blank drawing.*

2. Choose the **External References Palette** button from the **Palettes** panel to display the **EXTERNAL REFERENCES** palette. In this palette, choose the **Attach DWG** option; the **Select Reference File** dialog box will be displayed.

   Select the drawing that you want to attach (BEARING) and then choose the **Open** button; the **Attach External Reference** dialog box will be displayed, as shown in Figure 18-6. In this dialog box, the name of the file that you have selected to be attached to the current drawing as an xref is displayed in the **Name** drop-down list. You can also specify the name of the file to be attached from the **Name** drop-down list.

> **Note**
> *AutoCAD also searches for the xref file in the paths defined in the **Project Files Search Path** folder in the **Files** tab of the **Options** dialog box. This folder does not have any path defined in it and displays **Empty** when the tree view is expanded. To define a search path, select **Empty** and choose the **Add** button in the dialog box. You can enter a project name here, if you want. Now, expand the tree view, select **Empty** again, and choose the **Browse** button; the **Browse for Folder** window*

is displayed. Select the folder that is to be searched for the file and choose the ***OK*** *button. Then, choose the* ***Apply*** *button and the* ***OK*** *button from the* ***Options*** *dialog box to exit it.*

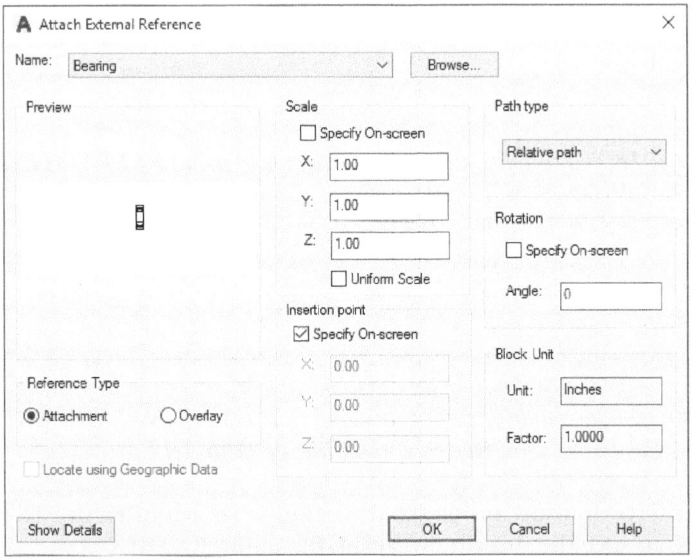

Figure 18-6 *The* ***Attach External Reference*** *dialog box*

In the **Reference Type** area, select the **Attachment** radio button, if it is not selected by default. The **Overlay** option is discussed later in this chapter. The **Path type** drop-down list is used to specify whether you want to attach a drawing with full path, relative path, or no path. If you select the **Full path** option, the precise location of the xreffed drawing is saved. If you select the **Relative path** option (if not selected by default), the position of the xreffed drawing with reference to the host drawing is saved. If you select the **No path** option, AutoCAD will search for the xreffed drawing in only that folder in which the host drawing is saved. You can also specify the insertion point, scale factors, and rotation angle in the respective **X**, **Y**, **Z**, and **Angle** edit boxes or select the **Specify On-screen** check boxes to use the pointing device to specify them on the screen. By default, the scale factors in **X**, **Y**, and **Z** edit boxes is 1 and the rotation angle is 0. The **Block Unit** area provides information regarding the units of the inserted block. The **Unit** edit box displays the unit of the block. The **Factor** edit box displays the scale factor, depending on the unit of the block and that of the current drawing. If you choose the **Show Details** button, the path of the file is displayed adjacent to **Found in**. Also, the saved path of the file is displayed adjacent to **Saved path**. Choose the **OK** button from the **Attach External Reference** dialog box to accept the default values and exit the dialog box. Specify the insertion point; the drawing is attached to the current drawing, but it appears faded. After attaching the BEARING drawing as an xref, save the current drawing with the file name SHAFT, as shown in Figure 18-7. You can control the fading intensity

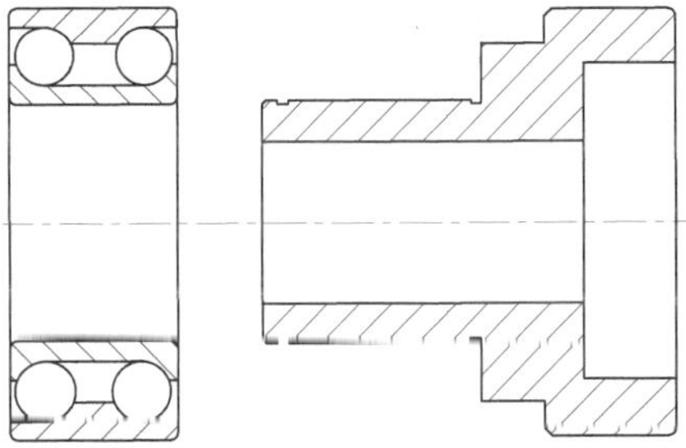

Figure 18-7 *Attaching the BEARING drawing as an xref*

of the attached objects by using the options from the **Fade control** area of the **Display** tab in the **Options** dialog box. In this area, you can either use the slider bar to increase or decrease the fading intensity or you can enter a value in the edit box. You can also use the **XDWGFADECTL** variable to control the fading intensity of other objects while editing them. By default, the fading intensity value is set to 50.

Note

In AutoCAD 2018, you can also control the Path type by using ***REFPATHTYPE*** *system variable. This system variable has three values which are given next:*

0=No path
1=Relative path (default value)
2=Full path

You can also change the Path type of an existing xreffed drawing by first invoking a shortcut menu by right-clicking on the name of xreffed drawing from ***EXTERNAL REFERENCES*** *palette and then choosing the desired path type from the* ***Change Path Type*** *cascading menu.*

3. Open the BEARING drawing and make the changes shown in Figure 18-8 (draw polylines on the sides). Now, save the drawing with the file name BEARING.

4. Open the SHAFT drawing. In the **EXTERNAL REFERENCES** palette, you will notice that the message **Needs reloading** is displayed in the **Status** column of the BEARING drawing. Right-click on the BEARING and choose **Reload**; the modified BEARING drawing is automatically updated, refer to Figure 18-9. This is the most useful feature of external reference. You could also have inserted the BEARING drawing as a block, but if you had updated the BEARING drawing, the drawing in which it was inserted would not have been updated automatically.

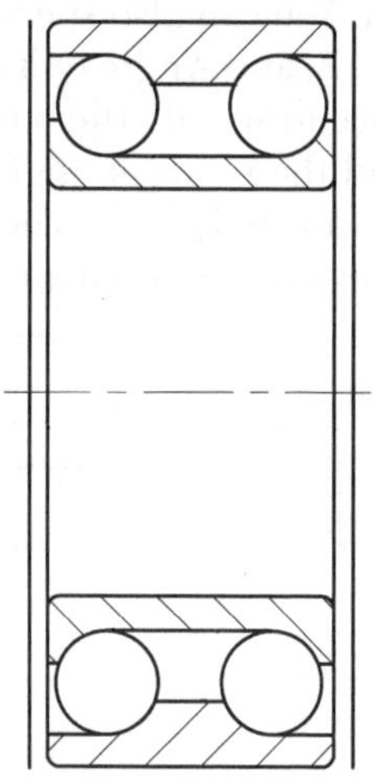

Figure 18-8 *The modified xref BEARING drawing*

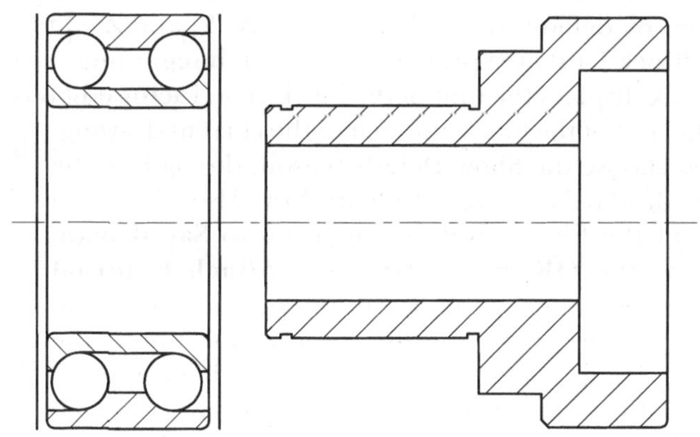

Figure 18-9 *BEARING drawing automatically updated after loading the SHAFT drawing*

When you attach an xref drawing, AutoCAD remembers the name of the attached drawing. If you xref the drawing again, AutoCAD displays a message as given next.

Xref "BEARING" has already been defined.
Using existing definition.
Specify insertion point or [Scale/X/Y/Z/Rotate/PScale/PX/PY/PZ/PRotate]: *Specify the location to place another copy of the xref.*

Note

If the external reference drawing that you want to attach is currently being edited, AutoCAD will attach the drawing that was last saved through the ***Save, Write Block,*** *or* ***Exit Autodesk AutoCAD 2018*** *buttons.*

Points to Remember about Xref

1. When you enter the name of the xref drawing, AutoCAD checks for block names and xref names. If a block exists with the same name as the name of the xref drawing in the current drawing, the **Attach** tool is terminated and an error message is displayed.

2. When you xref a drawing, the objects that are in the model space are attached. Any objects that are in the paper space are not attached to the current drawing.

3. The layer 0, DEFPOINTS, and the linetype CONTINUOUS are treated differently. The current drawing layers 0, DEFPOINTS, and linetype CONTINUOUS will override the layers and linetypes of the xref drawing. For example, if the layer 0 of the current drawing is white and the layer 0 of the xref drawing is red, the white color will override the red.

4. The xref drawings can be nested. For example, if the BEARING drawing contains the reference INRACE and you xref the BEARING drawing to the current drawing, the INRACE drawing is automatically attached to the current drawing. If you detach the BEARING drawing, the INRACE drawing gets detached automatically.

5. You can rename an xref under the **File References** column name in the list box of the **EXTERNAL REFERENCES** palette by double-clicking on the xref. You can now enter a new name. An AutoCAD warning is displayed: **Caution! "XXXX" is an externally referenced block. Renaming it will also rename its dependent symbols**.

6. When you xref a drawing, AutoCAD stores the name and path of the drawing by default. If the name of the xref drawing or the path where the drawing was originally stored has changed or you cannot find it in the path specified in the **Options** dialog box, AutoCAD cannot load the drawing, plot it, or use the **Reload** option of the **EXTERNAL REFERENCES** palette.

Detaching an Xref Drawing (Detach Option)

The **Detach** option can be used to detach or remove the xref drawings. If there are any nested xref drawings defined with the xref drawings, they are also detached. Once a drawing is detached, it is erased from the screen. To detach an xref drawing, select the file name in the **EXTERNAL REFERENCES** palette list box to highlight it and then right-click on it, a flyout will be displayed. Next, choose the **Detach** option from the flyout, the xref is completely removed from the current drawing.

Updating an Xref Drawing (Reload Option)

When you load a drawing, AutoCAD automatically loads the referenced drawings. The **Reload** option of the **EXTERNAL REFERENCES** palette lets you update the xref drawings and nested xref drawings at any time. You do not need to exit the drawing editor and then reload the drawing. To reload the xref drawings, invoke the **EXTERNAL REFERENCES** palette, select the xreffed drawing in the list box, and then right-click on it to choose the **Reload** option from the shortcut menu. AutoCAD will scan for the referenced drawings and the nested xref drawings and load the most recently saved version of the drawing.

You can reload all the attached xref drawings at one time by selecting **Reload All References** from the drop-down list of the **Refresh** button on the upper left corner of the **EXTERNAL REFERENCES** palette.

The **Reload** option is generally used when the xref drawings are currently being edited and you want to load the updated drawings. The xref drawings are updated based on what is saved on the disk. Therefore, before reloading an xref drawing, you should make sure that the xref drawings that are being edited have been saved. If AutoCAD encounters an error while loading the referenced drawings, the **External References** tool is terminated, and the entire reload operation is canceled.

Unloading an Xref Drawing (Unload Option)

The **Unload** option allows you to temporarily remove the definition of an xref drawing from the current drawing. However, AutoCAD retains the pointer to the xref drawings. When you unload the xref drawings, the drawings are not displayed on the screen. You can reload the xref drawings by using the **Reload** option.

Tip

It is recommended that you unload the referenced drawings if they are not being used. After unloading the xref drawings, the drawings load much faster and need lesser memory.

Adding an Xref Drawing (Bind Option)

The **Bind** option lets you convert the xref drawings to blocks in the current drawing. The bound drawings, including the nested xref drawings (that are no longer xrefs), become a permanent part of the current drawing. The bound drawing cannot be detached or reloaded. You can use this option when you want to send a copy of your drawing to a customer for review. Because the xref drawings are a part of the existing drawing, you do not need to include the xref drawings or the path information. You can also use this option to safeguard the master drawing from accidental editing of the piece parts. To bind the xref drawings, select the file names in the **EXTERNAL REFERENCES** palette and then right-click and choose the **Bind** option from the shortcut menu; the **Bind Xrefs/DGN underlays** dialog box is displayed, as shown in Figure 18-10. AutoCAD provides two methods to bind the xref drawing in the **Bind Type** area of the dialog box. These methods are discussed next.

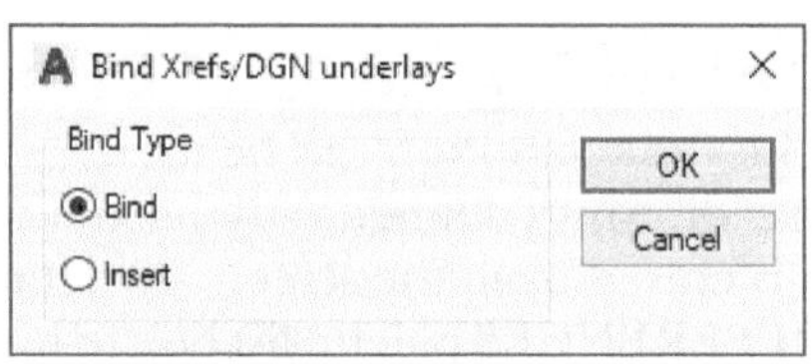

*Figure 18-10 The **Bind Xrefs/DGN underlays** dialog box*

Bind

When you use the **Bind** radio button, AutoCAD binds the selected xref definition to the current drawing. All the xrefs are converted to blocks and the named objects are renamed. For example, if you xref the drawing Bearing with a layer named Object, a new layer Bearing|Object is created in the current drawing. When you bind this drawing, the xref dependent layer Bearing|Object will become a locally defined layer Bearing0Object, refer to Figure 18-11. If the Bearing0Object layer already exits, AutoCAD will automatically increment the number, and the layer name becomes Bearing1Object.

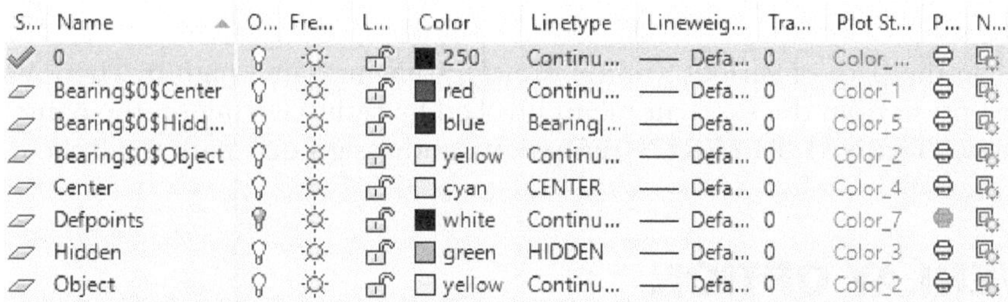

S...	Name	O...	Fre...	L...	Color	Linetype	Lineweig...	Tra...	Plot St...	P...	N...
	0				250	Continu...	Defa...	0	Color_...		
	Bearing0Center				red	Continu...	Defa...	0	Color_1		
	Bearing0Hidd...				blue	Bearing|...	Defa...	0	Color_5		
	Bearing0Object				yellow	Continu...	Defa...	0	Color_2		
	Center				cyan	CENTER	Defa...	0	Color_4		
	Defpoints				white	Continu...	Defa...	0	Color_7		
	Hidden				green	HIDDEN	Defa...	0	Color_3		
	Object				yellow	Continu...	Defa...	0	Color_2		

Figure 18-11 *Partial view of the* ***LAYER PROPERTIES MANAGER***

Insert

When you use the **Insert** radio button, AutoCAD inserts the xref drawing. The xrefs get converted into blocks. For example, if you xref the drawing Shaft with a layer named Object, a new layer Shaft|Object is created in the current drawing. If you use the **Insert** option to bind the xref drawing, the layer name Shaft|Object is renamed as Object. If the object layer already exists, then the values set in the current drawing override the values of the inserted drawing.

Editing an XREF's Path

By default, AutoCAD saves the path of the referenced drawing and displays it in the **Saved Path** column of the **EXTERNAL REFERENCES** palette. As mentioned earlier, when AutoCAD loads the drawing containing a referenced file, and if it is not able to find the file at the location specified in the **Saved Path** column of the **EXTERNAL REFERENCES** palette, it searches for the file in the current directory, and in the **Support File Search Path** locations specified in the **Files** tab of the **Options** dialog box. If a file with the same name is found, it is loaded. Now, when you invoke the **EXTERNAL REFERENCES** palette, you will notice that if you select an xref name in the list box to highlight it, the path displayed in the **Found At** column for the xref file is different from the one displayed in the **Saved Path** edit box. To update the path of the xref file, choose the Browse button. The new path is saved and displayed in the **Found At** column.

If AutoCAD is unable to locate the specified file even in the directories specified in the **Files** tab of the **Options** dialog box, it will display an error message saying that it cannot find the specified file. The path of the file is displayed as a marker text in the current drawing. Now, when you invoke the **EXTERNAL REFERENCES** palette, the status of the drawing is shown as **Not Found**. To specify a new path for the xref file, click in the **Saved Path** field; the path will be highlighted and the Browse button will be displayed next to the path. Click on this button; the **Select new path** dialog box will be displayed. Using this dialog box, you can locate the drawing to be used as xref. Once you have found the file, choose the **Open** button to return to the **EXTERNAL REFERENCES** palette. The new path is displayed in the **Found At** column and the **Saved Path** edit box. The specified xref file is reloaded and replaces the marker text in the drawing, when you choose the **OK** button in the **EXTERNAL REFERENCES** palette. If you remember the new location of the xref file, you can also enter it in the **Saved Path** edit box. For example, if a drawing, which was originally in the C:\CAD\Proj1 subdirectory, has been moved to C:\Parts directory, the path must be edited so that AutoCAD is able to load the xref drawing.

In AutoCAD 2018, you can assign new path to the xreffed file whose path is missing by choosing the **Select New Path** option from the shortcut menu invoked by right clicking on the name of xreffed drawing from **EXTERNAL REFERENCES** palette. You can also assign the same path to every file whose path is missing using this tool.

You can change the path of various xreffed drawings having same path by choosing the **Find and Replace** option from the shortcut menu invoked by right-clicking on the name of xreffed drawing from **EXTERNAL REFERENCES** palette and assign new path to all the drawings at once.

THE OVERLAY OPTION

As discussed earlier, when you attach an xref to a drawing, the **Attach External Reference** dialog box is displayed. The **Reference Type** area of this dialog box has two radio buttons, **Attachment** and **Overlay**. You can select any of these radio buttons to xref a drawing. The **Attachment** radio button is selected by default. The advantage of selecting the **Overlay** radio button is that you can access the desired drawing instead of the drawing along with its xreffed attachments. For example, consider three people working on three different drawings that are a part of the same project. The first designer is working on the layout of walls of a room, the second designer is working on the furniture layout of the room, and the third on the electrical layout of that room. The names of the drawings are WALLS, FURNITURE, and ELECTRICAL, respectively. Assume that the designer working on the walls layout selects the **Attachment** radio button to xref the FURNITURE drawing so that he or she can check the furniture layout according to the wall structure. After insertion, the WALLS drawing will comprise the wall structure (current drawing) along with the furniture layout (xreffed drawing). Now, if the designer working on the electrical layout xrefs the WALLS drawing to check the location of electrical fittings with respect to the walls, he/she will get the drawing that has the furniture layout as well as the wall layout. This is because the FURNITURE drawing was xreffed in the WALLS drawing by selecting the **Attachment** radio button.

In this example, the designer working on the ELECTRICAL drawing may not require the FURNITURE drawing. This is because at this stage, the designer will be more interested in checking the electrical fittings with respect to the wall structure. So the furniture layout that is xreffed with the wall structure needs to be avoided. This can be done by selecting the **Overlay** radio button while X-referencing the FURNITURE drawing in the WALLS drawing. This means that the designer working on the wall structure needs to xref the furniture layout by selecting the **Overlay** radio button. Now, if the wall structure is xreffed in some other drawing, the furniture layout will not appear.

One of the problems of using the **Attachment** option is that you cannot have a circular reference. For example, assume you are designing the plant layout of a manufacturing unit. One person is working on the floor plan, refer to Figure 18-12, and the second person is working on the furniture layout in the offices, refer to Figure 18-13. The names of the drawings are FLOORPLN

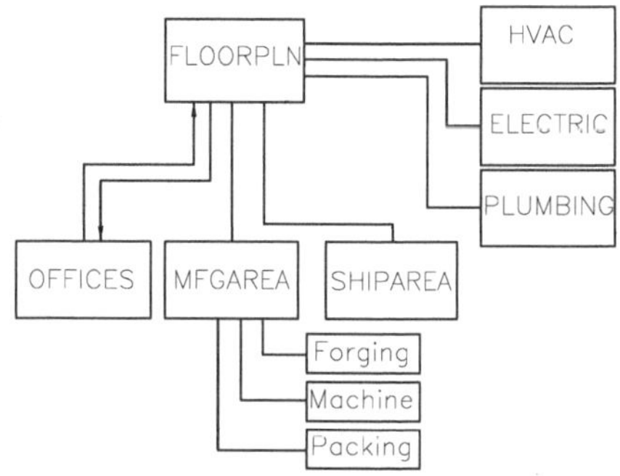

Figure 18-12 *Hierarchy of FLOORPLAN drawing*

and OFFICES, respectively. The person working on the office layout uses the **Attachment** option to insert the FLOORPLN drawing so that he or she has the latest floor plan drawing. The person who is working on the floor plan wants to reference the OFFICES drawing.

Now, if the **Attachment** option is used to reference the drawings, AutoCAD displays an error message. This is because by attaching the OFFICES drawing, a circular reference is created. The AutoCAD message displayed is "**Circular references detected. Continue?**", as shown in Figure 18-14. If you choose the **No** button, the **External References Palette** tool is canceled and no drawing is referenced. But if you choose the **Yes** button, the following message **Breaking circular reference from "offices" to "current drawing"** is displayed at command line and the particular file you wanted to reference gets referenced.

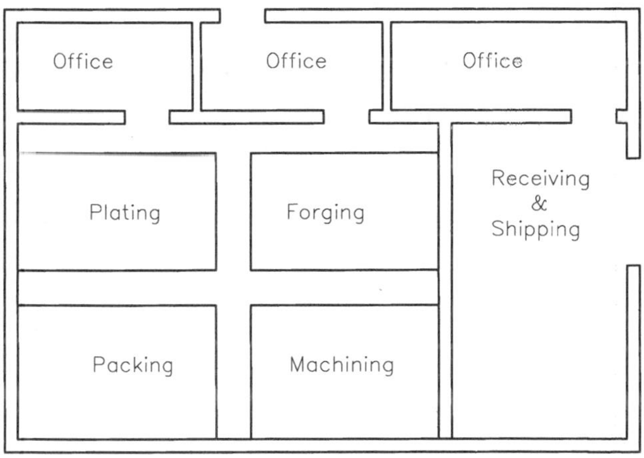

Figure 18-13 *Hierarchy of OFFICES drawing*

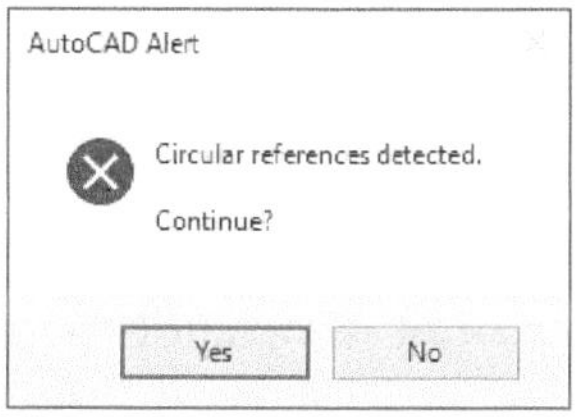

Figure 18-14 *The* ***AutoCAD Alert*** *message box*

However, to overcome this problem of circular reference, you can use the **Overlay** option to overlay the OFFICES drawing. This is a very useful option because the **Overlay** option lets different operators avoid circular reference and share the drawing data without affecting the drawing. Overlaying allows you to view a referenced drawing without having to attach it to the current drawing. This option can be invoked by selecting the **Overlay** radio button in the **Attach External Reference** dialog box, which is displayed after you have selected a drawing to reference. Also, when a drawing that has a nested overlay is overlaid, the nested overlay is not visible in the current drawing. This is another difference between attaching an xref and overlaying an xref to a drawing. This feature is especially useful when you want to reference a drawing that another user who is referencing your drawing does not need. Although the attachment will reference the nested reference too, the overlay option ignores nested references.

In AutoCAD, you can change an external referenced file from attachment to overlay and vice-versa. To do so, select the file from the **EXTERNAL REFERENCES** palette and right-click on it; a shortcut menu will be displayed, refer to Figure 18-15. Hover the cursor on the **Xref Type** option in the shortcut menu; two options are displayed, **Attach** and **Overlay**. Select the option as per requirement. The selected file will become attachment or overlay as per the option selected. You can change the type of multiple reference files by selecting all of them and then right-clicking on them.

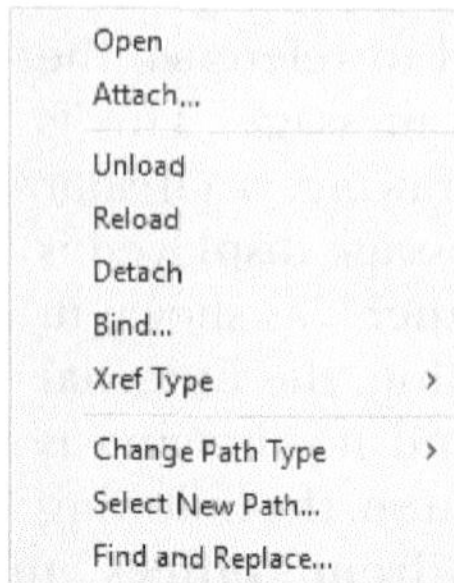

Figure 18-15 *The shortcut menu*

Example 1 — Attachment and Overlay

In this example, you will use the **Attachment** and **Overlay** options to attach and reference the drawings. Two drawings, PLAN and PLANFORG are given. The PLAN drawing, refer to Figure 18-16, consists of the floor plan layout, and the PLANFORG drawing, refer to Figure 18-17 has the details of the forging section only. The CAD operator who is working on the PLANFORG drawing wants to xref the PLAN drawing for reference. Also, the CAD operator working on the PLAN drawing should be able to xref the PLANFORG drawing to complete the project. The following steps illustrate how to accomplish the defined task without creating a circular reference.

Download these files from *http://www.cadcim.com*. The path of the file is as follows: Textbooks>CAD/CAM>AutoCAD>AutoCAD 2018: A Problem-Solving Approach, Basic and Intermediate >Input Files.

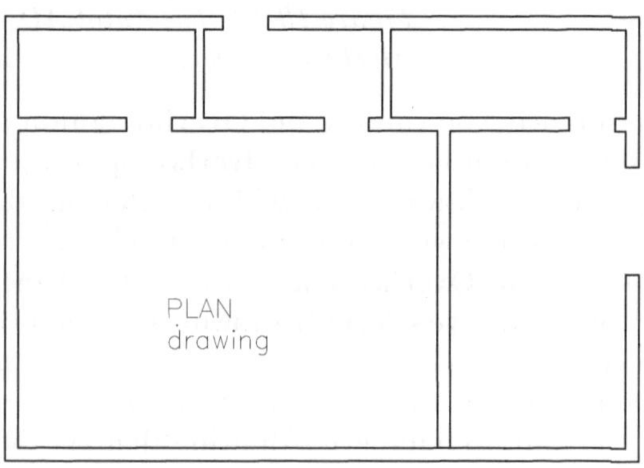

Figure 18-16 *The PLAN drawing*

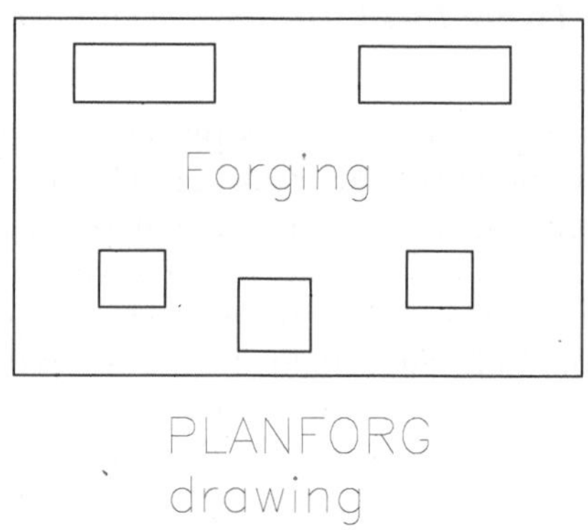

Figure 18-17 *The PLANFORG drawing*

How circular reference is caused?

1. Open the drawing PLANFORG and then choose the **External References Palette** button from the **Palettes** panel in the **View** tab. Next, choose the **Attach DWG** option from the

EXTERNAL REFERENCES palette; the **Select Reference File** dialog box is displayed. Select the PLAN drawing from the list box of the **Select Reference File** dialog box and choose the **Open** button; the **Attach External Reference** dialog box is displayed. In this dialog box, the name of the PLAN drawing is displayed in the **Name** edit box, and the **Attachment** radio button is selected by default in the **Reference Type** area. Choose the **OK** button to exit the dialog box and specify an insertion point on the screen. Now, the drawing consists of the PLANFORG and PLAN. Save the drawing.

2. Open the drawing file PLAN. Next, choose the **External References Palette** button and attach the PLANFORG drawing to the PLAN drawing using the same steps as described in Step 1. AutoCAD will display the message that the circular reference has been detected and will ask you if you want to continue. If you choose **Yes** in the AutoCAD message box, the circular reference is broken and you are allowed to reference the specific drawing.

   The possible solution for the operator working on the PLANFORG drawing is to detach the PLAN drawing. This way the PLANFORG drawing does not contain any reference to the PLAN drawing and would not cause any circular reference. The other solution is to use the **Overlay** option, as follows :

How to prevent circular reference?

3. Open the PLANFORG drawing, refer to Figure 18-18 and select the **Overlay** radio button in the **Attach External Reference** dialog box, which is displayed after you have selected the PLAN drawing to reference. The PLAN drawing is overlaid on the PLANFORG drawing, refer to Figure 18-19. Save the drawing.

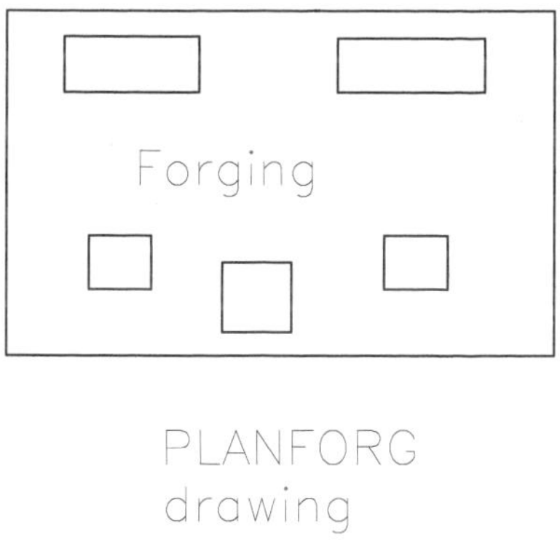

Figure 18-18 *The PLANFORG drawing*

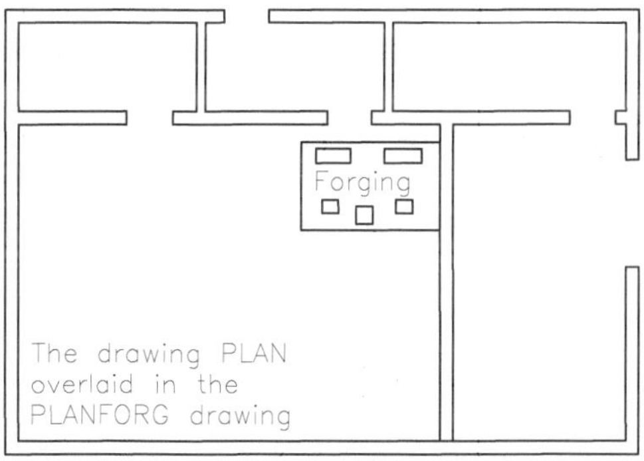

Figure 18-19 *The PLANFORG drawing after overlaying the PLAN drawing*

4. Open the drawing file PLAN, refer to Figure 18-20, and select the **Attachment** radio button in the **Attach External Reference** dialog box, which is displayed when you select the PLANFORG drawing in the **Select Reference File** dialog box to attach it as an xref to the PLAN drawing. You will notice that only the PLANFORG drawing is attached, refer to Figure 18-21. The drawing that was overlaid in the PLANFORG drawing (PLAN) does not appear in the current drawing. This way, the CAD operator working on the PLANFORG drawing can overlay the PLAN drawing, and the CAD operator working on the PLAN drawing can attach the PLANFORG drawing, without causing a circular reference.

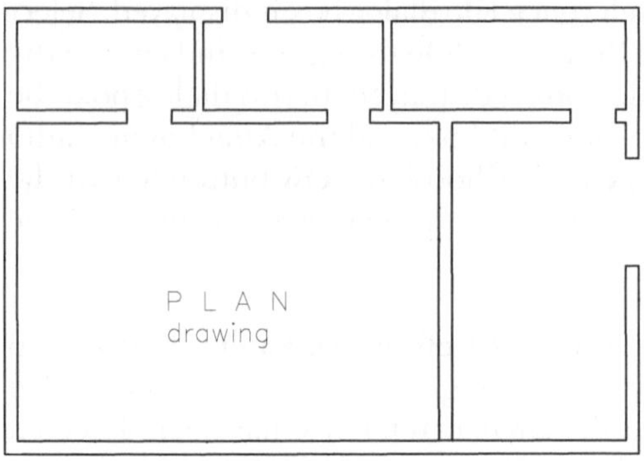

Figure 18-20 The PLAN drawing

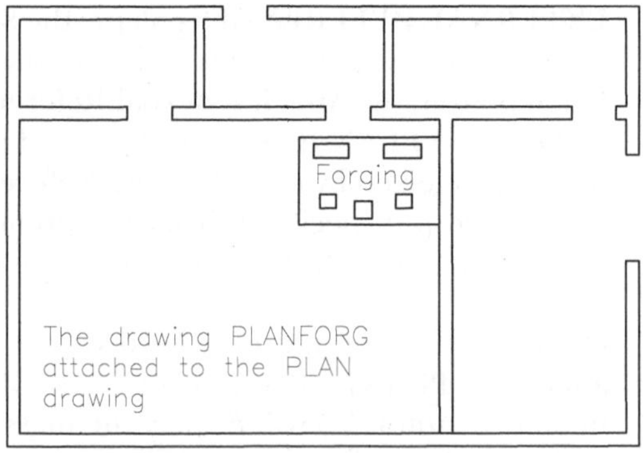

Figure 18-21 The PLAN drawing after attaching the PLANFORG drawing

ATTACHING FILES TO A DRAWING

Ribbon: Insert > Reference > Attach **Command:** ATTACH

You can use the **Attach** tool in the **Reference** panel, refer to Figure 18-22, to attach a DWG, DGN, DWF, PDF, Autodesk Point Cloud files, Navisworks files, or image file without invoking the **EXTERNAL REFERENCES** palette. Using this tool, you can attach a drawing file easily, since most of the xref operations involve simply attaching a drawing file. When you invoke this tool, AutoCAD displays the **Select Reference File** dialog box. To attach a *.dwg, .dgn, .dwf, .pdf, .rcp, rcs, .nwc, .nwd,* or image file, specify it in the **Files of type** drop-down list in the **Select Reference File** dialog box; the corresponding files will be listed in the dialog box. Select the drawing file to be attached and choose the **Open** button; the **Attach External Reference** dialog box is displayed. Select the **Attachment** radio button (if not selected by default) under the **Reference Type** area. You can specify the insertion point, scale, and rotation angle on screen or in the respective edit boxes.

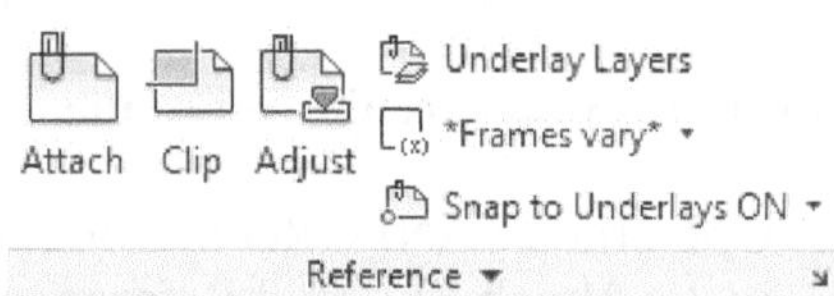

*Figure 18-22 The **Attach** tool in the **Reference** panel*

Note

*1. To select a .dgn, .dwf, .pdf, or image file, specify the file type in the **Files of type** drop-down list in the **Select Reference File** dialog box; the files will be attached as an underlay. Underlays are discussed in the next section.*

*2. AutoCAD maintains a log file (.xlg) for xref drawings if the **XREFCTL** system variable is set to 1. This file lists information about the date and time of loading and other xref operations to be completed. This .xlg file is saved in the current drawing with the same name as the current drawing and is updated each time the drawing is loaded or any xref operations are carried out.*

WORKING WITH UNDERLAYS

You can attach a DWF, DGN, or PDF file as an underlay to the current drawing file. The underlay files are not a part of original drawing files. Therefore, if you add a file as an underlay, it does not increase the file size of the current drawing. The procedure to add a file as an underlay is similar to attaching a drawing file using the **Attach** tool. After you select the file to attach, the **Attach <XXXX> Underlay** dialog box will be displayed, where <XXXX> is the file type. Figure 18-23 shows the **Attach PDF Underlay** dialog box that is displayed on selecting a pdf file from the **Select Reference File** dialog box.

If the selected *.pdf* file has multiple pages, all pages of the pdf file are listed in the **Select one or more pages from the PDF file** area. Select the pages to be attached from this area. If you have selected multiple pages as well as the **Specify on-screen** check box from the **Insertion point** area, then you are prompted to specify different insertion points for different pages.

The files attached as an underlay behave like blocks. The general modify commands like move, copy, rotate, mirror, and so on can be applied on them. However, you cannot bind a file that is attached as an underlay or modify the attached file in the current drawing file.

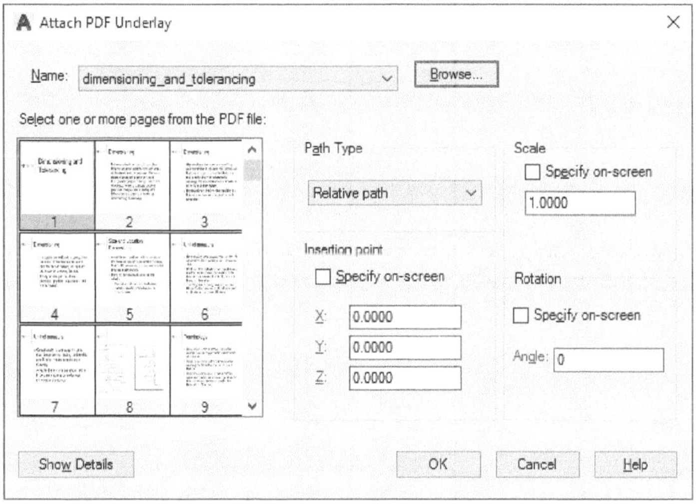

*Figure 18-23 The **Attach PDF Underlay** dialog box*

Editing an Underlay

As discussed earlier, you cannot edit a file that is attached as an underlay. However, you can control the appearance of the underlay by adjusting the contrast, fade, and monochrome display. To do so, select the attached object; a contextual tab will be displayed. Figure 18-24 shows the **PDF Underlay** tab that is displayed on selecting a PDF file.

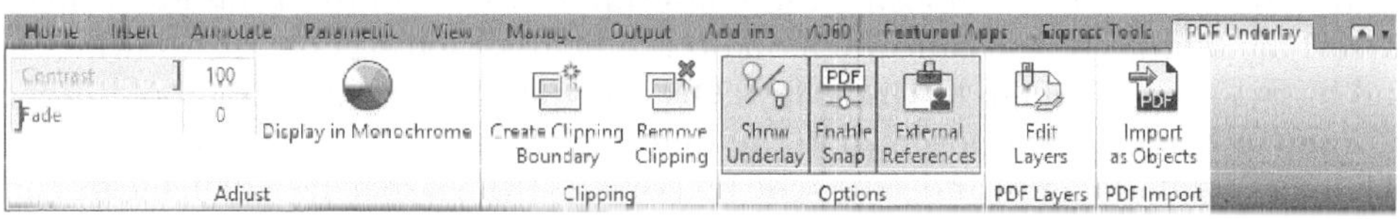

*Figure 18-24 The **PDF Underlay** tab*

You can use the options in this contextual tab to adjust the fade, contrast, and monochrome display of the underlay. You can create a new clipping boundary similar to that of an attached drawing. By default, the **Enable Snap** button is chosen in the **Options** panel. Therefore, you can snap entities in the underlaid object. If you deselect this button, you cannot snap entities in the underlaid objects. You can use the **Show Underlay** button from the **Options** panel to display/hide the underlaid objects. Both **Enable Snap** and **Show Underlay** are toggle buttons. If the attached underlay has layers, you can hide/display the selected layers. To do so, choose the **Edit Layers** button from the **PDF Layers** panel of the **PDF Underlay** contextual tab; the **Underlay Layers** dialog box will be displayed, as shown in Figure 18-25. If multiple drawings are attached as an underlay, all file names will be listed in the **Reference Name** drop-down list. Select the file from the **Reference Name** drop-down list for which you need to hide the layers; the corresponding layers will be listed in the list box. Click on the bulb icon of the layer to be hidden. Alternatively, select the layer from the list box and right-click; a shortcut menu will be displayed. Choose the **Layer(s) Off** option to hide the selected layer. To hide multiple layers, press the CTRL key and select the layers to be hidden. Next, choose **Layer(s) Off**. Then, choose the **OK** button to exit the **Underlay Layers** dialog box.

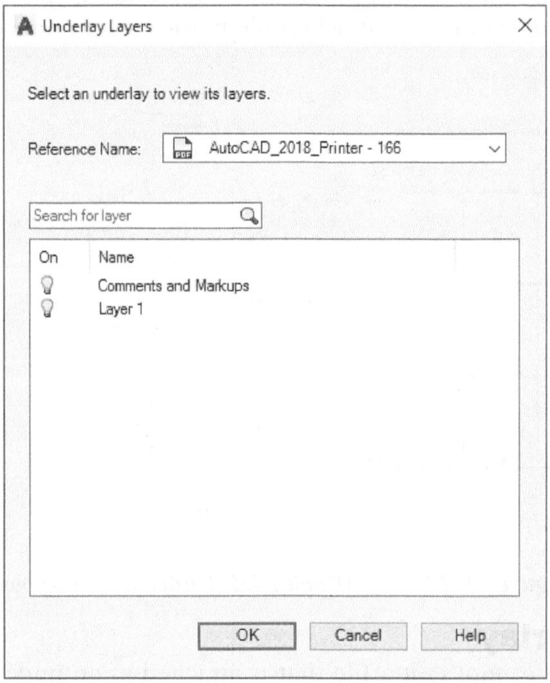

*Figure 18-25 The **Underlay Layers** dialog box*

If you have attached a file as an underlay, you can invoke the **Underlay Layers** dialog box without invoking the contextual tab by choosing the **Underlay Layers** tool from the **Reference** panel in the **Insert** tab. Similarly, you can switch on/off the OSNAP settings for the drawing that are underlaid by choosing the **Snap to Underlays ON / Snap to Underlays OFF** tool, respectively from the **Snap to Underlays** drop-down in the **Reference** panel. You can import the geometry, fills and hatches, raster images, and TrueType text objects from a specified PDF file by choosing the **Import as Objects** button from the **PDF Import** panel of the **PDF Underlay** contexual tab.

Note

*If there are more underlays of different file types and you have set different osnap setting for each file type, then the **Underlay Osnap's Vary** tool will be activated in the **Snap to Underlays** drop-down in the **Reference** panel. However, if you choose the **Snap to Underlays ON / Snap to Underlays OFF** tool, the corresponding osnap setting will be applied to all underlays.*

OPENING AN XREFFED OBJECT IN A SEPARATE WINDOW

If you are in the host drawing and you want to open a selected xreffed object in a separate window without using the **Select File** dialog box, you can use the **Open Reference** tool available in the **External Reference** contextual tab which is displayed on selecting an external reference. Select the xreffed object that you want to open in a separate window. When you select the desired xref, AutoCAD opens the DWG file of the xreffed object in a separate window. You can now make the desired changes in the DWG file of the xreffed object. Save the changes and then close the drawing. When you open the host drawing, you will notice that the **Manage xrefs** displays a message that the external reference file has changed and the xreffed drawing needs to be reloaded. Reload the xreffed drawing using the **EXTERNAL REFERENCES** palette and you will notice that the host drawing is updated.

USING THE DesignCenter TO ATTACH A DRAWING AS AN XREF

The **DESIGNCENTER** can also be used to attach an xref to a drawing. To do so, choose the **DesignCenter** button from the **Palettes** panel in the **View** tab; the **DESIGNCENTER** palette will be displayed. In the **DESIGNCENTER** palette, choose the **Tree View Toggle** button, if it is not chosen already, to display the tree pane. Expand the **Tree view** and double-click on the folder whose contents you want to view. The contents of the selected folder are displayed in the palette. From the thumbnails of drawings displayed on the right-side of the palette, right-click on the drawing to be attached as an xref; a shortcut menu is displayed, refer to Figure 18-26. Choose **Attach as Xref** from the shortcut menu; the **Attach External Reference** dialog box will be displayed. Alternatively, you can also use the right mouse button to drag and drop the drawing into the current drawing; a shortcut menu will be displayed. Choose the **Create Xref** option to insert the drawing as an xref.

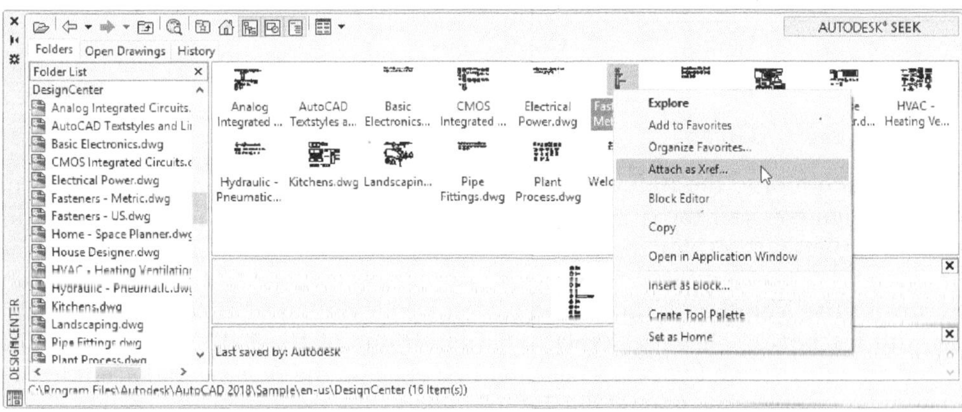

Figure 18-26 The shortcut menu displayed

In the **Attach External Reference** dialog box, the **Name** drop-down displays the name of the selected file to be inserted as an xref. Select the **Attachment** radio button in the **Reference Type** area, if not already selected. Specify the **Insertion point**, **Scale**, and **Rotation** in the respective edit boxes or select the **Specify On-screen** check boxes to specify this information on the screen.

Choose the **OK** button to exit the dialog box; the selected object is attached as an xref to the current drawing.

ADDING XREF DEPENDENT NAMED OBJECTS

Menu Bar: Modify > Object > External Reference > Bind
Toolbar: Reference > Xbind **Command:** XB/XBIND

You can use the **Xbind** tool to add the selected named objects such as blocks, dimension styles, layers, line types, and text styles of the xref drawing to the current drawing. The following example describes the use of this command.

1. Load the drawing Bearing that was created earlier. Make sure the drawing has the following layer setup. Otherwise, create the following layers using the **LAYER PROPERTIES MANAGER**.

Layer Name	Color	Linetype
0	White	Continuous
Object	Red	Continuous
Hidden	Blue	Hidden2
Center	White	Center2
Hatch	Green	Continuous

2. Draw a circle and create it as a block with the name SIDE. Save the drawing as Bearing.

3. Start a new drawing with the following layer setup:

Layer Name	Color	Linetype
0	White	Continuous
Object	Red	Continuous
Hidden	Green	Hidden

4. Use the **Attach** tool in the **Reference** panel to attach the Bearing drawing to the current drawing. When you xref the drawing, the layers will be added to the current drawing, as discussed earlier in this chapter.

5. Now, invoke the **Xbind** tool; the **Xbind** dialog box is displayed. This dialog box has two areas with list boxes. They are **Xrefs** and **Definitions to Bind**. If you want to bind the blocks defined in the xref drawing Bearing, first click on the plus sign adjacent to the xref Bearing; the icons for the named objects in the drawing are displayed in a tree view, refer to Figure 18-27. Click on the plus sign next to the Block icon. AutoCAD lists the blocks defined in the xref drawing (Bearing). Select the block Bearing|SIDE and then choose the **Add** button. The block name will be added to the **Definitions to Bind** list box. Choose the **OK** button to exit the dialog box. AutoCAD will bind the block with the current drawing and a message is displayed at the command prompt: **1 Block(s) bound**. The name of the block will change to Bearing0SIDE. You can invoke the **Block Definition** dialog box by choosing

the **Create Block** tool in the **Block Definition** panel and check the **Name** drop-down list to see if the block with the name Bearing0SIDE has been added to the drawing. If you want to insert the block, you must enter the new block name (Bearing0SIDE). You can also rename the block to another name that is easier to use.

If the block contains a reference to another xref drawing, AutoCAD binds that xref drawing and all its dependent symbols to the current drawing also. Once you bind the dependent symbols, AutoCAD does not delete them, not even when the xref drawing is detached. For example, the block Bearing0SIDE will not be deleted even when you detach the xref drawing or end the drawing session.

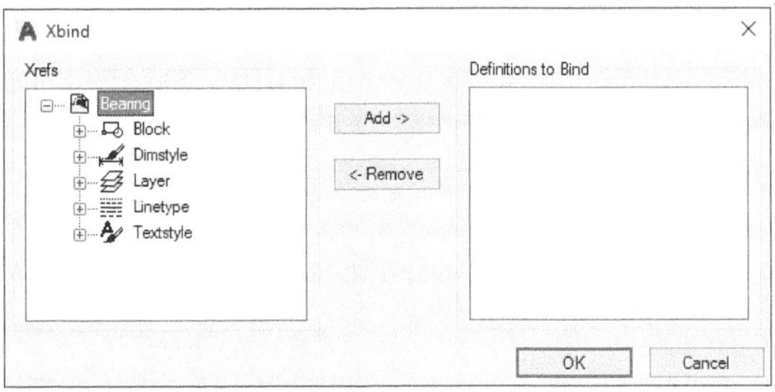

Figure 18-27 *The* ***Xbind*** *dialog box*

You can also use the **-XBIND** command to bind the selected dependent symbols of the xref drawing using the command prompt.

6. Similarly, you can bind the dependent symbols, Bearing|Standard (textstyle), Bearing|Hidden, and Bearing|Object layers of the xref drawing. Click on the plus signs adjacent to the respective icons to display the contents and then select the layer or textstyle you want to bind and choose the **Add** button. The selected named objects are displayed in the **Definitions to Bind** list box. If you have selected a named object that you do not want to bind, select it in the **Definitions to Bind** list box and choose the **Remove** button. Once you have finished selecting the named objects that you want to bind to the current drawing, choose the **OK** button. A message indicating the number of named objects that are bound to the current drawing is displayed at the command prompt.

Once bound, the layer names will change to Bearing0Hidden and Bearing0Object. If the layer name Bearing0Hidden was already there, the layer will be named Bearing1Hidden. These two layers become a permanent part of the current drawing. Even if the xref drawing is detached or the current drawing session is closed, the layers are not discarded.

CLIPPING EXTERNAL REFERENCES

Ribbon: Insert > Reference > Clip **Command:** CLIP

The **Clip** tool (Figure 18-28) is used to trim an xref after it has been attached to a drawing to display only a portion of the drawing, refer to Figure 18-29. After you have attached an xref to a drawing, you can trim it to display only a portion of the drawing by using the **Clip** tool. However, clipping xref does not modify the referenced drawing. On invoking the **Clip** tool, you are prompted to select an object to clip. Select a DWG, DGN, IMAGE, or PDF; the respective clipping options will be displayed.

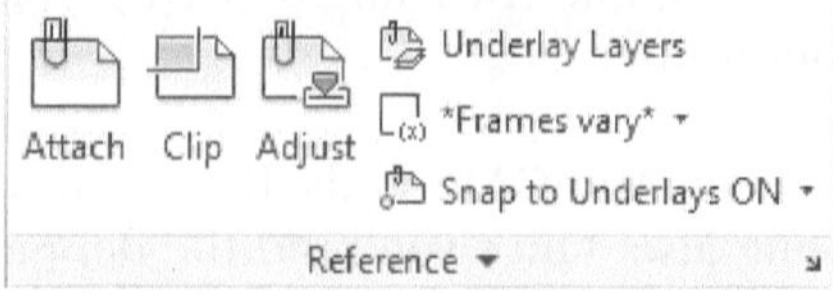

*Figure 18-28 The **Clip** tool in the **Reference** panel*

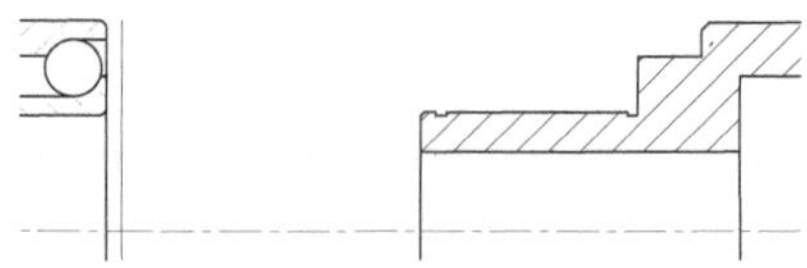

*Figure 18-29 Using the **Clip** tool to clip*

You can also invoke the **Clip** tool by selecting an xref and then right-clicking in the drawing area to display a shortcut menu. Next, choose the corresponding clip command from it. For example, to clip an attached *.dwg* file, select the attached *.dwg* file, right-click, and choose the **Clip Xref** option; the following prompt sequence will be displayed.

Enter clipping option [ON/OFF/Clipdepth/Delete/generate Polyline/New boundary] <New>: *Press ENTER to specify a new clip boundary or enter an option.*
Specify clipping boundary or select invert option: [Select polyline/Polygonal/Rectangular/Invert clip] <Rectangular>: *Press ENTER to select the **Rectangular** option, and then specify two corners of the rectangular boundary.*

You can also right-click in the drawing area at the enter clipping option prompt to display a shortcut menu. This shortcut menu displays all the options available at the command prompt that can be selected here. All the clipping options available are discussed next.

New boundary

The clipping boundary can be specified by using the **Rectangular**, **Polygonal**, or **Select polyline** option. The **Rectangular** option generates a rectangular boundary and the **Polygonal** option allows you to specify a boundary of any shape. You can draw a boundary using the **Polyline** tool or the **Polygon** tool and then, use the **Select polyline** option to select this polyline as the clipping boundary. The **Invert clip** option inverts the direction of the clipping. For example, if the objects outside the clipping boundary are hidden, by default, the **Invert clip** option will hide the objects inside the clipping boundary and display the objects outside the boundary. After selecting the **Invert clip** option, you need to redefine the clipping boundary using any one of the options discussed above. The **Invert clip** option can only be used with the 2D Wireframe visual style. If a boundary already exists, AutoCAD will ask you if the old boundary should be deleted. You can enter **YES** if you want to delete the old boundary and define a new one. If you enter **NO**, the old boundary is retained and the **Clip Xref** tool exits.

ON/OFF

The **ON/OFF** option allows you to specify whether to display the clipped portion or not. When the clipping boundary is off, you can see the complete xref drawing and when it is on, the drawing that is within the clipping polygon is displayed.

Delete

The **Delete** option completely deletes the predefined clipping boundary and the entire xref gets displayed. The **Erase** tool cannot be used to delete the clipping boundary.

generate Polyline

If you have a clipped boundary, select this option to create a polyline coinciding with the boundary of the clipped xref drawing. You can edit the polyline boundary without affecting the clipped drawing. For example, if you stretch the boundary, it does not affect the xref drawing. The edited boundary can be used later to specify a new clipping boundary.

Clipdepth

This option allows you to define the front and back clipping planes for 3D xref objects or blocks. The objects between the front and back planes will be displayed, refer to Figure 18-30 and Figure 18-31. You will be able to understand this option better after you have dealt with 3D drawings in the **Advanced AutoCAD 3D: A Problem-Solving Approach (3D and Advanced)** book. In the figures that follow, the clipping boundary is defined aligned to the front face of the object, and therefore, the clipping planes will get defined parallel to it. The xref must contain a clip boundary before specifying a clip depth. If you use the **Clipdepth** option, it prompts you to specify a front clip point and a back clip point. Specifying these points, creates a clipping frame passing through them and parallel to the clipping boundary. If the front clipping plane is specified behind the back clipping plane, AutoCAD displays an error message and the clipdepth is also not applied. The **Distance** option for specifying the front or back clip points creates a clipping plane at a specified distance from the clipping boundary parallel to it. The **Remove** option removes both the front and back clipping planes and the entire object is visible.

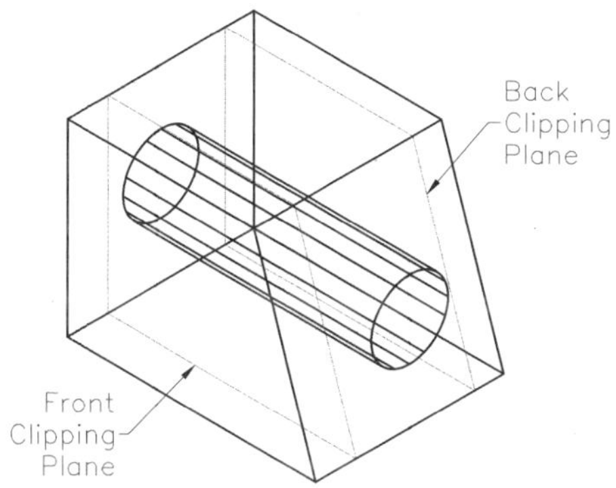

Figure 18-30 *3D xref object before clipping*

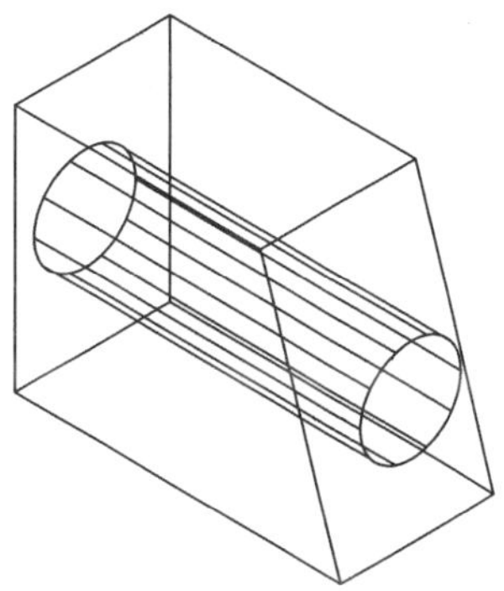

Figure 18-31 *3D xref object after clipping*

Similarly, you can clip the other underlaid xrefs. The options available for clipping the underlaid Xrefs are **ON**, **OFF**, **Delete**, and **New Boundary**. These options are the same as discussed above.

DISPLAYING CLIPPING FRAME

You can select the appropriate option from the **Frames** drop-down list in the **Reference** panel of the **Insert** tab, refer to Figure 18-32, to turn on or off the display of clipping boundary of all clipped Xrefs. If there are multiple underlays of different file types and you have set different frame settings for each file type, then the **Frames vary** button will be displayed in the **Reference** panel of the **Insert** tab. You can also use the **FRAME** system variable to turn on or off the display of clipping boundary of all clipped xrefs. When the value of **FRAME** system variable is 0, the clipping boundary will neither be displayed or plotted. When it is 1, the clipping boundary will be displayed and plotted. When it is 2, the clipping boundary will be displayed, but not plotted. When it is 3 (default), the settings vary for all the clipping boundaries. To control the display of frames of individual attached Xrefs, you need to invoke the individual system variables like **XCLIPFRAME**, **DGNFRAME**, **PDFFRAME**, and **IMAGEFRAME**.

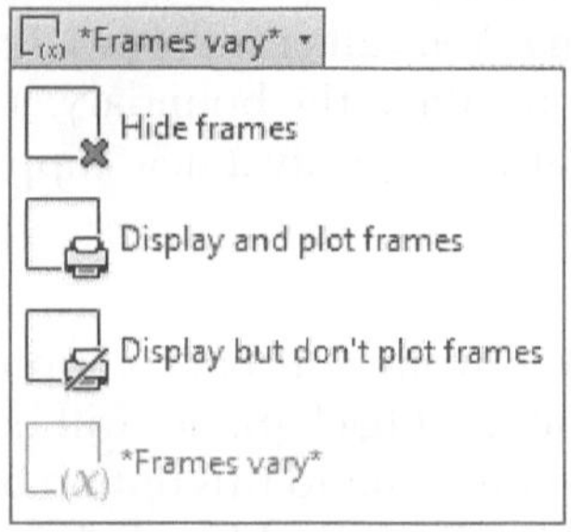

*Figure 18-32 Options in the **Frame** drop-down list*

DEMAND LOADING

The demand loading feature loads only that part of the referenced drawing that is required in the existing drawing. For example, demand loading provides a mechanism by which objects on frozen layers are not loaded. Also, only the clipped portion of the referenced drawing can be loaded. This makes the xref operation more efficient since less disk space is used, especially when the drawing is reopened. Demand loading is enabled by default. You can modify its settings in the **External References (Xrefs)** area of the **Open and Save** tab of the **Options** dialog box, refer to Figure 18-33. You can select any of the three options available in the **Demand load Xrefs** drop-down list in this dialog box. These options are **Disabled**, **Enabled**, and **Enabled with copy**. These options correspond to a value of **0**, **1**, and **2** of the **XLOADCTL** system variable, respectively, and are discussed next.

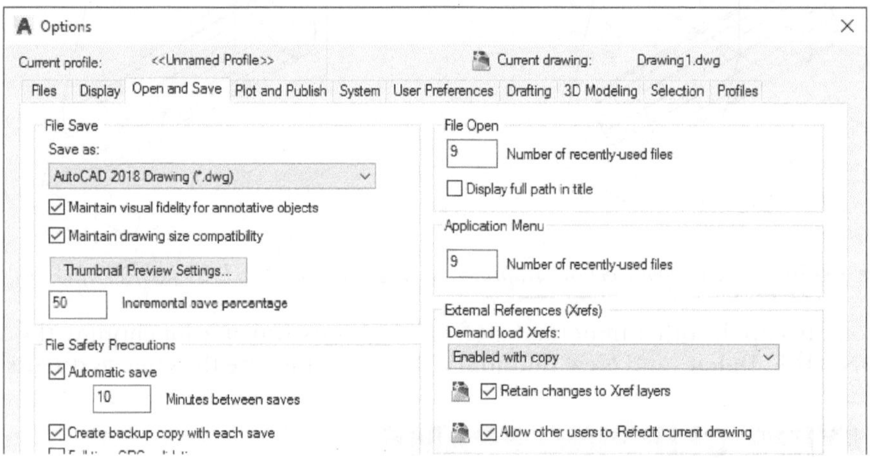

*Figure 18-33 Partial view of the **Options** dialog box with the **Open and Save** tab chosen*

Setting	Value of XLOADCTL	Features
Disabled	0	1. Turns off demand loading. 2. Loads entire xref drawing file. 3. The file is available on the server and other users can edit the xref drawing.
Enabled	1	1. Turns on demand loading. 2. The referenced file is kept open. 3. Makes the referenced file read-only for other users.
Enabled with copy	2	1. Turns on demand loading with the copy option. 2. A copy of a referenced drawing is opened. 3. Other users can access and edit the original referenced drawing file.

You can also set the value of **XLOADCTL** at the command prompt. When you are using the **Enabled with copy** option of demand loading, the temporary copies of the xref are saved in the AutoCAD temporary files directory (defined in the **Temporary External Reference File Location** folder in the **Files** tab of the **Options** dialog box) or in a user-specified directory. The **XLOADPATH** system variable creates a temporary path to store demand loaded Xrefs.

Spatial and Layer Indexes

As mentioned earlier, the demand loading improves performance when the drawing contains referenced files. To make it work effectively and to take full advantage of demand loading, you must store a drawing with Layer and Spatial indexes. The layer index maintains a list of objects in different layers and the spatial index contains lists of objects based on their location in 3D space.

Layer and spatial indexes are created using the **Save Drawing As** dialog box. Choose the **Options** option from the **Tools** drop-down to display the **Saveas Options** dialog box. Choose the **DWG Options** tab if it is not already chosen and select the type of index from the **Index type** drop-down list. **None** is the default option selected in the drop-down list. As a result, no indexes are created. The other options available are: **Layer**, **Spatial**, and **Layer & Spatial**. Once you have selected the type of index to create, choose the **OK** button to exit the dialog box and choose the **Save** button in the **Save Drawing As** dialog box to save the drawing with the indexes. The **INDEXCTL** variable also controls the creation of layer index and spatial index and its value can be set using the command prompt. The following are the settings of the **INDEXCTL** system variable, and they correspond to the **Index type** options available in the **DWG Options** tab of the **Saveas Options** dialog box.

Setting	Features	Index Type option
0	No index created	None
1	Layer index created	Layer
2	Spatial index created	Spatial
3	Layer and spatial index created	Layer and Spatial

EDITING REFERENCES IN-PLACE

Ribbon: Insert > Reference > Edit Reference **Command:** REFEDIT
Toolbar: Refedit > Edit Reference In-Place

Often you have to make minor changes in the xref drawing if you want to save yourself from the trouble of going back and forth between drawings. In this situation, you can use in-place reference editing to select the xref, modify it, and then save it after modifications. This feature of AutoCAD has already been discussed in detail with reference to blocks in Chapter 16, Working with Blocks. The following steps explain the referencing editing process.

1. To edit in-place, select an external referenced object; the **External Reference** contextual tab will be added to the **Ribbon**, as shown in Figure 18-34. Choose the **Edit Reference In-Place** tool from the **Edit** panel; the **Reference Edit** dialog box will be displayed.

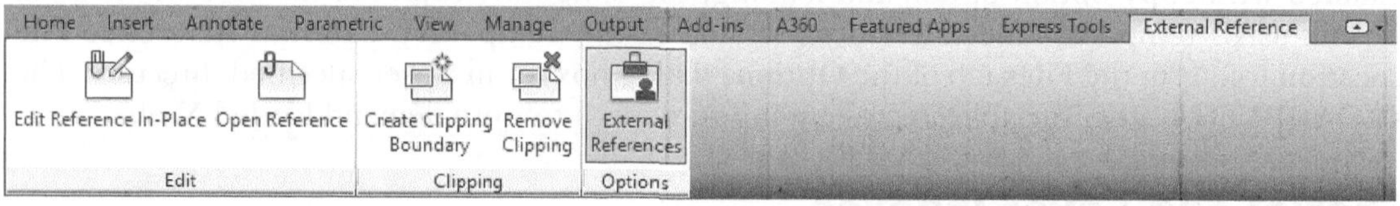

Figure 18-34** The **Edit Reference** contextual tab added to the **Ribbon

2. In the **Reference name** list box of the **Reference Edit** dialog box, the selected reference and its nested references are listed. Select the specific xref you wish to edit from the list.

3. In the **Settings** tab of the dialog box, select both the **Create unique layer, style, and block names** and the **Lock objects not in working set** check boxes. The **Display attribute definitions for editing** check box is disabled by default. In the **Identify Reference** tab of the dialog box, select the **Prompt to select nested objects** radio button. Choose the **OK** button to return to the current drawing. At the **Select nested objects:** prompt, select the objects you want to modify and press ENTER. The objects that have not been selected for modifications will become faded. The fading is controlled by the **XFADECTL** system variable or by using the **Xref display** slider bar in the **Display** tab of the **Options** dialog box. You can add or remove objects to the working set by choosing the respective tools in the **Edit Reference** panel or by using the **REFSET** command. Once you have defined a working set, all the standard AutoCAD commands can be used to modify them.

4. When you choose the **Save Changes** tool in the **Edit Reference** panel, AutoCAD displays a message: **All references edits will be saved**. Choose the **OK** button to return to the drawing area. The modifications made are saved in the drawing as well as in the current drawing as a

reference. On choosing the **Discard Changes** tool in the **Edit Reference** panel, the changes made will not be saved and the current drawing is redisplayed.

Note

*In the **External References (Xrefs)** area of the **Open and Save** tab of the **Options** dialog box, if you select the **Allow other users to Refedit current drawing** check box, the current drawing can be edited in-place by other users even when it is open and is being referenced by another file. This option is selected by default and can also be controlled by the **XEDIT** system variable. The default value of **XEDIT** is 1 and can be changed using the command prompt.*

Self-Evaluation Test

Answer the following questions and then compare them to those given at the end of this chapter:

1. The ________ are entries such as blocks, layers, and text styles.

2. If you use the **Insert** tool to insert a drawing, the information about the named objects is lost if the names are ________, and if the names are ________, the drawing will be imported.

3. The __________ option from the **Attach** drop-down list of the **EXTERNAL REFERENCES** palette is used to attach an xref drawing to the current drawing.

4. The ________ feature loads only that part of the referenced drawing that is required in the existing drawing.

5. The ________ option can be used to overcome the problem of circular reference.

6. After selecting the ________ option, the xref is completely removed from the current drawing.

7. If an assembly drawing has been created by inserting a drawing, the drawing will be updated automatically if a change is made in the inserted drawing. (T/F)

8. The external reference facility helps you keep a drawing updated no matter when the changes were made in the piece part drawings. (T/F)

9. Objects can be added to a dependent layer. (T/F)

10. The **Overlay** option ignores the nested references. (T/F).

Review Questions

Answer the following questions:

1. Which of the following features is used to reference an external drawing without making this drawing a permanent part of the existing drawing?

   (a) demand loading (b) external reference
   (c) external clipping (d) insert drawing

2. If an xref has nested references that cannot be found, which of the following will be displayed under the status heading of the **List View** button in the **EXTERNAL REFERENCES** palette?

   (a) **Orphaned** (b) **Not found**
   (c) **Unreferenced** (d) **Unresolved**

3. Which of the following system variables, when set to 1, will allow AutoCAD to maintain a log file (*.xlg*) for xref drawings?

   (a) **XLOADCTL** (b) **XLOADPATH**
   (c) **XREFCTL** (d) **INDEXCTL**

4. Which of the following system variables, when set to 0, will not allow the clipping boundary to be displayed?

   (a) **XCLIPFRAME** (b) **XLOADCTL**
   (c) **INDEXCTL** (d) **XREFCTL**

5. In the __________ drawings, the information regarding dependent symbols is not lost.

6. AutoCAD maintains a log file for xref drawings, if the __________ variable is set to 1.

7. It is possible to edit xrefs in-place using the __________ tool.

8. You can use the __________ tool to add the selected dependent symbols from the xref drawing to the current drawing.

9. If the xref drawings get updated, changes are not automatically reflected in the assembly drawing when you open an assembly drawing. (T/F)

10. There is a limit to the number of drawings you can reference. (T/F)

11. It is not possible to have nested references. (T/F)

12. Like blocks, the xref drawings can be scaled, rotated, or positioned at any desired location. (T/F)

13. You can change the color, linetype, or visibility (on/off, freeze/thaw) of a dependent layer. (T/F)

Exercise 1 *Bind Xref*

In this exercise, you will start a new drawing and xref the drawings as Part-1 and Part-2, refer to Figure 18-35 and Figure 18-36. For assembly, refer to Figure 18-37. You will also edit one of the piece parts to correct the size and use the **Bind Xref** option to bind some of the dependent symbols to the current drawing. The parameters of layers for Part-1, Part-2 and ASSEM1 are as follows:

For Part-1, set up the following layers:

Layer Name	Color	Linetype
0	White	Continuous
Object	Red	Continuous
Hidden	Blue	Hidden2
Center	White	Center2
Dim-Part1	Green	Continuous

For Part-2, set up the following layers:

Layer Name	Color	Linetype
0	White	Continuous
Object	Red	Continuous
Hidden	Blue	Hidden
Center	White	Center
Dim-Part2	Green	Continuous
Hatch	Magenta	Continuous

For ASSEM1, set up the following layers:

Layer Name	Color	Linetype
0	White	Continuous
Object	Blue	Continuous
Hidden	Yellow	Hidden

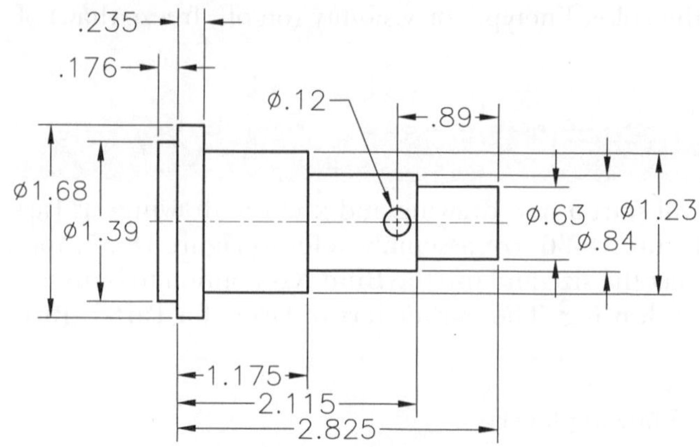

***Figure 18-35** Drawing of Part-1*

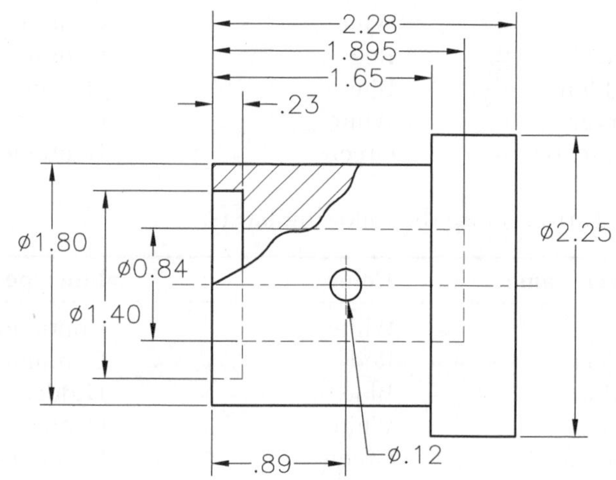

***Figure 18-36** Drawing of Part-2*

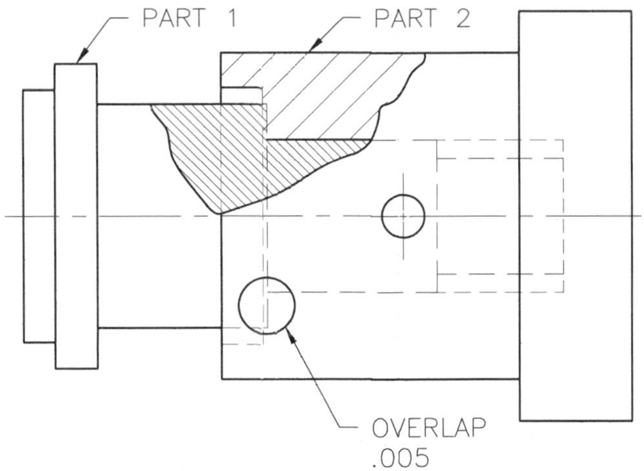

Figure 18-37 *Assembly drawing after attaching Part-1 and Part-2*

Answers to Self-Evaluation Test

1. named objects, **2.** duplicated, unique, **3.** **Attach DWG**, **4.** demand loading, **5.** **Overlay**, **6.** **Detach**, **7.** F, **8.** T, **9.** F, **10.** T

Chapter 19

Working with Advanced Drawing Options

Learning Objectives

After completing this chapter, you will be able to:

- *Define multiline style and specify the properties of multilines using the Multiline Style command*
- *Draw various types of multilines using the MLINE command*
- *Edit multilines using the MLEDIT command*
- *Draw NURBS splines using the Spline tool*
- *Edit NURBS splines using the Edit Spline tool*

Key Terms

- *Multiline*
- *MLEDIT*
- *Revision Cloud*
- *Wipeout*
- *Spline*
- *Fit Points*
- *CV*
- *Knots*
- *Kink*
- *Weight*

UNDERSTANDING THE USE OF MULTILINES

The Multiline feature allows you to draw composite lines that consist of multiple parallel lines. These parallel lines are called elements. You can draw these lines using the **MLINE** command. But before drawing multilines, you need to set the multiline styles. This can be accomplished by using the **MLSTYLE** command. You can also edit multilines by using the **MLEDIT** command.

DEFINING A MULTILINE STYLE

Menu Bar: Format > Multiline Style	**Command:** MLSTYLE

You can create a multiline style by using the **MLSTYLE** command. You can specify the number of elements in a multiline and the properties of each element. The style also controls the start and end caps, the start and end lines, and the color of multilines and fill. When you invoke the **Multiline Style** tool from the **Format** menu or by using the **MLSTYLE** command, AutoCAD displays the **Multiline Style** dialog box, as shown in Figure 19-1. Using this dialog box, you can set the spacing between parallel lines, specify linetype pattern, set colors, solid fill, and capping arrangements. By default, the multiline style (STANDARD) has two lines that are offset at 0.5 and -0.5.

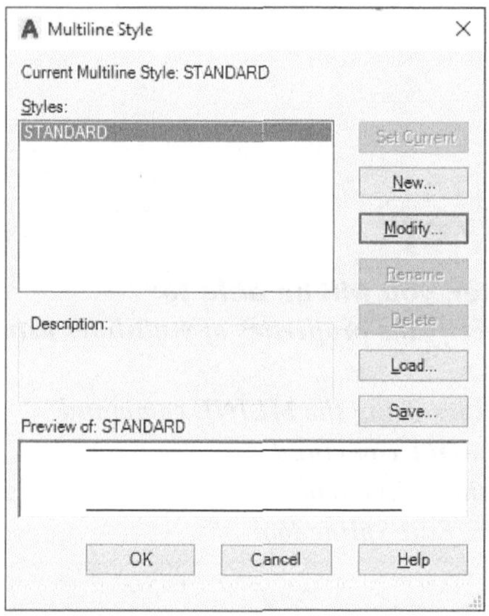

***Figure 19-1** The **Multiline Style** dialog box*

Note

You cannot modify a multiline style being used in the current drawing. You first need to delete the multiline from all the places where it is used and then you can modify its style.

Styles List Box

The **Styles** list box displays the names of the styles. By default, the **STANDARD** style is available in this list box. If several styles have been defined, all of them will be listed in this list box.

Set Current

If several styles have been defined, select a style from the **Styles** list box and choose the **Set Current** button to make the style as the current style. The current multiline style is saved in the **CMLSTYLE** system variable.

New

The **New** button is chosen to create a new multilinestyle. On choosing this button, the **Create New Multiline Style** dialog box will be displayed, as shown in Figure 19-2. The **New Style Name** edit box is used to specify the name of the new multiline style that you want to define. The **Start With** drop-down list will be available only if some styles have already been defined. You can select an existing style as a reference to create the new style. The new style will start with the properties associated with the style selected from the **Start With** drop-down list. As soon as you specify the name of the new style, the **Continue** button is highlighted. To create a new style, enter the name of the new style in the **New Style Name** edit box and then choose the **Continue** button; the **New Multiline Style** dialog box will be displayed, as shown in Figure 19-3.

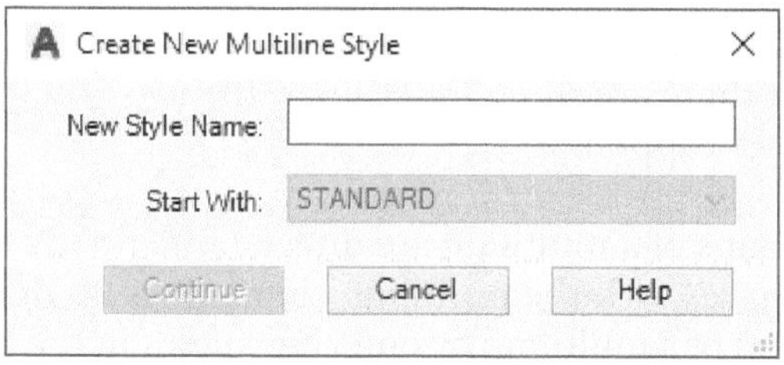

***Figure 19-2** The **Create New Multiline Style** dialog box*

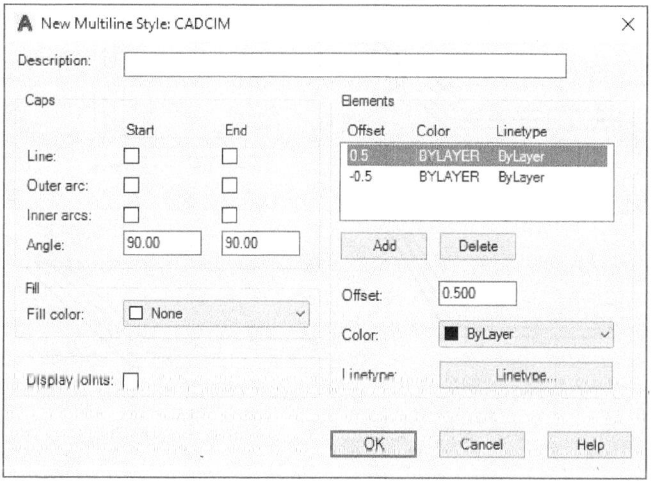

***Figure 19-3** The **New Multiline Style** dialog box*

The title bar of the **New Multiline Style** dialog box displays the name of the new style. By default, some properties in the dialog box are defined at some preset values. These values correspond to the selection made in the **Start With** drop-down list of the **Create New Multiline Style** dialog box.

Description

This edit box is used to specify the description of the new multiline style. Giving information in this edit box is optional so you can leave it blank if you want.

Caps Area

The options under this area are used to set the type and location of the start and end caps of the multilines. These options are discussed next.

Line: Selecting the **Start** and **End** check boxes of this option caps the multiline with a line at the start point and the endpoint, refer to Figure 19-4.

Outer arc: Selecting the **Start** and **End** check boxes of this option draws a semicircular arc between the endpoints of the outermost lines, refer to Figure 19-4.

Inner arcs: This option is used to draw a semicircular arc between the two innermost lines at the start point and endpoint of a multiline. The arc is drawn between the even-numbered inner lines, refer to Figure 19-4. For example, if there are two inner lines, an arc will be drawn at their ends. On the other hand, if there are three inner lines, the two outer lines are capped with the arc and the middle line is not capped.

Angle: By default, the end caps of a multiline are drawn tangentially to the multiline elements, that is, the angle the cap makes with the multiline elements is 90 degree. You can control the cap angle at the start and end of a multiline by entering angles in the corresponding **Angle** edit boxes, refer to Figure 19-4. This angle can be between 10 degree and 170 degree.

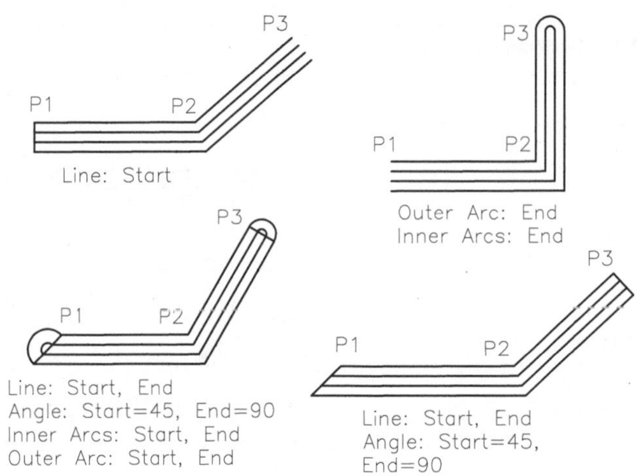

Figure 19-4 Drawing multilines with different end cap secifications

Fill Area

The options under this area are used to fill the multiline with a specified color. By default, **None** is selected in the **Fill color** drop-down list. As a result, there is no fill effect in the multiline. To specify a fill color, select it from this drop-down list. On selecting the **Select Color** option, the **Select Color** dialog box will be displayed which can be used to select additional colors.

Display joints

If you select the **Display joints** check box, AutoCAD will draw a line across all elements of the multiline at the vertex points, where the multiline changes direction. The joints of the multiline are also called miter joints. If you draw only one multiline segment, no line is drawn at the miter joint.

Elements Area

The options in this area modify the element properties of the multiline style. The element properties include the number of lines, color, and linetype of the lines comprising the multiline. The following options are available for setting the properties of the individual lines (elements) that constitute the multiline.

Offset, Color, and Linetype: This list box displays the offset, color, and linetype of each line that constitutes the current multiline style. The lines are always listed in the descending order, based on the offset distance. For example, a line with a 0.5 offset will be listed first and a line with a 0.25 offset will be listed next. You can select an element to be modified from the list box; the selected element is highlighted.

Add: This button allows you to add new lines to the current line style. When you choose the **Add** button, AutoCAD inserts a line with the **Offset** = 0.0, **Color** = BYLAYER, and **Linetype** = Bylayer. The new element gets added between two existing elements. After the line is added, you can change its offset distance, color, or linetype. The offset distance can be entered in the **Offset** edit box. Similarly, you can select the options in the **Color** drop-down list to specify a color for the selected element of the multiline. Also, you can choose the **Linetype** button to display the **Select Linetype** dialog box. You can use this dialog box and its options to load and select the linetype you want to apply to the selected element of a multiline.

Delete: This button allows you to delete a selected element from the multiline style. The highlighted element is removed from the **Elements** list box.

Offset: This edit box allows you to change the offset distance of the selected line in the **Elements** list box. The offset distance is defined with respect to the origin (0,0). The offset distance can be a positive or a negative value, which enables you to center the lines.

Color: This drop-down list allows you to assign a color to the selected line. When you select the **Select Color** option from this drop-down list, AutoCAD displays the **Select Color** dialog box. You can select a color from the dialog box or enter a color number or name in the **Color** edit box.

Linetype: This button allows you to assign a linetype to the selected line. When you choose this button, AutoCAD displays the **Select Linetype** dialog box. After selecting a linetype in this dialog box, choose the **OK** button to exit. You can also choose the **Load** button in the **Select Linetype** dialog box to display the **Load or Reload Linetypes** dialog box, where you can select the linetype that you want to use. The selected linetype is displayed in the **Loaded linetypes** list box of the **Select Linetype** dialog box. You can now select the specific linetype and apply it to a selected element of a multiline.

After you have added the elements to a multiline and set their properties, choose the **OK** button to exit the **New Multiline Style** dialog box. An image of the current multiline style is displayed in the **Preview of** area in the **Multiline Style** dialog box. The new style is now listed in the **Style** list box.

Load

Choose this button from the **Multiline Style** dialog box to load a multiline style from an external multiline library file (*acad.mln*). On choosing this button, the **Load Multiline Styles** dialog box will be displayed, as shown in Figure 19-5. This dialog box displays all multiline styles available in the current *mln* directory. If the style is saved in another directory or file, choose the **File** button to display the **Load Multiline Style From File** dialog box and then select the multiline file that you want to load. Once the file is loaded, all styles saved under it are displayed in the list box. You can select the style and then choose the **OK** button to make it current.

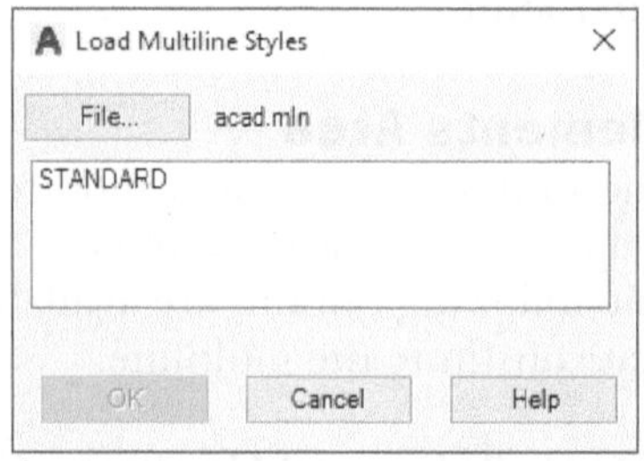

***Figure 19-5** The **Load Multiline Styles** dialog box*

Save

This button lets you save a multiline style to an external file (*.mln*). When you choose this button, AutoCAD displays the **Save Multiline Style** dialog box. This dialog box lists the names of the available predefined multiline style files (*.mln*). From the file listing, select or enter the name of the file where you want to save the current multiline style and choose the **Save** button. By default, the multiline styles get saved in the *acad.mln* file at the location *C:\Users\<user name>\AppData\Roaming\Autodesk\AutoCAD 2018\R22.0\enu\Support*.

Rename

This button allows you to rename the current multiline style. To do so, select the multiline style to be renamed and choose the **Rename** button; the text will be displayed in an edit box. Rename the text and click once on the list box. Note you cannot rename the **STANDARD** multiline style.

Preview of Area

The **Multiline Style** dialog box also displays the current multiline configuration in the **Preview of** area. The panel will display the color, linetype, caps and relative spacing of the lines. As you select another multiline style, the image in the preview area also gets updated accordingly. The name of the multiline style whose preview is being shown is displayed above the **Preview of** area.

DRAWING MULTILINES

Menu Bar: Draw > Multiline **Command:** MLINE/ML

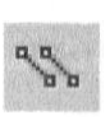

The **MLINE** command is used to draw multilines. The following is the prompt sequence for the **MLINE** command:

Specify start point or [Justification/Scale/STyle]: *Select a start point or enter an option.*
Specify next point: *Select the second point.*
Specify next point or [Undo]: *Select the next point.*
Specify next point or [Close/Undo]: *Select the next point, enter **U**, or enter **C** for close.*

When you invoke the **MLINE** command, it always displays the current status of the multiline justification, scale, and style name. Remember that all line segments created in a single **MLINE** command are a single entity. The options provided under this command are discussed next.

Justification Option

The justification determines how a multiline is drawn between the specified points. Three justifications are available for the **MLINE** command. They are **Top**, **Zero**, and **Bottom**.

Top

This justification produces a multiline in which the top line coincides with the points you selected on the screen. Since the line offsets in a multiline are arranged in descending order, the line with the largest positive offset will coincide with the selected points. This is the default justification option, refer to Figure 19-6.

Zero

This option will produce a multiline in which the zero offset position of the multiline coincides with the selected points. Multilines will be centered if the positive and negative offsets are equal, refer to Figure 19-6.

Bottom

This option will produce a multiline in which the bottom line (the line with the least offset distance) coincides with the selected point when the line is drawn from left to right, refer to Figure 19-6.

Scale Option

The **Scale** option is used to change the scale of a multiline. For example, if the scale factor is 0.5, the distance between the lines (offset distance) will be reduced to half, as shown in Figure 19-7. Therefore, the width of the multiline will be half of what was defined in the multiline style. A negative scale factor will reverse the order of the offset lines. The multilines will now be drawn such that the line with the maximum negative offset distance is at the top and the line with the maximum positive offset distance is at the bottom. For example, if you enter a scale factor of -0.5, the order in which the lines are drawn will be reversed, and the offset distances will be reduced by half. Here it is assumed that the lines are drawn from left to right. If the lines are drawn from right to left, the offsets are reversed. Also, if the scale factor is 0, AutoCAD forces the multiline into a single line. However, the line will still possess the properties of a multiline. This scale factor does not affect the linetype scale factor (**LTSCALE**).

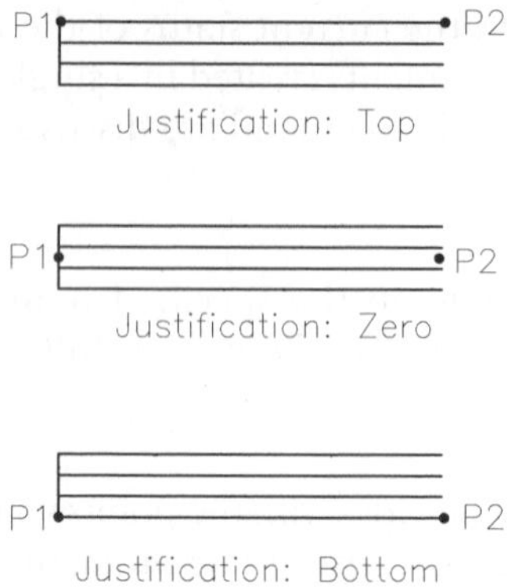

***Figure 19-6** Justifications in multilines*

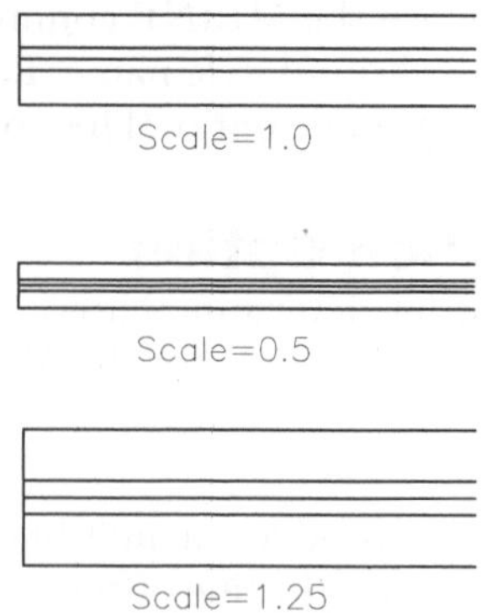

***Figure 19-7** Different multiline scales*

STyle Option

The **STyle** option allows you to change the current multiline style. The style must be defined before using the **STyle** option.

Note

All options explained above are available at the dynamic prompt. To access the options through dynamic prompt, press the down arrow key whenever dynamic prompting is available at the cursor. Now, select the option using the cursor.

EDITING MULTILINES BY USING GRIPS

Multilines can be easily edited using grips. When you select a multiline, the grips appear at the endpoints, based on the justification used while drawing multilines. For example, if the multilines are top-justified, the grips will be displayed at the endpoint of the first (top) line segment. Similarly, for zero and bottom-justified multilines, the grips are displayed on the centerline and bottom line, respectively.

Note

*Multilines do not support certain editing tools such as **Break**, **Chamfer**, and **Fillet**. However, tools such as **Copy**, **Move**, **Rotate**, **Mirror**, **Stretch**, **Scale**, and **Explode** as well as most object snap modes can be used with multilines.*

EDITING MULTILINES BY USING DIALOG BOX

Menu Bar: Modify > Object > Multiline	**Command:** MLEDIT

When you invoke the **MLEDIT** command, AutoCAD displays the **Multilines Edit Tools** dialog box, as shown in Figure 19-8. This dialog box contains five basic editing tools. To edit a multiline, first select the editing operation you want to perform by clicking on the image tile. Once you have selected the editing option, AutoCAD will prompt you to select the first and second multilines. After editing one set of multilines, you will be prompted again to select the first multiline or undo the last editing. Press ENTER to exit this command after you have finished the editing.

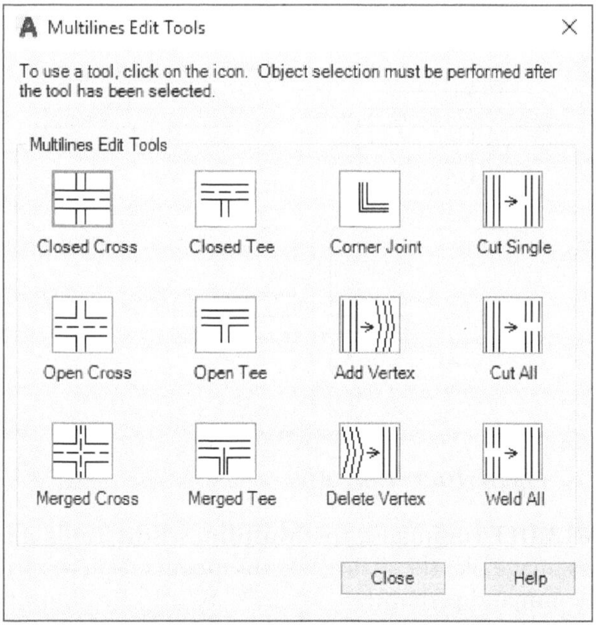

Figure 19-8 *The* ***Multilines Edit Tools*** *dialog box*

The following is the list of options for editing multilines:

Cross Intersection
Closed Cross (CC), Open Cross (OC), Merged Cross (MC)

Tee Intersection
Closed Tee (CT), Open Tee (OT), Merged Tee (MT)

Corner Joint (CJ)

Adding and Deleting Vertices
Add Vertex (AV), Delete Vertex (DV)

Cutting and Welding Multilines
Cut Single (CS), Cut All (CA), Weld All (WA)

Cross Intersection (CC/OC/MC)

Using options in the **Multilines Edit Tools** dialog box, you can create three types of cross intersections: closed, open, and merged. You must be careful about the order in which you select multilines for editing. The order in which multilines are selected determines the edited shape of a multiline, refer to Figure 19-9. The cross intersection can belong to a self-intersecting multiline or two different multilines.

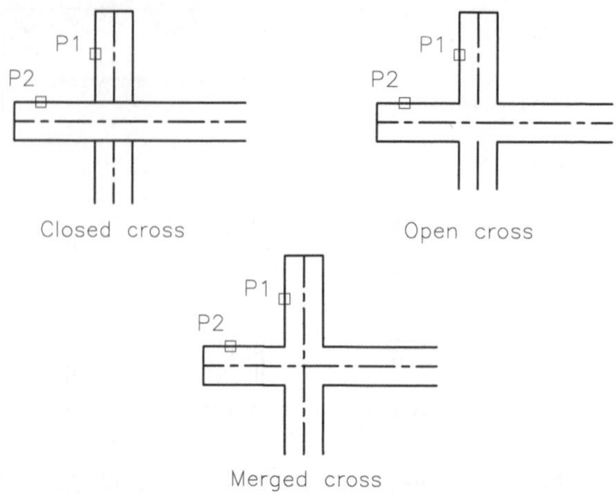

Figure 19-9 *Three types of cross intersections*

When you invoke the **MLEDIT** command, the **Multilines Edit Tools** dialog box is displayed. Choose the **Closed Cross** image tile; the dialog box disappears from the screen and the following prompts appear in the command prompt:

Select first mline: *Select the first multiline.*
Select second mline: *Select the second multiline.*
Select first mline or [Undo]: *Select another multiline, press ENTER to end the command, or enter **U** to undo the last operation.*

If you enter **U**, AutoCAD will undo the last editing operation and prompt you to select the first multiline. However, if you do not enter **U** and select another multiline, AutoCAD will prompt you to select the second multiline.

Tee Intersection (CT/OT/MT)

Using options in the **Multilines Edit Tools** dialog box, you can create three types of tee-shaped intersections: closed, open, and merged. Similar to the cross intersection, in this type of intersection also, you have to be careful how you select the objects because the order in which you select them determines the edited shape of a multiline, refer to Figure 19-10. The prompt sequence for the tee intersection is the same as that for the cross intersection.

When you invoke the **MLEDIT** command, the **Multilines Edit Tools** dialog box will be displayed. Choose the **Closed Tee** image tile; the dialog box disappears from the screen and the following prompts appear in the command prompt.

Select first mline: *Select the first multiline.*
Select second mline: *Select the intersecting multiline.*
Select first mline or [Undo]: *Select another multiline, enter **U** to undo the last operation, or press ENTER to end the command.*

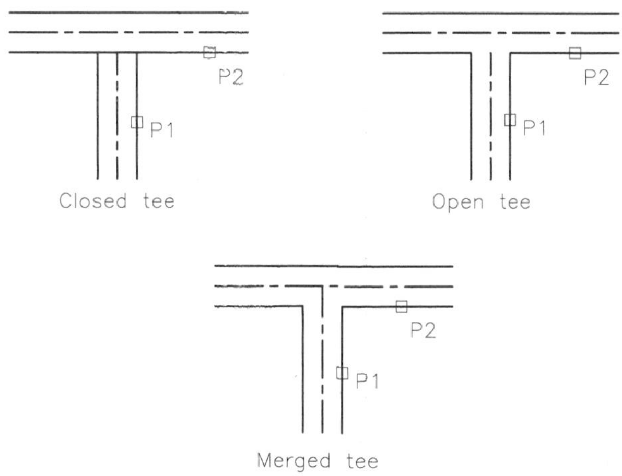

Figure 19-10 *Three types of tee intersections*

Corner Joint (CJ)

The **Corner Joint** option is used to create a corner joint between the two selected multilines. The multilines must be two separate objects (multilines) or self-intersecting multilines, refer to Figure 19-11. When you specify two multilines, AutoCAD trims or extends the first multiline to intersect with the second one. The prompt sequence that follows when you invoke this option is given next.

Select first mline: *Select the multiline to trim or extend.*
Select second mline: *Select the intersecting multiline.*
Select first mline or [Undo]: *Select another multiline, enter **U** to undo the last operation, or press ENTER to end the command.*

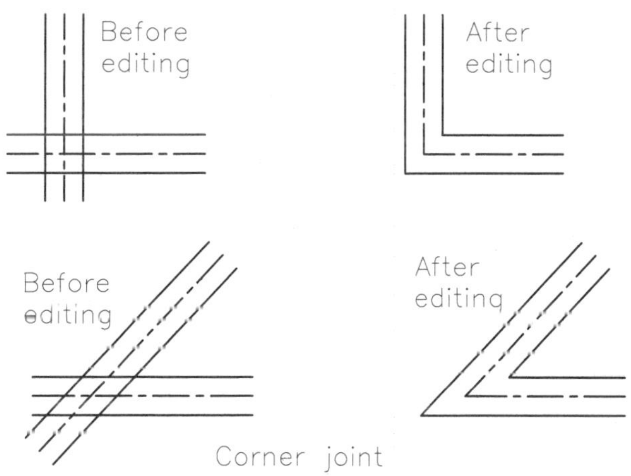

Figure 19-11 *Editing corner joints*

Adding and Deleting Vertices (AV/DV)

You can use the **MLEDIT** command to add or delete the vertices of a multiline, refer to Figure 19-12. When you select a multiline for adding a vertex, AutoCAD inserts a vertex point at the point where you clicked on the object while selecting it. Later, you can move the vertex by using grips. Similarly, you can also use the **MLEDIT** command to delete vertices by selecting the object whose vertex point you want to delete. AutoCAD removes the vertex that is nearest to the point where you click to select the multiline segment.

When you invoke the **MLEDIT** command, the **Multilines Edit Tools** dialog box is displayed. Choose the **Add Vertex** image tile; the dialog box is removed from the screen and the following prompts appear in the command prompt.

Select mline: *Select the multiline for adding vertex.*
Select mline or [Undo]: *Select another multiline for modifications; enter **U** to undo the last operation, or press ENTER to exit the command.*

A same prompt sequence appears at the command prompt when you use the **Delete Vertex** option.

Cutting and Welding Multilines (CS/CA/WA)

You can also use the **MLEDIT** command to cut or weld multilines. When you cut a multiline, it does not create two separate multilines. They continue to be a part of the same object (multiline). You can cut away an area from any of the elements of a multiline or from the entire multiline. Also, the points selected for cutting the multiline do not have to be on the same element of the multiline, refer to Figure 19-13. You can select the two points that define the cut on different elements of the multiline. While cutting a single element of the multiline, if you select the two cut points on different elements, the element you selected first gets cut by the distance defined by the two points.

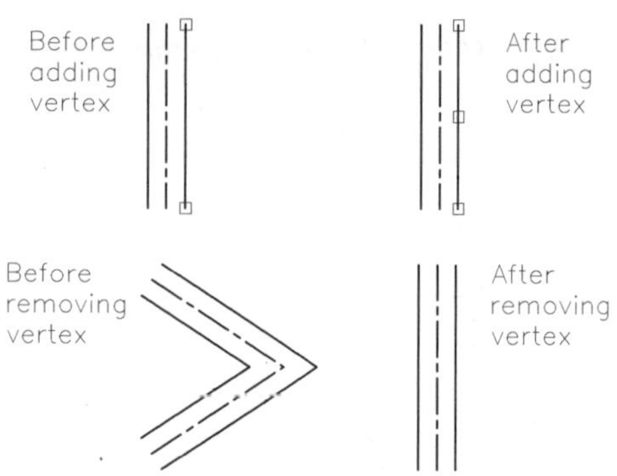

Figure 19-12 *Adding and deleting vertices*

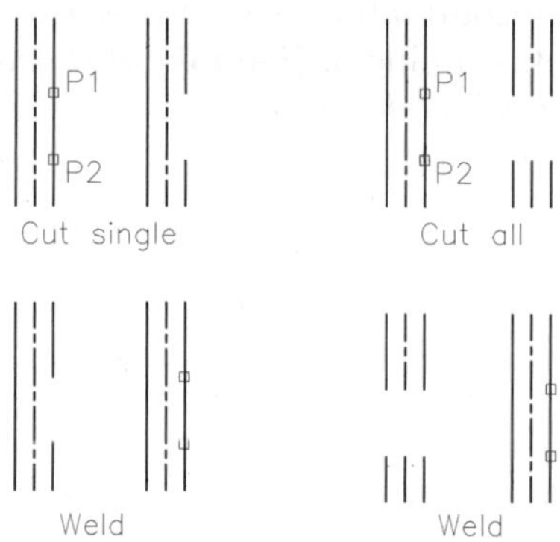

Figure 19-13 *Cutting and welding multilines*

In the **Multilines Edit Tools** dialog box, choose the **Cut Single** image tile; the dialog box is removed from the screen, and the following prompts appear at the command prompt.

Select mline: Select the multiline.
(The point where you select the multiline specifies the first cut point.)
Select second point: *Select the second cut point.*
Select mline or [Undo]: *Select another multiline to cut, enter **U** to undo the last operation, or press ENTER to exit the command.*

The **Weld All** option reconnects the multilines that have been cut by using the **Cut Single** or **Cut All** option of the **MLEDIT** command (Figure 19-13). You cannot weld or join separate multilines.

In the **Multilines Edit Tools** dialog box, choose the **Weld All** image tile; the dialog box is removed from the screen, and the following prompts appear at the command prompt.

Select mline: *Select the multiline.*
Select second point: *Select a point on the other side of the cut.*
Select mline or [Undo]: *Select another multiline to modify, enter **U** to undo the last operation, or press ENTER to exit the command.*

Note

*The following system variables store values for various aspects of multilines. The **CMLJUST** variable stores the justification of the current multiline (0-Top, 1-Middle, 2-Bottom). The **CMLSCALE** variable stores the scale of the current multiline (Default scale = 1.0000) and the **CMLSTYLE** variable stores the name of the current multiline style (Default style = STANDARD).*

Tip

*You can also edit multilines by entering the **-MLEDIT** command at the pointer input. On doing so, all the options are displayed at the dynamic prompt, refer to Figure 19-14.*

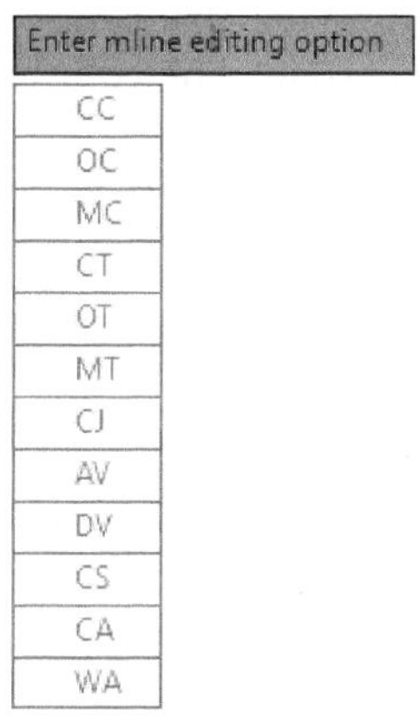

Figure 19-14 *Dynamic prompt for the **-MLEDIT** command*

Example 1 — Multiline

In this example, you will create a multiline style that represents a wood-frame wall system. The wall system consists of ½" wallboard, 4 X ½" wood stud, and ½" wallboard.

1. Enter **MLSTYLE** at the command prompt to display the **Multiline Style** dialog box. Also, the current style **STANDARD** is displayed in the **Styles** list box.

2. Choose the **New** button to invoke the **Create New Multiline Style** dialog box. Enter **MYSTYLE** in the **New Style Name** edit box and choose **Continue** to display the **New Multiline Style: MYSTYLE** dialog box.

3. Enter **Wood-frame Wall System** in the **Description** edit box.

4. Select the **0.5** line definition in the **Elements** list box. In the **Offset** edit box, replace **0.500** with **1.00**. This redefines the first line which will now be 1.00" above the centerline of the wall.

5. Select the **-0.5** line definition in the **Elements** list box. In the **Offset** edit box, replace **-0.500** with **-1.00**. This redefines the second line which will now be placed 1.00" below the centerline of the wall.

6. Choose the **Add** button; a new line is added with offset value of 0 and is highlighted in the **Elements** list box.

7. In the **Offset** edit box, replace **0.000** with **1.50**.

8. Select **Yellow** from the **Color** drop-down list.

9. Repeat steps 6 through 8, but this time use the value **-1.50** in place of **1.50** in step 7 to add another line to the current multiline style. The color of this line should be red.

10. Choose the **OK** button and return to the **Multiline Style** dialog box. The new multiline style is displayed in the **Preview of** area.

11. Choose the **Set Current** button to make the **MYSTYLE** as current style.

12. Choose the **OK** button from the **Multiline Style** dialog box to return to the drawing area. To test the new multiline style, use the **MLINE** command and draw a series of lines, refer to Figure 19-15.

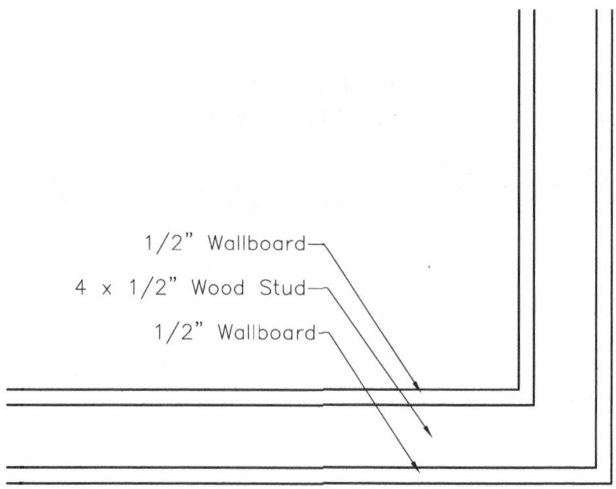

Figure 19-15 *Multiline style created for Example 1*

CREATING REVISION CLOUDS

Ribbon: Home > Draw > Revision Cloud drop-down or
Annotate > Markup > Revision Cloud drop-down
Tool Palettes: Draw > Revision Cloud **Toolbar:** Draw > Revision Cloud
Menu Bar: Draw > Revision Cloud **Command:** REVCLOUD

Revision cloud is the sequential arc of polylines and is used to create a cloud-shaped object. Revision clouds can be used to highlight the details of a drawing. The tools to draw a revision cloud are grouped in the **Revision Cloud** drop-down of the **Draw** panel in the **Ribbon**, refer to Figure 19-16. Remember that the tool that was used last to create a revision cloud will be displayed in this drop-down. The different methods to draw a revision cloud are discussed next.

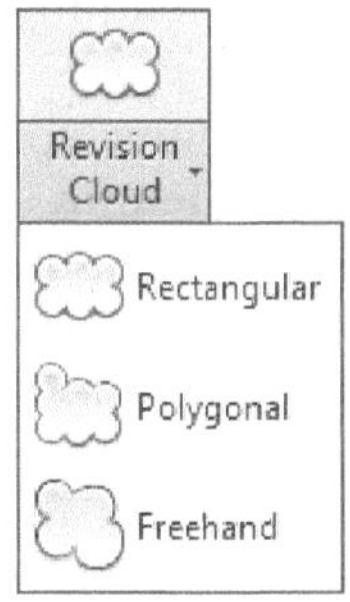

***Figure 19-16** The tools in the **Revision Cloud** drop-down*

Rectangular Revision Cloud

To draw a rectangular revision cloud, choose the **Rectangular Revision Cloud** tool from the **Revision Cloud** drop-down in the **Draw** panel; you will be prompted to specify the first point. Specify the first point or enter coordinates. Next, specify the opposite corner point of the rectangle. The prompt sequence that will follow when you choose this tool is as follows:

Specify first corner point or [Arc length/Object/Rectangular/Polygonal/Freehand/Style/Modify] <Object>: *Specify first corner point of rectangle.*
Specify opposite corner: *Specify opposite corner point of rectangle.*

Polygonal Revision Cloud

To draw a polygonal revision cloud, choose the **Polygonal Revision Cloud** tool from the **Draw** panel, refer to Figure 19-16. You will be prompted to specify the first point, specify the first point; you will be prompted to specify the next point. Keep specifying the points until the desired polygonal revision cloud is created. Press ENTER to terminate the command. The prompt sequence that will follow when you choose this tool from the **Draw** panel is as follows:

Specify start point or [Arc length/Object/Rectangular/Polygonal/Freehand/Style/Modify] <Object>: *Specify the start point of the revision cloud.*
Specify next point: *Specify the next point of the revision cloud.*
Specify next point or [Undo]: *Specify the next point of the revision cloud.*
Specify next point or [Undo]: *Specify the next point of the revision cloud, or press ENTER to exit the tool.*

Freehand Revision Cloud

To draw a freehand revision cloud, choose the **Freehand Revision Cloud** tool from the **Draw** panel, refer to Figure 19-16. You will be prompted to specify the first point, specify the first point. Now, as you move the cursor, different arcs of the cloud with varied radii are drawn. When the start point and endpoint meet, the revision cloud is completed and you get a message that the revision cloud has been created. The prompt sequence that will follow when you choose this tool from the **Draw** panel is as follows:

> Specify first point or [Arc length/Object/Rectangular/Polygonal/Freehand/Style/Modify] <Object>: *Specify the start point of the revision cloud.*
> Guide crosshairs along cloud path...
> Revision cloud finished.

While making any type of the revision cloud, you can define the length of the arcs to be drawn using the **Arc length** option from the command prompt. The arcs drawn using this option will be of constant length. You can convert a closed loop into a revision cloud using the **Object** option. Note that the selected closed loop should be a single entity such as an ellipse, a circle, a rectangle, a polyline, and so on. The **Style** option is used to define the arc style for the revision cloud. The default style is **Normal** that creates a revision cloud similar to the one shown in Figure 19-17. You can change the style to **Calligraphy** to create a revision cloud similar to the one shown in Figure 19-18.

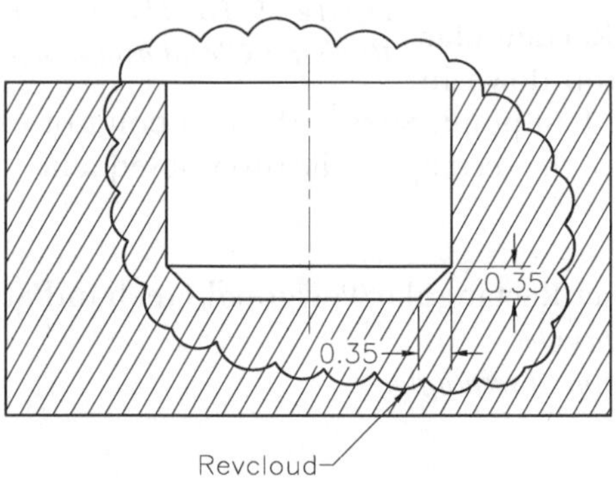

Figure 19-17 *Revcloud*

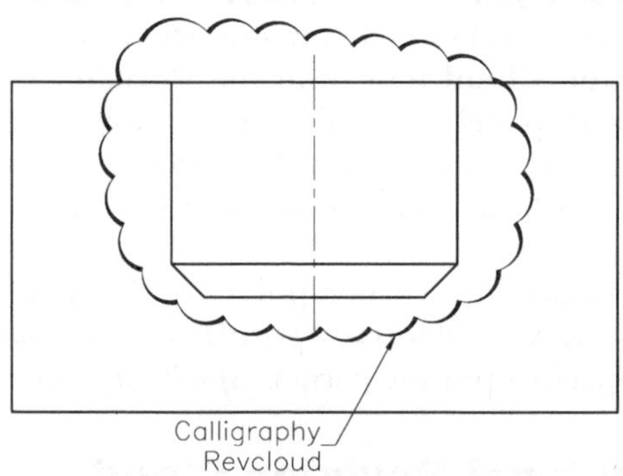

Figure 19-18 *Calligraphy revcloud*

Note

*The **REVCLOUD** stores the last used arc length in the system registry. This value is multiplied by the **DIMSCALE** value to provide consistency when the program is used with drawings that have different scale factors.*

CREATING WIPEOUTS

Ribbon: Home > Draw > Wipeout or Annotate > Markup > Wipeout
Command: WIPEOUT

The **Wipeout** tool is used to create a polygonal area to cover the existing objects with the current background color. The area defined by this tool is governed by the wipeout frame. The frame can be turned on and off for editing and plotting the drawings, respectively. This tool can be used to add notes and details to a drawing. The prompt sequence that will follow when you choose the **Wipeout** tool from the **Draw** panel is as follows:

> Specify first point or [Frames/Polyline] <Polyline>: *Specify the start point of the wipeout.*
> Specify next point: *Specify the next point of the wipeout.*

Specify next point or [Undo]: *Specify the next point of the wipeout.*
Specify next point or [Close/Undo]: *Specify the next point of the wipeout or press ENTER.*

Figure 19-19 shows a drawing before creating a wipeout and Figure 19-20 shows a drawing after creating the wipeout.

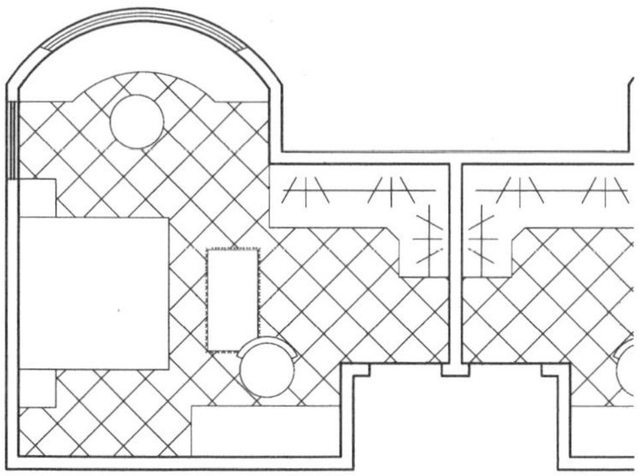

Figure 19-19 *Drawing before creating a wipeout*

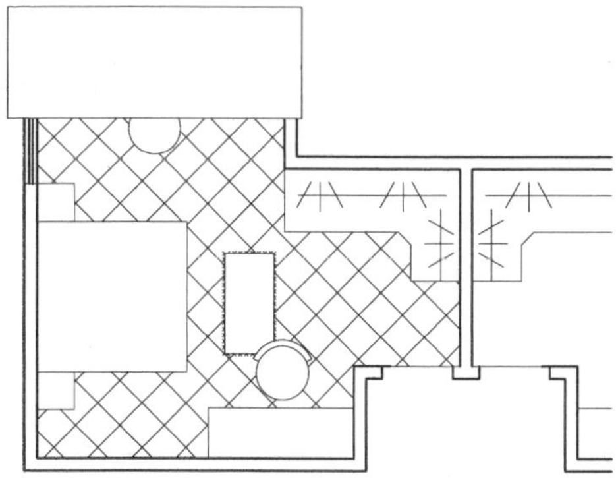

Figure 19-20 *Drawing after creating a wipeout*

If you do not want the frame of the wipeout to be displayed, enter **F** at the **Specify first point or [Frames/Polyline] <Polyline>** prompt and turn the frame off. The display of frames of all existing wipeouts will be turned off. Also, the display of frames of all new wipeouts will be turned off.

CREATING NURBS

Ribbon: Home > Draw > Spline Fit	**Menu Bar:** Draw > Spline > Fit Points	
Tool Palettes: Draw > Spline	**Toolbar:** Draw > Spline	**Command:** SPLINE/SPL

The NURBS is an acronym for **Non-Uniform Rational Bezier-Spline**. These splines are considered true splines. In AutoCAD, you can create NURBS using the **Spline** tool. The spline created with the **Spline** tool is different from the spline created using the **Polyline** tool. The non-uniform aspect of the spline enables the spline to have sharp corners because the spacing between the spline elements that constitute a spline can be irregular. Rational means that irregular geometry such as arcs, circles, and ellipses can be combined with free-form curves. The Bezier-spline (B-spline) is the core that enables accurate fitting of curves to input data with Bezier's curve-fitting interface. Not only are spline curves more accurate compared to smooth polyline curves, but they also use less disk space.

The prompt sequence to draw a spline with six fit points is given below.

Choose the ***Spline*** *tool.*

Specify first point or [Method/Knots/Object]: *Select point P1*
Enter next point or [start Tangency/toLerance]: *Select point P2.*
Enter next point or [end Tangency/toLerance/Undo]: *Select point P3.*
Enter next point or [end Tangency/toLerance/Undo/Close]: *Select point P4*
Enter next point or [end Tangency/toLerance/Undo/Close]: *Select point P5.*

Enter next point or [end Tangency/toLerance/Undo/Close]: *Select point P6 and press ENTER to end the process of point specification.*

Options for Creating Splines

On invoking the **Spline** tool, the following options are displayed for creating the splines:

Object

This option allows you to change a 2D or 3D spline fitted polyline into a NURBS feature. The original splined polyline is deleted if the system variable **DELOBJ** is set to 1, which is the default value of the variable. You can change a polyline into a splined polyline using the **Spline** option of the **Edit Polyline** tool.

Method

In AutoCAD, you can create a spline by specifying fit points or control vertices. By default, a spline is created by specifying the fit points. Fit points are the points through which the spline will pass. Control vertices determine the shape of the curve. To set the method to create a spline, enter **M** at the **Specify first point or [Method/Knots/Object]** prompt. Then, you need to specify the method at the **Enter spline creation method [Fit/CV] <Fit>:** prompt. Figure 19-21 shows the spline created by using the **Fit** method. Figure 19-22 shows the spline created by using the **CV** method.

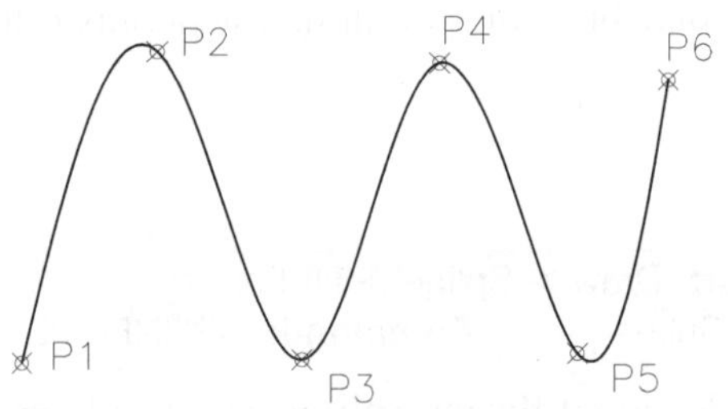

Figure 19-21 *Spline drawn by using the* ***Fit*** *method*

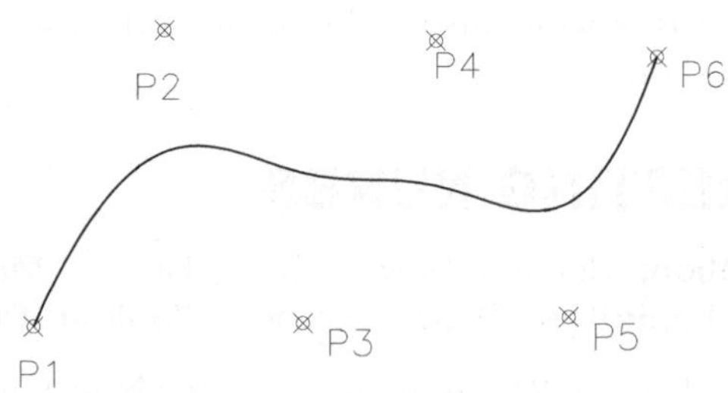

Figure 19-22 *Spline drawn by using the* ***CV*** *method*

Note

On selecting a spline, a grip will be displayed at the start point. Left-click on the grip; a shortcut menu will be displayed. Now, you can choose an appropriate option to display the fit points or the control vertices, as shown in Figure 19-23.

Knots

If you have selected the **Fit** method, the **Knots** option will be displayed at the command prompt, as given below.

Enter spline creation method [Fit/CV] <CV>: **FIT**
Current settings: Method=Fit Knots=Uniform
Specify first point or [Method/Knots/Object]:

You can specify three types of knots: **Chord**, **Square root**, and **Uniform**. Figure 19-24 shows the splines formed by using three different knot options.

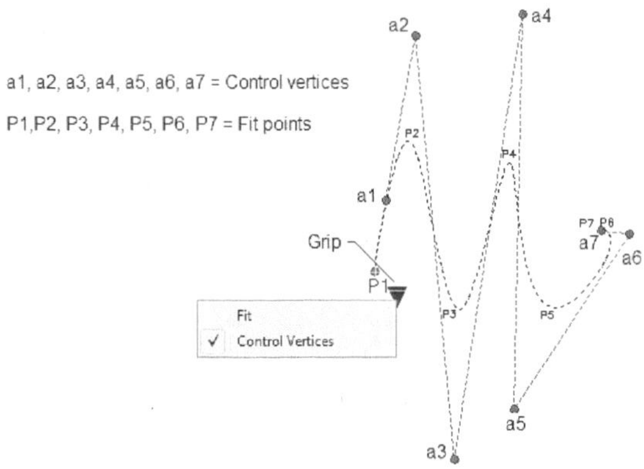

Figure 19-23 Control vertices and fit points of a spline

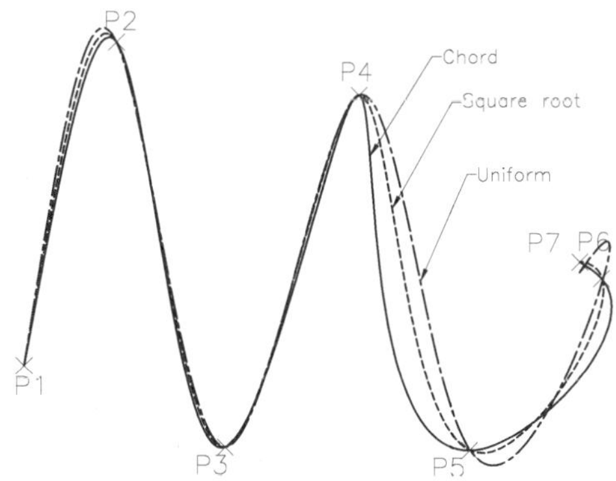

Figure 19-24 Splines with different knot options

Degree

If you have selected the **CV** method, then the **Specify first point or [Method/Degree/Object]** prompt will be displayed. Enter **D** at the command prompt and specify the degree.

Close

This option allows you to create closed NURBS. When you use this option, AutoCAD will automatically join the endpoint of the spline with the start point.

Tolerance

This option is used to control the fit of the spline between specified points. By default, this value is zero; as a result, the spline passes through the points by which it is created. Using this option, you can specify the tolerance values that will govern the spline creation, refer to Figure 19-25. The splines will be offset from the specified point by a distance equal to the tolerance value. The smaller the value of the tolerance, the closer the spline will be to the specified points.

Start and End Tangency

This option is used to control the tangency of a spline at its start point and the endpoint. On entering **T** at the **Enter next point or [start Tangency/toLerance]** or **Enter next point or [end Tangency/toLerance/Undo/Close]** prompt, you will be prompted to specify the tangent. Specify a point; the tangency will be determined by the slope of the spline at the specified point. Remember that after specifying the start point of the spline, you need to specify the start tangency. If you specify the second point, the default value will be used for the tangency. Similarly, you need to specify the end tangency after specifying the last point of the spline. Figure 19-26 shows a spline with start and end tangencies. The virtual tangent line is for reference.

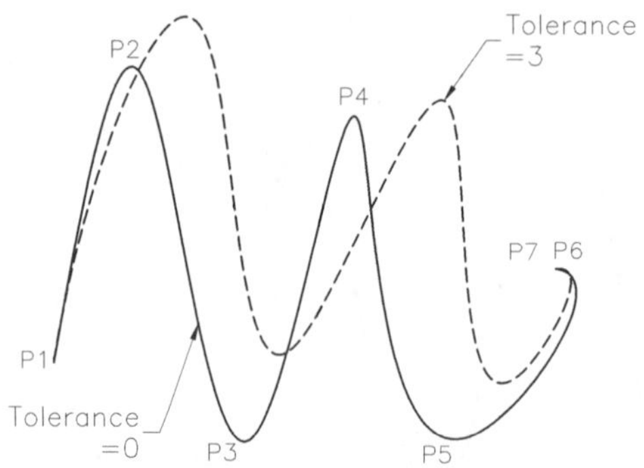

*Figure 19-25 Creating a spline with the **Tolerance** of 0 and 3*

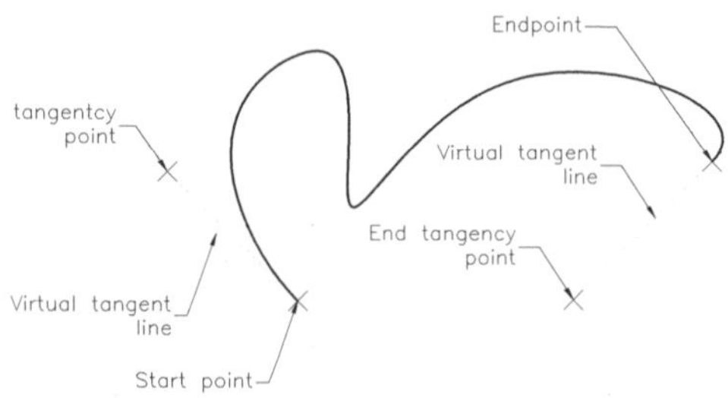

***Figure 19-26** Spline with start and end tangencies*

EDITING SPLINES

Ribbon: Home > Modify > Edit Spline **Menu Bar:** Modify > Object > Spline
Tool Palettes: Modify > Edit spline **Toolbar:** Modify II > Edit Spline
Command: SPLINEDIT/SPE

The NURBS can be edited using the **Edit Spline** tool. Using this tool, you can fit data in a selected spline, close or open a spline, move vertex points, and refine or reverse a spline. Apart from the ways mentioned in the preceding command box, you can choose the options available in the **Spline** cascading menu that will be displayed when you select a spline and right-click. The prompt sequence that will follow when you choose the **Edit Spline** tool in the **Modify** panel is given next.

Select spline: *Select the spline to be edited if not selected already using the above-mentioned shortcut menu.*
Enter an option [Close/Join/Fit data/Edit vertex/convert to Polyline/Reverse/Undo/eXit] <eXit>: *Select any one of the options.*

Options for Editing Splines

On invoking the **Edit Spline** tool, the following options are displayed for editing the splines:

Fit data

When you draw a spline, the spline fits as per the specified points (data points). The **Fit data** option allows you to edit these points. You can add, delete, or move the data points. These data points or control points are also referred to as fit points. For example, if you want to redefine the start and end tangents of a spline, select the **Fit data** option and then select the **Tangents** option. The prompt sequence that will follow when you invoke this option is given next.

Select spline: *Select the spline to be edited.*
Enter an option [Close/Join/Fit data/Edit vertex/convert to Polyline/Reverse/Undo/eXit] <eXit>: **F** Enter
Enter a fit data option [Add/Close/Delete/Kink/Move/Purge/Tangents/toLerance/eXit] <eXit>: **T** Enter

The start and end tangent points can be selected or their coordinates can be entered. The options available within the **Fit data** option are as follows:

Add: You can use this option to add new fit points to the spline. When you invoke this option, you will be prompted to specify the existing fit point on the spline. After selecting the existing fit point, you will be prompted to specify the location of the new control points. The fit point you select and the next fit point appear as selected grips. You can now add a fit point between these two selected fit points, as shown in Figure 19-27. If you select the start point or endpoint of the spline, only they get highlighted. When you select the start point of the spline, you are prompted to specify whether you want to add the new fit point before or after the start point of the spline. AutoCAD will continue prompting for the location of new control points until you press ENTER at the **Specify new fit point to add <exit>** prompt.

Close/Open: This option is used to close an open spline or open a closed spline, refer to Figure 19-28. If the spline is open, the **Close** option is available and if the spline is closed, the **Open** option is displayed.

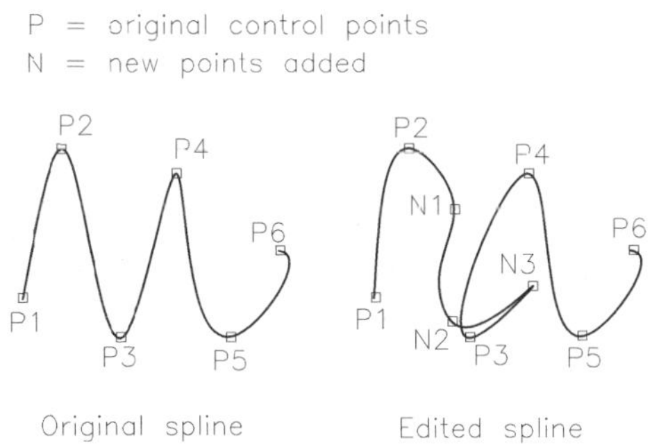

Figure 19-27 The original spline and the edited spline after adding fit points

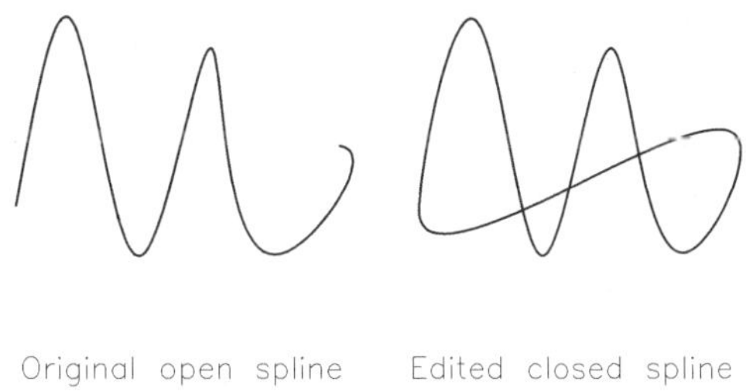

Figure 19-28 An open spline and a closed spline

Delete: This option is used to delete a selected fit point from a spline. You can continue deleting fit points from a spline until only two fit points are left in the spline.

Kink: This option is used to add a knot and a fit point to the selected point. On selecting this option, you will be prompted to specify a point on the spline. Select a point; a kink will be added.

Move: You can move fit points by using this option. When you select this option, the start point of the spline is selected and the following prompt sequence appears:

> Specify new location or [Next/Previous/Select point/eXit] <N>: *Select a new location for the start point using the mouse pick button or enter any one of these options.*

You can enter **N** if you want to select the next point, **P** if you want to select a previous point, or **S** if you want to select any other point, and **X** if you want to exit the tool. Figure 19-29 shows the movement of data points in a spline. Remember that this option is used to move only the data points on the spline and not the control points on the Bezier control frame.

Purge: This option is used to remove fit point data from a spline. This reduces the file size, which is useful when a drawing, for example, a landscape contour map, contains large number of splines. Purging simplifies the spline definition and the drawing file size.

Tangents: This option is used to modify the tangents of the start and endpoints of a selected spline, refer to Figure 19-30. When you select this option, you will be prompted to specify the start and end tangents of the spline. You can specify the start and end tangents or use the systems default tangents.

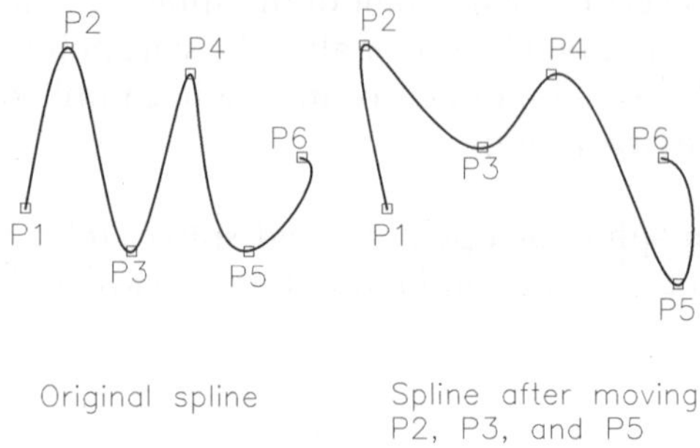

Figure 19-29 The original spline and the edited spline after moving the data points

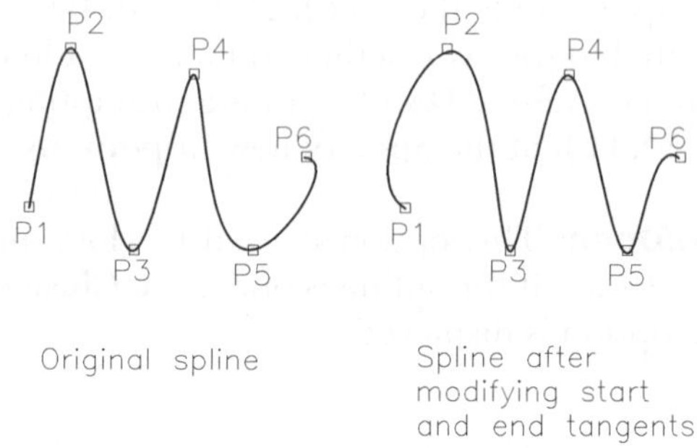

Figure 19-30 The original spline and the spline after modifying the start and end tangents

toLerance: This option is used to modify the fit tolerance values of a selected spline. As discussed, while creating the splines, different tolerance values produce different splines. A smaller tolerance value creates a spline that passes very closely through the definition points of a spline. When you invoke this option, you will be prompted to specify the tolerance value for the spline.

eXit: Choose this option to exit the **Fit data** option of editing splines.

Close/Open

This option is used to close an open spline or open a closed spline. When you select the **Close** option, AutoCAD lets you open, edit the vertex, convert spline to polyline, or reverse the spline.

Edit Vertex

This option is used to refine a spline by adding more control points in it, elevating the order, or adding weight to vertex points. The prompt sequence that will follow when you invoke this option is given next.

Enter an option [Open/Fit data/Edit vertex/convert to Polyline/Reverse/Undo/eXit] <eXit>: ***E*** Enter
Enter a vertex editing option [Add/Delete/Elevate order/Move/Weight/eXit] <eXit>:

The options in this prompt are discussed next.

Add: This option is used to add more control points on the spline. When you invoke this option, you will be prompted to specify the location of the new point on the spline. You can directly specify the location of the new point using the left mouse button. A new control point will be added at the specified location.

Delete: This option is used to delete a selected fit point from a spline.

Elevate order: This option is used to increase the order of a spline curve. The order of a curve can be defined as the highest power of the algebraic expression that defines the spline plus 1. For example, the order of a cubic spline will be 3 + 1 = 4. Using the **Elevate order** option, you can increase this order for a selected spline. This results in more control points on the curve and a greater possibility of controlling the spline. The value of the spline order varies from 4 to 26. You can only increase the order and not decrease it. For example, if a spline order is 18, you can elevate its order to any value greater than 18, but not less than 18.

Move: When you draw a spline, it is associated with the Bezier control frame. The **Move** option allows you to move the vertices of the control frame. The **Move** option is similar to the **Move** option of **Fit data** for editing the splines. The prompt sequence that follows when you invoke this option is given next.

> Enter an option [Close/Join/Fit data/Edit vertex/convert to Polyline/Reverse/Undo/eXit] <eXit>: **E** [Enter]
> Enter a vertex editing option [Add/Delete/Elevate order/Move/Weight/eXit] <eXit>: **M** [Enter]
> Specify new location or [Next/Previous/Select point/eXit] <N>:

Weight: You can also add weight to any of the control vertices of a spline by using this option. When weight is added to a particular vertex, the spline gets pulled more towards it. Similarly, a lower value of weight of a particular spline vertex will result in the spline getting pulled less towards that particular vertex. In other words, adding weight to a particular point will force the selected point to maintain its tangency with the point. The more weight added to the point, the more is the distance through which the spline will remain tangent to the point. By default, the spline gets pulled equally towards the vertices of the spline. The default value of weight provided to each control point is 1.0 and can have only positive values. Once you have added the weight to a point, you can proceed to the next point. You can also directly select the point to which the weight has to be added. The prompt sequence for using this option is given next.

> Enter an option [Close/Join/Fit data/Edit vertex/convert to Polyline/Reverse/Undo/eXit] <eXit>: **E** [Enter]
> Enter a vertex editing option [Add/Delete/Elevate order/Move/Weight/eXit] <eXit>: **W** [Enter]
> Enter new weight (current = 1.0000) or [Next/Previous/Select point/eXit] <N>: **S** [Enter]
> Specify existing fit point on spline <exit>: *Select a fit point*
> Enter new weight (current = 1.0000) or [Next/Previous/Select point/eXit] <N>: **3** [Enter]
> Enter new weight (current = 1.0000) or [Next/Previous/Select point/eXit] <N>: **Exit** [Enter]

Join

If a spline, line, or an arc is joined to the spline that is being edited, then you can use this option to join those entities to the spline. On choosing this option, you will be prompted to select an open curve. Select the curves to be joined and press ENTER; all curves will be joined to the spline and knot and fit points will be added at the joining point. The prompt sequence for using this option is given next.

Enter an option [Close/Join/Fit data/Edit vertex/convert to Polyline/Reverse/Undo/eXit]
<eXit>: **J**
Select any open curves to join to source: *Select an object. 1 found*
Select any open curves to join to source: *Select an object. 1 found, 2 total*
Select any open curves to join to source:
2 objects joined to source

Reverse

This option is used to reverse the spline direction. This implies that when you apply this option to a spline, its start point becomes its endpoint and vice versa.

convert to Polyline

This option is used to convert a spline into a polyline. On specifying this option, you will be prompted to specify a precision value. Specify a value between 0 and 99, and then press ENTER; the spline will be converted into a polyline. The precision value determines the accuracy of the resulting polyline.

Undo

This option will undo the previous editing operation applied to a spline within the current session of the **Edit Spline** tool. You can continue to use this option till you reach the spline as it was when you started to edit it.

EDITING SPLINES USING 3D EDIT BAR

Command: 3DEDITBAR

The **3DEDITBAR** command is used to edit a spline by using the Move gizmo. To edit a spline using this command, select the spline and right click; a shortcut menu will be displayed. Choose the **Spline > 3D Edit Bar** option from the shortcut menu; you will be prompted to select a point on the curve. Select a point on the curve at the position where you want to modify the spline; the Move gizmo will be displayed with one extra arrow tangential to the curve at the selected point. This arrow can be used to change the tangent direction as well as the magnitude of tangency at the point. Using this arrow, you can dynamically edit the spline.

Self-Evaluation Test

Answer the following questions and then compare them to those given at the end of this chapter:

1. When you use the **Inner arcs** option for multilines, a capping arc is drawn between the __________ numbered inner lines.

2. The **Multilines Edit tools** dialog box consists of __________ basic editing tools.

3. The __________ option of the **Fit data** option of the **Edit Spline** tool is used to reduce the file size by removing the fit data of the selected splines.

4. The __________ system variable stores the justification of the current multiline.

5. The name of the multiline style that you enter in the **New Style Name** edit box of the **Create New Multiline style** dialog box can have up to thirty-one characters including spaces. (T/F)

6. The **Zero** option is used to create a multiline so that the zero offset position of the multiline coincides with the selected points. (T/F)

7. Multilines cannot be edited using grips. (T/F)

8. While using the **Top** justification option to draw a multiline, the line with the largest positive offset coincides with the points selected on the screen. (T/F)

9. When a multiline is cut, two separate multilines are created. (T/F)

10. You cannot weld or join separate multilines. (T/F)

Review Questions

Answer the following questions:

1. In which file are the multiline styles saved by default?

   (a) *acad.mln* (b) *acad.pat*
   (c) *acad.mpr* (d) *acad.plt*

2. Which of the following is the default value of the start and end angles for multilines?

   (a) 90 (b) 180
   (c) 45 (d) 0

3. Which of the following tools does not work on multilines?

   (a) **Mirror** (b) **Fillet**
   (c) **Stretch** (d) **Explode**

4. Which of the following options can be used to reverse the direction of spline creation while editing a spline?

   (a) **Fit data** (b) **Refine**
   (c) **Reverse** (d) **Weight**

5. AutoCAD forces a multiline to turn into a single line if the scale factor of the multiline is________.

6. The current multiline style is saved in the __________ system variable and the default value is **STANDARD**.

7. The three justifications thet are available for the **MLINE** command are __________, __________, and __________.

8. Using options of the **MLEDIT** command, you can create three types of cross intersections: __________, __________, and __________.

9. If the value of **Fit tolerance** of a spline is __________, the spline passes exactly through the fit points of the spline.

10. You need to set the degree of a spline if you are drawing the spline by using the __________ method.

11. By default, the *.mln* files are saved at *C:\Users\<user name>\AppData\Roaming\Autodesk\AutoCAD 2018\R20.1\enu\Support*. (T/F)

12. Once the **Purge** option of **Fit data** is used on a spline, the **Fit data** option is no longer available for the particular spline. (T/F)

13. You can break or trim a multiline. (T/F)

14. You cannot change the lineweights of the lines that constitute a multiline. (T/F)

Exercise 1

Create the drawing shown in Figure 19-31.

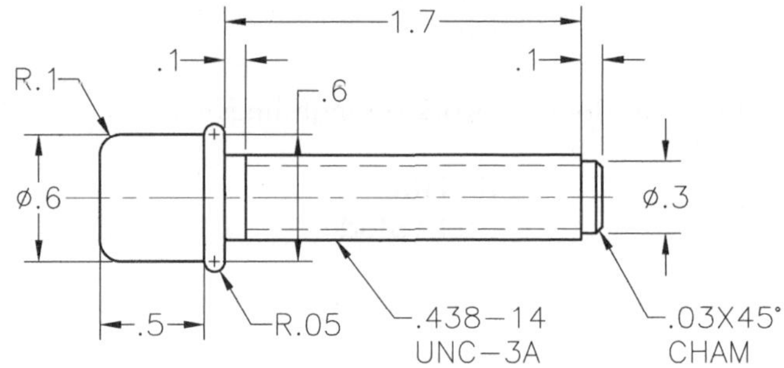

Figure 19-31 *Drawing for Exercise 1*

Exercise 2

Create the drawing shown in Figure 19-32. Use the **MLINE** command to draw the walls. The wall thickness is 12 inches. Assume the missing dimensions.

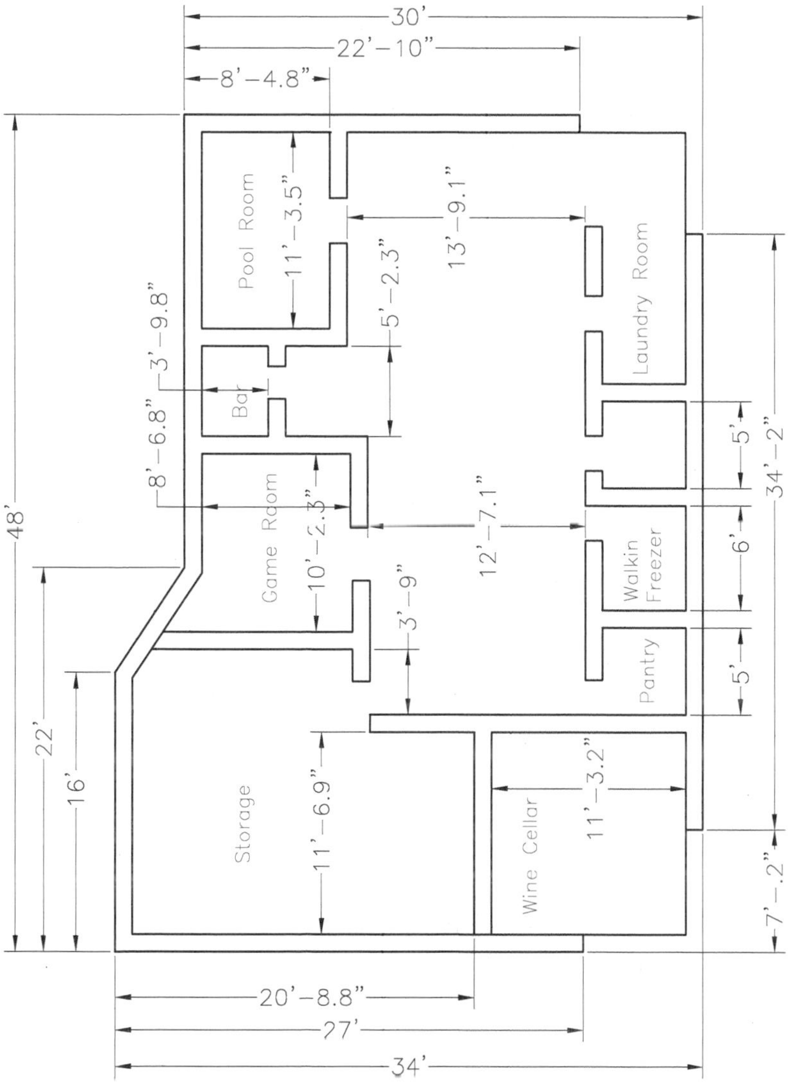

Figure 19-32 Drawing for Exercise 2

Problem-Solving Exercise 1

Create the drawing shown in Figure 19-33. Some of the reference dimensions are given in the drawing. Assume the missing dimensions.

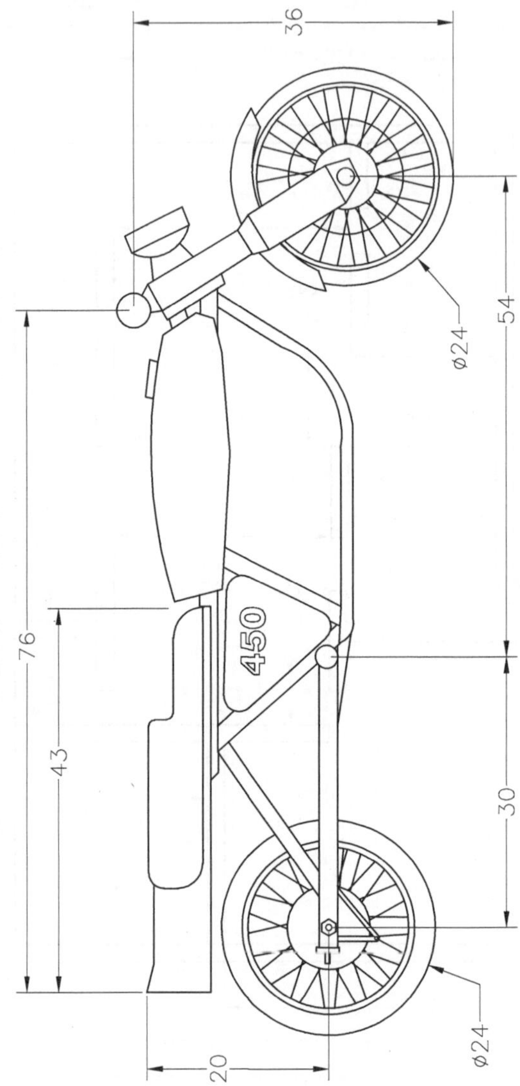

Figure 19-33 *Drawing for Problem-Solving Exercise 1*

Problem-Solving Exercise 2

Create the drawing shown in Figure 19-34. Some of the reference dimensions are given in the drawing. Assume the missing dimensions.

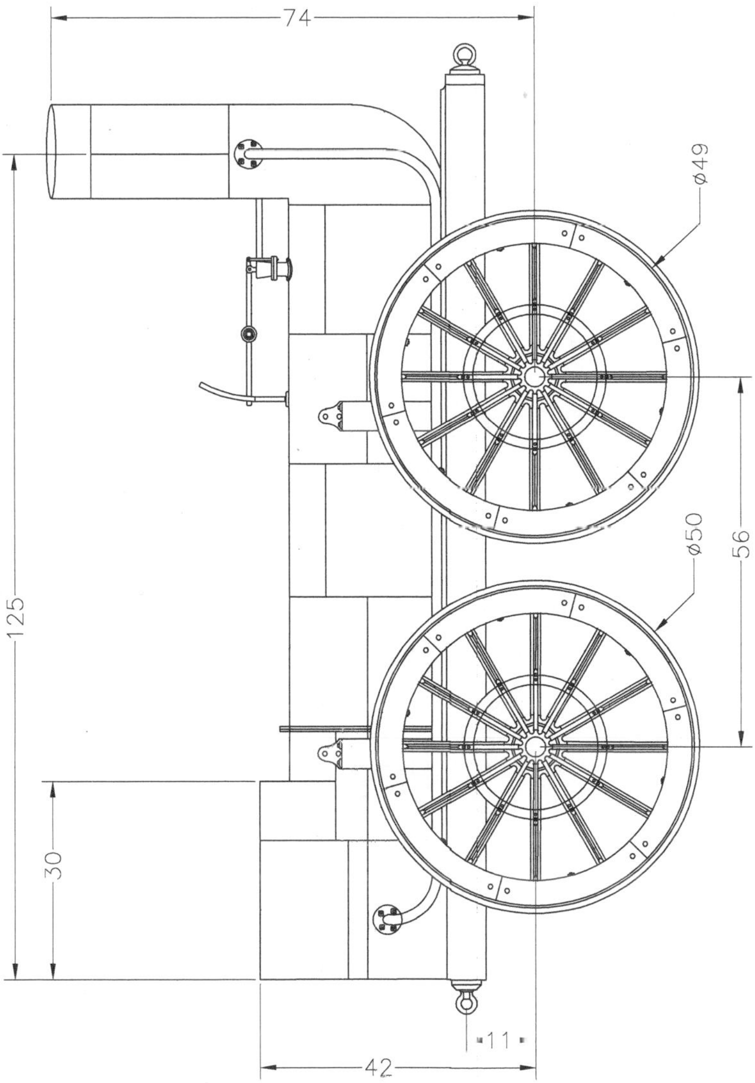

Figure 19-34 *Drawing for Problem-Solving Exercise 2*

Problem-Solving Exercise 3

Create the drawing shown in Figure 19-35. Some of the reference dimensions are given in the drawing. Assume the missing dimensions.

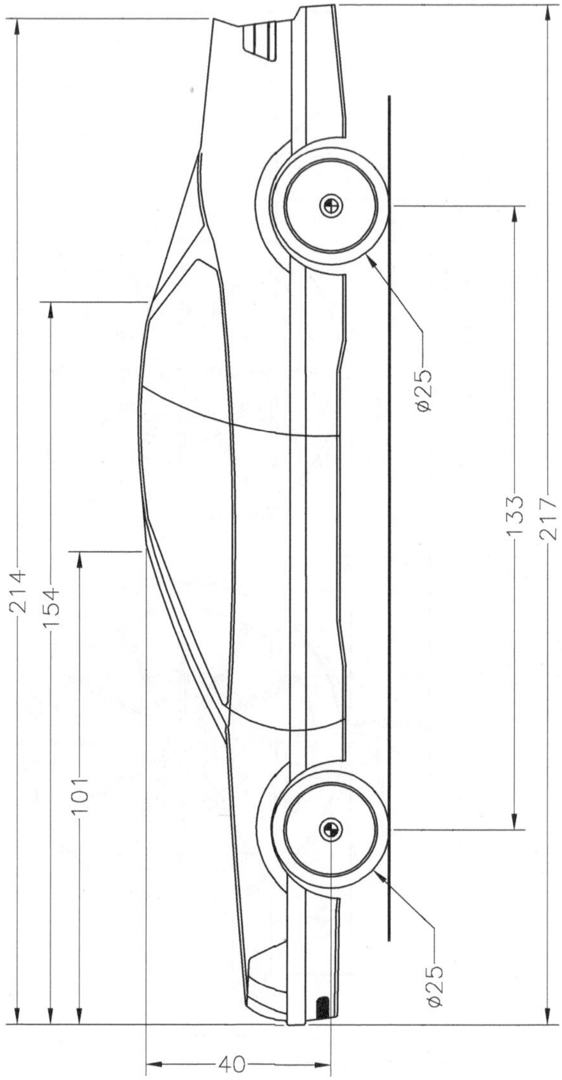

***Figure 19-35** Drawing for Problem-Solving Exercise 3*

Problem-Solving Exercise 4

Create the drawing shown in Figure 19-36. Some of the reference dimensions are given in the drawing. Assume the missing dimensions.

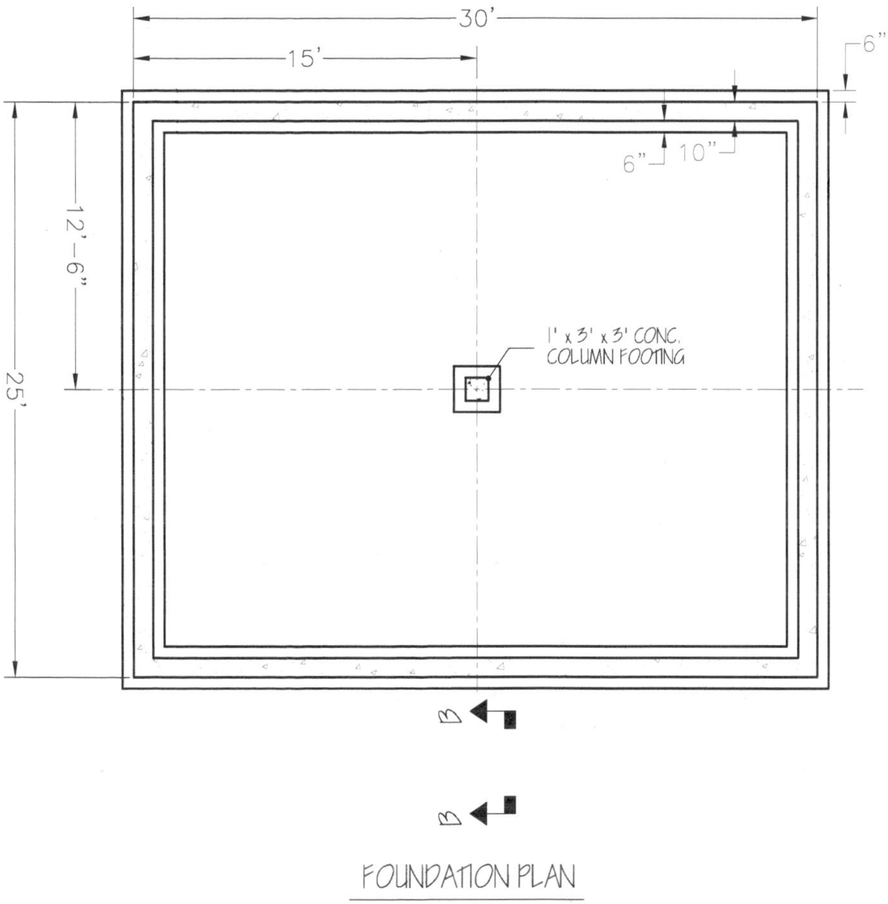

Figure 19-36 *Drawing for Problem-Solving Exercise 4*

Problem-Solving Exercise 5

Create the drawing shown in Figure 19-37. Some of the reference dimensions are given in the drawing. Assume the missing dimensions.

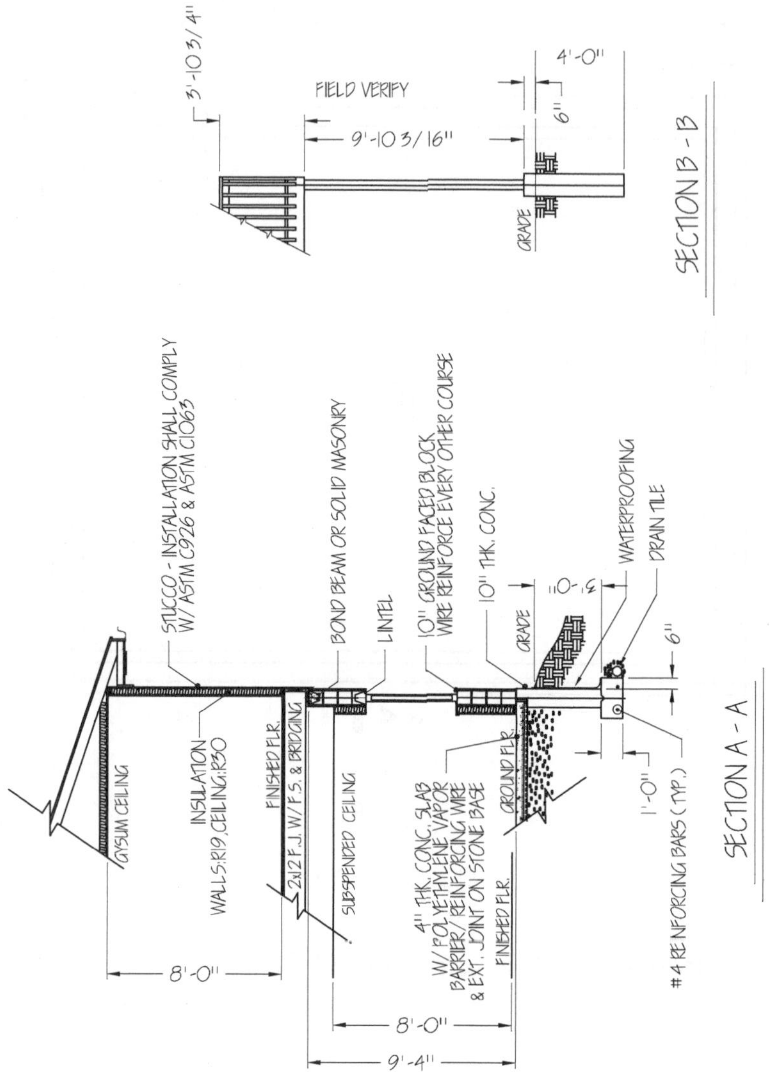

Figure 19-37 *Drawing for Problem-Solving Exercise 5*

Problem-Solving Exercise 6

Create the drawing shown in Figure 19-38. Some of the reference dimensions are given in the drawing. Assume the missing dimensions.

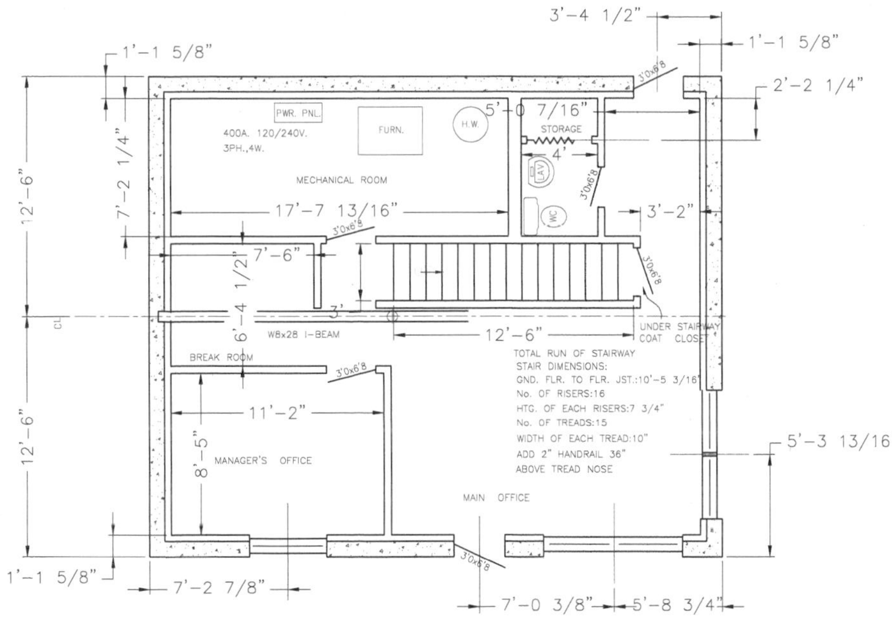

Figure 19-38 Drawing for Problem-Solving Exercise 6

Problem-Solving Exercise 7

Create the drawing shown in Figure 19-39. Some of the reference dimensions are given in the drawing. Assume the missing dimensions.

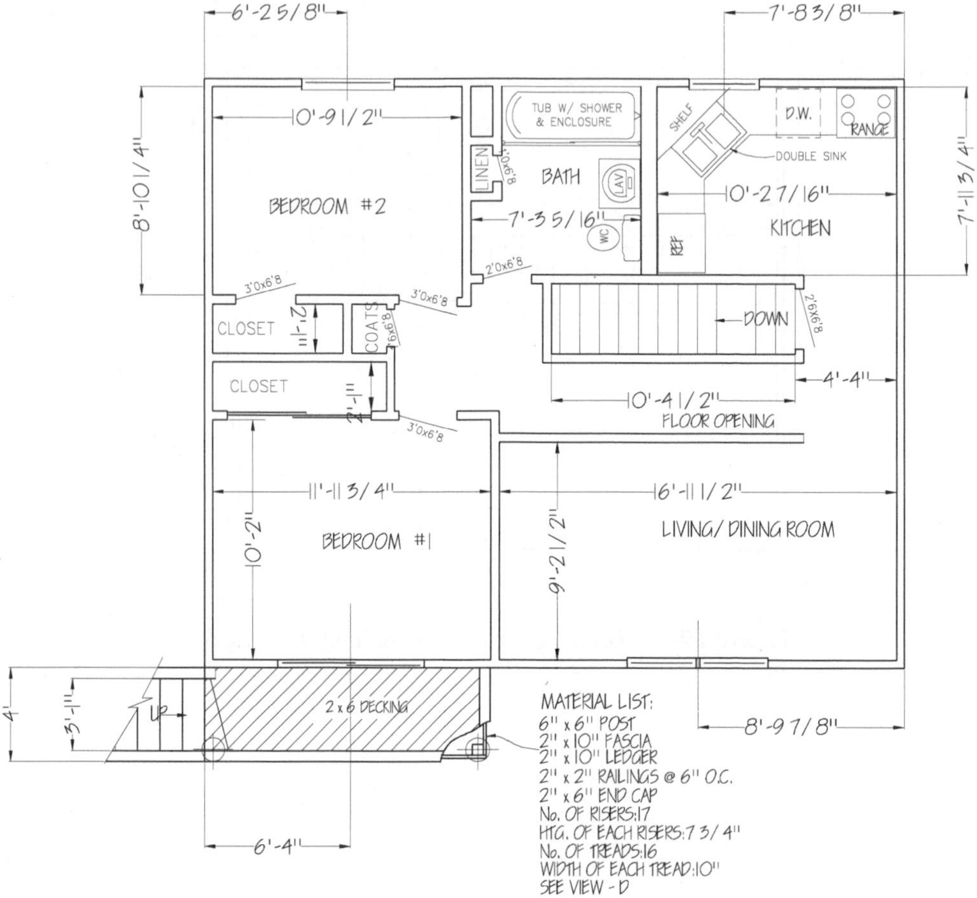

Figure 19-39 Drawing for Problem-Solving Exercise 7

Answers to Self-Evaluation Test

1. even, 2. five, 3. **Purge**, 4. **CMLJUST**, 5. T, 6. T, 7. F, 8. T, 9. F, 10. T

Chapter 20

Grouping and Advanced Editing of Sketched Objects

Learning Objectives

After completing this chapter, you will be able to:
- *Group sketched objects*
- *Select and cycle through defined groups*
- *Change properties and location of sketched objects*
- *Perform editing operations on polylines*
- *Explode compound objects and undo previous commands*
- *Rename the named objects and remove unused named objects*

Key Terms

- *Group*
- *Explode*
- *Polyline Edit*
- *SPLINETYPE*
- *Undo*
- *Redo*
- *Rename*
- *Purge*

GROUPING SKETCHED OBJECTS USING THE OBJECT GROUPING DIALOG BOX

Ribbon: Home > Groups > Group Manager **Command:** CLASSICGROUP

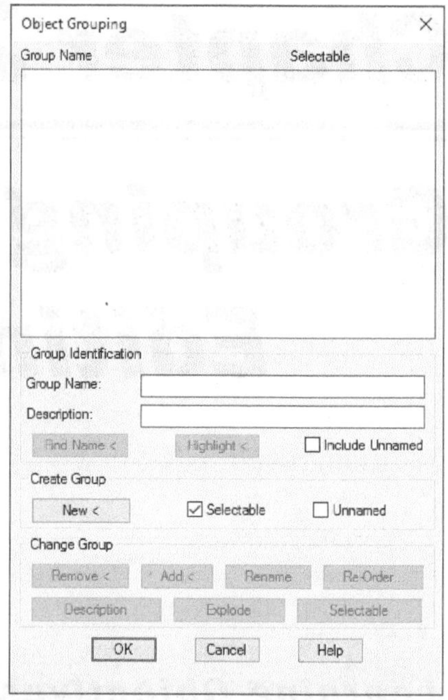

*Figure 20-1 The **Object Grouping** dialog box*

In AutoCAD, you can group sketched objects using the **Object Grouping** dialog box, as shown in Figure 20-1. To invoke the **Object Grouping** dialog box, you need to choose the **Group Manager** tool from the **Groups** panel in the **Home** tab. You can use the **Object Grouping** dialog box to group AutoCAD objects and assign a name to the group. Once you have created groups, you can select the objects by the group name. The individual characteristics of an object are not affected by forming groups. Groups enable you to select all the objects in a group together for editing. It makes the object selection process easier and faster. Objects can be members of several groups. Also, a group can contain several smaller groups. This may be referred to as nested groups.

Although an object belongs to a group, you can still select an object as if it does not belong to any group. Groups can be selected by entering the group name or by selecting an object that belongs to the group. You can also highlight the objects in a group or sequentially highlight the groups to which an object belongs. The options in the **Object Grouping** dialog box are discussed next.

Group Name List Box

The **Group Name** list box in the **Object Grouping** dialog box displays the names of the existing groups. The list box also displays whether a group is selectable or not, under the **Selectable** column. A selectable group is the one in which all members of the group are selected on selecting a single member. However, the members that are in frozen or locked layers are not selected. You can also make a group non-selectable; which helps you to select the objects in the group individually.

Group Identification Area

The options under the **Group Identification** area are as follows:

Group Name

The **Group Name** edit box displays the name of the selected group. You can also use the **Group Name** edit box to enter the name of a new group. You can enter any name, but it is recommended that you use a name that reflects the type of objects in the group. For example, the group name WALLS can include all lines that form walls. Group names can be up to thirty-one characters long and can include letters, numbers, and special characters ($, _, and -). Group names cannot have spaces.

Description

The **Description** edit box displays the description of the selected group. It can be used to enter the description of a group.

Find Name

The **Find Name** button is used to find the group name or names associated with an object. When you choose this button, the dialog box temporarily disappears from the screen and AutoCAD prompts you to **Pick a member of a group**. Once you select the object, the **Group Member List** dialog box will be displayed, as shown in Figure 20-2, showing the group name(s) to which the selected object belongs.

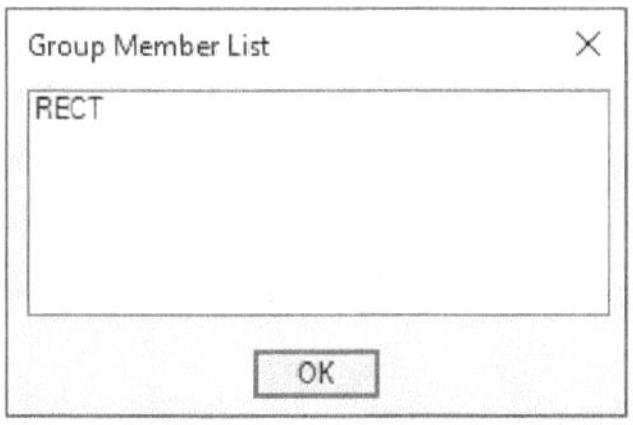

***Figure 20-2** The **Group Member List** dialog box*

Highlight

The **Highlight** button is used to highlight the objects in the selected group name. This button is available only when you select a group from the **Group Name** list box. When you choose the **Highlight** button, the objects that are members of the selected group are highlighted in the drawing and the **Object Grouping** message box is displayed, as shown in Figure 20-3. Choose the **Continue** button or press ENTER to return to the **Object Grouping** dialog box.

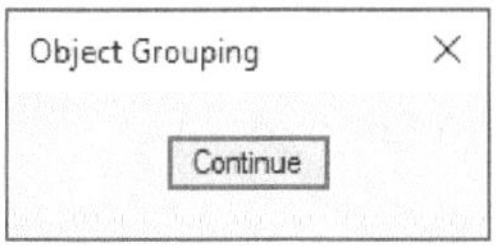

***Figure 20-3** The **Object Grouping** message box*

Include Unnamed

The **Include Unnamed** check box is used to display the names of the unnamed groups in the **Object Grouping** dialog box. The unnamed groups are created when you select the **Unnamed** check box in the **Create Group** area or when you copy the objects that belong to a group. AutoCAD automatically groups and assigns a name to the copied objects. The format of the name is A*n* (for example, *A1, *A2, *A3). If you select the **Include Unnamed** check box, the unnamed group names (*A1, *A2, *A3, ...) will also be displayed in the **Group Name** list box of the dialog box. The unnamed groups can also be created by not assigning a name to the group (see **Unnamed** in the next section, "**Create Group** Area").

Create Group Area

The options under this area are discussed next.

New

The **New** button is used to create a new group. To create a group, enter the name of the group in the **Group Name** edit box and then choose the **New** button; the **Object Grouping** dialog box will be temporarily closed and you will be prompted to select the objects to be included in the group. After selecting the objects, right-click; the dialog box will be displayed again and a new group will be created from the selected objects. The new group name is now displayed in the **Group Name** list box of the dialog box. The group names in the **Group Name** list box are listed alphabetically.

Selectable

The **Selectable** check box allows you to define a group as selectable. A selectable group has a property that if you select any one object in the group, the entire group will be selected. If you clear this check box while defining a group, the new group created will not be selected at once. Therefore, you need to select all members of the group individually as the entire group will not be selected upon selecting the individual entities of the group.

Even if a group is defined as selectable, and the **PICKSTYLE** system variable is set to 0, you will not be able to select the entire group by selecting one of its members. You will be able to individually select members of the group. You can also turn the group selectability on or off by selecting or clearing the **Object grouping** check box in the **Selection modes** area of the **Selection** tab of the **Options** dialog box or by using the SHIFT+CTRL+A toggle keys.

Unnamed

When you create a group, you can assign it a name or leave it unnamed. If you select the **Unnamed** check box, AutoCAD will automatically assign a group name to the selected objects and these unnamed groups will be listed in the **Group Name** list box. To view the name of the unnamed group, the **Include Unnamed** check box should be selected. The format used for assigning a name is A*n* (*A1, *A2, *A3 ...), where *n* is a number which increments by 1 with each newly added unnamed group.

Change Group Area

All the options under this area, other than the **Re-Order** button, will be available only when you highlight a group name by selecting it in the **Group Name** list box of the dialog box. The options in this area are used to modify the properties of the existing group. These options are as follows.

Remove

The **Remove** button is used to remove objects from the selected group. Once you select the group name from the **Group Name** list box and then choose the **Remove** button; the dialog box will be temporarily closed and AutoCAD will display the following prompts at the command prompt.

Select objects to remove from group...
Remove objects: *(Select the objects that you want to remove from the selected group.)*

Also, all objects belonging to the selected group will be highlighted. As you select the objects to be removed from the group, they no longer appear highlighted. Note that even if you remove all objects from the group, the group name will still exist, unless you use the **Explode** option to remove the group definition (discussed later in this section). If you remove objects and then add them later in the same drawing session, the objects retain their order in the group.

Add

The **Add** button is used to add objects to the selected group. When you select this option, AutoCAD will prompt you to select the objects you want to add to the selected group. The prompt sequence in this case will be similar to that of the **Remove** option. Similar to removing an object, all objects belonging to the selected group are highlighted and as soon as you select an object to be added to the group, it also gets highlighted.

Rename

The **Rename** button is used to rename the selected group. To rename a group, first select the group name from the **Group Name** list box, enter the new name in the **Group Name** edit box, and then choose the **Rename** button. AutoCAD will rename the specified group. You can use this option to rename unnamed groups that were discussed earlier.

Re-Order

The **Re-Order** button is used to change the order of the objects in the selected group. The objects are numbered in the order in which you select them when selecting objects for the group. Sometimes, while creating a tool path, you may want to change the order of these objects to get a continuous tool motion. You can do this using the **Re-Order** button. This option is also useful in some batch operations where one object needs to be on top of another object for display reasons. When you choose the **Re-Order** button, AutoCAD displays the **Order Group** dialog box, as shown in Figure 20-4, where you can change the order of the group members.

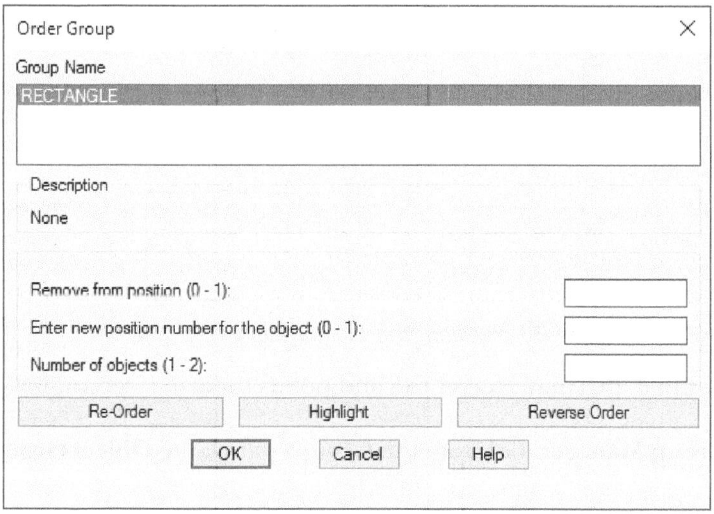

*Figure 20-4 The **Order Group** dialog box*

Description

The **Description** button is used to change the description of the selected group. To change the description of a group, first select the group name from the **Group Name** list box, enter the new description in the **Description** text box, and then choose the **Description** button. AutoCAD will update the description of the specified group.

Explode

The **Explode** option is used to delete group definition of the selected group. The objects that were in the group become regular objects without a group reference. If you had made copies of the group that was exploded in a drawing, they shall remain as unnamed groups in the drawing. You can select the **Include Unnamed** check box in the **Group Identification** area of the **Object Grouping** dialog box to view the names of the unnamed groups in the **Group Name** list box. You can then select them in the list box and explode them or rename them as required.

Selectable

The **Selectable** button is used to change the selectable status of the selected group. To change the selectable status of the group, first select the group name from the **Group Name** list box, and then choose the **Selectable** button. This button acts like a toggle key between the options of selectable and non-selectable. If the selectable status for a group is displayed as "**Yes**", you can choose the **Selectable** button to change it to "**No**". Selectable implies that the entire group gets selected when one object in the group is selected. If the selectable status is "**No**", you cannot select the entire group by selecting one object in the group.

Example 1 — Reorder Group

In this example, you will draw a rectangle representing a toolpath. The rectangle should comprise of four individual lines. Group all lines by selecting them in the order shown in Figure 20-5(a). Then, highlight the order, and re-order the group, as shown in Figure 20-5(b).

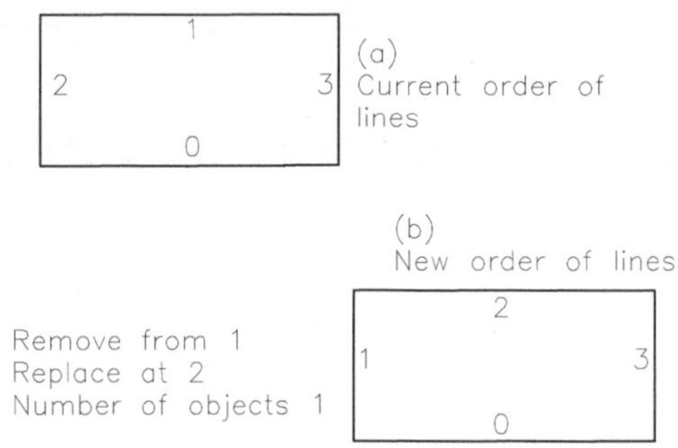

Figure 20-5 *Changing the order of group objects*

1. Draw four lines that are connected at the end points to form a rectangle.

2 Choose the **Group Manager** tool from the **Groups** panel; the **Object Grouping** dialog box is displayed.

3. Type **G1** in the **Group Name** edit box and choose the **New** button; the **Object Grouping** dialog box will disappear and you will be prompted to select the objects for grouping.

4. Select the lines in the order specified in Figure 20-5(a) and right-click; the **Object Grouping** dialog box is displayed again.

5. Make the group (G1) current by selecting it in the **Group Name** list box and choose the **Re-Order** button in the dialog box; the **Order Group** dialog box is displayed.

6. Select the group G1 in the **Group Name** list box, if not already selected, and choose the **Highlight** button; the **Object Grouping** dialog box is displayed, as shown in Figure 20-6. You can use the **Next** and **Previous** buttons to highlight the grouped objects in the order of selection.

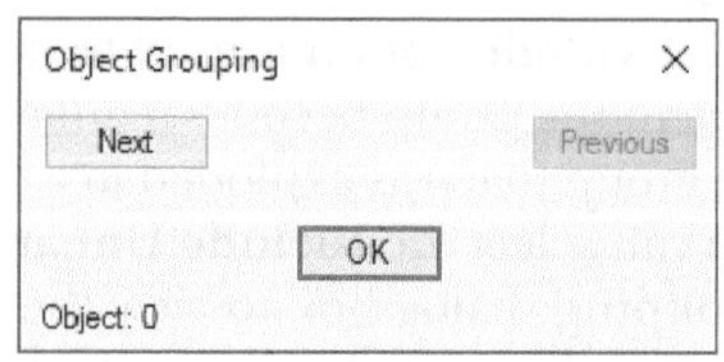

Figure 20-6 *The **Object Grouping** dialog box*

You will notice that the order of selection is not proper. As these lines represent a tool path, you need to reorder the objects, as shown in Figure 20-5(b).

7. To get a clockwise tool path, you must switch object numbers 1 and 2. You can do so by entering the necessary information in the **Order Group** dialog box. Enter **1** in the **Remove from position (0-3)** edit box and **2** in the **Enter new position number for the object (0-3)** edit box. Enter **1** in the **Number of objects (1-4)** edit box because there is only one object to be replaced.

8. After entering the information, choose the **Re-Order** button to define the new order of the objects. You can confirm the change by choosing the **Highlight** button again and cycling through the objects.

GROUPING SKETCHED OBJECTS USING THE GROUP BUTTON

Ribbon: Home > Groups > Group	**Command:** GROUP/G
Toolbar: Group > Group	

In AutoCAD, you can group objects by using the **Group** tool from the **Groups** panel of the **Home** tab. The prompt sequence to create a group is given next:

*Choose the **Group** tool.*
Select objects or [Name/Description]: **N** Enter
Enter a group name or [?]: *Enter the group name* Enter
Select objects or [Name/Description]: *Select the objects to be grouped.*
Select objects or [Name/Description]: Enter
Group "*group name*" has been created.

You can also group the objects by using the shortcut menu. Select the objects to be grouped, and right-click in the drawing area; a shortcut menu will be displayed. Choose **Group** > **Group** from the shortcut menu; the selected objects will be grouped as *Unnamed group*.

Later on, you can ungroup them using **Ungroup** option from the same shortcut menu.

SELECTING GROUPS

You can select a group by name by entering **G** at the **Select objects** prompt. For example, if you have to move a particular group, choose the **Move** tool from the **Modify** panel in the **Home** tab and then enter the following prompt sequence:

Select objects: **G** Enter
Enter group name: *Enter the group name*
n found
Select objects: Enter

Instead of entering **G** at the **Select Objects** prompt, if you select any member of a selectable group, all the group members get selected. Make sure that the **PICKSTYLE** system variable is set to 1 or 3. Also, the group selection can be turned on or off by pressing SHIFT+CTRL+A. If the group selection is off and you want to erase a group from a drawing, choose the **Erase** tool from the **Modify** panel. The prompt sequence for erasing the group is given next.

Select objects: *Press SHIFT+CTRL+A*
<Groups on> *Select an object that belongs to a group. (If the group has been defined as selectable, all objects belonging to that group will be selected.)*

If the group has not been defined as selectable, you cannot select all objects in the group, even if you turn the group selection on by pressing the SHIFT+CTRL+A keys. This setting can also be changed in the **Selection** tab of the **Options** dialog box. You can select or clear the **Object grouping** check box in the **Selection modes** area of the dialog box to turn group selectability on or off.

> **Tip**
> *The keyboard shortcut SHIFT+CTRL+A is used as a toggle key to turn the group selection on or off.*

CHANGING PROPERTIES OF AN OBJECT

AutoCAD provides you different options for changing the properties of an object. These options are discussed next.

Using the PROPERTIES Palette

Ribbon: View > Palettes > Properties	**Toolbar:** Standard > Properties
Quick Access Toolbar: Properties (*Customize to Add*)	**Command:** PROPERTIES/PR/CH

The categories displayed in the **PROPERTIES** palette depend on the type of object selected. The **General** category displays the general properties of objects, such as color, layer, linetype, linetype scale, plot style, lineweight, hyperlink, and thickness. The procedure to change the general properties of objects using the **PROPERTIES** palette has already been discussed earlier in Chapter 4. In this chapter, the **Geometry** category containing properties that control the geometry of an object will be discussed. Depending on the type of object selected, the **Geometry** category will contain a set of different properties. If you have selected many types of objects in a drawing, the drop-down list at the top of the **PROPERTIES** palette will display all the type of selected objects. If you select a type of object from the drop-down list, the corresponding categories of the object properties will be displayed in the palette. You can also invoke the **PROPERTIES** palette from the shortcut menu displayed on selecting the object.

Selecting a Line

If you have selected a line in the drawing, the **PROPERTIES** palette appears similar to what is shown in Figure 20-7, where you can change the properties of the selected object.

Start X/Start Y/Start Z: The **Start X/Start Y/Start Z** fields in the **Geometry** category display the start point coordinates of the selected line. You can enter new values in these fields or use the Pick Point button that appears in the field you click in. When you choose the Pick Point button, a rubber-band line gets attached to the cursor on its start point and the endpoint of the line is fixed. You can now move the cursor and specify a new start point for the line.

End X/End Y/End Z: Similar to the start point, you can also modify the location of the endpoint of a line by entering new coordinate values in the **End X**, **End Y**, **End Z** fields. You can also choose the Pick Point button in the respective fields and select a new location for the endpoint of the selected line. The Pick Point button appears in the fields when you click on them.

Note

*The **Delta X, Delta Y, Delta Z, Length,** and **Angle** fields are not available for change but the values in these fields get updated as the start and endpoints of the line are changed.*

Selecting a Circle

When you select a circle, the **Geometry** category displays the categories as shown in Figure 20-8. You can modify the values in these fields. The effects of modifying the values are discussed next.

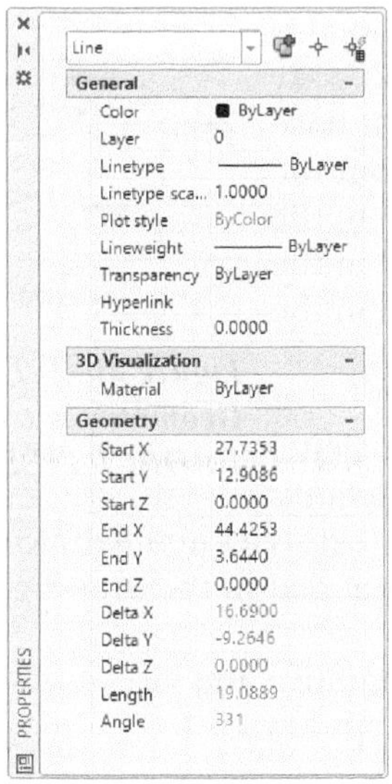

*Figure 20-7 The **PROPERTIES** palette for a line*

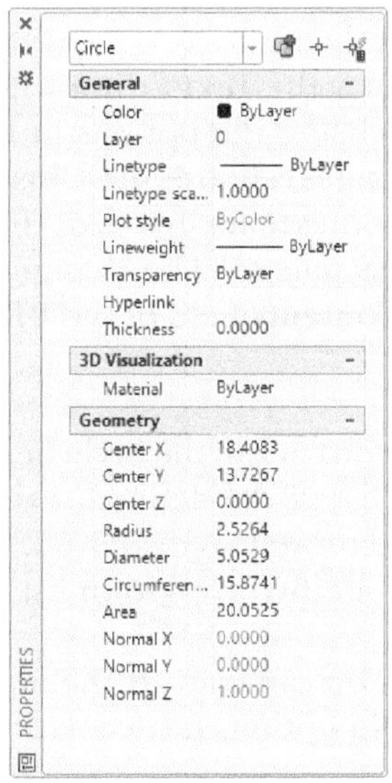

*Figure 20-8 The **PROPERTIES** palette for a circle*

Center X/Center Y/Center Z: Here, under the Center X/Center Y/Center Z fields of the Geometry category, you can specify a new location of the center point of the circle by entering new coordinate values in the Center X, Center Y, and Center Z fields. When you click in any of these fields; the Pick Point button is displayed. You can choose this button to locate a new location of the center point of the circle. The circle will be drawn at the new location with the same radius as specified before. It is as if the circle has moved from the old location to a new one.

Radius/Diameter: You can enter a new value for the radius or diameter of the circle in the **Radius** or **Diameter** fields respectively. The circle's radius or diameter is modified as per the new values you have entered. As you modify the values of the radius or the diameter, the values in the **Circumference** and **Area** fields get modified accordingly.

Note

*You can also enter new values of the circumference or area in the **Circumference** and **Area** fields, respectively, if you want to create a circle with a given value of circumference or area. You will notice that the radius and diameter values are modified accordingly. The **Normal X, Normal Y,** and **Normal Z** fields are not available for modifications.*

Selecting the Multiline Text

If you select multiline text written in a drawing and invoke the **PROPERTIES** palette, refer to Figure 20-9, apart from the **General** category, three more categories of properties are displayed: **Text**, **3D Visualization**, and **Geometry**. The properties in the **Text** and **Geometry** categories and how they can be modified are discussed next.

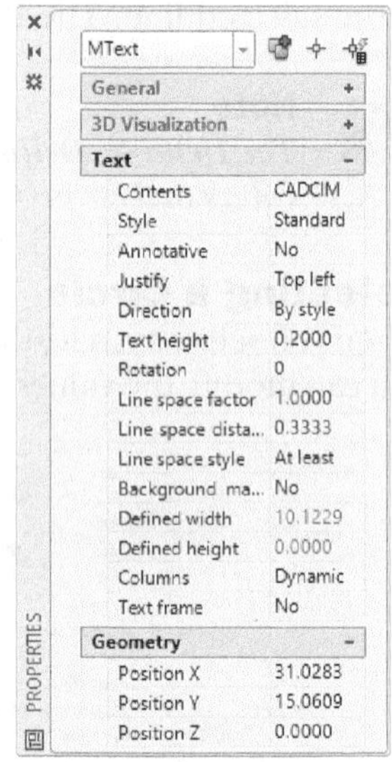

*Figure 20-9 The **Text** and **Geometry** categories of the **PROPERTIES** palette*

Contents: The current contents of the text are displayed in the **Contents** field under the **Text** category of the **PROPERTIES** palette. To modify the contents, click in the field and the button is displayed at the right-corner of the field. You can then choose this button to display the **Text Editor** where you can make the necessary modifications using the options in the dialog box. Once you have made the changes, choose the **Close Text Editor** button from the **Text Editor** contextual tab to exit the text editing and return to the **PROPERTIES** palette. The changes you made are reflected in the value of the **Contents** field of the **PROPERTIES** palette and in the drawing.

Style: When you click in the **Style** field in the **PROPERTIES** palette, a drop-down list of the defined text styles is displayed. By default, only the Standard style is displayed. If you had defined more text styles in the drawing, they can be selected from the drop-down list and applied to the current text in the drawing.

Annotative: You can convert the non-annotative text to annotative and vice-versa by selecting the **Yes** and **No** options respectively from the **Annotative** drop-down list.

Justify: All the text justification options are available in the **Justify** drop-down list. This drop-down list will be available when you click in the **Justify** field. By default, the Top left justification is applied to the text. You can select a text justification from the drop-down list to be applied to the selected text in the drawing.

Direction: This drop-down list displays the possible directions for the text. This option is generally available for the multiline text objects.

Text height: You can enter a new value for the height of the selected text in the drawing. The default text height is 0.2. But, you can make the text smaller or larger in the drawing by simply entering a new value in the **Text height** field of the **PROPERTIES** palette.

Rotation: This field displays the current angle of the selected text and is 0 degree by default. You can change the angle of rotation of the text by entering an angle by which you want to rotate the selected text in the **Rotation** field and then pressing ENTER. The effect is immediately visible in the drawing.

Line space factor: The effect of changing the value of this field is more evident when you have selected a paragraph or multiline text. This value controls the spacing between the lines in a paragraph or multiline text. A scale factor of 1 is the default value. You can increase or decrease the spacing between the lines of the selected paragraph text by entering a new scale factor of your choice and pressing ENTER. The result is immediately visible in the drawing.

Line space distance: This field is used to modify the distance between the spacing of each line of the multiline text. Click in this field and enter the new value in it.

Line space style: This field when selected displays two line spacing options in the corresponding drop-down list. They are **Exactly** and **At least**. **At least** is the default option.

Background mask: This field specifies whether or not any background mask is assigned to the multiline text.

Columns: Columns are of three types, None, Static, or Dynamic. To edit the column settings, choose the button; the **Column Settings** dialog box will be displayed. You can change the column settings through this dialog box.

Defined width/Defined height: These fields display the defined width/height of the text window in the **In-Place Text Editor**. These fields will be available, when you choose the **None** option from the **Columns** field. To change the values of these fields, click in the field and enter the new value in it.

Position X/Position Y/Position Z: You can change the location of the insertion point of the selected text by entering new *X*/*Y*/*Z* coordinates for the text in these fields. You can also use the Pick Points button that is displayed in these fields when you click in them. When you choose the Pick Points button, a rubber-band line is attached between the cursor and the selected text and you can move the cursor and specify a new location for the text on the screen. The values of the three fields get updated automatically.

Selecting the Annotative Block Reference

When you select a block in the drawing and invoke the **PROPERTIES** palette, apart from the **General** category, three more categories containing the properties of the block are available. They are **Geometry**, **3D Visualization**, and **Misc**. The properties under these categories are discussed next.

Position X/Position Y/Position Z: In the **Position X/Position Y/Position Z** fields of the **Geometry** category, you can enter new *X*, *Y*, and *Z* coordinates respectively for the selected block. The block reference shall move to the new location as you specify the coordinates. You can also click in any one of the fields to display the Pick Points button and choose it to specify a new location for the block on the screen.

Scale X/Scale Y/Scale Z: You can specify new X, Y, and Z scale factors for the selected block in the **Scale X**, **Scale Y**, and **Scale Z** fields, respectively. The current scale factors for the block are displayed in the **Scale X**, **Scale Y**, and **Scale Z** fields and as you change them, the modifications are reflected in the drawing.

Name: This field under the **Misc** category displays the name of the selected block reference and is not available for modifications.

Rotation: This field specifies the current rotation angle of the selected block. You can specify a new angle of rotation for the selected block in this field. After specifying an angle, when you press ENTER, the selected block in the drawing is rotated through the specified angle.

Annotative: This field specifies whether the block is annotative or non-annotative. This information is read-only.

Annotative scale: This field displays the current annotation scale of the drawing. You can add more annotation scales to the drawing in the **Annotation Object Scale** dialog box that will be displayed when you choose the button from the **Annotative scale** field.

Match orientation to layout: This field displays whether or not the orientation of the text used in the block is forced to align with the orientation of the floating viewports. This information is read-only.

Block Unit: This field specifies the unit of the block.

Unit factor. This field specifies the conversion factor between the block unit and the drawing unit.

Selecting the Annotative Attribute

When you select an attribute before converting it into a block, apart from the **General** category, the other three categories under which the properties of an attribute are displayed are **Text**, **3D Visualization**, and **Misc**. Editing of an attribute has already been discussed in Chapter 17.

Tag: You can modify the text of the tag by entering a new value in the **Tag** field under the **Text** category. After you have modified the tag text and pressed ENTER, the old attribute text in the drawing is replaced by the new text.

Annotative: This field specifies whether the attribute is annotative or non-annotative. Select the appropriate option from the **Annotative** drop-down list to change the annotative property of the attributes.

Annotative scale: This field displays the current annotation scale of the drawing. You can add more annotation scales to the drawing in the **Annotation Object Scale** dialog box that will be displayed when you choose the button from the **Annotative scale** field.

Prompt: You can also change the text of the prompt and enter a new prompt value in the **Prompt** field.

Value: This field displays the default value of the selected attribute. You can change this default value by entering a new value in the **Value** field.

Style: When you click in this field, the **Style** drop-down list is available. You can select a style for the attribute text from this drop-down list. Only the text styles that already have been defined are available in this drop-down list and can be selected.

Justify: You can select an attribute text justification from the **Justify** drop-down list.

Paper text height: This field displays the height of the annotative text that is to be maintained on the paper.

Model text height: This field displays the height of the text that is to be displayed in the model space. The **Model text height** value depends on the **Paper text height** value and the **Annotative scale**.

Height: You can change the height of the selected non-annotative attribute text by entering a new value in this field.

Rotation: You can rotate the selected attribute text by specifying an angle in the **Rotation** field.

Width factor: You can modify the width factor of the attribute text by entering a new value in the **Width factor** field of the **PROPERTIES** palette.

Obliquing: The attribute text can also be made slanting by entering an angle value in the **Obliquing** field of the **PROPERTIES** palette.

Direction: This field displays the flow direction of the attribute text.

Boundary Width: This field displays the width of the text window in the **In-Place Text Editor**. The value displayed here is the relative value, specifying a value less than **1** will decrease the boundary width and a value more than **1** will increase the boundary width. The value in the **Boundary Width** will be available only if the **Multiple lines** check box is selected in the **Mode** area of the **Attribute Definition** dialog box. You can also select the **Yes** option from the **Multiple lines** drop-down list in the **Misc** area of the **PROPERTIES** Palette.

Text alignment X/Text alignment Y/Text alignment Z: The **Text alignment X/Text alignment Y/Text alignment Z** fields of the **Text** category display the *X*, *Y*, and *Z* coordinates of the alignment point of the selected attribute. Note that these fields will be available only if you modify the properties such as the text alignment of the attributes, while defining them. If these fields are available and you click on them, the Pick Point button appears in the field. You can use this button to specify the new location of the attribute.

Note

If you modify the text alignment of the first attribute and define the remaining attributes below this attribute, the remaining attributes will also have the ***Text Alignment*** *fields active.*

Misc: As discussed earlier, under the **Misc** category, you can redefine the attribute modes that have been defined at the time of the attribute definition. You can also make the attribute text appear upside-down or backwards by selecting **Yes** from the **Upside down** drop-down list and the **Backward** drop-down list, respectively.

Note

Choose the ***QuickCalc*** *button from the respective fields to open the Quick Calculator. Using the Quick Calculator, you can enter the numerical values as mathematical equations. These equations may include scientific calculations. You can also perform units conversion using the Quick Calculator.*

Exercise 1 — Properties

Draw a hexagon on OBJ layer in red color. Let the linetype be hidden. Now, use the **PROPERTIES** palette to change the layer of the hexagon to some other existing layer, the color to yellow, and the linetype to continuous. Also, in the **PROPERTIES** palette, under the **Geometry** category, specify a vertex in the **Vertex** field or select one using the arrow (Next or Previous) buttons and then relocate it. The values of the **Vertex X** and **Vertex Y** fields change as the coordinate values of the vertices change. Also, notice the change in the value in the **Area** field. You can also assign a start and end lineweight to each of the hexagon segments between the specified vertices. Use the **Tools > Inquiry > List** tool from the menu bar to verify that the changes have taken place.

EXPLODING COMPOUND OBJECTS

Ribbon: Home > Modify > Explode	**Toolbar:** Modify > Explode
Menu Bar: Modify > Explode	**Command:** EXPLODE/X

The **Explode** tool is used to split compound objects such as blocks, polylines, regions, polyface meshes, polygon meshes, multilines, 3D solids, 3D meshes, bodies, or dimensions into the basic objects that make them up, refer to Figure 20-10. For example, if you explode a polyline or a 3D polyline, the result will be ordinary lines or arcs (tangent specification and width are not considered). When a 3D polygon mesh is exploded, the result is 3D faces. Polyface meshes are turned into 3D faces, points, and lines. Upon exploding 3D solids, the planar surfaces of the 3D solid turn into regions, and non-planar surfaces turn into bodies, multilines are changed to lines. Regions turn into lines, ellipses, splines, or arcs. On exploding, 2D polylines lose their width and tangent specifications and 3D polylines explode into lines. When a body is exploded, it changes into single-surface bodies, curves, or regions. When a leader is exploded, the components are lines, splines, solids, block inserts, text or multiline text, tolerance objects, and so on. Multiline text explodes into a single line text. This tool is especially useful when you have inserted an entire drawing and you need to alter a small detail. After you invoke the **Explode** tool, you are prompted to select the objects you want to explode. After selecting the objects, press ENTER or right-click to explode the selected objects and then end the command.

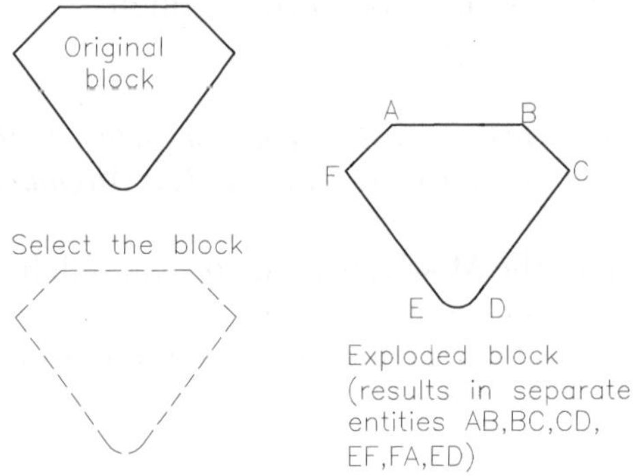

Figure 20-10 *Use of the* ***Explode*** *tool*

When a block or dimension is exploded, there is no visible change in the drawing. The drawing remains the same except that the color and linetype may have changed because of floating layers, colors, or linetypes. The exploded block is turned into a group of objects that can be modified separately. To check whether the explosion of the block has taken place, select any object that was a part of the block. If the block has been exploded, only that particular object will be highlighted. With the **Explode** tool, only one nesting level is exploded at a time. Hence, if there is a nested block or a polyline in a block and you explode it, the inner block or the polyline will not be exploded. Attribute values are deleted when a block is exploded, and the attribute definitions are redisplayed.

Note

*Remember that the blocks inserted using the **MINSERT** command and x-refs cannot be exploded.*

Tip

*If you want to insert a block in the form of its separate components while using the **INSERT** tool, select the **Explode** check box in the **Insert** dialog box. Also, if you are using the **-INSERT** command, type * prior to the block name at the **Enter block name or [?]:** prompt, the block will be inserted in the drawing as separate component object, and not as an entire block.*

EDITING POLYLINES

A polyline can assume various characteristics such as width, linetype, joined polyline, and closed polyline. You can edit polylines, polygons, or rectangles to attain the desired characteristics using the **Edit Polyline** tool. In this section, we will be discussing how to edit simple 2D polylines. The following are the editing operations that can be performed on an existing polyline using the **Edit Polyline** tool. These operations are discussed in detail later in this chapter.

1. A polyline of varying widths can be converted to a polyline of uniform width.
2. An open polyline can be closed and a closed one can be opened.
3. You can remove bends and curved segments between two vertices to make a straight polyline.
4. A polyline can be split up into two and individual polylines or polyarcs connected to one another can be joined into a single polyline.
5. After invoking the **Edit Polyline** tool, if you select an entity that is not a polyline, you are prompted to specify whether you want the entity to be converted into a polyline. You can avoid this prompt by setting the value of the **PEDITACCEPT** variable to 1.
6. Multiple polylines can be edited.
7. The appearance of a polyline can be changed by moving and adding vertices.
8. Curves of arcs and B-spline curves can be fitted to all vertices in a polyline, with the specification of the tangent of each vertex being optional.
9. The linetype generation at the vertices of a polyline can be controlled.
10. Multiple polylines can be joined together to form a single polyline.

Editing Single Polyline

Ribbon: Home > Modify > Edit Polyline	**Toolbar:** Modify II > Edit Polyline
Menu Bar: Modify > Object > Polyline	**Command:** PEDIT/PE

You can edit a single polyline by using the **Edit Polyline** tool. To invoke this tool, choose the **Edit Polyline** tool from the expanded **Modify** panel of the **Home** tab; the following prompt sequence is displayed:

Select polyline or [Multiple]:

If the selected entity is not a polyline, the following message will be displayed at the command prompt.

Object selected is not a polyline.
Do you want to turn it into one? <Y>:

If you want to turn the object into a polyline, respond by entering Y or by simply pressing ENTER. To let the object be as it is, enter N. If you enter N, then AutoCAD will prompt you to select another polyline or object to edit. As mentioned earlier, you can avoid this prompt by setting the value of the **PEDITACCEPT** variable to **1**. The subsequent prompts and editing options depend on the type of polyline that has been selected. AutoCAD provides you the option of either selecting a single polyline or multiple polylines. In this case, a single 2D polyline is selected, and its prompt sequence is given next.

Enter an option [Close/Join/Width/Edit vertex/Fit/Spline/Decurve/Ltype gen/Reverse/Undo]: *Enter an option or press ENTER to end command.*

Note
Depending on the type of polyline selected, the options of ***Edit Polyline*** *tool get changed. In this chapter, the* ***2D polyline*** *options have been discussed.*

The options available in the **Single** polyline selection method are discussed next.

Close (C) Option
This option is used to close an open polyline. The **Close** option creates the segment that connects the last segment of the polyline to the first. You will get this option only if the polyline is not closed. Figure 20-11 illustrates this option.

Open (O) Option
If you close an open polyline, the **Close** option will be replaced by the **Open** option. Enter **O** for open; the closing segment will be removed, refer to Figure 20-11.

Join (J) Option
This option appends lines, polylines, or arcs whose endpoints meet a selected polyline at any of its endpoints and adds (joins) them to it, refer to Figure 20-12. This option can be used only if a polyline is open. After this option has been selected, AutoCAD prompts you to select objects. Once you have chosen the objects to be joined to the original polyline, AutoCAD examines them

to determine whether any of them has an endpoint in common with the current polyline, and joins such an object with the original polyline. The search is then repeated using new endpoints. They will not join if the endpoint of the object does not exactly meet the polyline. The line touching a polyline at its endpoint to form a T will not be joined. If two lines meet a polyline in a Y shape, only one of them will be selected, and this selection depends upon the sequence of selecting the lines. If you select the two lines, the first selected line will get joined to the polyline.

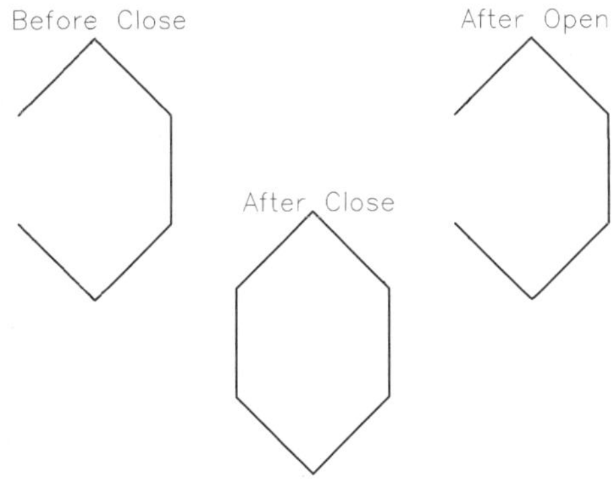

Figure 20-11 *The* ***Close*** *and* ***Open*** *options*

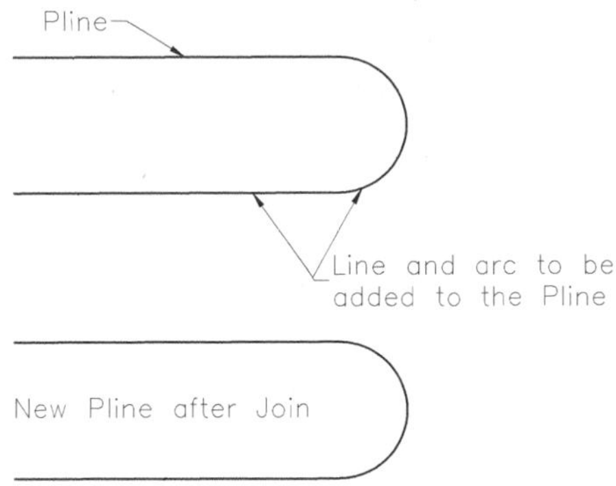

Figure 20-12 *Using the* ***Join*** *option*

Width (W) Option

The **W** option allows you to define a new, unvarying width for all segments of a polyline, refer to Figure 20-13. It changes the width of a polyline with a constant or a varying width. The desired new width can be specified either by entering the width using the keyboard or by specifying the width as the distance between the two specified points. Once the width has been specified, the polyline assumes it. Here, you will change the width of the given polyline in figure from 0.20 to 0.5, refer to Figure 20-14. On invoking the **Edit Polyline** tool, the following prompt is displayed:

Select polyline or [Multiple]: *Select a polyline.*
Enter an option [Close/Join/Width/Edit vertex/Fit/Spline/Decurve/Ltype gen/Reverse/Undo]: **W** Enter
Specify new width for all segments: **0.5** Enter

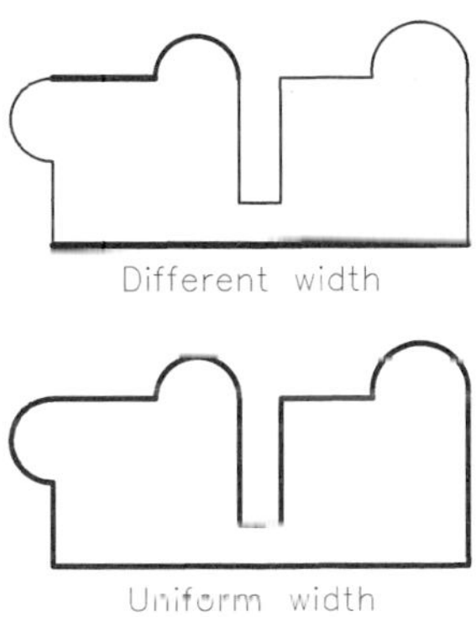

Figure 20-13 *Making the width of a polyline uniform*

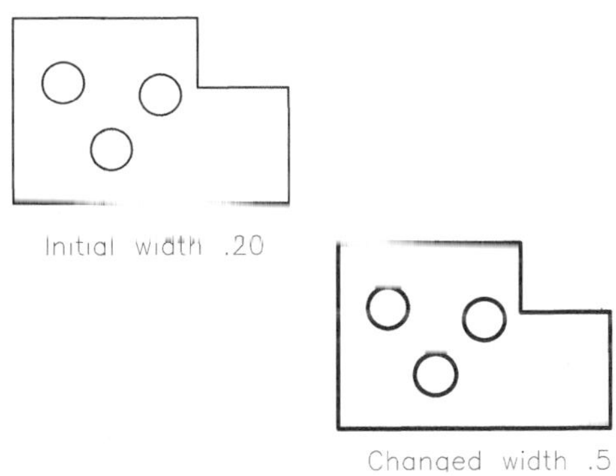

Figure 20-14 *Changing the width of all segments*

Note

*Circles drawn using the **Circle** tools cannot be changed to polylines. However, for polycircles drawn by using the **Arc** option of the **Polyline** tool (by drawing two semicircular polyarcs) or by using the **Donut** tool, you can modify the thickness using the **Width** option of the **Edit Polyline** tool.*

Edit vertex (E) Option

The **Edit vertex** option lets you select vertex of a polyline and perform different editing operations on the vertex and the segments following it. A polyline segment has two vertices. The first one is at the start point of the polyline segment; the other one is at the endpoint of the segment. When you invoke this option, an X marker appears on the screen at the first vertex of the selected polyline. If a tangent direction has been specified for this particular vertex, an arrow is generated in that direction. After this option has been selected, the next prompt appears with a list of options for this prompt. The prompt sequence, after you invoke the **Edit Polyline** tool, is given next.

Select polyline or [Multiple]: *Select the polyline to be edited.*
Enter an option [Close/Join/Width/Edit vertex/Fit/Spline/Decurve/Ltype gen/Reverse/Undo]: **E** Enter
Enter a vertex editing option [Next/Previous/Break/Insert/Move/Regen/Straighten/Tangent/Width/eXit]<N>: *Enter an editing option or press ENTER to accept default.*

All the options for the **Edit vertex** option are discussed next.

Next and Previous Options: These options move the X marker to the next or the previous vertex of a polyline. The default value in the **Edit vertex** option is one of these two options. The option selected as default is the one you chose last. In this manner, the **Next** and **Previous** options help you to move the X marker to any vertex of the polyline by selecting one of these two options, and then pressing ENTER to reach the desired vertex. These options cycle back and forth between the first and last vertices, but cannot move past the first or last vertex, even if the polyline is closed, refer to Figure 20-15.

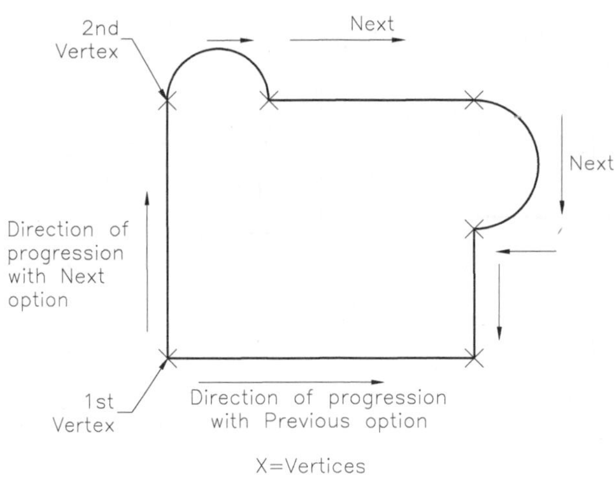

***Figure 20-15** The **Next** and **Previous** options*

The prompt sequence for using the **Edit vertex** option, after you invoke the **Edit Polyline** tool, is given next.

Select polyline or [Multiple]: *Select the polyline to be edited.*
Enter an option [Close/Join/Width/Edit vertex/Fit/Spline/Decurve/Ltype gen/Reverse/Undo]: **E** Enter
Enter a vertex editing option [Next/Previous/Break/Insert/Move/Regen/Straighten/Tangent/Width/eXit] <N>: *Enter N or P to move to the next or previous vertices respectively.*

Break Option: With the **Break** option, you can remove a portion of the polyline, as shown in Figure 20-16 or break it at a single point. You can specify the vertices within which the polyline would be removed. By specifying two different vertices, all the polyline segments and vertices between the specified vertices are erased. If one of the selected vertices is at the endpoint of the polyline, the **Break** option will erase all the segments between the first vertex and the endpoint of the polyline. The exception to this is that AutoCAD does not erase the entire polyline, if you specify the first vertex at the start point (first vertex) of the polyline and the second vertex at the endpoint (last vertex) of the polyline. If both vertices are at the endpoint of the polyline, or only one vertex is specified and its location is at the endpoint of the polyline, no change is made to the polyline. The last two selections of vertices are treated as invalid by AutoCAD, which acknowledges this by displaying the message ***Invalid***.

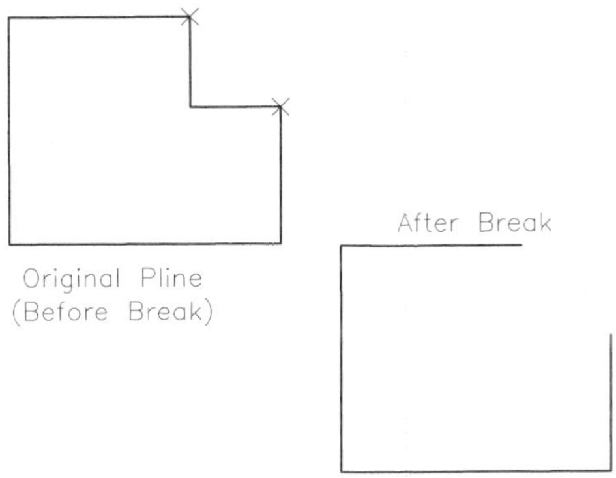

Figure 20-16 *Using the **Break** option*

To use the **Break** option, first you need to move the marker to the first vertex where you want the split to start. The placement of the marker can be achieved with the help of the **Next** and **Previous** options. Once you have selected the first vertex to be used in the **Break** operation, invoke the **Break** option by entering **B** at the command prompt. AutoCAD takes the vertex where the marker (X) is placed as the first point of the breakup. The next prompt asks you to specify the position of the next vertex for the breakup. You can enter **G** at this prompt if you want to split the polyline at one vertex only. Otherwise, use the **Next** or **Previous** option to specify the position of the next vertex and then enter **G**. On doing so, the polyline segments between the two selected vertices will be erased. The prompt sequence for using this option, after you have invoked the **Edit Polyline** tool, is given next.

Select polyline or [Multiple]: *Select the polyline to be edited.*
Enter an option [Close/Join/Width/Edit vertex/Fit/Spline/Decurve/Ltype gen/Reverse/Undo]: **E** Enter

Enter a vertex editing option [Next/Previous/Break/Insert/Move/Regen/Straighten/Tangent/Width/eXit]<N>: *Enter N or P to locate the first vertex for the **Break** option.*
Enter a vertex editing option [Next/Previous/Break/Insert/Move/Regen/Straighten/Tangent/Width/eXit]<N>: **B** Enter

Once you invoke the **Break** option, AutoCAD treats the vertex where the marker (X) is displayed as the first point for splitting the polyline. The next prompt issued is given next.

Enter an option [Next/Previous/Go/eXit] <N>: *Enter **G** if you want to split the polyline at one vertex only or move the X marker using the **Next** or **Previous** option to specify the position of the next vertex for breakup.*

After you have specified the next position of the X marker using the **Next** and **Previous** options, entering **GO** deletes the polyline segment between the two markers specified. Now, exit the enter a vertex editing option prompt using the **eXit** option.

Insert Option: The **Insert** option is used to define a new vertex and add it to the polyline, refer to Figure 20-17. You can invoke this option by entering I for Insert. You should invoke this option only after you have moved the marker (X) to the vertex after which the new vertex is to be added. The new vertex is inserted immediately after the vertex with the X mark. After you invoke the **Edit Polyline** tool, the prompt sequence for using the **Insert** option will be as follows:

Select polyline or [Multiple]: *Select the polyline to be edited.*
Enter an option [Close/Join/Width/Edit vertex/Fit/Spline/Decurve/Ltype gen/Reverse/Undo]: **E** Enter
Enter a vertex editing option [Next/Previous/Break/Insert/Move/Regen/Straighten/Tangent/Width/eXit]<N>: *Move the marker to the vertex after which the new vertex is to be inserted.*
Enter a vertex editing option[Next/Previous/Break/Insert/Move/Regen/Straighten/Tangent/Width/eXit]<N>: **I** Enter
Specify location for new vertex: *Move the cursor and click to specify the location of the new vertex or enter the coordinates of the new location.*

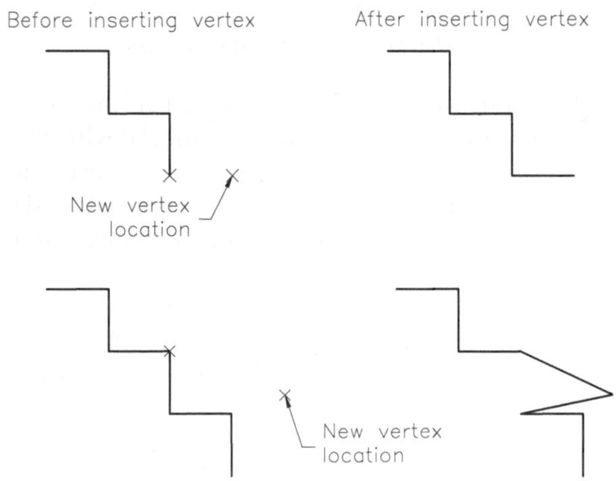

Figure 20-17 *Using the **Insert** option to define new vertex points*

Tip

In AutoCAD, you can insert vertex by using the shortcut menu. To do so, select a polyline; the grips will be displayed. Hold the cursor on one of the grips; a shortcut menu will be displayed. Choose the ***Add Vertex*** *option and click on the drawing area to add new vertex. You can also stretch the selected arc or convert the line to arc or vice versa by selecting appropriate option from the shortcut menu.*

Move option: This option is used to move the X-marked vertex to a new position, refer to Figure 20-18. Before invoking the **Move** option, you must move the X marker to the vertex you want to relocate by selecting the **Next** or **Previous** option. The prompt sequence for relocating a vertex after you invoke the **Edit Polyline** tool is given next.

Select polyline or [Multiple]: *Select the polyline to be edited.*
Enter an option [Close/Join/Width/Edit vertex/Fit/Spline/Decurve/Ltype gen/Reverse/Undo]: **E** Enter
Enter a vertex editing option [Next/Previous/Break/Insert/Move/Regen/Straighten/Tangent/Width/eXit]<N>: *Enter* ***N*** *or* ***P*** *to move the X marker to the vertex you want to relocate.*
Enter a vertex editing option [Next/Previous/Break/Insert/Move/Regen/Straighten/Tangent/Width/eXit]<N>: **M** Enter
Specify new location for marked vertex: *Specify the new location for the selected vertex by using the pick button of your pointing device or by entering its coordinate values.*
Enter a vertex editing option [Next/Previous/Break/Insert/Move/Regen/Straighten/Tangent/Width/eXit]<N>: *Enter an option or enter* ***X*** *to exit.*

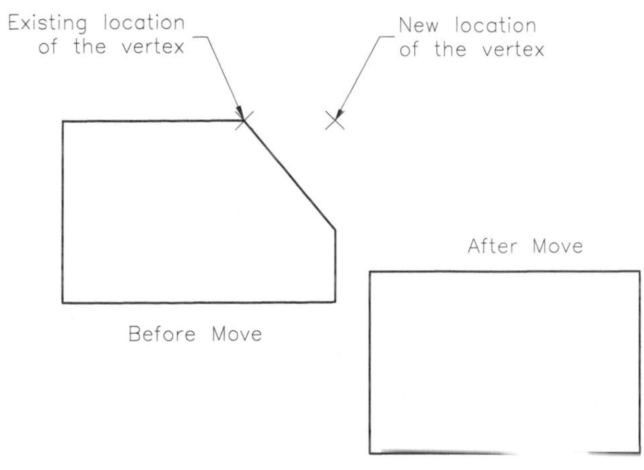

Figure 20-18 *The* ***Move*** *option*

Regen Option: The **Regen** option regenerates the polyline to display the effects of edits you have made, without having to exit the vertex mode editing. It is used most often with the **Width** option.

Straighten Option: The **Straighten** option is used to straighten polyline segments or arcs between specified vertices, refer to Figure 20-19. It deletes the arcs, line segments, or vertices between the two specified vertices and substitutes them with one polyline segment.

The prompt sequence to use this option after you invoke the **Edit Polyline** tool is given next.

Select polyline or [Multiple]: *Select the polyline to be edited.*
Enter an option [Close/Join/Width/Edit vertex/Fit/Spline/Decurve/Ltype gen/Reverse/Undo]: **E** Enter
Enter a vertex editing option [Next/Previous/Break/Insert/Move/Regen/Straighten/Tangent/Width/eXit]<N>: *Move the marker to the desired vertex from where you want to start applying the **Straighten** option with the **Next** or **Previous** option.*
Enter a vertex editing option [Next/Previous/Break/Insert/Move/Regen/Straighten/Tangent/Width/eXit]<N>: **S** Enter
Enter an option [Next/Previous/Go/eXit] <N>: *Move the marker to the next desired vertex, until you reach the vertex you want to straighten.* Enter an option [Next/Previous/Go/eXit] <N>: **G** Enter

The polyline segments between two marker locations are replaced by a single straight line segment. If you specify a single vertex, the segment following the specified vertex is straightened, if it is curved.

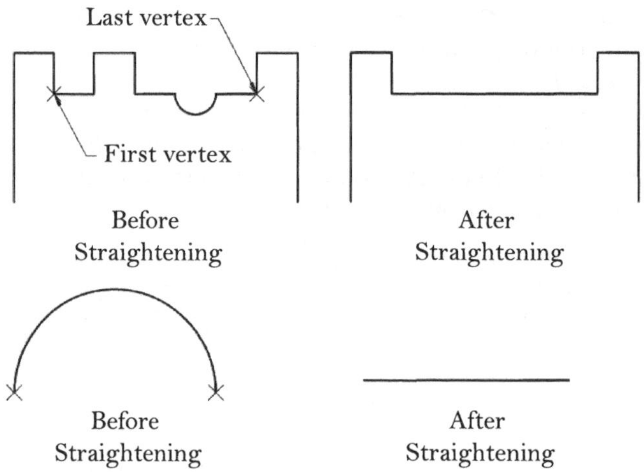

Figure 20-19 *Using the **Straighten** option to straighten polylines*

Tangent option: The **Tangent** option is used to associate a tangent direction to the current vertex (marked by X). The tangent direction is used in the curve fitting or the **Fit** option of the **Edit Polyline** tool. This option is discussed in detail in the subsequent section on curve fitting. The prompt issued on using the **Tangent** option is given next.

Specify direction of vertex tangent: *Specify a point or enter an angle.*

You can specify the direction of the vertex tangent by entering an angle at the previous prompt or by selecting a point to express the direction with respect to the current vertex. You can then move the marker to another vertex using the **Next** or **Previous** option and change its direction of tangent or enter X to exit the **Enter a vertex editing option** prompt.

Width option: The **Width** option allows you to change the width at the start and end points of a polyline segment that follows the current vertex, refer to Figure 20-20. By default, the ending width is equal to the starting width and hence, you can get a polyline segment of uniform width by pressing ENTER at the **Specify ending width for next segment <starting width>** prompt. You can also specify different starting and ending widths to get a varying-width polyline. The prompt sequence is given next.

> Enter an option [Close/Join/Width/Edit vertex/Fit/Spline/Decurve/Ltype gen/Reverse/Undo]: **E** Enter
> Enter a vertex editing option [Next/Previous/Break/Insert/Move/Regen/Straighten/Tangent/Width/eXit]<N>: *Move the marker to the starting vertex of the segment whose width is to be altered, using the **Next** or **Previous** option.*
> Enter a vertex editing option [Next/Previous/Break/Insert/Move/Regen/Straighten/Tangent/Width/eXit]<N>: **W** Enter
> Specify starting width for next segment <current>: *Enter the revised starting width.*
> Specify ending width for next segment <starting width>: *Enter the revised ending width or press ENTER to accept the default option of keeping the ending width of the segment equal to the starting width.*

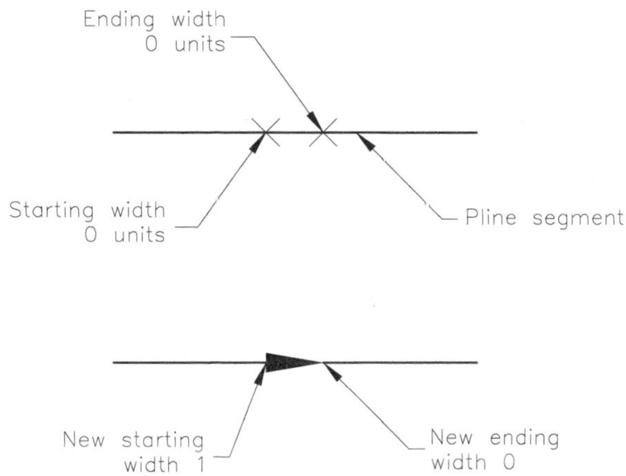

Figure 20-20 *Using the **Width** option to change the width of a polyline*

If no difference is noticed in the appearance of the polyline, you may need to use the **Regen** option. The segment with the revised widths is redrawn after invoking the **Regen** option or when you exit the vertex mode editing.

eXit Option. This option lets you exit the vertex mode editing and return to the **Edit Polyline** prompt.

Fit Option

The **Fit** or **Fit curve** option is used to generate a curve that passes through all the corners (vertices) of the polyline, using the tangent directions of the vertices, refer to Figure 20-21.

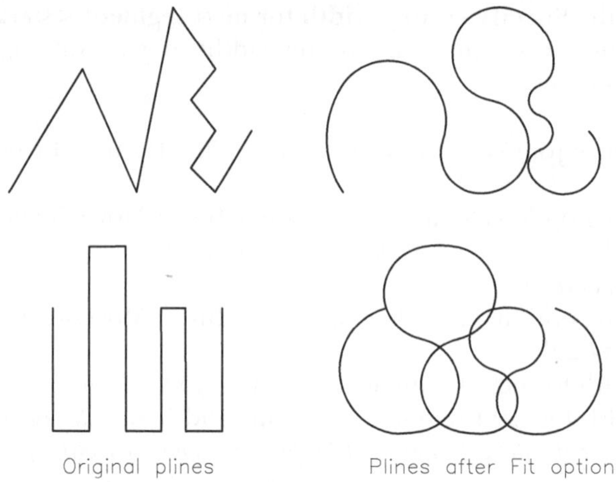

Figure 20-21 *Curves generated using the* ***Fit*** *option*

The curve is composed of a series of arcs passing through the corners (vertices) of the polyline. This option is used when you draw a polyline with sharp corners and you need to convert it into a series of smooth curves. An example of this is a graph. In a graph, we need to show a curve by joining a series of plotted points. The process involved is called curve fitting; therefore, this option is known as **Fit**. The vertices of the polyline are also known as the control points. The closer these control points are, the smoother is the curve. Therefore, if the **Fit** option does not give optimum results, insert more vertices into the polyline or edit the tangent directions of vertices and then use the **Fit** option on the polyline. Before using this option, you may give each vertex a tangent direction.

The curve is then constructed according to the tangent directions you have specified. The following prompt sequence illustrates the **Fit** option after you invoke the **Edit Polyline** tool.

Select polyline or [Multiple]: *Select the polyline to be edited.*
Enter an option [Close/Join/Width/Edit vertex/Fit/Spline/Decurve/Ltype gen/Reverse/Undo]: **F** Enter

If the tangent directions need to be edited, use the **Edit vertex** option of the **Edit Polyline** tool. Move the X marker to each of the vertices that need to be changed. Now, you can invoke the **Tangent** option, and either enter the tangent direction in degrees or select points. The chosen direction is expressed by an arrow placed at the vertex. The prompt sequence to use the **Tangent** option of the **Edit Polyline** tool is given next.

Select polyline or [Multiple]: *Select the polyline to be edited.*
Enter an option [Close/Join/Width/Edit vertex/Fit/Spline/Decurve/Ltype gen/Reverse/Undo]: **E** Enter
Enter a vertex editing option [Next/Previous/Break/Insert/Move/Regen/Straighten/Tangent/Width/eXit]<N>: **T** Enter
Specify direction of vertex tangent: *Specify a direction in + or - degrees, or select a point in the desired direction. Press ENTER.*

Once you specify the tangent direction, use the **eXit** option to return to the previous prompt and use its **Fit** option.

Tip

*In AutoCAD, after applying the **Fit** option to a polyline, you can change the tangent direction by using the tool tip. To do so, select a polyline; the grips will be displayed. Move the cursor near one of the grips; a tooltip will be displayed. Choose the **Tangent Direction** option and specify the new direction in the drawing area.*

Spline Option

The **Spline** option, refer to Figure 20-22, also smoothens the corners of a straight segment polyline, as does the **Fit** option, but the curve passes through only the first and the last control points (vertices), except in the case of a closed polyline. The spline curve is stretched toward the other control points (vertices) but does not pass through them, as in the case of the **Fit** option. The greater the number of control points, the greater the force with which the curve is stretched toward them. The prompt sequence on invoking the **Edit Polyline** tool is as follows:

Select polyline or [Multiple]: *Select the polyline.*
Enter an option [Close/Join/Width/Edit vertex/Fit/Spline/Decurve/Ltype gen/Reverse/Undo]: **S** Enter

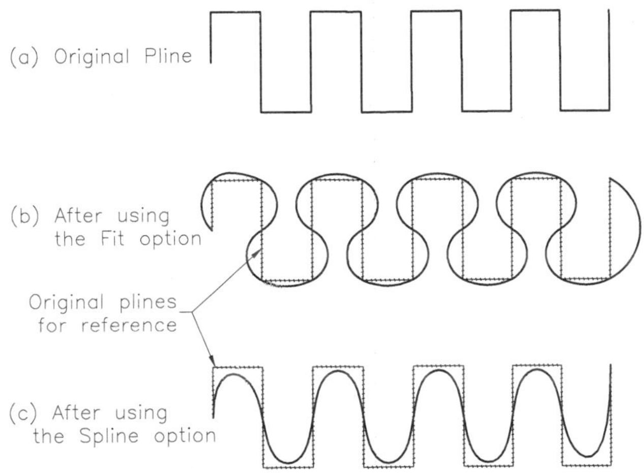

Figure 20-22 *Smoothening the corners using the **Spline** option*

The generated curve is a B-spline curve. The frame is the original polyline without any curves in it. If the original polyline has arc segments, these segments are straightened when the spline's frame is formed. A frame that has width produces a spline curve that tapers smoothly from the width of the first vertex to that of the last. Any other width specification between the first width specification and the last is neglected. When a spline is formed from a polyline, the frame is displayed as a polyline with a zero width and a continuous linetype. Also, AutoCAD saves its frame so that it may be restored to its original form. Tangent specifications on control point vertices do not affect spline construction.

By default, the spline frames are not shown on the screen, but you may want them displayed for reference. In this case, the system variable **SPLFRAME** needs to be manipulated. The default value for this variable is zero. If you want to see the spline frame as well, set it to 1.

Now, whenever the **Spline** option is used on a polyline, the frame will also be displayed. Most editing tools such as **Move**, **Erase**, **Copy**, **Mirror**, **Rotate**, and **Scale** work similarly for both the Fit curves and Spline curves. They work on both the curve and its frame, whether the frame is visible or not. The **Extend** tool changes the frame by adding a vertex at the point the last segment intersects with the boundary. If you use any of the previously mentioned tools and then use the **Decurve** option to decurve the spline curve and later use the **Spline** option again, the same spline curve is generated. The **Break**, **Trim**, and **Explode** tools delete the frame. The **Divide**, **Measure**, **Fillet**, **Chamfer**, **Area**, and **Hatch** tools recognize only the spline curve and do not consider the frame. The **Stretch** tool first stretches the frame and then fits the spline curve to it.

When you use the **Join** option of the **Edit Polyline** tool, the spline curve is decurved and the original spline information is lost. The **Next** and **Previous** options of the **Edit vertex** option of the **Edit Polyline** tool move the marker only to the points on the frame, whether visible or not. The **Break** option discards the spline curve. The **Insert**, **Move**, **Straighten**, and **Width** options refit the spline curve. Object Snaps consider the spline curve and not the frame; therefore, if you wish to snap to the frame control points, restore the original frame.

There are two types of spline curves: **Quadratic B-spline** and **Cubic B-spline**. These types of curves pass through the first and the last control points, which is the characteristic of the spline curve. Cubic curves are very smooth. A cubic curve passes through the first and last control points, and the curve is closer to the other control points. Quadratic curves are not as smooth as the cubic ones, but they are smoother than the curves produced by the **Fit curve** option. A quadratic curve passes through the first and last control points, and the rest of the curve is tangent to the polyline segments between the remaining control points, refer to Figure 20-23.

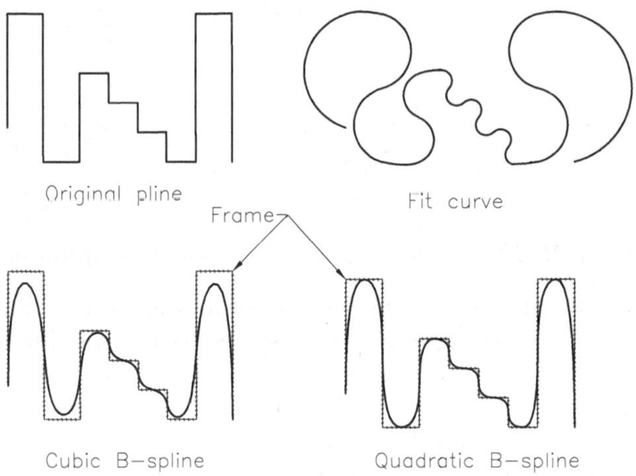

***Figure 20-23** Comparison of fit curve, quadratic B-spline, and cubic B-spline*

Generation of different types of spline curves: If you want to edit a polyline into a B-spline curve, you are first required to enter a relevant value in the **SPLINETYPE** system variable. A value of 5 produces the quadratic curve, whereas a value of 6 produces a cubic curve. The default value is 6, which implies that when we use the **Spline** option of the **Edit Polyline** tool, a cubic curve is produced by default. You can change the value of the **SPLINETYPE** variable using the command prompt.

In case you are editing 3D polygon meshes, the smoothness of the meshes is controlled by the **SURFTYPE** variable. The value of the variable can be set on the command prompt. You can select the type of polygon mesh you want when you are using the **Smooth Surface** option of the **Edit Polyline** tool.

SPLINESEGS. The system variable **SPLINESEGS** governs the number of line segments used to construct the spline curves, and therefore you can use this variable to control the smoothness of the curve. The default value for this variable is 8. With this value, a reasonably smooth curve that does not need much regeneration time is generated. The greater the value of this variable, the smoother will be the curve. But greater the regeneration time, the more space will be occupied by the drawing file.

Figure 20-24 shows cubic curves with different values for the **SPLINESEGS** variable.

Decurve Option

The **Decurve** option straightens the curves generated after using the **Fit** or **Spline** option on a polyline. On using this option, the curves return to their original shape, refer to Figure 20-25. The polyline segments are straightened using the **Decurve** option. The vertices inserted after using the **Fit** or **Spline** option are also removed. Information entered for the tangent reference is retained for use in future fit curve operations. You can also use this tool to straighten out any curve drawn with the help of the **Arc** option of the **Polyline** tool. Enter **D** at the **Enter an option [Close/Join/Width/Edit vertex/Fit/Spline/Decurve/Ltype gen/Reverse/Undo]** prompt to invoke the **Decurve** option of the **Edit Polyline** tool.

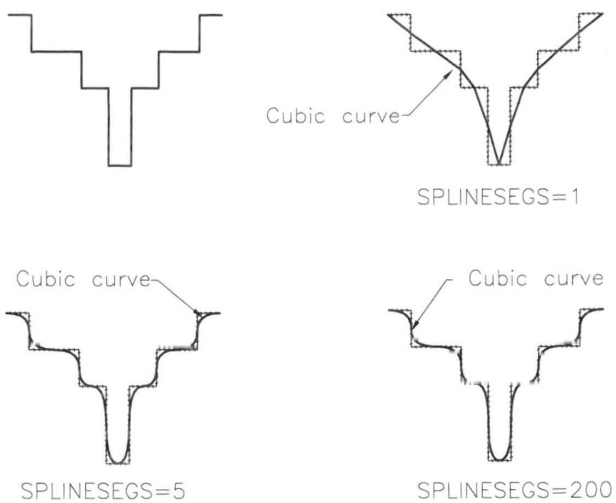

Figure 20-24 *Using the* ***SPLINESEGS*** *variable*

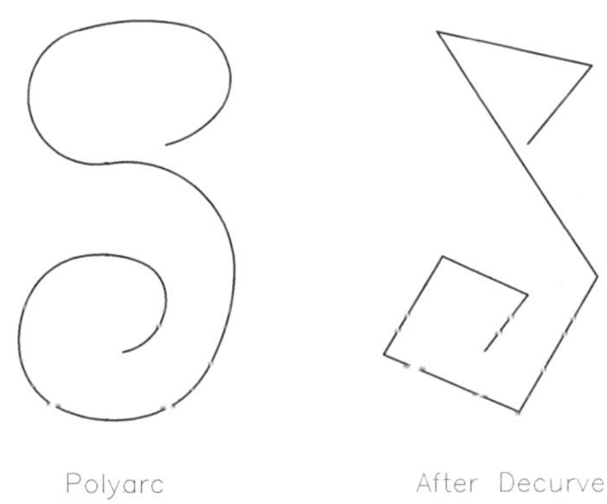

Figure 20-25 *Using the* ***Decurve*** *option*

Note

If you use editing tools such as the ***Break*** *or* ***Trim*** *on spline curves, the* ***Decurve*** *option cannot be used.*

Ltype gen Option

You can use this option to control the linetype pattern generation for linetypes other than Continuous with respect to the vertices of the polyline. This option has two modes: ON and OFF. If turned off, the break in the noncontinuous linetypes will be avoided at the vertices of the polyline and a continuous segment will be displayed at the vertices, refer to Figure 20-26. If turned on, this option generates the linetype in a continuous pattern such that the gaps may be displayed at the vertices. This option is not applicable to polylines with tapered segments.

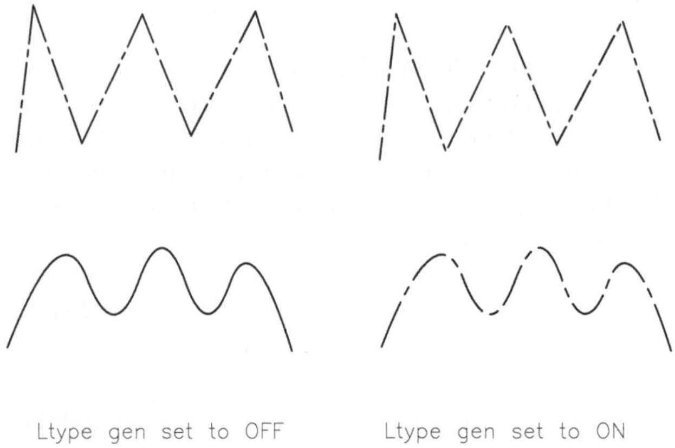

***Figure 20-26** Using the **Ltype gen** option*

The command prompt displayed when you select a polyline and invoke the **Ltype gen** option of the **Edit Polyline** tool is given next.

Enter polyline linetype generation option [ON/OFF] <Off>: *Enter **ON** or press ENTER to accept the default value.*

The linetype generation for new polylines can also be controlled with the help of the **PLINEGEN** system variable, which acts as a toggle function. The default value of this variable is off. Entering the value **ON** turns on the **Ltype gen** option. Alternatively, select the appropriate option in the **Linetype generation** field in the **Misc** area of the **PROPERTIES** palette with the polyline selected.

Reverse Option

The **Reverse** option is used to change the start point of the polyline. On entering **R** and pressing ENTER at the **Enter an option [Close/Join/Width/Edit vertex/Fit/Spline/Decurve/Ltype gen/Reverse/Undo]** command prompt, the start point of the polyline will be changed. This can be confirmed by using the **Edit vertex** option of the **Edit Polyline** tool before and after using the **Reverse** option.

Undo (U) Option

The **Undo** option negates the effect of the most recent polyline editing operation. You can go back as far as you need to in the current polyline editing session by using the **Undo** option repeatedly until you get the desired screen. If you started editing by converting an object into a polyline, and you want to change the polyline back to the object from which it was created, the **Undo** option of the **Edit Polyline** tool will not work. In this case, you will have to exit to the command prompt and use the **Undo** tool to undo the operation.

Editing Multiple Polylines

Selecting the **Multiple** option of the **Edit Polyline** tool allows you to select more than one polyline for editing. You can select the polylines using any of the objects selection techniques. After the objects to be edited are selected, press ENTER or right-click to proceed with the command. The prompt sequence that will follow is given next.

Enter an option [Close/Open/Join/Width/Fit/Spline/Decurve/Ltype gen/Reverse/Undo]:

Join

This option is used to join more than one polylines that may or may not be in contact with each other. Even the polylines that are not coincident can be joined using this option. The polylines are joined using a specified distance value called the **Fuzz distance**. After you select the **Join** option, the sequence of prompt is as follows.

Enter fuzz distance or [Jointype] <current>: *Enter a distance or **J** for changing the **Jointype**.*

The prompt sequence to follow when you enter **J** at the above prompt is given next.

Enter join type [Extend/Add/Both] <Extend>:

Extend: This option is used to extend or trim the selected polylines at the endpoints that are nearest to each other, refer to Figure 20-27. Keep in mind that the segments of the selected polylines that are nearest to each other should not be parallel. This means that the segments that are nearest to each other should intersect at some point when extended.

Add: This option is used to join the selected polylines by drawing a straight line between the nearest endpoints, refer to Figure 20-28. The fuzz distance should be greater than the actual distance between the two endpoints to be joined.

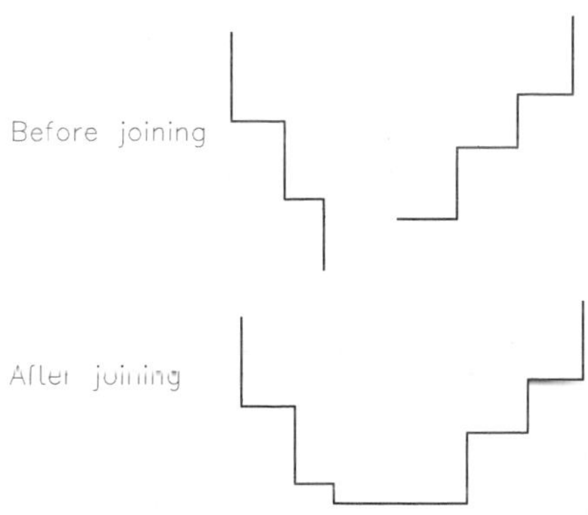

Figure 20-27 *Joining two polylines using the **Extend** option*

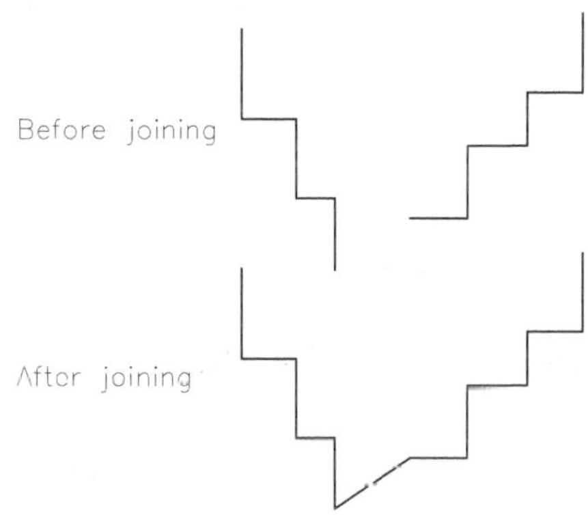

Figure 20-28 *Joining two polylines using the **Add** option*

Both: This option joins the endpoints by extending or trimming if possible; otherwise, it adds a line segment between the two endpoints.

Exercise 2 **Edit Polyline**

a. Draw a line from point (0,0) to point (6,6). Convert the line into a polyline with a starting width 0.30 and an ending width 0.00.

b. Draw different polylines of varying width segments and then use the **Join** option to join all the segments into one polyline. After joining the segments, make their width uniform with the **Width** option.

Exercise 3 **Edit Polyline**

a. Draw a staircase-shaped polyline and use the different options of the **Edit Polyline** tool to generate a fit curve, a quadratic B-spline, and a cubic B-spline, and then convert the curves back to the original polyline.

b. Draw square-wave-shaped polylines, and use different options of the **Edit vertex** option to navigate around the polyline, split the polyline into two at the third vertex, insert more vertices at different locations in the original polyline, and convert the square-wave-shaped polyline into a straight-line polyline.

UNDOING PREVIOUS COMMANDS

Quick Access Toolbar: Undo **Toolbar:** Standard > Undo **Command:** UNDO/U

In AutoCAD, their are many tools with the **Undo** option, which can be used to undo (nullify) the changes made within these commands. The **Undo** option is used to undo a previous command or to undo more than one command at a time. This command can be invoked by entering **UNDO** at the command prompt. **Undo** is also available in the **Quick Access Toolbar**, the **Edit** menu, and the **Standard** toolbar. The **Undo** tool in the **Quick Access Toolbar** can only undo the previous command and only one command at a time. If you right-click in the drawing area; a shortcut menu will be displayed. Choose **Undo**. It is equivalent to **UNDO > 1** or to enter **U** at the command prompt. The **U** command can undo only one operation at a time. You can use **U** as many times as you want until AutoCAD displays the message: **Nothing to undo**. When an operation cannot be undone, a message is displayed but no action takes place. External commands such as **PLOT** cannot be undone.

Undoing Previous Commands using the Quick Access Toolbar

Click the arrow on the **Undo** tool in the **Quick Access Toolbar**; the **Undo** list box will be displayed. All commands used recently will be listed in the **Undo** list box. Select the commands that you want to undo by placing the cursor in the list box and moving downward. The Commands selected are highlighted in blue color, as shown in Figure 20-29. The Status Bar below the **Undo** list box displays the number of commands selected. Click the left mouse button to confirm the selections.

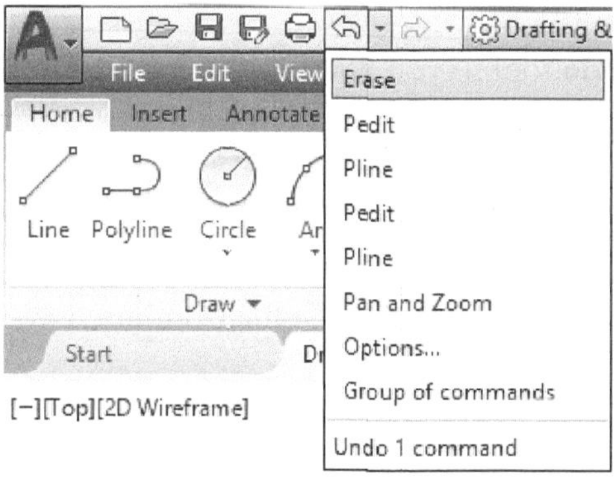

*Figure 20-29 The **Undo** list box*

Undoing Previous Commands using the Command Prompt

To Undo previous commands using the command Line, enter **UNDO** at the command prompt (if you are working in dynamic mode, the command will be entered at pointer input). The prompt sequence for the **UNDO** command is given next.

Command: **UNDO**
Enter the number of operations to undo or [Auto/Control/BEgin/End/Mark/Back] <1>: *Enter a positive number, an option, or press ENTER to undo a single operation.*

Various options of this command are discussed next.

Number (N) Option

This is the default option. This number represents the number of previous command sequences to be deleted. For example, if the number entered is 1, the previous command is undone; if the number entered is 4, the previous four commands are undone, and so on. This is identical to invoking the **U** command four times, except that only one regeneration takes place. AutoCAD allows you to know which commands were undone by displaying a message after you press ENTER. The prompt sequence is given next.

Command: **UNDO**
Enter the number of operations to undo or [Auto/Control/BEgin/End/Mark/Back]<1>:3 Enter
PLINE LINE CIRCLE

Control (C) Option

This option allows you to determine how many of the options are active for the **Undo** tool. You can disable the options you do not need. With this option, you can even disable the **Undo** tool. To access this option, type C. You will get the following prompt.

Enter an UNDO control option [ALL/None/One/Combine/Layer] <All>: *Enter an option or press ENTER to accept the default option.*

ALL

The **All** option activates all the features (options) of the **Undo** tool.

None (N)

This option turns off the **Undo** tool. If you have used the **BEgin** and **End** options or the **Mark** and **Back** options to create **Undo** information, all of that information is undone. The prompt sequence for invoking the **Control** option is as follows.

Command: **UNDO**
Enter the number of operations to undo [Auto/Control/BEgin/End/Mark/Back] <1>: **C** Enter
Enter an UNDO control option [ALL/None/One/Combine/Layer] <All>: **N** Enter

If you try to use the **Undo** tool now, AutoCAD gives you the following message.

U command disabled. Use **UNDO** command to turn it on.

The prompt sequence for the **UNDO** command after issuing the **None** option is given next.

Command: **UNDO**
Enter an UNDO control option [All/None/One/Combine/Layer] <All>: *Enter O or press ENTER to accept the default option.*

To enable the **UNDO** options again, you must enter the **All** or **One** (one mode) option.

One (O)

This option restrains the **UNDO** command to a single operation. All **UNDO** information saved earlier during editing is scrapped. The prompt sequence is as follows.

Enter the number of operations to undo or [Auto/Control/BEgin/End/Mark/Back] <1>: **C** Enter
Enter an UNDO control option [All/None/One/Combine/Layer] <All>: **O** Enter

If you then enter the **UNDO** command, you will get the prompt that is given next.

Command: **UNDO**
Enter an option [Control] <1>: *Press ENTER to undo the last operation or enter* **C** *to select another control option.*

In response to this last prompt, you can now either press ENTER to undo only the previous command, or go into the **Control** options by entering C. AutoCAD acknowledges undoing the previous command with messages given next.

Command: **UNDO**
Enter an option [Control] <1>: Enter
CIRCLE
Everything has been undone

Tip

*AutoCAD stores all information about all the **UNDO** operations performed in a drawing session. When you use the **None** control option of the **UNDO** command, this information is removed and the disk space is made available. In case of limited disk space, it may be a good idea to use the **One** suboption of the **UNDO Control** command. Using **One** control option, you can **UNDO** commands and at the same time make the disk space available.*

Combine

This option allows you to combine all the consecutive **Zoom** and **Pan** operations as a single operation while using the **UNDO** and **REDO** commands.

Layer

This option allows you to combine layer property actions as a single action.

Auto (A) Option

Enter **A** to invoke this option. The following prompt is displayed:

Enter UNDO Auto mode [ON/OFF] <On>: *Select ON or OFF or press ENTER to accept the default setting.*

This option is turned on by default and every menu item is a single operation. When you use the **Begin** and **End** options to group a series of commands as a single operation, entering **U** at the command prompt removes the objects individually and not as a group, if the **Auto** option is turned on. But if the **Auto** option is turned off, entering **U** at the command prompt will remove the entire group of objects you had grouped using the **Begin** and **End** options in one single operation.

Also, if you have put a marker in between the start and end operations and if **Auto** is On, the group of commands till the marker is undone altogether on using the **Back** option. This group of commands is considered to be a single group and is undone as a single command Although entering **U** at the command prompt removes the objects individually until the marker is encountered. But if the **Auto** option is turned off, entering **U** at the command prompt, or using the **Back** option of the **UNDO** command, undoes the entire group of operations irrespective of the marker being there.

BEgin (BE) and End (E) Options

A group of commands is treated as one command for the **U** and **UNDO** commands (provided the **Auto** option is turned off) by embedding the commands between the **BEgin** and **End** options of the **UNDO** command. If you anticipate the removal of a group of successive commands later in a drawing, you can use this option, since all of the commands after the **BEgin** option and before the **End** option are treated as a single command by the **U** command (if the **Auto** option is turned Off). For example, the following sequence illustrates the possibility of removal of two commands.

Command: **UNDO**
Enter the number of operations to undo or [Auto/Control/BEgin/End/Mark/Back] <1>: **BE** [Enter]

Command: **CIRCLE**
Specify center point for circle or [3P/2P/Ttr (tan tan radius)]: *Specify the center.*
Specify radius of circle or [Diameter] <current>: *Specify the radius of the circle.*
Command: **PLINE**
Specify start point: *Select the first point.*
Specify next point or [Arc/Halfwidth/Length/Undo/Width]: *Select the next point.*
Specify next point or [Arc/Close/Halfwidth/Length/Undo/Width]: *Press ENTER.*
Command: **UNDO**
Enter the number of operations to UNDO or [Auto/Control/BEgin/End/Mark/Back]: **E** Enter
Command: **U**

To start the next group after having finished specifying the current group, use the **End** option to end the operation. Another method is to enter the **BEgin** option to start the next group while the current group is active. This is equivalent to issuing the **End** option followed by the **BEgin** option. The group is complete only when the **End** option is invoked to match a **BEgin** option. If **U** or the **UNDO** command is issued after the **BEgin** option has been invoked and before the **End** option has been issued, only one command is undone at a time until it reaches the juncture where the **BEgin** option has been entered. If you want to undo the commands issued before the **BEgin** option was invoked, you must enter the **End** option so that the group is complete.

Mark (M) and Back (B) Options

The **Mark** option installs a marker in the Undo file. The **Back** option allows you to undo all the operations until the mark. In other words, the **Back** option returns the drawing to the point where the previous mark was inserted. For example, if you have completed a portion of your drawing and do not want anything up to this point to be deleted, you can insert a marker and then proceed. Then, even if you use the **Back** option, it will work only until the marker. You can insert multiple markers, and with the help of the **Back** option, you can return to the successive mark points. The following prompt sequence is used to introduce a mark point:

Command: **UNDO**
Enter the number of operations to undo or [Auto/Control/BEgin/End/Mark/Back]: **M** Enter

The prompt sequence for using the **Back** option is given next.

Command: **UNDO**
Enter the number of operations to undo or [Auto/Control/BEgin/End/Mark/Back]: **B** Enter

Once all the marks have been exhausted with the successive **Back** options, any further invoking of the **Back** option displays the message: **This will undo everything. OK? <Y>**. If you enter Y (Yes) at this prompt, all operations carried out since you entered the current drawing session will be undone. If you enter N (No) at this prompt, the **Back** option will be disregarded.

You cannot undo certain commands and system variables, for example, **DIST**, **LIST**, **DELAY**, **NEW**, **OPEN**, **QUIT**, **AREA**, **HELP**, **PLOT**, **QSAVE** and **SAVE**, among many more. Actually, these commands have no effect that can be undone. Commands that change operating modes (**GRID**, **UNITS**, **SNAP**, **ORTHO**) can be undone, though the effect may not be apparent at first. This is the reason why AutoCAD displays the command names as they are undone.

REVERSING THE UNDO OPERATION

Quick Access Toolbar: Redo **Toolbar:** Standard > Redo **Command:** REDO

If you right-click in the drawing area, a shortcut menu is displayed. Choose **Redo** to invoke the **REDO** command. The **REDO** command brings back the process you removed previously using the **U** and **UNDO** commands. This command undoes the last **UNDO** command performed, provided it is entered immediately after the **UNDO** command. On using this command, the objects previously undone reappear on the screen. Click on the **Redo** button in the **Quick Access Toolbar**; the **Redo** drop-down is displayed, refer to Figure 20-30. It lists the commands that have been recently undone. Select the commands that you want to **Redo** and click the left mouse button to confirm the selection.

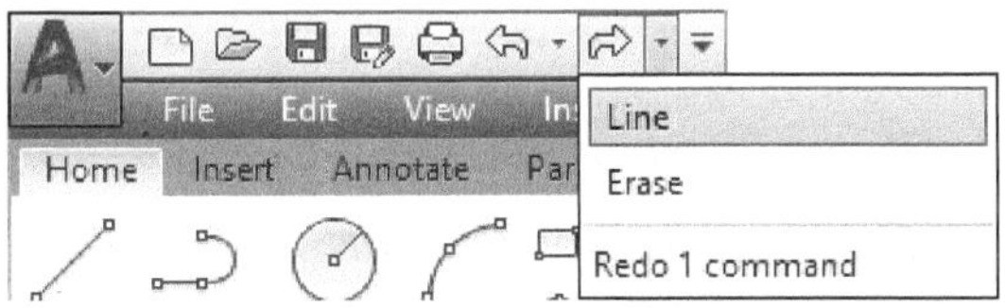

*Figure 20-30 The **Redo** drop-down*

Note

*Consecutive **Zoom** and **Pan** operations can be undone or redone by using the **Undo** or **Redo** command only once so that the drawing returns to the initial zoom state. To disable this feature, clear the **Combine zoom and pan commands** check box in the **Undo/Redo** area of the **User Preferences** tab of the **Options** dialog box.*

RENAMING NAMED OBJECTS

Menu Bar: Format > Rename **Command:** RENAME

You can edit the names of the named objects such as blocks, dimension styles, layers, linetypes, styles, UCS, views, and viewports using the **Rename** dialog box. You can select the named object from the list in the **Named Objects** area of the dialog box. The corresponding names of all the objects of the specified type that can be renamed are displayed in the **Items** area. For example, if you want to rename the layer named HID to HIDDEN, the process will be as follows:

1. Enter **RENAME** at the command prompt and then press ENTER; the **Rename** dialog box will be displayed, as shown in Figure 20-31.

2. Select **Layers** in the **Named Objects** list box, if not already selected. All the layer names in the current drawing that can be renamed are displayed in the **Items** list box.

3. Select **HID** in the **Items** list box to highlight it. HID will be displayed in the **Old Name** edit box.

4. Enter **HIDDEN** in the **Rename To** edit box, and choose the **OK** button.

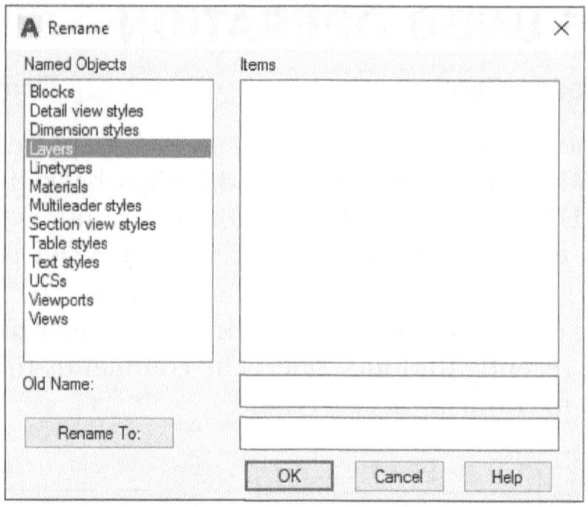

Figure 20-31 *The **Rename** dialog box*

Now, the layer named **HID** will be renamed to **HIDDEN**. You can view the change in the **Layer** drop-down list in the **Layers** panel of the **Home** tab or invoke the **LAYER PROPERTIES MANAGER** to notice this change. You can rename blocks, dimension styles, linetypes, styles, UCS, views, and viewports in the same way.

Note

*1. The **RENAME** command cannot be used to rename drawing files created using the **Insert > Block Definition > Create Block > Write Block** method. You can change the name of a drawing file by using the **Rename** option of your Operating System.*

*2. The Layer **0** and the **Continuous** linetype cannot be renamed and, therefore, do not appear in the **Items** list box of the **Rename** dialog box.*

REMOVING UNUSED NAMED OBJECTS

Application Menu: Drawing Utilities > Purge
Menu Bar: File > Drawing Utilities > Purge **Command:** PURGE

This is another editing operation used for deletion and it was discussed earlier in relation to blocks. You can delete unused named objects such as blocks, layers, dimension styles, linetypes, text styles, shapes, and so on with the help of the **PURGE** tool. When you create a new drawing or open an existing one, AutoCAD records the named objects in that drawing and notes other drawings that reference the named objects. Usually only a few of the named objects in the drawing (such as layers, linetypes, and blocks) are used. For example, when you create a new drawing, the prototype drawing settings may contain various text styles, blocks, and layers which you do not want to use. Also, you may want to delete particular unused named objects such as unused blocks in an existing drawing. Deleting inactive named objects is important and useful because doing so reduces the space occupied by the drawing. With the **PURGE** tool, you can select the named objects you want to delete. You can invoke this tool at any time in the drawing session. On invoking the **PURGE** command, the **Purge** dialog box is displayed, as shown in Figure 20-32.

View items you can purge

When this radio button is selected, AutoCAD displays the tree view of all the named objects that are in the current drawing and those that can be purged. When this radio button is selected, the **Items not used in drawing** area, and the two check boxes, **Confirm each item to be purged** and **Purge nested items**, are displayed in the dialog box. These options are discussed next.

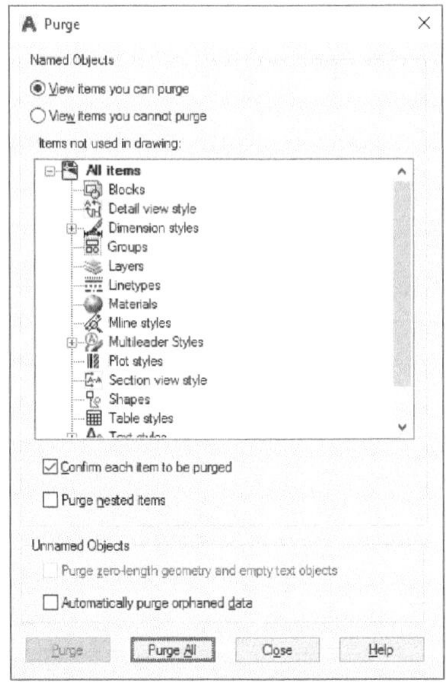

*Figure 20-32 The **Purge** dialog box with items that can be purged*

Items not used in drawing

This area lists all the named objects that can be purged. You can list the items of any object type by choosing the plus (+) sign or by double-clicking on the named object in the tree view. Select the items to be purged. You can select more than one item by holding down the SHIFT or the CTRL key.

Confirm each item to be purged

This check box is selected to confirm before purging the selected item. The **Confirm Purge** dialog box is displayed when items are selected to be purged and after the **Purge** or **Purge All** button is chosen. You can confirm or skip the items to be purged in this dialog box.

Purge nested items

This check box, when selected, removes all the nested items not in use. This removes the nested items only when you choose the **Purge All** button or select blocks.

Purge zero - length geometry and empty text objects

While drawing a line, arc, or polyline if the same point is selected as the start and the end point by mistake, then a zero length geometry will be created. Also, if there is only empty space created by mistake while creating a text, then the **Purge zero-length geometry and empty text objects** check box will be available. You can purge the zero length geometry or the empty spaces by selecting this check box.

View items you cannot purge

This radio button is used to display the tree view of the items that you cannot purge. These are the items that are used in the current drawing or are the default items that cannot be removed, refer to Figure 20-33. Selecting this radio button displays the tree view in the **Items currently used in drawing** area of the dialog box. When you select an object in this tree view, information about why you cannot purge this object is displayed below the tree view.

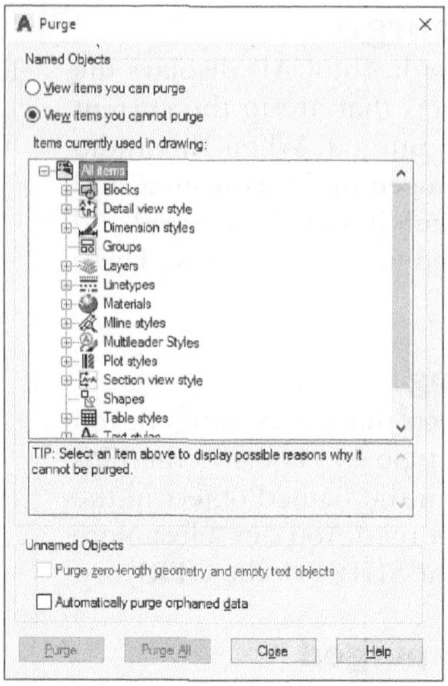

Figure 20-33 *The **Purge** dialog box with items that cannot be removed*

Note

1. *The **Entire Drawing** option of the **Write Block** dialog box, which is invoked on using the **WBLOCK** command or the **-WBLOCK** option, has the same effect as the **PURGE All** command. The only difference is that in this case the unused named objects are removed automatically without any verification, though this method is much faster as compared to the previous one.*

2. *Standard objects created by AutoCAD (such as layer 0, STANDARD text style, Dimension style, and linetype CONTINUOUS) cannot be removed by the **PURGE** command, even if these objects are not used.*

SETTING SELECTION MODES USING THE OPTIONS DIALOG BOX

Application Menu: Options **Command:** OPTIONS/OP

When you select a number of objects, the selected objects form a selection set. You can specify the objects to be selected in the **Options** dialog box which is invoked by choosing the **Options** button from the **Application Menu**, as shown in Figure 20-34. Five selection modes are provided in the **Selection** tab of this dialog box. You can select any one of these modes or a combination of various modes.

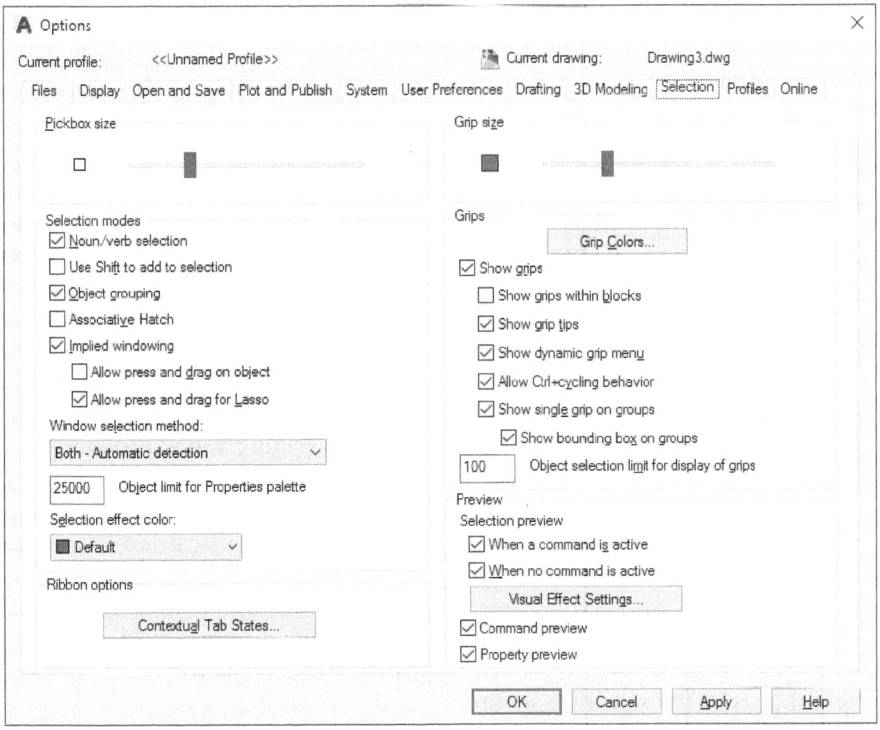

*Figure 20-34 The **Selection** tab of the **Options** dialog box*

Noun/verb selection

By selecting the **Noun/verb selection** check box, you can select the objects (noun) first and then specify the operation (verb) (command) to be performed on the selection set. This mode is active by default. For example, if you want to move some objects when the mode **Noun/verb selection** is enabled, first select the objects to be moved, and then invoke the **MOVE** command. The objects selected are highlighted automatically when the **MOVE** command is invoked and AutoCAD does not issue any **Select objects** prompt. The following are some of the commands that can be used on the selected objects when the **Noun/verb selection** mode is active.

ARRAY **BLOCK** **CHANGE** **CHPROP** **COPY**
DVIEW **EXPLODE** **ERASE** **LIST** **MIRROR**
MOVE **PROPERTIES** **ROTATE** **SCALE** **WBLOCK**

The following are some of the commands that are not affected by the **Noun/verb selection** mode. You are required to specify the objects (noun) on which an operation (command/verb) is to be performed, after specifying the command (verb).

BREAK **CHAMFER** **DIVIDE** **EDGESURF** **EXTEND**
FILLET **MEASURE** **OFFSET** **REVSURF** **RULESURF**
TABSURF **TRIM**

When the **Noun/verb selection** mode is active, the **PICKFIRST** system variable is set to 1 (On). In other words, you can also activate the **Noun/verb selection** mode by setting the **PICKFIRST** system variable to 1 (On).

Use Shift to add to selection Option

The next option in the **Selection modes** area of the **Selection** tab of the **Options** dialog box is **Use Shift to add to selection**. Selecting this option establishes the additive selection mode, which is the normal method of most Windows programs. In this mode, you have to hold down the SHIFT key when you want to add objects to the selection set. For example, suppose X, Y, and Z are three objects on the screen and you have selected the **Use Shift to add to selection** check box in the **Selection modes** area of the **Options** dialog box. Select object X. It is highlighted and put in the selection set. After selecting X, and while selecting object Y, if you do not hold down the SHIFT key, only object Y is highlighted and it replaces object X in the selection set. On the other hand, if you hold down the SHIFT key while selecting Y, it is added to the selection set (which contains X), and the resulting selection set contains both X and Y. Also, both X and Y are highlighted. To summarize the concept, objects are added to the selection set only when the SHIFT key is held down while objects are selected. Objects can be discarded from the selection set by reselecting these objects while the SHIFT key is held down.

If you want to clear an entire selection set quickly, draw a blank selection window anywhere in a blank drawing area. You can also right-click to display a shortcut menu and choose **Deselect All**. All selected objects in the selection set are discarded from it.

When the **Use Shift to add to selection** mode is active, the **PICKADD** system variable is set to 0 (Off). In other words, you can activate the **Use Shift to add to selection** mode by setting the **PICKADD** system variable to off.

Implied windowing

By selecting this option, you can automatically create a Window or Crossing selection when the **Select objects** prompt is issued. The selection window or crossing window, in this case, is created in the following manner: At the **Select objects** prompt, select a point in the empty space on the screen. This becomes the first corner point of the selection window. After this, AutoCAD prompts you to specify the other corner point of the selection window. If the first corner point is to the right of the second corner point, a Crossing selection is defined; and if the first corner point is to the left of the second corner point, a Window selection is defined. The **Implied windowing** check box is selected by default.

If this option is not active, or if you need to select the first corner in a crowded area where selecting would select an object, you need to specify Window or Crossing at the **Select objects** prompt, depending on your requirement.

When the **Implied windowing** mode is active, the **PICKAUTO** system variable is set to 1 (On). In other words, you can activate the **Implied windowing** mode by setting the value of the **PICKAUTO** system variable to 1 (On).

Press and drag

This selection mode is used to govern the way you can define a selection window or a crossing window. When you select this option, you can create the window by pressing the pick button to select one corner of the window and continuing to hold down the pick button and dragging the cursor to define the other diagonal point of the window. When you have the window you want, release the pick button. If the **Press and drag** mode is not active, you have to select twice to specify the two diagonal corners of the window to be defined. This mode is not active by default. This implies that to define a selection window or a crossing window, you have to select twice to define their two opposite corner points.

When the **Press and drag** mode is active, the **PICKDRAG** system variable is set to 1 (On). In other words, you can activate the **Press and drag** mode by setting **PICKDRAG** to On.

Object grouping

This turns the automatic group selection on and off. When this option is on and you select a member of a group, the whole group is selected. You can also activate this option by setting the value of the **PICKSTYLE** system variable to 1. (Groups were discussed earlier in this chapter.)

> **Tip**
> *You can clear the **Object grouping** check box in the **Selection Modes** area of the **Selection** tab of the **Options** dialog box to be able to select the objects of a group individually for editing without having to explode the group.*

Associative Hatch

If the **Associative Hatch** check box is selected in the **Selection modes** area of the **Selection** tab of the **Options** dialog box, the boundary object is also selected when an associative hatch is selected. You can also select this option by setting the value of the **PICKSTYLE** system variable to 2 or 3. It is recommended that you select the **Associative Hatch** check box for most drawings.

Pickbox Size

The **Pickbox** slider bar controls the size of the pickbox. The size ranges from 0 to 50. The default size is 3. You can also use the **PICKBOX** system variable.

Window selection method

This drop-down list can be used to control the selection method. During the window selection, you can control the window behaviour in the following two ways:

Click and Click. Using this method, you can define the selection window by clicking in the screen to specify the start point and endpoint of the window.

Press and drag. Using this method, you can define the selection window by clicking on any position in the drawing screen and dragging the cursor according to requirement.

You can also use both options by selecting **Both - Automatic detection** from the **Window selection method** drop-down list.

Self-Evaluation Test

Answer the following questions and then compare them to those given at the end of this chapter:

1. A group of commands is treated as one command for the **U** and **UNDO** commands by embedding them between the __________ and __________ options of the **UNDO** command.

2. If the **Press and Drag** mode is not active, you have to select __________ to specify the two diagonal points of a selection window.

3. The _________ option in the prompt of the **Edit Polyline** tool can be used to change the starting and ending widths of a polyline separately to a desired value.

4. The __________ option of the **Edit Polyline** tool is used to select more than one polyline.

5. You can move the first and last vertices in a closed polyline by using either the ______ option or the __________ option.

6. While using the _______ tool, if you select a line or an arc, AutoCAD provides you with the option of converting them into a polyline first.

7. Even if a group is defined as selectable and the **PICKSTYLE** system variable is set to 0, you cannot select the entire group by selecting one of its members. (T/F)

8. The **PROPERTIES** palette is used to change the properties associated with an object. (T/F)

9. The **PROPERTIES** palette can be used to modify the geometry of objects apart from their general properties. (T/F)

10. The **RENAME** command can be used to change the name of a drawing file created by using the **Write Block** tool. (T/F)

Review Questions

Answer the following questions:

1. In which of the following notations will the name of a group be displayed in the **Group Name** list box if you make a copy of the group without naming it?

   (a) $A1 (b) @A1
   (c) %A1 (d) *A1

2. Which of the following options is used to delete a selected group from a drawing?

   (a) **Remove** (b) **Reorder**
   (c) **Explode** (d) **Rename**

3. Which of the following system variables controls the smoothness of a curve?

   (a) **SPLINETYPE** (b) **SPLINESEGS**
   (c) **PLINEGEN** (d) **PICKFIRST**

4. Which of the following options of the **Edit Polyline** tool can straighten a curve drawn with the help of the **Polyline** tool?

   (a) **Join** (b) **Close**
   (c) **Decurve** (d) None of these

5. Which of the following properties cannot be changed using the **CHANGE** command?

   (a) **Lineweight** (b) **Color**
   (c) **Plotstyle** (d) **Thickness**

6. The ________ command can be used to change the name of a block.

7. If the __________ option of the **UNDO** command is set to off, any group of commands grouped together using the **Begin** and **End** options of the **UNDO** command are undone together.

8. Circles drawn using the **Circle** tool can be changed to _________.

9. The __________ option in the **Group** tool is used to change the order of the objects in the selected group.

10. You can select a group by entering _________ at the command prompt.

11. The __________ option of the **UNDO** command disables the **UNDO** and **U** commands entirely.

12. When you use the **Group** tool to form object groups, AutoCAD allows you to sequentially highlight the groups of which the selected object is a member. (T/F)

13. The standard objects created by AutoCAD (such as layer 0, STANDARD text style, and linetype CONTINUOUS) cannot be removed by using the **PURGE** tool. (T/F)

14. If you explode an object, it remains identical to its original geometry; only the color and linetype may change because of floating layers, colors, or linetypes. (T/F)

15. The **PURGE** tool has the same effect as that of the **WBLOCK Entire drawing** or the **-WBLOCK** method. The only difference is that with the **PURGE** tool, deletion takes place automatically. (T/F)

Exercise 4 Properties and Edit Polyline

Draw part (a) in Figure 20-35 and then using the **Properties** and relevant **Edit Polyline** tool options, convert it into parts (b), (c), and (d). The linetype used in part (d) is HIDDEN.

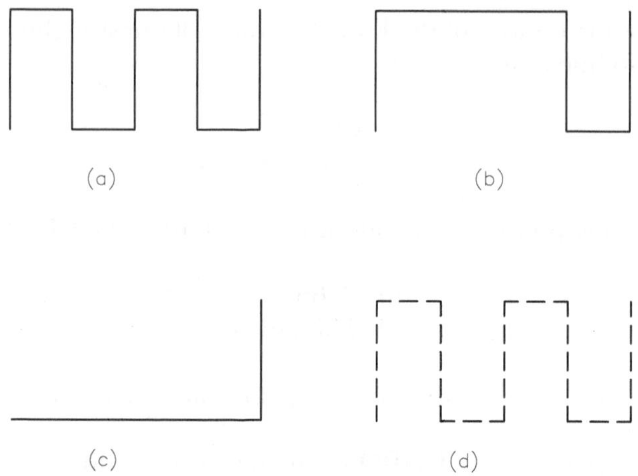

Figure 20-35 *Drawing for Exercise 4*

Exercise 5 Edit Polyline

Draw the sketch shown in Figure 20-36 using the **Line** tool. Change the object to a polyline with a width of 0.05.

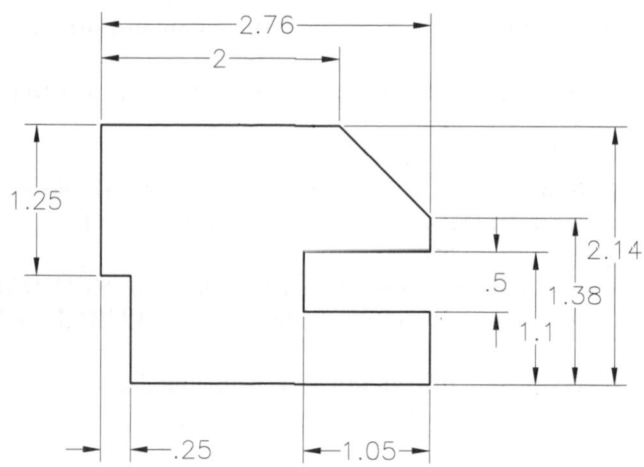

Figure 20-36 *Drawing for Exercise 5*

Exercise 6 — Edit Polyline

Draw part (a) of Figure 20-37 and then using the relevant **Edit Polyline** tool options, convert it into drawing (b).

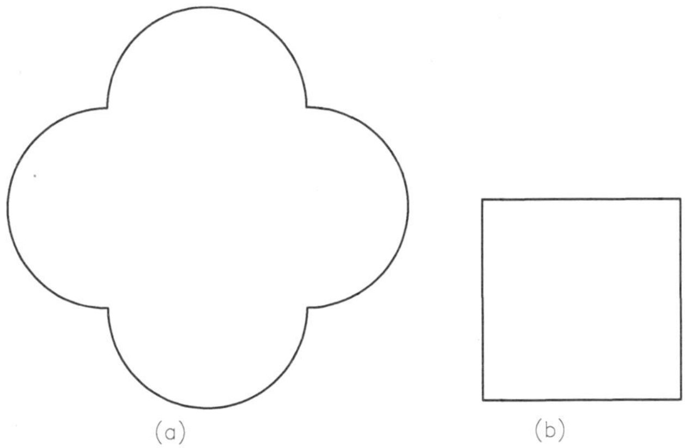

Figure 20-37 *Drawing for Exercise 6*

Exercise 7 — Edit Polyline

Draw part (a) of Figure 20-38 and then using the relevant **Edit Polyline** tool options, convert it into drawings (b), (c), and (d). Identify the types of curves.

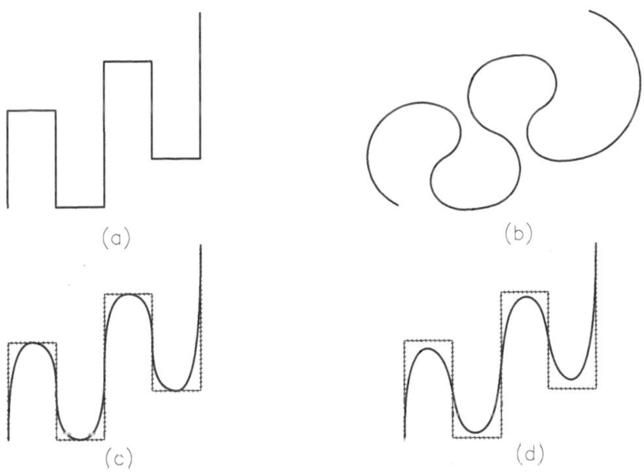

Figure 20-38 *Drawing for Exercise 7*

Exercise 8 Edit Polyline

Draw part (a) of Figure 20-39 and then using the relevant **Edit Polyline** tool options, convert it into drawing (b).

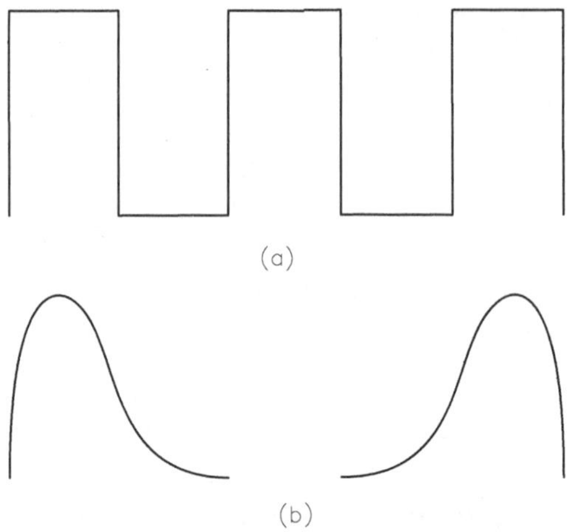

Figure 20-39 *Drawing for Exercise 8*

Exercise 9 Edit Polyline

Draw the part (a) of Figure 20-40 and change it into the figure shown in part (b) by using the appropriate commands. You can also use grips to obtain this illustration.

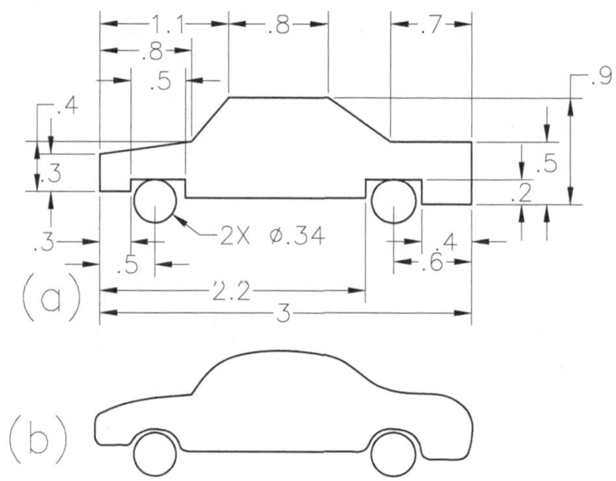

Figure 20-40 *Drawing for Exercise 9*

Exercise 10 — *Edit Polyline*

Create the drawing shown in Figure 20-41. Use the splined polylines to draw the break lines. Dimension the drawing as shown.

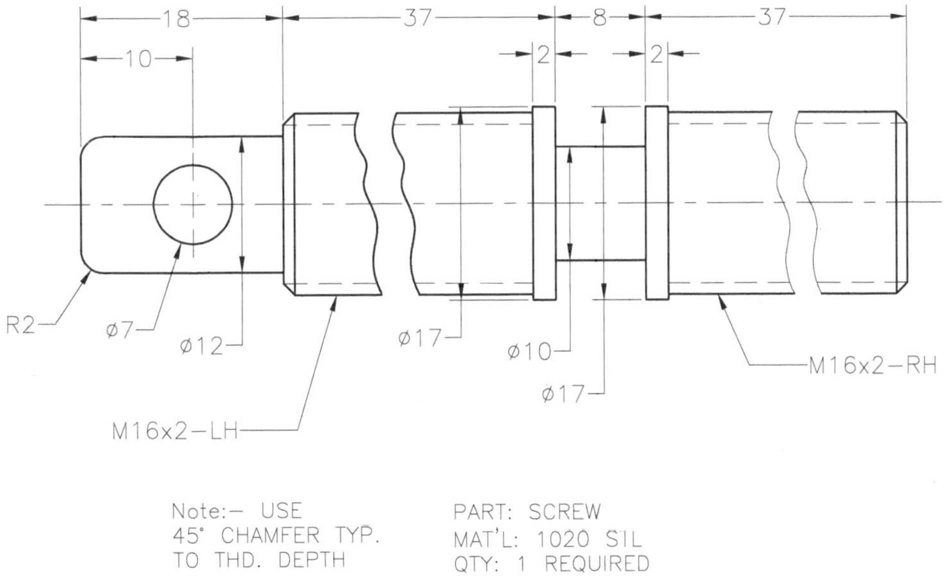

Figure 20-41 *Drawing for Exercise 10*

Answers to Self-Evaluation Test

1. Begin, **End**, **2.** Twice, **3.** Width, **4. Multiple**, **5. Next**, **Previous**, **6. Edit Polyline**, **7.** T, **8. T**, **9.** T, **10.** F

Chapter 21

Working with Data Exchange & Object Linking and Embedding

Learning Objectives

After completing this chapter, you will be able to:

- *Import and export .dxf files using the Save As and Open tools*
- *Import files*
- *Convert scanned drawings into the drawing editor using the DXB file format*
- *Attach the raster images to the current drawing*
- *Edit raster images*
- *Understand the embedding and linking functions of the OLE feature of Windows*
- *Use DWG Convert and CONTENT EXPLORER*

Key Terms

- *DXF Files*
- *DXB Files*
- *ACIS Files*
- *DWG Convert*
- *PDF Files*
- *3D Studio Files*
- *DGN Files*
- *BMP Files*
- *Attach Image*
- *EPS Files*
- *OLE Objects*
- *Draw Order*

UNDERSTANDING THE CONCEPT OF DATA EXCHANGE IN AutoCAD

Different companies have developed different softwares for applications such as CAD, desktop publishing, and rendering. This non-standardization of software has led to the development of various data exchange formats that enable the transfer (translation) of data from one data processing software to the other. This chapter will cover various data exchange formats provided in AutoCAD. AutoCAD uses the *.dwg* format to store drawing files. This format is not recognized by some other CAD softwares. To address this problem, AutoCAD provides various data exchange formats such as DXF (Data Interchange Format) and DXB (Drawing Interchange Binary).

CREATING DATA INTERCHANGE (DXF) FILES

The DXF file format generates a text file in ASCII code from the original drawing. This allows any computer system to manipulate (read/write) data in a DXF file. Usually, the DXF format is used for CAD packages based on microcomputers. For example, packages like SmartCAM use DXF files. Some desktop publishing packages, such as PageMaker and Ventura Publisher also use DXF files.

Creating a Data Interchange File

Using the **Save** or **Save As** tool, you can create an ASCII file with a *.dxf* extension from an AutoCAD drawing file. Once you invoke any of these tools, the **Save Drawing As** dialog box will be displayed. Next, choose the **Options** option from the **Tools** drop-down to display the **Saveas Options** dialog box, as shown in Figure 21-1. In this dialog box, choose the **DXF Options** tab and enter the degree of accuracy for the numeric values. The default value for the degree of accuracy is sixteen decimal places. You can enter a value between 0 and 16 decimal places.

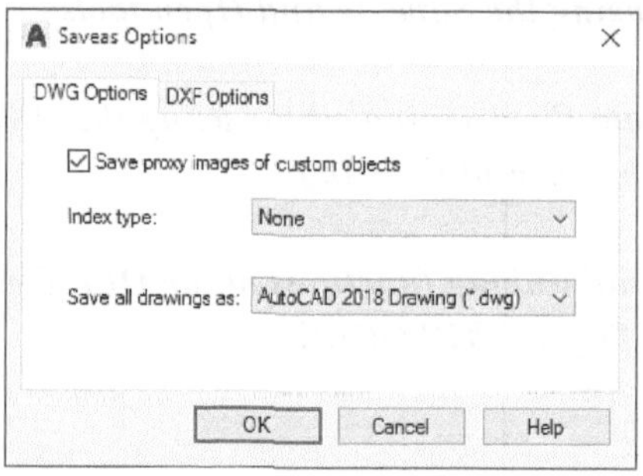

***Figure 21-1** The **Saveas Options** dialog box*

In the **DXF Options** tab, you can also select the **Select objects** check box which allows you to specify the objects to be included in the DXF file. In this case, the definitions of the named objects such as block definitions, text styles, and so on are not exported.

Select the **ASCII** radio button. Choose the **OK** button to return to the **Save Drawing As** dialog box. Choose the **Save** button here. Now, an ASCII file with a *.dxf* extension has been created and this file can be accessed by other CAD systems. This file contains data on the objects specified. By default, DXF files are created in the ASCII format. However, you can also create binary format files by selecting the **BINARY** radio button in the **Saveas Options** dialog box. Binary DXF files are more efficient and occupy only 75 percent of the ASCII DXF file. You can access a binary format file more quickly than an ASCII format file.

Note

You can also create a DXF file by using the ***-WBLOCK*** *command. When you execute this command, the* ***Create Drawing File*** *dialog box will be displayed, where you can enter the name of the file in the* ***File name*** *edit box and select any version of DXF [*dxf] from the* ***Files of type*** *drop-down list. By default, the DXF file to be created assumes the name of the drawing file from which it will be created.*

Information in a DXF File

The DXF file contains data of the objects which are specified using the **Select objects** check box in the **Saveas Options** dialog box. You can change the data in this file as per your requirement. To examine the data in this file, load the ASCII file in the word processing software. A DXF file is composed of the following parts:

Header

In this part of the drawing database, all variables in the drawing and their values are displayed.

Classes

This section deals with the internal database.

Tables

All named objects such as linetypes, layers, blocks, text styles, dimension styles, and views are listed in this part.

Blocks

The objects that define blocks and their respective values are displayed in this part.

Entities

All entities in the drawing, such as lines, circles, and so on are listed in this part.

Objects

Objects in the drawing are listed in this part.

Converting DXF Files Into Drawing Files

You can import a DXF file into a new AutoCAD drawing file with the **Open** tool. After you invoke the **Open** tool, the **Select File** dialog box is displayed. From the **Files of type** drop-down list, select the **DXF (*.dxf)** option. In the **File name** edit box, enter the name of the file you want to import into AutoCAD or select the file from the list. Choose the **Open** button. Once this is done, the specified DXF file is converted into a standard DWG file, regeneration is carried out, and the file is inserted into the new drawing. Now, you can perform different operations on this file just as with the other drawing files.

Tip

A data interchange file (DXF) can also be inserted into the current drawing using the ***Insert*** *tool.*

Importing CAD Files

Ribbon: Insert > Import > Import drop-down > Import
Menu Bar: File > Import **Command:** IMPORT

You can import any surface, solid, 2D and 3D wire geometry from the supported file formats to AutoCAD. In AutoCAD, you can import IGES, CATIA, Rhino, Pro/ENGINEER and many other file formats. To import a CAD geometry to AutoCAD, choose the **Import** tool from the **Import** drop-down of the **Import** panel; the **Import File** dialog box will be displayed. From the **Files of type** drop-down list, select the required format. Next, browse to the required file and then choose the **Open** button from the dialog box; the **Import - Processing Background Job** message box will be displayed stating that the import job is processing in the background. Next, close the message box. The details of the progress can be seen on the bottom-right corner of the screen. After the processing gets completed, a link will be displayed as pop-up. Click on the link to import the CAD geometry into AutoCAD; the inserted part geometry will be placed as a block reference.

OTHER DATA EXCHANGE FORMATS

The other formats that can be used to exchange data from one data processing format to the other are discussed next.

DXB File Format

Menu Bar: Insert > Drawing Exchange Binary **Command:** DXBIN

AutoCAD offers another file format for data interchange, DXB. This format is much more compressed than the binary DXF format and is used when you want to translate a large amount of data from one CAD system to another. For example, when you scan a drawing, a DXB file is created. This file has a huge amount of data in it. To import a DXB file, enter the **DXBIN** command at the command prompt; the **Select DXB File** dialog box will be displayed. In the **File name** edit box, enter the name of the file (in DXB format) you want to import into AutoCAD. Choose the **Open** button. Once this is done, the specified DXB file will be converted into a standard DWG file and is inserted into the current drawing.

Note

Before importing a DXB file, you must create a new drawing file. No editing or drawing setup (limits, units, and so on) can be performed on this file. This is because if you import a DXB file to an old drawing, the settings (definitions) of layers, blocks, and so on, of the file being imported are overruled by the settings of the file to which you are importing the DXB file.

Creating and Using an ACIS File

Application Menu: Export > Other Formats **Command:** EXPORT, ACISOUT

Trimmed NURBS, regions, and solids can be exported to an ACIS file with an ASCII format. To do so, choose **Export > Other Formats** from the **Application Menu**; the **Export Data** dialog box will be displayed. Enter a file name in the **File name** edit box. From the **Files of type** drop-down list, select **ACIS (*.sat)** and then choose the **Save** button; you will be prompted to select the objects. Select the solids, regions, or ACIS bodies that you want to add to the file and press ENTER. AutoCAD appends the file extension *.sat* to the file name. You can also use the **ACISOUT** command to perform this function. It prompts you to select objects before the **Create ACIS File** dialog box is displayed on the screen. Keep in mind that only solids, regions, or ACIS bodies can be selected to add to the *.sat* file.

To import an ACIS file, choose the **Import** tool from the **Import** drop-down of the **Import** panel in the **Insert** tab; the **Import File** dialog box will be displayed. In the **Files of type** drop-down list, select the *.sat* file format. Next, select a file to be imported and choose the **Open** button; the file will be inserted. Alternatively, enter **ACISIN** at the command prompt and import the file using the **Select ACIS File** dialog box.

Importing PDF Files

Ribbon: Insert > Import > Import drop-down > PDF Import **Command:** PDFIMPORT

You can import the geometry, raster images, fills, and true type text objects from a PDF file into the current drawing as AutoCAD objects. To do so, choose the **PDF Import** tool from the **Import** drop-down of the **Import** panel in the **Insert** tab; the **Select PDF File** dialog box will be displayed. Select a PDF file to import and choose the **Open** button; the **Import PDF** dialog box will be displayed, as shown in Figure 21-2.

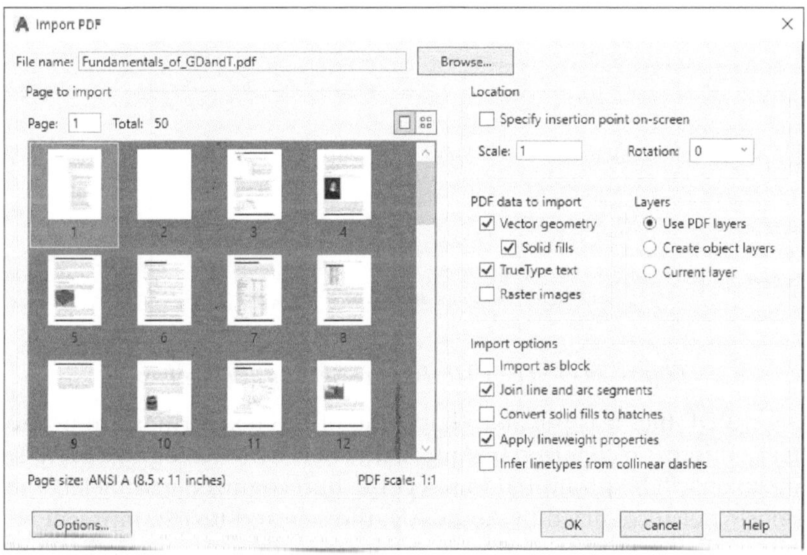

***Figure 21-2** The **Import PDF** dialog box*

Enter the page number in the **Page** edit box under the **Page to import** area of the **Import PDF** dialog box. To specify the scale, rotation and point of insertion of the imported geometry choose the respective options under the **Location** area. You can also choose the type of data to be imported using the options available in the **PDF data to import** area. To specify the layers in which the PDF data is to be imported, choose the options under the **Layers** area. The options under the **Import options** area are discussed next.

You can join 2D solids with the coincident edges and convert them to hatch objects by choosing the **Convert solid fills to hatches** check box. Choose the **Apply lineweight properties** check box to apply the lineweights of the PDF to the extracted geometry. You can choose the **Infer linetypes from collinear dashes** check box to collect collinear dash and dot segments and replace them with a single polyline. If you uncheck this box, each segment in a dashed line is imported as a separate polyline. Choose the **Options** button at the bottom of the **Import PDF** dialog box; the **Options** dialog box will be displayed. In the **Options** dialog box, you can specify the file location for image files that are extracted from the PDF and attached to the drawing.

Alternatively, you can import different objects from the previously attached PDF by entering the **PDFIMPORT** command at the command bar. On doing so, you will be prompted to select PDF underlay. Select an attached PDF from the drawing area; you will be prompted to specify a rectangular or polygonal boundary around the objects that you want to import or choose the **All** option from the command prompt to import all the objects in the overlay. Choose the **Settings** option from the command prompt to invoke the **PDF Import Settings** dialog box, as shown in Figure 21-3. The options in this dialog box are same as discussed for the **Import PDF** dialog box. After selecting the boundary you can choose the options in the command prompt to keep, detach, or unload the PDF underlay after the objects are imported into the current drawing.

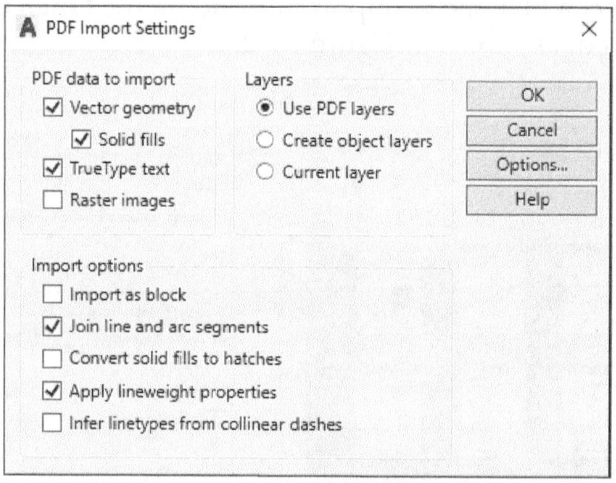

***Figure 21-3** The **PDF Import Settings** dialog box*

While importing a PDF file, it is possible that some of the text strings are not recognized by AutoCAD. To make this text recognized by AutoCAD, choose the **Recognize SHX Text** tool from the **Import** panel; you will be prompted to select the unrecognized text. Select the text stamps that were previously not recognized by AutoCAD; the selected text stamps will be recognized. This tool recognizes the text by comparing its geometry with some pre-defined text styles. You can also set the list of text styles by using the **PDF Text Recognition Settings** dialog box. To invoke this dialog box, choose the **Recognition Settings** tool from the **Import** panel; the **PDF Text Recognition Settings** dialog box will be displayed, as shown in Figure 21-4. You can select any text style and add or remove more text styles by choosing required options from the **SHX fonts to compare** area of this dialog box.

In the **Create text on** area, you can create the recognized text on the set layer or on the same layer by selecting the **Current layer** or **Same layer as geometry** radio buttons, respectively. Also, you can set the percentage for matching geometry to the defined text style from the **Recognition threshold** slider in the **Conversion settings** area.

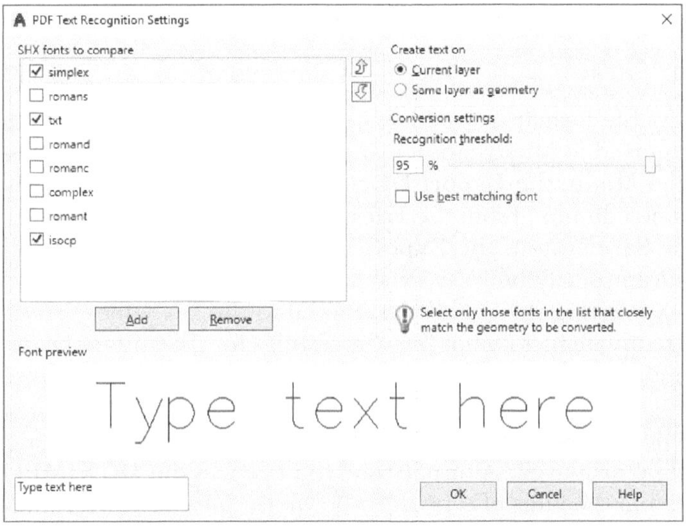

*Figure 21-4 The **PDF Text Recognition Settings** dialog box*

Tip

*You can also access the PDF import options by choosing the **Import as Objects** tool in the **PDF Import** panel of the **PDF Underlay** contextual tab which will be displayed on selecting the object.*

Importing 3D Studio Files

Menu Bar: Insert > 3D Studio **Command:** 3DSIN

You can import 3D geometry, views, lights, and objects with surface characteristics created in 3D Studio and saved in *.3ds* format. To do so, choose the **3D Studio** tool from the **Insert** menu; the **3D Studio File Import** dialog box will be displayed. Select the file you wish to import and choose the **Open** button. You can use the **3DSIN** command to import 3D Studio file.

Creating and Using a Windows Metafile

Application Menu: Export > Other Formats **Command:** EXPORT, WMFOUT

The Windows Metafile format (WMF) file contains screen vector and raster graphic formats. In the **Export Data** dialog box or in the **Create WMF File** dialog box, enter the file name. Select **Metafile (*.wmf)** from the **Files of type** drop-down list. The extension *.wmf* is appended to the file name. Next, save the settings and then select the objects you want to save in this file format.

The **WMFIN** command invokes the **Import WMF** dialog box. Select the *.wmf* file you want to import and choose the **Open** button. Specify an insertion point, rotation angle, and scale factor. Specify the scaling by entering a scale factor using the **Corner** option to specify an imaginary box whose dimensions correspond to the scale factor, or by using the **X**, **Y**, or **Z** option to specify 3D scale factors. You can also import a *.wmf* file by using the **Import File** dialog box that will be displayed on choosing the **Import** tool from the **Import** panel in the **Insert** tab.

Creating and Using a V8 DGN File

Application Menu: Export > DGN	**Command:** EXPORT, DGNEXPORT

The **V8 DGN** (*.DGN*) file format is used by the Microstation software. A **.dwg* file created in AutoCAD can be exported to Microstation using this format. To do so, choose **Export > DGN** from the **Application Menu**; the **Export DGN File** dialog box will be displayed. Enter a file name in the **File name** edit box. From the **Files of type** drop-down list, select **V8 DGN (*.dgn)** and then choose the **Save** button; the **Export DGN Settings** dialog box will be displayed. In this dialog box, you can specify how the externally referenced files in the current drawing are taken care of while converting the current drawing into the DGN file. You can also specify the seed files (standard template files containing the settings for the units to be used for conversion, working units, resolution of the drawing, and so on) to be used for conversion in this dialog box.

To import a DGN file, choose **Open > DGN** from the **Application Menu**; the **Import DGN File** dialog box will be displayed. Alternatively, you can use the **DGNIMPORT** command to import a DGN file. From the **Files of type** drop-down list, select the **MicroStation DGN (*.dgn)** option, if it is not selected by default. Next, select or enter the name of the design file and choose the **Open** button; the **Import DGN Settings** dialog box will be invoked. You can exchange the data of the drawing files and design files using the **Export/Import DGN Settings** dialog box. For example, you can translate DGN elements to DWG objects, Levels to Layers, Line Styles to Linetypes, Cells to Blocks, Sheet Model to DWG Layouts, etc. You can save and reuse, modify, rename or delete the mapping translations using the **DGNMAPPING** command.

Creating a BMP File

Application Menu: Export > Other Formats	**Command:** EXPORT, BMPOUT

This is used to create bitmap images of the objects in your drawing. In the **Export Data** dialog box, enter the name of the file, select **Bitmap (*.bmp)** from the **Files of type** drop-down list and then choose the **Save** button. Select the objects you wish to save as bitmap and press ENTER. Entering **BMPOUT** displays the **Create Raster File** dialog box. Enter the file name and choose the **Save** button. Select the objects to be saved as bitmap. The file extension *.bmp* is appended to the file name.

RASTER IMAGES

A raster image consists of small square-shaped dots known as pixels. In a colored image, the color is determined by the color of pixels. The raster images can be moved, copied, or clipped. They will used as a cutting edge with the **Trim** tool. They can also be modified by using grips. You can also control the image contrast, transparency, and quality of the image. AutoCAD stores images in a special temporary image swap file whose default location is the Windows Temp directory. You can change the location of this file by modifying it under **Temporary Drawing File Location** in the **Files** tab of the **Options** dialog box.

The images can be 8-bit gray, 8-bit color, 24-bit color, or bitonal. When the image transparency is set to On, the image file formats with transparent pixels is recognized by AutoCAD and transparency is allowed. The transparent images can be in color or grayscale. AutoCAD supports many formats and some of them are given next.

Image Type	File Extension	Description
BMP	*.bmp*	Windows and OS/2 Bitmap Format
JFIF or JPEG	*.jpg, jpeg*	Joint Photographics Expert group
PCX	*.pcx*	Picture PC Paintbrush Picture
PNG	*.png*	Portable Network Graphic
TARGA	*.tga*	True Vision Raster based Data format
TIFF/LZW	*.tif, .tiff*	Tagged Image File Format

When you store images as Tiled Images, that is, in the Tagged Image File Format (TIFF), you can edit or modify any portion of the image; only the modified portion is regenerated, thus saving time. Tiled images load much faster as compared to the untiled images.

Attaching Raster Images

Ribbon: Insert > Reference > Attach **Tool Palettes:** Draw > Attach Image
Toolbar: Reference > Attach Image or Insert > Attach Image **Command:** IMAGEATTACH

Attaching raster images to a drawing does not make them part of the drawing. To attach an image, choose the **Attach** tool from the **Reference** panel; the **Select Reference File** dialog box will be displayed, as shown in Figure 21-5. Select the image to be attached; a preview of the selected image will be displayed in the **Preview** area of the dialog box. Next, choose the **Open** button; the **Attach Image** dialog box will be displayed, as shown in Figure 21-6. The name of the selected image is displayed in the **Name** drop-down list. You can select another file by using the **Browse** button. The **Name** drop-down list displays the names of all the images in the current drawing. Select the **Specify on-screen** check boxes to specify the **Insertion point**, the **Scale**, and **Rotation** angle on the screen. Alternatively, you can clear these check boxes and enter values in the respective edit boxes. On choosing the **Show Details** button, the **Attach Image** dialog box is expanded and it provides the image information such as the Horizontal and Vertical resolution values, current AutoCAD unit, and Image size in pixels and units. Choose the **OK** button to return to the drawing screen.

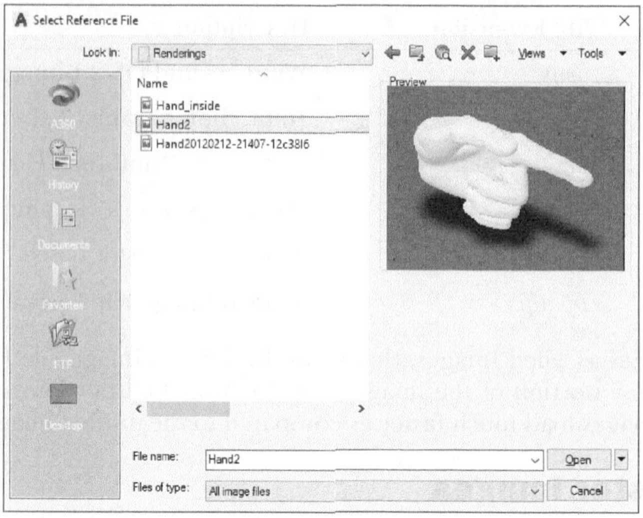

Figure 21-5 *The* ***Select Reference File*** *dialog box*

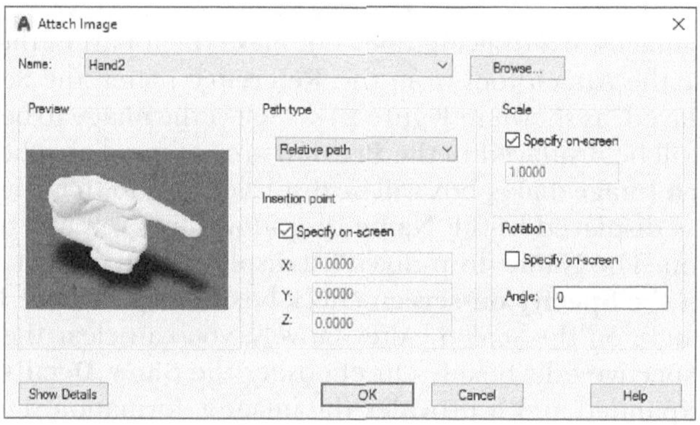

Figure 21-6 *The* ***Attach Image*** *dialog box*

You can also attach and scale an image from the Internet. In the **Select Reference File** dialog box, choose the **Search the Web** button. Once you have located the image file you wish to attach to the current drawing, enter the URL address in the **Look in** drop-down list and the image file name in the **Name or URL** edit box. Choose the **Open** button. Specify the insertion point, scale, and rotation angle in the **Attach Image** dialog box. You can also right-click on the image you wish to attach to the current drawing and choose **Properties** from the shortcut menu to display the **Properties** palette. From here, you can select, cut, and paste the URL address in the **File name** edit box of the **Select Reference File** dialog box.

Managing Raster Images

Enhanced

Ribbon: View > Palettes > External References Palette	**Command:** IMAGE
Toolbar: Reference > External References	**Menu Bar:** Insert > External References

Choose the **External References Palette** button from the **Palettes** panel; the **EXTERNAL REFERENCES** palette will be displayed, refer to Figure 21-7. If the image has not been inserted earlier, right-click in the **File References** area and choose the **Attach Image** option from the shortcut menu. You can view the image information either as a list or as a tree view by choosing the respective buttons located at the right corner of the **File References** head of the **EXTERNAL REFERENCES** palette. The **List View** displays the names, loading status, size, date last modified on, and search path of all images in the drawing. The **Tree View** displays images in hierarchal structure. These images show its nesting levels within blocks and Xrefs. The **Tree View** does not display the status, size, or any other information about an image file. You can rename an image file in this dialog box.

Figure 21-7 The ***EXTERNAL REFERENCES*** *palette*

Preview

To display the **Preview** area, choose the **Preview** button located at the right corner of the **Details** area. In this area, you can see the preview of the image. This area displays the preview of the image file attached to the current drawing and the file details of the attached image file. To get the file details, choose the **Details** button located adjacent to the **Preview** button. The information about the image file such as file name, saved path, and so on will be listed, as shown in Figure 21-8. Once you have referenced an image file to the current drawing, you can replace it with another image file by using the **Saved Path** edit box. To do so, choose the Browse [...] button in the corner of the edit box to display the **Select Image File** dialog box. Browse and select the image file and then choose the **Open** button. Now, the new path will be displayed in the **Found At** and **Saved Path** edit boxes.

Figure 21-8 The ***Details*** *area of the* ***EXTERNAL REFERENCES*** *palette*

> **Tip**
> *You can also use the command prompt for managing the image files using the* ***-IMAGE*** *command. Except the* ***Open*** *option, all the other options of the* ***EXTERNAL REFERENCES*** *palette will be available in the command prompt.*

When you select the name of the attached image and right-click on it, a shortcut menu will be displayed. The options in this shortcut menu are discussed next.

Open

This option enables you to open the attached image in its default viewing software from its current location in the AutoCAD file.

Attach

This option allows you to attach an image file with the current drawing. You can also attach an image file by choosing the **Attach Image** option from the flyout on the upper left corner of the **EXTERNAL REFERENCES** palette; the **Select Reference File** dialog box will be displayed. Select the file that you want to attach to the drawing and the selected image is displayed in the **Preview** box. Choose the **Open** button; the **Attach Image** dialog box is displayed. The name of the file, its path, and extension are displayed in the **Attach Image** dialog box. You can use the **Browse** button to select another file. Choose the **OK** button in the **Attach Image** dialog box and specify a point to insert the image. Next, AutoCAD will prompt you to enter the scale factor. You can enter the scale factor or specify a point on the screen.

Detach

This option detaches the selected and all associated raster images from the current drawing. Once the image is detached, no information about the image is retained in the drawing.

Reload

The **Reload** option simply reloads an image. The changes made to the image since the last insert will be loaded on the screen.

Unload

The **Unload** option unloads an image. An image is unloaded when it is not needed in the current drawing session. When you unload an image, AutoCAD retains information about the location and size of the image in the database of the current file. Unloading a file does not unlink the file from the drawing and the image frame is displayed. If you reload the image, the image will appear at the same point and in the same size as the image was before unloading. Unloading the raster images enhances AutoCAD performance. Also, the unloaded images are not plotted. If multiple images are to be loaded and the memory is insufficient, AutoCAD automatically unloads them.

Change Path Type

The **Change Path Type** option is used to change the path type from where the image can be imported. You can set three types of paths by selecting the desired option from the **Change Path Type** cascading menu invoked by clicking on the **Change Path Type** option in the shortcut menu. The options in this cascading menu are discussed next.

Make Absolute: This option is used to set full path of the attached image which includes drive, url, or network server location.

Make Relative: This option is used to set most flexible path because it does not save drive name. Therefore, by using this option, you can easily move your file in different drawings with same folder structure without breaking the reference.

Remove path: This option is used when you do not want to set any path. On selecting this option, you can move your drawing wherever you want without facing any problem.

Select New Path

The **Select New Path** option is used to change the current path of the attached image whose referenced path has been changed. Also, you can attach a different image by using this option.

Find and Replace

This option is used to simultaneously change the path of all the attached images having same path from one location to another.

EDITING RASTER IMAGE FILES

Raster image files can be easily edited. The different methods to edit a raster image files are discussed next.

Clipping Raster Images

Ribbon: Insert > Reference > Clip	**Toolbar:** Reference > Clip Image
Menu Bar: Modify > Clip > Image	**Command:** IMAGECLIP

The **Clip** tool is used to clip the boundaries of images and to provide a desired shape to them. To invoke this tool, select the image to be clipped; the **Image** tab will be added to the **Ribbon**. Choose the **Create Clipping Boundary** tool; you will be prompted to specify the boundary. Specify a rectangular or polygonal boundary; the image will be clipped at the specified boundary. Also, an arrow will be displayed pointing inside the clipping boundary. Click on the arrow to flip the clipping direction.

You can also invoke this tool by selecting and right-clicking on an image to be clipped and choose **Image > Clip** from the shortcut menu displayed.

After choosing this tool, AutoCAD will prompt you to select the image to be clipped. Select the raster image by selecting the edge of the image. The image boundary must be visible to select it. The clipping boundary must be specified in the same plane as the image or a plane that is parallel to it. The following prompt sequence is displayed when you choose the **Clip** tool from the **Reference** panel.

Select object to clip: *Select the boundary of an image.*
Enter image clipping option [ON/OFF/Delete/New boundary] <New>:

New boundary

This option is used to define a boundary for clipping the image. When you invoke this option, you are prompted to specify whether or not you want to delete the old boundary, if a boundary already exists. If you enter **No** at the **Delete old boundary? [No/Yes] <Yes>** prompt, this command will end. You can enter **Yes** to specify the new clipping boundary. The boundary can be defined in a rectangular shape or a polygonal shape.

ON

This option is used to turn the image clipping on. The image will be clipped using the last boundary.

OFF

This option is used to turn the image clipping off. If you have a clipped image, you can redisplay the entire image.

Delete

This option is used to delete the existing clipping boundary.

One such clipping is shown in Figures 21-9 and 21-10. Figure 21-9 shows the actual image and Figure 21-10 shows the clipped image where the clipping boundary is created by using the midpoints of all the four sides of the image.

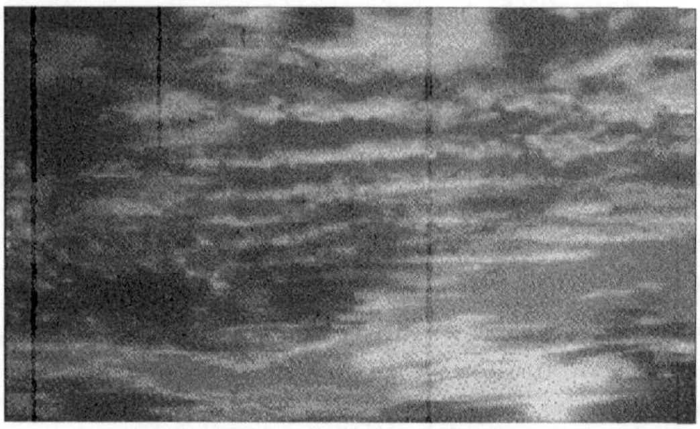

Figure 21-9 *Image before clipping*

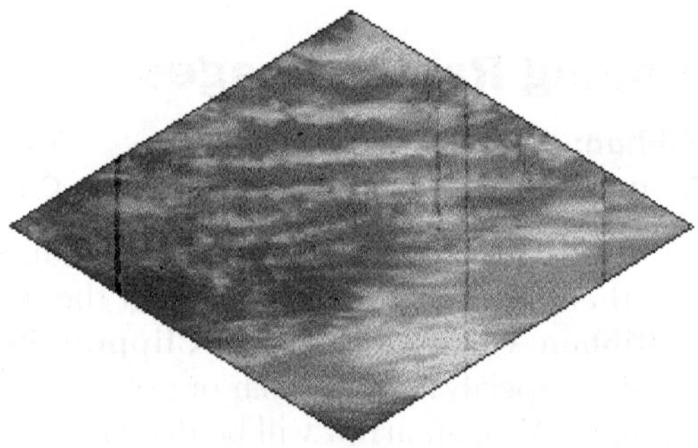

Figure 21-10 *Image after clipping*

Tip

*You can improve the performance by turning off the highlighting of an image. This can be done by clearing the **Highlight raster image frame only** check box in the **Display** tab of the **Options** dialog box. You can also use the **IMAGEHLT** system variable. By default, **IMAGEHLT** is set to 0, that is, only the raster image frame will be highlighted.*

Adjusting Raster Images

Ribbon: Insert > Reference > Adjust
Menu Bar: Modify > Object > Image > Adjust
Toolbar: Reference > Adjust Image
Command: IMAGEADJUST/ADJUST

The **Adjust** tool allows you to adjust the brightness, contrast, and fade of a raster image. On selecting an attached image, the **Image** tab will be added to the **Ribbon**. Adjust the brightness, contrast, and fade using the corresponding option in the **Adjust** panel of the **Image** tab.

Alternatively, choose the **Adjust Image** tool from the **Reference** toolbar to invoke the **Image Adjust** dialog box, as shown in Figure 21-11. This dialog box is used to adjust an image. As you adjust the brightness, contrast, or fade, the changes are dynamically made in the image. If you choose the **Reset** button, the values will be returned to the default values (Brightness= 50, Contrast= 50, and Fade= 0). You can also choose **Properties** in the shortcut menu to display the **PROPERTIES** palette. In this palette, you can enter new values of brightness, contrast, and fade. If you choose the **Adjust** tool from the **Reference** panel, you need to set the values in the command prompt.

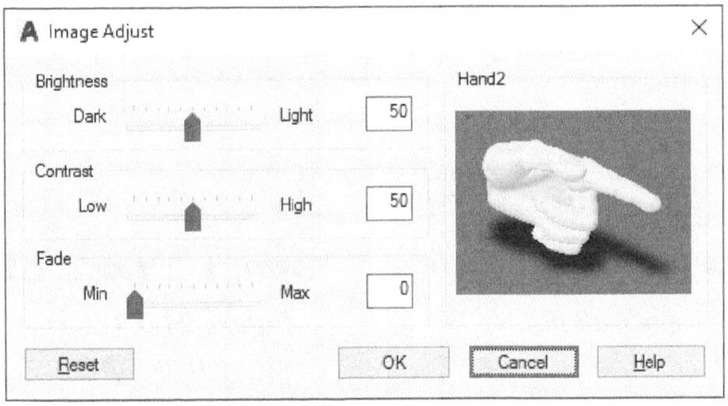

*Figure 21-11 The **Image Adjust** dialog box*

Modifying the Image Quality

Menu Bar: Modify > Object > Image > Quality **Command:** IMAGEQUALITY
Toolbar: Reference > Image Quality

The **Quality** tool allows you to control the quality of the image that affects the display performance. To control the quality, choose the **Quality** tool from **Modify > Object > Image** in the Menu bar; you will be prompted to specify the quality of image. A high-quality image takes a longer time to display. When you change the quality, the display changes immediately without causing a **REGEN**. The images are always plotted using a high-quality display. Although draft quality images appear grainier, they are displayed more quickly.

Modifying the Transparency of an Image

Toolbar: Reference > Image Transparency **Command:** TRANSPARENCY
Menu Bar: Modify > Object > Image > Transparency

When you attach an image with transparent background to a drawing, the transparent background turns opaque. To control the transparency of the attached image, select it; the **Image** tab will be added to the **Ribbon**. Choose the **Background Transparency** button from the **Image** tab to turn on the transparency of the image; the background of the image will become transparent. The **TRANSPARENCY** command can also be used to control the transparency of an image. Figure 21-12 shows two images one over the other with the transparency of the top image turned off. Figure 21-13 shows the figure with the transparency of the top image turned on. You can also right-click on an image and choose **Properties** from the shortcut menu displayed. In the **PROPERTIES** palette, select an option from the **Background Transparency** drop-down list displayed under the **Misc** list.

Note

You have to choose images in such a way that they can give the effect of transparency. Dull and opaque images will not give the effect of transparency.

Figure 21-12 *Image with the transparency off*

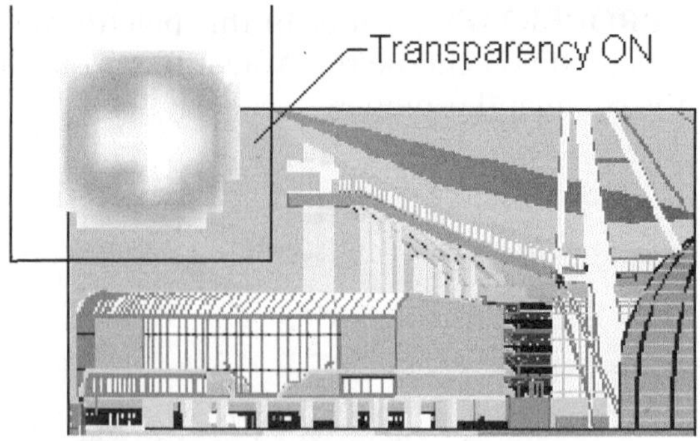

Figure 21-13 *Image after turning the transparency on*

Controlling the Display of Image Frames

Menu Bar: Modify > Object > Image > Frame **Command:** IMAGEFRAME
Toolbar: Reference > Image Frame

The **FRAME** tool is used to turn the image boundary on or off. This tool can be invoked from **Modify > Object > Image** menu. If the image boundary is off, the image cannot be selected with the pointing device and therefore cannot be accidentally moved or modified.

CHANGING THE DISPLAY ORDER

Ribbon: Home > Modify > Draw Order drop-down
Command: DRAWORDER/DR **Toolbar:** Draw Order

The tools in the **Draw Order** drop-down, refer to Figure 21-14, of the **Modify** panel are used to change the display order of the selected images and other objects.

If you choose the **Bring to Front** tool, the selected object will be moved to the front of all entities. If you choose the **Send to Back** tool, the selected object will be moved behind all entities. If you choose the **Bring Above Objects** tool, the selected object will be moved above the referenced objects. If you choose the **Send Under Objects** tool, the selected object will be moved under the referenced objects.

The **Bring Text to Front** tool can be used to bring entire text to the front of all entities. If you choose **Bring Dimensions to Front**, all dimensions will come to front of all the entities. The **Send Hatches to Back** tool is used to send all the hatches to the back of all entities.

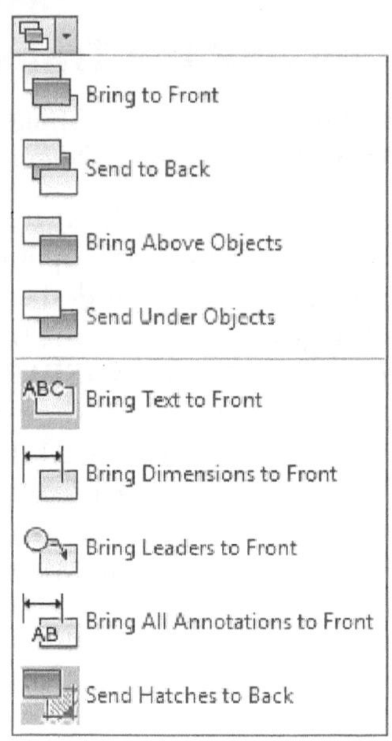

Figure 21-14 *Tools in the* ***Draw Order*** *drop-down*

Other Editing Operations

You can also perform other editing operations such as copy, move, and stretch to edit a raster image. Remember that you can also use the image as the trimming edge for trimming objects. However, you cannot trim an image. You can insert the raster image several times or make multiple copies of it. Each copy can have a different clipping boundary. You can also edit the image using grips. You can use the **Properties** palette to change the image layer, boundary linetype, and color, and perform other editing commands such as changing the scale, rotation, width, and height by entering new values in the respective edit boxes. You can also display an image or turn off the display by selecting options from the **Show image** drop-down list in the **Misc** field of the **Properties** palette. If you select **Yes**, the image is displayed and if you select **No**, the display of the image is turned off. You can turn off the display of the image when you do not need it, thus improving the performance.

Scaling Raster Images

The scale of the inserted image is determined by the actual size of the image and the unit of measurement (inches, feet, and so on). For example, if the image is 1" X 1.26" and you insert this image with a scale factor of 1, its size on the screen will be 1 by 1.26 AutoCAD units. If the scale factor is 5, the image will be five times larger. The image that you want to insert must contain the resolution information (DPI). If the image does not contain this information, AutoCAD treats the width of the image as one unit.

DWG Convert

Application Menu: Save As > DWG Convert **Command:** DWGCONVERT
Menu Bar: File > DWG Convert

The **DWG Convert** tool is used to convert a single or batch of the AutoCAD drawing files into any older version of AutoCAD drawing format. You can do the conversion by following the procedure given next.

Invoke the **DWG Convert** dialog box by choosing the **DWG Convert** tool from the **File** menu; the **DWG Convert** dialog box will be displayed, as shown in Figure 21-15. Choose the **Add file** button from the bottom of the **Files Tree** area; the **Select File** dialog box will be displayed. Next, browse to the required location, select the required file/files, and then choose the **Open** button; the selected files will be displayed in tree form in the **Files Tree** area of the **DWG Convert** dialog box. Also, a check box will be displayed on the left of each drawing file. By default, all the check boxes are selected. You can clear the check box corresponding to the files that are not to be converted. You can also view the selected files along with their details such as their path and location, version, size, date, and so on in the form of a table by choosing the **Files Table** tab. If you want to save the current file list, then choose the **Save list** button; the **Save Conversion List** dialog box will be displayed. Save the file list in the desired folder.

You can select the version of output file from the **Select a conversion setup** area; the description of the conversion setup will be displayed in the **Setup description** area. You can also specify the conversion settings, if required, by choosing the **Conversion Setups** button. This is discussed in the next head. Now, choose the **Convert** button located at the lower right corner of the dialog box; the **Conversion Package Creation is in Progress** window will be displayed and in a few moments the files will be converted. Exit the dialog box by choosing the **Close** button.

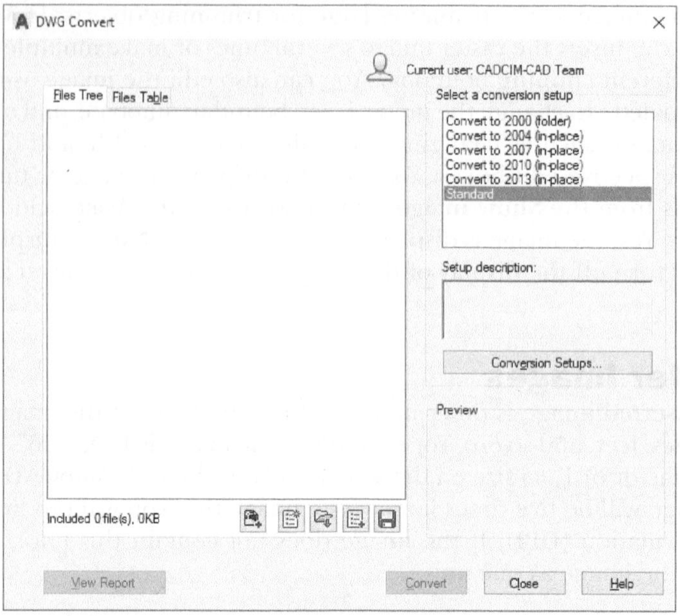

*Figure 21-15 The **DWG Convert** dialog box*

You can also open any previously saved file list by using the **Open list** button. If you choose this button, the **Open Conversion List** dialog box will be displayed. Browse to the required file and choose the **Open** button; all files in the conversion list will be imported in the **Files Tree** area of the **DWG Convert** dialog box. Later on, you can replace this list with a new list using the **Append list** button.

Conversion Setup Options

The **Conversion Setups** options are used to control the output of the files to be converted. To modify the conversion settings, choose the **Conversion Setups** button from the **DWG Convert** dialog box; the **Conversion Setups** dialog box will be displayed, as shown in Figure 21-16. The options in this dialog box are discussed next.

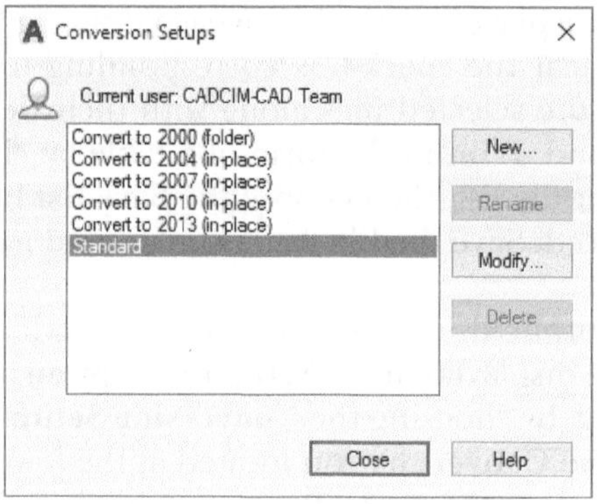

*Figure 21-16 The **Conversion Setups** dialog box*

New

This button is used to create a new conversion scheme. On choosing this button, the **New Conversion Setup** dialog box will be displayed, as shown in Figure 21-17. You can enter the name of new conversion setup in the **New Conversion setup name** edit box. Next, select an option from the **Based on** drop-down list. Finally, choose the **Continue** button; the **Modify Conversion Setup** dialog box will be displayed. This dialog box is discussed later in this chapter.

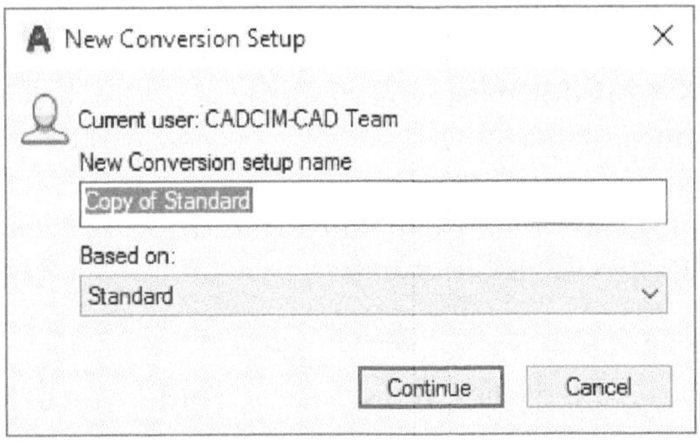

*Figure 21-17 The **New Conversion Setup** dialog box*

Rename

This button is used to rename the selected conversion setup.

Modify

This button is used to modify the existing conversion settings according to the desired output. On choosing the **Modify** button, the **Modify Conversion Setup** dialog box will be displayed, as shown in Figure 21-18. Using this dialog box, you can modify conversion settings. The options in this dialog box are discussed next.

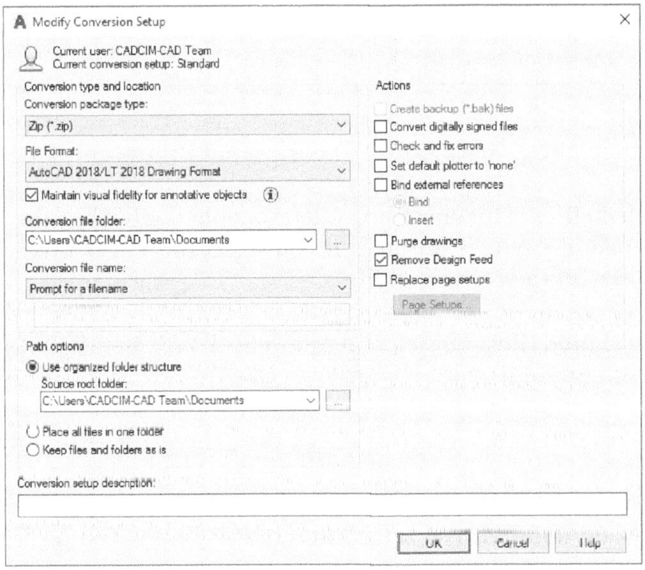

*Figure 21-18 The **Modify Conversion Setup** dialog box*

Conversion type and location Area

The options under the **Conversion package type** drop-down list in this area are discussed next.

In-place (overwrite files): This option is used if you want the converted files to be in the same directory, in which the source files are present. If you want to overwrite the existing files, this option also allows the software to overwrite the previous files with the converted new files.

Folder (set of files): This option is used if you want the converted files to be saved in the specified directory. On selecting this option, the **Conversion file folder** drop-down list will be activated. Using this drop-down list, you can browse to the desired folder where you want to save the converted files.

Zip (*.zip): This option is used to bind all converted drawing files into a zip file, which can be uncompressed to the specific location later.

Path options Area

The **Path options** area will be enabled when you select the **Folder (set of files)** or **Zip (*.zip)** option from the **Conversion package type** drop-down list. In the **Path options** area, there are three radio buttons that are explained next.

Use organized folder structure: On selecting this radio button, you can store the converted files in the specified folder in same organized way as they are present in the source folder (in **Source root folder** drop-down).

Place all files in one folder: On selecting this radio button, you can save all converted files in one folder which is specified as output folder.

Keep files and folder as is: On selecting this radio button, the files are saved in the way they were originally present. In other word, the hierarchy remains the same as of original file location.

Actions Area

In the **Actions** area, there are 8 check boxes. Description of these check boxes is given next.

Create backup(*.bak) files: This check box will be enabled only when the **In-place (overwrite files)** conversion package type is selected. If you select this check box, then the backup file will also be created with the converted file.

Convert digitally signed files: On selecting this check box, the digitally signed files will be included in the conversion list.

Check and fix errors: If you select this check box, the errors will automatically be fixed during the conversion.

Set default plotter to 'none': If you select this check box, the plotter for all converted files will be set to **None**.

Bind external references: You can bind the external referenced files with the converted drawing files using this check box. This option has two radio buttons, **Bind** and **Insert**. **Bind** is used to bind the external referenced file as external object. **Insert** is used to bind the external reference as internal object of the drawing.

Purge drawings: Select this check box if you want to purge the drawings.

Remove Design Feed: This check box is selected by default and is used to remove design feed data from the specified drawing.

Replace page setups: Select this check box if you want to replace the page setup of the converted drawing files with a pre-stored template. To get a pre-stored template, choose the **Page Setups** button after selecting the check box; the **Page Setups** dialog box will be displayed. Choose the **Browse** button, and then select a pre-stored template.

Conversion setup description Area

This area is located at the bottom of the dialog box. You can enter the description of the conversion setup in the **Conversion setup description** edit box in this area.

Delete

This button is used to delete any of the conversion setup in the list.

WORKING WITH POSTSCRIPT FILES

Application Menu: Export > Other Formats **Menu Bar:** File > Export
Command: EXPORT, PSOUT

PostScript is a page description language developed by Adobe Systems. It is mostly used in DTP (desktop publishing) applications. AutoCAD allows you to work with PostScript files. You can create and export PostScript files from AutoCAD, so that these files can be used for DTP applications. PostScript images have a higher resolution than raster images. The extension for these files is *.eps* (Encapsulated PostScript).

Creating PostScript Files

As just mentioned, any AutoCAD drawing file can be converted into a PostScript file. This can be accomplished by using the **PSOUT** command. When you invoke this command, the **Create PostScript File** dialog box is displayed, as shown in Figure 21-19. You can also use the **Export** tool to display the **Export Data** dialog box. The options are similar in both the dialog boxes.

In the **File name** edit box, enter the name of the PostScript (EPS) file you want to create. Select **Encapsulated PS (*.eps)** from the **Files of type** drop-down list. Next, choose the **Save** button to accept the default setting and create the PostScript file. You can also choose the **Options** option from the **Tools** flyout of the **Create PostScript File** dialog box to change the settings through the **PostScript Out Options** dialog box and then save the file. The **PostScript Out Options** dialog box, as shown in Figure 21-20, provides the options given next.

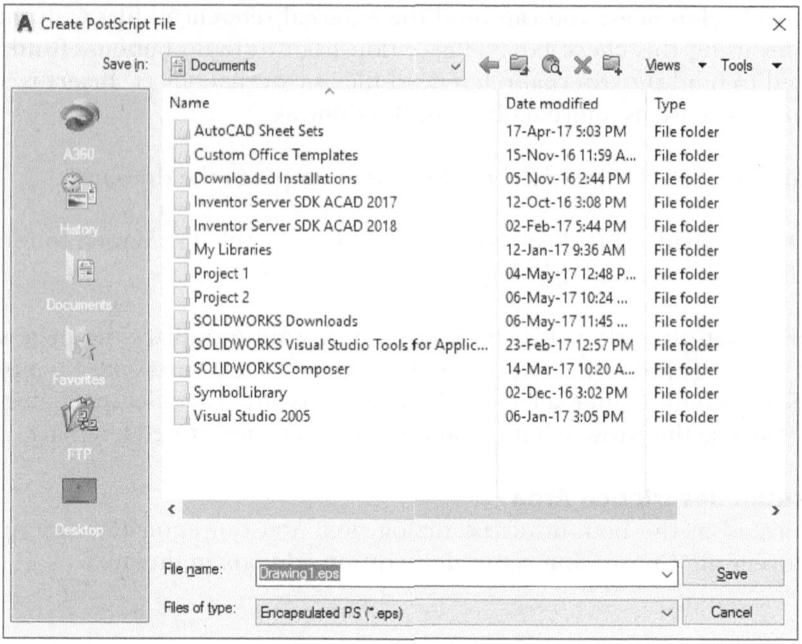

*Figure 21-19 The **Create PostScript File** dialog box*

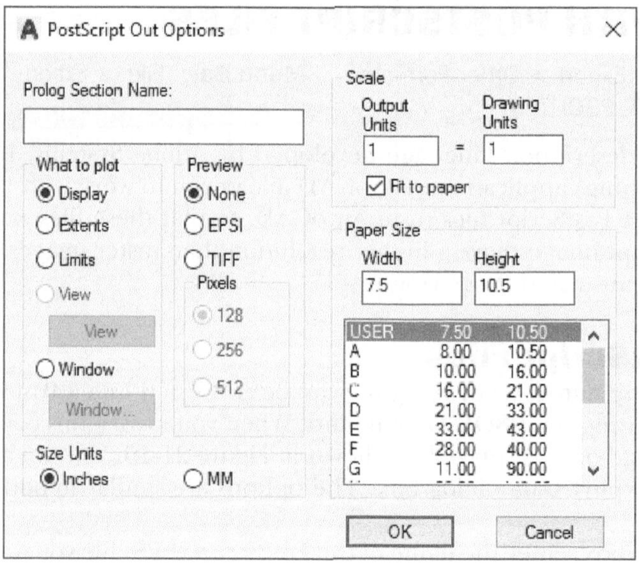

*Figure 21-20 The **PostScript Out Options** dialog box*

Prolog Section Name

In this edit box, you can assign a name for a prolog section to be read from the *acad.eps* file.

What to plot Area

The **What to plot** area of the dialog box has the following options:

Display: If you select this radio button when you are in the model space, the display in the current view is saved in the specified EPS file. Similarly, if you are in the layouts, the current viewport is saved in the specified EPS file.

Extents: If you use this option, the PostScript file will contain the section of the AutoCAD drawing that currently holds objects. In this way, this option is similar to the **Zoom Extents** option. If you add objects to the drawing, they are also included in the PostScript file to be created because the extents of the drawing are also altered. If you reduce the drawing extents by erasing, moving, or scaling objects, then you must use the **Zoom Extents** or **Zoom All** option. Only then does the **Extents** option of the **PSOUT** command calculate the extents of the drawing to be exported. If you are in the model space, the PostScript file is created in relation to the model space extents; if you are in the paper space, the PostScript file is created in relation to the paper space extents.

Limits: With this option, you can export the whole area specified by the drawing limits. If the current view is not the plan view [viewpoint (0,0,1)], the **Limits** option exports the area just as the **Extents** option would.

View: Any view created with the **VIEW** command can be exported with this radio button. This radio button will be available only when you have created a view using the **VIEW** command. Select the **View** radio button to invoke the **View Name** dialog box from where you can select the view.

Window: In this option, you need to specify the area to be exported with the help of a window. When this radio button is selected, the **Window** button is also available. Choose the **Window** button to display the **Window Selection** dialog box where you can choose the **Pick** button and then specify the two corners of the window on the screen. You can also enter the coordinates of the two corners in the **Window Selection** dialog box.

Preview Area

The **Preview** area of the dialog box has two types of formats to preview images: **EPSI** and **TIFF**. If you want a preview image with no format, select the **None** radio button. If you select **TIFF** or **EPSI**, you are required to enter the pixel resolution of the screen preview in the **Pixels** area. You can select a preview image size of 128 X 128, 256 X 256, or 512 X 512.

Size Units Area

In this area, you can set the paper size units to **Inches** or **MM** by selecting their corresponding radio buttons.

Scale Area

In this area, you can set an explicit scale by specifying how many drawing units are to be output per unit. You can select the **Fit to paper** check box so that the view to be exported is made as large as possible for the specified paper size.

Paper Size Area

You can select a size from the list or enter a new size in the **Width** and **Height** edit boxes to specify a paper size for the exported PostScript image.

OBJECT LINKING AND EMBEDDING (OLE)

With Windows, it is possible to work with different Windows-based applications by transferring information between them. You can edit and modify the information in the original Windows application, and then update this information in other applications. This is made possible by creating links between different applications and then updating those links, which in turn update or modify the information in the corresponding applications. This linking is a function of the OLE feature of Microsoft Windows. The OLE feature can also join together separate pieces of information from different applications into a single document. AutoCAD and other Windows-based applications such as Microsoft Word, Notepad, and Windows WordPad support the Windows OLE feature.

For the OLE feature, you should have a source document where the actual object is created in the form of a drawing or a document. This document is created in an application called a server application. AutoCAD for Windows and Paintbrush can be used as server applications. Now this source document is to be linked to (or embedded in) the compound (destination) document, which is created in a different application, known as the container application. AutoCAD for Windows, Microsoft Word, and Windows WordPad can be used as container applications.

Clipboard

The transfer of a drawing from one Windows application to another is performed by copying the drawing or the document from the server application to the Clipboard. The drawing or document is then pasted in the container application from the Clipboard. Hence, a Clipboard is used as a medium for storing the documents while transferring them from one Windows application to another. The drawing or the document on the Clipboard stays there until you copy a new drawing, which overwrites the previous one, or until you exit Windows. You can save the information present on the Clipboard with the *.clp* extension.

Object Embedding

You can use the embedding function of the OLE feature when you want to ensure that there is no effect on the source document even if the destination document has been changed through the server application. Once a document is embedded, it has no connection with the source. Although editing is always done in the server application, the source document remains unchanged. Embedding can be accomplished by means of the following steps. In this example, AutoCAD for Windows is the server application and MS Word is the container application.

1. Create a drawing in AutoCAD (the server application).

2. Open MS Word (container application).

3. It is preferable to arrange both the container and server windows so that both are visible, as shown in Figure 21-21.

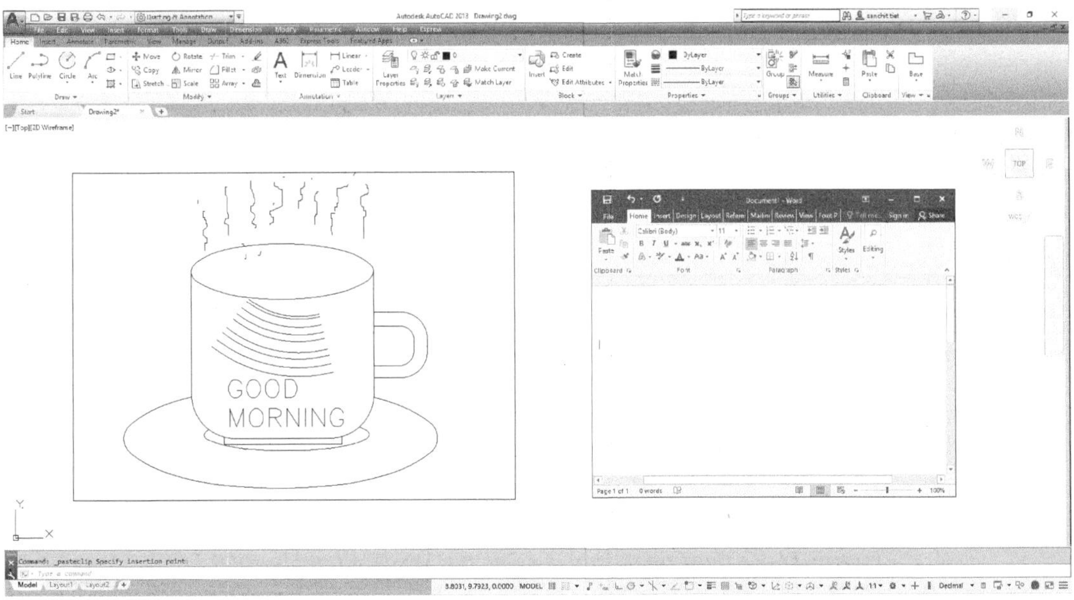

Figure 21-21 *AutoCAD graphics screen with the MS Word window*

4. In AutoCAD, copy the drawing using the CTRL+C keys; the **copyclip** tool is invoked. This tool can be used to embed drawings. You can also invoke this tool from the **Edit** menu, or by entering **COPYCLIP** at the command prompt. The next prompt, **Select objects**, allows you to select the entities you want to transfer. You can either select the full drawing by entering **ALL** or select some of the entities by selecting them. You can use any of the object selection methods for selecting objects. With this command, the selected objects are automatically copied to the Windows Clipboard.

5. After the objects are copied to the Clipboard, make the MS Word window active. To get the drawing from the Clipboard to the MS Word application (client), you need to paste it into the Word application. Choose the **Paste Special** tool from **Home > Clipboard > Paste** drop-down, refer to Figure 21-22; the **Paste Special** dialog box will be displayed, as shown in Figure 21-23. In this dialog box, select the **Paste** radio button (default) for embedding, and then choose the **OK** button. The drawing is now embedded in the MS Word window.

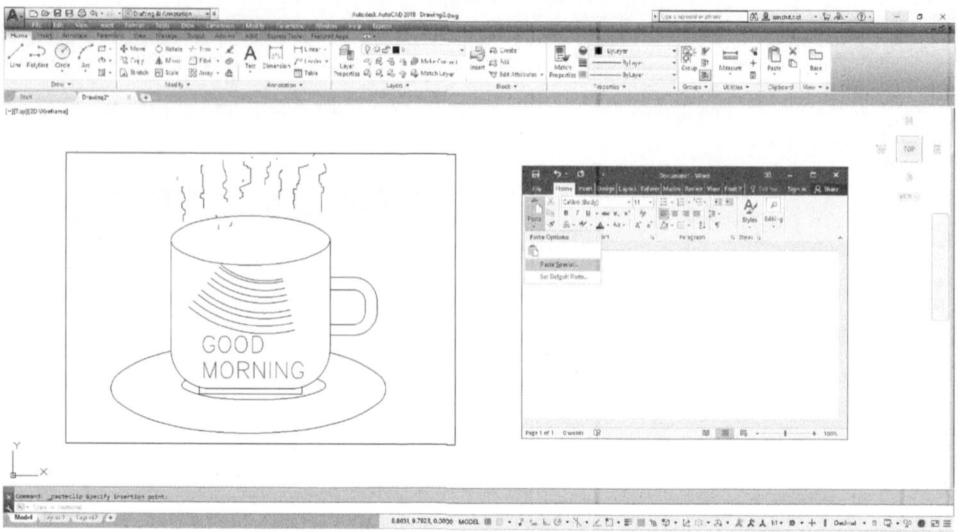

Figure 21-22 Pasting a drawing into the MS Word application

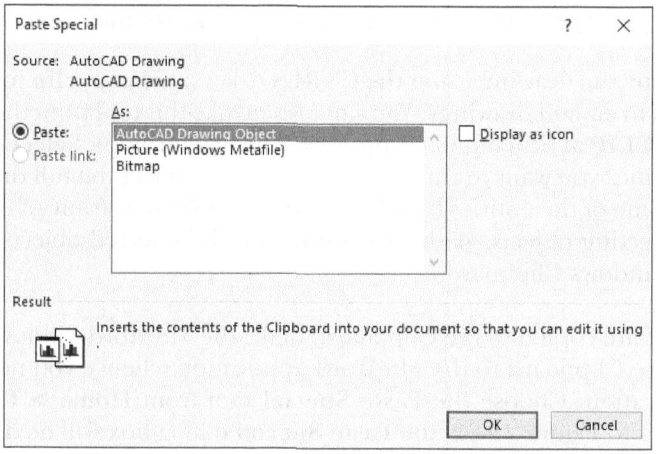

*Figure 21-23 The **Paste Special** dialog box*

6. Your drawing is now displayed in the MS Word window, but it may not be displayed at the proper position. You can get the drawing displayed in the current viewport by moving the scroll bar up or down in the MS Word window. You can also save your embedded drawing by choosing the **Save** button in MS Word. On doing so, the **Save As** dialog box is displayed where you can enter a file name. Save the file and then exit AutoCAD.

7. Now, you need to edit the embedded drawing. Editing is performed in the server application, which in this case is AutoCAD. You can get the embedded drawing into the server application (AutoCAD) directly from the container application (MS Word) by double-clicking on the drawing in MS Word. The other method of editing an embedded drawing is by right-clicking on it and then choosing **AutoCAD Drawing Object > Edit** from the shortcut menu.

8. Now, you are in AutoCAD, with your embedded drawing displayed on the screen, but as a temporary file with a file name such as [Drawing in Document]. Here, you can edit the drawing by changing the color and linetype or by adding and deleting the text, entities, and so on. In this example, the plate have been hatched.

9. After you have finished modifying your drawing, choose the **Update Microsoft Word** option from the **File** menu in the server (AutoCAD), refer to Figure 21-24. To display the menu bar, click on the down arrow in the **Quick Access Toolbar** and select **Show Menu Bar**. AutoCAD automatically updates the drawing in MS Word (container application). Now, you can exit this temporary file in AutoCAD.

Figure 21-24 *Updating the AutoCAD drawing in Microsoft Word*

Note

Do not zoom or pan the drawing in the temporary file. If you do so, this will be included in the updating and the new file will display only that portion of the drawing that lies inside the original area.

10. This completes the embedding function. Now, you can exit the container application. While exiting it, a message box asking whether or not to save changes in MS Word is displayed.

Linking Objects

The linking function of OLE is similar to the embedding function. The only difference is that here a link is created between the source document and the destination document. If you edit the source, you can simply update the link, which automatically updates the client. This allows you to place the same document in a number of applications, and if you make a change in the source document, the clients will also change by simply updating the corresponding links. Consider AutoCAD for Windows to be the server application and MS Word to be the container application. Linking can be performed by means discussed next.

1. Open a drawing in the server application (AutoCAD). If you have created a new drawing, then you must save it before you can link it with the container application. Next, open MS Word (container application).

2. It is preferable to arrange both the container and the server windows so that both are visible.

3. In AutoCAD, choose the **Copy Link** option from the **Edit** menu of the menu bar to invoke the **COPYLINK** command. This command can be used for linking the drawing. This command copies all objects that are displayed in the current viewport directly to the Clipboard. Here, you cannot select objects for linking. If you want only a portion of the drawing to be linked, you can zoom into that view so that it is displayed in the current viewport prior to invoking the **COPYLINK** command. This command also creates a new view of the drawing having the name OLE1.

4. Make the MS Word window active. To get the drawing from the Clipboard to the MS Word (container) application, choose the **Paste Special** tool from **Home > Clipboard > Paste** drop-down; the **Paste Special** dialog box will be displayed. In this dialog box, select the **Paste link** radio button for linking. Choose the **OK** button. Note that the **Paste link** radio button in the **Paste Special** dialog box will not be available if you have not saved the drawing.

5. The drawing is now displayed in the MS Word window and is linked to the original drawing. You can also save your linked drawing by choosing the **Save** button from the **Quick Access Toolbar** in MS Word. It displays the **Save As** dialog box where you can enter a file name.

6. You can now edit your original drawing. Editing can be performed in the server application, which, in this case, is AutoCAD for Windows. You can edit the drawing by changing the color and linetype or by adding and deleting text, entities, and so on. Next, save your drawing in AutoCAD by using the **Save** tool. You can now exit AutoCAD.

7. You will notice that the drawing is automatically updated, and the changes made in the source drawing are present in the destination drawing also. If the drawing is not updated automatically, right-click on the drawing and then choose the **Update Link** option from the shortcut menu displayed. Automatic updating is possible if the **Automatic** radio button is selected in the **Links** dialog box, refer to Figure 21-25. The **Links** dialog box can be invoked by choosing **Linked AutoCAD Drawing Object > Links** from the shortcut menu displayed on right clicking on the drawing in the Word application.

8. Exit the container application after saving the updated file.

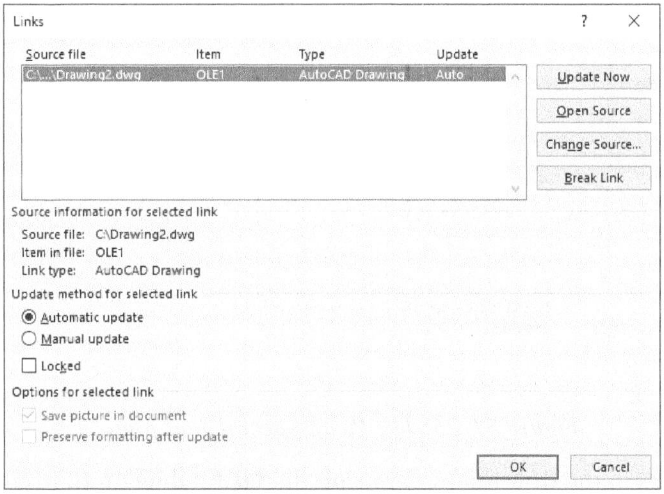

Figure 21-25 *The **Links** dialog box*

Note

The dialog box may be different in your case as it depends on the version of MS Word being used currently.

Linking Information to AutoCAD

You can also embed and link information from a server application into an AutoCAD drawing. You can also drag selected OLE objects from another application into AutoCAD, provided this application supports Microsoft ActiveX and the application is running and visible on the screen. Dragging and dropping is like cutting and pasting. If you press the CTRL key while you drag the object, it is copied to AutoCAD. Dragging and dropping an OLE object into AutoCAD embeds it into AutoCAD.

Linking Objects to AutoCAD

Start any server application such as MS Word and open a document in it. Select the information you wish to use in AutoCAD with your pointing device and choose the **Copy** tool to copy this data to the Clipboard. Open the AutoCAD drawing to which you want to link this data. Choose the **Paste Special** tool from **Home > Clipboard > Paste** drop-down or use the **PASTESPEC** command; the **Paste Special** dialog box will be displayed, as shown in Figure 21-26. In the **As** list box, select the data format you wish to use. Select the **Paste Link** radio button to paste the contents of the Clipboard into the current drawing. If you select the **Paste** radio button, the data will be embedded and not linked. Choose the **OK** button to exit the dialog box. Specify the insertion point; the data will be displayed in the drawing.

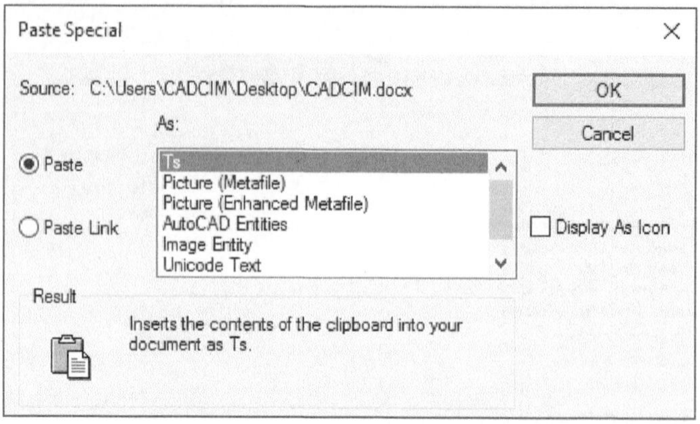

*Figure 21-26 The **Paste Special** dialog box*

You can insert objects in the drawing by choosing the **OLE Object** tool from the **Data** panel of the **Insert** tab, or by choosing the **OLE Object** tool in the **Insert** toolbar. This command links an entire file to a drawing from within AutoCAD. On invoking this command, the **Insert Object** dialog box is displayed, as shown in Figure 21-27.

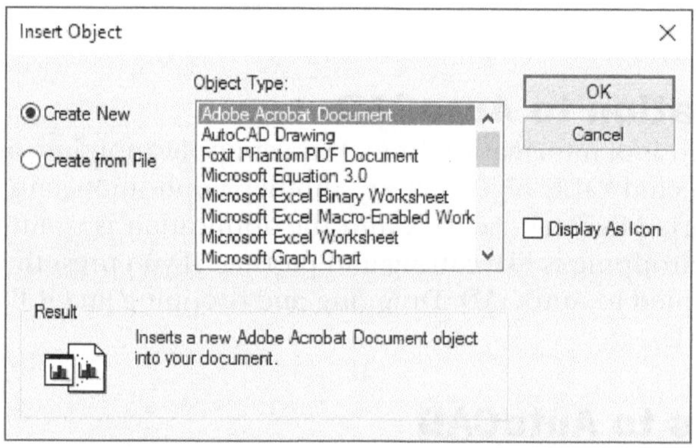

*Figure 21-27 The **Insert Object** dialog box*

Select the **Create from File** radio button. Also, select the **Link** check box. Choosing the **Browse** button displays the **Browse** dialog box. Select a file you want to link from the list box or enter a name in the **File name** edit box and choose the **Open** button. The path of the file is displayed in the **File** edit box of the **Insert Object** dialog box. If you select the **Display As Icon** check box, an icon is displayed in the dialog box as well as in the drawing. Choose the **OK** button to exit the dialog box; the selected file is linked to the AutoCAD drawing.

Whenever the server document changes, AutoCAD updates links automatically. But, you can use the **Links** dialog box to change these settings, refer to Figure 21-28. This dialog box can be displayed by choosing the **OLE Links** tool from the **Edit** menu. In the **Links** dialog box, select the link you want to update and then choose the **Update Now** button. Next, choose the **Close** button. If the server file location changes or if it is renamed, you can choose the **Change Source** button in the **Links** dialog box to display the **Change Source** dialog box. In this dialog box, locate the server file name and location and choose the **Open** button. You can also choose the **Break Link** button in the **Links** dialog box to disconnect the inserted information from the server application. This is done when the linking between the two is no longer required.

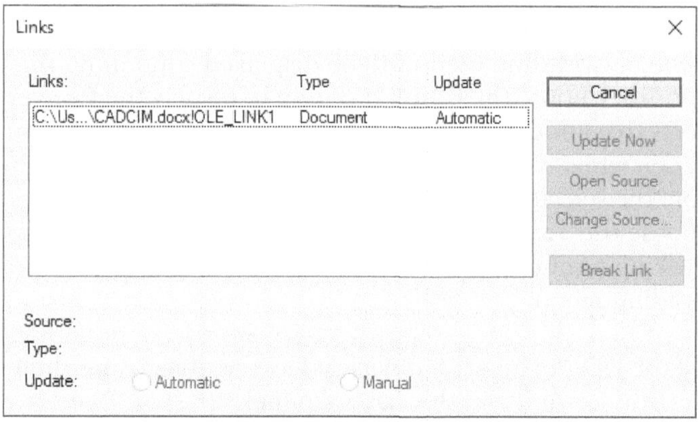

*Figure 21-28 The **Links** dialog box*

Embedding Objects into AutoCAD

Open the server application and select the data you want to embed into the AutoCAD drawing. Copy this data to the Clipboard by choosing the **Copy** tool in the toolbar or **Copy** from the **Edit** menu. Open the AutoCAD drawing and choose **Paste** from the AutoCAD **Edit** menu. You can also use the **PASTECLIP** command. Specify the insertion point; the selected information is embedded into the AutoCAD drawing.

You can also create and embed an object into an AutoCAD drawing. To do so, choose the **OLE Object** tool from the **Data** panel of the **Insert** tab; the **Insert Object** dialog box will be invoked. In this dialog box, select the **Create New** radio button and select the application you wish to use from the **Object Type** list box. Choose the **OK** button, the selected application opens. Now, you can create the information you wish to insert in the AutoCAD drawing and save it before closing the application. You can edit information embedded in the AutoCAD drawing by double-clicking on the inserted OLE object; the server application will open. The modifications made in the server application get automatically reflected in the AutoCAD drawing.

Working with OLE Objects

Select an OLE object and right-click to display a shortcut menu. Next, choose the **Properties** option from the shortcut menu; the **PROPERTIES** palette will be displayed. Specify a new height value and a new width value in the **Height** and **Width** edit boxes in the **Geometry** area. Enter a value in percentage of the current values in the **Scale height %** and **Scale width %** edit boxes. If you select the **Yes** option in the **Lock aspect** field, whenever you change the height or the width from the **Scale height %** and **Scale width %** edit boxes, the respective width or height changes automatically to maintain the aspect ratio. If you want to change only the height or the width, select **No** for this field.

The pointing device can be used to modify and scale an OLE object in the AutoCAD drawing. Selecting the object displays the object frame and handles. These handles allows you to move and stretch a frame. Stretching the object's frame does not scale objects proportionately.

Select an OLE object and right-click to display a shortcut menu. You can choose **Clipboard > Cut** to remove an object from a drawing and paste it on the Clipboard. The **Copy** option is used to place a copy of the selected object on the Clipboard. The **Erase** option is used to remove an object from a drawing but it does not place the object on the Clipboard. Choose the **OLE** option from the shortcut menu; a cascading menu will be displayed containing the **Open**, **Reset**, **Text Size**, and **Convert** options. Choose the **Convert** option to display the **Convert** dialog box where you can convert objects from one type to another. Choose the **Open** option to open an object in the Server application where you can edit and update it in the current drawing. Choose the **Reset** option to restore the selected OLE objects to their original size, that is, the size they were in when inserted. Choose the **Text Size** option to resize the text. You can set the draw order of the object by first invoking a shortcut menu and then choosing the corresponding option from the **Draw Order** cascading menu.

If you want to change the layer of an OLE object, select the object, and then select the required layer from the **Layer** drop-down list in the **Layers** panel.

The **OLEHIDE** system variable controls the display of OLE objects in AutoCAD. The default value is 0, which makes all OLE objects visible. The different values and their effects are as follows:

0 All OLE objects are visible
1 OLE objects are visible in paper space only
2 OLE objects are visible in model space only
3 No OLE objects are visible

The **OLEHIDE** system variable affects both screen display and printing.

Self-Evaluation Test

Answer the following questions and then compare them to those given at the end of this chapter:

1. You can import a DXB file into an AutoCAD drawing file by using the __________ command.

2. The __________ system variable controls the display of OLE objects in AutoCAD.

3. If you import a DXB file into an old drawing, the settings of layers, blocks, and so on of the file being imported are __________ by the settings of the file into which you are importing the DXB file.

4. The __________ is used as a medium of storing documents while transferring them from one Windows application to the other.

5. You can get an embedded drawing into the Server application directly from the container application by __________ on the drawing.

6. The **Copy** tool copies a drawing from the __________ to the Clipboard.

7. The DXF file format generates a text file in ASCII code. (T/F)

8. You can directly open a DXF file in AutoCAD by using the **Open** tool. (T/F)

9. An image attached to AutoCAD cannot be detached. (T/F)

10. A file in the container application is automatically modified only when a link is maintained between the server application and the container application. (T/F)

Review Questions

Answer the following questions:

1. Which of the following tools can be used to open a DXF format file?

   (a) **Open** (b) **New**
   (c) **Save** (d) None of these

2. Which of the following tools is used to add an image to the drawing as an external reference?

   (a) **Attach** (b) **Insert**
   (c) **Adjust** (d) **Create Block**

3. In which of the following panels, the options are used to modify the brightness of an image?

   (a) **Options** (b) **Visual Styles**
   (c) **Clipping** (d) **Adjust**

4. The __________ tool is used to modify frames by retaining only the desired portion of the images.

5. The __________ tool is used to create an ASCII format file with the *.dxf* extension from the AutoCAD drawing files.

6. Binary DXF files are __________ efficient and occupy only 75 percent of the ASCII DXF file.

7. File access for files in binary format is __________ than for the same file in ASCII format.

8. If the **OLEHIDE** system variable value is __________, the OLE objects are visible in the paper space only.

9. When you select an image file to attach, the __________ dialog box is displayed where you can define the insertion point, scale factor, and rotation angle for the image.

10. The clipping boundary for the raster images can be of __________ or the __________ shape.

11. In AutoCAD, you can clip the boundary of an image and give it the desired shape. (T/F)

12. The scanned files can be imported into the current session of AutoCAD using the **Attach** tool. (T/F)

13. You can export an AutoCAD drawing into 3D Studio MAX. (T/F)

14. Raster images can be attached using the **Attach** tool. (T/F)

Exercise 1

In this exercise, you will create a cup and a plate, refer to Figure 21-29 for dimensions. Assume the missing dimensions. Below the cup and plate, enter the following text in MS Word: **These objects are drawn in AutoCAD**. Then using OLE, paste the text into the current drawing.

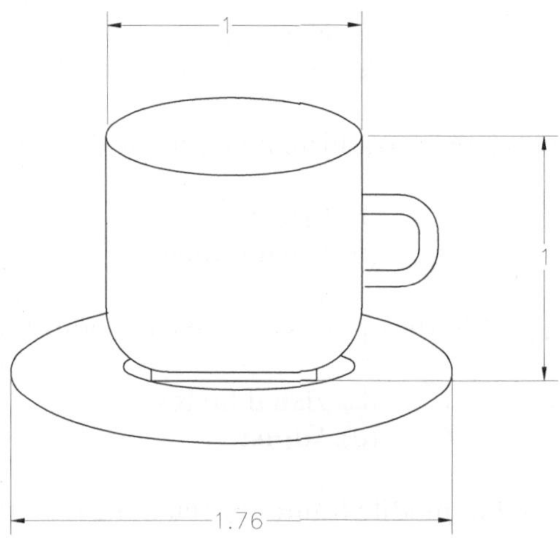

Figure 21-29 *Dimensions for Exercise 1*

Answers to Self-Evaluation Test

1. DXBIN, **2. OLEHIDE**, **3.** overruled, **4.** Clipboard, **5.** double-clicking, **6.** current display, **7.** T, **8.** T, **9.** F, **10.** T

Chapter 22

Conventional Dimensioning and Projection Theory Using AutoCAD

Learning Objectives

After completing this chapter, you will be able to:

- *Understand the dimensioning units*
- *Understand about basic dimensioning rules*
- *Understand the dimensioning of cylindrical features, holes, rounds, fillets, chamfers, and repetitive features*
- *Understand reference dimensions*
- *Understand working drawings, detail drawings, and assembly drawings*
- *Understand the arrangement of projected views*
- *Understand about the X, Y, and Z axes, the XY, YZ and XZ planes, and parallel planes*
- *Draw orthographic projections and position views*
- *Dimension a drawing*
- *Draw sectional views using different types of sections*
- *Hatch sectioned surfaces*
- *Use and draw auxiliary views*

Key Terms

- *Dimensioning Rules*
- *Reference Dimensions*
- *Cylindrical Features*
- *Dimensioning fillets and chamfers*
- *Dimensioning Components*
- *Detail Drawing*
- *Assembly Drawing*
- *Bill of Materials*
- *Full Section*
- *Half Section*
- *Broken Section*
- *Revolved Section*
- *Offset Section*
- *Aligned Section*
- *Hatch Lines*
- *Auxiliary Views*

DIMENSIONING

Dimensioning is one of the most important elements in a drawing. When you dimension a drawing, you not only provide information of the size of a part, but also a series of instructions to a machinist, an engineer, or an architect. The way the part is positioned in a machine, the sequence of machining operations, and the location of different features of the part depend on how you dimension it. For example, the number of decimal places in a dimension (2.000) determines the type of machine to be used for the machining operation. The machining cost of such an operation is significantly higher than those that have dimension upto only one digit after the decimal (2.0). If you are using a computer numerical control (CNC) machine, then locating a feature may not be a problem, but the number of pieces that you can machine without changing the tool depends on the tolerance assigned to a dimension. A closer tolerance (+.0001, -.0005) will definitely increase the tooling cost and ultimately the cost of the product. Similarly, if a part is to be forged or cast, the radius of the edges and the tolerance you provide to these dimensions determine the cost of the product, the number of defective parts, and the number of parts you get from the die.

While dimensioning, you must consider the manufacturing process involved in making a part and the relationships that exist among different parts in an assembly. If you are not familiar with any operation, get help. You must not assume things when dimensioning or making a piece part drawing. The success of a product, to a large extent, depends on the way you dimension a part. Therefore, never underestimate the importance of dimensioning in a drawing.

DIMENSION UNITS

Generally, metric system of dimensioning is considered as the official standard of measurement for engineering drawings, but most of the drawings in North America are still dimensioned in decimal inches. So, you should be familiar with all dimensioning systems that are used in the interpretation of an engineering drawing. The dimensions used in this book are primarily decimal inch. However, metric dimensions are used very frequently. To make information more clear, engineering drawings should contain one of the following notes:

- Unless Otherwise Specified, All Dimensions Are in Millimeters
- Unless Otherwise Specified, All Dimensions Are in Inches

The Inch and Metric unit system is discussed next.

Inch Units

An inch is a unit of length in the imperial and United States customary systems of measurement. Historically, an inch was also used in a number of other systems of units. Traditional standards for the exact length of an inch have varied in the past, but since July 1959, when the international yard was defined as 0.9144 metres, the international inch has been exactly 25.4 mm. There are 12 inches in a foot and 36 inches in a yard.

The Decimal-Inch System

In the Decimal-Inch system, the parts are designed in basic decimal increments (preferably .02 inch) and the values are expressed as two numbers after the decimal, as shown in Figure 22-1. Using the .02 value as the increment the second value after the decimal will be an even number or zero. In some cases to meet the design requirements you can also use the values other than the increment of .02 inch, such as .25 inch or .29 inch. Whenever greater accuracy is required, the dimensions are expressed as values upto three or four decimal places, such as 1.6587 or 5.9876. In Decimal-Inch dimensioning system, the numbers to the right of the decimal point indicate the degree of precision. For the dimensions less than 1 there will not be a zero before the decimal point.

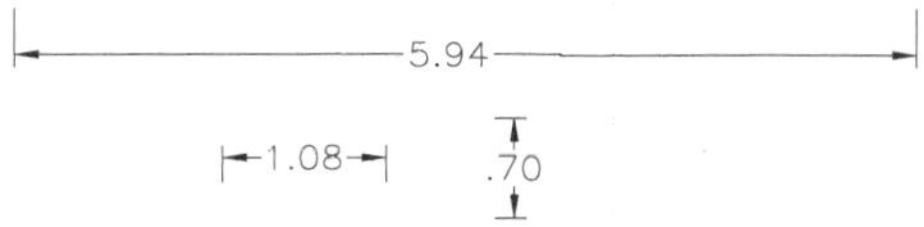

Figure 22-1 *Dimensions in the Decimal-Inch system*

The Fractional-Inch System

In the Fractional-Inch system, the parts are designed in common fractions, refer to Figure 22-2. The smallest fraction used is 1/64th of an inch. Sizes other than common fractions are expressed as decimals. This system of dimensioning was replaced by the Decimal-Inch dimensioning system of engineering drawings over 50 years ago. But, you should be aware of this unit system because some tools like drills, reamers, and pipes are being manufactured using Fraction-Inch system.

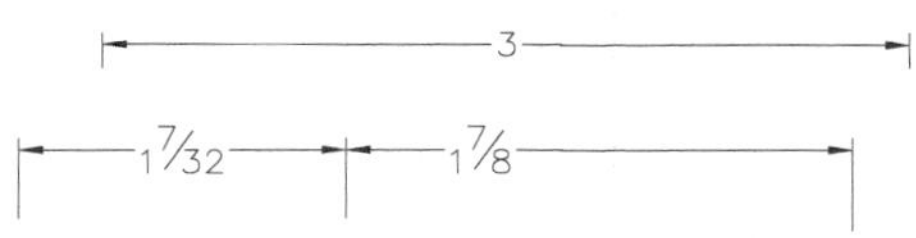

Figure 22-2 *Dimensions in the Fractional-Inch system*

SI (Metric) Units

The standard metric units used in an engineering drawing are the millimeters for linear measurements and the micrometers for surface roughness, refer to Figure 22-3. In the metric system of dimensioning, the numbers to the right of the decimal point indicate the degree of precision. Whole dimensions in a drawing do not require a zero to the right of the decimal point. For example, the dimension of 5 mm will be expressed as 5 not 5.0, unless and until the part to be manufactured requires that specific precision. For expressing large dimensions a space should be used to separate groups of three numbers in metric values, such as 54 487 or 4.524 47.

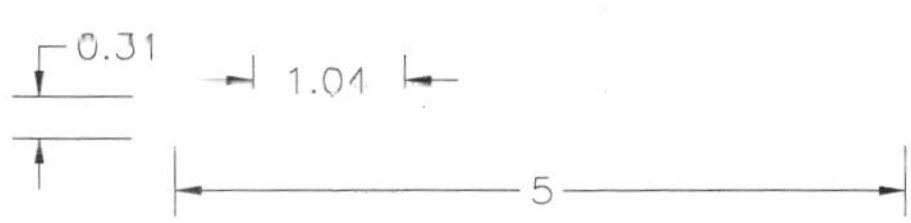

Figure 22-3 *Dimensions in the Metric (Millimeters) system*

DIMENSIONING COMPONENTS

A dimension consists of the following components, refer to Figure 22-4:

- Extension line
- Arrows or tick marks
- Dimension line
- Leader lines
- Dimension text

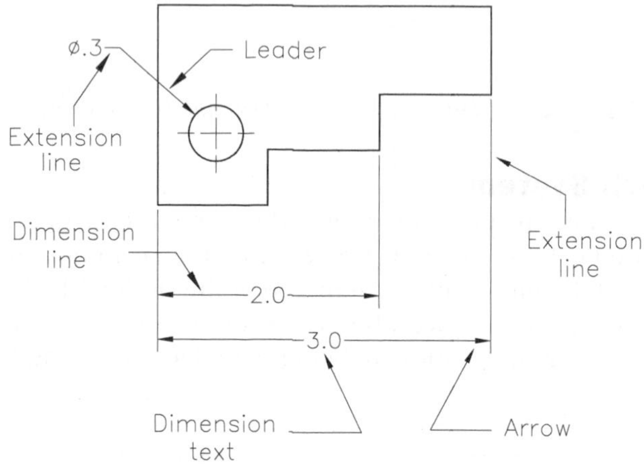

***Figure 22-4** Dimensioning components*

The extension lines are drawn to extend the points that are dimensioned. The length of the extension lines is determined by the number of dimensions and the placement of the dimension lines. These lines are generally drawn perpendicular to the surface. The dimension lines are drawn between the extension lines at a specified distance from the object lines. The dimension text is a numerical value that represents the distance between the points. The dimension text can also consist of a variable (A, B, X, Y, Z12,...). In such a case, the value assigned to it is defined in a separate table. The dimension text can be centered around or on the top of the dimension line. Arrows or tick marks are drawn at the end of the dimension line to indicate the start and end of the dimension. Leaders are used for dimensioning a circle, arc, or any nonlinear element of a drawing. They are also used to attach a note to a feature or to give the part numbers in an assembly drawing.

COMMON RULES FOR DIMENSIONING

1. Place dimensions in the view that best shows the shape of the object, refer to Figure 22-5. Sometimes dimensions can placed between views according to the availability of space between the views.

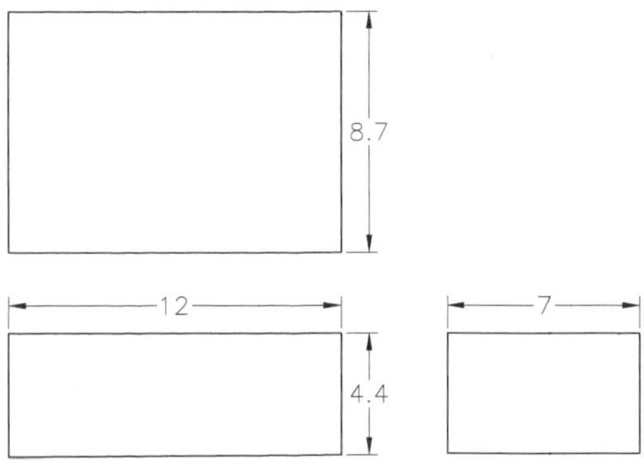

Figure 22-5 *Dimensions placed in appropriate views*

2. Place dimensions between the views when possible, refer to Figure 22-6.

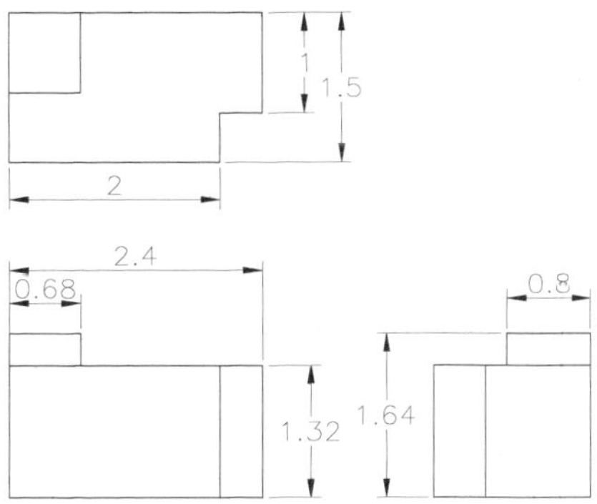

Figure 22-6 *Place dimensions between views*

3. You should make the dimensions in a separate layer/layers. This makes it easy to edit or control the display of dimensions (freeze, thaw, lock, and unlock). Also, the dimension layer/layers should be assigned a unique color so that at the time of plotting, you can assign the desired pen to plot the dimensions. This helps in controlling the line width and the contrast of dimensions at the time of plotting.

4. The distance of the first dimension line should be at least 0.375 units (10 units for metric drawing) from the object line. In CAD drawing, this distance may be 0.75 to 1.0 units (19 to 25 units for metric drawings). Once you decide on the spacing, it should be maintained throughout the drawing.

5. The distance between the first dimension line and the second dimension line must be at least 0.25 unit. In CAD drawings, this distance may be 0.25 to 0.5 unit (6 to 12 units for metric drawings). If there are more dimension lines (parallel dimensions), the distances between them must be the same (0.25 to 0.5 unit). Once you decide on the spacing (0.25 to 0.5), the same spacing should be maintained throughout the drawing. An appropriate snap setting is useful for maintaining this space. If you are using baseline dimensioning, you can use AutoCAD's **DIMDLI** variable to set the spacing. The dimensions must be placed in such a way so that they are not crowded, especially when there is not much space, refer to Figure 22-7.

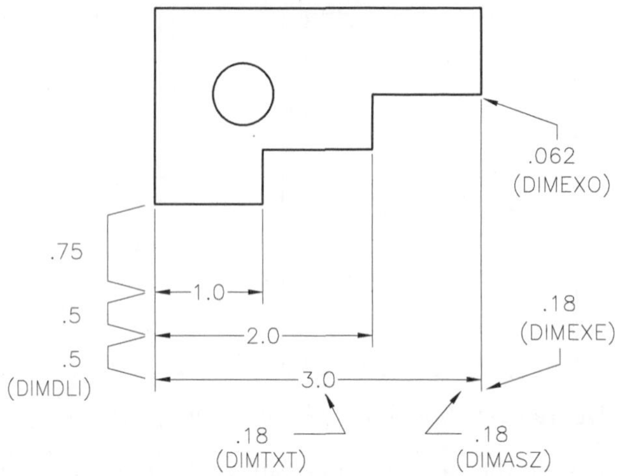

Figure 22-7 *Arrow size, text height, and spacing between dimension lines*

6. For parallel dimension lines, the dimension text can be staggered if there is not enough room between the dimension lines to place the dimension text. You can use the AutoCAD Object Grips feature or the **DIMTEDIT** command to stagger the dimension text, refer to Figure 22-8.

7. All dimensions should be given outside the view. However, the dimensions can be shown inside the view if they can be easily understood there and cause no confusion with the other dimensions or details, refer to Figure 22-9. In case of large drawings, dimensions can be placed on the view to improve clarity.

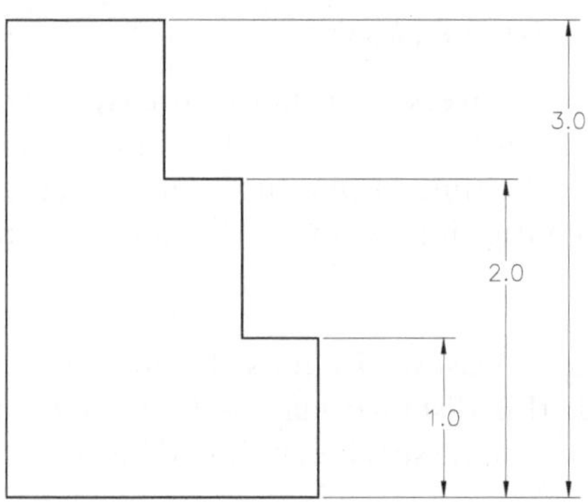

Figure 22-8 *Staggered dimensions*

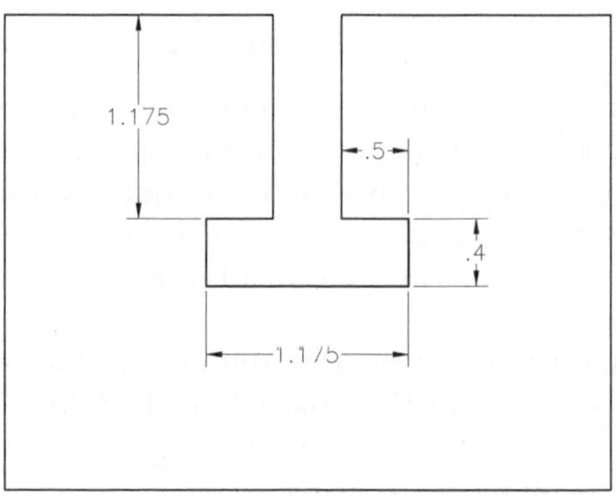

Figure 22-9 *Dimensions inside the view*

8. Dimension lines should not cross the extension lines, refer to Figure 22-10. You can accomplish this by giving the smallest dimension first and then the next largest dimension, refer to Figure 22-11.

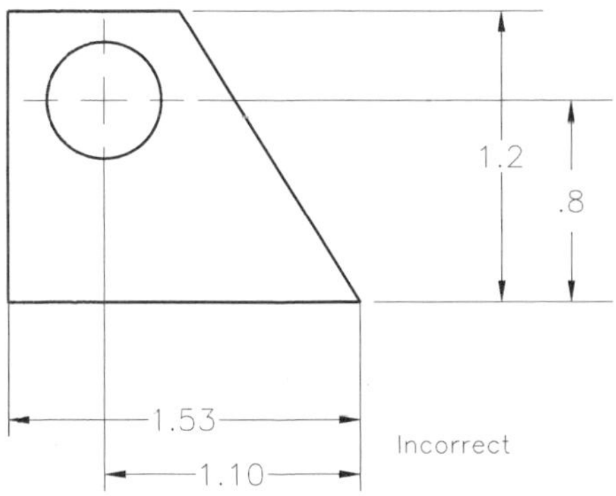

Figure 22-10 Dimensions placed incorrectly

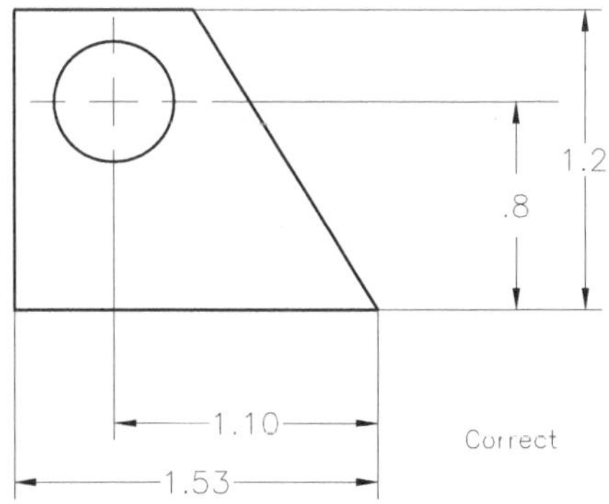

Figure 22-11 Dimensions placed correctly

9. If you decide to have the dimension text aligned with the dimension line, then the entire dimension text in the drawing must be aligned, refer to Figure 22-12. Similarly, if you decide to have the dimension text horizontal or above the dimension line, then to maintain uniformity in the drawing, the entire dimension text must be horizontal, refer to Figure 22-13 or above the dimension line, refer to Figure 22-14.

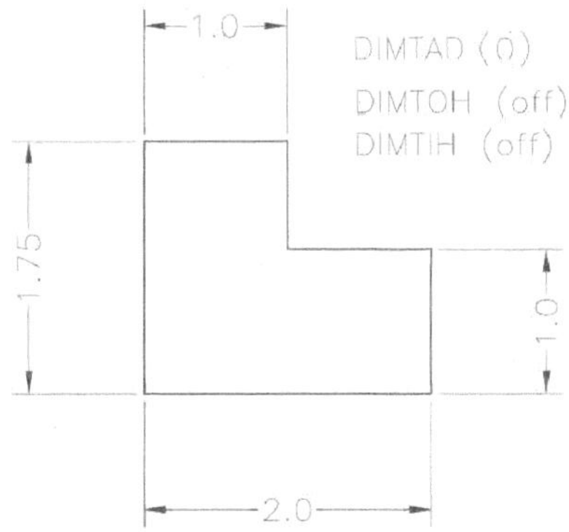

Figure 22-12 Dimension text aligned with the dimension line

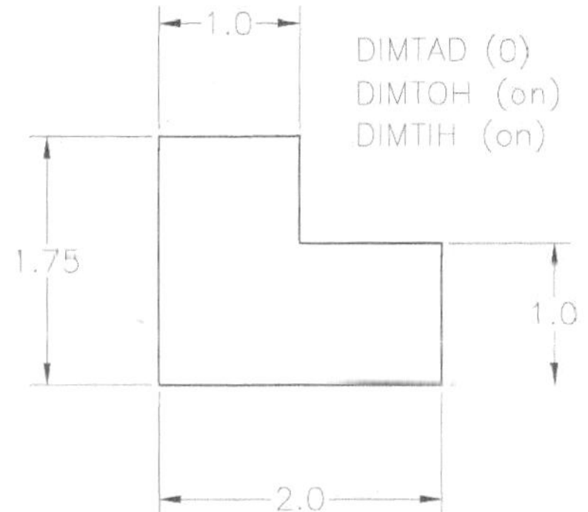

Figure 22-13 Horizontal dimension text

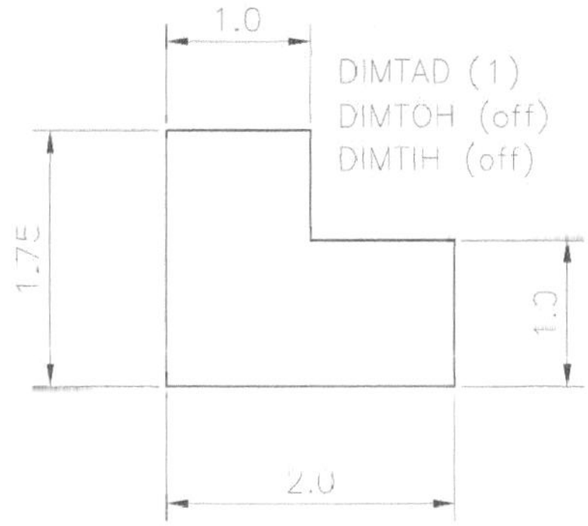

Figure 22-14 Dimension text above the dimension line

10. If you have a series of continuous dimensions, they should be placed in a continuous line, refer to Figure 22-15. Sometimes you may not be able to apply the dimensions in a continuous line even after adjusting the dimension variables. In that case, apply the dimensions that are parallel, refer to Figure 22-16.

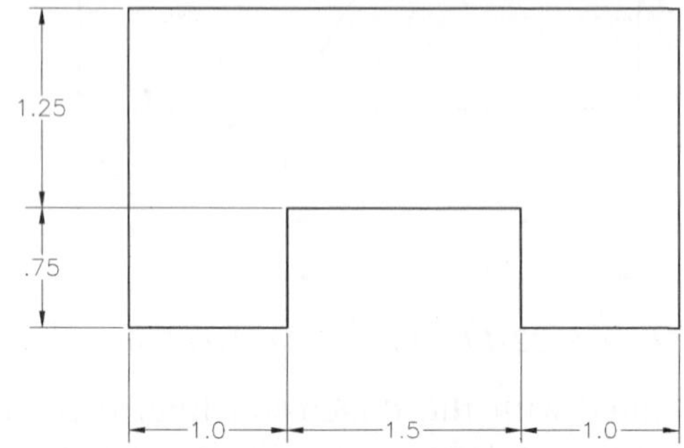

Figure 22-15 Continuous dimensions

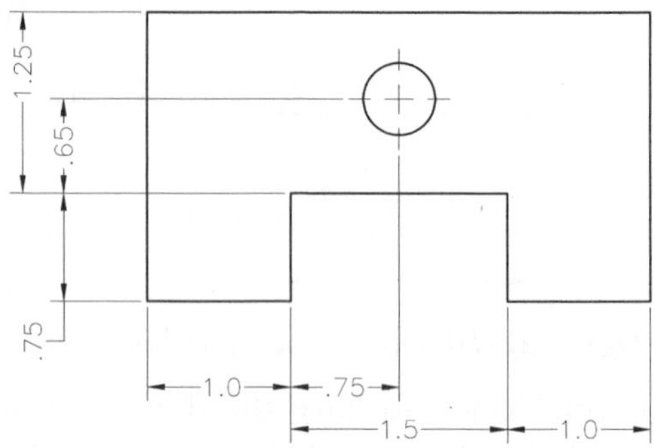

Figure 22-16 Parallel dimensions

11. You should not dimension with the hidden lines. The dimension should be given where the feature is visible, refer to Figure 22-17. However, in some complicated drawings, you might be justified to dimension a detail with a hidden line.

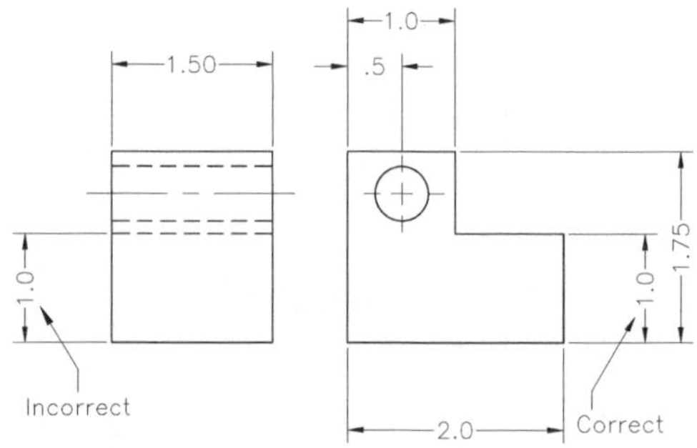

Figure 22-17 Undimensioned hidden lines

12. The dimensions must be given where the feature that you are dimensioning is obvious and shows the contour of the feature, refer to Figure 22-18.

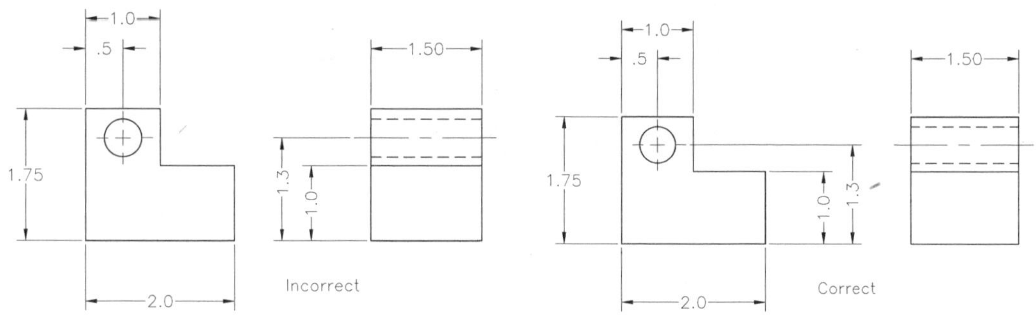

Figure 22-18 Dimensions given where they are obvious

13. The dimensions must not be repeated, as shown in Figure 22-19, as it makes difficult to update them.

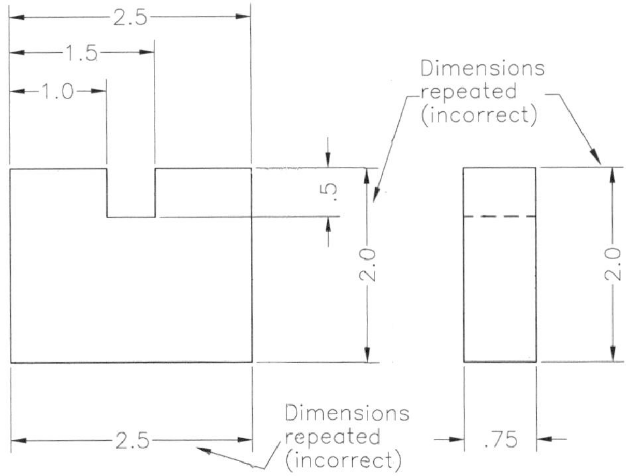

Figure 22-19 *Incorrect method of dimensioning*

14. The dimensions must be given depending on how the part will be machined, and also on the relationship that exists between the different features of the part, refer to Figure 22-20.

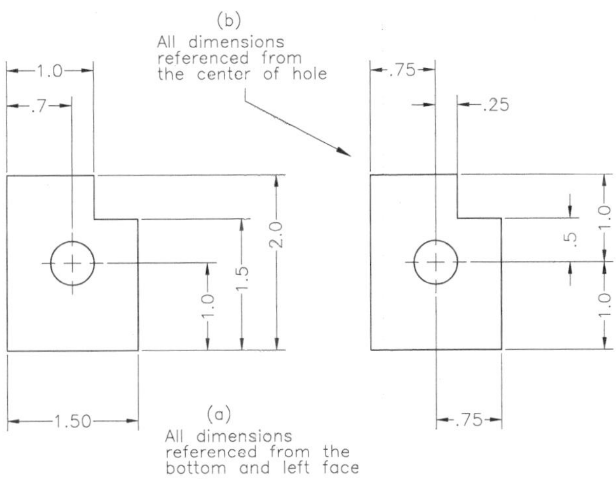

Figure 22-20 *Different dimensioning styles*

15. The dimensions enclosed in parenthesis can be identified as reference dimensions, refer to Figure 22-21. A reference dimension is placed on a drawing for information purpose only. Reference dimensions are not used for manufacturing of the part therefore it must be clearly labeled. Previously, reference dimensions were identified by placing the abbreviation REF after or below the dimension.

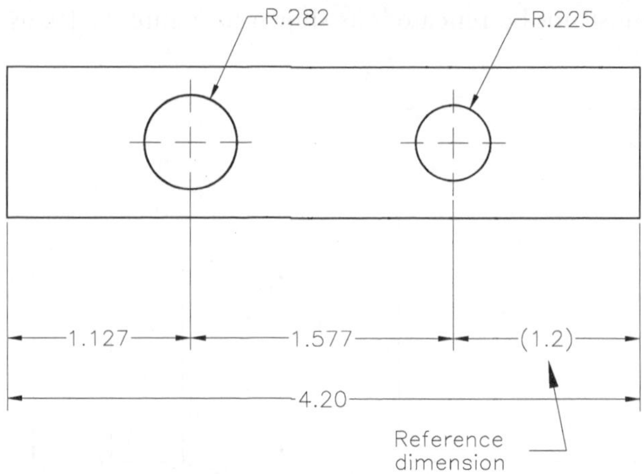

Figure 22-21 *Reference dimension marked in parenthesis*

16. If you give continuous (incremental) dimensions for dimensioning various features of a part, the overall dimension must be omitted or given as a reference dimension, refer to Figure 22-22. Similarly, if you give the overall dimension, one of the continuous (incremental) dimensions must be omitted or given as a reference dimension. Otherwise, there will be a conflict in tolerances. For example, the total positive tolerance on the three incremental dimensions shown in Figure 22-22 is 0.06. Therefore, the maximum size based on the incremental dimensions is (1 + 0.02) + (1 + 0.02) + (1 + 0.02) = 3.06. Also, the positive tolerance on the overall 3.0 dimension is 0.02. Based on this dimension, the overall size of the part must not exceed 3.02. This causes a conflict in tolerances with incremental dimensions because the total tolerance is 0.06, whereas with the overall dimension, the total tolerance is only 0.02.

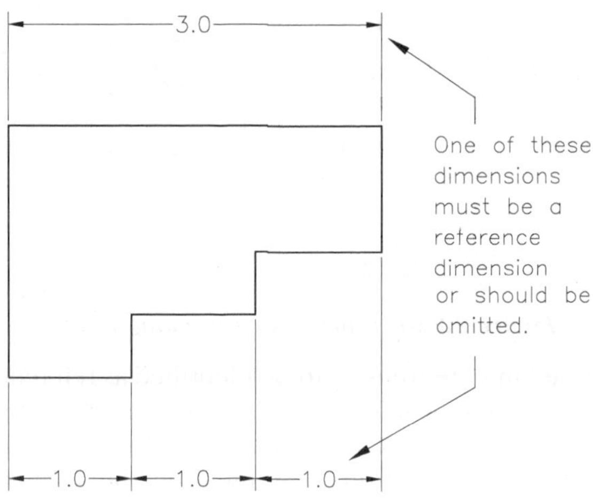

Figure 22-22 *Referencing or omitting a dimension*

17. If the dimension of a feature appears in a section view, you must not hatch the dimension text, refer to Figure 22-23. You can accomplish this task by selecting the dimension object while defining the hatch boundary. You can also accomplish this by drawing a rectangle

around the dimension text and then hatching the area after excluding the rectangle from the hatch boundary.

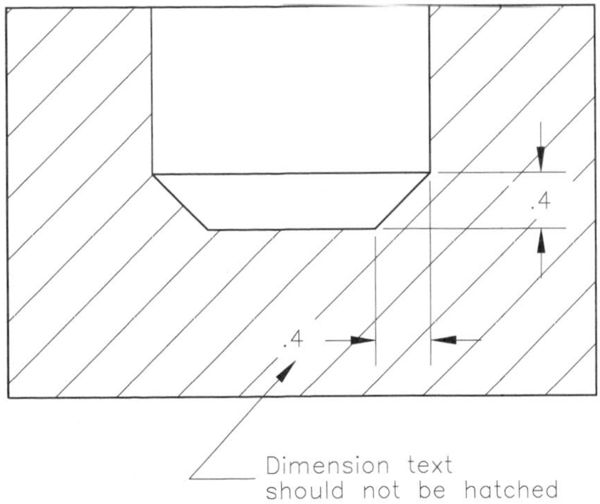

***Figure 22-23** Dimension text excluded from hatching*

18. While dimensioning a circle, the diameter should be preceded by the diameter symbol, refer to Figure 22-24. AutoCAD automatically puts the diameter symbol in front of the diameter value. However, if you override the default diameter value, you can use %%c followed by the value of the diameter (%%c1.00) to put the diameter symbol before the diameter dimension.

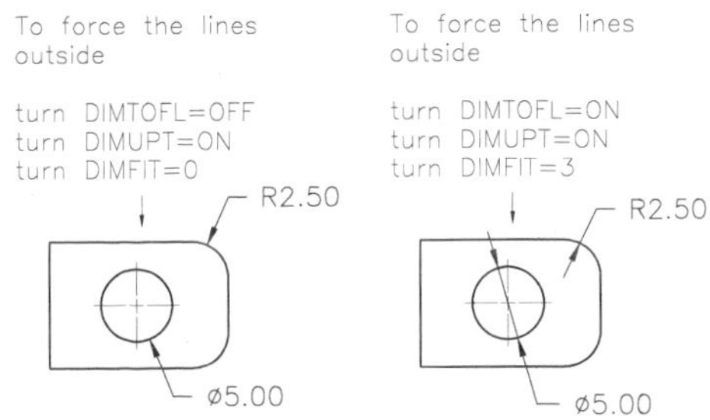

***Figure 22-24** Diameter should be preceded by the diameter symbol*

19. Cylindrical features should be dimensioned by the method shown in Figure 22-25. The circle must be dimensioned as a diameter, never as a radius. Where the diameters of a number of concentric cylinders are to be given, they must be shown on the end view, refer to Figure 22-26.

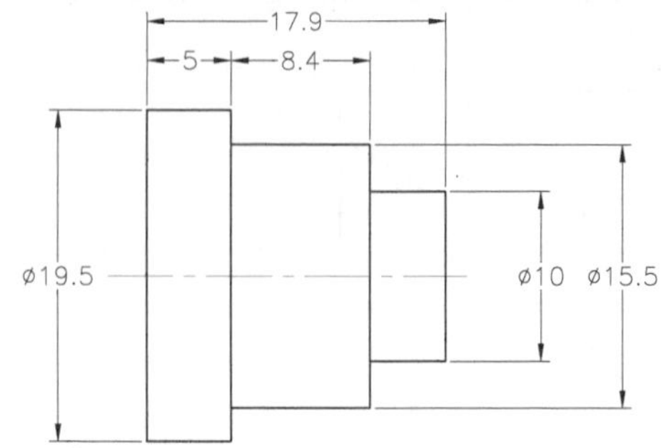

Figure 22-25 Dimensioning of cylindrical features

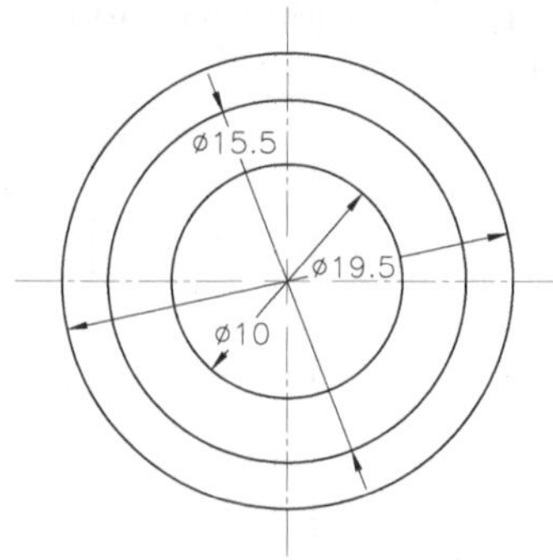

Figure 22-26 Dimensioning diameters on end view

20. For dimensioning a circular arc, letter R is added before the radius dimension, as shown in Figure 22-27. Also, the center of the arc should be indicated by a small cross. You can use the **DIMCEN** variable in AutoCAD to control the size of the cross. If the value of this variable is 0, AutoCAD does not draw the cross in the center when you dimension an arc or a circle.

21. The preferred method for designating the size of holes is shown in Figure 22–28. While dimensioning a hole feature a leader is used and the symbol Ø precedes the size of the hole. When two or more holes of the same size are required, the number of holes is specified. If a blind hole is required, the depth of the hole is specified by the depth symbol in the dimensioning note; otherwise, it is assumed that all holes shown are through holes. The degree of accuracy to which a hole is to be machined is specified on the drawing. The use of operational names such as *turn, bore, grind, ream, tap*, and *thread* with dimensions should be avoided.

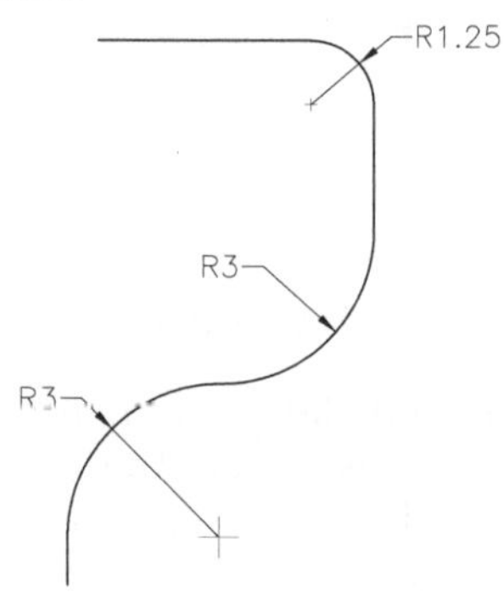

Figure 22-27 Dimensioning of arcs

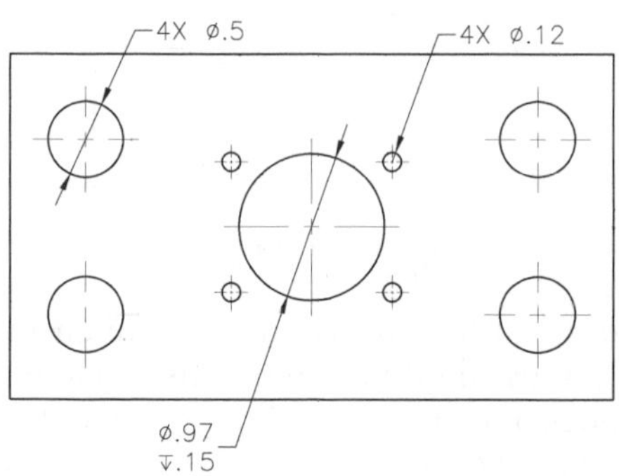

Figure 22-28 Dimensioning of holes

22. A dimension that is not to be scaled should be indicated by drawing a straight line under the dimension text, refer to Figure 22-29. This line can be drawn by using the **TEXTEDIT** command. If you invoke this command, AutoCAD will prompt you to select an annotative object. Select the object; the **Text Editor** will be displayed and a new **Text Editor** tab will be added to the **Ribbon**. Select the text (< >), and then choose the **U** button in the **Formatting** panel of the **Text Editor** tab to underline the text.

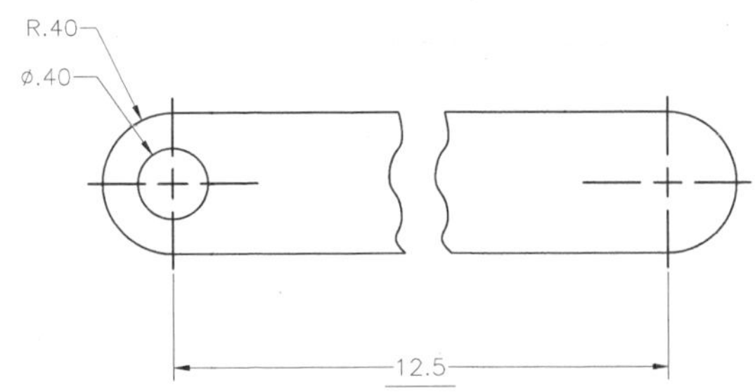

Figure 22-29 Specifying dimension that is not to be scaled

Dimensioning of Rounds, Fillets, and Chamfers

A round, or radius, or chamfer is applied on the outer surface of a part to improve its appearance and to avoid formation of a sharp edge that might chip off under a sharp blow or cause interference. It is also a safety feature. In a fillet, additional material is allowed in the inner intersection of two surfaces, as shown in Figure 22-30. If all the fillets and rounds have equal dimension then a general note, such as ROUNDS AND FILLETS R10 or ROUNDS AND FILLETS R10 UNLESS OTHERWISE SPECIFIED, is normally used on the drawing instead of placing individual dimensions.

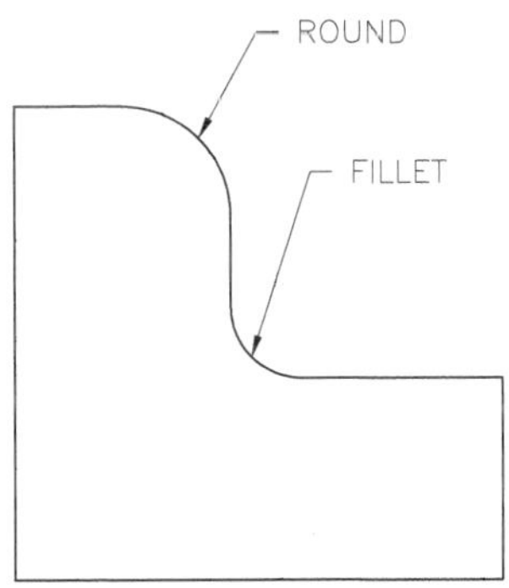

Figure 22-30 Fillets and rounds

A chamfer can be dimensioned by specifying the chamfer angle and the distance of the chamfer from the edge. It can also be dimensioned by specifying the distances, as shown in Figure 22-31.

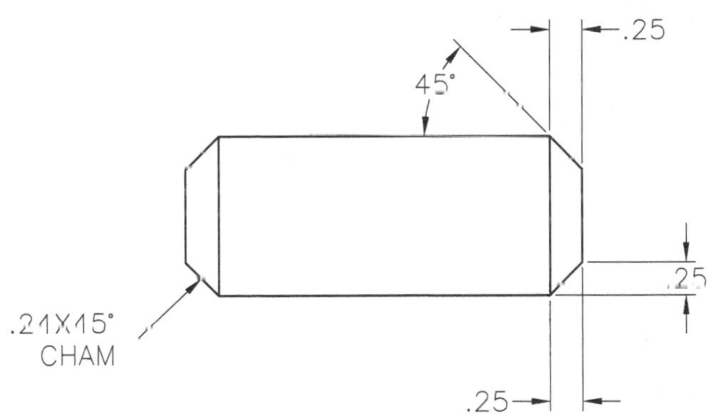

Figure 22-31 Different ways of specifying a chamfer

Dimensioning of Repetitive Features

Repetitive features and dimensions may be specified on a drawing by the use of an X preceded by the number to indicate the "number of times" or "places" for which they are required. A space is inserted between X and the specified dimension, as shown in Figure 22-32. If there are similar repetitive features of different sizes, some other form of indication may be required in order to ensure the legibility of drawing, as shown in Figure 22-33.

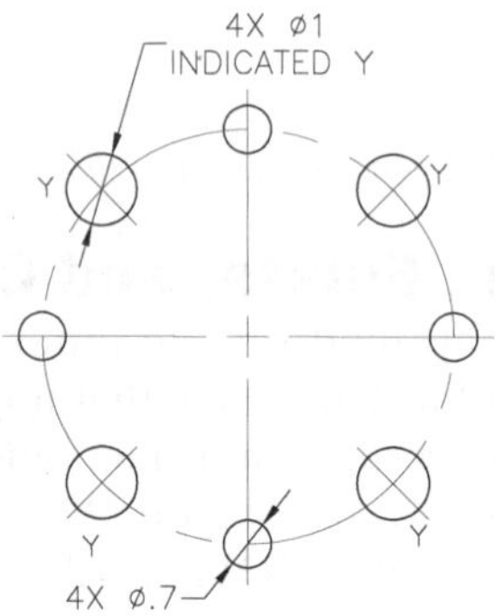

Figure 22-32 Dimensioning of repetitive features with different sizes

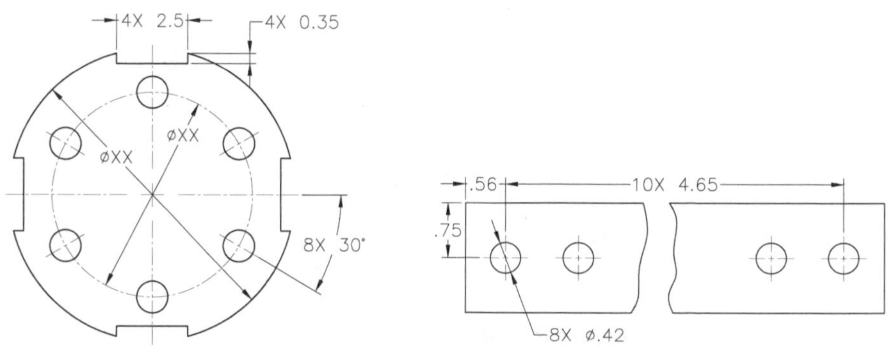

Figure 22-33 Dimensioning of repetitive features

WORKING DRAWINGS

A working drawing is a drawing that provides information and instructions for the manufacturing or construction of parts, machines, or structures. A working drawing is intended to provide the description about shape, dimensions or size, and specifications of the product. Because working drawings may be sent to another plant, another company, or even to another country to manufacture, construct, or assemble the final product, the drawing should qualify the drawing standards of the respective plant, company, or country.

Generally, working drawings are classified into two groups:

Detail Drawing

A detail drawing is the drawing of a single part that includes a complete and exact description of its form and shape. Detail drawings provide necessary information for manufacturing of parts for some specific product or structure, refer to Figure 22-34. Each detail drawing must be drawn and dimensioned to completely describe the size and shape of the part. It should also contain information that might be needed in manufacturing the part. The finished surfaces and all the necessary operations should be indicated by using symbols or notes on the drawing. The material of which the part is made and the number of parts that are required for the production of the assembled product must be given in the title block. Detail drawings should also contain part numbers. This information is used in the bill of materials and the assembly drawing. The part numbers make it easier to locate the drawing of a part. Regardless of the part's size, you should make a detail drawing of each part on a separate drawing. When required, these detail drawings can be inserted in the assembly drawing by using the **External References** tool from the **Reference** panel of the **Insert** tab.

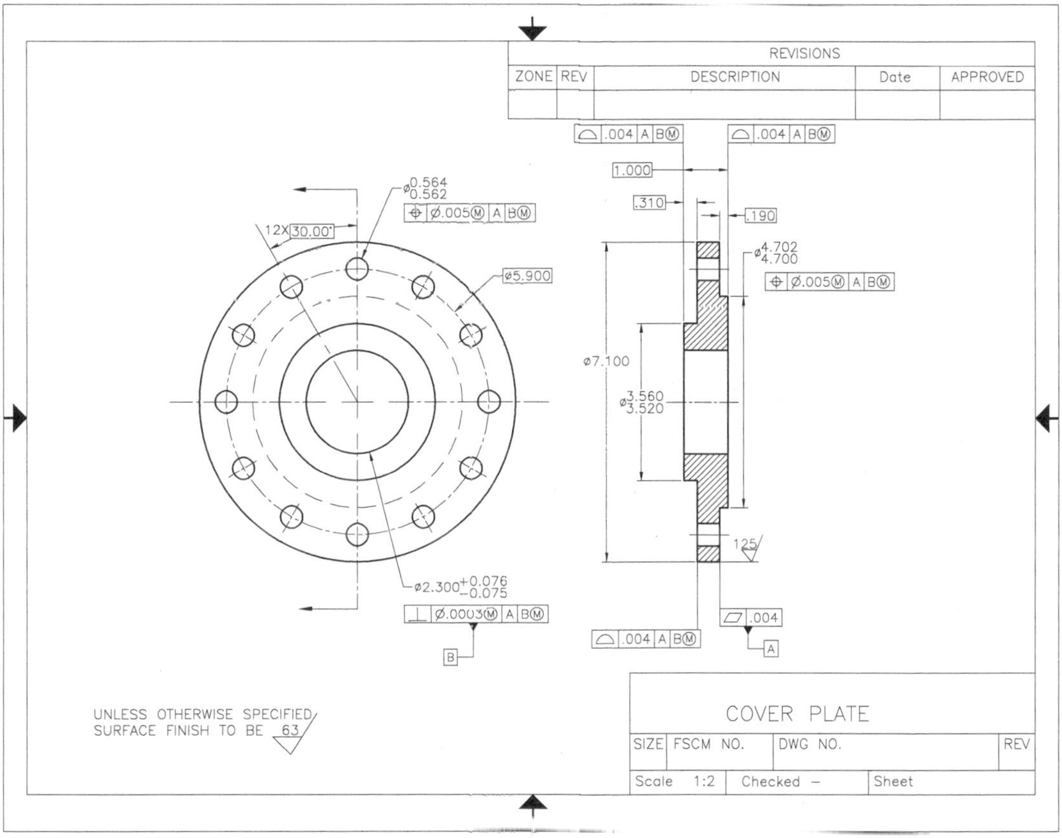

Figure 22-34 Detail drawing of Cover Plate

Assembly Drawing

An assembly drawing is the presentation of a product or structure put together, showing all parts in their operational positions. These drawings provide necessary information about the assembly of parts and structures, refer to Figure 22-35. Assembly drawings may include instructions, lists of component parts, reference numbers, references to detail drawings or shop drawings, and specifications. The main view may be drawn in full section so that the assembly drawing shows nearly all the individual parts and their locations. Additional views should be drawn only when some of the parts cannot be seen in the main view. The hidden lines, as far as possible, should be omitted from the assembly drawing because they clutter it and might cause confusion. However, a hidden line may be drawn if it helps to understand the product. Only assembly dimensions should be shown in the assembly drawing. Each part can be identified on the assembly drawing by the number used in the detail drawing and in the bill of materials. The part numbers should be given as shown in Figure 22-35. A part number consists of a text string for the detail number, a circle (balloon), a leader line, and an arrow or dot. The text should be made at least 0.2 inches (5 mm) high and enclosed in a 0.4 inch (10 mm) circle (balloon). The center of the circle must be located not less than 0.8 inches (20 mm) from the nearest line on the drawing. Also, the leader line should be radial with respect to the circle (balloon). The assembly drawing may also contain an exploded isometric or isometric view of the assembled unit.

BILL OF MATERIALS

A bill of materials is a list of parts placed on an assembly drawing just above the title block. The bill of materials contains the part number, part description, material, quantity required, and drawing numbers of the detail drawings, refer to Figure 22-35. If the bill of materials is placed above the title block, the parts should be listed in ascending order so that the first part is at the bottom of the table. The bill of materials may also be placed at the top of the drawing. In that case, the parts must be listed in descending order with the first part at the top of the table. This structure allows room for any additional items that may be added to the list.

MULTIVIEW DRAWINGS

When designers design a product, they visualize its shape in their minds. To represent that shape on paper or to communicate the idea to people, they must draw a picture of the product or its orthographic views. Pictorial drawings, such as isometric drawings, convey the shape of the object, but it is difficult to show all features and dimensions in an isometric drawing. Therefore, in industry, multiview drawings are the accepted standards for representing products. Multiview drawings are also known as orthographic projection drawings. To draw different views of an object, it is very important to visualize the shape of the product. The same is true when you look at different views of an object to determine its shape. To facilitate visualizing the shapes, you must picture the object in 3D space with reference to the *X*, *Y*, and *Z* axes. These reference axes can then be used to project the image into different planes. This process of visualizing objects with reference to different axes is, to some extent, natural in human beings. You might have noticed that sometimes, when looking at objects that are at an angle, people tilt their heads. This is a natural reaction, an effort to position the object with respect to an imaginary reference frame (*X*, *Y*, and *Z* axes).

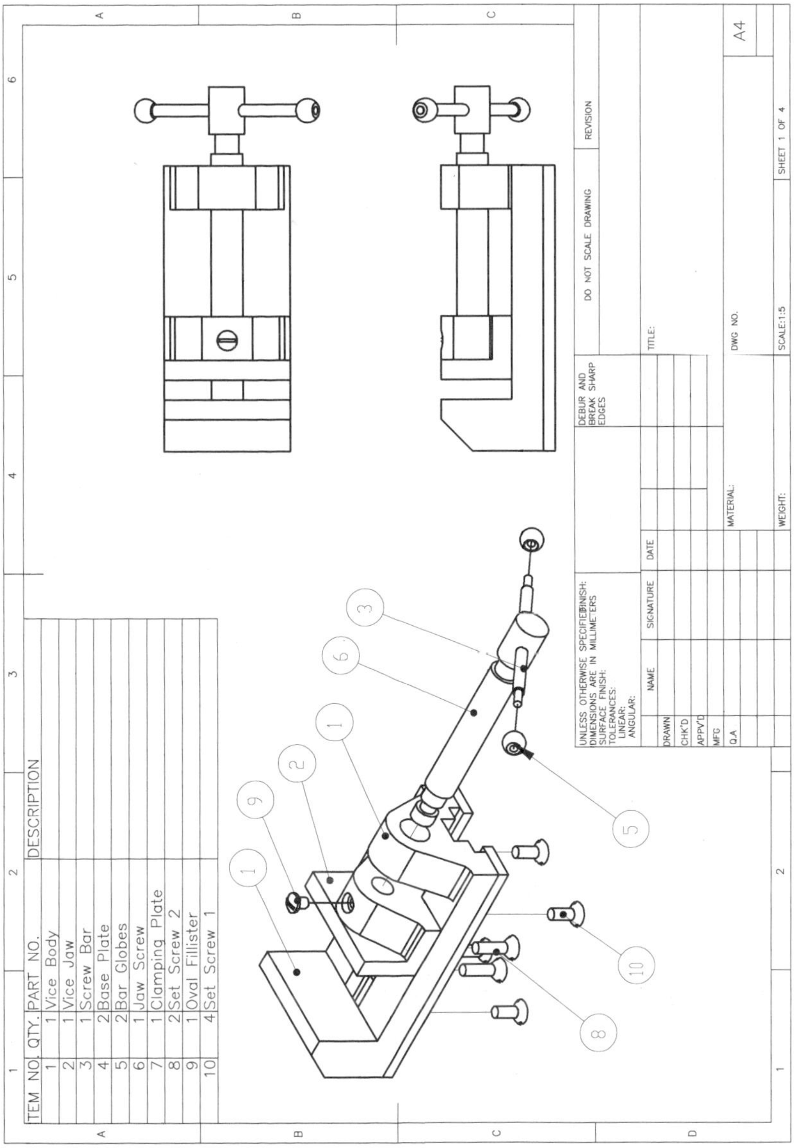

***Figure 22-35** Assembly drawing with title block and bill of materials*

UNDERSTANDING THE X, Y, AND Z AXES

To understand the *X*, *Y*, and *Z* axes, imagine a flat sheet of paper on the table. The horizontal edge represents the positive *X* axis, and the other edge along the width of the sheet, represents the positive *Y* axis. The point where these two axes intersect is the origin. Now, if you draw a line perpendicular to the sheet passing through the origin, the line defines the positive *Z* axis, refer to Figure 22-36. If you project the *X*, *Y*, and *Z* axes in the opposite direction beyond the origin, you will get the negative *X*, *Y*, and *Z* axes, refer to Figure 22-37.

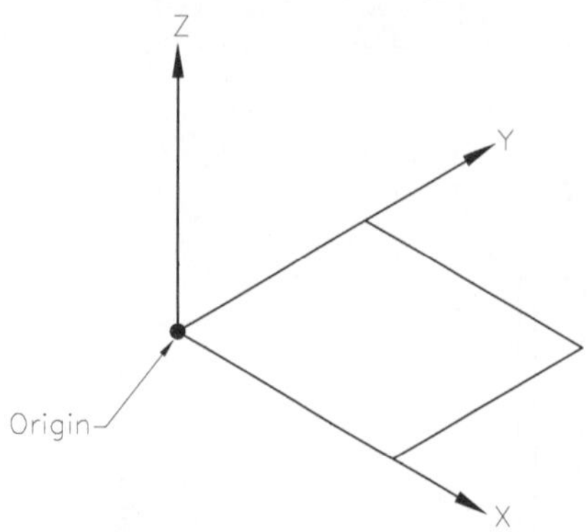

Figure 22-36 X, Y, and Z axes

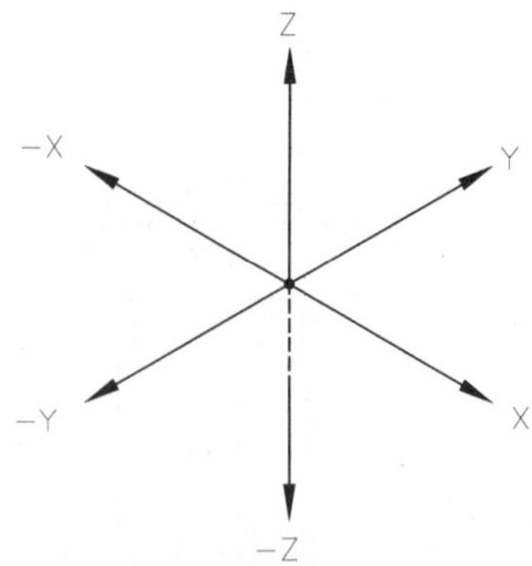

Figure 22-37 Positive and negative axes

The space between the *X* and *Y* axes is called the *XY* plane. Similarly, the space between the *Y* and *Z* axes is called the *YZ* plane, and the space between the *X* and *Z* axes is called the *XZ* plane, refer to Figure 22-38. A plane parallel to these planes is called a parallel plane, refer to Figure 22-39.

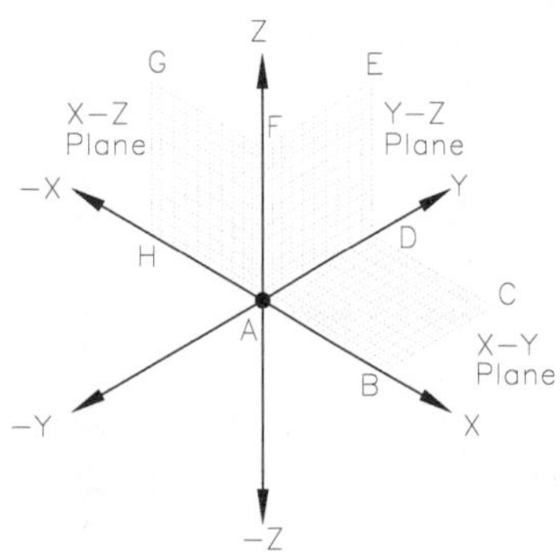

Figure 22-38 XY, YZ, and XZ planes

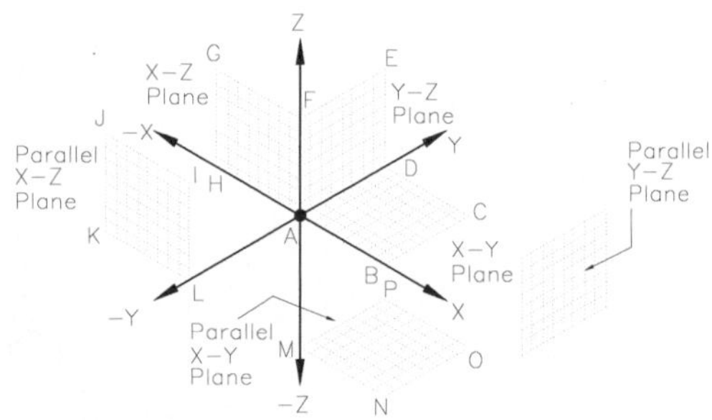

Figure 22-39 Parallel planes

ORTHOGRAPHIC PROJECTIONS

The first step in drawing an orthographic projection is to position the object along the imaginary *X*, *Y*, and *Z* axes. For example, if you want to draw orthographic projections of the step block shown in Figure 22-40, position the block such that the far left corner coincides with the origin, and then align it with the *X*, *Y*, and *Z* axes.

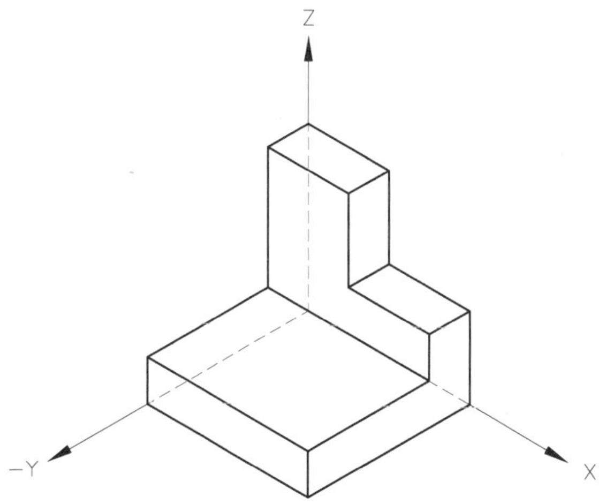

Figure 22-40 *Aligning the object with the X, Y, and Z axes*

Now, you can look at the object from different directions. Looking at the object along the negative *Y* axis and toward the origin is called the front view. Similarly, looking at it from the positive X direction is called the right side view. To get the top view, you can look at the object from the positive *Z* axis, refer to Figure 22-41.

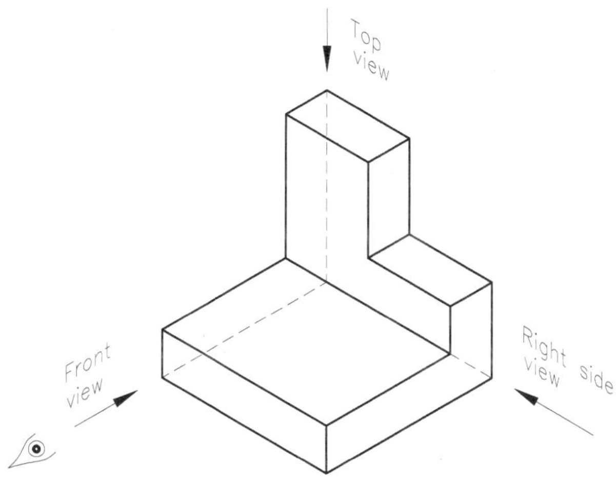

Figure 22-41 *Viewing directions for Front, Side, and Top views*

To draw the front, side, and top views, project the points onto the parallel planes. For example, to draw the front view of the step block, imagine a plane parallel to the *XZ* plane located at a certain distance in front of the object. Now, project the points from the object onto the parallel plane, refer to Figure 22-42, and join them to complete the front view.

Repeat the same process for the side and top views. To represent these views on paper, position them, as shown in Figure 22-43.

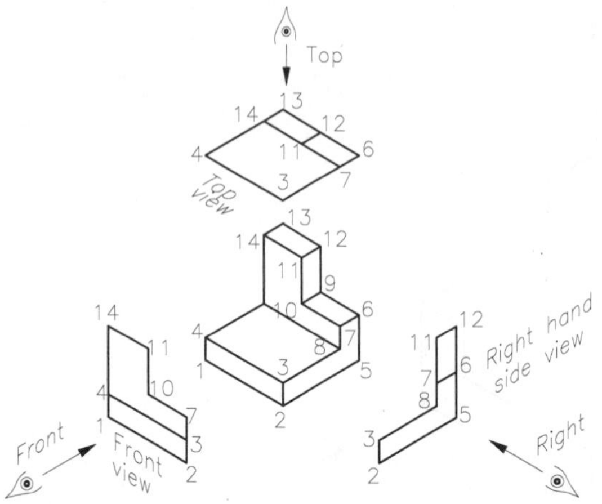

Figure 22-42 *Projecting points onto parallel planes*

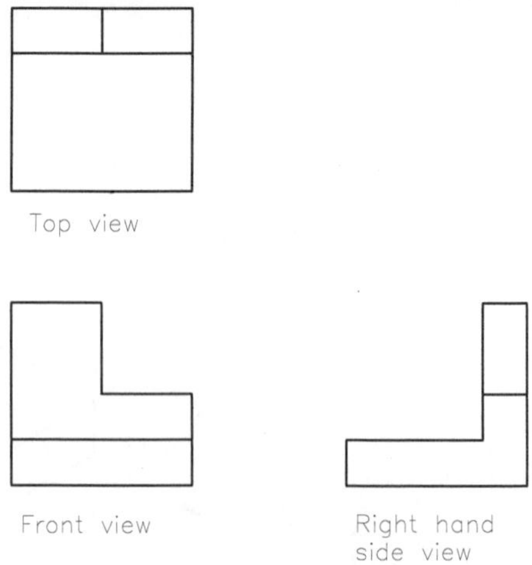

Figure 22-43 *Representing views on paper*

Another way of visualizing different views is to imagine the object enclosed in a glass box, refer to Figure 22-44.

Now, look at the object along the negative *Y* axis and draw the front view on the front glass panel. Repeat the process by looking along the positive *X* and *Z* axes, and draw the views on the right side and the top panel of the box, refer to Figure 22-45.

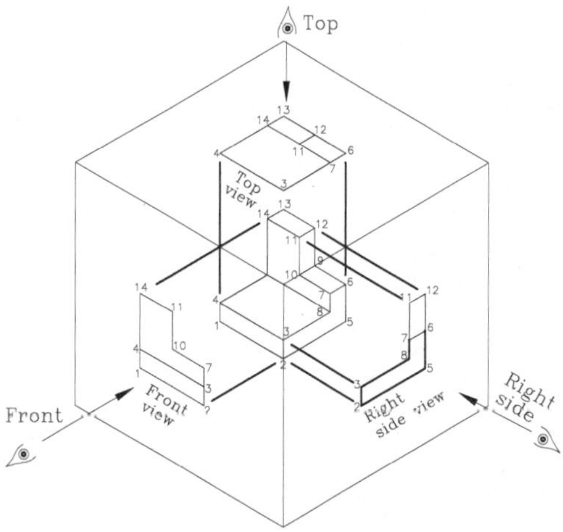

Figure 22-44 *Objects inside a glass box*

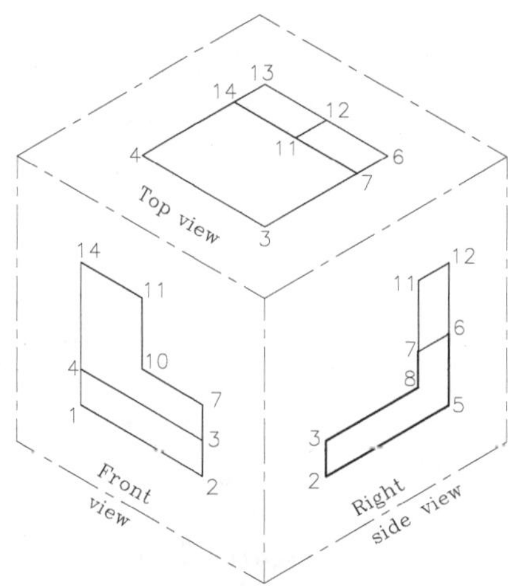

Figure 22-45 *Front, top, and side views*

To represent the front, side, and top views on paper, open the side and the top panels of the glass box, refer to Figure 22-46. The front panel is assumed to be stationary.

After opening the panels through 90 degree, the orthographic views will appear, as shown in Figure 22-47.

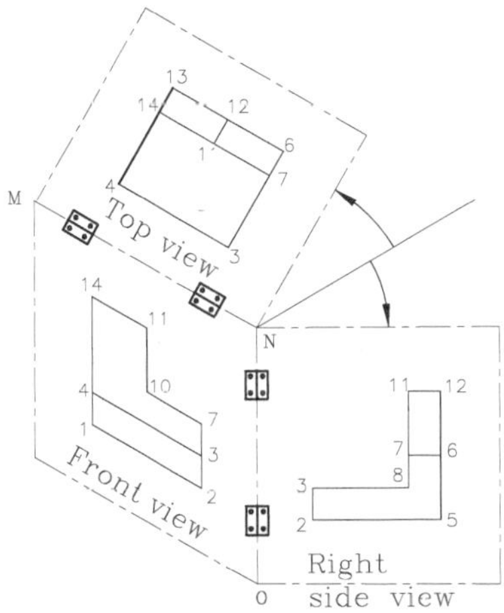

Figure 22-46 Opening the side and top panels

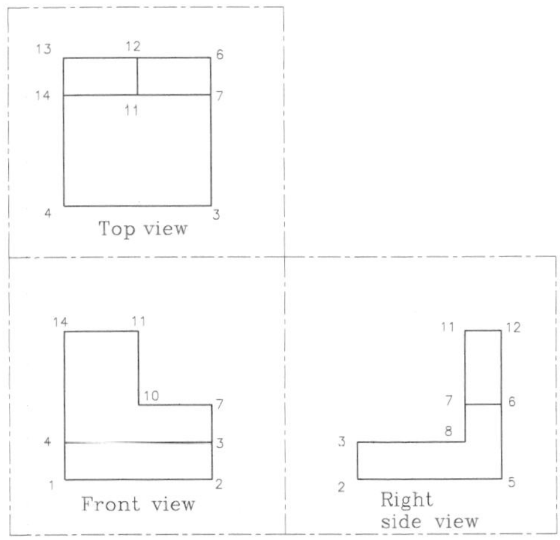

Figure 22-47 Views after opening the panels

POSITIONING ORTHOGRAPHIC VIEWS

Orthographic views must be positioned, as shown in Figure 22-48. The right side view must be positioned directly on the right side of the front view. Similarly, the top view must be directly above the front view. If the object requires additional views, they must be positioned, as shown in Figure 22-49.

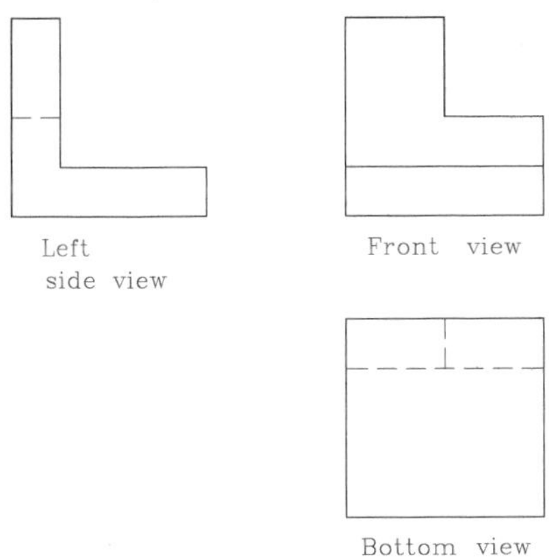

Figure 22-48 Positioning orthographic views

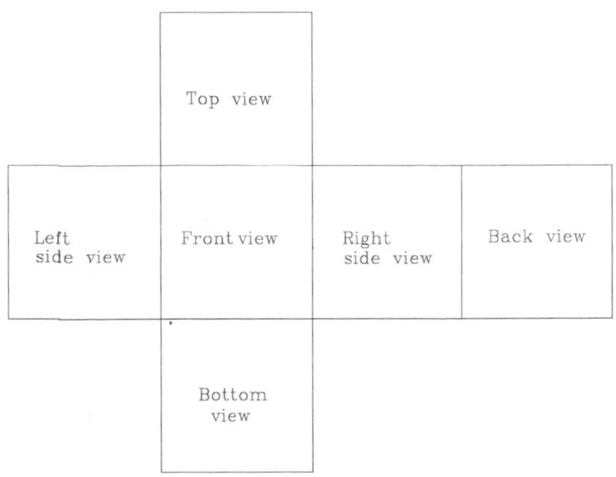

Figure 22-49 Standard placement of orthographic views

The different views of the step block are shown in Figure 22-50.

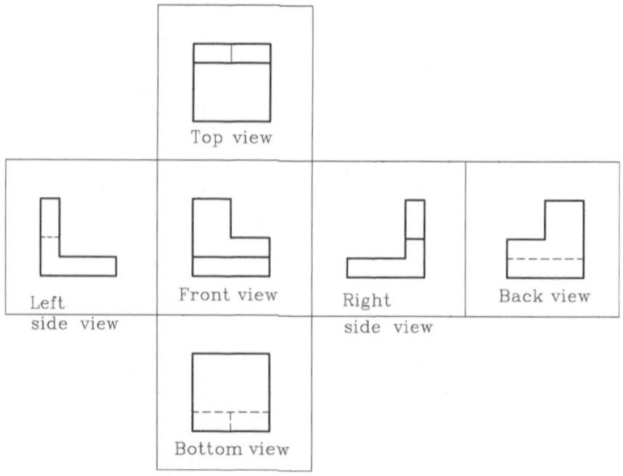

Figure 22-50 Different views of the step block

Example 1 Orthographic Views

In this example, you will draw the required orthographic views of the object shown in Figure 22-51. Assume the dimensions of the drawing.

Drawing the orthographic views of an object involves the following steps:

1. Look at the object and determine the number of views required to show all its features. For example, the object in Figure 22-51 requires three views only (front, side, and top).

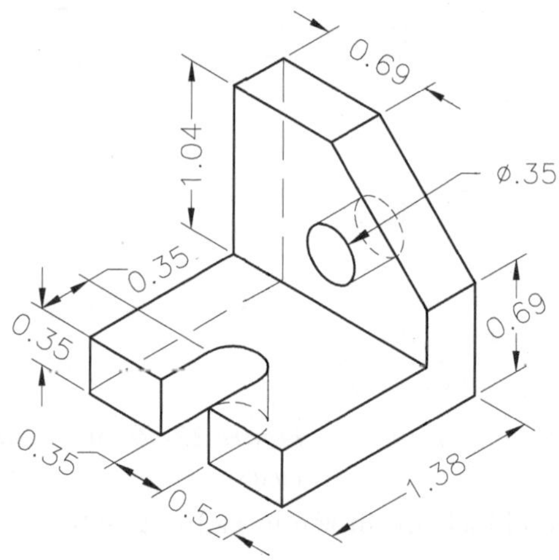

Figure 22-51 Step block with hole and slot

2. Based on the shape of the object, select the side that you want to show as the front view. In this example, the front view, i.e. the view along -y axis, is the one that shows the maximum number of features or that gives a better idea about the shape of the object. Sometimes, the front view is determined by how the part will be positioned in an assembly.

3. Picture the object in your mind and align it along the imaginary X, Y, and Z axes, refer to Figure 22-52.

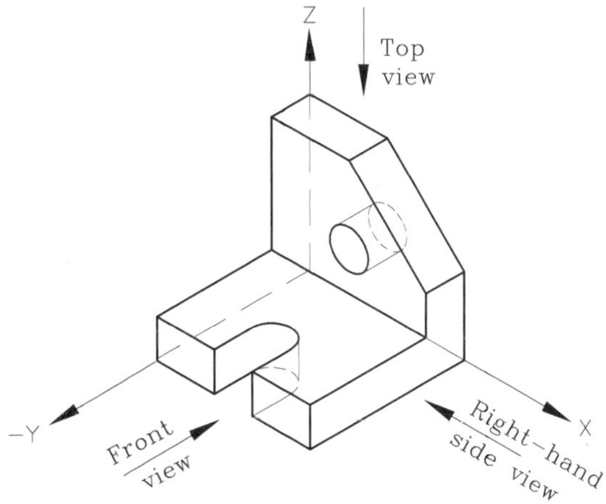

Figure 22-52 *Align the object with the imaginary X, Y, and Z axes*

4. Look at the object along the negative Y axis and project the image on the imaginary XZ parallel plane, refer to Figure 22-53.

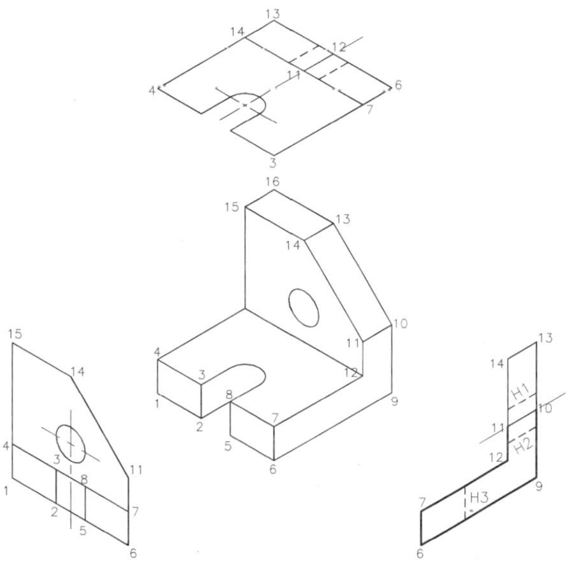

Figure 22-53 *Project the image onto the parallel planes*

5. Use the projection on imaginary XZ parallel plane to draw the front view of the object. If there are any hidden features, they must be drawn with hidden lines. The holes and slots must be shown with center lines.

6. To draw the right side view, look at the object along the positive *X* axis and project the image onto the imaginary YZ parallel plane

7. Use the projection on imaginary YZ parallel plane to draw the right side view of the object. If there are any hidden features, they must be drawn with hidden lines. The holes and slots, when shown in the side view, must have one center line.

8. Similarly, draw the top view to complete the drawing. Figure 22-54 shows different views of the given object.

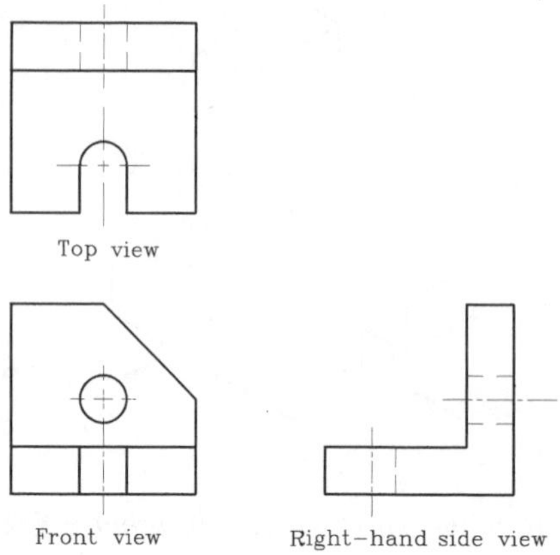

Figure 22-54 Front, side, and top views

Exercises 1 through 4 — Orthographic Views

Draw the required orthographic views of the objects shown in Figure 22-55 through Figure 22-58. The distance between the dotted lines is 1 unit.

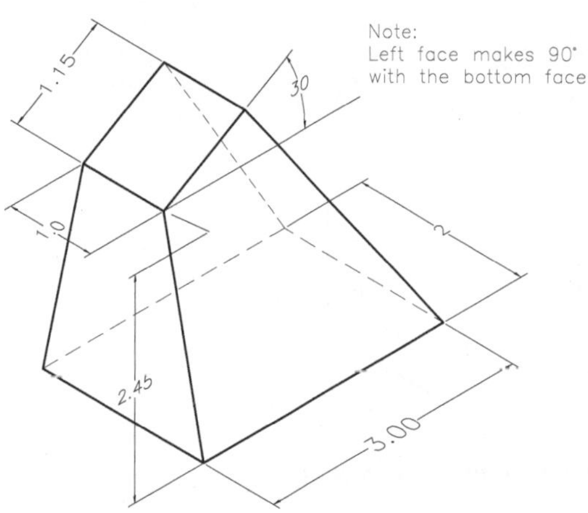

***Figure 22-55** Drawing for Exercise 1 (the object is shown as a surface wireframe model)*

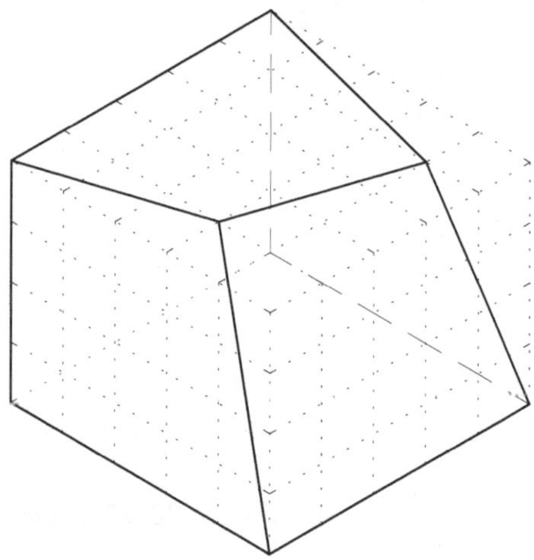

***Figure 22-56** Drawing for Exercise 2*

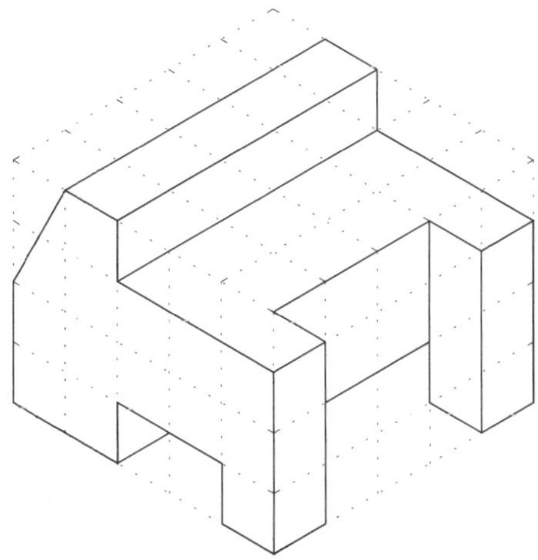

Figure 22-57 *Drawing for Exercise 3*

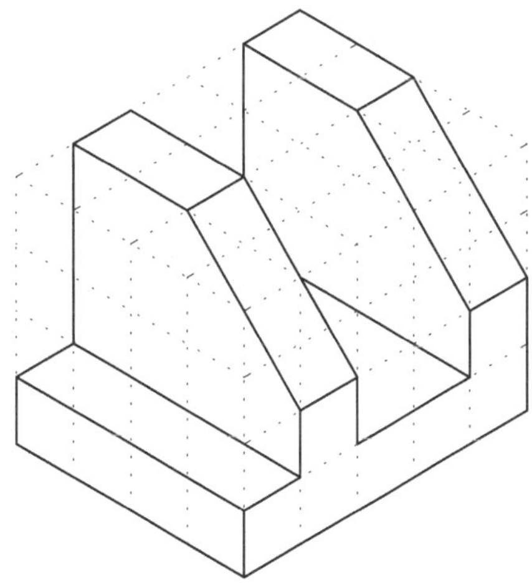

Figure 22-58 *Drawing for Exercise 4*

Exercises 5 through 10 Orthographic Views

Draw the required orthographic views of the following objects and then give the required dimensions, refer to Figures 22-59 through 22-64.

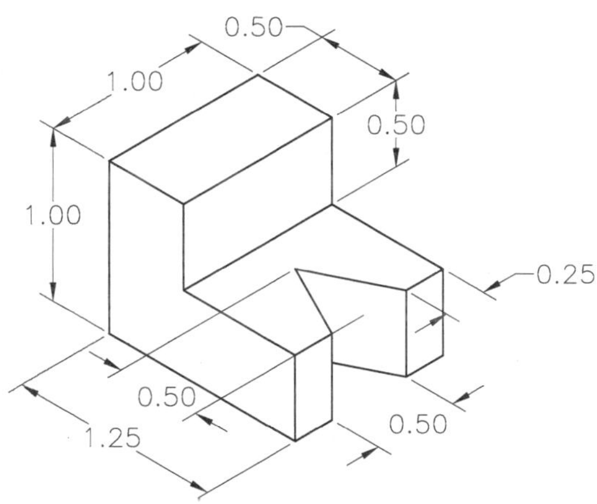

Figure 22-59 *Drawing for Exercise 5*

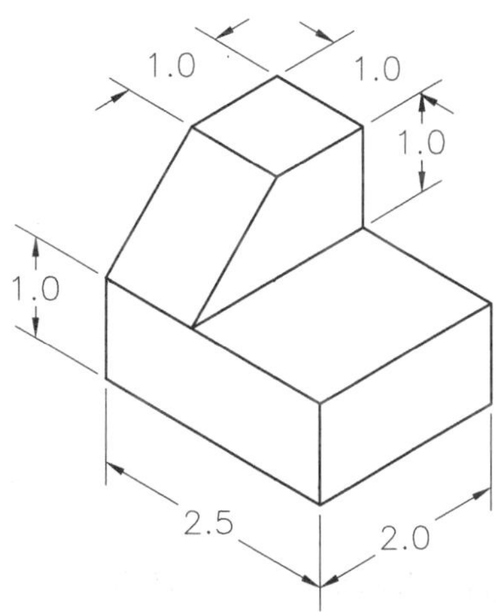

Figure 22-60 *Drawing for Exercise 6*

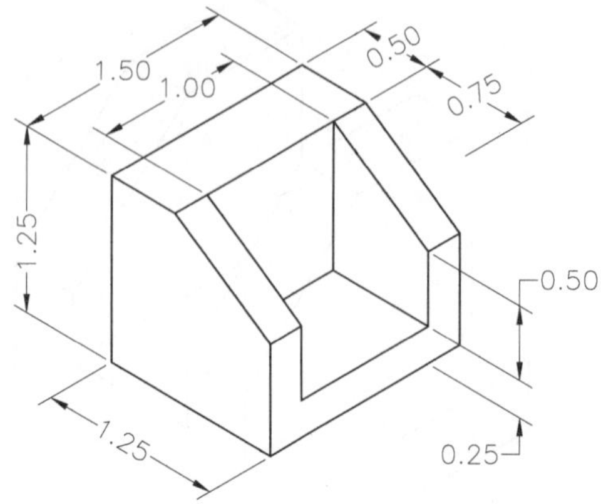

Figure 22-61 Drawing for Exercise 7

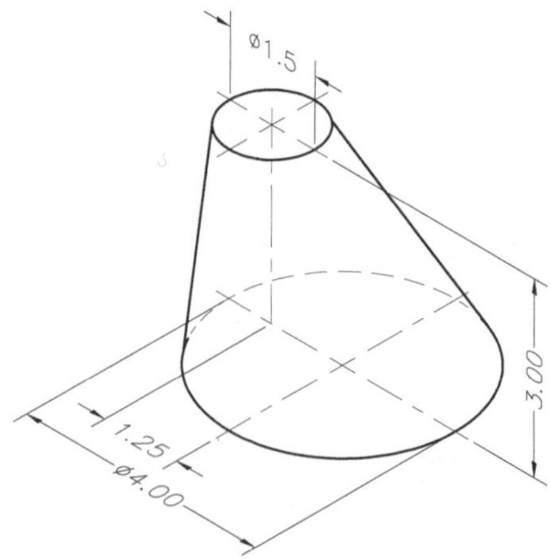

Figure 22-62 Drawing for Exercise 8

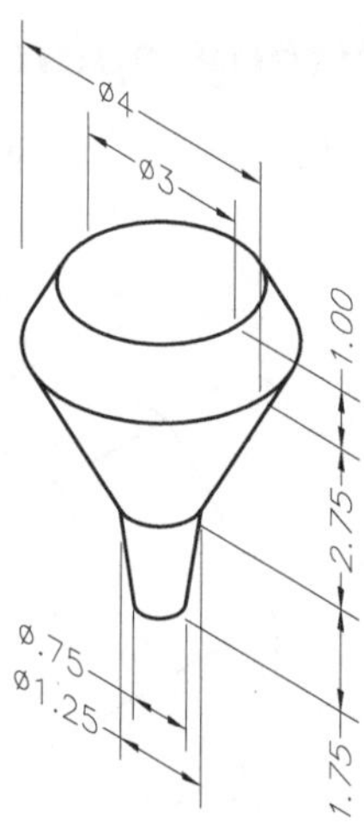

Figure 22-63 Drawing for Exercise 9

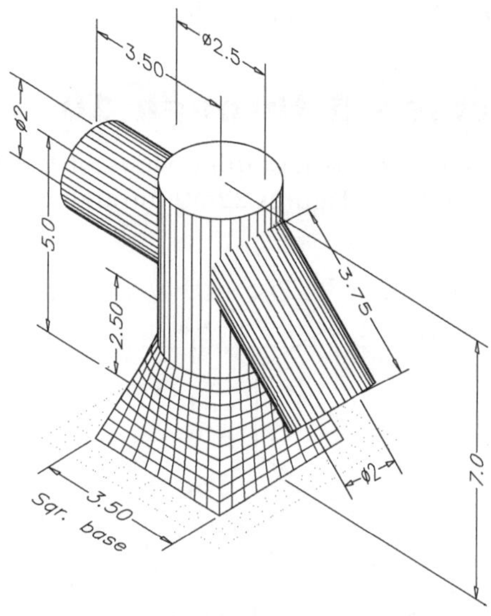

Figure 22-64 Drawing for Exercise 10 (assume the missing dimensions)

SECTIONAL VIEWS

In the principal orthographic views, the hidden features are generally shown by hidden lines. In some objects, the hidden lines may not be sufficient to represent the actual shape of the hidden feature. In such situations, sectional views can be used to show the features of the object that are not visible from outside. The location of the section and the direction of sight depend on the shape of the object and the features that need to be shown. Several ways to cut a section in the object are discussed next.

Full Section

Figure 22-65 shows an object that has a drilled counterbore hole with taper. In the orthographic views, these features will be shown by the hidden lines, refer to Figure 22-66.

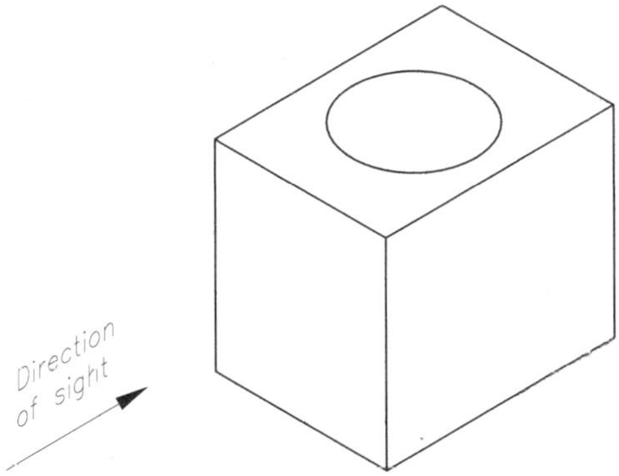

Figure 22-65 *Rectangular object with hole*

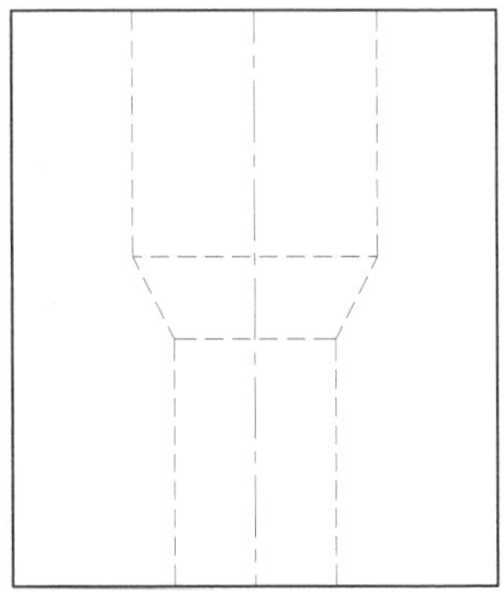

Figure 22-66 *Feature shown with hidden lines*

To better represent the hidden features, the object must be cut so that the hidden features are visible. In the full section, the object is cut along its entire length. To get a better idea of a full section, imagine that the object is cut into two halves along the centerline, as shown in Figure 22-67. Now, remove the left half and look at the right half in the direction that is perpendicular to the sectioned surface. The view you get after cutting the section is called a full section view, refer to Figure 22-68.

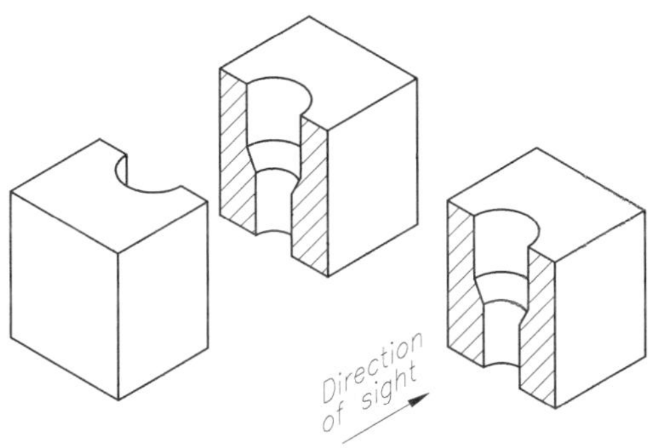

Figure 22-67 *One-half of the object removed*

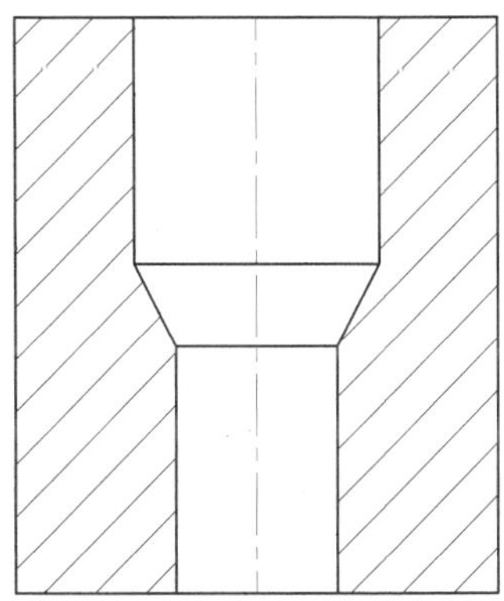

Figure 22-68 *Full section view*

In this section view, the features that would be hidden in a normal orthographic view are visible. Also, the part of the object where the material is actually cut is indicated by section lines. If the material is not cut, the section lines are not drawn. For example, if there is a hole, no material is cut when the part is sectioned, and so the section lines must not be drawn through that area of the section view.

Half Section

If the object is symmetrical, it is not necessary to draw a full section view. For example, in Figure 22-69, the object is symmetrical with respect to the centerline of the hole, so a full section is not required. But, in some objects it may help to understand and visualize the shape of the hidden details better to draw the view in half section. In half section, one-quarter of the object is removed, as shown in Figure 22-70. To draw a view in half section, imagine one-quarter of the object removed, and then look in the direction that is perpendicular to the sectioned surface.

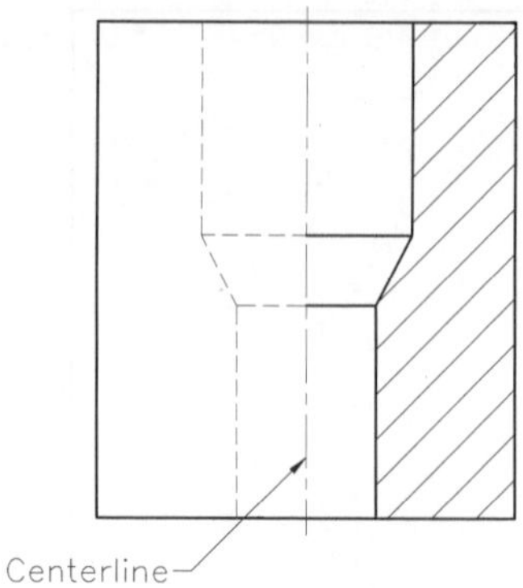

Figure 22-69 *Front view in half section*

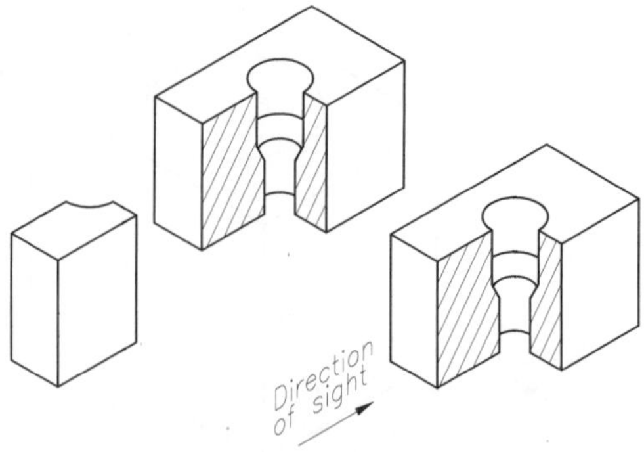

Figure 22-70 *One-quarter of the object removed*

You can also show the front view with a solid line in the middle, as shown in Figure 22-71. Sometimes the hidden lines, representing the remaining part of the hidden feature, are not drawn, refer to Figure 22-72.

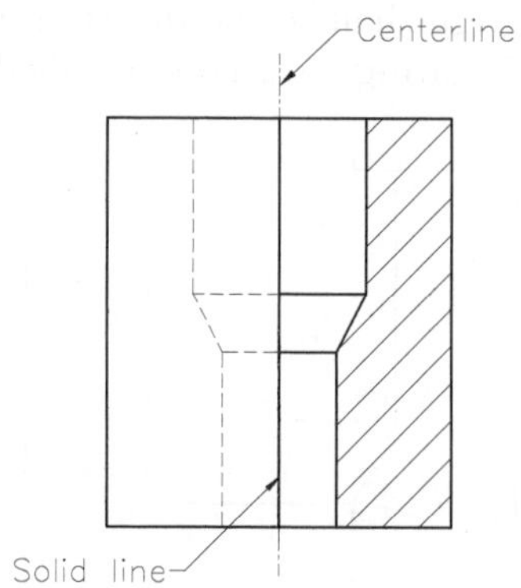

Figure 22-71 *Front view in half section*

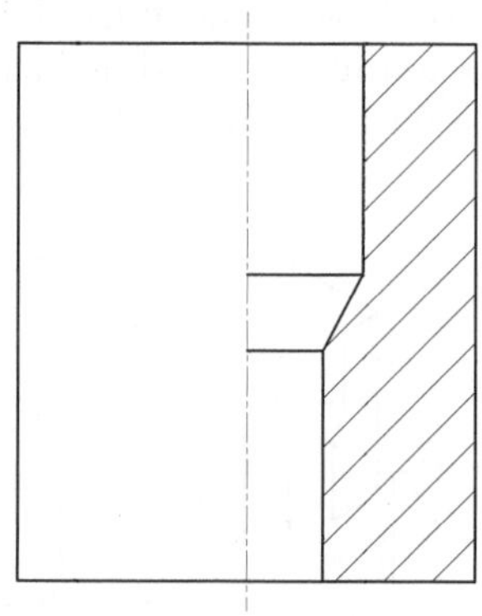

Figure 22-72 *Front view in half section with the hidden features not drawn*

Broken Section

In the broken section, only a small portion of the object is cut to expose the features that need to be drawn in the section. The broken section is designated by drawing a thick line in the section view, refer to Figure 22-73.

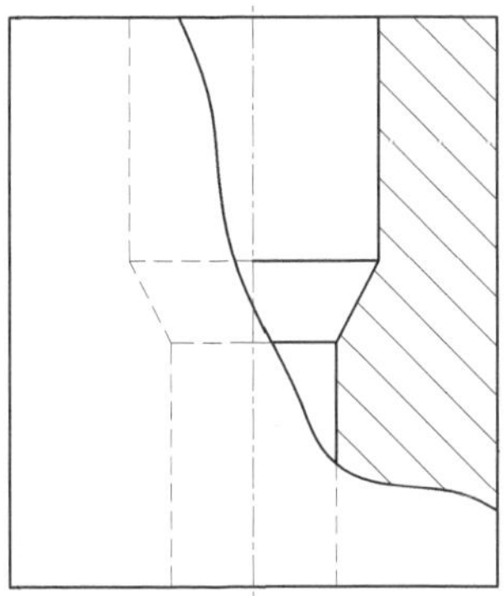

Figure 22-73 *Front view with broken section*

Revolved Section

The revolved section is used to show the true shape of the object at the point where the section is cut. The revolved section is used when it is not possible to show the features clearly in any principal view. For example, for the object shown in Figure 22-74, it is not possible to show the actual shape of the middle section in the front, side, or top view. Therefore, a revolved section is required to show the shape of the middle section.

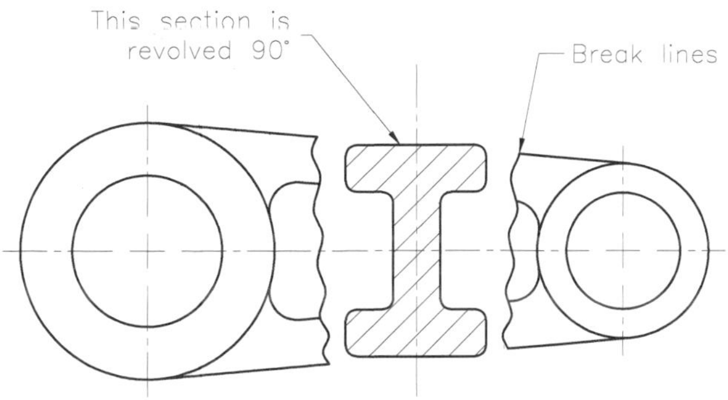

Figure 22-74 *Front view with the revolved section*

The revolved section involves cutting an imaginary section through the object and then looking at the sectioned surface in a direction that is perpendicular to it. To represent the shape, the view is revolved through 90 degrees and drawn in the plane of the paper, refer to Figure 22-74. Depending on the shape of the object, and for clarity, it is recommended to provide a break in the object so that its lines do not interfere with the revolved section.

Removed Section

The removed section is similar to the revolved section, except that it is shown outside the object. The removed section is recommended when there is not enough space in the view to show it or if the scale of the section is different from the parent object. The removed section can be shown by drawing a line through the object at the point where the revolved section is required and then drawing the shape of the section, as shown in Figure 22-75.

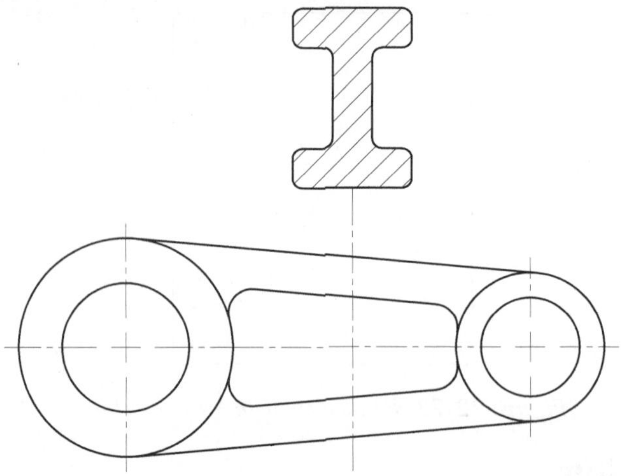

Figure 22-75 Front view with the removed section

The other way of showing a removed section is to draw a cutting plane line through the object where you want to cut the section. The arrows should point in the direction, in which you are looking at the sectioned surface. The section can then be drawn at a convenient place in the drawing. The removed section must be labeled, as shown in Figure 22-76. If the scale has been changed, it must be mentioned with the view description.

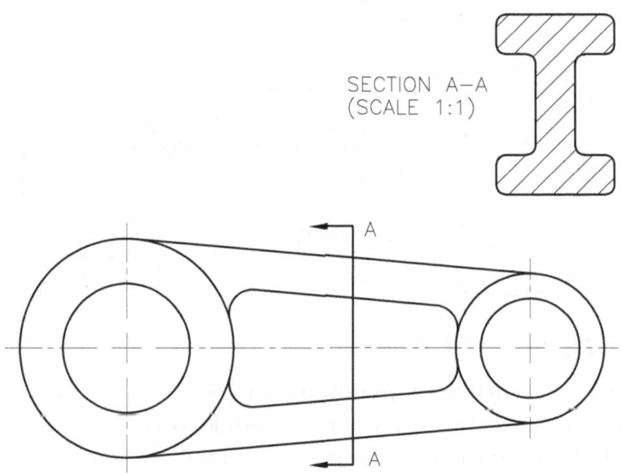

Figure 22-76 Front view with the removed section drawn at a convenient place

Offset Section

The offset section is used when the features of the object that you want to section are not in one plane. The offset section is designated by drawing a cutting plane line that is offset through the center of the features that need to be shown in the section, refer to Figure 22-77. The arrows indicate the direction in which the section is viewed.

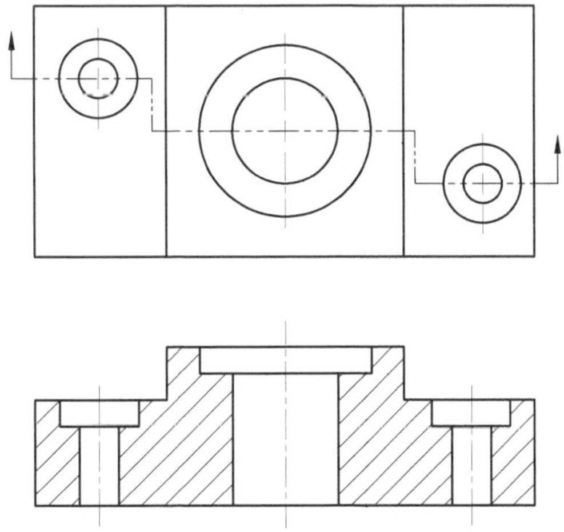

Figure 22-77 Front view with offset section

Aligned Section

In some objects, cutting a straight section might cause confusion in visualizing the shape of the section. Therefore, the aligned section is used to represent the shape along the cutting plane, refer to Figure 22-78. Such sections are widely used in circular objects that have spokes, ribs, or holes.

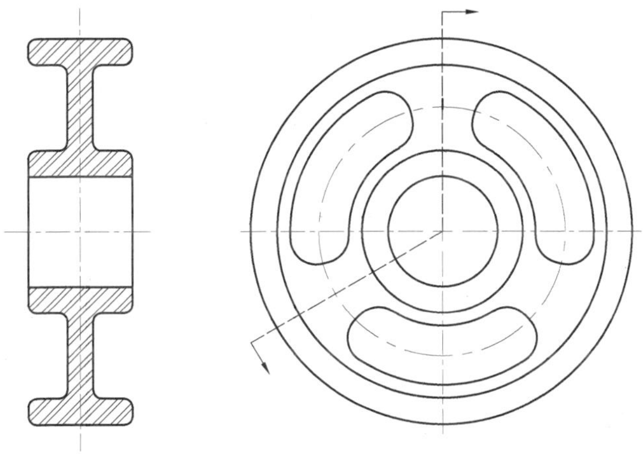

Figure 22-78 Side view in section (aligned section)

Cutting Plane Lines

Cutting plane lines are thicker than object lines, refer to Figure 22-79. You can use the **Polyline** tool to draw the polylines of the desired width, generally 0.005 to 0.01. However, for drawings that need to be plotted, you should assign a unique color to the cutting plane lines and then assign that color to the slot of the plotter that carries a pen of the required tip width.

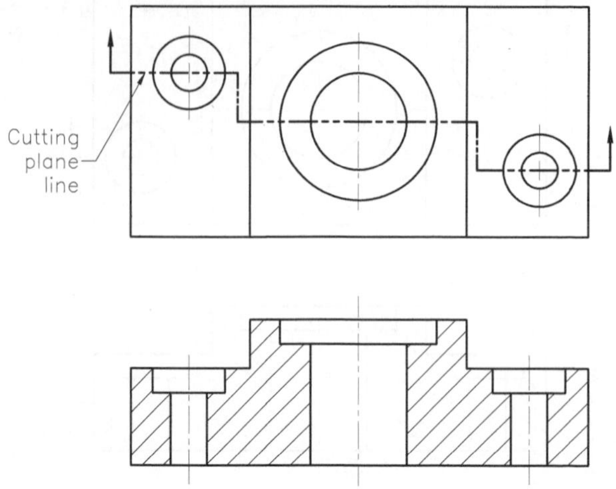

Figure 22-79 Cutting plane lines

In the industry, generally three types of lines are used to show the cutting plane for sectioning. The first line consists of a series of dashes 0.25 units long. The second type consists of a series of long dashes separated by two short dashes, refer to Figure 22-80. The length of the long dash can vary from 0.75 to 1.5 units, and the short dashes are about 0.12 units long. The space between the dashes should be about 0.03 units. Third, sometimes the cutting plane lines might clutter the drawing or cause confusion with other lines in the drawing. To avoid this problem, you can show the cutting plane by drawing a short line at the end of the section, refer to Figure 22-80 and Figure 22-81. The line should be about 0.5 units long.

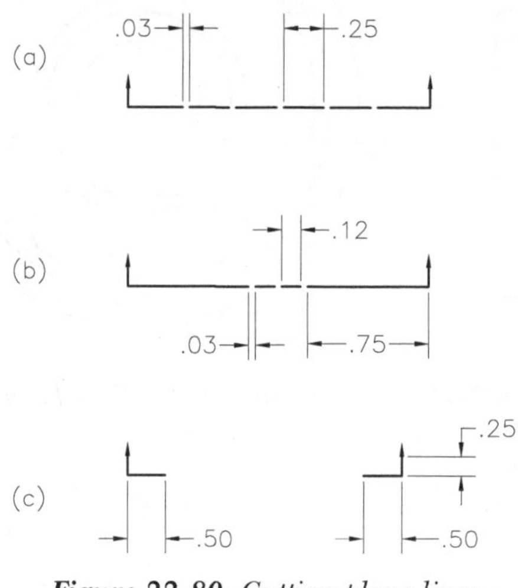

Figure 22-80 Cutting plane lines

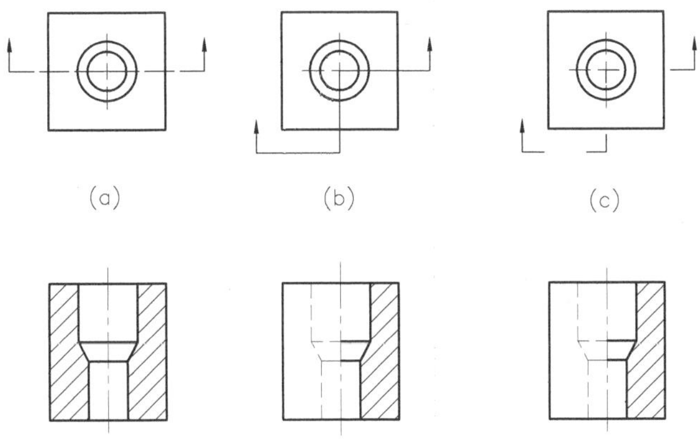

Figure 22-81 *Application of cutting plane lines*

Note

In AutoCAD, you can define a new linetype that you can use to draw the cutting plane lines. Add the following lines to the ***Aclt.lin*** *file, and then load the linetypes before assigning it to an object or a layer.*

```
*CPLANE1,___ ___ ___ ___
 A,0.25,-0.03
 *CPLANE2,___ ___ ___ ___
 A,1.0,-0.03,0.12,-0.03,0.12,-0.03
```

Spacing for Hatch Lines

The spacing between the hatch (section) lines is determined by the space that is being hatched, refer to Figure 22-82. If the hatch area is small, the spacing between the hatch lines should be smaller compared to a large hatch area.

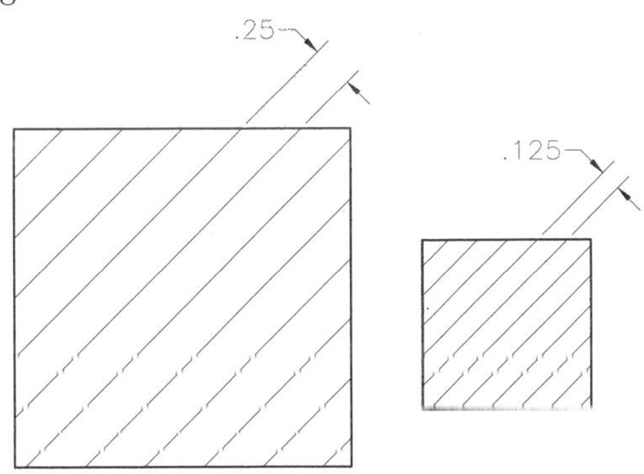

Figure 22-82 *Hatch line spacing*

In AutoCAD, you can control the spacing between the hatch lines by specifying the scale factor at the time of hatching. If the scale factor is 1, the spacing between the hatch lines is the same as defined in the hatch pattern file for that particular hatch. For example, in the following hatch pattern definition, the distance between the lines is 0.125.

***ANSI31, ANSI Iron, Brick, Stone masonry**
45, 0, 0, 0, .125

When the hatch scale factor is 1, the line spacing will be 0.125; if the scale factor is 2, the spacing between the lines will be 0.125 x 2 = 0.25.

Direction of Hatch Lines

The angle for the hatch lines should be 45 degrees. However, if there are two or more hatch areas next to one another representing different parts, the hatch angle must be changed so that the hatched areas look different, refer to Figure 22-83.

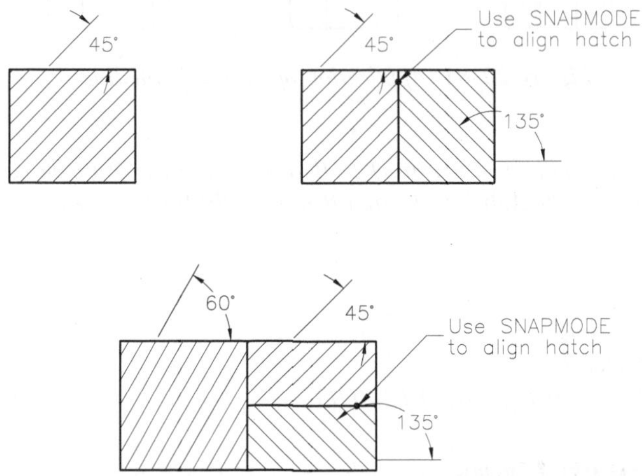

Figure 22-83 Hatch angle for adjacent parts

Also, if the hatch lines fall parallel to any edge of the hatch area, the hatch angle should be changed so that the lines are not parallel or perpendicular to any object line, refer to Figure 22-84.

Figure 22-84 Hatch angle

Points to Remember

1. Some parts, such as bolts, nuts, shafts, ball bearings, fasteners, ribs, spokes, keys, and other similar items, if sectioned, should not be shown in the section. In case of ribs, if the cutting plane passes through the center plane of the feature, they should not be section-lined. If the cutting plane passes crosswise through ribs, they must be section-lined.

2. Hidden details should not be shown in the section view unless the hidden lines represent an important detail or help the viewer to understand the shape of the object.

3. The section lines (hatch lines) must be thinner than the object lines. You can accomplish this by assigning a unique color to the hatch lines and then assigning the color to that slot on the plotter that carries a pen with a thinner tip.

4. The section lines must be drawn on a separate layer for display and editing purposes.

Exercises 11 and 12 — Section Views

In the following drawings, refer to Figures 22-85 and 22-86, the views have been drawn without a section. Draw these views in the section as indicated by the cutting plane lines in each object.

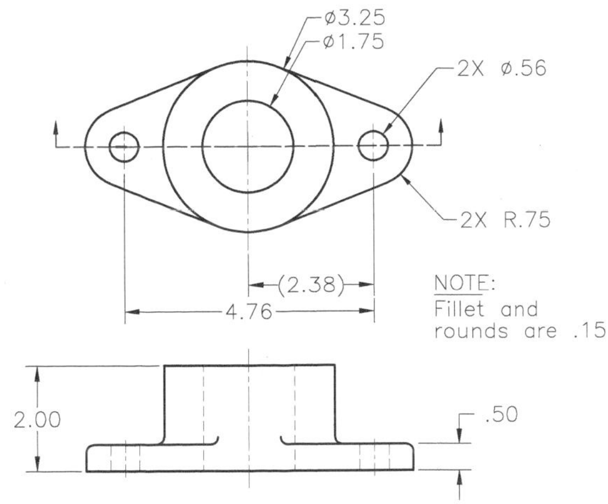

Figure 22-85 *Drawing for Exercise 11*

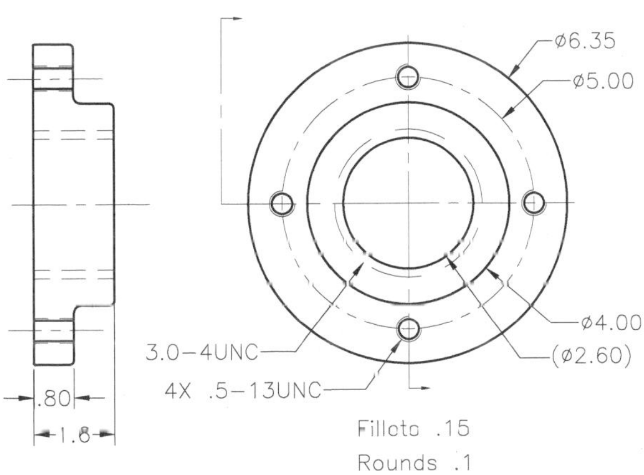

Figure 22-86 *Drawing for Exercise 12*

Exercises 13 and 14 — Section Views

Draw the orthographic views of the objects shown in Figures 22-87 and 22-88. The required view should be the front section view of the object such that the cutting plane passes through the holes. Also, draw the cutting plane lines in the top view.

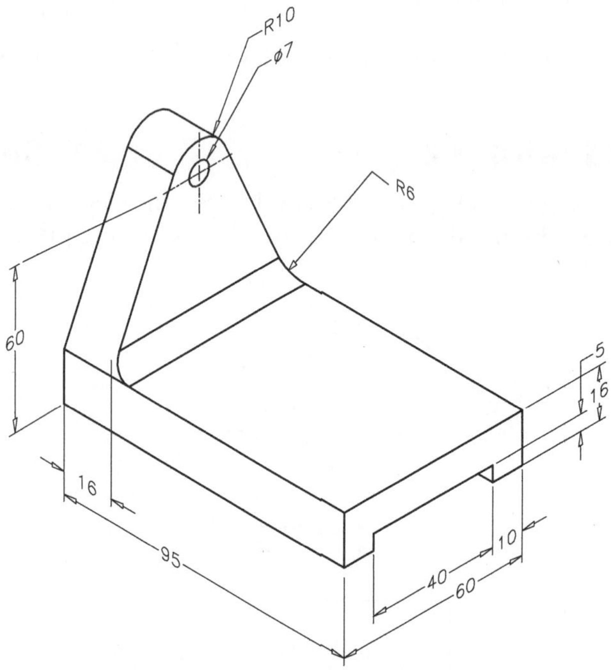

Figure 22-87 Drawing for Exercise 13

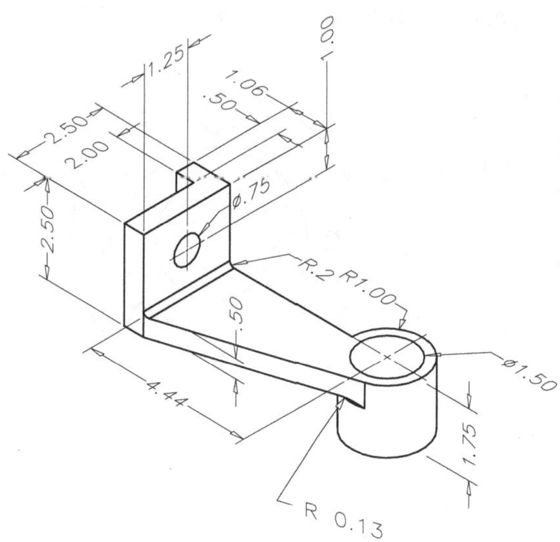

Figure 22-88 Drawing for Exercise 14

Exercise 15 Section View

Draw the required orthographic views of the object shown in Figures 22-89 and 22-90 with the front view in the section. Also, draw the cutting plane lines in the top view to show the cutting plane. The material thickness is 0.25 units. (The object has been drawn as a surfaced 3D wiremesh model.)

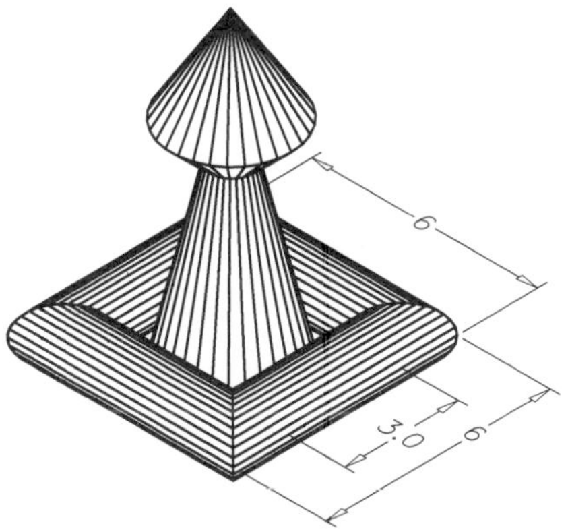

Figure 22-89 Isometric view of the model

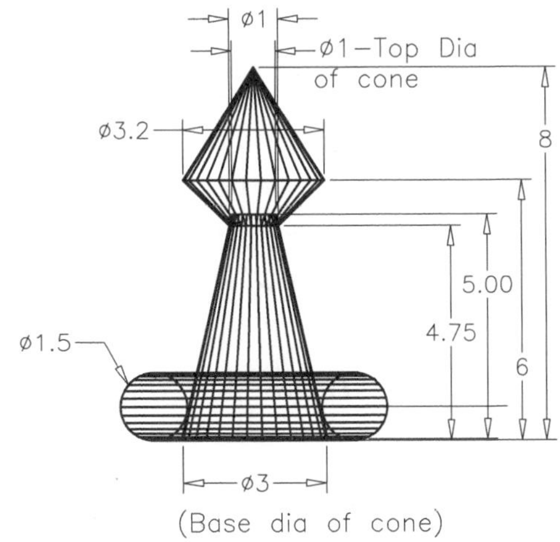

Figure 22-90 Front view of the model

AUXILIARY VIEWS

As discussed earlier, most objects generally require three principal views (front view, side view, and top view) to show all features of the object. Round objects may require just two views. Some objects have inclined surfaces. It may not be possible to show the actual shape of the inclined surface in one of the principal views. To get the true view of the inclined surface, you must look at the surface in a direction that is perpendicular to the inclined surface. Then you can project the points onto the imaginary auxiliary plane that is parallel to the inclined surface. The final view after projecting the points is called the auxiliary view, as shown in Figures 22-91 and 22-92.

The auxiliary view in Figure 22-92 shows all the features of the object as seen from the auxiliary view direction. For example, the bottom left edge is shown as a hidden line. Similarly, the lower right and upper left edges are shown as continuous lines. Although these lines are technically correct, the purpose of the auxiliary view is to show the features of the inclined surface. Therefore, in the auxiliary plane, you should draw only those features that are on the inclined face, as shown in Figure 22-93. Other details that will help you to understand the shape of the object may also be included in the auxiliary view. The remaining lines should be ignored because they tend to cause confusion in visualizing the shape of the object.

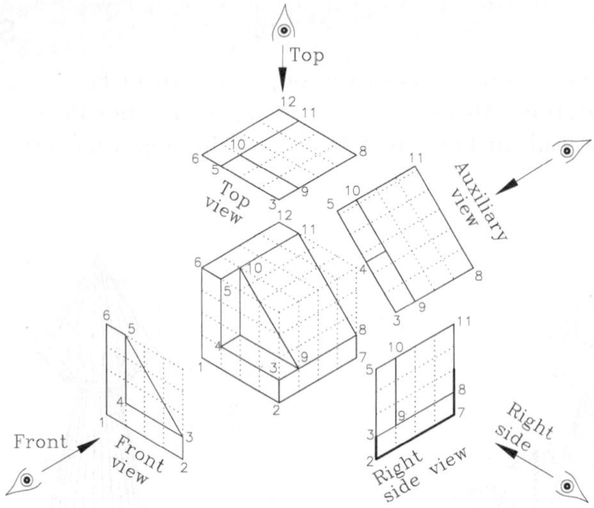

Figure 22-91 Points projected on the auxiliary plane

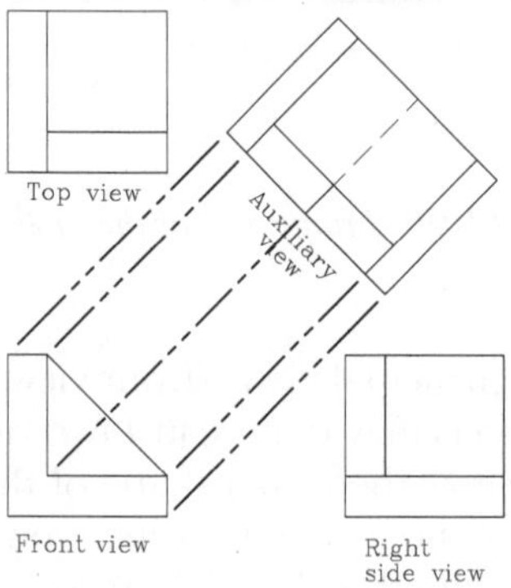

Figure 22-92 Auxiliary, front, and side views

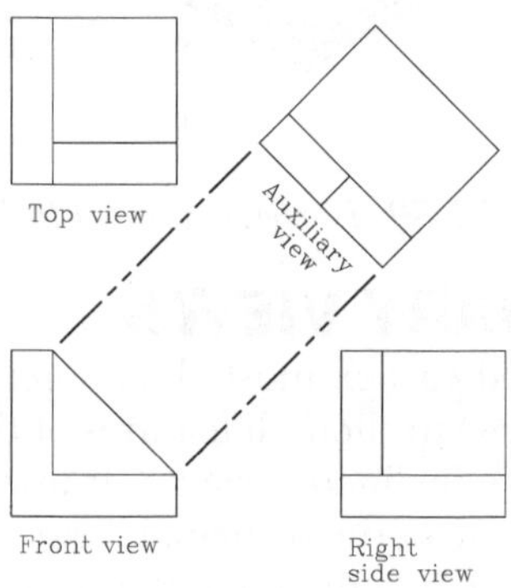

Figure 22-93 Features on the inclined plane in an auxiliary view

How to Draw Auxiliary Views

The following example illustrates how to use AutoCAD to generate an auxiliary view.

Draw the required views of the hollow triangular block that has a hole in the inclined face, as shown in Figure 22-94. (The block has been drawn as a solid model.)

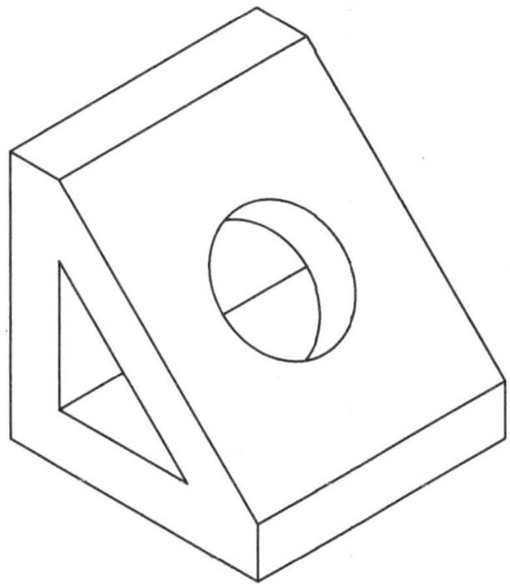

Figure 22-94 *Hollow triangular block*

The following steps are involved in drawing different views of this object.

1. Draw the required orthographic views: the front view, side view, and the top view as shown in Figure 22-95. The circles on the inclined surface appear like ellipses in the front and top views. These ellipses may not be shown in the orthographic views because they tend to clutter them, refer to Figure 22-96.

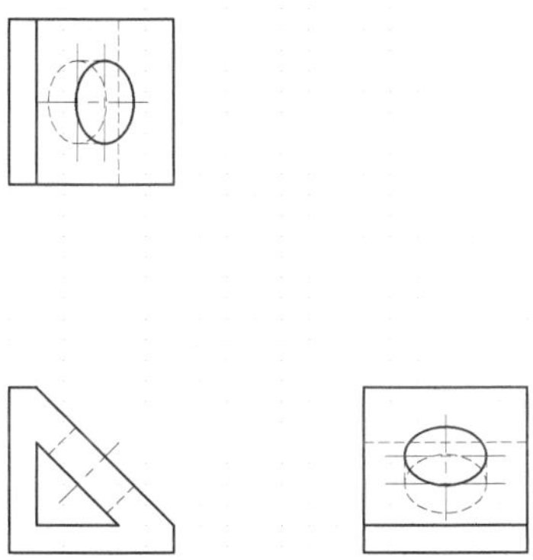

Figure 22-95 *Front, side, and top views*

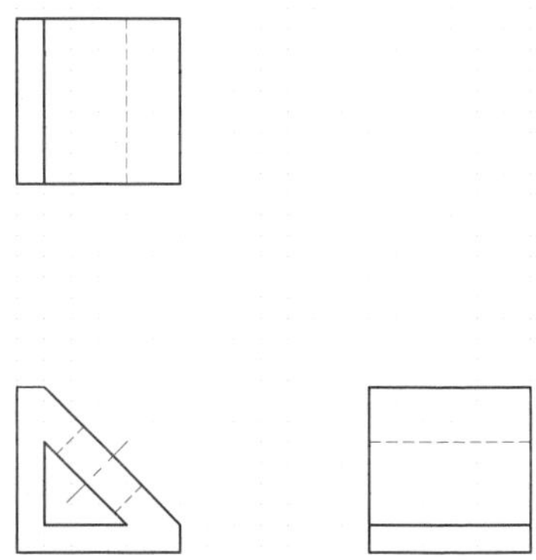

Figure 22-96 *The ellipses are not visible in the orthographic views*

2. Determine the angle of the inclined surface. In this example, the angle is 45 degrees. Use the **SNAP** command to rotate the snap by 45 degrees, refer to Figure 22-97 or rotate the UCS by 45 degrees around the *Z* axis.

   Command: **SNAP** [Enter]
   Specify snap spacing or [ON/OFF/Aspect/Style/Type] <0.5000>: **R** [Enter]
   Specify base point <0.0000,0.0000>: *Select P1.*
   Specify rotation angle <0>: **45** [Enter]

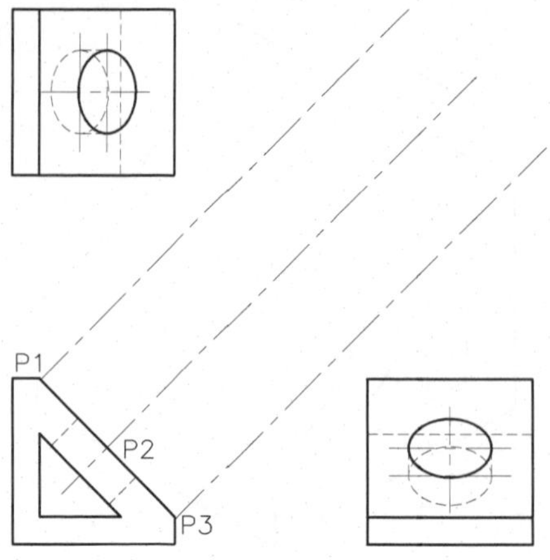

Figure 22-97 Grid lines at 45-degree

Using the rotate option, the snap will be rotated by 45 degrees and the grid lines will also be displayed at 45 degrees (if the **GRID** is on). Also, one of the grid lines will pass through point P1 because it was defined as the base point.

3. Turn **ORTHO** on, and project points P1, P2, and P3 from the front view onto the auxiliary plane. Now, you can complete the auxiliary view and give the dimensions. The projection lines can be erased after the auxiliary view is drawn, refer to Figure 22-98.

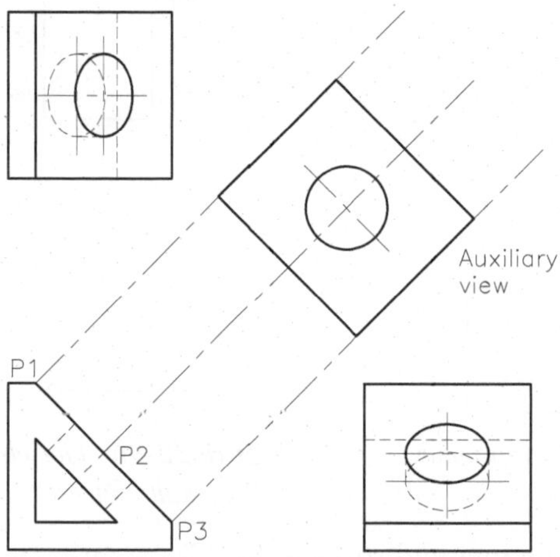

Figure 22-98 Auxiliary, front, side, and top views

Exercise 16 — Orthographic Views

Draw the orthographic and auxiliary views of the object are shown in Figure 22-99. The object is drawn as a surfaced 3D wiremesh model.

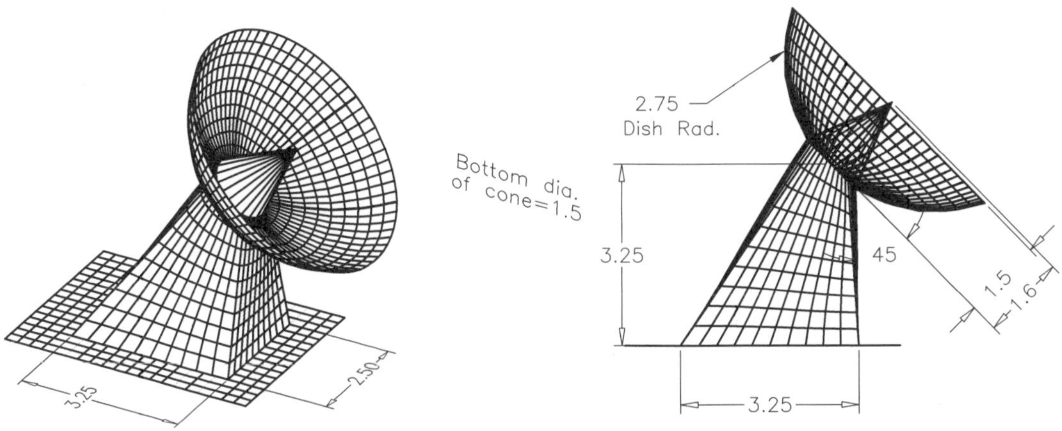

Figure 22-99 Dimensions for the mesh model

Exercises 17 and 18 — Orthographic Views

Draw the orthographic and auxiliary views of the objects shown in Figure 22-100 and Figure 22-101. The objects are drawn as 3D solid models and are shown at different angles (viewpoints are different).

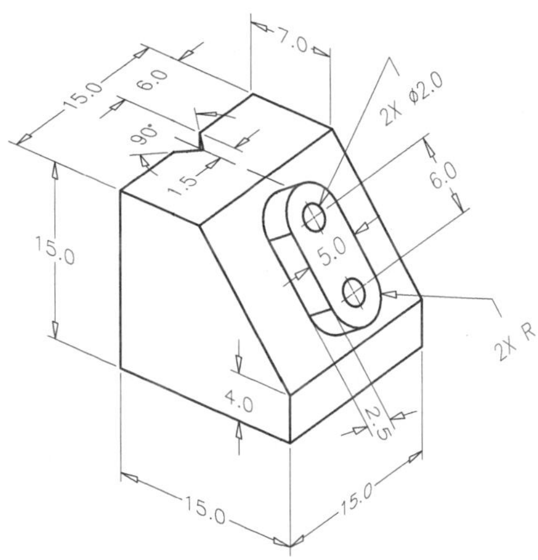

Figure 22-100 Drawing for Exercise 17

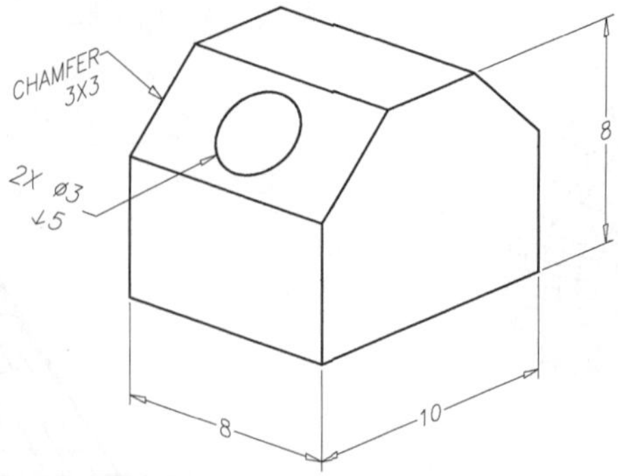

Figure 22-101 *Drawing for Exercise 18*

Self-Evaluation Test

Answer the following questions and then compare them to those given at the end of this chapter:

1. A line perpendicular to the *X* and *Y* axes defines the __________ axis.

2. The circle must be dimensioned as a __________ never as a radius.

3. If you give continuous (incremental) dimensioning for dimensioning various features of a part, the overall dimension must be omitted or given as a __________ dimension.

4. The removed section is similar to the __________section except that it is shown outside the object.

5. In AutoCAD, you can control the spacing between the hatch lines by specifying the __________ at the time of hatching.

6. The distance between the first dimension line and the second dimension line must be __________ to __________units.

7. The reference dimension must be enclosed in __________.

8. The front view shows the maximum number of features or gives a better idea about the shape of the object. (T/F)

9. The number of decimal places in a dimension (for example, 2.000) determines the type of machine that will be used for performing the machining operation. (T/F)

10. The dimension layer/layers should be assigned a unique color so that at the time of plotting you can assign a desired pen to plot the dimensions. (T/F)

11. All dimensions should be placed inside the view. (T/F)

12. The dimensions can be placed inside the view if they can be easily understood and cause no confusion with the other object lines. (T/F)
13. If the object is symmetrical, it is not necessary to draw a full section view. (T/F)
14. While dimensioning, you must consider the manufacturing process involved in making a part and the relationship that exists between different parts in an assembly. (T/F)
15. A dimension must be assigned where the feature is visible. However, in some complicated drawings, you might be justified to dimension a detail with a hidden line. (T/F)

Review Questions

Answer the following questions:

1. Multiview drawings are also known as __________ drawings.
2. The distance of the first dimension line should be __________ to __________ units from the object line.
3. For parallel dimension lines, the dimension text can be __________ if there is not enough room between the dimension lines to place the dimension text.
4. While dimensioning a circle, the diameter should be preceded by the __________.
5. While dimensioning an arc or a circle, the dimension line (leader) must be __________.
6. In the __________ section, the object is cut along the entire length.
7. The part of the object where the material is actually cut is indicated by drawing __________ lines.
8. The __________ section is used to show the true shape of the object at the point where the section is cut.
9. The __________section is used when the features of the object that you want to section are not in one plane.
10. The section lines must be drawn on a separate layer for __________ and __________purposes.
11. In a broken section, only a __________ of the object is cut to __________ the features that need to be drawn in section.
12. The assembly drawing is used to show the __________ and their __________ in an assembled product or a machine unit.
13. The space between the *X* and *Y* axes is called the *XY* plane. (T/F)

14. A plane that is parallel to the *XY* plane is called a parallel plane. (T/F)

15. If you look at the object along the negative *Y* axis and toward the origin, you will get the side view. (T/F)

16. The top view must be directly below the front view. (T/F)

17. Before drawing orthographic views, you must look at the object and determine the number of views required to show all features of the object. (T/F)

18. By dimensioning, you not only modify the size of a part, but also give a series of instructions to a machinist, an engineer, or an architect. (T/F)

19. You can change grid, snap or UCS origin, and snap increments to make it easier to place the dimensions. (T/F)

20. You should not dimension with hidden lines. (T/F)

21. A dimension that is not to be scaled should be indicated by drawing a straight line under the dimension text. (T/F)

22. Dimensions must be given where the feature that you are dimensioning is obvious and shows the contour of the feature. (T/F)

23. In radial dimensioning, you should place the dimension text vertically. (T/F)

24. If the dimension of a feature appears in a section view, you must hatch the dimension text. (T/F)

25. Dimensions must not be repeated as it makes their updation difficult. (T/F)

26. Cutting plane lines are thinner than object lines. You can use the **Polyline** tool to draw the polylines of the desired width. (T/F)

27. The spacing between the hatch (section) lines is determined by the space being hatched. (T/F)

28. The angle for the hatch lines should be 45-degree. However, if there are two or more hatch areas next to one another representing different parts, the hatch angle must be changed so that the hatched areas look different. (T/F)

29. Some parts, such as bolts, nuts, shafts, ball bearings, fasteners, ribs, spokes, keys, and other similar items that do not show any important feature, if sectioned, must be shown in section. (T/F)

30. Section lines (hatch lines) must be thicker than object lines. (T/F)

Exercises 19 through 24

Draw the required orthographic views of the following objects (the isometric view of each object is given in Figures 22-102 through 22-107). Also, dimension the drawings.

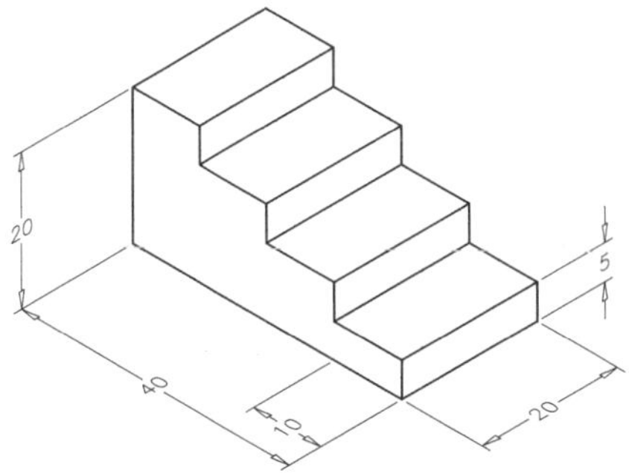

Figure 22-102 Drawing for Exercise 19

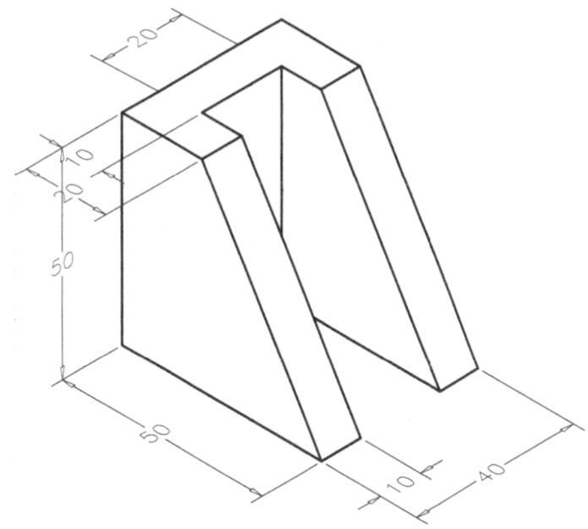

Figure 22-103 Drawing for Exercise 20

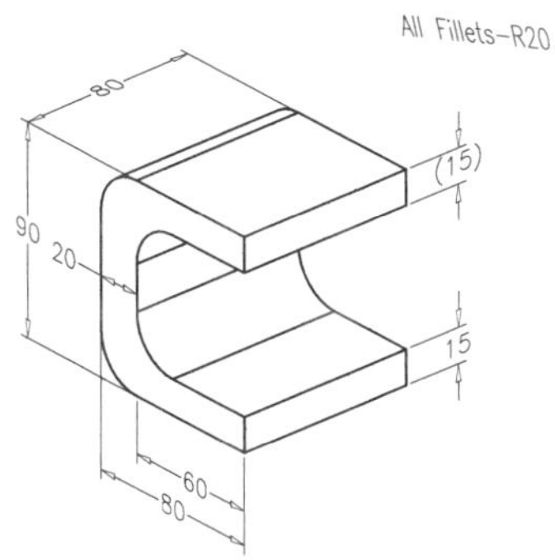

Figure 22-104 Drawing for Exercise 21

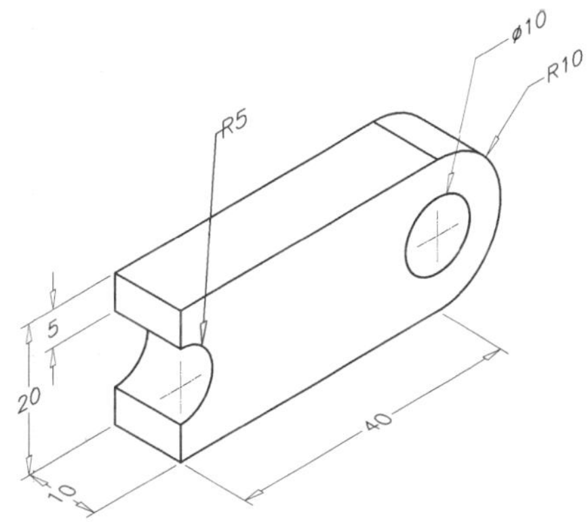

Figure 22-105 Drawing for Exercise 22

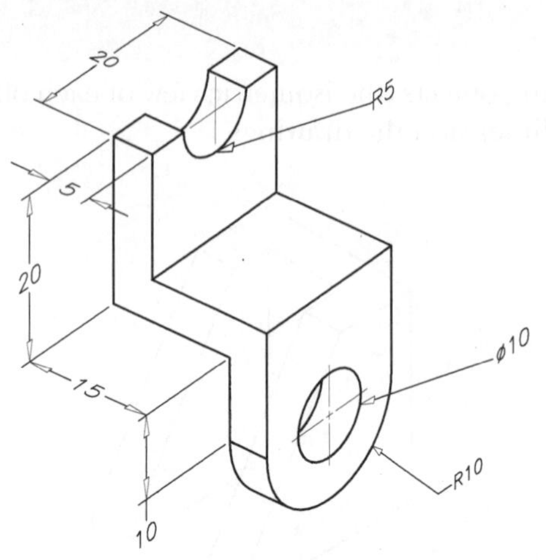

Figure 22-106 *Drawing for Exercise 23*

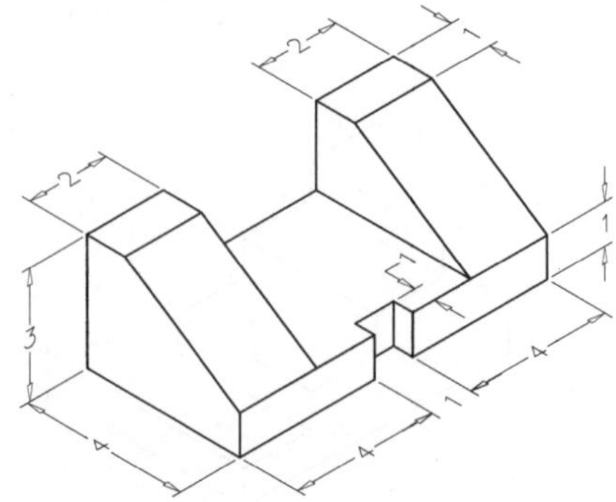

Figure 22-107 *Drawing for Exercise 24*

Answers to Self-Evaluation Test

1. Z, **2.** diameter, **3.** reference, **4.** revolved, **5.** scale factor, **6.** 0.25, 0.5, **7.** parentheses, **8.** T, **9.** T, **10.** T, **11.** F, **12.** T, **13.** T, **14.** T, **15.** T

Chapter 23

Concepts of Geometric Dimensioning and Tolerancing

Learning Objectives

After completing this chapter, you will be able to:

- *Understand tolerances and allowances*
- *Understand tolerancing methods*
- *Understand datums, features, and material condition modifiers*
- *Understand geometric characteristics symbols*
- *Understand the form, orientation, position, profile, and runout tolerances*
- *Understand fits*

Key Terms

- *Basic Size*
- *Limit Dimensioning*
- *Plus and Minus Tolerancing*
- *Tolerances*
- *Geometric Characteristics*
- *Maximum Material Condition (MMC)*
- *Least Material Condition (LMC)*
- *Regardless of Feature Size*
- *Feature Control Frame*
- *Form Tolerances*
- *Profile Tolerances*
- *Orientation Tolerances*
- *Location Tolerances*
- *Runout Tolerances*
- *Inch Fits*
- *Metric Fits*

HISTORY OF TOLERANCES AND ALLOWANCES

The history of engineering drawing extends over a period of 6000 years but the practice of tolerancing and dimensioning was introduced for the first time only about 80 years ago. Gradually, engineers and designers realized that exact dimensions and shapes could not be attained in shaping physical objects. Therefore, a feasible scheme of interchangeable manufacturing that was crucial to mass production methods was established. During this era, skilled handicrafters, designers, and engineers took pride in the ability to work with exact dimensions. This meant that objects were dimensioned more accurately than they could be measured. However, the use of modern measuring instruments showed deviations from the sizes which were earlier believed to be exact.

At the starting of industrial age it was realized that variations in the sizes of parts had always been present and such variations could be restricted but not avoided. The slight variation in the size which a part was originally intended to have could be tolerated without impairment of its correct functioning. It became evident that interchangeable parts need not be identical parts, but rather it would be sufficient if the significant sizes that controlled their fits lay between definite limits. The problem of manufacturing interchangeable parts was resolved by holding the parts between two limiting sizes lying so closely that any intermediate size is acceptable.

The concept of limits essentially means that a precisely defined basic condition is replaced by two limiting conditions and any result lying on or between these two limits is acceptable.

In order to calculate limits and tolerances, following definitions must be clearly understood.

Basic Size (Basic Dimension)

Basic size or basic dimension is theoretically the exact value of dimension for which the limits are derived with the help of allowance and tolerance.

Limits of Dimension

The limits of dimension are the maximum and minimum values permitted for a specific dimension.

Allowance

The allowance is the intentional difference applied in the basic size of mating parts. Allowance can also be defined as the minimum clearance (positive allowance) or maximum interference (negative allowance) between the mating parts.

Tolerance

Tolerance is the total permissible variation in a given dimension. It is the difference between maximum and minimum limits.

METHODS OF TOLERANCING

Tolerances are expressed using one of the two methods: limit dimensioning or plus and minus tolerancing. These methods apply to both inch and metric drawings.

Limit Dimensioning

In the limit dimensioning method, only the maximum and minimum dimensions are specified. When dimensions require greater accuracy than a general note provides, individual tolerances or limits are shown for that dimension. During placement of dimensions, the larger dimension is placed above the lower dimension, refer to Figure 23-1. When limit dimensions are used for diameter or radial features and are placed above each other, only one diameter or radius symbol is used which is located at midheight, refer to Figure 23-1.

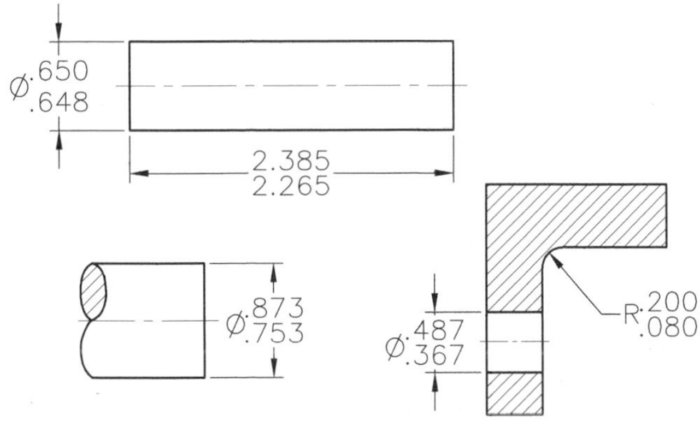

Figure 23-1 *Placement of limit dimensions*

If a maximum dimension has digits to the right of the decimal point, you need to add zeros to the minimum dimension after the decimal point and vice versa. This means that both the limits are expressed to the same number of decimal places, as shown in Figure 23-2.

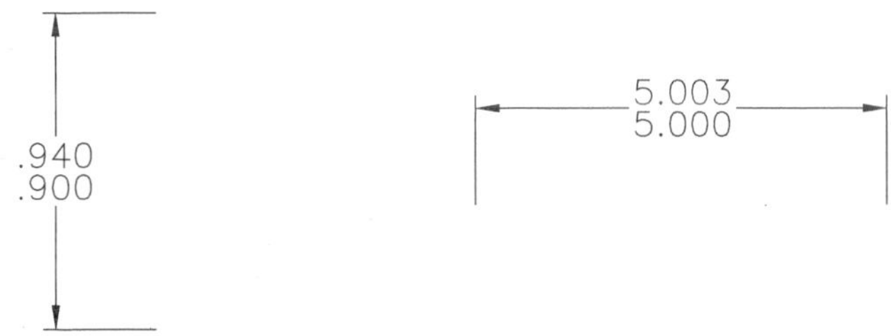

Figure 23-2 *Limit dimensioning with equal digits after the decimal*

When a dimension is shown with a leader and is placed in one line, the smaller size is shown first and a small dash separates the two limits, refer to Figure 23-3.

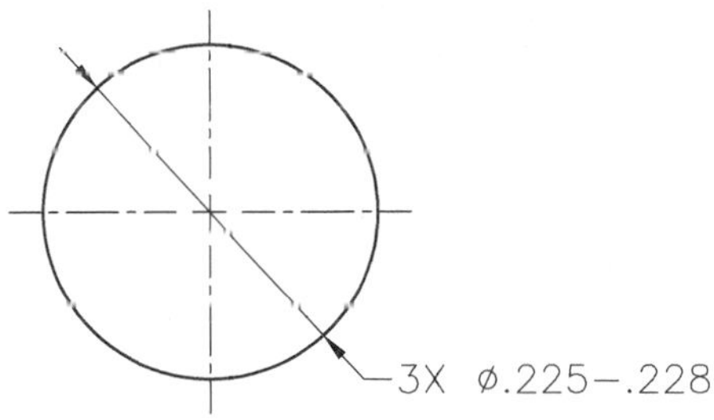

Figure 23-3 *Limit dimensioning of a circular feature*

For the case where only one limit is important and any variation from that limit in the other direction may be permitted, the MAX (maximum) or MIN (minimum) can be specified with the dimension value, as shown in Figure 23-4.

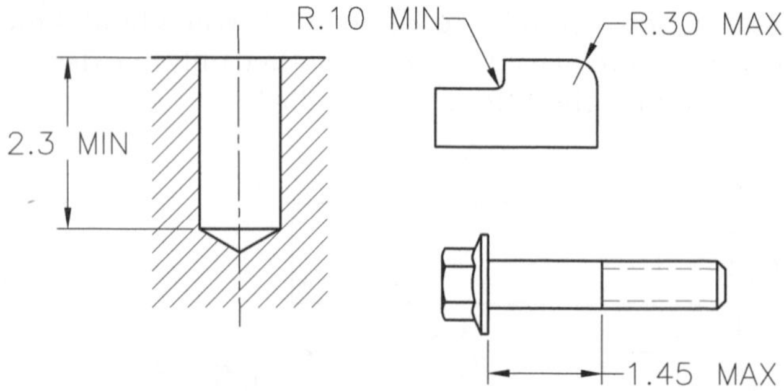

Figure 23-4 *Limit dimensioning with single limit*

Plus and Minus Tolerancing

In this method, the dimension is mentioned first and it is followed by a plus and minus tolerance expression. If the tolerance is expressed in plus and minus values then it is called bilateral tolerance, refer to Figure 23-5. The values of plus and minus limits need not be the same for bilateral tolerance.

If the tolerance is expressed with one value in plus or minus and the second one in zero then it is called as unilateral tolerance. A unilateral tolerance is the one that is applied in one direction such that the permissible variation in the other direction is zero, refer to Figure 23-5.

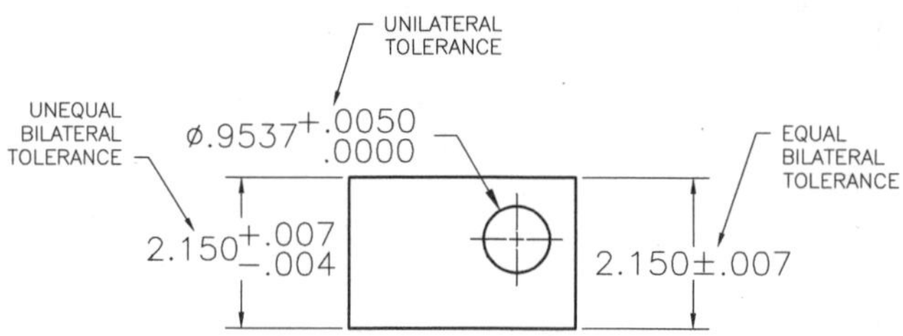

Figure 23-5 *Plus and minus tolerancing*

GEOMETRIC TOLERANCES

The intent of an engineering drawing is to convey information of the manufactured part from the designer to the manufacturer and inspector. Hence, an engineering drawing must contain all information necessary for the correct manufacturing of the part. It must also enable the inspector to determine precisely whether the finished parts are acceptable or not. Therefore, each drawing must convey three essential types of information: the material to be used, the size or dimensions of the part, and the shape or geometric characteristics of the part. The drawing must also specify the permissible variation of size and form.

A geometric tolerance is the maximum permissible variation of form, profile, orientation, or location of a feature from is indicated or specified in the drawing of that part. The tolerance value specifies that a feature would be allowed to have any variation of form or take up any position within the specified geometric tolerance zone. The tolerance value represents the width or diameter of the tolerance zone within which the point, line, or surface of the feature should lie. For example, a line controlled in a single plane by a straightness tolerance of .005 inch must lie within .005 inch wide zone, as shown in Figure 23-6.

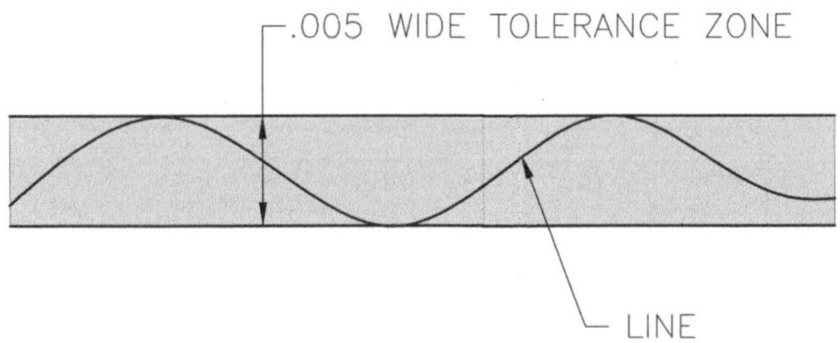

Figure 23-6 *Tolerance zone for straightness of a line*

The actual size of a feature must be within the size limits specified on the drawing. Each measurement made at any cross-section of the feature must not be greater than the maximum limit of size nor smaller than the minimum limit of size, refer to Figure 23-7(a) and Figure 23-7(b).

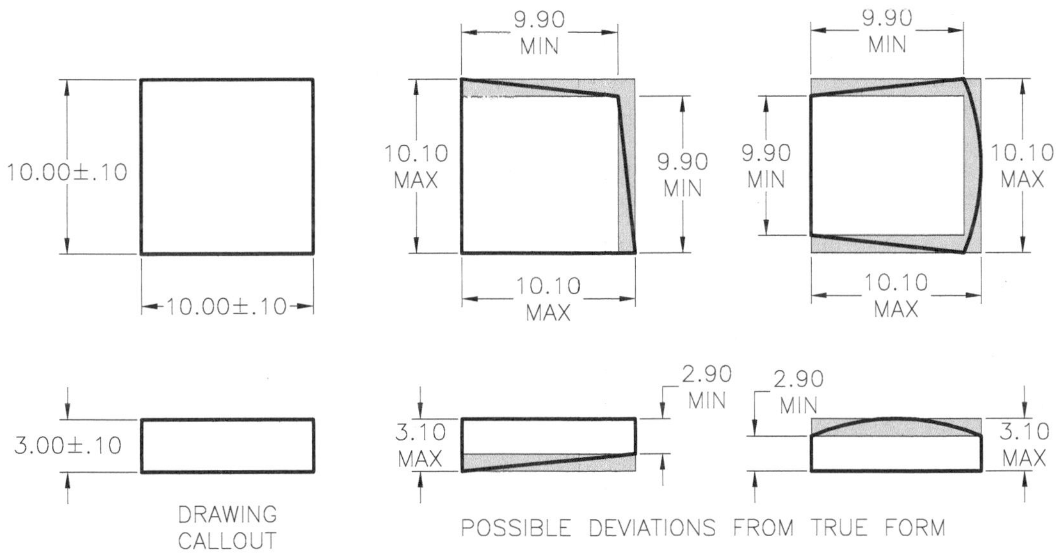

Figure 23-7(a) *Deviation of shape for flat features*

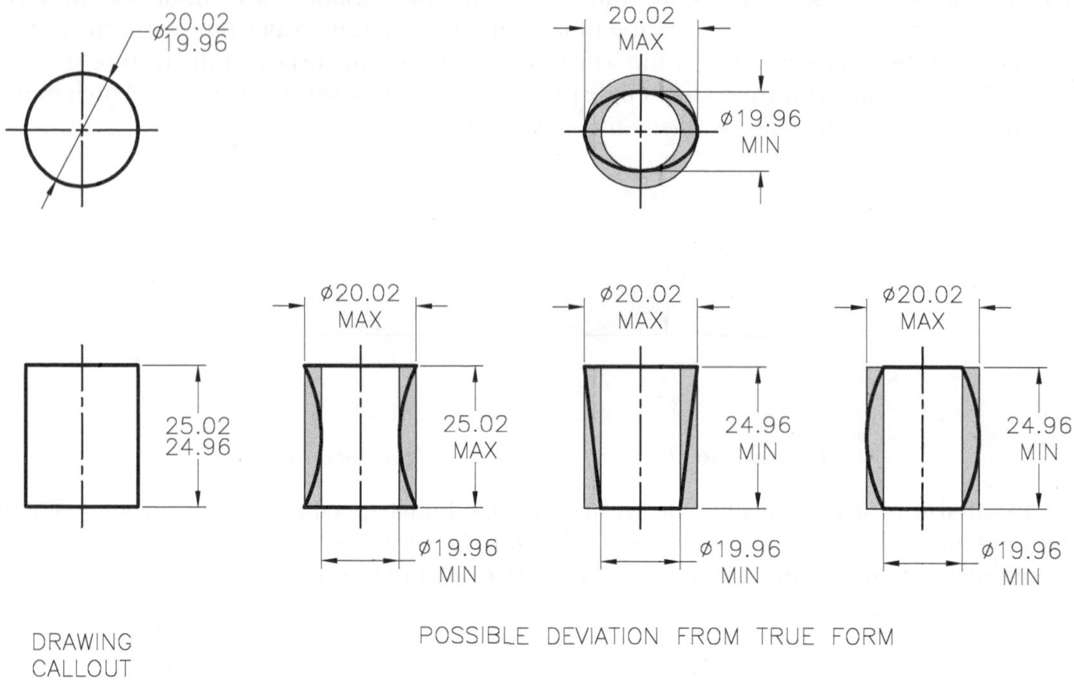

Figure 23-7(b) *Deviation of shape for cylindrical features*

Although each part is manufactured within the prescribed tolerance zones, the parts may not fit together because of deviation from their geometric form.

In order to meet functional requirements, it is often necessary to control the errors of form, including roundness and flatness as well as deviation from true size. To avoid any bending or deformation between mating parts, such as holes and shafts, it is usually necessary to ensure that they do not interfere the boundary of perfect form at their maximum material condition (the smallest hole or the largest shaft). Figure 23-8 shows deviation of form at the maximum material condition for shaft and holes.

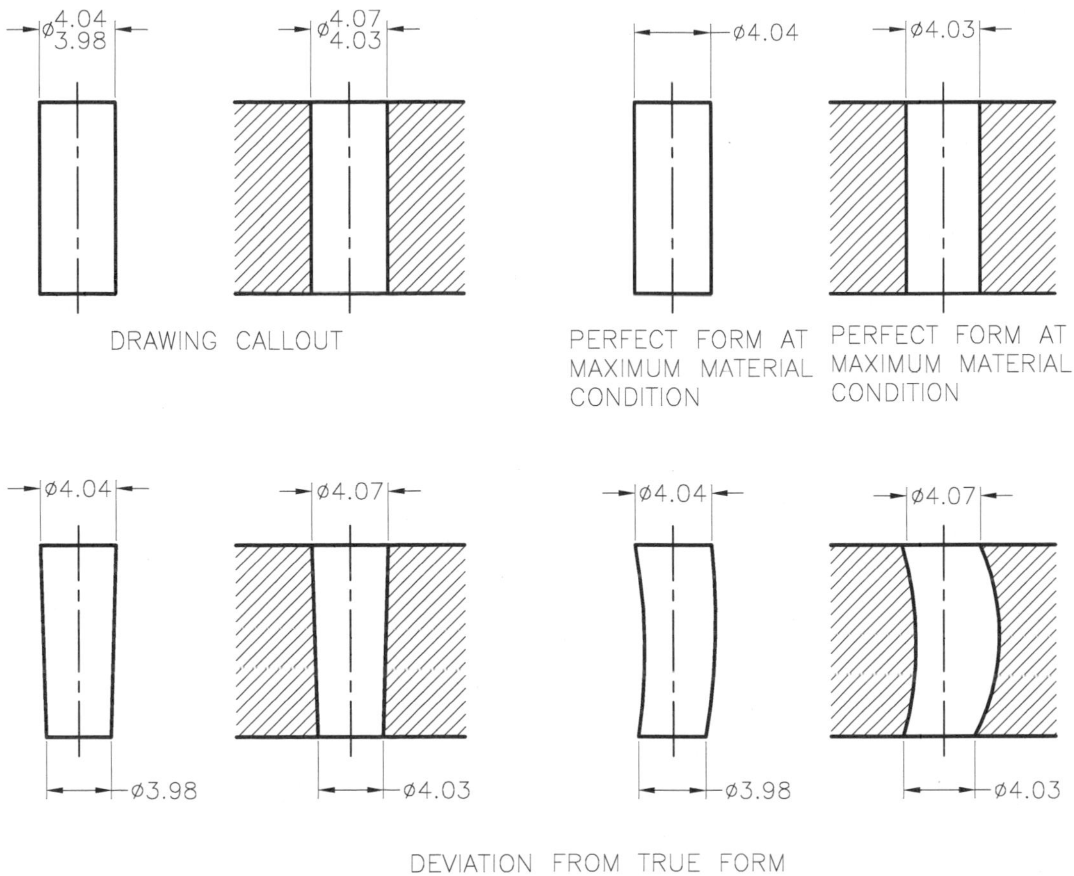

Figure 23-8 *Deviation of form at the maximum material condition*

Datums

Datums are imaginary references which are used to establish the location or geometric relationship between features of a part. The design of a part consists of many datums, each of which is a geometrically perfect form. A datum can be a straight line, a circle, a flat plane, a sphere, a cylinder, a cone, or a single point. As established from actual features, datums are assumed to be "exact" for the purpose of computation or reference.

Features

Features are real geometric shapes that make up the physical characteristics of a part. Features are specific component portions of a part which may include one or more surfaces such as holes, screw threads, profiles, faces, or slots.

Datum Reference Frame

Engineering, Manufacturing, and Inspection, all share a common three plane concept. These three planes are mutually perpendicular, perfect in dimension and orientation, and are exactly 90 degrees to each other. In geometric tolerancing, it is referred as Datum Reference Frame. The DRF consists of a system of features which are considered as the basis for dimensions for manufacturing and inspection. It provides complete orientation or a skeleton to which the part requirements are attached. The three main features of the datum reference frame are the planes, axes, and points.

Figure 23-9 shows a rectangular part fitted into the corner represented by the intersection of the three datum planes. The datum planes are imaginary and therefore perfect. They are considered as absolute reference base. There is a primary, a secondary, and a tertiary datum plane for each part. The part will vary from these planes even though the variation may not be visible to naked eyes.

Figure 23-10 shows a cylindrical part resting on a flat surface of the primary plane and the center of the cylinder is aligned with the vertical datum axis formed by the intersection of other two planes.

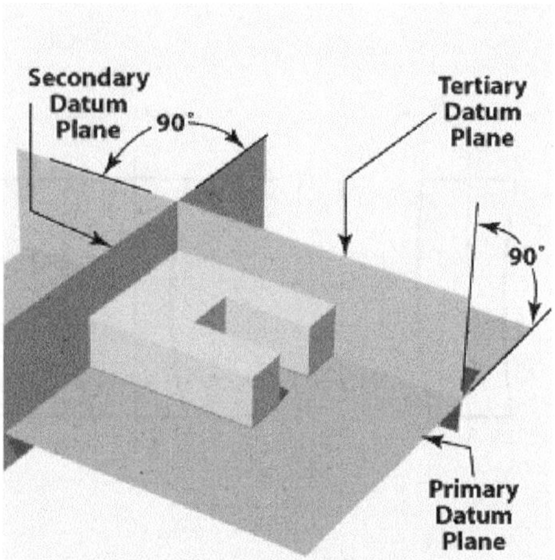

Figure 23-9 The datum reference frame with a rectangular plate

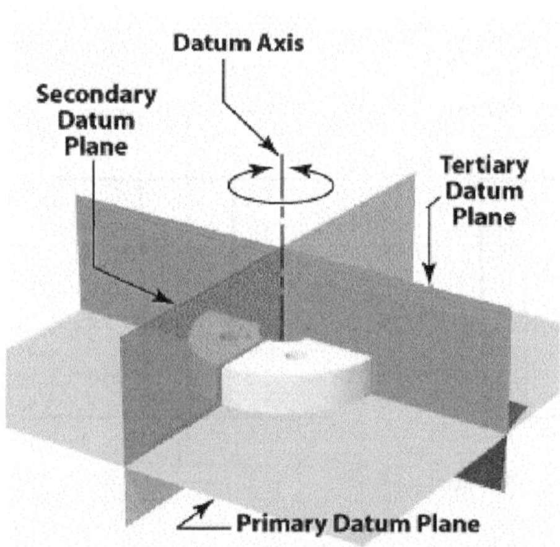

Figure 23-10 The datum reference frame with a circular plate

Material Condition Modifiers

Material condition modifiers tremendously impact the applied tolerance or datum reference. These modifiers can only be applied to features and datums that specify the size of the part. Examples of these features are holes, slots, pins, and tabs. If modifiers are applied to the features that are without size, they have no impact. However, if no modifier is specified in the feature control frame, the default modifier is regardless of feature size (RFS). The three types of material condition modifiers are explained next.

- **Maximum Material Condition (MMC)**

  This is a condition of a part feature where the part contains the maximum amount of material or the minimum hole-size and maximum shaft-size.

- **Least Material Condition (LMC)**

  This is the opposite of the MMC concept. This is a part feature which contains the least amount of material or the largest hole-size and smallest shaft-size.

- **Regardless of Feature Size (RFS)**
  When MMC or LMC is not specified with a geometric tolerance for a feature of size, no relationship is supposed to exist between the feature of size and the geometric tolerance. In other words, the tolerance applies regardless of feature size.

  In this case, the geometric tolerance controls the form, orientation, location of the axis, or median plane of the feature.

Feature Control Frame

The current method uses feature control frame to specify geometric tolerances. A feature control frame consists of a rectangular box divided into two or more compartments containing the geometric characteristic symbol followed by the tolerance value or description, modifiers, and any applicable datum feature references, as shown in Figure 23-11. If the tolerance zone is cylindrical, then a diameter symbol has to be added before the tolerance value followed by a material condition symbol. Other compartments are added when there is a requirement of composite tolerancing for a geometric feature.

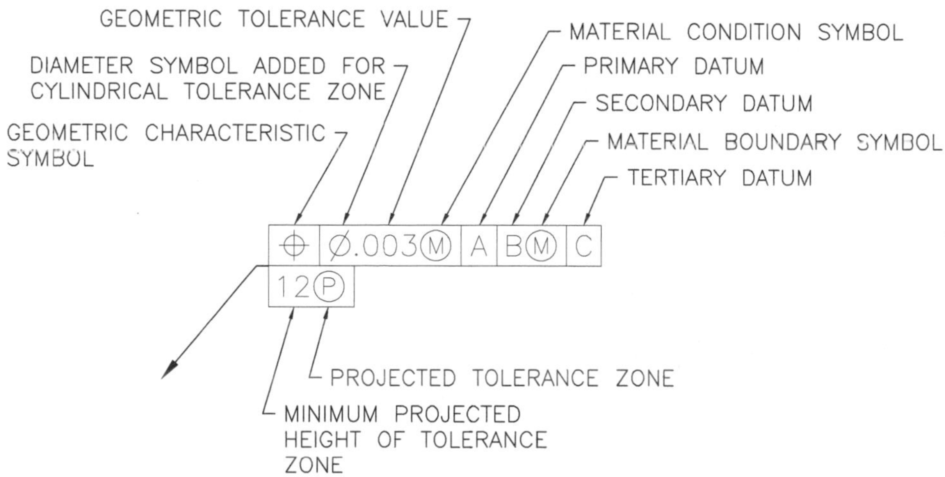

Figure 23-11 *The feature control frame*

Supplementary symbols, such as datum systems, datum targets, least and maximum material conditions, and projected tolerance zones are used in order to facilitate this precise interpretation of an engineering drawing. It is not always required to use geometric tolerances for every feature of a part.

Generally, if each feature meets all dimensional tolerances, form variations will be adequately controlled by the accuracy of the manufacturing process and the equipment used. A geometric tolerance is also used to state functional or interchangeability requirements of the manufactured part.

System of Geometric Tolerancing

The system of geometric tolerancing offers precise interpretation of drawing requirements. The geometric characteristics of a part that are controlled by using geometric tolerancing are represented by a symbol. The following table shows different characteristics and their symbols.

FEATURES	TYPES OF TOLERANCE	CHARACTERSTICS	SYMBOL
INDIVIDUAL FEATURES	FORM	STRAIGHTNESS	—
		FLATNESS	▱
		CIRCULARITY(ROUNDNESS)	○
		CYLINDRICITY	⌭
INDIVIDUAL OR RELATED FEATURES	PROFILE	PROFILE OF A LINE	⌒
		PROFILE OF A SURFACE	⌓
RELATED FEATURES	ORIENTATION	ANGULARITY	∠
		PERPENDICULARITY	⊥
		PARALLELISM	//
	LOCATION	POSITION	⌖
		CONCENTRICITY	◎
		SYMMETRY	⌯
	RUNOUT	CIRCULAR RUNOUT	↗*
		TOTAL RUNOUT	⌰*

ARROWHEADS MAY BE FILLED OR NOT

FORM TOLERANCES

Form tolerances are used to control the form characteristics of the manufactured part. These characteristics include straightness, flatness, circularity, and cylindricity. Form tolerances are applicable to single feature or elements of single feature and, as such, do not require locating dimensions. The form tolerance must be less than the size tolerance. Form and orientation tolerances critical for the function and interchangeability of parts are specified where the tolerances of size and location do not provide sufficient control. A tolerance of form may be specified where no tolerance of size is given, for example, controlling the flatness of parts after assembly.

Straightness

Straightness is a condition in which the elements of a surface or the axes of a surface are in a straight line. The geometric characteristic symbol used for indicating straightness is a horizontal line. A straightness tolerance refers to a tolerance zone within which the considered element of the surface or center line must lie. The straightness tolerance is applied to the view where the elements to be controlled are represented by a straight line.

The straightness tolerance is specified on a drawing by means of a feature control frame, which is directed by a leader to the line requiring control. In Figure 23-12(A), the symbol of straightness states that the line shall be straight within .08 in. This means that the line shall be contained within a tolerance zone consisting of the area between two parallel straight lines in the same plane separated by the specified tolerance value refer to Figure 23-12(B). Theoretically, straightness of a line can be measured by keeping a straightedge in contact with the line and then determining the space between the straightedge and the line. If the space does not exceed the specified tolerance then the edge is considered straight.

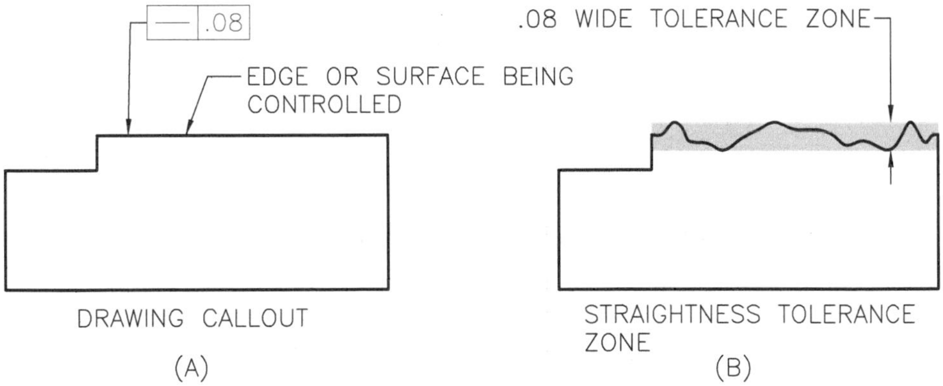

Figure 23-12 *Straightness tolerance applied to a flat surface*

For cylindrical parts or curved surfaces that are straight in one direction, the feature control frame should be directed to the side view where line elements appear as a straight line, as shown in Figure 23-13(A). Straightness of a cylindrical surface means that each line element of the surface shall be contained within a tolerance zone that consists of the space between two parallel lines, separated by the specified tolerance, when the part is rolled along one of the planes, refer to Figure 23-13(B). Theoretically, this could be measured by rolling the part on a flat plate and measuring the space between the part and the plate, refer to Figure 23-14.

The straightness tolerance applied to surface controls surface elements only. Therefore, it will only control the bending or a wavy condition of the surface, but it will not necessarily control the straightness of the axis or the conicity of the cylinder.

The straightness tolerance can be applied to a conical surface in the same manner as for a cylindrical surface, refer to Figure 23-15. In this way it will ensure that the rate of taper is uniform. For controlling the actual rate of taper, or the taper angle, the tolerance must be applied separately.

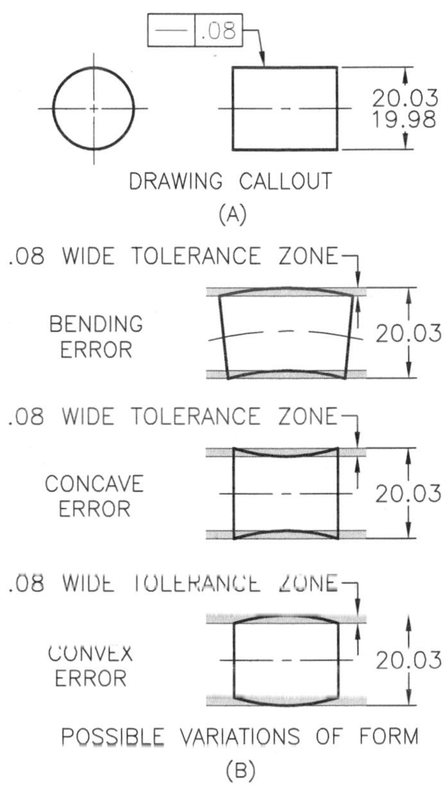

Figure 23-13 *Straightness tolerance applied to a cylindrical feature*

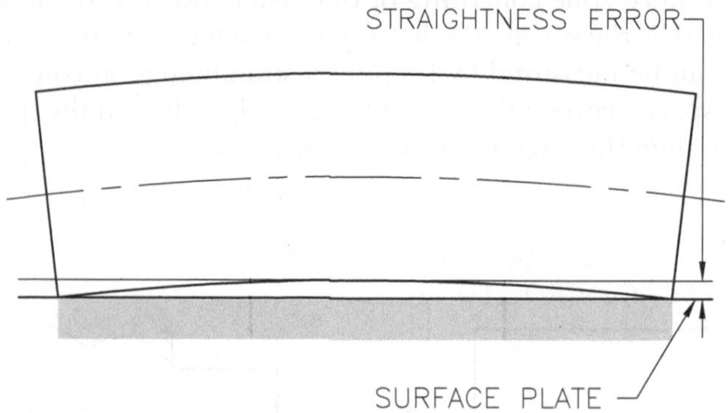

Figure 23-14 *Measuring the straightness of a cylindrical surface*

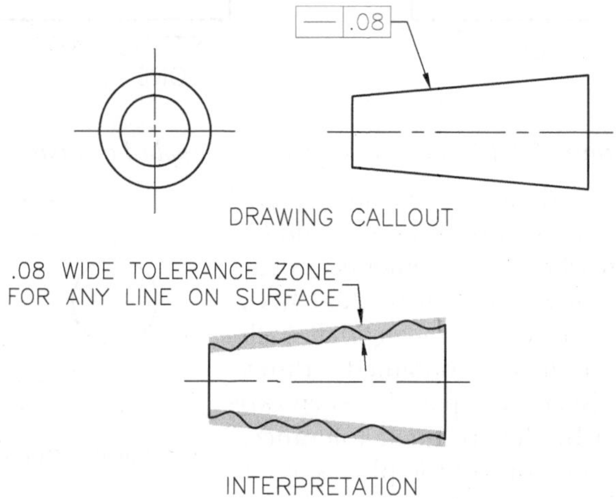

Figure 23-15 *Straightness tolerance applied for conical feature*

The straightness tolerance applied to a flat surface indicates the controlling of straightness is in one direction only. Therefore, in this case, it must be directed to the line on the drawing which represents the surface to be controlled and the direction in which control is required, refer to Figure 23-16(A). It is then interpreted to mean that each line element on the surface in the indicated direction shall lie within the specified tolerance zone, refer to Figure 23-16(C).

Different straightness tolerances may be specified in two or more directions when required. However, if the same straightness tolerance is required in two coordinate directions on the same surface, a flatness tolerance is used instead of a straightness tolerance. It is not necessary to indicate the tolerances in all three views. The straightness tolerances may be shown on a single view by indicating the direction with short lines terminated by arrowheads, as shown in Figure 23-16(B).

Straightness may be applied on unit basis for limiting unexpected surface variation within a relatively short length of the feature. When using a unit control on a feature of size, a maximum limit is typically specified to restrict the relatively large theoretical variations. If straightness for the total length is not specified then the straightness per unit length given is used alone.

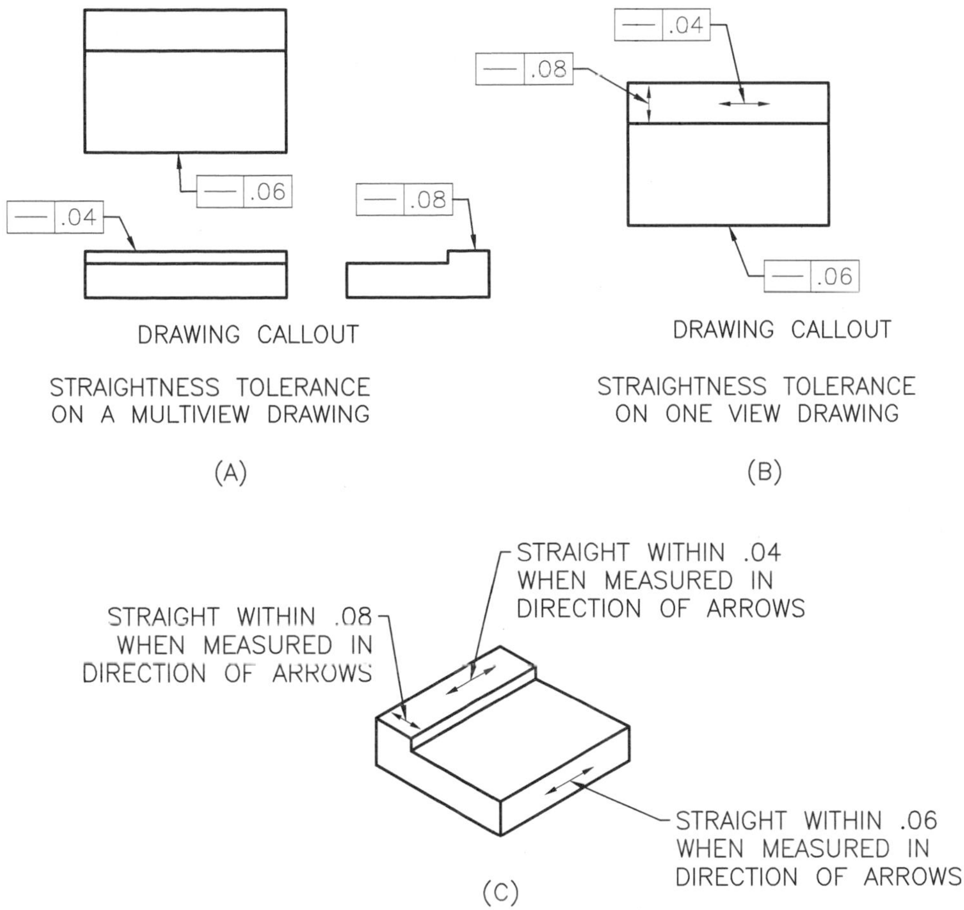

Figure 23-16 *Straightness tolerance in multiple directions*

Flatness

Flatness of a surface is a condition in which all surface elements lie in one plane. A flatness tolerance specifies a tolerance zone defined by two parallel planes within which all points on the surface must lie. These two parallel planes must lie within the limits of the size. These planes may be oriented in any manner to contain the surface but it is not necessary that they should be parallel to the base. The symbol for flatness is a parallelogram with angles of 60°.

When a flatness tolerance is specified on a surface, the feature control frame is attached to a leader and is directed to the surface or to an extension line of the surface. It is placed in a view where the surface elements to be controlled are represented by a line, refer to Figure 23-17.

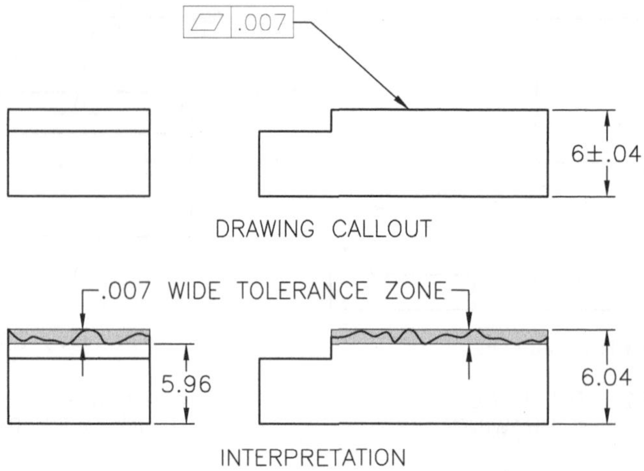

Figure 23-17 *Flatness tolerance applied to a surface*

If a surface is associated with a size tolerance then the flatness tolerance must be less than the size tolerance and it should be contained within the limits of the specified size. When flatness tolerances are applied to opposite surfaces of a part and the size tolerances are also shown, as shown in Figure 23-18, the flatness tolerance must be less than the size tolerance and lie within the limits of size.

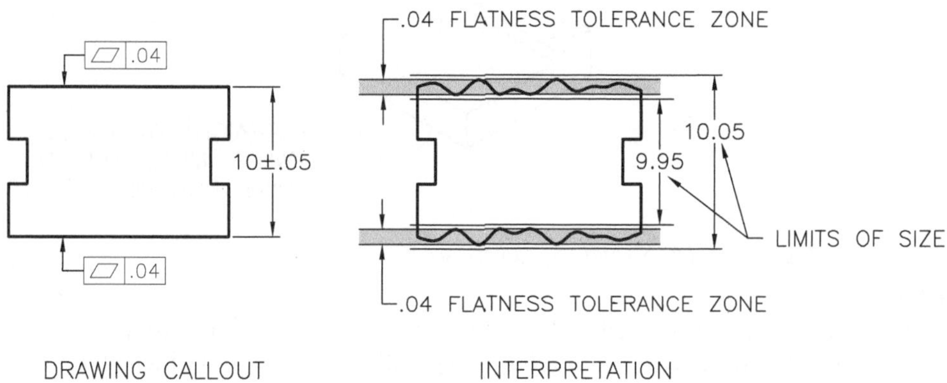

Figure 23-18 *Flatness tolerance within limits of size*

For limiting any unexpected surface variation within a relatively small area of the feature, flatness may be applied on unit basis. The unit variation is used either in combination with a specified total variation, or alone. It is expected to specify the maximum limit to restrict the relatively large theoretical variations. Since flatness involves surface area, the value of the tolerance is specified to the left of the area separated by a slash, refer to Figure 23-19.

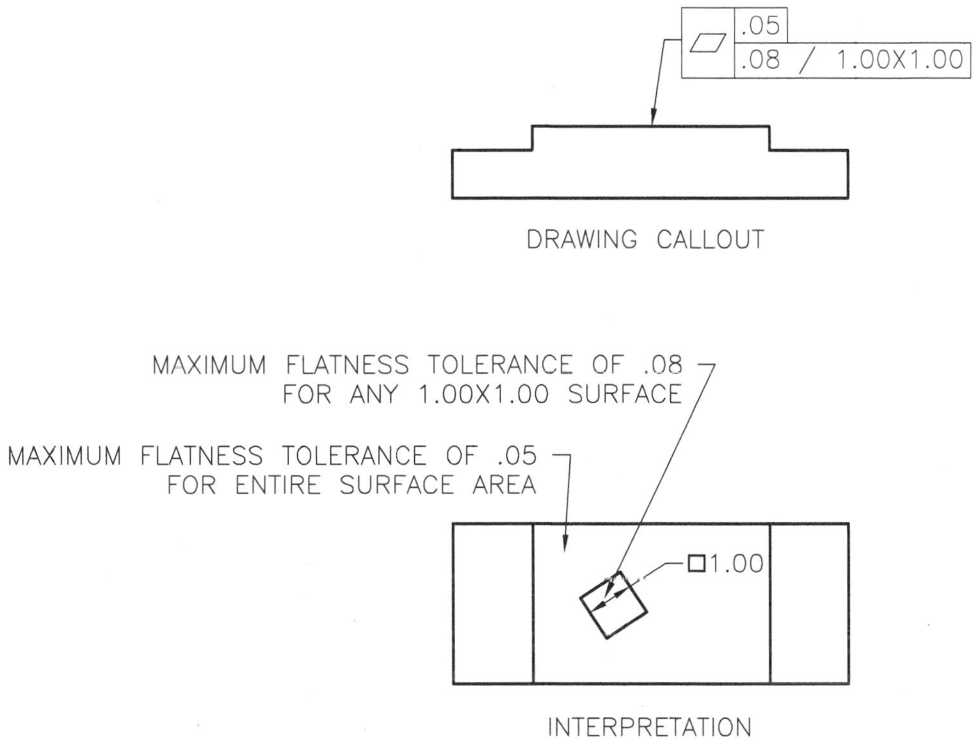

Figure 23-19 *Overall flatness tolerance combined with a flatness of unit area*

Circularity (Roundness)

Circularity is a condition on a surface of revolution (cylinder, cone, sphere) where all points of the surface are intersected by any plane perpendicular to a common axis (cylinder, cone) or a plane passing through a common center (sphere) are equidistant from that axis or center. Circularity is similar to straightness with the only difference that in circularity the line representing straightness is wrapped around a circular cross-section.

Common type of circularity errors of a circular line on the periphery of a cross-section of a circular feature may occur in the form of ovality, lobing or as random irregularities. Possible deviations from a true circle are shown in Figure 23-20.

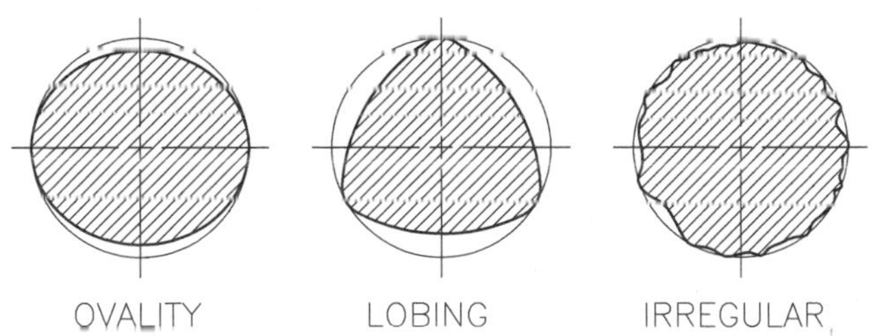

Figure 23-20 *Common types of circularity errors*

The symbol used for circularity is a circle. The circularity tolerance is specified by using this symbol in the feature control frame, as shown in Figure 23-21. A circularity tolerance specifies a tolerance zone bounded by two concentric circles within which each circular element of the surface must lie, refer to Figure 23-21.

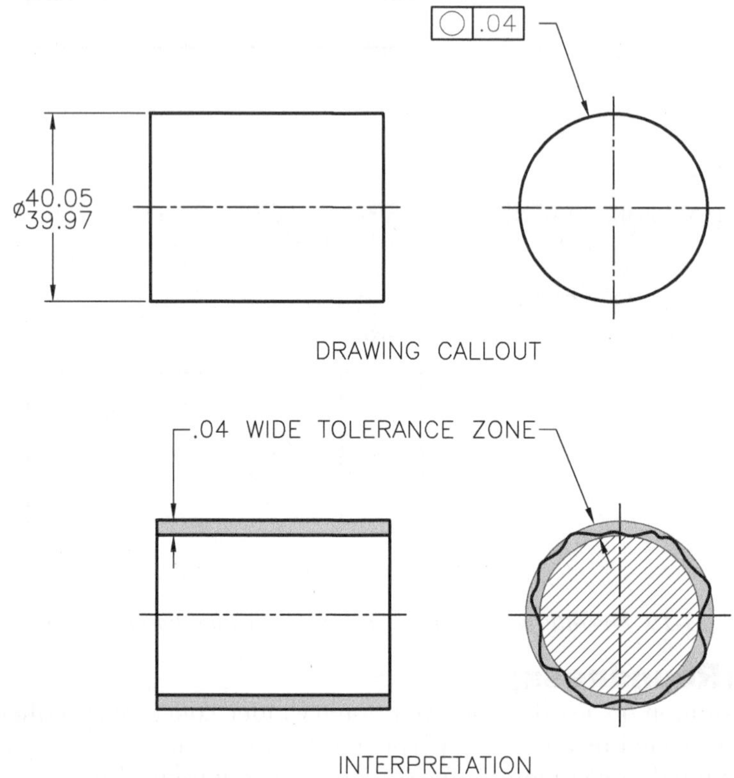

***Figure 23-21** Circularity tolerance applied to a cylindrical feature*

Circularity of non-cylindrical parts refers to conical parts and other features that are circular in cross-section but have variable diameters. Because many sizes of circles may be involved in the end view, it is usually good practice to apply the circularity tolerance to the side views, as shown in Figure 23-22.

As circularity is a form of tolerance, it is not related to datums and may be specified by using the circularity symbol in the feature control frame. Circularity is expressed on an RFS basis. The absence of a modifying symbol in the feature control frame means that RFS applies to the circularity tolerance. A circularity tolerance cannot be modified on an MMC basis because it controls surface elements only. The circularity tolerance must be less than half the size tolerance because it must lie in a space equal to half the size tolerance.

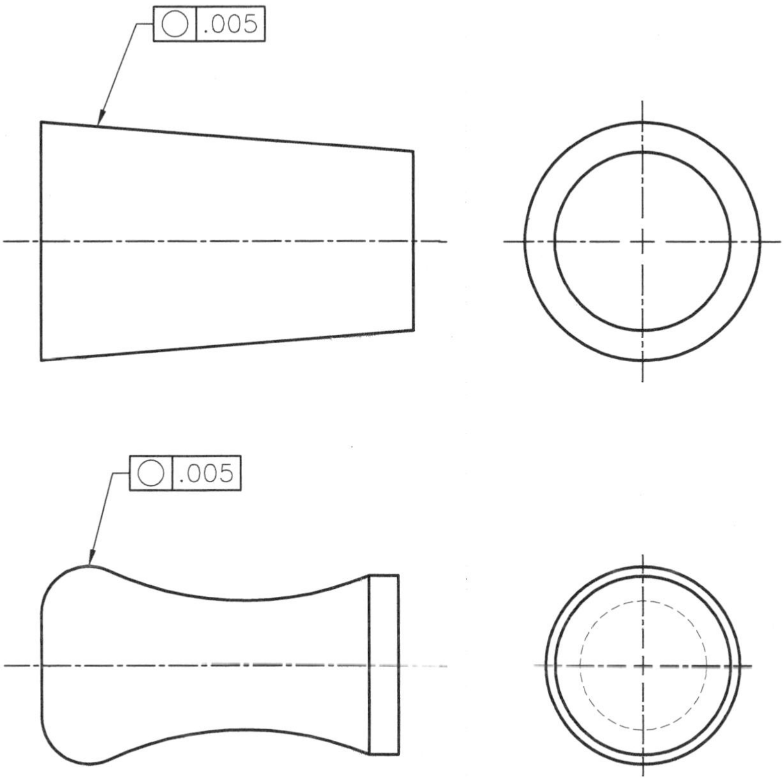

Figure 23-22 *Circularity tolerance applied to non cylindrical feature*

Cylindricity

Cylindricity is a condition of a surface in which all points on the surface are at same distance from a common axis. It is like a flatness tolerance wrapped around a cylinder. The cylindricity tolerance is a composite control of form that includes circularity, straightness, and parallelism of the surface element of a cylindrical feature.

The geometric characteristic symbol for cylindricity consists of a circle with two tangent lines at 60°. A cylindricity tolerance that is measured radially specifies a tolerance zone bounded by two concentric cylinders within which the surface must lie. So the cylindricity tolerance must be within the specified limits of size. In an engineering drawing, cylindricity tolerance can be simultaneously applied for end view or side view, as shown in Figure 23-23.

The cylindricity tolerance must be less than half of the size tolerance. Since each part is measured for form deviation, it is obvious that the total range of the specified cylindricity tolerance will not always be available. The cylindricity tolerance zone is controlled by the measured size of the actual part. The part size is first determined then the cylindricity tolerance is added as a refinement to the actual size of the part. Figure 23-24 shows some permissible form errors for the part shown in Figure 23-23.

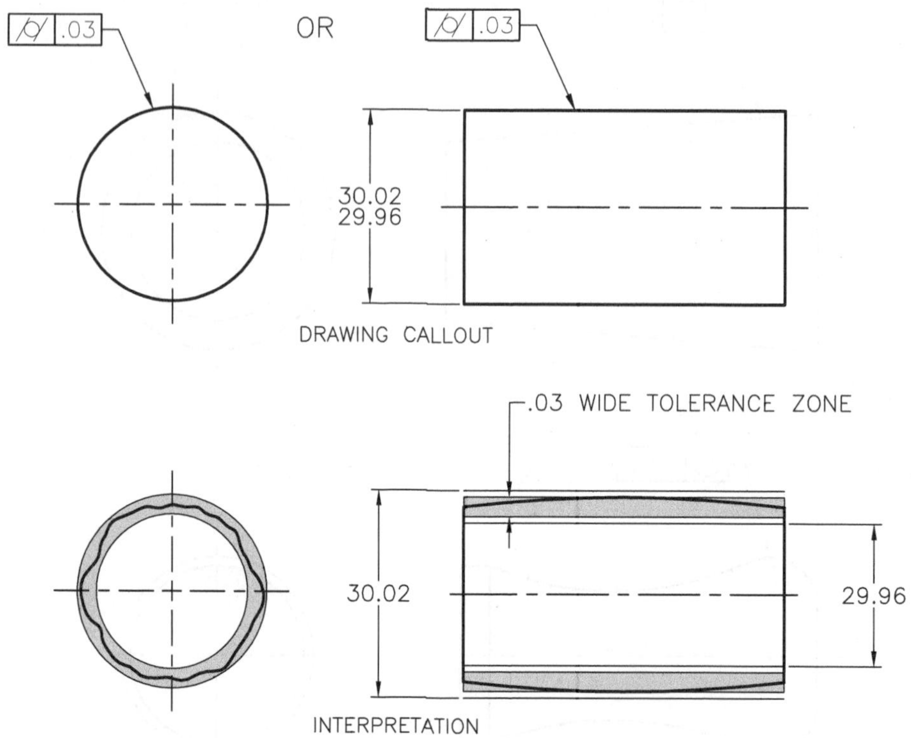

Figure 23-23 *Cylindricity tolerance applied to a cylindrical feature*

Cylindricity tolerances can be applied only to cylindrical surfaces, such as round holes and shafts. No specific geometric tolerances have been devised for other circular forms which require the use of several geometric tolerances. A conical surface, for example, must be controlled by a combination of tolerances for circularity, straightness, and angularity. Since cylindricity is a form tolerance much like the flatness tolerance, it controls surface elements only and cannot be modified on MMC basis. The absence of a modifying symbol in the feature control frame indicates that RFS applies.

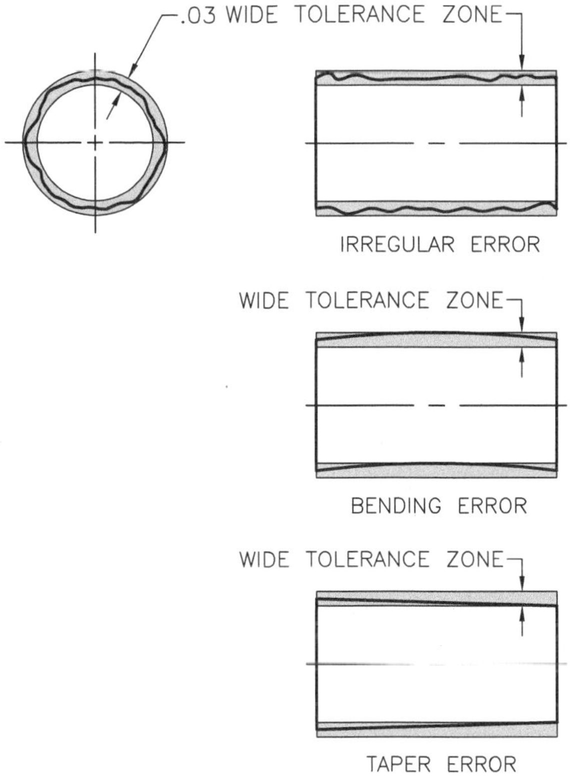

Figure 23-24 *Possible errors in a cylindrical feature*

PROFILE TOLERANCES

A profile is the outline form or shape of a line or surface. A line profile represents the edge of a part or it may refer to line elements of a surface in a single direction, such as the outline of cross-sections through the part. A surface profile represents the form or shape of a complete surface in three dimensions.

Profile tolerances are used to control the position of lines and surfaces that are neither flat nor cylindrical. The elements of a line profile may be straight lines, arcs, or other curved lines. The elements of a surface profile may be flat surfaces, spherical surfaces, cylindrical surfaces, or surfaces composed of various line profiles in two or more directions. A profile tolerance specifies a uniform boundary along the true profile within which the elements of the surface must lie. MMC is not applicable to profile tolerances. Where used as a refinement of size, the profile tolerance must be contained within the limits of size.

There are two geometric characteristics symbols for profiles. One is for line and one for surfaces. Separate symbols are needed because it is often necessary to differentiate between line elements of a surface and the complete surface itself. The symbol for the profile-of-a-line consists of a semicircle with a diameter equal to twice the size of the letters used in the whole drawing. The symbol for profile-of-a-surface is identical to profile-of-a-line except that the semicircle is closed by a straight line at the bottom, refer to Figure 23-25.

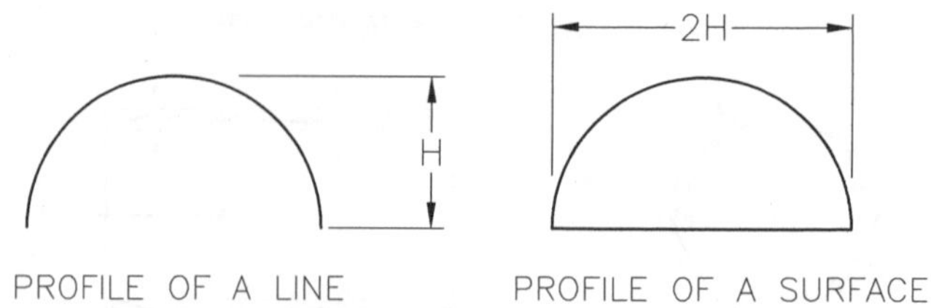

Figure 23-25 Symbols used for profile

Profile-of-a-line Tolerance

The profile-of-a-line tolerance may be directed to a line of any length or shape. Datums will not be used when only requirement is the profile shape taken cross-section by cross-section. Profile-of-a-line tolerancing is used where it is not desirable to control the entire surface of the feature as a single entity. The profile-of-a-line tolerance is specified in the usual manner by including the symbol and tolerance in a feature control frame directed to the line that is to be controlled, refer to Figure 23-26. The tolerance zone established by the profile-of-a-line tolerance is two dimensional, extending along the length of the considered feature. If the line on the drawing to which the tolerance is directed represents a surface, the tolerance applies to all line elements of the surface parallel to the plane of the view on the drawing, unless otherwise specified. The tolerance indicates a tolerance zone consisting of the area between two parallel lines, separated by the specified tolerance which are themselves parallel to the basic form of the line being toleranced.

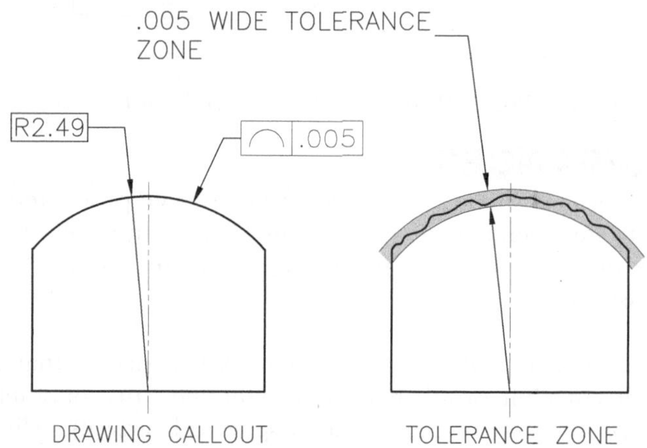

Figure 23-26 Profile-of-a-line tolerance

Profile-of-a-surface Tolerance

If a profile of line tolerance is applied to the whole surface then it is known as profile-of-a-surface tolerance. The tolerance zone established by the profile-of-a-surface tolerance is three dimensional, extending along the length and width or circumference of the considered feature or features. The profile-of-a-surface tolerance indicates a tolerance zone having the same form as the basic surface with a uniform width equal to the specified tolerance within which the entire surface must lie, refer to Figure 23-27.

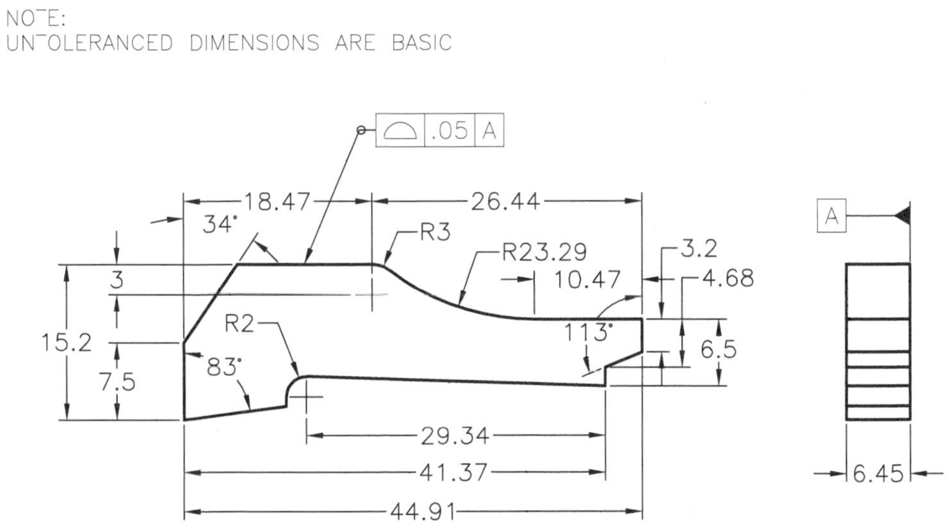

Figure 23-27 *Specifying the profile-of-a-surface tolerance*

Different profile tolerances may be applied on segments of a profile according to the requirement, as shown in Figure 23-28. Profile-of-a-surface tolerance is used to control form or combinations of size, form, and orientation. If it is used for the refinement of size, the profile tolerance must be contained within the size limits. Profile-of-a-surface tolerance may be applied to parts of any shape including parts having a constant cross-section, parts having a surface of revolution, or parts having a profile tolerance applied all over. Although the profile tolerance may be directed to the surface in either view, it is usually directed to the view showing the shape of the profile.

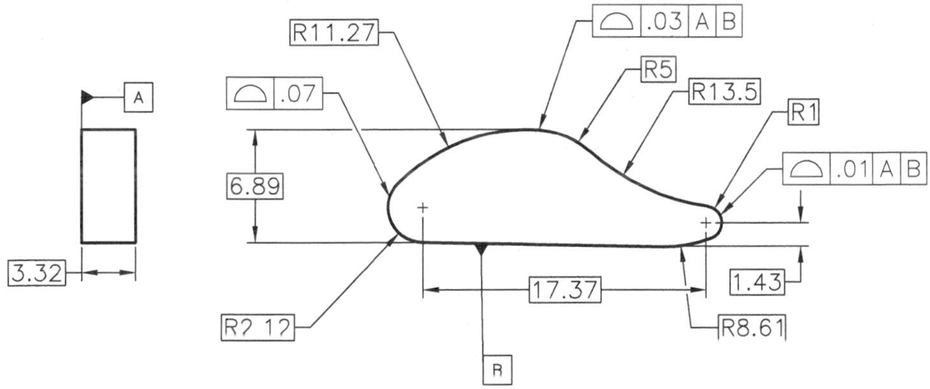

Figure 23-28 *Specifying different profile tolerances on a segment of a profile*

The basic rules for profile-of-a-line tolerancing apply to profile-of-a-surface tolerancing as well. However, in most cases, the profile-of-a-surface tolerance requires reference of datums in order to provide proper orientation of the profile. This is specified by indicating suitable datum with the feature. The criterion that distinguishes whether a profile tolerance is being applied to position or to orientation is whether the profile is related to the datum by a basic dimension or by a toleranced dimension.

Profile tolerancing may be used to control the form and orientation of plane surfaces. Profile-of-a-surface tolerance is used to control a plane surface inclined to a datum feature, as shown in Figure 23-29.

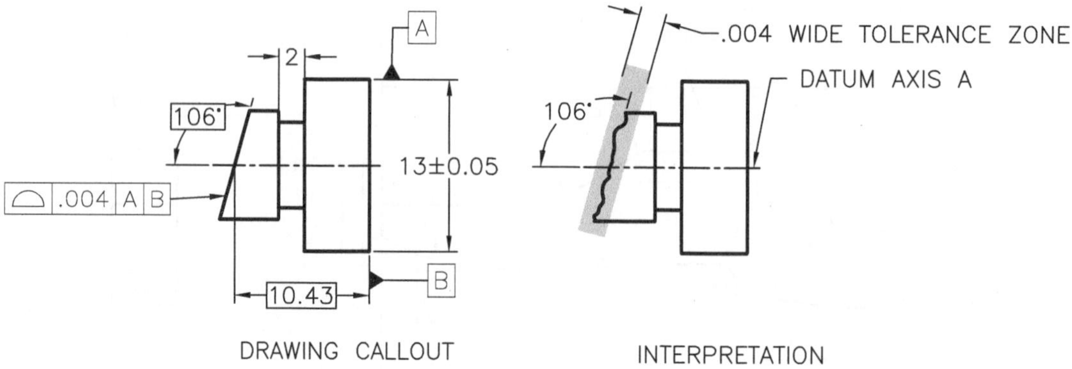

Figure 23-29 Profile-of-a-surface tolerance zone

ORIENTATION TOLERANCES

Orientation refers to the angular relationship that exists between two or more lines, surfaces, or other features. An orientation tolerance controls parallel, perpendicular, and all other angular relationships. As orientation refers to a certain degree, the limits of size controls the form and parallelism, and the tolerances of location controls the orientation. The extent of this control should be considered before specifying the form or orientation tolerances. The general geometric characteristic for orientation is termed as angularity. This term may be used to describe angular relationships of any angle between straight lines or surfaces with straight line elements, such as flat or cylindrical surfaces. For two specific type of angularity, special terms are used. They are perpendicularity and parallelism. Perpendicularity (squareness) is used for features that are related to each other by a 90° angle, and parallelism for features related to one another by an angle of zero.

A tolerance of form or orientation may be specified where the tolerances of size and location do not provide sufficient control. Note that an orientation tolerance, when applied to a planar surface, controls flatness to the extent of the orientation tolerance. When the flatness control in the orientation tolerance is not sufficient, a separate flatness tolerance should be considered. An orientation tolerance does not control the location of features.

The three geometric symbols for orientation tolerances are shown in Figure 23-30. The proportions for the symbols are based on the height of the letters used in the drawing.

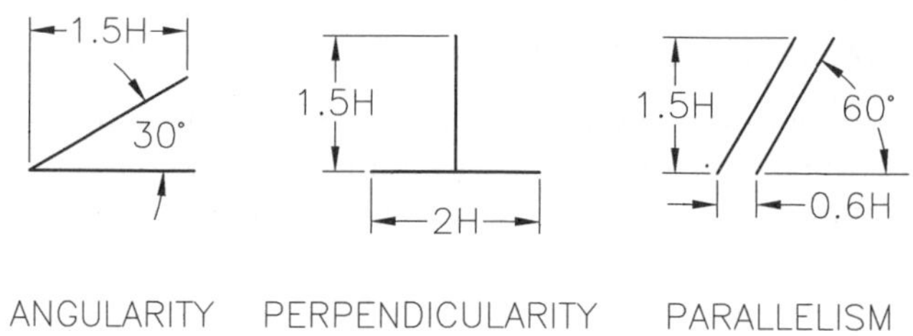

Figure 23-30 Symbols used for Orientation tolerances

Angularity Tolerance

Angularity refers to the angular relation of a surface or axis (at an angle other than 0° and 90°) with respect to a datum plane or datum axis. The angularity tolerance is a three-dimensional quantity and the shape of the tolerance zone depends on the shape of the feature. If applied to a flat surface, the tolerance zone is specified by two imaginary planes, parallel to the ideal angle and spaced apart at the prescribed distance, refer to Figure 23-31. If angularity is applied to a hole, it references to an imaginary cylinder around the ideal angle but the center axis of the hole must stay within that imaginary cylinder, refer to Figure 23-32.

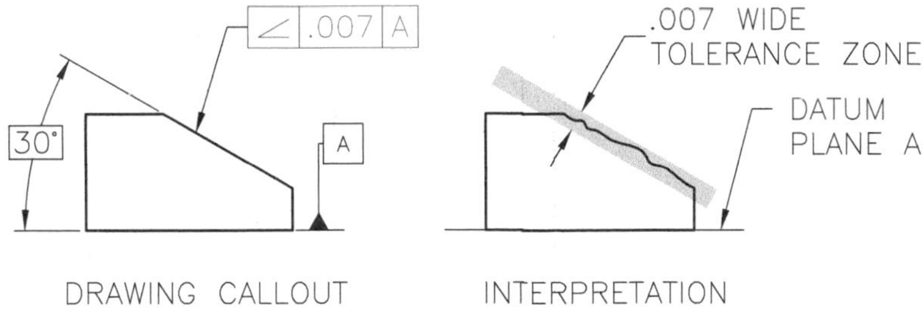

Figure 23-31 Angularity tolerance applied to a surface

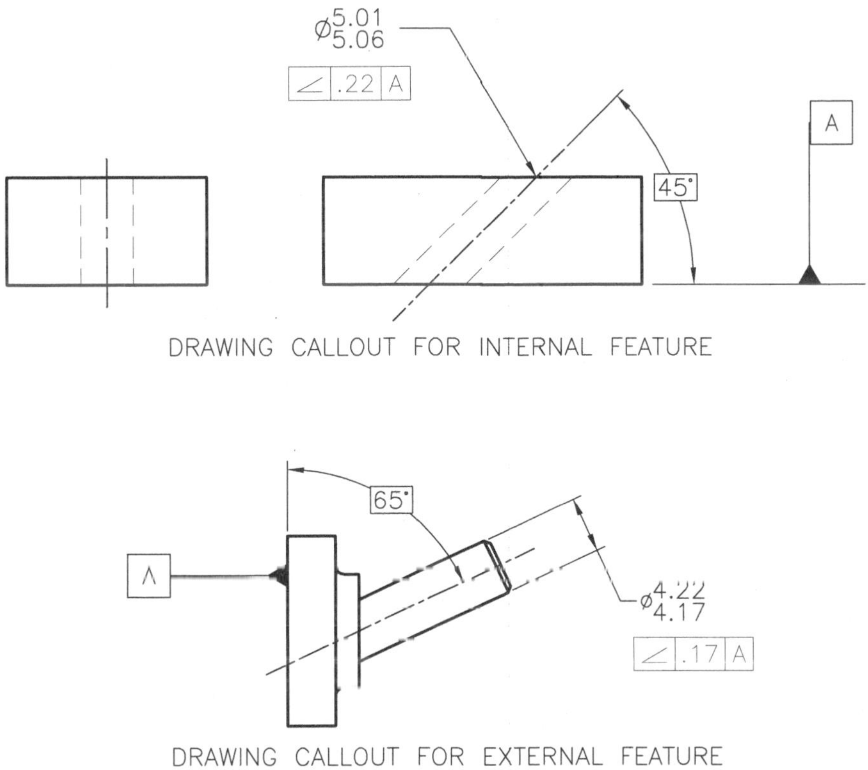

Figure 23-32 Angularity tolerance applied to cylindrical features

For geometric tolerancing of angularity, the angle between the datum and the controlled features should be stated as a basic angle. Therefore, it should be enclosed in a rectangular frame (basic dimension symbol) to indicate that the general tolerance note does not apply, refer to Figures 23-31 and 23-32. However, for perpendicularity (90°) or parallelism (0°) the angle need not be stated.

Perpendicularity Tolerance

Perpendicularity is the condition where a surface subtends 90° angle to a datum plane or axis. The perpendicularity tolerance for a feature specifies a tolerance zone defined by two parallel planes perpendicular to a datum plane or axis. The surface or axis of the considered feature must lie within this specified zone.

The perpendicularity tolerance specifies one of the following tolerance zones:

1. A cylindrical tolerance zone perpendicular to a datum plane or axis within which the center line of the considered feature must lie, refer to Figure 23-33.

2. A tolerance zone defined by two parallel planes perpendicular to a datum axis or plane within which the surface of the considered feature must lie, refer to Figure 23-34.

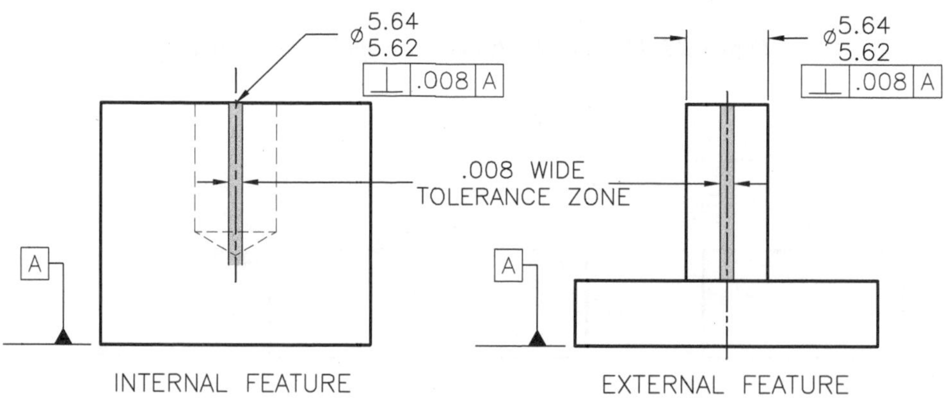

Figure 23-33 *Perpendicularity tolerance zone in cylindrical features*

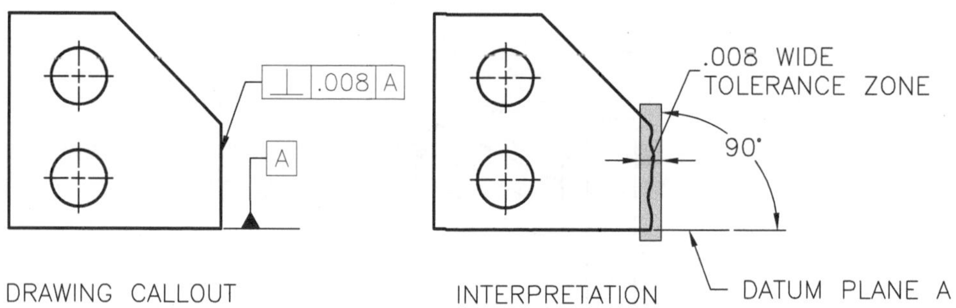

Figure 23-34 *Perpendicularity tolerance applied to flat surface*

Parallelism Tolerance

Parallelism refers to condition where a feature is parallel to the reference datum plane. Parallelism can also be stated as the condition of a surface equidistant at all points from a datum plane. The parallelism tolerance for a flat surface or a cylindrical feature specifies a tolerance zone defined by two planes or lines parallel to a datum plane or axis. For a flat surface, line elements of the surface must lie within the specified tolerance zone, refer to Figure 23-35. For a cylindrical feature, the axis of the feature must lie within the specified cylindrical tolerance zone, refer to Figure 23-36.

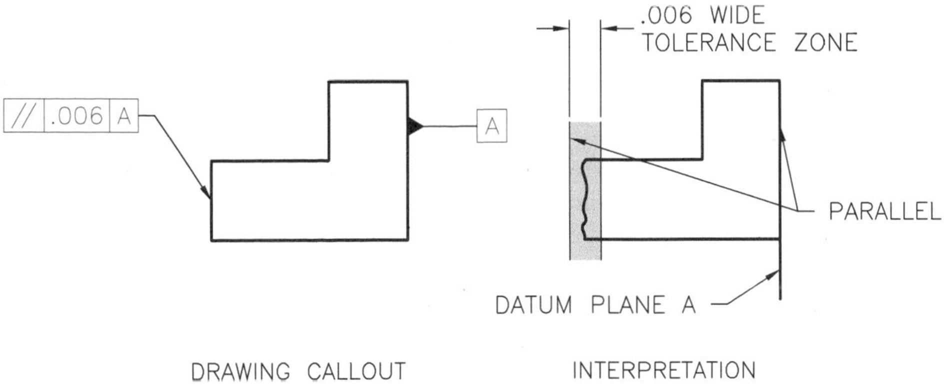

Figure 23-35 *Parallelism tolerance applied to flat surfaces*

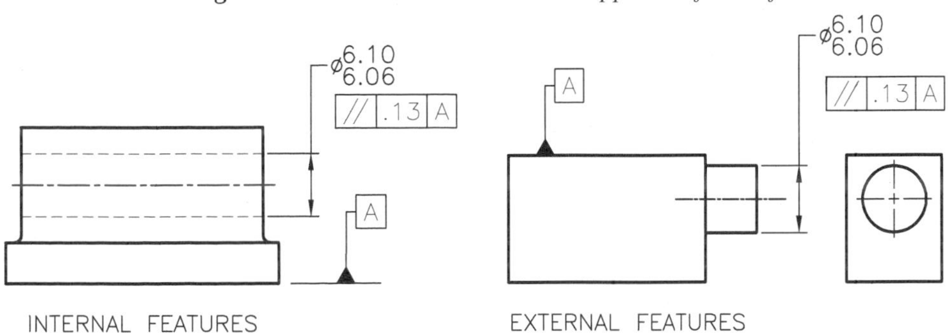

Figure 23-36 *Parallelism tolerance applied to cylindrical features*

Note

Flatness and parallelism are sometimes confused with each other. However, flatness is not related to another datum and it looks at the feature independently. Parallelism relates the inspected feature to another datum plane. Whenever an orientation tolerance is applied to a flat surface, it indirectly defines the flatness of the feature.

LOCATION TOLERANCES

Location tolerances include position, concentricity, and symmetry tolerances. Position tolerance is used to control coaxiality of features, the center distance between features, and the location of features as a group. Concentricity and symmetry tolerances are used to control the center distance of feature elements. The geometric characteristics symbols for the location tolerances are in the proportion of the text height used in the drawing, as shown in Figure 23-37.

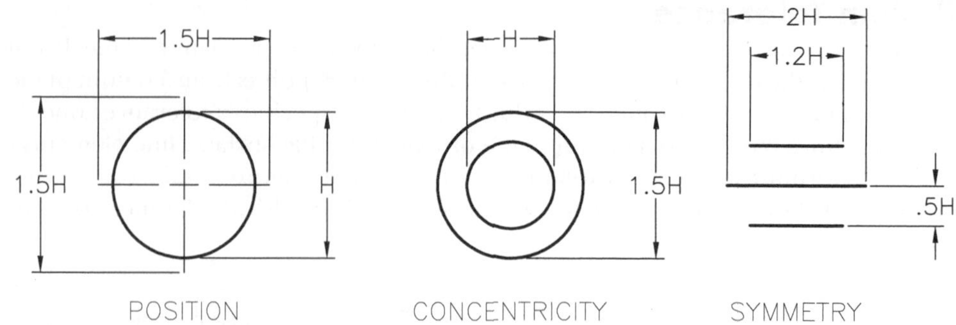

Figure 23-37 Geometric characteristics symbols for location tolerances

Position Tolerance

Position is the location of one or more features of size relative to one another or to one or more datum references. The position tolerance is likely one of the most common of the location tolerances and probably used more than any other geometric tolerance. The ideal or exact location of the feature is called the true position. The actual location of the feature is compared to the true position and involves one or more datums to determine the true position. The exact location of a feature is defined by basic dimensions which is shown in a rectangular box and is established with reference to datum planes or axes, as shown in Figure 23-38.

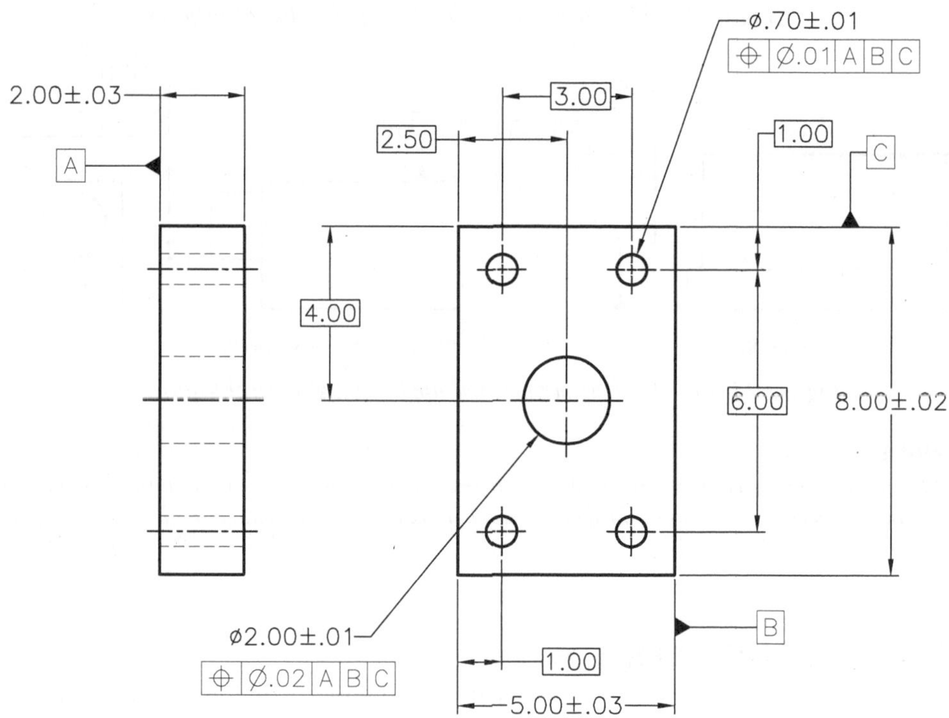

Figure 23-38 Position tolerance applied on hole features

A position tolerance locates center points, axes and median planes of the features. It has nothing to do with the size, shape, or angle of a feature. The position tolerance involves the location of center axis of the hole and the axis of the hole must be within the imaginary cylinder around the intended true position of the hole, as shown in Figure 23-39. If the toleranced feature is rectangular, the tolerance zone will be defined by two imaginary planes at a specified distance from the ideal true position.

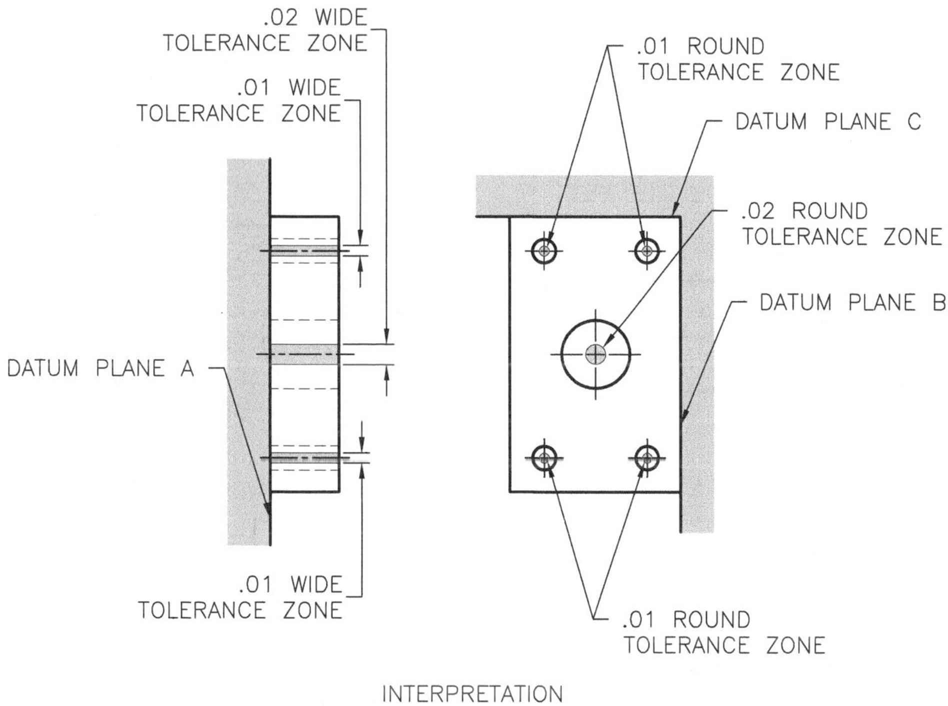

Figure 23-39 Interpretation of true position

Concentricity Tolerance

Concentricity is a condition where the median points of all diametrically opposed elements of a surface of revolution (or the median points of corresponding elements of two or more radially disposed features) are congruent with a datum axis or center point, refer to Figure 23-40. This tolerance is not used very often because median points are difficult to establish due to irregularities of form. The only reason to use this tolerance is to control the error of balance that can exist if the mass center is not close to the axis of rotation or center plane.

The concentricity tolerance is a cylindrical (or spherical) tolerance zone whose axis (or center point) coincides with the axis (or center point) of the datum feature(s), refer to Figure 23-40. Concentricity is measured using the median points of multiple diameters within the cylindrical tolerance zone. The median points of all corresponding elements of the feature(s) being controlled, regardless of feature size, must lie within the cylindrical (or spherical) tolerance zone.

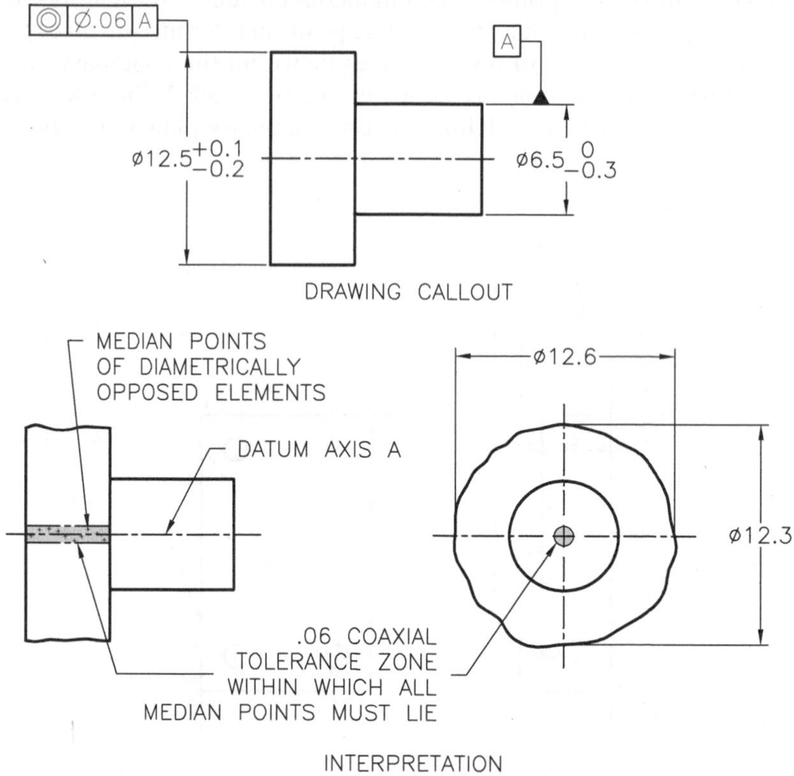

Figure 23-40 *Concentricity tolerance applied to a cylindrical feature*

Symmetrical Tolerance

Symmetry is a condition where the median points of all opposite or corresponding elements of two or more features (surfaces) are congruent with a datum axis or center plane, as shown in Figure 23-41.

Symmetry is much like concentricity except that it controls rectangular features and involves reference of two datum planes. Both of these control the median points of a feature of size. Concentricity is applied to circular features whereas symmetry is applied to non circular features. The tolerance zone is equally disposed about the datum plane. The median points of the toleranced feature, regardless of its feature size must lie within the tolerance zone which is defined by two parallel planes for symmetry, refer to Figure 23-41.

Note

Both symmetry and concentricity tolerances are difficult to measure and increase the cost of inspection. However, when a certain characteristic like balancing of a part is a primary concern, these tolerances are very effective.

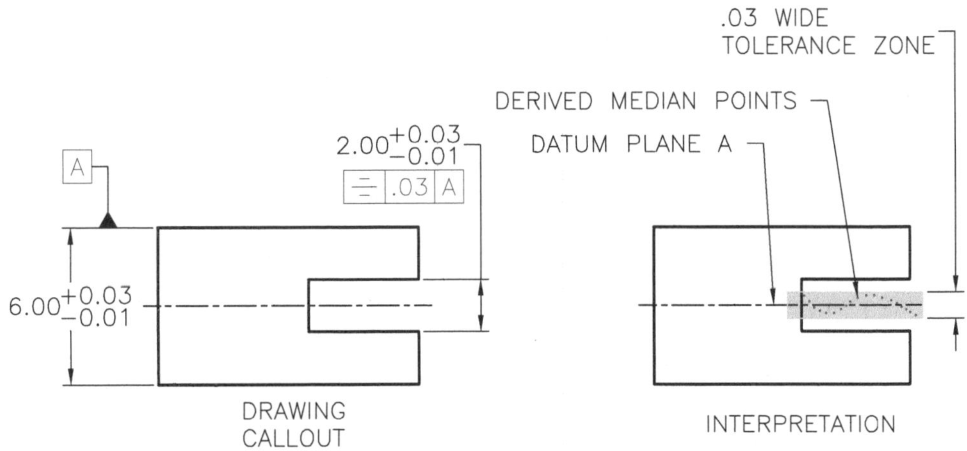

Figure 23-41 *Symmetry tolerance applied to a rectangular feature*

RUNOUT TOLERANCES

Runout tolerances are three-dimensional in nature and are only applied to cylindrical parts that rotate about an axis. Runout tolerances are used to control the relationship of a feature relative to a datum axis which is established between two diameters that are axially separated. Runout tolerances are composite tolerances used to control the relationship of one or more cylindrical features during a full 360^0 rotation about the datum axis.

There are two types of runout tolerances used in the drawings: circular runout and total runout. Both circular and total runout reference a cylindrical feature to a center datum-axis and simultaneously control the location, form, and orientation of the feature. The type of runout tolerance used depends on design requirements and manufacturing considerations. Geometric characteristics symbols used for runout tolerancing are shown in Figure 23-42.

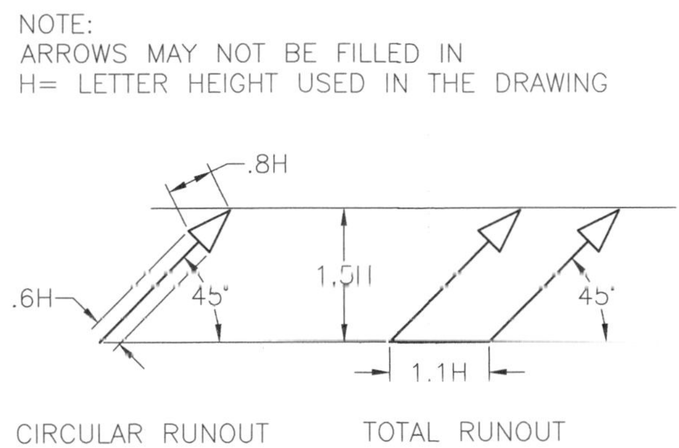

Figure 23-42 *Geometric characteristics symbols for runout tolerances*

Circular Runout

Circular runout provides control of circular elements of a surface. The tolerance is applied independently at any cross-section as the part is rotated 360°. If applied to surfaces that are constructed around a datum axis, circular runout controls variations such as circularity and coaxiality. When applied to surfaces constructed at right angles to the datum axis, circular runout controls wobble at all diametral positions.

For inspecting the circular runout, the part must be rotated about the datum axis. A calibrated instrument is placed against the surface of the rotating part to detect the highest and lowest points. The surface must remain within two imaginary circles having their centers located at the center axis, as shown in Figure 23-43.

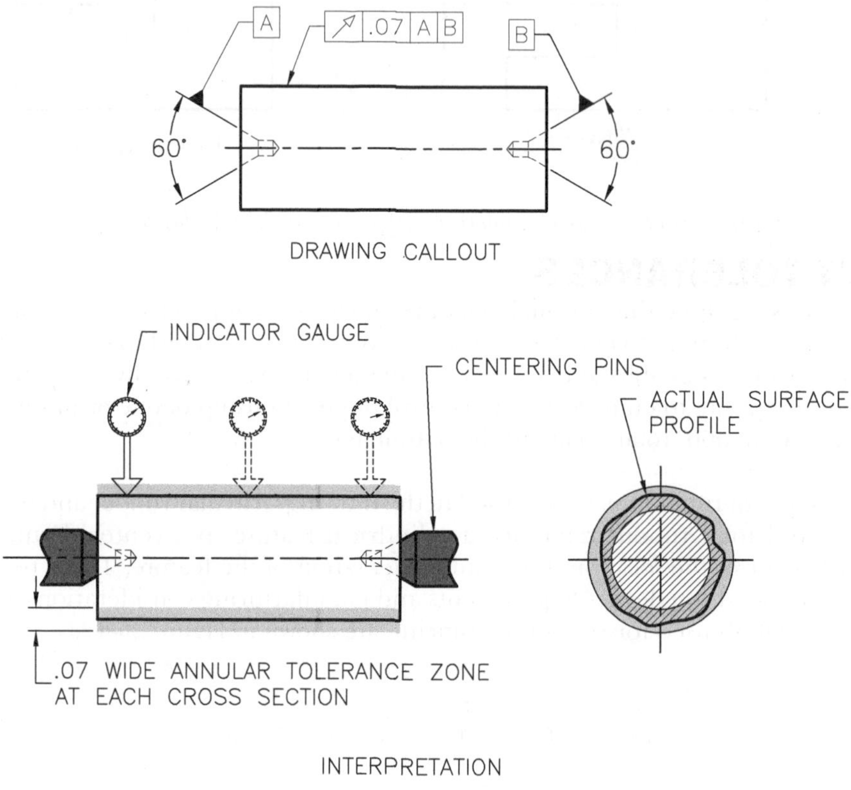

Figure 23-43 *Circular runout for cylindrical feature*

Figure 23-43 shows a surface measured at several points indicated by three different positions of the indicator gauge. At each position, the indicator movement during one revolution of the part must not exceed the specified tolerance. For a cylindrical feature, runout error is caused by eccentricity and errors of roundness. It is not affected by taper (conicity) or errors of straightness of the straight line elements such as barrel shaping.

A part where tolerance is applied to a surface at right angle to the datum axis is shown in Figure 23-44(A). In this case, an error generally termed as wobble will be shown when the surface is flat but not perpendicular to the axis, refer to Figure 23-44(B). Error will be shown if the surface is convex or concave or perfect, as shown in Figure 23-44(C). Circular runout can also be applied to curved surfaces. Unless otherwise specified, measurement is always done normal to the surface.

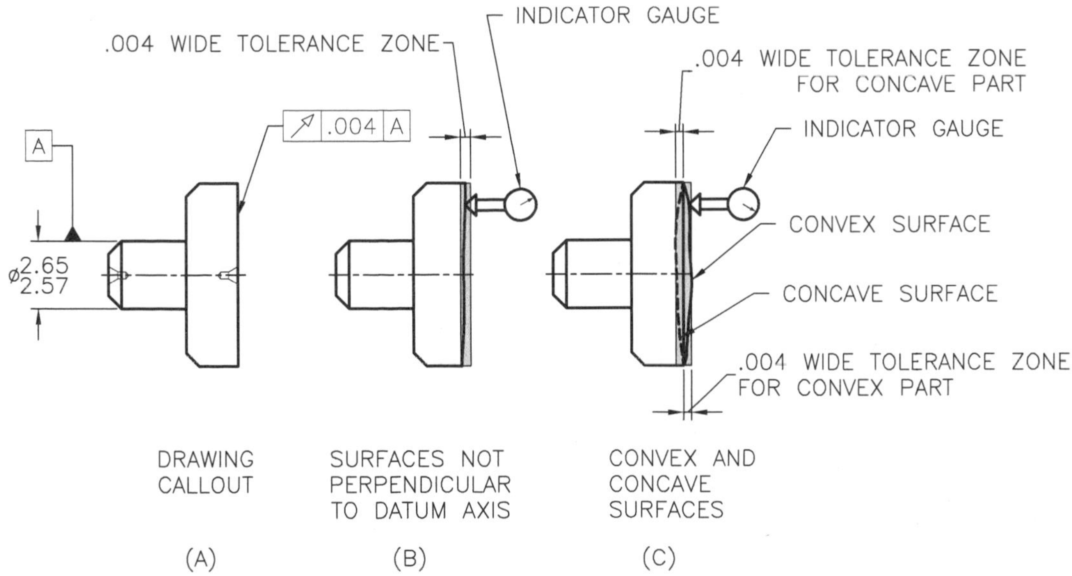

Figure 23-44 *Circular runout for flat surfaces perpendicular to datum axis feature*

If a runout tolerance is applied to a specific portion of a surface, a thick chain line is also drawn adjacent to the surface profile to show the desired length. Basic dimensions are used to define the extent of the portion as indicated in Figure 23-45.

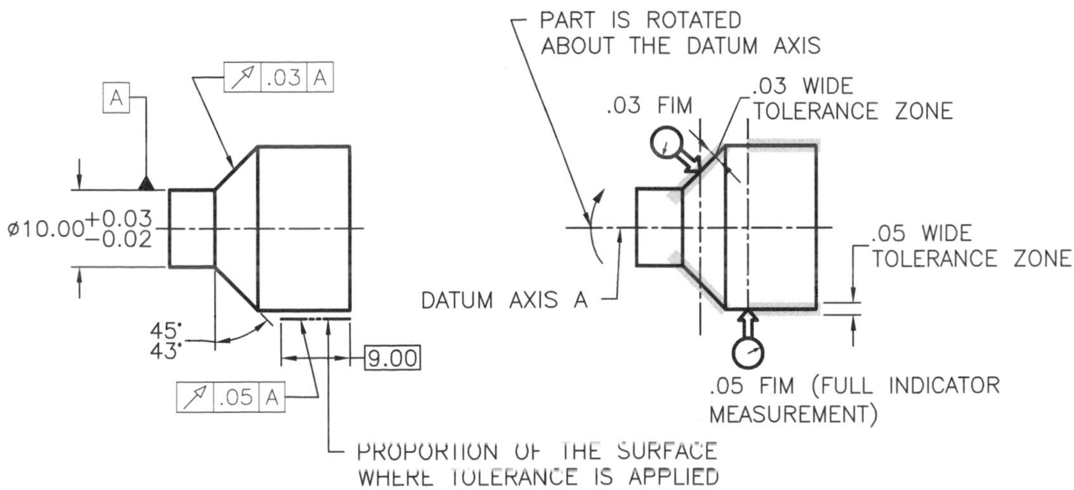

Figure 23-45 *Circular runout applied to a specific portion of surface*

When runout tolerance is directed to a surface, it is applied to the full length of the surface until there is an abrupt change in the surface profile. If a control with the same tolerance is applied to more than one portion of a surface, additional leaders and arrowheads may be used. If different tolerance values are required, separate tolerances must be specified. If only part of a surface or several consecutive portions require the same tolerance, the length on which the tolerance need to apply can be indicated, as shown in Figure 23-46.

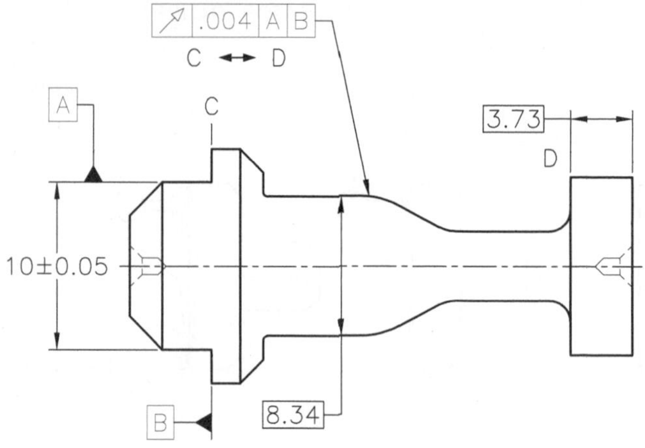

Figure 23-46 Circular runout applied to specified length of the part

Total Runout

Total runout is the runout of a complete surface and not merely of each circular element of the part. The tolerance zone is specified by two concentric cylinders separated by the specified tolerance value and coaxial with the datum axis, as shown in Figure 23-47. A total runout may be applied to surfaces at various angles, therefore it also controls the profile of the surface in addition to runout.

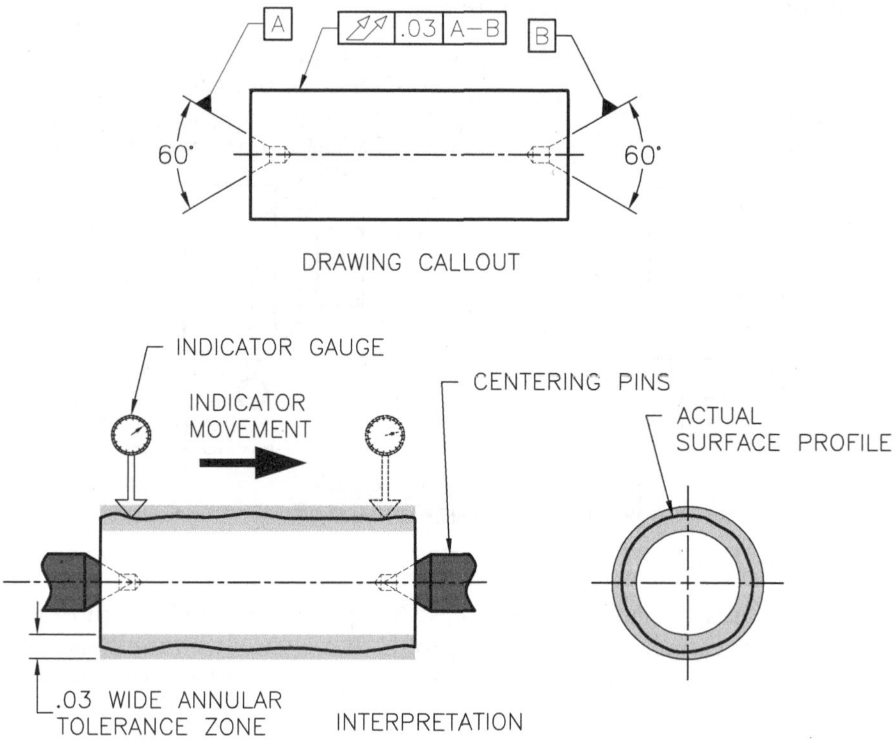

Figure 23-47 Measurement of tolerance zone for total runout

Unlike circular tolerance which is only affected by the errors of eccentricity and roundness, total runout is also affected by straightness and conicity of the surface.

For measuring total runout of a cylindrical surface, the indicator is traversed over the full surface while the part is revolved about its datum axis. Measurements are made over the whole surface without resetting the indicator. However, for measurement purposes, the indicator gauge must be capable of following the true profile direction of the surface.

The measuring process is comparatively simple for straight surfaces, such as cylindrical surfaces and flat faces. For conical surfaces, the datum axis can be tilted to the taper angle so that the measured surface becomes parallel to a surface plate. Total runout is the difference between the lowest indicator reading at any position and the highest reading at the same position or at any other position on the same surface.

FITS

Fit is a specific combination of tolerances and allowances in the design of mating parts. When two parts are assembled, the relation resulting from the difference between their sizes before assembly is called a fit. In a general term, fit is the degree of tightness or looseness between two mating parts.

A fit system is the system of standard allowance to suit specific range of basic size. Proper selection of these standard allowances ensures specific classes of fit in mating parts. System of fits can be classified into two systems:

Hole Basis System

In the hole basis system, the size of the hole is kept constant and shaft sizes are varied to obtain various types of fits, refer to Figure 23-48. In this system, lower deviation of hole is kept zero, which means the minimum limit of the hole is same as the basic size. The maximum limit of the hole and the maximum and minimum limits for the shaft are then varied to give desired type of fit. The hole basis system is commonly used compared to shaft basis system. It is more convenient to make holes of fixed size as the tools like drills, taps and reamers have the standard size and are easily available for producing holes. On the other hand, size of the shaft produced by turning or grinding can be very easily varied.

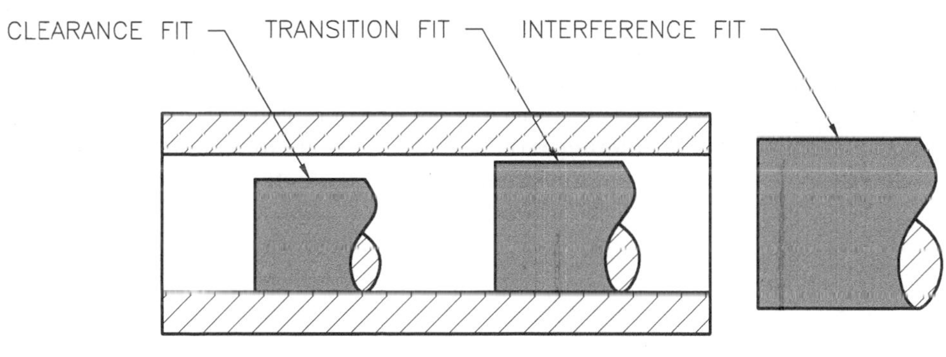

Figure 23-48 Hole basis system of fits

Shaft Basis System

In the shaft basis system, the size of the shaft is kept constant and fits are obtained by varying the size of the hole, refer to Figure 23-49. Shaft basis system is used when the ground bars or drawn bars are readily available. These bars do not require further machining and fits are obtained by varying the sizes of the hole. In this system, the upper deviation (fundamental deviation) of shaft is kept zero which means the maximum limit of the shaft is considered as the basic size and fits are obtained by varying the minimum limit of shaft or both the limits of the hole.

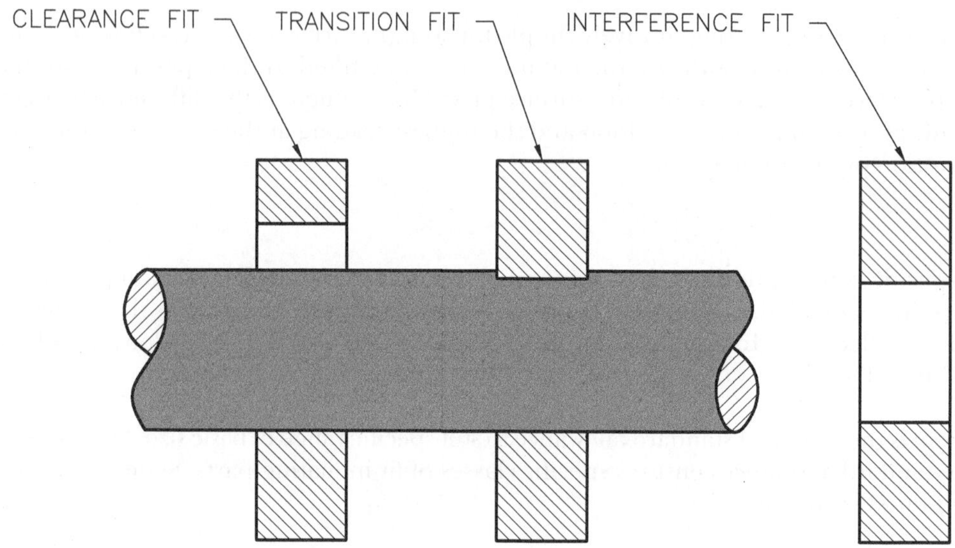

Figure 23-49 *Shaft basis system of fits*

Based on hole and shaft system, fits are categorized into the following three types.

- Clearance fit
- Interference fit
- Transition fit

Clearance Fit

Clearance fit is the difference between the sizes of the hole and the shaft. Clearance fits have limits of size specified in such a manner that there will always remain a clearance between the two mating parts. When it is desirable for the shaft to rotate or slide freely within the hole, clearance fits are maintained between the mating parts. Clearance fits are intended for accurate assembly of parts and bearings. The parts having clearance fits can be assembled by hand because the hole is always larger than the shaft. The tolerances on both the parts are maintained in such a manner that the hole diameter will always be larger than the shaft diameter, as shown in Figure 23-50.

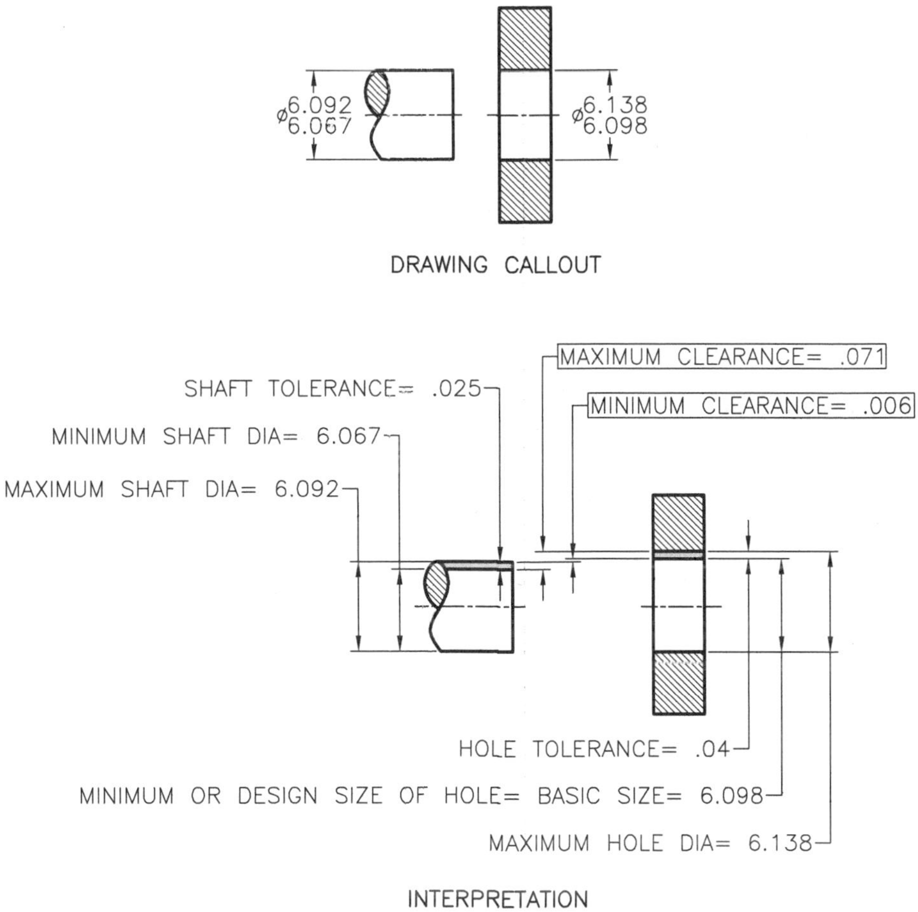

Figure 23-50 *Calculation of clearance fit*

The clearance may be the maximum clearance or the minimum clearance. The minimum clearance fit is the difference between the minimum size of the hole and the maximum size of the shaft.

Minimum clearance = Minimum hole diameter - Maximum shaft diameter

The maximum clearance fit is the difference between the maximum size of the hole and the minimum size of the shaft.

Maximum clearance = Maximum hole diameter - Minimum shaft diameter

Clearance fit is classified into three categories.

Loose Fit

It is used between those mating parts where precision is not required. It provides minimum allowance and generally used on loose pulleys such as agricultural machineries, and so on.

Running Fit

For a running fit, the dimension of shaft should be smaller enough to maintain a film of oil for lubrication. Generally, it is used in bearing pair, and so on.

Slide Fit or Medium Fit

It is used on those mating parts where higher level of precision is required. It provides medium allowance and is used in tool slides, slide valve, automobile parts, and so on.

Note
Maximum clearance in a loose or sliding fit is always greater than zero. On the other hand, in a tight fit, both the maximum and minimum clearance are negative.

Interference Fit

Interference fits have limits of size specified in such a manner that the mating parts always have interference between them. In a general term, the hole will be always smaller than the shaft. In such a fit, the tolerance zone of the hole will always be lower than the tolerance zone of the shaft. Interference fits are used for permanent assemblies of parts which require rigidity and alignment, such as dowel pins and bearings in castings. Parts are usually assembled together by pressure or heat expansion. The tolerances on each part are maintained in a way that the shaft diameter will be larger than the hole diameter, as shown in Figure 23-51.

Maximum interference is arithmetical difference between the minimum size of the hole and the maximum size of the shaft.

Maximum interference = Maximum shaft diameter - Minimum hole diameter

Minimum interference is the difference between the maximum size of the hole and the minimum size of the shaft.

Minimum interference = Minimum shaft diameter - Maximum hole diameter

Note
Interference fit has a negative allowance which means that interference exists between maximum limit of hole and minimum limit of the shaft.

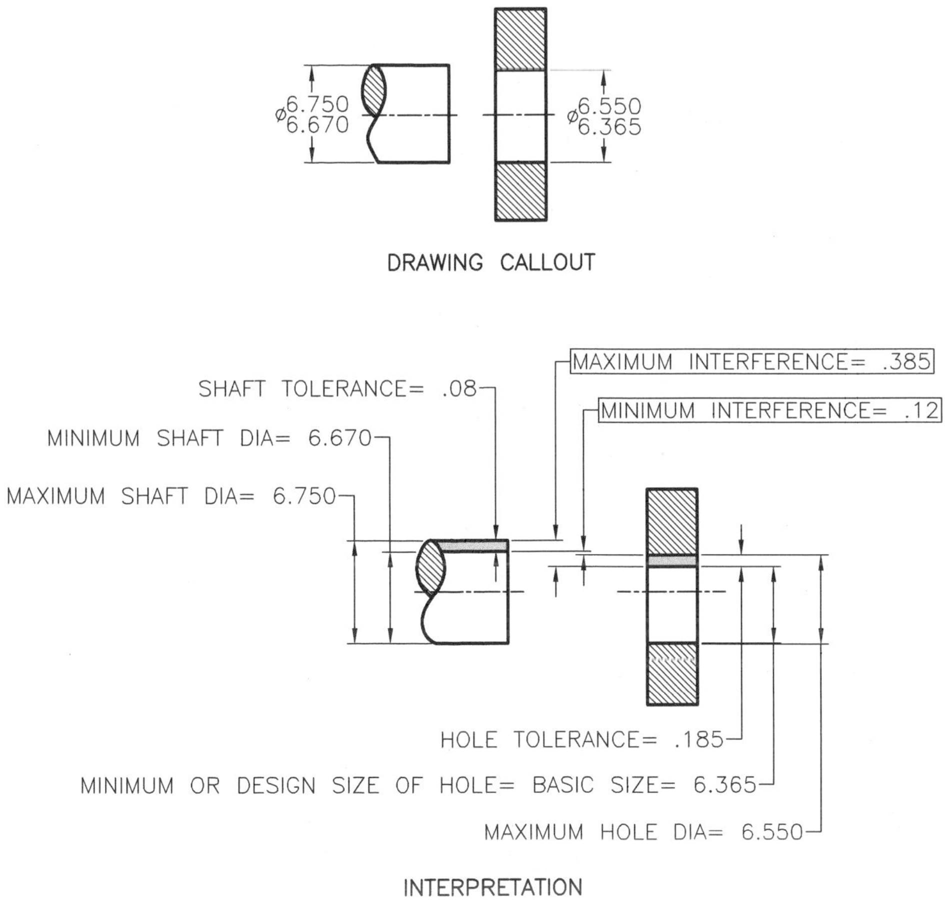

***Figure 23-51** Calculation of interference fit*

Interference fit is classified into three categories.

Shrink Fit or Heavy Force Fit

It refers to maximum negative allowance. In an assembly of a hole and a shaft, the hole is expanded by heating and then rapidly cooled in its position. It is used in fitting of rims, seating rings and so on.

Medium Force Fit

These fits have medium negative allowance. In this fit considerable pressure is required to assemble a hole and the shaft. Force fit is generally used in car wheels, armature of dynamos and so on.

Tight Fit or Press Fit

One part can be assembled into the other with a hand hammer or by light pressure. A slight negative allowance exists between two mating parts. It gives a semi-permanent fit and is used on a keyed pulley and shaft, rocker arm, and so on.

Transition Fit

Transition fits have limits of size specified in such a manner that either a clearance or an interference may result depending on the actual value of the individual tolerances of the mating components. Transition fits are a compromise between clearance and interference fits. They are used for applications where accurate location is important but either a small amount of clearance or interference is permissible. When in an assembly of hole and shaft, hole is machined to its smallest size and the shaft is machined to its largest size, the result will be an interference fit, as shown in Figure 23-52. When the hole is at its maximum size and the shaft is at its smallest size, the result will be a clearance fit.

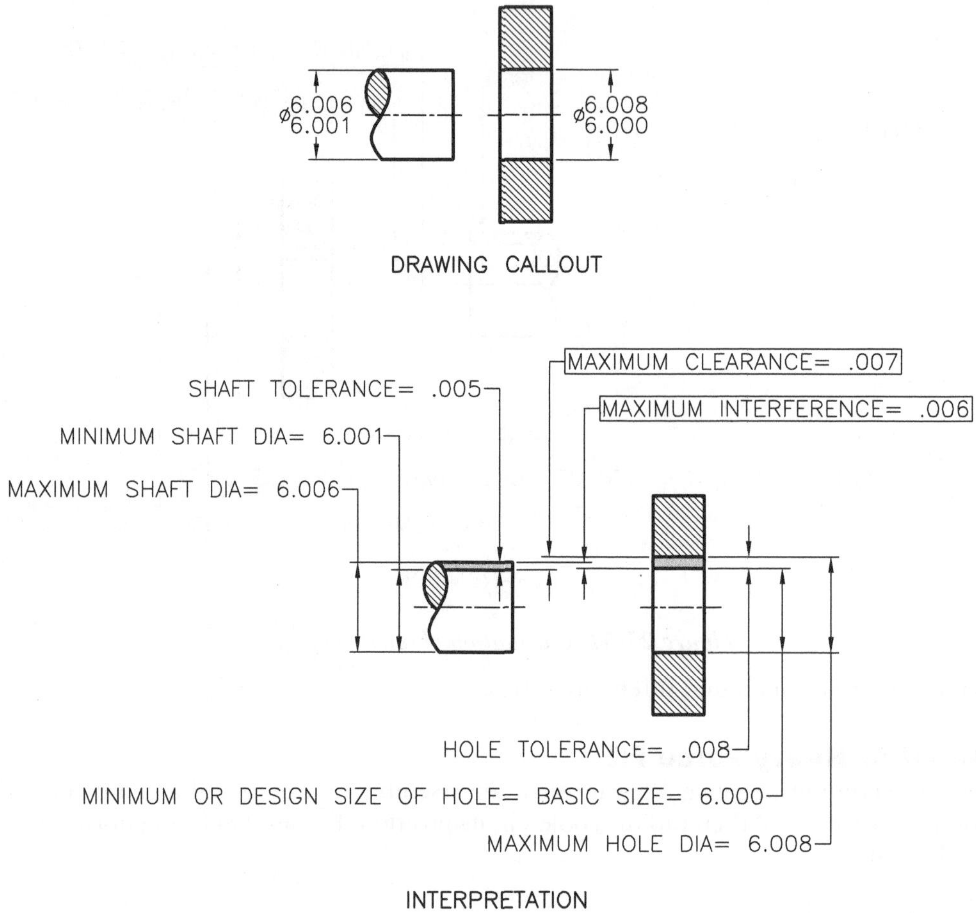

Figure 23-52 *Calculation of transition fit*

Transition fit is sub-classified into three categories.

Push Fit

In this type of fit zero allowance and a light pressure is required in assembling the hole and the shaft. The moving parts show least vibration with this type of fit. It is also known as snug fit. This type of fit is used in automobiles and plastic components.

Force Fit or Shrink Fit

Force fit is used when two mating parts are to be rigidly fixed such that one cannot move without the other. To assemble a hole and a shaft, either requires high pressure to force the shaft into the hole or the hole to be expanded by heating. This type of fit is used in railway wheels, and so on.

Wringing Fit

A slight negative allowance exists between two mating parts in this fit. It requires pressure to force the shaft into the hole and gives a light assembly. It is used in fixing keys, pins, and so on.

STANDARD OF FITS

There are some standards designated for the fits that are used worldwide for designing purpose. The standard of fits provides preferred tolerances for limits and fits of non threaded cylindrical features and defines specific sizes, fits, tolerances, and allowances to use wherever they are applicable. Based on the standards, fits are categorized as inch fits and metric fits. These fits are discussed next.

Standard Inch Fits

The American National Standards Institute published the standard named "Preferred Limits and Fits for Cylindrical Parts" (ANSI B4.1-1967) to define terms and recommended standard allowances, tolerances, and fits for mating parts. The tabular data is provided in thousandths (.001) of an inch. Standard fits are designated by the means of symbols and specifications as shown in Figure 23-53.

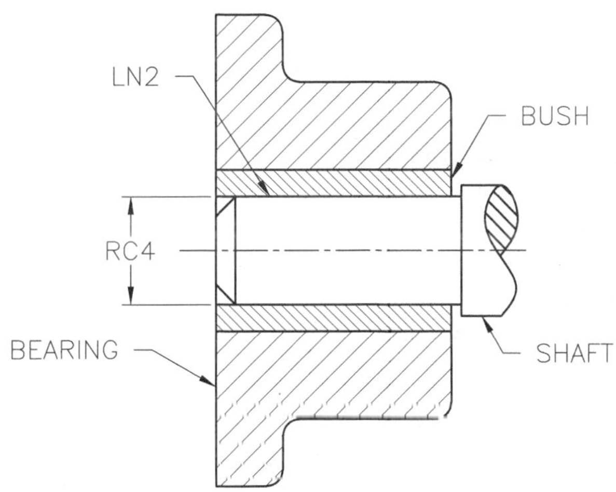

Figure 23-53 Designation of standard inch fit

The letter symbols used for standard inch fits are:

RC - Running and sliding fit
LC - Locational clearance fit
LT - Locational transition fit

LN - Locational interference fit
FN - Force or shrink fit

These letter symbols are used in conjunction with numbers representing the class of fit; for example, FN4 represents a class 4 force fit. Each of these symbols (two letters and a number) represents a complete fit for which the minimum and maximum clearance or interference and the limits of size for the mating parts are given directly in ANSI B4.1 chart.

Running and Sliding Fits

Running and sliding fits are intended to provide a smooth running performance with suitable lubrication allowance.

RC1 Precision Sliding Fit

This fit is intended for an accurate location of parts that must assemble without perceptible play for high precision work such as gauges.

RC2 Sliding Fit

This fit is intended for accurate location, but with greater maximum clearance than class RC1. In this type of fit parts can move and turn easily but are not intended to run freely.

RC3 Precision Running Fit

This fit is the closest fit that can be expected to run freely. It is intended to precision work for oil-lubricated bearings at slow speeds and light journal pressures.

RC4 Close Running Fit

This fit is intended chiefly as a running fit for grease or oil-lubricated bearings on accurate machinery with moderate surface speeds and journal pressures where accurate location and minimum play are desired.

RC5 and RC6 Medium Running Fits

These fits are intended for higher running speeds and/or where temperature variations are likely to be encountered.

RC7 Free Running Fit

This fit is intended for use where accuracy is not essential and/or where large temperature variations are likely to be encountered.

RC8 and RC9 Loose Running Fits

These fits are intended for use where materials made to commercial tolerances are involved such as cold-rolled shafting, tubing, and so on.

Locational Clearance Fits

Locational clearance fits are intended for parts that are normally stationary but can be freely assembled or disassembled. These are classified as follows:

LC1 to LC4

These fits have zero clearance, but in practice the probability is that the fit will always have a clearance.

LC5 and LC6

These fits have a minimum clearance intended for close location fits for non-running parts.

LC7 to LC11

These fits have progressively larger clearances and tolerances and are useful for various loose clearances for assembly of bolts and similar parts.

Locational Transition Fits

Locational transition fits are a compromise between clearance and interference fits for application where accuracy of location is important but either a small amount of clearance or interference is permissible. These are classified as follows:

LT1 and LT2

These fits average a slight clearance between parts. A light push is required to fit.

LT3 and LT4

These fits with no clearance and are used where some interference can be tolerated.

These are sometimes referred to as an easy keying fit and are used for shaft keys and ball race fits. Assembly is generally done by pressure or hammer blows.

LT5 and LT6

These fits average a slight interference although appreciable assembly force will be required.

Locational Interference Fits

Locational interference fits are used where accuracy of location is the prime importance and for parts requiring rigidity and alignment with no special requirements for bore pressure. These are classified as follows:

LN1 And LN2

These are light press fits with very small minimum interference suitable for parts, such as dowel pins, which are assembled with an arbor press of steel, cast iron, or brass. Parts can normally be dismantled and reassembled.

LN3

This is suitable as a heavy press fit in steel and brass, or a light press fit in more elastic materials and light alloys.

LN4 to LN6

While LN4 can be used for permanent assembly of steel parts, these fits are primarily intended as press fits for soft materials.

Force or Shrink Fits

Force or shrink fits constitute a special type of interference fit. In this kind of fit, the interference varies almost directly with diameter and the difference between its minimum and maximum limits is kept as small as possible to maintain the resulting pressures within reasonable limits.

These fits are classified as follows:

FN1 Light Drive Fit
This fit requires light assembly pressure and produces more or less permanent assemblies. It is suitable for thin sections or long fits or for cast-iron external members.

FN2 Medium Drive Fit
This fit is suitable for heavier steel parts or as a shrink fit on light sections.

FN3 Heavy Drive Fit
This fit is suitable for heavier steel parts or as a shrink fit in medium sections.

FN4 And FN5 Force Fits
This fit is suitable for parts that can be highly stressed.

Example 1

For a shaft of 2 inch diameter RC6 fit is assigned. In the table of ANSI B4.1 (Running and sliding fits) for the range of nominal sizes between 1.97 to 3.15 the limit for hole and shaft in the column of RC6 Medium running fit is given as, Hole = +3.00 and 0, Minimum Clearance = 2.50, and Shaft = – 2.5 and – 4.3. These values are taken as thousandths of an inch.

Hence, tolerances for the hole and the shaft will be:

Hole $Ø2.0025^{+.0030}_{\ \ 0000}$ inch

Shaft $Ø2.000^{-.0025}_{-.0043}$ inch

Minimum Clearance = .0025 inch

Example 2

For a 1.15 inch hole with RC7 fit, value in the column of RC7 is given as, Hole = +2.00 and 0, Clearance = +2.5, and Shaft = – 2.5 and – 3.7. Hence, tolerances will be:

Hole $Ø1.1500^{.0020}_{.0000}$ inch

Shaft $Ø1.1475\pm^{-.0025}_{-.0037}$ inch

Minimum Clearance = .0025 inch

Standard Metric Fits

The system of preferred metric limits and fits was developed by the International Organization for Standardization (ISO) and is known as the ANSI B4.2 standard. It is approved and adopted for metric drawings. Metric system of fits designates symbols that are used to define specific dimensional limits on drawings. The system is specified for holes, cylinders, and shafts and is also applicable to fits between parallel surfaces such as keys and slots.

International Tolerance Grade or IT Grade

International Tolerance (IT) Grade establishes the magnitude of the tolerance zone or the amount of part size variation allowed for dimensions of internal and external features. The smaller the grade number, the smaller the tolerance zone, refer to Figure 23-54.

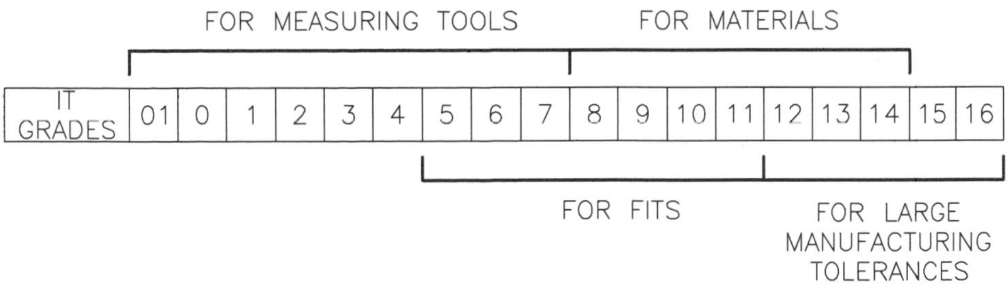

Figure 23-54 *Application of International Tolerance (IT) grades*

Grades 1 through 4 are very precise grades intended primarily for gauge making and similar precision work. Grade 4, however can also be used for very precise production work. Grades 5 through 16 represent a progressive series suitable for cutting operations, such as turning, boring, grinding, milling, and sawing. Grade 5 is the most precise grade obtained by fine grinding and lapping while 16 is the coarsest grade for rough sawing and machining. Grades 12 through 16 are intended for large manufacturing operations such as cold heading, pressing, rolling, and other forming operations.

Symbols for Metric Fits

By combining the IT grade number and the tolerance position letter, the tolerance symbol is established that identifies the actual maximum and minimum limits of the part. The toleranced sizes are thus defined by the basic size of the part added up with the symbol comprising a letter and number, refer to Figure 23-55.

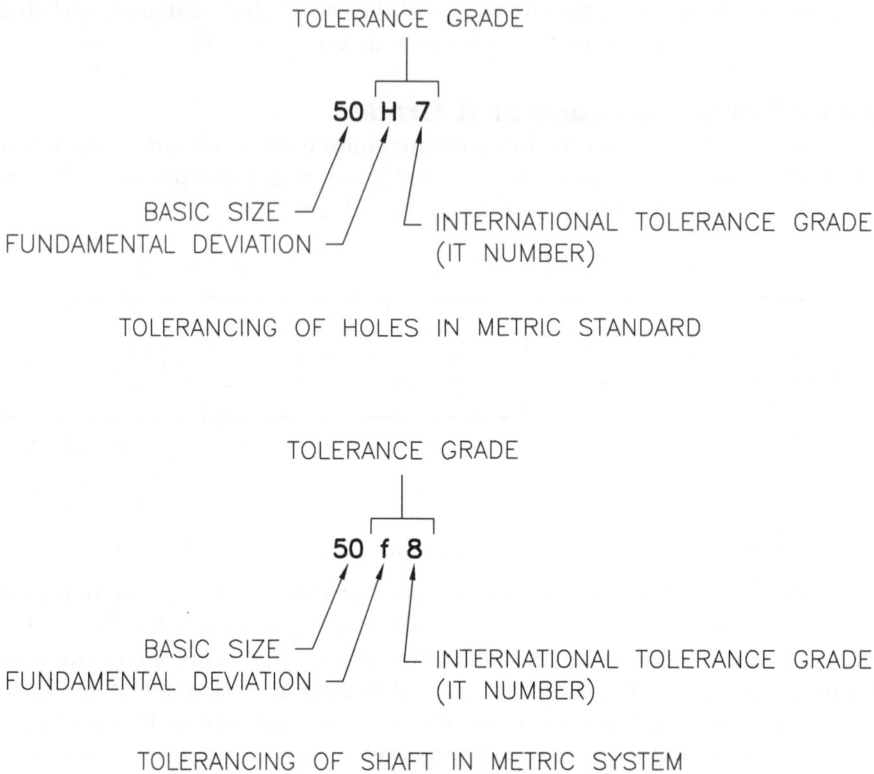

Figure 23-55 *Tolerancing of features in Metric system*

Hole basis fits have a fundamental deviation of "H" on the hole, and shaft basis fits have a fundamental deviation of "h" on the shaft. Normally, the hole basis system is preferred over the shaft basis system because it is easier to produce holes of fixed size rather than producing shafts of fixed size.

A fit is specified by the basic size common for both hole and shaft followed by a symbol corresponding to each component with the internal part symbol preceding the external part symbol, refer to Figure 23-56.

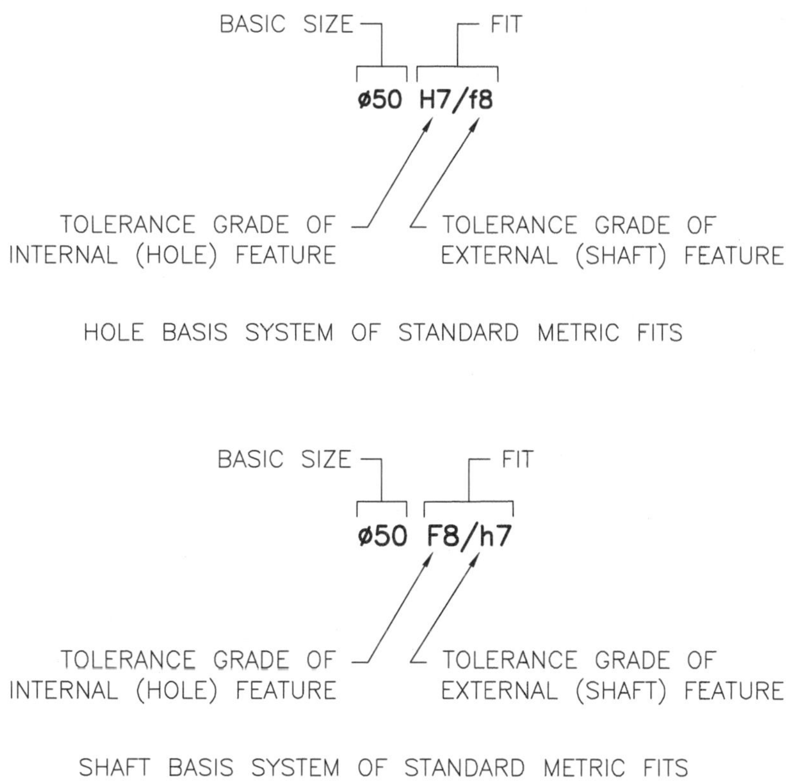

Figure 23-56 *Symbols used in standard metric fits*

Metric Standard Hole Basis Fits System

In the hole basis fits system, the minimum size of the hole is considered as the basic size.

For example, for a Ø16 H7/g6 fit, which is a Preferred Hole Basis Clearance Fit, refer to ANSI B4.2 (Preferred hole basis metric fits), the limits for the hole and shaft will be as follows:

Hole limits = Ø16.000 and Ø16.018
Shaft limits = Ø15.994 and Ø15.983

Minimum clearance = 0.006
Maximum clearance = 0.035

If a Ø40 H7/s6 Preferred Hole Basis Interference Fit is required, refer to ANSI B4.2 (Preferred hole basis metric fits), the limits for the hole and shaft will be as follows:

Hole limits = Ø40.000 and Ø40.025
Shaft limits = Ø39.957 and Ø40.059

Minimum interference = 0.018
Maximum interference = –0.059

Metric Standard Shaft Basis Fits System

The shaft basis fits system is recommended where more than two fits are required on the same shaft. Tolerances for holes and shafts are same as those for a basic hole system, however, the basic size becomes the maximum shaft size.

For example, for a Ø16 D9/h9 fit, which is a Preferred Shaft Basis Clearance Fit, refer to ANSI B4.2 (Preferred shaft basis metric fits), the limits for the hole and shaft will be as follows:

Hole limits = Ø16.050 and Ø16.093
Shaft limits = Ø15.957 and Ø16.000
Minimum clearance = 0.050
Maximum clearance = 0.136

According to metric standard hole and metric standard shaft basis system, the preferred hole and shaft fits are shown in Figure 23-57.

	ISO SYMBOL		DESCRIPTION	
	HOLE BASIS	SHAFT BASIS		
CLEARANCE FITS	H11/c11	C11/h11	LOOSE RUNNING FIT FOR WIDE COMMERCIAL TOLERANCES OR ALLOWANCES ON EXTERNAL MEMBERS.	MORE CLEARANCE
	H9/d9	D9/h9	FREE RUNNING FIT NOT FOR USE WHERE ACCURACY IS ESSENTIAL, BUT GOOD FOR LARGE TEMPERATURE VARIATIONS, HIGH RUNNING SPEEDS, OR HEAVY JOURNAL BEARINGS.	
	H8/f7	F8/h7	CLOSE RUNNING FIR FOR RUNNING ON ACCURATE MACHINES AND FOR ACCURATE LOCATION AT MODERATE SPEEDS AND JOURNAL PRESSURES.	
	H7/g6	G7/h6	SLIDING FIT NOT INTENDED TO RUN FREELY, BUT TO MOVE AND TURN FREELY AND LOCATE ACCURATELY.	
	H7/h6	H7/h6	LOCATIONAL CLEARANCE FIT PROVIDES SNUG FIT FOR LOCATING STATIONARY PARTS, BUT CAN BE FREELY ASSEMBLED AND DISASSEMBLED.	
TRANSITION FITS	H7/k6	K7/h6	LOCATIONAL TRANSITION FIT FOR ACCURATE LOCATION, A COMPROMISE BETWEEN CLEARANCE FIR AND INTERFERENCE FIT.	
	H7/n6	N7/h6	LOCATIONAL TRANSITION FIT FOR MORE ACCURATE LOCATION WHERE GREATER INTERFERENCE IS PERMISSIBLE.	MORE INTERFERENCE
INTERFERENCE FITS	H7/p6	P7/h6	LOCATIONAL INTERFERENCE FIT FOR PARTS REQUIRING RIGIDITY AND ALIGNMENT WITH PRIME ACCURACY OF LOCATION BUT WITHOUT SPECIAL BORE PRESSURE REQUIREMENTS.	
	H7/s6	S7/h6	MEDIUM DRIVE FIT FOR ORDINARY STEEL PARTS OR SHRINK FITS ON LIGHT SECTIONS, THE TIGHTEST FIT USABLE WITH CAST IRON.	
	H7/u6	U7/h6	FORCE FIT SUITABLE FOR PARTS SUITABLE FOR PARTS THAT CAN BE HIGHLY STRESSED OR FOR SHRINK FITS WHERE THE HEAVY PRESSING FORCES REQUIRED ARE IMPRACTICAL	

***Figure 23-57** Description of preferred metric fits*

Example 3

A 50 mm shaft rotates in a bearing. The tolerance for both shaft and bearing is 0.075 mm and the required allowance is 0.10 mm. Determine the dimensions of the shaft and the bearing bore using the hole basis system.

In the hole basis system, hole dimension is the basic size. Hence,

Minimum limit or basic size of the hole= 50 mm

Maximum limit of the hole= Minimum limit of hole + Tolerance
= 50+.075 = 50.075 mm

Maximum limit of the shaft = Minimum limit of the hole - allowance
= 50 – 0.10 = 49.90 mm

Minimum limit of shaft= Maximum limit of shaft – Tolerance
= 49.90 – 0.075 = 49.825 mm

Example 4

For a clearance fit, the limits for a hole and a shaft are specified as:

Shaft = $\text{Ø}50^{-0.005}_{-0.018}$ and Hole = $\text{Ø}50^{-0.020}_{-0.000}$

Determine:
(a) Basic size
(b) Shaft and hole tolerances
(c) Limits for shaft and hole
(d) Maximum and minimum clearance

From the given data

(a) Basic size = 50 mm

(b) Shaft tolerance = 0.018 – 0.005 = 0.013 mm
Hole tolerance = 0.020 mm

(c) Maximum limit of shaft = 50 – 0.005
= 49.995 mm
Minimum limit of shaft = 50 – 0.018
= 49.982 mm

Maximum limit of hole = 50 + 0.020
= 50.020 mm
Minimum limit of hole = 50 mm

(d) Maximum clearance = Maximum limit of hole – Minimum limit of shaft
= 50.020 – 49.982 = .038 mm

Example 5

A hole and shaft have a basic size of 25 mm refer to Figure 23-58. A clearance fit of maximum clearance of 0.02 mm and a minimum clearance of 0.01 mm is applied between the parts. If the hole tolerance is to be 1.5 times the shaft tolerance then determine the limits for hole and shaft using:

(a) Hole basis system
(b) Shaft basis system

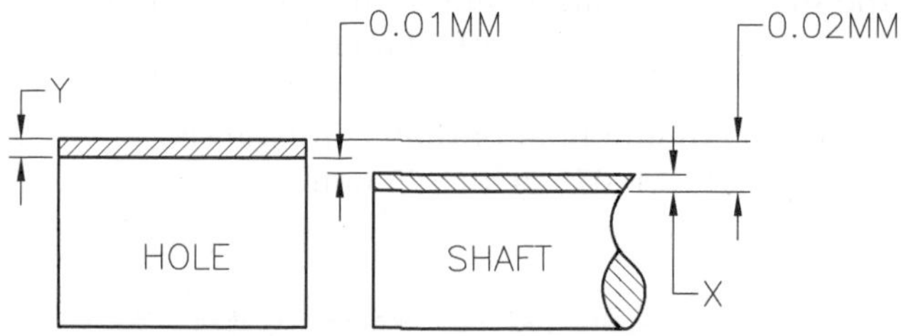

Figure 23-58 *Figure for Example 5*

If X is the tolerance in the shaft and Y is the tolerance in the hole, then

$$Y + 0.01 + X = 0.02$$
$$1.5X + 0.01 + X = 0.02$$

On solving both equations, X = 0.004 and Y = 0.006

(a) Using the hole basis system.

The lower limit of the hole will be the basic size. Hence,

Minimum limit of the hole = 25 mm (Basic Size)
Maximum limit of the hole = Basic size + Tolerance
= 25 + .006 = 25.006 mm

Maximum limit of the shaft = Minimum limit of the hole – Minimum clearance
= 25 – 0.01 = 24.99 mm
Minimum limit of the shaft = Maximum limit of the shaft – Tolerance
= 24.99 – 0.004 = 24.986 mm

(b) Using the shaft basis system.

The maximum limit for the shaft will be the basic size. Hence,

Maximum limit of the shaft = Basic size of shaft = 25 mm
Minimum limit of the shaft = 25 – 0.004 = 24.996 mm

Maximum limit for the hole = 25.01+ 0.006 = 25.016 mm
Minimum limit for the hole = 25+ 0.01 = 25.01 mm

Self-Evaluation Test

Answer the following questions and then compare them to those given at the end of this chapter:

1. In the limit dimensioning method, only the __________ and __________ dimensions are specified.

2. The __________ of a dimension is theoretically the exact value of dimension.

3. The __________ of a dimension is the total permissible variation in its size.

4. __________ are imaginary references used for locating features.

5. __________ is a condition in which the elements of a surface or its axes are in a straight line.

6. __________ is a condition of a surface in which all the points on the surface are at same distance from a common axis.

7. __________ are used to control the form characteristics of a manufactured part.

8. __________ of a surface is a condition in which all surface elements are in one plane.

9. The cylindricity tolerance must be greater than half of the size tolerance. (T/F)

10. Cylindricity tolerances can be applied only to cylindrical surfaces, such as round holes and shafts. (T/F)

Review Questions

Answer the following questions:

1. Which of the following is an interference fit?

   (a) **Push fit** (b) **Force fit**
   (c) **Wringing fit** (d) **Slide fit**

2. In which of the following components, the slide fit is applied?

   (a) **Keyed Pulleys** (b) **Seating Rings**
   (c) **Slide Valves** (d) **Bearings**

3. Location tolerances include the __________, __________, and __________ tolerances.

4. A force fit is used when the two mating parts are to be __________.

5. An orientation tolerance controls __________, __________, and all other angular relationships.

6. A condition of a part feature where the part contains the maximum amount of material is called as __________.

7. The maximum clearance fit is the difference between the __________ size of the hole and the __________ size of the shaft.

8. In the shaft basis system, the size of the shaft is kept constant. (T/F)

9. The maximum clearance in a loose or sliding fit is always greater than zero. (T/F)

10. It is possible to obtain an exact dimension. (T/F)

Exercise 1

The size of a shaft of 30 mm basic size is given as 30±0.04 mm. Find the tolerance.

Exercise 2

A 50 mm diameter shaft is made to rotate in the bush. The tolerances for both shaft and bush are 0.050 mm. Determine the dimension of the shaft and bush to give a maximum clearance of 0.075 mm with the hole basis system.

Exercise 3

Refer to the data available in ANSI B4.2 (Description of preferred fits) and determine the type of fits produced by the mating of holes and shafts for the following sizes.

(a) 30mm H_7/f_6

(b) 23mm U_7/h_6

(c) 30mm P_8/h_5

Exercise 4

A journal and bearing assembly has the following sizes:

Journal = $Ø40^{-0.001}_{-0.002}$

Bearing = $Ø40^{+0.001}_{-0.002}$

Determine the tolerance on journal, tolerance on bearing, minimum clearance, maximum clearance, and type of fit.

Exercise 5

Determine the limits of size, the value of minimum and maximum clearance or interference, and the type of fit for the parts shown in Figure 23-59.

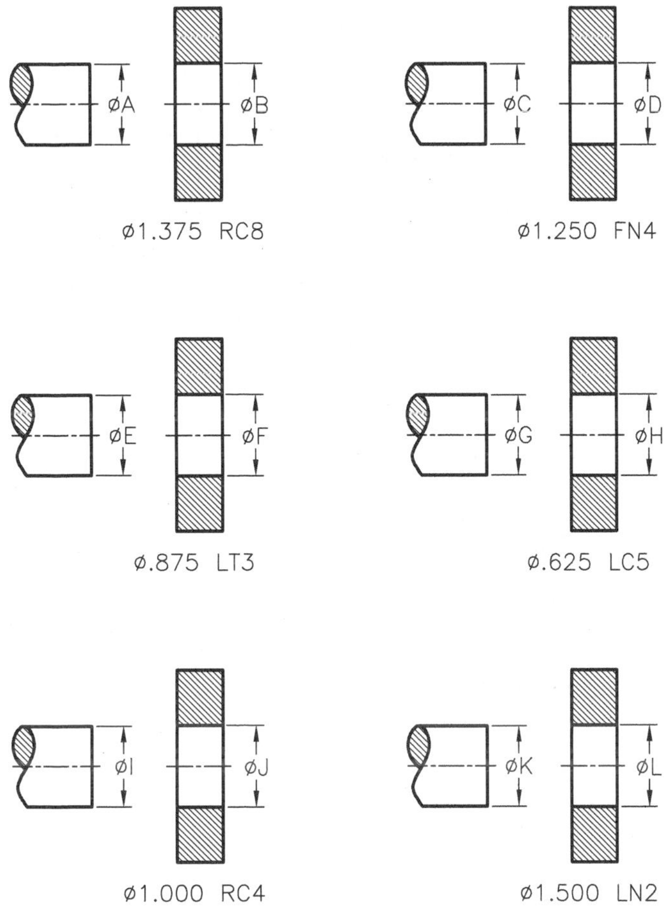

Figure 23-59 *Figure for Exercise 5*

Exercise 6

Draw orthographic views of the sketch shown in Figure 23-60 and add the following geometric tolerances to the appropriate views.

(a) Surfaces A, B, and E are to be datums A, B, and E respectively.
(b) Surface C is to be parallel with datum A within .004 inch and to be flat within .005 inch.
(c) Surface D is to be parallel within .003 inch with datum A and to be flat within .003 inch.
(d) Surface F is to have an angularity within .008 inch with datum A.

(e) Surface G is to be perpendicular within .002 inch with datum A also apply a flatness tolerance of .003 inch on the same surface.
(f) The bottom surface D is to be flat within .002 inch.

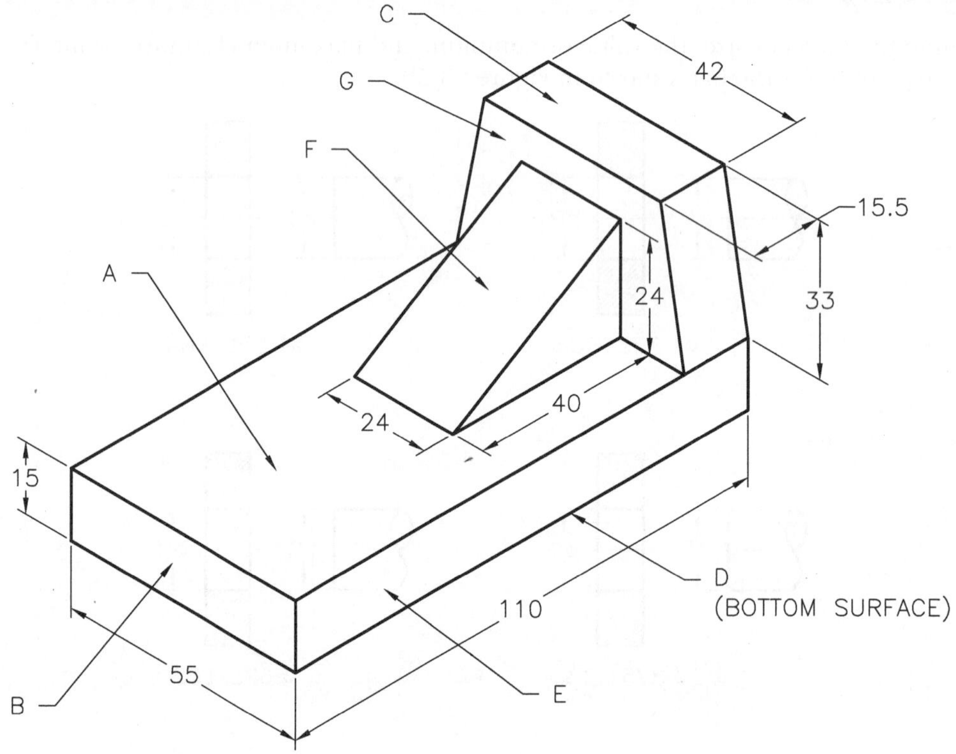

Figure 23-60 Figure for Exercise 6

Exercise 7

In Figure 23-61, Part A must fit in Part B so that the maximum clearance does not exceed .005 inch. Find out the maximum and minimum limits for Part B. Flatness tolerance of .002 inch is to be added to the surfaces of both parts.

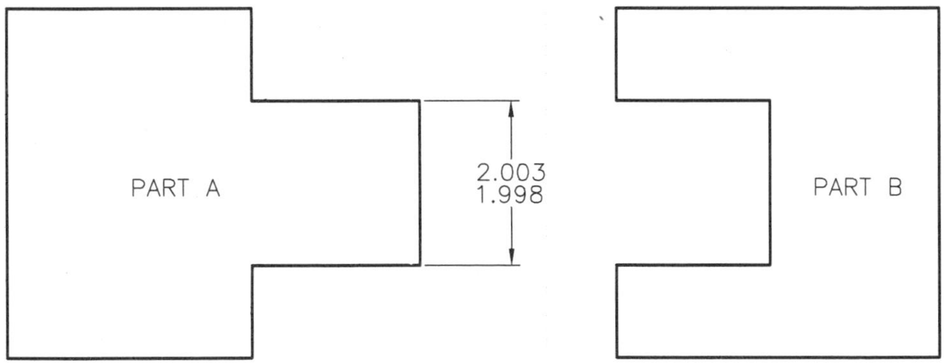

Figure 23-61 Figure for Exercise 7

REFERENCES

ASME B4.1-1967 (R2009) Preferred Limits and Fits for Cylindrical Parts
ASME B4.2-1978 Preferred Metric Limits and Fits
ASME Y14.5-2009 Dimensioning and Tolerancing

Answers to Self-Evaluation Test

1. maximum, minimum, **2.** basic size, **3.** tolerance, **4.** Datums, **5.** Straightness, **6.** Cylindricity, **7.** Form tolerances, **8.** Flatness, **9.** F, **10.** T

Chapter 24

Isometric Drawings

Learning Objectives

After completing this chapter, you will be able to:

- *Understand isometric drawings, isometric axes, and isometric planes*
- *Set isometric grid and snap*
- *Draw isometric circles in different isoplanes*
- *Dimension isometric objects*
- *Write text in isometric styles*

Key Terms

- *Isometric Planes*
- *Isometric Axes*
- *Isometric Snap*
- *Isometric Grid*
- *Iso Circles*
- *Isometric Text*

ISOMETRIC DRAWINGS

Isometric drawings are generally used to help visualize the shape of an object. For example, if you are given the orthographic views of an object, as shown in Figure 24-1, it takes time to put information together to visualize the shape. However, if an isometric drawing is given, as shown in Figure 24-2, it is much easier to understand the shape of the object. Thus, isometric drawings are widely used in industry to help in understanding products and their features.

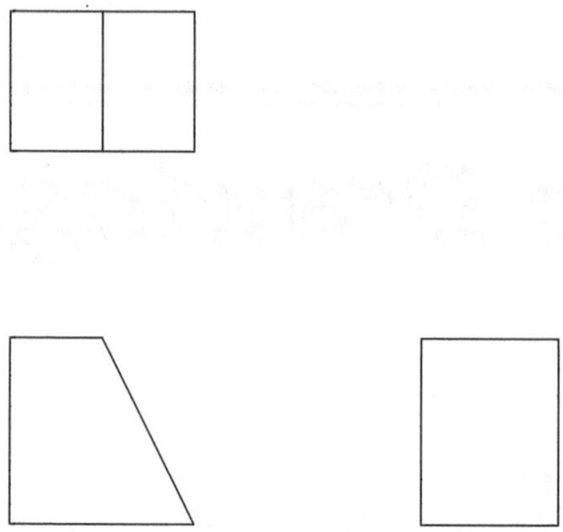

Figure 24-1 *Orthographic views of an object*

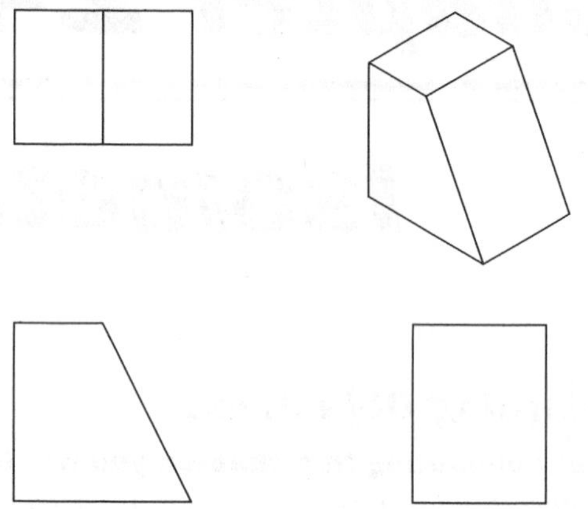

Figure 24-2 *Orthographic views with an isometric view*

An isometric drawing should not be confused with a three-dimensional (3D) drawing. An isometric drawing is just a two-dimensional (2D) representation of a 3D drawing on a 2D plane. A 3D drawing is the 3D model of an object on the X, Y, and Z axes. In other words, an isometric drawing is a 3D drawing on a 2D plane, whereas a 3D drawing is a true 3D model of the object. The model can be rotated and viewed from any direction. A 3D model can be a wireframe model, surface model, or solid model.

ISOMETRIC PROJECTIONS

The word "isometric" means equal measurement. The angle between any of the two principal axes of an isometric drawing is 120 degrees, refer to Figure 24-3. An isometric view is obtained by rotating the object by 45 degree angle around the imaginary vertical axis, and then tilting the object forward through a 35°16' angle. If you project the points and edges on the front plane, the projected length of the edges will be approximately 82 percent (isometric length/actual length = 9/11), which is shorter than the actual length of the edges. However, isometric drawings are always drawn to a full scale because their purpose is to help the user visualize the shape of the object. Isometric drawings are not meant to describe the actual size of the object. The actual dimensions, tolerances, and feature symbols must be shown in the orthographic views. Also, you should avoid showing any hidden lines in the isometric drawings, unless they show an important feature of the object or help in understanding its shape.

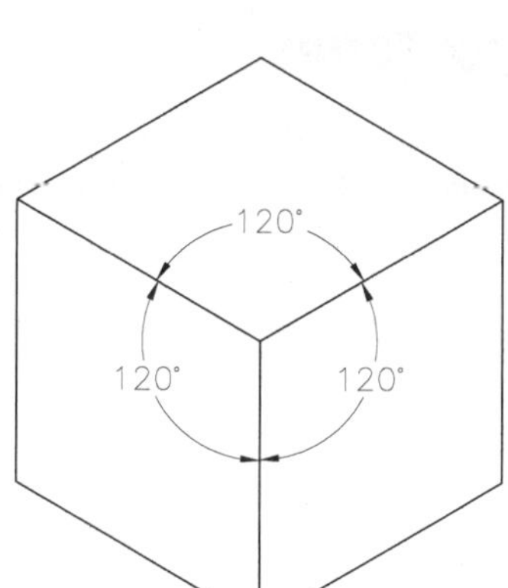

Figure 24-3 *Principal axes of an isometric drawing*

ISOMETRIC AXES AND PLANES

Isometric drawings have three axes: right horizontal axis (P0,P1), vertical axis (P0,P2), and left horizontal axis (P0,P3). The two horizontal axes are inclined at 30 degrees to the horizontal or X axis (X1,X2). The vertical axis is at 90 degrees, as shown in Figure 24-4.

When you draw an isometric drawing, the horizontal object lines are drawn along or parallel to the horizontal axis. Similarly, the vertical lines are drawn along or parallel to the vertical axis. For example, to make an isometric drawing of a rectangular block, the vertical edges of the block are drawn parallel to the vertical axis. The horizontal edges on the right side of the block are drawn parallel to the right horizontal axis (P0,P1), and the horizontal edges on the left side of the block are drawn parallel to the left horizontal axis (P0,P3). It is important to remember that the angles do not appear true in isometric drawings. Therefore, the edges or surfaces that are at an angle are drawn by locating their endpoints. The lines that are parallel to the isometric axes are called isometric lines. The lines that are not parallel to the isometric axes are called non isometric lines.

Similarly, the planes can be isometric planes or non isometric planes.

Isometric drawings have three principal planes, namely isoplane right, isoplane top, and isoplane left, as shown in Figure 24-5. The isoplane right (P0,P4,P10,P6) is defined by the vertical axis and the right horizontal axis. The isoplane top (P6,P10,P9,P7) is defined by the right and left horizontal axes. Similarly, the isoplane left (P0,P6,P7,P8) is defined by the vertical axis and the left horizontal axis.

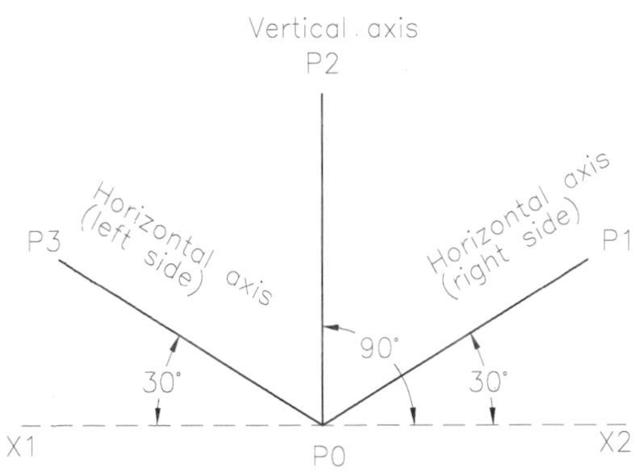

Figure 24-4 Isometric axes

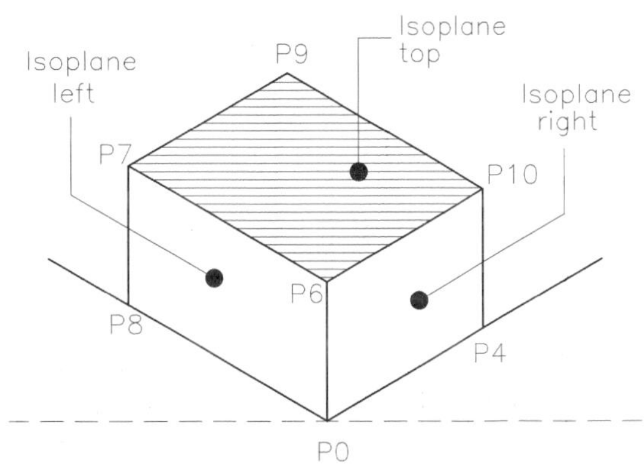

Figure 24-5 Isometric planes

SETTING THE ISOMETRIC GRID AND SNAP

You can use the **SNAP** command to set the isometric grid and snap. The isometric grid lines are displayed at 30 degree angle to the horizontal axis. Also, the distance between the grid lines is determined by the vertical spacing which can be specified by using the **GRID** or **SNAP** command. The grid lines coincide with three isometric axes which make it easier to create isometric drawings. The following command sequence and Figure 24-6 illustrate the use of the **SNAP** command to set the isometric grid and snap of 0.5 unit:

Command: **SNAP**
Specify snap spacing or [ON/OFF/Aspect/Legacy/Style/Type] <0.5000>: **S**
Enter snap grid style [Standard/Isometric] <S>: **I**
Specify vertical spacing <0.5000>: *Enter a new snap distance.*

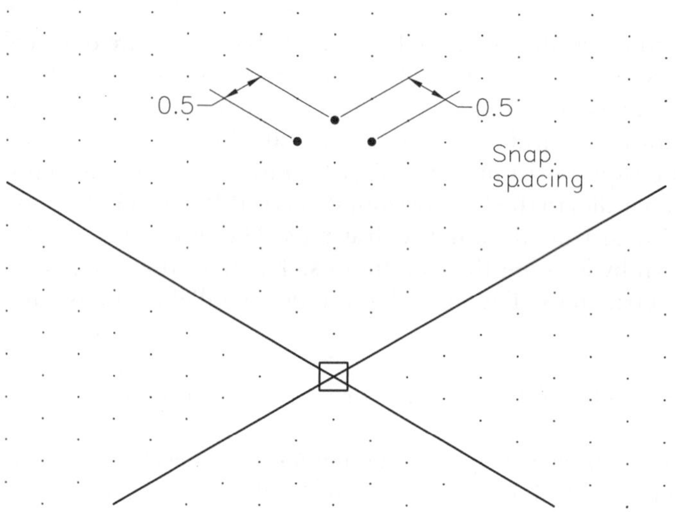

Figure 24-6 *Setting the isometric grid and snap in dotted grid*

Note

*1. When you use the **SNAP** command to set the isometric grid, the grid lines may not be displayed. To display the grid lines, turn the grid on by choosing the **Grid Display** button from the Status Bar or press F7.*

2. You cannot set the aspect ratio for the isometric grid. Therefore, the spacing between the isometric grid lines will be the same.

You can also set the isometric grid and snap by using the **Drafting Settings** dialog box shown in Figure 24-7. You can invoke this dialog box by right-clicking on **SNAPMODE**, **GRIDMODE**, **Polar Tracking**, **Object Snap**, **3D Object Snap**, **Object Snap Tracking**, **Dynamic Input**, **Quick Properties**, or **Selection Cycling** button available in the Status Bar and then choosing **Settings** from the shortcut menu displayed. You can also invoke this dialog box by entering **DSETTINGS** at the Command prompt.

The isometric snap and grid functions can be turned on/off by choosing the **Grid On (F7)** check box located in the **Snap and Grid** tab of the **Drafting Settings** dialog box. The **Snap and Grid** tab also contains the radio buttons to set the snap type and style. To display the grid on the screen, make sure the grid is turned on.

When you set the isometric grid, the display of crosshairs also changes. The crosshairs are displayed at an isometric angle and their orientation depends on current isoplane. You can toggle between isoplane right, isoplane left, and isoplane top by pressing the CTRL and E keys (CTRL+E) simultaneously or by using the function key, F5. You can also toggle among different isoplanes by entering the **ISOPLANE** command at the Command prompt:

Command: **ISOPLANE**
Enter isometric plane setting [Left/Top/Right] <Top>: **T**
Current Isoplane: **Top**

***Figure 24-7** The **Drafting Settings** dialog box*

The Ortho mode is useful while drawing in the Isometric mode. In the Isometric mode, Ortho aligns with the axes of the current isoplane.

Example 1 — *Isometric Drawing*

In this example, you will create the isometric drawing shown in Figure 24-8.

1. Use the **SNAP** command to set the isometric grid and snap. The snap value is 0.5 unit.

   Command: **SNAP**
   Specify snap spacing or [ON/OFF/Aspect/Legacy/Style/Type] <0.5000>: **S**
   Enter snap grid style [Standard/Isometric] <S>: **I**
   Specify vertical spacing <0.5000>: **0.5** *(or press ENTER)*

2. Change the isoplane to the isoplane left by pressing the F5 key. Choose the **Line** tool and draw lines between the points P1, P2, P3, P4, and P1, as shown in Figure 24-9.

Tip
*You can increase the size of the crosshairs using the **Crosshair size** slider bar in the **Display** tab of the **Options** dialog box.*

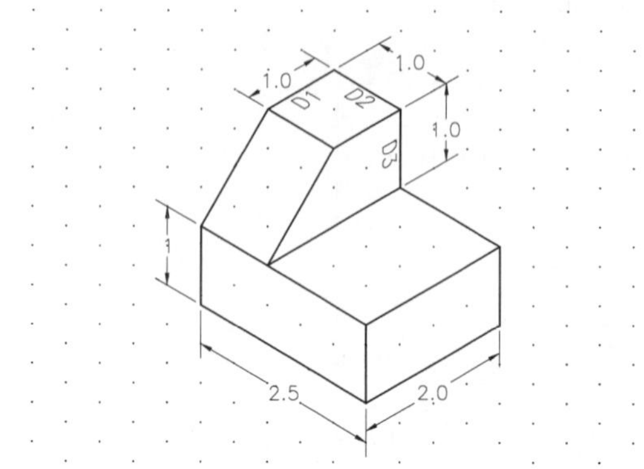

Figure 24-8 Isometric drawing for Example 1

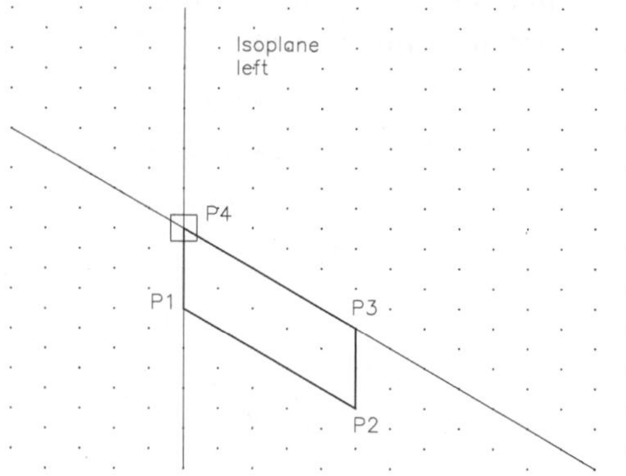

Figure 24-9 Drawing the bottom left face

3. Change the isoplane to the isoplane right by pressing the F5 key. Invoke the **Line** tool and draw the lines, as shown in Figure 24-10.

4. Change the isoplane to the isoplane top by pressing the F5 key. Invoke the **Line** tool and draw the lines, refer to Figure 24-11.

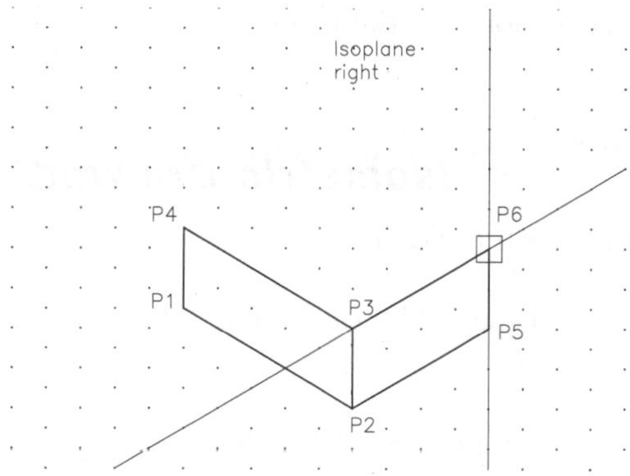

Figure 24-10 Drawing the bottom right face

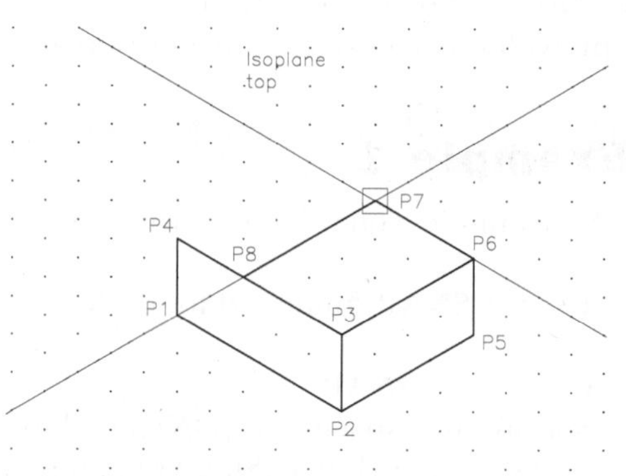

Figure 24-11 Drawing the top face

5. Similarly, draw the remaining lines, refer to Figure 24-12.

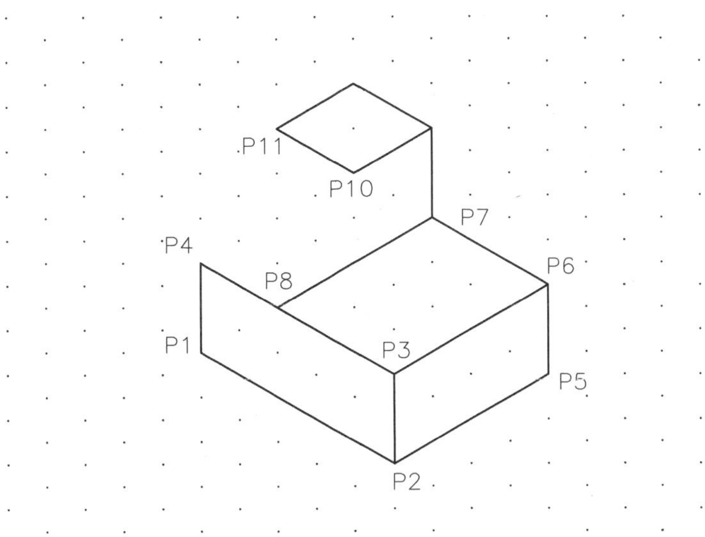

Figure 24-12 Drawing the remaining lines

6. The front left end of the object is tapered at an angle. In isometric drawings, oblique surfaces (surfaces at an angle to the isometric axis) cannot be drawn like other lines. Make sure that the Endpoint Object Snap is on, and then locate the endpoints of the lines that define the oblique surface. Next, draw the lines between those points. To complete the drawing shown in Figure 24-8, draw a line from P10 to P8 and from P11 to P4, refer to Figure 24-13.

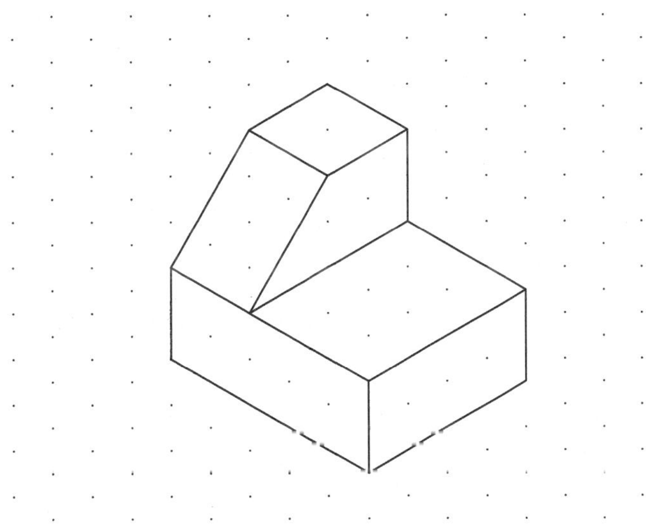

Figure 24-13 Isometric drawing with the tapered face

DRAWING ISOMETRIC CIRCLES

The isometric circles are drawn by using the tools available in the **Ellipse** drop-down and then selecting the **Isocircle** option. To draw an isometric circle, choose the **Axis, End**, or **Elliptical Arc** tool from the **Ellipse** drop-down. As soon as you select any of these options, the **Isocircle** option will be available in the Command prompt. Select the **Isocircle** option from the Command prompt; you will be prompted to specify the center of isocircle. Specify the center of the isocircle.

On specifying the center, you will be prompted to specify the radius of the isocircle. Once you specify the radius and press enter, isocircle will be created.

Note that you must have the Isometric Snap on while using the Ellipse tools to display the **Isocircle** option. If the isometric snap is not ON, you cannot draw an isometric circle. Before entering the radius or diameter of the isometric circle, you must make sure that you are in the required isoplane.

For example, to draw a circle in the right isoplane, you must toggle through the isoplanes until the required isoplane (right isoplane) is displayed. You can also set the required isoplane as the current plane before choosing the **Ellipse** tool. The crosshairs and the shape of the isometric circle will automatically change as you toggle through different isoplanes. As you enter the radius or diameter of the circle, AutoCAD draws the isometric circle in the selected plane, refer to Figure 24-14.

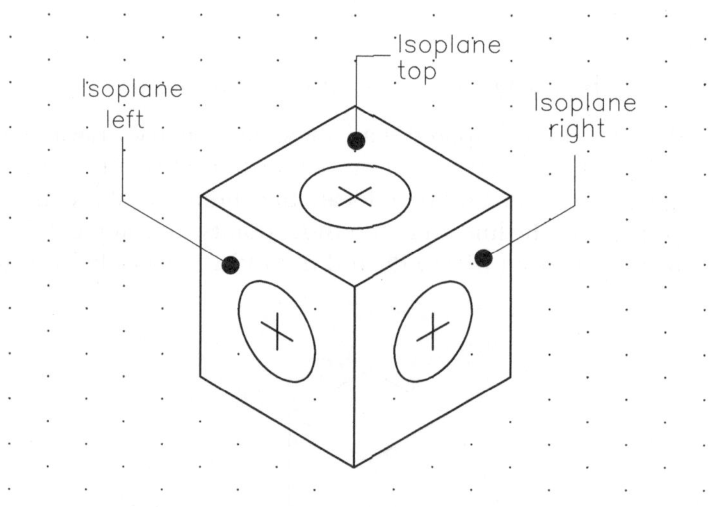

Figure 24-14 *Isometric circles drawn*

The prompt sequence used to draw an isometric circle after choosing the **Axis, End** tool from the **Ellipse** drop-down is as follows:

Specify axis endpoint of ellipse or [Arc/Center/Isocircle]: **I** Enter
Specify center of isocircle: *Select a point.*
Specify radius of isocircle or [Diameter]: *Enter circle radius,* Enter

Creating Fillets in Isometric Drawings

To create fillets in isometric drawings, you first need to create an isometric circle and then trim its unwanted portion. Remember that there is no other method to directly create an isometric fillet.

Dimensioning Isometric Objects

Isometric dimensioning involves two steps: (1) dimensioning the drawing using the standard dimensioning tools, (2) editing the dimensions to change them to oblique dimensions.

Example 2 *Dimensioning*

The following example illustrates the process involved in dimensioning an isometric drawing. In this example, you will dimension the isometric drawing created in Example 1.

1. Dimension the drawing given in Example 1, as shown in Figure 24-15. You can use the aligned or linear dimensions to dimension the drawing. Remember that when you select the points, you must use the **Intersection** or **Endpoint** object snap to snap the endpoints of the object you are dimensioning. AutoCAD automatically leaves a gap between the object line and the extension line, as specified by the **DIMGAP** variable.

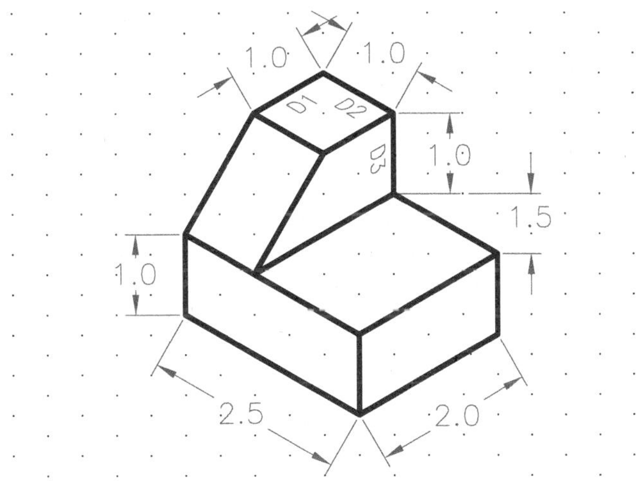

Figure 24-15 *The dimensioned isometric drawing before using the* ***Oblique*** *tool*

2. The next step is to edit the dimensions. You can choose the **Oblique** tool from the **Dimensions** panel of the **Annotate** tab. After selecting the dimension that you want to edit, you are prompted to enter the oblique angle. The oblique angle is determined by the angle that the extension line of the isometric dimension makes with the positive *X* axis. The following prompt sequence is displayed when you invoke this option from the **Ribbon**:

   Select objects: *Select the dimension (D1).*
   Select objects: *Press ENTER.*
   Enter obliquing angle (Press ENTER for none): **150** Enter

For example, the extension line of the dimension labeled D1 makes a 150 degree angle with the positive X axis, refer to Figure 24-16(a), therefore, the oblique angle is 150 degrees. Similarly, the extension lines of the dimension labeled D2 and D3 make a 30 degree angle with the positive X axis, refer to Figure 24-16(b) and (c), therefore, the oblique angle is 30 degrees. After you edit all dimensions, the drawing should appear as shown in Figure 24-17.

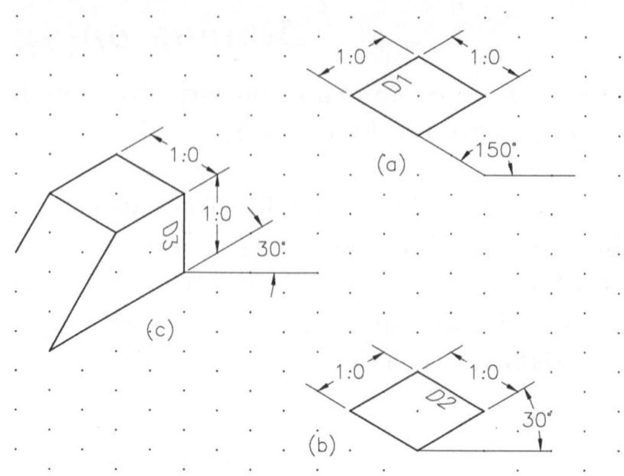

Figure 24-16 Determining the oblique angle

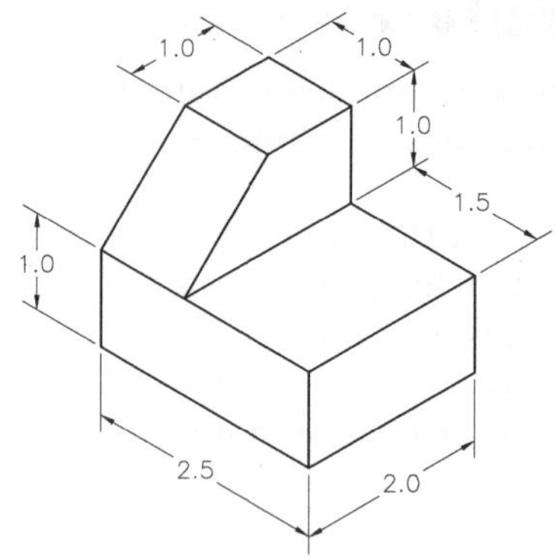

Figure 24-17 Object with isometric dimensions

ISOMETRIC TEXT

You cannot use regular text when placing the text in an isometric drawing because the text in an isometric drawing is obliqued at a positive or negative 30 degree angle. Therefore, you must create two text styles with oblique angles of positive 30 degrees and negative 30 degrees. You can use the **-STYLE** command or the **Text Style** dialog box to create a new text style. Figure 24-18 shows the **Text Style** dialog box with a new text style, **ISOTEXT1** and its corresponding values.

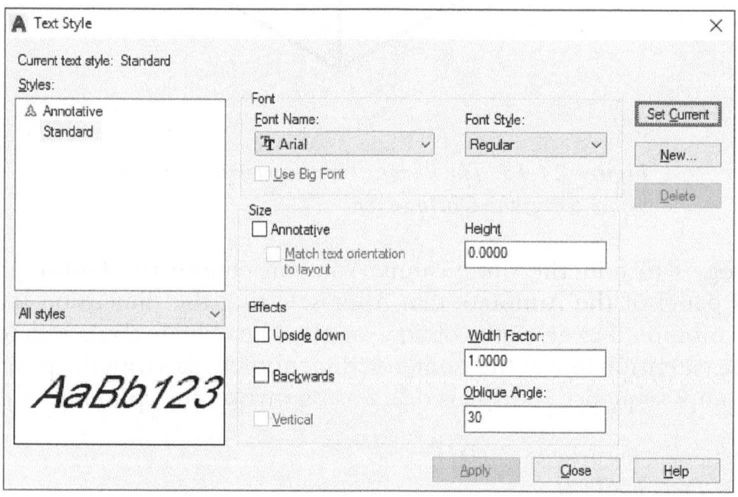

Figure 24-18 The **Text Style** dialog box

Similarly, you can create another text style, **ISOTEXT2**, with a negative 30 degrees oblique angle. When you place the text in an isometric drawing, you must also specify the rotation angle for the text. The text style and the text rotation angle depend on the placement of the text in the isometric drawing, as shown in Figure 24-19.

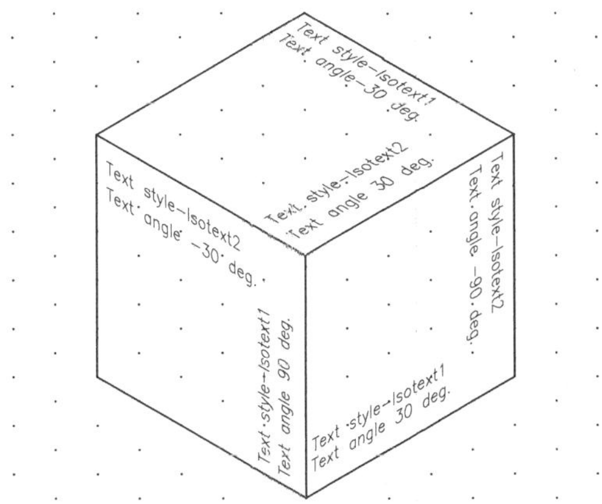

Figure 24-19 *Text style and rotation angle for isometric text*

Self-Evaluation Test

Answer the following questions and then compare them to those given at the end of this chapter:

1. The word "isometric" means __________. The three angles between the three principal axes of an isometric drawing measure __________ degree each.

2. The ratio of isometric length to the actual length in an isometric drawing is approximately __________.

3. The angle between the right isometric horizontal axis and the X axis is __________ degree.

4. Isometric drawings have three principal planes: isoplane right, isoplane top, and __________.

5. To toggle among isoplane right, isoplane left, and isoplane top, you can use __________ key combination or __________ function key.

6. The lines that are not parallel to the isometric axes are called __________.

7. You can only use the aligned dimension option to dimension an isometric drawing. (T/F)

8. The isometric snap must be turned on to display the **Isocircle** option while using the **Ellipse** tool. (T/F)

9. While placing text in an isometric drawing, you need to specify the rotation angles. (T/F)

10. You should avoid showing any hidden lines in isometric drawings. (T/F)

Review Questions

Answer the following questions:

1. The __________ view is generally used to help in visualizing the shape of an object.

2. An isometric view is obtained by rotating an object by __________ degrees around the imaginary vertical axis and then tilting the object forward through a __________ angle.

3. The isometric snap and grid can be turned on/off by selecting the __________ check box.

4. Isometric drawings have three axes: right horizontal axis, vertical axis, and __________.

5. The lines parallel to the isometric axis are called __________.

6. You can use the __________ command to set the isometric grid and snap.

7. Isometric grid lines are displayed at __________ degrees to the horizontal axis.

8. You can also set the isometric grid and snap by using the **Drafting Settings** dialog box, which can be invoked by entering __________ at the Command prompt.

9. Isometric circles are drawn by using the Ellipse tools and then selecting the __________ option.

10. To place text in an isometric drawing, you must create two text styles with oblique angles of __________ degree and __________ degree.

11. You should avoid showing hidden lines in isometric drawings unless they help in understanding its shape. (T/F)

12. Angles do not appear true in isometric drawings. (T/F)

13. You can set the aspect ratio for the isometric grid. (T/F)

14. You can draw an isometric circle without turning the isometric snap on. (T/F)

15. Only the aligned dimensions can be edited to change them to oblique dimensions. (T/F)

EXERCISES 1 through 4

Draw the following isometric drawings, refer to Figures 24-20 through 24-23. The dimensions can be determined by counting the number of grid lines. The distance between the isometric grid lines is assumed to be 0.5 unit. Dimension the drawing, as shown in Figure 24-23.

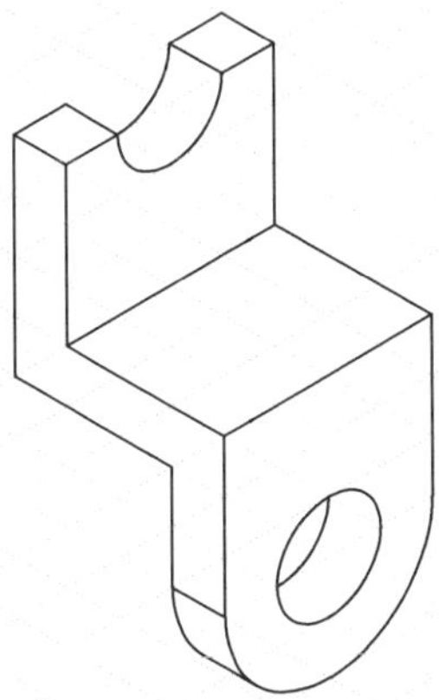

Figure 24-20 Drawing for Exercise 1

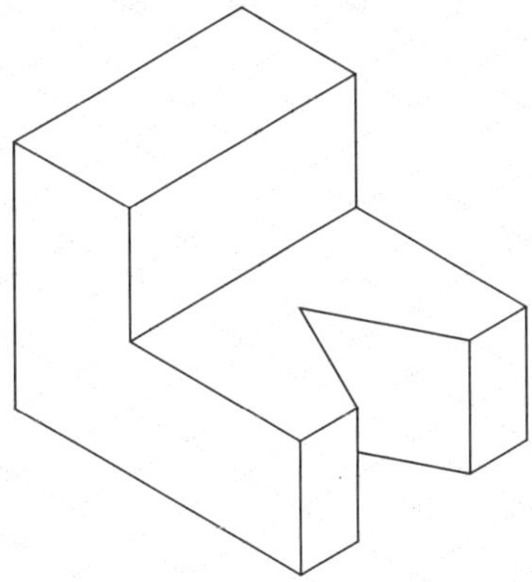

Figure 24-21 Drawing for Exercise 2

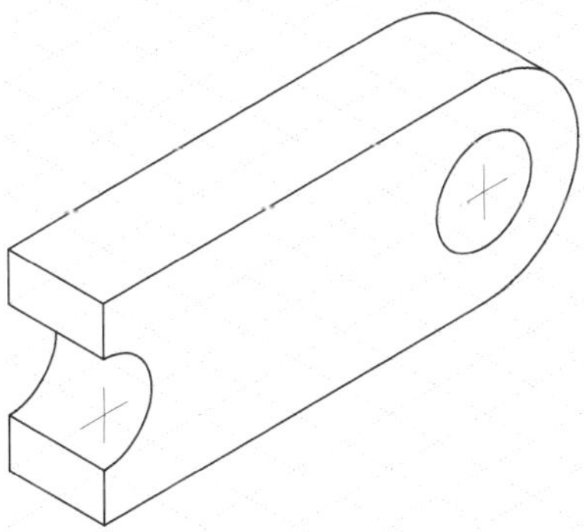

Figure 24-22 Drawing for Exercise 3

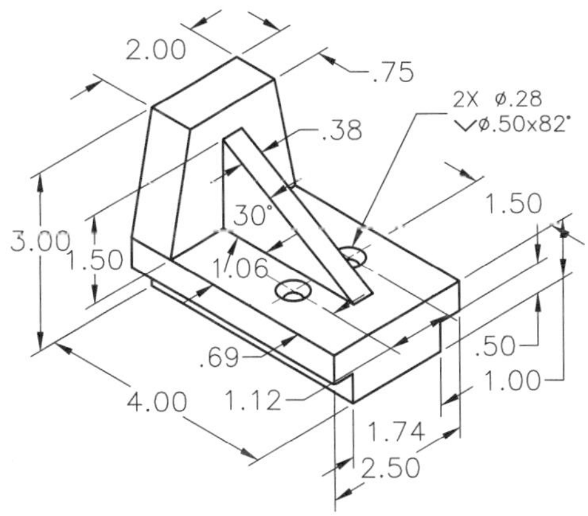

Figure 24-23 Drawing for Exercise 4

Answers to Self-Evaluation Test

1. equal measurement, 120, **2.** 9/11, **3.** 30, **4.** isoplane left, **5.** CTRL+E, F5, **6.** non isometric lines, **7.** T, **8.** T, **9.** T, **10.** T

Index

Symbols

2D Object Snap 1-8
2-Point tool 2-26
3D Object Snap button 1-8
3-Point tool 2-26, 3-2
-ATTEDIT command 17-40
-PURGE command 16-51
-WBLOCK command 21-3, 16-51

A

Absolute Coordinate System 2-9
ACISOUT command 21-4
Add option 5-4
Add-A-Plot Style Table Wizard 14-18
Add-A-Plotter Wizard 14-10
Add/Delete Scales tool 7-3
Add Folder Options dialog box 17-19
Add Leaders tool 8-42
Add Page Setup dialog box 14-3
Add Parameter Properties dialog box 16-32, 16-53
Add Plot Style dialog box 14-23
Add Vertex option 6-12
Adjust Space tool 8-29
Adjust tool 21-14
Advanced Setup wizard 1-21, 15-4
Aligned Section 22-31
Aligned tool 8-14
Alignment Parameter 16-28
Align tool 8-42
All option 5-4
Angle Format 2-31
Angular tool 8-19
ANNOAUTOSCALE system variable 7-4
ANNORESET command 7-5
Annotational Constraint 11-15
Annotation Object Scale dialog box 7-4
Annotation Scale 1-9
Annotation Visibility 1-9
Annotative Dimensions 8-56
Application Menu 1-12
ARC command 3-2
Arc drop-down 3-2
Arc Length tool 8-15
AREA System Variable 6-26
Area tool 6-23
Array Action 16-24
Associative Dimensions 8-6
Associative Hatch 12-11, 20-41
ATTACH command 18-16
Attach External Reference dialog box 18-7
Attach Image dialog box 21-10
Attach Option 18-6
Attach PDF Underlay dialog box 18-17
Attach tool 18-16, 21-9
ATTDEF command 17-2
ATTDIA system variable 17-8
ATTEXT command 17-30
ATTIPE system variable 17-4
ATTREDEF command 17-45
Attribute Definition dialog box 17-2
Attribute Extraction dialog box 17-31
ATTSYNC command 17-12
Auto option 5-6
AutoCAD HELP 1-35
Autodesk Seek design content 6-20
Automatic Timed Save 1-27
AutoScale 1-9
AutoStack Properties dialog box 7-25
Auxiliary Views 22-37
Axis, End tool 3-15

B

Background Mask dialog box 7-14
BACKGROUNDPLOT system variable 14-8, 14-27
Backup Files 1-28
Baseline tool 8-17
Basepoint Parameter 16-32
BEDIT command 16-14

Bind option 18-10
Bind Xrefs/DGN underlays dialog box 18-10
Block Attribute Manager dialog box 17-11
Block Authoring Palettes 16-18, 16-33
BLOCK command 16-2
Block Definition dialog box 16-3
Block Editor 16-15
Block Editor tab 16-16
Block Editor tool 16-14
Block Properties Table dialog box 16-52
BMPOUT command 21-8
Boundaries panel 12-7
BOUNDARY command 12-28
Boundary Creation dialog box 12-29
Boundary tool 12-28
Box option 5-6
Break at Point tool 5-50
Break tool 5-50, 8-30
Bullets and Numbering option 7-18

C

Cell Border Properties dialog box 7-43
Center 3-3
Center, Diameter tool 2-25
Center Mark tool 8-25, 8-26
Center, Radius tool 2-25
Center, Start, Angle tool 3-8
Center, Start, End tool 3-7
Center, Start, Length tool 3-8
Center tool 3-15
CHAMFER 5-20
CHAMFERA system variable 5-21, 5-23
CHAMFERB system variable 5-21, 5-23
CHAMFERC system variable 5-23
CHAMFERD system variable 5-23
Chamfer tool 5-20
CHAMMODE system variable 5-23
Check Spelling dialog box 7-50
Check Spelling tool 7-50
Circle drop-down 2-25
Clean Screen button 1-10
CLIP command 18-21
Clipdepth 18-23
Clip tool 18-21, 21-13
CMLJUST system variable 19-13
CMLSCALE system variable 19-13
CMLSTYLE system variable 19-3, 19-13
Coincident tool 11-4
Collect tool 8-45
Collinear constraint 11-6
Column Settings dialog box 7-20
Compare Dimension Styles dialog box 10-33
Concentric constraint 11-6
Constraint Settings dialog box 11-9, 11-13, 11-18
Constraints to Blocks 16-51
Construction Line tool 3-29
Continue tool 3-9, 8-18
CONVERT command 12-29
Convert to Arc option 6-12
Convert to Line option 6-12
Coordinate Systems 2-9
COORDS system variable 1-6
Copy tool 5-8
Cpolygon option 5-3
Create New Dimension Style dialog box 10-3, 10-34
Create New Drawing dialog box 1-19, 15-3
Create New Multiline Style dialog box 19-3
Create New Table Style dialog box 7-38
Create PostScript File dialog box 21-18, 21-19, 21-22
Create Sheet Set wizard 6-45
Create Block tool 16-2
Current Plot Style dialog box 14-24
Custom Arrow Block dialog box 10-9
CVPORT system variable 13-5

D

Data Extraction - Additional Settings dialog box 17-20
DATAEXTRACTION command 17-17
Data Extraction wizard 17-17, 17-21, 17-29
DBLIST command 6-28
DCTCUST system variable 7-51
DCTMAIN system variable 7-51
DDEDIT command 17-7
DDPTYPE command 3-27
Decurve option 20-27
Define Attributes tool 17-2
DEFPOINTS layer 8-7
DELOBJ system variable 19-18
DesignCenter tool 6-17, 16-34
Detach option 18-9

DGNEXPORT command 21-8
DGNFRAME system variable 18-24
Diameter tool 8-23
Dictionaries dialog box 7-51
DIMADEC system variable 8-9
DIMANGULAR command 8-19
DIMARC command 8-15
DIMASSOC system variable 8-7
DIMASZ system variable 10-9
DIMAUNIT system variable 10-22
DIMBASELINE command 8-17
DIMBREAK command 8-30
DIMCEN system variable 8-5, 8-25, 10-10
DIMCENTER command 8-25
DIMCLRD system variable 8-49, 10-4
DIMCLRT system variable 8-49
DIMCONTINUE command 8-18
DIMDEC system variable 8-9, 10-20
DIMDIA command 8-23
DIMDISASSOCIATE command 8-6, 8-34
DIMDLE system variable 10-5
DIMDLI system variable 22-5
DIMEDIT command 9-5
Dimensional Constraint 11-15
Dimension, Dimjogline tool 8-25
Dimension drop-down 8-10
Dimension Edit tool 9-5
Dimensioning 22-25
Dimension Input Settings dialog box 2-4
Dimension Line 8-3
Dimension Style Families 10-28
Dimension Style Manager dialog box 10-2
Dimension Text 8-3
Dimension Text Edit tool 9-7
Dimension Update tool 9-8
DIMEXO system variable 10-6
DIMFRAC system variable 10-20
DIMGAP system variable 8-49, 10-14
DIMINSPECT command 8-32
DIMJOGGED command 8-23
DIMJOGLINE command 8-25
DIMLFAC system variable 10-21
DIMLINEAR command 8-10
DIMLUNIT system variable 10-20
DIMLWD system variable 10-4
DIMORD command 8-26, 8-27, 8-28
DIMPOST system variable 10-20
DIMRAD command 8-24
DIMREASSOCIATE 8-34
DIMRND system variable 10-20
DIMSCALE system variable 10-18
DIMSE1 system variable 8-24
DIMSE2 system variable 8-24
DIMSPACE command 8-29
DIMSTYLE command 10-2
DIMTAD system variable 10-13
DIMTIH system variable 8-28, 10-15
DIMTM system variable 10-25, 10-26
DIMTOH system variable 8-28, 10-15
DIMTOLJ system variable 10-27
DIMTOL system variable 10-25
DIMTP system variable 10-25, 10-26
DIMTXSTY system variable 8-49
DIMTXT system variable 8-49
Direct Distance Entry 2-18
Direction Control dialog box 2-33, 15-7
Distance tool 6-26
DIVIDE command 5-53
Divide tool 3-28, 5-53
DONUT command 3-25
DONUTID system variable 3-25
DONUTOD system variable 3-25
Drafting Settings dialog box 24-5
DRAGMODE system variable 16-10
Drawing Properties dialog box 6-30
Drawing Recovery Manager 1-28
Drawing Recovery message box 1-29
Drawing Units dialog box 2-31, 15-7
DRAWORDER command 21-16
Draw Order drop-down 21-16
DTEXT command 7-6
DWGPROPS command 6-30
DXBIN command 21-4
DXF files 21-2
Dynamic Blocks 16-16
Dynamic Input button 1-7

E

EDGEMODE system variable 5-29
Edit Attribute Definition dialog box 17-7
Edit Attributes dialog box 17-9, 17-38
Edit Block Definition dialog box 16-15
Edit Drawing Scales dialog box 7-3
Edit Hatch tool 12-21

Edit Reference Panel 16-48
Edit Reference tool 16-45, 17-45, 18-26
Edit Spline tool 19-20
Edit tool 17-7
Ellipse drop-down 3-14
Elliptical Arc tool 3-16
End 3-3
Enhanced Attribute Editor dialog box 17-37
Equal constraint 11-7
Equations 11-22
ERASE command 2-21
Erase tool 2-21
EXPLMODE system variable 16-48
EXPLODE command 20-14
Explode tool 20-14
EXPORT command 21-4, 21-7, 21-21
Extend tool 5-28
Extension Lines 8-4
External References palette 18-5, 21-11
External References Palette button 18-4, 21-10
EXTNAMES system variable 16-3
Extract Data tool 17-17

F

Fence option 5-5
Field dialog box 7-21
Fillet/Chamfer drop-down 5-17
FILLETRAD system variable 5-17
Fillet tool 5-17
FILLMODE system variable 3-26, 12-4
Find and Replace dialog box 7-22, 7-52
Find and Replace option 18-12
FIND command 7-52
Find Text search box 7-52
Fit data 19-20
Fix tool 11-4
Flip Action 16-29
Flip Parameter 16-29
Font drop-down list 7-14
Frame drop-down list 18-24
FRAME system variable 18-23
Full Section 22-26
Fully-Defined Sketch 11-16

G

GDT 8-47
Geometric Tolerance dialog box 8-48
GFANG system variable 12-16
GFNAME system variable 12-16
Gizmo 1-9
Gradient Pattern 12-16
GRAPHSCR command 6-23
Grid 1-7
GRIPBLOCK system variable 6-4
GRIPCOLOR system variable 6-4
GRIPCONTOUR system variable 6-4
GRIPHOT system variable 6-4
GRIPHOVER system variable 6-4
Grips 6-2
GRIPSIZE system variable 6-4
GRIPS system variable 6-4
GRIPTIPS system variable 6-4
Group option 5-5

H

Half Section 22-27
Hatch and Gradient dialog box 12-14
Hatch Angle 12-9
Hatch Creation tab 12-3
Hatch Edit dialog box 12-21
Hatch Editor tab 12-20
Hatch Pattern Type dialog box 12-23
Hatch tool 12-3
Hatch Transparency 12-9
Horizontal constraint 11-2
HPANG system variable 12-9
HPBOUND system variable 12-29
HPDOUBLE system variable 12-10
HPNAME system variable 12-8, 12-13
HPSCALE system variable 12-10
Hyperlink 6-13

I

ID Point tool 6-27
IMAGEADJUST command 21-14
Image Adjust dialog box 21-15
IMAGECLIP command 21-13
IMAGE command 21-10
IMAGEFRAME command 21-16
IMAGEFRAME system variable 18-24

Image Frame tool 21-16
IMAGEHLT system variable 21-14
Image Quality tool 21-15
Image Transparency tool 21-15
Import Page Setups dialog box 14-17
INDEXCTL system variable 18-25
Infer Constraints button 1-7
Insert a Block in a Table Cell dialog box 7-44
Insert dialog box 16-6
Insert Formula Column dialog box 17-26
Insert Layout(s) dialog box 13-23
Insert Object dialog box 21-30
Insert Table dialog box 7-33
Insert tool 16-5, 16-7
Inspection Dimension dialog box 8-32
Inspect tool 8-32
INSUNITS system variable 16-9, 16-12, 16-44
Isometric Circles 24-7
Isometric Drafting 1-7
Isometric Drawings 24-2
Isometric Grid 24-3
Isometric Projections 24-2
Isometric Snap 24-3
ISOPLANE command 24-4

J

Jogged tool 8-23
JOIN command 5-53
Join tool 5-53
Join Viewports tool 13-5
JUSTIFYTEXT command 7-31
Justify tool 7-31

K

Kink 19-21

L

Last option 5-2
LASTPOINT system variable 6-27
LAYOUT command 13-21
LAYOUTWIZARD command 13-24
Leader Settings dialog box 8-36
Lengthen tool 5-31
LIMITS command 15-6
Line tool 2-6
Linear Parameter 16-22
Linear tool 8-10
Line Spacing flyout 7-18
Link External Data dialog box 17-23
Links dialog box 21-29
List tool 6-27
Load Multiline Styles dialog box 19-6
Lock UI 1-9
Lookup Action 16-31
Lookup Parameter 16-31
LTSCALE system variable 13-20
LWDISPLAY system variable 17-15

M

Manage Cell Content dialog box 7-46
Manage Cell Styles dialog box 7-41
Manage Custom Dictionaries dialog box 7-51
Manage Plot Styles tool 14-17
Manage Xrefs icon 1-10
Match Properties tool 6-14
Material Condition dialog box 8-50
Measure drop-down 6-23
Measure tool 3-28
MINSERT command 16-41
MIRROR command 5-48
Mirroring the Objects by Using Grips 6-10
Mirror tool 5-48
MIRRTEXT system variable 5-50
MLEADERALIGN command 8-42
MLEADER command 8-39
MLEADEREDIT command 8-42
MLEADERSTYLE command 10-34
MLEDIT command 19-8
MLINE command 19-6
MLSTYLE command 19-2
Model Space 1-7
Move Action 16-20
Move tool 5-7
Moving the Objects by Using Grips 6-6
MTJIGSTRING system variable 7-12
Multileader Style Manager dialog box 10-34, 10-35
Multileader tool 8-39
Multilines Edit Tools dialog box 19-9
Multilines tool 19-6
Multiline Style dialog box 19-2
Multiline Text tool 7-11, 17-46
Multiple option 5-6

Multiple Points tool 3-28
Multiple tool 17-40
MVSETUP Command 13-26

N

Named tool 13-2, 13-5, 13-8
Navigation Bar 1-5
Nesting of Blocks 16-39
New Dimension Style dialog box 10-3, 10-4
New Excel Data Link dialog box 7-34
New Multiline Style dialog box 19-3
New Page Setup dialog box 14-15
New Parameter dialog box 16-53
New Text Style dialog box 7-48
New tool 1-18
New View / Shot Properties dialog box 6-42
New Visibility State dialog box 16-30

O

Object option 5-7
Object Grouping dialog box 20-2
Object Linking and Embedding (OLE) 21-24
OBJECTSCALE command 7-3
Object Selection Methods 2-22
Offset Section 22-30
Offset tool 5-11
OLEHIDE system variable 21-32
OPTIONS command 6-3
Options dialog box 2-42, 6-3
Order Group dialog box 20-5
Orthographic Projections 22-18
Ortho Mode 1-7
OSOPTIONS system variable 12-17
Over-defined sketch 11-16
Overlay Option 18-12

P

PAGESETUP command 13-24, 14-13
Page Setup dialog box 14-15
Page Setup Manager dialog box 14-14
Page Setup Manager tool 14-14
PAN command 6-39
Pan tool 2-30, 6-39
Paragraph dialog box 7-16
Parallel constraint 11-5
Parameter drop-down 16-17
Parameter Sets 16-33
Parameters Manager palette 11-23
PARTIALOAD command 1-31
Partial Open dialog box 1-31
Paste as Block tool 5-11
PASTEBLOCK command 5-11
PASTEORIG command 5-11
PASTESPEC command 21-29
Paste Special dialog box 21-30
Paste to Original Coordinates tool 5-11
Path Array 5-45
PCINWIZARD command 14-13
PDFIMPORT command 21-6
PDF Text Recognition Settings dialog box 21-6
PDMODE system variable 5-51
PDSIZE system variable 5-51
PEDIT command 20-16
PERIMETER system variable 6-26
Perpendicular constraint 11-5
PICKADD system variable 20-40
PICKBOX system variable 20-41
PICKDRAG system variable 20-41
PICKFIRST system variable 6-11, 20-40
PICKSTYLE system variable 20-4, 20-7, 20-41
PLINE command 3-20
PLINEGEN system variable 20-28
Plot 2-39
PLOT command 14-2
Plot dialog box 14-2
Plot Styles window 14-18
Plot Style Table Editor 14-19
Plotter Configuration Editor dialog box 14-12
PLOTTERMANAGER command 14-10
Plot tool 14-2
Point Parameter 16-18, 16-20
Point Style dialog box 3-27
Point Style tool 3-27
Polar Parameter 16-24
Polar Stretch Action 16-25
Polar Tracking 1-7
Polygon tool 3-18
Polyline tool 3-20
PostScript Out Options dialog box 21-22
Previous option 5-2
PROJMODE system variable 5-29
PROPERTIES command 6-13, 9-8
Properties palette 6-14, 7-30, 17-8, 20-8

Property Lookup Table dialog box 16-32
Property Settings dialog box 6-15
PSETUPIN command 14-16
PSLTSCALE system variable 13-20
PSOUT command 21-21
PURGE command 16-38, 20-36

Q

QDIM command 8-9
QLEADER command 8-35
QNEW 1-18
QSELECT command 6-15
Quick Dimension tool 8-9
Quick Select dialog box 6-16
Quick Select tool 6-15
QuickSetup wizard 1-23

R

Radius tool 8-24
Raster Images 21-8
RAY command 3-31
Ray tool 3-31
Reassociate tool 8-6, 8-34
Recognize SHX Text tool 21-6
Rectangle tool 3-10
Rectangular Array 5-33
REDO command 20-35
REDRAWALL command 6-31
REDRAW command 6-31
REFEDIT command 16-45, 17-45, 18-26
Reference Edit dialog box 16-46
REFPATHTYPE system variable 18-8
REFSET command 16-48
REGENALL command 6-31
REGENAUTO system variable 17-42
REGEN command 6-31
Relative Coordinate System 2-12
Relative Polar Coordinates 2-16
Relative Rectangular Coordinates 2-12
Reload option 18-10
Remove Leader tool 8-42
Remove option 5-4
Remove Vertex option 6-12
RENAME command 16-50, 20-35
Rename dialog box 16-50, 20-36
REVCLOUD command 19-15
Revolved Section 22-29
Ribbon 1-11
Rotate Action 16-27
Rotate tool 1-6, 5-13
Rotating the Objects by Using Grips 6-7
Rotation Parameter 16-27

S

SAVEAS command 1-24
Saveas Options dialog box 21-2
Save Block As dialog box 16-16
SAVE command 1-24
Save Drawing As dialog box 1-25
Scale Action 16-23
SCALE command 5-15
Scale tool 5-15, 7-30
Scaling the Objects by Using Grips 6-9
Select a Data Link dialog box 7-34
Select Annotation Scale dialog box 16-12
Select File dialog box 1-30
Selection Cycling button 6-17
Selection list box 6-17
Select New Path option 18-12
Select Page Setup From File dialog box 14-16
Select Plot Style dialog box 14-24
Select Reference File dialog box 21-10
Select template dialog box 1-18
Set Base Point tool 16-45
Sheet List Table dialog box 7-54
Sheet Set Manager 6-52, 7-54
Shortcut Menu 1-13
ShowMotion 1-6
Sign Convention 2-16
Single option 5-6
Single Line tool 3-32, 7-6
Single tool 17-36
Smooth constraint 11-8
SNAPBASE system variable 12-11
Snap Mode 1-7
Sort Columns dialog box 17-25
SPACETRANS command 13-30
SPELL command 7-50
SPLFRAME system variable 20-26
SPLINE command 19-17
SPLINEDIT command 19-20, 19-24
SPLINESEGS. The system variable 20-27
Spline tool 19-17
SPLINETYPE system variable 20-26

Stack Properties dialog box 7-25
Standard Template Drawings 15-2
Start, Center, End tool 3-3
Start, Center, Angle tool 3-3
Start, Center, Length tool 3-5
Start, End, Angle tool 3-5
Start, End, Direction tool 3-5
Start, End, Radius tool 3-7
STARTUP system variable 1-19, 15-2
Status Bar 1-6
STATUS command 6-29
SteeringWheels 1-5
Stretch Action 16-21
Stretching the Objects by Using Grips 6-5
Stretch tool 5-30
STYLE command 7-47
STYLESMANAGER command 14-17
SUbobject option 5-7
Symbol dialog box 8-49
Synchronize Attributes tool 17-12

T

Table Cell tab 7-42
TABLEINDICATOR system variable 7-44
TABLESTYLE command 7-38
Table Style dialog box 7-38
Table Style tool 7-38
Table tool 7-32
Tangent constraint 11-6
Tan, Tan, Radius tool 2-27
Tan, Tan, Tan tool 2-28
Template Options dialog box 15-5
TEXT command 7-6
Text drop down 7-6, 7-12
TEXTFILL system variable 7-51
TEXTQLTY system variable 7-51
TEXTSCR command 6-23
Text Style dialog box 7-48, 24-10
Text to Mtext Settings dialog box 7-32
Tiled Viewports 13-2
TILEMODE system variable 13-2
TIME command 6-28
TOLERANCE command 8-48
Tolerance tool 8-48
Tool Palettes 16-34
Tool Palettes button 12-18
TOOLPALETTES command 12-18
Tool Properties dialog box 12-19, 16-36
Tooltip Appearance dialog box 2-5
TRANSPARENCY command 21-15
Trim drop-down 5-25
TRIMMODE system variable 5-20
Trim tool 5-24

U

Under-defined sketch 11-16
Underlay Layers dialog box 18-18
Undo option 5-6
UNDO command 20-30
Units for Lighting 2-33
Unload option 18-10
Update tool 9-8

V

Vertical constraint 11-3
VIEW command 6-41
ViewCube 1-6
View Manager dialog box 6-41
Viewports dialog box 13-4
Visibility Parameter 16-30
Visibility States dialog box 16-30
VISRETAIN system variable 18-3
VPCLIP command 13-14
VPLAYER command 13-16
VPORTS command 13-5, 13-8

W

WBLOCK command 16-43
WIPEOUT command 19-16
Wipeout tool 19-16
WMFIN command 21-7
WPolygon option 5-3
Write Block dialog box 16-43

X

XBIND command 18-20
Xbind dialog box 18-21
Xbind tool 18-20
XCLIPFRAME system variable 18-24
XEDIT system variable 18-27
XFADECTL system variable 16-47, 18-26
XLOADCTL system variable 18-24
XLOADPATH system variable 18-25

XPLODE Command 16-48
XREF command 18-4
XREFCTL system variable 18-16
XY Parameter 16-26

Z

ZOOM command 6-32
Zoom drop-down 6-32
Zoom Extents tool 2-29
Zoom In 6-38
Zoom In tool 2-30
Zoom Out 6-38
Zoom Out tool 2-30
Zoom Previous tool 2-30, 6-36
Zoom Realtime tool 2-30, 6-32
Zoom tool 1-6
Zoom Window tool 2-29